Race,
Racism, and American Law

This book is dedicated to all those who throughout America's history have risked its wrath to protest its faults. Courageous black athletes mounted a famous protest against racism at the 1968 Olympic games. That protest, like so many that preceded it, constituted a prophecy:

> The dramatic finale of an
> Extraordinary achievement
> Performed for a nation which
> Had there been a choice
> Would have chosen others, and
> If given a chance
> Will accept the achievement
> And neglect the achievers.
> Here, with simple gesture, they
> Symbolize a people whose patience
> With exploitation will expire with
> The dignity and certainty
> With which it has been endured . . .
> Too long.

DB

ASPEN PUBLISHERS

Race,
Racism, and American Law
Sixth Edition

Derrick Bell

Wolters Kluwer
Law & Business

AUSTIN   BOSTON   CHICAGO   NEW YORK   THE NETHERLANDS

Aspen Publishers
Attn: Permissions Department
76 Ninth Avenue, 7th Floor
New York, NY 10011-5201

To contact Customer Care, e-mail customer.care@aspenpublishers.com,
call 1-800-234-1660, fax 1-800-901-9075, or mail correspondence to:

Aspen Publishers
Attn: Order Department
PO Box 990
Frederick, MD 21705

Printed in the United States of America.

1 2 3 4 5 6 7 8 9 0

ISBN 978-0-7355-7574-5

Library of Congress Cataloging-in-Publication Data

Bell, Derrick A.
  Race, Racism, and American law / Derrick Bell. — 6th ed.
    p. cm.
  Includes index.
  ISBN 978-0-7355-7574-5
  1. African Americans — Civil rights. 2. Civil rights — United States. I. Title.

KF4757.B35 2008
342.7308'73 — dc22   2008023630

About Wolters Kluwer Law & Business

Wolters Kluwer Law & Business is a leading provider of research information and workflow solutions in key specialty areas. The strengths of the individual brands of Aspen Publishers, CCH, Kluwer Law International and Loislaw are aligned within Wolters Kluwer Law & Business to provide comprehensive, in-depth solutions and expert-authored content for the legal, professional and education markets.

CCH was founded in 1913 and has served more than four generations of business professionals and their clients. The CCH products in the Wolters Kluwer Law & Business group are highly regarded electronic and print resources for legal, securities, antitrust and trade regulation, government contracting, banking, pension, payroll, employment and labor, and healthcare reimbursement and compliance professionals.

Aspen Publishers is a leading information provider for attorneys, business professionals and law students. Written by preeminent authorities, Aspen products offer analytical and practical information in a range of specialty practice areas from securities law and intellectual property to mergers and acquisitions and pension/benefits. Aspen's trusted legal education resources provide professors and students with high-quality, up-to-date and effective resources for successful instruction and study in all areas of the law.

Kluwer Law International supplies the global business community with comprehensive English-language international legal information. Legal practitioners, corporate counsel and business executives around the world rely on the Kluwer Law International journals, loose-leafs, books and electronic products for authoritative information in many areas of international legal practice.

Loislaw is a premier provider of digitized legal content to small law firm practitioners of various specializations. Loislaw provides attorneys with the ability to quickly and efficiently find the necessary legal information they need, when and where they need it, by facilitating access to primary law as well as state-specific law, records, forms and treatises.

Wolters Kluwer Law & Business, a unit of Wolters Kluwer, is headquartered in New York and Riverwoods, Illinois. Wolters Kluwer is a leading multinational publisher and information services company.

Summary of Contents

Contents

Chapter 4

Fair Employment Laws and Their Limits   *149*

Chapter 5

Discrimination in the Administration of Justice — 229

Contents

Chapter 6
Voting Rights and Democratic Domination   *341*

Chapter 7

Property Barriers and Fair Housing Laws 425

Chapter 8
Interracial Intimate Relationships and Racial Identification　　497

Chapter 9
Public Facilities: Symbols of Subordination　　555

Chapter 10

The Parameters of Racial Protest   595

Contents

Chapter 11
Racism and Other "Nonwhites"   *683*

Preface to the Sixth Edition

Thirty-five years after publication of the first edition of this text in 1973, the pessimism expressed there during what many believed were the closing phases of the long civil rights crusade, unfortunately has proven all too accurate. Overt expressions, actions, and policies growing out of beliefs in white superiority or racial priority have diminished. We have learned that this progress has often occurred for reasons without the involvement of lawmakers in the legislatures or the courts. Indeed, hard won victories in the courts and statutes have often failed to provide expected gains.

The contemporary illustration of a history-long pattern is Brown v. Board of Education, a decision that on its 50th anniversary in 2004, had not been reversed, but was deemed irrelevant by all save those who continued to believe that through reverence, its revival might be achieved. Such continued faith in what was a viable precedent, does not provide either guidance of what went wrong, nor offer direction as to more promising new strategies.

Chapter 1, American Racism and the Relevance of Law, takes a detailed look at a 1935 essay by Ralph Bunche, A Critical Analysis of the Tactics and Programs of Minority Groups. Dr. Bunche, writing three-quarters of a century ago, expressed insights and offered suggestions of real value in understanding current resistance and the limited ability of law to alter deeply held views by much of the public. Given widespread opposition to judicially recognized racial injustice, the courts and the law generally have little alternative to reversing or seriously limiting reforms.

Dr. Bunche would not be surprised by the popular rationale that further civil rights policies are no longer needed because racism is a thing of the past and continuing complaints of discrimination are simply whining by those minorities who prefer preferences over performance. The courts to a large extent are now handing down decisions in race cases that reflect this belief. The Supreme Court's current policy of applying its strict scrutiny yardstick to any racial classification overturns the traditional view that this tough-to-overcome hurdle was intended to protect discrete and insular minorities from discrimination fostered by hostile majorities. Now, turning this standard on its head, the Court — in most instances — is protecting members of the majority against modest policies intended to ameliorate generations of overt racial prejudice.

Ignored in the rush to proclaim color blindness as the judicial panacea to claims of racial injustice is the fact that virtually all policies adopted as protections against racial injustices suffered by blacks and other people of color in this country actually prove of more value to whites. The widespread opposition to affirmative action, an opposition not eased by either court decisions that have rendered such policies very difficult to maintain, or the fact that whites in general, and particularly white women, have benefited from policies of affirmative action far more than have people of color. Now, as a century ago, the idea that racial remedies for blacks also help whites remains a difficult one to convey. Racial issues in law rather than moving toward resolution have been inundated with the fictions that contradict racial reality.

As this edition is readied for publication, Senator Barack Obama seems on the verge of becoming the first black to gain the nomination for president by a major political party. In the process, his well-organized campaign has gained tremendous support from all segments of the population, an event that many felt would not happen in their lifetimes. That said, it is unlikely, even if Senator Obama survives the many challenges to his nomination and election, that this historical first will alter significantly the continuing racial barriers that most people of color face in all the areas reviewed in this edition.

Chapter 2, Race and American History, contains a detailed review of how racial laws and policies in this country have led many to wonder with Tilden J. LeMelle whether in the absence of recognition that racist practices are seen as a threat "a society such as the United States is really capable of legislating and enforcing effective public policy to combat racial discrimination in the political process and elsewhere." He says "history presents no instances where a society in which racism has been internalized and institutionalized to the point of being an essential and inherently functioning component of that society ever reforms, particularly a culture from whose inception racial discrimination has been a regulative force for maintaining stability and growth and for maximizing other cultural values."

Chapter 3, The Quest for Effective Schools, substantially revises the education materials in previous editions to focus on recent decisions, including the 2007 *Seattle-Louisville* cases that subjected to quite strict scrutiny and then rejected the modest efforts school districts attempted to gain some racial diversity in its schools. There is more coverage of school desegregation alternatives in private and public settings, including innovative approaches to motivating and teaching students whose economic and cultural backgrounds have provided little understanding of how scaling seemingly impassable barriers can be achieved.

Chapter 4, Fair Employment Laws and Their Limits, reviews both the continuing and growing racial disparities in every area of the job market. Discrimination in employment is ever present if harder to discern. Victims are finding Title VII and other antidiscrimination policies harder than ever to utilize effectively. Case development has shown a greater willingness to protect defendants than to recognize the more subtle but still effective means of discrimination. As a result, employment cases are harder to bring and even harder to win.

The chapter refers to studies showing that these laws are only minimally effective in reducing prejudice and enhancing opportunity for black workers. Most such claims, when resolved by courts, are dismissed on pretrial motions. When employment discrimination plaintiffs do get their claims to a jury, they fare worse than plaintiffs in other civil actions. This ill fate continues on appeal, with federal appellate courts reversing plaintiffs' victories at a higher rate than defendants' wins in employment discrimination cases. As a result, lawyers are reluctant to take these cases on a contingency basis. Although the Court's 2007 decision, Ledbetter v. Goodyear Tire & Rubber Co., is an exception, defendants are usually more willing to negotiate and settle job bias claims brought by white women.

Chapter 5, Discrimination in the Administration of Justice, has shown little change for the better since the Fifth Edition. Given their percentages in the population, a disproportionate number of those sentenced to death are black and Latino. Even so, public support for the death penalty has diminished as a result of the use of DNA evidence that has freed defendants who had served many years while awaiting execution.

Beyond the death penalty, though, the statistics show a continuing pattern of bias. The number of blacks and Latinos serving often-lengthy prison sentence have increased. Almost 1 in 4 black men between the ages of 20 and 30 are under the supervision of the criminal justice system on any given day. For white men in the same age group, the corresponding statistic is 1 in 16. Black persons are more likely than whites to have been shot at by police, 18 times more likely to be wounded and 5 times more likely to be killed. Prosecutors are more likely to pursue full prosecution, file more severe charges, and seek more stringent penalties in cases involving defendants of color, particularly where the victim is white. Minority offenders are also sentenced to prison more often and receive longer terms than whites convicted of similar crimes and with similar records. As of 2007, more than 60 percent of the people in prison are now racial and ethnic minorities. For black males in their twenties, 1 in every 8 is in prison or jail on any given day. Of the 2.2 million incarcerated individuals, 900,000 are black. These trends have been intensified by the disproportionate impact of the "war on drugs," in which three-fourths of all persons in prison for drug offenses are people of color. The chapter covers the generally harsh decisions that explain these statistics. Calls for legislative reform are resisted by officials who fear they will face "soft on crime" charges that may endanger their reelection.

Chapter 6, Voting Rights and Democratic Domination, records the continuing frustration by courts seeking judicially manageable standards for determining the validity of electoral districts apportioned equally through computerized techniques capable of effectively gerrymandering lines to favor one political party over the other. And, as indicated by its decision in Georgia v. Ashcroft, the Court is looking more broadly in determining whether redistricting plans adopted to ensure the effective inclusion of black votes can meet that standard without the creation of safe-black districts. In the area of individual voting rights, it appears that the Supreme Court's approval of a state's requirement that perspective voters produce a government issued photo ID at the polling place, Crawford v. Marion County Election Board, 553 U.S. _____ (2008), will be the first of several challenges to proposed state laws proposed to prevent voter fraud, but Opponents of Voter ID laws, enacted or being considered in several states, maintain that they will discourage voting and in particular black and Latino voting for reasons quite similar to those that led to invalidation of poll taxes.

Chapters 7, 8, 9, and 10 cover developments in the areas of Property Barriers and Fair Housing Laws, Interracial Intimate Relationships and Racial Identification, Public Facilities, and The Parameters of Racial Protest. In each area, despite surface compliance with antidiscrimination policies, there remain serious problems of exclusion, discrimination, and exploitation operating just below the surface with effects that are both serious and extremely resistant to traditional litigation approaches. Most civil rights advocates would agree that laws intended to bar racial bias for those seeking to buy or lease personal residences have not been very effective, relying as most do on action by those alleging discrimination. The once steadfast resistance to interracial sex and marriage has lessened steadily over the years, but problems remain in policy differences on interracial adoption. The relative openness of most places of public accommodation is evidence that the fear of economic loss and the hope for gain is a more powerful engine of change than either law or public resistance. And racial protests that have always walked the fine line between activities that gain attention while saying within boundaries that lawyer can argue are constitutionally protected, have a difficult time during times of war when all but the most peaceful (and likely ineffective) protests can be deemed unpatriotic and unworthy of protection.

Chapter 11, Racism and Other "Nonwhites," has been updated with further coverage given the treatment of Indians and policies ranging from genocide to subjugation and exploitation. It covers as well the racial experience of Chinese, Japanese, and Mexican Americans in this country as well as the continuing racial problems faced by the Aborigines in Australia and the Maori in New Zealand. In addition, the section titled, "September 11, 2001," added in the Fifth Edition, has been updated to address racial components of anti-terrorist policies instituted by the Bush Administration in the wake of the one of the most devastating attacks in American history. These policies have included overt racial profiling with race and ethnicity used as proxies for affiliation with terrorism. There have been large numbers of immigration-based detentions, including purely preventive based detentions, of persons from certain countries or ethnic or religious backgrounds. The federal government has also imprisoned a large number of foreign persons in Guantanamo Bay, Cuba, and in unknown locations abroad without formal charges or access to lawyers. In addition, the government has also failed to extend traditional legal procedures to U.S. citizens being held as enemy combatants. It has detained foreign nationals and a small number of U.S. citizens, and has also conducted secret wiretapping and secret searches without a showing of probable cause or criminal wrongdoing.

As in past editions, most of the Sixth Edition chapters contain racism hypos, hypothetical cases providing a detailed set of facts that can provide the basis for simulated appellate case arguments with students representing each side. This is an excellent way to facilitate discussion of both the depths and the parameters of racial issues in each of the subject areas. Utilizing this approach serves as a vehicle for teachers at both the law school and undergraduate levels who want to lift the teaching of race relations law beyond the reading of cases and discussion about what the cases meant.

Beginning with the Second Edition, published in 1980, I reduced edited cases to summaries, recognizing that legal opinions in the racial field often reflect rather than set society's patterns and practices. This editorial change (cushioned by a companion volume of edited Leading Civil Rights Cases) reflected my concern that for all the furor they sometimes cause and all the change in racial patterns and policies attributed to them, the studying in detail of the usually lengthy and often multiple opinions in race cases seldom furthers understanding of what the Court has done and why it has done it. Any concern that students are shortchanged by not having the full or only lightly edited opinions of major cases available is resolved by the ready availability of the full opinions on the data bases or from the Supreme Court's website, www.supremecourtus.gov

The key question in the Sixth Edition remains that of the First: What does it mean to say that racism is a permanent feature of American society? Is there an inchoate property right in whiteness? In short, are there components of racial thought, belief, and identification that are critical to the maintenance of social stability in a society marked by enormous disparities in income, wealth, and opportunity? When the poor white person boasts: "Every morning, when I wake up, I thank God that I'm white!," what exactly is he thankful for?

Whatever the answer, it is now apparent that racism is no longer definable by views and actions that are blatantly prejudiced. Rather, as psychology Professor Beverly Daniel Tatum explains, racism is a system of apparent advantage based on race that benefits all whites whether or not they seek it. Except in response to the most overt discrimination, racial remedies, whether judicial or legislative, that appear to interfere with this advantage are opposed when suggested and resisted when approved. This is the answer to the question posed in the Preface of the First Edition where I wondered why the hard-won decisions protecting basic rights of black citizens from racial discrimination are abandoned or become obsolete before they are effectively enforced. My question, pertinent then even in the midst of the greatest surge of positive civil rights gains in American history, has become critically important given the overturning and reinterpreting of the legal precedents even the most pessimistic among us viewed as permanent.

Finally, the Sixth Edition continues the effort of its predecessors to make clear that racism burdens whites as well as blacks and racial remedies benefit all groups. The nineteenth-century Populist leader, Tom Watson, put it well in 1892 when, as a staunch advocate of a union between Negro and white farmers, he wrote: You are kept apart that you may be separately fleeced of your earnings. You are made to hate each other because upon that hatred is rested the keystone of the arch of financial despotism which enslaves you both. You are deceived and blinded that you may not see how this race antagonism perpetuates a monetary system which beggars you both. I have cited Tom Watson in each of the previous editions. It remains a message worthy of being both heard and taught.

In a later era, Dr. Ralph Bunche urged that the only realistic program for any minority group in modern America that can resolve this self-destructive antagonism is one based upon an intelligent analysis of the problems of the group in terms of the broad social forces which determine its condition. Certainly no program of opportunism and no amount of idealism can overcome or control these forces. The only hope for the improvement in the condition of the masses of any American minority group is the hope that can be held out for the betterment of the masses of the dominant group. Their basic interests are identical and so must be their programs and tactics.

Derrick Bell

June 2008

Acknowledgments

Once again, former students have provided essential research and writing. Chief among them is Ellen Joy Radice, J.D. 2003, Harvard Law School, who researched and drafted substantial versions of several chapters. Other contributions were made by former NYU law students, Margo Kaplan, J.D. 2004, Sarah Blanton, J.D. 2007, and Ana E.J. Jung, LL.M 2007. My thanks to Craig Gurian, Executive Director of the Anti-Discrimination Center of Metro New York, for reviewing and making suggestions for Chapter 7. Gail Thomas and Naomi Nurse helped with the administrative work.

Excerpts from the following materials appear with the kind permission of the copyright holders.

Bell, Derrick, Bakke, Minority Admissions, and the Usual Price of Racial Remedies, 67 Calif. L. Rev. 1 (1979). Copyright © 1979, California Law Review, Inc., Reprinted by Permission.

Bell, Derrick, Black Colleges and the Desegregation Dilemma, prepared for inclusion in a 1980 report on black colleges by the Ford Foundation's Private Black Colleges Program, Morris T. Keeton, Director.

Bell, Derrick, Brown v. Board of Education and the Interest-Convergence Dilemma, 93 Harv. L. Rev. 518 (1980). Copyright © 1980 by the Harvard Law Review Association. Reprinted by permission.

Bell, Derrick, Racial Remediation: An Historical Perspective on Current Conditions, 52 Notre Dame Lawyer 5 (1976). Reprinted with permission. Copyright © by the Notre Dame Lawyer, University of Notre Dame.

Bell, Derrick, The Legacy of W.E.B. Du Bois: A Rational Model for Achieving Public School Equity for America's Black Children, 11 Creighton L. Rev. 409 (1978).

Bell, Derrick, The Racial Imperative in American Law, originally published in The Age of Segregation: Race Relations in the South, 1890-1945, published by the University Press of Mississippi in 1978. This material is used with the permission of the University Press of Mississippi.

Bunche, Ralph J., A Critical Analysis of the Tactics and Programs of Minority Groups. The Journal of Negro Education, Vol. 4, No. 3, The Courts and the Negro Separate School (July 1935). Reprinted by permission of the JSTOR Archive, a trusted digital repository providing for long-term preservation and access to leading academic journals and scholarly literature from around the world.

Freeman, Alan, Legitimizing Racial Discrimination Through Antidiscrimination Law: A Critical Review of Supreme Court Doctrine, 62 Minn. L. Rev. 1049 (1978).

Frymer, Paul, Uneasy Alliances: Race and Party Competition in America, Princeton University Press (1999). Copyright © 1999 by Princeton University Press. Reprinted by permission of Princeton University Press.

Newton, Nell Jessup, Federal Power over Indians: Its Sources, Scope, and Limitations, 132 U. Pa. L. Rev. 195 (1984). Copyright © 1984 University of Pennsylvania Law Review.

Sturm, Susan and Guinier, Lani, The Future of Affirmative Action: Reclaiming the Innovative Ideal, 84 Calif. L. Rev. 953, 957 (July 1996). Copyright © 1996, California Law Review, Inc. Reprinted by permission.

Williams, Patricia, The Alchemy of Race and Rights, Harvard University Press, 58-59 (1991). Reprinted by permission.

The pen and ink drawing in the Dedication is by Bernice Loss. It is based on a photograph of the 1968 Olympic victory of John Carlos and Tommie Smith and was used in the Loss work by permission of United Press International.

Chapter 1

American Racism and the Relevance of Law

For weal or for woe, the destiny of the colored race in this country is wrapped up with our own; they are to remain in our midst, and here spend their years and here bury their fathers and finally repose themselves. We may regret it. It may not be entirely compatible with our taste that they should live in our midst. We cannot help it. Our forefathers introduced them, and their destiny is to continue among us; and the practical question which now presents itself to us is as to the best mode of getting along with them.[1]

§1.1 THE CURRENT RELEVANCE OF DR. RALPH BUNCHE'S RACIAL ASSESSMENT

The year was 1866. Speaking to his Senate colleagues, Senator Jacob Merritt Howard, abolitionist and key architect of the Fourteenth Amendment, urged Radical and Conservative Republicans alike to confront the challenge posed by the presence of the former slaves "in our midst." Grudging rather than generous, conciliatory rather than crusading, Senator Howard's statement contemplated sanctuary rather than equality for those formerly enslaved and now an unwelcome addition to the citizenry.

Senator Howard's candidly expressed apprehension about the prospect of blacks living free in white America continues to echo through contemporary civil rights decisions in which the measure of relief from discrimination blacks are able to gain is determined less by the character of harm suffered by blacks than the degree of disadvantage the relief sought will impose on whites. This unacknowledged formula, seldom mentioned outside academic settings, has resulted in an increasing number of black people being left outside the law's protection and placed at risk at a time when this country's economic and political policies are in great turmoil.

That the current status of blacks leaves little room for optimism and the future, barring unforeseen developments, could prove far worse would not be a surprise to

---

1. II Encyclopedia of the American Constitution 761 (Leonard W. Levy, Kenneth L. Karst & Dennis J. Mahoney eds., 1986).

Dr. Ralph J. Bunche, who as a young political scientist in 1935 predicted that the Constitution was an unreliable source for protection of black peoples' rights and lives. Referring to John Stuart Mill's treatise, *Representative Government*, Bunche felt the British philosopher and political economist had been proven wrong in asserting as to different racial groups of whites, that it was impossible to build up a democracy out of the intermingling of racially differentiated peoples. Bunche, though, found much evidence supporting Mill's statement

> when related to the intermixture of white and black populations in the same society. Throughout the world today, wherever whites and blacks are present in any significant numbers in the same community, democracy becomes the tool of the dominant elements in the white population in their ruthless determination to keep the blacks suppressed.[1]

Providing reason for Senator Howard's pessimism, Dr. Bunche wrote:

> The significant fact is that democracy, while never offered in any large measure to the black populations of the world, has been extended to the great masses of the working-class population only so long as it was employed by them as a harmless device involving no real threat to the increasing control of the society by the ruling classes. Minority populations, and particularly racial minorities, striving to exist in any theoretically democratic modern society, are compelled to struggle strenuously for even a moderate participation in the democratic game. Minority groups are always with us. . . . [W]hatever the nature of the minority group, its special problems may always be translated in terms of political, economic, and social disadvantages. Group antagonisms develop, which are fed by mythical beliefs and attitudes of scorn, derision, hate, and discrimination. These serve as effective social barriers and fix the social, and hence, the political and economic status of the minority population. The mental images or verbal characterizations generally accepted as descriptive of the members of the particular racial group, . . . give rise to stereotypes which are of the greatest significance in race relations. These race distinctions, along with similar class and caste distinctions, are so thoroughly rooted in our social consciousness as to command serious attention in any consideration of programs whose objective is equitable treatment for minority racial groups.[2]

§1.1   1. Ralph J. Bunche, A Critical Analysis of the Tactics and Programs of Minority Groups, in *The Journal of Negro Education,* Vol. 4, No. 3, The Courts and the Negro Separate School (July 1935), pp. 308-320. In 1948, Bunche was on a United Nations peace-keeping mission. Count Folke Bernadotte, the mediator he had been assisting, was assassinated. Bunche stepped in and spent the next six months helping to develop armistice agreements that were signed by Israel and Egypt, Jordan, Lebanon, and Syria. In 1950 Bunche was persuaded to accept the Nobel Peace Prize; he initially refused, feeling the honor belonged not to an individual, but to the United Nations. See, http://spotlight.ucla.edu/alumni/ralph-bunche.

   See also Amy L. Chua, The Paradox of Free Market Democracy: Rethinking Development Policy, 41 Harv. Int'l L.J. 287, (2000). In explaining how democracy can coexist within a capitalist society, Professor Chin cites, *inter alia,* racism (and the creation of a large racial underclass) has arguably made poor and working-class whites feel better about their relative plight, giving them a consoling sense of superiority and status vis-à-vis African Americans, Hispanic Americans, and other groups of color perceived (in many senses correctly) as "the sediment of the American stratificational order." Id. at 306.

   2. To see how the generally believed stereotypes of Indians as uncivilized savages totally ignorant of the value of the lands they occupy, gained acceptance and provided support for Supreme Court decisions from Chief Justice John Marshall to Chief Justice William Rehnquist, see Robert Williams, Like a Loaded Weapon (2005), discussed in Chapter 11.

The perceived economic competition blacks pose for whites, particularly those in the working class, Bunche contends, means that racial prejudice is explainable in economic terms. In addition, "The cultural, political and economic degradation of the Negro also gave the poor-whites their sole chance for 'status.'"[3] While deemed the "minority class," blacks are that in only the narrow racial sense, and otherwise are "subject to the same divisive influences impinging upon the life of every other group in the nation." This poses a dilemma for black leadership that, Bunche complains have eschewed class concerns and:

> traditionally put its stress on the element of race; it has attributed the plight of the Negro to a peculiar racial condition. Leaders and organizations alike have had but one end in view — the elimination of "discrimination against the race."
>
> This attitude has been reflected in the tactics that they have employed to correct abuses suffered by their group. They have not realized that so long as this basic conflict in the economic interests of the white and black groups persists, and it is a perfectly natural phenomenon in a modern industrial society, neither prayer, nor logic, nor emotional or legal appeal can make much headway against the stereotyped racial attitudes and beliefs of the masses of the dominant population. The significance of this to the programs of the corrective and reform organizations working on behalf of the group should be obvious. The most that such organizations can hope to do is to devote themselves to the correction of the more flagrant specific cases of abuse, which because of their extreme nature may exceed even a prejudiced popular approval; and to a campaign of public enlightenment concerning the merits of the group they represent and the necessity for the establishment of a general community of interest among all groups in the population.[4]

The political and economic opportunity that minority groups struggle for, Bunche argued, received more lip service than support from democratic liberalism as those principles were applied in countries whose economies were so ordered that "great masses of the populations were presupposed to be non-property-holding workingmen, whose opportunities for obtaining property became progressively less easy, and whose economic status was increasingly less certain as a result of technological and financial developments within the economic structure, resulting in periodic unemployment, loss of income and dissipation of meager savings."[5] While the American Dream was energized here by the presence of the frontier with free land and rich natural resources, the opportunity to "go West" was never widely open to the Negro population, a fact that forestalled development of class stratification and consciousness of it as found among whites.

The assumptions of political freedom for individuals: equality before the law, the right to free speech, press, religion, assemblage and movement, and

3. See, e.g., David Roediger, The Wages of Whiteness: Race and the Making of the American Working Class (1991).

4. Bunche, supra note 1, at 311.

5. Id at 312. Bunche cites without explanation a lengthy internal conflict within the NAACP during the mid-1930s over whether its efforts should be directed toward challenging the legality of racial segregation through the courts, the view of lawyers and much of the group's board of directors, or of improving the economic status of Negroes through building business enterprises and internal self organization to push for nondiscriminatory public policies though not necessarily through erad-ication of the color-line. See, Mark Tushnet, The NAACP: Legal Strategy Against Segregated Edu-cation, 1925-1950, 6-12 (1987 ed.).

participation in government through the ballot, were systematically denied to blacks when Bunche wrote his essay in the mid-1930s, and even 70 some years later, cannot be assumed, particularly the right to vote without that vote being challenged, denied, or diluted. To gain their civil rights, Bunche listed the available options. He argued that violence was not available both because of numbers, and the scattered nature of the population. Significantly, he adds that as the failed efforts of Communists to organize blacks for revolutionary activities show clearly: "the Negro masses are so lacking in radical class consciousness; they are so conservative and deeply imbued with a peasant psychology and the lingering illusion of the American Dream, that any possibility of large-scale identification of the Negro population with revolutionary groups can be projected only in the future."[6]

At the time in which he was writing, Bunche saw little hope in racial separation such as the Marcus Garvey "back to Africa" Movement, economic passive resistance of the Gandhi mode such as boycotts of the "don't buy where you can't work" variety, and non-violent resistance that had not then had success in India with its much greater potential. Its most serious flaw, Bunche felt, was the fact that "the Negro is not out of a job simply because he is a Negro, but, rather because the economic system finds itself incapable of affording an adequate number of jobs for all—in fact, its productive system is so organized that it must have a marginal labor supply. But the most serious defect in the rationalization of this tactic is in the fact that such programs widen still further the already deplorable gap between the white and black working-classes of the nation, by boldly placing the competition for jobs on a strictly racial basis. If the doctrine were carried out to its logical conclusion, it would necessarily advocate that Negro workers be organized as a great strike-breaking group."[7] Based on this view, Bunche on one hand might have predicted the opposition by many whites to affirmative action programs that led to the eventual denial of their validity by the courts. Because, as with affirmative action programs, whites would perceive them as in economic competition with them, Bunche dismissed as unrealistic the then attractive views of Booker T. Washington that blacks might develop a separate economic community within the white world outside that controls credit, basic industry, and the state. On the other hand, black groups, particularly churches, have made impressive gains in building and operating schools, health clinics, senior citizen housing, drug rehabilitation programs, and other much-needed facilities in black communities.[8] These efforts offer services that neither government nor private enterprise are providing and thus are not viewed as a threat to major industries.

Bunche argues that there are political barriers facing those who place reliance on the ballot and the courts as the means to gain social justice for blacks. He explains:

> The inherent fallacy of this belief rests in the failure to appreciate the fact that the instruments of the state are merely the reflections of the political and economic

6. Bunche, supra note 1, at 312.
7. Id at 314.
8. See, e.g., John J. DiIulio, Jr., Living Faith: The Black Church Outreach Tradition, Jeremiah Project Report, No. 3, 1998, http://www.manhattan-institute.org/html/jpr-98-3.htm.

ideology of the dominant group, that the political arm of the state cannot be divorced from its prevailing economic structure, whose servant it must inevitably be.

Leaders of the American Negro such as the National Association for the Advancement of Colored People, have conducted a militant fight under this illusory banner. They have demanded full equality for the Negro, involving the eradication of all social, legal, and political restrictions tending to draw a line of distinction between the black citizen and the white. The Negro, like the white American, is to quaff the full draught of eighteenth-century democratic liberalism. The Negro individual citizen must have every right boasted by the individual white citizen, including the franchise, freedom of economic opportunity (consisting chiefly of the right to employment without discrimination), the right to accommodations in public places and on common carriers, the right to voluntary choice of his place of residence without involuntary segregation, the right to jury service, and equal expenditures of public funds for education and other public services."[9]

When he wrote, 90 percent of Southern blacks were barred from the ballot. Today, blacks' right to vote is more established in law than protected in fact. Chapter 6 reviews a seemingly endless array of tactics used to limit the black vote and its significance on elections. The assumption, then as now, that the Constitution will protect the rights set out in its provisions, Bunche contends ignores the quite significant fact that the Constitution is a very flexible instrument and that, in the nature of things, it cannot be anything more than the controlling elements in the American society wish it to be. In other words, this charter of the black man's liberties can never be more than our legislatures, and, in the final analysis, our courts, wish it to be. And, what these worthy institutions wish it to be can never be more than what American public opinion wishes it to be. Unfortunately, so much of American public opinion is seldom enlightened, sympathetic, tolerant or humanitarian. Too often (in Bunche's day and not impossible in ours) it resembles mob violence.[10]

Because so much of white society ranges from uncaring to hostile, Bunche finds that civil rights groups look for support from aspects of the dominant society with civil libertarian leanings, efforts that "depend upon its ability to create a sympathetic response to its appeals among influential elements in the controlling population."[11] Success in the long run, Bunche asserts, requires black groups to soften their militancy and conform to the genteel programs that cultivate the good will of the white upper classes. This results in the civil rights groups being

> forced into a policy of conciliation with the enlightened, i.e., the ruling interests, in the dominant group. They must rely upon sympathetic understanding and fair play in their campaigns for social justice, . . . They can be militant, but only politely so; they can attack, but not too harshly; they must entreat, bargain, compromise and capitulate in order to win even petty gains. They must politely play the game according to the rules even though they have no stakes.[12]

This assessment would seem harsh and inaccurate during the civil rights era of the post-*Brown* 1950s and 1960s, but in more recent decades, funding and support

9. Bunche, supra note 1, at 315.
10. Id at 316.
11. Id.
12. Id.

from government, corporate, and foundation sources has been harder to come by even though civil rights policies have relied on seeking progress through the courts and legislatures as opposed to more militant direct action measures that they generally neither defend nor support.

Dr. Bunche saved his most trenchant criticism for the courts and the faith that civil rights groups place in them. Again, his condemnation would seem inappropriate given the civil rights victories racked up during the civil rights era. Many of those gains, though, have been watered down, reinterpreted, and overruled with the result that Bunche's assessment gains a validity that it actually never lost. He contends that:

> the Negro in the United States is a special ward of the Supreme Court. The Negro has had countless experiences which sufficiently establish the fact that he has rights only as this august tribunal allows them, and even these are, more often than not, illusory. It is only inadvertently that the courts, like the legislatures, fail to reflect the dominant mass opinion. It must be futile, then, to expect these agencies of government to afford the Negro protection for rights which are denied to him by the popular will. Moreover, even could we optimistically hope that the Supreme Court, in its theoretical legal detachment, would go counter to the popular will and wipe out the proscriptions imposed on the Negro, as it appeared to do in the *Scottsboro* cases,[13] the condition of the group could not be greatly changed. In the first place, American experience affords too many proofs that laws and decisions contrary to the will of the majority cannot be enforced. In the second place, the Supreme Court can effect no revolutionary changes in the economic order, and yet the status of the Negro, as that of other groups in the society, is fundamentally fixed by the functioning and the demands of that order. The very attitudes of the majority group which fix the Negro in his disadvantaged position are part and parcel of the American economic and political order.[14]

Bunche reviews the laws and decisions as they stood when he was writing. Many of those rulings upholding racial segregation were struck down thorough reinterpretations of the Civil War Amendments, thereby rendering his examples of the subordination of black rights to Court rulings both outdated as to the cases he discusses, but very relevant to current legal precedents. For today, as then, there is "the tendency of the Supreme Court to detach itself from political reality when questions involving Negro rights are concerned and to resort to legal fictions. . . ." Citing an early case upholding the Texas Primary that denied blacks access to the vote, Bunche could as well be speaking of the Court's decisions in several of the voter apportionment decisions discussed in Chapter 6. In his view, even

> winning . . . minor and too often illusory victor[ies] now and then, are essentially inefficacious in the long run. They lead up blind alleys and are chiefly programs of escape. No minority group should relent in the most determined fight for its rights, but its leadership should recognize the limitations of opportunistic and socially blind policies. The only realistic program for any minority group in modern America is one

---

13. Powell v. Alabama, 287 U.S. 45 (1932); Norris v. Alabama, 294 U.S. 587 (1935). In these *cause célèbre* cases, the Court established the right to counsel in state and federal courts by overturning convictions of nine young blacks convicted of raping a white woman on a freight train.

14. Bunche, supra note 1, at 317.

which is based upon an intelligent analysis of the problems of the group in terms of the broad social forces which determine its condition. Certainly no program of opportunism and no amount of idealism can overcome or control these forces.[15] The only hope for the improvement in the condition of the masses of any American minority group is the hope that can be held out for the betterment of the masses of the dominant group. Their basic interests are identical and so must be their programs and tactics.[16]

Here, Bunche advocates what he believes is the only meaningful strategy for the advancement of blacks without mentioning either the failures of the Populist Movement of the 1890s, about which he certainly knew, nor the Poor People's March that Martin Luther King, Jr. was seeking to organize at his death in 1968. Yet Dr. Bunche would be pleased to cite the Texas ten percent plan as an example of blacks and poorer whites coming together to support a legislative initiative that would aid both.

In the wake of a court decision, Hopwood v. Texas,[17] barring Texas colleges from considering race or ethnicity in their admissions process, the Texas legislature enacted legislation requiring Texas flagship colleges to admit students from any Texas high school who had graduated in the upper ten percent of their class. The plan assured continued racial diversity, but also enabled whites from rural high schools to gain admission to the top Texas schools from which they had been rejected in favor of applicants with more impressive credentials based on traditional measures who had not been among the top ten percent in their more competitive high schools. Complaints from the University of Texas and from parents in suburban districts led to a major effort to scale back the plan in 2007, but again white legislators from rural districts joined with black and Latino colleagues to defeat the change.[18] Professors Lani Guinier and Gerald Torres view the Texas ten percent plan as representing the

---

15. Contemporary scholars have suggested more circumspectly what Bunche said directly. Judge Richard Posner, a major constitutional scholar, wrote:

> Almost a quarter century as a federal appellate judge has convinced me it is rarely possible to say with a straight face of a Supreme Court constitutional decision that it was decided correctly or incorrectly. He says that is because the most important pronouncements of the Court were invariably political in nature, rather than strictly legal. Such cases can be decided only on the basis of a political judgment, and a political judgment cannot be called right or wrong by reference to legal norms.

Richard A. Posner, Foreword: A Political Court, 119 Harv. L. Rev. 32 (2005).

Yale Law Professor Bruce Ackerman, a major figure in constitutional law, agreed with the dissent of Justice Stevens who condemned the majority's decision in Bush v. Gore to halt the Florida recount as a blatantly partisan act, without any legal basis whatsoever. Ackerman's agreement was reluctant because, he wrote, "this view goes against the grain of my entire academic career, which has been one long struggle against the slogan that law is just politics." Bruce Ackerman, The Court Packs Itself, Vol. 12, No. 3 The American Prospect 48 (Feb. 12, 2001).

And Justice Sandra Day O'Connor wrote that "real change comes principally from attitudinal shifts in the population at large. Rare indeed is the legal victory in court or legislature that is not a careful byproduct of an emerging social consensus." Sandra Day O'Connor, The Majesty of the Law: Reflections of a Supreme Court Justice, 166 (2003).

16. Bunche, supra note 1, at 320.

17. 78 F.3d 992 (5th Cir. 1996).

18. Inside Higher Ed., http://www.insidehighered.com/news/2007/05/29/percent. Rep. Helen Giddings was quoted in Texas press accounts as saying that under the current system, "You don't have to be an athlete today, you don't have to be related to a large donor today, you don't have to be wealthy today, you don't have to be a legacy today. You have to perform."

kind of shared interest between blacks and whites that can further social and economic policies of value to both.[19]

As this volume goes to press, Senator Barack Obama appears to have adopted Dr. Bunche's position as he seeks the Democratic nomination to run for president of the United States. His campaign urges voters to unite across traditional lines of race and party by emphasizing the similarity of their needs, the dangers they face, and the potential in unity for achieving reforms both abroad and at home.

§1.2   COLOR-BLIND CONSTITUTIONALISM:
A REDISCOVERED RATIONALE

Dr. Bunche's prophetic essay reviewed in the previous section accurately predicted the adoption and later the rejection of constitutional interpretations seemingly intended to remedy racial injustices. The cases discussed in this section are reviewed in more detail in the chapters that follow, but it is worthwhile to compare Bunche's analysis with this summary of how under public pressure, the Court has reinterpreted the Fourteenth Amendment back to its once colorblind roots. While from its enactment in 1866 until more than three decades into the 20th century, the Fourteenth Amendment had provided scant protection against the prejudicial policies and practices that so circumscribed black lives, the potential for improvement came, significantly enough, in one of a series of "New Deal" cases in which the Court began rejecting the "right of contract" ideology of the Lochner era.[1] In United States v. Carolene Products Co.,[2] the Court in upholding a challenged federal law enacted to protect public health, indicated that such economic regulations need meet only a minimum standard of rational review meaning it was neither arbitrary nor irrational. In its now famous footnote 4, Justice Harlan Stone suggested that the Court might apply a more exacting standard in reviewing legislation aimed at discrete and insular minorities who lack the normal protections of the political process. Also it provided that this heightened scrutiny, later designated as strict scrutiny, would be applied to legislation within a specific prohibition of the Constitution and the first ten amendments deemed protected under the Fourteenth Amendment.

In its first application of the strict scrutiny standard, Korematsu v. United States,[3] the Court found that the government had shown a compelling state interest justifying the relocation of Japanese Americans during World War II. Some two decades later in Loving v. Virginia,[4] the Court applied the strict scrutiny standard

---

19. See Lani Guinier & Gerald Torres, The Miner's Canary: Enlisting Race, Resisting Power, Transforming Democracy (2002).

§1.2   1. Lochner v. New York, 198 U.S. 45 (1905). The fiction that workers and company owners stood on mutual ground when negotiating job contracts was not unlike the fiction in Plessy v. Ferguson that "separate but equal" provided blacks with all the protection required of the states.

2. 304 U.S. 144 (1938).

3. 323 U.S. 214 (1944).

4. 388 U.S. 9 (1967).

to invalidate a law barring marriage between two races. For more than a decade thereafter, few racial classifications deemed to disadvantage blacks or other minorities were able to show the compelling state interest required to survive. Classifications that disadvantaged blacks but did not mention race directly and arguably were intended to achieve some legitimate non-racial goal were another matter. They are usually approved unless the civil rights challengers are able to introduce proof that they were intentionally intended to discriminate, a very difficult task.[5] Before long, the only challenged racial classifications were by whites to affirmative action policies. These challenges contended that, far from benign, affirmative action programs are invidious measures anathema to the principles of equality embodied in the Fifth and Fourteenth Amendments of the Constitution. These arguments began to prevail as the Court determined to apply the strict scrutiny standard to racial classifications whether they were overtly intended to discriminate or were efforts to remedy past discriminatory patterns.[6] As a result, any white claiming that an affirmative action policy is a form of reverse discrimination can challenge that policy and, in effect, becomes the "discrete and insular minority" entitled to special judicial protection. While a consensus in support of certain race-based affirmative action programs among business, military, and civic leaders was crucial to the closely divided 5-4 decision upholding the University of Michigan Law School's admissions program,[7] the Court's new majority, following Justice O'Connor's retirement, has now concluded that the validity of all racial classifications must be measured by the strict scrutiny standard.[8] Currently the Court's equality jurisprudence resonates with the rhetoric of "color-blindness." In the idealized color-blind environment envisioned by the Court majority, race loses its legal, social, and political significance. Lawmakers, they find, have no reason to pass race-based laws and policies even for racial remediation reasons because social inequality would reflect merit alone rather than any degree of individual or systematic racial discrimination. But even the current Court, distrustful as it is of all racial classifications, recognizes, at least theoretically, compelling reasons for narrowly tailored race-based measures. Still, because race-specific antidiscrimination strategies are so difficult to justify under strict scrutiny, critical race theorists argue that jurisprudence based on color-blindness serves to reify rather than repair existing racial disparities. Their writings expose how the rules governing equal protection review actually disadvantage communities of color.[9]

---

5. See, e.g., Washington v. Davis, 426 U.S. 229 (1976); McCleskey v. Kemp, 481 U.S. 279 (1987).

6. See, e.g., Adarand Constructors, Inc. v. Pena, 515 U.S. 200 (1995).

7. Grutter v. Bollinger, 539 U.S. 306 (2003).

8. Parents Involved v. Seattle School District No. 1; Meredith v. Jefferson County Board of Education, No. 05-908, 551 U.S. __ (2007).

9. See, e.g., Tanya Kateri Hernandez, Multiracial Discourse: Racial Classifications in an Era of Color-Blind Jurisprudence, 57 Md. L. Rev. 97 (1998); Neil Gotanda, A Critique of "Our Constitution Is Color-Blind," 44 Stan. L. Rev. 1 (1991); Duncan Kennedy, A Cultural Pluralist Case for Affirmative Action in Legal Academia, 1990 Duke L.J. 705; Garry Peller, Race-Consciousness, 1990 Duke L.J. 758; Derrick Bell, Xerces and the Affirmative Action Mystique, 57 Geo. Wash. L. Rev. 1597 (1989); Charles Lawrence III, The Id, the Ego, and Equal Protection: Reckoning with Unconscious Racism, 39 Stan. L. Rev. 317 (1987).

Critical race theorists view the intent requirement as a double-edged sword. Kimberle Crenshaw acknowledges the need to subject overt acts of discrimination to constitutional review in order to discourage the express exploitation of minorities.[10] She recognizes as well that the adoption of formal race-neutrality eventually made it impossible for southern state legislators to continue a post-Reconstruction Jim Crow regime bent on expressly denying persons of color the same opportunities as whites to vote, attend school, obtain employment, own a home, enter business transactions, or engage in any number of social, political, or economic activities. In this respect, the prohibition on intentional discrimination is a positive advancement. That said, Crenshaw is concerned that the intent requirement makes it difficult to address the conditions of inequality that arise when lawmakers pursue legitimate race-neutral objectives despite their impact on minorities. One example might be a municipality's decision to locate a toxic waste dump in a community with particularly low property values. This might make sense from an economic perspective, but it poses problems from an equality perspective if such areas are disproportionately inhabited by persons of color.

Another concern is that the intent requirement makes it nearly impossible to challenge the most potent forms of racial discrimination that emerge from the subconscious level. The influence of unconscious racism is the theme of Charles Lawrence III's seminal work, "The Id, the Ego, and Equal Protection: Reckoning with Unconscious Racism."[11] To Lawrence, the requirement of intent is misplaced because society already discourages overt acts of discrimination. As a result, conscious acts of racial bias are rare, readily identified, and easily remedied. White supremacy nonetheless continues in the form of government decisions influenced by racial myths and stereotypes. Despite the damage these decisions inflict on persons of color, however, they are difficult to identify and even harder to remedy through an equal protection claim absent some indication of conscious motivation.[12] Lawrence uses the case of Arlington Heights v. Metropolitan Housing Development Corp.[13] to make his point. In that case, a predominantly white upper-middle-class suburb blocked the construction of a low-income housing development by refusing to amend a single-family zoning restriction to permit construction of multifamily dwellings. A group of black plaintiffs sued town officials because the zoning decision effectively excluded racial minorities from the neighborhood. The Supreme Court agreed that the zoning decision had that effect but rejected the equal protection claim because the plaintiffs did not show that town officials acted with the intent to maintain a segregated community. Subtler forms of racial bias nonetheless could have been at play.[14] As Lawrence explains, perhaps town officials predicted that aesthetics, economic stability, and environmental benefits associated with single-family zoning would stabilize, if not increase, property values. When it came time to vote on the proposed zoning

---

10. Kimberle Crenshaw, Race, Reform and Retrenchment: Transformation and Legitimation in Anti-Discrimination Law, 101 Harv. L. Rev. 1331, 1376-1382 (1988).
11. Lawrence, supra note 9.
12. Id. at 318-344.
13. 429 U.S. 252 (1977).
14. Lawrence, supra note 9, at 347-349.

amendment, town officials most likely acted in their own interest by ignoring or at least dismissing any concern that existing zoning patterns discouraged integration from poor minorities.

A racist subtext might be operating in another manner. Suppose again that town officials were genuinely interested in increasing property values and maintained the restriction on multifamily units in order to discourage integration from poor residents. The problem occurs if they reflexively associated poverty with minorities but would have lifted the zoning restriction had they associated poverty with a certain subpopulation of whites.[15] Race may even be a factor if the zoning restriction was preserved simply because residents never expressed an interest in the construction of multifamily units. It could be that white residents chose not to champion multifamily zoning for fear that the construction of such homes would encourage integration from racial minorities. In none of these scenarios are town officials consciously concerned with a sudden influx of minority residents, but to Lawrence, the influence of unconscious racial bias is apparent. Because this bias occurs outside the realm of the conscious, however, it is difficult to identify and thus evades review under a jurisprudence that requires proof of intent.

Other scholars have examined the workings of unconscious racism in additional contexts.[16] Tanya Kateri Hernandez used McCleskey v. Kemp[17] as her backdrop for examining how unconscious racism impacts the criminal justice system to the detriment of black defendants.[18] In *McCleskey*, a black defendant charged with murdering a white victim claimed that Georgia's capital sentencing process discriminated against persons of color in violation of the Eighth and Fourteenth Amendments. To support his claim, McCleskey introduced the "Baldus Study," which analyzed the effect of over 230 variables on capital sentencing outcomes in more than two thousand Georgia murder cases. According to the study, the likelihood that a black defendant would receive the death penalty increased significantly when the victim was white.[19] Even the Court acknowledged that the presence of a white victim was the most influential factor leading to the imposition of a death sentence. Nonetheless, it brushed aside the connection as a mere "discrepancy that appears to correlate with race" and rejected McCleskey's claim because he could not identify a causal connection between racial bias and the outcome of his case specifically.[20]

Hernandez's criticism demonstrates how the preoccupation with intentional discrimination overlooks how investigators, jurors, prosecutors, and legislators are influenced by racial stereotypes. In *McCleskey*, police officers might have embraced the myth of black criminality and chosen, intentionally or not, to dismiss leads pointing to other suspects. Jurors influenced by the same precept might have

---

15. Id. at 243-244.
16. See, e.g., Timothy Davis, Racism in Athletics: Subtle Yet Persistent, 21 U. Ark. L. Rev. 881 (1999); Angela J. Davis, Prosecution and Race: The Power and Privilege of Discretion, 67 Fordham L. Rev. 13 (1998); Richard Delgado, Words That Wound: A Tort Action for Racial Insults, Epithets and Name-Calling, 17 Harv. C.R.-C.L. L. Rev. 133 (1982).
17. 481 U.S. 279 (1987).
18. Hernandez, supra note 9.
19. *McCleskey*, supra note 5, at 287.
20. Id. at 312.

returned a guilty verdict without adequately weighing exculpatory evidence. Alternatively, they might have intended to return a death sentence only if the crime turned out to be excessively violent or the defendant impervious to rehabilitation. Confronted by a black defendant, they might have been convinced that such was the case with McCleskey. The prosecutor's decision to seek the death penalty also might have been driven by a subconscious aversion to black defendants if she would have pursued a less drastic course in a case involving a white defendant and black victim. Even legislators supporting Georgia's capital sentencing statute might have been influenced by racial bias. Perhaps they saw death as an appropriate punishment for hardened criminals who commit heinous crimes but subconsciously associated that criteria with black defendants. They might have rejected capital punishment altogether had they envisioned its implementation against whites, or at least taken steps to ensure that it was administered fairly. Taken together, Hernandez suggests, these scenarios reflect government action that, while neutral on its face, is influenced significantly by racial stereotypes. She agrees with Lawrence, however, that the requirement of intent places these decisions beyond the reach of constitutional adjudication.

An additional concern is that the rule of consistency functions as an agent of white privilege because it undermines the most effective means of promoting racial equality. Demanding strict judicial scrutiny of all race-based classifications does more than just ignore precedent and the obvious difference between benign and invidious motives — points raised by the dissenting Justices in Adarand, Croson, and Gratz. According to critical race scholars, any rule that takes the same approach to invidious and benign racial classifications stabilizes existing racial disparities by making it exceedingly difficult for lawmakers to compensate victims of discrimination or promote diversity through direct race-based subsidies.

The late scholar Alan David Freeman accused the Court of taking a "means-oriented" approach to equal protection by improperly focusing on the types of laws enacted rather than the consequences of or purpose behind those laws.[21] If, as he explained, in all but the most limited of circumstances, attempts to promote equality must be race-neutral, this strategy effectively prohibits race-specific measures that operate to maintain white supremacy vis-à-vis the subordination of persons of color. It ignores the power of race-neutral rules that hasten the same result by operating on a playing field that is already skewed against minorities. On its face, a college admissions program that relies on grade point averages and standardized test scores is facially neutral but significantly advantages whites who consistently outperform nonwhites on these measures. This, of course, is less attributable to the inherent ability of white applicants than it is to the fact that, statistically, access to quality secondary educational institutions and the financial means to enroll in expensive test prep courses is more readily available to whites than nonwhites. Under the Court's consistency rule, this type of program would be labeled nondiscriminatory even though it creates racial disparities in higher education.

21. Alan David Freeman, Legitimizing Racial Discrimination Through Antidiscrimination Law: A Critical Review of Supreme Court Doctrine, in Critical Race Theory: The Key Writings That Formed the Movement 29 (Kimberle Crenshaw et al. eds., 1995) [hereinafter Key Writings].

Neil Gotanda weaves threads of Freeman's critique into his own criticism of consistency.[22] Like Freeman, Gotanda agrees that strict scrutiny, while an effective means of combating race-specific subordination strategies, does not address race-neutral agents of inequality. He attributes the Court's desire to subject all race-based classifications to a uniform standard to its "formal" understanding of race as a neutral concept devoid of any social or political meaning. Under this approach, race is perceived as nothing more than an arbitrary means of categorizing persons who share similar attributes such as skin color or ancestry. If this were true, a uniform strict scrutiny rule would be appropriate because racial identity would seldom provide any basis for allocating social, economic, educational, or occupational opportunities. Gotanda's concern is that approaching both benign and invidious race-based classifications with heightened suspicion treats race-neutrality as a present-day norm rather than a normative ideal yet to be achieved. In Gotanda's mind, this approach ignores the reality that race has been used as an agent of oppression against people of color but not whites. Gotanda explained the very different significance of race specifically for black and white citizens as follows:

> The history of segregation is not the history of blacks creating racial categories to legitimate slavery, nor is it a history of segregated institutions aimed at subordinating whites. Indeed, racial categories themselves, with the metaphorical themes of white racial purity and nonwhite contamination, have different meanings for blacks and whites. If judicial review is to consider the past and continuing character of racial subordination, then an affirmative action program aimed at alleviating the effects of racial subordination should not automatically be subject to the same standard of review as Jim Crow segregation laws. Judicial review using historical-race should be asymmetric because of the fundamentally different histories of whites and blacks.[23]

Gotanda finds the call for formal equality particularly ironic since that very concept gave rise to the racist "separate but equal" doctrine articulated in the 1896 case of Plessy v. Ferguson.[24] There, the Court upheld against an equal protection challenge a Louisiana statute that segregated black and white passengers on public train cars, reasoning that the statute subjected both groups to an equivalent restriction. Rather than single out one group of passengers for pernicious treatment, the statute merely required blacks to sit in one section of the train and whites to sit in another. The Court even went so far as to chastise blacks for reading too much into the segregation statute:

> [T]he underlying fallacy of the plaintiff's argument [consists of] the assumption that the enforced separation of the two races stamps the colored race with a badge of inferiority. If this be so, it is not by reason of anything found in the act, but solely because the colored race chooses to put that construction upon it.[25]

As the lone dissenter, Justice John Harlan rejected the formalist rationale invoked by the majority because he understood the equal protection guarantee to pertain to

22. Gotanda, supra note 9.
23. Id. at 49.
24. 163 U.S. 537 (1896).
25. Id. at 551.

actual real-life circumstances. To Harlan, the statute's obvious objective undermined that guarantee:

> Everyone knows that the statute in question had its origins in the purpose, not so much to exclude white persons from railroad cars occupied by blacks, as to exclude colored people from coaches occupied by or assigned to white persons. . . . The thing to accomplish was, under the guise of giving equal accommodation for whites and blacks, to compel the latter to keep to themselves while traveling in railroad passenger coaches.[26]

Justice Harlan considered racial segregation to be inherently subordinating even if it was the product of a race-neutral classification. Indeed, it was the specific subordinating purpose of the statute that influenced his now famous words:

> [I]n view of the Constitution, in the eye of the law, there is in this country no superior, dominant, ruling class of citizens. There is no caste here. Our Constitution is color-blind, and neither knows nor tolerates classes among citizens.[27]

Fifty years later, a unanimous Court would seize on Justice Harlan's rationale to strike down racially segregated public school systems in Brown v. Board of Education.[28] According to Gotanda, *Brown* followed the premise of Harlan's dissent in standing for the proposition that racial classifications, when used for the specific purpose of subordinating individual members of a particular racial category, violate equal protection. In this regard, it provided the original rationale for strict scrutiny. To say that either *Brown* or the *Plessy* dissent supports the broader proposition that race is always an irrelevant group characteristic, and, therefore, any use of race demands strict scrutiny, denies the distinct purpose and effect of the segregated policies under review in those cases.

Nonetheless, this is precisely what some members of today's Court have done. Although the unanimous decision in *Brown* and Justice Harlan's dissent in *Plessy* both turned on the purpose of the statute in question, the ideal of color-blindness is cited as justification for presuming that all classifications based on race are impermissible, even when the purpose of the classification is benign. For Gotanda, this approach misses the mark. Because the subordination of minority groups provided the rationale for skeptical review of race-based classifications in *Brown* and *Plessy*'s dissent, it does not necessarily follow that race-based classifications designed for the opposite purpose warrant the same level of scrutiny. Gotanda therefore views the consistency rationale as a violation of the central tenet of *Brown* that is eerily reminiscent of the mind-set that gave rise to the separate but equal doctrine Harlan repudiated in *Plessy*.

A third criticism of contemporary equality jurisprudence focuses on the protected expectations of "innocent" third parties. As discussed above, this concern is articulated in the second prong of strict scrutiny requiring narrow tailoring in the form of attempted "race-neutral alternatives." To critical race theorists, however,

---

26. Id. at 557.
27. Id. at 559.
28. 347 U.S. 483 (1954).

the concern for nonminority interests is nothing more than a strategy for protecting white privilege.[29] Professor Ann Ayers's scholarship raises this point.[30] Consider a race-neutral low-interest start-up loan program offered by a municipality to finance new businesses. Even if the program is intended to generate business competition from minority entrepreneurs as a remedy for past discrimination, entrepreneurs of any race would be eligible to apply for the subsidy. The remedy provided in the form of business start-up proceeds now becomes available to nonminorities who not only have never suffered race-based harm, but who very well might have benefited, albeit unwittingly, from discrimination against minorities. The program would nonetheless likely pass constitutional review as a facially neutral alternative to a race-specific remedy, even though it provides broader benefit than a race-specific program. It is in this manner, Ayers claims, that race-neutral solutions undermine the purpose of narrow tailoring, which is to streamline remedies to deserving victims.

Despite this seeming contradiction between the goal of narrow tailoring and the requirement of race-neutral alternatives, strict scrutiny requires lawmakers to consider programs that do not specifically rely on race to further compelling goals. Class-based remedies are one type of program that has gained attention. In the context of a university admissions program, for example, special consideration might be given to underprivileged applicants generally, regardless of their racial background. This approach would eliminate the burden nonminorities experience from race-based programs. The Court's decision in *Croson* implicitly endorsed class-based affirmative action when it suggested several race-neutral options the city council might have tried to increase minority contracting opportunities.

Given the correlation between race and income potential, it seems likely that class-based remedies provide a viable race-neutral mechanism for redressing the effects of prior discrimination. Still, many scholars find class-based remedies problematic in part because they are incapable of addressing the real conditions of minority exclusion.[31] Specifically, they argue that class-based affirmative action programs fail to take into account that race remains the best measure of social disadvantage — an even better measure than poverty. While it is true that poverty disproportionately affects persons of color, more whites than nonwhites actually live in poverty. As a result, class-based initiatives are more likely to benefit whites than persons in any other racial group.

Class-based programs might also rest on misperceptions about the dynamics of discrimination because it suggests that class is a more appropriate basis for affirmative action than race. This argument assumes that economic disadvantage poses a greater obstacle to achievement and is more difficult to transcend than the effects of racial bias. But empirical support has been cited for the opposite

29. Thomas Ross, Innocence and Affirmative Action, 43 Vand. L. Rev. 297, 299-300 (1990); Alan David Freeman, in Key Writings at 29.

30. Ann Ayers, Narrow Tailoring, 43 UCLA L. Rev. 1781, 1784-1793 (1996).

31. See, e.g., Richard Delgado, Ten Arguments Against Affirmative Action — How Valid?, 50 Ala. L. Rev. 135 (1998); Katheryn K. Russell, Affirmative (Re)Action: Anything But Race, 45 Am. U. L. Rev. 803 (1996); Jerome McCristal Culp, Jr., Colorblind Remedies and the Intersectionality of Oppression: Policy Arguments Masquerading as Moral Claims, 69 N.Y.U. L. Rev. 162 (1994).

conclusion.[32] Further, an argument can be made that a class-based approach prioritizes the integration of poor whites into the mainstream of society over middle class nonwhites, even though the law has expressly denied benefits from minorities of every economic background.[33]

In a similar vein, it is questionable whether any benefit would accrue from a class-based admission program if the policy selects from the pool of minority applicants those candidates with the smallest intersection of race and poverty. That is, a middle class Latina applicant would likely appear more qualified than a lower class Latina applicant owing to superior schooling and perhaps broader life experiences.[34] Accordingly, even though students with more diverse backgrounds in terms of race and class would be included in the applicant pool, they would likely be passed over for "more qualified" candidates. In this respect, class-based affirmative action programs disregard the intersection of race and poverty and thus support an "intra-race version of the status quo."[35] In the end, while class-based affirmative action programs might promote a measure of racial integration, they fail to address intraracial class distinctions. Class-based programs therefore provide one example of how race-neutral strategies protect the interests of nonminorities but fail to address systems of minority subordination.

Moving beyond a careful look at the relevant case decisions in the race area, it is appropriate to ask "Where do we stand in this first decade of the twenty-first century?" Professor Cheryl Harris, in a lengthy and insightful book review of *The Miner's Canary* by Professors Lani Guinier and Gerald Torres,[36] finds that the authors enter the "political debate about race at a particularly stark moment for progressive legal scholars and activists." She writes:

> For those who are committed to identifying and repairing deeply entrenched racial inequality, the ground is exceptionally hard. Indeed, this moment parallels another troubling period in American history and jurisprudence — that following Reconstruction and culminating in Plessy v. Ferguson.
>
> In at least two respects, contemporary race jurisprudence approximates the jurisprudence of the *Plessy* era. First, the current Court seems to have adopted the specific forms of racial erasure prominent in the period of so-called Southern redemption. It has called upon and resuscitated interpretations of the Equal Protection Clause that assign the federal government a subordinate role relative to the states in protecting the right to be free from discrimination.[37]

To support her statement, Harris reviews the Court's ruling in United States v. Morrison[38] striking down a section of the Violence Against Women Act that authorized civil actions against perpetrators of gender-motivated violence. By a 5-4 margin, the Court, asserting both dual federalism and state sovereignty concerns, found the federal government lacked the power to enforce antidiscrimination

32. See Delgado, supra note 31, at 140-141.
33. See Russell, supra note 31, at 809.
34. Id.
35. See Culp, supra note 31, at 178.
36. Cheryl Harris, Mining in Hard Ground (Book Review), 116 Harv. L. Rev. 2487 (2003).
37. Id. at 2489-2492. Harris's lengthy footnotes to the cited material are omitted.
38. 529 U.S. 598 (2000).

laws against individuals as opposed to state actors. Ignoring a voluminous record of the state's failure to protect victims of sexual assault, the Court reached back to the Civil Rights Cases,[39] which invalidated a public accommodations law as authority for its reading of the Fourteenth Amendment in *Morrison*. Harris continues:

> In so doing, the Court has embraced as well the same states' rights logic that constituted the bedrock of the segregationist platform. Second, like the *Plessy* Court in 1896, the current Court insists that all racial identities are symmetrical and hold no social significance. Indeed, under a regime of colorblindness, this Court has naturalized and evacuated race as a matter of law. The result is that the Court now treats all race-conscious efforts to eradicate racial inequality as conceptually equivalent to acts designed to install racial hierarchy.[40]

The implications of Professor Harris's assessment are staggering. I have revised a hypothetical used in an earlier edition of this text as a vehicle to explore what a state might do in an effort to remedy the harm its citizens are convinced was perpetrated by affirmative action programs on "innocent whites."

§1.3 Racism Hypo: The Freedom of Employment Act[1]

In the light of Professor Harris's summary of how the Supreme Court has reinterpreted legal doctrine, might a state utilize current understandings that have rendered all affirmative action programs vulnerable to enact a statute to even the playing field for white victims of race-based programs? Assume that the economy is in decline and the unemployment rolls have been growing at a rapid clip.

Its preamble advises that "The Freedom of Employment Act" will allay growing racial hostility by eliminating policies that undermine fundamental principles of fair play in a misguided and socially disruptive effort to remedy instances of past racial discrimination, problems that mostly disappeared with the enactment of civil rights laws three decades earlier. As introduced, the "corrective legislation" contains three provisions: First, it bans all affirmative action programs, including preferential recruitment, hiring, promotions, or other employment policies, practices, rules, and regulations, based in whole or in part on race, ethnicity, or proxy stand-ins for race.

Second, the measure establishes a rebuttable presumption that all persons of the African race or of Hispanic ethnicity who obtained their positions on or after January 1, 1970, did so through reasons that included consideration of their race or ethnicity and thus are suspect job holders who were actual or potential beneficiaries of affirmative action policies. As such, they hold their positions unfairly and without proof that their qualifications were superior to nonminority applicants who were not eligible for fair consideration under affirmative action policies.

---

39. 109 U.S. 3 (1883).
40. Harris, supra note 36, at 2491-2492.
§1.3 1. Derrick Bell, Gospel Choirs: Psalms of Survival in an Alien Land Called Home 74-76 (1996).

Under the legislation, such positions are rendered "vulnerable to challenge" by nonminority individuals (job challengers) not eligible for affirmative action preferences and presumed harmed by them. If any such challenger can show that he or she had superior training or experience at the time the job was filled, the presumed affirmative action beneficiary holding the position must, upon formal demand, vacate the position within 30 days. Judicial review, after the exhaustion of extensive administrative remedies, is available, but the cost must be borne by the suspect job holder. Job holders who contest bona fide challenges and are subsequently held not entitled to the jobs they hold, are liable for damages to the job challenger in the amount of job salary from the date 30 days after the challenge was filed.

Third, all those who held or were eligible to hold affirmative action positions are, upon surrender of those positions, required to find work within 30 days or be subject to induction into what is called "special service" and assigned to work deemed in the national interest. The government, at its discretion, can assign inducted workers to civilian employers with labor-intensive work deemed in the public interest, like environmental clean-up operations, farming (particularly harvests of fruits and vegetables), mining, reforestation projects, and the maintenance of parks and other public facilities.

This special service would be more like the military than the Civilian Conservation Corps of the 1930s. All those found physically and mentally able must go. The terms of service are for three years, except that failing to locate a job within 30 days of mustering out results in automatic extensions of service for another three years. This would not be slavery. Inducted workers will receive the minimum wage, and although deemed on duty at all times, they will normally work eight-hour days and will receive room, board, and recreational facilities at no cost.

A "dream team" of civil rights lawyers is organized to challenge the various provisions of the statute under existing legal precedents.

The state attorney general is assigned to defend the measure.

Assume that the district court granted a summary judgment motion submitted by the state, the court of appeals affirmed, and the Supreme Court has granted review. What arguments might be effective against the act?

Chapter 2

Race and American History

§2.1 AN OVERVIEW OF BLACK HISTORY

The materials in this chapter provide a foundation for the Ralph Bunche essay, an edited portion of which is set out in Chapter 1. There is little doubt though even less general acknowledgement that recognition, maintenance, and protection of slavery were the essential quid pro quo for the establishment of the world's first constitutional government committed to the protection of basic rights of liberty. As historian David Brion Davis put it, "Americans bought their independence with slave labor."[1] In a description of racial attitudes at the beginning of this nation that have a disturbingly contemporary ring, Professor Davis said, "What distinguished American colonists was their magnificent effrontery. They rejoiced to find their ideals of freedom and equality reflected in the actual social order, but resolutely denied that the social order rested on a 'mudsill' of slavery. . . ."[2] Reluctantly, most Americans reading these materials will accept them as "history," or even "unhappy history," but they will conclude with unjustified relief that it is of only peripheral relevance to current problems. While the facts in the Afrolantica hypo set out in §2.16 are in the realm of the fantastic, the effective planning of future strategies will require an assessment of future possibilities for African Americans quite like those debated by lawyers for Quad A and KFM. More indirectly, the debate assumes the presence of unacknowledged forces with strengths exceeding the authority of the Civil War Amendments and the civil rights statutes of both the nineteenth century and the twentieth century that dilute the protection from discrimination people of color can expect from laws and policies nominally intended to have this purpose.

The thrust of Ralph Bunche's essay is that blacks are uniquely destined to repeat history whether or not they earlier learned its lessons. The first Reconstruction experience, as bitter as it was, did not enable avoidance of what has become a

---

§2.1 1. David B. Davis, The Problem of Slavery in the Age of Revolution: 1770-1820, at 260, 262 (1975) (quoting Edmund S. Morgan, and stating that whites' "rhetoric of freedom was functionally related to the existence and in many areas to the continuation of Negro Slavery").
2. Id. at 261.

19

quite similar withdrawal of the rights and opportunities gained during the second Reconstruction of the 1960s.

But beyond the ebb and flow of racial progress lies the still viable and widely accepted (though seldom expressed) belief that America is a white country and blacks, particularly blacks as a group, are not entitled to the concern, resources, or even empathy that would be extended to similarly situated whites. Benjamin Franklin, though president of the Pennsylvania Abolition Society, wanted to send away all blacks and preserve America for "the lovely White and Red." Most antebellum abolitionists shared Franklin's view. Few were able to imagine a black, even one of the stature of Frederick Douglass's as the equal of themselves. It was this inability that led William Lloyd Garrison to split with Douglass, assertedly over policy differences, but actually over Douglass' insistence that blacks, not their white friends, should chart the course of their freedom efforts. Conflicts of precisely this character helped split the 1960s civil rights movement.

The materials that follow provide illustrations of these themes and others that will be recognizable both in the issues covered in subsequent chapters and in current racial developments too recent to be included here. A knowledge of history is an aid in identifying the continuing problems of race. History has thus far given little hope that any lasting solutions will be found soon. It is not that the white majority is rigidly opposed to enjoyment by blacks of rights and opportunities that whites accept as a matter of course; it is rather that for a complex of racial reasons, whites are not willing to alter traditional policies and conduct that effectively deprive blacks of these rights and opportunities. And it is this unwillingness that gives continuing validity to the observation of Reinhold Niebuhr made in 1932:

> It is hopeless for the Negro to expect complete emancipation from the menial social and economic position into which the white man has forced him merely by trusting in the moral sense of the white race. . . . However large the number of individual white men who do and who will identify themselves completely with the Negro cause, the white race in America will not admit the Negro to equal rights if it is not forced to do so. Upon that point one may speak with a dogmatism which all history justifies.[3]

A final question: What is it about Dr. Niebuhr's dire prediction that renders it as accurate a warning today as it was when it was written in 1932, long before this country adopted any of the myriad of civil rights laws and precedents? The history revealed here suggests three points about race and racism in American policy-making that are part of the answer.

1. What appears to be progress toward racial justice is, in fact, a cyclical process. Barriers are lowered in one era only to reveal a new set of often more sophisticated but no less effective policies that maintain blacks in a subordinate status. Their status as slaves from the seventeenth through much of the nineteenth centuries evolved into segregation after a brief Reconstruction period. And the post-*Brown* period in the mid-twentieth

---

3. Reinhold Niebuhr, Moral Man and Immoral Society 252-253 (1932).

century has brought us the "eerily awful equal opportunity era": "eerie" because some blacks seem to be making substantial moves into the mainstream; "awful" because so many blacks have disappeared into poverty with all its afflictions.

2. Significant progress for blacks is achieved when the goals of blacks coincide with the perceived needs of whites. For example, blacks gained their freedom when Abraham Lincoln recognized that ending slavery would help preserve the Union; job opportunities for blacks always improve during the labor shortages that exist during times of war. Alas, these gains seldom survive the crisis that created them.

3. Serious differences between whites are often resolved through compromises that sacrifice the rights of blacks. When the disputed presidential election of 1876 threatened a renewed civil war, a compromise was effected that withdrew Northern troops from the South condemning the newly freed blacks to their former masters. And when working class whites insisted on official segregation as the price of their continued support of elite policymakers, they gained a shaky status at the expense of blacks that the Supreme Court ratified in 1896. Of course, the classic sacrifice of blacks was that made by the Framers to secure Southern support for the Constitution. The original Constitution contained no less than several provisions intended to recognize and protect property in slaves. To say the least, this was a serious contradiction in a document intended to insure basic liberties to all.

§2.2 THE EMANCIPATION PROCLAMATION

What may be the earliest federal action on behalf of blacks, the Emancipation Proclamation, came in the only way that it could come, by executive action. It was generally assumed that the courts could not have ended slavery, which was condoned and protected in the Constitution (see §2.5). Congress feared the political consequences of abolishing slavery, and even Abraham Lincoln was far from enthusiastic about the executive order, which, with more than a little reluctance, he finally issued on January 1, 1863.[1] There is adequate evidence that Lincoln hated slavery. "If slavery is not wrong," he said, "nothing is wrong. I cannot remember when I did not so think and feel."[2] He had argued against slavery and denounced the Supreme Court's *Dred Scott* decision in his famous 1858 senatorial campaign debates with Stephen Douglas. As president, Lincoln both deplored slavery and urged the federal government to cooperate with states that moved toward gradual abolition through the establishment of a fund to compensate

§2.2   1. Lincoln's motivations are reviewed in Irving Dillard, The Emancipation Proclamation in the Perspective of Time, 23 Law in Transition 95 (1963).
2. Id. at 96.

the loss slave owners would suffer if their slaves were freed.[3] But when, during the Civil War, field commanders on their own initiative issued orders freeing slaves in the areas of their military operations, Lincoln vetoed their actions. In his view, the question of emancipation was political and not military. Abolitionists, who had been urging Lincoln to end slavery, denounced his action overruling field commanders. In a famous response to one of them, Horace Greeley, editor of the *New York Tribune*, Lincoln indicated that his primary goal was to win the war and preserve the Union. He wrote Greeley:

> I would save the Union. I would save it the shortest way under the Constitution. The sooner the national authority can be restored, the nearer the Union will be "the Union as it was." If there be those who would not save the Union unless they could at the same time save slavery, I do not agree with them. If there be those who would not save the Union unless they could at the same time destroy slavery, I do not agree with them. My paramount object in this struggle is to save the Union, and is not either to save or to destroy slavery. If I could save the Union without freeing any slave, I would do it; and if I could save it by freeing all the slaves, I would do it; and if I could save it by freeing some and leaving others alone, I would also do that. What I do about slavery and the colored race, I do because I do believe it helps to save the Union. I shall do less whenever I shall believe that what I am doing hurts the cause, and I shall do more whenever I shall believe doing more will help the cause. I shall try to correct errors when shown to be errors, and I shall adopt new views so fast as they shall appear to be true views.
>
> I have here stated my purpose according to my view of official duty; and I intend no modification of my oft-expressed personal wish that all men everywhere could be free.[4]

Lincoln's response to Greeley is significant for more than its candor. Here was, for perhaps the first and last time, a president of the United States acknowledging that the civil rights of blacks, even the basic right not to be a slave in a society dedicated to individual liberty, must take a lower priority to the preservation of the Union. The statement is important even considering the serious crisis posed by the Southern rebellion and the general belief of the time that blacks were not the intellectual or moral equals of whites. But in this instance, as in many others, the weight of events helped tilt the scales of self-interest toward the black cause.

The year 1862 was a difficult one for Lincoln. The war dragged on. Casualties and costs mounted. Military advisers urged emancipation as a means of disrupting the Southern economy, which, with its white manpower in arms, relied on slaves to keep the farms and plantations going. There were indications that foreign powers

3. Id. A joint resolution for compensated emancipation was passed by Congress in early 1862, but by that point in the hostilities, there was little interest in it. Congress did approve a measure freeing slaves in the District of Columbia and providing funds to send them abroad if deemed advisable.

4. Id. at 97-98. See also Speeches and Letters of Abraham Lincoln, 1832-1865 at 194-195 (Mervin Roe ed., 1919). Earlier, in his first inaugural speech, Lincoln had denied any purpose, legal right, or inclination "to interfere with the institution of slavery in the States where it exists." Id. at 165. Lincoln's position, that whether for political or legal reasons it was best not to interfere with slavery, quite likely reflected the prevailing view in the North. Abolitionists and blacks continued to press the matter, but the majority of whites were opposed to their position. The prevailing view in the North was that the Civil War was intended to preserve the Union, not to end slavery.

might both recognize the Confederacy and supply it with financial aid and arms. Foreign abolitionists might oppose such plans if the North abolished slavery.[5] In the North, where enlistments had flagged and there was much resistance to conscription, Lincoln was aware that a document purporting to end slavery would open the way for enlisting thousands of blacks in the Union Army. Perhaps with all these matters in mind, Lincoln told a delegation of church people who had come to plead for the outright, uncompensated emancipation of all slaves, "I view the matter as a practical war measure to be decided upon according to the advantages or disadvantages it may offer to the suppression of the rebellion."[6] In September 1862, Lincoln issued what he characterized as a preliminary proclamation. In this document, he warned that on January 1, 1863, he would free the slaves in those areas which by that date had not rejected the Confederacy "by simply again becoming good citizens of the United States."[7] On the first day of the new year, Lincoln issued the Emancipation Proclamation.[8] It was clear to Lincoln and other federal policymakers that the Emancipation Proclamation served the best interests of the country, and it was issued primarily for that purpose. Blacks, though, were no less overjoyed because the formal end to slavery was a fortuitous dividend of a policy adopted for other reasons. One black preacher reflected the feelings of the black community in an exuberant, if unrealistic welter of biblical metaphor. "Sound the loud timbrel o'er Egypt's dark sea, Jehovah hath triumphed, His people are free."[9] Actually, as a legal matter the proclamation freed no slaves — its terms having been carefully limited to those areas still under the control of the Confederacy, and thus beyond the reach of federal law. Slaveholding territories that had sided with the Union were specifically excluded. But Lincoln's dramatic action had a symbolic effect that far exceeded its legal force. Blacks made no distinction between the areas covered by the proclamation and those excluded from its impact. Slaves did not revolt on a wholesale basis, but as word of the Emancipation filtered down to them, increasing numbers simply slipped away or became disloyal, particularly when Union troops approached.[10] On the political front, the Emancipation did open the way for the enlistment of blacks, and by war's end there were more than 200,000 blacks serving in the Union Army.

As has so frequently been the case, the self-interest advantages of an action nominally taken to benefit blacks were lost on the mass of working class whites. Even the September 1862 preliminary proclamation had sparked an adverse political reaction across the country. The political backlash cost Lincoln's Republican Party heavily in the midterm elections of 1862. Less than a week after Lincoln

---

5. John Hope Franklin & Alfred A. Moss, Jr., From Slavery to Freedom 283-284 (8th ed. 2000). Professor Franklin has reviewed Lincoln's changing viewpoint on the Emancipation Proclamation and the effect of the document on blacks, the nation, and the world in John Hope Franklin, The Emancipation Proclamation (1963).

6. Dillard, supra note 1, at 98.

7. Id.

8. Proclamation of January 1, 1863. No. 17, 12 Stat. 1268 (1863).

9. Frederick Douglass, Life and Times of Frederick Douglass 351-355 (Collier ed. 1962).

10. See Franklin & Moss, supra note 5, at 225-230; J. G. Randall & David Donald, The Civil War and Reconstruction 385 (2d ed. 1961).

signed the preliminary measure, the legislature in his home state of Illinois condemned the act as "unwarrantable in military as in civil law" and as "a gigantic usurpation, at once converting the war, professedly commenced by the administration for the vindication of the authority of the Constitution into the crusade for the sudden, unconditional and violent liberation" of the slaves.[11]

Republicans slowly regained political support, but the adverse reaction of whites to the idea of fighting a war to free blacks remained a bitter and not infrequently violent one. In July 1863, the drawing of the first names in New York under the new federal Selective Service Law sparked several days of riots in which blacks were lynched and beaten. The rioters first sacked, then burned, the Colored Orphan Asylum, and committed many other atrocities.[12] The draft riots combined the bitterness of whites over being sent off to fight a war to free blacks with frustration over their economic situation. Just prior to the riots, 3,000 longshoremen had gone on strike for higher wages. In keeping with the usual practice, employers replaced the strikers with blacks, who under ordinary circumstances would have been barred from these jobs. The government worsened matters by drafting the unemployed whites into a war to help win the freedom of slaves, who the white workers feared would become strikebreakers, and the violent reaction followed.[13] This hostility to blacks persisted to the end of the war.

A number of possible points are suggested by the Emancipation Proclamation history period. First, blacks are more likely to obtain relief for even acknowledged racial injustice when that relief also serves, directly or indirectly, to further ends that policymakers perceive are in the best interests of the country. Second, blacks, as well as their white allies, are likely to focus with gratitude on the relief obtained, usually after a long struggle. Little attention is paid to the self-interest factors without which no relief might have been gained. Moreover, the relief is viewed as proof that society is indeed just, and that eventually all racial injustices will be recognized and remedied. Third, the remedy for blacks appropriately viewed as a "good deal" by policy-making whites often provides benefits for blacks that are more symbolic than substantive; but whether substantive or not, they are often perceived by working class whites as both an unearned gift to blacks and a betrayal of poor whites. As will be shown in §2.8, this sense that working class white interests have been subordinated to those of blacks has a lengthy history.

None of this is self-evident. Not every advance in the status of blacks can be characterized by the three points set out above. The fact is, though, that the racial injustices visited upon blacks are so immense, and the effort required to bring amelioration of the condition in any of the several areas of concern including education, employment, voting, public accommodations, and housing, is so great, that when a barrier is breached, the gain is eagerly accepted as proof of progress in the long, hard struggle to eliminate racial discrimination. Most Americans, black and white, view the civil rights crusade as a long, slow, but always upward pull that must, given the basic precepts of the country and the commitment of its people to equality and liberty, eventually end in the full enjoyment by blacks of all rights and

11. J. G. Randall, Constitutional Problems Under Lincoln 100 (1951).
12. Randall & Donald, supra note 10, at 316-317.
13. Franklin & Moss, supra note 5, at 279.

privileges of citizenship enjoyed by whites. But even a rather cursory look at American political history suggests that in the past, the most significant political advances for blacks resulted from policies that were intended to, and had the effect of, serving the interests and convenience of whites rather than remedying racial injustices against blacks. And, all too often, from the draft riots that followed the issuance of the Emancipation Proclamation in 1863 to the "white backlash" that followed the civil rights gains made by blacks a century later, a great mass of whites have perceived civil rights for blacks not as a benefit for whites as is often the case, but rather as a societal setback that must be opposed politically and, if conditions are favorable, violently.

§2.3 ABOLITION OF SLAVERY IN NORTHERN STATES

The pattern of motivations that led Lincoln to issue the Emancipation Proclamation in 1863, and the black-white responses to his action, were foreshadowed by abolition policies in the Northern states a half-century earlier.

In his book, North of Slavery, Leon F. Litwack, reports that in the Northern states, slavery was abolished by constitutional provisions in Vermont (1777), Ohio (1802), Illinois (1818), and Indiana (1816); by a judicial decision in Massachusetts (1783); by constitutional interpretation in New Hampshire (1857); and by gradual abolition acts in Pennsylvania (1780), Rhode Island (1784), Connecticut (1784 and 1797), New York (1799 and 1817), and New Jersey (1804).

In varying degrees, abolition in the North was the result of several factors: idealism stemming from the Revolution, with its "rights of man" ideology; the lesser dependence of the Northern economy on a large labor force; its relatively small investment in slaves combined with the great hostility of the white laboring class to the competition of slaves; the fear of slave revolts; and a general belief that there was no place for "inferior" blacks in the new societies.

Even so, abolition was not accomplished without a major effort in most states, and idealism usually was the makeweight for a decision already based on more pragmatic grounds. As de Tocqueville observed, "In the United States people abolish slavery for the sake not of the Negroes but of the white men."[1] Vermont had only a few slaves, and its constitution explicitly outlawed slavery in 1777. Although New Hampshire also had but few slaves, a petition for freedom to the legislature in 1779 was considered "not ripe." Judicial interpretations of the state's 1783 constitution asserted the end of slavery, but confusion on the subject was not finally resolved until 1857, when a statute banned slavery.

In Massachusetts, efforts to specifically ban slavery in the constitution of 1780 failed, but the state's high court interpreted that constitution to include such a provision in the famous *Quock Walker* case of 1783.[2] According to

§2.3 1. Alexis de Tocqueville, Democracy in America 344 (Anchor Books ed. 1969).
2. For a discussion of the historical import of the *Quock Walker* case, see David B. Davis, The Problem of Slavery in the Age of Revolution: 1770-1823, at 508 (1975).

Chief Justice William Cushing: "Although slavery had been tolerated in Massachusetts, it was incompatible with the new spirit 'favorable to the natural rights of mankind.'"

Where slavery was more firmly entrenched, as in Pennsylvania, Rhode Island, Connecticut, New York, and New Jersey, the efforts of abolitionists met with more opposition. Each of these states adopted gradual abolition statutes designed to lessen the burden that abolition would place on the slave owner. In Pennsylvania, an act of March 1, 1780, c. 146, provided that no person born in the state after the date of enactment should be deemed a slave, but that such children would be considered as "indentured servants" of their parents' master until age 28. The statutes of the other states were quite similar.[3]

The delayed effective date, according to some historians, was not the result of anti-black vindictiveness. Rather, it was the solution to the problem that plagued all abolition movements: Who will pay the price of freedom? Under gradual emancipation statutes, the slaves were forced to pay through their labor almost 100 percent of their market value during the long years as "indentured servants."[4]

Commenting on this nineteenth-century precedent for the "all deliberate speed" principle, one writer observed: "Freedom was thus conferred upon a future generation and the living were given merely the consolation of a free posterity."[5]

But freedom even for those blacks who were emancipated under these statutes left much to be desired. They were no longer slaves, but they certainly were not citizens. Indeed, their intermediate status carried with it many of the obligations, but few of the privileges, of citizenship. The freedmen could not vote, but they were taxed. They could not serve on juries, and, excluded from the militia in peacetime, they were required under a 1707 Massachusetts act to perform menial service on the parade ground or to labor on the roads in lieu of military service.[6]

From an economic standpoint, the freedmen were relegated to domestic work, while slaves were involved in every form of employment. Prejudice was strong; blacks were not only excluded from jobs considered appropriate for white workmen, but they were often the victims of insult and physical attack. Blacks were segregated in the worst areas of the towns where they lived, their children were often barred from the public schools, and on certain occasions they were even forbidden to appear in public places.[7]

Obviously, Northern states did not intend abolition of slavery to be equated with acceptance of blacks. "Until the post-Civil War era, in fact, most northern whites would maintain a careful distinction between granting Negroes legal protection — a theoretical right to life, liberty, and property — and political and social equality."[8] Partial recognition of that character was no boon. Blacks know now and

---

3. Arthur Silversmith, The First Emancipation: The Abolition of Slavery in the North 4, 124-132 (1967).

4. See Robert Fugal & Stanley Engelmann, Philanthropy at Bargain Prices: Notes on the Economics of Gradual Emancipation, 3 J. Legal Stud. 377 (1974). See also Donald L. Robinson, Slavery in the Structure of American Politics, 1765-1820 at 30, 37 (1971).

5. Winthrop D. Jordan, White Over Black 345 (1968).

6. Lorenzo Greene, The Negro in Colonial New England, 1620-1776, at 332-333 (1942).

7. Id.

8. Leon F. Litwack, North of Slavery 15 (1961).

likely recognized then that the power to withhold political and social equality meant that legal protection too could be suspended or withdrawn whenever the grantors deemed it in their self-interest to do so.

§2.4   SLAVERY IN AMERICA

The slavery era is one of the most thoroughly canvassed areas of American history. Courses detailing the law's involvement with the "peculiar institution" are offered at some law schools, and several additions to the literature have increased our understanding of a practice with roots as old as the society.[1] The Kerner Commission succinctly set out slavery's origins and development.

> Twenty years after Columbus reached the New World, African Negroes, transported by Spanish, Dutch and Portuguese traders, were arriving in the Caribbean Islands. Almost all came as slaves. By 1600, there were more than half a million slaves in the Western Hemisphere.
> In Colonial America, the first Negroes landed at Jamestown in August, 1619. Within 40 years, Negroes had become a group apart, separated from the rest of the population by custom and law. Treated as servants for life, forbidden to intermarry with whites, deprived of their African traditions and dispersed among Southern plantations, American Negroes lost tribal, regional and family ties.
> Through massive importation, their numbers increased rapidly. By 1776, some 500,000 Negroes were held in slavery and indentured servitude in the United States. Nearly one of every six persons in the country was a slave.[2]

Beginning with the early colonial period and extending up to the time of the Civil War, there was a vast amount of litigation at both the state and federal levels involving blacks. In virtually all of the cases, blacks were the subjects and not the parties in the litigation.[3] They were property subject to ownership; and the law, reflecting as it did then the prevailing belief in the inherent inferiority of all blacks, experienced little difficulty in treating them as "chattels personal."[4]

There were contradictions involved in holding "chattels personal" responsible for acts requiring the free will of humans, while at the same time denying to those "chattels" the basic due process rights the law guaranteed to all humans. This resulted in analytical contortions by courts of the period that would be humorous

§2.4   1. Nathan Huggins, Black Odyssey (1990); A. Leon Higginbotham, Jr., In the Matter of Color: Race and the American Legal Process: The Colonial Period (1978); Herbert Guttmann, The Black Family in Slavery and Freedom, 1750-1925 (1974); Eugene D. Genovese, Roll, Jordan, Roll: The World the Slaves Made (1974); Eugene D. Genovese, The Political Economy of Slavery (1965); David B. Davis, The Problem of Slavery in the Age of Revolution (2d ed. 1999); David B. Davis, The Problem of Slavery in Western Culture (1970); Eric Williams, Capitalism and Slavery (4th ed. 1966).
2. Rep. of Natl. Commn. on Civil Disorders, Rejection and Protest: An Historical Sketch 95 (1968).
3. Helen T. Catterall, Judicial Cases Concerning American Slavery and the Negro, vols. I-V (1936).
4. Kenneth M. Stampp, The Peculiar Institution 197-236 (1956).

were the legal fictions adopted and suspended not so arbitrarily and predictably used to protect the slave system, usually but not always at the expense of the slaves.[5] As will be made clear in the next section, Northern judges, some with strong commitments to the abolition of slavery, seldom fared better in solving the moral dilemmas posed by the law.

§2.5 SLAVERY AND THE CONFLICT OF LAWS

Slavery decisions almost uniformly favored the "peculiar institution" and gave precedence to the interests of slave owners over those of slaves seeking freedom through litigation. The constitutional provisions protecting slavery (see §2.7) certainly limited the Court's discretion in this field, but the decisions went beyond even constitutional requirements in what were apparently conscious efforts to protect all property rights, including those in humans. And with isolated exceptions, slaves could expect little assistance from even the greatest of antebellum jurists who, despite dicta-wringing over the moral evil of slavery, found it necessary to "follow the law."[1] The Supreme Court provided little leadership in this controversial area, and Chief Justice John Marshall made a point of avoiding substantive decisions in slavery cases whenever possible.[2] Marshall's major aim was to secure the Supreme Court's position as constitutional arbiter in the federal system. The Court did not wish to unduly provoke Congress, which could easily curtail the Court's authority by reduction of its appellate jurisdiction. Then too, whatever the scruples about slavery among the Court's members, they were uniform in their commitment to the protection of property rights. Slaves, of course, were a critically important form of property. Thus, as Professor Donald Roper describes it, Marshall's approach to slavery questions was cautious.[3] For example, he reports that after a federal judge had created great hostility toward the court in South Carolina by holding a state statute regulating and restricting the movement of free Negro seamen void as in conflict with the commerce clause of the U.S. Constitution,[4] Marshall wrote to Justice Story that he earlier had avoided a similar situation in Virginia involving a case with a statute quite like that of South Carolina. He reported, "a case has been brought before me in which I might have considered its constitutionality, had I chosen to do so; but it was not

---

5. Judge A. Leon Higgenbotham, Jr., loses few opportunities to point out the hypocrisy that was the necessary component of so many slave decisions in, In the Matter of Color (1978). See also Eugene D. Genovese, Roll, Jordan, Roll: The World the Slaves Made 25-49 (1974). For a generally sympathetic perspective on the quality of justice meted out by Southern judges in slave cases, see A. E. Keir Nash, Fairness and Formalism in the Trials of Blacks in the State Supreme Courts of the Old South, 56 Va. L. Rev. 64 (1970).

§2.5 1. The moral-legal dilemma is examined extensively in Robert M. Cover, Justice Accused: Antislavery and the Judicial Process (1975).

2. Donald N. Roper, In Quest of Judicial Objectivity: The Marshall Court and the Legitimization of Slavery, 21 Stan. L. Rev. 532 (1969).

3. Id. at 533.

4. Elkison v. Deliesseline, 8 F. Cas. 493 (No. 4366) (C.C.S.C. 1823).

absolutely necessary, and as I am not fond of butting a wall in sport, I escaped on the construction of the act."[5]

The South Carolina statute that was voided in the Elkison v. Deliesseline case was a measure typical of those enacted by Southern states to discourage nonslave blacks from entering their territories and becoming, by their presence and status, disruptive forces and living reminders that slavery was not the only possibility for black people. Under the provisions of the act, if any vessel came into a port or harbor of the state bringing a free colored person, such person was to become an absolute slave, and, without even a trial, be sold. Feeling ran so high over the statute that one attorney defending it likened importation of free blacks to that of "clothes infested with the plague, or wild beasts from Africa. . . ."[6]

The Northern states, for reasons that differed from those in the South far less than could be gauged by their rhetoric, also opposed the importation into their states of slaves by their masters. These states had abolished slavery in order to protect jobs for free whites, lessen the fear of slave rebellions, and reduce the likelihood of a large black population. Unlike South Carolina, whose statute threatened slavery even for a free sailor coming into a port of that state, most Northern states permitted a slave owner to pass through the territory and even to remain for a limited period of time without losing property rights in slaves who accompanied him or her. There was no general agreement as to how long this limited period of time might run, and as hostilities between North and South grew more bitter, the time allotted became shorter and shorter. When a slave sought his or her freedom on the basis that the sojourn in a free state had exceeded this "reasonable length," attorneys representing the slave generally invoked the doctrine of a famous English precedent, Somerset v. Stewart.[7] In the Somerset case, Lord Mansfield resolved a lengthy litigation over the status of a slave who was brought by his master to England, escaped, and was recaptured. Mansfield found no statutes authorizing slavery, a status which he said constituted "so high an act of dominion," and was "so odious, that nothing can be suffered to support it, but positive law."[8] Thus, Somerset was freed, and the rule was established that a slave became free upon setting foot in a free jurisdiction.[9]

5. Roper, supra note 2, at 534.

6. 8 F. Cas. at 496.

7. 98 Eng. Rep. 499 (K.B. 1772). The litigation and the decision's significance is reviewed in detail in A. Leon Higgenbotham, Jr., In the Matter of Color: Race and the American Legal Process: The Colonial Period 313-368 (1978).

8. 98 Eng. Rep. at 510.

9. One writer argues that the Somerset decision was poorly reported and generally misconstrued to hold that Lord Mansfield had freed all 14,000 black slaves then in England, a result sought by Somerset's attorneys, but that the decision was limited to a finding that Stewart could not remove Somerset from England against his will in the absence of positive law. The broader interpretation of the decision was generally accepted in America, where its effect was to stimulate passage of fugitive slave legislation. The influence of the Somerset decision is reflected in the euphemistic clauses in the Northwest Ordinance, passed by Congress in July 1787, to the effect that while slavery was to be barred from the territories, "any person escaping into the same, from whom labor or service is lawfully claimed in any one of the original states, such fugitive may be lawfully reclaimed and conveyed to the person claiming his or her labor service. . . ." Article 6, and Article 4 §2 cl. 3 of the Federal Constitution, the fugitive slave provision. Jerome Nadelhaft, The Somerset Case and Slavery: Myth, Reality, and Repercussions, 51 J. Negro Hist. 193 (1966).

Conflicts of law arose when a free state determined that a slave within its borders had been held there sufficiently long to invoke the *Somerset* precedent, and overruled the slave status recognized by the master's domicile.[10] Until the 1830s, litigation in this field was marked by the willingness of free states to recognize the bondage of slaves sojourning within their borders for limited periods of time, and a similar willingness of slave states to recognize the freedom acquired by former slaves who had remained beyond some reasonable time limit in a free state.

The tacit accommodation between the courts of the North and the South did not last. Beginning around 1830 and accelerating during the 1840s and 1850s, courts in both regions took increasingly divergent attitudes toward the legal status of slavery and, predictably, became less willing to accept the contrary policies or laws of sister states. Abolitionists in the North were becoming more outspoken and militant in their views. They rejected the *Somerset* doctrine, which would recognize slavery if authorized by positive law, and they denounced the Constitution to the extent that it condoned and protected slavery. Rather, they appealed to and urged compliance with a higher law that did not recognize the legitimacy of institutionalized evil, even when allowed by statute. For their part, Southerners were now convinced that slavery must not die out, and that their economic survival depended on its maintenance and expansion.[11]

As sectional conflict became more intense, states that had earlier accommodated the interests of sister states began to refuse to recognize the enslaved status of anyone within their borders, even of those slaves merely passing through the state with their masters or fleeing in violation of federal law.[12] Similarly, Southern states refused to recognize even the permanent freedom of blacks born in free states or the emancipating effects of a slave's prolonged residence in a free state. Louisiana adopted a statute that established that emancipation could not be effected by a slave's residence in another state.[13] Finally, though, the change in position was accomplished solely by the judiciary overturning earlier cases in which the emancipation by residence in a sister state had been recognized. Thus, in Missouri, which had earlier been especially sensitive to its relations with neighboring Illinois, a free state, the state supreme court in Scott v. Emerson overturned a considerable body of case law to hold that a slave was not rendered free as a result of having spent four years in nonslave areas.[14]

While Lord Mansfield in 1772 was at least limiting the power of slave owners in England, Virginia (whose population of 200,000 slaves roughly equaled the white population) by the same year had passed 33 acts to prohibit the importation of slaves, all of which were rejected by England. Benjamin Franklin probably typified the reaction of many Americans to the *Somerset* decision when he wrote to a friend: "I have made a little extract . . . of the number of slaves imported and perishing with some close remarks on the hypocrisy of this country [England] which encourages such a detestable commerce by laws for promoting the Guinea trade, while it piqued itself on its virtue, love and liberty, and the equity of its courts, in setting free a single Negro." Peter M. Bergman, The Chronological History of the Negro in America 46 (1969).

10. Note, American Slavery and the Conflict of Laws, 71 Colum. L. Rev. 74 (1971).
11. Bergman, supra note 9, at 39-40.
12. Id. at 43.
13. Id.
14. 15 Mo. 576 (1852).

The Missouri court, in explaining its rejection of the earlier rules, candidly pointed to the change in political climate:

> Times are not now as they were when the former decisions on this subject were made. Since then not only individuals but States have been possessed with a dark and fell spirit in relation to slavery, whose gratification is sought in the pursuit of measures, whose inevitable consequences must be the overthrow and destruction of the government. Under such circumstances it does not behoove the State of Missouri to show the least countenance to any measures which might gratify this spirit.[15]

§2.6 THE *DRED SCOTT* CASE

Emerson v. Scott was the first phase of the famous decision in Dred Scott v. Sandford.[1] As indicated above, the case raised the substantive issue of whether the slave Dred Scott's temporary residence in free territory in the state of Illinois sufficed to free him under the common law doctrine of the *Somerset* case. The Supreme Court found that Scott was not a citizen of Missouri within the meaning of the Constitution and thus could not invoke the diversity jurisdiction of the federal courts. But rather than settle the case on this procedural ground, the Court reiterated former law that Scott's four-year residence in Illinois had not altered his slave status, and invalidated the Missouri Compromise of 1820 (equally dividing new states between slave and free) on the ground that it violated substantive rights in property under the Fifth Amendment's due process clause.

Chief Justice Taney utilized the debater's technique in framing the question in *Dred Scott* so as to leave little alternative as to the answer. He wrote:

> The question is simply this: Can a negro whose ancestors were imported into this country, and sold as slaves, become a member of the political community formed and brought into existence by the Constitution of the United States, and as such become entitled to all the rights, and privileges, and immunities, guaranteed by that instrument to the citizen?[2]

---

15. Id. at 586.

§2.6 1. 60 U.S. (19 How.) 393 (1857). Professor Don E. Fehrenbacher has published the definitive work covering every aspect of this landmark litigation in The *Dred Scott* Case: Its Significance in American Law and Politics (1978).

2. 60 U.S. at 403. Professor Fehrenbacher notes that the actual question before the Court was whether Dred Scott, if he was a free Negro, could be regarded as a citizen of Missouri, at least to the extent of being eligible to bring suit in a federal court under the diverse citizenship clause. The trial court had held that any resident capable of owning property was to this extent a citizen. Another criterion, Professor Fehrenbacher suggests, was whether free Negroes were citizens of the state to the extent of being able to bring suit in the courts of that state, which they most certainly were. Scott had previously brought such a suit for his freedom and had lost, but not on the jurisdictional issue. Scott v. Emerson, 15 Mo. 576 (1852). But Chief Justice Taney redefined the whole problem, shifting the ground of inquiry from state citizenship to federal citizenship, simultaneously making the right to bring suit in federal courts dependent upon the confirmation of all rights enjoyed under the federal constitution. Fehrenbacher, supra note 1, at 341-342.

He distinguished the condition of American Indians who, "although they were uncivilized, they were yet a free and independent people, associated together in nations or tribes, and governed by their own laws." The Indian governments, he reasoned, were treated as foreign governments, and even though Indian tribes are now under the subjection of the white race and "it has been found necessary, for their sake as well as our own, to regard them as in a state of pupilage," they can, like other subjects of a foreign government, be naturalized and become citizens of a state, and of the United States.[3]

Blacks, on the other hand, were not included and were not intended to be included under the word "citizens" in the Constitution, and thus can claim none of the rights and privileges of that document. Rather, he said that blacks were always considered "a subordinate and inferior class of beings," they had been subjugated by the dominant race, and, whether emancipated or not, they remained subject to their authority. They had, he found, no rights or privileges but those whites might choose to grant them.

The states, he argued, could not confer national citizenship, and the Constitution limited its grant of the rights and privileges of citizenship to those recognized as citizens of the several states at the time the Constitution was adopted.[4] He then cited several historic facts which he deemed proofs that the states did not intend to include blacks among their citizens. For example, he concedes that the language in the Declaration of Independence is broad, but insists the status of blacks at the time indicates they were not seen as equals.

In the statement for which the decision is most frequently remembered, Chief Justice Taney said:

> They had for more than a century before been regarded as beings of an inferior order, and altogether unfit to associate with the white race, either in social or political relations; and so far inferior that they had no rights which the white man was bound to respect; and that the negro might justly and lawfully be reduced to slavery for his benefit. . . . This opinion was at that time fixed and universal in the civilized portion of the white race. It was regarded as an axiom in morals as well as in politics, which no one thought of disputing, or supposed to be open to dispute; and men in every grade and position in society daily and habitually acted upon it in their private pursuits, as

---

Indeed, Taney complicated matters by restating the issue as one of "whether the descendants of such slaves, when they shall be emancipated, or who are born of parents who had become free before their birth, are *citizens of a State;* in the sense in which the word 'citizen' is used in the Constitution of the United States." 60 U.S. at 403.

3. Id. at 403-404. Professor Fehrenbacher notes that Chief Justice Taney, for no logical reason, abruptly turned aside to introduce a paradox: the American Indian, though not included in the "political community" of the United States, and, in fact, "under subjection to the white race," had nevertheless in some instances been admitted to federal citizenship. Taney did not make clear why American aborigines so subjugated could nevertheless be members of a foreign nation sufficiently to become citizens while a race transplanted from Africa could not.

4. Of course, when the Constitution was put into effect, as Professor Fehrenbacher points out, supra note 1, at 343, a large majority of American citizens — namely, women and children — were not members of the sovereign people in the sense of holding power and participating in government through their elective representatives. Moreover, many adult male citizens were barred from constituent membership by property and religious qualifications for voting.

well as in matters of public concern, without doubting for a moment the correctness of this opinion.[5]

Colonial legislation that generally barred marriage between whites and blacks showed, in his view, "too plainly to be misunderstood, the degraded condition of this unhappy race." These laws were intended to provide "a perpetual and impassible barrier" between the white race and the black so as to prevent intermarriages that were regarded as "unnatural and immoral." He noted that the prohibition applied both to free negroes and slaves, and that the stigma was fixed upon the whole race.[6]

The Constitution, he found, not only contained no provisions specifically including blacks among those it deemed the "people of the United States," but contained two clauses that point directly to the Negro race as a separate class of persons. One clause reserves to the initial states the right to import slaves until the year 1808. In the other clause, the states pledge to protect the property of the master by delivering up any slave who may have escaped from his service and be found within their respective territories. With an understatement that does not characterize his opinion, Chief Justice Taney said, "Certainly these two clauses were not intended to confer on them or their posterity the blessings of liberty, or any of the personal rights so carefully provided for the citizen."[7]

While some states ended slavery because such labor was unsuited to the climate and unprofitable to the master, the change in their status had not changed public opinion regarding the former slaves. There was no indication that the people in those states regarded those who were emancipated as entitled to equal rights with themselves. In support of this conclusion, Taney reviewed statutes from

5. 60 U.S. at 407. It is estimated that the clause in this paragraph regarding blacks having no rights that the white man was bound to respect created more controversy than the decision itself. Professor Fehrenbacher reviews the discussion, and concludes that "the notorious clause" does not, as some of Chief Justice Taney's defenders claim, cease to be outrageous when it is read in context. In fact, free Negroes in the United States could not lawfully be hunted down and reduced to slavery, and many states regarded this practice as kidnapping and made it punishable accordingly. As for free Negroes, Professor Fehrenbacher indicates that a list of their legal rights was at least as lengthy as a list of their disabilities. In some respects, such as property rights, a black man's status was superior to that of a married white woman, and it was certainly far above that of a slave. He could marry, enter into contracts, purchase real estate, bequeath property, and seek redress in the courts. To say otherwise, Fehrenbacher concludes, was a gross perversion of the facts. Fehrenbacher, supra note 1, at 349.

6. The two laws referred to were enacted in 1717 in Maryland and 1705 in Massachusetts, both long before the Declaration of Independence. Taney, of course, argues that both laws "were still in force when the Revolution began, and are a faithful index to the state of feeling toward the class of persons of whom they speak, and of the position they occupied throughout the thirteen colonies. . . ." But, of course, this argument proves too much in that miscegenation laws (see Chapter 8) remained in effect in several states until 1967.

7. Professor Fehrenbacher reminds the reader that both clauses were aimed at the African slave trade and the recovery of fugitive slaves, and neither had any legal bearing on the legal status of free Negroes. He also points out that Chief Justice Taney conveniently ignored another provision in the Constitution, Article I, §2, apportioning representation and direct taxation among the states according to the number of "free persons" in each, plus three-fifths of the number of slaves. He argues that this provision plainly separated slaves from free blacks, and appeared to make the latter a part of the "people" upon whom the federal government was to be founded. Fehrenbacher, supra note 1, at 352.

Massachusetts and Connecticut abolishing slavery, but providing for restrictions on the activities of blacks not applicable to whites.[8]

In New Hampshire, only free white citizens were entitled to be enrolled in the state militia, and Connecticut barred the establishment in that state of any school for the instruction of persons of the African race not inhabitants of the state. Chief Justice Taney said it would be impossible to enumerate all the various laws marking the depressed condition of the black race that were passed after the Revolution, and before and since the adoption of the Constitution.

It was argued that in the power granted to Congress to establish rules of naturalization, it was understood that the word is confined to persons born in a foreign country, under a foreign government. Congress, thus, had no power to raise to the rank of citizen anyone born in the United States who from birth or parentage, by the laws of the country, belonged to an inferior and subordinate class. And, in the Naturalization Law of 1790, Congress confined the right of becoming citizens "to aliens being free, white persons." The Constitution does not limit congressional power in this respect, Chief Justice Taney argued, but the language of the law shows that citizenship at that time was understood to be confined to the white race.

In 1792, Congress enacted the first militia law directing every "free able-bodied white male citizen" to be enrolled in the militia.

Congress in 1813 provided that following the end of the war with Great Britain, "it shall not be lawful to employ on board of any public or private vessels of the United States, any person or persons except citizens of the United States, or persons of color, natives of the United States." Taney notes the distinction between persons of color and citizens.

In the congressional charter to the city of Washington, issued in 1820, the corporation is authorized "to restrain and prohibit the nightly and other disorderly meetings of slaves, free negroes, and mulattoes." Again, it was contended that this legislation was aimed expressly at blacks, whether slave or free. Taney saw this as further proof that neither group were viewed as citizens of the United States. About that time an attorney general of the United States had decided that the words "citizens of the United States" were used in the acts of Congress in the same sense as in the Constitution; and that free persons of color were not citizens within the meaning of the Constitution and laws.

In summary, Chief Justice Taney refused to concede that blacks were citizens, even in a limited sense. The Constitution treated blacks as property and granted them no rights, leaving it to the states to deal with the race, as "each State may think justice, humanity, and the interests and safety of society require." Taney

---

8. "The historical inaccuracy of this passage could perhaps be attributed to a combination of ignorance and willfulness. Appeals to conscience were prevalent in the early abolition movement, and there is no reason to believe that they were any more rhetorical than the appeals to interests that often accompanied them." Id. at 353. Professor Fehrenbacher acknowledges that it was easier to consult conscience in the Northern states where investments in slavery were limited, but he condemns as "Taney's fundamental error" the flat assertion that abolition in the North did not reflect any change in attitude toward the black race. He said, "Evidence to the contrary is overwhelming." In the ferment of the revolutionary era, the anomaly of slavery in civilized society caused a great deal of soul searching that was not less impressive because "they did not then and there embrace interracial equality. . . ." Id. at 354-355.

argued that no change in public opinion or feeling in relation to this unfortunate race should tempt a court to give to the words of the Constitution a more liberal construction in their favor than they were intended to bear when the instrument was framed and adopted. While the Constitution might be amended, the Chief Justice concluded that "while it remains unaltered, it must be construed now as it was understood at the time of its adoption. . . . Any other rule of construction would abrogate the judicial character of this court, and make it the mere reflex of the popular opinion or passion of the day."[9]

Far from settling the slavery issue, the *Dred Scott* decision set off a storm of criticism of and acclaim for the case and the Court. Republican Senator Seward, in a major speech on the Senate floor, called the decision a "pro-slavery conspiracy."[10] He concluded: "Dred Scott, who had played the hand of dummy in this interesting political game, unwittingly, yet to the complete satisfaction of his adversary, was voluntarily emancipated; and thus received from his master, as a reward, the freedom which the court had denied him as a right." Actually, in 1846 Scott had sought to purchase his and his family's freedom and was turned down. He then petitioned a local court for his freedom on the grounds of residence in Illinois and the Minnesota Territory. Scott and his family were manumitted in May 1857. He worked as a hotel porter in St. Louis, but died of tuberculosis a year later.[11]

A convention of blacks met in Philadelphia to denounce the *Dred Scott* decision.[12] But the very excessiveness of the decision's language likely spurred those opposed to slavery to redouble their efforts to abolish the institution. One writer maintains that *Dred Scott* was not the "classically worst" assertion of judicial supremacy, but was rather a "sincere" judicial effort to solve a nation-wrecking problem. He concludes: "The Court's fault, if it may be so described, lay in accepting the buck which Congress and the statesmen had passed, and in failing to anticipate the partisan, political use which its efforts could be made to serve."[13]

The debate continues. Government Professor Mark A. Graber points out that, prior to the passage of the Civil War Amendments, descendants of American slaves could not be U.S. citizens. In Graber's view, Chief Justice Taney's conclusions were

---

9. Point by point, Professor Fehrenbacher provides historical facts and a careful analysis of Chief Justice Taney's reasoning that devastates the famous opinion in a chapter that is well worth reading. Even so, the reality of life in antebellum America for the black — free or slave — may have been much closer to Taney's assertions than to Fehrenbacher's criticism of those assertions. If the North could no longer countenance slavery, but was not ready to recognize the freedmen as equals in terms of rights and opportunities, then the abolition acts, given the fear and distaste felt for blacks, amounted to not much more than compulsory unemployment laws.

It is interesting to note that Frederick Douglass described Taney's statement regarding blacks having no rights the white man was bound to respect as a "historical fact." Frederick Douglass, Life and Times of Frederick Douglass 293 (Collier ed. 1962).

10. Congressional Globe 35-1, p. 941, as cited in Fehrenbacher, supra note 1, at 473-474, 698 n.65.

11. Fehrenbacher, supra note 1, at 568.

12. Peter M. Bergman, The Chronological History of the Negro in America 212 (1969).

13. Wallace Mendelson, Dred Scott's Case — Reconsidered, 38 Minn. L. Rev. 16, 28 (1953). See also Edward S. Corwin, The Dred Scott Decision in the Light of Contemporary Legal Doctrine. 17 Am. Hist. Rev. 52 (1911).

well within the mainstream of antebellum constitutional thought.[14] The failed compromise of black rights in the *Dred Scott* case led to one of the most destructive wars in history. The Union was saved at a terrible cost in blood, and the industrial system, freed of its plantation competition, was able to advance its exploitation of labor, white as well as black.

The decision to go to war to save the Union was far from universally accepted in the North, particularly among Democrats. When Lincoln broadened the war's rationale by issuing the Emancipation Proclamation, opposition grew stronger even among Republicans. Given its cost in lives and its aftermath, in which freed blacks were left more vulnerable to white vengeance and exploitation than they had been under slavery, there is reason to conclude that those who opposed the war, urging that the South be allowed to secede and go in peace, may have had a point. The plantation system's reliance on slave labor could not long compete with the swiftly developing industrial system. Economic need might well have overcome political pride, leading to the Confederacy's failure and forcing its members to seek readmission to the Union.

It is interesting to compare *Dred Scott*, the decision everyone loves to hate, with Brown v. Board of Education, the decision that virtually everyone admires. Slavery advocates applauded the *Dred Scott* decision that sacrificed black rights but that enraged abolitionists and Northern industrialists, whose efforts pushed the nation toward the Civil War that no one wanted. Racial reform advocates hailed the *Brown* decision that sought to overturn past compromises of black rights, but the decision enraged large numbers of whites who mounted a political rebellion that over the years seriously undermined the Court's good intentions. Both cases indicate how difficult it is to rearrange racial compromises that harm blacks who feel the pain and working class whites who are oblivious of their loss.

§2.7   SLAVERY AND THE FOUNDING FATHERS

By 1776, when the American colonies were ready in the name of individual rights to rebel against English domination, slavery had been established for more than a century. The Revolutionary period thus revealed an increase in the general ambivalence of the white majority as to the status of blacks. Clearly, there was a contradiction between the recognition of individual rights demanded by white Americans for themselves and the suppression of those rights for blacks, free and slave, living in their midst. As lawyer-historian Staughton Lynd concludes in *Slavery and the Founding Fathers*,[1] the contradictions are best explained by the almost universal belief in Negro inferiority. In his original draft of the Declaration of Independence, Thomas Jefferson, a slaveholder himself, included a paragraph

14. Mark A. Graber, Desperately Ducking Slavery: Dred Scott and Contemporary Constitutional Theory, 14 Const. Comment. 271, 280-281 (1997).

§2.7   1. Staughton Lynd, Slavery and the Founding Fathers, in Black History (M. Drimmer ed., 1968).

critical of King George's sanction of the slave trade. This was not merely an act of hypocrisy or a makeweight argument to justify the document as an effort to include blacks within the class petitioning for relief from English oppression. Rather, Virginia had long been concerned about the potential for revolt resulting from the sizable percentage of slaves in its population. Prior efforts to limit importation of slaves had been regularly rejected by England. Perhaps the section reflected what Jefferson considered just and what he believed would gain the support of those who professed the concept of liberty. However, at the insistence of Southern representatives in the Continental Congress, the key section on slavery was struck from the declaration.

It was perhaps prophetic that the ringing, seemingly unequivocal words of the declaration — "We hold these Truths to be self-evident, that all Men are created equal" — in fact contained reservations; for Jefferson, their author, never deviated from his lifelong conviction that the Negro must be freed so as "to be removed beyond the reach of mixture" so that he would not stain "the blood of his master."[2] During the eighteenth century, most of the colonies levied taxes on the importation of slaves and enjoyed a comfortable revenue from this source. But one by one, many of the colonies imposed statutory restrictions on the importation of slaves or banned the trade entirely. In the main, these statutes reflected the colonists' constant fear of slave insurrections. In the Northern colonies, the acts were also the result of the opposition of white immigrants to slave labor and, to some extent, the activities of abolitionists.

At the first Continental Congress meeting in 1774, efforts to halt the importation of slaves came to little, and, as already seen, the criticism of the slave traffic included in Jefferson's first draft of the Declaration of Independence was stricken. By the close of the Revolutionary War, the pressures to fully reopen the profitable African slave trade were great, particularly since, as a result of the fighting, the slaves, "by pillage, flight, and actual fighting, had become so reduced in numbers . . . that an urgent demand for more laborers was felt in the South."[3]

There was virtually no action taken against the slave trade by the Congress of the Confederation. Indeed, the only legislative activity in regard to the trade prior to 1778 was taken by the individual states. During this period, Connecticut, Vermont, Pennsylvania, Delaware, and Virginia had by law prohibited the further importation of slaves, and importation had practically ceased in all the New England and Middle states, including Maryland.[4]

The Founding Fathers, in establishing the framework of the new federal government, handled the question of slavery as an economic and political rather than a moral matter, particularly so in light of the sensitivity of Southern delegates, who would brook no interference with their institution. Even so, the delegates apparently recognized that slavery was, in the final analysis, incompatible with the doctrines of freedom and liberty that characterized this "Revolutionary Generation" at the close of the eighteenth century. As Professor Lynd points out in his article, and as the following relevant slavery provisions of the Constitution reflect,

---

2. Winthrop D. Jordan, White Over Black 546 (1968). See chapter 6, reviewing Jefferson's now-acknowledged long-term sexual relationship with Sally Hemings, one of his slaves.

3. W. E. B. Du Bois, The Suppression of the African Slave Trade 49 (1896).

4. Id. at 48-51.

the delegates artfully avoided use of the term "slavery," referring instead to "persons" whom the states shall think it proper to import, or "persons" bound to service or labor.

Article I

Section 2. Clause 3. Representatives and direct Taxes shall be apportioned among the several States which may be included within this Union, according to their respective Numbers, which shall be determined by adding to the whole Number of free Persons, including those bound to Service for a Term of Years, and excluding Indians not taxed, three-fifths of all other Persons. . . .

Section 9. Clause 1. The Migration or Importation of such Persons as any of the States now existing shall think proper to admit, shall not be prohibited by the Congress prior to the Year one thousand eight hundred and eight, but a Tax or duty may be imposed on such Importations, not exceeding ten dollars for each Person. . . .

Article IV

Section 2. Clause 1. The Citizens of each State shall be entitled to all Privileges and Immunities of Citizens in the several States. . . .

Section 2. Clause 3. No person held to Service or Labour in one State, under the Laws thereof, escaping into another, shall, in Consequence of any Law or Regulation therein, be discharged from such Service or Labour, but shall be delivered up on Claim of the Party to whom such Service or Labour may be due.

Professor Lynd has examined and found wanting the traditional explanation that Northerners did not make more of an issue of slavery at the Constitutional Convention because they were confident it would die away gradually of its own accord.[5] He points out that they certainly were aware that slavery was flagrantly at odds with the principles of the American Revolution. The delegates were deeply involved in sectional conflict that evolved into a straightforward contest for national power. There was a common belief that within the next few decades, the Southern states would expand into western areas and be the dominant group in the new federal government. The South, for its part, was willing to strengthen the federal government if it were assured of controlling it. For this reason, the South agreed to the plan of giving each state equal representation in the Senate. For their part, the Northern states agreed to this plan because of their current superiority. Similarly, the South won the right to include slaves in apportioning representation, and the admission of new states represented in Congress on the same basis as the old states.

Professor Lynd points out that there is adequate evidence that Northern delegates knew that the South would never abandon slavery, but they recognized that without the South's support a strong federal government would be impossible. They also turned aside from an attack on slavery because of their commitment to private property. On this point, both Northern and Southern delegates held similar views. Thus, Gouverneur Morris, one of the convention's most outspoken opponents of slavery, declared in the convention debates of July 5 and 6, "Life and

5. Lynd, supra note 1, at 119.

liberty were generally said to be of more value, than property," but that "an accurate view of the matter would nevertheless prove that property was the main object of Society."[6] The unfathomable dilemma for abolitionists, though, was stated succinctly by another delegate, Charles Cotesworth Pinckney: "Property in slaves should not be exposed to danger under a Government instituted for the protection of property."[7] This was not merely a theoretical consideration for the North. As Madison recalled as late as 1833, the desire to compromise on the slavery issue was also motivated by the interests many Northerners had in the issue as merchants, ship-owners, and manufacturers. But personal interest aside, as Professor Lynd points out, "The belief that private property was the indispensable foundation for personal freedom made it more difficult for Northerners to confront the fact of slavery squarely."[8]

The other factor that Professor Lynd suggests led the North to acquiesce in a federal government that permitted slavery grew out of the difficulty even the most liberal of the Founding Fathers had in imagining a society in which whites and blacks would live together as fellow citizens. As Jefferson suggested, honor and intellectual consistency drove the Fathers to favor abolition; personal distaste, to fear it. At another point, Jefferson wrote: "Nothing is more certainly written in the book of fate, than that these people are to be free; nor is it less certain that the two races, equally free, cannot live in the same government."[9] Even Benjamin Franklin, the future president of the Pennsylvania Abolition Society, urged in 1751 that America not "darken its people" by importing Africans.

> . . . the Number of purely white People in the World is proportionably very small. All Africa is black or tawny. Asia chiefly tawny. America (exclusive of the new Comers) wholly so. And in Europe, the Spaniards, Italians, French, Russians and Swedes, are generally of what we call a swarthy Complexion; as are the Germans also, the Saxons only excepted, who with the English, make the principal Body of White People on the Face of the Earth. I could wish their Numbers were increased. And while we are, as I may call it, *Scouring* our Planet, by clearing America of Woods, and so making this Side of our Globe reflect a brighter Light to the Eyes of Inhabitants in Mars or Venus, why should we in the Sight of Superior Beings, darken its People? why increase the Sons of Africa, by Planting them in America, where we have so fair an Opportunity, by excluding all Blacks and Tawneys, of increasing the lovely White and Red?[10]

In summary, Professor Lynd concludes:

> Unable to summon the moral imagination required to transcend race prejudice, unwilling to contemplate social experiments which impinged on private property, the Fathers, unhappily, ambivalently, confusedly, passed by on the other side. Their much-praised deistic coolness of temper could not help them here. The compromise

6. Id. at 131.
7. Id.
8. Id.
9. Id. at 129.
10. Id. at 130.

of 1787 was a critical, albeit characteristic, failure of the American pragmatic intelligence.[11]

§2.8   THE ORIGIN AND DEVELOPMENT OF SLAVERY COMPROMISE[1]

There was political precedent even for the Founding Fathers' decision to sublimate the rights of blacks to the interests of whites. Historians have debated for decades whether American slavery took root in the seventeenth century as an outgrowth of racism or economic necessity, but in a new look at the subject, Professor Edmund Morgan joins the growing group of his peers who find elements of both prejudice and profit in this labor-intensive slavery equation, with the emphasis on the latter.[2] The coming of tobacco to Virginia in 1617 turned a struggling colony into a get-rich-quick society. To cultivate crop, servants that were indentured to their masters for a period of years were imported in great numbers. Most were young and male. Life was so hard that in the early years few survived their years of servitude. Some blacks were brought to the colony, both as slaves and servants, and generally worked, ate, and slept with the white servants.[3]

As the years passed, more and more servants lived to gain their freedom, despite the practice of extending terms for any offense, large or small.[4] They began farms of their own and increasingly resisted the policies of the larger, more established planters. For their part, the established growers began about 1660 to rely on black slaves for their labor needs. Slaves were more expensive initially, but their terms did not end, and their owners gained the benefits of the slaves' offspring.[5]

The fear of slave revolts increased as reliance on slavery grew and racial antipathy became more apparent. Fear and racism tended to lessen the economic and political differences between rich and poor whites. Both tended to look on royal officials and tax collectors as their common oppressors. They joined forces to

---

11. Id. at 131. Pursuant to the compromises worked out in the Constitutional Convention, the Second Congress enacted a fugitive slave law in 1793. The constitutionality of the act was upheld by the Supreme Court in Prigg v. Pennsylvania, 41 U.S. (16 Pet.) 539 (1842). The act was amended and strengthened as part of the Missouri Compromise of 1850. See Albert P. Blaustein & Robert L. Zangrando, Civil Rights and the American Negro 127 (1968).

§2.8   1. This section is excerpted from Derrick Bell, Racial Remediation: An Historical Perspective on Current Conditions, 52 Notre Dame Law. 5, 17-18 (1976).

2. Edmund S. Morgan, American Slavery, American Freedom (1975).

3. Id. at 154-155. Records of the time reveal little evidence of the racial prejudice that was to develop later.

4. Id. at 216-218.

5. Id. at 295-315. Masters substituted the fear of pain and death for the extension of terms as an incentive to force the slaves to work. Murder and dismembering of slaves was condoned, if not as common as the frequently administered beatings. Blacks, Morgan writes, were thought of as "a brutish sort of people." He concludes: ". . . whether or not race was a necessary ingredient of slavery, it *was* an ingredient. . . . The only slaves in Virginia belonged to alien races from the English. And the new social order that Virginians created after they changed to slave labor was determined as much by race as by slavery." Id. at 315 (emphasis supplied).

protest import taxes on tobacco, the profits from which sustained both. Thus, the rich began to look to their less wealthy neighbors for political support against the English government and in local elections.[6]

Wealthy whites retained all their former prerogatives, but the creation of a black subclass enabled poor whites to identify with and support the policies of the upper class. With the safe economic advantage provided by their slaves, large landowners were willing to grant poor whites a larger role in the political process. Thus, paradoxically, slavery for blacks led to greater freedom for poor whites.[7]

In the main, poor whites in the seventeenth century were ready to trade their economic demands for racism, and even two hundred years later in the post–Civil War period, the efforts of some leaders of the Populist Party to unite poor Southern whites and blacks against the ruling Bourbons were shattered by the continued inability of poor whites to surrender racism even for responsive political power.[8] Their susceptibility had not lessened midway through the twentieth century, as Dr. Martin Luther King's Southern Christian Leadership Conference discovered during the 1968 Poor People's Campaign.[9]

A final example of black rights becoming grist in the mill of white interest occurred more than a century ago during the hotly disputed Hayes-Tilden presidential election of 1876. In the following year, a possible second Civil War was

6. Id. at 364-366.

7. In explaining the paradox of slave owners espousing freedom and liberty, Morgan writes: "Aristocrats could more safely preach equality in a slave society than in a free one. Slaves did not become leveling mobs, because their owners would see to it that they had no chance to. The apostrophes to equality were not addressed to them. And because Virginia's labor force was composed mainly of slaves, who had been isolated by race and removed from the political equation, the remaining free laborers and tenant farmers were too few in number to constitute a serious threat to the superiority of the men who assured them of their equality. . . ." "This is not to say that a belief in republican equality had to rest on slavery, but only that in Virginia (and probably in other southern colonies) it did. The most ardent American republicans were Virginians, and their ardor was not unrelated to their power over the men and women they held in bondage." Id. at 380-381.

8. The nineteenth-century parallels with Professor Morgan's origin of slavery compromise theory are striking. The Populists were unable to control the Negro vote and were appalled at Democratic Party tactics that included forcing blacks to vote repeatedly for Democratic candidates. The Populists joined the movement for complete disfranchisement of blacks in order to reunite the white South. Professor John Hope Franklin commented on the result: "The poor, ignorant white farmers reverted to their old habits of thinking and acting, comforted in their poverty by Conservative assurances that Negro rule must be avoided at any cost. . . . The poor whites could say with one of their leaders that the Negro question was an everlasting, overshadowing problem that served to hamper the progress of poor whites and prevent them from becoming realistic in social, economic, and political matters." John Hope Franklin, From Slavery to Freedom 272 (4th ed. 1974). See also C. Vann Woodward, Origins of the New South, 1877-1913 (1951).

But the effect on poor whites is best described by Tom Watson, a Populist leader, who in 1892 as a staunch advocate of a union between Negro and white farmers wrote: "You are kept apart that you may be separately fleeced of your earnings. You are made to hate each other because upon that hatred is rested the keystone of the arch of financial despotism which enslaves you both. You are deceived and blinded that you may not see how this race antagonism perpetuates a monetary system which beggars both." Tom Watson, The Negro Question in the South, in Stokely Carmichael & Charles V. Hamilton, Black Power: The Politics of Liberation in America 68 (1967).

9. See Jules Archer, 1968 Year of Crisis 50-51 (1968); Charles Fager, Uncertain Resurrection: The Poor People's Washington Campaign (1969); Max Hastings, The Fire This Time: America's Year of Crisis 77-82 (1968).

averted by a compromise that even conservative historians now concede was a shameful moment.[10]

By 1876, the demolition of Radical Reconstruction was already well advanced. The federal government had proven itself unwilling or unable to halt the violence and terrorism by which Southern whites regained political control in most Southern states. The Democrats had regained great strength both in the South and much of the North. They fully expected that their presidential candidate Samuel J. Tilden, the reform governor of New York, would be elected. Republicans were divided by scandal and disparate views on economic issues; but all had tired of their lengthy involvement in Southern affairs and were more than ready to bury the hatchet on terms that would insure continued development of business interests in the South.

When the election returns were counted, Tilden had a plurality of 250,000 votes in the nation, and appeared to have won the electoral count by one vote. But the returns from three Southern states, South Carolina, Florida, and Louisiana (the last three states in which blacks still played a major political role) were challenged. Recounts of the votes did not resolve the challenge which then was submitted to a special electoral commission composed of 5 members from the Senate, 5 from the House, and 5 members of the Supreme Court. As it turned out, 8 of the 15 were Republicans and each disputed issue was resolved in favor of the Republicans by a strictly party vote of 8 to 7.

But the Democrats need not have accepted this resolution. They did so because of several understandings between Democratic and Republican leaders that if the Republican Hayes was elected, the national administration would withdraw the remaining federal troops from the South and would do nothing to prevent popularly elected Democratic governors from taking office in the three states (Florida, South Carolina, and Louisiana) still controlled by Republicans. It was also agreed that Hayes would include Southern Democrats in his cabinet and would support efforts of Southern capitalists to obtain subsidies for railroad construction in the South. President Hayes willingly carried out these promises to the Southerners. The demise of blacks as a political force proceeded rapidly thereafter.[11]

The loss of protection for their political rights presaged the destruction of economic and social gains that blacks in some areas had achieved. Blacks lost

---

10. In the mammoth Reconstruction literature with its many views on Radical Republican motivations, the accomplishments of the experiment, and the reasons for its failures, a fair sample of these views, with special focus on the myriad of factors contributing to the Hayes-Tilden Compromise, can be found in Lerone Bennett, Black Power USA: The Human Side of Reconstruction (1967); Hodding Carter, The Angry Scar (1959); W. E. B. Du Bois, Black Reconstruction in America (1935); J. G. Franklin & David Donald, The Civil War and Reconstruction (2d ed. 1961); Paul Haworth, The Hayes-Tilden Disputed Presidential Election of 1876 (1906); Rayford Logan, Betrayal of the Negro (1954); Kenneth Stampp, The Era of Reconstruction, 1865-1877 (1965); J. G. Randall, Reconstruction: After the Civil War (1961); C. Vann Woodward, Reunion and Reaction (1951).

11. Blacks made impressive gains in the post-bellum period. Personal and real property holdings, skilled jobs, businesses acquired and money saved by blacks are recorded in Charles Wesley, Negro Labor in the United States 1850-1925, at 138-147 (1927). Detailed information concerning the achievements by blacks in the crafts and the professions can be obtained from the many studies of reconstruction in particular states. See, e.g., Joel Williamson, After Slavery: The Negro in South Carolina During Reconstruction, 1861-1877, at 161-163 (1965).

businesses and farms, progress in the public schools was halted, and the Jim Crow laws that would eventually segregate blacks in every aspect of public life began to emerge.[12] As Professor C. Vann Woodward put it:

> The determination of the Negro's "place" took shape gradually under the influence of economic and political conflicts among divided white people — conflicts that were eventually resolved in part at the expense of the Negro. . . . [Documenting the acquiescence of Northern liberals in the compromise that included the acceptance of the Southern view of racial superiority, Woodward concludes:] Just as the Negro gained his emancipation and new rights through a falling out between white men, he now stood to lose his rights through the reconciliation of white men.[13]

§2.9 THE PRINCIPLE OF THE INVOLUNTARY SACRIFICE

The degree to which his contemporaries accept the basic thesis of Professor Morgan's explanation of how black slavery opened the way for less-well-off whites to gain greater rights and more equality than otherwise would have been possible is more than a little unsettling to even the militant civil rights lawyer. Can the properly esteemed Professor C. Vann Woodward be correct when he writes that "political democracy for the white man and racial discrimination for the black were often

---

In politics, blacks held many local and state offices throughout the South, and between 1870 and 1901 the South sent 20 blacks to the House of Representatives and 2 blacks to the Senate. Samuel Denny Smith, The Negro in Congress 1870-1901, at 4-5 (1940).

In education, Southern state legislatures with sizeable black representation structured the first public school systems in much of the South. Dr. W. E. B. Du Bois states, "[i]t is fair to say that the Negro carpetbag governments established the public schools of the South." W. E. B. Du Bois, Black Reconstruction in America 664 (1935). Dr. Du Bois indicates that there were many germs of a Southern public school system before the Civil War, but the public schooling in its modern sense "was founded by the Freedmen's Bureau and missionary societies, and that the state public school system was formed mainly by Negro Reconstruction governments." Id. For a detailed discussion, see id. at 637-639. See also Horace Bond, The Education of the Negro in the American Social Order (1966).

12. For example, at the end of the Civil War black artisans outnumbered whites by five to one, but by 1890 they made up only a small proportion of the labor force. C. Vann Woodward, Reunion and Reaction (1951).

13. C. Vann Woodward, The Strange Career of Jim Crow 7, 53 (3d rev. ed. 1974).

Southern leaders in the post-Reconstruction era enacted segregation laws mainly at the insistence of poor whites who needed these barriers to retain a sense of superiority over blacks. Professor Woodward writes, "[i]t took a lot of ritual and Jim Crow to bolster the creed of white supremacy in the bosom of a white man working for a black man's wages." Woodward, Reunion and Reaction (1951).

The political phenomenon uncovered by Morgan at the country's birth remained viable 200 years later. Professor Woodward observes that "[t]he barriers of racial discrimination mounted in direct ratio with the tide of political democracy among whites." He concludes: "It is one of the paradoxes of Southern history that political democracy for the white man and racial discrimination for the black were often products of the same dynamics." Id.

Another historian has accepted the Morgan thesis in a major study of slavery during the early years of the American Republic. David B. Davis, The Problem of Slavery in the Age of Revolution: 1770-1823, at 260-264 (2d ed. 1999).

products of the same dynamics"?[1] Is it more than a clever play on words when he suggests that Jim Crow laws were intended "to bolster the creed of white supremacy in the bosom of a white man working for a black man's wages"?[2] But how else explain actions like those of Louisiana governor Francis Tillou Nicholls who, following his inauguration in 1877, denounced racial bigotry, appointed blacks to office, and attracted many to his party. Then, in 1890, he signed into law the state's first railroad segregation statute. Two years later, Nicholls, now the state's Chief Justice, upheld the law's constitutionality in a decision destined to be affirmed by the Supreme Court in Plessy v. Ferguson.[3] Professor Woodward explains that by late 1892, the wave of Populist radicalism was reaching its crest in the South, and Nicholls' flip-flop on Negro rights "typified the concessions to racism that conservatives of his class were making in their efforts to divert poor-white farmers from economic reform."[4]

As we have seen, Nicholls's behavior set no new precedent. Rather, it followed a well-used pattern of racial politics observable before and, regrettably, long after his use of it. Thanks to Professor Morgan, we know how the practice got started. Its purposes are clear, but why is it so successful decade after decade? By now, its use and predictable outcome have an almost ritualistic character. Perhaps in this ritual we shall find an answer. At the least, discussion of the principle of involuntary sacrifice may help lead us to a satisfactory and rational explanation for behavior that, transferred to any other political arena, would be condemned as despicable.

In classical literature the lamb, goat, or virgin is sacrificed so that man and his gods may establish or reestablish their relationship. For humans, the surrender of something of value serves as a symbol of their seriousness. The ultimate example is God's command to Abraham to take his only son, Isaac, and offer him as a burnt offering to prove his fidelity. A less drastic parallel is the tradition of negotiators to signal to one another that they are serious and ready to reach a solution through compromise by surrendering a bargaining point they badly wanted to win, or one they had convinced the other side they badly wanted to win.

In the resolution of racial issues in America, black interests are often sacrificed so that identifiably different groups of whites may settle a dispute and establish or reestablish their relationship. We have observed the phenomenon at work in seventeenth-century Virginia and in the settlement of the sectional differences that enabled the Constitution to be signed by the delegates and ratified by the states. Arguably, Chief Justice Taney tried to use the technique in his *Dred Scott* opinion, but the sacrifice of black interests in that situation was so heavy-handed that it damaged many white interests as well. In the Hayes-Tilden Compromise of 1877, on the other hand, the sacrificial technique worked to perfection.

In myth and in America, the symbol set for involuntary sacrifice sometimes goes free, and may actually benefit from the resolution reached. In the biblical

---

§2.9   1. C. Vann Woodward, The Strange Career of Jim Crow (3d rev. ed. 1974).
2. Id.
3. 163 U.S. 537 (1896).
4. C. Vann Woodward, The Case of the Louisiana Traveler, in Quarrels That Have Shaped the Constitution 150, 151 (John A. Garraty ed., 1964).

story, an angel of Jehovah stayed Abraham's hand as he was about to slay his son, indicating that his willingness to sacrifice the boy was proof of his devotion. And in America, the Emancipation Proclamation represented Lincoln's conclusion that the more usual compromise of sacrificing black interests would not be possible. Rather than a bargain with the slaveholding states, the proclamation represented a bargain with the abolitionists here and abroad, with Lincoln's military commanders, and with the more radical elements of his Republican Party. Blacks, as a consequence, gained a symbolic but important benefit. When the war ended, this benefit paid even more valuable dividends in the form of the Civil War Amendments and the civil rights acts enacted by Congress to give the amendments meaning. Here too, though, self-interest motivations and involuntary sacrifice policies were much in evidence.

§2.10 THE CIVIL WAR AMENDMENTS AND CIVIL RIGHTS ACTS[1]

The military expediency that so influenced the decision to issue the Emancipation Proclamation and recruit black soldiers during the Civil War posed a dilemma for federal policymakers at the close of the war. As one Republican congressman bluntly put it, "[m]en who have handled muskets do not willingly become slaves."[2] Black leaders had urged the enlistment of blacks to give validity to Frederick Douglass's assertion: "He who fights the battles of America may claim America as his country and have that claim respected."[3]

Historians have cited humanitarian concerns, political realities, and a desire to punish the South as factors explaining the enactment of the civil rights amendments.[4] But Dr. Mary Frances Berry suggests that necessity and self-interest in utilizing large numbers of black troops during the conflict largely determined the measures aimed at securing emancipation and granting citizenship and suffrage during the postwar years.[5]

§2.10 1. This section is excerpted from Derrick Bell, Racial Remediation: An Historical Perspective on Current Conditions, 52 Notre Dame Law. 5, 9-11 (1976).

2. Mary Frances Berry, Toward Freedom and Civil Rights for the Freedmen: Military Policy Origins of the Thirteenth Amendment and the Civil Rights Act of 1866, at 9 (1975) (unpublished manuscript, Dept. of History, Howard University).

3. Id. at 19.

4. In the decades following Reconstruction, historians and much of the country viewed the era with regret, and those responsible for it with contempt. Radical Republicans were condemned as self-seeking scoundrels. Blacks were dismissed as ignorant clowns, totally unfit for citizenship. In recent years, more moderate views of the period have gained general acceptance. Some historians now argue that principle was a major motivation of Radical Republican policies. See, e.g., Cox & Cox, Negro Suffrage and Republican Politics: The Problem of Motivation in Reconstruction Historiography, 33 J. S. Hist. 303 (1967); Kincaid, Victims of Circumstance: An Interpretation of Changing Attitudes Toward Republican Policy Makers and Reconstruction, 57 J. Am. Hist. 48 (1970).

5. Berry, supra note 2, at 7-8. She reports that the campaign to enact the Thirteenth Amendment abolishing slavery began in 1864 while large numbers of black soldiers were engaged in combat. All black regiments were involved daily in the war's final battles when the Thirteenth Amendment was reconsidered by Congress early in 1865. In those debates, Republican congressman Henry Wilson supported the measure with the statement: "[W]e owe it to the course of the country, to

Enactment of the Thirteenth Amendment ended the Constitution's protection of slavery, but did not resolve the issue of the newly freed slaves' political status.[6] Opposition to black suffrage was great, and its proponents settled on the Civil Rights Act of 1866 as a means of protecting black civil rights against state and private interference.[7] But before the year ended, a majority of Congress recognized that the right to a lawsuit offered scant protection against the newly enacted Black Codes, race riots, and widespread white terror and intimidation.

Even so, Dr. Berry reports that the federal government intensified its efforts to discharge black soldiers who during the early months of 1866 outnumbered white troops three to one in some parts of the South.[8] In addition to charges of incompetence and insubordination, Union generals charged that black troops were hostile

liberty, to justice, and to patriotism to offer every inducement to every black man who can fight the battle of the country to join our armies." Arguments like Wilson's prevailed, and the Thirteenth Amendment was passed and signed by President Lincoln on February 1, 1865. At that point there were 200,000 blacks in the army, including the all-black XXI Army Corps of 32 black regiments. Black troops made up large contingents in almost every successful battle during the last year of the war. Id. at 11.

6. The Thirteenth Amendment provides:

"Section 1. Neither slavery nor involuntary servitude, except as a punishment for crime whereof the party shall have been duly convicted, shall exist within the United States, or any place subject to their jurisdiction." "Section 2. Congress shall have power to enforce this article by appropriate legislation."

7. Section 1 of the Civil Rights Act of 1866 provides:

"Be it enacted by the Senate and House of Representatives of the United States of America in Congress assembled, That all persons born in the United States and not subject to any foreign power, . . . are hereby declared to be citizens of the United States; and such citizens, of every race and color, without regard to any previous condition of slavery or involuntary servitude, . . . shall have the same right in every State and Territory in the United States, to make and enforce contracts, to sue, be parties, and give evidence, to inherit, purchase, lease, sell, hold, and convey real and personal property, and to full and equal benefit of all laws and proceedings for the security of person and property, as is enjoyed by white citizens, and shall be subject to like punishment, pains, and penalties, and to none other, any law, statute, ordinance, regulation, or custom, to the contrary notwithstanding."

The Fourteenth Amendment enacted by Congress in June 1866 (and finally ratified in 1868) was designed to end doubt about the constitutionality of the Civil Rights Act of 1866. Primary responsibility for the protection of black rights, however, was left to the states. All persons born in the United States were made citizens, but deprivations of citizenship rights were negatively stated rather than in positive form as in the Civil Rights Act of 1866. Section 1 of the Fourteenth Amendment provides:

"No state shall make or enforce any law which shall abridge the privileges or immunities of citizens of the United States; nor shall any state deprive any person of life, liberty, or property, without due process of law; nor deny to any person within its jurisdiction the equal protection of the laws."

8. Berry, supra note 2, at 15. Dr. Berry explains that after the Civil War ended, white troops were rapidly mustered out because they were anxious to go home, and any delay was questioned. Black troops, on the other hand, were more willing to remain in the service. Their terms had not expired and most had neither homes nor employment to which to return. Id. at 13.

As an example, Berry reports: "The order to muster out numerous white volunteer regiments in August 1865, left General Stonemen in Tennessee, two batteries of white artillery, and thirteen black regiments of all arms. Five of these black regiments were ordered to Alabama, where at that moment white troops were in the majority, so that General Woods could muster out five white regiments. In December 1865, when the states formally ratified the Thirteenth Amendment, only one of twelve infantry regiments in Mississippi was white, and in the following month there were 6,550 white and 17,768 black volunteers in Texas and Louisiana. Not until November of 1866 was black military

and insulting to Southern whites, threatening to white women, and encouraged militancy and insolence among civilian blacks.[9] It was clear that black troops invited to perform courageously during a time of national need were not expected to exhibit concern for black liberty when the crisis for the whites was over.

Even without Dr. Berry's theory, it is beyond dispute that the Republicans recognized that unless some action was taken to legitimate the freedmen's status, Southerners would utilize violence to force blacks into slavery, thereby renewing the economic dispute that had led to the Civil War. To avoid this result, the Fourteenth and Fifteenth Amendments and Civil Rights Acts of 1870-1875 were enacted.[10] They were the work of the Radical Reconstructionists, some of whom were deeply committed to securing the rights of citizenship for the freedmen. For most Republicans, however, a more general motivation was the desire to maintain Republican Party control in the Southern states and in Congress.

Within a decade it became apparent that the Thirteenth Amendment abolishing slavery was obsolete. Southern planters could achieve the same benefits with less burden through the sharecropping system and stark violence. The Fifteenth Amendment, politically obsolete at its birth, was not effectively enforced for almost a century. The Fourteenth Amendment, unpassable as a specific protection for black rights, was enacted finally as a general guarantee of life, liberty, and property of all "persons." Corporations, following a period of ambivalence,[11] were deemed persons under the Fourteenth Amendment,[12] and for several generations received far more protection from the courts[13] than did blacks.

According to research in a Harvard Law Review case review,[14] In the first seventy years of the Amendment, the Court struck down 232 state laws pursuant to its commands;[15] 179 of these cases were decided in favor of corporations — including 55 cases in favor of the burgeoning railroad industry.[16] Thus, even though the Fourteenth Amendment was designed as a refuge for the least powerful Americans, the Supreme Court, under relentless pressure from the corporate bar, turned it into a boon for railroads, monopolies, utility companies, bankers, and other large commercial interests.

---

strength, after muster-out, at a low enough level to make black military presence in the South a nonthreatening issue, and even then the presence of black veterans remained threatening."

9. In September 1865, all black regiments raised in the North were ordered mustered out on the theory that because they were unfamiliar with Southern racial ways, they posed a greater source of difficulty. Union generals moved black troops from urban to remote areas. Those who could not soon be relieved of military duties were assigned to the West where they could be occupied with fighting Indians and defending the frontier. Id. at 16-17.

10. Adopted in 1870, the Fifteenth Amendment prohibited the denial of the right to vote to U.S. citizens because of "race, color, or previous condition of servitude." Congress was empowered to enforce the provision "by appropriate legislation." The fate of post-Civil War laws is reviewed in Gressman, The Unhappy History of Civil Rights Legislation, 50 Mich. L. Rev. 1323 (1952).

11. Slaughter-House Cases, 83 U.S. (16 Wall.) 36 (1873).

12. Santa Clara County v. Southern Pac. R.R., 118 U.S. 394 (1886).

13. See, e.g., Allgeyer v. Louisiana, 165 U.S. 578 (1897); Lochner v. New York, 198 U.S. 45 (1905); Coppage v. Kansas, 236 U.S. 1 (1915); Adkins v. Children's Hospital, 261 U.S. 525 (1923).

14. 121 Harv. L. Rev. 275 (2007)

15. See, Felix Frankfurter, Mr. Justice Holmes and the Supreme Court 139.

16. Statistics are calculated from case summaries provided in id. app. 1.

Indeed, blacks became victims of judicial interpretations of the Fourteenth Amendment and legislation based on it so narrow as to render the promised protection meaningless in virtually all situations.[17]

§2.11 THE LESSONS OF THE FIRST RECONSTRUCTION

The period from the end of the Civil War to 1877 saw the basic rights of blacks to citizenship established in law, but precious little accomplished to ensure their political and economic rights. Without the latter, the former proved, then as so often today, all but worthless.

The Freedmen's Bureau was established by Congress in 1865, and helped with some of the basic needs of the former slaves, but Thaddeus Stevens's plan to give land to blacks was never adopted. As Lerone Bennett recounts the history:

> . . . To Stevens, more than to any other man, the freedmen owed their undying faith in the magical phrase, "Forty Acres and a Mule." In and out of Congress, the crusty old Pennsylvanian demanded that large plantations be broken up and distributed to the freedmen in forty-acre lots. Congress refused to budge and Stevens, always a realist, admitted that the dream was stillborn. He was 74, old and gnarled like an oak tree, on the day he rose in the House and pronounced the eulogy. "In my youth," the Great Commoner said, "in my manhood, in my old age, I had fondly dreamed that when any fortunate chance should have broken up for a while the foundation of our institutions [that we would have] so remodeled all our institutions as to have freed them from every vestige of human oppression, of inequality of rights. . . . This bright dream has vanished 'like the baseless fabric of a vision.'"[1]

If broken promises had been the only failures of the Reconstruction era and its aftermath, the plight of blacks and the complexity of racial issues today, despite the heritage of slavery, would be far less serious. Historians, many of them alerted by the decline of the post-World War II "Second Reconstruction" effort, are taking a close look at the physical violence, economic devastation, and total white domination that so quickly wiped out the impressive gains in income, education, property holdings, and political influence made during the First Reconstruction. Research emphasis until

---

17. See, e.g., United States v. Reese, 92 U.S. 214 (1876); United States v. Cruikshank, 92 U.S. 542 (1876); Civil Rights Cases, 109 U.S. 3 (1883); United States v. Harris, 106 U.S. 629 (1883); Plessy v. Ferguson, 163 U.S. 537 (1896); James v. Bowman, 190 U.S. 127 (1903).

The Court did recognize the Civil War Amendments' protection against exclusion of blacks from juries, Strauder v. West Virginia, 100 U.S. 303 (1880); Ex parte Virginia, 100 U.S. 339 (1880). Convictions under civil rights acts for blatant violation of federal rights usually including violence were upheld in a few cases. Ex parte Yarbrough, 110 U.S. 651 (1884); United States v. Waddell, 112 U.S. 76 (1884); Logan v. United States, 144 U.S. 263 (1892).

§2.11 1. Lerone Bennett, Jr., Before the Mayflower 189 (1961). Bennett reports that Charles Sumner fought hard for the measure in the Senate, but without success. Land that had been given to blacks was reclaimed and returned to its former owners, who had been pardoned by President Andrew Johnson.

recently has been on the loss of federal support, the political trickery that cost blacks their suffrage rights, and the constant economic squeeze that tenant farming and share-cropping made possible.

Economic and political suppression would have been ineffective had it not been for the wholesale and brutal violence that rendered thousands of ex-slaves literally unable to know on which side of emancipation they had fared worst. Professor Leon Litwack writes in *The Aftermath of Slavery*:

> How many black men and women were beaten, flogged, mutilated, and murdered in the first years of emancipation will never be known. Nor could any accurate body count or statistical breakdown reveal the barbaric savagery and depravity that so frequently characterized the assaults made on freedmen in the name of restraining their savagery and depravity — the severed ears and entrails, the mutilated sex organs, the burnings at the stake, the forced drownings, the open display of skulls and severed limbs as trophies. . . .
>   Neither a freedman's industriousness nor his deference necessarily protected him from whites if they suspected he harbored dangerous tendencies or if they looked upon him as a "smart-assed" nigger who needed chastisement.[2]

Rayford W. Logan, another historian, described the post-Reconstruction years for black people as "The Nadir."[3] The portrayal is not extravagant. It defines the depths to which blacks were reduced, and the nature of the betrayal and brutality which brought the freedmen low. The law's involvement in that downfall and its consequences could not have been greater. Our question is, why? Why were three constitutional amendments and a series of statutes specifically intended to protect the rights of the freedmen so easily swept aside? More specifically, during the far from gentle slide back toward a condition which, when measured purely in terms of physical protection, was no better than slavery, why were courts so unable to safeguard black rights?

An explanation requires placing post-Reconstruction courts in the context of their more general functioning at that time.[4] In the final decades of the nineteenth century, American courts had become first the espousers and then the creators and propagators of a conservative ideology that permeated all aspects of American life. Called upon to decide pressing questions concerning the relations of labor and capital, the power of state legislatures, and the rights of big business, the courts foreswore impartiality and came down heavily on the side of economic interests. The shift from a stand of noninterference in questions of economic and legislative

---

2. Leon F. Litwack, Been in the Storm So Long: The Aftermath of Slavery 276-277 (1969). Whatever other criticisms can be made about Robert W. Fogel & Stanley L. Engerman, Time on the Cross: The Economics of American Negro Slavery (1974), its authors observed correctly that "one of the worst consequences of the traditional interpretation of slavery is that it has diverted attention from the attack on the material conditions of black life that took place during the decades following the end of the Civil War." Id. at 260-261.

3. Rayford W. Logan's Betrayal of the Negro (1965) originally appeared as The Negro in American Life and Thought: The Nadir, 1877-1901 (1954).

4. The explanation offered here is excerpted from a lengthy study of the post-Reconstruction era, Derrick Bell, The Racial Imperative in American Law, in The Age of Segregation: Race Relations in the South, 1890-1945, at 3, 7-9 (Robert Haws ed., 1978).

policy mirrored other changes that were occurring in American society during this era.[5]

In the 1880s, American society was rife with social tensions. There were cries from the society's lower-income echelons for free silver, labor rights, a graduated income tax, and protection against the trusts.[6] These demands were countered by an ideology that embraced the established order of things and the immutability of prevailing social patterns. The ideas of Charles Darwin, Herbert Spencer, William Graham Sumner, and other influential social scientists were combined to champion a system that supported natural rights and racial purity, and that equated wealth and power with virtue.[7] Immigrants in the North and blacks in the South were seen as corrupting forces or entities to be discounted in the formulation of public policy. Popular democracy and, with it, universal suffrage became suspect, and a return to property and literacy qualification was urged.[8]

The Supreme Court, sympathetic to conservative interests through the pattern of its past decisions, its duties as preserver of the law, and its specific composition at the time, became in these decades the major protector of propertied interests.[9] Courts formulated due process and freedom of contract doctrine to shield business from state regulation, denied rights to labor, outlawed the federal income tax, and watered down the Sherman Anti-Trust laws.[10] Having recast its image and reputation after the debacle of *Dred Scott*, the Court expanded its role from interpreter to a principal maker of law, and became the central paradox in a paradoxical age of conservative reform. It espoused individual rights at the expense of the individual and acted in behalf of public interest through the protection of private enterprise.

Within this framework, racial law became an important conduit for the preservation and legitimation of the established order. Shaken by fears of a powerful

5. See Arnold Paul, Conservative Crisis and the Rule of Law: Attitudes of Bar and Bench, 1887-1895, at 19-81 (1969); Robert McCloskey, American Conservatism in the Age of Enterprise 72-126 (1951); Robert Harris, The Quest for Equality 57-108 (1960); and Charles Warren, III, The Supreme Court in United States History 255-343 (1922).

6. For a discussion of the major issues of the day, see C. Vann Woodward, Origins of the New South 369-395 (1951); Harold Faulkner, The Quest for Social Justice, 1898-1914 (1931); Robert Wiebe, The Search for Order 1877-1920 (1967).

7. See C. Vann Woodward, The Strange Career of Jim Crow 103 (3d rev. ed. 1974); Logan, Betrayal of the Negro, supra note 3, at 165-174; Thomas Gosset, Race: The History of an Idea in America 144-175, 253-309 (1963).

8. See discussion of Northern newspapers' positions on suffrage issue, 1890-1901, in Logan, Betrayal of the Negro, supra note 3, at 195-217. For other discussions of the suffrage issue in the North and West, see Forrest Wood, Black Scare, The Racist Response to Emancipation and Reconstruction 80-102 (1968); David Southern, The Malignant Heritage: Yankee Progressives and the Negro Question 1901-1914 (1968); and Barbara Solomon, Ancestors and Immigrants: A Changing New England Tradition (1956).

9. The judges, as members of the legal profession, had had a legal education conservative in nature and had generally gone on to practice law for corporate powers. Thus their professional development took a conservative bent. Moreover, in its decisions, the Court had been generally called upon to preserve the status quo, to prevent either state or federal government from taking action. It had generally tended toward the exercise of "negative power." See McCloskey, supra note 5, at 75-77 (1951).

10. E.g., Lochner v. New York, 198 U.S. 45 (1905) (business protected from state regulation); In re Debs, 158 U.S. 564 (1895) (denied rights to labor); Pollock v. Farmers Loan & Trust Co., 157 U.S. 429 (1895) (prohibition of federal income tax); and United States v. E. C. Knight Co., 156 U.S. 1 (1895) (weakened Sherman Anti-Trust Act).

coalition of white Populists and blacks, white conservatives in the South turned to disfranchisement as well as legal separation in social and economic spheres. Race distinction, an instrument of popular suppression in other eras of American history, was once more brought forth by an elite wishing to maintain power. Here, too, the courts were the espousers of conservative sentiment. Though eager to countermand state regulation in the economic realm, the justices were satisfied to leave state regulation of race relations untrammeled during these years. The Court first reduced privileges and immunities under federal protection. Later, it invalidated the public accommodation provisions of the 1875 Civil Rights Act, and finally formulated the separate but equal doctrine that sustained segregation for three generations.[11] Court policy thus followed the swing toward conservatism evidenced in the political and economic realms. The courts, and along with them the rule of law, became not impartial arbiters of societal relations but instead the mirror and enforcer of property interests.

In the sections that follow, further consideration will be given to the law's role in the systematic subjugation of a people so recently declared free and entitled by federal statute to the same rights in all important endeavors as those "enjoyed by white citizens."[12] But without in any way minimizing the anarchy that prevailed in much of the South even before the removal of the last federal forces, it must be said that some blacks made progress that, under the circumstances, must be deemed miraculous. Indeed, as some historians are perhaps too quick to point out, the gains in education, property ownership, and income made by the freedmen during the First Reconstruction compare far more favorably than one might expect with the advances made by their descendants a century later during the Second Reconstruction.

Professor James M. McPherson, noting how many of his history students assumed that blacks had done no more than survive the First Reconstruction, reports that black literacy increased from 10 percent in 1860 to 30 percent in 1880.[13] During the same period, the number of black children attending school increased from 2 to 34 percent. The proportion of white children rose only from 60 to 62 percent during that time. McPherson concedes these figures are "minimal and shameful" by today's literacy standards, but he says, "[i]n no other period of American history has either the absolute or relative rate of black literacy and school attendance increased so much as in the 15 years after 1865."[14]

In the area of politics, fewer than 1 percent of black adult males were eligible to vote. One million were eligible three years later, and 700,000 voted in the 1872 presidential election. No black man held public office in 1867, but by 1870 at least 15 percent of all Southern public officials were black. Professor McPherson notes

11. Reduction of privileges and immunities under federal protection: Slaughterhouse Cases, 83 U.S. (16 Wall.) 36 (1873); United States v. Reese, 92 U.S. 214 (1876): United States v. Cruikshank, 92 U.S. 542 (1876). Invalidation of public accommodation provisions: Civil Rights Cases, 109 U.S. 3 (1883). Formulation of separate but equal doctrine: Plessy v. Ferguson, 163 U.S. 537 (1896).

12. Similar language is found in both the April 9, 1866, and the May 31, 1870, civil rights acts now codified in 42 U.S.C. §§1981 and 1982 (1970).

13. James M. McPherson, Comparing the Two Reconstructions, Princeton Alumni Weekly 16, 18 (Feb. 26, 1979).

14. Id. at 18.

by way of comparison that in 1979, 14 years after the passage of the Voting Rights Act of 1965, fewer than 3 percent of Southern officeholders were black. In land-ownership, only 20 percent of the black farm operators owned their own land in 1880, while two-thirds of the white farmers owned their land, the average value of which was more than double that owned by blacks. Blacks were clearly on the bottom of the economic ladder, but the 20 percent who did own land represented an increase from zero in 1865, greater than in any comparable period of American history.[15]

Professor McPherson argues that these gains, inadequate though they were, were seen as revolutionary by poor whites who launched a violent counter-revolution that undercut but did not totally eliminate black gains. He notes a marked similarity in the response of even liberal whites to progress made by blacks during the Second Reconstruction. Their reaction or "backlash" has taken the form of "white flight," abandonment of poverty programs, the erection of suburban housing barriers, and the prevalence of a sense that the federal government tried to force racial change too quickly. Even considering this country's far greater knowledge and resources in the twentieth century, he finds it "remarkable that our ancestors accomplished so much and we so little."[16]

§2.12 UNDERSTANDING RACISM BASED ON THE NINETEENTH-CENTURY EXPERIENCE

If the slavery era proved the ability of blacks to simply survive, the Reconstruction era and its aftermath proved their ability to improve conditions despite severe adversity. But courage and effort aside, it does not require an unreasonable reading of history to conclude that the degree of progress blacks have made away from slavery and toward equality has depended on whether allowing blacks more or less opportunity best served the interests and aims of white society. We have seen, for example, that the major liberating events in black history have, in fact, been motivated less by black suffering than by the pragmatic advantage they offered white society; moreover, under our principle of involuntary sacrifice (§2.9), major conflicts between opposing white groups have been resolved through compromises that victimized blacks (e.g., the colonial decision to legitimize slavery, the Found-ing Fathers' agreement to recognize and protect slavery in the Constitution, and the Hayes-Tilden Compromise of 1877). To the extent that resolutions of differences occur between poor and wealthy whites, the poor whites often achieve a larger voice in the political process through specific laws and policies that reduce the status of blacks.

The significance of these findings in planning strategies for racial remediation depends on the degree to which they will remain viable factors in future racial

15. Id. at 18-19.
16. Id. at 20.

policy-making. It is hard to imagine that still unrevealed problems will not lend themselves to solutions that either improve or diminish the value of black rights. It is even more difficult to imagine a future time when the racial motivations that underlay so much past and present policymaking will disappear. Little that has happened in the twentieth century does more than reinforce the conclusions drawn out of the experience of the nineteenth.

Certainly, there was little indication in this history to justify placing much faith in the law, and yet in the nineteenth century blacks continued, with scant success, to look to the courts to remedy those aspects of societal racism the practice of which contravened constitutional protections and applicable statutory provisions. No less a judicial personage than Justice Oliver Wendell Holmes explained why this faith was misplaced.

In Giles v. Harris,[1] the plaintiff charged that the disfranchising clauses of the Alabama Constitution were designed to prevent blacks from voting, and thus violated the Fourteenth and Fifteenth Amendments. The Supreme Court responded first with sophistry, indicating that a court of equity cannot enforce registration under statutory provisions that the plaintiff himself is contending are invalid. The Court added that a court of equity could not enforce political rights, and on this technical ground denied the request for an injunction requiring the state to permit six thousand blacks to vote. Plaintiffs had alleged "that the great mass of the white population intends to keep the blacks from voting." If that were the case, Justice Holmes, speaking for the Court, responded, it would do little good to give black voters an order that would be ignored at the local level. Then virtually conceding the Court's impotency in political cases, Holmes added, "Apart from damages to the individual, relief from a great political wrong if done, as alleged, by the people of a state and the state itself, must be given by them or by the legislative and political department of the Government of the United States."[2]

Considering the almost nonexistent leverage blacks of the period exercised at either the legislative or executive levels, in substantial part because of practices precisely like those challenged by the plaintiffs in the *Giles* case, Justice Holmes's decision represented judicial abstention with a vengeance. On the other hand, what alternative did Justice Holmes have available? His observation that the Court could do nothing if "the great mass of the white population intends to keep the blacks from voting," was not a pretty truth; but it was the truth. And, in the final analysis, a court's power to issue and enforce orders is limited to those orders that at least a substantial percentage of the people want or will permit to be carried out.

In litigation involving racial issues, the last three or four decades have shown an impressive number of areas where courts are willing and able to enforce orders protecting the basic rights of blacks over frequently ardent resistance of substantial percentages of whites. But as we shall see, the contemporary protection of black rights, like that granted in the nineteenth century, may well be closely connected with the defense of interests that are perceived, at least by whites in policymaking positions, as important to them.

§2.12 1. 189 U.S. 475 (1903). For discussion of this case, see Charles S. Mangum, Jr., The Legal Status of the Negro 402 (1940).
2. 189 U.S. at 488.

Self-interest has been described by one writer as the most basic and important force underlying white policy and action vis-à-vis blacks. Such action more often than not serves the interests of the actors or is accounted for by an incorrect perception of objective interest. Values and morals (i.e., the American creed) do under certain conditions prompt and guide the action, but they appear to be powerless to motivate any large segment of whites to action in unison against their perceived interests.[3] I have reduced my sense of how the nation's obsession with racism is combined with its ambivalent commitment to both self-interest and equality for all to a useful (though somewhat simplistic and sardonic) formula:

$$\text{White Racism v. Justice} = \text{White Racism}$$
$$\text{White Racism v. White Self-Interest} = \text{Justice}$$

The elimination of racism as a policy factor in public and private decisions would seem in the interest of every American, white as well as black. But racial subordination has served so many white interests well that some social scientists doubt that it can be eliminated. Public policy expert Tilden J. LeMelle doubts

> . . . whether a society such as the United States is really capable of legislating and enforcing effective public policy to combat racial discrimination in the political process and elsewhere. He says history presents no instances where a society in which racism has been internalized and institutionalized to the point of being an essential and inherently functioning component of that society ever reforms, particularly a culture from whose inception racial discrimination has been a regulative force for maintaining stability and growth and for maximizing other cultural values. He doubts whether such a society of itself can even legislate (let alone enforce) public policy to combat racial discrimination. He sees the United States acting effectively against racism only when that racism is perceived as posing a serious threat to the country rather than serving as the useful regulator it has been.[4]

When written in the 1970s, Professor LeMelle's assessment must have seemed harsh and pessimistic, but considered against the retrenchment of subsequent years, its accuracy is reflected in the widespread opposition to black gains, all too easily condemned as the result of reverse discrimination. The sense of so many whites that their racial standing is more important than social improvement poses a serious barrier for those urging social reform in the areas of housing, poverty, public health, and prison reform. Economist Robert Heilbroner believes that race is one reason the United States lags behind countries like Norway, Denmark, England, and Canada in addressing social needs.

> [In these countries,] there is no parallel to the corrosive and pervasive role played by race in the problem of social neglect in the United States. It is the obvious fact that the persons who suffer most from the kinds of neglect (mentioned above) are disproportionately Negro. This merging of the racial issue with that of neglect serves as a rationalization for the policies of inaction that have characterized so much of the

3. Norval D. Glenn, The Role of White Resistance and Facilitation in the Negro Struggle for Equality, in Power and the Black Community 414 (Sethard Fisher ed., 1970).
4. Tilden J. LeMelle, Foreword to Richard M. Burkey, Racial Discrimination and Public Policy in the United States 38 (1971).

American response to need. Programs to improve slums are seen by many as programs to "subsidize" Negroes; proposals to improve conditions of prisons are seen as measures to coddle black criminals; and so on. In such cases, the fear and resentment of the Negro takes precedence over the social problem itself. The result, unfortunately, is that the entire society suffers from the results of a failure to correct social evils whose ill effects refuse to obey the rules of segregation.[5]

The views on the subject could be extended indefinitely. The phenomenon of racism in America, clearly present in the colonial seventeenth century, was brought to full development during the nation's birth and growth to maturity in the eighteenth and nineteenth. It continues as a major force in even the twenty-first though it cannot be easily cabined by definition or illustration. Perhaps an analogy will set the stage for group discussion and heightened individual insight.[6]

In reviewing a book on pre-Civil War judges who, despite their moral opposition to slavery, handed down decisions that upheld slavery, I suggested that most whites view the racial plight of blacks as an injustice that should be corrected. But on a priority scale, the elimination of racism would rate only a step or two higher than the campaign to end the senseless slaughter of the oceans' great whales.[7] In other words, racial equality, like whale conservation, should be advocated, but with the understanding that there are clear and rather narrow limits as to the degree of sacrifice or the amount of effort that most white Americans are willing to commit to either crusade.

Indeed, the country is unlikely to be invaded by a school of great whales, but because many whites fear inroads by blacks in their schools, jobs, and neighborhoods, a public opinion poll might even give a higher priority to whale conservation than to racial remediation. In a sense, this fear, not unlike the fear of slave revolts, has survived its antebellum origins. Mixed with guilt and that intangible aversion to color that Winthrop Jordan found in even the Elizabethan Englishmen,[8] the fear continues to evoke an irrational dread that inundation will follow if blacks are released from the subordinate position where, despite all the civil rights efforts, they remain.

Fear of inundation by blacks should be added to the two, already identified, components of racism: (1) the inherent sense that white people represent a higher and better order of humanity than do blacks; and (2) the feeling that while blacks are citizens, have made many contributions, and should not be discriminated against, America is not simply a country consisting of a white majority; it is a white country, which means that flourishing black institutions of any kind are unnatural, suspect, and not to be encouraged.

In our time, we have placed our faith and hopes on integration to eliminate racial discrimination. But consider the very definition of integration. Irrationally, an

5. Robert Heilbroner, The Roots of Social Neglect in the United States, Is Law Dead? 288, 296 (Eugene Rostow ed., 1971).

6. The analogy discussion was excerpted from Derrick Bell, Racial Remediation: An Historical Perspective on Current Conditions, 52 Notre Dame Law. 5, 23-25 (1976).

7. Robert M. Cover, Justice Accused: Antislavery and the Judicial Process (1975), reviewed, Bell, 76 Colum. L. Rev. 350, 357-358 (1976).

8. Winthrop D. Jordan, White Over Black 3-43 (1968).

"integrated" school, work force, or neighborhood is one with no more than a 25 percent black population. If the percentage is substantially greater, it is no longer a legitimately integrated setting for most white Americans, and is referred to as a "changing" school, a neighborhood in danger of "tipping," or a "racially imbalanced" job unit.

Consider also that racial integration is resisted until it occurs on a basis that insures white dominance and control. When blacks turn their energies from white-dominated integration and toward the establishment of strong, viable black institutions, they incur opposition and hostility that increases in direct proportion to their success. When the ventures fail, as so many do under this pressure, the society in general, including all too many blacks, breathes a sigh of relief. Once again the society can relax and indulge itself in the subtle satisfactions of black subordination.

Thus, white dominance over blacks is not only profitable, it is also, for the reasons just listed, comforting, and because of the ancestral fears of inundation, essential. This is not to say that blacks as individuals cannot achieve and prosper in this country, and receive general acclaim for those achievements. Successful blacks serve white interests by providing the rationalizing link between the nation's espousal of racial equality and its practice of racial dominance. The unspoken and totally facetious maxim is that with self-improvement the opportunity is available for all blacks to be successful. But success for individual blacks demands exceptional skills exercised diligently in settings where their efforts will further or, at least, not threaten white interests. Obviously, no more than a small percentage of blacks is likely to be graced by so felicitous a set of circumstances.

§2.13 REPARATIONS FOR RACISM

While not intended, it is likely that the just-completed discussion of the efficacy of law in eradicating manifest racism in the society leads inevitably to the question, what else is there? One answer espoused by some advocates is racial reparations based on the injustices blacks have experienced in this country. Such reparations might be seen as one means of financing entry into first-class citizenship, or they might be viewed as recognition that neither entry nor acceptance will be possible for blacks, and that they had better simply get "paid off" for the exploitation they and their forebears have suffered on account of their race and color.

The Civil Liberties Act of 1988,[1] which provided $20,000 and an apology to people of Japanese ancestry who were interned during World War II, revitalized the movement for African American reparations.[2] Grass roots reparations activism

§2.13   1. Wartime Relocation of Civilians, 102 Stat. 903, Pub. L. 100-383 (Aug. 10, 1988), 50 U.S.C.A. App. §1989 (Restitution for World War II Internment of Japanese-Americans and Aleuts, or "The Civil Liberties Act of 1988").

2. Vincene Verdun, 67 Tul. L. Rev. 597 (1993), If the Shoe Fits Wear It: An Analysis of Reparations to African Americans.

is being furthered by the National Coalition of Blacks for Reparations (N'Cobra) and other organizations seeking to use the Japanese reparations precedent to support requests for a total of $4 trillion in reparations to descendants of African American slaves.[3] Two legislators, Congressman John Conyers and Massachusetts State Senator William Owens, have each introduced reparations legislation, both thus far without further legislative action.[4]

Professor Vincene Verdun notes that the consistent plea for reparations for over 130 years carries a mysterious and even irrational aura from the perspective of many Americans arising out of perceptions that include: reparations are unlikely ever to be awarded, since after all no relief has been given for the past 130 years; reparations are undeserved by African Americans because they were never slaves since all ex-slaves have been dead for at least a generation; white Americans living today have not injured African Americans and should not be required to pay for the sins of their slave master forefathers; it is impossible to determine who should get what and how much; or that African Americans must become self-reliant and determine their own fate and stop waiting for relief from external sources. Opponents of reparations to African Americans are so overwhelmingly entrenched in the rightness of their position that they conceptualize the cry for reparations as frivolous, meritless, and divisive.

But, according to Professor Verdun, the reparations movement cannot be easily dismissed or discredited, in part because so many of its supporters are part of the American mainstream. For the same reason, the movement cannot be classified as radical or extremist. A movement that has been sustained through several generations, and has won the support of knowledgeable and reputable people throughout history, including members of Congress, businesspeople, professionals, academicians, attorneys, educators, and the hard-working masses, cannot be dismissed as frivolous. Proponents of reparations pursue their cause with fervor equivalent to that of its opponents, and stand firm in the following assertions: (1) reparations were given to Jews by Germany and to the American Indians and Japanese Americans by the United States, which is precedent for the payment of reparations to African Americans; (2) slaves were not paid for their labor for over 265 years, depriving

---

3. See Reparations Sought for Black Americans, Los Angeles Times, Dec. 10, 1990, at 1.

4. The Conyers bill, which would create a commission to study the institution of slavery subsequent de jure and de facto racial and economic discrimination against African Americans, and the impact of these forces on living African Americans, was first introduced on November 20, 1989. H.R. 374-5, 101st Cong., 1st Sess., 135 Cong. Rec. H9154 (1989). The bill did not come out of the House Committee on Judiciary. Conyers reintroduced the bill on April 10, 1991, H.R. 1684, 102d Cong., 1st Sess., 137 Cong. Rec. H2134 (1991), and the bill, with 25 cosponsors, was again referred to the House Judiciary Committee. The Conyers bill was supported by resolutions from the state legislature of Louisiana and the city councils of Inglewood, California, Detroit, Michigan, and Washington, D.C. A resolution, with 22 supporters, memorializing the Congress of the United States to pass the Conyers bill was introduced in the Michigan House of Representatives. Organizations that have publicly announced support of the Conyers bill include Detroit chapters of the National Association for the Advancement of Colored People and the American Civil Liberties Union, as well as the Southern Christian Leadership Council.

The Owens bill, which provides for payment of reparations for slavery, the slave trade, and invidious discrimination against the people of African descent born or residing in the United States, was introduced on January 30, 1991, S. 298, 191 Mass. S.B. 298, and was referred to the Joint Committee on Federal Financial Assistance.

the descendants of slaves of their inheritance; (3) the descendants of the slavemasters inherited the benefit derived from slave labor that properly belongs to the descendants of slaves;[5] (4) the U.S. government promised ex-slaves 40 acres and a mule and broke that promise;[6] and (5) systematic and government-sanctioned economic and racial oppression since the abolition of slavery impeded and interfered with the self-determination of African Americans and excluded them from sharing in the growth and prosperity of the nation.

Unfortunately, the proponents and opponents of reparations maintain diametrically opposed points of view, and both groups are deeply entrenched in the "rightness" of their positions. Opponents of reparations, who are usually white, frequently approach the issue of reparations from the dominant perspective, that is, a system of values and perceptions common to the group that exercises economic, political, and ideological control over society.[7] Proponents of reparations, usually black, evaluate them on the basis of a consciousness (the African American consciousness) spawned from generations of survival as an oppressed people in a hostile environment and rooted in the heritage of the African culture that survived the trip across the Atlantic Ocean and the institution of slavery. The differences in these two value systems and the perspectives they engender are the foundation for the polarity between opponents and proponents of reparations.

Professor Arnold Schuchter, in a lengthy study of the subject, warns those who would take the reparations idea seriously that since the claim for redress will be in the form of an argument based on morality, disappointment must be expected. Writing of the motivations and the performance of Germany in paying $820 million in reparations to Israel for the resettlement of five hundred thousand Jews, Professor Schuchter concludes his review of the German reparations experience in language providing a valuable message to blacks who — despite

---

5. This position has a foundation in the law of trusts. The descendants of slave masters are analogous to the trustees, the descendants of slaves to the beneficiaries of the trust, and the withheld wages of slaves represent the corpus. The beneficiaries have a right to demand that the corpus and any profits derived from the use of the corpus be turned over to them by the trustee.

6. The 40 acres and a mule may be more symbolic in its origins than substantive. Although legislation was available to provide land to freedmen and land was divided up by the Freedmen's Bureau in 20- and 40-acre plots, none provided for mules for freedmen. The promise could have been derived from the efforts of the War Department to make provisions for the thousands of freedmen that joined General Tecumseh Sherman in his successful march across Georgia in late 1864 and early 1865. Sherman, acting under the authorization of the War Department, assigned each head of family of the freedmen 40 acres of land and provided them with a possessory title (which was later revoked by President Andrew Johnson when he restored the lands to the dispossessed white planters) to land bordering the Atlantic Ocean in the Southern states of South Carolina and Florida. Sherman ordered General Saxton to lend animals that were too broken down for military service to Negroes so that they could work the land. See Claude F. Oubre, Forty Acres and a Mule 1, 18-19 (1978).

7. Race, class, or gender does not absolutely determine if an individual will analyze issues from the dominant perspective. However, a member of the dominant group (e.g., a white, heterosexual, middle-class, Christian male) is more likely to have been indoctrinated into the values and norms that establish the dominant perspective than a poor black female.

All proponents of reparations are not African Americans, nor do they necessarily perceive issues from the consciousness of an African American. There are other ideological bases for supporting reparations from within the dominant perspective. See, e.g., Boris I. Bittker, infra note 9, and Graham Hughes, Reparations for Blacks, 43 N.Y.U. L. Rev. 1063 (1968) (individual whites are guilty of inertia for not taking positive steps to improve the position of black people).

their increasing strength and militancy — must call still on the morality of the majority:

> Moral commitment to redress of historic wrongs against humanness can be badly compromised in the political and legislative process by which moral commitment is translated into programs and financial support. Frequently, the nature of the compromise is not at all obvious and tends to be obscured by moral rhetoric. Often we only hear the "good" reason, while the "real" reason for political action that shows up in legislation contradicts that "good" reason. Consequently, we are caught off guard, and the legislative actions supposedly designed to correct social and political injustice actually result in greater injustice. Avoiding this outcome requires continuous and highly skilled scrutiny of the political and legislative process in order to catch contradictions between principle and outcome at the time of decision-making. Those who choose to assert their will to establish a radically different moral and political direction in America, to eradicate racism, segregation, and social injustice, will have to institutionalize their commitment in a highly pragmatic and organized process of political surveillance, advocacy and action.[8]

Professor Schuchter's advice seems sound, but minority groups will likely have difficulty following it for precisely the same reason that the legal process is so uncertain a protector of their rights. The absence of real economic and political power, the determination, conscious and unconscious, of whites to maintain dominance over all institutions of importance to them and to exhibit aggressive concern whenever any black enterprise appears to be gaining real self-sufficiency, all of these factors militate against the likelihood that a viable reparations scheme will get beyond the not unimpressive hand-outs made by some major church groups following James Forman's dramatic presentation of a "Black Manifesto" demanding $500 million from America's churches and synagogues. See details at §12.4.

Forman's protest did prompt Professor Boris Bittker to take the matter of reparations seriously. The result[9] was a thorough examination of the many legal difficulties that would attend a suit intended to obtain reparational remedies for blacks either as individuals or as a class. In reviewing his book,[10] I suggested that:

> Professor Bittker has succeeded perhaps too well. His book is intended as a summary review rather than an in-depth analysis of the issues; an approach that permits a great deal of glossing over of difficult legal problems. Even so, it becomes clear that, short of a revolution, the likelihood that blacks today will obtain direct payments in compensation for their subjugation as slaves before the Emancipation Proclamation, and their exploitation as quasi-citizens since, is no better than it was in 1866, when Thaddeus Stevens recognized that his bright hope of "Forty Acres and a Mule" for every freedman had vanished "like the baseless fabric of a vision."[11]

8. Arnold Schuchter, Reparations 243-244 (1970).
9. Boris I. Bittker, The Case for Black Reparations (1973).
10. Derrick Bell, Book Review, 9 Harv. C.R.-C.L. L. Rev. 156 (1976).
11. Lerone Bennett, Before the Mayflower 189 (1961).
    The vision was not Stevens's alone. Harvard College Professor Ewart Guinier, in his review of the Bittker book, reminds us that the passionate black writer, David Walker, had protested the lack of compensation for the labor of slaves in 1829, and that after the Civil War, Bishop Henry McNeal Turner called for reparations on numerous occasions. Professor Guinier also cites reparations calls made in more recent years by Whitney Young, Martin Luther King, and the Newark Black Power Conference of 1967. Ewart Guinier, Book Review, 82 Yale L.J. 1719, 1721 (1973).

There is an air of mystery about visions that can be translated into energy, action, and on occasion success. Indeed, faith may be the definition for the human attraction that mystery provides to an otherwise preposterous idea. Visions of this character can seldom survive clinical examination. They are irrational by nature, and wilt under legal analysis. Thus, Professor Bittker's exploratory surgery of black reparations "using the tools of his [lawyer's] trade"[12] predictably exposes some serious legal and political difficulties while giving little attention to the pressures, moral and political, that, when applied by those whose faith in a cause exceeded their belief in the law, have spawned other legally acceptable reparations programs in this country and elsewhere.[13]

Professor Bittker is aware that the lawmaking process is affected by many societal factors. He suggests early in the book that perhaps the student who questioned him about the law and black reparations was really implying "that our system of law is shaped by political and economic power and that it serves those who possess that power, not those who live their lives outside the mainstream of American society."[14] However, he decided to take the question at its face value, a decision that made his work more manageable from the standpoint of legal analysis, but divorced the discussion from the reality of factual situations in which serious reparations proposals would be likely to arise.[15]

In closing my review, I concluded that even if Professor Bittker had devised a foolproof legal theory for black reparations litigation, few judges or legislators would be moved in the absence of some dramatic event, major crisis, or tragic circumstance that conveyed the necessity or at least the clear advantages of adopting a reparations scheme. At that point, Professor Bittker's suggestions and concerns would be helpful in evolving a workable plan.

Legal analysis cannot give life to a process that must evolve from the perceptions of those responsible for the perpetuation of racism in this country. Suggestions to the contrary, even those made in good faith, constitute less a contribution to legal scholarship than the ultimate in societal conceit.[16]

Despite the many legal and political obstacles to reparations, it is once again the subject of media attention and several law review articles.[17] Randall Robinson

---

12. Bittker, supra note 9, at 7.

13. Professor Bittker cites several examples including the Indian Claims Commission, 25 U.S.C. §70a (1946), and the Federal Compensation Law under which West Germany paid reparations to Nazi victims. Bittker, supra note 9, at 22, 177.

14. Bittker, supra note 9, at 4.

15. Bell, supra note 10, at 157-158.

16. Id. at 165.

17. See, e.g., Alfred Brophy, Some Conceptual and Legal Problems in Reparations for Slavery, 58 N.Y.U. Ann. Surv. Am. L. 497 (2003); Chad Bryan, Commentary: Precedent for Reparations? A Look at Historical Movements for Redress and Where Awarding Reparations for Slavery Might Fit, 54 Ala. L. Rev. 599 (2003); Robert Westley, Reparations and Symbiosis: Reclaiming the Remedial Focus, 71 UMKC L. Rev. (2002); Robert Westley, Many Billions Gone: Is It Time to Reconsider the Case for Black Reparations? 19 B.C. Third World L.J. 429 (1998); Watson Branch, Reparations for Slavery: A Dream Deferred, 3 San Diego L.J. 177 (2002); Edberto Roman, Reparations and the Colonial Dilemma: The Insurmountable Hurdles and Yet Transformative Benefits, 13 Berkeley La Raza L.J. 369 (2002); Kevin Hopkins, Forgive the U.S. Our Debts? Righting the Wrongs of Slavery, 89 Geo. L.J. 2531 (2001).

in his book, *The Debt: What America Owes to Blacks,*[18] ably restates the arguments for reparations. Robinson and other commentators are aware of both the tremendous legal barriers they face in the courts and the overwhelming opposition of the public. Some writers suggest reparations can avoid continuing racially divisive outcomes by avoiding attempts to compensate individual victims, a route earlier commentators view as filled with procedural land mines. Rather, they say, the focus should be on repairing the past wrongs by building mutual, interracial trust, respect, and a sense of shared destiny. To this end, one quite optimistic commentator suggests that reparations take the form of "subsidies to black-owned businesses, investment in education programs and scholarships for black youths, training programs for black workers, affirmative action programs, resources for community-based organizations in predominantly black communities, and development and implementation of programs designed to educate the country about the legacy of slavery. Conceived and implemented in this manner, reparations can serve to bridge the color line, rather than to widen the divide."[19]

Hidden by the often outraged opposition to reparations is the fact that this country compensates for generalized loss all the time: Certainly large corporations make reparations under bankruptcy laws, restructuring, tax provisions, and — in the case of some worthy corporations such as Chrysler or Lockheed — through outright government grants. There are differences between the Japanese reparations program and that sought by blacks, but even so, there are supportive reasons — the eligibility of heirs and the education fund — for feeling that the Japanese precedent might be helpful to black reparations' advocates.

Harvard law professor Charles Ogletree and a host of other lawyers filed a reparations suit against the City of Tulsa and the state of Oklahoma on behalf of hundreds of survivors of the total destruction of Greenwood, the prosperous black section of that city, in 1921.[20] Plaintiffs filed litigation following failure of negotiations for a reparations settlement. The history is clear. In 1921, a young black man who had accidentally stepped on the toe of a white female elevator operator was charged with molesting her. Fearing he might be lynched, armed black men volunteered to help the sheriff protect the youth. A scuffle with whites resulted, shooting started, and two blacks and ten whites were killed. When the outnumbered blacks retreated to the black community, whites looted hardware and sporting goods stores, arming themselves with rifles, revolvers, and ammunition. Large groups of whites and blacks fired on each other. Whites then decided to invade what they called "Niggertown" and systematically wipe it out.

To accomplish this end, more than ten thousand armed whites gathered. Sixty to eighty automobiles filled with armed whites formed a circle around the black section, while airplanes were used to spy on the movements of blacks and — according to some reports — to drop bombs on the blacks. Black men and

---

18. Randall Robinson, The Debt: What America Owes to Blacks (2000).

19. Note, Bridging the Color Line: The Power of African-American Reparations to Redirect America's Future, 115 Harv. L. Rev. 1689 (2002).

20. Alexander v. Oklahoma, Civ. No. 4:03cv00133 (N.D. Oklahoma 2003). See Tatsha Robertson, Quest for Vindication Survivors of 1921 Tulsa Race Riots Hail Suit for Reparations, Boston Globe, Feb. 26, 2003, at A1.

women fought valiantly but vainly to defend their homes against the hordes of invaders who, after looting the homes, set them on fire. Blacks seeking to escape the flames were shot down.

Fifty or more blacks barricaded themselves in a church where they resisted several massed attacks. Finally, a torch applied to the church set it ablaze, and the occupants began to pour out, shooting as they ran. Several blacks were killed. The entire black area became a smoldering heap of blackened ruins. Hardly a shanty, house, or building was left standing throughout the area. Domestic animals wandering among the wreckage gave the only signs of life in the desolation. Unofficial estimates put the death toll at 50 whites and from 150 to 200 blacks, many of whom were buried in graves without coffins. Other victims incinerated in the burning houses were never accounted for.[21]

In recent years, the City of Tulsa raised a memorial to the victims of the massacre, but the city actively defended against the litigation. The judge in the case granted the plaintiffs' request to take depositions of some of their clients, all of whom are in their 80s or older, in order to preserve critical testimony about the tragedy. The interest-convergence potential in this case is present, but city and state officials have not recognized that, if the reparations suit is successful, it could cost them many millions of dollars and, even if defendants prevail, the cost in prestige and lost business resulting from resurrecting these events could be very large. Reparations is an area of racial controversy in which there is more white resistance than even to affirmative action. The Tulsa litigation, though, by narrowing the usually broad coverage of reparations claims to a specific and undeniable racial attack that caused the deaths of countless blacks and the destruction of a whole community, quiets opponents and exerts pressure for relief. Both the district court and the 10th Circuit Court of Appeals on September 8, 2004, ruled against the plaintiffs on statute of limitations grounds.[22]

According to Randall Robinson: "The issue here is not whether or not we can, or will, win reparations. The issue rather is whether we will fight for reparations, because we have decided for ourselves that they are our due."[23] Here is the activist strategy for responding to the restraints of racial fortuity. It is based on the conviction that a cause is worth pursuing despite the obstacles of law and public opinion. The pursuit can create conditions that convince policymakers, unmoved by appeals to simple justice, that relief is a prudent necessity.

§2.14 EMIGRATION AS AN ANSWER

We would be hard-pressed to uncover current barriers to the long-sought ideal — racial equality — that were not well known at the country's birth. Most whites

21. See Derrick Bell, Nigger Free, in Gospel Choirs: Psalms of Survival in an Alien Land Called Home 125-127 (1996).
22. http://ca10.washburnlaw.edu/cases/2004/09/04-5042.htm. See Charles J. Ogletree, Jr., Tulsa Reparations: The Survivors' Story, http://www.bc.edu/schools/law/lawreviews/meta-elements/journals/bctwj/24_1/03_FMS.htm.
23. Robinson, supra note 18, at 206.

could not conceive of blacks as their equals, and most of those who worked to end slavery during the early decades of the nineteenth century did so to open the way for returning them to Africa.[1] Thus, the Afrolantica Opportunity Racism Hypo (§2.2) represents no more than an allegorical answer to a continuing need.

By the 1830s, the white colonization movement had placed some 1,400 blacks in Liberia. Then the movement declined. It gained some support during the 1850s when it was endorsed by the Republican Party. Abraham Lincoln included a provision of $100,000 for the voluntary emigration of freedmen to Haiti and Liberia in an 1862 bill later enacted, emancipating slaves in the District of Columbia. In the same year, he called a group of black leaders to the White House and urged them to support colonization, stating: "Your race suffer greatly, many of them, by living among us, while ours suffer from your presence. In a word we suffer on each side. If this is admitted, it affords a reason why we should be separated."[2]

By the 1850s several black leaders had also become so discouraged with discrimination, exclusion, and hostility that they supported the emigration idea, although some favored Central America or Haiti over Africa.[3] Emigration plans were revived around the turn of the century, during the period when blacks were lynched, burned, tortured, and disenfranchised in record numbers.[4]

§2.14   1. By 1816, the American Colonization Society had become the best known of several movements to colonize blacks. To win support for their goals, these groups generally painted a dreary picture of black degradation and wretchedness. They opposed equal rights for blacks and preached the inherent inferiority of the race.

Blacks repudiated the Colonization Society and the idea of African colonization, maintaining that America was their country too. There were exceptions. Paul Cuffe, a black shipowner from Massachusetts, was, despite business success, the constant victim of discrimination. He was jailed as a result of his refusal to pay taxes, which he withheld in protest over the denial of the vote and other privileges of citizenship denied blacks. Finally, determining to "emancipate" Africa and provide a haven for those American blacks who wanted to go there, Cuffe led voyages of blacks to Sierra Leone from 1811 to 1816, at his own expense. (The British had established a colony in Sierra Leone, where they hoped to resettle several hundred destitute and friendless blacks who had come to England after having fought for Great Britain during the Revolutionary War in return for their freedom.) Cuffe's movement ended with his death in 1817. Sheldon Harris, Paul Cuffe: Black America and the Africa Return (1972).

2. John Hope Franklin, From Slavery to Freedom 281 (3d ed. 1967).

3. The black leader, physician, and journalist Martin R. Delany favored emigration.

Considerable effort was expended in support of these plans, and early in 1861 a ship with 2,000 black emigrants aboard sailed from Philadelphia to Haiti. William Z. Foster, The Negro People in American History 173 (1954).

Frederick Douglass, who represented the majority of the black leadership, opposed emigration, asserting: "We are Americans. We are not aliens. We are a component part of the nation. . . . We have no disposition to renounce our nationality." Leon F. Litwack, North of Slavery 259 (1961). Those favoring emigration held a convention in 1854, but it won little black support, and even that lessened when the Civil War raised hope in blacks that slavery and inequality might be ended.

4. Bishop Henry M. Turner, a leader of the movement who looked longingly to Africa as the only possible place of Negro freedom, wrote, "We were born here, raised here, fought, bled and died here, and have a thousand times more right here than hundreds of thousands of those who help to snub, proscribe and persecute us, and that is one of the reasons I almost despise the land of my birth." Edwin Redkey, Black Exodus 32 (1969). Some blacks did go to Africa during these years. See authorities collected in E. Osofsky, Come Out from Among Them: Negro Migration and Settlement, 1890-1914 (1966).

Then, in the period following World War I, blacks again turned to emigration, this time forming what John Hope Franklin has called the largest black mass movement in American history. Once more despair was the chief motivation, as lynching, antiblack rioting, and racial discrimination of every form took their toll on even the most optimistic blacks. In the 1920s Marcus Garvey, a charismatic Jamaican immigrant, founded the Universal Negro Improvement Association, which in a few years raised $10 million and attracted at least half a million members. Garvey told blacks that racial prejudice was so much a part of the white man's civilization that it was futile to appeal to his sense of justice and his high-sounding democratic principles. Garvey bought and equipped ships, but in 1925, following a controversial prosecution, entered federal prison for two years, convicted of mail fraud. He was pardoned in 1927 and deported as an undesirable alien. He tried to revive his movement, but failed.[5]

Of course, while organized emigration efforts have not met with broad success, blacks have constantly migrated from one portion of the country to another, seeking opportunity and acceptance. The escapes from slavery via the Underground Railroad brought countless blacks to the North, and took many to Canada. After the Civil War, scores of blacks headed west to Kansas, Texas, and California. There were major movements from South to North during both world wars. The emigrees were all seeking employment, a better life, and racial equality.[6] Black nationalist groups traditionally have made emigration or separation a major goal. Paradoxically, the black-led emigration efforts, including contemporary efforts by Black Muslims and other militant nationalists to establish black communities in this country, have met with the most severe opposition and harassment from whites, particularly law enforcement officials.[7]

Most serious black emigration efforts have come in periods of severe racial repression. The stringent provisions of the 1850 Fugitive Slave Act, for example, created chaos among the 100,000 fugitive slaves, as well as among free blacks then living in the North. The result was a veritable exodus to Canada with several hundred blacks departing within days after the new measure became law.[8]

Some contemporary black writers see a return of outright repression on the horizon for American blacks. They assert that blacks were imported for their labor and that racism served to justify the exploitation. With automation, black labor is no longer necessary, but racism remains, and like the Indian the black may be headed for extermination.[9] While he does not predict black genocide, black writer-philosopher Julius Lester has urged blacks to consider emigration. In his view,

5. Franklin, supra note 2, at 489-493. See also Elton Fax, Garvey (1972); Edmund Cronon, Black Moses: The Story of Marcus Garvey and the Universal Negro Improvement Association (1969); Marcus Garvey, Philosophy and Opinions of Marcus Garvey (1992).
6. See Arna Bontemps & Jack Convoy, Anyplace But Here (1997); George Groh, The Black Migration (1972).
7. See, e.g., Wallace v. Brewer, 315 F. Supp. 431 (M.D. Ala. 1970).
8. William Foster, The Negro People in American History 171-172 (1954). Similarly, blacks in the deep South banded together and headed for Kansas and Oklahoma to escape the post-Reconstruction violence. See Nell Painter, The Exodusters (1976).
9. See, e.g., Sidney Willhelm, Who Needs the Negro? (Anchor ed. 1971); Samuel F. Yette, The Choice: The Issue of Black Survival in America (1971).

300 years of experience have taught us that integration, no matter how hard blacks try, simply won't work. Mr. Lester writes:

> An ethnic or religious minority lives at the mercy of the majority which defines and governs the entire society. The minority is even dependent upon the majority for its physical existence, because, at any juncture in history, the majority can make the minority the scapegoat for whatever problems the society may be confronting and attempt to eradicate it. This happened to the Jews and Gypsies of Europe for many centuries and it is happening today to the Vietnamese minority in Cambodia.
>
> Having absolutely no power and being totally dependent on the goodwill of the majority, the minority can seek its survival in one of three ways: (1) try to assimilate by adopting the customs, mores, culture, values, etc., of the majority, as the European immigrant groups to America did successfully, and as blacks have tried to do; (2) try to be as unobtrusive and separate as possible, while remaining a part of and being governed by the political and economic apparatus of the majority, as the Chinese have done in America and Southeast Asia, and as the Indians have done in Africa; or (3) separate geographically from the majority and become an independent political and economic unit, as in the case of Pakistan, a Moslem state, and Israel, a Jewish one.[10]

Blacks, according to Lester, have put most of their effort into assimilation or integration, although this required a denial of selfhood. But emulation of whites has not led to assimilation. At best, some middle class blacks have become "acceptable" to liberal whites. Civil rights laws are generally unenforced and their penalties are not severe. Moreover, Lester claims, even when the laws were obeyed white attitudes toward blacks did not change. Persecution in many forms, overt and subtle, continues. A revolution is not on the horizon, and even if it were, Lester fears it could well replace one racist society with another. He concludes that the only viable alternative for blacks is to separate themselves from the United States.

Lester reports that most modern-day blacks simply laugh at his emigration proposal, but the cyclical nature of black history, and the very clear justification and support for such ideas as recently as the depression of the 1930s, provide a somber response that is far from funny. It is not impossible that the presently emerging nonwhite nations in Africa, Asia, and South America may reach a stage of development and stability sufficient to encourage American blacks to emigrate. It is hard to imagine that conditions here will become so oppressive that more than 20 million blacks (who, with all their problems, are the world's most well-to-do nonwhites) would pull up stakes and leave. It is even harder to imagine how white society would survive their departure. A massive black emigration would certainly pose a serious ideological crisis for the country. More importantly, could the capitalist class structure maintain itself without the scapegoat role that blacks have filled for three hundred years? The answer may lie in the fact that militant black groups espousing emigration or the establishment of separate black states seem to attract far more official hostility than do integrationists.[11]

---

10. Julius Lester, The Necessity for Separation, Ebony, Aug. 1970, at 166-169. See also Carl T. Rowan, The Coming Race War in America (1996).

11. I have explored these issues in fictional settings. See Derrick Bell, Faces at the Bottom of the Well: The Permanence of Racism 158 (1992), and Gospel Choirs: Psalms of Survival in an Alien Land Called Home 17 (1996).

Assuming that the country never has to face the trauma a mass departure of blacks would likely evoke, will the price of their continued presence be a permanent assignment as scapegoat, or, as discussed in §2.9, the involuntary sacrifice role? Slavery has ended. Public, and a great deal of private, discrimination has been made unlawful. But thus far none of these developments have broken the double fetters forged in a Virginia colony so long ago for whites and blacks. As Professor Morgan concludes in *American Slavery, American Freedom*, it is this question that he leaves with his readers.

> Eventually, to be sure, the course the Virginians charted for the United States proved the undoing of slavery. And a Virginia general gave up at Appomattox the attempt to support freedom with slavery. But were the two more closely linked than his con-querors could admit? Was the vision of a nation of equals flawed at the source by contempt for both the poor and the black? Is America still colonial Virginia writ large? More than a century after Appomattox, the questions linger.[12]

§2.15 A NEW RACIAL REALISM

In *The New American Dilemma*,[1] Professor Jennifer Hochschild utilizes Professor Edmund Morgan's findings[2] as she examines what she calls the "anomaly thesis."[3] This is the philosophy incorporated in Gunnar Myrdal's massive midcentury study, *An American Dilemma*.[4] According to Dr. Myrdal, racism was simply the failure of liberal democratic practices (re black rights) to coincide with liberal demo-cratic theory. Dr. Myrdal assumed, and two generations of civil rights advocates accepted, the idea that the standard practices of American policymaking were adequate to the task of abolishing racism and that white America did, in fact, want to abolish racism.

Reviewing the modest progress in school desegregation over almost four dec-ades, Professor Hochschild concludes that the anomaly thesis simply cannot explain the persistence of racial discrimination.[5] Rather, she finds the continued viability of racism supports arguments "that racism is not simply an excrescence on a funda-mentally healthy liberal democratic body but is part of what shapes and energizes the

---

12. Edmund S. Morgan, American Slavery, American Freedom 387 (1975).

§2.15   1. Jennifer L. Hochschild, The New American Dilemma (1984).

2. Edmund S. Mogan, American Slavery, American Freedom (1975).

3. Racial discrimination "is a terrible and inexplicable anomaly stuck in the middle of our liberal democratic ethos." Hochschild, supra note 1, at 3.

4. Gunnar Myrdal, An American Dilemma (1944). "The Negro problem in America represents a moral lag in the development of the nation and a study of it must record nearly everything which is bad and wrong in America. . . . However, . . . not since Reconstruction has there been more reason to anticipate fundamental changes in American race relations, changes which will involve a devel-opment toward the American ideals." Id. at xix.

5. Id. at 203.

body."[6] Under this view, "liberal democracy and racism in the United States are historically, even inherently, reinforcing; American society as we know it exists only because of its foundation in racially based slavery, and it thrives only because racial discrimination continues. The apparent anomaly is an actual symbiosis."[7]

Professor Hochschild looks at writings supporting the symbiosis thesis, including Professor Morgan's relationship between slavery and the development of a republican ideology of freedom and to contemporary Marxist accounts of the functional utility of racism within a capitalist economy. History, she points out, reveals several occasions in which blacks have served as bargaining chips in facilitating the settlement of differences between segments of the white society. Even traditional liberal views regarding the need of symmetry in legal principles serve to protect and perpetuate racist policies and practices.

If Professor Hochschild is correct, then her "new dilemma" explains the intractable nature of the dilemma Mr. Myrdal (and most of us) saw as the barrier to full equality for blacks. She suggests that rather than being understood as the tension between liberal democratic theory and liberal democratic practice, the American dilemma must be understood as the more fundamental problem of reconciling liberalism with democracy. If most white citizens choose not to grant the citizens of color their full rights, then perhaps democracy must give way to liberalism.

But how do you invoke the equality policy choice in a majoritarian, democratic state where racial equality is the oft-heralded ideal but power-based majoritarianism is the ongoing societal stabilizing fact? More crucially, how do you convince white Americans that the nation's most pressing social problems will never be addressed meaningfully as long as the needed reforms can be stigmatized by opponents as aid for unworthy black folks?

The racial diversion ploy works for conservative politicians for the same reasons that Professor Morgan argues it worked in seventeenth-century America and has worked as an insulator against social change ever since. In 1990, North Carolina Senator Jesse Helms used the phenomenon against his black Democratic challenger. Trailing late in the race, Senator Helms aired a series of television ads designed to fuel white fears that affirmative action policies supported by his opponent were being used to take jobs from whites. He gained sufficient support by this tactic to win reelection.

Helms's tactics in more or less blatant forms enabled Republicans to become the dominant political force in the South and, increasingly, across the country. They have achieved this position not by championing social reform, but by claiming that the Democratic Party was the party for "special interests," meaning, of course, the party for blacks. This position, along with attacks on big government, has enabled Republicans to dominate Southern politics at least since Ronald Reagan's election to the presidency in 1980. And like their Democratic predecessors, they have maintained control by making vague promises regarding needed social reforms while emphasizing their determination to protect whites against "liberal" — read black — threats from school integration to affirmative action.

6. Id. at 5.
7. Id. at 5.

Sadly, much of the Democratic leadership, while absolutely dependent on black votes, particularly in national elections, goes to great lengths to avoid acknowledging this reliance. Indeed, Democrats also seek elusive white votes by claiming they are not catering to "special interests."

The continued success of tactics now three hundred years old raises a fundamental question that civil rights adherents have avoided: Given racism's important stabilizing role in this country, can it ever be made less than the basis of black subordination in compromises between differing white groups, the real reason why whites gain priority to scarce resources, or the factor that enables whites to bond as whites across great chasms of opportunity, wealth, and well-being? Those who urge emigration would not be guilty of exaggeration were they to argue as follows:

> Black people will never gain full equality in this country. Even our most successful efforts will produce no more than temporary "peaks of progress." Given this unassailable truth, blacks need to acknowledge the permanence of their subordinate status. That acknowledgment sidetracks both despair and unrealistic strategies, the failure of which breeds despair. Acknowledgment, moreover, frees blacks to imagine and implement racial strategies that can bring personal fulfillment and, on occasion, even triumph.

At the least, blacks need to examine what it was about their reliance on racial remedies that may have prevented them from recognizing that these legal rights could do little more than bring about the cessation of one form of discriminatory conduct that soon appeared in a more subtle though no less discriminatory form. This examination requires the redefinition of racial equality goals and opportunity to which blacks have adhered for more than a century.

Reform of our civil rights thinking is as badly needed as was our thinking about jurisprudence prior to the advent of the legal realists. Indeed, racial realism is to race relations what legal realism is to jurisprudential thought. The legal realists were a group of scholars in the early part of the twentieth century who challenged the classical structure of law as a formal group of "common law" rules that, if properly applied to any given situation, would lead to a right — and therefore a just — result.

The legal realists cut through the carefully constructed spheres of "private" and "public," the distinction on which many cases were won or lost. As one commentator put it:

> [T]he realists undermined all faith in the objective existence of "rights" by challenging the coherence of the key legal categories that gave content to the notion of bounded public and private spheres. . . . There will be a right if, and only if, the court finds for the plaintiff or declares the statute unconstitutional. Rights are not a preexisting fact of nature, to be found somewhere "out there," but are a function of legal decision-making itself. What the court cites as the reason for the decision — the existence of a right — is, in fact, only the result.[8]

8. Elizabeth Mensch, The History of Mainstream Legal Thought, in The Politics of Law 13, 22-23 (David Kairys ed., rev. ed. 1990).

Traditional civil rights law is also highly structured and founded on the belief that the Constitution was intended — at least after the Civil War Amendments — to guarantee equal rights to blacks. This belief in eventual racial justice, and the litigation and legislation based on that belief, was always dependent on the ability of its advocates to adhere to equality ideology while rejecting discriminatory experience. This choice had to survive the undeniable fact that the Framers initially opted to protect property, including enslaved Africans in that category. The political motivations for the Civil War Amendments almost guaranteed that when political needs changed, the protection provided the former slaves would not be enforced. The pattern of periodic protection of black rights is now predictable. Both the historic pattern and its contemporary replication require review of the racial equality ideology. Civil rights advocates must replace it with an approach that recognizes the real role of racism in our society and seeks to deflect and frustrate its many manifestations.

§2.16   Racism Hypo: African Americans and the Afrolantica Opportunity[1]

As is usually the case with new discoveries, the first oceanographers who reported strange movement in the middle of the Atlantic and suggested that the long lost continent of Atlantis might resurface were dismissed as cranks and publicity seekers. When the first rumblings in the ocean some 900 miles due east of South Carolina grew into an insistent churning that made the waters over the giant site unnavigable, the ridicule heaped on the scientists changed to praise and then to ever more insistent requests that the scientists explain the strange phenomenon.

The ancients accepted as unseen fact what modern scientists refused to believe even as its huge mass became clear on their radar screens. Plato described the "lost continent" in two dialogues, *Timaeus* and *Critias*, and the legend of its existence persisted throughout the Middle Ages and even after the Renaissance. Variously called Atlantis, Atalantica, or Atalantis, the continent was said to be situated in the Atlantic Ocean. It disappeared beneath the waves at some unrecorded point in history.

Now, in the first decade of the twenty-first century, over a period of several months, the huge mass began rising slowly from the ocean depths. Then, in a spectacular display of nature's power, it roared into view with the power of a volcano erupting. For several days the area was cloaked in boiling hot steam and impenetrable mists. When the air finally cleared after several weeks, there lay a new land complete with tall mountains sheltering fertile valleys, rich plains already lush with vegetation, and beautiful beaches interspersed with deepwater harbors. From all indications, the land — roughly the size of New England — was uninhabited, though observers could see from afar that fish filled its streams and animals in great abundance roamed its fields.

§2.16   1. This hypo is based on "The Afrolantica Awakening in Derrick Bell, Faces at the Bottom of the Well: The Permanence of Racism 32 (1992).

The United States and several other countries wasted no time in dispatching representatives to "claim" the land or portions of it. The task proved harder than it looked. The first explorers landed by helicopter and barely escaped with their lives: They experienced severe problems in breathing and managed to take off just before they would have lost consciousness. Subsequent attempts to land either by air or by water also failed even though the landing parties were equipped with space suits and breathing apparatus that had sustained human life on the moon. On the new continent, it was the weight of the atmosphere that threatened human life. One survivor explained that it was like trying to breath under the heavy pressures at the bottom of the sea.

Remarkably, none of the independent adventurers who tried to land on the new land died. Somehow, gasping for breath, they managed to make their escape though the experience was sufficiently painful and scary that none of the survivors wanted to try a second time. The frustration throughout the world was great. Here was an exciting new land mass that seemed to be aching for exploration and (of course) development, and no human seemed able to survive on its inviting but inhospitable shores.

Then came the discovery. A team of four U.S. Navy divers tried to reach the new land underwater. A submarine entered a deep harbor and emitted the divers through a special chamber. They swam underwater through the harbor and into the mouth of a large river that emptied into the harbor. All seemed to go well until the divers were about a half-mile up the river. Then, suddenly, they began to experience the breathing difficulties that had plagued earlier explorers. They turned immediately and started back to the submarine, but they had gone too far; long before they reached the harbor, they began to lose consciousness. The crew chief, Ensign Marcia Shufford, alone managed to link the three helpless team members together with a slender cable and towed them to safety. Shufford had not experienced the breathing problems her crewmates complained of and, in fact, felt increasingly invigorated by the new land's waters.

Back on the submarine, the divers were revived and hailed their crew chief as a hero. Shufford declined the honors and reported that she had not felt any breathing problems. Quickly arranged medical checks found her quite normal. The only difference between Shufford and the members of her crew (and indeed all those who had tried to explore the new land) was her race: Shufford was an African American. Neither the military nor government officials viewed this fact as significant. After all, peoples of color from other countries, including Africa, had tried to land on the new land with the usual near calamitous results. But just in case, the next helicopter exploratory party consisted entirely of African American men and the pilot, an African American woman.

They landed cautiously on the land that the media had dubbed "Afrolantica," but soon found they did not need breathing equipment. In fact, all experienced what became known as the "Afrolantica High": a feeling of well-being, exhilaration, and heightened self-esteem. This, they explained on their return, was not an alcohol or drug-induced feeling of escape, but rather, an experience of being unburdened, of liberation. All agreed that on Afrolantica, they felt truly free.

In the period of renewed racial hostility sweeping the country, the linking of Afrolantica and freedom for blacks came easily. Here, many thought, is the long-sought promised land. This view grew as more and more African Americans visited the new land and found it both habitable and inviting. Biblical parallels with the Hebrews' experiences in the Book of Exodus became common. As one black put it after a trip to the new land, "After wandering in the American wilderness for not 40 but almost 400 years, suffering the destruction of slavery, the second-class status of segregation, and now the hateful hypocrisy of the equal opportunity era, the Lord has sent us a home that is as hostile to others as America has been to us. Let us go and show there what we might have done here."

The leader's enthusiasm was shared by some but far from all African Americans. As a spokesperson for the opposing view explained, "Emigrating to Afrolantica would be like leaving civilization and returning to the wilderness. Life here is hard, but we will not surrender our labors and those of generations that came before us and for whom life was even harder than it is for us. America, like it or not, is our land too. We would like to visit Afrolantica, but our home is here."

African American Advocates for Afrolantica (Quad A) introduced legislation in Congress that would provide each African American citizen wishing to emigrate to Afrolantica with a $20,000 "Reparations Subsidy" to finance the move that would be repaid if the recipient sought to return in less than ten years. Opponents, organized under what they called the "Keep the Faith Movement" (KFM), now claim the legislation would be both bad policy and unconstitutional because it would create and offer benefits based on the race of the recipient without citing a compelling state interest to justify a suspect racial classification.

Both sides believe the historical materials set out in this chapter support their arguments. Quad A supporters view this history as an "endless cycle" of racial oppression that wanes and waxes under the influence of the political and economic needs of the nation's white majority. Acknowledging improvements in the lives of some African Americans, Quad A maintains that their subordinated status has not changed and will not change because it is a major source of social stability in a nation where most working class whites are disadvantaged by their class status.

KFM advocates maintain African Americans must not give up their long equality struggle that transformed the Constitution from a document primarily protective of property and those who own it to a shield for the protection of individual rights that, though flawed, is the envy of the free world. The eras of slavery and segregation are important history, but they are *history* and not precise predictors of the future for African Americans. While the plight of the black underclass is cause for the deepest concern, an increasing number of whites are now experiencing the debilitating burdens of poverty. The nation must soon consider legislation like that enacted during the Great Depression that will ease if not eliminate poverty, improve education, and guarantee employment opportunities for all. Having worked so hard to bring about these reforms, African Americans would be foolish to leave the American table just at the time when the long-awaited banquet is about to be served.

Following the implementation of an elaborate selection process, almost 1,000 representatives of every stratum of black America have come together in a major meeting to discuss the two positions and perhaps evolve a consensus view for decision and action.

Counsel for both sides should expect questions from the convention. How should African Americans view this question if they are members of the middle class? Members of the underclass?

How will the current Supreme Court rule on a Fourteenth Amendment challenge to the Reparations Subsidy?

If most African Americans reject the temptation of a new if uncertain life in Afrolantica and remain loyal to America, will this country's response take the form of gratitude-based efforts to eliminate all forms of racial discrimination, or will the nation continue its policies that assume a dominant place for whites and a subordinate role for peoples of color? Consider all these questions in the light of the historical materials in this chapter. An examination of history will not guarantee infallible answers but will teach many lessons that should be considered in the decision-making process.

Chapter 3

The Quest for Effective Schools

§3.1 THE *SEATTLE-LOUISVILLE* DECISION

In the summer of 2007, nearly fifty years after it decided Brown v. Board of Education, the Supreme Court once again issued a decision that would radically alter the role of race in public schooling. In Parents Involved in Community Schools v. Seattle School District No. 1[1] (hereinafter the *"Seattle-Louisville* decision"), the Supreme Court declared unconstitutional race-conscious admission and transfer plans that for the past five decades had been vital to eradicating segregation, facilitating integration, and preventing resegregation. The plurality opinion, authored by Chief Justice Roberts, and a concurrence by Justice Thomas, denied any compelling interest in remedying segregation where it was not the result of an explicit government policy. Justice Kennedy, the emergent swing vote of the Roberts court, refused to join the plurality's conclusion that there was no compelling state interest in combating de facto segregation, but nonetheless joined them in finding that the plans under review were not narrowly tailored. In its wake, the *Seattle-Louisville* decision has left schools struggling to determine how best to address the issue of racial integration in their schools.

§3.1.1 The Seattle and Louisville Plans

In response to segregated school populations, Seattle's black parents and the NAACP repeatedly urged the school board to change policies that were creating segregated schools,[2] twice filing lawsuits against the board. Throughout this time, the school responded with several race-conscious plans.[3] In 1999, the school board

---

§3.1 1. 551 U.S. _____, 127 S. Ct. 2738 (2007).

2. In 1958, black parents whose children attended Harrison Elementary school, which had a black student population of over 75 percent, wrote the Seattle board of education complaining that boundaries for the school were set to exclude black children from the neighboring white school. See id. at 2803.

3. In 1963 the school board adopted a new race-based transfer amid black parents' and the NAACP's protests that school boundary lines and transfer policies that kept schools segregated. In 1969, the NAACP filed a federal lawsuit claiming that the board had unconstitutionally established

created the plan before the Supreme Court, in which students ranked their choice in schools and the district gave first preference to those who had siblings at the school. Second preference was given to those students whose race was underrepresented in the school only if the minority/majority enrollment ratio fell outside a thirty percent range of the minority/majority population ration within the district. Students were free to transfer from the school in which they were initially placed to a different school of their choice without regard to their race.[4]

Segregation in Louisville also endured long after the *Brown* decision, resulting in a 1975 desegregation order from the district court. The court adopted a complex, race-conscious plan that used racial percentage guidelines and busing to achieve integration.[5] Over the course of the following decades, the school board constantly revised its racial guidelines and its methods of maintaining school populations within them, falling in and out of compliance with the court order.[6] In 1996, the school board instituted the plan at issue, which prohibited the transfer of any student if the transfer would lead to a school population falling outside the guidelines set to reflect the district's population ratio of black students to non-black students.[7] In 2000, the District Court dissolved the 1975 court order.[8]

§3.1.2   The Legal Standard

At the outset, the Justices differed in what standard should be applied to the plans. The majority applied strict scrutiny, maintaining that "because racial classifications are simply too pernicious to permit any but the most exact connection between justification and classification, distributions of government burdens or benefits based on individual racial classifications are reviewed under strict scrutiny."[9] A dissent authored by Justice Breyer and joined by Justices Stevens, Souter, and Ginsburg (hereinafter "the Breyer dissent") argued that while strict scrutiny was applicable where the government used racial classifications to exclude and separate races, strict scrutiny was not merited in government actions that sought to bring about inclusion and remedy inequalities based on race. The Breyer dissent cited the Court's long history of approving race-conscious measures to integrate

---

and maintained racially segregated schools through certain "rules and regulations." The school board once again responded with a plan that used "explicitly racial criteria" and used busing to integrate schools. In 1977, the NAACP filed a second legal complaint alleging that the school board "created or perpetuated unlawful racial segregation" through certain policies and procedures, such as school-transfer criteria and district drawing. The federal Department of Health, Education and Welfare's Office for Civil Rights entered into a settlement agreement with the school board for a new plan that included mandatory busing based on minority representation percentages in schools. In 1988, this plan was replaced with the plan that allowed students to choose their schools, subject to racial constraints. See id.

4. See id. at 2747.
5. See id. at 2806.
6. See id. at 2806-2808.
7. See id. at 2808-2809.
8. See id.
9. Id. at 2742 (quoting Fullilove v. Klutznick, 448 U.S. 448, 537 (Stevens, J., dissenting)) (internal quotation marks and citations omitted).

schools, stemming from the principle asserted in Swann v. Charlotte-Mecklenburg Board of Education:

> School authorities are traditionally charged with broad power to formulate and implement educational policy and might well conclude, for example, that in order to prepare students to live in a pluralistic society each school should have a prescribed ratio of Negro to white students reflecting the proportion for the district as a whole. To do this as an educational policy is within the broad discretionary powers of school authorities.[10]

The Breyer dissent argued that, even in the cases cited by the plurality as demonstrating that strict scrutiny was applied to the use of race for inclusive purposes, strict scrutiny was applied differently depending on the context of the race-conscious measures. "Rather, [previous cases] apply the strict scrutiny test in a manner that is 'fatal in fact' only to racial classifications that harmfully *exclude*; they apply the test in a manner that is *not* fatal in fact to racial classifications that seek to *include*."[11] The plurality opinion, the Breyer dissent argued, would ignore this vital distinction and "transform the 'strict scrutiny' test into a rule that is fatal in fact across the board" depriving local government of "the longstanding legal right to use race-conscious criteria for inclusive purposes in limited ways.[12] The Breyer dissent argued that courts need not blindly adhere to an identically-strict legal test for the multitude of contexts in which race-conscious measures may arise.[13] "In a word," the Breyer dissent concluded, "the school plans under review do not involve the kind of race-based harm that has led this Court, in other elements, to find the use of race-conscious criteria unconstitutional"; while they required careful review, strict scrutiny was unnecessary and improper.[14] The plurality dismissed this view as placing too much confidence in a judge's ability to determine the benign from the invidious.[15] In the plurality's view, a court determining the level of scrutiny to apply should concern itself only with determining *whether* race is a factor in a policy, and ignore *why*.

§3.1.3 Applying Strict Scrutiny

Applying strict scrutiny, the majority first considered the issue of a compelling state interest. The majority noted that the Court had recognized two

---

10. Swann v. Charlotte-Mecklenburg Bd. of Educ., 402 U.S. 1, 16 (1971)
11. Id. at 2817.
12. Id. at 2817-2818.
13. For example, race-conscious government action arises in the context of "census forms, research expenditures for diseases, assignments of police officers patrolling predominantly minority-race neighborhood, efforts to desegregate racially segregated schools, policies that factor minorities when distributing goods or services in short supply, actions that create minority-majority electoral districts, peremptory strikes that remove potential jurors on the basis of race, and others." Id. at 2718.
14. The dissent noted that it was this context-specific analysis of the Court's jurisprudence that led Judge Kozinski in the Ninth Circuit to apply a standard of review that was less than strict in analyzing the Seattle policies. Id. at 2819.
15. See id. at 2763.

compelling state interests in the use of racial classifications in schools: (1) remedying the effects of past intentional discrimination, and (2) diversity in higher education.[16] The majority found that the former interest could not be established absent a showing of "de jure" segregation through segregation laws or a court-ordered desegregation decree.[17] Because Seattle lacked either and Louisville's court order had been dissolved, the majority found this interest absent. The majority also held that the schools lacked the compelling state interest in diversity that the Court has recognized in Grutter v. Bollinger,[18] reasoning that *Grutter* only allowed schools to consider race in admissions as one of numerous factors contributing to diversity and that, in any event, this interest was unique to higher education.[19]

The plurality went even further than the majority, broadly rejecting race-conscious government action and strictly adhering to colorblind constitutionalism. The plurality embraced as the "ultimate goal . . . eliminating entirely from governmental decision making such irrelevant factors as a human being's race."[20] Interpreting the plans at issue as furthering "racial balance, pure and simple,"[21] the plurality rejected them as hindering the goal of colorblind government decision making. In the plurality's view, while exceptions may be made in narrow circumstances where de jure segregation has taken place, any race-conscious measure is by definition unconstitutional because the ultimate goal of the Fourteenth Amendment is a colorblind government.

In finding a compelling state interest, the Breyer dissent rejected the majority's reliance on the distinction between *de jure* and *de facto* segregation. The Breyer dissent argued that the distinction between *de facto* and *de jure* segregation has been used by the Court to determine what schools *must* do to remedy segregation rather than to limit what they *may* do.[22] It dismissed the majority's reliance on a distinction that is so often illusory, considering the subtle forms of segregation that governments may employ without passing a law. Moreover, the majority's logic would punish schools for taking the initiative to cure such invidious

16. See id. at 2752-2753.

17. See id.

18. 539 U.S. 306 (2003). Given the strong dissents in *Grutter* and the changes in the Court's composition since that decision, it is more than doubtful that a future case with similar facts would approve that limited use of racial criteria. See, Derrick Bell, Diversity's Distractions, 103 Colum. L. Rev. 1622 (2003). Its loss may be less than its defenders predict. As I concluded the Columbia piece:

> Diversity then is less a means of continuing minority admissions program in the face of widespread opposition than it is a shield behind which college administrators can retain policies of admission that are woefully poor measures of quality, but convenient vehicles for admitting the children of wealth and privilege. Justice O'Connor is comfortable with having elites handle admissions and then legitimate their choices with a critical mass of people of color. Justice Thomas knows that this process is not based on merit, but his view of the Fourteenth Amendment is impotent to address the unfairness. And so in the wake of the Michigan affirmative action case, the overwhelming majority of those admitted to the most selective institutions will be those applicants whose often impressive credentials have been enhanced with money and privilege.

19. 127 S. Ct. at 2753-2754.

20. Id. at 2758 (quoting Richmond v. J.A. Croson Co., 488 U.S. 469, 495 (1989)).

21. Id. at 2753.

22. See id. at 2823-2824.

discrimination without being compelled by a court order. In the case of Louisville, where such a court order was dissolved, the majority would require race-conscious measures the day before the dissolution and prohibit them the day after.[23] The Breyer dissent also rejected the majority's distinction between the interest in diversity at the higher education level and the interests in desegregation in schools; it was, the Breyer dissent noted, precisely this interest that was the focus of *Brown*.[24]

In contrast to the plurality, the Breyer dissent interpreted the Fourteenth Amendment as requiring racial equality, a goal often hindered by colorblind constitutionalism. It identified a compelling state interest in "the school districts' interest in eliminating school-by-school racial isolation and increasing the degree to which racial mixture characterizes each of the district's schools and each individual student's public school experience."[25] The Breyer dissent noted that this compelling interest is often given numerous labels — "diversity," "racial balancing" or "integration" — but that, regardless of its name, it is comprised of three essential elements: (1) a historical and remedial element in rectifying the consequences of prior segregation, (2) an educational element in overcoming the adverse educational effects of segregated schools, and (3) a democratic element "in producing an educational environment that reflects the 'pluralistic society' in which our children will live."[26] As Justice Breyer wrote:

> The compelling interest at issue here, then, includes an effort to eradicate the remnants, not of general "societal discrimination," . . . but of primary and secondary school segregation . . . ; it includes an effort to create school environments that provide better educational opportunities for all children; it includes an effort to create citizens better prepared to know, to understand, and to work with people of all races and backgrounds, thereby furthering the kind of democratic government our Constitution foresees. If an educational interest that combines these three elements is not "compelling," what is?[27]

The Court next considered whether, if a compelling state interest existed, the plans at issue were narrowly tailored to achieve those interests. The majority held that the plans were not narrowly tailored as evidenced by the minimal impact they had on student assignments.[28] Ultimately, the racial tie-breaker affected only fifty-two students in Seattle and accounted for three percent of assignments in Louisville schools.[29] The majority was quick to note that greater use of race would not be preferable; moreover, it did not state that it would have found the policies narrowly tailored if they had an substantial impact on admissions. The majority also found that the districts failed to demonstrate that they had given "serious, good faith consideration of workable race-neutral alternatives."[30]

---

23. See id. at 2824.
24. See id. at 2822-2823.
25. Id. at 2820.
26. Id. at 2820-2822.
27. Id. at 2823.
28. See id. at 2759-2760.
29. See id. at 2760.
30. Id.

The plurality opinion imposed the additional requirements to demonstrate narrow tailoring. The plurality argued that the plans were not narrowly tailored because the school districts failed to demonstrate that the specific racial balance imposed by the plans were necessary to achieve the educational and social benefits of racial diversity.[31] In order to be narrowly tailored, such plans would need to be tied to "pedagogic concept of the level of diversity needed to obtain the asserted educational benefits" — because the plans were tied to the racial demographics of the general population, they failed this test.[32]

The Breyer dissent found the plans narrowly tailored based on five features: (1) their limited use of race, which diminished over time, (2) their reliance on non-race-conscious elements where possible, (3) the way that the school districts developed and modified the plans over time, (4) the plans' comparison with prior plans, and (5) the absence of "reasonably evident alternatives."[33] Specifically, the court noted that the race-conscious criteria set the outer bounds of broad ranges of racial percentages in a larger plan that relied primarily on non-racial elements such as student choice.[34] In contrast to the majority, the Breyer dissent argued that the small effect that race-conscious elements had on admissions demonstrated that the plans had been narrowly tailored to limit the use of race.[35] The Breyer dissent noted that the plans at issue were in fact more narrowly tailored than those the Court approved in *Grutter*. Unlike in *Grutter*, the plans at issue only considered race in a small fraction of the applications and, where students did not receive their school of choice based on race, they were assigned to another of the districts' substantially equal schools.[36] The Breyer dissent also relied on the lengthy historical development of the plans, in which school districts experimented with several types of race-conscious and non-race-conscious plans before developing the plans at issue.[37] Notably, both districts had attempted to achieve integration through non-race-conscious means such as redrawing districts, new school construction, and unrestricted voluntary transfers; all such efforts had failed.[38]

> The school boards' widespread consultation, their experimentation with numerous other plans, indeed, the forty-year history . . . make clear that plans that are less explicitly race-based are unlikely to achieve the boards "compelling" objectives. . . . Having looked at dozens of amicus briefs, public reports, news stories, and the records of this Court's prior cases, which together span fifty years of desegregation history in school districts across the Nation, I have discovered many examples of districts that sought integration through explicitly race-conscious methods, including mandatory busing. Yet, I have found *no* example or model that would permit this Court to say to Seattle and Louisville: "Here is an instance of a desegregation plan that is likely to achieve your objectives and also makes less use of race-conscious

31. See id. at 2655-2656.
32. Id.
33. Id. at 2829-2830.
34. See id. at 2824-2823.
35. See id. at 2823.
36. See id.
37. See id. at 2825-2827.
38. See id. at 2828.

criteria than your plans." And if the plurality cannot suggest such a model — and it cannot — then it seeks to impose a "narrow tailoring" requirement that in practice would never be met.[39]

The Breyer dissent also took issue with the plurality's insistence that the racial balance correspond to a level necessary to achieve educational benefits rather than population demographics. This reasoning, the Breyer dissent argued, imposed upon the plaintiffs a burden "to prove that *no other set of numbers will work*," a test contradicted by cases in which the Court "explicitly permitted districts to use target ratios based upon the district's underlying population."[40] The Breyer dissent also noted that similar target percentages were supported by research demonstrating that they reduced the risk of "white flight."[41]

§3.1.4 Justice Kennedy's Concurrence

Though the plurality and the Breyer dissent argue passionately about the role of race in school admissions, it is Justice Kennedy's more equivocal concurrence that may possibly provide guidance for courts and schools in the future. Justice Kennedy was the swing vote for the majority holding that strict scrutiny should be applied and that, applying strict scrutiny, the schools had failed to demonstrate that their plans were narrowly tailored to achieve the asserted compelling state interests. However, Justice Kennedy refused to join the plurality holding that diversity could not be a compelling state interest, and set forth a lengthier discussion of the types of admission plans that would be acceptable to achieve this compelling state interest. Thus, schools looking to tailor their admission plans to the decision will likely look to Justice Kennedy's concurrence to determine whether a majority of the Court would find that their plans survive strict scrutiny.[42]

Justice Kennedy rejected the plurality's adherence to colorblind constitutionalism, arguing that, "[i]n the real world, it is regrettable to say, it cannot be a universal constitutional principle."[43] Kennedy defended schools' ability to adopt

39. Id. at 2826-2827.

40. See id. at 2827.

41. See id. at 2827-2828.

42. Organizations that support race-conscious plans to achieve diversity are already looking to the Kennedy concurrence as controlling. In an interview following the issuance of the decision, Theodore Shaw of the NAACP Legal Defense Fund stated:

> I am grateful for the sliver of hope that Justice Kennedy's opinion holds out . . . . Justice Kennedy's opinion made it clear that he refused to join the plurality opinion written by the chief justice, insofar as it indicated that race can never be considered. And it laid out a number of things which could be done that might help ameliorate racial segregation. And I suspect that there are other things he would also accept. And he's the key vote here, so the window is open . . . . And I think that, ultimately, this is more of a Bakke type 4-4-1 split than a 5-4 split, in which [Kennedy's] decision will ultimately rule the day.

PBS Online Newshour: Court Strikes Down Racial Criteria in School Diversity Plans (originally aired June 28, 2007) (transcript available at www.pbs.org/newshour/bb/law/jan-june07/integration_06-28.html).

43. Id. at 2792.

race-conscious measures to encourage diversity and prevent resegregation.[44] However, Justice Kennedy refused to condone measures that identified individual students based on their race; he limited schools concerned with the racial balance of their student body to "devis[ing] race-conscious measures to address the problem in a general way and without treating each student in different fashion solely on the basis of a systematic, individual typing by race."[45] Justice Kennedy reserved the use of individual racial classifications for schools that have engaged in de jure segregation and are therefore required "to resort to extraordinary measures including individual student and teacher assignment to schools based on race."[46] Otherwise, Justice Kennedy's concurrence prohibited the use of racial classifications "absent some extraordinary showing" that he left undefined.[47]

For schools who have not engaged in de jure segregation, Justice Kennedy offered acceptable measures to achieve racial diversity, such as "strategic site selection of new schools; drawing attendance zones with general recognition of the demographics of neighborhoods; allocating resources for special programs; recruiting students and faculty in a targeted fashion; and tracking enrollments, performance, and other statistics by race."[48] However, as Justice Breyer noted in his dissent, such measures were either tried without success by the school districts or were simply unsuitable for the districts' needs.[49] Justice Kennedy also suggested that race may be used as one of many factors in a merit-based admissions policy like *Grutter*; however, as Justice Breyer and other commentators have noted, such admissions systems are impractical at the elementary and secondary school level.[50]

§3.1.5   The Road from *Seattle-Louisville*

Much of the debate in the *Seattle-Louisville* decision is less about whether schools can achieve substantive equality than the message they send when they attempt to do so. The plurality sought to achieve equality by requiring schools to

44. See id. at 2791-2792.
45. Id. at 2792.
46. Id. at 2793.
47. Id. at 2796.
48. Id. at 2792.
49. Seattle had built one new high school in the 44 years before the decision, which served only 300 students. Louisville had attempted redrawing attendance zones on a racial basis, but achieved success only when it was combined with forced busing. Seattle and Louisville had both experimented with allocating resources for special programs such as magnet schools, but the limited desegregation effect of those efforts extended only to those few schools to which additional resources were granted. Tracking is of little use because "tracking reveals the problem; it does not cure it." Id. at 2828 (Breyer, J., dissenting).
50. See id. at 2829 ("The context here does not involve admission by merit; a child's academic, artistic, and athletic "merits" are not at all relevant to the child's placement. These are not affirmative action plans, and hence "individualized scrutiny" is simply beside the point."); see also Richard Kahlenberg, How to Keep *Brown* Alive, Slate, June 29, 2007, available at www.slate.com/id/2169443 (the analogy to college admissions, where officers look closely at the qualities of individual candidates to judge their merit, falls apart when applied to large public-school systems that assign thousands of students each year for reasons that have nothing to do with the complex calculations of selective admissions in higher education).

pretend race does not exist.[51] Justice Kennedy agreed with the use of race-conscious measures to achieve race-conscious ends, as long as those measures avoid identifying any individual child by race. In the words of one legal scholar, "[t]he new harm of racial classification that the court's conservatives now fetishize is something that afflicts all Americans, regardless of race. This harm is not substantive . . . Rather it is entirely about how people — often white people — *feel* when the government takes their race into account in decision-making."[52]

Schools are already feeling the effects of the decision. For example, a city of 55,000 in New York has been forced to reconsider an admission plan that has resulted in integrated schools of equally high quality and which has successfully staved off white flight for the past eighteen years.[53] It is substantially similar to those at issue in the *Seattle-Louisville* decision, as are dozens of other plans in numerous cities, such as Cambridge, Massachusetts, Milwaukee, Wisconsin, and San Jose, California.[54] In one such city, the *Seattle-Louisville* decision has resuscitated a legal challenge in which judgment had previously been rendered in favor of the defendant.[55]

Schools attempting to follow the nebulous standards set by the Kennedy concurrence face a daunting challenge. They must tread a tightrope of achieving integration without appearing conscious of the race of their students. Instead, schools will look to proxies for race, even where such proxies have proved impractical or ineffective in the past.[56]

§3.2 THE STRUGGLE FOR EQUAL EDUCATION IN THE NINETEETH AND EARLY TWENTIETH CENTURIES

The *Seattle-Louisville* decision is the latest, and perhaps most devastating, obstacle in the two-century struggle of African Americans to obtain effective public

51. In the words of one legal scholar:

> A majority of the justices seem to believe that striking down these plans would relocate school assignments to some race-neutral Garden of Eden, a wondrous, mythical place in which race plays no role in which public school pupils attend . . . . For the justices to assume that race comes into play for the first time when these school boards attempt to lessen racial separation is to make an assumption tragically blind to the role of race in America.

Walter Dellinger, A Supreme Court Conversation, Slate, June 29, 2007, available at www.slate.com/id/2168856.

52. Risa Goluboff, The Battle Over *Brown*, Slate, July 2, 2007, available at www.slate.com/id/2169616. Indeed, immediately after the decision was issued, the lawyer for the conservative Pacific Legal Foundation issued a press release stating that "[w]ith these decisions, an estimated 1,000 school districts around the country that are sending the wrong message about race to kids will have to stop. Press Release, PLF Hails U.S. Supreme Court Decisions on Education Race Cases, June 28, 2007, available at http://www.pacificlegal.org/?mvcTask=pressReleases&id=817.

53. See Joseph Berger, A Successful Plan for Racial Balance Now Finds Its Future Uncertain, N.Y. Times, Aug. 22, 2007, at B7.

54. See id.

55. Motion for Relief from Final Judgment, Comfort v. Lynn School Committee, No. 99-cv-11811 (D. Mass. July 3, 2007).

56. See Jeffrey Rosen, Can a Law Change a Society?, N.Y. Times, July 1, 2007.

school for their children. Tracing these efforts over the generations reveals a pattern of dissatisfaction first with integrated, then with separated schools, quite like the ebb and flow of the earth's oceans influenced by the far-off moon. In ancient times, man was aware of the tides, but did not know that the rising and receding of mighty waters were influenced by the earth's distant lunar satellite. In a similar way, the forces which caused black parents to oscillate between segregated and integrated educational tactics have been hidden or disguised.[1]

§3.2.1 Roberts v. City of Boston

When public schools opened in Boston in the late eighteenth century, black children were neither barred nor segregated. But by 1790, racial insults and mistreatment had driven out all but three or four black children.[2]

In 1806, blacks and liberal whites opened a black school in the home of Primus Hall, son of black Revolutionary War veteran and community leader Prince Hall. For what was to prove the first, but not the last time, educational equality seemed to lie with the separate rather than the integrated school. Although initially financed by blacks with the help of whites, the school later received support from the Boston School Committee, which exercised ever greater control over the school as its contributions increased. As the School Committee's heavy-handed policy making increased, so did complaints about the poor quality of instruction and poor conditions in the black schools. Many black parents, forgetting the mistreatment of black children in white schools fifty years earlier, became convinced that they had a new and better idea — integrated schools. Thus motivated, a suit to desegregate Boston's public schools was filed in state court.

In Roberts v. City of Boston,[3] the Massachusetts court found School Committee's segregation policy reasonable, despite evidence of the inferiority of the black schools and harms of segregation put forth by the plaintiffs. The court reasoned that, because the feelings of prejudice by whites were rooted deep in community opinion and feelings, the court concluded they would influence white actions as effectually in an integrated as in a separate school. Plaintiffs had argued that under the constitution and laws of Massachusetts, all persons, without distinction of age or sex, birth or color, origin or condition, are equal before the law. The court responded that the broad general principle did not guarantee the same treatment for all, but only that the law would equally protect the rights of all as those rights are determined and regulated.

---

§3.2   1. This discussion is based on material contained in Derrick Bell, The Legacy of W. E. B. Du Bois: A Rational Model for Achieving Public School Equity for America's Black Children, 11 Creighton L. Rev. 409 (1978).

2. White, The Black Leadership Class and Education in Antebellum Boston, 42 J. Negro Educ. 505 (1973).

3. 59 Mass. (5 Cush.) 198, 201-204 (1850).

Chief Justice Shaw's views were harsh, but some blacks of the period shared his doubts. One of them, Thomas P. Smith, in a speech delivered before "the colored citizens" of Boston in December, 1849, predicted accurately:

> Were the [black] school abolished, of course the whole mass of colored children of various ages and conditions, with very few exceptions, would be precipitated into one or two schools at the West end, where the great body of our people live. Suppose those schools to be full, as they are; in that case the colored ones could not be admitted, unless some of the present ones are excluded. That would not be done. Then other school-houses would have to be built, of course, for the accommodation of these very children, and when finished they would enter, and there be alone in their glory, as at present; having made much trouble and expense, and really accomplished nothing.[4]

Five years later, school integration advocates won when the Massachusetts legislature enacted a law barring the exclusion of any child from the public schools on account of race.[5] But there was a high price for victory. Black schools were closed and black teachers dismissed. School officials feared that white parents would not send their children to the former nor allow them to be instructed by the latter. Textbook aid provided to black children under segregation was also ended, and after a decade or so, state officials conceded that Boston's public schools had again become identifiable by race.

§3.2.2 The Impact of the *Roberts* Precedent

The *Roberts* decision rather than its subsequent legislative repeal became a major precedent in nineteenth century school litigation. Many state courts, even after the Civil War amendments were adopted, found that classification based on race was not an "abridgement of rights protected by the Thirteenth and Fourteenth Amendments."[6] But most courts also held that racial classification was only reasonable where separate schools were in fact provided for blacks. Where only one public school was maintained in a district, blacks could not be excluded.[7]

Sometimes the disparities between schools provided for blacks and those provided for whites became too much even for nineteenth-century courts. A federal court used the equal protection clause to void a Kentucky statute which directed that school taxes collected from whites be used to maintain white schools, and taxes from blacks to operate black schools, which resulted

---

4. Address by Thomas P. Smith, Delivered Before the Colored Citizens of Boston in Opposition to the Abolition of Colored Schools, December 24, 1849. The role Smith played in opposing school integration is discussed in White, supra note 2, at 513.

5. Mass. Laws 1855 ch. 256, §1. See Stanley Schultz, The Culture Factory: Boston Public Schools, 1789-1860, 204-205 (1973).

6. Ward v. Flood, 48 Cal. 36, 17 Am. Rep. 405 (1874) (San Francisco).

7. See, e.g., State ex rel. Pierce v. Union Dist. Sch. Trustees, 46 N.J. 76 (1884) (Burlington); Commonwealth ex rel. Brown v. Williamson, 30 Leg. Int. 406 (1873) (Wilkes Barre, Pa.); State ex rel. Stoutmeyer v. Duffy, 7 Nev. 342, 8 Am. Rep. 713 (1872); People ex rel. Workman v. Board of Educ., 18 Mich. 400 (1869) (Detroit).

in a greatly inferior education for black children.[8] Other courts reached similar conclusions.[9]

There were also courts that refused to follow the *Roberts* decisions, and held that where local officials segregated their schools without legislative authority, mandamus would lie ordering the admission of black children to white schools.[10]

However, few courts in the North shared these views, and in the South when public schools slowly began during the Reconstruction period, often organized by blacks, they were generally operated on a segregated basis. Legal efforts to attack separate schools directly were foreclosed by the Supreme Court with its Plessy v. Ferguson decision.[11] Justice Brown in the *Plessy* case relied heavily on Roberts v. City of Boston, arguing (erroneously, as we know from the legislative overturning of the *Roberts* result) that if school segregation was permissible in one of the states "where the political rights of the colored race have been longest and most earnestly enforced," then segregation of public streetcars should be deemed reasonable under the Fourteenth Amendment.[12]

§3.2.3   Cumming v. Richmond County Board of Education

Three years after *Plessy,* the Court dashed expectations that it would seriously enforce the "equal" part of its "separate but equal" standard in Cumming v. Richmond County Board of Education.[13]

In *Cumming,* three black parents and taxpayers sought, in 1897, to enjoin a Georgia school board from collecting school tax levies from them for a high school for black children that the board had closed. The board decided, for "purely economic reasons," to discontinue the black high school and open four primary schools in the same building. The U.S. Supreme Court unanimously refused to establish standards that would satisfy the "separate but equal" formula.

The Court reasoned that, given the limited resources available, granting the plaintiffs relief would impair the white high school or force its closure, thus taking educational privileges from white children without giving to colored children the additional opportunities furnished in high school. The Court also concluded that the school board's decision to provide primary school education for three hundred children in place of high school education for sixty was reasonable and not made so as to discriminate against the black children.[14]

---

8. Claybrook v. City of Owensboro, 16 F. 297 (D. Ky. 1883).
9. Davenport v. Cloverport, 72 F. 689 (D. Ky. 1896). See also McFarland v. Goins, 96 Miss. 67, 50 So. 493 (1909); Williams v. Board of Educ. of Fairfax Dist., 45 W. Va. 199, 31 S.E. 985 (1898). But see Chrisman v. City of Brookhaven, 70 Miss. 477 (1892), which approved a bond issue for $15,000, of which $3,000 was for building a school for blacks, and $12,000 was for a white school.
10. Clark v. Board of Directors, 24 Iowa 266 (1868); People ex rel. Workman v. Board of Educ., supra note 7, at 442.
11. 163 U.S. 537 (1896).
12. Id. at 544.
13. 175 U.S. 528 (1899).
14. Id. at 543-543.

Although blacks continued to challenge applications of the separate but equal doctrine, litigation could not bring equality for blacks under the easily evaded "separate but equal" standard in a society whose attitude toward the education of blacks ranged from apathy to outright hostility. At the time of the 1954 decision in Brown v. Board of Education, the South as a whole was spending on the average $165 a year for a white pupil, and $115 for a black.[15]

§3.3 EXTRACTING EQUALITY FROM THE "SEPARATE BUT EQUAL" DOCTRINE

Construction of the long and laboriously prepared road leading to the Supreme Court's repudiation of state-sanctioned segregation has been amply recorded by contemporary historians.[1] Paving the way were the "graduate school desegregation cases," in which the Supreme Court held that the *Plessy* rationale was violated by denying blacks admission to state-run graduate programs, even though the state was willing to pay tuition to out-of-state schools or admission was provided to allegedly equal segregated facilities within the state.[2] However, in these cases, the Court granted relief without reaching the issue of the constitutionality of separate but equal educational facilities. The NAACP had won several battles but not the war — the overriding goal remained the total destruction of the *Plessy* precedent. Thus, while their clients received all they could hope for in terms of relief, the lawyers were not satisfied. In the years after *Brown,* it could be said that these roles were reversed. Legal rights were obtained, but educational needs too often remained unmet. Why this was so is a question that subsequent sections attempt to address.

§3.4 BROWN V. BOARD OF EDUCATION

As with other landmark cases, the Supreme Court's 1954 decision in Brown v. Board of Education[1] has taken on a life of its own, with meaning and significance,

15. Anthony Lewis, The School Desegregation Cases, Portrait of a Decade 17 (1965). See also Louis Harlan, Separate and Unequal (1968).

§3.3 1. See, e.g., Richard Kluger, Simple Justice (1976); Loren Miller, The Petitioners: The Story of the Supreme Court of the United States and the Negro (1966).

2. In Missouri ex rel. Gaines v. Canada, 305 U.S. 337 (1938); Pearson v. Murray, 169 Md. 478, 182 A. 590 (1936); and Sipuel v. Board of Regents of the Univ. of Okla., 332 U.S. 631 (1948).

See Mark Tushnet, The NAACP: Legal Strategy Against Segregated Education 1925-1950 (1987) (a general discussion of the NAACP's strategy leading up to *Brown*); Robert Carter, The NAACP's Legal Strategy Against Segregated Education, 86 Mich. L. Rev. 1083 (1988) (discussing the organization's gradual and incremental approach).

§3.4 1. 347 U.S. 483 (1954).

as we have come to learn, beyond its facts and perhaps greater than its rationale. Four school desegregation cases were consolidated in *Brown*. The facts and local conditions were different, but all posed a common legal question: whether public schools could be operated on a racially segregated basis without violating the equal protection clause. School boards relied on the "separate but equal" doctrine announced by the Supreme Court in Plessy v. Ferguson.[2] Plaintiffs argued that segregated public schools were not "equal," could not be made "equal," and thus denied equal protection of the laws.

§3.4.1   The *Brown* Opinions

In earlier cases attacking segregation at the college and graduate school level, the Court had struck down segregation provisions which failed to provide equal education for blacks, while specifically avoiding the issue of whether segregation itself was unconstitutional.[3] Finally addressing the question, the Court searched diligently in the legislative history of the Fourteenth Amendment for the framers' view on this issue. and found that the evidence "inconclusive."

Thus, Chief Justice Warren decided that the Court could not "turn the clock back to 1868 when the Amendment was adopted, or even to 1896 when Plessy v. Ferguson was written." Rather, public education had to be considered "in the light of its whole development and its present place in American life throughout the Nation. Only in this way can it be determined if segregation in public schools deprived these plaintiffs of the equal protection of the laws."[4]

Then, in terms that have been frequently quoted, Chief Justice Warren described the importance of public education:

> Today, education is perhaps the most important function of state and local governments. Compulsory school attendance laws and the great expenditures for education both demonstrate our recognition of the importance of education to our democratic society. It is required in the performance of our most basic public responsibilities, even service in the armed forces. It is the very foundation of good citizenship. Today it is a principal instrument in awakening the child to cultural values, in preparing him for later professional training, and in helping him to adjust normally to his environment. In these days it is doubtful that any child may reasonably be expected to succeed in life if he is denied the opportunity of an education. Such an opportunity, where the state has undertaken to provide it, is a right which must be made available to all on equal terms.[5]

Chief Justice Warren then addressed the major issue in the case: "Does segregation of children in public schools solely on the basis of race, even though the physical facilities and other 'tangible' factors may be equal, deprive the children of the minority group of equal educational opportunities? We believe that it does."

---

2. 163 U.S. 537 (1896).
3. See, e.g., Sweatt v. Painter, 339 U.S. 629 (1950); McLaurin v. Oklahoma State Regents, 339 U.S. 637 (1950).
4. 347 U.S. at 492-493.
5. Id. at 493.

The opinion first referred to the earlier challenges to segregation at the college and graduate level, and emphasized those intangible aspects of an education which are essential to the provision of "equal educational opportunities. . . ." Chief Justice Warren found:

> Such considerations apply with added force to children in grade and high schools. To separate them from others of similar age and qualifications solely because of their race generates a feeling of inferiority as to their status in the community that may affect their hearts and minds in a way unlikely ever to be undone.[6]

With this background, the opinion concluded: "Whatever may have been the extent of psychological knowledge at the time of Plessy v. Ferguson, this finding is amply supported by modern authority. Any language in Plessy v. Ferguson contrary to this finding is rejected." "In the field of public education," the Court held, "the doctrine of 'separate but equal' has no place. Separate educational facilities are inherently unequal."

As lawyer-historian Loren Miller has written, "The harsh truth is that the first *Brown* decision was a great decision; the second *Brown* decision was a great mistake."[7] In Brown v. Board of Education (No. II),[8] the Supreme Court, having decided that segregated education denied the constitutional guarantee of equal protection, addressed itself to the question of what remedy should be granted. Rejecting petitioners' requests for immediate relief, the Court opted for a procedure that would permit the individual resolution of administrative and academic problems involved in compliance. Again speaking for a unanimous Court, Chief Justice Warren said:

> Full implementation of these constitutional principles may require solution of varied local school problems. School authorities have the primary responsibility for elucidating, assessing, and solving these problems: courts will have to consider whether the action of school authorities constitutes good faith implementation of the governing constitutional principles. Because of their proximity to local conditions and the possible need for further hearings, the courts which originally heard these cases can best perform this judicial appraisal. Accordingly, we believe it appropriate to remand the cases to those courts.[9]

Chief Justice Warren urged that traditional equitable principles be applied to resolve difficulties in implementation, keeping in mind the plaintiffs' personal interests in admission to public schools as soon as practicable on a

---

6. Id. at 494.

7. Loren Miller, The Petitioners: The Story of the Supreme Court of the United States and the Negro 351 (1966).

8. 349 U.S. 294 (1955).

9. Id. at 299. Professor Alexander Bickel thought the delay inherent in the "all deliberate speed" approach defensible. "It went without saying also that while the vitality of constitutional principles as reflected in specific court orders ought, to be sure, not be allowed to yield simply because of disagreement with them, disagreement is legitimate and relevant and will, in our system, legitimately and inevitably cause delay in compliance with law laid down by the Supreme Court, and will indeed, if it persists and is widely enough shared, overturn such law." Bickel, The Decade of School Desegregation: Progress and Prospects, 64 Colum. L. Rev. 193, 196 (1964).

nondiscriminatory basis. The Court expected a "prompt and reasonable start toward full compliance, with defendants carrying the burden of showing that requests for additional time are necessary in the public interest and consistent with good faith compliance at the earliest practicable date." The Court returned the cases to the district courts with the admonition that orders and decrees be entered to admit plaintiffs to public schools on a racially nondiscriminatory basis "with all deliberate speed. . . ."

§3.4.2 Robert L. Carter: An Advocate's Analysis of *Brown*

Commenting on this decision more than a decade later, Robert L. Carter, by then the former NAACP General Counsel, surmised that although the Court denied that its "all deliberate speed" formula was intended to do more than allow time for necessary administrative changes which transformation to a desegregated school system required, "it is clear that what the formula required was movement toward compliance on terms that the white South could accept."[10] Carter reminded that until *Brown II,* constitutional rights had been defined as personal and present, and under the guise of "judicial statesmanship," the Warren Court sacrificed individual and immediate vindication of the newly discovered right of blacks to a desegregated education in favor of a remedy more palatable to whites.

In spite of belated efforts in 1964 and 1965, in which the Court stated that "[d]elays in segregating school systems are no longer tolerable," very little school desegregation took place. The eleven states of the old Confederacy had a mere 1.17 percent of their black students attending school with white students by the 1963-1964 school year. In the following year, the percentage had risen to 2.25 percent, and with the help of the Civil Rights Act of 1964 and guidelines for desegregation devised by the United States Department of Health, Education and Welfare, the percentage reached 6.01 percent.

In summarizing the first decade after *Brown,* Mr. Carter does not minimize the effect of the decision which he credits with fathering "a social upheaval the extent and consequences of which cannot even now be measured with certainty." He notes, however, that the pre-existing pattern of white superiority and black subordination remains unchanged. . . . Few in the country, black or white, understood

---

For a discussion of the debate over "all deliberate speed," see Paul Gerwitz, Remedies and Resistance, 92 Yale L.J. 585, 609-628 (1983). More than a dozen years later, Lewis Steel, an attorney for the NAACP, criticized the "all deliberate speed" formulation as evidence of the Supreme Court's willingness to sacrifice the rights of blacks to protect the interests of whites. Steel said the Court's tolerance of delay in implementing *Brown* "made clear that it was a white court which would protect the interests of white America in the maintenance of stable institutions." Lewis Steel, Nine Men in Black Who Think White, N.Y. Times, Oct. 15, 1968, at 53, col. 2. The NAACP Board summarily fired Steel the day after the article's publication. See N.Y. Times, Oct. 29, 1968, at 43, col. 2. General Counsel, Robert L. Carter, unable to gain a hearing for Mr. Steel, resigned and his legal staff did the same. For further details, see Robert L. Carter, A Matter of Law, A Memoir of Struggle in the Cause of Equal Rights, 199-202 (2005).

10. Robert Carter, The Warren Court and Desegregation, 67 Mich. L. Rev. 237, 243 (1968).

in 1954 that racial segregation was merely a symptom, not the disease; that the real sickness is that our society in all of its manifestations is geared to the maintenance of white superiority. . . ."[11]

§3.5 THE *GREEN/SWANN/KEYES* BREAKTHROUGH

After years of slogging through what civil rights lawyers described as "trench warfare," the school desegregation forces finally won several major legal victories beginning in the last years of the 1960s.

§3.5.1 Green v. County School Board of New Kent County

From the standpoint of those who believed that the *Brown* mandate could not be implemented unless public schools were rendered nonidentifiable by race, the Court's 1968 decision in Green v. County School Board of New Kent County[1] was considered as important a victory as *Brown.* In the *Green* case, the Court virtually eliminated "freedom-of-choice" plans as a sufficient desegregation technique.

Justice Brennan explained that *Brown II* imposed an affirmative duty on school districts to take whatever steps were necessary to convert a dual-school system into a "unitary system in which racial discrimination would be eliminated root and branch."[2] The Court did not hold that freedom of choice plans could have no place in an effective desegregation program, but that "in desegregating a dual system a plan utilizing 'freedom of choice' is not an end in itself. . . ."[3] And, if other means of desegregating the schools are reasonably available, including rezoning of schools, freedom-of-choice plans must be held unacceptable. As the Civil Rights Commission reports show, "freedom of choice" was never more than a theoretical concept for most blacks, who feared, frequently with justification, that the exercise of their constitutional right to send their children to a formerly all-white school would cost them their jobs or much more. In a typical case, Chief Judge Haynsworth of the Fourth Circuit reviewed events in a school district which, after ignoring the *Brown* decision for a decade, adopted a freedom-of-choice plan in 1963.

> There followed . . . numerous acts of violence and threats directed against Negro members of the community, particularly those requesting transfers of their children into formerly all-white schools. Shots were fired into houses, oil was poured into wells, and some of the Negro leaders were subjected to a barrage of threatening telephone calls. Violence was widely reported in the local press, and an implicit threat

11. Id. at 247.
§3.5 1. 391 U.S. 430 (1968).
2. Id. at 437-438.
3. Id. at 440. While acknowledging that there might be instances in which freedom of choice could produce results, the Court noted that to date such plans had not indicated their effectiveness as a tool of desegregation.

was carried home to everyone by publication of the names of Negro applicants for transfer.[4]

§3.5.2   The Nixon Retreat and the Court's Response

Public opposition to school desegregation was growing and played a major role in the 1968 presidential election, in which Richard Nixon gained the White House on the basis, according to many, of a campaign that conveyed the message that he would oppose further school desegregation progress. His new administration adopted policies that slowed the federal government's participation in the school desegregation campaign.[5] In Alexander v. Holmes County Board of Education,[6] the Supreme Court entered the controversy over the government's "retreat." For the first time since *Brown,* the government's position opposed that of counsel for the black plaintiffs. On a motion from the Department of Justice and the recommendation of the Secretary of HEW, the Fifth Circuit suspended its order to desegregate 33 Mississippi school districts in the forthcoming school year and postponed the date for the submission of plans. The Supreme Court, in a per curiam decision, stated:

> [T]he Court of Appeals should have denied all motions for additional time because continued operation of segregated schools under a standard of allowing "all deliberate speed" for desegregation is no longer constitutionally permissible. Under explicit holdings of this Court the obligation of every school district is to terminate dual school systems at once and to operate now and hereafter only unitary schools.[7]

§3.5.3   Swann v. Charlotte-Mecklenburg Board of Education

The *Green* and *Alexander* decisions left considerable confusion in their wakes regarding what techniques federal courts could employ to carry through the affirmative duties of desegregation. At the outset of Swann v. Charlotte-Mecklenburg Board of Education[8] Chief Justice Burger noted that it was time to formulate more specific guidelines utilizing the lower courts' experience in the day-to-day implementation of *Brown*'s broad constitutional commands.

Considering the problem of student assignment, Chief Justice Burger noted four areas of major concern:

(1) *Racial Balances or Racial Quotas.* Here, the emphasis is on elimination of discrimination inherent in a dual school system and not with the elimination of

---

4. Coppedge v. Franklin County Bd. of Educ., 394 F.2d 410 (4th Cir. 1968).

5. There was to be less emphasis on "deadlines, coercion and punishment," a statement interpreted by civil rights adherents as a "scuttling" of the guidelines and of HEW's enforcement program. In the next year or so, civil rights personnel resigned at both HEW and the Justice Department. The events are recorded in Leon Panetta & Peter Gall, Bring Us Together, The Nixon Team and the Civil Rights Retreat (1971); and Jack Greenberg, Revolt at Justice, 1 Washington Monthly 32 (Dec. 1969).

6. 396 U.S. 19 (1969).

7. Id. at 20. The Court also cited Green v. New Kent County, supra, and Griffin v. School Bd., 377 U.S. 218, 234 (1964), in support of its action.

8. 402 U.S. 1 (1971).

the many other societal factors that may result in racial discrimination. The Court concluded that the 71 percent to 29 percent racial ratio set by the district court was appropriate as "a starting point in the process of shaping a remedy, rather than an inflexible requirement."

(2) *One-Race Schools.* If a plan will leave any one-race schools, the school board carries the burden of showing that the one-race status is not the result of continuing discrimination, present or past.

(3) *Remedial Altering of Attendance Zones.* As an interim corrective measure for a proved violation, altered attendance zones would be approved even though they may be administratively awkward, inconvenient, and even bizarre in some situations.

(4) *Transportation of Students.* Chief Justice Burger warned that an objection to transportation of students may have validity when the time or distance of travel is so great as to risk either the health of the children, or significantly impinge on the educational process.

Finally, Chief Justice Burger added:

> It does not follow that the communities served by such systems will remain demo-graphically stable, for in a growing, mobile society, few will do so. Neither school authorities nor district courts are constitutionally required to make year-by-year adjustments of the racial composition of student bodies once the affirmative duty to desegregate has been accomplished and racial discrimination through official action is eliminated from the system.[9]

§3.6　THE ROAD FROM *SWANN*

Although the *Swann* guidelines were ambiguous, the decision represented the high-water mark of judicial support for school desegregation remedies that rely on mandatory reassignments on the basis of race.[1] Based on this judicial "green light," lower courts began entering system-wide desegregation orders in school cases across the country.[2] But, by the end of the 1976 term, the Supreme Court had either vacated or remanded orders for system-wide school desegregation plans in

---

9. Id. at 30-31.

§3.6 1. The Court's intent is more pronounced in the companion case of Davis v. Board of School Commissioners: "Having once found a violation, the district judge or school authorities should make every effort to achieve the greatest possible degree of actual desegregation, taking into account the particularities of the situation. . . . The measure of any desegregation plan is its effectiveness." 402 U.S. 33, 37 (1971). See also McDaniel v. Barresi, 402 U.S. 39 (1971) (where the Court held that in the remedial process, assigning students on the basis of race would almost invari-ably be required); North Carolina State Bd. of Educ. v. Swann, 402 U.S. 43 (1971) (where the Court struck down a statute that prohibited assignment or involuntary busing of students on account of race in order to create a racial balance); Lee v. Nyquist, 318 F. Supp. 710 (W.D.N.Y. 1970), aff'd, 402 U.S. 935 (1971).

2. A selection of the cases and the issues resolved therein in 2 Emerson, Haber, & Dorsen's Political and Civil Rights in the United States 688-690 (1979).

four cases.[3] In each of the remands, the Supreme Court pointedly referred the lower courts to the invidious purpose-and-intent standards of liability in the Washington v. Davis[4] and Village of Arlington Heights v. Metropolitan Housing Development Corp.[5] decisions.

Outside the courtroom, white children, the prospective objects of the school desegregation orders, were leaving the public schools or moving to the suburbs at a rapid rate.[6] The cities in which white flight occurred indicated the existence of a tipping point — reached when approximately 25 to 50 percent of the student body was black — at which white families began to migrate to the suburbs to avoid racial mixing and what they feared would lead to educational decay. An increasing issue for the Court was the degree to which a school system must risk losing more of an already declining white school population in order to affect a maximum amount of racial balance within all the schools.

Some argue that the white exodus was a demographic phenomenon with little or no connection to school desegregation orders, while others have attacked the Court for doing more harm than good. Busing, in particular, has met with intense and well-publicized hostility for encouraging white families to flee to the suburbs to avoid its reach, resulting in urban schools that are even more racially isolated than before busing. Busing, combined with white fear of racial mixing, has led to racially separate housing patterns within cities. Whites, running from the blacks in the inner cities, have hid in the suburbs behind an impressive array of economic, social, and legal barriers. Local governments have been active accomplices, through mortgaging practices, the location of public housing and urban renewal projects, and zoning regulations. Racial isolation in housing has both created single-race schools and insulated these schools from challenges. Eventually, school boards are able to explain away single-race schools as the result of "natural" separation rather than official discrimination and to thereby avoid desegregation decrees.

In Milliken v. Bradley,[7] the Court allayed middle class fears that the school bus would become the Trojan horse of their suburban Troys by holding that the district court was in error when it ordered 53 suburban school districts to participate

---

3. Austin Indep. Sch. Dist. v. United States, 429 U.S. 990 (1976); United States v. Bd. of School Commrs. of City of Indianapolis, 429 U.S. 1068 (1976); School Dist. of Omaha v. United States, 433 U.S. 667 (1977); Brennan v. Armstrong (Milwaukee), 433 U.S. 672 (1977).

4. 426 U.S. 229 (1976).

5. 429 U.S. 252 (1977).

6. By the late 1970s, roughly half of all nonwhite children in the nation resided in the 20 to 30 largest school districts. The minority children averaged 60 percent of the school population in these districts, only a few of which contained a majority of white students. In the ten largest districts, the minority percentage averaged 68.2 percent.

In Los Angeles, for example, civil rights officials agreed to drop a 25-year-old desegregation suit because the proportion of white students in the district had dropped to 17 percent from more than 65 percent when the lawsuit was initiated in 1963. Adelson, Desegregation Lawsuit Ending After 25 Years, N.Y. Times, June 22, 1988, at B6, col. 2. It is estimated that in the years following court-ordered busing in Boston, 60 percent of public school families avoided participation in the plan by moving or enrolling their children in parochial schools. See Paul Gerwitz, Remedies and Resistance, 92 Yale L.J. 585, 628-630 (1983).

7. 418 U.S. 717 (1974).

in the desegregation of the predominantly black Detroit school system.[8] *Milliken* held that a court could not impose a multidistrict remedy to a single district de jure segregation problem without a finding that the other school districts included somehow participated in a segregation scheme and without those districts having the opportunity to be heard.

Chief Justice Burger stated that remedies that reach across school district lines must be firmly founded on proof of wrong. As applied in the instant case, "it must first be shown that there has been a constitutional violation within one district that produces a significant segregative effect in another district."[9]

In his dissent, Justice Douglas feared that "We take a step that will likely put the problems of the Blacks and our society back to the period that antedated the 'separate but equal' regime of Plessy v. Ferguson." Both Justices White and Marshall wrote separate dissents.[10]

The initial hope that metropolitan plans could be forced on resisting, suburban, mainly white school districts evaporated for all save the most committed civil rights proponents of integrated schools. In their view, the most substantial impediment to school desegregation is the court's short-sighted acquiescence to patterns of residential segregation.[11] Whites had every incentive to flee the inner city while racism and the perceived (and usually actual) inferiority of black schools keep white families from moving into predominantly black neighborhoods. Thus, courts' tolerance of residual school segregation created an inescapable cycle of racial separation.

§3.6.1 Tracking and Disenchantment

As these and other effects of court ordered desegregation continued, pressure mounted on all sides against the integration effort. In the 1980s it was the

---

8. The Detroit public school population was already 63.8 percent black in 1970 and was growing at a rate greater than the city's black population. Given the prospect of an increased white exodus, a remedial plan consolidating the Detroit system with the 53 surrounding suburban districts was deemed by the district court, the only solution. Bradley v. Milliken, 345 F. Supp. 914 (E.D. Mich. 1972), aff'd, 484 F.2d 215, 250 (6th Cir. 1973).

9. 418 U.S. 717, 744-745 (1974). Chief Justice Burger said that there was no evidence of significant violations in the 53 outlying districts.

10. The Court's dissenters were joined by most of the legal commentators. See, e.g., Charles Lawrence, Segregation "Misunderstood": The *Milliken* Decision Revisited, 12 U.S.F. L. Rev. 15 (1977); Robert Sedler, Metropolitan Desegregation in the Wake of *Milliken* — On Losing Big Battles and Winning Small Wars: The View Largely from Within, 1975 Wash. U. L.Q. 535 (1976); Taylor, The Supreme Court and Urban Reality: A Tactical Analysis of Milliken v. Bradley, 21 Wayne L. Rev. 751 (1975).

11. Gerwitz, supra note 6, at 628-665 (1983); Hankins, The Constitutional Implications of Residential Segregation — To Boldly Go Where Few Courts Have Gone, 30 How. L.J. 481, 486 (1987) (noting that "[o]ne of the most significant obstacles preventing effective school desegregation is residential racial separation"); Note, Unitary School Systems and Underlying Vestiges of State Imposed Segregation, 87 Colum. L. Rev. 794, 808-809 (1987) (arguing that "residential segregation as a vestige of unconstitutional school segregation may become the last barrier to widespread declarations of unitariness"); Note, School Desegregation: An Encore of "Separate But Equal" — Jenkins v. Missouri, 20 Creighton L. Rev. 1055, 1085 (1987) (describing failure to grant interdistrict relief as "separatism [which] propagates the inherent inequality condemned in *Brown I*"); Note, Housing Discrimination as a Basis for Interdistrict School Desegregation Remedies, 91 Yale L.J. 340, 346 (1983).

disillusionment of black parents with a remedy that disproportionately burdened blacks that most dramatically shifted the political landscape regarding busing.[12] Black children were shuffled in and out of predominantly white schools to take the places vacated by whites fleeing to outlying suburbs. In these white schools, black children all too often met naked race-hatred and a curriculum blind to their needs. Black parents, who often live far from the schools where their children are sent, had no input into the school policies and little opportunity to involve themselves in school life.[13]

One of the most disturbing and frustrating aspects of the integration experience for young black children is "tracking." History shows that white students are admitted to accelerated schools and programs, and black children are relegated to inferior schools or low tracks.[14] Tracking internalizes the bias and stigma of segregation, nullifying the benefits of intraschool integration.[15]

Reflecting the evolving judicial temperament, school systems that isolate minority students in separate tracks met with judicial hostility in the 1960s and 1970s, only to be insulated from court challenges in the 1980s.[16] Courts refused to intervene in tracking programs on the grounds that these programs are matters of educational policy best left to the school administrators and teachers.

The acceptance of tracking systems that effectively segregate black students is another example of judges' willingness to overlook race discrimination that results from facially nonracial factors. Even more disturbing, however, is the judges' willingness to tolerate racial discrimination that inevitably results from tracking. Low-level tracks teach black students the insidious and lasting "meta-lesson" that they are intellectually inferior to white students and must accustom themselves to occupying the lowest rung in the social and economic hierarchy.[17]

12. According to a Gallup poll conducted in 1981, half of the black population in the United States believed that busing to achieve school integration "has caused more difficulties than it is worth." Half of Blacks in Poll Question Busing's Value, N.Y. Times, Mar. 2, 1981, at B4, col. 1. See also Lena Williams, Controversy Reawakens as Districts End Busing, N.Y. Times, Mar. 25, 1986, at A24, col. 1. In DeKalb County, Georgia, a poll of black residents commissioned by the DeKalb Chamber of Commerce found that 87.6 percent of black parents surveyed would not support mandatory busing to achieve racial balance in the schools. See Jordan, Is Desegregation Working for Blacks?, Boston Globe, Jul. 1, 1990, at 89.

13. See, e.g., Riddick v. School Bd. of Norfolk, 784 F.2d 521 (4th Cir. 1986) (noting "dramatic drop" in parental involvement as a result of busing).

14. See Note, Teaching Inequality: The Problem of Public School Tracking, 102 Harv. L. Rev. 1318 (1989); Jeannie Oakes, Keeping Track: How Schools Structure Inequality 65-67 (1985) (finding "minority students . . . in disproportionately small percentages in high-track classes and in dispro-portionately large percentages in low-track classes").

15. See, e.g., Braddock & McPartland, The Social and Academic Consequences of School Desegregation, Equity and Choice, Feb. 1988, at 66-67; West, "Tracking" Hampers Minorities' Access to Math, Science Careers, Study Finds, Educ. Week, Sept. 26, 1990, at 8.

16. Compare McNeal v. Tate County Sch. Dist. 508 F.2d 1017 (5th Cir. 1975); United States v. Tunica County Sch. Dist., 421 F.2d 1236 (5th Cir.) (reversing district court's approval of student assignments on the basis of achievement scores), cert. denied, 398 U.S. 951 (1970); Singleton v. Jackson Mun. Separate Sch. Dist., 419 F.2d 1211, 1219 (5th Cir.) (holding that testing cannot be employed until the school system has achieved unitary status), vacated in part and rev'd in part sub nom. Carter v. West Felicana Parish Sch. Bd., 396 U.S. 226 (1969).

17. See Teaching Inequality, supra note 14, at 1319, 1329, 1332-1333 (describing tracking as a "self-fulfilling prophecy").

In addition to tracking, desegregation plans requiring that parents send their children far from home were viewed by some black parents as coercive and potentially harmful as the freedom-of-choice plans rejected by the Court two decades earlier. The 1980s saw a growing disenchantment with mandatory integration as the linchpin of an educational policy for black children. Many parents, advocates, scholars, and judges came to see a singular focus on racial balance in public schools as actually counterproductive.[18]

Pressure was also coming from the political arena, particularly the executive branch. The Justice Department did not aggressively prosecute schools not in compliance with desegregation orders, and it encouraged districts that felt they had achieved unitary status to seek dissolution of their orders.[19]

§3.6.2 Judicial Retreat

Two considerations likely influenced the Court heavily at this time. First was the serious and steadily growing opposition to busing in general as a means of effecting school desegregation and, in particular, the overwhelming opposition to busing children between the inner city and the suburbs. Second was that studies of the educational effects of school desegregation had been inconclusive as to the value either in education or in socialization for black or white children.[20]

This resistance triggered judicial debate on the process by which school cases can be jettisoned from court's dockets. What has been settled, though, is the fact that school districts can be relieved of their obligation to integrate their public schools even though substantial racial separation continues or will emerge in the absence of a positive duty.

In Board of Education of Oklahoma City Public Schools v. Dowell,[21] the Supreme Court held that formerly segregated school districts may be released from court-ordered busing even if some segregation persists, so long as all "practicable" steps to eliminate the vestiges of discrimination have been taken.[22] Justice Rehnquist stated that the school desegregation plans need not stay in effect unless "the purposes of the litigation as incorporated in the decree . . . have not been fully achieved." Since the purpose of the litigation was to ensure compliance with the Fourteenth Amendment, the District Court's finding that the school system is unitary and likely to remain so shows that the aim of the litigation had been achieved if the Board had complied in good faith with the desegregation decree

18. See Equal Educational Opportunity: The Status of Black Americans in Higher Education, 1975-1977, Howard University, Inst. for the Study of Educ. Policy 107 (1980).

19. Early in Reagan's first term, Secretary of Education T. H. Bell announced that the federal role in enforcing antidiscrimination laws in schools should be drastically reduced, leaving primary responsibility for compliance with the states. See Hunter, Bell Will Not Push Lawsuits on Busing, N.Y. Times, Mar. 16, 1981, at A15, col. 1; Norman, The Strange Career of the Civil Rights Division's Commitment to Brown, 93 Yale L.J. 983, 985-988 (1984).

20. See Nancy St. John, School Desegregation Outcomes for Children (1975).

21. 498 U.S. 237.

22. See also Flax v. Potts, 864 F.2d 1157 (5th Cir. 1989), a Fifth Circuit case that portended the Supreme Court's own backsliding.

since it was entered and if the vestiges of past discrimination had been eliminated to the extent practicable. In his dissent, Justice Marshall pointed out the tragic illogic of the Court's willingness to acquiesce to private causes of segregation such as racially isolated residential patterns.

Consequently, the courts have taken almost every opportunity to release school districts from court ordered desegregation — even where a substantial number of racially identifiable schools remain or would emerge. Once a desegregation decree is dissolved, plaintiffs must make a showing of intentional discrimination to merit renewed judicial supervision.[23] That is a nearly impossible showing to make, because residential segregation means that substantial resegregation of schools will emerge from "natural" causes, without evidence of a segregative intent by the school board and thus without remedy. In a twist of bitter irony, white flight became a freewheeling argument to block desegregation in almost every context.[24]

§3.6.3   Changing Ideology

Perhaps the most fundamental change of the decade was the dissolution of the ideological justification for desegregation.

The desire to refocus the thrust of school desegregation caused a search for a new ideological underpinning. Some, like the plurality opinion in the *Seattle-Louisville* decision, have read *Brown* to require only an end to intentional discrimination against black children. This symbolic but empty victory condemns but does not cure the effects of segregation and does nothing to dislodge the hold of prior discrimination.

Others, such as the dissenting Justices in the *Seattle-Louisville* decision, argued that the purpose of desegregation is to ensure equal education opportunities for black students. However, not all proponents of this view agree on the means to achieve this end. Robert Carter argued that if equal educational opportunity can be achieved without integration, *Brown* has been satisfied. Others would claim that the inescapable conclusion of the Court's decision in *Brown* is that racial separation is itself an injury, regardless of parity in the facilities.

Those who focused on quality of education and challenged proponents of racial balance remedies in the courts had a difficult time being heard.[25] When groups not committed to racial balance obtained a court order for some

---

23. Pasadena City Bd. of Educ. v. Spangler, 427 U.S. 424 (1976). See also City of Mobile v. Borden, 446 U.S. 55, 74 (1980) (plurality opinion) (while a history of discrimination should not be ignored, it "cannot in the manner of original sin condemn governmental action that is not itself unlawful").

24. See, e.g., *Flax*, supra note 22, at 1161 & n.11 ("while 'white flight' cannot be used as a justification for avoiding the affirmative duty to desegregate; a school district — especially one nearing a declaration of unitary status — has a legitimate interest in retaining a sufficient number of white students to provide an integrated educational experience for the students") (citations omitted).

25. The discussion that follows is adopted from Derrick Bell, Serving Two Masters: Integration Ideals and Client Interests in School Desegregation Litigation, 85 Yale L.J. 470, 484-487 (1976).

other form of relief, they usually faced intervening civil rights organizations with more expertise and resources. This sometimes resulted in open confrontations between NAACP and local blacks who favored plans oriented toward improving educational quality.

§3.6.4 The Racial Balance Debate Revisited

The NAACP and other major civil rights groups did not change their views as to the value of integration policies throughout the 1970s, despite growing resistance and the increased difficulty of effectively integrating large urban school systems with their steadily decreasing percentages of white students. In a controversial law review article, it was suggested that civil rights lawyers had become more committed to their belief in integration than they were to the educational interests of their clients.[26] A reassessment of school desegregation strategies was appropriate because, as argued in the article:

> The great crusade to desegregate the public schools has faltered. There is increasing opposition to desegregation at both local and national levels (not all of which can now be simply condemned as "racist"). While the once vigorous support of federal courts is on the decline, new barriers have arisen — inflation makes the attainment of racial balance more expensive, the growth of black populations in urban areas renders it more difficult, and increasing numbers of social science studies question the validity of its educational assumptions.
>
> Civil rights lawyers dismiss the new obstacles as legally irrelevant. Having achieved so much by courageous persistence, they have not wavered in their determination to implement *Brown* using racial balance measures developed in the hard-fought legal battles of the last two decades. This stance involves great risk for clients whose educational interests may no longer accord with the integration ideals of their attorneys. . . . Now that traditional racial balance remedies are becoming increasingly difficult to achieve or maintain, there is tardy concern that racial balance may not be the relief actually desired by the victims of segregated schools.[27]

For many civil rights workers, success in obtaining racially balanced schools became a symbol of the nation's commitment to equal opportunity — not only in education, but in housing, employment, and other fields where the effects of racial discrimination are still present. One commentator, Dean Earnest Campbell, observed, "[T]he busing issue has acquired meanings that seem to have little relevance for the education of children in any direct sense."[28] Any retreat on busing was deemed an abandonment of this commitment and a return to segregation. Indeed, some leaders saw busing as a major test of black political strength.

26. Id.
27. Id. at 471-472. The article reviewed the development of school desegregation strategies, their early effectiveness, and the commitment of civil rights organizations to them even when it meant opposing local black groups who preferred relief they hoped would improve the educational quality of the public schools. Alternative types of relief were discussed along with a review of procedural rules that might facilitate bringing such views before the courts.
28. Earnest Campbell, Defining and Attaining Equal Educational Opportunity in a Pluralistic Society, 26 Vand. L. Rev. 461, 478 (1973).

§3.6.5   School Desegregation's Gains and Losses

Despite all the obstacles, school desegregation advocates can take credit for the thousands of children — white as well as black — who attended racially desegregated schools and felt advantaged by their experiences. For many of these students, studies indicate that desegregation increases the academic achievement of black students. Black children attending desegregated schools perform better on standardized achievement and IQ tests and are more likely to complete high school and to enroll in and graduate from college than black students in single-race schools. This means, of course, that desegregation may improve substantially the opportunities available for black adults in every arena.[29]

Unfortunately, the benefits of desegregation that some have experienced were neither widespread nor permanent. As indicated in the earlier sections, racial hostility as well as the economic and housing barriers have combined to limit integrated schooling to those black and Latino families able to live in mainly white, middle class areas. As a result, there is a steady decline in the number of children able to obtain a racially integrated education in American schools. A study issued in early 2003 by the strongly pro-integration Harvard Civil Rights Project[30] reports that, as of the 2000-2001 school year, white students, on average, attend schools where 80 percent of the student body is white. Minority students are increasingly attending schools that are virtually all nonwhite. Quite often in these schools devastating poverty, limited resources, and social and health problems of many types are concentrated. The nation's largest city schools are, almost without exception, overwhelmingly nonwhite. In suburban districts that were virtually all white three decades ago, serious patterns of segregation have emerged as more and more nonwhites move into suburban areas.

More striking than nationwide statistics, Jonathan Kozol focuses on the schools in the Mott Haven section of the Bronx and reports that in the elementary schools serving the neighborhood, among 11,000 children, only 26 are white. This segregation rate of 99.2 percent leaves two-tenths of one percentage point as the distinction between legally enforced segregation in the South of 50 years ago and the socially and economically enforced apartheid in this New York City school district today.[31]

29. See, e.g., Taylor, *Brown*, Equal Protection, and the Isolation of the Poor, 95 Yale L.J. 1700, 1710-1711 nn.36-42 (1986); T. Cook, Black Achievement and School Desegregation 9, 85 (1984); Mahard & Crain, Research on Minority Achievement in Desegregated Schools, in The Consequences of School Desegregation 124 (Christine Russell & Willis Hawley eds., 1983); Willis Hawley & Smylie, The Contribution of School Desegregation to Academic Achievement and Racial Integration, in Eliminating Racism: Profiles in Controversy 284-285 (Phyllis Katz & Dalmas Taylor eds., 1988); Braddock & McPartland, The Social and Academic Consequences of School Desegregation, Equity & Choice, Feb. 1988, at 8-9 (desegregation increases the likelihood of attendance at four-year and desegregated colleges).

30. Erica Frankenberg, Chungmei Lee, & Gary Orfield, A Multiracial Society with Segregated Schools: Are We Losing the Dream? (2003).

31. Jonathan Kozol, Ordinary Resurrections 31 (2000). For a depressing review of segregation and inadequacies in schools across the country, see Jonathan Kozol, Savage Inequalities: Children in America's Schools (1991).

The academic status of all black children, including those attending integrated schools, is not encouraging. Despite evidence that integration has improved the performance of minority students, shocking disparities still mark the educational attainments of black students and white students. Black students are twice as likely as white students to drop out of high school.[32] On standardized achievement tests in reading, black nine-year-olds scored an average of ten points lower than white nine-year-olds. As many as 40 percent of minority youths are functionally illiterate.[33]

Conditions for Latino children are even more dreary. Segregated both by race and poverty, and with a developing pattern of linguistic segregation, Latinos have by far the highest school dropout rates. The Supreme Court did not recognize the entitlement of Latino children to desegregation until 1973.[34] Latinos often asked for bilingual education as part of the segregation remedy as a means of gaining equal access to the curriculum and eventually full integration.[35] While the federal government provided support for this movement, it likely prompted a strong anti-bilingual movement among many whites that — even as the segregation of Latino children increased — succeeded in California, Arizona, and Massachusetts through voter referenda to outlaw bilingual education.

The unhappy fact is that the quality of education is shockingly bad in many, perhaps most, schools attended by poorer black and Spanish-speaking children in what are nominally desegregated schools. Facilities are often inadequate to awful, and because of many factors, whites make up the majority of the faculty and administrators. Many white teachers are dedicated and work hard along with their similarly dedicated black and Hispanic colleagues, but the barriers in their way are many, and some otherwise productive teachers of all races simply give up. Some leave teaching; others remain in their jobs but limit their functioning to trying to maintain order, reasoning that their students don't seem to want to learn so why even try to teach them. Such attitudes, of course, soon become self-fulfilling.

§3.7 THE NEUTRAL PRINCIPLE OF RACE IN *BROWN*

Initially, the proponents of the *Brown* decision viewed its essence to be in that portion of Chief Justice Warren's opinion where he found that "[t]o separate [black children] from others of similar age and qualifications solely because of their race generates a feeling of inferiority as to their status in the community that may affect their hearts and minds in a way unlikely ever to be undone."[1] The general sense

---

32. College Entrance Examination Board, Equality and Excellence: The Educational Status of Black Americans 12 (1985).

33. N. Francis, Equity and Excellence in Education, in Association of Black Foundation Executives Conference Proceedings 73 (Apr. 26, 1985).

34. Keyes v. School Dist. No. 1, Denver, 413 U.S. 189 (1973).

35. See United States v. Texas, 466 F.2d 518 (5th Cir. 1972).

§3.7   1. Brown v. Board of Educ., 347 U.S. 483, 494 (1954).

was that, without this "racial stigma by separation" argument, the Court's *Plessy* precedent might have limited relief to an order requiring equalization of resources and facilities in all-black schools. Implementation of *Brown II*'s "all deliberate speed" mandate went slowly in those early years, with far more resistance than compliance. And it was at this point that Professor Herbert Wechsler, a scholar of prestige and influence, presented the Oliver Wendell Holmes Lecture at Harvard Law School, raising a criticism of the *Brown* decision that gained renewed importance when the Court's once strong support for school desegregation faded to scepticism.[2]

Professor Wechsler had no difficulty with the Court's departure from earlier decisions that had approved segregated schools. That the departure disturbed settled patterns in a portion of the country did not, he felt, constitute legitimate criticism. He was bothered neither by the uncertain position of the Fourteenth Amendment's framers on school segregation, nor the view that the issue should have been remitted to the Congress.

Disclaiming adherence to either those "who perceive in law only the element of fiat, in whose conception of the legal cosmos reason has no meaning or no place," or those who "frankly or covertly make the test of virtue in interpretation whether its result in the immediate decision seems to hinder or advance the interests or the values they support,"[3] Professor Wechsler saw the need for criteria of decision that could be framed and tested as an exercise of reason, and not merely adopted as an act of willfulness or will. He believed, in short, that courts could engage in a "principled appraisal" of legislative actions that exceeded a fixed "historical meaning" of constitutional provisions without, as Judge Learned Hand feared, becoming "a third legislative chamber."[4] The largely instrumental principles of politics that may be trimmed or shaped by the legislator to match prevailing popular winds must be eschewed by the judicial process. Instead, Professor Wechsler said, courts "must be genuinely principled, resting with respect to every step that is involved in reaching judgment on analysis and reasons quite transcending the immediate result that is achieved."[5]

Applying those standards which Professor Wechsler said should include constitutional and statutory interpretation, the subtle guidance provided by history, and appropriate but not slavish fidelity to precedent, he found difficulty with Supreme Court decisions where principled reasoning was in his view either deficient or, in some instances, nonexistent.[6] The *Brown* opinion apparently was included in the latter category.

Professor Wechsler reviewed and rejected the possibility that *Brown* was based on a declaration that the Fourteenth Amendment barred all racial lines in legislation. He doubted that the evidence of racial harm caused by segregation,

2. Herbert Wechsler, Toward Neutral Principles of Constitutional Law, 73 Harv. L. Rev. 1 (1959). This discussion is based on Derrick Bell, *Brown* and the Interest-Convergence Dilemma, 93 Harv. L. Rev. 518 (1980).
3. Wechsler, supra note 2, at 11.
4. Id. at 16.
5. Id. at 15.
6. Id. at 19.

disputed as it was by state witnesses, and enabled the decision to turn on the facts. Rather, the *Brown* decision must have rested on the view "that racial segregation is, in principle, a denial of equality to the minority against whom it is directed. . . ."[7] Assuming this basis for the Court's decision, he questioned the soundness of the proof presented to reach a decision contrary to those reached by legislatures, and involving an inquiry into the motives of the legislature generally foreclosed to the courts.

Venturing on with great courage, if a rather appalling underestimation of the realities of racial discrimination, Professor Wechsler suggested that assuming facilities were equal, the legal issue in state-imposed segregation was not one of discrimination at all, but "the denial by the state of freedom to associate, a denial that impinges in the same way on any groups or races that may be involved."[8] He then suggested that "if the freedom of association is denied by segregation, integration forces an association upon those for whom it is unpleasant or repugnant." And concluding with a question that challenged legal scholars (and which has returned in altered but still identifiable form to haunt and perhaps enlighten us), he asked:

> Given a situation where the state must practically choose between denying the association to those individuals who wish it or imposing it on those who would avoid it, is there a basis in neutral principles for holding that the Constitution demands that the claims for association should prevail? I should like to think there is, but I confess I have not written the opinion. To write it is for me the challenge of the school segregation cases.[9]

§3.7.1 Scholarly Responses to Professor Wechsler

Those legal scholars who accepted Professor Wechsler's challenge had little difficulty in finding a neutral principle on which the *Brown* decision could be based.[10] Indeed, from the hindsight of an era of the greatest racial consciousness-raising the country has ever known, much of Professor Wechsler's concern seems, to put it kindly, bizarre. To doubt, even for the purposes of debate, that racial segregation is harmful to blacks, and to suggest that the harm done to them is no less severe than that suffered by whites, is to discuss a world that does not exist now and could not possibly have existed then. And then, to surmise that what blacks really sought in *Brown* was the right to associate with whites as opposed to the right not to be excluded from schools designated by the states for whites only, exhibits a character of racial conceit that threatens to drown all substance in Professor Wechsler's position in a flood of now obsolete social myths.

---

7. Id. at 33.
8. Id. at 34.
9. Id.
10. Charles Black, The Lawfulness of the Segregation Decisions, 69 Yale L.J. 421 (1960); Louis Pollack, Racial Discrimination and Judicial Integrity: A Reply to Professor Wechsler, 108 U. Pa. L. Rev. 1 (1959); Michael Heyman, The Chief Justice, Racial Segregation, and the Friendly Critics, 49 Cal. L. Rev. 104 (1961).

But Wechsler's search for a neutral principle on which *Brown* might be based remains important, precisely because those suggested by the legal scholars are not deemed legitimate by large segments of the American people. One would have thought, for example, that Yale's Professor Charles Black correctly cited racial equality as the principle which properly underlay the *Brown* opinion.[11] In Professor Black's view, Professor Wechsler's question is "awkwardly simple." He states it in the form of a syllogism. His major premise is that "the equal protection clause of the fourteenth amendment should be read as saying that the Negro race, as such, is not to be significantly disadvantaged by the laws of the states," His minor premise is that "segregation is a massive intentional disadvantaging of the Negro race, as such, by state law."[12] Professor Black's conclusion is that the equal protection clause clearly bars racial segregation which he finds harms blacks and benefits whites in ways too numerous and obvious to bear citation.[13]

Logically, the argument is persuasive and under that logic, Professor Black has no trouble urging that "[w]hen the directive of equality cannot be followed without displeasing white[s], then something that can be called a 'freedom' of the white[s] must be impaired."[14] It is precisely here, though, that many whites part company with Professor Black. They may agree in the abstract that blacks are citizens and are entitled to constitutional rights, but few understand that racial segregation was far more than a series of now-obsolete customs that can be dropped without any change in the status or condition of whites.

This seems to be the point at which Professor Wechsler has perhaps unwisely obscured with his discussion of rights of association and nonassociation. There is now, thanks to the work of civil rights lawyers, a recognized freedom of association protecting the right to join with others to seek goals independently protected by the First Amendment.[15] The Court, on the other hand, has not really recognized a right of state-protected nonassociation, although in rejecting an argument to this effect advanced by a racially segregated private academy,[16] there was some suggestion that a group of whites who organized privately without publicly seeking students and without receiving state aid, might be able to exclude blacks, just as the public accommodations section of the Civil Rights Act of 1964 excludes bona fide private clubs from its coverage.[17] Self-segregation of that type is a long way from the

11. Black, supra note 10.
12. Id. at 421.
13. Id. at 425-426.
14. Id. at 429.
15. See, e.g., NAACP v. Button, 371 U.S. 415 (1963); Shelton v. Tucker, 364 U.S. 479 (1960); NAACP v. Alabama ex rel. Patterson, 357 U.S. 449 (1958). In these cases, the Supreme Court recognized the right of blacks to associate together to litigate and petition for civil rights free of interference by state agencies seeking membership lists. But the Court has not protected goals of associations which members would be free to pursue independently where those goals were not recognized as rights under the First Amendment. See Laurence Tribe, American Constitutional Law 700-710 (1978).
16. Runyon v. McCrary, 427 U.S. 160 (1976).
17. Id. There is, of course, a right of nonassociation where nonmembership is connected with freedoms of belief and association. On this basis, patronage discharges solely for nonaffiliation with a particular political party were invalidated in Elrod v. Burns, 427 U.S. 347 (1976). And flag salute requirements were banned as in violation of rights to freedom of expression. West Virginia State Bd. of Educ. v. Barnette, 319 U.S. 624 (1943).

structured societal advantage and superior status granted whites by law before *Brown*.

It would seem then that Professor Wechsler's critique was essentially normative. That is, he was writing about *Brown* in the realm of pure reason and expressed concern that no neutral principle could be found to mediate the conflict between "racial equality" (desired by blacks), and "nonassociational freedom" (the white-oriented freedom not to associate with blacks). On its own terms, in the realm of the normative, of the ideal, of what ought to be, that critique was false as Charles Black, among others, demonstrated. On another level, however, the positivistic level, that is, the description of "what the world is," Professor Wechsler's analysis may lead the way to a new perspective on the turbulent conflict that led to *Brown* and which continues to deeply trouble the society a quarter of a century later. To the extent that this conflict is between "racial equality" and "associational freedom," used here as a proxy for all those things whites will have to give up in order to achieve a racial equality that is more than formal, it is clear that the conflict will never be mediated by a "neutral principle." If it is to be resolved at all, it will be determined by the existing power relationships in the society and the perceived self-interest of the white elite. And it may well be that Professor Wechsler's criticism received as much fanfare as it did and continues to haunt American jurisprudence as it does because it expressed, albeit in a masked and intellectually acceptable form, a deeper truth, a positivistic truth, about the subordination of law to interest-group politics in issues involving race.[18]

§3.7.2 White Self-Interest as a Support for *Brown*

To recall the era of Jim Crow in America is to conclude that Professor Wechsler's concern could not have been the loss by whites of the right not to associate with blacks. During that time, racial association in the South was seldom a problem because the status relationships between the races were so clear. *Brown* upset the legal rationale for the well-settled status of blacks on the bottom and whites somewhere above. While Wechsler felt that there must be a basic common neutral principle which all would see and accept as legitimate for equalizing black-white status, thereby justifying the result in *Brown,* it was certainly no more than we have come to expect from courts if he were seeking a judicial acknowledgement of the benefits, vested interests, and relied-on expectations whites had enjoyed under the legal blessing of *Plessy*. All of these benefits might well be characterized as the interest by whites in superior societal status. It would have then been necessary to weigh this interest against the disadvantages suffered by blacks because of its existence.

Whites simply cannot envision the personal responsibility and the potential sacrifice inherent in Professor Black's conclusion that true equality for blacks will require the surrender of racism-granted privilege for whites. To the extent that Professor Wechsler recognized and challenged his colleagues to bridge this gap

---

18. I am indebted to Yale law professor Owen Fiss for his aid in developing this argument.

with a neutral principle which all would perceive as legitimate, he placed more reliance on the intellectual process than history and experience indicate it can bear.

Almost a half century has passed since Professor Wechsler stirred controversy and turmoil with his analysis of the *Brown* decision. We now know that despite his misgivings, the Supreme Court ignored or at least was undeterred by all manner of public resistance to the implementation of *Brown,* and that its support wavered at a point when considerable progress had been made, and when resistance to further progress was arguably no greater than it had been in those first turbulent years after 1954. The question is whether anything in Professor Wechsler's search for a "neutral principle" on which *Brown* could be decided explains the Supreme Court's almost fervent fidelity to *Brown* until the mid-1970s, and the slow but steady erosion of the Court's commitment observable in its decisions since that time. In response, it is necessary to consider the possible white self-interest factors in the *Brown* decision.

The *Brown* decision represented an unstated understanding that legally sanctioned segregation no longer furthered and in fact was now harmful to the interests of those whites who make policy for the country. Recall the discussion in Chapter 2, suggesting that black progress throughout the history of this country was tied to policy change which furthered the interests of whites, or some of them. These policy changes were generally asserted as being for the benefit of blacks, and seldom were the white self-interest motivations acknowledged. Abraham Lincoln's indication to Horace Greeley that he would end slavery to the degree that such action would help save the Union, §2.2 supra, was the classic example. That lesson of history is almost definitively illustrated by the *Brown* decision.

As indicated in §3.2.1, blacks had been seeking the end of segregated schools in litigation stretching back to 1850, and in the Massachusetts school desegregation case, Roberts v. City of Boston,[19] had advanced without success arguments about the inequality, unfairness, and socially stigmatizing effects of segregation, arguments that were quite similar to those which won approval in *Brown.* The separate-but-equal doctrine was formulated out of the rejection of these arguments and the Court in Plessy v. Ferguson even cited the *Roberts* case to illustrate the by-then long-settled reasonableness of state-mandated classifications based on race.[20]

The greater receptivity of the Court to the plaintiffs' arguments in *Brown* can't be explained, as Professor Wechsler pointed out, by the evidentiary record in the school cases of harm done to blacks by segregated schools.[21] That evidence was controverted by experts for the states.[22] Until *Brown,* black claims that segregated public schools were inferior had been met by orders requiring merely that facilities be made equal.[23] Courts had been unwilling to substitute their judgments for those

19. 59 Mass. (5 Cush.) 198 (1850).
20. 163 U.S. 537, 544-545 (1896).
21. Wechsler, supra note 2, at 32-33.
22. Id. The efforts by the NAACP to prove the damage done to blacks by separate schools, and school board efforts to show that segregated schools helped rather than harmed blacks, are both documented in Richard Kluger, Simple Justice, 315-366, 400-424, 439-450, 482-507 (1976).
23. The cases are collected in Leflar & Davis, Segregation in the Public Schools — 1953, 67 Harv. L. Rev. 377, 430-435 (1954), and Larson, The New Law of Race Relations, 1969 Wis. L. Rev. 470, 482-483 n.27.

of the legislatures as to the wisdom of school segregation policies.[24] The decision in *Brown* to break with its long-held position on these issues, despite the language of the opinion, can't be understood without some consideration of the decision's impact on interests other than those of long-suffering black children and their parents.

Brown, while taking from whites the benefits of segregation referred to by Professor Black, has proved of greater value to whites than blacks. Certainly, it has been a great blessing to whites in policy-making positions able to benefit from the economic and political advances at home and abroad that followed abandonment of apartheid in our national law.

First, the decision in *Brown* provided immediate credibility to America's struggle with communist countries to win the hearts and minds of emerging Third World peoples. This benefit was not unforeseen. Specific arguments to this effect were advanced by both NAACP lawyers and the federal government's brief.[25] And following the decision, the point was not lost on the news media. *Time* magazine, predicting that *Brown*'s international impact would be scarcely less important than that for black children, wrote: "In many countries, where U.S. prestige and leadership have been damaged by the fact of U.S. segregation, it will come as a timely reassertion of the basic American principle that 'all men are created equal.' "[26] This view was impressively substantiated by the legal historian Mary Dudziak's book, *Cold War Civil Rights*, based on her untiring searches through literally thousands of official government documents as well as international newspapers and news releases.[27]

Second, *Brown* offered much-needed reassurance to American blacks that the precepts of equality and freedom so heralded during World War II might yet be given meaning at home. If so talented and successful a black as Paul Robeson could in 1949 predict that blacks would not fight for this country in a war with Russia, need his prediction have been accurate to prompt thoughtful men to consider the prudence of narrowing the gap between American ideals and their reality as experienced by blacks, virtually all of whom had more reason for disenchantment with the society than did Mr. Robeson?[28]

Third, for those who view America as a land where the words "principle" and "profit" are virtually interchangeable, there certainly were those who recognized that the South could not be industrialized, could not make the transition from

24. Some nineteenth-century courts refused to approve public schools segregated by local authorities without legislative authority. See §3.2.

25. See quotes and citations in Derrick Bell, Racial Remediation: An Historical Perspective on Current Conditions, 52 Notre Dame Law. 5, 12 (1976).

26. Id. at 12 n.31.

27. Mary Dudziak, Cold War Civil Rights: Race and the Image of American Democracy 18-78 (2000). For a detailed review of the Dudziak book, see Richard Delgado, Explaining the Rise and Fall of African American Fortunes — Interest Convergence and Civil Rights Gains, 37 Harv. C.R.-C.L. L. Rev. 369 (2002).

28. Dorothy Butler Gilliam, Paul Robeson: All-American (1976). In an unwritten speech before the Partisans of Peace's World Peace Congress in Paris, Robeson said, "It is unthinkable . . . that American Negroes would go to war on behalf of those who have oppressed us for generations . . . against a country [the Soviet Union] which in one generation has raised our people to full human dignity of mankind."

a rural, plantation society to the Sunbelt with all its potential and profit, if it remained a section divided by state-sponsored segregation.

§3.7.3   Poor White Status and Opposition to *Brown*

For those whites who saw these benefits, as well as those who long had abhorred the moral evil of segregation, the principle of racial equality was adequate justification for the constitutionally sanctioned change mandated by *Brown.* But poorer whites neither recognized nor believed that they would profit directly from school desegregation. To the contrary, they relied (as had generations before them) on the expectation that white elites would protect their long-held entitlement to a place in the society superior to blacks. Historians have traced this arrangement back one hundred years before the Constitution, which document, of course, made the inferior status of blacks relative to whites perfectly clear.

Segregated schools and facilities were established by legislatures at the insistence of the white working classes who saw color barriers as official confirmation that the establishment would maintain them in a permanent societal status superior to that designated for blacks.[29] Historian John Hope Franklin notes how the Populist movement collapsed in the 1890s as poor whites heeded Conservative assurances that "Negro rule" must be avoided at all costs.[30] The issue of race, as Professor Franklin quoted a dejected leader of poor whites, "was an everlasting, overshadowing problem which served to hamper their progress and prevent them from becoming realistic in social, economic and political matters."[31] Little has changed. Today, many poorer whites who oppose all social reform as "welfare programs for blacks" have employment, education, and social service needs that differ from the condition of poor blacks by a margin that, without a racial scorecard, becomes difficult to measure.

When segregation practices were finally condemned by the Supreme Court, the outcry was greatest among poorer whites who feared loss of control over their public schools and other facilities that by any standard were inferior when compared with similar institutions serving upper-class whites. As the school desegregation campaigns moved North, the similar reactions and resistances belied the earlier belief that only ignorant rednecks would violently oppose a federal court order. We now know more clearly that many whites at any class level will oppose any school remedy or minority admissions plan, particularly if it threatens their perceived status and prerogatives. It is an opposition which is deeply held and is now merging with the long-held beliefs that in this country individuals rise or fall on their individual merits. Arguments by Professor Owen Fiss and others that group remedies are required to rectify harm done on a group basis[32] are having little impact. The law and constitutional interpretation are conformed to a societal view of racial policy-making which alone explains otherwise irrational decisions.

29. See C. Vann Woodward, The Strange Career of Jim Crow 6 (3d rev. ed. 1974).
30. John Hope Franklin, From Slavery to Freedom 272 (4th ed. 1974).
31. Id.
32. Owen Fiss, Groups and the Equal Protection Clause, 5 Phil. & Pub. Aff. 107 (1976).

§3.7.4 Judicial Supremacy and Enforcement of *Brown*

Enforcement of *Brown* protected interests in judicial supremacy. By 1959, when Professor Wechsler's speech was published, it was apparent that compliance with the *Brown* mandate to desegregate the public schools would not come easily or soon. In a word, opposition to *Brown* was rampant throughout the South. Its adherents were on the defensive and not only the decision, but also the legitimacy of the Court that issued that decision were placed in question. It was during this period that the controversy over the *Brown* decision underwent a subtle but significant shift.

The correctness of *Brown,* the issue of paramount importance to blacks, was subsumed by the massive resistance movement to the question of judicial supremacy, a matter of far more concern to the Court and much of the country. The Supreme Court was aware of the danger and lost little time in seeking a firmer basis on which to ground school orders than the rights of blacks provided.

It was not likely by accident that the Supreme Court began its dramatic per curiam opinion in the 1958 *Little Rock, Arkansas* case. "As this case reaches us, it raises questions of the highest importance to the maintenance of our federal system of government."[33] Reaching back to Marbury v. Madison,[34] the Court reaffirmed and positively expanded Chief Justice Marshall's statement that "[i]t is emphatically the province and duty of the judicial department to say what the law is."[35]

Brown might not have been a wise or proper decision, but few who believed so wanted to go to war or seriously endanger the federal system to correct the Court's error. Even Professor Wechsler's criticism of *Brown* concluded with a denial that he intended to offer "comfort to anyone who claims legitimacy in defiance of the courts." Such defiance, he said, was the "ultimate negation of all neutral principles."[36]

For some time then, the danger to federalism posed by secessionist-oriented resistance to *Brown* by southern state and local officials provided a quantum of support that lasted a good 15 years until school desegregation efforts moved north and west. Decisions in school cases during this period were oriented toward countering defiance of the *Brown* ruling, rather than obtaining compliance with it.[37]

When the Court, in obvious frustration with the slow pace of school desegregation, announced in 1968 what Justice Powell later termed "the *Green/Swann* doctrine of 'affirmative duty' . . . ,"[38] placing on school boards the duty to disestablish their dual-school systems,[39] even those orders retained the anti-defiance form. They were intended more to condemn school board evasion than to guarantee that at long last black children would obtain the "equal educational opportunity" promised them in *Brown*. Even so, the demise of long-effective barriers to

---

33. 358 U.S. at 4.

34. 1 Cranch 137, 2 L. Ed. 60 (1803).

35. 358 U.S. at 18.

36. Wechsler, supra note 2, at 35.

37. See cases cited at §3.4.

38. Keyes v. School Dist. No. 1, Denver, Colo., 413 U.S. 189, 224 (1973) (Justice Powell, concurring in part and dissenting in part).

39. The doctrine evolved from Supreme Court decisions in Green v. School Bd. of New Kent County, 391 U.S. 430 (1968), and Swann v. Charlotte-Mecklenburg Bd. of Educ., 402 U.S. 1 (1971).

desegregation, including pupil assignment schemes,[40] and "freedom of choice" plans,[41] seemed to herald more progress. The affirmative duty standard initially adopted in a case involving a small two-school district in rural Virginia,[42] and then applied in Charlotte, North Carolina, a fairly large, southern urban district,[43] and finally held applicable to Denver, Colorado, an urban district outside the South,[44] led civil rights lawyers to believe that final victory, if not yet in hand, was at least in sight. Behind them lay years of effort in several hundred school cases, most of them hotly contested at every stage.[45]

The school desegregation techniques which won Supreme Court approval, though, were anti-defiance remedies. Balancing the student and teacher populations by race in each school as a rough measure of compliance, eliminating one-race schools, redrawing school attendance lines, and transporting students to achieve racial balance, the *Green/Swann* remedies, all were effective preventatives for official foot-dragging and evasion. But they did not in themselves guarantee black children either better or less discriminatory schooling than they had obtained in pre-*Brown* schools.

When civil rights lawyers set their sights on desegregating whole metropolitan areas, including the suburban districts where so many white parents sought sanctuary when school desegregation threatened urban and often predominantly minority districts, the Supreme Court drew the line. First in interdistrict[46] and then in intradistrict suits,[47] the Court began erecting a series of barriers to the forms of traditional relief it earlier had approved.

The Court's wavering support for racial balance remedies reflects a pragmatic weighing of black-versus-white interests. It may not satisfy Professor Wechsler's desire for a normative standard, but the Court by that point was rather clearly balancing the interests asserted by plaintiffs in school desegregation cases against other well-settled and highly valued interests. The predictable result of this balancing is based on the traditional priority of white over black interests.

In the transition from pure anti-defiance remedies to Justice Powell's "affirmative duty" plans, Chief Justice Burger cautioned in the *Charlotte* case that "[t]he reconciliation of competing values in a desegregation case is, of course, a difficult task with many sensitive facts. . . ."[48] "Competing values" must refer to the conflicting interests of civil rights lawyers who contend that *Brown* requires a rough balance of races in each school and whites who prefer to retain existing school policies sans, of course, any overt racial discrimination. In the *Detroit*

40. These plans, requiring black children to run a gantlet of administrative proceedings in order to obtain assignment to a white school, won early judicial approval in Shuttlesworth v. Birmingham Bd. of Educ., 162 F. Supp. 372 (N.D. Ala.), aff'd, 358 U.S. 101 (1958), and Covington v. Edwards, 264 F.2d 780 (4th Cir.), cert. denied, 361 U.S. 840 (1959).

41. Green v. School Board of New Kent County, 391 U.S. 430 (1968).

42. Id.

43. Swann v. Charlotte-Mecklenburg Bd. of Educ., 402 U.S. 1 (1971).

44. Keyes v. School Dist. No. 1, Denver, Colo., 413 U.S. 189 (1973).

45. The post-*Brown* legal campaign is reviewed in Stephen Wasby, Anthony D'Amato, and Rosemary Metrailer, Desegregation from *Brown* to *Alexander* (1977).

46. Milliken v. Bradley, 418 U.S. 717 (1974). See §3.6.

47. See §3.6.

48. 402 U.S. at 31.

case,[49] Chief Justice Burger, and then in the *Dayton* case,[50] Justice Rehnquist, wrote majority opinions which elevated the concept of "local autonomy" over the public schools to "a vital national tradition."[51]

It was under the banner of local control that Union troops were withdrawn from the South in the late 1860s. But surrender to history-influenced paranoia is hardly justified. The Court has affirmed on several occasions the right of parents to retain a strong voice in their children's education, overruling in the process state policies intended to facilitate understanding and the assimilation of students from heterogeneous backgrounds.[52] Private schooling or flight to all-white suburbs remains an alternative available to some whites, but avoidance does not eliminate the "conflicting values" as to whether and when parents must be left to such alternatives.

Over the years since the *Swann* decision, a majority of the Court concluded that local educational interests should prevail in the absence of proof of discriminatory school policies so overt and perverse that the school patrons must be held to have known of them and to have acquiesced in their operation. Local control principles were abandoned by the Court majority when a minority of white parents asserted that modest desegregation policies in Seattle and Louisville were unjustified racial classifications.

§3.7.5   Racial Interest-Convergence Principles

The cases do not expressly balance the interests of minority plaintiffs seeking to maintain the validity of *Swann*-type remedies intended to integrate the schools, against the interests of whites who oppose these remedies. But it is possible to discern the outline of a school desegregation principle which, while hardly neutral, is a statement of the general applicability sought by Professor Wechsler almost a half-century ago. It relies as much on political history as legal precedent and emphasizes the world as it is rather than how we might like it to be. Translated from judicial activity in racial cases both before and after *Brown,* it provides that:

> In the absence of overt racial discrimination of a character that shocks the public conscience, the Fourteenth Amendment, standing alone, will not authorize judicial relief providing an effective remedy for blacks where the remedy sought threatens the superior societal status of middle and upper-class whites. It follows that the availability of Fourteenth Amendment protection in racial cases is not actually determined by the character of harm suffered by blacks or the quantum of liability proved against whites. Rather, racial remedies are the outward manifestations of unspoken and

---

49. Milliken v. Bradley, 418 U.S. 717, 741 (1974). Chief Justice Burger said, "No single tradition in public education is more deeply rooted than local control over the operation of schools; local autonomy has long been thought essential both to the maintenance of community concern and support for public schools and to quality of the educational process."

50. Dayton Bd. of Educ. v. Brinkman, 433 U.S. 406 (1977).

51. Id. at 410.

52. See, e.g., Pierce v. Society of Sisters, 268 U.S. 510 (1925); Meyer v. Nebraska, 262 U.S. 390 (1923); Bartels v. Iowa, 262 U.S. 404 (1923); cf. San Antonio Indep. Sch. Dist. v. Rodriguez, 411 U.S. 1 (1973).

perhaps unconscious judicial conclusions that the remedies, if granted, will secure or advance societal interests deemed important by the upper classes.

Racial justice or its appearance may, from time to time, be counted among the interests deemed important by the courts and the society's policymakers. Poorer whites, viewing any remedy for blacks as an unfair preference, will challenge all racial remedies, even those which, sooner or later, improve their status as much or more than that of blacks. Most racial remedies, however, when measured by their actual potential, will prove of more symbolic than substantive value to blacks.

Professor Wechsler's assumption that whites had "nonassociational rights" which could not be ignored if the *Brown* decision was to survive, has been proven correct. For a historic and constitutionally recognized preference for white interests over black rights when the two converge is the neutral principle which gave birth to *Brown* and led eventually to its demise.

Whites in high policy-making positions, including those who sit on federal courts, can take no comfort in conditions in dozens of inner-city school systems where the great majority of nonwhite children attend classes as segregated and ineffective as those so soundly condemned by Chief Justice Warren in the *Brown* opinion. Where remedies for such conditions are focused on gaining real educational effectiveness, as opposed to racial balance-oriented relief, deemed by many as the equivalent of, if not superior to educationally effective schools, the Supreme Court has shown in its second *Detroit* decision a willingness, bordering on eagerness, to support and encourage what it called there "educational components."[53]

To school integration advocates, it may seem a step backward toward the *Plessy* "separate but equal" era, but they forget that prior to *Brown,* the racial separation in black schools was required by law. Effective schooling was not required and was generally discouraged. Even so, some black schools through great effort achieved academic distinction. Forgotten as well were the outstanding black high schools like Dunbar and Armstrong in Washington, D.C.; Frederick Douglass, one in Baltimore and another with the same name in St. Louis; Booker T. Washington in Atlanta; and Crispus Attucks in Indianapolis. Some dating back to the 1890s, these schools, staffed with talented teachers, often with doctoral degrees, turned out black graduates who went on to impressive careers.

Writer Jill Nelson interviewed Benjamin J. Henley Jr. and Charles S. Lofton, two retired Dunbar High School teachers.[54] Native Washingtonians, between them they had worked in the D.C. public schools for nearly a century. Each came from families in which memories of slavery were very much alive, and a sense of history and education were viewed as essential to upward mobility. They were school-mates at Dunbar High School in the 1920s, during the school's long heyday as an elite public institution that trained some of black America's finest minds. Teachers at Dunbar inspired them to join their profession. Lofton told Nelson, "Integration, with all the good it brought, was also the beginning of the end of Dunbar, and

---

53. Milliken v. Bradley II, 433 U.S. 267 (1977). See also Zelman v. Simmons-Harris, 534 U.S. 1077 (2002) (approving tuition vouchers in the Cleveland public schools).

54. Jill Nelson, Retired Educators Recall 50 Years of Change in D.C. Schools, Washington Post, Apr. 22, 1989.

Negro education as he'd known it. I wouldn't want it to go out that I'm not for integration — I am," he said. "I'm not for what it did to Dunbar and to students."

No less effort will be required to achieve effective black schools today. Indeed, while integrated schools are resisted by poorer white parents, policies necessary to obtain effective schools threaten the self-interest of teacher unions, and others with vested interests in the status quo. But successful independent black schools may be a lesson that effective schooling for blacks must precede, rather than come as the result of integration.

§3.8   Hypo: Using Income to Achieve Integration

Parents Opposed to Income-Based Assignments vs. The Centerville School Board

Centerville is a small Mid-Atlantic city with a population of 100,000. Approximately 35 percent of the population is black or Latino. The Centerville school district consists of five elementary schools, five secondary schools, and the African American Academy, which provides both elementary and secondary education.

The neighborhoods of Centerville are extremely segregated. Because of this segregation, a school-assignment policy based on geographic proximity has resulted in heavily segregated schools. The Centerville school district assigns students to all schools based on geographic proximity, with the exception of the African American Academy located in the black community and enrolls students whose parents want its rather strict but academically successful regimen. Because the neighborhoods of Centerville are extremely segregated, this has resulted in highly segregated schools.

In recent years, some parents, teachers and school officials, have become concerned that such racial isolation has led to educational and social problems within the schools and the city. Those few white families living within predominantly black school zones overwhelmingly request transfers to predominantly white schools. Schools with predominantly minority students contend that they receive inadequate funding — particularly compared to predominantly white schools. Students that comprise the minority at each school tend to fare worse than their counterparts at the school, and argue that it is because they receive less attention and must study a curriculum that focuses on the perspective of the dominant race in the school population and — in the case of Latino students — adapt to a new language without appropriate resources and attention.

Recently, parents and teachers have complained that team rivalry between the schools has taken on racial overtones; at sports events, signs and taunts about the rival teams often refer to negative stereotypes about the race of the rival school's student population. In response to these issues that are worsening, the Centerville Board of Education met to consider how it could use its admissions and transfer policies to achieve more integrated schools. After several closed meetings reviewing extensive studies including counsel from legal and educational experts, the board settled on a plan that would assign all students based on their household income. Students are grouped into three categories of household income. For a given school, school assignments are made by randomly selecting one student from each of the income categories — one student from the highest income category, then one student from the lowest income category, then one student from the middle income category. The cycle is then repeated until all slots in the school are full. Because selection from each category is random, student choice is not taken into consideration.

The population of Centerville, which generally identifies as relatively liberal, greeted the plan with overwhelming support. The plan achieves an effectively integrated school system in the first few months of its institution. Soon thereafter, however, four white families who live in a predominately white neighborhood file suit against the school district. Of the four families, three of the families' children must travel significant distances to get to school, resulting in a one-hour commute each way. Moreover, the plan has resulted in siblings being split, creating additional problems for the parents, who must monitor their children in different schools.

The white families allege that the plan is unconstitutional under the *Seattle-Louisville* decision. They argue that the plan seeks to accomplish racial balancing, an impermissible goal given that Centerville has never engaged in de jure segregation. They also argue that the board has attempted to surreptitiously use race-conscious measures without appearing to do so by using economic indicators as a proxy for race, a transparent attempt to circumvent *Seattle-Louisville*'s prohibition of such race-conscious measures. In fact, they argue, the plan is even worse than the one at issue in *Seattle-Louisville*, which at least took into account students' choice and sibling attendance. Moreover, they argue that the plan could not possibly be narrowly tailored, considering that the school board did not even attempt other, non-race-conscious means before instituting the plan. They also argue that there is no evidence that the plan will adequately address the educational and social problems it seeks to resolve; hence, it cannot be narrowly tailored; indeed, many families believe that racial tensions have worsened within schools.

Soon after the complaint was filed, a group of 15 black families were granted a motion to intervene. The black families live in a predominately black neighborhood, and their children had attended the African American Academy, which is now subject to the new school admission plan. Before the creation of the plan, the African American Academy had used a merit-based admissions policy similar to the one the Court approved in *Grutter*. Because few white students had sought admission, the school's student body was composed almost entirely of black students from the lowest income category. Utilizing teaching policies that have succeeded in other inner-city schools (see §3.9), these students consistently scored higher than the district's average on all standardized tests, and the school's percentage of students who continued on to college was above average for district schools. The new plan has made it impossible for the school to continue to function, and the school will likely abandon its mandate of providing quality education to low-income black students. Plans have already been put into action to rename the school Anthony Kennedy Academy.

Like the white plaintiffs, the black plaintiffs argue that the plan is unconstitutional in light of *Seattle-Louisville,* because it is directly aimed at created racially balanced schools. Along with the white plaintiffs, they also argue that the plan is an attempt to surreptitiously thwart *Seattle-Louisville* by using household income as a proxy for race. As a result, they argue, their school is forced to abandon a constitutional admissions system for a thinly disguised version of the race-based admissions plan *Seattle-Louisville* overturned. They also argue that, by doing so, the plan is specifically designed to deprive black students of the educational opportunities of African American Academy.

In response, the board has argued that the *Seattle-Louisville* decision left open the question of whether racial balancing may be pursued in the absence of de jure segregation. Specifically, they note that Justice Kennedy's concurrence acknowledges that such a goal may be a compelling state interest, as long as students are not identified and assigned schools depending on their race. They argue that the plan avoids such race-conscious decision-making, and thus comports with the mandates of *Seattle-Louisville*.

The federal district court issued a lengthy opinion, in which it concluded that strict scrutiny was not applicable because the plan was not a racial classification, but rather affected racial balanced incidentally as it sought to resolve issues resulting from economic privilege and pressures. Applying the rational basis test, the district court found that the plan served the rational basis of achieving socioeconomic diversity.

The plaintiffs appealed and the court of appeals reversed. Looking to the records of the district's meetings and the problems that led to the creation of the plan, the court of appeals concluded that the district clearly intended to racially desegregate students, using household income as a proxy. Applying strict scrutiny, the court of appeals held that, even if racial balance is a compelling state interest, the plans at issue are merely racial classifications disguised as race-neutral measures. It held that such measures are unconstitutional in light of the *Seattle-Louisville* decision. The court of appeals also held that, even if the measures were not equivalent to the racial classifications rejected by the majority in the *Seattle-Louisville* decision, the school board still failed to demonstrate that the plans were narrowly tailored to achieve the interests at stake. The court of appeals cited case studies in which school districts had attempted to achieve racial balancing through assignments based on household income, only to have those plans fail as schools became resegregated in a matter of years. Moreover, the court of appeals noted that there was no conclusive evidence that the plans would achieve the purported social and educational benefits of integration.

The Supreme Court granted certiorari.

Law firm A will represent the group of white parents challenging the plan.

Law firm B will represent the group of black parents challenging the plan.

Law firm C will represent the school district.

§3.9   SINGLE-RACE SCHOOLS: RETROGRADE OR RENAISSANCE?

Disenchantment with desegregation as a means of solving educational inequalities has surfaced in yet another resurgence of the idea of single-race schools. The ineffectiveness of existing arrangements for schooling many black children has caused educators to cast about for new solutions. Many have become convinced that the problem of low achievement and high drop-out rates stems from the schools themselves. The racism which appears to be entrenched in American public schools, rearing its head in segregated schools and classrooms and in the lowered expectations of black children, has convinced many that the only option for black children is to leave the system entirely.

To be immersed in and judged by a system which fails to recognize the culture and needs of black students may be worse than being left out entirely — or racially segregated by law for that matter. Separate schools seek to rectify this one-sidedness by gearing themselves specifically towards the needs and experiences of black children. They respond to the social ills disproportionately visited upon blacks — discrimination, joblessness, poverty, and crime, to name a few — by fostering a sense of pride in self that leads to motivation to accomplish in areas for which there are few models in their home communities. Developing necessary skills than can be perceived as steps toward a life beyond what they once thought was available to them.

Predictions of failure in an ostensibly color-blind educational system were borne out in the decades after *Brown.* Rather than recognizing that the different life histories of black children raised in the inner cities required specialized approaches, many school principles felt it was best to "treat all kids just alike." Black children were expected to perform the same as middle-class whites with curricula geared for middle-class whites. Sociologist Ray Rist, who spent a school year with young black children bused to a wealthy white school, found the results of this even-handed integration to be disastrous.[1] The insensitivity of the school system to the particular needs of black children has convinced many of the unwillingness and inability of an integrated school system to educate black children.

In addition, single-race schools promise opportunities not only for black students but also for black school administrators and teachers. Integrative remedies have generally entailed closing black schools, firing black teachers, and demoting black principals. The hostility of white-dominated school systems to the admission of black students is surpassed only by their unwillingness to countenance the employment of black people in positions of authority in the schools. Separate schools, it is hoped, will offer new opportunities for professionals excluded from facilities which remain segregated in their faculties and administrative hierarchies.

Despite their promises for the future, history offers important warnings regarding the prospects of single-race schools. All-black public schools before *Brown,* with many exceptions, were inadequate in facilities, equipment, teacher salaries, and other necessities for effective schooling.[2] Today, a half-century after *Brown,* evidence shows that predominantly black schools all too often have higher student-faculty ratios, less-experienced and lower-paid teachers, inferior facilities, and lower-quality course offerings and extracurricular programs than white schools.[3]

---

§3.9   1. Ray Rist, The Invisible Children: School Integration in American Society (1978).

2. See, e.g., James Anderson, The Education of Blacks in the South 1860-1935 (1988); Ron Edmonds, Effective Education for Minority Pupils: *Brown* Confounded or Confirmed, in Shades of *Brown:* New Perspectives on School Desegregation 118-119 (Derrick Bell ed. 1980).

3. Norfolk, Virginia, and Little Rock, Arkansas both experimented, under court supervision, with all-black schools that received a proportionately higher share of funding in order to remedy

The advocates of single-race schools must also allay fears that encouraging racial separation will encourage both racism and separatism.

An aspect of schooling lost sight of during the long years of desegregation efforts is the role of school in sustaining a community. Mrs. Hall, a teacher at the Fairmont Elementary School in St. Louis, explains: "A community is only as good as the school that is in it. The basis of the Black community used to be the Black Church. Fairmont has served an essential role, just as the Black Church has played in the African American community."[4]

The 1954 decision in *Brown* was the culmination of two decades of active struggle against legal segregation in all aspects of American society. The implementation of *Brown,* however, resulted in the disproportionate busing of black children into predominantly white and often hostile schools; in addition, many black schools were closed, a policy that perpetuated the stigma that all-black schools were not the good institutions that some were, despite their intentional fiscal, social, and political neglect by racist school boards and state officials.[5]

Many of today's black schools are private and operate out of churches, community centers, or rented buildings. Others are public. They may be co-ed or open to only boys or girls. Dr. Gail Foster, for many years an advocate for independent schools, issued a study more than a decade ago reporting that African Americans created close to 400 schools nationally, enrolling some 52 thousand students.[6] She studied 70 independent black schools in the New York–New Jersey area, serving 12,000 students, most in elementary grades, although some schools cover the intermediate grades. They survived, Foster found, both because of the inadequacy of the public schools but also because parents view them "as models of the type of curriculum and pedagogy — infused with community values, culture, and expectation for children — that should be a fundamental part of any school reform effort.[7]

On a visit to a Solomon Schechter School in Queens, part of a nationwide network of 70 Conservative Jewish schools, Foster found that students come from a range of observant families. Visiting classes and speaking to the principal, she found that Conservative Jewish schools that emphasize culture, Jewish heritage, and the Israeli homeland are much like independent black schools that emphasize the role of African ancestry and the contributions of black people.

---

historic inequalities. In both cities, black schools lost funding and deteriorated in quality as soon as the courts withdrew from the system. See also Note, Unitary School Systems and Underlying Vestiges of State-Imposed Segregation, 87 Colum. L. Rev. 794, 801 (1987); Camp, Thompson & Crain, Within-District Equity: Desegregation and Microeconomic Analysis, in The Impacts of Litigation and Legislation on Public School Finance 273, 282-286 (Julie Underwood & Deborah Verstegen eds., 1990) (citing recent studies which found that predominantly minority public schools tend to receive fewer resources than other schools in the same district). See also United States v. Yonkers Bd. of Educ., 837 F.2d 1181 (2d Cir. 1987) (discussing the inferior and generally overcrowded facilities and low levels of faculty experience at schools with higher minority populations).

4. Jerome E. Morris, A Pillar of Strength: An African American School's Communal Bond with Families and Community since *Brown,* 33 Urban Educ., Jan. 1999.

5. Id.

6. School Directory, Institute for Independent Education ii (1995).

7. Gail Foster, Historically Black Independent Schools, in City Schools 291 (Diane Ravitch & Joseph Viteritti eds., 2000).

This emphasis spurs some black parents to choose black independent elementary schools out of concern for the psychological well-being of their children. Foster explains that they are frightened by the "crisis of self-hatred" so prevalent among African American youth attending neighborhood public schools where preparation for and interest in learning is minimal. To avoid this environment, those black parents who are able move to the suburbs or enroll their children in expensive private schools. Even in these settings, black parents have reason for concern that they have escaped the ghetto only to find little affirmation of or role models for African Americans in the school's outlook or its curriculum. Indeed, they may find a character of racism that is no less damaging because it is unthinking.

Most independent schools that are primarily African American eagerly welcome children of other cultures and races. Some have even given their schools names such as "Learning Tree Multi-Cultural School," or "Mrs. Black's School for All Children. Foster points out that when whites avoid our private schools blacks are accused of segregation, but the fact that such schools tend to be 100 percent black is a white parental choice, not the result of a racially exclusive policy by the schools.

These schools are designed to respond to the social ills disproportionately visited upon blacks — discrimination, joblessness, poverty, and crime, to name a few — by fostering a sense of cultural pride, providing students with positive black role models, and teaching the particular skills black children need to survive using pedagogical models that will attract and hold their interest. The different life histories of black children raised in the inner cities require specialized approaches.

Dr. Deborah Prothrow-Stith has diagnosed inner-city violence as a major "public health" problem and, in response, has developed an intervention program for the public school system to help prevent teenage violence.[8] Although programs such as these need not necessarily be instituted in single-sex schools, some educators insist that these reforms will be more effective if targeted at males, the most frequent perpetrators of street violence. Although young girls may also benefit from violence intervention programs, their different roles in the perpetuation of violence suggest that different programs, tailored to their specific needs, might be more appropriate.

High levels of violence, teenage pregnancy, and other social problems correlate with low academic performance. To the extent that single-sex education can improve academic performance, supporters maintain that such schools can be an important method of addressing these correlated problems. Beyond the issue of the value of separating by sex as well as race, several reasons explain why single-sex schools may serve all elementary and secondary schoolchildren better than do coeducational classrooms. Research indicates that teachers are biased against boys in elementary grades and against girls in secondary grades. According to this theory, girls in elementary school are asked to read aloud more than are boys — perhaps from the sexist notion that reading is a feminine activity — and, in high school, boys are encouraged to participate more actively in science and math.

8. Deborah Prothrow-Stith & Michaele Weissman, Deadly Consequences 163-164 (1991).

Furthermore, teachers praise girls for good manners in elementary school in a way that might dampen active learning skills later in their education. The rebellious spirit that teachers tolerate from elementary school boys, however, later serves them well when they become more active classroom participants. The availability of role models in single-sex elementary and secondary schools may well counter these tendencies, leading boys to see reading as more "masculine" and girls to see science and math as more accessible.

None of these arguments persuades those who view single-sex schools as an invidious form of gender segregation, even though some of the most prestigious prep schools in the country are single-sex. Simply referring to them as African American schools, whether for girls or boys, also engenders negative reactions. But, as Professor Pamela Smith notes, Catholic schools or Jewish yeshivas are not labeled segregative. Like these schools, the schools attended by African American children are characterized by the communities they serve. The label "all African American" is not a racial classification; it merely refers to the community served by the school. A better label, she admits, might be "inner-city schools," but Smith contends that the label alone should not trigger heightened constitutional scrutiny simply because the schools cater to African Americans, traditionally members of a suspect class.[9]

Independent black schools, while facing a host of economic and educational issues, continue to flourish because, as Foster explains, their curriculum and instruction reflect their assumption of the responsibility to provide students with the skills and attitudes needed to uplift not only students but also communities. Setting high standards for students, these schools view students as a critical part of the solution to the problems that plague their communities. Expulsion of students is more rare than at other schools, for part of their commitment is an expression of the schools' underlying reverence for their students, even those who are difficult and slow.

Despite their potential and the enthusiastic community support they engendered, these schools have been fiercely opposed. Often the resistance has come from those who remain committed either to the *Brown* ideal of integration or to the maintenance of the status quo.[10]

§3.10   Racism Hypo: Debating the *Brown* Decision the Court Might Have Written[1]

Over the decades, the *Brown* decision, like other landmark cases, has gained a life quite apart from the legal questions it was intended to settle. The passage

9. Pamela J. Smith, Comment: All-Male Black Schools and the Equal Protection Clause: A Step Forward Toward Education, 66 Tul. L. Rev. 2003 (1992).

10. See generally Robin D. Barnes, Symposium: Group Conflict and the Constitution: Race, Sexuality, and Religion: Black America and School Choice: Charting a New Course, 106 Yale L.J. 2375, 2377 (1997); Note, Inner-City Single-Sex Schools: Educational Reform or Invidious Discrimination?, 105 Harv. L. Rev. 1741 (1992).

§3.10   1. The material in this section is based on Derrick Bell, Silent Covenants: Brown v. Board and the Quest for Racial Justice (2004).

of time has calmed both the ardor of its admirers and the ire of its detractors. Today, of little use as legal precedent, it has gained in reputation as a measure of what law and society might be. That noble image, dulled by resistance to any but minimal steps toward compliance, has transformed *Brown* into a magnificent mirage, the legal equivalent of that city on a hill to which all aspire without any serious thought that it will ever be attained.

The earlier sections in this chapter should be of assistance in considering whether the decision set out below might have furthered the schooling of black children more effectively than the one the Court issued a half century ago. In addition, compare the reasoning of the alternative decision with that set out in *Brown* and developed over the years by desegregation advocates. Advocates for both sides can bring focus to what should prove a vigorous discussion.

The Supreme Court of the United States
May 17, 1954

Today, we uphold our six decades old decision in Plessy v. Ferguson, 163 U.S. 537 (1896). We do so with some reluctance and in the face of the arguments by the petitioners that segregation in the public schools is unconstitutional and a manifestation of the desire for dominance whose depths and pervasiveness this Court can neither ignore nor easily divine. Giving full weight to these arguments, a decision overturning *Plessy*, while it might be viewed as a triumph by Negro petitioners and the class they represent, will be condemned by many whites. Their predictable outraged resistance could undermine and eventually negate even the most committed judicial enforcement efforts.

No less a personage than Justice Oliver Wendell Holmes acknowledged the limits of judicial authority when, speaking for the Court in a 1903 voting rights case from Alabama, he denied the relief sought by black voters because if, as the black petitioners alleged, the great mass of the white population intends to keep the blacks from voting, it would do little good to give black voters an order that would be ignored at the local level. "Apart from damages to the individual," Holmes explained, "relief from a great political wrong, if done, as alleged by the people of a state and the state itself, must be given by them or by the legislative and political department of the Government of the United States."[2]

While giving racial discrimination the sanction of law, Justice Holmes refused either to interfere or to acknowledge the status-affirming role for whites reflected in their refusal to grant blacks even the basic citizenship right to vote. The Court in Plessy v. Ferguson had done the same seven years earlier when by distinguishing between the denial of political rights and the separation of the races on a social basis, the Court rejected Homer Plessy's argument that this law-enforced separation branded blacks with a "badge of inferiority."[3]

Respondents' counsel, John W. Davis, a highly respected advocate, urges this Court to uphold "separate but equal" as the constitutionally correct measure of racial status because, as he put it so elegantly: "Somewhere, sometime to every principle comes a moment of repose when it has been so often announced, so confidently relied upon, so long continued, that it passes the limits of judicial discretion and disturbance."

2. Giles v. Harris, 189 U.S. 475, 488 (1903).
3. Plessy v. Ferguson, 163 U.S. 537, 552 (1896).

Elegance, though, must not be allowed to trample further long-suppressed truth. The "separate" in the "separate but equal" standard has been rigorously enforced. The "equal" has served as a total refutation of equality. Within the limits of judicial authority, the Court recognizes these cases as providing an opportunity to test the legal legitimacy of the "separate but equal" standard, not, as petitioners urge, by overturning *Plessy*, but by ordering for the first time its strict enforcement.

Counsel for the Negro children have gone to great lengths to prove what must be obvious to every person who gives the matter even cursory attention: With some notable exceptions, schools provided for Negroes in segregated systems are unequal in facilities — often obscenely so. Unfortunately, this Court in violation of *Plessy*'s "separate but equal" standard, rejected challenges to state-run schools that were both segregated and ruinously unequal.

Hardly three years after setting the "separate but equal" standard, this Court diluted the equal prong with "practical considerations." When black parents sought to enjoin a Georgia school board from collecting school tax levies from them for a black high school it had closed while continuing to operate the white high school, Justice Harlan, speaking for the Court, reasoned that enjoining the board from operating a high school for whites would deprive whites of a high school education without regaining the black high school that had served 60, and that had been turned into a primary school for 300 children. Given the board's limited resources, he found their decision reasonable.[4]

Justice Harlan returned to his dissenting role in race cases when the Court upheld a Kentucky statute subjecting to a heavy fine Berea College, a private college that admitted both white and black students.[5] Because the state had chartered the private school and could revoke the charter, it could also amend it to prohibit instruction of the two races at the same time and in the same place. Justice Harlan pointed out that the precedent could bar minority association with whites in churches, markets, and other public places, a warning that by 1908 had become fact in many jurisdictions.[6]

In recent years, this Court, acknowledging the flouting of the "separate but equal" standard at the graduate school level, ordered black plaintiffs into previously all-white graduate programs. In Sweatt v. Painter,[7] the most significant of these cases, Texas denied admission to a black law school applicant, Herman Marion Sweatt. When Sweatt filed suit, the state sought to meet the separate but equal standard by setting up a small law school in three basement rooms eight blocks from the University of Texas Law School. It would have no regular faculty or library and was not accredited. This Court, in ordering Sweatt's admission, considered both its inadequate facilities and the intangible assets of the white law school, including its reputation, the value of interaction with its faculty, student body, and alumni that includes most of the state's lawyers and judges.

---

4. Cumming v. Richmond County Bd. of Educ., 175 U.S. 528 (1899).

5. Berea College v. Kentucky, 211 U.S. 45 (1908). See also Gong Lum v. Rice, 275 U.S. 78 (1927) (the Court rejected the challenge of Chinese parents whose child was assigned to a Negro school).

6. C. Vann Woodward, The Strange Career of Jim Crow (2d rev. ed. 1966).

7. 339 U.S. 629 (1950). See also McLaurin v. Oklahoma State Regents, 339 U.S. 637 (1950); Sipuel v. Oklahoma, 332 U.S. 631 (1948); Missouri ex rel. Gaines v. Canada, 305 U.S. 337 (1938).

Encouraged by those decisions, petitioners now urge that we extend those holdings to encompass segregation in literally thousands of public school districts. In support, their counsel speak eloquently both of the great disparities in resources and of the damage segregation does to Negro children's hearts and minds. We recognize and do not wish to rebut petitioner's evidence of this psychological damage.

Rather, we suggest that segregation perpetuates the sense of white children that their privileged status as whites is deserved in fact rather than bestowed by law and tradition. We hold that racial segregation afflicts white children with a lifelong mental and emotional handicap that is as destructive to whites as the required strictures of segregation are damaging to Negroes.

Again, it would seem appropriate to declare wrong what is clearly wrong. Given the history of segregation and the substantial reliance placed on our decisions as to its constitutionality, though, a finding by this Court in these cases that state-supported racial segregation is an obsolete artifact of a bygone age, one that no longer conforms to the Constitution, will set the stage not for compliance but for levels of defiance that will prove the antithesis of the equal educational opportunity the petitioners seek.

The desegregation of public schools is a special matter, the complexity of which is not adequately addressed in the petitioners' arguments. In urging this Court to strike down state-mandated segregation, the petitioners ignore the admonishment of W. E. B. Du Bois, one of the nation's finest thinkers. Commenting on the separate school–integrated school debate back in 1935, Dr. Du Bois observed that "Negro children needed neither segregated schools nor mixed schools. What they need is education."[8]

We are aware as well that despite the tremendous barriers to good schools posed by the *Plessy* "separate but equal" standard, some black schools, through great and dedicated effort by teachers and parents, achieved academic distinction. Many of the most successful blacks today are products of segregated schools and colleges. In urging what they hope will be a brighter tomorrow, petitioners need not cast aside the miracles of achievement attained in the face of monumental obstacles. While truly harmed by racial segregation, there is far too much contrary evidence for this Court to find that Negroes are a damaged race.

We conclude that Dr. Du Bois is right as an educational matter and that as a legal matter his still accurate admonition can be given meaning within the structure of the Plessy v. Ferguson holding. The three phases of relief that we will describe below focus attention on what is needed now by the children of both races. It is the only way to avoid a generation or more of strife over an ideal that, while worthwhile, will not provide the effective education petitioners' children need and that existing constitutional standards, stripped of their racist understandings, should safeguard.

While declaring racial segregation harmful to Negro children, the unhappy fact is that as the nation's racial history makes clear, racial division has been a source of much undeserved benefit to whites and a great deal of misery to Negroes. And as is always the case, oppression is harmful to the oppressor

---

8. W. E. B. Du Bois, Does the Negro Need Separate Schools?, 4 J. Negro Educ. 328 (1935); see generally Derrick Bell, The Legacy of W. E. B. Du Bois: A Rational Model for Achieving Public School Equity for America's Black Children, 11 Creighton L. Rev. 409 (1977).

as well as the oppressed. We accept the expert testimony submitted in this case that a great many white as well as Negro children have been harmed by segregation.

Pressured by this litigation, the school boards assure this Court that they are taking admittedly tardy steps to equalize facilities in Negro schools. We find these measures worthwhile but woefully inadequate to remedy injustices carried on for most of a century. This being the case, more important than striking down Plessy v. Ferguson is the need to reveal its hypocritical underpinnings by requiring its full enforcement for all children, white as well as black. Full enforcement requires more than either equalizing facilities or, as in the case of Delaware, one of the five cases before the Court, ordering plaintiffs because of the inadequacy of the Negro schools to be admitted into the white schools.

Realistic rather than symbolic relief for segregated schools will require a specific, judicially monitored plan designed primarily to provide the educational equity long denied under the separate but equal rhetoric. This Court finds that it has the authority to grant such relief under the precedent of Plessy v. Ferguson. As a primary step toward the disestablishment of the dual school system, this Court will order relief that must be provided to all children in racially segregated districts in the following components.

1. *Equalization.* Effective immediately on receipt of this Court's mandate, lower courts will order school officials of the respondent school districts to take the following actions:
   (A) Ascertain through appropriate measures the academic standing of each school district as compared to nationwide norms for school systems of comparable size and financial resources. These data, gathered under the direction and supervision of the district courts, will be published and made available to all patrons of the district, white as well as black.
   (B) All schools within the district must be fully equalized in resources, physical facilities, teacher-pupil ratios, teacher training, experience, and salary with the goal of each district, as a whole, measuring up to national norms within three years. School districts will report progress to the court annually.

2. *Representation.* The battle cry of those who fought and died to bring this country into existence was "taxation without representation is tyranny." Effective relief in segregated school districts requires no less than the immediate restructuring of school boards and other policy-making bodies to insure that those formally excluded by race from representation have persons selected by them in accordance with the percentage of their children in the school system. This restructuring must take effect no later than the start of the 1955-1956 school year.

3. *Judicial oversight.* To effectuate the efficient implementation of these orders, federal district judges will establish three-person monitoring committees with the Negro and white communities, each selecting a monitor and a third person with educational expertise selected by an appropriate federal agency. The monitoring committees will work with school officials to prepare the necessary plans and procedures enabling the school

districts' compliance with phases one and two. The district courts will give compliance oversight priority attention and will address firmly any actions intended to subvert or hinder the compliance program.

School districts that fail to move promptly to comply with the equalization standards set out above will be deemed in noncompliance and following a judicial determination to this effect, courts will determine whether such noncompliance with the "separate but equal" standard justifies relief such as we have ordered in the graduate school cases, including orders to promptly desegregate their schools by racially balancing the student and faculty populations in each school.

In this Court's view, the petitioners' goal — the disestablishment of the dual school system — will be more effectively achieved for students, parents, teachers, administrators, and other individuals connected directly or indirectly with the school system by these means rather than by a ringing order for immediate desegregation that we fear will not be effectively enforced and will be vigorously resisted. Our expectations in this regard are strengthened by the experience in the Delaware case, where school officials unable to finance the equalization of separate schools opted to desegregate those schools.

We recognize that this decision neither comports with the hopes for orders requiring immediate desegregation by petitioners or the states' contentions that we should simply reject those petitions and retain the racial status quo. Our goal, though, is not to determine winners and losers. It is rather our obligation to unravel the nation's greatest contradiction as it pertains to the public schools. Justice John Marshall Harlan, while dissenting in *Plessy*, perhaps unwittingly articulated this contradiction in definitive fashion when he observed:

> The white race deems itself to be the dominant race in this country. And so it is, in prestige, in achievements, in education, in wealth and in power. So, I doubt not, it will continue to be for all time, if it remains true to its great heritage and holds fast to the principles of constitutional liberty. But in view of the Constitution, in the eye of the law, there is in this country no superior, dominant, ruling class of citizens. There is no caste here. Our Constitution is color-blind, and neither knows nor tolerates classes among citizens.[9]

The existence of a dominant white race and the concept of color-blindness are polar opposites. The Fourteenth Amendment's equal protection clause cannot easily ferret out the racial injustice masquerading in seemingly neutral terms like "separate but equal" and "color-blindness." It has proven barely adequate as a shield against some of the most pernicious modes of racial violence and economic domination. The clause, perhaps unfortunately given its origins, most comfortably serves to adjudicate relationships between legally recognized categories of business or other entities (rather than squarely addressing the validity of the state's exercise of coercion against a whole group).

This Court does not ignore the value of simply recognizing the evil of segregation, an evil Negroes have experienced firsthand for too long. There is, we also agree, a place for symbols in law for a people abandoned by law for much of the nation's history. We recognize and hail the impressive manner in which

9. 163 U.S. at 559.

Negroes have taken symbolic gains and given them meaning by the sheer force of their belief in the freedoms this country guarantees to all. Is it not precisely because of their unstinting faith in this country's ideals that they deserve better than a well-intended but empty and likely unenforceable expression of equality, no matter how well meant? Such a decision will serve as sad substitute for the needed empathy of action called for when a history of racial subordination is to be undone.

The racial reform-retrenchment pattern so evident in this Court's racial decisions enables a prediction that when the tides of white resentment rise and again swamp the expectations of Negroes in a flood of racial hostility, this Court and likely the country will vacillate and then, as with the Emancipation Proclamation and the Civil War Amendments, rationalize its inability and — let us be honest — its unwillingness to give real meaning to the rights we declare so readily and so willingly sacrifice when our interests turn to new issues, more pressing concerns.

It is to avoid still another instance of this by now predictable outcome that we reject the petitioners' plea that the Court overturn *Plessy* forthwith. Doing so would systematically gloss over the extent to which *Plessy*'s simplistic "separate but equal" form served as a legal adhesive in the consolidation of white supremacy in America. Rather than critically engaging American racism's complexities, this Court would substitute one mantra for another: where "separate" was once equal, "separate" would be now categorically unequal. Rewiring the rhetoric of equality (rather than laying bare *Plessy*'s white supremacy underpinnings and consequences) constructs state-supported racial segregation as an eminently fixable aberration. And yet, by doing nothing more than rewiring the rhetoric of equality, this Court would foreclose the possibility of recognizing racism as a broadly shared cultural condition.

Imagining racism as a fixable aberration, moreover, obfuscates the way in which racism functions as an ideological lens through which Americans perceive themselves, their nation, and their nation's Other. Second, the vision of racism as an unhappy accident of history immunizes "the law" (as a logical system) from anti-racist critique. That is to say, the Court would position the law as that which fixes racism rather than that which participates in its consolidation. By dismissing *Plessy* without dismantling it, the Court might unintentionally predict, if not underwrite, eventual failure. Negroes, who despite all, are perhaps the nation's most faithful citizens, deserve better.[10]

§3.11 SCHOOL FINANCE

For years, advocates assumed that integration, on its own, would improve the educational prospects of black children, but time proved that the persistent educational gap between black and white students is only indirectly traceable to segregation. Instead, the substantial disparities in the resources provided to black students relative to white students was thought to be part of the problem. Therefore,

---

10. I owe credit for the thoughts and language in the last few paragraphs to Nirej Sekhon, a former student, currently a Stanford Law School Fellow.

according to some school advocates, priority should be given to "desegregating not the students but the money."[1]

With this shifting of consciousness, school finance become an important legal issue in public schooling. The judicial and political climate that caused courts to abandon desegregation decrees also prompted advocates of black children and parents to seek other avenues of relief.[2] Even the NAACP, which stalwartly defended mandatory desegregation as the linchpin of school strategies, began to look to funding as an essential element of obtaining equal educational opportunities for black students.[3]

In the first major school finance case, the California Supreme Court struck down the state system for funding public education as unconstitutional.[4] The California finance scheme relied on local property taxes as a major source of school revenue, with the balance drawn from a state foundation program which provided a minimum amount of guaranteed support for all districts. Despite state aid, disparities between school districts were still enormous. At one end of the spectrum, one district spent $577.49 per pupil in 1968-1969, while another was able to expend $1,231.72 per student. The assessed valuation per pupil in the first district was only $3,706 versus $50,885 per child in the second district.

Children and parents who resided in Los Angeles County brought a class action to challenge the constitutionality of the state finance system. Plaintiffs represented all children in the state "except children in that school district, the identity of which is presently unknown, which school district affords the greatest educational opportunity of all school districts." The California Supreme Court found that the state finance system "invidiously discriminates against the poor" in violation of the equal protection clause of the Fourteenth Amendment "because it makes the quality of a child's education a function of the wealth of his parents and neighbors." Education, the Court held, is a fundamental right "which cannot be conditioned on wealth."

The fundamental problem with the California scheme was that it did not offer poor districts the same opportunity to *choose* their educational priorities. Although, theoretically, districts with lower tax bases can simply tax themselves at higher rates to produce more revenue, there is no conceivable means by which East Los Angeles can produce the same amount of money as Beverly Hills. Rejecting the argument that the state finance system enhances local autonomy, the Court agreed that the system actually lessens the choice of the poor district which "cannot freely choose to tax itself into an excellence which its tax rolls cannot provide."

Despite the obvious applicability of its Fourteenth Amendment arguments to racial classifications, the Court nowhere in its opinion addressed the role of race in

---

§3.11   1. See also Julius Chambers, Adequate Education for All: A Right, An Achievable Goal, 22 Harv. C.R.-C.L. L. Rev. 55 (1977).

2. Id.

3. See id. at 72-73 (counsel to the NAACP Legal Defense Fund argued that while "I have not meant to suggest the abandonment of our traditional arsenal of weapons to advance educational opportunity," "we cannot afford to overlook new ways in which to remedy the immediate harm now befalling so many poor and black students").

4. Serrano v. Priest, 96 Cal. Rptr. 601, 487 P.2d 1241 (Cal. 1971).

the legislative proportioning of benefits and burdens. Although the property-poor communities which suffered under the California system were assuredly, at least in some cases, communities of color, the Court did not develop or even refer to a racial critique of the finance system.

Whatever *Serrano*'s achievements or shortcomings, the Supreme Court closed the door to federal challenges of school financing. In 1973, in San Antonio School District v. Rodriguez,[5] the Court upheld the constitutionality of the Texas financing scheme that unfairly allocated educational resources across the state. The Texas system permitted wide variations in funding among school districts since it was funded, in part, by revenues realized from wildly disparate local property tax bases. The state maintained a minimum foundation program which ensured districts the funding necessary for basic expenses but did not significantly ameliorate disparities in interdistrict per-pupil wealth and expenditures.

Mexican American parents of children attending public schools in an urban school district in San Antonio instituted a class action on behalf of school children throughout the state who were members of status minority groups, were poor and resided in school districts with a low property tax base. Declining to apply strict scrutiny to the Texas system in the absence of a suspect classification or a deprivation of a fundamental right, the Court rejected plaintiffs' claim that the finance system discriminated against minority and poor students. "[This] large, diverse, and amorphous class," the Court wrote, "unified only by the common factor of residence in districts that happen to have less taxable wealth than other districts" lacked the traditional indicia of "suspectness" necessary to trigger strict scrutiny equal protection analysis. Furthermore, because there is no "explicit or implicit" constitutional right to a public education, the Court found that education may not be considered a fundamental right. Not surprisingly, the Texas system survived the deferential review undertaken by the Court, which found that the reliance of local wealth was rationally related to its purpose of assuring a basic education for every child in the state while fostering local control of public schools.[6]

States, however, as did California, have relied on their own constitutional provisions to invalidate school finance schemes which have the effect of discriminating against black students. Several states have rejected *Rodriguez* and declared education to be a fundamental right subject to strict judicial scrutiny under the state equal protection provisions. Others have based constitutional challenges on state provisions guaranteeing an efficient, adequate, or thorough system of public education to all residents.[7] To date, there have been decisions in school finance cases in 38 states. Eighteen states have struck down school finance schemes either on state equal-protection grounds or under state constitutional provisions mandating equal or adequate education.[8]

5. 411 U.S. 1 (1973).

6. Id. at 49, 53. See also Danson v. Casey, 399 A.2d 360, 367 (1979) (recognizing the "concept of local control [of schools] to meet diverse local needs").

7. See infra note 11. Forty-eight state constitutions explicitly recognize a right to education, and many contain requirements that the education is provided on an equal, general, or efficient basis. See Chambers, supra note 1, at 63.

8. For details on all the state school finance litigation, see James E. Ryan, *Sheff,* Segregation, and School Finance Litigation, 74 N.Y.U. L. Rev. 529, n.15 (May 1999).

In Edgewood Independent School District v. Kirby,[9] the Supreme Court of Texas ruled that Texas's school financing system violated the state constitutional requirement that an "efficient" system of public education be established for the "general diffusion of knowledge."[10] Texas financed public schools through local revenues supplemented by state and federal funds. Because property wealth differs substantially between localities, this funding system produced "glaring disparities" between districts. The Texas Supreme Court took the bold step of equating the constitutional guarantee of efficiency with the requirement of equality in practice. The financing system, according to the court, provided only a "limited" and "unbalanced" diffusion of knowledge, which was "directly contrary to the constitutional vision of efficiency." Even additional state aid to property-poor school districts would not be sufficient to remedy the constitutional deficiencies: "[a] band-aid will not suffice; the system itself must be changed."

The historical imbalances in the resources provided to black schools and to white schools raises other issues critical to effective desegregation remedies. Achievement lags of black students have caused many to realize that simply integrating the schools will not be enough to eliminate the vestiges of a discriminatory system. Having denied black children access to effective schools for centuries, we cannot expect that these children can now be thrown into the schools to compete with white students on an equal basis. Since the skewed level of preparedness is a vestige of the system of separate and unequal schools — no less so than racial imbalance in student assignment — the Constitution may require that courts order increased funding for black schools and the establishment of remedial programs for black students as elements of an appropriate remedy.[11]

The various school-finance litigations, whatever the state, have two things in common: First, none of the courts make the connection between unequal funding and race; and second, there is reason to doubt that equalizing funding without more makes a substantive difference. The latter problem should come as little surprise. Schools in poor, segregated neighborhoods that have been marginalized for decades will not suddenly achieve high-quality education and produce students competitive with those of the traditionally privileged schools just because they are now given equal funding. That is like expecting a Pinto to keep up with a Porsche simply because they are given the same quality fuel. Remediation for present-day inequities cannot compensate for ancient injuries.

It is, though, a start. In June 2005, New York's highest court determined in litigation begun 10 years earlier that the state's funding process shortchanged the students in New York City and failed to provide them with "a sound basic education,"[12] as required by the state constitution. At the time of trial, the New York City public school system comprised nearly 1,200 schools serving 1.1 million children and employing a staff of over 135,000, including 78,000 teachers.

9. 777 S.W.2d 391 (Tex. 1989).

10. Tex. Const., art. VII, §1.

11. See, e.g., Comment, Eliminating the Continuing Effects of the Violation: Compensatory Education as a Remedy for Unlawful School Segregation, 97 Yale L.J. 1173, 1192 (1988); Comment, Unitary School Systems and Underlying Vestiges of State-Imposed Segregation, 87 Colum. L. Rev. 794, 801 (1987).

12. Campaign for Fiscal Equity, Inc. v. State, 86 N.Y.2d 307 (1995).

Some 84 percent of city school-children were racial minorities, 80 percent were born outside the United States, and 16 percent were classified as Limited English Proficient (LEP, persons who speak little or no English). Most of the state's students in each of these categories (upwards of 73 percent) were eligible for the federal free or reduced lunch program; 442,000 city schoolchildren came from families receiving Aid to Families with Dependent Children; and 135,000 were enrolled in special education programs.

The court found that tens of thousands of the city's students are assigned to overcrowded classrooms led by unqualified, inexperienced teachers. More than a third of these students are functionally illiterate, and only half of them graduate on time. Thirty percent never finish high school. As of the 1996-1997 school year, the state provided 39.9 percent of all public school funding — $10.4 billion out of a total of $26 billion — while districts provided 56 percent and the federal government 4 percent. These figures represented an investment of $9,321 per pupil, $3,714 of it by the state. Per-pupil expenditures in the New York City public schools, at $8,171, were lower than in three-quarters of the state's districts, including all the other "large city" districts. The state's dollar contribution to this figure was also lower, at $3,562, than its average contribution to other districts; and the city's, at about $4,000, was likewise lower than the average local contribution in other districts.

The Court gave the governor and the legislature 400 days to ascertain the actual cost of providing a sound basic education and then ensure that every school district has the resources necessary to provide it. Leaving deliberately unclear who will pay for any needed budget increases, the court added that the distribution of the tax burden between the city and the state is "now in the realm of politics and not law." It appears that years of litigation in the courts and predictable foot-dragging in the legislature lie ahead.

§3.12   CHARTER SCHOOLS AND SCHOOL VOUCHERS

In addition to major reform within the existing school system, some school advocates have urged publicly funded alternatives to the existing systems, including charter schools and vouchers that enable parents to choose among available private schools. In either approach, minority parents and inner-city community groups seeking alternatives to traditional public schools have found allies among conservatives. Opposition to these new educational options tends to come from civil rights groups, public school officials, teachers' unions, and parents concerned with one more financial drain on the public schools.

§3.12.1   Charter Schools

Legislation, now enacted in at least 30 states, enables a designated granting body or "agency" to give permission and public funds to entities that apply for charters with the purpose of establishing and operating primary and secondary schools free from many of the statutory and regulatory constraints of the existing education code, that is, free from the centralized control and bureaucracy of the existing public school district. Charter schools, representing a new way of fulfilling various state constitutional mandates to provide free public education to the young, will likely play a prominent role in public education during the coming decade. They appear to further the political agendas of many and, according to supporters, hold great promise for developing innovative approaches to public education while challenging school systems to improve their performance.[1]

Charter advocates contend that charter school administrators should be provided with a budget equal to the average per pupil expenditures prevailing in the district or state in which their schools are chartered and should be given five years or so (depending on state law that in some states provides 10-15 years) to justify the charter by demonstrating improvement in student performance. Supporters contend that with these resources charter school teachers and staff will be more motivated than are their counterparts at traditional public school administrators to produce effective educational results. All families, not just the wealthy, should be able to choose the schools their children will attend, advocates argue, dismissing as paternalism the concern that low-income parents will not make appropriate choices for their children.

Those who generally oppose charter schools view the movement with alarm. They fear it will simply increase school choice for already privileged students and their parents, those who have the information and social savvy to exploit the new schooling opportunities.[2] Opponents also predict that charter schools will discriminate, either explicitly or implicitly, by race or socioeconomic status and, if necessary, to further the movement, will disadvantage already disadvantaged students as they drain already strapped school systems of much-needed funds and support. They also make the point that charter schools don't necessarily have to admit children with learning disabilities or English language learners to the degree that traditional public schools do. This enables them to use the funding they receive for specialized programs not available in the public schools. They can then look more successful because they need not cope with the variety of complicated issues that challenge traditional public schools.

This argument formed the basis of an equal-protection challenge to Colorado's School Act, filed by a group of Latino parents who sought to enjoin the Pueblo, Colorado, school board from closing two neighborhood public schools and opening a new charter school. The closings required some children to ride buses or to cross busy intersections to reach new, overcrowded schools. Plaintiffs claimed that the decision to close schools in the predominantly Latino neighborhood in

---

§3.12   1. See, e.g., Karla A. Turekian, Note and Comment: Traversing the Minefields of Education Reform: The Legality of Charter Schools, 29 Conn. L. Rev. 1365 (1997); Kevin S. Huffman, Note: Charter Schools, Equal Protection Litigation, and the New School Reform Movement, 73 N.Y.U. L. Rev. 1290 (1998).

2. This concern seems to be belied by the facts. According to one study, nearly two-thirds of charter school students nationwide are nonwhite, and more than half come from low-income families. See Richard C. Seder, Allow Charter Schools to Reach Their Full Potential, Christian Sci. Monitor, Oct. 3, 1997, at 18.

conjunction with state approval and oversight of the new charter school was racially discriminatory. In upholding the dismissal of claims, the Tenth Circuit determined that the plaintiffs had failed to demonstrate discriminatory intent or purpose under either the Fourteenth Amendment or Title VI of the 1964 Civil Rights Act.[3]

The result reflects the difficulty of challenging charter schools under current standards requiring proof that discrimination is intentional.[4] A further difficulty lies in proving that the charter school's actions are those of the state, since the Court currently seems determined to insulate the government from liability if actors causing the purported harm are not directly functioning as the state.[5] Until the issue is resolved by the Supreme Court, it will remain unclear whether charter schools are state actors. Charter schools, then, are options that allow students to exit schools that don't serve them. Parents, regardless of race, seek schools providing a high-quality education in a setting with shared community values, safety, proximity, and respect for parents. Indeed, shared values and proximity are more important to parents than educational outcomes, a reason, Dr. Foster suggests, why voucher and charter schools get consistently high marks from parents, even when academic performance is moderate or low.

Few major studies have attempted to answer the question of how these alternative, mainly minority schools work. Despite the obstacles, some of these schools have proven successful. One of these is the Frederick Douglass Academy in Harlem. The school sends a very high percentage of its students to four-year colleges and is considered to be one of the top public schools in the country, based on its course offerings and student performances on Advanced Placement Exams. The school's population is roughly 80 percent African American and 15 percent Hispanic. In terms of the economic backgrounds from which the students come, approximately 90 percent are eligible for free lunch, and yet the students manage to succeed.[6]

In Boston, the MATCH Charter Public High School boasts that 100 percent of its students passed the MCAS in 2007 with a score of Proficient or Advanced making it the #1 high school among 400 in Massachusetts in math. Similarly, 100 percent of the members of MATCH's first three graduating classes have been admitted to 4-year colleges. The student body is 69 percent African American, 23 percent Hispanic, 4 percent Asian, and 3 percent White with 70 percent of the students qualifying for reduced price lunch, the measure of poverty. In November, 2007, the MATCH School was named one of 53 National Charter Schools of the Year by the Center for Education Reform.[7]

3. Villanueva v. Carere, 85 F.3d 481 (10th Cir. 1996).

4. See, e.g., Washington v. Davis, 426 U.S. 229 (1976); McCleskey v. Kemp, 481 U.S. 279 (1987).

5. Rendell-Baker v. Kohn, 457 U.S. 830 (1982) (a private school designed to educate troubled children and which received more than 90 percent of its funds from government sources allegedly fired teachers in violation of their due process rights; the Court found that the school was not a state actor, reasoning that "acts of such private contractors do not become the acts of the government by reason of their significant or even total engagement in performing public contracts").

6. According to the the the New York Cit Schools Annual School Report, available at http://www.nycenet.edu, there are now about six Frederick Douglass Academies in the various boroughs of New York City, all seeking to emulate the success of the original Harlem school.

7. MATCH Charter Public High School, http://www.matchschool.org.

To quote a gospel song, these schools serving children with many disadvantages are constantly climbing the rough side of the mountain. After a rocky start a decade ago, the African American Academy in Seattle became a public school model. Its staff and 465 students gained a new, $23.3 million, 100,000 square-foot building located on a twelve-acre site. The Academy uses the same curriculum as the Seattle public schools but blends African and African American history into daily lessons. The gap in achievement with white schools is closing slowly, a sign that the school is meeting a major challenge, given that 84 percent of its students are eligible for free and reduced-price lunches; only 19 percent of the students live with both parents, the lowest rate in the district; and, the school estimates, 40 percent of the students live with relatives or foster parents.[8]

In recent years, though, the school's performance and its reputation have declined. Critics cite to numerous reasons why the Academy has not lived up to its promise. Enrollment has declined by more than a third over the last six years. With a new principal and additional funding of $460,000, the Board is giving the school another year to improve.[9] As the comparison of the Seattle school with its counterparts in New York and Boston indicates, charter programs are by no means uniform, varying greatly from state to state. The differences lead to wide variations in accessibility by poor parents. Black educators seeking to gain state approval for such programs often experience serious political obstacles. It is thus better not to favor voucher or charter programs in general, but rather to support or oppose them after reviewing the enabling laws. For example, a voucher law that allows a school to charge more tuition than the amount of the voucher is quite different from one that prohibits such charges.

§3.12.2   Tuition Vouchers

Tuition voucher arrangements, both the most popular and likely the most controversial of educational alternatives to emerge in the last decade, allow parents to select a public or private school of their choice.[10] Voucher programs allow a state to write checks to parents for all or part of the private or public-school tuition for elementary or secondary schooling. In some cases, parents endorse the check to the public or private school of their choice; in other cases, states send a check, payable to the parent, directly to the school. Voucher legislation is under consideration in at least 23 states and has been adopted in Arizona, Maine, Wisconsin, Ohio, Pennsylvania, and Vermont.

---

8. Sara Gonzales, For African Americans, a School to Call Home, Seattle Times, June 16, 1999; Linda Shaw, Seattle's African American Academy: Rescuing the Dream, Seattle Times, Feb. 14, 1999.

9. Emily Heffter, Seattle's African American Academy Gets One More Try, Seattle Times, Aug. 27, 2007.

10. See Frank R. Kemerer, The Constitutionality of School Vouchers, 101 Ed. Law. Rep. 17 (1995); Carol L. Ziegler & Nancy M. Lederman, School Vouchers: Are Urban Students Surrendering Rights for Choice?, 19 Fordham Urb. L.J. 813 (1992); Greg D. Andres, Comment, Private School Voucher Remedies in Education Cases, 62 U. Chi. L. Rev. 795 (1995).

Educators supporting voucher programs hold that, by allowing parents to choose the schools for their children, a more market-oriented educational system will be created. This system will bring both private and public schools into competition, thus increasing the quality of education for all.[11] Opponents respond by arguing that vouchers will not alter the educational advantages available to well-off parents, but, rather, will enhance them by siphoning needed resources from already poorly funded schools. Opponents see, moreover, that the real beneficiaries of vouchers are the pervasively sectarian schools funding of which they assert will be in clear violation of the First Amendment's establishment clause. Opponents have already challenged plans that would permit the use of vouchers at such schools. Milwaukee and Cleveland each have taxpayer-funded voucher programs, allowing public funds for religious schools. Both plans have been challenged in court.

The Milwaukee Parental Choice Plan (MRCP) permits states to give selected students up to $2,500 per year to use at private schools. Tuition checks made out to parents are mailed directly to the participating schools, at which the parents have enrolled their children. Participating schools must comply with federal antidiscrimination provisions in Title VI and must follow state reporting requirements. Students are chosen through a lottery from families with incomes below 175 percent of the poverty level, a level that allows 15,000 Milwaukee students (about 15 percent of the school population) to leave public schools for private schools. Of the private schools participating, 89 percent are sectarian. The Wisconsin Supreme Court found that the state's voucher program is a "neutral" effort to help parents pay for education and that is not seeking to advance religion, since poor parents are given money to send their children to either a sectarian or a nonsectarian school. Thus, funds reach sectarian schools only through intervening choices made by individual parents.[12]

The Cleveland plan is similar to that in Milwaukee in that eligible parents have an average income of under $10,000 per year, receive vouchers of up to $2,500 per year, and may use them in sectarian schools. In May 1997, about 80 percent of the 2,000 students in the program used the vouchers to attend religious schools, most of them Catholic. At that point, a state appeals court blocked the program from expanding beyond 2,000 students, finding that it infringed on the establishment clause. But the Supreme Court gave its approval in a five-to-four vote, even though, by this point, 96 percent of the students taking part in the program used the vouchers to attend religious schools.[13] A factor was that the voucher program was one of a number of efforts over the years to provide options for Cleveland's poor parents in a demonstrably failing system. Among the 50 largest school districts in the country, Cleveland had the lowest overall graduation rate, with 28 percent.[14]

11. See Milton Friedman, Capitalism and Freedom 93-96 (1962).
12. The Milwaukee plan is Jackson v. Benson, 578 N.W.2d 602 (Wis. 1998), cert. denied, 119 S. Ct. 466 (1999). The Cleveland plan is Simmons-Harris v. Goff, 684 N.E.2d 705 (Ohio 1999). See Joseph P. Viteritti, Choosing Equality: Religious Freedom and Educational Opportunity under Constitutional Federalism, 15 Yale L. & Pol'y Rev. 113, 156 (1996).
13. Zelman v. Simmons-Harris, 534 U.S. 1077 (2002).
14. High School Graduation Rates in the United States (Jay P. Greene ed., Nov. 2001).

Writing for the majority, Chief Justice Rehnquist concluded that the program was enacted for a valid secular reason and did not violate the establishment clause by promoting religion, the decision on where to spend the vouchers being left to the parents. In a concurring opinion, Justice O'Connor expanded further on the theme of "parental choice," noting the array of options that Cleveland offered to parents who preferred to stay in the public school system. In dissent, Justice Souter, joined by the three other moderate members of the Court, argued that public school options could not be considered in assessing parental choice or else "there will always be a choice and the voucher can always be constitutional." He also stressed that the Court had never before upheld such a substantial transfer of taxpayer dollars to religious institutions, transfers he deemed a "dramatic departure from basic Establishment Clause principle."

Because the close five-to-four Cleveland voucher decision was so dependent on the specific history of that case, it is unlikely that opponents to these plans will concede defeat. Future efforts will be motivated by concern that vouchers will benefit the non-needy while taking funds from public school systems; they will permit subtle but still substantial discrimination; and, like the Milwaukee and Cleveland plans permitting the use of vouchers in religious schools, they will violate the establishment clause of the First Amendment.[15] If raised in the early 1970s, these arguments would likely have been deemed correct, based on the Court's invalidation on establishment grounds of a New York school voucher plan[16] and the then rigorous application of the standards in Lemon v. Kurtzman.[17] These required (1) that the statute must have a secular legislative purpose; (2) that its principal or primary effect must be one that neither advances nor inhibits religion; and (3) that the statute must not foster "an excessive government entanglement with religion."

In analyzing aid to parochial schools, courts have focused their analyses on the second and third prongs of the *Lemon* test, noting that most state programs satisfy the first prong in that education is a legitimate secular purpose. Critics, though, argue that vouchers fail the second prong because they are not neutrally provided; their use is contingent on attending private school, most of which are religious and "pervasively sectarian." Parents do choose, but the choice is not a meaningful one when about three-fourths of the private schools available are sectarian. Vouchers are more like direct subsidies than an "incidental" benefit, and covering as they do elementary and secondary schools, the aid will cover younger children who are more susceptible to religious indoctrination.

Opponents also contend that voucher programs fail the "excessive entanglement" or third prong of *Lemon,* because constant government surveillance will be required to insure that funds are not spent for religious purposes. In addition, annual funding decisions will inevitably be guided by deeply rooted and divergent religious beliefs, leading to continuous religion-based fighting over state funds.

---

15. "Congress shall make no law respecting an establishment of religion." U.S. Const. amend. I.

16. Committee for Pub. Educ. and Religious Liberty v. Nyquist, 413 U.S. 756 (1973) (a group of laws authorizing funding to nonpublic, mainly Catholic schools, recognizing that they had assumed a heavy burden of education youth).

17. 403 U.S. 602 (1971).

Voucher proponents point out that the current Court, as reflected in the Cleveland voucher case, has moved beyond a rigorous application of the *Lemon* standards and, in recent cases, has adopted a "benign neutrality" toward religion.[18] These cases are distinguishable from voucher plans in that they do not approve a neutral service and tend to be heavily skewed toward religion. Thus, the Court should not distinguish *Lemon* and *Nyquist* in order to approve these school funding devices.[19] Vouchers may conflict with state constitutions, 24 of which, as well as Puerto Rico's, contain explicit prohibitions against spending public funds on sectarian education.[20]

Against these barriers of precedent, modern voucher programs have several factors that weigh in favor of judicial approval. States enacting these programs have taken steps to address the *Lemon* standards by having parents choose their schools and by having checks written to parents to be sent to their chosen schools for endorsing. Aid is limited to the lesser of the state's public schools' per-student expenditures or a particular private schools' per-student expenditures related solely to educational programming. This weakens the charge that vouchers are subsidizing religious training. No special supervisory functions are included in the programs beyond those required of all schools.

As is evident from the very existence of the *Lemon* test, the idea of an impenetrable wall of separation between church and state is archaic. The role of religious institutions in American education, healthcare, and other social programs has not been characterized by proselytizing and coercion, but rather can be said to have greatly benefited the state, relieving it of burdens that it might otherwise have had to bear, without jeopardizing religious freedom. Permitting that sector of the population arguably most in need of the educational benefits offered by religious institutions to avail itself of those opportunities need not be seen as advancing religion, particularly where the voucher programs are neutral as to particular religions. Finally, given the thrust of recent cases in which protecting free speech rights of religious organizations far outweigh establishment concerns, it may be

---

18. See, e.g., Mueller v. Allen, 463 U.S. 388, 394 (1983) (Court considered several factors in upholding state income-tax deductions for educational expenses for children in private school, including the availability of a variety of deductions for all taxpayers, not just those with school children, and expressly distinguished deductions from the tax benefits in Committee for Public Educ. and Religious Liberty v. Nyquist, 413 U.S. 756 (1973), concluding the tax benefits there were actually tuition grants to parents of children attending private schools); Witters v. Washington Dept. of Services for the Blind, 474 U.S. 481, 488 (1986) (Court held state-funded scholarships for disabled students to pay Bible college tuition constitutional, generally deeming academic learning at the college level less of an establishment-clause danger because of age and maturity of students, and the plan did not create "financial incentive[s] for students to undertake sectarian education"); Zobrest v. Catalina Foothills Sch. Dist., 509 U.S. 1 (1993) (Court considered a number of factors in holding that a state-funded sign-language interpreter could assist hearing-impaired child in sectarian school, including lack of bias toward religion in statute approving the funding (the Federal Individuals with Disabilities Education Act), the purchase of a neutral service, translation, and the absence of any relationship between qualification for the aid and attendance at a private school).

19. See Harlan A. Loeb & Debbie N. Kaminer, God Money and Schools: Voucher Programs Impugn the Separation of Church and State, 30 J. Marshall L. Rev. 1, 9-10, 30-31 (1996).

20. See id. at 33.

that voucher plans must include sectarian schools to avoid charges that their exclusion violates the free-exercise clause.[21]

While the legal issues do not involve race directly, the outcome of the tuition voucher litigation will be of great importance to the thousands of black parents who have enrolled their children in private — often sectarian schools — at their own expense as well as the many more who would if they could afford to do so. And perhaps reflecting their frustration with the perceived inadequacies of the public schools, a 1996 Gallop Poll reported that 72 percent of black parents interviewed supported school vouchers, as compared to the general public, which split 48 percent to 48 percent. And when it was split by age group, 86.5 percent of those black parents age 26 to 35 supported private school vouchers.[22]

Even considering the disappointments of the school desegregation experience, however, prudence dictates careful review before jeopardizing the existing school system with all the problems that beset those schools serving poor minority children. Professor Molly O'Brien provided substance to these concerns by pointing out that the history of tuition vouchers does not emanate from the race-neutral, theory-driven school reform idea attributed to libertarian economist Milton Friedman.[23] Rather, several years before his 1955 essay proposing the radical restructuring of public education, a tuition grant plan had already been considered by the Georgia legislature and other southern states, all part of the race-baiting politics of the pre-*Brown* South, when the prospect of court-ordered desegregation spurred a movement to abandon public schooling in favor of a private system funded by vouchers.

While acknowledging that notions of individual autonomy and "choice" have strong appeal in American culture, Professor O'Brien found little or no evidence to suggest that many parents or students objected to the system of student placement before court-ordered desegregation. Similarly, she found available data on school achievement does not support a theory of public school decline. In her view, "the school tuition voucher movement was conceived at the margin of race/class

21. See, e.g., Rosenberger v. Rector and Visitors of Univ. of Va., 515 U.S. 819 (1995) (public university may not refuse on establishment-clause grounds to pay costs of printing student publication promulgating Christian faith if the school funds other student group publications; refusal denies students' freedom of speech, and payment does not violate Establishment Clause); Capitol Square Review & Advisory Bd. v. Pinette, 515 U.S. 753 (1995) (Court refused to allow state officials to bar the Ku Klux Klan's private religious display of a cross in a public plaza, explaining that the possibility some viewers might falsely assume official endorsement of the display was insufficient to permit restrictions on private speech.); Lamb's Chapel v. Center Moriches Union Free Sch. Dist., 508 U.S. 384 (1993) (allowing church access to public school premises for after-hours film series on family issues from a religious perspective would not have violated the establishment clause; banning the series based on the religious content of the speech was not a content-neutral regulation and therefore violated the pastor's and the church's free-speech rights and violated free speech); Widmar v. Vincent, 454 U.S. 263 (1981) (a state university, which makes its facilities generally available for the activities of registered student groups, violates the free-exercise clause by closing its facilities to a registered student group desiring to use the facilities for religious worship and religious discussion); Board of Educ. of Westside Community Sch. v. Mergens, 496 U.S. 226 (1990) (applying the Widmar v. Vincent result to high schools).

22. James Brooke, Minorities Flock to Cause of Vouchers for Schools, N.Y. Times, Dec. 27, 1997, at A1.

23. Molly Townes O'Brien, Private School Tuition Vouchers and the Realities of Racial Politics, 64 Tenn. L. Rev. 359 (1997).

conflict, nurtured in the context of a struggle to gain financing for public education from a fiscally conservative power structure, and born out of the racial politics of the Deep South."[24]

The advocates of tuition vouchers in Milwaukee, Cleveland, and the several states where they are under consideration view them as providing schooling options for poor parents, rather than as means of white flight. But even such laudable motives cannot guarantee that the familiar pattern of civil rights progress will not again unfold: That is to say, can these option plans achieve and maintain a base that is equally nonthreatening and beneficial to both whites and blacks? This concern is not a call for rejection of vouchers and other public school alternatives, but it suggests a counsel of caution based on policy priorities in racial matters quite evident in historical developments and still present today. Professor Jim Ryan articulates the need for caution, noting that it is one thing for academics to debate how vouchers will or will not work in theory and another to review how actual plans are funded and implemented.[25]

> For private school choice to work, sufficient resources and sufficient attention to detail will be necessary to ensure that the theoretical underpinnings have a realistic chance of being translated into a workable plan. And this commitment, I think, will have to be a sustained one, to ensure that the inevitable problems that arise in the implementation of a voucher plan are confronted and overcome. Voucher plans will also require the commitment and resources of both those within and outside of the community. Despite the success of some non-public school programs, there is a basis for concern to the extent that these schools fit within the history of urban and suburban relations with a trend of suburban absolution and apartheid, wherein suburbanites have successfully managed to reduce their responsibility for and involvement in urban problems, particularly with regard to schools. Evidence of this trend is apparent in both the desegregation and school finance contexts, and could eventually undermine the alternative school movement.[26]

24. Id. at 364.

25. Jim Ryan, School Choice: School Choice and the Suburbs, 14 J.L. & Pol. 459, 465-466 (1998).

26. Professor Ryan cites as exemplars Milliken v. Bradley, 418 U.S. 717 (1974), where the Court ignored rather obvious evidence of government-sponsored or government-encouraged housing segregation that rendered desegregation of the heavily black Detroit school district impossible. The decision freed the courts and white America from responsibility for black ghettos and for the children now condemned to ghetto schools. Milliken v. Bradley II, 433 U.S. 267 (1977), can be seen as softening the blow by requiring states to provide additional resources to inner-city schools.

In the school-finance litigation, Ryan sees a similar barrier created between cities and suburbs as civil rights lawyers opt for equity or "adequacy" over equality suits. The goal of so-called adequacy suits in school finance litigation is to secure sufficient resources to give every student an adequate education. Adequacy suits presuppose, however, that certain districts will be able to provide more than an adequate education. "Adequacy arguments are likely to prove far less threatening than equality arguments because they don't invoke the image of leveling off — where the worst and best are placed on the same footing." Ryan quotes Professor Peter Enrich, who writes, "adequacy arguments, unlike equality arguments, do not ask judges, lawyers and legislators to sacrifice their own children's education for the sake of a societal norm." Like *Milliken II* remedies, then, adequate financing provides some funds to poor school districts, but not enough to threaten the funds that are available for more affluent districts. Adequate financing allows suburban and urban districts to remain separate in terms of financing in a way that equal resources would not. See Peter Enrich, Leaving Equality Behind: New Directions in School Finance Reform, 48 Vand. L. Rev. 101, 166-183 (1995).

§3.13   BLACK COLLEGES AND THE DESEGREGATION DILEMMA[1]

Most Americans view black colleges, whether publicly or privately funded, as exemplars of the familiar advice that blacks should pull themselves up the way white ethnic immigrants supposedly did in the late nineteenth and early twentieth centuries. And, indeed, while the range of quality in mainly black schools is as great as in their mainly white counterparts, these schools offer support systems both academically and psychologically that can provide a much needed benefit as indicated by the fact that students at black colleges are more likely to complete school than are their counterparts at predominantly white schools.

Even so, the Supreme Court's attraction to color-blindness as the appropriate standard in all race cases while deeming all racial classification as suspect, theoretically places in some risk the opportunities of black students to obtain a college education in black colleges. And yet the demand heard frequently two decades ago for conversion of " 'white colleges and black colleges to just colleges' . . . threatens to deny black colleges their continuing role in affording higher education to blacks" is seldom heard today perhaps in part because decisions like *Bakke* and *Grutter* limit the ability of other institutions to assume that function.[2]

While integrationists castigate black colleges as segregated outposts in a desegregated world, black colleges, unlike most of their once totally segregated white counterparts, have always enjoyed the somewhat dubious benefits of a white presence. Most black colleges have had some white faculty, and have often been controlled by mainly white boards of directors. The state colleges have always been dominated by their state legislatures. White students have never been excluded by black colleges outside the deep South, and since 1954 they have been admitted throughout the South as well. Indeed, a few former black colleges are now mainly white. Black professional schools now have 40 to 50 percent white students.

It is clear that many whites enroll in black colleges, particularly at the professional level, because they can't get into white schools. Nevertheless, they present paper criteria superior to those held by many black applicants who may not be admitted anywhere. In this day of extreme competition for professional school admission, one should not assume that all these rejected black applicants are unqualified. And yet, after *Bakke* and the University of Michigan cases, *Grutter* and *Gratz*, discussed earlier, it is far from clear that black colleges can give absolute preferences to black applicants, despite their historical mission to educate

---

§3.13   1. In earlier editions, this discussion was based on a paper, Derrick Bell, Black Colleges and the Desegregation Dilemma, prepared for inclusion in a report on black colleges by the Council for the Advancement of Experiential Learning (M. Keeton ed., 1980). In the last decade, the complex problems facing historically black colleges have been more political and economic than legal. They are important to the growth and the survival of these schools but are beyond the scope of this text. Thus, in this section, I will review the major cases that, as will be obvious, have not resolved and arguably have worsened the dilemmas facing institutions that are both proudly and efficiently serving black students in a nation transfixed with the soothing unrealities of color-blindness.

2. Gil Kujovich, Equal Opportunity in Higher Education and the Black Public College: The Era of Separate But Equal, 72 Minn. L. Rev. 29, 169-170 (1987).

blacks and the increased efficiency and dedication they are bringing to that task. While, in *Grutter,* the Supreme Court allowed race to be considered as one factor in an admissions program designed to provide diversity to college classes, black colleges may not consider race to show a preference for black applicants. Given their historic mission to lift up the black masses, it would be the supreme irony if black colleges were barred from deemphasizing racial diversity in favor of a reasonable priority for minority children of the poor, the oppressed, and other blacks from disadvantaged backgrounds—students who have no opportunity to take advantage of those seats often set aside in white colleges for "the affluent who may bestow their largess on the institutions, and to those having connections with celebrities, the famous, and the powerful."[3]

In response to integration advocates, the black college presidents, sensing the danger from a too enthusiastically applied desegregation scheme, formed, in 1969, the National Association for Equality in Higher Education (NAFEO). In an early case threatening the continued existence of black colleges,[4] the NAFEO filed an amicus brief disagreeing with the civil rights plaintiffs as to the need to establish a unitary system. The issue, as NAFEO saw it, was not equal educational opportunity but the achievement of equality of educational attainment. This goal required the continuing existence and enhancement of public black colleges—institutions of higher learning well-endowed to serve their students and the communities from which they come.

Traditional Fourteenth Amendment suits have created crises to the extent that they impose similar standards of performance on black colleges as on their white counterparts. Even though the Supreme Court indicated soon after *Brown* that the "all deliberate speed" standard was not applicable in graduate schools where blacks were to be admitted immediately "under the rules and regulations applicable to other qualified candidates,"[5] most southern states continued to refuse blacks admission to state-run colleges and graduate schools, precipitating lengthy and often dramatic legal battles. The courageous plaintiffs in those cases are still remembered: Autherine Lucy and later Vivian Malone in Alabama; Horace Ward and later Hamilton Holmes and Charlayne Hunter in Georgia; and, of course James Meredith and later Cleveland Donald in Mississippi.

On the other hand, black educators feared that merger-type relief would transform a black institution into a predominantly white college that would basically serve the educational needs of the white community. At the college level, black educators suggested, desegregation should include nondiscriminatory admission and the equalizing of facilities but should not require consolidations or merger requirements that would destroy the identity of the black schools. Rather, black colleges should receive adequate budgets and be given the primary responsibility for those aspects of education of particular interest to the black community, such as social welfare, community planning, and community health. But, of course, these suggestions appeared contradictory to many integration advocates who by the early

---

3. Regents of Univ. of Cal. v. Bakke, 438 U.S. 265, 404 (1978).
4. Adams v. Richardson, 351 F. Supp. 636 (D.C. 1972), modified and aff'd, 480 F.2d 1159 (D.C. Cir. 1973).
5. State of Florida ex rel. Hawkins v. Board of Control, 350 U.S. 413, 414 (1956).

1970s were anxious to apply the Supreme Court's "neither white school nor Negro school" standard at the college level.

When courts tired of the delaying tactics of public school boards, and began ordering desegregation plans designed to effect the "root and branch" disestablishment of the dual school system, a similar attitude took hold regarding litigation at the college level with results that gave substance to the worst fears of black college educators. As they had warned, desegregation, like segregation before it, evolved into simply another technique for preserving white control and dominance.

In Tennessee, after several years in which it became apparent that plans featuring joint, cooperative, and exclusive programming would not integrate mainly black Tennessee State University (TSU) the court in February 1977 ordered the merger of the traditional all black college with the nearby University of Tennessee at Nashville (UT-N), an institution that had begun as a two-year, non-degree-granting extension college offering no advanced courses, and which had grown to a major, degree-granting institution that remains about 90 percent white.[6] The merger plan calls for the expansion of the mainly black TSU to encompass the mainly white UT-N, but to provide for desegregation through a series of planned steps of both faculty and student bodies. The district court rejected arguments seeking to distinguish college desegregation requirements from those of the public schools. It also did not see as controlling the expressed concern of some witnesses that blacks hold few positions on governing boards in the state system, and that merger would result in black administrators losing control of TSU.[7]

On appeal, the Sixth Circuit approved the merger plan.[8] In dissent, Judge Engel noted that TSU continues to draw black students from throughout the state of Tennessee, and he asked "if a student elsewhere in the state has the right, as he now has in Tennessee, to enroll in a regional college of his choice without impediment because of his race, is it wrong for him to prefer to go to a college such as TSU if he prefers?"[9] He expressed sympathy for those witnesses who urged that the merger would cause TSU to lose its identity as a respected and longstanding black university.

Rigid application of public school desegregation standards to college desegregation problems has lead to decisions like Craig v. Alabama State University,[10] in which the court found in favor of white teachers who charged the mainly black college had engaged in a pattern of reverse discrimination against whites in hiring, promotion, and tenure. Four of 56 administrative staff and 36 of 196 full-time faculty were white. The court enjoined all discrimination based on race, and denounced the black college president as an "administrative tyrant"

6. Geier v. Blanton, 427 F. Supp. 644 (M.D. Tenn. 1977).
7. Id. at 661. These fears are not without basis. According to Roy S. Nicks, chancellor of the State Board of Regents of Tennessee, the merger order will mean the end of efforts to preserve black leadership and presence at TSU. Nicks, asked in an interview, "Is TSU going to be allowed to control?," responded "The judge settled that, they're not. The Board of Regents is, and the Board of Regents is not dominated by blacks." Brown, Black College Survival, N.Y. News World Forum (Dec. 13, 1978).
8. Geier v. University of Tenn., 597 F.2d 1056 (6th Cir. 1979).
9. Id. at 1074.
10. 451 F. Supp. 1207 (M.D. Ala. 1978).

who "utilized his powers over the employment process to maintain a nearly dictatorial grip over the internal life of the university." The decision reflected no sense that a priority, or at least a preference, for black teachers and staff at a black college might be justified by educational considerations, or that the matter might be an issue worthy of discussion.

A coalition of black citizens in Mississippi attempted to avoid this result, whom they challenged the public higher education establishment in Mississippi.[11] Seeking to enjoin disparities in funding, resources, and control between white and black schools, the black group made it clear in a position paper released when the suit was filed that their goal was to expand the definition of "equal educational opportunity" to preserve and strengthen black colleges. They rejected simply dismantling the dual system because it is only one branch of the evil of racism. In their view:

> If a White teacher is a racist in his heart, he will find a way to discriminate against a Black student in a perfectly integrated setting. An educational institution can be no more compassionate and sympathetic than the individual educators and students who comprise it.[12]

The *Ayers* group acknowledged that some black students can make great strides in an integrated school system, but noted that others will benefit from the sympathetic intellectual environment of a majority black institution.[13] While challenges to dual systems of state institutions of higher education continued, the pace over the years has slowed substantially. In Bazemore v. Friday,[14] the Supreme Court determined that a less rigorous standard would govern desegregation cases in the context of higher education than in lower schools.[15]

The reach of the Supreme Court's decision in *Bazemore* is by no means certain. The Sixth Circuit has limited *Bazemore*'s reach to membership in

---

11. Ayers v. Lynch, No. C.A. 75-9-N (N.D. Miss. 1975).

12. Ayers v. Waller: Towards a Substantive Definition of Equal Educational Opportunity. A Position Paper of the Black Mississippian's Council on Higher Education adopted at Statewide Assembly, May 10, 1973.

13. The group hoped the case would move "beyond the superficiality of liberal 'racialism' and seek to correct the historical educational injustices of segregation while avoiding the contemporary educational injustices of integration." Id.

14. 478 U.S. 385 (1986). *Bazemore* involved the issue of whether 4-H clubs run through an extension program operated by North Carolina State University were subject to an affirmative duty of integration. The clubs had maintained racially segregated branches that remained racially identifiable even after they were merged in 1963. The district court found that formally nonracial admissions and employment policies adopted after the merger satisfied the Fourteenth Amendment.

The Supreme Court concurred with the district court's judgment, holding that the extension service complied with its constitutional obligations by discontinuing its prior discriminatory practices and adopting a neutral admissions policy. The Court focused on the choice available to potential members — who were fully free either to join or abstain from membership in these voluntary associations — in distinguishing *Bazemore* from lower school cases.

15. Id. at 408 (White, J., concurring). Justice White's concurrence was incorporated into the Court's per curiam opinion. Id. at 387. See also Ayers v. Allain, 914 F.2d 676 (5th Cir. 1990); Alabama State Teacher's Assn. v. Alabama Pub. Sch. & College Auth., 289 F. Supp. 784 (M.D. Ala. 1968) (holding that *Green* is not strictly applicable to higher education because of the greater freedom in choosing a college).

voluntary associations within a university rather than to admission to a university itself.[16] Under a consent decree governing desegregation of Tennessee's public universities, defendants were to select 75 black students yearly for entry into professional programs. Reading *Bazemore* to require only that states establish neutral admissions standards, the United States challenged this provision as an unnecessary burden on the equal protection rights of nonminority students. The Sixth Circuit held that the district court was entitled to impose affirmative remedies to remove the vestiges of prior discrimination and that the admission goals were a permissible remedy. The court reasoned that a university education, while voluntary, is a prerequisite to many careers and therefore distinct from the extracurricular 4-H clubs in *Bazemore*. A state's interest in educating its citizens, the court concluded, required the application of *Green* to university enrollment.

The Fifth Circuit, on the contrary, offered a scathing treatment of racial balance remedies in the university setting. Stating that the role of choice in college enrollment patterns makes a qualitative difference in the nature of higher education, the court held in Ayers v. Allain[17] that universities are only obligated to discontinue prior discriminatory practices and adopt good faith race-neutral policies. Limited in its judicial imagination to the remedies traditionally applied in public school cases — busing and zoning, for instance — the court found mandatory affirmative desegregation to be unavailing in the university context. In its distaste for the remedies, the court adopted a legal standard which would almost always deny any liability.

The court easily dismissed the remedies proposed by the plaintiffs, such as merging existing universities and dismantling duplicative programs. These alternatives, the court wrote, "impose a regime of imperatives and uniformity on what are in essence diverse institutions and in so doing . . . destroy the choices available to both black and white citizens of Mississippi." Comparing the proposed state-imposed integration of Mississippi universities with their prior segregation, the court added that "[u]nder *Bazemore* latter-day Merediths are not routed to what the government deems the appropriate institution, but may attend any institution they wish. Under *Green* . . . they may attend only the institutions that a federal judge has meticulously selected, grafted and pruned for them."

The court's decision faithfully reflects the mindset of the Reagan judiciary, which jealously guards the "choices" available to whites while neglecting the rights of blacks to be free from racial discrimination and isolation. It is not difficult to imagine the ease with which the Fifth Circuit's reasoning may be adopted by federal courts evaluating the constitutionality of integration plans in magnet school districts. Any limits placed on the attendance choices of white students for the sake of integration will be met with cries that students have been deprived of their rights to enter particular programs because of their race. What is forgotten, though, is that any desegregation plan necessarily eliminates choice — most importantly, the often-exercised choice of whites to attend schools which exclude blacks.

16. Geier v. Alexander, 801 F.2d 799 (6th Cir. 1986). See also United States v. Louisiana, 692 F. Supp. 642, 656 (E.D. La. 1988) (holding that the obligation to achieve nonracially identifiable colleges must be the same as for primary and secondary schools).
17. 914 F.2d 676 (5th Cir. 1990) (en banc).

The Supreme Court granted certiorari in United States v. Mabus and Ayers v. Mabus, cases involving the desegregation of Mississippi colleges.[18] The issue to be resolved by the Court is whether desegregation in the context of higher education is governed by the *Bazemore* or by the *Green* standard. The Court of Appeals had adopted the freedom of choice model endorsed by *Bazemore,* and the government, along with a group of private plaintiffs, filed an appeal.

Three states, Mississippi, Alabama, and Louisiana, have had major desegregation litigation concerning public higher education. In these cases, courts tried to reconcile the role of the historically black institutions of higher education — tenaciously defended by black students and alumni — with the constitutional mandate of desegregation. Unfortunately, the mandates of an ostensibly color-blind interpretation caused courts, all the way up to the Supreme Court, to deny requests for special treatment of black colleges, whether in increased funding or in set-asides for black students and faculty.

In these states, predominantly black colleges and white colleges existed nearly side by side and yet duplicated many facilities and course offerings. The black schools, without exception, were more limited in their curricula and resources than were their neighboring white brethren. The district courts believed that unifying the fragmented systems that perpetuated separate and unequal schools was a necessary first step in integrating the schools. Only when disparities in the system were erased by leveling the boundaries between schools would white students be attracted to black schools and integration be achieved. But the judges were confronted with a surprising revelation: Neither the white nor the black institutions sought integration.

The black plaintiffs feared the consequences of assimilation. Having only one system would ensure the political dominance of whites and therefore, as history counsels, the subordination of the needs of blacks students. Just as black teachers were driven out of the public schools in the years after *Brown,* it was expected that black administrators will find themselves without a role in a unitary system. Thus, although resource-inferior, the black universities at least ensured black citizens control over their own institutions. The absence of white students and trustees meant that the state would leave interested blacks to shape their own institutions. All that the black plaintiffs wanted was the opportunity to do it well by being given adequate funding.

Similarly, blacks in Alabama asked the court to consider a desegregation order which required the increased funding of historically black institutions of higher education in the state. In United States v. Alabama,[19] a lawsuit originally filed by the United States in 1983, the class of black intervenors alleged that Alabama continued to maintain a racially dual system of higher education and that black universities were continually under funded relative to white institutions. They contended that these practices deny the state's black citizens "an equal opportunity to preserve and develop their own traditions, values and cultural

---

18. 499 U.S. 958 (1991).
19. 828 F.2d 1532 (11th Cir. 1987), cert. denied, 487 U.S. 1210 (1988).

identities."[20] Furthermore, they argued that the unique educational role of black universities as repositories of history and culture mandates that the schools survive integration with their black character and heritage intact. Rather than countenancing segregation, the maintenance of historically black institutions on a par with white institutions would promote educational equality by erasing the stigma of inferiority associated with predominantly black educational institutions. Finally the intervenors quoted a 1984 article:

> The value of these [black] institutions for those they serve stems from participation in their inception and maintenance. . . . By contrast, the heart of the injury in state-compelled racially segregated schooling is the element of involuntariness or powerlessness in the subjection of blacks to a discriminatory school system over which they have no effective influence and that expresses a racial hierarchy.[21]

Unfortunately, the Supreme Court did not have the type of vision for which the Mississippi and Alabama groups hoped. In United States v. Fordice,[22] the Supreme Court granted *certiorari* in the Mississippi litigation in order to settle a conflict between the Fifth and Sixth Circuits. The Sixth Circuit limited *Bazemore*'s reach to membership in voluntary associations within a university rather than to admission to the university itself, holding that the district court was entitled to impose affirmative remedies to remove the vestiges of prior discrimination.[23] The Fifth Circuit, on the contrary, argued that the role of choice in college enrollment patterns makes a qualitative difference in the nature of higher education and held that universities are only obligated to discontinue prior discriminatory practices and adopt good faith race-neutral policies.[24]

The Supreme Court had to decide this issue in the context of the Mississippi system in which there were five predominantly white and three predominantly black public institutions of higher education. Not surprisingly, the three universities classified as "comprehensive," with the most funding and the best program offerings, were all predominantly white. Moreover, the one school classified as "urban," with programs limited to its urban location, was predominantly black. The remaining two white and two black schools were all classified as "regional," with more limited missions than the comprehensive universities; however, funding at all five white schools was higher than at any of the three black institutions.

Based on the factual findings of the district court, the Supreme Court found that many of the policies of the current system, even if racially neutral on their face, had a segregative effect, and that these policies were traceable to past policies

20. United States v. Alabama, Amended Complaint of Plaintiffs Knight et al. and Plaintiffs-Intervenors Sims et al., at 22 (N.D. Ala. May 13, 1988).

21. Brief of Plaintiffs-Intervenors — Appellees Knight et al., at 53 n.11, quoting Shane, School Desegregation Remedies and the Fair Governance of Schools, 132 U. Pa. L. Rev. 1041, 1084 (1984).

22. 505 U.S. 717, 729 (1992).

23. Geier v. Alexander, 801 F.2d 799 (6th Cir. 1986). See also United States v. Louisiana, 692 F. Supp. 642, 656 (E.D. La. 1988) (holding that the obligation to achieve nonracially identifiable colleges must be the same as for primary and secondary schools).

24. Ayers v. Allain, 914 F.2d 676, 687 (5th Cir. 1990) (en banc).

intended to keep black and white students in separate schools. Consequently, the Court held:

> That college attendance is by choice and not by assignment does not mean that a race-neutral admissions policy cures the constitutional violation of a dual system. . . . [T]here may still be state action that is traceable to the State's prior de jure segregation and that continues to foster segregation. . . . If policies traceable to the de jure system are still in force and have discriminatory effects, those policies too must be reformed to the extent practicable and consistent with sound educational practices.[25]

The Court identified four such aspects of the Mississippi system, though it made clear that this was by no means an exhaustive list. These four policies were: relative admission standards, program duplication, different school mission assignments, and continued operation of all eight public universities.[26] With respect to admissions standards, the Court noted that a prospective student needed a 15 on the American College Test (ACT) to gain automatic admission to any of the five white colleges (with the exception of the Mississippi University for Women, which required an 18). At the three black schools, was a score of only 13 was required, even though students scoring 13 or 14 were usually excluded from the white universities. The Court then noted, "In 1985, 72 percent of Mississippi's white high school seniors achieved an ACT composite score of 15 or better, while less than 30 percent of black high school seniors earned that score."[27] The Court had no difficulty tracing this policy to the past dual system, and, moreover, it found that the state had provided no reasonable justification for these separate standards. In fact, it noted that the exclusive use of ACT scores, without the consideration of grades, was particularly unjustified, given that the ACT's administering organization itself said that would be "foolish" and that the grade differential between blacks and whites in the state was much narrower than the ACT differential.[28]

The Supreme Court's review of dual admissions standards may end up helping many black students get into the better, predominantly white schools from which they had previously been excluded. But the Court's focus on the other three policies may, at the same time, serve to dismantle or even eliminate many public black institutions of higher education. Eliminating program duplication will mean that black students who want the more comfortable and supportive surroundings of a predominantly black college may be forced into a white-dominated institution in order to find their academic program. Even more troublesome is the prospect of forced mergers and closures of black institutions. The Supreme Court stated "as the District Court recognized, continuing to maintain all eight universities in Mississippi is wasteful and irrational."[29] The Court failed to address

---

25. United States v. Fordice, 505 U.S. 717, 729 (1992).

26. Id. at 733.

27. Id. at 733.

28. Id. at 736-737. "43.8 percent of white high school students and 30.5 percent of black students averaged at least a 3.0, and 62.2 percent of whites and 49.2 percent of blacks earned at least a 2.5 grade point average." Id. at n.10.

29. Id. at 741.

the reality that if any institution were to be closed, it would be a historically black school, and if a black and a white university were to merge, the white administration and culture would surely dominate. The Court, however, explicitly left any decisions about closure and merger to the district court and remand and added that it may not be necessary if other changes were sufficient.[30]

The Supreme Court made clear that it was not concerned with the continued support of black universities, as such. The goal was integration, no matter how much its attainment might end up disadvantaging the very people it was intended to help. With one swift stroke, in the last paragraph of the decision, the Court dashed the hopes of the groups from Mississippi and Alabama who had expected that the Court would understand what forced integration in higher education would mean for black students. The majority stated, "If we understand private petitioners to press us to order the upgrading of Jackson State, Alcorn State, and Mississippi Valley State solely that they may be publicly financed, exclusively black enclaves by private choice, we reject that request."[31] The Court left open the possibility of increased funding for these institutions on remand, but only for the purpose of promoting integration (presumably, by improving the facilities and making the predominantly black schools more attractive to white students). Once again, black students can only hope to see benefits from changes made for the sake of white students.

One black scholar, Alex Johnson, was very critical of the *Fordice* decision.[32] He concludes that "given this society's past and present, the only appropriate result in *Fordice* should have been the maintenance, at an improved funding level, of predominantly or historically black colleges, while at the same time preserving equal opportunity for African Americans to attend predominantly white educational institutions."[33] Johnson argues that, since the *Brown* decisions, the Supreme Court has based its decisions on an "idealized" integrationism that ignores the social realities of race in America and the position of African-American students. He states, that, "Only by acknowledging and accommodating the reality of the unique and separate African American culture or nomos will the process of integration ever move forward to accomplish the ideal state of integration sought by *Brown* and its progeny."[34]

The maintenance and improvement of black colleges, Johnson argues, are important for several reasons. First, they provide a more comfortable and supportive environment for students who have lived and been educated in segregated and disadvantaged environments. Ironically, programs that courts may consider as inferior or too remedial may actually be necessary transitional steps for students from poor educational backgrounds. Besides these programs, black colleges offer the support of being around others from a similar background, what Johnson calls

---

30. Id. at 742.
31. Id. at 743.
32. Alex M. Johnson, Jr., Bid Whist, Tonk, and United States v. Fordice: Why Integrationism Fails African-Americans Again, 81 Cal. L. Rev. 1401 (1993).
33. Id. at 1403.
34. Id. at 1403.

the African American nomos, and an administration that is a part of and appreciates that culture. As Johnson states:

> Predominantly or historically black colleges are in a unique position to respect and acknowledge the differential treatment that African-American students have received in secondary and elementary education. These colleges are in a unique position to provide the nurturing environment in which these same students can ameliorate the effects of their past educational disadvantages. . . . In this sense, predominantly or historically black colleges can be regarded as equalizing entitlements accorded African-American students on the basis of their history, their present position in society, and their anticipated future position in society.[35]

Most of all, Johnson stresses that for African American students integration must be voluntary and on their own terms. The alternative is to force these students to attend white-dominated institutions for which they are ill-equipped both culturally and educationally. The greatest tragedy is that while these students are being told by society that they have been given an equal opportunity and that their success or failure is completely up to them, in reality, they are being set up to fail. The Court's idealized vision of integrationism thus creates a new badge of inferiority for African American students. Johnson describes the resulting victimization cycle:

> First, as a result of the inferior education they receive in segregated primary and secondary schools, many African-American students are ill-prepared to compete academically with whites in an "integrated" environment. When these African-American students are forced to compete with white students for places or resources in the integrated environment mandated by the Court in *Fordice,* they find themselves at a competitive disadvantage. The students who are the victims of the initial discriminatory acts that led the Court to order integration are victimized again. The Court's failure to order equalization of funding as the remedy for the State's actions — actions which placed them at a competitive disadvantage in the first place — forces them to compete on what, ostensibly, is now a "level playing field," but which in reality is something quite different.[36]

Fortunately, *Fordice* has not been the unmitigated disaster that Johnson feared. After the case was remanded and the parties were still not able to settle, the district court ordered a remedy that did not include the closure or merger of any of the historically black institutions.[37] On appeal, the Fifth Circuit did not disturb that result. The Fifth Circuit also upheld the lower court's implementation of new, universal admissions standards for the eight universities. While these new standards will make it easier for black students to attend the historically white institutions, they will likely reduce the total number of black students accepted into the system through regular admission.[38] In addition, new programs were added to two

35. Id. at 1465 (footnotes omitted).
36. Id. at 1433.
37. Ayers v. Fordice, 879 F. Supp. 1419 (N.D. Miss. 1995) (*Ayers II*).
38. Ayers v. Fordice, 111 F.3d 1183 n.23 (5th Cir. 1997), citing *Ayers II*, 879 F. Supp. at 1479. Both the district and appellate courts felt that the yet to be established "spring screening and summer remedial" program would compensate for this reduction in regular admissions. The program screens

of the black universities, but unequal levels of funding were held to be justified by the different sizes of the schools. Several issues, however, were left for reevaluation on remand: clarification on the issue of the proposed mergers; elimination of duplicate programs in the event no mergers took place; and determination of whether unjustified inequality in equipment exists between the black and white universities. Similar outcomes have followed litigation in Alabama and Louisiana.[39]

These lower court decisions, however, are no reason to forget Professor Johnson's concerns. *Fordice* leaves lower courts with a great deal of discretion, more than enough to completely undermine public black universities. That no court has yet struck the death blow for these institutions provides little long-term security. Indeed, the lower courts have paid more than lip-service to the Supreme Court's idealized integrationism when they maintain that the goal is not to support the historically black universities but to achieve a color-blind society.

§3.14   Racism Hypo: Excluded White Applicants v. Howard University School of Dentistry

Howard University is a predominantly black, federally funded university located in Washington, D.C., that was established shortly after the Civil War to educate the freedmen in the arts, sciences, and the professions. It has gained a national reputation for its performance over the decades and the achievements of its graduates. The Howard School of Dentistry has not been noted for its research capabilities, but it has long held a deserved reputation as producing dentists who are highly skilled at the technical aspects of their profession. Graduates of the school are usually able to make bridges, dentures, and other dental appliances with greater skill and accuracy than can the laboratories where most dentists have such appliances made.

While the School of Dentistry recognizes its obligation to train black dentists, a responsibility which it carried almost alone during the pre-*Brown* years when most dental schools in the country would not accept blacks or would accept only token numbers of them, the enrollment during the 1960s and 1970s was often predominantly white. This change in enrollment pattern was due in part to the greater willingness of predominantly white schools to accept black applicants, but was mainly a result of the great increase in applicants for professional schools, and the willingness of many white applicants to obtain their educations at a black school when they were not accepted at predominantly white schools.

During the last decade or more, Howard's School of Dentistry has received so many white applicants, and the paper credentials submitted by some of these

students in the spring who did not gain regular admission for a summer program designed to prepare them socially and academically for undergraduate education. Those who successfully complete the program are granted admission. The district court will monitor the success of the program. Id. at 1200-1201.

39. 900 F. Supp. 272 & 9 F.3d 1159.

applicants have been so high, that but for a unique admissions process, the School of Dentistry would be virtually all-white.

A few years ago, the school's faculty developed and adopted a new "Potential for Effective Practice" test (PEP), a professional aptitude test that measures with amazing accuracy technical performance in dental school and the student's potential for providing quality dental care after admission to practice. Most black dentists serve patient loads that are predominantly black, and the PEP is geared for measuring effective performance in black community practices. Those who prepared the test designed questions that measure attitudes, outlooks, expectations, and responses, with the result that those who have grown to maturity as minorities in the society usually score far higher than those who have lived their lives as members of the majority group. The qualities measured by the test, however, translate into character traits of perseverance, acceptance, commitment, and skills application that in fact are found in those black practitioners who are successful in practice.

Experience with the PEP test reveals that blacks and other minorities score an average of 200 points above most but not all white applicants. Careful studies have been made, but the initial findings remain unchanged. Experts surmise that the varied array of survival skills that enable minority students to reach professional school are also the characteristics that are essential to success in practice. As it turns out, the gap between scores of blacks and whites on the PEP test is the exact reverse of that evidenced in the traditional standardized test, a test, like most standardized tests, deemed valid.

The Howard Dental School has been utilizing the PEP as a critical factor in its admissions process for two years. During that time, the racial characteristic of its enrollment has changed dramatically, with the result that 90 percent of its entering students are blacks, Latinos, and American Indians, and only 10 percent are white. This litigation was initiated in federal court by a group of white applicants who were denied admission based on their PEP test scores. They assert that by traditional standards of undergraduates' grades and scores on nationally recognized dental aptitude tests, they were more qualified than virtually all of the black students admitted to the school.

The plaintiffs charge that Howard's reliance on the PEP test violates their rights under the Fourteenth Amendment and the Civil Rights Acts of 1866 and 1964. They seek an injunction against the continued use of the PEP test and wish to have their applications judged on the standards in use at Howard prior to the adoption of the PEP test. The plaintiffs contend that they are no less entitled to injunctive relief if, as they concede, Howard University adopted the PEP test in good faith, and without any invidious intent to discriminate against applicants on the basis of race and color. They concede further that a shortage of black and other minority dentists does exist, that this shortage is due at least in part to societal discrimination, but they deny that the remedy adopted by university officials is appropriate, necessary, or in conformance with standards set by the Supreme Court in *Bakke, Grutter, Gratz,* and the *Seattle-Louisville* school decisions. See the discussion in §1.2 Color-Blind Constitutionalism: A Rediscovered Rationale.

The case has been set for hearing on plaintiffs' motion for preliminary injunction on facts stipulated above.

Law firm A will represent the excluded white applicants.

Law firm B will represent Howard University.

Chapter 4

Fair Employment Laws and Their Limits

§4.1 EMPLOYMENT DISCRIMINATION AND ITS IMPACT ON THE ECONOMIC STATUS OF BLACKS

§4.1.1 The Current Economic Status of Blacks

Throughout much of the 1990s, the problem of the persistent and widening racial gap in unemployment was eclipsed, first, by the nation's obsession with and opposition to affirmative action and, later, by the political diversion of welfare reform. Notwithstanding that minuscule numbers of blacks benefited from either affirmative action or governmental welfare policies, civil rights advocates during the last decade were challenged by the need to confront the pervasive perception that blacks were doing well by reaping unjust deserts. Thus, proponents of black rights who advocated addressing the pressing need for more job opportunities for minority workers were too often met with the discordant refrains that either the vast majority of black people lacked skill and initiative and possessed no "personal responsibility" or that far too many unqualified blacks had attained status and success through special pleading and programs operating at the expense of more qualified white counterparts.

This debate placed both proponents and opponents of expanded economic opportunity for blacks squarely on the horns of a dilemma. Neither camp was willing to disavow black progress altogether. For proponents to do so would be tantamount to conceding the uselessness of the very policies they had so vigorously defended. Self-proclaimed fair-minded opponents, on the other hand, dreaded being characterized as callous or, worst yet, racist. But to an even greater degree, opponents realized that ignoring black progress undercut their own emphasis on the values of hard work and personal responsibility. Thus, in the 1990s, and through the next decade, the existence of a growing black middle class filled the vacuum and took center stage. For the civil rights advocate, the black middle class represented continuing promise for the future. For those unconvinced of the lingering effects of employment discrimination, past and present, the black middle class represented the absolute success, and thus obsolete utility, of antidiscrimination and remedial governmental policies.

But today, as in previous decades, for blacks as a whole, their economic status reflects a continuing pattern of economic disadvantage due to discrimination.

Literary genius Richard Wright wrote more than 50 years ago about the recurrent myth that the salvation of blacks lies with its emerging middle class, and his comments remain equally applicable today:

> [T]hose few Negroes who have lifted themselves, through personal strength, talent, or luck, above the lives of their fellow-blacks — like single fishes that leap and flash for a split second above the surface of the sea — are but fleeting exceptions to that vast, tragic school that swims below in the depths, against the current, silently and heavily, struggling against the waves and vicissitudes that spell a common fate.[1]

Wright's observations are supported by David H. Swinton, Dean of the Business School at Jackson State University and Professor of Economics, whose 1991 study rebutted the general view of black progress:

> Both in absolute terms and in comparison to white Americans, blacks have high unemployment rates, low rates of employment, inferior occupational distributions, and low wages and earnings. Blacks have low incomes and high poverty rates. They own little wealth and small amounts of business property. . . . [And] no significant progress is being made to improve the status of blacks and to close the gaps. Thus, the disparities in all the above-mentioned measures of economic status have persisted at roughly the same level for the last two decades, and many indicators of inequality have even drifted upwards during this period.[2]

The much-heralded emergence of the black middle class is, in fact, a myth: the *only* group of blacks to even approach what might be termed "progress" in an income sense climbed *out* of the middle class and into the more than $50,000 a year category, while unprecedented numbers of blacks fell out of the middle class and into deep poverty.[3] Indeed, in the late nineties, "[a]lthough the number of blacks living in poverty is at an all-time low, more than twice as many African Americans still live below the poverty line than whites do — 28 percent versus 11 percent."[4]

The economic situation of African Americans has been exasperated by the recession of the early twenty-first century. The progress shown by the African American community in the 1990s was mostly a result of the general rosy picture

§4.1 1. Twelve Million Black Voices: Text by Richard Wright, Photo direction by Edwin Rosskam (1941), preface, p. xix.

2. David H. Swinton, The Economic Status of African Americans: "Permanent" Poverty and Inequality in The State of Black America 1991, at 25 (Janet Dewart ed., 1991).

3. Id. at 37. See, e.g., Cecelia Conrad & Malinda Lindquist, The Economic Status of African Americans: A Year-End Review, in FOCUS, The Monthly Magazine of the Joint Center for Political and Economic Studies, Dec. 1997 (noting that "within the African American community . . . the gap between the haves and have-nots is likely to grow"). From 1967 to 1996, the percentage of blacks earning over $50,000 climbed from 1.7 percent to 7.4 percent. Id. But, as implied by the title and opening line of Ellis Cose's important study, The Rage of a Privileged Class: Why Are Middle-Class Blacks Angry? Why Should America Care? (1993), far from reveling in their economic gain, middle class blacks are "in excruciating pain" over "the broken covenant, of the pact ensuring that if you work hard, get a good education, and play by the rules, you will be allowed to advance and achieve to the limits of your ability." Id. at 1.

4. Isabelle DePommereau, Why Black Financial Progress Is Running into Speed Bumps, *Christian Science Monitor*, Feb. 4, 1998, at 5.

of the American economy during that decade — across the board, incomes rose, unemployment dropped, and poverty decreased. The new millennium began with a pending recession that was hastened by the traumatic events of September 11. African Americans have experienced the resulting economic downturn particularly hard in comparison to other racial groups.[5] Whatever gains African Americans made in the economic boom of the 1990s have been eroded in the tough economy of the early 2000s.

In comparison to the 1990s, when the median income of black families rose from $27,311 (in 1991) to $34,616 (in 2000), in 2001 the black community saw a 2.9 percent decline in median income to $33,598. Figures for that same year indicate that the median income declined among all families in America generally but at a much less steep rate of 1.4 percent and only by 0.8 percent among non-Hispanic whites.[6] More recent Census Bureau figures report that median income in the black community fell from $29,939 (in 2001) to $29,026 (in 2002), an additional 3 percent decline. Again, the median income among all American families declined at a much less steep rate — 1.1 percent — than that of black families and particularly in comparison to the median income decline of non-Hispanic white families — 0.3 percent.[7]

Poverty rates for black families fell to a historic low of 19.3 percent in 2000. However, between 2000 and 2001, the black family poverty rate rose to 20.7 percent[8] and to 22.7 percent by the end of 2001 — outpacing rates for all other racial groups.[9] Moreover, poverty rates for all African American families with children rose 5.1 percent, from 25.3 to 26.6 percent, and rose 29.9 percent among married African American couples with children, from 6.7 to 8.7 percent.[10] Recent Census Bureau figures show that poverty rates continued to rise in 2002 with blacks again suffering the worst increases of poverty among all racial groups — rising to 24.1 percent in comparison to the 8 percent of non-Hispanic whites in poverty.[11]

Part of the reason for the racial economic disparities can be attributed to the disparities in the unemployment levels between the racial groups. Unemployment rose among black workers from 7.5 percent in December 2000 to 10.2 percent a year later. In contrast, while the unemployment rate also rose among white workers, it rose from 3.5 percent in December 2000 to 5.2 percent a year later.[12] In good times or in bad, the African American unemployment rate is consistently

5. Roderick Harrison, Census Shows Despite a Decade of Economic Gains, Race and Gender Gaps Persist, The Crisis, July 1, 2003. Data is based on The Black Population in the United States issued by the Census Bureau, Apr. 2002; Lynette Clemetson, More Americans in Poverty in 2002, Census Study Says, N.Y. Times, Sept. 27, 2003, at A1. Data is based on the Census Bureau's annual Current Population Survey, Sept. 2003.

6. Harrison, supra note 5.

7. Clemetson, supra note 5.

8. Harrison, supra note 5.

9. Clemetson, supra note 5, at A10.

10. Harrison, supra note 5.

11. Clemetson, supra note 5, at A10.

12. IMDiversity, Black Leaders Decry Higher Jobless Rate, Wall St. J. Executive Career Site, Jan. 23, 2002.

approximately double that of whites.[13] "The cause of higher unemployment rates includes less work experience and seniority, lower education and other skill levels, persistent discrimination and more difficulty gaining employment through informal networks and in growing suburban areas. All together, this means that blacks remain 'last in, first out' in any downturn."[14]

The unemployment problem is even worse for black teenagers. In the third quarter of 2006, the unemployment rate for teenagers between the ages of 16 and 19 was 13 percent for white teens and 32.7 percent for black teens.[15] The irony of the situation is that "[t]he persistent high level of joblessness among black youth not only denies these young people work experience that is needed to enhance their employment opportunities as adults, but it also deprives their families of vital income support." The high unemployment rate among black teenagers has led to increased apathy, disillusionment, and loss of confidence.[16]

The incomes of the lowest two-thirds of black families have deteriorated substantially, so much so that this backslide has more than offset proportional gains at the highest levels of income. And even at the upper end, where some progress may have been made, had parity with whites existed, there would have been many more black families in the $50,000 plus bracket.[17] Moreover, it has become increasingly clear that, as one author summarizes, "Even among blacks and whites of comparable income, occupational, and educational attainments, racial differences in wealth holding are astounding and enduring."[18] In fact, whites at the poverty level possess financial assets that almost equal those of blacks at the highest income levels.[19] Within the black community, according to urban sociologist and economist William Julius Wilson, 50 percent of the total income is earned by the richest fifth of African Americans, while 40 percent of all black children live in poverty.[20] Swinton notes discouragingly:

> Poorer blacks continue to be relatively poorer in comparison to poorer whites. . . . The
> most important conclusion, however, is that the unequal status of blacks at all positions

13. See, e.g., Unemployment Rate Dips for Blacks, NPR News and Notes, Feb. 8, 2007, transcript available at http://www.npr.org/templates/story/story.php?storyId=7272202; Julianne Malveaux, The Real Deal on Black Unemployment, Black Issues in Higher Education, Aug. 12, 2004; T. Shawn Taylor, Job Losses Hit Blacks Hard, Chi. Trib., Aug. 17, 2003.

14. Taylor, supra note 13, quoting Harry J. Holzer, Professor of Public Policy at Georgetown University.

15. United States Bureau of Labor Statistics, Unemployment Rates By Age, Sex, Race, and Hispanic or Latino Ethnicity, available at http://www.bls.gov/web/cpseed16.pdf.

16. Marjorie Hunter, Recession Kills Black Teen-Ager Hopes, N.Y. Times, May 19, 1975, at 1, col. 7; see also Carl Rowan, Offer Jobs, Not Prisons for Youths, Chi. Sun-Times, May 12, 1993, at 33.

17. Herbert Hill, The Economic Status of Black Families in the State of Black Americ 1971, at 28-29 (James Williams ed., 1979).

18. Taunya Banks, Book Review: "Nondiscriminatory" Perpetuation of Racial Subordination, 76 B.U. L. Rev. 669, 673 (1996) (reviewing Melvin L. Oliver & Thomas M. Shapiro, Black Wealth/White Wealth (Routledge, N.Y., 1995)).

19. Melvin L. Oliver & Thomas M. Shapiro, Black Wealth/White Wealth 101 (paperback ed., 1997). Oliver and Shapiro conclude that "Blacks and whites with equal incomes possess very unequal shares of wealth." Id.

20. Salim Muwakkil, The Hardest Sell in the Black Community, Chi. Trib., July 6, 1998, at 11-21. Swinton, supra note 2, at 40.

of the black income distribution appears to be a permanent feature of the American economy.[21]

In short, the overall record is not advancement, but retrogression, with little hope of significant improvement. Past and present discrimination is the key to the division between the economic advance for whites and economic stagnation for blacks.

§4.1.2 The Insidious Causes and Devastating Impact of Employment Discrimination

That the economic disadvantage of blacks is directly attributable to racial discrimination in employment and other critical areas should be obvious. Since the days of slavery, most blacks in this country have been second class workers, limited, for the most part, to the most unskilled, unattractive, and poorly paid occupations. Blacks traditionally have been severely underrepresented among the ranks of professionals, managers, sales workers, craftsmen, and foremen.[22] In contrast, blacks have been heavily concentrated in unskilled positions, such as factory workers and laborers. African Americans tend to be the last hired in a booming economy, and the first to lose their jobs in economic downturns.[23] Bernard Anderson, a professor at the Wharton School of the University of Pennsylvania, has compared the relationship between blacks and the United States Economy as that of a caboose to a train — making gains when the train as a whole speeds up, but never catching up to the engine.[24] Moreover, recent changes in the economy, including down-sizing, out-sourcing, and consolidations and mergers are disproportionately affecting African Americans, further widening the racial gap in employment, income, and well-being.

A recent Northwestern University sociology experiment found that the disadvantage of being a young black male job applicant was "equivalent to forcing a white man to carry an 18-month prison record."[25] In the controlled experiment involving 350 different employers, students posing as job applicants applied to low-wage, entry-level positions throughout the Milwaukee area. Not surprisingly, white male applicants without a crime record fared best while black male applicants with a crime record fared the worst. But the most surprising outcome was that

---

21. Swinton, supra note 2, at 40.

22. Sally Tidwell, Economic Costs of American Racism, in The State of Black America 1991, at 228 (Janet Dewart ed., 1991) ("Not only are African Americans much more likely than whites to be unemployed, but they are also much more likely to be employed in lower status, lower paying occupations, and are correspondingly less likely to hold the more prestigious and rewarding positions in the occupational structures. Racism and discrimination in economic life continue to cost African Americans dearly. . . .")

23. See Stephanie Armour, Job Hunt Gets Harder for African Americans, USA Today, Dec. 9, 2002, at B1.

24. NPR News & Notes, Unemployment Rate Dips for Blacks, Feb. 8, 2007, transcript available at http://www.npr.org/templates/story/story.php?storyId=7272202.

25. David Wessel, Racial Discrimination Is Still at Work, Wall St. J., Sept. 4, 2003, at A2. See also DeWayne Wickham, Race Seems to Trump Schooling, USA Today, Sept. 9, 2003, at A13.

white ex-cons were called back 17 percent of the time while black crime-free applicants were called back just 14 percent of the time. Additionally, while acknowledging a criminal background cut white applicant chances by half, acknowledging a criminal background cut a black applicant's chances by two-thirds. This latter result is particularly disturbing because of the increasing number of black males projected to carry criminal backgrounds in the coming generation.[26] "Employers don't spend a lot of time screening applicants. They want a quick signal whether the applicant seems suitable. Stereotypes among young black men remain so prevalent and so strong that race continues to serve as a major signal of characteristics of which employers are wary."[27]

In another experiment conducted by economists from MIT and the University of Chicago, researchers responded to help-wanted ads with resumes that were either likely to be identified by employers as having commonly African American names or more commonly identified white names. They found that resumes with common white-sounding names such as "Emily Walsh" were 50 percent more likely to receive callbacks than resumes with black-sounding names such as "Lakeisha Washington." Essentially, they concluded, putting a white-sounding name on the resume "is worth as much as an extra eight years of work experience."[28] When researchers tweaked the resumes to make them better, by adding more experience or additional skills for instance, the slightly better resumes yielded 30 percent more callbacks for resumes with white-sounding names after the enhancements. However, when researchers enhanced the resumes of black applicants, the better resumes only yielded 9 percent more callbacks.[29]

These studies illustrate why racial discrimination remains the major factor in explaining the economic disadvantage of blacks today. The Joint Center for Economic and Political Studies found that "[e]ven after controlling for differences in skill, the persistence of wage disparities underscores the role of discrimination."[30]

Discrimination against black workers may appear in many contexts. Most obviously, an employer may decide to fire or simply not to hire a black worker who is just as productive as a white worker who holds the position. Or an employer may choose to promote a white worker rather than to promote an equally qualified black worker to a higher position with an increased wage and status. Finally, employers may pay black workers less than white workers of similar productivity within the same occupation.[31]

---

26. Wessel, supra note 25. Nearly 17 percent of black men have spent time in jail. Bureau of Justice Statistics estimate that 30 percent of African American boys turning 12 this year will have a criminal record in their lifetimes.

27. Wessel, supra note 25.

28. Id.

29. Id.

30. Cecilia Conrad & Malinda Lindquist, Prosperity and Inequality on the Rise, in FOCUS, The Monthly Magazine of the Joint Center for Political and Economic Studies, May 1998. See also Robert W. Fairlie & William A. Sundstrom, The Emergence, Persistence, and Recent Widening of the Racial Unemployment Gap, 52 Ind. & Lab. Rel. Rev. 252, 268 (1999) (noting the likely role of biased hiring & layoff decisions as well as weakened enforcement of antidiscrimination laws in the racial disparity in unemployment).

31. See William Julius Wilson, When Work Disappears: The World of the New Urban Poor 111-146 (1997).

Job discrimination often combines with other forms of racial discrimination, such as residential segregation, to trap blacks in a cycle of economic disadvantage. Thus, in recent years blacks have been trapped by housing discrimination, forcing them to live in central city ghettos.[32] As most new employment opportunities have been located in the suburbs rather than in the central city, blacks are at a severe disadvantage in the job market.[33] For many blacks living in inner-city ghettos, the *search* for suburban employment itself often presents practical transportation barriers.[34] Inner-city transportation systems rarely provide reliable ingress and egress between the center city and the suburbs. Thus, for inner-city residents who are unlikely to own automobiles, access to employment opportunities, even those for which they qualify, is severely restricted. Moreover, because of the concomitant social decay in jobless environments, one resident in a study lamented "Taxis don't want to come over here to get you and bring you back either."[35] At least one suburban employer noted his concern over frequent absenteeism for the inner-city employee unable to get to work.[36] One commentator summarized the plight of inner-city blacks seeking jobs:

> [E]mployers make assumptions about the inner-city black workers *in general* and reach decisions based on those assumptions before they have had a chance to review systematically the qualifications of an individual applicant. The net effect is that many black inner-city applicants are never given the chance to prove their qualifications on an individual level because they are systematically screened out by the selective recruitment process. Statistical discrimination, although representing elements of class bias against poor workers in the inner city, is clearly a matter of race. The

32. Terry Williams & William Kornblum, A Portrait of Youth: Coming of Age in Harlem Public Housing in The State of Black America 1991, at 188-193 (Janet Dewart ed., 1991). Modern trends replicate past fallout. "Housing segregation in the United States developed slowly and deliberately. In fact, prior to 1900, African Americans were scattered widely throughout white neighborhoods. . . . However, as African Americans moved north into industrial communities after World War I and II, the picture of the urban ghetto began to develop." Marc Seitles, Comment: The Perpetuation of Residential Racial Segregation in America: Historical Discrimination, Modern Forms of Exclusion, and Inclusionary Remedies, 14 J. Land Use & Envtl. Law 89, 91 (1998). Cf. Phyliss Craig-Taylor, To Be Free: Liberty, Citizenship, Property and Race, 14 Harv. BlackLetter L.J. 45 (1998) (tracing roots of housing and property discrimination against blacks). The intra-metropolitan residential pattern of blacks is a direct result of discrimination and the segregation of blacks into central city ghettos; it affects their employment opportunities and is the principal cause of most urban problems.

33. Wilson, supra note 31, at 54. In When Work Disappears, Wilson writes, "[t]he growing suburbanization of jobs has aggravated the employment woes of poor inner-city workers. Most ghetto residents cannot afford an automobile and therefore have to rely on public transit systems that make the connection between inner-city neighborhoods and suburban job locations difficult and time-consuming." Id. Some employers, concerned with tardiness or absenteeism, are reluctant to hire them based upon this reality alone, while others advance a host of stereotypes, including theft, fear of lawsuits, bad work ethic, and so on, to account for their reluctance to hire inner-city blacks. Id. at 111-146. Even black entrepreneurs have begun to locate their businesses outside the inner city. See Scott Cummings, African American Entrepreneurship in the Suburbs: Protected Markets and Enclave Business Development, 65 J. Am. Planning Assoc., Jan. 1, 1999, at 50 encouraging black businessmen to shun business activity within the ethnic enclave.

34. William Julius Wilson, When Work Disappears: The World of the New Urban Poor 41 (1996).

35. See id. at 11.

36. See id. at 114.

selective recruitment patterns effectively screen out far more black workers from the inner city than Hispanic or white workers from the same type backgrounds. But race is also a factor, even in those decisions to deny employment to inner-city black workers on the basis of objective and thorough evaluation of their qualifications. The hard and soft skills among inner-city blacks that do not match the current needs of the labor market are products of racially segregated communities, communities that have historically featured widespread social constraints and restricted opportunities.[37]

Caught in the vise-like grip of job discrimination and housing discrimination, the urban black faces a grim situation with little hope for escape.

Other more insidious causes of employer discrimination stem from the decline in unionization and the outsourcing of middle-income jobs.[38] The disappearance of these jobs, in combination with the fact that blacks tend to be the first fired from positions, has pushed more and more blacks into low-income jobs.[39] Even public-sector jobs that cannot be outsourced to other countries are increasingly outsourced to private contractors, which are not necessarily subject to the same guidelines on equal opportunities employment as federal agencies.[40]

Immigration is another complex issue in black unemployment. The success stories of numerous immigrant groups has prompted the question of why African Americans have not been able to achieve similar success. However, immigration itself is part of the answer to that question. Historically, employers have shown a preference for immigrant workers over African Americans. During the industrial revolution, the North's need for cheap labor was satisfied by the influx of 25 million European immigrants, while blacks — through employer preferences, racist union practices, and nepotism, were categorically excluded from the industrial sector save for a few menial, dangerous jobs that immigrants spurned.[41] When immigration was cut off by the First World War, a massive migration of blacks to cities in the North and West resulted in the most significant economic advance for blacks since the abolition of slavery.[42]

History has continued to repeat itself with the influx of immigrants over the past few decades. Employers seeking workers that are deemed better, more willing workers than blacks and, some might feel, easier to exploit, choose immigrant workers over United States workers, particularly African Americans. Vulnerable immigrant workers have fewer legal rights and are more susceptible to exploitation because they face deportation. Immigrant workers working legally in the United States contend with an employer's threats to family members or friends who may be in the country illegally. Those holding temporary work visas are prohibited from working for any employer but the one that sponsored the visa, giving employers discretion over the deportation of the worker. Moreover, regardless of their legal

37. Wilson, supra note 34, at 136-137.

38. See id.; see NPR News & Notes, Many Black Workers Stuck in Dead End Jobs, Sept. 4, 2007, transcript available at http://www.npr.org/templates/story/story.php?storyId=14156279.

39. Id. See also Kimbriell Kelly, 36 Chi. Rep. 8 (2007).

40. Amelia Gruber, Civil Rights Group Joins Unions in Fight Against Job Competitions, Jan. 20, 2004, at www.govexec.com/dailyfed/0104/012004a1.htm.

41. Stephen Steinberg, Immigration, African Americans, and Race Discourse, 15 New Labour Forum 48 (2006).

42. See id.

status, immigrant workers often lack the cultural capital to understand and enforce their rights. They also lack the social benefits, such as welfare and unemployment benefits, that would allow them to seek another job if their employer violates their rights.[43]

These vulnerabilities, while not accurate in every circumstance, contribute to employer perceptions of immigrant workers as easier to exploit.[44] By contrast, African Americans are perceived as lazy and unreliable, and their assertions for increased pay or other improvements are perceived as "whining," "attitude," and poor work ethics.[45]

Indeed, these attitudes have been adopted by studies that purport to demonstrate that immigration does not exacerbate African-American unemployment, and rather place blame on African-American culture for creating workers that are less attractive to employers. In a review of such studies, Stephen Steinberg notes that experts have explained the fact that immigrants have higher employment rates than blacks, not on racism, but on "network hiring" and "social capital, . . . the supposition that immigrants have the requisite abilities and work habits that blacks lack."[46] Steinberg argues that this reasoning ignores the inherent racist reasoning behind these justifications in order to place blame on African Americans:

> Network hiring is a device that employers use to prevent blacks from even getting their foot in the door. This is racism, plain and simple! It is a working-class variant of "the old-boy network" that hiring is a mechanism of discrimination, and indeed one that employers use precisely because it insulates them from allegations of racism since they are not directly implicated in the recruitment of workers.
>
> The concept of "social capital" presumes that immigrants have traits that blacks lack. When employers use these prejudgments as the basis of hiring decisions, they are engaged in acts of prejudice. . . . [Social capital is used as] a smoke screen for shifting the blame for discrimination from employers who actually make the hiring decisions to hapless blacks who are denied employment. This illogical argument is advanced even though no evidence is proffered to validate the supposition that there are not black workers in abundance who have precisely the traits that are ascribed to immigrants and who could be readily hired, but for the prejudgments of employers.[47]

As a result, employment decisions are made based on racist attitudes and the eagerness to exploit the most vulnerable workers. "[E]mployer preferences for the most exploitable workers place all low-wage workers in a difficult position that is mediated by legal status, social institutions, and stereotypes."[48]

Faced with a shrinking job market confined to low-wage jobs, African Americans face few options. One is to accept low-paying, often unregulated work, competing in a race to the bottom with immigrant labor to be the group most easily exploited by employers. This problem is exacerbated by welfare reform policies

---

43. Rachel Bloomekatz, Rethinking Immigration Status Discrimination and Exploitation in the Low-Wage Workplace, 54 U.C.L.A. L. Rev. 1963, 1973-1977 (2007).

44. See id. at 1979-1980.

45. See id. at 1980; Steinberg, supra note 41.

46. See Steinberg, supra note 41.

47. Id.

48. Bloomekatz, supra note 43, at 1982-1983.

such as abrupt or arbitrary benefit cutoffs, or "work first" policies that require beneficiaries to take the first job offered, despite the limited number and quality of jobs available to them.[49] Similarly, those coming out of prison face the stigma of ex-offender status, in addition to being legally barred from certain jobs.[50]

These limited options have far-reaching implications on the lives of African Americans. A recent survey by the National Employment Law Project compared the concerns of unemployed African Americans with those of unemployed whites. While 46 percent of unemployed whites were very concerned that they would be forced to take a job that paid less than their previous job, 63 percent of African Americans shared this fear.[51] Eighty percent of unemployed African Americans reported having had trouble paying bills for electricity or gas, phone, rent or mortgage, health care, auto loans, or other loans, compared with 60 percent of unemployed whites.[52] As a result, 33 percent of unemployed African Americans reported having had to move or move in with friends or relatives, compared with 24 percent of unemployed whites. While African Americans and whites were equally likely to report increased stress on their families due to unemployment, this stress is more likely to translate into material difficulties for African Americans. For example, 25 percent of African Americans were forced to cut child or elder care from their budgets, compared with 6 percent of whites; 67 percent of African Americans reported having to cut spending on food, compared with 52 percent of whites; 61 percent of African Americans reported having to cut spending on kids, compared with 41 percent of whites, and 29 percent of African Americans were forced to interrupt their education, compared to 18 percent of whites.[53]

Perhaps the most disturbing result of these limited employment options is the crisis in health care available to African Americans. The NELP study found that 70 percent of unemployed African Americans were concerned that they would have to take a job that did not provide health insurance, compared to 56 percent of unemployed whites.[54] Indeed, between 2000 and 2003, African Americans experienced a 3.7 percentage point decline in employer-sponsored health care coverage.[55] The number of uninsured African Americans increased by over 14 percent between 2000 and 2004, with the majority of uninsured individuals belonging to working families.[56] Because African Americans are more likely to work in nonstandard job environments, such as temporary agencies or independent contracting, they are less likely to receive insurance coverage through their employers.[57]

---

49. See Siobhán McGrath & Nina Martin, Unregulated Work, Dollars & Sense 15, 18 (Sept./Oct. 2005), available at http://www.brennancenter.org/dynamic/subpages/download_file_8410.pdf.
50. See id.
51. National Employment Law Project, Unemployed in America: A Look at Unemployed African Americans, Survey Among 413 Unemployed Adults Conducted April 17-28, 2003.
52. See id.
53. See id.
54. See id.
55. See Families USA, Improving Health Coverage and Access for African Americans, Minority Health Initiatives 1 (Jan. 2006), available at http://www.familiesusa.org/assets/pdfs/minority-health-tool-kit/AfrAm-fact-sheet.pdf.
56. See id.
57. See id. at 3.

Moreover, African Americans are less likely to have steady employment, which is often a prerequisite to health coverage.[58]

The diminishing health care coverage has resulted in diminishing access to health care among African Americans and, not surprisingly, health disparities between African Americans and whites. Among African Americans, 34 percent report having no regular doctor, compared to 24 percent of whites.[59] African Americans are more likely to use the emergency room for ailments such as asthma, and their mortality rate from the disease is three times higher than it is for whites.[60] Death rates for heart disease among Africans Americans are nearly twice as high as the rates for whites, yet African Americans are less likely to receive bypass surgery than whites.[61]

It is not easy to overstate the adverse effect on an individual or a group of long-term unemployment. In a society where both well-being and worth are judged by what one has and what one does, the denial of the opportunity to work inevitably results in the loss of motivation to work and lays the basis for these predictable syndromes: individual despair, family dissolution, aberrant behavior, and welfare dependency; all of which in the public mind boomerang back to blacks as characteristics that manifest their inferiority, inability, or at least unreadiness, for opportunities that whites takes for granted.[62]

Professor William Julius Wilson portrays a devastating picture of the nation's urban centers. In most urban ghettos, jobs have virtually disappeared, leaving residents either jobless or in search of employment in neighboring suburbs.[63] The jobless are usually low-skilled and uneducated men. Without jobs to support their families, inner-city men often spiral into cycles of crime, domestic violence, alcoholism, and despair.

If it is appropriate to consider long-term unemployment a serious disease, it may prove useful, in considering the sections which follow, to imagine that all upper-middle-class white youths from ages 16 to 19 were suddenly struck down with a disease that left them with characteristics similar to those so observable in most of the country's black ghettos: apathy, a lack of marketable skills, a poor outlook on life, a tendency to sublimate life's troubles in alcohol and drugs, or a tendency to resolve them with criminal behavior. If such a disaster occurred, is it possible to imagine an effort so large or so expensive that this country would not wish to undertake it immediately if it promised to return the afflicted white youth to their former status of health and well-being. However, if one then considers the reasons why such an effort *would* be willingly mounted to help whites, but is not

---

58. See id.
59. See id. at 1.
60. See id. at 2.
61. See id.
62. See Wilson, supra note 34, at 73. ("[W]ork is not simply a means to make a living and support one's family. It also constitutes a framework for daily behavior and patterns of interaction because it imposes disciplines and regularities. Thus, in the absence of regular employment, a person lacks not only a place in which to work and the receipt of regular income but also a coherent organization of the present — that is, a system of concrete expectations and goals.")
63. See Wilson, supra 34, at 3-6, 25-50.

even seriously considered for blacks, it is possible to gain some perspective on the factors that undermine fair employment practice laws at their inception, as they are administered, and as they are interpreted by the courts.

Professor Wilson states that the civil rights strategy of the 1960s was premised on the proposition that government, through the enactment and enforcement of antidiscrimination legislation, could best ensure blacks access to equal opportunities and social and political progress. Programs based upon such a premise, however, were simply inadequate to eradicate the cumulative effects of pervasive and persistent discrimination. "Long periods of racial oppression can result . . . in a system of inequality that lingers even after racial barriers come down. . . . [T]he most disadvantaged minority individuals, crippled by the cumulative effects of both racial and class subjugation, disproportionately lack the resources to compete effectively in a free and open market."[64]

Still, Wilson concludes that "as long as minorities are underrepresented in higher-paying and desirable positions in society, affirmative action programs will be needed."[65] Affirmative action policies directed solely at addressing the needs of the economically disadvantaged in society would benefit both poor blacks and poor whites and especially those living below the poverty line. But the elimination of all policies based on race would result in "the systematic exclusion of many middle-income blacks" from further advancement into high caliber educational, professional, and economic institutions or positions. In Wilson's view, "conventional measures of performance" are insensitive to the cumulative effects of racism and discrimination, which are often manifested in subtle ways and result in the "under-representation of blacks in positions of high status and their overrepresentation in positions of low status."[66] Professor Wilson proposes, rather, specific measures to confront both the economic and the race-based discrimination confronting the urban poor. He concludes that, "since race is one of the components of 'disadvantage,' the ideal affirmative action program would emphasize flexible criteria of evaluation based on both need and race. . . . Now more than ever, we need broader solutions than those we have employed in the past."[67]

More than a decade has passed since the publication of Professor Wilson's book and, if anything, the status of poverty level blacks, conditions have worsened without meaningful relief beyond the earnest efforts by local churches and community agencies. To literally add insult to injury, some academics and well-known public figures, have been critical of actions and behaviors of some members

---

64. See id. at 196. Affirmative action was an outgrowth of the recognition of and concern for the plight of the least prepared black Americans. To supplement Title VII of the Civil Rights Act of 1964, black leaders urged adoption of affirmative action programs in education, employment, and public contracts. This, too, proved an ineffective strategy for reaching the masses of economically and educationally disadvantaged blacks. Even those disadvantaged to whom it did provide opportunity were from "low socioeconomic backgrounds with the greatest educational and social resources." Id. at 197. Wilson suspects, however, that for the inner city ghetto dweller, affirmative action has not resulted in heightened hopes or concrete opportunities.

65. See id. at 198.

66. See id. at 198-199.

67. Id. at 199.

of these groups. Sociologist Stephen Steinberg understands the temptation to condemn the often indefensible, but explains:

> You know, it's easy to see where people . . . are coming from. It's always tempting to get up on a pulpit and just shout, as Nancy Reagan did: Don't take drugs, don't drop out of school. But in making this sort of moral condemnation, they fail as social scientists to really get into the experience and the mind-set of the people they're talking about, and to ask why people engage in self-destructive behavior. We're failing to see that there is a whole generation of black youth consigned once again to the periphery jobless, without hope. And then we use their reactions, whether it's cultural or behavioral, to impugn them.[68]

§4.2 COMPETING THEORIES ON THE EFFICACY OF LEGAL RESTRAINTS FOR EMPLOYMENT DISCRIMINATION

Given the long history of employment discrimination and its impact on the economic status of blacks in this country, it is not surprising that a compelling case may be made for imposing legal restraints on employment discrimination. Objections to the use of antidiscrimination laws have been both practical and ideological. While some argue that laws designed to enhance the economic status of blacks have been largely ineffective,[1] they express no fundamental opposition to using governmental authority to combat discrimination in employment. In their view, prohibition of discrimination is consistent with the color-blind concept on which society is, or should be, based.

In addition to the basic conflict between those who favor antidiscrimination laws and those who do not, there exists a more subtle debate about how to best design and implement anti-bias laws in the employment field. As discrimination has shifted from the overt to more subtle forms, new approaches are receiving attention.

Professor Susan Sturm argues for a regulatory approach to solve the bias that continues to persist in the workplace.[2] She contends that while traditional anti-discrimination laws have helped reduce the overt forms of discrimination — or first-generation discrimination, as she titles it — they do not address the more

---

68. David Glenn, A Sociologist Offers a Harsh Assessment of How His Discipline Treats Race Relations, The Chronicle of Higher Educ., p. A13, (Nov. 16, 2007).

§4.2 1. See David Strauss, Symposium: The Law and Economics of Racial Discrimination in Employment: The Case for Numerical Standards, 79 Geo. L.J. 1619 (1991); see also Leroy D. Clark, Symposium: The Law and Economics of Racial Discrimination in Employment: The Law and Economics of Racial Discrimination in Employment by David A. Strauss, 79 Geo. L.J. 1695 (1991) (arguing that antipathy for racial minorities continues to affect employment decisions and proposing legislative solutions); Jerome Culp, Small Numbers, Big Problems, Black Men, and the Supreme Court: A Reform Program for Title VII after *Hicks*, 23 Cap. U. L. Rev. 241 (1994) (concluding that Title VII has done little to improve the economic condition of black men, and suggesting an administrative alternative to judicial relief).

2. Susan Sturm, Second Generation Employment Discrimination: A Structural Approach, 101 Colum. L. Rev. 458 (2001).

subtle forms of discrimination that have become more common in its place. "Second-generation" claims of discrimination and bias involve the patterns of workplace interactions and socializing that continue to exclude non-dominant groups. Informal interactions influence opportunities for advancement and shape an organizational structure that still excludes minorities. Professor Sturm cites a common claim of hostile workplace environment where co-workers may not have the formal power to hire or fire, but are able to marginalize a co-worker. Second-generation discrimination is much more complex and therefore harder to resolve with clear simplified legal rules. Because second-generation discrimination is more structural and cultural, it often cannot be traced back to a single bad actor. The discriminatory impact can be understood only in relation to broader patterns of conduct and not by segregating individual behavior into discrete legal claims. "Comments or behavior occurring in conjunction with sex segregation and marginalization may be discriminatory, while the same statements may produce little gender exclusion in a more integrated context."[3]

Professor Sturm argues that second-generation problems require problem solving rather than fixed legal rules that discourage actual problem solving. For one, rules are too inflexible. "Any rule specific enough to guide behavior will inadequately account for the variability, change and complexity characteristic of second generation problems."[4] Legal rules also discourage structural change by creating an incentive to prevent legal exposure rather than to adopt long-term strategies that address the discrimination. "Employers producing information that reveals problems or patterns of exclusion increase the likelihood that they will be sued. Thus, lawyers counsel clients not to collect data that could reveal racial or gender problems."[5] Finally, she argues that a rules-enforcement approach places the focus on the invisible legal boundary that must not be crossed. Thus the only cases that are discussed by employers and in the public mindset are those cases that are so egregious as to warrant legal sanction and that clearly cross the line. Professor Sturm advocates a structural approach where the judiciary is responsible for articulating general legal norms that encourage a problem-solving regime implemented by employers. For instance, in the example of hostile work environment, the Supreme Court in various cases has formulated an open-ended doctrine where the conduct is discriminatory if it is perceived as hostile or reasonably would be perceived as such. As a consequence, Professor Sturm argues the Court left the task of defining sexual harassment to the fact-specific, problem-solving process. Furthermore, the Court imposed employer liability unless the employer has exercised reasonable care to eliminate the harassment when it might occur, thus adopting an approach that encourages the development of workplace solutions. She also argues for the inclusion of nongovernmental organizations — problem-solving lawyers, psychologists, human resource professionals, consulting organizations — mediating the relationship between the two structures. There are, of course, those who oppose the very concept of antidiscrimination laws regardless of the form they take. Critics of the application of antidiscrimination laws in

3. Id. at 471.
4. Id. at 475.
5. Id. at 476.

employment generally begin with a presumption that private conduct should normally be left free of government coercion. Because business decisions involve subjective matters of individual taste, government coercion necessarily impinges on individual freedom. The most vocal proponent of this view in recent years is Professor Richard Epstein. Professor Epstein maintains that "[a]n antidiscrimination law is the antithesis of freedom of contract, a principle that allows all persons to do business with whomever they please for good reason, bad reason, or no reason at all."[6] Within the labor market, Professor Epstein argues that there are "good reasons for expecting *rational* discrimination to persist in private markets," including racial discrimination,[7] and that antidiscrimination laws impose greater costs, economic and social, than they do benefits.

Like early opponents of legal restraints on labor, Professor Epstein doubts that the economic disadvantage of blacks is attributable to employment discrimination. For example, he argues that the minimum wage rates forced by the Fair Labor Standards Act,[8] along with union bargaining power, have the effect of putting a premium on skilled labor.[9] As labor costs increase due to minimum wage rates, employers will tend to hire fewer workers who are unskilled, less educated, or less experienced. Thus, he argues, the minimum wage rate works against disadvantaged black workers by allowing employers to use subjective criteria, such as racial prejudice, in selecting workers.

Evaluating studies that conclude that racial discrimination may result in lower wages for black workers or segregation within the market, Professor Epstein attributes the results to the very existence of antidiscrimination laws.[10] In short, the constant risk of litigation compels employers to make economic judgments that will minimize their costs and maximize their profits. This reality may lead to less hiring and fewer promotions or to hiring in lower wage jobs.

Professor Epstein maintains that "free entry and multiple employers provide ample protection for all workers, even those faced with policies of overt and hostile discrimination by some employers."[11] Under an employment regime free of government intervention, Professor Epstein posits that the opportunities for all workers, including victims of discrimination, will expand.[12] Finally, this regime of limited government may legitimately include any voluntary affirmative action programs in the private, but not the public, sphere.[13]

---

6. Richard A. Epstein, Forbidden Grounds: The Case Against Employment Discrimination Laws 3 (1992).

7. Id. at 76-78.

8. 29 U.S.C. §§201-219 (1976).

9. Epstein, supra note 6, at 74.

10. Citing Professor Sovern's contemporaneous assessment of the efficacy of employment discrimination legislation, Professor Epstein argues that unwavering, uncritical support of the antidiscrimination principle has persisted in allegiance to historical conditions that no longer exist. Id. at 7.

11. Id. at 59.

12. Id. at 30, 72-78. Traditional critics of laws against discrimination were less sanguine about the notion that some forms of discrimination have "survival value" and would resist being driven from the market.

13. Id. at 9, 412-437. Consistent with his view of freedom of contract, Professor Epstein argues that "in the context of private employment those who want to practice affirmative action should be free to do so, for whatever reason, and for the benefit of whichever groups they choose." Id. at

Epstein's arguments, including his use of a "right to contract," are right out of the nineteenth century, but if his subtext is that anti-employment bias laws just don't work, then the sections that follow illustrate all to clearly that antidiscrimination laws do not provide a comprehensive remedy for racial discrimination in employment opportunity. Too often the legal requirements of such claims are too burdensome for plaintiffs and fail to address the nuances of employment discrimination. This may explain why antidiscrimination claims so often fail. In the 40-plus years since the implementation of the first major national prohibition against race discrimination in employment, numerous interdisciplinary studies have been conducted and support conclusions that these laws are only minimally effective in reducing prejudice and enhancing opportunity for black workers.[14]

Studies of empirical data concerning judicial treatment of employment discrimination claims have found that most such claims, when resolved by courts, are dismissed on pretrial motions.[15] When employment discrimination plaintiffs do get their claims to a jury, they fare worse than plaintiffs in other civil actions.[16] This ill-fate continues on appeal, with federal appellate courts reversing plaintiffs' victories at a higher rate than defendants' wins in employment discrimination cases.[17]

Based largely on anecdotal evidence, practitioners and scholars have long believed that plaintiffs alleging race or national origin discrimination in employment do more poorly than individuals alleging other forms of discrimination by their employers. This perception has been confirmed by some empirical studies of litigation outcomes.[18]

---

412. Governmental entities and officials, however, do not enjoy the same "[u]nbounded contractual freedom" as private employers; they must act "[a]t all times . . . as trustees for the public whom they serve and as contracting partners with employers and other parties." Id. at 421. Because of the fundamental differences in its obligations, the government's options in adopting affirmative action programs, though not nonexistent, are narrowly circumscribed.

14. Much of this discussion is taken from Anajana Samat, J.D., N.Y.U. 2003, Employment Discrimination Litigation: An Overview of Precedent & Practice (Sept. 2007), on file with author.

15. Wendy Parker, Lessons in Losing: Race Discrimination in Employment, 81 Notre Dame L. Rev. 889 (2006); Pat K. Chew, Freeing Racial Harassment from the Sexual Harassment Model, 85 Or. L. Rev. 615 (2006); but see Kevin M. Clermont & Stewart J. Schwab, Proceedings: How Employment-Discrimination Plaintiffs Fare in the Federal Courts of Appeals, 1 J. of Empirical Legal Studies 429 (Spring 2004) ("pretrial and trial win rates are similar across types of discrimination cases, such as Title VII, the ADA, and the ADEA — despite the differing nature of, and resulting reaction to, suits based on race, sex, disability, and age. . . .").

16. Parker, supra note 15, at 922; Clermont & Schwab, supra note 15, at 444 (reviewing Administrative Office data on civil litigation outcomes in all federal district courts for years 1979 through 2000 and finding "employment discrimination plaintiffs have won 4.23% of their pretrial adjudications, while other plaintiffs have won 22.23% of their pretrial adjudications."); Michael Selmi, *Why Are Employment Discrimination Cases So Hard to Win?*, 61 La. L. Rev. 555, 557 (2001); Ann C. McGinley, *Credulous Courts and the Tortured Trilogy: The Improper Use of Summary Judgment in Title VII and ADEA Cases*, 34 B.C. L. Rev. 203, 220-221 (1993).

17. Clermont & Schwab, supra note 15, at 450 (reviewing Administrative Office data concerning years 1988 through 2000 and finding that appellate courts reversal rates of plaintiff wins versus defendant wins was 54% versus 11% in appeals from pretrial dispositions, and 43% versus 8% in appeals from the trial phase).

18. E.g., Parker, supra note 15, passim; Chew, supra note 15, at 631 (comparison of study of federal sexual harassment cases between 1986 and 1996 with study of all federal racial harassment cases between 1976 and 2002 showed that plaintiffs' success rate was 48.2% in sexual harassment cases but only 21.5% in racial harassment cases.)

In one recent survey of federal case filings and selected published opinions, Professor Wendy Parker found that race discrimination plaintiffs had lower success rates than almost all other employment discrimination claimants.[19] In her survey of employment discrimination cases filed in the Eastern District of Pennsylvania and the Northern District of Texas, Professor Parker found that whenever judges resolved race claims, plaintiffs almost always lost.[20] She further found that judges dismissed more race cases on pretrial motions than gender discrimination cases, even though the latter were more likely to settle (statistically) than race cases. The most common defenses raised by employers to race discrimination claims were, in order of frequency, failure to state a prima facie case; existence of a legitimate, nondiscriminatory reason for the allegedly adverse employment action; and failure to follow EEOC rules or procedures.[21] With the exception of the latter procedural defense, a finding in favor of a defendant on either of the first two meant the judge believed that, "as a matter of law reasonable jurors could not find for plaintiff."[22]

In all likelihood, in the course of ruling on an employer's pretrial dispositive motion, judges are required to draw some inferences to fill in the holes and accept or reject one or the other party's position. Given that courts are ruling in favor of defendants at such high rates, in effect, they are calling close cases, making inferences, or otherwise reading evidence to be either insufficient to support a claim of discriminatory motive or sufficient to prove the existence of a legitimate nondiscriminatory reason for adverse actions. Professor Parker interprets such judicial action to be a sign of judicial *agreement* with (and not merely judicial deference to) employers' race-neutral explanations for their adverse treatment of plaintiffs. She terms this phenomenon an "anti-race plaintiff ideology among federal judges" whereby courts regard and treat "race and national origin discrimination cases fairly alike, no matter who the plaintiffs and defendants are, no matter what their respective arguments are, and no matter what the race and gender of the judge are."[23]

In earlier work, Professor Michael Selmi expressed his view that judges, like all human beings, are operating with a particular "way of seeing things" or "bias."[24] In the case of federal judges dealing with race discrimination claims, this worldview, as Professor Selmi explains, is one that can be analogized to that of the "anti-affirmative action mindset, one that views both the persistence of

---

19. Parker, supra note 15. Interestingly, Professor Parker found that plaintiffs alleging age discrimination fared just as well — or rather, poorly — as those claiming race discrimination. Id. at 928 & n.186. Professor Parker based her findings on an examination of two data sets. As part of the "national study," she examined reported opinions from federal district courts that were published either by the court or by Westlaw in 2003 and that involved Title VII race or national origin discrimination claims. Her "case filing study" extended to all cases filed in the Eastern District of Pennsylvania and the Northern District of Texas in 2002 that were designated as employment discrimination cases by the court clerk and included a Title VII race or national origin claim. In this latter set, Professor Parker looked not just at opinions to find cases, but any matter that had a docket sheet.

20. Id. at 894.

21. Id. at 908 n.92.

22. Id. at 896.

23. Id. In reaching this conclusion, Parker first explains why race neutral explanations for such outcomes are inadequate, especially since they do not explain why race plaintiffs do so much worse than other employment discrimination plaintiffs. Id. at 921-928.

24. Selmi, supra note 16, at 563.

discrimination and the merits of the underlying claims with deep skepticism."[25] As an example of how one's preconceived notions "about the world — about the prevalence of discrimination and its role in shaping events" — impacts judicial decision making, Professor Selmi points to the *Hicks* decision:

> In that case, Melvin Hicks, who was the only African American supervisor on staff, was disciplined and ultimately fired after several confrontations with his boss, who was white. As the trial court found, Hicks was disciplined for infractions of his subordinates contrary to common practice, and Hicks was also singled out following a change in management. The new management wanted to reassert control of the prison facility in response to a report suggesting that having too many African-American supervisors might have had a deleterious affect on discipline among the inmates, a majority of whom were African-American. Despite its finding that the employer's proffered reasons were pretextual, the district court found that the under-lying rationale was personal animus between Hicks and his supervisors, rather than racial animus. Surely the evidence could have been interpreted to find that the source of the personal bias was racial animosity, conscious or otherwise, though this possibility never seems to have been explored by the district court. It was, however, expressly mentioned by Justice Souter in dissent, suggesting that a different judge, working through a different mindset, one where discrimination may be more readily accepted as an explanation, would have interpreted the evidence differently.[26]

Plaintiffs bringing race discrimination claims thus may be losing at such disproportionate rates because they suffer from multiple layers of institutional and attitudinal bias. As a baseline matter, the *McDonnell Douglas* framework, discussed in more detail below, "permits courts to 'believe' the defendants on mere articulation and to 'disbelieve' plaintiffs who must leap a higher hurdle to create a jury issue on pretext."[27] On a motion for summary judgment, the employment discrimination plaintiff must deal with an added disadvantage, namely, the practice of breaking down the evidentiary record into its component parts, thereby permitting courts to lose sight of the larger picture presented by the evidence. In effect, on a defendant's Rule 56 motion, courts are "dissecting the plaintiff's evidence into small 'segments,' rigorously scrutinizing each segment of evidence to declare it 'insufficient,' and then declaring that plaintiff has not raised a genuine issue of material fact at all."[28] Add to all this Professor Selmi's suggestion that "courts appear hesitant to draw inferences of racial discrimination based on cir-cumstantial evidence, even though courts have long recognized that race discrim-ination is generally subtle in form and dependent on circumstantial evidence,"[29] and you have a setting that is stacked against a plaintiff alleging she was discrim-inated against on account of her race by her employer.

---

25. Id. at 562.

26. Id. at 563-564 (footnotes omitted).

27. Jeffrey A. Van Detta, "Le Roi Est Mort; Vive Le Roi!": An Essay on the Quiet Demise of McDonnell Douglas and the Transformation of Every Title VII Case after Desert Palace, Inc. v. Costa into a "Mixed-Motives" Case, 52 Drake L. Rev. 71, 106 (2003) (discussing McGinley, supra note 16, at 220-221).

28. Van Detta, supra note 27, at 106 (citing and discussing McGinley, supra note 16).

29. Selmi, supra note 16, at 564 (footnote omitted).

§4.3 FAIR EMPLOYMENT LAWS: AN OVERVIEW

§4.3.1 Title VII

Until the passage of Title VII of the Civil Rights Act of 1964,[1] blacks had little effective legal machinery for dealing with employment discrimination. Prior to Title VII, efforts were made to combat job bias under federal labor relations laws, see §4.7, infra. Some complaints of employment discrimination were addressed to administrative civil rights agencies. These agencies often viewed themselves as mediators between employers and black workers. Agencies during this period simply failed to act as law enforcement agencies enforcing the legal rights of blacks. For these reasons, the public policy against discrimination, though established well before Title VII in a variety of state laws, executive orders, and court decisions, remained unenforced.[2]

Thus, the passage of Title VII marked a turning point in employment discrimination law. Title VII established the Equal Employment Opportunities Commission (EEOC), an executive agency empowered to receive, file, and investigate complaints of discrimination from individuals, and to conciliate complaints by voluntary means.[3] Charges of discrimination had to be filed with the EEOC within 90 days after the incident; where local fair employment remedies were available, the plaintiff had to pursue those remedies first.[4] Title VII provided that plaintiffs could bring an action in federal district court after receiving a letter from the EEOC authorizing the suit.[5] In addition, the United States Attorney General was authorized to sue in order to remedy a "pattern and practice" of discrimination.[6] Substantively, Title VII barred discriminatory acts and practices by private employers or unions with more than 25 workers or members, and which engaged in an industry affecting interstate commerce.[7] A key section provides that it is unlawful for an employer "to fail or refuse to hire or to discharge any individual, or otherwise to discriminate against any individual with respect to his compensation, terms, conditions, or privileges of employment, because of such individual's race, color, religion, sex, or national origin."[8]

In 1972, Title VII was amended. Under the amended version, the EEOC itself may now bring a federal court action to remedy discrimination.[9] Several procedural changes were made: Filing times for plaintiffs were extended, while

§4.3 1. 42 U.S.C. §§2000e et seq. (1976).

2. See Herbert Hill, The New Judicial Perception of Employment Discrimination — Litigation Under Title VII of the Civil Rights Act of 1964, 43 U. Colo. L. Rev. 243-247 (1972). Twenty states and seven major cities had enforceable fair employment practice laws at the time Title VII was passed. See Paul H. Norgren, Fair Employment Practice Laws, in Employment, Race, and Poverty 542 (Arthur M. Ross & Herbert Hill eds., 1967).

3. 42 U.S.C. §§2000e-4, 2000e-5(b) (1970).

4. Id. at §2000e-5(e).

5. Id. at §2000e-5(f)(1).

6. Id. at §2000e-6.

7. Id. at §2000e-2(a), (c).

8. Id. at §2000e-2 (1976).

9. Id. at §2000e-5(f)(1).

the time within which the EEOC must complete its investigation was shortened.[10] And as will be discussed, Title VII was further amended in 1991.

§4.3.2   Section 1981

The Civil Rights Act of 1870, as codified at 42 U.S.C. §1981,[11] provides that all persons shall have certain equal rights, including the right "to make and enforce contracts." As interpreted by the Supreme Court, §1981 applies to both private and public discrimination,[12] thereby preserving "the right to contract for employment."[13]

Thus, §1981 provides an alternative remedy to Title VII, giving the plaintiff a separate, wholly independent cause of action.[14] That Title VII and §1981 are separate, distinct, and independent was confirmed by the Supreme Court in Johnson v. Railway Express Agency.[15] In holding that the filing of a claim with the EEOC pursuant to Title VII does not toll the statute of limitations under §1981, the Court noted that Congress clearly indicated its approval of the two statutes as separate sources of relief for victims of employment discrimination. Clearly, Title VII was not intended to deprive black workers of other remedies for employment discrimination, such as §1981. Nor was it intended that plaintiffs be required to complete Title VII's filing procedures with the EEOC before bringing an action under §1981 in federal district court. Thus, the Court in *Johnson* established §1981 as a viable tool in employment discrimination litigation strategy.[16] In this respect, *Johnson* is much like the Court's decision in Alexander v. Gardner-Denver Co.,[17] preserving alternative strategies for black workers.

As one more example of whites benefiting from civil rights provisions intended to protect blacks, the Court has chosen to extend the protection of §1981 to whites as well as blacks broadening the language of the section, providing that "[a]ll persons . . . shall have the same right . . . to make and enforce contracts . . . as is enjoyed by white citizens."[18] Similarly, the protection of Title VII has been extended to white workers, as that statute prohibits discrimination because of an individual's race, without reference to whites or blacks.[19] In

---

10. Id. at §2000e-5(b), (e).

11. Id. at §1981 (1976).

12. See Jones v. Alfred Mayer Co., 392 U.S. 409 (1968).

13. Id. at 442 n.78; see also Brady v. Bristol-Myers, Inc., 459 F.2d 621 (8th Cir. 1972); Caldwell v. National Brewing Co., 443 F.2d 1044 (5th Cir. 1971); Young v. International Tel. & Tel. Co., 438 F.2d 757 (3d Cir. 1971); Boudreaux v. Baton Rouge Marine Contracting Co., 437 F.2d 1011 (5th Cir. 1971); Sanders v. Dobbs Houses, Inc., 431 F.2d 1097 (5th Cir. 1970), cert. denied, 401 U.S. 948 (1971); Waters v. Wisconsin Steel Works, 427 F.2d 476 (7th Cir.), cert. denied, 400 U.S. 911 (1970); Mizell v. North Broward Hosp. Dist., 427 F.2d 468 (5th Cir. 1970).

14. See, e.g., Long v. Ford Motor Co., 496 F.2d 500 (6th Cir. 1974); DeMatteis v. Eastman Kodak Co., 511 F.2d 306 (2d Cir. 1975).

15. 421 U.S. 454 (1975).

16. In fact, most race discrimination complaints contain both Title VII and §1981 counts, perhaps to deal with the possibility that the coverage of one may be broader than the other.

17. 415 U.S. 36 (1974). This case is discussed further in §4.7.3.

18. 42 U.S.C. §1981 (1976).

19. Id. at §2000e-2(a)(1).

McDonald v. Santa Fe Trail Trans. Co.,[20] the Court extended the protection of §1981 to whites, rejecting the argument that the phrase "as is enjoyed by white citizens" necessarily limited §1981 to the protection of nonwhites against racial discrimination. The Court focused on the legislative history of the Civil Rights Act of 1866, finding an intent to proscribe racial discrimination against all citizens, rather than an intent to assure specified civil rights to the formerly enslaved blacks.[21] In the Court's view, §1981's major thrust is banning the use of race as a consideration in employment, rather than ensuring that blacks achieve equality in the job market. For the many blacks who are unemployed or underpaid, the equal treatment strategy of fair employment laws such as Title VII and §1981 provides only faint hope for achieving their ultimate goal—equal employment.

§4.4 TITLE VII AND DISPARATE TREATMENT

§4.4.1 Establishing a Prima Facie Case

Initially, Title VII's prohibition of discrimination because of an individual's race gave little guidance as to how exactly a black worker was to prove a case in court. The Supreme Court was left with the task of developing the mechanism for establishing a prima facie case of racial discrimination. In McDonnell Douglas Corp. v. Green,[1] the Court outlined the procedures for proving a case of disparate treatment, that is, when an employer has treated a black worker and a white worker disparately.

The plaintiff in a Title VII case initially was required to establish a prima facie case of racial discrimination. In a critical passage, the Court declared that:

> [t]his may be done by showing (i) that he belongs to a racial minority; (ii) that he applied and was qualified for a job for which the employer was seeking applicants; (iii) that, despite his qualifications, he was rejected; and (iv) that, after his rejection, the position remained open and the employer continued to seek applicants from persons of complainant's qualifications.[2]

In short, the Court provided that wherever the employer could assert a legitimate reason for its employment decision, a black worker would have the

---

20. 427 U.S. 273 (1976).

21. Discrimination on the basis of national origin is also covered by Title VII and §1981. At least with respect to Title VII, Congress intended to protect within the category "national origin," members of groups of persons of common ancestry, heritage, or background. The EEOC position is that Title VII's national origin protection may extend to a protected class defined by a variety of factors, including religion, membership in associations, ethnic stereotypes, and food, irrespective of ethnic origin. See generally Espinoza v. Farah Mfg., 414 U.S. 86 (1973) (Title VII does not prohibit employer's policy against employment of aliens); Frontera v. Sindell, 522 F.2d 1215 (6th Cir. 1975) (§1981 does not require that Civil Service examination be administered in Spanish to Spanish-speaking applicants); Guerra v. Manchester Terminal Corp., 498 F.2d 641 (5th Cir. 1974) (§1981 covers discrimination based on workers' status as aliens).

§4.4 1. 411 U.S. 792 (1973). See Roy L. Brooks, The Structure of Individual Disparate Treatment Litigation after *Hopkins*, 6 Lab. L. 215 (1990).

2. 411 U.S. at 802.

opportunity to use a variety of evidence in showing that the employer's reason was in fact a pretext.[3]

§4.4.2   Rebutting a Prima Facie Case

Once the plaintiff in a Title VII suit has established a prima facie case of employment discrimination, *McDonnell Douglas* provides that the employer shall be given the opportunity to show a legitimate, nondiscriminatory reason for his employment decision. In Furnco Construction Corp. v. Waters,[4] the Supreme Court further explained how an employer might rebut a prima facie case of employment discrimination.

In *Furnco*, the employer hired only bricklayers that he knew to be experienced and competent or persons who had been recommended to him. The black plaintiffs were not hired, even though they were fully qualified and had attempted to get jobs by appearing at the job site gate. *Furnco* developed two themes in explaining the rebuttal of a *McDonnell Douglas* prima facie case. First, the employer need only articulate a legitimate nondiscriminatory motive in rebutting the plaintiff's case. Moreover, the employer need not show that he adopted a hiring procedure that maximized the hiring of minority employees; the employer need only articulate some legitimate nondiscriminatory reason for his decision. The Court warned that courts should not become involved in determining the best hiring procedures for employers. Second, the employer may introduce statistics showing that he has a racially balanced work force. While such statistics are not conclusive, under the *Furnco* rule they are at least entitled to consideration.

Interestingly, the Court's opinion in *Furnco* seemingly allowed the employer to continue his practice of hiring acquaintances of the supervisor, rather than hiring qualified applicants at the job site. It takes little imagination to see how the employer's practice might perpetuate past discrimination against blacks, in effect establishing and reinforcing an "old boy network" of bricklayers. Moreover, the Court's decision provided considerable leeway to employers who already have an apparently racially balanced work force; these employers may decide to engage in questionable employment practices, with the knowledge that they will later be able to rely on their favorable statistics in case of subsequent suits.

---

3. On remand, the district court concluded that the black worker was not reemployed because of his participation in the illegal stall-in and not because of his race or legitimate civil rights activities. The court held that these reasons were not mere pretext, but were the real reasons for plaintiff's rejection by the company. Green v. McDonnell Douglas Corp., 390 F. Supp. 501 (E.D. Mo. 1975). Plaintiff showed that on three occasions during the previous several years, traffic on the roads to the company plant had been slowed as a result of strike activities, and no disciplinary action had been taken. The employer responded that on these occasions blacks as well as whites took part in the activities and that agreements with the union provided for no disciplinary measures, with only one exception. Plaintiff's efforts to show that nonwhites were underrepresented in the company's work force did not impress the district court, and his charges that more nonwhites than whites were disciplined by the company were deemed unsupported because of incomplete statistics.

4. 438 U.S. 567 (1978).

§4.4.3 St. Mary's Honor Center v. Hicks

In St. Mary's Honor Center v. Hicks,[5] the Court emphasized the need for the factfinder actually to determine that the employer discriminated against the plaintiff. That finding may be premised on an inference of discrimination adduced from the plaintiff's evidence, as well as the factfinder's rejection of the employer's explanation. Regardless, the Court emphasized, no liability may exist without an ultimate finding of discrimination. Mr. Hicks had made out a prima facie case of racial discrimination and had demonstrated that the employer's reasons for discharging him were lies. However, the Court held that he was not entitled to judgment as a matter of law. The Court ruled that the employer had introduced two nondiscriminatory reasons for the discharge. Giving no weight to the employer's credibility, the Court found that the employer had satisfied its burden of production, which served to rebut the prima facie case and destroy the presumption of discrimination.[6]

In what would become one of many divided opinions in employment discrimination jurisprudence, the majority of the Court concluded that there is a significant difference between, on the one hand, finding that an employer was not actually motivated by the lawful reason it offers in court or that its explanation simply was not believable and, on the other hand, finding that an employer was motivated by unlawful discriminatory animus.[7] This distinction, according to the Court, was the result of the particular allocation of burdens between the parties: at all times, the plaintiff has the "ultimate burden of persuading the court that she has been the victim of intentional discrimination."[8] Thus, even if the plaintiff affirmatively musters evidence showing the falsity of the employer's alleged reasons for its conduct, the plaintiff may nonetheless fail on her claim if, for example, the factfinder determines the plaintiff has not established that discriminatory animus motivated the employer.

As a practical matter, the *Hicks* opinion meant that, while a plaintiff is not required to present additional proof of discrimination to successfully reply to a defendant's reasons, a plaintiff may lose even if the factfinder finds the employer's explanation for its conduct not credible. By making it harder for plaintiffs to prevail on pretext alone, *Hicks* has been criticized for downplaying the continued prevalence of discrimination.[9] In addition, *Hicks* seems to run counter to the main

---

5. 509 U.S. 502 (1993).

6. 505 U.S. at 509. In his dissent, Justice Souter wrote: "The Court today decides to abandon the settled law that sets out this structure for trying disparate-treatment Title VII cases, only to adopt a scheme that will be unfair to plaintiffs, unworkable in practice, and inexplicable in forgiving employers who present false evidence in court." Id. at 533. "What is more," the Justice added, "the Court is throwing out the rule for the benefit of employers who have been found to have given false evidence in a court of law." Id. at 537.

For a review of cases in which courts have acted sternly against employment-discrimination plaintiffs who file false charges, see Stephen Plans, Truth: The Lost Virtue in Title VII Litigation, 29 Seton Hall L. Rev. 599 (1998).

7. Id. at 514-515 ("Nothing in law would permit us to substitute for the required finding that the employer's action was the product of unlawful discrimination, the much different (and much lesser) finding that the employer's explanation of its action was not believable.").

8. Texas Dep't of Community Affairs v. Burdine, 450 U.S. 248 (1981).

9. Deborah A. Calloway, St. Mary's Honor Center v. Hicks: Questioning the Basic Assumption, 26 Conn. L. Rev. 997 (1994).

purpose of the burden-shifting framework.[10] As explained by the Supreme Court, the framework serves to narrow the court's inquiry by eliminating the most likely nondiscriminatory, legitimate explanations for an employer's conduct. However, under *Hicks*, the burden-shifting fails to accomplish this goal since pretext is even harder to eliminate and remains part of the court's evaluation of the evidence.[11]

§4.4.4   Disparate Treatment Cases: A Plaintiffs' Quagmire

In May 2007, the Supreme Court decided Ledbetter v. Goodyear Tire & Rubber Co.,[12] in which the sole female supervisor at an Alabama Goodyear plant sued for sex discrimination. Ledbetter argued that she had been discriminated against throughout the course of her 19-year career with Goodyear, in that she received smaller raises than the men received. Goodyear argued that her claim was time-barred because Title VII requires suits to be filed within 180 days of the violation. The Supreme Court rejected Ledbetter's argument that each paycheck that she received that was less than what her male counterparts were receiving was a new violation in favor of a narrow reading of the statute that prohibited her claim. The decision distinguishes wage-discrimination claims from hostile work environment claims, holding that the latter consists of a discrete action rather than a series of actions that culminates in a violation.[13] It therefore effectively prohibits plaintiffs from basing their claim on wage discrimination that occurred 180 days before their claim was filed. In a dissent read from the bench, Justice Ginsburg observed that the decision would create an insurmountable obstacle for potential plaintiffs, as "Pay disparities often occur, as they did in Ledbetter's case, in small increments; only over time is there strong cause to suspect that discrimination is at work."[14] Thus, racial minorities who are victim to a pattern of incrementally small wage raises compared to white employees would find themselves time-barred due to the very nature of the discrimination.

Ledbetter represents just one of the many obstacles facing plaintiffs attempting to adapt Title VII law to the practical realities of workplace discrimination. This task has proven particularly daunting for black plaintiffs. As a general observation, there have been far fewer racial discrimination than sex discrimination cases decided under Title VII between 2000 and 2003. However, the fact that race is still a factor in the work place is uncontroverted, and the Department of Labor's most recent Glass Ceiling Report found that despite the efforts of some companies to remove barriers that minorities face in reaching middle and upper level management positions, the glass ceiling still exists in a majority of companies.[15] Although there have been a few significant decisions that should generally

10. Kenneth R. Davis, The Stumbling Three-Step, Burden-Shifting Approach in Employment Discrimination Cases, 61 Brook. L. Rev. 793 (1995).

11. *Burdine*, 450 U.S. at 256.

12. 127 S. Ct. 2162 (2007).

13. See id. at 2175-2176.

14. Id. at 2178-2179 (Ginsburg, J., dissenting).

15. Department of Labor, Office of Federal Contract Compliance Programs, Third Glass Ceiling Report (2000).

benefit plaintiffs in Title VII actions, it is likely that, as Professor Susan Sturm suggests in §4.2.1, modern employment discrimination on the basis of race has become too subtle to be effectively remedied under Title VII. Other commentators have also concluded that Title VII was created to deal with overt discrimination and is incapable of dealing with second-generation discrimination, which is more complex and involves unconscious bias.[16] Further, whereas Title VII case law requires a fairly direct link between evidence of an employer's animus against a minority group and an employment action against a plaintiff, it is also no longer assumed by psychology that discrimination takes place at the time the employment decision is made. Rather, social cognitive theory shows that perception and judgment errors distort seemingly objective data upon which a much earlier employment decision may be based.[17]

Courts have not been attuned to these psychological findings. In several cases, the plaintiff has shown direct evidence of offensive comments about a protected group in the work place, but the comments are considered "stray remarks" that are not relevant or linked to an adverse employment action against a member of the protected group. In one Sixth Circuit case, the court actually found that insults such as "nigger" were more indicative of a personality conflict than racial animus.[18] Some commentators assert that these cases fail to see that the "stray remarks" are likely indicative of an employer's attitude toward a particular group, which could easily give rise to unconscious discrimination against employees who are members of these groups. Thus, writing off unfair treatment against an employee as based on a personality conflict does not account for the likelihood that the personality conflict may be based on bias against a particular race or gender.[19] Rather, courts should look at personal animosity as evidence of discrimination rather than its antithesis.[20] Some lower courts have done so, others have not. In their holdings on the evidentiary value of remarks by management personnel, some courts allow remarks as probative evidence of discrimination, some courts may or may not label the comments "stray remarks," some courts bar stray remarks pursuant to Rule 403 of the Federal Rules of Evidence, and other courts have labeled comments "stray remarks" but admitted them into evidence anyway.[21]

The First Circuit, for instance, may allow a comment as probative evidence as long as the temporal connection between the statement and decision are not remote,

16. See, e.g., Susan Sturm, Second Generation Employment Discrimination: A Structural Approach, 101 Colum. L. Rev. 458 (2001); Rebecca H. White & Linda H. Krieger, Whose Motive Matters? Discrimination in Multi-Actor Employment Decision Making, 61 La. L. Rev. 495 (2001).

17. See Chad Derum & Karen Engle, 81 Tex. L. Rev. 1177, 1189 (2003) (citing Linda Hamilton Krieger, The Content of Our Categories: A Cognitive Bias Approach to Discrimination and Equal Employment Opportunity, 47 Stan. L. Rev. 1161 (1995)).

18. See, e.g., Sweezer v. Michigan Dept. of Corr., 229 F.3d 1154 (6th Cir. 2000); see also Gorley v. Metro-North Commuter R.R., No. 99 Civ. 3240 (NRB), 2000 WL 1876909 (S.D.N.Y. Dec. 22, 2000) (offensive comments about Hispanics and blacks were considered stray comments unrelated to the employment action); Padilla v. Carrier Air Conditioning, 67 F. Supp. 2d 650, 660 (E.D. Tex. 1999) (offensive remarks about blacks, such as a supervisor's claim that her dog was trained to bite blacks, were sporadic comments not violative of Title VII).

19. Ann C. McGinley, Viva La Evolucion! Recognizing Unconscious Motive in Title VII, 9 Cornell J.L. & Pub. Pol'y 415, 475-477 (2000).

20. Derum & Engle, supra note 17, at 1243.

21. Edward T. Ellis, Evidentiary Issues in Employment Cases, SJ012 ALI-ABA 1035 (2003).

it was made by an actual decision-maker, and the comment is related to the employment decision in question.[22] Similarly, the Fifth Circuit held that stray remarks may be sufficient evidence if they are made by a decision-maker, are related to the employment decision in question, are proximate in time to the adverse action, and are related to the protected class of individuals of which the alleged victim is a member. The Seventh Circuit has also allowed stray remarks to be entered as evidence when they are made by decision-makers and are close in time to and related to the challenged employment action. In contrast, the Sixth Circuit seems to require only that the stray remarks be made by a decision-maker in order for them to be considered.[23] Other courts differ on their definition of "stray remarks," and by definition stray remarks are not admissible. In the Ninth Circuit, the court has labeled comments not related to the decision-making process or tied to the adverse employment action as "stray remarks" and, as a consequence of the categorization, not allowed their admissibility. The Tenth Circuit has similarly held that stray remarks are isolated comments unrelated to the decision-making process for the particular employment action and thus are not admissible. Likewise, the Eleventh Circuit has held that remarks related to the employment decision and made by a decision-maker are not stray remarks and therefore are not admissible.[24]

In the Eighth Circuit, the courts have allowed comments not directly related to the employment action where the comment reflects discriminatory animus or a biased corporate culture. However, the Court stated these comments were more than just stray remarks because they reflect discriminatory animus.[25] Some courts in the Third Circuit have also held that comments reflecting discriminatory animus and made in regards to the employment decision complained of are not just stray remarks, which would not ordinarily be given value. But the Third Circuit has allowed a remark to be entered into evidence even though it was made by a non-decision-maker two years before the challenge employment decision because it was evidence of a biased corporate culture.[26] Connected to the uncertainty as to the weight to be given to stray remarks, commentators have discussed the inability of Title VII to combat the problem of unconscious bias.[27] Some argue that whereas the Title VII model used to presume an illegitimate discriminatory motivation for an employer's actions, there has been a doctrinal shift and courts are beginning to presume that personal animosity is the likely motivating factor.[28] The "personal animosity" concept as distinct from racial animosity emerged in the Supreme Court's decision in St. Mary's Honor Center v. Hicks, but commentators such as Derum and Engle argue that there has recently been a dramatic shift toward this concept, and that it is now exceedingly difficult for Title VII plaintiffs to win because employers have been rid of their responsibility to justify discriminatory actions.[29]

22. Id. at 1038.
23. Id. at 1040.
24. Id. at 1041.
25. Id.
26. Id. at 1039.
27. See, e.g., McGinley, supra note 19.
28. See generally Derum & Engle, supra note 17.
29. 509 U.S. 502 (1993).

As a result, Title VII is now less effective in combating unconscious discrimination. Whereas earlier courts were willing to "sweep broadly" and find discrimination without direct evidence of discriminatory intent, modern courts are hesitant to interfere with or question employers absent direct evidence of such intent.[30] This trend is troubling because "smoking gun" direct evidence of discriminatory intent is incredibly difficult to find. Moreover, the trend has continued even after the Supreme Court's decision in Reeves v. Sanderson Plumbing Products, Inc.[31] (discussed below) because plaintiffs may not win as a matter of law by showing that the employer's offered reason is incredible, and courts continue to interject the personal animosity presumption as a legitimate explanation for seemingly discriminatory treatment, even when there is no evidence of such personal animosity and when personal animosity is not directly asserted by employers.[32] Even if there is evidence of personal animosity, such cases ignore that unconscious discrimination may motivate animosity against a particular employee, assuming instead that there is a clear dichotomy between discrimination based on an impermissible criteria and discrimination based on personal animosity. Although earlier cases such as *McDonnell Douglas*, *Furnco*, and *Burdine* indicated the Court's willingness to treat Title VII as a deterrent mechanism that would find discrimination based on circumstantial evidence even where the employers may have been acting properly, "many courts now prefer to risk false-negative over false-positive findings of discrimination." [33]

The Supreme Court's decision in Desert Palace v. Costa appears contrary to this trend. There, the Court upheld a jury's finding of liability against an employer based on circumstantial evidence.[34] The ruling is potentially important because of the particular difficulty in finding direct evidence of discriminatory intent in the employment context, but the decision could turn on the outrageous nature of the facts. Plaintiff was the only female employee of a Caesars Palace Hotel warehouse, where she operated fork lifts and other heavy machinery. Although her job performance was considered "excellent" she received many informal rebukes, was denied privileges given to her male co-workers, was more harshly disciplined, and received disproportionately less overtime.[35] For example, whereas men who missed work for medical reasons were given overtime to make up the time, the plaintiff was suspended by a warehouse supervisor when she missed work while undergoing surgery to remove a tumor.[36] Supervisors also reputedly

---

30. Derum & Engle, supra note 17, at 1190-1193 (describing the tension between Title VII and employment-at-will doctrine, which states that employers may hire or fire employees without cause). In line with employment-at-will doctrine, cases that find that the plaintiffs suffered an adverse employment action due to personal animosity rather than illegal bias reflect a deference to employers and a judicial belief that they should not be forced to articulate precise reasons for their actions. Id. at 1237. The authors do note that even a complete reversal of at-will employment that would require employers to legitimize their decisions would not solve the unconscious bias problem because seemingly objective measures of merit would still be tainted by unconscious bias. Id. at 1194.

31. 530 U.S. 133 (2000).

32. Derum & Engle, supra note 17, at 1225.

33. Id. at 1182.

34. 123 S. Ct. 2148 (2003).

35. 299 F.3d 838, 844-845 (9th Cir. 2002).

36. Id.

used sex-based verbal slurs against the plaintiff and suspended her when she complained to management about them.

Eventually, the plaintiff was discharged and the hotel cited disciplinary problems. The hotel argued that she was fired because of a physical altercation with another employee. However, plaintiff provided evidence, including union reports and photographs of her injuries, that in fact she was the one victimized by this employee. Further, although she was fired because of the altercation, the other employee was merely suspended. The district court jury found for the plaintiff, and a three-judge panel on the Ninth Circuit reversed, arguing that a mixed motive jury instruction (as opposed to a pretext jury instruction) should not have been given because the plaintiff had failed to present substantial direct evidence of discriminatory animus. The full Ninth Circuit vacated this decision and held for the plaintiff, becoming the only circuit to not require plaintiffs to provide direct evidence of discrimination in mixed motive cases.[37] The Supreme Court affirmed, holding that although Justice O'Connor's controlling concurrence in Price Waterhouse v. Hopkins seemed to require direct evidence that discriminatory animus was a but-for cause of an employment action in a mixed motive case, subsequent amendments to Title VII in 1991 made clear that the plaintiff need prove only that a protected classification was a motivating factor. Further, the Court found that an employer's evidence that the same employment decision would have been made without consideration of the plaintiff's sex is not a defense to liability but rather an affirmative defense with respect to the scope of remedies (they may avoid damages but not awards such as injunctions, attorneys' fees, and declaratory relief).

Another potentially significant Supreme Court employment discrimination case is Reeves v. Sanderson Plumbing Products, Inc.[38] The *Reeves* plaintiff was a 57-year-old employee who supervised workers at the manufacturing company he had been with for 40 years. He was terminated and replaced by a younger person after an investigation into his timekeeping practices. The plaintiff brought an age discrimination suit, offering into evidence disparaging comments that his supervisor made about his age (which even included explicit statements that the plaintiff was "too damn old to do the job").[39] Although the district court found for the plaintiff, the Fifth Circuit reversed and directed a verdict for the employer. The Fifth Circuit held that the plaintiff had merely disproved the employer's proffered explanation but had not offered enough evidence to allow a jury to find age as the real reason for his termination. The decision was in line with several other circuits that required Title VII plaintiffs to show something more than the prima facie case (that they were a qualified member of a protected class and suffered an adverse employment action),[40] and that

---

37. Courts that did require a heightened showing of direct evidence included the First, Fourth, Eighth, and Eleventh Circuits. See Mohr v. Dustrol, Inc., 306 F.3d 636, 640-641 (8th Cir. 2002); Fernandes v. Costa Bros. Masonry, Inc., 199 F.3d 572, 580 (1st Cir. 1999); Trotter v. Board of Trustees of Univ. of Ala., 91 F.3d 1449, 1453-1454 (11th Cir. 1996); Fuller v. Phipps, 67 F.3d 1137, 1142 (4th Cir. 1995).

38. 530 U.S. 133 (2000).

39. Id. at 149-150.

40. The importance of whether an employment action is characterized as "adverse" was highlighted in Ali v. Alamo Rent-a-Car Inc., 8 Fed. Appx. 156 (4th Cir. 2000), upheld by 246 F.3d 662 (2001), cert denied, 534 U.S. 944 (2001). There the Fourth Circuit denied the Title VII

the employer's proffered explanation was false in order to avoid a directed verdict. Under such a "pretext-plus" analysis, an employer who proffered a nondiscriminatory explanation for a plaintiff's discharge or lack of promotion eliminated any presumption of discrimination, even if this explanation was likely false. Under the facts of *Reeves*, the Fifth Circuit found that the evidence of disparaging comments about the plaintiff's age, absent an presumption, could not be linked to his termination.

The Supreme Court reversed the Fifth Circuit and clarified the *McDonnell Douglass* burden-shifting model. The Court held that a plaintiff's prima facie case in conjunction with sufficient evidence for a jury to reject the employer's nondiscriminatory reason for the employment action may be enough to sustain liability under Title VII. An employer's dishonesty about the reason for termination may be considered affirmative evidence of guilt because the employer is in the best position to explain the true reason for its action. Thus, although the presumption of discrimination does drop out of the picture when the employer proffers an explanation, the probative value of the discredited explanation here was too strong to avoid a jury decision and a finding for the employee as a matter of law.

As a result of *Reeves*, it will be easier for Title VII plaintiffs to reach a jury if they can discredit the employer's nondiscriminatory explanation.[41] However, some post-*Reeves* cases seem to maintain the pretext-plus requirement despite the Supreme Court's indication that disproving an employer's proffered explanation should be enough to avoid summary judgement.[42] Moreover, the *Reeves* Court did not rule out the possibility that in cases where no rational factfinder will be able to hold for the plaintiff, a directed verdict could be proper even against a plaintiff who disproves the employer's explanation.[43] It is also clear that a plaintiff who satisfies the prima facie case cannot win as a matter of law simply by proving that the employer's proffered reason was false.

Protection from sexual harassment has been extended to bystanders by the Second Circuit in Leibowitz v. New York City Transit Authority.[44] The court held that an employee whose only alleged injury was the indirect result of the harassment of others had standing under Title VII, although because the plaintiff in this instance was not present when the sexual harassment occurred and was not aware

---

claim of a woman who was transferred from her position at Alamo Rent-a-Car because she refused to stop wearing a head scarf in accordance with her religious beliefs. The court found that an "adverse" employment action is a prerequisite to any religious accommodation claim and that the plaintiff's transfer in this case was not adverse.

41. For example, in McGuinness v. Lincoln Hall, 263 F.3d 49 (2d Cir. 2001), the court held that summary judgment should not be found against a white plaintiff who showed that she had received a less favorable severance package than a similarly situated black employee because he had discredited the employer's proffered explanation for the disparity. The employer argued that the black employee had received the more favorable severance package because he had negotiated for it and because he faced poor job prospects due to a seasonal lull in hiring, but the plaintiff brought forth statements in a deposition of the black former employee that he had been offered the better severance package without negotiation.

42. See Vadie v. Mississippi State Univ., 218 F.3d 365, 373 n.23 (5th Cir. 2000) (stating that a plaintiff who wishes to avoid summary judgment must create an issue of fact as to the employer's proffered explanation and also create a reasonable inference that impermissible discriminatory intent motivated the employer).

43. 530 U.S. at 148.

44. 252 F.3d 179 (2d Cir. 2001).

of it firsthand, she failed to prove that the work place environment was hostile to her. Also, the Ninth Circuit has extended Title VII's protection from retaliation on behalf of an employee who alleges discrimination to co-worker retaliation that rises to the level of an adverse work environment.[45] Finally, many employers, such as those that have less than 15 employees, are not bound by Title VII. However, four circuits have held that at-will employees may sue for racially discriminatory discharge under 42 U.S.C. §1981.[46] This statute, enacted to bar racial discrimination in the formation of enforcement of private contracts, has since been amended to cover wrongful termination claims based on racial discrimination.

§4.5   TITLE VII AND DISPARATE IMPACT

As with most regulatory measures, passage of Title VII did not ensure the immediate end of all racial discrimination in employment; but, predictably, overt refusals to hire or upgrade for racial reasons were transformed into special "qualifications" involving education, training, experience, residency, seniority, test scores, family connections, and even arrest records and wage garnishments.

Cases in which plaintiffs rely upon statistical proof of the discriminatory effect of an employer's hiring practices have come to be known as "disparate impact" cases.[1] In disparate impact cases, a plaintiff may introduce statistics, for example, that an employer's use of a certain qualification excludes minority workers from a job or that members of a minority race are underrepresented in the employer's work force. Contrast this with the disparate treatment cases, discussed in the preceding section, in which minority workers allege that an employer has treated them differently from white workers. In disparate impact cases the employers may be facially neutral, "fair in form, but discriminatory in operation." In what was for years a landmark case, Griggs v. Duke Power Co.,[2] the Supreme Court first established that Title VII prohibits neutral employment practices in disparate impact cases. In *Griggs*, black employees at the respondent's Dan River power-generating facility in North Carolina brought a class action under Title VII. The employees challenged the imposition of educational requirements as a condition of employment and transfer within the company. Prior to the effective date of Title VII, the respondent had openly discriminated in hiring. Blacks were assigned only to the labor department, where the highest-paying jobs paid less than the lowest-paying jobs in the other four departments.

---

45. See Fielder v. UAL Corp., 281 F.3d 973 (9th Cir. 2000).

46. See Lauture v. International Bus. Mach. Corp., 216 F.3d 258 (2d Cir. 2000); Perry v. Woodward, 199 F.3d 1126, 1133 (10th Cir. 1999); Spriggs v. Diamond Auto Glass, 165 F.3d 1015, 1018-1019 (4th Cir. 1999); Fadeyi v. Planned Parenthood Ass'n of Lubbock, Inc., 160 F.3d 1048, 1051-1052 (5th Cir. 1998).

§4.5   1. See Elaine Shoben, Probing the Discrimination Effects of Employee Selection Procedures with Disparate Impact Analysis Under Title VII, 56 Tex. L. Rev. 1 (1977).

2. 401 U.S. 424 (1971).

Beginning in 1965, the respondent ceased to restrict blacks to the labor department, but conditioned employment in any other department on graduation from high school and on satisfactory performance on two professionally prepared aptitude tests. Initially, completion of high school was made the prerequisite of transfer from labor and coal handling to "inside" departments; then the company allowed incumbent employees who had not graduated from high school to qualify for transfer by passing the aptitude tests. The test standards were more stringent than the high school education requirement. According to the 1960 census, only 12 percent of black males in North Carolina had graduated from high school, compared to 34 percent of white males. The aptitude tests, neither of which measured the ability to learn or perform a particular job, were among those found by the EEOC in 1966 to discriminate against blacks in that a disproportionately high number of blacks failed. In one case, 58 percent of whites passed the tests used by respondent, as compared with only 6 percent of the blacks. White employees who had been hired prior to the adoption of the educational requirements were permitted to continue working in the "inside" departments and were promoted, whether or not they had graduated from high school.

The Court in *Griggs* began by reviewing the objective of Title VII, which was to achieve equality of employment opportunities and to remove barriers favoring white employees. In light of this objective, "practices, procedures, or tests neutral on their face, and even neutral in terms of intent, cannot be maintained if they operate to 'freeze' the status quo of prior discriminatory employment practices." Thus, the testing process used by the employer had the effect of excluding blacks who had received inferior education in segregated schools. Applying Title VII to the employer's testing process, Congress required "the removal of artificial, arbitrary, and unnecessary barriers to employment when the barriers operate invidiously to discriminate on the basis of racial or other impermissible classification."

The Court explained that Title VII was directed at the consequences of employment practices, not the motivation. The employer must show the relationship between the requirement and job, not an easy task in light of the inherent inadequacy of testing devices and degree requirements. Chief Justice Burger said, "History is filled with examples of men and women who rendered highly effective performance without the conventional badges of accomplishment in terms of certificates, diplomas, or degrees. Diplomas and tests are useful servants, but Congress had mandated the common-sense proposition that they are not to become masters of reality."[3] Neither the high school completion requirement nor the

---

3. Writing for the Court, Chief Justice Burger used a childhood fable to illustrate his point:

Congress has now provided that tests or criteria for employment or promotion may not provide equality of opportunity merely in the sense of the fabled offer of milk to the stork and the fox. On the contrary, Congress has now required that the posture and condition of the jobseeker be taken into account. It has — to resort again to the fable — provided that the vessel in which the milk is proffered be one all seekers can use. The Act proscribes not only overt discrimination but also practices that are fair in form, but discriminatory in operation. The touchstone is business necessity. If an employment practice which operates to exclude Negroes cannot be shown to be related to job performance, the practice is prohibited.

Id. at 431.

general intelligence test in *Griggs* were related to successful job performance. In fact, evidence showed that employees who had not met these qualifications performed their work satisfactorily, and even were often promoted.

Griggs left many questions unanswered for later disparate impact cases. *Griggs* did not specify exactly how much of an adverse impact upon a minority group would constitute a Title VII violation. While *Griggs* involved practices which virtually excluded blacks from higher-paying jobs, many other cases involve only partial exclusion or underrepresentation of minority workers. Moreover, *Griggs* left open the choice of what groups should be analyzed in measuring disparate impact: Should a court compare the number of minority workers hired with the number of minority members in the general population? In the applicant pool? In the local community? In the occupation?

§4.6 THE EROSION OF PLAINTIFFS' EMPLOYMENT DISCRIMINATION REMEDIES AND THE 1991 AMENDMENTS

§4.6.1 Undermining *Griggs* and Then Some: Wards Cove v. Antonio

Reflecting the loss of interest in civil rights from 1965 when *Griggs* was decided, the Court's 1989 decision in Wards Cove Packing Co. v. Antonio,[1] sharply altered and nearly demolished *Griggs*. On the evidentiary front, *Wards Cove* required plaintiffs in disparate impact cases to isolate the "qualified" applicants in the labor pool of the surrounding area and then to compare these numbers against those actually hired out of the group. Racial stratification, where numbers of whites in certain jobs (or all jobs) are compared to numbers of blacks in certain jobs (or no jobs), would no longer control the inquiry into whether or not an employer's policy discriminates on the basis of race. In short, the evidentiary requirements of *Wards Cove* forced plaintiffs into at least two inimitable evidentiary challenges: first, to go beyond accessible workplace distributions, and further, to go beyond even less accessible labor pool distributions (the pool examined must be "qualified"); and second, to bear the burden, tacitly, of "proving" the existence of qualified-but-discouraged-or-rejected applicants *even if* the workplace is totally segregated and the labor pool has been historically stratified because of racism.

The *Wards Cove* plaintiffs were a class of predominantly Filipino and Alaskan native workers at defendant-petitioners' salmon canneries who filed a Title VII suit in 1974 under both a disparate impact and a disparate treatment theory. They alleged that defendants' hiring and promotion practices — separate hiring channels, a lack of objective hiring criteria, a rehire preference, nepotism, and not promoting from within — denied them employment in the higher paid "noncannery" jobs because of race.

"Cannery workers" were mostly nonwhite, and their jobs were classified as unskilled. They were hired through an agreement with a largely nonwhite union

§4.6   1. 490 U.S. 642 (1989).

local and from the Alaskan native population living near the canneries. "Noncannery workers," on the other hand, were predominantly white, and most of their jobs were classified as skilled. Virtually all noncannery jobs were better paid than the cannery jobs. Employees were hired through a more informal process, and recruited by white supervisors through word of mouth.

In a five-to-four decision the Court held that a mere showing that nonwhites were overrepresented in the lower paid cannery jobs, and underrepresented in the higher-paid noncannery jobs, based on statistical evidence of a lower percentage of minority workers in the at-issue, higher-paying jobs, was not sufficient by itself to make out a disparate impact claim.[2] Justice White wrote for the Court that "[i]t is . . . a comparison . . . between the racial composition of the qualified persons in the labor market and the persons holding at-issue jobs . . . that generally forms the proper basis for the initial inquiry in a disparate impact case." As to skilled non-cannery workers, the Court stated that if the lower representation of nonwhites resulted from the dearth of qualified nonwhite applicants, the employer's employ-ment practices could not be said to have caused the alleged disparate impact.[3]

As to unskilled noncannery workers, the Court found that the racial imbalance was not improper where there was no showing of barriers or practices that deterred qualified nonwhite applicants for those positions.[4] The Court further stated that using cannery workers as a potential labor pool for the unskilled noncannery jobs was not appropriate where those workers neither had applied nor would apply for the jobs in question, where many persons who were not cannery workers would be qualified for those positions, and where the nonwhite "over-representation" in the cannery jobs was largely the result of the hiring agreement with the predominantly nonwhite union local.

The majority also laid down stricter causation requirements for a prima facie case of disparate impact. Adopting the plurality portion of Justice O'Connor's opinion in Watson v. Fort Worth Bank & Trust,[5] the *Wards Cove* majority ruled that "[a]s a general matter, a plaintiff must demonstrate that it is the

---

2. Id. at 650, 655.

3. Id. at 651-652. "If the absence of minorities holding such skilled positions [as accountants, managers, boat captains, electricians, doctors and engineers, and the many other 'skilled' non-cannery positions] is due to a dearth of qualified nonwhite applicants (for reasons which are not the [defendants'] fault), [defendants'] selection methods and employment practices cannot be said to have had a disparate impact on non-whites." Id.

4. Id. at 653. "[R]acial imbalance in one segment of an employer's work force does not, without more, establish a prima facie case of disparate impact with respect to the selection of workers for the employer's other positions. . . . [Where] there are no barriers or practices deterring qualified non-whites from applying for non-cannery positions, . . . if the percentage of selected applicants who are nonwhite is not significantly less than the percentage of qualified applicants who are nonwhite, the employer's selection mechanism probably does not operate with a disparate impact on minorities."

5. 487 U.S. 977, 994 (1988). "[W]e note that plaintiff's burden in establishing a prima facie case goes beyond the need to show that there are statistical disparities in the work force. The plaintiff must begin by identifying the specific employment practice that is challenged. . . . Especially in cases where an employer combines subjective criteria with the use of more rigid standardized rules or tests, the plaintiff is in our view responsible for isolating and identifying the specific employment practices that are allegedly responsible for any observed statistical disparities." Id., quoted at 490 U.S. 642, 656 (1989).

application of a specific and particular employment practice that has created the disparate impact under attack. Such a showing is an integral part of the plaintiff's prima facie case in a disparate-impact suit under Title VII."[6] Finally, the Court held that once plaintiffs have established a prima facie case that a specific challenged practice has created the disparate impact, the employer's burden is merely to produce evidence of the business necessity of the challenged practice. Relying again on the *Watson* plurality opinion, the Court ruled that the "ultimate burden of proving that discrimination against a protected group has been caused by a specific employment practice remains with the plaintiff at all times."[7] Thus, plaintiff's burden is to prove that the proffered business justification was not the reason for the adoption of the challenged practice that caused disparate impact. "The touchstone of this inquiry [that the challenged practice serves a legitimate employment goal of the employer] is a reasoned review of the employer's justification for his use of the challenged practice." *Wards Cove*'s majority opinion seriously undermined the principle of disparate impact adopted by the Court in the landmark decision in *Griggs*. Justice Stevens' dissent reviews the law prior to and after the *Wards Cove* decision.

> [I]ntent plays no role in the disparate-impact inquiry. The question, rather, is whether an employment practice has a significant, adverse effect on an identifiable class of workers — regardless of the cause or motive for the practice. The employer may attempt to contradict the factual basis for this effect; that is, to prevent the employee from establishing a prima facie case. But when an employer is faced with sufficient proof of disparate impact, its only recourse is to justify the practice by explaining why it is necessary to the operation of business. Such a justification is a classic example of an affirmative defense. . . .
>
> Failing to explore the interplay between these distinct orders of proof, the Court announces that our frequent statements that the employer shoulders the burden of proof respecting business necessity "should have been understood to mean an employer's production — but not persuasion — burden." Our opinions always have emphasized that in a disparate-impact case the employer's burden is weighty. "The touchstone," the Court said in *Griggs*, "is business necessity." Later, we held that prison administrators had failed to "rebut the prima facie case of discrimination by showing that the height and weight requirements are . . . essential to effective job performance," Dothard v. Rawlinson. I am thus astonished to read that the "touchstone of this inquiry is a reasoned review of the employer's justification for his use of the challenged practice. . . . There is no requirement that the challenged practice be . . . essential[.]" This casual — almost summary — rejection of the statutory construction that developed in the wake of *Griggs* is most disturbing. I have always believed that the *Griggs* opinion correctly reflected the intent of the Congress that enacted Title VII. Even if I were not so persuaded, I could not join a rejection of a consistent interpretation of a federal statute. Congress frequently revisits this statutory scheme and can readily correct our mistakes if we misread its meaning. . . .

---

6. 490 U.S. at 657. The Court stated that even if plaintiffs showed nonwhite underrepresentation under the standards set out above, to make out a prima facie case they would still be required to "demonstrate that the disparity they complain of is the result of one or more of the employment practices they are attacking here, specifically showing that each challenged practice has a significantly disparate impact on [their] employment opportunities. . . ."

7. Id. at 659, *quoting* Watson v. Fort Worth Bank & Trust, 487 U.S. 977, 997 (1988).

Congress did indeed respond in 1991 by amending Title VII, rejecting *Wards Cove*'s allocation of the burden of production and persuasion, as discussed below in section 4.6.4.

> Also troubling, however, was the Court's apparent redefinition of the employees' burden of proof in a disparate-impact case. No prima facie case will be made, it declares, unless the employees " 'isolate and identify the specific employment practices that are allegedly responsible for any observed statistical disparities.' " This additional proof requirement is unwarranted. It is elementary that a plaintiff cannot recover upon proof of injury alone; rather, the plaintiff must connect the injury to an act of the defendant in order to establish prima facie that the defendant is liable. Although the causal link must have substance, the act need not constitute the sole or primary cause of the harm. *Cf.* Price Waterhouse v. Hopkins.[8] Thus in a disparate-impact case, proof of numerous questionable employment practices ought to fortify an employee's assertion that the practices caused racial disparities. Ordinary principles of fairness require that Title VII actions be tried like "any lawsuit." The changes the majority makes today, tipping the scales in favor of employers, are not faithful to those principles.[9]

§4.6.2 The Legacy of Washington v. Davis and the Search for Discriminatory Purpose

Washington v. Davis[10] is a pivotal decision for those seeking to recognize the limits of employment civil rights law enforcement. Although it was an employment discrimination case, the direct issue involved the equal protection clause, not Title VII or §1981. Two black police officers charged that the District of Columbia's police department engaged in discriminatory hiring and promotion practices. More specifically, the plaintiffs challenged the use of a civil service written exam designed to test verbal ability, vocabulary, reading, and comprehension. Using *Griggs* as a guideline, the appeals court found that the use of the invalidated test directly violated the standards set forth in *Griggs*. Four times as many blacks as whites failed the test, the court reasoned, and the test had not been shown to be an adequate measure of job performance; because discriminatory impact was evident, it was irrelevant whether there was discriminatory *intent*.

The Supreme Court reversed the court of appeals. It held that Title VII standards set in *Griggs* were inapplicable to equal protection cases.[11] The Court, using

---

8. Price Waterhouse v. Hopkins, 490 U.S. 228 (1989).

9. Wards Cove Packing Co. v. Antonio, 490 U.S. 642, 672-673 (1989) (citations and footnotes omitted).

10. 426 U.S. 229 (1976).

11. The plaintiffs had to bring suit challenging an employment policy under the equal protection clause because the government was the defendant-employer and nothing on the books would permit plaintiffs to bring suit under the Title VII *Griggs* disparate impact standards. Title VII did not apply because it had not yet been extended to federal employees at the time the suit was initially filed. Ironically, *Davis* had no direct impact upon employment opportunity for minority workers employed by the government, despite the fact that this was the group to whom the holding was directed. Title VII was amended in 1972, subsequent to the filing of the Davis action in 1970; the amendment overturned the problem that the Davis plaintiffs faced (having to use the equal protection clause because Title VII did not apply to government workers) and made Title VII applicable to government

as "precedent" voting rights[12] and school discrimination[13] cases, held that there must be "discriminatory racial purpose" before it could be said that a policy violated the equal protection clause. The *Davis* majority announced that even if a policy had a disparate effect on black Americans, that policy must be upheld by courts if (1) the policy was race-neutral on its face and (2) the policy served a legitimate public function.

In sum, then, *Davis* mandated that in the absence of proof of discriminatory purpose, courts were barred from ordering relief. In effect, policies challenged as racially biased were, from *Davis* on, tested under the least restrictive "reasonable basis" test of the equal protection clause. By refusing to extend the *Griggs* standard to equal protection cases — by requiring instead near-impossible proof of discriminatory intent — the Court dealt a severe blow to minority groups seeking to challenge discriminatory state action on equal protection grounds. The impact of this case would surface in housing, criminal justice,[14] and education[15] cases and, in a discouraging employment case where the Court revisited *Davis* and further tightened its daunting standards.[16]

The legacy *Davis* left may be better understood by trying to uncover what motivated the Court to bar application of discriminatory impact standards. The *Davis* court explained its refusal to accept a disproportionate impact test in equal protection analysis because it feared such a test "would be far reaching and would raise serious questions about, and perhaps invalidate, a whole range of tax, welfare, public service, regulatory, and licensing statutes."[17] Speculatively worrying about a "slippery slope," the Court declared in addition that a disparate impact test for equal protection analysis would render suspect *any* difference in treatment among racial classes.[18]

That fear emerged in a context more serious, in a vital sense, than employment discrimination: a case challenging the application of the death penalty to black defendants convicted of murdering white victims. In McCleskey v. Kemp,[19] the Court's "sky is falling" concern surfaced to deny a black capital defendant the right to challenge his death sentence despite massive statistical evidence that Georgia's jury verdict sentences had put many more black than white defendants to death. The defendant challenged his death sentence on the grounds that Georgia's death penalty *in operation* placed a dramatically higher value on white lives than black lives. In a five-to-four decision, the Court found the study failed to meet its burden that McCleskey had to show that "racial considerations played a part in

employers. See 42 U.S.C. §2000e-5(f)(1) (state and local government employees may use Title VII) and §2000e-16 (federal employees).

12. See Wright v. Rockfeller, 376 U.S. 52 (1964).

13. See Keyes v. School Dist. No. 1, 413 U.S. 189, 205 (1973).

14. See, e.g., McCleskey v. Kemp, 481 U.S. 279 (1987).

15. See, e.g., Wygant v. Jackson Bd. of Educ., 476 U.S. 267 (1986).

16. See Richmond, Va. v. J.A. Croson Co., 488 U.S. 469 (1989).

17. 426 U.S. at 248 (citing Frank I. Goodman, De Facto School Segregation: A Constitutional and Empirical Analysis, 60 Cal. L. Rev. 275 (1972) (arguing against discriminatory purpose standard and for a prohibition of de facto segregation)).

18. 426 U.S. at 240-241 (citing Jefferson v. Hackney, 406 U.S. 535, 548 (1972)).

19. 481 U.S. 279 (1987).

his sentence."[20] The absence of proof of specific, demonstrable, invidious intent on the part of the Georgia lawmakers hence made the state's rebuttal of McCleskey's discrimination claim unnecessary. The fact that the facially neutral Georgia law permitted the death penalty to be imposed on those who committed crimes such as McCleskey's — with no statutory racial specification or explicit jury intent in McCleskey's case — was deemed sufficient to justify the state's action.

As in *Davis*, the Court feared that reliance on a statistical study could pose a far-reaching threat to the criminal sentencing system that would extend to non-capital sentencing. The majority worried that courts might have to evaluate statistical sentencing disparities that correlated with the race or sex of actors other than the defendant or the victim in the criminal justice system, such as the prosecutor, the defense counsel, or the judge. Even the defendant's physical appearance and other "arbitrary variables" influencing the jury's decision might come under scrutiny, the majority declared. In dissent, Justice Brennan characterized the majority's fear as "a fear of too much justice. . . . The prospect that there may be more widespread abuse than [even] McCleskey documents may be dismaying, but it does not justify complete abdication of our judicial role." Were the racial roles reversed (i.e., were disproportionate numbers of whites being executed for similar crimes), it is hard to imagine that *McCleskey* would have denied such whites a fair chance at life. One wonders: If McCleskey were a white defendant convicted of killing a black during a felony in a state where whites were the victims of a justice system controlled by blacks, would the (white) Court's concern about the potential disruptive outcome of a reversal carry the same convincing weight? We in modern America for some years now have been witnessing the shift of the Court's racial shield from minorities to whites. In other words, the presumption — despite staggering evidence — seems now to be that nondiscrimination is the norm and that, in the absence of strong proof of fairly blatant discriminatory intent, the equal protection shield now protects both whites in general (as in *Washington* and *McCleskey*) and individual whites who allege disadvantage by the operation of racial remediation plans.

A key example of the latter protection is found in a series of decisions invalidating affirmative action plans. In Wygant v. Jackson Board of Education,[21] the white plaintiffs challenged a school board's bargaining agreement that was reached with the teacher's union. The plaintiffs challenged the agreement's layoff provision, claiming that they were laid off because of their race in violation of the Fourteenth Amendment's equal protection clause. (The bargaining agreement provided that in case teacher layoff became necessary, the least senior teacher would be let go first, except that at no time would there be a greater percentage of minority personnel laid off than the extant percentage of minority personnel employed at the time of the layoff.) The issue, the plurality of a divided Court decided, was whether the equal protection clause allowed school boards to extend preferential protection against layoffs to some of its employees because of their race or national origin.

20. Id. at 292.
21. 476 U.S. 267 (1986). The adverse impact of these "anti-affirmative action" cases on equal protection jurisprudence is discussed in Chapters 1 and 3.

Such a preference, the plurality emphasized, based on racial or ethnic criteria, required a thoroughly searching investigation to ensure consonance with constitutional guarantees. This thorough examination has two prongs: First, *any* racial classification (even for the benefit of a disadvantaged group) "must be justified by a compelling governmental interest."[22] Second, the means chosen by the State to effectuate its purpose must be "narrowly tailored to the achievement of that goal."[23] The Court went on to hold that the board's layoff plan was too intrusive, and that the plan did not satisfy the second prong of the "permissible racial classification" test. Employing rhetoric of "innocent parties" (the white plaintiffs) who would be unfairly burdened by the plan, the plurality concluded, "We have previously expressed concern over the burden that a preferential layoff scheme imposes on innocent parties. . . . [L]ayoffs impose the entire burden of achieving racial equality on particular individuals, often resulting in serious disruption of their lives. That burden is too intrusive."

The reasoning behind this conclusion sheds light on the influential *Davis* legacy. First, the Court noted that while race-conscious remedial action may be necessary to carry out the mandate of Brown v. Board of Education (to eliminate every vestige of racial segregation and discrimination in the schools), such a command may come into conflict with another constitutional duty required by the Fourteenth Amendment, namely, to "do away with all governmentally imposed distinctions based on race." Even though conflict may arise between the two imperatives, the plurality noted, the Court had recognized that to remedy the effects of prior discrimination, it might be necessary to take race into account — in short, a dedication to eradicating racial discrimination might entail that "innocent" persons be called upon to bear some of the burden of the remedy. By setting up inevitable tension, the Court emphasized that substantive equal protection (which would not bar *all* governmentally imposed distinctions based on race, merely those which replicated discrimination against disadvantaged groups) was as elusive a theory of justice as ever.

The plurality's second move demonstrates, even more clearly, which way the racial shield of equal protection had come to face: In the second line of reasoning, the Court distinguished between race-conscious *hiring* and race-conscious *firing*. With a wave of its judicial hand, the plurality declared that race-conscious firing was worse than race-conscious hiring, saying "[t]hough hiring goals may burden some innocent individuals, they simply do not impose the same kind of injury that layoffs impose. Denial of a future employment opportunity is not as intrusive as loss of an existing job."[24] But this reasoning does not explain why it is better for innocent blacks (i.e., "innocent" in the sense that they did nothing to deserve past discrimination barriers which precluded large-scale employment of minorities and hence are likely to be last hired and first fired) to be fired because race-conscious

22. Id. at 274, citing Palmore v. Sidoti, 466 U.S. 429, 432 (1984).
23. Id. at 274, citing Fullilove v. Klutznick, 448 U.S. 448, 480 (1980).
24. Id. at 282-283. "We have previously expressed concern over the burden that a preferential layoff scheme imposes on innocent parties. . . . In cases involving valid hiring goals, the burden to be borne by innocent individuals is diffused to a considerable extent among society generally. Though hiring goals may burden some innocent individuals, they simply do not impose the same kind of injury that layoffs impose. Denial of a future employment opportunity is not as intrusive as loss of an existing job." Id.

hiring criteria cannot, any longer, be backed up by race-conscious *firing* criteria (in order to achieve the good of compensatory hiring policies). For whites who hold proportionally more jobs with proportionally more seniority, it is true that race-conscious firing would be worse than race-conscious hiring — they already have jobs, or a good chance at getting one, if employment history is to be believed, and they already have tenure. But for blacks, the firing/hiring question is a distinction without a difference. The shield of racial equality turns now one way, now another, depending on a fine-tuned distinction that ultimately serves to destroy the shield's efficacy.

Third, *Wygant* fed into the slippery slope fear of *Davis* when the plurality noted, "The role model theory employed by the district court [to support a holding favorable to the plan] has no logical stopping point, and allows the Board to engage in discriminatory hiring and layoff practices long past the point required by any legitimate remedial purpose." Implicit in this fearful statement is a normativity, which *assumes that discrimination against whites is the thing to be feared.* The equal protection clause, originally enacted to combat discrimination by whites against nonwhites, was employed in *Wygant* to combat "discrimination" against whites.

The legacy of *Davis* and its progeny had disturbing results in the employment context. One strategy to open equal employment opportunity for minority workers that extended beyond securing entry-level jobs for victims of discrimination seemed to present itself in affirmative action measures directed towards benefiting minority businesses. Minority businesses are likely to employ high proportions of minority managers and supervisors. Measures that assist minority business are therefore likely to assist minority workers in, or seeking, managerial or supervisory jobs. Such assistance is badly needed; fair employment laws are likely to be most effective at protecting minority workers in low-level blue-collar positions, and least effective at giving minorities a fair opportunity to enter upper-level management or supervisory positions.

A prime example of this affirmative action strategy was the ten percent set-aside of the Public Works Employment Act of 1977.[25] Under §103(f)(2) of this Act, at least 10 percent of each federal grant for state and local public works projects had to be used to purchase services of minority business enterprises (MBEs). The seminal case dealing with this set-aside provision, Fullilove v. Klutznick,[26] appeared as good news on the MBE horizon. In that case, a plurality of the Supreme Court upheld the Public Works Act's MBE provision, which the Second Circuit had upheld despite the newness and sparseness of the legislation. The Court urged deference to congressional power, and different groups of Justices emphasized different standards of review. Commentary on *Fullilove* was mixed. The plurality opinion had produced much confusion. One commentator hailed the court's incomprehensible affirmative action policy as a deliberate and practical choice that allowed it to uphold affirmative action plans for the present while preserving the freedom to reconsider such policies in the future.[27]

25. 42 U.S.C.A. §6705(f)(2) (Supp. 1978).

26. 448 U.S. 448 (1980), aff'g Fullilove v. Kreps, 584 F.2d 600 (2d Cir. 1978).

27. Comment, Reverse Racial Preferences Under the Equal Protection Clause: Round II, Fullilove v. Klutznick, 19 Am. Bus. L.J. 197 (1981).

It appears that the commentator was prescient indeed. Another MBE case, City of Richmond v. Croson, was considered by the Supreme Court and — in circumstances that seemed to beg the Court to uphold the MBE provision instituted by the City of Richmond — came to represent the demolishing of *Fullilove*'s promising precedent. The City of Richmond had relied on *Fullilove*'s holding when it decided to erect a plan requiring prime contractors awarded city construction contracts to subcontract at least 30 percent of the dollar amount of each contract to one or more MBE's. The Supreme Court called Richmond's reliance on *Fullilove* "misplaced." Reaffirming the *Wygant* plurality's finding that the strict scrutiny standard must be applied to *all* race conscious legislation (no matter the target group or the affected group), the Court in *Croson* announced that all racial classifications (including those designated as "benign" or "remedial") must be deemed suspect and subject to the strict scrutiny standard. "We thus reaffirm," the *Croson* majority noted, "the view expressed by the plurality in *Wygant* that the standard of review under the Equal Protection Clause is not dependent on the race of those burdened or benefited by a particular classification."[28]

The Court rejected Richmond's plan. It was an "unyielding racial quota," the majority declared, not justified even by past discrimination in the entire construction industry. The Court rejected any compelling governmental interest on the part of the city of Richmond, holding that its inclusivity of races other than African American when such other races had not been demonstrated to have been discriminated against, betrayed the real motivation (administrative efficiency) of the government. The Court also decided that the plan was not narrowly tailored enough, that the 30 percent quota rested upon "a completely unrealistic assumption that minorities will choose to enter construction in lockstep proportion to their representation in the local population." And then, reminiscent of *Davis, McCleskey*, and *Wygant*, the sky began to fall, according to Justice O'Connor:

> To accept Richmond's claim that past societal discrimination alone can serve as the basis for rigid racial preferences would be to open the door to competing claims for "remedial relief" for *every* disadvantaged group. . . . Courts would be asked to evaluate the extent of prejudice and consequent harm suffered by various minority groups. Those whose societal injury *is thought* to exceed some *arbitrary* level of tolerability then would be entitled to preferential classification (citation omitted). We think such a result [i.e., preferentiality] would be contrary to both the *letter* and the *spirit* of a constitutional provision whose central command is equality. [Emphasis supplied.][29]

Many commentators, the Court dissenters included, were astonished by the *Croson* decision. Justice Marshall, joined by Justices Brennan and Blackmun, marveled that Richmond, a city which was the capital of the Confederacy, had taken forthright steps to combat the effects of racial discrimination in its midst. He

---

28. 488 U.S. 469, 501-503 (1989). The Court found such reliance misplaced on two theories. First, the *Fullilove* decision did not apply "strict scrutiny" or another traditional method of equal protection review. And second, Congressional authority to enact remedies for racial discrimination under §5 of the Fourteenth Amendment and the commerce clause has no counterpart for state and local government entities. Id. at 487, 490.

29. 488 U.S. 469, 505-506 (1989).

deplored the majority for frustrating this effort, and noted that such frustration would likely condemn similar efforts in other cities. A more apposite standard of review, he argued, would be that of *Fullilove* (which the majority had flatly rejected): That "race-conscious classifications designed to further remedial goals must serve important governmental objectives and must be substantially related to achievement of those objectives in order to withstand constitutional scrutiny."[30] Richmond had a strong and compelling reason to end discrimination in construction contracting, and proffered plenty of proof of past discrimination to support its remedial plan.

Justice Marshall continued pointedly,

> Today, for the first time, a majority of this Court has adopted strict scrutiny as its standard of Equal Protection Clause review of race-conscious remedial measures. This is an unwelcome development. A profound difference separates governmental actions that themselves are racist, and governmental actions that seek to remedy the effects of prior racism, or to prevent neutral governmental activity from perpetuating the effects of such racism.[31]

Marshall's final challenge, in *Croson*, was even more pointed. He wondered how, if the Court majority really believed that groups like Richmond's whites were entitled to suspect class status, the Court's decisions denying suspect status to women, and to persons with incomes below average, could stand on anything but "shaky ground."

The following year, the Court, in a five-to-four decision in Metro Broadcasting, Inc. v. Federal Communications Commission,[32] did hold that congressionally approved affirmative action programs need only meet intermediate scrutiny. But, as Professor Erwin Chemerinsky notes,[33] the majority opinion in *Metro Broadcasting* was written by Justice Brennan and joined by Justices White, Marshall, Blackmun, and Stevens. The dissent was comprised of Justices O'Connor, Kennedy, Scalia, and Rehnquist. Between *Metro Broadcasting*, in 1990, and Adarand Constructors, Inc. v. Pena,[34] in 1995, four of the Justices in the majority, but none of those in dissent, resigned. In *Adarand*, the four dissenters from *Metro Broadcasting* were joined by Justice Thomas to create a majority that overruled *Metro Broadcasting* and enabled a conclusion that "federal racial classifications, like those of a State, must serve a compelling governmental interest, and must be narrowly tailored to further that interest."[35]

---

30. Id. at 535, citing University of Cal. v. Bakke, 438 U.S. 265, 359 (1979).

31. Id. at 551-552.

32. 497 U.S. 547 (1990) (upholding FCC policies that gave a preference to minority-owned businesses in broadcast licensing, and finding that "benign race-conscious measures mandated by Congress — even if those measures are not 'remedial' in the sense of being designed to compensate victims of past governmental or society discrimination — are constitutionally permissible to the extent that they serve important governmental objectives within the power of Congress and are substantially related to the achievement of those objectives." 497 U.S. at 564-565).

33. Erwin Chemerinsky, Constitutional Law Principles and Policies 587 (1997).

34. 515 U.S. 200 (1995).

35. Id. at 225.

Writing for the plurality in *Adarand*, Justice O'Connor, while adopting strict scrutiny as the appropriate test for all affirmative action, said that such programs might pass judicial review if they furthered a compelling interest and satisfied the "narrow tailoring" test as set out in previous cases.[36] Justice Scalia, writing separately, argued that the government never could have a compelling interest in using racial classifications to remedy prior discrimination. And Justice Thomas espoused the view that all discrimination, whether malicious or benign, is noxious.[37]

Thus, in *Adarand*, the Supreme Court overruled the intermediate standards of review used in *Metro Broadcasting* but did not decide whether diversity is a compelling governmental interest under the strict scrutiny test. Leonard Baynes writes that "by not specifically overruling the standard of review used in *Metro Broadcasting*, the Court left open the possibility that diversity — at least in some manifestation — might still be a sufficient ground for an affirmative action program."[38] The author argues that given the legal landscape, employers, specifically the FCC, should retain its diversity rationale but combine that rationale with evidence of discrimination. He suggests three things to survive a legal challenge:

1. minority-owned telecommunications businesses in pursuit of licenses are more likely to be discriminated against by bankers, venture capitalists, and others;
2. minority and women-owned businesses are more likely to have a different customer base or broadcasting format; and
3. this different customer base and broadcasting format causes these businesses to be discriminated against by others.[39]

Martha R. Mahoney attacks the *Croson* and *Adarand* decisions for their unwillingness to discuss class. She argues that "[h]idden assumptions about class and status helped the Court develop the rule that 'race classification demands strict scrutiny' rather than 'equal protection demands an exploration of power, harm, and interest.' "[40] She explains that in *Croson*, set-aside programs are "precisely the areas in which whiteness reproduces itself in private clubs and social networks, even after previously excluded groups achieve political power." Mahoney argues that

> [t]o reach the *Croson* holding, the Court had to overlook class, the social nature of work, the meaning of racial subordination and privilege, and questions of the ongoing reproduction of power — as well as distinguishing away the entire history of subordination in Richmond, Virginia as unreachable "societal" discrimination.
>
> The contractor cases [*Adarand* and *Croson*] can only be explained through understanding class as well as whiteness. Courts do not protect inchoate opportunity for working people. . . . The Court has found opportunity insufficiently certain to

36. Id. at 237.
37. Id. at 241 (Justice Thomas concurring in part and concurring in the judgment).
38. Leonard M. Baynes, Life After *Adarand*: What Happened to the *Metro Broadcasting* Diversity Rationale for Affirmative Action in Telecommunications Ownership?, 33 U. Mich. J.L. Reform 87, 113 (1999-2000).
39. Id. at 127-128.
40. Martha R. Mahoney, Class and Status in American Law: Race, Interest, and the Anti-Transformation Cases, 76 S. Cal. L. Rev. 799, 856 (2003).

create standing when the plaintiffs are African Americans. Yet opportunity for white businessmen seemed so tangible that the Court granted standing even in the absence of criteria on which it insists in other cases.

She concludes that

> When either whiteness or class is ignored, white workers are placed in an inherently more reactionary position than when both are considered together. If we notice only whiteness, then working class whites see only those aspects of self shared with more elite whites, and fail to see those aspects of self shared with people of color.[41]

In another article, Reshma M. Saujani takes advantage of the Court's unwillingness to distinguish between different types of racial classification in *Adarand* to propose that the Court look at unconscious racism, arguing that

> If the Court no longer distinguishes between "invidious" and "benign" racial discrimination, it similarly should not distinguish between "conscious" and "unconscious" intent, especially if unconscious intent can be measured. Justice Thomas should take the same uncompromising position as he did in *Adarand*, that "good intentions cannot provide refuge from the principle that under our Constitution, the government may not make distinctions on the basis of race." If the government's good intentions cannot protect its benign racial classifications, then their embedded bad intentions should not protect racial decisions that may be invidious.[42]

She suggests that courts use the Implicit Association Test, a computer-based test developed by Yale and University of Washington psychologists that can discern an unconscious racist motive when the record seems to indicate no animus on the part of the decision-maker but the policy choice has a racially disparate impact.

§4.6.3 Further Erosion: Prelude to the 1991 Amendments

Prior to the 1988 Court Term, civil rights adherents were worried but still cautiously optimistic in their assessment of the Court's employment decisions. The *Davis-Wygant-Croson* case line portended heightened difficulty for plaintiffs, but still many pro-plaintiff doctrines prevailed. There remained hope that even ideological conservatives would not countenance policies that denied individuals a chance to work at their highest levels of effectiveness. Those hopes were shattered by *Watson, Patterson, Wards Cove*, Martin v. Wilks, *Lorance*, and several other decisions.

As important as the substance of the decisions (summarized below) are the messages the cases send between the lines to people of color who still rely on the law to provide at least partial insulation from injury by a society where racism thrives. There exist also, between the lines, messages to those who are anxious to reestablish, in law as well as fact, the unchallenged dominance of whites over blacks in this country.

41. Id. at 891.
42. Reshma M. Saujani, "The Implicit Association Test": A Measure of Unconscious Racism in Legislative Decision Making, 8 Mich. J. Race & L. 395, 422 (2003).

A.   Watson v. Fort Worth Bank and Trust

In Watson v. Fort Worth Bank and Trust,[43] the petitioner, a black woman, brought suit charging that she had been rejected in favor of white applicants for four promotions to supervisory positions in respondent bank's employee structure. The bank had not developed precise and formal selection criteria for the positions. Instead it relied on the subjective judgment of white supervisors who were acquainted with the candidates and with the nature of the jobs. The Court held that subjective or discretionary employment practices challenged as violating Title VII may, in appropriate cases, be analyzed under the disparate impact approach. However, the Court also held that the plaintiff must demonstrate the discriminatory effect of *specific practices* on the protected group members.

In *Watson*, the Court foreshadowed its reflexive fear of quotas by seizing on the subjectivity of the criteria under challenge. Justice O'Connor, writing for a plurality of the Court (joined by the Chief Justice and Justices White and Scalia), expressed concern that the extension of disparate impact analysis to subjective employment criteria could increase the risk that employers would adopt surreptitious numerical goals and quotas in order to avoid liability. Presumably, she reasoned, such strategic employers would believe that, because disparate impact analysis inevitably focuses on statistical evidence and because statistical evidence cannot practically be rebutted by the kind of counter-evidence typically used to defend objective criteria, the threat of ruinous litigation would require the employer to somehow ensure that no plaintiff could establish a prima facie case under disparate impact theory. Justice O'Connor feared that precluding the establishment of a plaintiff's case would come in the form of clandestine quotas, and that such a result would be contrary to Congress's clearly expressed intent in 42 U.S.C. §2000e-2(j) (that no employer shall be required to grant preferential treatment to any protected individual or group because of a numerical imbalance in its work force).

B.   Martin v. Wilks

In, Martin v. Wilks,[44] the plaintiffs were white firefighters who wished to intervene in a consent decree agreed on by the City of Birmingham and the Jefferson County Personnel Board. They claimed that, because the city and board were making promotional decisions in accordance with consent orders, the plaintiffs were being denied promotions on the basis of race in favor of "less qualified" blacks. In a five-to-four decision upholding the Eleventh Circuit ruling, the Supreme Court held that respondent white firefighters who had failed to intervene in earlier employment discrimination proceedings were not precluded from challenging employment decisions pursuant to the consent decree. Chief Justice Rehnquist, writing for the majority, rejected the position taken by most courts of appeal that respondents, having failed to intervene timely in the initial

43. 487 U.S. 977 (1988).
44. 490 U.S. 755 (1989).

proceedings, were barred from making an impermissible collateral attack on the consent order.

A dissenting Justice Stevens reminded the majority that,

> The predecessor to this litigation was brought to change a pattern of hiring and promotion practices that had discriminated against black citizens in Birmingham for decades. The white respondents in this case are not responsible for that history of discrimination, but they are nevertheless beneficiaries of the discriminatory practices that the litigation was designed to correct. Any remedy that seeks to create employment conditions that would have obtained if there had been no violations of law will necessarily have an adverse impact on whites, who must now share their job and promotion opportunities with blacks.[45]

C. Patterson v. McLean Credit Union

Another 1989 case that dealt with post-hiring employment problems involved a black woman plaintiff and §1981. Unlike Martin v. Wilks, however, in Patterson v. McLean Credit Union,[46] the Court came down decisively on the side of the defendant-employers. At issue was whether §1981 provided employees protection from racial harassment in the workplace. The Court held that racial harassment relating to the conditions of employment was not actionable under §1981 because that law does not apply to conduct which occurs *after* formation of a contract, nor does it apply to conduct that does not interfere with the right to enforce established contract obligations.

The *Patterson* case involved the following facts: Petitioner Brenda Patterson, a black woman, was employed for ten years until she was laid off as a teller and file coordinator by respondent McLean Credit Union. She brought action under §1981, alleging that during her employment, respondent subjected her to various forms of racial harassment, denied her wage increases, failed to offer her training for higher-level jobs, failed to promote her to accounting clerk, and discharged her, all because of her race. As summarized by the court of appeals, Ms. Patterson testified that her supervisor "[p]eriodically stared at her for several minutes at a time; that he gave her too many tasks, causing her to complain that she was under too much pressure; that among the tasks given her were sweeping and dusting, jobs not given to white employees. On one occasion, she testified, [her supervisor] told [her] that blacks are known to work slower than whites. According to [petitioner, her supervisor] also criticized her in staff meetings while not similarly criticizing white employees." Despite her evidence, the district court dismissed her claim and the court of appeals affirmed. The Supreme Court granted certiorari to decide

---

45. Justice Stevens notes unapologetically and wisely, "It is inevitable that nonminority employees or applicants will be less well off under an affirmative action plan than without it, no matter what form it takes. For example, even when an employer simply agrees to recruit minority job applicants more actively, white applicants suffer the 'nebulous' harm of facing increased competition and the diminished likelihood of eventually being hired." Id. at 792, n.31 (citing Maimon Schwarzchild, Public Law by Private Bargain: Title VII Consent Decrees and the Fairness of Negotiated Institutional Reform, 1984 Duke L.J. 887, 909-910).

46. 491 U.S. 164 (1989).

whether petitioner's claim of racial harassment was actionable under §1981. And, after oral argument, the Court decided sua sponte to review whether to reconsider the interpretive coverage given §1981 in Runyon v. McCrary.[47] Although the Court declined to expressly overrule *Runyon*, they narrowed §1981's coverage considerably. Speaking for the majority, Justice Kennedy focused on the term "make and enforce contracts" in the section and found that "Section 1981 cannot be construed as a general proscription of racial discrimination in all aspects of contract relations. . . ." Justice Kennedy distinguished between the *formation* stage of the contract (for employment) and the *post-formation* stage. He asserted that §1981 extended only to the formation of a contract, but not to problems that might arise later from the conditions of continuing employment. With that, the Court found that Ms. Patterson's racial harassment claims related to conditions of employment rather than formation of contract, and hence were not actionable under §1981.

In Martin v. Wilks, the Court insisted on the flexibility of procedure in order to allow white plaintiffs to intervene in a situation where normally intervention would be absolutely barred by collateral attack doctrine. In *Patterson*, by contrast, the Court insisted on the narrowness of procedural remedy, in a situation where the distinction between "formation" and "post-formation" of an employment contract betrayed a rigidly formal orientation in the context of a black woman challenging poor treatment after hiring. This extremely narrow interpretation of §1981 stands in stark contrast to the procedural expansiveness with which the Court treated the white plaintiffs' claim.

D.   Lorance v. AT&T Technologies[48]

In this Title VII case, Justice Scalia in a five-to-three decision ruled that under §703(h) of Title VII,[49] the operation of a facially neutral seniority system having disparate impact on men and women was not unlawful unless discriminatory intent were proven. Moreover, a claim of discrimination based on a seniority system begins to run at the time of the adoption of the seniority system.

The issue in the case was whether Title VII required a challenge to a new seniority system at the time of the system's adoption. The issue arose because AT&T and a local branch of the AFL-CIO had altered, through collective bargaining agreements, the determination and privileges of a worker's seniority. Before 1979, the agreements had determined a worker's seniority on the basis of years of plantwide service. In addition, plantwide seniority was transferable upon promotion to a more skilled "tester" position. A new agreement executed in 1979 changed the seniority system; it made seniority in the more skilled tester positions dependent upon the amount of time actually spent as a tester, not just in plantwide service. In 1982, petitioners (women employees who were promoted to tester positions between 1978 and 1980) received demotions during an economic

47. 427 U.S. 160 (1976).
48. 490 U.S. 900 (1989).
49. 42 U.S.C. §2000e-2(h).

downturn that they would not have sustained had the former seniority system remained in place.

They brought suit, charging that respondents had violated Title VII of the Civil Rights Act of 1964 by adopting the new seniority system with the purpose and effect of protecting incumbent testers (jobs traditionally dominated by men) from female employees who had greater plantwide seniority and who were becoming testers in increasing numbers. The district court granted summary judgment for respondents on the ground that the petitioners' charges had not been filed within the required period "after the alleged unfair labor practice occurred."[50] The court of appeals affirmed.

The Supreme Court concluded that the limitations period of §706(e) commenced to run, in this case, in 1979 when the changed seniority rule went into effect. This ruling, the Court held, struck a balance between the interest in having valid claims vindicated, and the interest in not adjudicating stale claims.

E. *Price Waterhouse v. Hopkins*[51]

Once the defendant presents evidence of a legitimate reason for its actions, the plaintiff must demonstrate that the legitimate nondiscriminatory motive put forth by the defendant is merely pretext for discrimination. The pretext analysis created a wealth of confusing and sometimes contradictory jurisprudence from the Court that Congress would later seek to clarify in the Civil Rights Act of 1991.

Under the burden-shifting framework, once the employer presents a nondiscriminatory reason for its actions, the plaintiff, if she elects to attack this reason, may present evidence that "a discriminatory reason more likely motivated the employer" or "that the employer's proffered explanation is unworthy of credence."[52] However, the court could conclude that her evidence is not sufficient to show the employer's reasons are pretextual but nevertheless also shows that race also played some role in the employer's decision-making process.[53] That is, when proof of an employer's reliance on unlawful considerations such as race is broad but stops just short of some "smoking gun" evidence, such evidence of pretext "allow[s] the trial court to credit her claim of [unlawful] motive without having to discredit the employer's reliance on a non-discriminatory reason."[54]

This is precisely what happened in Price Waterhouse v. Hopkins, in which the lower court concluded that although the record did not show that the employer's nondiscriminatory explanation was false, it did establish that gender stereotyping played *a* role in the employer's actions.[55] The Supreme Court granted certiorari to

---

50. §706(e) of Title VII, 42 U.S.C. §2000e-5(e).

51. 490 U.S. 228 (1989).

52. Id. (citing *McDonnell Douglas*, 411 U.S. at 804-805).

53. Steven J. Kaminshine, Disparate Treatment as a Theory of Discrimination: The Need for a Restatement, not a Revolution, 2 Stan. J. C.R. & C.L. 1, 20-21 (2005) (using Price Waterhouse v. Hopkins as example of judicial review of such facts and explaining that that case "presented a mixed-motive question . . . not because one of the parties alleged mixed motives or litigated on that basis, but because the proof allowed for mixed-motive findings.").

54. Id. at 22.

55. See discussion in Kaminshine, supra note 53, at 20-21.

resolve uncertainty concerning the burdens on a plaintiff and defendant in cases involving proof of both lawful and unlawful motivations, but yielded no clear answer.

In this fractured decision, the plurality and two separately concurring Justices (White and O'Connor) agreed that if the evidence established that the employer had been motivated even in part by an unlawful motive, to avoid liability, the employer *might* then have to show that it would have acted in the same manner even if this factor were eliminated. The primary divide among these six Justices concerned the circumstances that would trigger the imposition of this burden on the employer.

Justice Brennan, writing for the plurality, concluded that Title VII's use of the phrase "because of" meant that an employer could not automatically evade liability if it had been motivated by both legitimate and unlawful considerations.[56] When the evidence supports the existence of multiple mixed motives on the part of the employer, "an employer shall not be liable if it can prove that, even if it had not taken gender into account, it would have reached the same decision regarding a particular person."[57] Justice O'Connor disagreed with the plurality's starting point and believed that the words "because of" as used in Title VII required a plaintiff to establish "but for" causation.[58] Thus, she did not believe that the *McDonnell Douglas* burden-shifting framework was per se inapplicable to the mixed motive context and would deviate from it only where the record contained "direct evidence" of unlawful motive. According to O'Connor's interpretation of Title VII, the analysis was to proceed as follows:

> First, the plaintiff must establish the *McDonnell Douglas* prima facie case. . . . The plaintiff should also present any direct evidence of discriminatory animus in the decisional process. The defendant should then present its case, including its evidence as to legitimate, nondiscriminatory reasons for the employment decision. . . . Once all the evidence has been received, the court should determine whether the *McDonnell Douglas* or *Price Waterhouse* framework properly applies to the evidence before it. If the plaintiff has failed to satisfy the *Price Waterhouse* threshold, the case should be decided under the principles enunciated in *McDonnell Douglas* and *Burdine*, with the plaintiff bearing the burden of persuasion on the ultimate issue whether the employment action was taken because of discrimination.[59]

§4.6.4   The Civil Rights Act of 1991 and Reformulated Legal Frameworks

The *Wards Cove* decision outraged the civil rights community that had championed employees' rights.[60] In response to *Wards Cove* and other Supreme Court decisions undermining earlier Title VII precedents, Senator Edward M. Kennedy (D-MA) and Representative Augustus F. Hawkins (D-CA) introduced companion

---

56. *Price Waterhouse*, 490 U.S. at 237-240.
57. Id. at 242.
58. Id. at 262-263.
59. Id. at 278-279.
60. The commentary has been vigorous in its criticism. See, e.g., Robert A. Robertson, The Civil Rights Act of 1991: Congress Provides Guidelines for Title VII Disparate Impact Cases, 3 Geo. Mason U. Civ. Rts. L.J. 1 (1992); Phillip S. Runkel, The Civil Rights Act of 1991: A Continuation of the *Wards Cove* Standard of Business Necessity? 35 Wm. & Mary L. Rev. 1177 (1994); Peter M.

bills in the Congress on February 7, 1990, that began the legislative effort to, among other things, substantially overrule *Wards Cove* and return the law to the disparate impact criteria set forth in Griggs v. Duke Power Co. and its progeny.

After the bill sailed through Congress, the President signed the measure on November 21, 1991. In enacting the Civil Rights Act of 1991, Congress expressly found that the 1989 Supreme Court decision of *Wards Cove* "weakened the scope and effectiveness of Federal civil rights protection" in the area of employment discrimination under Title VII of the Civil Rights Act of 1964.[61] With the enactment of the Civil Rights Act of 1991, Congress for the first time provided statutory guidelines for the adjudication of disparate impact cases under Title VII of the Civil Rights Act of 1964. The disparate impact statutory guidelines under the 1991 Act are set forth at 42 U.S.C. §2000e-2(k), which provides in relevant part:

> (k)(1)(A) An unlawful employment practice based on disparate impact is established under this title only if —
>
> (i) a complaining party demonstrates that a respondent uses a particular employment practice that causes a disparate impact on the basis of race, color, religion, sex, or national origin and the respondent fails to demonstrate that the challenged practice is job related for the position in question and consistent with business necessity; or
>
> (ii) the complaining party makes the demonstration described in subparagraph (C) with respect to an alternative employment practice and the respondent refuses to adopt such alternative employment practice.
>
> (B)(i) With respect to demonstrating that a particular employment practice causes a disparate impact as described in subparagraph (A)(i), the complaining party shall demonstrate that each particular challenged employment practice causes a disparate impact, except that if the complaining party can demonstrate to the court that the elements of a respondent's decision making process are not capable of separation for analysis, the decision making process may be analyzed as one employment practice.
>
> (ii) If the respondent demonstrates that a specific employment practice does not cause the disparate impact, the respondent shall not be required to demonstrate that such practice is required by business necessity.
>
> (C) The demonstration referred to by subparagraph (A)(ii) shall be in accordance with the law as it existed on June 4, 1989, with respect to the concept of "alternative employment practice."[62]

The guidelines provided plenty of room for disagreement concerning its proper construction, particularly the precise contours of pivotal terms, such as "job related for the position in question," "consistent with business necessity," and an employer's decision-making process that is "not capable of separation for analysis." In addition, the difficult task remained of determining what facts are sufficient to satisfy these disparate impact criteria.

Liepold, Stephen A. Sola, Reginald E. Jones, Civil Rights Act of 1991: Race to the Finish — Civil Rights, Quotas, and Disparate Impact in 1991, 45 Rutgers L. Rev. 1043 (1993); Alfred W. Blumrosen, Society in Transition IV: Affirmation of Affirmative Action Under the Civil Rights Act of 1991, 45 Rutgers L. Rev. 903 (1993); Theodore McMillian, The Civil Rights Act of 1991 — One Step Forward in a Long Road, 22 Stetson L. Rev. 69 (1992).

61. Civil Rights Act of 1991, Pub. L. No. 102-166, §§104-105 (1991).
62. 42 U.S.C. §2000e-2(k).

If the respondent fails to rebut the complaining party's statistical showing, and a prima facie case is established, the respondent must "demonstrate that the challenged practice is job related for the position in question and consistent with business necessity." Neither the term "job related" or "business necessity" is defined in the 1991 Act.

One of the stated purposes of the 1991 Act, however, was "to codify the concepts of 'business necessity' and 'job related' enunciated by the Supreme Court in *Griggs* and in other Supreme Court cases prior to *Wards Cove*."[63] In light of the 1991 statutory language and the Supreme Court cases prior to *Wards Cove*, the employer must show that there is a close nexus between the challenged employment practice and the requirements of performing the job in question and show, further, that the practice is consistent with business necessity. *Griggs*, of course, left the definition of business necessity unclear.

The *Wards Cove* standard of business necessity was far more deferential to employers than was the *Griggs* standard. After *Wards Cove*, a valid employment practice need not relate to job performance. Thus, an employment practice requiring a high school diploma for all positions in a company, similar to the challenged requirement in *Griggs*, could be invalid using the *Griggs* standard because having a high school diploma may in no way be related to the performance of certain unskilled manually intensive jobs. Under *Wards Cove*, however, if one of an employers' legitimate employment goals was to promote education in the community it serves, the practice of requiring a high school diploma for even unskilled positions could be valid, even if it disparately impacted a protected class. The *Griggs* decision addressed this argument and found it wanting, stating that such a goal would not justify disparate impact simply because it generally would improve the overall quality of the work force. Conceivably, using the *Wards Cove* standard of business necessity, the Court in *Griggs* would have reached a completely different decision. *Wards Cove*, then, is extremely important with regard to the ability of minority employees to protect themselves in the workplace, and civil rights advocates viewed the decision as a significant defeat in the battle against employment discrimination.

Professor Runkel notes,

> [W]hat is truly startling about the Civil Rights Act of 1991 is that so many observers confidently state that the Act overturns *Wards Cove*, even while noting the Act's ambiguity. These observers see litigation of the business necessity standard as inevitable but also see a return to *Griggs*, or to some standard very similar to *Griggs*, as equally inevitable.[64]

He continues by asking, "Regardless of the desirability of such an outcome, is such a conclusion really that obvious?" Runkel suggests that a more extensive look at this issue may reveal that the *Wards Cove* standard of business necessity is here to stay.

Not surprisingly, the lower courts have had difficulty defining the current (or pre–*Wards Cove*) business necessity standard. Linda Lye reviewed the published

---

63. Civil Rights Act of 1991 §3.
64. Runkel, supra note 60, at 196.

decisions from 1991 through 1997 in "Title VII's Tangled Tale: The Erosion and Confusion of Disparate Impact and the Business Necessity Defense,"[65] and found that four articulations of the standard, varying in stringency, have emerged. She labels these four articulations as follows: (1) necessity really means necessary to carry out a business practice the purpose is alleged to serve; (2) practice is demonstrably necessary to meet an important business goal; (3) practice is reasonably necessary to achieve an important business objective; and (4) practice bears a manifest relationship to employment and serve legitimate employment goals.[66]

Also notable is that the 1991 Civil Rights Act still places the burden of proving causation upon plaintiffs — just as *Wards Cove* had established. The Act also allows plaintiffs to lump together an array of inextricably interwoven employment policies or practices in appropriate cases — as did *Wards Cove*. This latitude may allow courts in some cases to find disparate impact when the employer vests total hiring discretion in a single individual unguided by identifiable, objective criteria. Thus, despite assertions that the 1991 Civil Rights Act overturns *Wards Cove*, under the language of the 1991 Civil Rights Act a mere showing of racial or sexual imbalance in a workforce will not suffice to put an employer on the defensive.

In addition to these changes, the 1991 Civil Rights Act reformulates standards of federal discrimination law that had been the subjects of several decisions of the United States Supreme Court that had made it more difficult for employee-plaintiffs to plead, prove, or recover for unlawful employment discrimination.

With regard to disparate impact discrimination, Congress also rejected the Court's holding in Watson that a plaintiff in a disparate impact case must show the discriminatory effect of specific practices on protected group members. The amendments state that "the complaining party shall demonstrate that each particular challenged employment practice causes a disparate impact, except that if the complaining party can demonstrate to the court that the elements of a respondent's decisionmaking process are not capable of separation for analysis, the decisionmaking process may be analyzed as one employment practice."[67]

Section 101 of the 1991 Civil Rights Act amends §1981 to provide: "For purposes of this section, the term 'make and enforce contracts' includes the making, performance, modification, and termination of contracts, and the enjoyment of all benefits, privileges, terms, and conditions of the contractual relationship." In Patterson v. McLean Credit Union,[68] the Supreme Court had narrowly construed the right "to make and enforce contracts" as that language is used in §1981, holding that §1981 "does not extend . . . to conduct by the employer after the contract relation has been established," unless a claim was for denial of a promotion that "involved the opportunity to enter into a new contract with the employer." Also, more than 20 years earlier, in Johnson v. Railway Express Agency, Inc.,[69] the Court had sanctioned use of this post–Civil War statute to fight private

65. 19 Berkeley J. Emp. & Lab. L. 315 (1998).
66. Id. at 349-352.
67. 42 U.S.C. 2000e-2(k)(1)(B)(i).
68. 491 U.S. 164 (1989).
69. 421 U.S. 454 (1975).

employment discrimination. In *Johnson*, the court approved a plaintiff's attempt to invoke the statute to remedy racially discriminatory seniority rules, job assignment, and the discharge of an employee.[70] In *Johnson*, the Court recognizes that Congress intended to supply aggrieved employees with this independent avenue of relief, and it allows that Johnson could have brought his claim were it not time-barred. The Court holds that EEOC proceedings do not toll the statute of limitations for bringing these suits, so Johnson did not obtain relief. In *Patterson*, the Court rejected a plaintiff's attempt to invoke the statute to remedy racial harassment and in the process significantly pruned the reach and effectiveness of §1981 to remedy racial discrimination in employment.

Further, §101 of the Act amends §1981 in apparent recognition that §1981 has been applied to private parties not because it expressly so provides. Now, the section provides that "[t]he rights protected by this section are protected against impairment by non-governmental discrimination and impairment under color of State law."

Congress also effectively overruled Martin v. Wilks by prohibiting challenges to consent decrees by individuals who had a reasonable opportunity to object to the decree or whose interests were adequately represented by another party.[71]

Beyond this, §112 of the 1991 Civil Rights Act overturns Lorance v. AT&T Technologies, Inc.[72] by amending §706(e) of Title VII of the Civil Rights Act of 1964[73] to provide as follows:

For purposes of this section, an unlawful employment practice occurs, with respect to a seniority system that has been adopted for an intentionally discriminatory purpose in violation of this title (whether or not that discriminatory purpose is apparent on the face of the seniority system), when the seniority system is adopted, when an individual becomes subject to the seniority system, or when a person aggrieved is injured by the application of the seniority system or provision of the system.

In *Lorance*, the Supreme Court had held time-barred a sex discrimination claim alleging that a facially neutral seniority system resulting in demotions for women was adopted with a discriminatory purpose. The Court held that Title VII's relatively brief charge-filing period for a claim having to do, as did this one, with the seniority system's intentionally discriminatory adoption began to run when the seniority system was adopted and not when the system later produced the plaintiff's demotions.

Congress also responded to *Price Waterhouse* in several ways. As an initial matter, Congress accepted the "same-decision defense," under which an employer may successfully prove that it would have made the same decision even if the protected characteristic had not been considered. But Congress also modified the decision in two important ways, both of which make individual disparate treatment law more favorable to plaintiffs.

70. Id. at 454-458.
71. 42 U.S.C. 2000e-2(n)(1)(B).
72. 490 U.S. 900 (1989).
73. 42 U.S.C. §2000e-5(e).

First, a new §703(m) rejects the "substantial factor" threshold test regarding an employer's state-of-mind, proposed by Justices O'Connor and White, accepting instead the "motivating factor" threshold proposed by the plurality. Thus, "an unlawful employment practice is established when the complaining party demonstrates that race, color, religion, sex, or national origin was a motivating factor for any employment practice, even though other factors also motivated the practice." Second, Congress limited the result, should an employer successfully carry its same-decision defense burden. Under the 1991 Act, the employer gains only a limitation on remedies and not a defense to liability. Section 706(g)(2)(B) provides that an employer, having successfully proven that it would have made the same decision even without consideration of the protected characteristic, is subject only to declaratory relief that it had discriminated, injunctive relief prohibiting such conduct in the future, and "attorney's fees and costs demonstrated to be directly attributable only to the pursuit of a claim under Section 703(m)." The new §§703(m) and 706(g)(2)(B) of Title VII apply to all individual disparate treatment cases, whether the claims are characterized as "*McDonnell Douglas*," "pretext," or "circumstantial evidence" cases or as "*Price Waterhouse*," "mixed-motives," or "direct evidence" cases. Where a plaintiff introduces evidence that is sufficiently "direct," the jury will be asked to determine if the plaintiff has proven that the protected characteristic was "a motivating factor" in the employer's decision. If so, the second question will be whether the defendant has proven that it would have made the same decision absent consideration of the prohibited characteristic; an answer in the affirmative will allow the defendant to escape having to provide the plaintiff with full legal and equitable remedies.[74]

Also, the 1991 Civil Rights Act overturns EEOC v. Arabian American Oil Co.[75] There, an American citizen working in Saudi Arabia filed a racial, religious, and ethnic discrimination claim against his employer, a Delaware corporation. The Court held that Title VII does not apply outside the United States. Section 109 of the 1991 Civil Rights Act amends both Title VII and the ADA to add to the definition of covered employees. Now, covered employees include U.S. citizens employed in foreign countries by U.S. companies.

74. For more criticism of the Act's power to alter disparate treatment jurisprudence over time, see William R. Corbett, The "Fall" of Summers, The Rise of "Pretext Plus," and the Escalating Subordination of Federal Employment Discrimination Law to Employment at Will: Lessons from *McKennon* and *Hicks*, 30 Ga. L. Rev. 305 (1996), in which Corbett cites Jerome McCristal Culp, Jr., Neutrality, the Race Question, and the 1991 Civil Rights Act: The "Impossibility of Permanent Reform," 45 Rutgers L. Rev. 965 (1993). "Shortly after passage of the 1991 Act, Professor Culp, predicting Congress would soon need to reform the law again, noted, 'Undoubtedly, these will be the Civil Rights Acts of 1998, 2005, and 2010.' He further predicted that, like the Civil Rights Act of 1991, none of these chimerical laws would permanently resolve race problems in our society. He premised this prediction on his belief that courts are unwilling to raise and address the 'race question,' which he formulates as, 'How does race alter the contours of legal reality?' " Corbett agrees with Culp: "If federal employment discrimination law is to retain (or regain) a role as a body of law embodying and serving public policy rather than being reduced to just another basis for tort recovery, Congress will have to step in again and again. Will Congress ever be able to effect the 'permanent' change that Culp deems impossible? I posit that such reform will not be possible until the Supreme Court stops subordinating federal employment discrimination law and its policies to the employment-at-will doctrine."

75. 499 U.S. 244 (1991).

§4.6.5   The Civil Rights Act of 1991 and Remedial Policies

The Civil Rights Act of 1991 allows victims of employment discrimination who bring claims under either Title VII of the Civil Rights Act of 1964 or the Americans with Disabilities Act to receive compensatory and punitive damages.[76] Before the Act, employees were awarded only equitable remedies, including reinstatement and back pay. The purpose of the Act was both to "create greater incentives for victims of discrimination to initiate cases by providing them with additional remedies" and as "a preventive measure, to force employers to address the potential consequences of large liability and to create more effective mechanisms for eliminating discriminatory conduct."[77]

The 1991 Civil Rights Act has changed the remedial policies underlying federal antidiscrimination legislation. It sets up a tort-like compensation scheme for intentional employment discrimination, complete with compensatory damages for emotional pain and suffering, punitive damages, and jury trials. The Act eliminates the conciliation/make-whole model[78] from the existing remedial schemes and chooses instead a modified tort model for all Title VII or ADA cases of intentional employment discrimination, whether based on race, color, religion, sex, national origin, or disability. At the same time, the Act leaves intact both the §1981 tort model for race discrimination claims and the ADEA's liquidated damages approach for age discrimination claims. Section 102 of the 1991 Civil Rights Act provides for jury trials upon demand; for compensatory damages for "future pecuniary losses, emotional pain, suffering, inconvenience, mental anguish, loss of enjoyment of life, and other nonpecuniary losses"; and for punitive damages where the employer engaged "in a discriminatory practice or discriminatory practices with malice or with reckless indifference to the federally protected rights of an aggrieved individual." Apparently, punitive damages cannot be sought for disparate impact discrimination.

The total compensatory damages awarded under the Act for future pecuniary losses, emotional pain, suffering, inconvenience, mental anguish, loss of enjoyment of life, and other nonpecuniary losses, and the amount of punitive damages

---

76. Civil Rights Act of 1991, 42 U.S.C. §1981a(a) (1994).

77. Kolstad v. American Dental Ass'n, 108 F.3d 1431, 1437 (D.C. Cir. 1997).

78. The conciliation/make-whole remedial approach is embodied in the centerpiece legislation effecting federal nondiscrimination law and policy in private employment: Title VII of the Civil Rights Act of 1964. Title VII prohibits discrimination on the basis of race, color, religion, sex, and national origin in a broad array of terms, conditions, and privileges of private employment. Title VII permits — indeed, requires — those aggrieved to seek mediation and conciliation of their charge through the Equal Employment Opportunity Commission (EEOC), an agency which Title VII also created. If no informal resolution is achieved, Title VII grants aggrieved persons access to the federal courts to seek relief to make them whole for the employment-related injury and litigation expenses they incur — plaintiffs may seek injunctive relief, orders requiring reinstatement to employment, declaratory relief, back pay, and attorneys fees. Because Title VII contains no jury trial provision, and because the types of relief granted by Title VII have usually been viewed as equitable in nature, courts have generally held that jury trials are unavailable for Title VII claims under either the statute itself or the Seventh Amendment. This same conciliation/make-whole remedial model was replicated by Congress in the Americans with Disabilities Act (ADA).

awarded under the Act, are capped by §102(b)(3) at levels which rise as the employer's workforce increases in size.

Against the backdrop of existing remedial schemes unaffected by the 1991 Civil Rights Act, then, the net effect of §102 is (1) to allow uncapped compensatory and punitive damages for intentional racial discrimination (since the caps do not apply if the employee-plaintiff can recover under §1981); (2) not to allow such damages for age discrimination or for any form of unintentional discrimination; and (3) to allow only capped compensatory and punitive damages for intentional sex, religious, and disability discrimination.

§4.6.6 Punitive Damages under the 1991 Act

In Kolstad v. American Dental Association,[79] the Supreme Court held that in order to obtain punitive damages, a plaintiff needed to show that the defendant had engaged in intentional discrimination "with malice or with reckless indifference to the federally protected rights of an aggrieved individual."[80] This repudiated several courts of appeals that had required plaintiffs to demonstrate a culpable state of mind and an independent showing of egregiousness of the defendant employer. Additionally, the Court modified the principles that allowed an employee to impute the discriminatory actions of an employee agent to his or her employer. The Court stated that "[a]n employer may not be vicariously liable for the discriminatory employment decisions of managerial agents where these decisions are contrary to the employer's good faith efforts to comply with Title VII."[81] However, the Court failed to define what constitutes "good faith efforts."[82]

In its annual review of major cases, the Harvard Law Review found that "[b]y allowing employers to avoid punitive damage for their agents' unlawful behavior without establishing a good-faith-effort standard, the Court rendered Title VII's most powerful deterrent mechanism — punitive damages — ineffectual."[83] The article explains that:

> The Court based its decision on the idea that the best way to induce compliance with Title VII is to provide employers with positive incentives. This opinion conflicts with Congress's decision that the best way to induce Title VII compliance is by providing a negative incentive — punishment — to those who engage in intentional discrimination. The difference in the two liability regimes is the amount of effort that employers will make to comply with Title VII by preventing unlawful discrimination.[84]

---

79. 527 U.S. 526 (1999).

80. Id.

81. Id. at 545.

82. See EEOC v. Wal-Mart Stores, Inc., 187 F.3d 1241 (10th Cir. 1999) ("*Kolstad* provides us no definitive standard for determining what constitutes good-faith compliance").

83. Leading Cases, Civil Rights Act of 1991 — Employer Liability for Punitive Damages in Title VII Claims, 113 Harv. L. Rev. 359, 359-360 (1999).

84. Id. at 367.

The article quotes employer law firm newsletters for employers celebrating the *Kolstad* decision. "As an employer, you can breathe a bit easier — you don't have to worry quite as much about large punitive damage awards if you've adopted and implemented antidiscrimination policies."[85]

Another law review article disagrees with the conclusion reached by the Harvard Law Review, finding that *Kolstad* has not made it more difficult to collect punitive damages. Rather, courts have "looked beyond whether an employer had a grievance procedure or an antidiscrimination policy, and analyzed whether these mechanisms were actually utilized, and whether they were effective in addressing the discrimination and harassment that occurred. Therefore, *Kolstad* has not limited plaintiffs' opportunities for punitive damages, as many commentators suggested it would."[86] Providing examples of cases decided post-*Kolstad*,[87] Kirshenbaum concludes that *Kolstad* has not reduced the chances for a plaintiff to receive punitive damages in an employment discrimination case.[88] In fact, it is likely to have the other effect:

> The first part of the *Kolstad* decision abrogated the egregiousness requirement that several circuits had previously adopted, and instituted a less strenuous intent standard that likely will permit many more claims of punitive damages to survive pretrial motions, and thus be tried to juries. Regarding the second part of the decision . . . if courts apply the good faith standard and review the employer's actual employment practices, rather than relying on the mere articulation of an anti-discrimination policy, the good faith standard will increase the opportunity for punitive damages in employment discrimination cases.[89]

---

85. Id. at n.62, citing High Court Ends Term with Important Rulings on ADA, Punitive Damages, Pa. Emp. L. Letter (Buchanan Ingersoll), July 1999, at 4; High Court Ends Term with Important Rulings on ADA, Punitive Damages, N.H. Emp. L. Letter (Sulloway & Hollis), Aug. 1999, at 6.

86. Andrea Meryl Kirshenbaum, Kolstad v. American Dental Ass'n: The Opportunity for Punitive Damages in Employment Discrimination Cases, 3 U. Pa. J. Lab. & Emp. L. 617, 629 (2001).

87. In Deffenbaugh-Williams v. Wal-Mart Stores, Inc., 188 F.3d 278 (5th Cir. 1999), the plaintiff, a white woman, brought suit under Title VII alleging that she had been discriminated against for dating an African-American male. Initially, the Fifth Circuit, awaiting the *Kolstad* decision, invited the EEOC to brief them on the impact of *Kolstad* and whether a new trial would be needed to determine punitive damages. However, after examining the decision, the court found that "*Kolstad*'s imputation holding was not such a sudden shift as to require, in fairness, giving Wal-Mart an opportunity to provide additional evidence." Id. The court upheld the jury's punitive damages verdict.

In Knowlton v. Teltrust Phones, Inc. 189 F.3d 1177, 11884 (10th Cir. 1999), the *Kolstad* decision influenced the court to reverse a directed verdict for the defendant that dismissed the plaintiff's punitive damages claim. The district court found that Knowlton had failed to prove actual malice or reckless indifference to her federally protected rights. However, the Tenth Circuit found that the employer had been "unmistakably aware" that Knowlton's supervisor was "rife with foul language [and] sexual innuendo" and remanded the issue of punitive damages to the district court to be decided by a jury.

In Cadena v. The Pacesetter Corp., 224 F.3d 1203 (10th Cir. 2000), the court found that even though a defendant in a Title VII discrimination suit maintains on paper a strong nondiscrimination policy and makes good faith efforts to educate its employees about that policy and Title VII, a plaintiff may still recover punitive damages if she demonstrates the employer failed to adequately address Title VII violations of which it was aware." The Tenth Circuit affirmed the lower court's award of $300,000 in compensatory and punitive damages.

88. Kirshenbaum, supra note 85, at 644-645.

89. Id. at 644-645.

§4.6.7 The Civil Rights Act of 1991 and Class Actions[90]

Employment discrimination class actions are affected in three ways by the Civil Rights Act of 1991:

1. The availability of substantial monetary damages to Title VII plaintiffs may destroy the homogeneity of remedy required to maintain a class action,[91] a concern that was not present when injunctive relief was the predominant remedy under the statute.
2. The individualized proof and liability issues may destroy the commonality necessary to maintain a class action under Rule 23(b)(3).
3. The availability of a jury trial under Title VII may raise Seventh Amendment bars to the bifurcation schemes that were traditionally used to manage class claims of discrimination.

In Allison v. Citgo,[92] plaintiffs alleged disparate impact and treatment in hiring, promotion, training, and compensation practices at Citgo's Lake Charles, Louisiana, facility. They sought declaratory, injunctive, and equitable relief as well as compensatory and punitive damages for a potential class of over 1,000 members. The district court and the Fifth Circuit denied class certification, finding that the requested compensatory damages would end up "predominating" in the action and each plaintiff would need "specific individualized" proof to establish damages — they would not flow automatically from a finding of liability to the class. The dissent argued that the majority had created a rule that would preclude class certification in Rule 23(b)(2) cases seeking certification.[93]

Similarly, in Lemon v. International Union of Operating Engineers,[94] the court held that the seeking of individual damages "jeopardizes [the] presumption of cohesion and homogeneity" by requiring "judicial inquiry into the particularized merits of each individual plaintiff's claim."[95] The court held that it would violate due process to deprive individual class members of the chance to opt out of such a class where money damages were at issue, precisely because of this divergence of interest. The court held that the trial judge had abused his discretion by certifying a Rule 23(b)(2) class without giving class members a chance to opt out and the court remanded without telling the lower court how the issue should be resolved.

Overall, Professor Piar argues that while the 1991 Act may limit class actions, it arguably makes it easier for individual plaintiffs to get access to courts.

---

90. For a thorough discussion of this topic, see Daniel F. Piar, The Uncertain Future of Title VII Class Actions After the Civil Rights Act of 1991, 2001 B.Y.U. L. Rev. 305.
91. Fed. R. Civ. Proc. 23(b).
92. 151 F.3d 402 (5th Cir. 1998).
93. Id. at 426-427 (Dennis, J., dissenting).
94. 216 F.3d 577 (7th Cir. 2000).
95. Id. at 580.

§4.6.8   The Threat of Rule 11 Sanctions and the 1993 Amendments

As if the Court's unpredictable reading of procedural requirements and statutory intent were not daunting enough, there is another factor plaintiffs must consider when trying to decide whether or not to pursue remedies for employment discrimination: The threat of sanctions for actually pursuing a Title VII claim (or any other employment discrimination remedy). Most familiarly known as Rule 11 sanctions, these can be brought against plaintiffs, counsel, and counsels' law firms.

What the courts give with one hand, they take away with the other. For a time, the Civil Rights Attorney's Fee Awards Act[96] made it easier for plaintiffs whose civil rights had been violated to find legal counsel willing to represent them, but Rule 11 of the Federal Rules of Civil Procedure now makes it harder and potentially dangerous for attorneys to bring innovative or unpopular civil rights cases.

Rule 11 requires courts to penalize lawyers (and, in some cases, clients) who file claims without a reasonable factual basis.[97] Designed to reduce the number of frivolous lawsuits in federal courts, Rule 11 became a powerful tool for deterring civil rights claims that, whatever their merits, are regarded as *per se* frivolous in a conservative judicial climate.[98] A University of Pennsylvania study of Rule 11 sanctions imposed in the Third Circuit concluded that plaintiffs in civil rights cases were sanctioned under this provision five times more often than plaintiffs in other types of cases.[99]

---

96. The Civil Rights Attorney's Fee Awards Act of 1976, Pub. L. No. 94-599, 42 U.S.C. §1988 (as amended 1991).

97. Fed. R. Civ. Proc. 11. The rule requires every lawyer who signs a pleading, motion, or other filing to certify that "to the best of the signer's knowledge, information, and belief formed after reasonable inquiry it is well grounded in fact and is warranted by existing law or a good faith argument for the extension, modification, or reversal of existing law, and that it is not interposed for any improper purpose, such as to harass or to cause unnecessary delay or needless increase in the cost of litigation."

The rule could potentially reach a great deal of innocent conduct by lawyers and litigants because it makes sanctionable conduct that is in good faith or only negligent, as well as willful or malicious filings. See, e.g., Eastway Constr. Corp. v. City of New York, 762 F.2d 243, 253 (2d Cir. 1985) ("No longer is it enough for an attorney to claim that he acted in good faith, or that he personally was unaware of the groundless nature of an argument of claim.").

98. See Lawrence Marcus, Rule 11: Does It Curb Frivolous Lawsuits or Civil Rights Claims?, Wash. Post, Apr. 12, 1991, at A17. See also Thomas E. Willging, The Rule 11 Sanctioning Process 75-76 (Federal Judicial Center, 1988); Georgene Vairo, Rule 11: A Critical Analysis, 118 F.R.D. 189, 200 (1988) (finding that plaintiffs, particularly civil rights plaintiffs, are sanctioned at a higher rate than defendants); Rampacek, Impact of Rule 11 Sanctions on Civil Rights Litigation, 3 Labor Law. 93 (1987); Carl Tobias, Reassessing Rule 11 and Civil Rights Cases, 33 How. L.J. 161 (1990).

Ironically, litigation over the propriety of Rule 11 sanctions may fill the court dockets emptied by the civil rights suits which Rule 11 has frozen out of the courts. One study reports that 668 Rule 11 decisions were reported in only four years. Vairo, supra, at 195.

99. S. Reporter, Rule 11 Transition (Report of the Third Circuit Task Force on Federal Rule of Civil Procedure, 1989). The study found that attorneys in civil rights were sanctioned in 47.1 percent of the cases in which the opposing party filed Rule 11 motions, while only 8.4 percent of attorneys in noncivil rights cases were sanctioned.

Julius Chambers, director-counsel of the NAACP Legal Defense and Education Fund, was recently fined $90,000 for bringing a Title VII claim on behalf of civilian employees of the Army. The lawsuit, which accused the Department of discrimination in virtually every aspect of civilian employment, was the largest class action employment discrimination case every filed against the Army. Blue v. U.S. Dep't of Army, 914 F.2d 525 (4th Cir. 1991), cert. denied sub nom. Chambers v.

Evidence of Rule 11's one-sidedness prompted one commentator to dub Rule 11 a "reverse-Robin Hood rule: It punishes the impoverished and unpopular and gives to the rich and respectable."[100] Rule 11's implication for civil rights claims is enormous. By requiring that plaintiffs have an evidentiary basis for their claim before even filing, Rule 11 effectively prevents plaintiffs from bringing claims that only discovery will bear out. Defendants often possess a monopoly over the material a plaintiff needs to prove its case — material that certainly will not be shared short of a court order. Rule 11 denies plaintiffs the ability to command the disclosure necessary to their case by making them subject to sanction for filing a claim without first obtaining disclosure. Consequently, defendants may immunize themselves from potential lawsuits merely by keeping a tight grasp on evidence of their wrongdoing.

Studies conducted show that Rule 11 disproportionately affected plaintiffs in civil rights cases.[101] Plaintiffs with low resources were deterred from filing suit for fear of harsh monetary sanctions. Lawyers with novel and potentially meritorious legal claims were reluctant to pursue these cases for fear that they could be deemed frivolous under Rule 11.[102] As Professor Carl Tobias describes:

> the 1983 version fostered much costly, unwarranted satellite litigation over its phrasing and the magnitude of sanctions that courts imposed while increasing incivility among lawyers. Rule 11 motions were filed and granted against civil rights plaintiffs more frequently than any other class of litigant, and numerous judges vigorously enforced the provision against the plaintiffs, levying large sanctions on them.[103]

This evidence prompted amendments to Rule 11 in 1993 that aimed to reduce its chilling effect on civil rights cases.[104] Some of the changes were aimed at reducing the unfettered discretion granted to federal court judges to determine Rule 11 violations, encouraging uniformity in sanctions, and deemphasizing harsh monetary penalties, including attorney's fee awards for the filing party. Perhaps, most significantly, the changes resulted in the creation of a safe harbor provision. The safe harbor provision intended to deter fewer plaintiffs from

---

U.S. Dept. of Army, 499 U.S. 959 (1991). At nearly the same time, civil rights lawyer William Kunstler and two other attorneys were fined more than $100,000 for filing a §1983 lawsuit on behalf of Native American rights advocates. Plaintiffs, who were facing criminal charges for allegedly taking hostages at a North Carolina newspaper, claimed that the prosecution was part of a government campaign to intimidate the activists. In re Kunstler, 914 F.2d 505 (4th Cir. 1990), cert. denied, 499 U.S. 965. See also Kamen v. American Tel. & Tel. Co., 791 F.2d 1006 (2d Cir. 1986); Quiroga v. Hasbro Inc., No. 90-5284 (3d Cir. Feb. 13, 1991); Lewis v. Brown & Root, Inc., 711 F.2d 1287 (5th Cir. 1983); Coleman v. General Motors Corp., 667 F.2d 704 (8th Cir. 1981) (both involving Rule 11 sanctions levied against Title VII plaintiffs).

100. Russ M. Herman, Rule 11 Is Prejudicial to Plaintiff, Nat'l L.J., July 24, 1989, at 17.

101. See Danielle Kie Hart, Still Chilling After All These Years: Rule 11 of the Federal Rules of Civil Procedure and Its Impact on Federal Civil Rights Plaintiffs After the 1993 Amendments, 37 Val. U. L. Rev. 1 (2002); Carl Tobias, The 1993 Revision of Federal Rule 11, 70 Ind. L.J. 171, 176-188 (1994); Eric Yamamoto & Danielle Kie Hart, Rule 11 and State Courts: Panacea or Pandora's Box? 13 U. Haw. L. Rev. 57 (1991); Carl Tobias, Rule 11 and Civil Rights Litigation, 37 Buff. L. Rev. 485 (1988-1989); William Schwarzer, Rule 11 Revisited, 101 Harv. L. Rev. 1013 (1988).

102. Tobias, supra note 97.

103. Id. at 171.

104. 1993 Amendment of Fed. R. Civ. P. 11; 1983 Amendment of Fed. R. Civ. P. 11.

pursuing their claims. It shielded the targets of sanctions by setting a limited time period for a party to file a Rule 11 claim and a 20-day withdrawal period granting immunity to a party against whom a Rule 11 sanction was filed.

In a law review article examining the impact of the 1993 amendments for civil rights litigators, Professor Danielle Kie Hart argues that the 1993 amendments have not been successful.[105] In analyzing Rule 11 decisions by federal courts after the 1993 changes, she concludes that judges continue to have discretion under Rule 11 to exert unpredictable and harsh penalties and that "Rule 11's chilling effects continue to exist in practice."[106] She calls for further study and advocates for federal courts to employ "high sanctioning thresholds," granting Rule 11 sanctions only "under exceptional circumstances."[107] Professor Hart's overriding concern is for the "enduring value in access to court for civil rights plaintiffs and, indeed, for all non-mainstream or marginalized litigants asserting novel theories that challenge existing power structures."[108]

Coupled with the general threat that Rule 11 poses to civil rights litigation efforts, the case of Harris v. Marsh,[109] illustrates the foreboding litigation picture victims of employment discrimination face.[110]

Efficiency reforms, though, "make expendable those raising difficult and often tenuous claims that demand the reordering of established political, economic and social arrangements, that is, those at the system's and society's margins."[111]

105. Hart, 37 Val. U. L. Rev. 1, supra note 100.
106. Id. at 112.
107. Id. at 121.
108. Id. at 6.
109. 679 F. Supp. 1204 (E.D.N.C. 1987), aff'd in part and rev'd in part sub nom. Blue v. United States Dep't of the Army, 814 F.2d 525 (4th Cir. 1990), cert. denied sub nom. Chambers v. United States Dep't of the Army, 111 499 U.S. 959 (1991).
110. The lower court had invoked a number of different yet overlapping legal theories to justify imposition of sanctions on two Title VII plaintiffs, their counsel, and counsel's law firm, including Federal Rules of Civil Procedure 11 and 16, the "bad faith" exception to the American Rule, and 28 U.S.C. §1927. When the lower court imposed the sanctions, it ordered not only that defendant be awarded payment for court costs and attorneys' fees, but also that the court *itself* be reimbursed for the expenses it incurred and the time it spent presiding over the litigation. Finally, it also directed that the NAACP Legal Defense Fund (the plaintiff's lawyers' firm) not pay any part of the sanctions for the lawyers involved in the case that were set at $17,000 and $13,000 fines, respectively, for bringing frivolous claims.
The court of appeals affirmed in part and reversed in part. Despite noting the dangers that Rule 11 poses for would-be civil rights litigants and despite a close examination of the record which led the appeals court to conclude, given a generous reading of plaintiff's allegations, that evidence of racial discrimination existed, the court was "constrained to uphold the district court's factual determinations." Professor Eric Yamamoto found that, while intended to increase judicial efficiency and discourage marginal litigants through punitive sanctions, federal procedural reforms have subtly yet measurably discouraged judicial access for those outside the political and cultural mainstream, particularly those challenging accepted legal principles and social norms. First, various indicators suggest that the reforms assume and facilitate a procedural system hospitable to litigants with disputes involving well-settled legal principles.
111. Professor Eric Yamamoto believes that litigation of marginal claims is an important mechanism of reform and that it has great social value even when the case is lost. He cites Fragante v. City and County of Honolulu, 888 F.2d 591 (9th Cir. 1989) as instructive in the employment discrimination context. There, an adult Filipino American, emigrated from the Philippines to Hawaii who spoke English grammatically and coherently, but with a strong accent. Based on those skills, he took the civil service exam in English, scoring highest among the test-takers, but was rejected for an

§4.7 UNIONS, LABOR RELATIONS LAW, AND ARBITRATION

§4.7.1 Racial Barriers to Unionization

African Americans suffer disproportionately from the recent decline in unionization. For much of the postwar period, unions represent a greater proportion of African-American workers than workers from other racial and ethnic backgrounds.[1] African-American workers are about 30 percent more likely than the rest of the workforce to be in a union today and, as recently as the mid-1980s, African-American workers were almost 50 percent more likely to be in a union or covered by a union at their workplace.[2] In a survey of data from the U.S. Census Bureau's Current Population Survey between 1979 and 2006, economists John Schmitt and Ben Zipperer found that, as union representation and union coverage have declined for the country as a whole, unionization rates for African-American have fallen more quickly than for the rest of the workforce.[3]

Although Schmitt and Zipperer found that part of the reason for the decline in unionization rates among African-Americans is related to the decline of U.S. manufacturing,[4] they found that the decline in manufacturing simply cannot explain the overall decline in African-American unionization. Since the early 1990s, the share of black workers in manufacturing has been falling more rapidly than the manufacturing share for the workforce as a whole.[5] Moreover, even within manufacturing, unionization rates have been declining. Now, manufacturing workers now are no more likely to be in a union than workers in the rest of the economy.[6] Meanwhile, unionization rates have held steady in the public sector for the past 25 years. This suggests that employer opposition to unions, not simply economic restructuring, lies behind the decline in overall unionization rates.[7]

---

entry-level clerical position with the City of Honolulu's Division of Motor Vehicles because of his very pronounced accent. Viewing his rejection as a manifestation of unconscious racism, he filed a Title VII suit, but lost at both the trial and appellate levels. The case, however, served to energize the Filipino community and became a rallying point for an expanded group who perceived the case to be a reflection of a larger discriminatory attitude that society and the established powers had not seriously acknowledged. The government agency revamped its interview procedures to ensure freedom from cultural bias in future decisions. The case also served as a catalyst for legislative lobbying efforts and stimulated public recognition of the existence of civil rights problems that were not being adequately addressed by government agencies. This contributed concretely to the legislative creation of a state civil rights commission with investigative and enforcement powers.

§4.7 1. See John Schmitt & Ben Zipperer, The Decline in African-American Representation in Unions and Manufacturing, 1979-2006, Center for Economic and Policy Research (Mar. 2007), available at http://www.cepr.net/documents/publications/african_americans_manufacturing_2007_03.pdf.

2. See id.

3. See id.

4. "For example, since the1960s, African-Americans were more likely to work in the heavily unionized automotive sector than white or Latino workers. As these sectors have declined in relative importance, unionization rates for blacks have also dropped." Id.

5. "From the end of the 1970s through the early 1990s, African-Americans were just as likely as workers from other racial and ethnic groups to have manufacturing jobs. Since the early 1990s, however, black workers have lost considerable ground in manufacturing. By 2006, blacks were about 15 percent less likely than other workers to have a job in manufacturing." Id.

6. Id.

7. See id.

Racially mixed labor forces are particularly vulnerable to anti-union employer tactics because employers are able to use race to divide voting units.[8] Historically, racially divisive tactics have been used to discourage union membership among both whites and blacks. For example, in one case an employer have threatened black workers that, if unionization occurred, the business would be turned over "to his son who didn't like colored people."[9] Employers have also incited racial animus on both sides, implying that blacks or whites would betray their race by joining a union that included other races in its membership.[10] Employers have also used the issue of desegregation, which unions often supported, to discourage white employees from voting for unionization.[11]

A recent study performed by the Center for Urban Economic Development of the University of Illinois at Chicago found that, of 62 union-representation campaigns launched in 2002, unions lost 62 percent of all campaigns where no single racial group represented more than 80 percent of the bargaining unit.[12] Employers in the surveyed campaigns "frequently used racially divisive messages . . . to break down union solidarity."[13] For example, in one situation, an organizer recalls:

> The boss skillfully organized the black workers against the union and against the Latino workers. Some key black leaders were promoted to supervisors. The boss then used the black supervisors to recruit black workers against the union. The employer organized a "vote no" committee. It included black workers in the bargaining unit but it was run by black supervisors. The committee effectively argued that the union would only support the Latino workers and the black workers would be left behind. They were successful in silencing some of the key pro-union black workers.[14]

§4.7.2   Labor Relations Law Remedies

Labor relations laws have been employed in attempts to prevent employers, or unions, from discriminating against black workers. The Railway Labor Act (RLA)[15] and National Labor Relations Act (NLRA)[16] have been used for these purposes. Under these acts, unions which represent a majority of employees in a collective bargaining unit serve as the exclusive representatives of all employees in the unit, regardless of whether or not they are union members.[17] The key point is that the courts have imposed a duty of fair representation upon the unions in

---

8. Chirag Mehta et al., Undermining the Right to Organize: Employer Behavior During Union Representation Campaigns 11 (American Rights at Work 2005), available at http://www.american-rightsatwork.org/resources/studies.cfm.

9. Fred A. Snow Co., 41 N.L.R.B. 1288, 1292 (1942); see also Charlotte LeMoyne, The Unresolved Problem of Race Hate Speech in Labor Union Elections, 4 Geo. Mason U. Civ. Rts. L.J. 77, 82 (1993).

10. See LeMoyne, supra note 9, at 83.

11. See id. at 95-96.

12. See id.

13. See id.

14. Id. at 12.

15. 45 U.S.C. §§151 et. seq. (1976).

16. 29 U.S.C. §§151 et. seq. (1968).

17. See §2, Fourth of the RLA; §9(a) of the NLRA.

representing employees; that is, the union "must represent the entire membership of the craft."[18] The Supreme Court has established that the union must "represent nonunion or minority union members of the craft without hostile discrimination, fairly, impartially, and in good faith."[19]

Applying the duty of fair representation to racial discrimination, courts have found that the duty is violated when a union causes an employer to discriminate against an employee on the basis of an invidious basis, such as race, in firings,[20] layoffs,[21] job classifications,[22] or other terms and conditions of employment.[23] In addition, a union may not: discriminate in its handling of grievances;[24] accept a discriminatory contract;[25] or have a segregated union membership.[26]

The history of civil rights lawyers efforts to utilize federal law to combat racial discrimination in the workplace is a lengthy one that resulted in as many setbacks as successes. The details are lengthy, complex, and their review beyond the scope of this text. Suffice to say that despite what might appear to be an effective coverage of the duty of fair representation, in fact the duty has had little impact on employment discrimination.[27]

§4.7.3 Arbitration Procedures

While the Supreme Court in Glover v. St. Louis San Francisco Railway Co.[28] allowed black workers to circumvent grievance-arbitration procedures in bringing

---

18. Steele v. Louisville & Nashville R.R., 323 U.S. 192, 204 (1944).

19. Id. Those familiar with the rampant racism that was an integral part of the development and growth of most American unions might wonder whether the doctrine of fair representation would be adequate to neutralize long-standing policies based on deeply ingrained feelings and beliefs. The history of racial discrimination in American unions is presented in William Gould, Black Workers and White Unions (1977); and Herbert Hill, Black Labor and the American Legal System (1977). See also Molly S. McUsic & Michael Selmi, Postmodern Unions: Identity Politics in the Workplace, 82 Iowa L. Rev. 1339, 1343-1351 (1997) (chronicling the historic exclusion of women and minorities from labor unions, but discouraging the formation of separate "identity caucuses" to advance the interests of racial and ethnic groups and women).

20. See Rolax v. Atlantic Coastline R.R., 186 F.2d 473 (4th Cir. 1950).

21. See Steele v. Louisville & Nashville R.R., 323 U.S. 192 (1944).

22. See Brotherhood of R.R. Trainmen v. Howard, 343 U.S. 768 (1952).

23. See Local 12, United Rubber Workers (Business League of Gladsen), 150 N.L.R.B. No. 18 (1964) (segregated lunch and work facilities).

24. See Conley v. Gibson, 355 U.S. 41 (1957).

25. See Central Ga. Ry. v. Jones, 229 F.2d 648 (5th Cir. 1965), cert. denied, 352 U.S. 848 (1956).

26. See Hughes Tool Co., 147 N.L.R.B. 1573 (1964).

27. For a history of pre-*Brown* efforts to utilize federal labor law, see Risa L. Goluboff, The Lost Promise of Civil Rights, (2007). See also William Gould, Black Power in the Unions: The Impact upon Collective Bargaining Relationships, 79 Yale L.J. 46 (1969); William Gould, Labor Arbitration of Grievances Involving Racial Discrimination, 118 U. Pa. L. Rev. 40 (1969).

28. 393 U.S. 324 (1969). The plaintiffs alleged a tacit understanding between the railroad employer and the union to avoid calling out black workers to work as carmen, thus leaving the blacks as carmen helpers for many years. Despite the complaints of the black workers to union officials, the union never filed a grievance on behalf of the workers, and in fact openly discouraged the blacks from pursuing further action. The Supreme Court held that the black workers need not exhaust their contractual remedies under the collective bargaining agreement, the union constitution, and the Railway Labor Act, before suing for damages and injunctive relief in court. The Court reasoned

their claims to court, it was unclear what would happen if black workers did, in fact, choose to press their claims through grievance and arbitration procedures. The entire relationship between fair employment laws and grievance-arbitration procedures was murky, at best. In particular, the question remained whether a black worker could later pursue his or her remedies under fair employment laws even after losing in grievance and arbitration procedures. To allow a subsequent remedy under fair employment laws would pose a potential threat to labor relations stability by undermining grievance and arbitration procedures. Nevertheless, in Alexander v. Gardner-Denver Co.,[29] the Supreme Court held that a black worker would not be foreclosed from pursuing his or her full remedies under fair employment laws even after previously taking the claim through a grievance and arbitration procedure and obtaining an adverse ruling. Since *Alexander*, however, the Court, while not overturning the decision, seriously undermined it in subsequent cases, some of which are discussed later in this chapter.[30]

---

that contractual or administrative remedies would not have to be exhausted where pursuing such remedies would be wholly futile. Where, as here, union officials seem to be acting in concert with the employer, black workers should not be required to submit their claims to "a group which is in large part chosen by the [defendants] against whom their real complaint is made."

29. 415 U.S. 36 (1974).

30. While the *Alexander* decision indicates a policy of affording black workers alternative, independent remedies for employment consideration, the Supreme Court has expressed little sympathy with self-help tactics where blacks resort to means outside of traditional fair employment laws or collective bargaining procedures. For example, an employer may discharge or refuse to hire a worker who has engaged in deliberate, unlawful activity against it, even where that activity is designed to protest discriminatory practices. See McDonnell Douglas Corp. v. Green, 411 U.S. 792 (1913). In Emporium Capwell Co. v. Western Addition Community Org., the Court expressed the view that the law provided adequate remedies for the resolution of employment discrimination complaints. 420 U.S. 50 (1975). The *Emporium* case involved two black department store employees concerned that their employment discrimination claims were not being adequately handled by union officials. The employees had complained to the union about the department store's alleged racial discrimination in promotion policies, but they refused to cooperate with the union's handling of the grievance, maintaining that it was not an individual matter and should be presented as a sort of class action. When the union insisted on proceeding on an individual case-by-case basis, the black employees walked out, effectively aborting the hearing.

Subsequently, the complaining blacks and other employees held a press conference and then distributed handbills to customers denouncing the company and calling for a boycott of the store. After a warning and a second handbilling incident, the two black complainants were discharged. A local civil rights group filed charges under the NLRA, and the Supreme Court agreed to consider whether the workers were protected under §7 of the National Labor Relations Act. 29 U.S.C. §157 (1975) (providing employees "the right to self-organization, to form, join, or assist labor organizations, to bargain collectively through representatives of their own choosing, and to engage in other concerted activities for the purpose of collective bargaining or other mutual protection," as well as the right to refrain from these activities).

The Court found against the black workers, noting that the collective bargaining agreement provided adequate remedies. 420 U.S. at 61-62. To allow the two employees to attempt to bargain with the employer on their own would create the possibility that an employer would face bargaining demands from a variety of groups. An employer may legitimately object to being forced to bargain on several fronts, and a union has an interest in presenting a united front.

The Court also rejected the argument that the workers were protected by Title VII's policy of protecting workers opposing unlawful discrimination from employer reprisals. See 42 U.S.C. §2000e-3 (1976).

The final result of *Emporium* is that black workers venture beyond filing claims under fair employment laws and arbitration-grievance procedures wholly at their own risk. An employer is free to fire employees who press their claims by picketing or protest. Thus, black workers must wind their way through the courts or union halls — discrimination claims are not to be heard on the streets.

The balance struck in *Alexander* was threatened by two later Supreme Court decisions on the enforceability of mandatory arbitration agreements in the employment context and by their progeny.[31] The first, Gilmer v. Interstate/Johnson Lane Corp.,[32] involved a claim under the Age Discrimination in Employment Act (ADEA).[33] Under the terms of Mr. Gilmer's employment as a manager of financial services, he was required to register as a securities representative. The registration application, in turn, provided that "[a]ny controversy between a registered representative and any member or member organization arising out of the employment or termination of employment of such registered representative," be resolved through arbitration.[34] After being terminated at the age of 62, Mr. Gilmer filed a timely age discrimination complaint with the EEOC and subsequently sought judicial relief in a federal forum. The employer argued that the arbitration clause in Mr. Gilmer's securities registration precluded the suit. Relying in part on *Alexander*, the Fourth Circuit rejected the employer's challenge and refused to compel arbitration.[35]

The Supreme Court, however, held that Mr. Gilmer's claim under the ADEA was subject to compulsory arbitration pursuant to the arbitration agreement in his registration application. In so ruling, the Court expressly distinguished *Alexander* and its progeny on three grounds:

> First, those cases did not involve the issue of the enforceability of an agreement to arbitrate statutory claims. Rather, they involved the quite different issue whether arbitration of contract-based claims precluded subsequent judicial resolution of statutory claims. Since the employees there had not agreed to arbitrate their statutory claims, and the labor arbitrators were not authorized to resolve such claims, the arbitration in those cases understandably was held to preclude subsequent statutory actions. Second, because the arbitration in those cases occurred in the context of a collective bargaining agreement, the claimants there were represented by their unions in arbitration proceedings. An important concern therefore was the tension between collective representation and individual statutory rights. . . . Finally, those cases were not decided under the FAA [Federal Arbitration Act], which . . . reflects a "liberal federal policy favoring arbitration agreements."[36]

Thus, the *Gilmer* Court concluded that the prior ruling in *Alexander* neither applied to the ADEA claim at issue nor was affected by the decision to enforce the arbitration agreement. In an important footnote in *Gilmer*, however, the Court retreated from its position in *Alexander* presumptively favoring the judicial forum over arbitration tribunals for the resolution of statutory, individual rights to be free of employment discrimination.[37]

31. The sanctity of the *Alexander* rule is also threatened by recent lower court decisions interpreting §118 of the Civil Rights Act of 1991. Section 118 is discussed in a later section of this chapter.

32. 500 U.S. 20 (1991).

33. 29 U.S.C. §§621 et seq.

34. 500 U.S. at 23.

35. 895 F.2d 195 (4th Cir. 1990). The Fourth Circuit also reviewed the legislative history of the ADEA and concluded that "Congress intended to protect ADEA claimants from the waiver of a judicial forum." Id. at 197.

36. 500 U.S. at 35.

37. The Court noted "[W]e are well past the time when judicial suspicion of the desirability of arbitration and of the competence of arbitral tribunals inhibited the development of arbitration as an

Gilmer, then, by its own terms, left *Alexander* intact: Prior labor arbitration does not preclude an individual's right to institute a subsequent discrimination action in a judicial forum. But the *Gilmer* Court, emphasizing that the arbitration agreement before it was neither between the employer and employee, nor the employer and a union, expressly left open the question whether a mandatory arbitration clause in an individual employment contract would prohibit resort to the judiciary. That question was addressed in Wright v. Universal Maritime Serv. Corp.[38]

Wright involved a general arbitration clause in a collective bargaining agreement (CBA). Almost three years after Mr. Wright had become disabled as a longshoreman and had sought and received a settlement for $250,000 for permanent disability, he returned, with his doctor's approval, to his union hiring hall to seek work from the stevedoring companies subject to the CBA. Mr. Wright worked several days without any complaint about his performance. When his prior settlement was discovered, however, the stevedoring companies refused Mr. Wright any further work. Although the union objected, citing the Americans with Disabilities Act (ADA), no grievance was brought by the union on Mr. Wright's behalf. Instead, like Mr. Gilmer, Mr. Wright completely bypassed the arbitration process, filed a claim with the EEOC, and subsequently brought suit in federal court charging a violation of the ADA. The stevedoring companies defended in part on the ground that Mr. Wright had failed to exhaust the arbitration remedy provided under the CBA. Again, the Supreme Court was asked to interpret the reach of *Alexander*.

Writing for a unanimous Court, Justice Scalia acknowledged tension between the *Alexander* and *Gilmer* lines of cases. On the one hand, the employee argued, consistent with both *Alexander* and *Gilmer* that an employee subject to an arbitration clause in a CBA retains his right to a federal forum for adjudication of statutory claims of discrimination even if the identical right can be waived in an individual employment contract or agreement. The employer, on the other hand, maintained that *Gilmer* "sufficiently undermined [*Alexander v.*] *Gardner-Denver* [such] that a union *can* waive employees' rights to a judicial forum." Attempting to reconcile the cases, the Court held that a union's waiver of its members' rights to a judicial forum for the adjudication of statutory employment discrimination claims must be "clear and unmistakable." The Court reasoned that the presumption of arbitrability applied in *Gilmer* extends to those situations where the issues under dispute are uniquely suited to interpretation by arbitrators. The Court stopped short, however, of reaffirming the *Alexander* preference for judicial resolution of discrimination claims, stating only that it would not *presume* such claims to be covered by a general arbitration agreement. Indeed, Justice Scalia writes, "whether or not [*Alexander v.*] *Gardner-Denver*'s seemingly absolute prohibition of union waiver of employees' federal forum rights survives *Gilmer*, [*Alexander v.*] *Gardner-Denver* at least stands for the proposition that the right to a federal

---

alternative means of dispute resolution." *Gilmer*, 500 U.S. at 34 n.5 (quoting Mitsubishi Motors Corp. v. Soler Chrysler-Plymouth, Inc., 473 U.S. 614, 626-627 (1985)).

38. 525 U.S. 70 (1998).

judicial forum is of sufficient importance to be protected against less-than-explicit union waiver in a CBA."[39] The resolution of whether such an explicit waiver would be enforceable, the Court left for another day.

The consequence of *Alexander, Gilmer*, and *Wright* for black laborers is that (1) a union-negotiated agreement to arbitrate contractual claims that also form the basis of a statutory right to be free of employment discrimination will not necessarily bar subsequent adjudication of such rights in a federal forum; (2) where the agreement to arbitrate, whether general or specific, is part of an *individual* employment arrangement, the federal presumption of arbitrability will render the agreement enforceable even as to statutory discrimination claims; (3) a nonspecific union-negotiated agreement to arbitrate will not be read to encompass, and thus to bar, an individual's right to judicial adjudication of statutory employment discrimination claims; *but* (4) the enforceability of a specific, explicit waiver of individual employees' rights to a judicial forum for employment discrimination claims contained in a CBA negotiated by a union is an open question. This question is one that threatens to engulf *Alexander*'s policy of affording workers alternative fora for relief from discriminatory employment practices.[40]

In Circuit City Stores, Inc. v. St. Clair Adams,[41] the Supreme Court finally faced the issue of compelling arbitration agreements in individual employment contracts. In a five-to-four decision, the Court upheld its decision in *Gilmer*, reaffirming its preference for arbitration proceedings as an alternative to litigation and expanding the scope of the Federal Arbitration Act (FAA) in holding that Congress intended the FAA to preempt state anti-arbitration laws.

The plaintiff, St. Clair Adams, signed an employment arbitration agreement as part of the terms of his employment in which he agreed to mandatory arbitration in the event of any employment disputes. Two years into his employment, Adams was discharged and sued in state court claiming age discrimination in violation of state law. Circuit City filed a motion to enjoin the state proceedings based upon the arbitration agreement.

The Supreme Court held that the FAA excludes review only of employment contracts of transportation workers. The Court did not address any possible policy implications of compelling arbitration in the context of an employment discrimination suit. Its decision rested almost completely on statutory interpretation. As in *Gilmer*, the Court in *Circuit City* ignored the earlier concern of *Alexander* that arbitration was an inappropriate forum to resolve discrimination disputes. However, Justice Kennedy noted that, "We have been clear in rejecting the supposition that the advantages of the arbitration process somehow disappear when transferred to the employment context. Arbitration agreements allow parties to avoid the costs of litigation, a benefit that may be of particular importance in

---

39. 525 U.S. at 80.

40. Numerous articles have been written on *Gilmer*, its interpretation by the lower courts, and its likely long-term effect on *Alexander*. See, e.g., Karen Halverson, Arbitration and the Civil Rights Act of 1991, 67 U. Cin. L. Rev. 445 (1999); T. Christopher Baile, Comment, Reconciling *Alexander* and *Gilmer:* Explaining the Continued Validity of Alexander v. Gardner-Denver Co. in the Context of Collective Bargaining Agreements, 43 St. Louis U. L.J. 219 (1999).

41. 532 U.S. 105 (2001).

employment litigation, which often involves smaller sums of money than disputes concerning commercial contracts."[42]

EEOC v. Waffle House, Inc.[43] answered the question whether the Supreme Court's broad reading of the federal arbitration laws in *Circuit City* precluded the EEOC from seeking judicial relief — such as back pay and damages — on behalf of the victim for violation of federal antidiscrimination laws. The Fourth Circuit had previously held that when the aggrieved parties were bound by arbitration agreements the FAA's purpose of favoring arbitration agreements outweighed the EEOC's right to litigate where it sought to defend primarily private interests. The Court further held the EEOC could seek only injunctive relief, rather than victim-specific relief, since then the EEOC's purpose of vindicating broad matters of the public interest could truly be served.[44]

In *Waffle House*, the EEOC was suing on behalf of a former employee, Eric Baker, who claimed he was terminated in violation of the Americans with Disabilities Act. The Supreme Court held that the EEOC, as a nonparty to the arbitration agreement, is not compelled to abide by it. Thus the EEOC has the authority to seek relief regardless of the forum the employee and employer choose. The Court first noted that since the ADA mirrored Title VII, the EEOC's enforcement powers under Title VII were the starting point for their analysis. The 1972 amendments to Title VII placed the primary burden of litigation on the EEOC, not on the victim, and the FAA did not trump this congressional intent. "If the EEOC could prosecute its claim only with Baker's consent, or if its prayer for relief could be dictated by Baker, the lower court's analysis might be persuasive. But once a charge is filed, the exact opposite is true under the ADA, which clearly makes the EEOC master of its own case and confers on the agency the authority to evaluate the strength of the public interest at stake."[45] Because of the statutory grant of authority independent from the victim, the Court concluded the EEOC cannot be compelled to relinquish that authority without its own consent.

The facts before the Court in *Circuit City* and *Waffle House* concerned the aggrieved parties' rights in the case of a dispute after having consented to an arbitration agreement. In EEOC v. Luce, Forward, Hamilton & Scripps, LLP,[46] the Ninth Circuit considered the issue of whether a mandatory arbitration agreement can be a compulsory condition of employment. Donald Lagatree was offered a full-time position as a legal secretary with the firm of Luce, Forward, Hamilton & Scripps, LLP ("Luce"). When he reported to work the first day, he was given an offer letter that set the terms of his employment. It included an arbitration clause that required Lagatree to agree to submit all potential claims related to his employment to arbitration. Lagatree strenuously objected to the clause. Luce responded by telling him the clause was nonnegotiable and terminating Lagatree for his refusal to sign the offer letter.

---

42. Id. at 122, 123.
43. 534 U.S. 279 (2002).
44. Id.
45. Id. at 291.
46. 345 F.3d 742 (9th Cir. 2003).

Lagatree sued Luce in state court alleging he was wrongfully terminated for refusing to waive his constitutional rights to a jury trial and judicial forum. The state court stated that in order for Lagatree's termination to be wrongful, the underlying right must be one that cannot be bargained away. The court held that since an individual's constitutional right to a jury trial and judicial forum can be circumvented by agreement, Lagatree was not wrongfully terminated.

The EEOC then sued Luce in federal court claiming unlawful retaliatory activity and seeking make-whole relief of lost wages and damages as well as permanent injunction precluding Luce from conditioning employment on a mandatory arbitration provision.[47] The district court held that res judicata precluded consideration of the EEOC's claim for make-whole relief. However, the court held that the EEOC was precluded only to the extent that it asserted claims on behalf of Lagatree in his individual capacity. The court reasoned that the EEOC's claim seeking injunctive relief is independent of its claim for an individual's private rights. The EEOC can seek injunctive relief pursuant to its objective in vindicating the public interest. Relying on prior precedent by the Ninth Circuit,[48] which held employers may not compel individuals to waive their Title VII rights to a judicial forum, the district court held the mandatory arbitration agreement could not be made a condition of employment. The court granted the injunction against Luce's use of the compulsory arbitration agreements.

The Ninth Circuit on review reversed the lower court based on its finding that *Circuit City*, which had been decided in the interim, had implicitly overruled the court's prior precedent finding mandatory arbitration agreements as a condition of employment unlawful.[49] The Court discussed the rationale behind its prior precedent, stating, "we thought it 'at least a mild paradox' that the Act, which expanded remedies for victims of discrimination, encouraged the use of a process whereby employers condition employment on their prospective employees' surrendering of their rights to a judicial forum."[50] However, the Ninth Circuit determined that the reasoning and language in *Circuit City* that "arbitration agreements can be enforced under the FAA without contravening the policies of congressional enactments giving employees specific protection against discrimination prohibited by federal law"[51] indirectly overturned the circuit court's conclusion that Congress precluded compulsory arbitration of Title VII claims. The court also concluded that since mandatory arbitration agreements as a condition of employment are not unlawful, Lagatree was not engaging in a protected activity for purposes of retaliation claims by refusing to sign the agreement.

On rehearing, a Ninth Circuit panel sitting en banc vacated the three-judge panel's ruling.[52] The court concluded that *Circuit City* had not overruled their prior

---

47. EEOC v. Luce, Forward, Hamilton & Scripps, LLP, 122 F. Supp. 2d 1080 (C.D. Cal. 2000).

48. Duffield v. Robertson Stepherts & Co., 144 F.3d 1182 (9th Cir. 1998) (holding that employers may not by conditioning employment on the execution of mandatory arbitration agreements compel individuals to waive their Title VII rights to a judicial forum).

49. EEOC v. Luce, Forward, Hamilton & Scripps, LLP, 303 F.3d 994 (9th Cir. 2002).

50. Id. at 1000.

51. Circuit City Stores, Inc., 532 U.S. at 122, 123.

52. EEOC v. Luce, Forward, Hamilton & Scripps, LLP, 345 F.3d 742 (9th Cir. 2003).

precedent but instead the prior precedent was wrongly decided and they overruled it themselves. The court reasoned that the conclusion that compulsory arbitration was inconsistent with Title VII was contrary to the Supreme Court's endorsement of arbitration in *Gilmer* and to their "stated position that arbitration affects only the choice of forum, not substantive rights."[53] The court reversed the judgment of the lower court as to injunctive relief insofar as the relief was based on the circuit court's prior precedent but remanded the case as to the issue of injunctive relief on the EEOC's retaliation claim.

In *Alexander*, the Court was willing to allow black workers alternative methods of pressing employment discrimination claims, allowing workers to pursue their claims in both the courts and collective bargaining procedures. Yet *Gilmer* and *Wright*, even though dealing with age and disability discrimination claims, respectively, nonetheless cast doubt on the longevity of that principle. Employers and unions alike may opt for mandatory, explicit, and binding arbitration of discrimination claims to avoid costly litigation. The escalating comfort with alternative dispute resolution of important public law rights, while providing for individual, confidential, and inexpensive resolution of such rights, may do little to decrease discrimination in the workplace.

When the consideration of claims of racial discrimination is consistent with the interests of the white majority, particularly in unions, blacks will be allowed to seek their remedies. Thus, it is consistent with the interests of white workers to allow blacks to file claims through the arbitration-grievance procedures. This remedy for black workers maintains or produces stability in labor relations, hence promoting the economic well-being of white workers and employers as well. But where the consideration of claims of racial discrimination is inconsistent with the interests of the white majority, blacks may be opposed in their attempts to remedy discrimination. Thus, it is inconsistent with the interest of employers and white workers to allow blacks to pursue judicial remedies, many of which may result in broad relief and threaten labor relations stability. In this light, *Gilmer* and *Wright* may be interpreted to preserve stability in labor relations at the expense of black workers who are the victims of discrimination.

The danger remains that white workers often remain the foes, rather than friends, of those who fight racial discrimination. As the labor movement has been institutionalized, and labor conflict regulated, the interests of the white union leadership have become vested. As union majoritarian rights become statutorily guaranteed, they are increasingly identified with those of the white employer. Conflict becomes disadvantageous for white workers; where possible, burdens are borne not by employers or white workers, but by black and other nonwhite workers.

The *appearance* of justice is critical to the maintenance of the status quo. Thus both union leaders and employers will favor limiting minority workers to procedures which the unions and employers themselves control. Black workers may be forced to rely solely on grievance-arbitration procedures, and forgo judicial remedies altogether, which at any rate all too often are burdensome, costly, and long.

---

53. Id.

The shortcomings of grievance-arbitration procedures are particularly evident when black workers seek group, rather than individual, remedies. Black workers have no way of ensuring that white union leaders will vigorously pursue remedies for all black workers who have been the victims of discrimination. To allow control by black workers over their own claims, either through self-help efforts or direct control of grievance-arbitration claims, would indeed pose some possibility of instability in labor relations. Instability is a price which white workers will resist, and black workers will demand, in order to remedy racial discrimination.

§4.8 BEYOND THE BLUE-COLLAR WORKER: THE UPPER LIMITS OF REMEDIES FOR EMPLOYMENT DISCRIMINATION

Throughout the history of Title VII, courts have manifested reluctance to extend its remedies beyond blue-collar workers. The practical effect of Title VII has been to begin opening job opportunities for minority workers at lower positions of employment, while many upper level positions remain untouched by its protection.

Early on, one circuit court suggested that as a job becomes more critical, the business necessity rule is more likely to be invoked.[1] Thus, according to this reasoning, in occupations important to health and safety, employers may set standards requiring skills greater than those absolutely necessary for the job. A different circuit, however, has interpreted the business necessity standard differently. The Third Circuit in Lanning v. SEPTA[2] found that under the Civil Rights Act of 1991, the *Spurlock* reasoning was no longer authoritative. Consequently, the business necessity standard adopted by the Act must "be interpreted in accordance with the standards articulated by the Supreme Court in *Griggs* and its pre-*Wards Cove* progeny, which demand that a discriminatory cutoff score be shown to measure the minimum qualifications necessary for the successful performance of the job in question in order to survive a disparate impact challenge."[3]

While in some cases the courts have allowed seemingly discriminatory practices under the business necessity rule, in others the courts have found Title VII altogether inapplicable. Courts, for example, have held that Title VII does not apply to professional licensing examinations, such as bar exams.[4] In Woodard v. Virginia Board of Bar Examiners,[5] for example, black plaintiffs argued that the

§4.8   1. Spurlock v. United Airlines, Inc., 475 F.2d 216 (10th Cir. 1972) (an airline's requirements that applicants for flight officer positions have a college degree and a minimum of 500 flight hours was justified under the business necessity rule, even though the requirements excluded minority applicants. The court was willing to give the employer substantial leeway, both because of the great expense involved in training pilots and the critical importance of their performance. Reasoning rejected by Lanning v. Southeastern Pa. Transp., 181 F.3d 478 (3d Cir. 1999).

2. 181 F.3d 478 (3d Cir. 1999).

3. Id. at 490.

4. See, e.g., Tyler v. Vickery, 517 F.2d 1089 (5th Cir. 1975); Murry v. Supreme Court, Mo. 72-2101 (9th Cir. 1973); Woodard v. Virginia Bd. of Bar Examiners, 454 F. Supp. 4 (E.D. Va. 1978), upheld by 598 F.2d 1345 (4th Cir. 1979).

5. 420 F. Supp. 211 (E.D. Va. 1976).

bar examiners' control over access to the job market for lawyers should make Title VII applicable to discrimination in the administration or scoring of the bar exam. The court rejected the argument, distinguishing professional licensing examinations from employment tests. Unlike employment examinations designed to test specific skills, "[s]uccessful passage of the bar examination is intended to reflect a mastery of a wide range of substantive knowledge with which to approach [legal] problems."[6]

Interestingly, the courts appear to provide greater protection to those already in the legal profession than to those seeking admission. In the well-publicized case of Lucido v. Cravath, Swaine & Moore,[7] a district court has held that Title VII applies to a law firm's decision whether to promote an associate to partner in the firm. The case involved a Catholic lawyer of Italian ancestry who alleged that he was unlawfully discriminated against because of his national origin or religion. The court held that the opportunity to become a partner in the law firm was a "term, condition or privilege of employment" and an "employment opportunity" within the scope of Title VII.[8] Thus, the paradoxical situation arises in which black plaintiffs cannot bring a Title VII claim challenging the discriminatory impact of bar examinations, while a white plaintiff can bring a Title VII claim challenging a law firm's partnership decision. Regardless of the law involved, this surely presents the paradox of fair employment laws being used to protect those already holding jobs, yet ignoring those seeking access to the job market.

Then, in Hishon v. King & Spalding,[9] a sex-based discrimination case under Title VII, the Supreme Court held that the ability to make partner was a part and parcel of the employment relationship, even though it was not required by an express or implied contract. Rejecting the law firm's "freedom of expressive association" argument, the Court said that the firm had not shown how its ability to fulfill protected functions would be inhibited by a requirement that it consider a woman lawyer for partnership on her merits. Similarly, as discussed earlier, the Court in Price Waterhouse v. Hopkins[10] found in favor of a woman seeking partnership in an accounting firm after being the victim of sexual harassment. Women and minorities continue to face subtle but real obstacles as they attempt to move up the corporate ladder or gain tenured positions. Most promotions come about as a result of a series of subjective decisions, susceptible to the influence of stereotypes and biases.[11] Professor Elizabeth Bartholet notes that "[s]ubjective systems . . . allow for the expression both of conscious bias and of the unconscious bias that is likely to result in the exclusion of persons who are visibly different from those doing the selecting."[12] Mary Radford also noted this phenomenon: "When looking for leaders in law firms, accounting firms, or news-rooms, decision-makers search

6. Id. at 214.

7. 425 F. Supp. 123 (S.D.N.Y. 1977).

8. 42 U.S.C. §2000e-2(a) (1976).

9. 467 U.S. 69, 78 (1984).

10. 490 U.S. 228 (1989).

11. Tracy Anbinder Baron, Keeping Women Out of the Executive Suite: The Courts' Failure to Apply Title VII Scrutiny to Upper-Level Jobs, 143 U. Pa. L. Rev. 267 (1994).

12. Elizabeth Bartholet, Application of Title VII to Jobs in High Places, 95 Harv. L. Rev. 947, 954, 955 (1982).

for more than just physical ability or technical competence. Personal attributes take on prime importance. Stereotypical notions of how persons of each gender should or will act (or look or dress) then become determinative."[13] Because upper-level jobs are more likely to be filled on the basis of subjective judgments, women vying for upper-level jobs are more likely to suffer the effects of unconscious biases than are women competing for lower-level jobs.

The Supreme Court denied certiorari in Ezold v. Wolf, Block, Schorr & Solis-Cohen,[14] in which a female was denied partnership. The trial court held the firm liable, because even though the firm provided evidence of uncomplimentary evaluations of Ezold's analytical ability, the court found that the firm had promoted men with overall evaluations lower that Ezold's, concluding that "the plaintiff was treated differently because of her gender."[15] However, the Third Circuit reversed, cautioning against "unwarranted invasion or intrusion" into "professional judgments about an employee's qualifications for promotion within a profession."[16] One law review argues that by "refusing to hear a further appeal, the Supreme Court effectively agreed."[17]

However, three years later, in the same trial court, in Masterson v. LaBrum & Doak,[18] the plaintiff prevailed in her lawsuit against a law firm when she did not make partner. The court determined that there was unequal information distributed to associates about the process of partnership selection. Unlike other associates in her class, Ms. Masterson was not informed that client development was a criterion for partnership selection and did not receive 1990 evaluations from upper management.

Teachers have not fared as well as lawyers in several Title VII cases. In Gray v. Board of Higher Education,[19] the plaintiff, a black professor at a state community college, initiated an action under the Reconstruction civil rights statutes, challenging his rejection for reappointment and tenure. He argued that he had never received an explanation for the decision. The court held that the Committee members were not required to disclose their reasoning because "it considered the confidentiality of the decisionmaking process to be essential to the peer review system for granting or withholding tenure."[20] The Second Circuit overturned the trial court and held that the plaintiff was entitled to the requested discovery; however, the court also indicated that in Title VII cases, there is a "qualified privilege" against a plaintiff's discovery. It suggested that "a meaningful written statement of reasons" was sufficient to be given to the unsuccessful candidate in order to protect "confidentiality

---

13. Mary F. Radford, Sex Stereotyping and the Promotion of Women to Positions of Power, 41 Hastings L.J. 471, 484 (1990).

14. 751 F. Supp. 1175 (E.D. Pa. 1990), rev'd, 983 F.2d 509 (3d Cir. 1992), cert. denied, 510 U.S. 826 (1994).

15. Id. at 1191-1192.

16. Ezold, 983 F.2d at 526-527.

17. Nancy L. Farrer, Of Ivory Columns and Glass Ceilings: The Impact of the Supreme Court of the United States on the Practice of Women Attorneys in Law Firms, 28 St. Mary's L.J. 529, 567 (1997).

18. 846 F. Supp. 1224 (E.D. Pa. 1993).

19. 692 F.2d 901 (2d Cir. 1982).

20. Harry F. Tepker, Jr., Title VII, Equal Employment Opportunity, and Academic Autonomy: Toward a Principled Deference, 16 U.C. Davis L. Rev. 1047, 1069 (1983).

and encourage a candid peer review process."[21] The Supreme Court rejected this reasoning in the University of Pennsylvania v. EEOC.[22] "[W]e cannot accept the University's invitation to create a new privilege against disclosure of peer review materials."

In Sweeney v. Board of Trustees of Keene State College,[23] the First Circuit had initially approved a finding of sex discrimination in the awarding of promotions and fixing of salaries of college professors. The court explicitly rejected a requirement that plaintiffs demonstrate discriminatory intent, noting that "[p]articularly in a college or university setting, where the level of sophistication is likely to be much higher than in other employment situations, direct evidence of sex discrimination will rarely be available."[24] Voicing an admirable willingness to apply Title VII to colleges and universities, the court declared:

> [W]e voice misgivings over one theme recurrent in [other] opinions: the notion that courts should keep "hands off" the salary, promotion, and hiring decisions of colleges and universities. This reluctance no doubt arises from the courts' recognition that hiring, promotion, and tenure decisions require subjective evaluation most appropriately made by persons thoroughly familiar with the academic setting. Nevertheless, we caution against permitting judicial deference to result in judicial adjudication of a responsibility entrusted to the courts by Congress.[25]

Despite the strength of the findings in the First Circuit opinion, the Supreme Court vacated and remanded the lower court opinion, drawing a distinction between the First Circuit's requirement that defendant "prove absence of discriminatory motive" and the *McDonnell Douglas* requirement that an employer "articulate some legitimate, nondiscriminatory reason."[26]

Speaking as the author of the Washington v. Davis opinion and thus entitled to more respect for his views than the Court's majority was willing to give him, Justice White explained that *Davis* held only that the test there involved, which sought to ascertain whether the applicant had the minimum communication skills necessary to understand the offerings in a police training course, could be used to measure eligibility to enter that program. *Davis* did not hold, according to Justice White, that: (1) a training course, the completion of which is required for employment, need not itself be validated in terms of job relatedness; and (2) a test which a job applicant must pass and which is designed to indicate his mastery of the materials or skills taught in the training course, can be validated without reference to the job.

Justice White was also critical of the lower court's finding that the state's use of the National Teachers' Examination (NTE) passed the business necessity test in that only two other states use the NTE for initial certification and South Carolina is the only state which uses the NTE in determining pay. Quoting *Griggs*, he said that

---

21. 692 F.2d at 907.
22. 493 U.S. 182 (1990).
23. 569 F.2d 169 (1st Cir.), vacated and remanded, 439 U.S. 24 (1978).
24. 569 F.2d at 175.
25. Id. at 176.
26. 439 U.S. 924 (1978).

tests, supposedly measuring an applicant's qualifications for employment, if they have a differential racial impact, must bear "some manifest relationship to the employment in question." And referring to *Davis* again, he found it insufficient for the employer "to demonstrate some rational basis for the challenged provisions."

While the Supreme Court neither approved nor disapproved the lower court's willingness to apply Title VII to colleges and universities, the decision is certainly an ominous sign for minority professors. Black teachers had reason for even more concern based on the Court's action in National Education Association v. South Carolina.[27] Dissenting for himself and Justice Brennan from a five-to-two summary affirmance (Justices Marshall and Blackmun took no part in the consideration or decision in the case), Justice White questioned the legal standards applied by the lower court, and urged a hearing on its decision that the NTE need not be validated against job performance and that the validation requirement was satisfied by a study which demonstrated only that a trained person could pass the test.

South Carolina for many years has used the NTE in hiring and classifying teachers despite the advice of its authors that it should not be used as the state uses it, and despite the fact that it serves to disqualify a greater proportion of black applicants than white and to place a greater percentage of black teachers in lower-paying classifications.[28] The lower court found that a validation test prepared by the test authors at the request of the state was sufficient to validate the NTE, even though the validation was not in relation to job performance and showed, at best, that the test measured familiarity of the candidate with the content of certain teacher training courses.[29]

Justice White might have questioned the lower court's finding that use of the NTE was not racially motivated, given the long history of segregated schools in South Carolina, and the use in many areas of the NTE to frustrate efforts to desegregate faculty as well as students.[30]

Decisions like *Sweeney* and *South Carolina* suggest that courts are far from enthusiastic at the prospect of applying Title VII to employment discrimination outside the context of blue-collar jobs. The one major exception to the pattern, *Lucido*, can perhaps best be interpreted as protecting employment opportunities for those already within the legal job market, an overwhelmingly white male group. For blacks and other nonwhites seeking access to higher-paying, higher-status

---

27. United States v. South Carolina, 445 F. Supp. 1094 (D.S.C. 1977), aff'd mem. sub nom. National Educ. Ass'n v. South Carolina, 434 U.S. 1026 (1978).

28. Justice White's concern was based on data predicting that "the new test score requirements contained in the 1976 revision of the State's plan will disqualify 83 percent of black applicants, but only 17.5 percent of white applicants; and 96 percent of the newly certified candidates permitted to teach will be white teachers." 434 U.S. at 1027, 1028.

29. The lower court accepted a study intended to demonstrate content validity by measuring the degree to which the content of the test matched the content of teacher training programs in South Carolina. Relying on Washington v. Davis, the court held that a positive relationship between the test and training course was sufficient to validate the former, wholly aside from its possible relationship to actual job performance.

To conduct the study, 456 experienced teacher-educators from the 25 training institutions in South Carolina were asked to assess the content validity of the NTE as compared to the curriculum in South Carolina schools, and to establish the minimum score requirement on each segment of the test.

30. See Baker v. Columbus Municipal Separate Sch. Dist., 462 F.2d 1112 (5th Cir. 1972).

positions, Title VII has not proved to be particularly useful. To the extent that the white elite still hold most of the more desirable positions of employment in this country, Title VII has posed little threat to the status quo. Unfortunately, readers of this chapter can be forgiven for concluding that Title VII has changed the status quo in the employment field far less than those who enacted it and those who have pursued remedies under it had hoped.

§4.9 EMPLOYMENT, RACE, AND GENDER: ARE YOU A BLACK, A WOMAN, OR WHAT?

There is now recognition that black women are uniquely vulnerable to discrimination because of the intersection between their race and gender. The focus of anti-discrimination law and policy on either race *or* gender obscures the barriers that black women face. Without a clear understanding of the harm, traditional race-sex thinking fails to address the complex intersection — not mere additive oppression — of race and gender discrimination that black women face. An intersectional-based theory is one that focuses on the relationship *between* various categories of subjectivity with a focus on how such categories interact.[1] These categories are not generally limited to race and gender, and many theorists analyze additional categories such as class and sexual orientation.[2]

The following anecdote captures the essence of the law's blindness to, and indifference towards, the intricate challenge black women face. During a talk on affirmative action, a white male faculty colleague observed that under the Court's cases, race-based remedies were tested under the strict scrutiny test. But policies challenged as sex discrimination had been measured by an intermediate scrutiny test. He therefore assumed that affirmative action policies intended to remedy sex discrimination against women would also be appraised under this lesser standard. He suggested that this distinction between policies designed to help blacks and those intended to aid women was somewhat paradoxical. "You mean white women," visiting professor Regina Austin interrupted. The colleague was taken aback. It was obvious that he had never realized that black women fall quite

---

§4.9   1. See generally Patricia Hill Collins, Black Feminist Thought: Knowledge, Consciousness, and the Politics of Empowerment (1990).

2. The category of "black women" is, however, often highlighted as a unique one in which the interrelationship between various forms of oppression may be highlighted and understood. Looking at the intersections of multiple categories, an intersectional theory recognizes that a black lesbian's experiences and social identity are constituted not merely by what it means to be black plus what it means to be a woman plus what it means to be a lesbian but, rather, by the complex interaction between these categories and their social meanings. The social position and subject space of any person is, according to an intersectional theory, comprised of the intersection of various categories, some of which are generally societally privileged and some of which are generally societally disadvantaged. Put in other terms, a heterosexual black woman may occupy a different subjective location than a black lesbian although the subjectivity of both are implicated by the interrelationship between being black and being female in this society.

literally into a "no man's" and "no woman's" land in race and sex discrimination law. The surprised colleague is not alone.

Professor Kimberle Crenshaw has called attention to employment discrimination cases where courts have refused to recognize black women as a distinctive class.[3] In Degraffenfield v. General Motors,[4] for example, five black women alleged that the employer's seniority system perpetuated the effects of past discrimination against black women. They showed that while General Motors hired white women for a number of years prior to the enactment of the Civil Rights Act of 1964, they had hired no black women prior to 1964. In addition, all black women hired after 1970 lost their jobs in a seniority-based lay-off during the 1973 recession.

The court rejected their claim. It stated:

> [P]laintiffs have failed to cite any decisions which have stated that black women are a special class to be protected from discrimination. . . . [T]hey should not be allowed to combine statutory remedies to create a new "super-remedy" which would give them relief beyond what the drafters of the relevant statutes intended. Thus this lawsuit must be examined to see if it states a cause of action for race discrimination, sex discrimination, or alternatively, either but not a combination of both.[5]

Then the court reasoned that there was no sex discrimination that the seniority system could conceivably perpetuate because General Motors had hired women — albeit white women. In terms of race discrimination, the court recommended that their suit be consolidated with another case against GM alleging race discrimination. The black women plaintiffs resisted the court's recommendation, pointing out that their action was not purely a race claim, but one specifically brought on behalf of black women alleging race *and* sex discrimination. The court, however, expressed reluctance to creating a new classification, "black women," whose members would have greater standing than, for example, a black male.[6] Some courts have accepted the idea that black women are protected by Title VII as a compound class, but the fact that there is a question as in *Degraffenfield* reflects the view that white women and their experiences are at the normative heart of sex discrimination doctrine.

3. Kimberle Crenshaw, Demarginalizing the Intersection of Race and Sex: A Black Feminist Critique of Antidiscrimination Doctrine, Feminist Theory, and Antiracist Politics, U. Chi. Legal F. (1989).

4. 413 F. Supp. 142 (E.D. Mo. 1976).

5. Id. at 413.

6. See also Moore v. Hughes, 708 F.2d 475 (9th Cir. 1983). The court refused to certify black females as class representatives in actions alleging race and sex discrimination, despite statistical evidence that established a significant disparity between men and women in supervisory jobs, and somewhat less of a disparity between black and white men. Because plaintiff had not charged discrimination because she was a female, "but only as a black female," the court had serious doubt that she could adequately represent white female employees. Id. at 480.

In Payne v. Travenol, 673 F.2d 798 (5th Cir. 1982), the court refused to certify black female plaintiffs to represent black males in a suit, even though all the evidence supported their race discrimination claim. Paradoxically, what the court had insisted in *Moore* (that black women were "too black" to deal effectively with claims of nonblack women) was precisely what the *Payne* court refused to recognize (that black women understand racism only too well — at least as well as their black male counterparts), although the court in *Payne* intimated that black women were too much *women* to represent a normatively male race discrimination claim).

§4.10   LITIGATION AROUND SEXUAL ORIENTATION

In the 1950s, President Eisenhower issued an executive order banning the employment of homosexuals, labeled as "sexual deviants," from the federal government. A half-century later, 14 states have statutes banning discrimination on the basis of sexual orientation. In three of those states the law also expressly bans discrimination on the basis of gender identity or expression. In addition, a number of counties and municipalities have bans on sexual orientation discrimination that may be far more stringent than the state law. For example, in Levin v. Yeshiva University,[1] the court held that lesbian medical students could assert disparate impact discrimination claims under the city ordinance but could not use the state law's sex discrimination ban to make the claim.

Title VII bans sex discrimination but does not define or specify the scope or meaning of "sex."[2] In DeSantis v. Pacific Telephone & Telegraph Company,[3] the Ninth Circuit held that Title VII was narrowly focused on discrimination against women or men and that sexual orientation claims were not cognizable under Title VII. But the Supreme Court's decision in Price Waterhouse v. Hopkins,[4] offered some hope for the gender nonconformity theory. The Court held that the plaintiff who was denied partnership for not being "feminine" enough was an example of sex discrimination based on gender nonconformity. Consequently, while a straightforward sexual orientation claim would be dismissed, lawyers could be creative in explaining how it fell under the "gender nonconformity" rubric. Further support was given by Oncale v. Sundowner Offshore Services, Inc.,[5] in which the Court accepted that a plaintiff could make a Title VII claim for suffering discrimination from co-workers of the same sex.

In Rene v. MGM Hotel Inc.,[6] a plaintiff alleged that he encountered a hostile work environment and was discriminated against because of his sexual orientation, a violation of Title VII. The district court issued summary judgment for the defendant, finding that "Title VII's prohibition of 'sex' discrimination applies only [to] discrimination on the basis of gender and is not extended to include discrimination based on sexual preference."[7] The Ninth Circuit, sitting en banc, reversed and remanded the case, although the majority was divided as to the reasoning. Writing for the plurality, Judge Fletcher focused on the physical nature of the conduct, finding that "an employee's sexual orientation is irrelevant for purposes of Title VII. . . . It is enough that the harasser engaged in severe or pervasive unwelcome physical conduct of a sexual nature."[8] Alternatively, Judge Pregerson's concurrence focused on the nature of the verbal abuse and described

---

§4.10   1. 96 N.Y.2d 484 (2001).

2. For a great overview on the topic, see Arthur S. Leonard, The Gay Rights Workplace Revolution, 30 Hum. Rts. 14 (2003).

3. 608 F.2d 437 (9th Cir. 1979).

4. 490 U.S. 228 (1989).

5. 523 U.S. 75 (1998).

6. 305 F.3d 1061 (9th Cir. 2002) (en banc).

7. Id. at 1064.

8. Id. at 1063-1064 (Pregerson, J., concurring).

the case as one of "actionable gender stereotyping harassment." He applied the reasoning from *Price Waterhouse* finding similarities between Rene who was treated "like a woman" and Hopkins who was considered "too macho" to make partner.

The dissent was straightforward, finding that "[i]f sexual orientation is to be a separate category of protection under Title VII, this is a matter for Congress to enact."[9] A casenote in the Harvard Law Review analyzes the Ninth Circuit's fragmented support and its "unsound solution that fails to adequately protect sexual minorities from workplace discrimination."[10]

> Both the plurality and the concurrence were clearly, and correctly, troubled by the possibility that the appalling abuse Rene suffered would go unsanctioned. If they failed to provide a remedy, the Ninth Circuit would have been giving license to homo-phobes to continue taking hits on gay colleagues. Yet the plurality's narrow focus on the nature of the harasser's physical conduct could exclude from Title VII protection gay plaintiffs who are victims of pervasive verbal harassment without physical touching, while the concurrence's narrow focus on the gendered nature of the harasser's verbal insults could exclude gay plaintiffs who are either verbally or physically assaulted by harassers who do not use gendered epithets.[11]

The decision implies it is okay to call a gay employee "faggot" but not "sweetheart." By denying certiorari, the Supreme Court has left many questions open.[12]

---

9. Id. at 1076 (Hug, J., dissenting).

10. Casenote, Ninth Circuit Extends Title VII Protection to Employee Alleging Discrimination Based on Sexual Orientation, 116 Harv. L. Rev. 1889, 1893 (2003).

11. Id. at 1896.

12. Recently, the Supreme Court declined to resolve the debate over the extent to which Price Waterhouse protects gays from harassment. In *Price Waterhouse*, described above, a woman had been denied a partnership in part because she failed to conform to stereotypes of femininity, including wearing make-up and being more submissive. Supreme Court held that employers may not take action against an employee for failure to conform to gender stereotypes. The Sixth Circuit, however, denied such protection to a gay former hospital employee who was harassed for not meeting his coworkers' expectations of how a man should act.[1] The Sixth Circuit held that the discrimination endured by the plaintiff was the result of his sexual orientation, not his gender, and was therefore not prohibited by Title VII. The perverse result is that straight men and women are protected by Title VII harassment based on their perceived failure to conform to sex stereotypes, while gay men and lesbians lack that protection in the Sixth Circuit purely as a result of their sexual orientation. As a result, defendants in Sixth Circuit sex-stereotyping cases have a potential defense that their discrimination against any employee was due to the employee's perceived sexual orientation.

Chapter 5

Discrimination in the Administration of Justice

§5.1 SUMMARY PUNISHMENT VIA RACIAL VIOLENCE

In the post-Reconstruction years, the law failed black people, not simply because it was inadequate, but because when they needed it most for their physical safety, it deserted them entirely. Laws that emasculated the right to vote posed an ominous handicap to their participation in government policy-making; laws that required segregation in public facilities constituted a humiliation to the spirit. But it was the absolute refusal of the law to protect them from random and organized violence that enabled the virtual re-enslavement of a race so recently freed.

The process by which the law's protection was withdrawn began immediately after the Civil War; really before it was received. For a period during the Reconstruction, there was a federal presence when civil rights statutes were enacted and federal troops were in view (if not always available). Then, when it was clear that the withdrawal of federal protection would mean horrible deaths and maimings for uncounted thousands of black people and lives for all filled with intimidation and threats of physical violence, the protection was withdrawn. The story of the oppression of blacks by armed force and vigilante violence has been told in literally hundreds of reports, histories, narratives, and studies.[1] The work of the organized

---

§5.1 1. One report places the number of lynchings of black persons between 1882 and 1968 at 3,446 — 73 percent of the total lynchings during that period. Robert L. Zangrandao, The NAACP Crusade Against Lynching 1909-1950 (1980). Professor Belknap argues that lynchers had "little to fear from those who administered the southern legal system." He quotes one Texas prosecutor who, speaking in 1935, dismissed lynching as "an expression of the will of the people." Michael R. Belknap, Federal Law and Southern Order 8-9 (1987).

Those nineteenth-century congressmen who urged support for the various civil rights acts spoke eloquently of the need to provide federal protection against the atrocities, many of which were detailed in a report nearly 600 pages long that reviewed the activities of the Ku Klux Klan and the inability of the state governments to cope with it. Justice Douglas quoted from a few of these speeches in Monroe v. Pape, 365 U.S. 167, 175 (1961).

"[Mr. Lowe of Kansas said:] 'While murder is stalking abroad in disguise, while whippings and lynchings and banishment have been visited upon unoffending American citizens, the local administrations have been found inadequate or unwilling to apply the proper corrective. Combinations, darker than the night that hides them, conspiracies, wicked as the worst of felons could devise, have gone unwhipped of justice. Immunity is given to crime, and the records of the public tribunals are searched in vain for any evidence of effective redress.'

terror groups, the Ku Klux Klan, the White Camellias, and the White League have all been well-documented. But the lynchings and whippings, the arson and random shootings, were just as frequently carried out by ad hoc mobs or even individuals.[2]

In addition to the lynchings, hundreds of blacks lost their lives in what are generally referred to as "race riots," but which in most instances were simply racial massacres. One of the bloodiest of these occurred in 1917 in East St. Louis, Illinois. Estimates of the number of blacks killed range from 40 to 200, and nearly 6,000 were driven from their homes. Petitions and protests (including in 1917 an NAACP-sponsored silent march down Fifth Avenue in New York, in which 10,000 persons protested against brutalities and lynchings) received major press coverage, but had little effect on lynchers and rioters and little more on the nation. The Congress never enacted an anti-lynching law, although efforts made by liberal congressmen date back to 1922. In that year, a Senate filibuster killed a House-passed measure that would have punished not only lynchers, but state officers who made no reasonable effort to prevent lynching; further, it would have required the county where the murder occurred to pay the victim's family $10,000.[3]

"Mr. Beatty of Ohio said: '. . . certain States have denied to persons within their jurisdiction the equal protection of the laws. The proof on this point is voluminous and unquestionable. . . . [M]en were murdered, houses were burned, women were outraged, men were scourged, and officers of the law shot down; and the State made no successful effort to bring the guilty to punishment or afford protection or redress to the outraged and innocent. The State, from lack of power or inclination, practically denied the equal protection of the law to these persons.' "

2. Justice Fortas reported in Price v. United States, 383 U.S. 787, 804 (1966), that in 1868 organizations with these romantic titles launched a wave of murders and assaults designed to keep blacks from the polls. The states themselves were helpless, despite the resort by some of them to such extreme measures as making it legal to hunt down and shoot any disguised man.

See Ralph Ginzburg, One Hundred Years of Lynchings (1969). In a compilation of the approximately 5,000 blacks lynched in the United States since 1859, the Ginzburg book reprints hundreds of newspaper reports of lynchings. Reading them explains how one presidential commission could report that murders in which the victims were riddled with bullets constituted some "of the less brutal lynchings of the past years because the victims in these cases were not mutilated or burned." To Secure These Rights, Report of the President's Committee on Civil Rights (1947).

Two early black historians, Carter Woodson and Charles Wesley, report that immediately after the Civil War, "Native whites undertook to 'manage' or 'control' the freedmen as they were handled when slaves. If the freedmen objected, they were beaten or killed. Referring to South Carolina, an authority said: 'The pecuniary value which the individual Negro formerly represented having disappeared, the maiming and killing of them seemed to be looked upon by many as one of those venial offenses which must be forgiven to the outraged feelings of a wronged and robbed people.' 'E. H. Johnson, a Virginia clergyman, killed a Negro soldier in 1865.' According to the Richmond Inquirer on November 3, 1866, 'J. C. Johnston, a law student of Lexington charged with killing a freedman, was acquitted.' For a trivial reason, one Queensbury, a planter in Louisa County, killed a Negro in his employ. Because of slight misunderstandings, R. N. Eastham of Rappahannock, and Washington Alsworth of Lunenburg killed Negroes in their service. On November 24, 1866, the Inquirer reported that Dr. James Watson, 'one of the most respectable gentlemen of Rockbridge County,' killed a Negro for driving into his vehicle. These criminals were not punished." Carter Woodson & Charles Wesley, The Negro in Our History 394 (1922).

3. Peter M. Bergman, The Chronological History of the Negro in America 403 (1969).

§5.2 CRIMINAL REMEDIES FOR CIVIL RIGHTS VIOLATIONS

To combat both organized and random white violence against blacks, Congress enacted two criminal statutes. In 1866 it enacted the section currently located at 18 U.S.C. §242 (1970). It was a narrow provision which forbade the deprivation "under color of any law" of several specifically enumerated rights, including the right "to make and enforce contracts, to sue, be parties, give evidence, and to the full and equal benefit of all laws and proceedings for the security of person and property as is enjoyed by white citizens," and the right to have no "punishment, pains, or penalties" imposed "by reason of . . . color or race, than is prescribed for the punishment of white persons."[1] Congress faced much criticism between 1866 and 1870, "because of the continued denial of rights to Negroes, sometimes accompanied by violent assaults."[2] Congress responded with the much broader Enforcement Act of 1870,[3] reenacting the narrow provisions of the Act of 1866 and in addition passing the predecessor of 18 U.S.C. §241, a conspiracy provision which protected all rights and privileges under the Constitution and laws of the United States rather than the specifically limited rights protected by the earlier act. In 1874 the specific enumeration of protected rights was eliminated for §242, which was expanded to protect "all rights, privileges, or immunities, secured or protected by the Constitution or laws of the United States." Thus the range of protected rights under §242 was expanded to be as broad as those protected under §241.

Section 242 now provides for a fine of up to $1,000 and imprisonment of up to one year for any person who, "under color of law" deprives another of these rights "by reason of his color, or race,"[4] unless the violation results in death of the victim, in which case the wrongdoer is subject to life imprisonment. Section 241 is aimed at organized group action, providing for up to 10 years' imprisonment or a fine of up to $10,000 for conspiracy "to injure, oppress, threaten, or intimidate any citizen in the free exercise or enjoyment of any right or privilege secured . . . by the Constitution or laws of the United States."[5] Unlike §242, §241 does not contain on its face any state action requirement. There have been few prosecutions under §§241 and 242, and even fewer developments in the interpretation of these statutes. In the only significant development, §241 was amended in 1988 to explicitly include within the statute's protection persons entering the United States illegally.[6]

---

§5.2 1. Act of April 9, 1866, §1, S2, 14 Stat. 27. For a comprehensive history of Reconstruction-era legislation, see Eric Foner, Reconstruction: America's Unfinished Revolution, 1863-1877 (1988).

2. United States v. Price, 383 U.S. 787, 802 (1966).

3. 16 Stat. 141, 144 (1870).

4. 18 U.S.C. §242 (1988).

5. 18 U.S.C. §241 (1988).

6. The legislative amendment codified the Ninth Circuit's decision that every inhabitant of the United States — whether legally or illegally residing in the country — is protected by §242. In United States v. Otherson, 637 F.2d 1276 (9th Cir. 1980), cert. denied, 454 U.S. 840 (1981), the court upheld the convictions under §242 of federal Border Patrol agents in California who routinely beat Mexican aliens while transporting them to processing centers. The lower court's interpretation of §241, which read to protect "citizens," was effectively overruled by the 1988 amendments to §241 that extended the statute's protection from only "citizen" to "inhabitant." 18 U.S.C.S. §241 (1988).

§5.3 INEFFECTIVE CRIMINAL PENALTIES

Until recently, the seemingly broad and protective statutes providing criminal penalties for civil rights violations offered little or no comfort to blacks. Their potential value as a deterrent was diluted both by a series of judicial opinions that narrowly circumscribed the conduct covered by the laws and by lax federal enforcement policies.[1]

A major obstacle to effective enforcement was the "color of law" provision found in §242, which in effect imposed a requirement of "state action" on the activity for which prosecution was sought. This created a vicious paradox: State officials who acted illegally (e.g., police officers who beat blacks) could defend themselves against federal prosecution by claiming they had not acted "under color" of state law but had in fact violated that law. Thus there was no state action and no violation of the statute. At the same time, the violator was secure in his knowledge that there was little or no chance of state prosecution.[2]

The legislative amendment conformed §241 to the scope of §242, which had always used the term "inhabitant."

§5.3   1. In United States v. Reese, 92 U.S. 214 (1876), two inspectors of a municipal election in Kentucky refused to receive and count in the election the vote of a black citizen. An action was brought under provisions of the Civil Rights Acts which prohibited interference with the right to vote. The Supreme Court held that the provisions were unconstitutional because they prohibited all interference with the right to vote; and thus exceeded the scope of the Fifteenth Amendment, which prohibited only interference based on race, color, or previous condition of servitude.

In United States v. Harris, 106 U.S. 629 (1883), 20 men seized 4 prisoners held by a county deputy sheriff in Tennessee and beat them severely, killing one of them. The Court ruled that, absent a finding of state action, an action under the provision of the Civil Rights Act that prohibited deprivation of equal protection of laws or equal privileges and immunities under the law could not stand. "It was never supposed that the section under consideration conferred on Congress the power to enact a law which would punish a private citizen for an invasion of the rights of his fellow citizen. . . ." 106 U.S. at 644.

Justice Harlan dissented in *Harris* and also in Baldwin v. Franks, 120 U.S. 678 (1887), in which the Court, citing *Harris*, directed the release of a defendant arrested for assaulting Chinese citizens and driving them out of a California town. The Court found that the Chinese citizens were protected under a treaty that might have afforded basis for federal protection, but the provision was deemed too broadly worded.

The Supreme Court did affirm convictions in Ex parte Yarbrough, 110 U.S. 651 (1884), in which the Court ruled that a Ku Klux Klansman who had forcefully prevented a black from voting in a congressional election in Georgia had violated a civil rights act. The provision, §5508 (a predecessor of 18 U.S.C. §241), was sustained as a valid exercise of the federal power to control elections that emanated from Art. 1, §4 of the Constitution. This was held to be the case also in Ex parte Siebold, 100 U.S. 371 (1880). However, in James v. Bowman, 190 U.S. 127 (1903), the Court ruled that another act of Congress, §5507, which covered all elections, was invalid. It held that the Fifteenth Amendment applied only to interference by states and that Art. 1, §4 extended to federal authorities and to federal elections.

The civil rights statutes were held to provide protection to a black who was attacked on a homestead on U.S. land. The statutes were said to protect the constitutional right to cultivate and enjoy that land. United States v. Waddell, 112 U.S. 76 (1884). In Logan v. United States, 144 U.S. 263 (1892), the Court held that prisoners who had been attacked while in the custody of a federal marshal had the constitutionally protected right to be safe while in federal custody. The Court stated, "The United States, having the absolute right to hold such prisoners, has an equal duty to protect them, while so held, against assault or injury from any quarter."

2. Screws v. United States, 325 U.S. 91 (1945), discussed in §5.4, is significant as a turning point in federal prosecutorial efforts in that the attempt to rely on such a defense failed.

This "state action" loophole was grafted by the Supreme Court onto §241, which on its face had no such requirement.

In United States v. Cruikshank,[3] the Court held that the deprivation of life, liberty, or property without due process was not covered by the statute if the deprivation was the result of acts of private individuals.[4] Congress could not constitutionally reach interference with the basic rights secured by the Fourteenth Amendment unless there was state action. Only the narrow exception of "positive" federal rights, like the right to vote, could be protected against private interference. In a final refusal to acknowledge as justices of the Supreme Court what they and all others of the time knew as men, the Court dismissed the charge that defendants had intended to prevent and hinder citizens of African descent and persons of color in the free exercise and enjoyment of their right and privileges under state and federal law, which rights and privileges are enjoyed by white persons. In short, the Court limited the facially broad provisions of §242 by requiring state action, except for a few limited exceptions, and the state action requirement was further limited by the interpretation given to "under color of law" in both §§241 and 242, that the wrongdoer was only covered if he acted in accordance with improper state law. Violation of state law in effect could immunize the criminal from federal prosecution. Given these severe judicially imposed limits, it is not surprising that few prosecutions were brought under either section.

Initially, there had been a major effort by the federal government in the post-Civil War period to enforce the Civil Rights Acts, in the hope that this would break the violent resistance to black citizenship. Thousands of prosecutions were brought, but only about 20 percent resulted in convictions. As the cases reviewed above indicate, the Supreme Court reversed some of them, and by their voiding of some and restrictive interpretation of other civil rights act provisions, discouraged vigorous enforcement.[5] Justice Blackmun calls the first 40 years of the twentieth century the "Dark Age of Civil Rights" because of the virtual absence of significant cases brought under the Civil Rights Acts.[6]

---

3. 92 U.S. 542 (1876).

4. The *Cruikshank* case arose out of a tragedy known both as the Grant Parish Massacre and the Colfax Massacre. In Louisiana during the elections of 1872 there were numerous disputes over the results of local elections. In the town of Colfax, where an election dispute over the positions of sheriff and judge had arisen, the sheriff, on the governor's orders, seized a building that was to be used as the courthouse. The seizure was made with the assistance of a posse of blacks. Rumors spread that the blacks were about to attack local whites, and on April 15, 1873, the courthouse was burned down and the blacks were shot as they came out. The governor took no action, but the Department of Justice investigator secured such evidence that 96 people were indicted under the Civil Rights Act of 1870 (now 18 U.S.C. §241). The Justice Department succeeded in arresting nine of them. They were found not guilty of murder but guilty of conspiracy to prevent blacks from the free exercise and enjoyment of rights and privileges granted and secured by the Constitution, including the rights to assemble peacefully for lawful purposes, to bear arms, vote, and not be placed in fear of bodily harm for voting. Homer Cummings & Carl McFarland, Federal Justice, Ch. XII 230 (1937). The Supreme Court reversed as to each count of the indictment.

5. See Robert K. Carr, Federal Protection of Civil Rights 40-55 (1947); Robert J. Kaczorowski, The Politics of Judicial Interpretation: The Federal Courts, Department of Justice and Civil Rights, 1866-1876 (1985) (arguing that through the Reconstruction legislation Congress intended to vest broad power in the national government to protect civil rights).

6. Harry A. Blackmun, Section 1983 and Federal Protection of Individual Rights — Will the Statute Remain Alive or Fade Away?, 60 N.Y.U. L. Rev. 1, 11 (1985).

By the end of the nineteenth century, the statutes were seldom used. Some revisions were made in the predecessors of §§241 and 242 in 1909, but during the next 30 years, no cases involving §242, and only four cases under the predecessor of §241, reached the Supreme Court, and none of them involved racial issues. In the lower courts, a typical case involved the forceful taking of some blacks from Tennessee to Missouri, where they were made to work, beaten, and denied wages. The white defendants were found guilty of conspiracy to deprive citizens of their right to be free from slavery and involuntary servitude.[7]

There was some increase in civil rights activity in the Department of Justice after Attorney General Frank Murphy created a Civil Section there in 1935. United States v. Classic[8] upheld an indictment under §§241 and 242 against election officials who made a false count in a federal primary election. And §241 was held an appropriate sanction for election officials who stuffed ballot boxes in federal elections.[9] But caution and restraint remained the key elements in the federal government's enforcement policy. Moderation, though, impressed neither the lawbreakers (as the statistics on lynching indicate) nor those members of the Supreme Court who viewed any prosecution under the civil rights statutes with the gravest suspicion.[10]

After the "Radical Reconstruction" of the 1860s, the end of the century saw a dramatic curtailment of government protection for the civil rights of black citizens

7. Smith v. United States, 157 Fed. 721 (8th Cir. 1907).

8. 313 U.S. 299 (1941).

9. United States v. Saylor, 322 U.S. 385 (1944).

10. For example, three Justices — Roberts, speaking for himself, Frankfurter, and Jackson — dissented from the Court's finding of liability in Screws v. United States, discussed in §5.4, because even though their review of the Justice Department's assurances of a moderate prosecutorial policy gave no cause for criticism, they remained concerned about the potential of the civil rights act to undermine federal-state balances. Justice Roberts wrote:

"The Department of Justice has established a policy of strict self-limitation with regard to prosecutions under the civil rights acts. When violations of such statutes are reported, the Department requires that efforts be made to encourage state officials to take appropriate action under state law to assure consistent observance of this policy in the enforcement of the civil rights statutes. All United States Attorneys have been instructed to submit cases to the Department for approval before prosecutions or investigations are instituted. The number of prosecutions which have been brought under the civil rights statutes is small. No statistics are available with respect to the number of prosecutions prior to 1939, when a special Civil Rights Section was established in the Department of Justice. Only two cases during this period have been reported: United States v. Buntin, 10 Fed. 730 (C.C.S.D. Ohio), and United States v. Stone, 188 Fed. 836 (D. Md.). Since 1939, the number of complaints received annually by the Civil Rights Section has ranged from 8,000 to 14,000, but in no year have prosecutions under both Sections 20 and 19, its companion statute, exceeded 76. In the fiscal year 1943, for example, 31 full investigations of alleged violations of Section 20 were conducted, and three cases were brought to trial. In the following fiscal year there were 55. Such investigations and prosecutions were instituted in 12 cases.

"Complaints of violations are often submitted to the Department by local law enforcement officials who for one reason or another may feel themselves powerless to take action under state law. It is primarily in this area, namely, where the official position of the wrongdoers has apparently rendered the State unable or unwilling to institute proceedings, that the statute has come into operation. . . .

"But such a 'policy of strict self-limitation' is not accompanied by assurance of permanent tenure and immortality of those who make it the policy. Evil men are rarely given power; they take it over from better men to whom it had been entrusted. There can be no doubt that this shapeless and all-embracing statute can serve as a dangerous instrument of political intimidation and coercion in the hands of those so inclined." 325 U.S. at 159-160.

and an escalation of racial violence.[11] The federal government's refusal to intervene in the violence prompted harsh criticism from many black leaders. Frederick Douglass, for one, chastised the government for failing to intervene on behalf of blacks: "If [the national government] has the right, and refuses to exercise it, it is a traitor to the citizen. If it has not this right, it is destitute of the fundamental quality of government."[12]

§5.4 SCREWS V. UNITED STATES

Race relations in this country are marked by the celebration of rare occurrences that, by all rights, should be commonplace. But on that standard, Screws v. United States is a landmark.[1] It represented the beginning of a slow decline in Court-imposed roadblocks to the federal criminal prosecution of private citizens and state officials charged with violating the civil rights of blacks.

In *Screws*, the Court dealt with an action arising out of what Justice Douglas called a "shocking and revolting episode in law enforcement." Robert Hall, a black, was arrested at his home late at night by Sheriff Screws of Baker County in Georgia and two other law officers on a warrant charging Hall with the theft of a tire. Between the time he was arrested and placed in jail, Hall was beaten by the officers with their fists and with a solid bar blackjack eight inches long and weighing two pounds, until he was unconscious. He died soon after his arrest.

An indictment was brought under §20 (now §242), charging that the defendants, acting under the color of state law, had "willfully" deprived the prisoner of the right not to be deprived of life without due process of law, the right to be given a trial, and the right to be punished in accordance with the laws of Georgia, and that the denial of these rights violated the Fourteenth Amendment.

---

11. See Michal R. Belknap, Federal Law and Southern Order: Racial Violence and Constitutional Conflict in the Post-Brown South 1-26 (1987) (discussing the violence and government inaction of the post-Reconstruction years); R. Logan, The Betrayal of the Negro 195-241(1965). Justice Blackmun reports that in these years of "reconciliation," "the Nation lost the urgency of its zeal to protect the individual rights and freedoms for which the war in part had been fought." Blackmun, supra note 6. He notes that federal prosecutions under the civil rights acts were drastically curtailed in the years after the Civil War, falling from 1,304 prosecutions in 1873 to 25 in 1878. Moreover, Congress surely and steadily rolled back the statutory protections afforded by Reconstruction legislation. In 1894 alone, Congress repealed 39 sections of the Revised Statutes concerning voting rights. Blackmun, supra note 6, at 11.

Protection of the rights of former slaves disappeared with the federal troops sent to guarantee these rights. By 1910, every southern state had imposed some combination of poll taxes or property or literacy requirements that effectively disenfranchised black voters. In 1896, 130,344 blacks were registered to vote in Louisiana. By 1900, only 5,320 blacks remained on the voting rolls. See Blackmun, supra note 6. See also Benno Schmidt, Principle and Prejudice: The Supreme Court and Race in the Progressive Era, 82 Colum. L. Rev. 835 (1982).

12. Frederick Douglass, 1 Denounce This So-Called Emancipation as a Stupendous Fraud, in 1 The Voice of Black America 562 (Eric Foner ed., 1975).

§5.4 1. Screws v. United States, 325 U.S. 91 (1945).

Defendants appealed from the guilty verdict returned by the jury in the federal district court. They argued that (1) §20 was unconstitutional under the due process clause of the Fifth Amendment because it was too vague and indefinite, and (2) the section requiring that their conduct was "under color of law" excludes their assault, which was not authorized by state law but rather was in itself a violation of state law. The majority of the Court rejected both arguments, although five members of the Court voted to return the case to the district court for a new trial with more specific instruction respecting the kind of intent required under the statute.

Justice Douglas, speaking for the majority in rejecting the defendants' "color of law" argument, conceded that, based on prior cases, a violation of local law does not necessarily mean that federal rights have been invaded even when a prisoner is assaulted, injured, or murdered:

> It is only state action of a "particular character" that is prohibited by the Fourteenth Amendment and against which the Amendment authorized Congress to afford relief. . . . In the present case, as we have said, the defendants were officers of the law who had made an arrest and by their own admissions made the assault in order to protect themselves and to keep the prisoner from escaping, i.e., to make the arrest effective. That was a duty they had under Georgia law. United States v. Classic is, therefore, indistinguishable from this case so far as "under color of state law" is concerned. In each officers of the State were performing official duties; in each the power which they were authorized to exercise was misused. We cannot draw a distinction between them unless we are to say that §20 is not applicable to police officers. But the broad sweep of its language leaves no room for such an exception. . . . (325 U.S. at 109-110.)[2]

Unhappily, as so often happens in civil rights landmark cases, the precedent was set, but the specific relief sought somehow slipped away. On retrial, following

---

2. Id. at 109-110. Justices Roberts, Frankfurter, and Jackson, in dissent, challenged the majority holding that the defendants had been acting under the color of state law. In their view, the federal government could intervene only when a specific state statute or an officer of the state acting under a state statute violated an individual's constitutional rights. They argued that a state official who was violating his own state law in his actions was not acting under the color of state law.

They also voiced concern about the overriding broadness of the statute. Since the statute did not specify what constitutional rights were protected, the dissenters argued that any time a state official did something wrong he was subject to a criminal action under the civil rights statute. To the point that the federal statute was needed because local officials might not act because of personal or political reasons the dissenters responded. "If it be significantly true that crimes against local law cannot be locally prosecuted, it is an ominous sign indeed. In any event, the cure is a reinvigoration of State responsibility. It is not an undue incursion of remote federal authority into local duties with consequent debilitation of local responsibility. . . ." 325 U.S. at 160-161.

Justice Murphy would have affirmed. In his dissent, he said there was no "reasonable doubt" that defendants knew their actions violated due process. He saw no real issue of warning, since "the Constitution, §20 and their own consciences" told them that they lacked any authority to take human life unnecessarily without due process in law. Justice Murphy felt that the really significant question was "whether law enforcement officers and those entrusted with authority shall be allowed to violate with impunity the clear constitutional rights of the marticulate and the friendless." He continued: "Too often unpopular minorities, such as Negroes, are unable to find effective refuge from the cruelties of bigoted and ruthless authority. States are undoubtedly capable of punishing their officers who commit such outrages. But where, as here, the states are unwilling for some reason to prosecute such crimes the federal government must step in unless constitutional guarantees are to become atrophied. . . . (325 U.S. at 138.)"

remand of the Screws case, defendants were acquitted by the jury.[3] The defeat likely defused whatever prosecutorial enthusiasm had been engendered by the Supreme Court's Screws decision.[4]

§5.5 INTERRACIAL LYNCHING AND THE REVITALIZATION OF SECTIONS 241 AND 242

On August 4, 1964, following a search of several weeks, the FBI found the bodies of three missing civil rights workers, of whom two, Michael H. Schwerner and Andrew Goodman, were white, and one, James E. Chaney, was black. The discovery climaxed a nation's horror and concern at what all feared had happened when the three were reported missing following their release from the Neshoba County jail. The details of the deaths, while far from pleasant, showed that these

3. See Robert K. Carr, Federal Protection of Civil Rights 114 (1947). The Justice Department's cautious policy about initiating prosecutions for violations of §§241 and 242 was based on the view (generally admirable for a prosecutor) that only those cases should be brought in which conviction was almost certain. Applying that standard to civil rights cases, however, meant that in addition to evidence of guilt (which might be substantial), consideration had to be given to the small likelihood that a jury would convict, and it can be presumed that many cases were dropped for this reason. Would there have been a deterrent effect on civil rights violations if the government had prosecuted cases where the evidence justified such actions, even if juries refused to convict out of sympathy with the defendants' acts?

For those who see serious ethical issues in the departure from the Justice Department's usual prosecutorial standards suggested in this question, it might be interesting to consider what the Department's policy would be if the racial roles were reversed, i.e., if a mainly black jurisdiction was blatantly violating the rights of whites and then refusing to convict those blacks charged with violations of federal civil rights statutes.

4. In their dissent in the Screws case, Justices Roberts, Frankfurter, and Jackson asserted that the ominous symptom of crimes against local law not being locally prosecuted could be "cured" not by reliance on "remote federal authority," which merely debilitates local responsibility, but by "a reinvigoration of State responsibility." Assuming that the justices were aware of the history of nonenforcement of the law in racial cases, their failure to suggest how such "reinvigoration of State responsibility" could be achieved renders their prescription an irresponsible one. The dissenters in Screws were all committed to the principles of federalism, but it is perhaps not unfair to wonder whether that commitment would have remained as staunch had the racial roles in Screws been reversed. A fictionalized version of the Screws case indicating that Mr. Hall was likely killed because of his independence, can be found in David Troutt, The Monkey Suit: and Other Short Fiction on African Americans and Justice (1997).

It should be noted that the difficulty of obtaining convictions for civil rights violations is not limited to the South. Northern cities that passed ordinances in the 1930s and 1940s providing criminal penalties for racial discrimination in public accommodations found that district attorneys would seldom prosecute the unpopular cases, and that when they did, juries generally refused to convict. Subsequent civil rights laws substituted injunctive relief and money damages for criminal provisions, which was followed in the Civil Rights Act of 1964. If federal civil rights statutes dropped criminal provisions and relied entirely on injunctive relief and money damages to the victims from both defendants and the county where the violation occurred, as in the anti-lynching bill passed by the House in 1922, serious racial violence might be further deterred. Certainly, findings of liability would be easier to obtain, and the monetary penalties might remove some violators from the status of community hero to which they are now elevated both by their deeds and the ensuing criminal prosecution by federal officials.

were not the least humane lynchings in the history of this most unhappy American pastime. The difference, of course, was that white blood was shed in the cause of blacks. The act came during a period of shocking assassinations — Medgar Evers, NAACP field secretary, in Mississippi in June 1963, and President John Kennedy in November 1963 — and the nation's guilt and outrage manifested itself in widespread demands that the guilty be prosecuted. Suddenly, the concern about federal intrusion on states' rights was cast aside (as it had been during the decade after the Civil War) both by the country and, as the *Price* opinion reflects, by the Supreme Court.

The Court abandoned past doubts as to the constitutionality of §§241 and 242 and expanded their reach in United States v. Price.[1] The facts revealed that the three civil rights workers had been released from confinement in the county jail in the middle of the night. The deputy sheriff who released them followed them, picked them up in an official automobile, and took them to a remote area where they were murdered by a group of 18 defendants, including 3 officials and 15 private persons. All 18 were charged under both §241 and §242. The nonofficial defendants claimed that charges under §242 against themselves should be dismissed since they had neither acted under state law nor acted in a manner abusive of any official capacity. The Court rejected this, stating that, given their close cooperation with officials, it was enough that they were "willful participants in joint activity with the State or its agents."[2]

Even if state action was assumed necessary for a violation of the Fourteenth Amendment, the joint action of private and official defendants was deemed sufficient to taint all with state action. The Court completely rejected contentions that due process violations were not included in §241's ambit, finding no support in the section's broad language and legislative history for the "positive federal rights" argument that only those rights provided by reason of federal power operating directly upon the citizen (such as voting) were protected. Rather, the Court held "we cannot doubt that the purpose and effect of §241 was to reach assaults upon rights under the entire Constitution, including the Thirteenth, Fourteenth, and Fifteenth Amendments."[3]

§5.5 1. 383 U.S. 787, 789 (1966). Destroying once and for all any action of constitutional limits on the type of rights protected (i.e., the "positive federal right" position), the Court stated, "We have no doubt of the power of Congress to enforce by appropriate criminal sanction every right guaranteed by the Due Process Clause of the Fourteenth Amendment."

2. 383 U.S. at 794. In a footnote to the just-cited quote, the Court explained:

"'Under color' of law means the same thing in §242 that it does in the civil counterpart of §242, 42 U.S.C. §1983 (1964 ed.). Monroe v. Pape, 365 U.S. 167, 185, 212 (majority opinion). . . . Recent decisions of this Court which have given form to the 'state action' doctrine make it clear that the indictments in this case allege conduct on the part of the 'private' defendants which constitutes 'state action,' and hence action 'under color' of law within §242. In Burton v. Wilmington Parking Authority, 365 U.S. 715, we held that there is 'state action' whenever the 'State has so far insinuated itself into a position of interdependence [with the otherwise "private" person whose conduct is said to violate the Fourteenth Amendment] that it must be recognized as a joint participant in the challenged activity, which, on that account, cannot be considered to have been so "purely private" as to fall without the scope of the Fourteenth Amendment.' 365 U.S., at 725."

3. 383 U.S. at 805. It was not until October 20, 1967, that Deputy Sheriff Price was convicted with six others in a federal district court (N.Y. Times, Oct. 21, 1967, at 1), and subsequently sentenced to six years in prison on December 29, 1967 (N.Y. Times, Dec. 30, 1967, at 1). Sheriff Rainey

In another important case decided the same day, United States v. Guest,[4] the Court held that Fourteenth Amendment rights to equal protection, as well as due process, were covered by §241. The prosecution concerned a conspiracy to prevent blacks from using public facilities owned or operated by or on behalf of the State of Georgia through a program of threats, intimidation, and violence. "[T]he action of the State need be [neither] exclusive [nor] direct," but could be "peripheral," or only "one of several cooperative forces leading to the Constitutional violation."[5] Since the extent of state involvement was unclear, and could range from mere private invocation of state police powers to active connivance to make false arrests, the indictment was sufficient to prevent dismissal, though it was possible that a bill of particulars or proof at trial would disclose no cooperative action between state and defendants. Finally, interference with the constitutional right to travel was held sufficient for a violation of §241 without any allegation of state action, since the right to travel was not subject to the Fourteenth Amendment state action requirement. Specific intent to interfere with that right was necessary for conviction.[6]

Justices Clark, Black, and Fortas concurred, but in an opinion by Clark, went on to say that in their opinion Congress could enact laws punishing all conspiracies to deny such rights as guaranteed by the Fourteenth Amendment, even in the absence of state interference with those rights. Justice Brennan, joined by the Chief Justice and Justice Douglas, went even further, and said that in his view §241 itself did not require state action, even for due process or equal protection claims.[7]

---

was acquitted on all charges. There was no attempt on the part of state officials to bring criminal charges against Price and Rainey.

4. 383 U.S. 745 (1966). Note in *Price*, the Court had held private persons operating in concert with public officials were persons acting under color of law for purposes of §242. In *Guest*, §241 was held to reach wholly private persons who interfere with the full enjoyment of federally protected rights.

5. 383 U.S. at 755-756.

6. Screws v. United States, 325 U.S. 91, 106-107 (1945).

7. Justice Douglas explained:

"Viewed in its proper perspective, §5 . . . [is] a positive grant of legislative power, authorizing Congress to exercise its discretion in fashioning remedies to achieve civil and political equality for all citizens. . . . I can find no principle of federalism nor word of the Constitution that denies Congress power to determine that in order adequately to protect the right to equal utilization of state facilities, it is also appropriate to punish other individuals — not state officers themselves and not acting in concert with state officers — who engage in the same brutal conduct for the same misguided purpose." 383 U.S. at 784.

In *Guest*, a majority of the justices concluded that Congress was not bound by state action in punishing interference with rights of due process or equal protection if it chose to expand its protection. The Court, though, did not accept Justice Brennan's invitation to rule that §241 reached private conspiracies aimed at Fourteenth Amendment rights.

Congress apparently acted on the suggestion in Justice Brennan's opinion that it should write a law that in more specific terms set out the rights intended to be protected. 18 U.S.C. §245 (1970), enacted as a part of the Civil Rights Act of 1968, prohibits a wide range of private conspiracies intended to interfere with the utilization of government facilities or federally protected rights.

There have been few reported federal prosecutions under §245, and none have reached the Supreme Court. The necessity of proving willful intent to deny civil rights is a likely obstacle. The difficult standard was met in United States v. Price, 464 F.2d 1217 (5th Cir. 1972), where the court affirmed a conviction under the section. Defendant had stopped George Smith, the black victim, who was driving with friends to a government recreational area; he directed at Smith vulgar expletives containing direct racial slurs, and then blocked his way, knocked him to the ground, beat him

Despite these successful prosecutions, the federal government was unwilling to intervene to protect the vast majority of civil rights workers and black citizens in the 1950s and 1960s. The federal prosecutions discussed above (which were the most blatant of attacks and, not coincidentally, involved white victims) were more than outweighed by the number of cases that were left unremedied.[8]

§5.6　CIVIL REMEDIES UNDER SECTION 1983

The Reconstruction civil rights acts contained, in addition to the criminal provisions discussed above, authorizations for victims of racial violence to seek damages and injunctive relief in federal courts. The most important surviving section, 42 U.S.C. §1983, has undergone fairly recent judicial reinterpretations. Section 1983 provides a civil action at law or equity for any person deprived "of any rights, privileges, or immunities secured by the Constitution and laws" by a wrongdoer acting "under color of any statute, ordinance, regulation, custom, or usage, of any State or Territory." Thus, there is a "state action" requirement similar to that found in §242 of the criminal statutes, and similar difficulties of construction arise.

In Monroe v. Pape,[1] the Court applied an analysis similar to that found in *Screws* to find that sufficient state action existed even when a state officer had misused his official powers or violated state law.[2] This was necessary to protect

---

unconscious, and threw him in a lake. The court termed "frivolous" defendant's assertion that, while the victim's race may have provoked the fight, the altercation only incidentally occurred on federal property and could have happened anywhere: "Here the circumstances under which defendant assaulted Smith were fully known to him and it is clear that the natural and probable consequences of his acts were to prevent Smith from enjoying the recreational facilities." 464 F.2d at 1218.

Prosecutions involving conduct prohibited by §245 are, perhaps because of the difficulties in proving willful deprivation of the rights infringed, likely to be brought under the more general provision of §241. See, e.g., Hayes v. United States, 464 F.2d 1252 (5th Cir. 1972). There, the court denied post-conviction relief to defendants. They were convicted under §241 and sentenced to ten years and $10,000 under one count, and one year and $1,000 under another, for bombing school buses used to transport black students to desegregated schools.

Section 245(b)(2)(F) did serve to codify the Supreme Court's decision in United States v. Johnson, 390 U.S. 563 (1968), where a divided Court had held that §241 provided a criminal sanction for the interference with the enjoyment of rights provided under Title II of the Civil Rights Act of 1964. There had been concern that such violations were subject to only a civil suit for an injunction as provided in §204 of that Act. 42 U.S.C. §2000a-3.

8. See Taylor Branch, Parting the Waters: America in the King Years 1954-63 (1989); Michal R. Belknap, Federal Law and Southern Order: Racial Violence and Constitutional Conflict in the Post-*Brown* South (1987) (arguing that a narrow conception of federal power caused the federal government to withhold its protection from black victims of white violence); Julius Chambers, Protection of Civil Rights: A Constitutional Mandate for the Federal Government, 87 Mich. L. Rev. 1599 (1989) (criticizing Belknap for his uncritical assessment of the Justice Department's inaction and arguing that the federal government had both the constitutional authority and obligation to protect the civil rights of black citizens).

§5.6　1. 365 U.S. 167 (1966).

2. The complaint alleges that 13 Chicago police officers broke into petitioners' home in the early morning, routed them from bed, made them stand naked in the living room, and ransacked every

plaintiffs when state laws themselves were adequate but were not enforced, or enforced in a racially biased manner. However, relying on legislative history, the Court went on to rule that the cause of action existed only against the individual violators, not the municipality that employed them (in this case Chicago), thereby creating absolute immunity from damage actions under §1983 for municipalities. This insulated local government from financial liability for the actions of its officers, removing an important incentive to ensure that they acted constitutionally. It also left plaintiffs in an unfortunate situation, since police officers were all too often judgment-proof.

§5.6.1 Severe Limitations on Municipal Liability in Cases after *Monroe*

In the wake of *Monroe*, lower courts were divided as to whether municipalities could be held liable under §1983 in equity. The Court resolved the issue in favor of municipal immunity in City of Kenosha v. Bruno.[3] This left the laws in a rather confused state, raising questions of what was a "municipality" for §1983 purposes. The courts construed the term broadly to include school districts,[4] state agencies,[5] and county boards of supervisors,[6] thus most local government bodies, except for a few government units whose activities are primarily proprietary, were immune under *Bruno*. It remained questionable to what extent officers acting in their official capacities could be enjoined, based on the theory that courts may enjoin officials from engaging in unconstitutional acts because such conduct is outside their legitimate authority. Thus such conduct is not action of the sovereign, but of the individual who, in effect, is acting on his own.[7] Given a similar set of problems the Court has held that the sovereign immunity provision of the Eleventh Amendment limits the power of the federal courts even in an action against an individual official if the state is the real party in interest.[8]

Even if injunctive relief is theoretically available, it is rarely granted in cases of official or police misconduct, at least in the absence of shocking facts and a sympathetic court. Even with shocking facts, a plaintiff has to surmount the

---

room, emptying drawers and ripping mattress covers. It further alleges that Mr. Monroe was then taken to the police station and detained on "open" charges for ten hours while he was interrogated about a two-day-old murder, that he was not taken before a magistrate though one was accessible, that he was not permitted to call his family or attorney, and that he was subsequently released without criminal charges being preferred against him. It is alleged that the officers had no search warrant and no arrest warrant and that they acted "under color of the statutes, ordinances, regulations, customs and usages" of Illinois and the City of Chicago.

3. 412 U.S. 507 (1973). This was not a racial case, but rather a suit by owners of a topless bar seeking review of the city's license denial. The lower courts did not seize upon this distinction, however, and routinely dismissed §1983 claims against municipalities. See, e.g., Dewell v. Lawson, 489 F.2d 877 (10th Cir. 1974); Harper v. Kloster, 486 F.2d 1134 (4th Cir. 1973).

4. Campbell v. Mason, 486 F.2d 554 (5th Cir. 1973); Kelley v. Wisconsin Interscholastic Athletic Ass'n, 367 F. Supp. 1388 (E.D. Wis. 1974).

5. Downs v. Department of Public Welfare, 368 F. Supp. 454 (E.D. Pa. 1973).

6. Cole v. Tuttle, 366 F. Supp. 1252 (N.D. Miss. 1973).

7. Ex parte Young, 209 U.S. 123 (1908).

8. Edelman v. Jordan, 413 U.S. 651 (1974). The state was the real party in interest because the equitable relief claimed consisted in part of payment of funds from the state treasury.

obstacle of standing. To obtain an injunction, plaintiffs must show that they have a "personal stake in the outcome" of the case.[9] Plaintiffs can demonstrate this personal stake solely with a showing of a direct and immediate threat of injury. The fact that they have been past victims of constitutional violations and that the municipality or its actors have not modified their behavior will not satisfy this standard.

In O'Shea v. Littleton,[10] black plaintiffs complained that they faced a county judge and magistrate who intentionally discriminated against blacks when setting bonds and sentencing defendants. The Court concluded that "past exposure to illegal conduct does not itself show a present case or controversy regarding injunctive relief . . . if unaccompanied by any continuing present adverse effects."[11] It is difficult to prove continuing present adverse effects, especially in the context of police brutality. In Rizzo v. Goode,[12] Rehnquist's opinion, based on his federalism concerns, held that what a small minority of police may do in the future because of their perception of the department's disciplinary policy is too speculative a basis on which to grant equitable relief.[13] While §1983, on its face, is the appropriate statute for challenging police departments and other local governmental agencies and for requesting equitable relief, the Court's jurisprudence has closed the avenue of relief. For a further discussion of limiting federal relief to a rising crisis, see §5.10 which addresses the increased national attention around racial profiling.

The Supreme Court has further limited the ability of plaintiffs to obtain relief under §1983. In Pierson v. Ray,[14] fifteen ministers conducting a sit-in in Jackson, Mississippi, were arrested and convicted of breach of the peace. Subsequently, they sued for damages under §1983. Their suit against the convicting judge was dismissed under the traditional shield of sovereign immunity, but the Fifth Circuit held the arresting officers liable under §1983 even though they had acted in good faith and with probable cause, since the statute several years later was declared unconstitutional, and thus the officers had deprived plaintiffs of rights under color of law. The Supreme Court reversed as to the police, stating:

> A policeman's lot is not so unhappy that he must choose between being charged with dereliction of duty if he does not arrest when he has probable cause, and being mulcted in damages if he does. . . . The same consideration would seem to require excusing him from liability for acting under a statute that he reasonably believes to be valid but that was later held unconstitutional on its face or as applied.[15]

While perhaps equitable as to the individual officer acting in good faith, this extension of immunity put plaintiffs in a very difficult position, since neither the

9. Baker v. Carr, 369 U.S. 186, 204 (1962).
10. 414 U.S. 488 (1974).
11. Id. at 495-496.
12. 423 U.S. 362 (1976).
13. See also City of Los Angeles v. Lyons, 461 U.S. 95 (1983) (holding that a victim of an illegal choke hold had no standing because he could not show a real threat that he would again be stopped by the police and be placed in the illegal choke hold).
14. 386 U.S. 547 (1967).
15. Id. at 555.

municipality (under *Monroe*) nor the individual (under *Pierson*) could be held liable in most cases.[16]

Even when no common law immunity is recognized, the "good faith" defense can make damages recovery in a §1983 suit extremely difficult, as indicated by the protracted litigation following the shootings at Jackson State College and Kent State University.[17] Some lower courts, though, have set limits on the defense. In Jenkins v. Averett,[18] a police officer's "gross and culpable negligence" in shooting an innocent youth was sufficient to defeat arguments of good faith.

The Supreme Court has since answered the question of whether police officers can raise a good faith defense to an action under §1983. In Malley v. Briggs,[19] when a police officer was alleged to have caused unconstitutional arrests by obtaining warrants without probable cause, the Court held that a police officer is entitled only to qualified and not absolute immunity under §1983. Therefore, the officer's conduct must be objectively reasonable; good faith reliance on a magistrate's judgment is no defense where the reliance is unreasonable.

---

16. On grounds of common law immunity, judges, legislators, prosecutors, and heads of executive departments may enjoy immunity from damages under §1983. See cases collected in 1 Emerson, Haber, & Dorsen's Political and Civil Rights in the United States, ch. XVII, §C (4th ed. 1979).

Reacting to allegations of shocking racial abuse in Cairo, Illinois, a small town with a large reputation for inhospitality to blacks, the Seventh Circuit found the judicial immunity defense was not available in actions seeking equitable relief. In Littleton v. Berbling, 468 F.2d 389 (7th Cir. 1972), black citizens of Cairo, Illinois, sought to enjoin state judges from discriminating against their class in setting bonds, sentencing, and assessing court costs, and to enjoin the state's attorney from abusing his authority by refusing to prosecute whites who committed crimes against blacks. The court held that "The legislative history of [§§1981 and 1983] makes clear that Congress meant to eliminate judicial immunity of state judges, at least as to suits seeking injunctive relief." It was further held that the exceptional circumstances of Younger v. Harris had been met, and injunctive relief was therefore warranted. The court of appeals provided guidelines for the trial judge, who was directed to grant relief if plaintiffs were able to prove their allegations at trial. It suggested: Should this be a block quote? "An initial decree might set out the general tone of rights to be protected and require only periodic reports of various types of aggregate data on actions on bail and sentencing and dispositions of complaints. Nevertheless, we have complete confidence in the district court's ability to set up further guides as required and if necessary to consider individual decisions. Difficulty of formulating a remedy if a complaint is proved following a trial cannot be grounds for dismissing the complaint ab initio. We cannot so easily belittle the powers of a court of equity nor the ability of district judges who have grappled with difficult remedies before, e.g., school desegregation orders, railroad reorganizations."

"We also are not unmindful of the possibility of a substantial additional burden being placed on the federal judiciary by our decision. However, if it can be alleged and proved, and the sweep of our decision is to be no broader, that the state officials consistently, designedly and egregiously have, under color of law, deprived an entire group of citizens of their civil rights, then the additional burden will necessarily have to be assumed. The civil rights of all persons, too often merely words in a constitutionally inspired century-old statute, deserve no lesser implementation than here accorded them." 468 F.2d at 415.

The Supreme Court did not agree. Ordering the suit dismissed, the Court found none of the plaintiffs had standing to sue in that none had themselves suffered an injury as a result of the challenged policies. Moreover, the Court found there were no allegations that any state criminal law was invalid on its face or as applied to plaintiffs. O'Shea v. Littleton, 414 U.S. 488 (1974).

17. Burton v. Waller, 502 F.2d 1261 (5th Cir. 1974) (good faith defense to shootings at Jackson State); Scheuer v. Rhodes, 416 U.S. 232 (1974), on remand (N.D. Ohio 1976) (unreported) (good faith defense for Kent State shootings), rev'd for new trial sub nom. Krause v. Rhodes, 570 F.2d 563 (6th Cir. 1977).

18. 424 F.2d 1228 (4th Cir. 1970).

19. 475 U.S. 335 (1986).

While quite clearly leaving open the extent to which a §1983 defendant can rely on a good faith defense, the Supreme Court had lowered the shield of absolute immunity to damages suits enjoyed by municipalities since Monroe v. Pape.

§5.6.2   Monell's Victory and the Court's Reshaping of Section 1983 Post-*Monell*

In Monell v. New York City Department of Social Services,[20] the Court reviewed the legislative history of the Civil Rights Act of 1871 and concluded that "Congress did intend municipalities and other local governmental units to be included among those persons to whom §1983 applies." As a result, the Court said such bodies can be sued directly under §1983 for monetary, declaratory, or injunctive relief where the challenged action "implements or executes a policy statement, ordinance, regulation, or decision officially adopted and promulgated by that body's officers."[21]

In City of Newport v. Facts Concert,[22] the Supreme Court limited relief under §1983 by finding that under most circumstances municipalities are exempt from punitive damages. In the opinion's footnote 29, the Court left open the possibility of punitive damages in "an extreme situation" where a municipality's "taxpayers are directly responsible for perpetrating an outrageous abuse of constitutional rights."[23] No court to date, however, has chosen to use this exception to grant punitive damages against a municipality.[24]

The Court did not completely define the extent to which a municipality could be held liable for acts of its employees, but it did offer some guidelines.[25] The Court was clear that a municipality would not be held liable under a theory of respondeat superior. Some municipal action, something more than simply

20. 436 U.S. 658 (1978).

21. Id. at 690. In *Monell*, female employees of New York City's Department of Social Services and Board of Education sought injunctive relief and back pay for periods of forced leave compelled by the defendants' official policy requiring pregnant employees to take unpaid leaves of absence before such leaves were required for medical reasons. Cf. Cleveland Bd. of Educ. v. LaFleur, 414 U.S. 632 (1974).

22. 453 U.S. 247 (1981).

23. Id. at 267 n.25. "It is perhaps possible to imagine an extreme situation where the taxpayers are directly responsible for perpetrating an outrageous abuse of constitutional rights. Nothing of that kind is presented by this case. Moreover, such an occurrence is sufficiently unlikely that we need not anticipate it here."

24. See Gloria Jean Rottell, Paying the Price: It's Time to Hold Municipalities Liable for Punitive Damages Under 42 U.S.C. §1983, 10 J.L. & Pol'y 189 (2001). She describes one case that could have applied the exception to grant punitive damages; see Ciraolo v. New York, 216 F.3d 236 (2d Cir. 2000). Id. at 215.

25. The Court did not address the question of whether some form of official immunity should be afforded to local governmental bodies, but the absolute immunity granted under Monroe was withdrawn. While welcoming the *Monell* decision, Professor Laurence Tribe fears the continuing cutbacks in the reach of §1983 due to the doctrine of Younger v. Harris, 401 U.S. 37 (1971), and its progeny, which greatly limits the power of federal courts to enjoin illegal state action if federal litigants have a parallel state proceeding deemed an adequate forum for airing their grievances. See also Paul v. Davis, 424 U.S. 693 (1976) (restricting the range of liberty and property interests protected by the Fourteenth Amendment); and Rizzo v. Goode, 423 U.S. 362 (1976) (limiting relief available against even repeated invasions of rights by police department, absent proof of high-level official encouragement of such misconduct).

employing a wrongdoer, must occur. Municipalities are not responsible for the actions of their employees unless the employees are acting under an official policy or a longstanding custom.

The Court continued to define the limits of *Monell* in Pembaur v. City of Cincinnati.[26] Writing for the Court, Justice Brennan argued that *Monell* does not require a pattern of unconstitutional activity as a predicate for a §1983 claim, but only limits recovery to cases in which the violation may be fairly attributed to the municipality. Thus, even a single act is sufficient to establish liability where — as in this case — the unconstitutional act is officially sanctioned or ordered.

The Supreme Court provided additional direction on the issue of when cities can be held liable for the acts of its employees in City of St. Louis v. Praprotnik.[27] In *Praprotnik*, the Court held that a municipality may not be held liable under §1983 for the isolated acts of its employees unless the plaintiff proves that the acts took place pursuant to an unconstitutional policy promulgated by officials having authority to make such a policy. So long as the final policy-making officials do not facilitate or endorse the unconstitutional acts of subordinate employees, plaintiff cannot prevail under §1983.

Then, in Daniels v. Williams,[28] the Supreme Court overruled Parratt v. Taylor,[29] which held that a prisoner's loss of property, even though negligently caused, amounted to a deprivation in the constitutional sense and was therefore actionable under §1983. Daniels involved a prison inmate injured when he fell over a pillow carelessly left on a stairway by a deputy. The prisoner claimed under §1983 that the deputy's conduct deprived him of his liberty interest in freedom from bodily injury without due process of law. Justice Rehnquist, writing for the Court, argued that due process guarantees historically applied only to "deliberate decisions of government officials to deprive a person of life, liberty or property." Daniels grows out of a fear that §1983 is being cast too broadly and that state officials will be liable under federal law wherever they cause a constitutionally cognizable injury.

Although negligence may not provide the basis for relief under §1983, unintentional conduct may still be sufficient to establish liability.[30] Geraldine Harris brought a claim under §1983 for maltreatment she suffered while in police custody. In Canton v. Harris, the Court rejected the city's contention that §1983 liability can be imposed only where the municipal policy in question is itself unconstitutional. Instead, Justice White held that the inadequacy of police training may serve as the basis for §1983 municipal liability where the failure to train amounts to "deliberate indifference to the rights of persons with whom the police come into contact." Justice White hedged potential liability by requiring that the deficiency in the training program be "closely related" to the ultimate injury. Thus, on remand, plaintiff must prove that a shortcoming in the training of police commanders

26. 475 U.S. 469 (1986).
27. 485 U.S. 112 (1988).
28. 474 U.S. 327 (1986).
29. 451 U.S. 527 (1981).
30. City of Canton v. Harris, 489 U.S. 378 (1989).

actually caused the officers' indifference to her medical needs. Lesser standards of fault and causation, the Court feared, would open municipalities to unprecedented §1983 liability, would result in de facto respondeat superior liability (a result rejected in *Monell*), would engage federal courts in an endless exercise of second-guessing municipal employee-training programs, and would implicate serious questions of federalism.

The Supreme Court limited the implication of Canton, though, in Board of County Commissioners v. Brown.[31] The plaintiff, a victim of police excessive force, sued the county, alleging that the sheriff had hired his deputy, knowing of his criminal record for assault, without investigating him further. According to the Court, the plaintiff must show that a municipal decision reflects deliberate indifference to the risk that a violation of a particular constitutional or statutory right will follow this particular decision. One of the opinion's greatest concerns was that cases alleging injury attributable to inadequate hiring decisions would lead to municipalities being held liable for injuries they did not cause. This, in turn, would lead to acceptance of the previously dismissed theory of respondeat superior.[32] In ignoring the real possibility of a policy maker's decision reaching the level of deliberate indifference to unconstitutional harm, the Court, as pointed out in Souter's dissent, has created yet another hurdle to municipal liability in §1983 actions.

In the same term as *Canton* the Supreme Court cut back the potential scope of §1983 in Will v. Michigan Department of State Police.[33] By a bare five-person majority, the Court held that a city is a "person" within the meaning of §1983, but remained firm in its conclusion that neither a state nor state employees sued in their official capacities are amenable to liability under §1983.[34] Constrained by a crabbed literalism in its statutory interpretation and by a narrow conception of the statute's historical purpose, Justice White argued that the term "person" did not, and was not intended to, include a state. In its everyday usage, he argued, the term "person" does not include a state. Employing logic of the most contorted and mystifying sort, Justice White argued that Congress' intent to provide a federal forum to complain of unconstitutional state action "does no more than confirm that the section is directed against state-action — action 'under color of' state law. It does not suggest that the State itself was a person that Congress intended to be subject to liability." Without more persuasive evidence of a contrary intent, the Court would not take the step of overriding the well-established common law doctrine of sovereign immunity to subject states to suit under §1983.

Justice Brennan, writing for the dissent, decried the majority's reliance on rules of statutory construction at the expense of the section's clear overriding purpose. Recounting the turbulent times which prompted the legislature to enact the Civil Rights Act of 1866, Justice Brennan found it difficult to believe that

31. 520 U.S. 397 (1997).
32. See Monell v. NYC Dept. of Social Servs., 436 U.S. 658 (1978).
33. 491 U.S. 58 (1989).
34. The question of whether states were subject to liability under §1983 was left open by Monell, the holding of which was limited to "local government units which are not considered part of the State for Eleventh Amendment purposes." 436 U.S. at 690 n.54.

Congress did not intend to alter the federal-state balance by making states accountable for their contribution to the upheaval. The inquiry that led the Court in *Monell* to extend §1983 to cities mandated the same result with regard to states. Justice Stevens, in a separate dissent, chastised the Court for its reliance on the apparent fiction that, absent consent, states may not be subject to liability when states are haled into federal court each day, through a variety of devices, to answer for their derelictions.

Yet even as recently as 2002, the Court in Gonzaga University v. Doe[35] further limited the scope of §1983 on state action, holding that spending legislation that provides federal funding to state actors does not automatically create rights enforceable under §1983. Congress, according to Chief Justice Rehnquist's majority opinion, must intend to create such rights through "clear" and "unambiguous" language.[36] The impact of the holding is profound. In §1983 cases, the right of an individual to sue is normally presumed with the burden on the defendant to show otherwise. With implied rights of action, the burden is on the plaintiff to show congressional intent to provide for private lawsuits. In merging both theories, the Court shifts the burden to the plaintiff and makes it more difficult to sue under §1983. Justice Stevens, in his dissent, argued that the majority was trying to import the implied right of action framework into the §1983 arena, undermining the "presumptive enforceability of rights under §1983."[37] Professor Bradford Mank suggests that *Gonzaga* be narrowly interpreted to allow plaintiffs to use legislative history and administrative regulations to show congressional intent to save the enforcement of statutory rights under §1983.[38]

Over the past 10 years, circuits have applied a state-created danger theory to find liability when a state actor subjects any person to a deprivation of a constitutionally protected right. Although the Supreme Court has left open this issue in previous decisions, the circuit courts have found liability when the use of state power has put a plaintiff in danger.[39] In these cases, "the court need only ask whether a state actor has 'warped' the actual course of events and thus caused an injury."[40] Only the Third and the Tenth Circuits have developed multipart tests to determine state-created danger, but with little Supreme Court guidance, these approaches can differ significantly. The Third Circuit's four-part test looks for the existence of "some relationship between the state and the plaintiff."[41] Whereas the five-prong test of the Tenth Circuit examines whether the plaintiff is "a member of a limited and specifically definable group."[42]

---

35. 536 U.S. 273 (2002).

36. Id. at 290.

37. Id. at 301-303 (Stevens, J., dissenting).

38. Bradford Mank, Suing Under Section 1983: The Future After Gonzaga University v. Doe, 39 Hous. L. Rev. 1417, 1420 (2003).

39. Recent Cases: Constitutional Law — Substantive Due Process — Fifth Circuit Rejects §1983 "State-Created Danger" Claim of Plaintiff Shot by an Undercover Informant Using a Gun on "Loan" from a City Officer, 116 Harv. L. Rev. 1912, 1918 (2003).

40. Id. at 1918.

41. Kneipp v. Tedder, 95 F.3d 1199, 1208 (3d Cir. 1996) (quoting Mark v. Borough of Hatboro, 51 F.3d 1137, 1152 (3d Cir. 1995)).

42. Uhlrig v. Harder, 64 F.3d 567, 574 (10th Cir. 1995).

Generally, §1983 is not available to redress private conduct. In Adickes v. S. H. Kress & Co.,[43] however, the Supreme Court held that damages might be recovered against a private store that denied service on the basis of race if such action were proved to have been "under color of any . . . custom or usage, of any state. . . ." The plaintiff, a white volunteer teacher at a "freedom school" for black children in Mississippi, sought service in defendant's store restaurant with six of her students. A waitress took the students' orders but refused to serve petitioner because she was a white person in the company of blacks. Upon leaving the store, the teacher was arrested by local police and charged with vagrancy. In her federal suit, she alleged that defendant's refusal had been pursuant to a custom of the community to segregate races in public eating places. The district court directed a verdict in favor of the store, and the court of appeals affirmed.

The Supreme Court reversed. The plaintiff, wrote Justice Harlan, could recover under §1983 if she could prove that the discrimination she suffered was with knowledge of, and pursuant to, a custom having the force of law by virtue of persistent official practices. Such a custom might be shown through direct police harassment involving groundless arrests on any charges. The majority rejected petitioner's contention (adopted by Justice Brennan) that the customs of the people, in addition to the customs of state officials, amounted to state action for purposes of §1983.[44]

Many of the Court's decisions show a willingness to dilute §1983 as a remedy for civil rights violations by extending it to more and more diverse causes of action. Also of note has been the growing controversy over §1983 as a vehicle for vindicating individuals' constitutional rights. Given the unimaginable number of individual grievances potentially actionable under §1983, it is not surprising that the statute has produced a substantial amount of litigation.[45] Critics contend that the cases brought under the statute are largely frivolous and dangerously

---

43. 398 U.S. 144 (1970).

44. Justice Harlan characterized the question in *Adickes* as being whether an individual who discriminates "under the compulsion of state law," 398 U.S. at 170, violates the Fourteenth Amendment. But in recent years, the Court had found state action not only when segregation was compelled, but when it was encouraged by statute.

The value of the *Adickes* opinion is further reduced by two disclaimers in the majority opinion's final footnote, 398 U.S. at 174 n.44.

First, the note suggests that a suit for damages may not be a "proper proceeding" under §1983 when the private discriminator is compelled by state law to discriminate.

Second, citing Pierson v. Ray, supra note 14, the majority states that it does not decide what, if any, defenses might be available to an action under §1983. Pierson held that a reasonable belief in the constitutionality of a statute under which arrests are made absolves police officers of liability for damages. Assuming that private individuals can raise similar defenses, a plaintiff would have the almost impossible task of proving that the individual acted with knowledge of, and pursuant to, a statute or custom, while having reason to know the statute or custom was unconstitutional. See 84 Harv. L. Rev. 71, 81-82 (1970).

45. Section 1983 has provided the basis for a broad range of cases, including litigation to overturn bans on lawyer advertising, Supreme Court of Va. v. Consumers Union of U.S., Inc., 446 U.S. 719 (1980); to challenge mandatory maternity leave policies, Cleveland Bd. of Educ. v. LaFleur, 414 U.S. 632 (1974); to establish the rights of a recipient of public assistance to pre-termination notice and hearing, Goldberg v. Kelly, 397 U.S. 254 (1970); to challenge loyalty oaths, Keyishian v. Board of Regents, 385 U.S. 589 (1967); and to establish the NAACP's authority to advise black persons of their legal rights, NAACP v. Button, 317 U.S. 415 (1963).

invasive of state autonomy.[46] Expressions of discontent have also surfaced in Supreme Court opinions, although so far primarily in dissenting opinions.[47]

Justice Blackmun, in a rare law review article, chastises the Court for its §1983 jurisprudence and argues that its uneasiness with the statute has caused it to abandon settled precedent. Complaining that "the Court appears inclined to cut back on Section 1983 in any way it can," he urges "that any restriction of what has become a major symbol of federal protection of basic rights not be made in irresponsible haste." He dismisses criticisms levied against §1983 as unproved and contrary to the legislative mandate which the statute embodies, and argues that those who claim that §1983 is being extended beyond its proper bounds fail to understand that §1983 was intended to increase federal power to protect individual rights in the face of lackadaisical or even oppressive state governments.[48] The narrow conception of federalism which underlies their opposition, Justice Blackmun continues, is without basis:

> When the Fourteenth Amendment became part of the Constitution, it committed this Nation to an order in which all governments, state as well as federal, were bound to respect the fundamental rights of individuals. That commitment, too, is part of "Our Federalism," no less than the values of state autonomy that the critics of Section 1983 so passionately invoke.[49]

46. See Harry A. Blackmun, Section 1983 and Federal Protection of Individual Rights — Will the Statute Remain Alive or Fade Away?, 60 N.Y.U. L. Rev. 1, 1-3 (1985) (noting the existence of the debate).

47. See, e.g., Pulliam v. Allen, 466 U.S. 522 (1984); Maine v. Thiboutot, 448 U.S. 1, 27 & n.16 (1980). As Justice Blackmun recounts, this criticism is by no means new. In the debate over the passage of §1983, opponents called the statute "one of the most dangerous that was ever introduced into the Senate of the United States." See Blackmun, supra note 46, at 6.

48. Blackmun, supra note 46, at 6. Justice Blackmun quotes as follows from Mitchum v. Foster, 407 U.S. 225, 242 (1972), in which the Supreme Court acknowledged the magnitude of the transformation required by §1983: "This legislative history makes evident that Congress clearly conceived that it was altering the relationship between the States and the Nation with respect to the protection of federally created rights; it was concerned that state instrumentalities could not protect those rights; it realized that state officers might, in fact, be antipathetic to the vindication of those rights; and it believed that these failings extended to the state courts. . . ."

"Section 1983 was thus a product of a vast transformation from the concepts of federalism that had prevailed in the late 18th century. . . . The very purpose of Section 1983 was to interpose the federal courts between the States and the people, as guardians of the people's federal rights — to protect the people from unconstitutional action under the color of state law. . . ."

49. Blackmun, supra note 46, at 28. Justice Blackmun cites a prophetic passage from Justice Harlan's dissent in the Civil Rights Cases: "I may be permitted to say that if the recent amendments are so construed that Congress may not, in its own discretion, and independently of the action or non-action of the States, provide, by legislation of a direct character, for the security of rights created by the national Constitution; if it be adjudged that the obligation to protect the fundamental privileges and immunities granted by the Fourteenth Amendment to citizens residing in the several States, rests primarily, not on the nation, but on the States; if it be further adjudged that individuals or corporations, exercising public functions, or wielding power under public authority, may, without liability to direct primary legislation on the part of Congress, make the race of citizens the ground for denying them that equality of civil rights which the Constitution ordains as a principle of republican citizenship; then, not only the foundations upon which the national supremacy has always securely rested will be materially disturbed, but we shall enter upon an era of constitutional law, when the rights of freedoms and American citizenship cannot receive from the nation that efficient protection which heretofore was unhesitatingly accorded to slavery and the rights of the master." 109 U.S. 3, 57 (1883).

§5.6.3 Pre-*Monell* Efforts to Achieve Municipal Liability

Unsurprisingly, the frustration engendered by *Monroe*, which opened the way for damages actions against police misconduct and then closed off the only meaningful source for realizing recovery, led civil rights lawyers to seek relief under the more generous language of 42 U.S.C. §1981. In two cases involving rather shocking fact situations, the Third Circuit responded favorably to these efforts.

Black plaintiffs in Mahone v. Waddle[50] alleged that Pittsburgh police officers, acting under the authority of city and state law and motivated by racial bias, subjected them to racial epithets, verbal harassment, and physical abuse by hands, fists, and nightsticks. Plaintiffs were falsely arrested and police gave false testimony against them. Their claim against the city was dismissed by the district judge. The court of appeals reversed on the basis of §1981, finding that it "has broad applicability beyond the mere right to contract" and that plaintiffs' exposure to officially inflicted punishment, pains, and penalties other than those to which white persons are subject falls within the broad language of both the "equal benefits and like punishment" clauses of §1981.[51] The court further noted Congress's intent "that the Civil Rights Act of 1866 would prohibit all racial discrimination, apparently including the type of racially motivated physical abuse and misuse of governmental power which is alleged in this instance."

The majority opinion addresses the dissent's concern that the Court's construction of §1981 will give rise to a federal cause of action for every racially motivated private tort by suggesting that the "equal benefit" and "like punishment clauses" reflect a concern with relations between the individual and state, not between two individuals. The majority opinion also refutes the argument that the municipal immunity recognized in §1983 and *Monroe* should be extended to §1981 cases, pointing out that the holding in *Monroe* was expressly limited to the narrow question whether the word "person" in §1983 includes municipal corporations. Section 1983 cannot be read as an implied repeal of §1981 insofar as municipal liability is concerned.

And, in Hail v. Pennsylvania State Police,[52] a black bank customer alleged a directive issued to banks by state officials ordering that the banks photograph suspicious black males or females coming on the premises violated his rights under §1981. He sought injunctive and declaratory relief as well as damages. The Circuit Court, having recently ruled on *Mahone*, reiterated its finding that §1981 is not confined to contractual matters when a governmental entity is involved, and that racially motivated misuse of governmental power falls within the ambit of its "equal benefit" and "like punishment" clauses.

---

50. 564 F.2d 1018 (3d Cir. 1977).

51. The plaintiffs in *Mahone* utilized generally ignored language in §1981, the whole of which reads: "All persons within the jurisdiction of the United States shall have the same right in every State and Territory to make and enforce contracts, to sue, be parties, give evidence, and to the full and equal benefit of all laws and proceedings for the security of persons and property as is enjoyed by white citizens, and shall be subject to like punishments, pains, penalties, taxes, licenses, and exactions of every kind, and to no other."

52. 570 F.2d 86 (3d Cir. 1978).

In the wake of *Monell*, future efforts to avoid the still unsolved questions of §1983's range and scope through the use of §1981 will likely result in decisions similar to those in the public accommodations field, where the specific limits of Title II are read into the broad coverage of §1981.[53]

§5.7   THE CIVIL RIGHTS ATTORNEY'S FEES AWARDS ACT OF 1976

Two significant cases have dealt with the issue of attorneys' fees awards under §1988. In the first case, Evans v. Jeff D.,[1] the Supreme Court held that §1988 does not make mandatory the award of attorneys' fees in every case the plaintiff wins. Consequently, a proposed settlement of a civil rights action is not rendered improper simply because it is conditioned upon a waiver of attorneys' fees.

This civil rights action had been brought by legal aid lawyers on behalf of a class of children institutionalized for mental disabilities. Just before trial, the state offered a full settlement, provided that the class surrender all claims to attorneys' fees and costs. While the legal aid society instructed the lead counsel to reject any offer contingent upon a fee waiver, the attorney determined that his professional duty to his clients required acceptance of the proposal, which he considered to be the best outcome for them. The attorney, however, submitted the settlement proposal to the district court along with a request that the court approve the settlement without the waiver because it created a conflict of interest and exploited his ethical obligation to his clients.

The district court accepted the settlement with the waiver provision. The Ninth Circuit reversed on the grounds that the strong federal policy embodied in §1988 required a fee award to prevailing plaintiffs, including those who won a favorable settlement. The Supreme Court again reversed. Justice Stevens wrote that §1988 did not erect an absolute barrier to fee waivers. While Congress "expected fee shifting to attract competent counsel to represent citizens deprived of their civil rights, it neither bestowed fee awards upon attorneys nor rendered them non-waivable or nonnegotiable; instead, it added them to the arsenal of remedies available to combat violations of civil rights."

The dissent, written by Justice Brennan, argued that attorneys' fees were not simply another remedy for victims of civil rights violations. The statute was enacted to provide economic incentives for lawyers to take civil rights cases — a purpose that is undermined when defendants can easily circumvent fee provisions by offering an attractive settlement package contingent upon a fee waiver. It is, Justice Brennan wrote, "embarrassingly obvious" that allowing defendants to slip through this gaping loophole in fee provisions will reduce the number of lawyers willing to take such cases and therefore make it harder for plaintiffs to obtain legal relief. Believing the majority to have threatened the legislative objective

---

53. See Runyon v. McCrary, 427 U.S. 160 (1976).
§5.7   1. 475 U.S. 717 (1986).

underlying §1988, Justice Brennan closed his dissent by asking Congress to "repair this Court's mistake."

Despite the result in the Evans case, it was not all bad news for civil rights litigants in this area of the Supreme Court's jurisprudence. In the other significant §1988 fee case, City of Riverside v. Rivera,[2] the Court decided that the amount of attorneys' fees available to the prevailing party in a civil rights action is not limited by the amount of damages recovered. While no rule commanded a majority of the Court, a plurality agreed that a proportionality rule was unwarranted (rejecting the position advocated by the government as amicus curiae). Civil rights cases provide important public benefits which may not be reflected in the damages award and justify fee awards in an amount sufficient to generate legal support for such cases. Consequently, the Court let stand a fee award seven times greater than the compensatory and punitive damages granted to the plaintiffs.

Other, less significant cases include North Carolina Department of Transportation v. Crest Street Community Council, Inc.,[3] in which the Court denied the plaintiff's request for attorneys' fees for costs incurred in preparing an administrative complaint and negotiating a settlement on the grounds that §1988 only authorizes awards for attorneys' fees expended to pursue court actions, and Hewitt v. Helms,[4] in which the Court held that a plaintiff is only entitled to collect attorneys' fees if he actually obtains some relief on the merits. In Hewitt, despite a lower court's ruling that a parole board had violated the plaintiff's due process rights and had amended its regulations as a result of the plaintiff's complaint, the fact that the plaintiff was released prior to the lawsuit's resolution (making moot any injunctive relief) and obtained no money damages means that he is not a prevailing party entitled to a fee award.

The Supreme Court has recently placed a further restriction on attorneys' fees[5] in Buckhannon v. West Virginia Department of Health and Human Resources.[6] The Court held that the "prevailing party" must secure a judicial decision or court-approved settlement to qualify for attorneys' fees.[7] Justice O'Connor rejected the more inclusive meaning of "prevailing party," accepted by the majority of appellate courts, awarded fees if the litigation resulted in the intended relief sought by the plaintiff. The Court's narrow definition of a prevailing party may serve to limit the number of civil rights cases that the private bar can afford to bring.[8] A more extensive description of the *Buckhannon* opinion is found in §6.6. In addition, the dangers to civil rights lawyers posed by Rule 11 sanctions is discussed at §4.6.8.

---

2. 477 U.S. 561 (1986).
3. 479 U.S. 6 (1986).
4. 482 U.S. 755 (1987).
5. David Luban, Taking Out the Adversary: The Assault on Progressive Public-Interest Lawyers, 91 Cal. L. Rev. 209, 240 (2003). See also Sylvia A. Law, In the Name of Federalism: The Supreme Court's Assault on Democracy and Civil Rights, 70 U. Cin. L. Rev. 367, 389-390 (2002).
6. 532 U.S. 598 (2001).
7. See also discussion in §5.7.
8. Mary D. Fan, Case Note: Textual Imagination, 111 Yale L.J. 1251 (2002).

§5.8   CIVIL REMEDIES UNDER SECTION 1985(3)

For almost all of its first one hundred years, §1985 remained largely unused. In 1882, the Supreme Court had struck down the criminal provisions of §1985(2).[1] The civil penalties of 42 U.S.C. §1985(3), analogous to the criminal provision 18 U.S.C. §241, provide a private cause of action for damages against any one who conspires to deprive, "either directly or indirectly, any person or class of persons of the equal protection of the laws, or of equal privileges and immunities under the laws," or any persons who "conspire to prevent by force, intimidation, or threat" to interfere with the right to vote. The case law under this section evolved similarly to that in the criminal context.

Collins v. Hardyman[2] had implied a "state action" requirement in the statute, even though no such limitation exists on the statute's face. The Supreme Court reversed its position in Griffin v. Breckenridge[3] holding that the statute was applicable to private conspiracies. While §1985(3) speaks in Fourteenth Amendment language of "equal protection," "[t]here is nothing inherent in the phrase that requires the action working the deprivation to come from the state." The Court, however, cautioned that the section is not to be read as a federal tort law. To avoid the "constitutional shoals" that would lie in the path of interpreting §1985(3) too broadly, full effect must be given "to the Congressional purpose by requiring, as an element of the cause of action, the kind of invidiously discriminatory motivation stressed by the sponsors . . . there must be some racial, or perhaps otherwise class-based, invidiously discriminatory animus behind the conspirators' action."

There is no indication in the *Griffin* decision that the compelling facts of that case and the absence of other avenues for effective relief in damages influenced the reconsideration of §1985(3)'s requirements. *Collins* involved the breaking up of a left-wing meeting by persons dressed in American Legion uniforms. The decision that there was no cause of action because defendants had not acted under "color of law" fit well into that anti-Red period in the nation's history.

On the other hand, *Griffin* was decided during the same calendar year as some of the Supreme Court's most expansive civil rights decisions.[4] It involved a group of blacks who, while driving along a Mississippi highway, were mistaken by whites for civil rights workers. The whites used their pickup truck to force the blacks' car to stop, ordered them out, and beat them seriously with iron clubs.

Whatever the value of the factual and chronological coincidences, the *Griffin* decision opened up far more issues than it resolved. For example, without deciding whether *Collins* was wrongly decided on its facts, the Court said §1985(3) was available to protect blacks against private conspiracies intended to prevent their exercise of rights under the Thirteenth Amendment and the privileges and immunities clause. It was unclear whether relief under the section could be had where

---

§5.8   1. United States v. Harris, 106 U.S. 629 (1882).

2. 341 U.S. 651 (1950).

3. 403 U.S. 88 (1971).

4. See Griggs v. Duke Power Co., 401 U.S. 424 (1971), and Swann v. Charlotte-Mecklenburg Sch. Bd., 402 U.S. 1 (1971).

private conspiracies deny rights protected against state interference by the Fourteenth Amendment.

This issue was resolved by the Burger Court in United Brotherhood of Carpenters & Joiners of America v. Scott.[5] The Court reinstated the state action requirement of *Collins* without expressly overruling *Griffin*. By excluding private conspiracies from the scope of §1985, the Court effectively deprived the statute of any force it once may have had.[6]

Scott involved an action by a construction company and two of its nonunion employees against local unions and residents who stood accused of attacking company workers and burning its office to the ground. Reversing the Fifth Circuit's contrary ruling, the Supreme Court held that a conspiracy to violate First Amendment rights does not violate §1985 unless the state was actively involved in the conspiracy or unless the conspiracy was aimed at influencing the state's activity. Justice White, who authored the majority opinion, characterized §1985 as a remedial statute which provides no greater rights than its underlying cause of action.[7] Therefore, because a Fourteenth Amendment claim hinges upon a showing of state action, a §1985 claim asserting a violation of equal protection must also be founded upon governmental involvement.

Calling the majority's opinion "crabbed and uninformed," Justice Blackmun wrote in dissent that the majority misinterpreted the legislative mandate of §1985. Section 1985, he argued, was drafted to safeguard individual rights not only from affirmative acts of the states, but also from the inaction of the state in the face of deprivations by others. The Reconstruction experience had taught legislators that

---

5. 463 U.S. 825 (1983).

6. See Comment, State Inaction and Section 1985(3): United Brotherhood of Carpenters & Joiners of America v. Scott, 71 Iowa L. Rev. 1271 (1986) (arguing that the Court erred in applying the Fourteenth Amendment's state action requirement to §1985, and thereby needlessly insulated private conspiracies from its reach); Ken Gormley, Private Conspiracies and the Constitution: A Modern Vision of 42 U.S.C. Section 1985(3), 64 Tex. L. Rev. 527, 532 (1985) (arguing that "the Scott decision threatens to send the conspiracy statute reeling back to the days of the 'Dreadful Decade,' when the statute had little or no practical importance"); Faunya Banks, Rethinking *Novotny* in Light of United Brotherhood of Carpenters & Joiners v. Scott: The Scope and Constitutionally Permissible Periphery of Section 1985(3), 27 How. L.J. 1497, 1500 n.10 (1984).

The Court's dicta in *Scott* further limited the remedial capacity of §1985 by excluding from the statute's protection conspiracies only affecting economic and commercial rights. Thus, after *Scott*, conspiracies directed at the deprivation of employment or interference with union activities and other basic economic rights are no longer actionable under §1985. In addition, lower courts following the Court's miserly interpretation of §1985 have restricted relief to the narrow class of people to whom §1985 already applies. See, e.g., Wilhelm v. Continental Title Co., 720 F.2d 1173, 1176 (10th Cir. 1983) ("In summary as to the *Scott* opinion, we find nothing therein to give any encouragement whatever to extend 1985 to classes other than those involved in the strife of the South in 1871 with which Congress was then concerned."), cert. denied, 465 U.S. 1103 (1984); D'Amato v. Wisconsin Gas Co., 760 F.2d 1474, 1486 (7th Cir. 1985) (refusing to extend §1985 to persons with disabilities); Fiske v. Lockheed Ga. Co., 568 F. Supp. 590 (N.D. Ga. 1983) (employees claiming to have been terminated because of their Socialist activities cannot maintain an action under §1985).

7. The Supreme Court had hinted at this result in dicta in Great Am. Fed. Sav. & Loan Ass'n v. Novotny, 442 U.S. 366 (1979). In *Novotny*, a white male loan officer sued his employer under §1985(3) claiming that he was terminated in violation of Title VII because he complained of the company's discrimination against women. The Supreme Court held that although §1985 is a remedial statute, it cannot be used to vindicate rights under Title VII since Title VII has its own complete remedial scheme. Id. at 376.

one of the greatest threats to the rights of former slaves was not state oppression but states' willingness to countenance the oppression of its black citizens by whites.[8] It is the possibility of nonenforcement by a state, not actual state action, that underlies §1985 relief.[9]

Today, §1985 lies dormant, except for the occasional and usually unsuccessful claim.[10] As in the pre-*Griffin* era, when courts made state action a gravamen of a §1985 cause of action, *Scott* threatens to render the statute virtually useless as a civil rights remedy. Any legislation that premises relief upon proving affirmative governmental complicity fails to reach the vast majority of conduct which threatens protected rights. As Professor Archibald Cox has written:

> The struggle for civil rights makes it all too plain that Equality requires more than abstractly equal status in terms of legal doctrine. . . . Bare legal rights . . . carry little meaning for the victim of intimidation and reprisals in a hostile community. . . . Any government committed to the promotion of racial equality and other human rights must concern itself, if it can, with the activities of private individuals.[11]

§5.9 CIVIL REMEDIES BASED DIRECTLY ON CONSTITUTIONAL AMENDMENTS

As the materials in the preceding sections have shown, individuals relying on §1983 or §1985(3) to recover damages for the violation of their constitutional rights face many obstacles, but they nevertheless travel a more certain path than would be the case if the suit were against federal officers, whose actions are not covered by either provision.

It has long been clear that a complaint alleging such violations should not be dismissed. The Supreme Court in 1946 held that a suit for damages against federal agents alleged to have invaded plaintiff's Fourth Amendment rights stated a constitutional claim within the jurisdiction conferred by 28 U.S.C. §1331(a).[1] While finding that the claim for damages "arises" under the Constitution in the strictly procedural sense that the district court must "entertain the suit," the Court, however, specifically declined to decide whether it "arises" in the substantive

---

8. See, e.g., Comment, A Construction of Section 1985(c) in Light of Its Original Purpose, 46 U. Chi. L. Rev. 402, 410-411 (1979); George C. Rable, But There Was No Peace: The Role of Violence in the Politics of Reconstruction 102-103 (1984). See also Griffin v. Breckenridge, 403 U.S. 88, 99 (1971).

9. 463 U.S. at 840-841, 851, 853-859 (Blackmun, J., dissenting). See also Note, State Inaction and Section 1985(3): United Brotherhood of Carpenters & Joiners v. Scott, 71 Iowa L. Rev. 1271, 1281 (1986); Gormley, supra note 6.

10. The vast majority of recent litigation under §1985 has concerned the obstruction of abortion clinics by anti-abortion groups. See, e.g., Roe v. Operation Rescue, 710 F. Supp. 577 (E.D. Pa. 1989); New York State Nat'l Org. for Women v. Terry, No. 88-3071 (S.D.N.Y. Jan. 10, 1989).

11. Archibald Cox, The Supreme Court 1965 Term Foreword: Constitutional Adjudication and the Promotion of Human Rights, 80 Harv. L. Rev. 91, 108 (1966).

§5.9 1. Bell v. Hood, 327 U.S. 678 (1946).

sense that it states a federal claim upon which relief could be granted. On remand, the district court, faced with the tough substantive question, concluded that the suit did not state a federal claim for relief.[2]

The Supreme Court was presented with the substantive issue for the first time in Bivens v. Six Unknown Named Agents of the Federal Bureau of Narcotics.[3] A majority found that violation of Fourth Amendment rights by federal agents is in itself an actionable offense for which the agents can be held personally liable in damages.[4]

Justice Harlan wrote a concurring opinion explaining that the Constitution had not limited to Congress the power to authorize a judicial remedy for the vindication of a federal constitutional right. Courts, he pointed out, often grant damages provisions if such relief is required to effectuate the government policy reflected in the statute. Interests protected by the Constitution, he reasoned, should be no less the subjects of judicial protection. Certainly, equitable relief is available to protect those interests without express congressional authorization. Nor need the plaintiff show that the remedy in damages is "essential," or "indispensable for indicating constitutional rights" as the government maintained. Such relief, Justice Harlan concluded, need only be "necessary" or "appropriate" to the vindication of the interest asserted.[5]

Sections 5.1 through 5.10 highlight the overarching trend of the Supreme Court to limit the impact of federal civil rights legislation and forestall unfettered civil rights litigation. Congress could have responded to the Court's decisions by clarifying its intent and changing legislation to guarantee relief for blatant civil rights violations. This raises questions for lawyers and legislatures about how to address the shortfalls of the legislation covered in earlier sections. Do we look to state constitutional protections and strengthening state civil rights legislation? Can we revive the potential of federal civil rights laws through amendment

2. Bell v. Hood, 71 F. Supp. 813 (S.D. Cal. 1947).

3. 403 U.S. 388 (1971). As in *Griffin*, *Monroe*, and *Mahone*, the *Bivens* breakthrough was spurred by shocking facts for which there appeared no other remedy. The plaintiff alleged that the narcotics agents entered his apartment and, without a warrant, arrested him for alleged narcotics violations. The agents manacled him in front of his wife and children, threatened to arrest his entire family, searched his apartment from stem to stern, then took the plaintiff to the federal courthouse where he was interrogated, booked, and subjected to a visual strip search.

4. Justice Brennan rejected government requests to dismiss the suit so that petitioner could file a tort suit for damages in the state court from which, the government admitted, the case would be removed to a federal court for decision on state law. The agents, Justice Brennan said, were more than private trespassers. They acted with federal power which, once granted, "does not disappear like a magic gift when it is wrongfully used." The Fourth Amendment serves as a limit on that power whether or not the state where it is abused provides a remedy.

5. To utilize the *Bivens* rule, plaintiffs must allege a statutory grant of jurisdiction. Most use federal question jurisdiction under 28 U.S.C. §1331(a), although it would seem that jurisdiction against state entities might be available without the necessity of alleging the $10,000 jurisdictional amount under 28 U.S.C. §1343(3). No jurisdictional amount need be alleged in suits against federal officials under §1331(a), as amended.

While several lower courts have recognized an implied cause of action under the First, Fourth, Fifth, Eighth, and Fourteenth Amendments by utilizing the *Bivens* rationale, it is not clear that the Supreme Court will extend *Bivens* beyond the Fourth Amendment.

It is also far from clear whether the Court will recognize an implied cause of action against a state or local defendant, although recent cases cast a dark shadow on that possibility.

under the current political climate? Does reform lie in the hand of lawyers, judges or communities? And given the history, is there much reason — save for infrequent occasions — for optimism from any of those who decide or influence policy-making?

§5.10   SOCIETAL LIMITS ON BASIC PROTECTIONS FOR BLACKS

A particularly virulent form of racial paranoia may be responsible for the feeling, but in reviewing the civil rights provisions covered in this chapter (all of which were born out of congressional concern for the rights of blacks but which now are intended to protect the constitutional rights of all), there seems to be at work an unseen but almost universally adhered-to understanding that the rights of blacks under these very statutes will receive protection only when that protection is in the interest of, or at least not greatly threatening to, the interests of whites.

Few will doubt that this was the case originally. Professor Mary Berry and others have convincingly shown that the post–Civil War Amendments and statutes were the product both of the committed concern of those horrified by the atrocities visited on the freedmen in that dreadful period and the desire to punish the South and keep its representatives from returning to and dominating the Congress. Sadly, there is scant room for debate as to which motivation was stronger. When fears of a Democratic Party takeover gave way to other concerns, blacks were left defenseless. The strong and seemingly clear language in the laws intended to protect not merely their rights but their very lives was diluted by a series of judicial rulings so burdened with sarcastic sophistry that, legally and morally, they made *Dred Scott* seem a model of logical and ethical adjudication.

All but the most perverse would prefer to forget rather than condemn this history but for the fact that the historic patterns remain in force. Certainly, modern courts acknowledge the presence and purpose of statutory protections, and even apply them — and vigorously too — in many cases (particularly those in which harm done to blacks has brought shock, embarrassment, even outrage to whites). We have seen such vigor in the *Screws* case, and especially in *Price*, where no effort was spared to bring those responsible for the Neshoba County murders at least to federal justice.

But where blacks allege harm that is as serious, though perhaps less dramatic; where, as so often is the case, the responsibility for the racial injustices is not the blatantly illegal acts of a few policemen but reflects policies authorized or condoned by the entire police force, often enough in conjunction with the full law enforcement establishment, the judicial response is listless, procedural, unresponsive. Reading Rizzo v. Goode,[1] or O'Shea v. Littleton,[2] the racially paranoid can

---

§5.10   1. 423 U.S. 362 (1976). Here, the Supreme Court barred enforcement of an injunction requiring controls on police conduct that the police department had worked out. Plaintiffs had proven their case, but the Court concluded that relief would be appropriate only if the high officials covered by the injunction were shown to have officially encouraged the misconduct.

2. 414 U.S. 488 (1974). The case is discussed in §5.6.1, note 16.

imagine the justices who joined the majority opinions writing to judicial colleagues of how they, like Chief Justice Marshall before them, had been able to escape an otherwise difficult ruling via a "Falstaffian tactic" because they, like he, are not "fond of butting a wall in sport. . . ."

Attempting to unravel the intricacies of standing and mootness through which the modern Court so often denies not simply justice but jurisdiction as well, one longs, almost, for the nineteenth-century candor of Justice Holmes admitting in Giles v. Harris, discussed in §2.14, that if all the whites in the area determine to deny the franchise to blacks, as the black petitioners alleged had happened, then the Court was powerless to intervene. The message is irresistible, revealing as it does the very essence of the democratic domination principle. Then and now, the power of the law to protect blacks from physical abuse and deprivation of even basic rights by either governmental officials or self-appointed racial regulators is limited. At some infinitely variable point — sometimes in matters of little moment, at others when the need for protection is critical to the maintenance of dignity, property, or even life itself — the legal provisions designed and enacted to protect black rights become suddenly, and without notice, inoperable.

Consider two cases. The first is Williams v. Alioto.[3] Understandably alarmed at a wave of what the media called "zebra killings" in which 17 whites were murdered, seemingly at random, by black assailants, the San Francisco Police Department issued composite sketches based on very general descriptions of the killers, ordering police to "stop and frisk" anyone that met the descriptions. Within a short time, over 600 blacks of every description were halted and searched. Finally, the practice was enjoined by the federal district court. But noting that the killers had been apprehended and less objectionable instructions on searches had been issued, the Ninth Circuit declared the issue moot and refused to review the civil liberties case.

No doubt, authorities would swear that had the zebra killers' victims been black and the suspects white, they would have followed identical procedures. Perhaps so. But suppose the random killings of whites had continued? Would the searches have been expanded as a result? Would curfews on blacks have been imposed? Recall that even warrantless door-to-door searches in black areas were not enjoined in Lankford v. Gelston, until long after they had been halted by the police.[4] Could blacks expect that injunction suits would prove of much use? Suits would be filed, and appropriately so, but depending on the sense of alarm generated, there is much in precedent and even more in the generally unrecorded behavior of courts in racial issues supporting the most pessimistic predictions for the success of those suits.

---

3. 15 Crim. L. Rep. 2187 (N.D. Cal 1974), vacated as moot, 549 F.2d 136 (9th Cir. 1977).
4. 364 F.2d 197 (4th Cir. 1966). Even the academic community is not immune from the irrational fear that if one black commits a crime, all must be deemed suspect. A former law student who served as a tutor in a Harvard undergraduate house reported that for a long period after an isolated crime in which two white students had been raped by two black men, all black male undergraduates were regarded with what she described as "fear and loathing" as well as suspicion by the Harvard-Radcliffe community. Matters reached such a point that someone called the Harvard Police to arrest a blind black student who had walked into the wrong house door by mistake.

One searches for a more definitive pattern of judicial behavior. Consider a second case, this time one that on its face did not seem to raise issues of crucial importance to whites. In Butler v. Cooper,[5] a §1983 suit was filed against various officials in the City of Portsmouth, Virginia, alleging a racially discriminatory conspiracy in the enforcement of the state's liquor laws. The plaintiff, a black widow, was arrested for selling two cans of beer in her home, and she established that 98 percent of the people arrested for selling legal whiskey without a license are black. Moreover, the city only engaged policemen to infiltrate and make arrests in black social clubs, while no white social club has ever been infiltrated by police. The court of appeals majority opinion found for the defendant Cooper and the Portsmouth Police Department, stating that a 98 percent black record of arrests was insufficient to show racially discriminatory enforcement of laws. The court failed to comment on the disparity between enforcement in white and black social clubs. These factors were brought out in a dissenting opinion by Judge Butzner.

None of this is to suggest that blacks can never expect justice in the courts; that the civil rights laws are never administered fairly; or that civil rights violators are never brought to account. Indeed, it is the fact that the legal process works well some of the time which renders its failures discussed here so disturbing. Blacks, paranoid or not, recognize the failures, and the reaction of whites to their recognition sometimes brings out another and usually more hostile form of the understanding.

Ealy v. Littlejohn[6] grew out of the failure of a Marshall County, Mississippi grand jury to charge anyone with the apparent murder of a young, black man who died while in police custody. In their frustration, blacks formed a citizens' association, instituted an economic boycott, and circulated a leaflet which was critical of local law enforcement officials and described the grand jury proceedings as a "farce." Responding to the group's accusations, the grand jury reconvened, purportedly to follow up on the association's claims that some members of the grand jury, as well as certain law enforcement officials, had not carried out their duties during the initial investigation.

In connection with this second investigation, members of the association were questioned, not only about the circumstances surrounding the death of the young man, but about the internal and financial operations of their organization as well. Subsequently, the association's members filed suit to enjoin the grand jury from inquiring into their internal operations. The court of appeals granted the requested relief, holding that the "grand jury had no right to intrude into [association] matters having not the remotest relationship to [the] tragic event and its investigation," and that the grand jury's inquiries into the "internal, structural, financial, and associational aspects" of the association "were posed in bad faith for the purpose of harassing those who, in the exercise of their First Amendment rights, had criticized [the district attorney] and had called the grand jury proceeding a farce."[7]

5. 554 F.2d 645 (4th Cir. 1977).
6. 569 F.2d 219 (5th Cir. 1978).
7. 569 F.2d at 229-230. The court found that plaintiffs' associational and free speech rights were abridged by questions relating to: (1) membership of the group; (2) those who associate with the group; (3) the group's meetings, persons who attend, and the matters discussed; (4) group financing

The Fifth Circuit's decision in *Ealy* corrected a serious misapplication of the grand jury process. The abuse was blatant and a source of great unease, not simply to the blacks harassed by it but also to all those involved in the administration of justice. (Senseless harm to blacks by an irresponsible few whites without any particular value and more than a little feeling of dislocation to whites at the policy-making level, has often been the real prerequisite for racial relief.) The formula didn't work in the non-licensed liquor prosecution case of *Butler*, but perhaps the court felt that the black social club proprietors there lacked clean hands and, as admitted violators, should not be granted relief from prosecution based on their equal protection claim.

But whatever difficulties were posed by the *Butler* case, the harder cases are those where recognition of legitimate rights asserted by blacks conflict with arguably valid interests of identifiable whites. That was the situation in the zebra killings case. Conflicting facts and interests of that character are at the root of the Racism Hypo that concludes this section.

Note: Increasing Public Support to End Racial Profiling

Racial profiling has come under intense scrutiny throughout the country. Even in the 2000 presidential campaign, both Republican and Democratic candidates alike renounced the practice as an unacceptable method of law enforcement.[8] President Bush, who has stated that "racial profiling is wrong," released an executive order to ban profiling by federal law enforcement agencies (except when needed for counter-terrorist activity). Race cannot be used as the only factor to identify a suspect, according to a Department of Justice policy, a statement that differs little from the current state of the law.[9] Advocates have criticized the administration's response as nothing more than "rhetorical smoke and mirrors."[10] The policy shows, however, that racial profiling has gained national attention as an undesirable practice. Yet, eradicating a practice that is integral to the daily behavior of local and national law enforcement officials, especially in light of current Supreme Court 4th Amendment jurisprudence may prove nearly impossible.

Although many argue that race should not be the primary basis for suspecting someone of criminal activity, profiling is an extremely subjective practice. Often law enforcement officials claim that race is justifiably and effectively used

---

and funding generally, or financing of the leaflet; and (5) the leaflet or any other printed or oral statement of any group member.

The court cited with approval Bursey v. United States, 466 F.2d 1059 (9th Cir. 1972), involving contempt charges brought against Black Panther newspaper staff members who refused to answer federal grand jury questions. The *Bursey* court enjoined the use of questions that, if answered, would reveal the details of a dissident group's funding. Such a disclosure would be "as effective a chilling device as is compulsory disclosure of its membership lists. . . ." 466 F.2d at 1088.

8. Eric Lichtblau, Bush Issues Racial Profiling Ban But Exempts Security Inquiries, N.Y. Times, June 18, 2003.

9. Id. See also Richard Schmitt, The Nation: New U.S. Guidelines Curb Racial Profiling: The Rules Are Lauded by Federal Officials But an ACLU Officer Calls Them Toothless, L.A. Times, June 18, 2003.

10. Mike Allen, Bush Issues Ban on Racial Profiling; Policy Makes Exceptions for Security, Wash. Post, June 18, 2003.

in police practice as only one of a number of factors.[11] In addition, officers need to articulate merely a reasonable suspicion, rather than probable cause, to stop a suspect, which has established a very low threshold for police conduct. The typical "driving while black" scenario arises when minor infractions, like a broken taillight or speeding, rather than the race of the suspect, become the easily articulated reason for justifying a police stop.

Studies throughout the past decade have revealed that police, whether as part of an official police policy or not, are using race as a marker of suspicious activity. Consequently, law enforcement disproportionately impacts minorities, which in turn yields resentment, distrust, and a lack of cooperation from targeted communities. For example, in New York, a study conducted by the state attorney general and Columbia's Center for Violence, Research and Prevention, found that crime rates and demographics could not explain the racial disparities in the New York Police Department's stop and frisks.[12] Although minorities make up only a quarter of the city's population, they represented more than half of the police stops.[13] In other urban areas of Maryland, Texas, Ohio, and New Jersey, reports present even greater disparities.[14] Police department data in Austin showed that for every 100 people ticketed, 73 were minorities, even though they constitute only 30 percent of the population.[15] In New Jersey, profiling has been dramatically documented through multiple studies, an intervention by the federal government and even police memoranda. The New Jersey legislature is the first to criminalize profiling in police searches and arrests.[16]

Legislative action may be the best recourse for curbing discriminatory policing given that legal challenges have not proven successful and often require proof of discriminatory intent, which is easy to overcome by offering objective reasons for the stop. The Supreme Court has restricted its interpretation of the Fourth Amendment dramatically. As Professor Taslitz describes, "The burden of this narrowing vision of Fourth Amendment rights has often fallen hardest on racial and ethnic minorities. The Court purports to endorse a color-blind search and seizure jurisprudence. Ignoring race, however, is often precisely what promotes racial disparities."[17]

---

11. See Andrew E. Taslitz, Stories of Fourth Amendment Disrespect: From Elian to the Internment, 70 Fordham L. Rev. 2257 (2002); Peter Lyle, Racial Profiling and the Fourth Amendment, 21 B.C. Third World L.J. 243, 262 (2001); David Cole, No Equal Justice: Race and Class in the American Criminal Justice System (1999); Angela J. Davis, Race, Cops, and Traffic Stops, 51 U. Miami L. Rev. 425, 427 (1997).)

12. Jerome H. Skolnick & Abigail Caplovitz, Guns, Drugs and Profiling: Ways to Target Guns and Minimize Profiling, 43 Ariz. L. Rev. 413, 426 (2001).

13. Id.

14. Jack Ludwig, Americans See Racial Profiling as Widespread, Gallup Poll Tuesday Briefing, May 13, 2003; David Kocieniewski, Study Suggests Racial Gap in Speeding in New Jersey, N.Y. Times, March 21, 2002, at B1; Andy Alford & Tony Plohetski, Traffic Stops Data Hint at Racial Bias, Austin Police Numbers Show Minorities More Likely to Be Searched, Whites More Likely to Have Contraband, Austin American-Statesman, Mar. 16, 2003; Mark Ferenchik, White Drivers Less Likely to Be Stopped by Police Here: But Even Researches Say Study Doesn't Prove That Officers Are Racially Profiling Motorists, Columbus Dispatch, June 26, 2003 at 1C.

15. Kocieniewski, supra note 14, at B1.

16. Alford & Plohetski, supra note 14, at A1.

17. Andrew Taslitz, Plugging into the Fourth Amendment's Matrix, Criminal Justice (Summer 2007) at 34; see also Andrew E. Taslitz, Racial Auditors and the Fourth Amendment: Data with

One recent case illustrates the difficulty of ending the practice on constitutional grounds. In Brown v. Oneonta,[18] an elderly, white woman was attacked in her home, and she related that the assailant cut himself with his knife in their struggle and determined that he was a black man based on her recollection of his hand and forearm. In a college town of over 10,000 residents and 7,500 students, African Americans comprised less than 300 residents and only 2 percent of the student population. The police began to stop all nonwhites on the street to observe their hands and acquired a list of all black college students to question each individually.

The Second Circuit found that the police action did not rise to an equal protection violation because defendants were not questioned based solely on their race, but on a number of factors including gender, age, and a cut on their hand. Thus the plaintiffs could not prove the discriminatory intent of the police. In addition, when a minority is found in such a small percentage, "it would be more useful for police to use race to find a black suspect than a white one."[19] The court recognized that the police action may create a "distrust of law enforcement," which can be addressed by the legislative branch. The decision was consistent with Supreme Court jurisprudence that holds racial animus irrelevant in the Fourth Amendment context of searches and seizures, "suggesting a high standard of proof to recover for racial profiling under the Fourteenth Amendment."[20] Professor Andrew Taslitz finds that the court's analysis informs the racial profiling debate:

> [It] proved so difficult for the Second Circuit despite the case's being an easier one than most instances of racial profiling. Profiling rarely involves a "sweep" of many young males . . . [M]ost profiling happens in a way that is less obvious to the public, such as a highway roadside stop where the suspect is unlikely to be observed by anyone but the police for any significant length of time.[21]

Given that a high threshold has been set for proving an unconstitutional case of racial profiling, some scholars have called for an end to race-based suspect descriptions.[22]

Racial profiling has a ripple effect that extends beyond the one individual who is stopped. In a recent article, Professor Taslitz argues that racial profiling is counter-productive when viewed from the collective impact on minorities. The formation of one's identity is intertwined with the groups that matter to them. As an

---

the Power to Inspire Political Action, 66 L. & Contemp. Probs. 221, 250 (2003) (summarizing data); see generally Tom R. Tyler & Yuen J. Huo, Trust in the Law: Public Cooperation with the Police and the Courts (2002) (analyzing racial minorities' attitudes toward the police).

18. 221 F.3d 329 (2d Cir. 2000). See also Morgan v. Woessner, 997 F.2d 1244, 1254 (9th Cir. 1993); United States v. Lawes, 292 F.3d 123, 127 (2d Cir. 2002).

19. Brown v. Oneonta, supra note 18, at 338.

20. Taslitz, supra note 11, at 2324.

21. Id. at 2326.

22. August Walker, The Color of Crime: The Case Against Race-Based Suspect Descriptions, 103 Colum. L. Rev. 662 (2003); R. Richard Banks, Race-Based Suspect Selection and Colorblind Equal Protection Doctrine and Discourse, 48 UCLA L. Rev. 1075 (2001).

extension of this, Taslitz explains that when a person feels unjustly treated by a police stop, this injustice is felt by their community. Therefore, Taslitz explains:

> When many persons of a certain race are regularly so stopped, the impact on the broader racial community is deeper. Minority communities sense, in a way that the Court does not, that strong Fourth Amendment protections are central to fostering respect for both individuals and their communities. At the same time, as grassroots activism and some community policing efforts have shown, respect-enhancing police actions improve law enforcement effectiveness. Citizens more actively and eagerly cooperate with a respectful police force. The result is crime reduction.[23]

One suggestion for ridding law enforcement of racial profiling comes from Professor Elizabeth Joh, who suggests replacing police officers with technology.[24] Professor Joh discusses "[r]ecent federal regulatory approval of the technical standards for the federal intelligent highway initiative shows that this is a real and practicable solution to the problem of police discretion in traffic stops."[25] Her article acknowledges the pitfalls of such technology, including increased enforcement of traffic laws on everyone regardless of race; but the solution "sidesteps entrenched difficulties in Fourth Amendment law and politics."[26]

African Americans have not been the only targets of policing because of their skin color. Professor Kevin Johnson compares police discrimination of African Americans to discrimination against Latinos in many urban areas, especially as a strategy for enforcement of immigration laws.[27] For undocumented citizens near the border, articulating a reason other than a person's ethnic appearance seems less important to the Supreme Court given that near the border "appearance is a relevant factor."[28] Johnson draws parallels between the psychological impact of such policies on both minority groups. Given "common interests in eliminating race profiling from all — criminal and immigration — law enforcement," he calls on African Americans and Latinos to find a common ground that will enable them to work together to fight police activity targeting their communities.[29]

After September 11, racial profiling was used significantly as a means for identifying "suspected terrorists." As a result of police sweeps, hundreds of Arab Americans and Arab immigrants were taken from their communities and detained without contact with family members or access to lawyers and information. The federal government devised a formalized registry system for immigrants from Arab countries suspected of supporting terrorist activity. Although the ACLU and other civil rights groups are exploring judicial remedies to discover the names of those detained in secret centers and their charges, the government's

---

23. Taslitz, supra note 17, at 34.
24. Elizabeth Joh, Discretionless Policing: Technology and the Fourth Amendment, 95 Cal. L. Rev. 195 (2007).
25. Id.
26. Id.
27. Kevin Johnson, The Case for African American and Latina/o Cooperation in Challenging Racial Profiling in Law Enforcement, 55 Fla. L. Rev. 341 (2003). See also Kevin Johnson, Immigration Reform, National Security after September 11, and the Future of North American Integration.
28. United States v. Brignoni-Ponce, 422 U.S. 873 (1975).
29. Johnson, supra note 27, at 363.

power to retain information under the guise of heightened national security seems boundless and is often supported by general public opinion. The complexity of racial identification and the broad leeway granted to national security enforcement in a time of crisis makes it easy for minorities, who have historically been unprotected in such circumstances, to serve as easily identifiable and tangible targets for national fear. The subject is covered in greater detail in §11.5.

§5.11   Racism Hypo: Black Plaintiffs v. Suburban Scene

Suburban Scene police attributed the first death to a possible suicide, though the typed note found near Jim Beardon's body made no sense. It said simply, "There is no hiding place down here!" There were no other clues.

Two weeks later, a similar message was pinned to Dean Rockwool's lapel. Rockwool, a popular political figure in Suburban Scene, was found seated at his desk one morning, quite dead. He had been working at his office late the previous night and, at some point, was shot in the back of the head.

Suburban Scene, the carefully planned community whose proud motto is "harmony through homogeneity," panicked. Both Beardon and Rockwool had been leaders in the successful campaign to defeat a low income housing project slated for construction in Suburban Scene. A public referendum had been required because the town zoning board had approved the project as a means of obtaining federal funds for a new town park and tennis courts.

Suburban Scene residents wanted the recreational facilities, but, as one speaker put it at a town meeting, "No federal money is worth it if we have to throw our town open to a lot of welfare cheats, muggers, drug addicts, and God knows what else. That's what I took on a whale-sized mortgage to get away from."

Few speakers were that candid, and the large audience listened respectfully as developers explained their efforts to make the new housing blend in. Civil rights representatives reported how badly inner-city people needed new housing. Then, at the special election, they defeated the housing project overwhelmingly. It had seemed, at the time, the right thing to do.

Now, the Suburban Scene town council ordered the voting machines used in the referendum election sealed and placed under constant guard. Then Mrs. Seeley was killed.

It could have been an accident. An elderly woman, Seeley had been returning home following a late meeting when her car left the road and struck a tree. Before she died, though, she told the state highway patrol she lost control of her car trying to elude a shiny, red and green van filled with young men who seemed to be following her. She thought the men were black.

At this point, the town council asked for state police help, and local sporting goods stores experienced a run on rifles, shotguns, and everything that would shoot. It was a newly purchased shotgun that killed the telephone repairman responding to a late-night emergency.

"I thought it was one of them," a distraught Suburban Scene homeowner explained. The repairman was black.

A special town meeting a few days later found residents applauding the police chief's suggestion that a special ordinance be adopted that would bar all blacks who were not residents of Suburban Scene from entering the town until the present emergency ended.

Drafting the measure was not easy, but it was quickly approved and placed in effect. Police were placed at roadblocks at all roadways leading into Suburban Scene. All black people unable to produce the special identification papers prepared for black residents were refused access. Black residents were outraged by the ordinance, but were even more incensed at the hostile behavior of some neighbors.

There have been no further incidents, but no progress has been made in efforts to solve the crimes. The ordinance has remained in effect, though its validity has been challenged in a suit filed on behalf of more than two hundred nonresident blacks. Some have been unable to get to their jobs in Suburban Scene, while others have alleged the ordinance is discriminatory and violates their right to travel. Damages sought by both groups total ten million dollars.

Citing the continuing danger, and urging patience and understanding on the plaintiffs, a federal district judge denied injunctive relief and dismissed the suit. The court of appeals has expedited the appeal.

Law Firm A will represent the black plaintiffs. Law Firm B will represent Suburban Scene.

§5.12 DISCRIMINATION IN THE CRIMINAL JUSTICE SYSTEM

§5.12.1 Death Penalty: An Overview

The death penalty is a form of violence committed through America's criminal justice system against the poor. As of January 1, 2007, 3,350 inmates were on death row.[1] The number of inmates on death row peaked at 3,593 inmates in 2000.[2] A disproportionate number of minorities, 42 percent, are on death row: 7 percent are Hispanic and 34 percent are black.[3] Since 1976 when the death penalty was declared constitutional, 1096 people[4] have been executed and 124 people have been released on overturned convictions.[5] Those being executed or awaiting their deaths are no different from those this country has historically executed. Almost every one is poor, over half are racial minorities, and most were sentenced to death for a crime against a white victim.[6] Beyond this, many suffer from severe mental impairments.

---

§5.12 1. NAACP Legal Defense and Education Fund, Inc., Death Row USA: Winter Report, A Quarterly Report of the Criminal Justice Project of the NAACP Legal Defense Fund and Education Fund (January 2007). See http://www.naacpldf.org/content/pdf/pubs/drusa/DRUSA_Winter_2007.pdf.

2. Id.

3. See Death Penalty Information Center Website at www.deathpenaltyinfo.org/article.php?scid=8&did=146.

4. Id. Also see NAACP 2007 Winter Report, supra note 1.

5. Death Penalty Information Center Statistics, http://www.deathpenaltyinfo.org/article.php?did=110&scid=/.

6. See Death Penalty Information Center articles, available at http://www.deathpenaltyinfo.org/article.php?scid=8&did=146, http://www.deathpenaltyinfo.org/article.php?did=205&scid=27, and http://www.deathpenaltyinfo.org/article.php?scid=6&did=111#ReleasedASK/.

Because application of the death penalty has proven far from flawless, over the past decade a moratorium movement in the United States has lead to increased scrutiny of death penalty convictions, a reevaluation in many state legislatures, and a chipping away at Supreme Court jurisprudence. This section examines some of the major problems plaguing the death penalty and discusses the movement that aims to reform and potentially abolish this practice.

Two of this country's foremost researchers on the links between capital punishment and race, David Baldus and George Woodworth, released a detailed report in 1998 about a study they did in Philadelphia that revealed the odds of receiving the death penalty to be four times greater for a black defendant than for a white one.[7] But despite such overwhelming evidence of racial bias, the response of the courts has been to deny relief on the grounds that patterns of racial discrimination are insufficient to prove discrimination in a particular case.[8]

Racial disparities in the application of the death penalty continue to persist. In 2007, 41.7 percent of the death row population was black, and one in three prisoners who have been executed were black.[9] The United States has executed 373 African American inmates since the reinstatement of the death penalty. The Department of Justice looked at its own statistics, finding that 75 percent of those executed by the federal government were racial minorities; over half were black.[10] From another vantage point of racial disparity, African Americans, who make up only 12 percent of the population, represent 50 percent of victims of murders in the United States. Professor Bryan Stevenson points out, though, that "eighty percent of those on death row are there for killing white people."[11] A 2007 study of 1560 individuals sentenced to death in 16 states found that African Americans on death row for killing white victims are more likely to be executed. "The disparity in execution rates based on the race of victims suggests our justice system places greater value on white lives, even after sentences are handed down," explains the study's co-author David Jacobs.[12]

Sadly, due process, equal protection of the law, and reliability in criminal adjudications are no longer as important as finality.[13] Our Supreme Court is so committed to limiting the appeals of condemned prisoners that it encourages states to get on with the killing. Even worse is that our Congress has stripped away the meaningful presence of habeas protection for condemned prisoners. This has been accomplished primarily by using procedural hurdles that often prove insurmountable barriers to justice.

---

7. David C. Baldus & George Woodworth, Racial Discrimination and the Death Penalty in the Post-*Furman* Era: An Empirical and Legal Overview, With Recent Findings from Philadelphia, 83 Cornell L. Rev. 1638 (1998).

8. NAACP 2007 Winter Report, supra note 1.

9. http://www.deathpenaltyinfo.org/article.php?scid=5&did=184/.

10. Bryan Stevenson, Will the Death Penalty Remain Alive in the Twenty-first Century? International Norms, Discrimination, Arbitrariness, and the Risk of Executing the Innocent, 2001 Wis. L. Rev. 1, at 14.

11. Id.

12. Study: Blacks Who Kill Whites Are Most Likely to Be Executed, http://researchnews.osu.edu/archive/dthrow.htm.

13. Stephen B. Bright, Casualties of the War on Crime: Fairness, Reliability and the Credibility of Criminal Justice Systems, 51 U. Miami L. Rev. 413 (1997).

Habeas is the mechanism by which a person convicted in state or federal court may petition the federal courts for review of a conviction or sentence on the grounds that it was unconstitutionally obtained. In the effort to increase the number and speed of executions, Congress strictly limited defendants' rights to habeas review by passing the Antiterrorism and Effective Death Penalty Act of 1996 (AEDPA),[14] meanwhile defunding death penalty resource centers. Legislators pushed AEDPA through Congress, in the wake of the tragedy of the Oklahoma City bombing, with such haste that few representatives understood its dramatic impact.[15] The power of AEDPA is in its nearly fatal stripping away of the strengths of the once great writ of habeas.

Under AEDPA, condemned prisoners face an unprecedented one-year statute of limitations for bringing a habeas claim.[16] This time limitation creates the possibility of fatal consequences for a client whose counsel misses the deadline. And the individual whose counsel misses the deadline apparently will be barred from ever seeking federal habeas review. Also, individuals without resources or representation are denied even the chance to present a single claim in federal court because, without a lawyer, they are unable to comply with the statute of limitations. So hundreds of inmates languish in prison without ever finding counsel to prepare a single federal habeas petition on their behalf.

The Act also prohibits federal courts from granting habeas relief except in very narrow circumstances.[17] Now, a federal court must be willing to call the lower court's opinion unreasoned and unprincipled in order to reverse.[18] This severely limits when a federal court can correct a flagrant misinterpretation of constitutional law by allowing almost any rational interpretation by a lower court to stand impenetrable.

Beyond this, AEDPA severely limits when a federal court may conduct even a much-needed evidentiary hearing,[19] and prohibits successive petitions for relief in all but the narrowest of circumstances.[20] Now, federal courts may only review successive petitions that go to factual innocence.[21] Previously, federal courts had discretion as to whether to hear a second petition on behalf of a defendant. The Supreme Court upheld the new provision restricting successive petitions in Felker v. Turpin.[22] Professor Stevenson explains that AEDPA's preclusion of successive petitions would "virtually exclude certain types of constitutional claims" relating to executions.[23] He looks to subsequent Supreme Court cases that review AEDPA provisions to argue that the Court has narrowly interpreted the statute to protect the "vitality of the writ."[24] In one case, the majority departed from the statute's text to

---

14. Antiterrorism and Effective Death Penalty Act (AEDPA), Pub. L. No. 104-132, 110 Stat. 1214 (1996).

15. Bryan Stevenson, The Politics of Fear and Death: Successive Problems in Capital Habeas Corpus Cases, 77 N.Y.U. L. Rev. 699 (2002).

16. ADEPA, supra note 14, at 1217.

17. Id. at 1215.

18. Id.

19. Id.

20. Id. at 1220-1221.

21. Id.

22. 518 U.S. 651 (1996).

23. Stevenson, supra note 15, at 704.

24. Id. at 776.

"guard against the 'far reaching and seemingly perverse' consequence of 'bar[ring] the prisoner from ever obtaining federal habeas review' of a claim."[25] For those on death row, a literal reading of AEDPA may create the perverse result that a defendant may not be able to raise constitutional claims that are not ripe until the successive petition.

Stevenson makes a compelling argument about the misdirected attack on successive habeas petitions. He explains that the judicial fears that prisoners and attorneys use successive petitions to manipulate the system prompted political action to clamp down on habeas petitions. Stevenson contends that although there are examples of abuse, they are rare. By the mid-1980s, however, the Court's frustration with last-minute filings and a rapidly increasing volume of filings became evident. This resentment translated into political pressure to limit successive petitions, which, in the words of Senator Orrin Hatch, let "anyone manipulate [them] to their own ends."[26]

Stevenson, however, presents an alternate story to show how this political momentum, which culminated in AEDPA, was based on an inaccurate portrait. As federal courts refused to recognize a constitutional right to counsel for death row inmates during collateral review, the number of people on death row increased from about 500 in the late 1970s to 2,500 by the late 1980s.[27] While demand for legal services exceeded the supply of lawyers, states pushed up execution time tables to appear tough on crime. Rather than manipulating the system, the few lawyers working on excessive caseloads turned to a case only when their time almost expired. Stevenson concludes that this reality, however, did not penetrate the images of "trickster" defense lawyers and "con man" prisoners advanced by federal judges. Yet these less sympathetic images fueled the dramatic changes, especially the restrictions on successive petitions that were written into AEDPA.

The stated objective of AEDPA was to hasten executions, but the resulting injustice has not been limited to inmates facing death sentences. Anyone unconstitutionally convicted of a crime faces these new barriers to habeas relief.

Another barrier is the defunding in 1996 of the postconviction defender organizations. Postconviction defender organizations exposed numerous cases of constitutional violations resulting in death sentences. Because these organizations successfully defended individuals whose death sentences had been unconstitutionally obtained, they have always been very unpopular with many death penalty advocates. Arguably, this unpopularity led to their defunding by Congress.[28]

Notably, many individuals could have avoided postconviction litigation entirely if they had been adequately represented at trial. Unfortunately, judges in many states appoint the least capable lawyers to capital cases, and states refuse to allow sufficient funding for an adequate defense.[29] A study of the Texas system, which has accounted for more than a third of all executions since 1976 with 405 as

---

25. Id. at 748, quoting Stewart v. Martinez-Villareal, 523 U.S. 637.
26. Id. at 748, quoting 137 Cong. Rec. 16,538 (1991) (statement of Sen. Hatch).
27. Id.
28. Stephen B. Bright, Does The Bill of Rights Apply Here Any More? Evisceration of Habeas Corpus and Denial of Counsel to Those Under Sentence of Death, 20-NOV Champion 25 (1996).
29. Stephen B. Bright, Counsel for the Poor: The Death Sentence Not for the Worst Crime But for the Worst Lawyer, 103 Yale L.J. 1835 (1994).

of September 2007[30] indicated that judges gave preference to counsel with reputations for closing cases quickly and appointed attorneys who had been subject to multiple disciplinary actions.[31] Inadequate legal representation is pervasive in the jurisdictions that account for most of the death sentences. According to the American Bar Association, "the inadequacy and inadequate compensation of counsel at trial" is one of the principal failings of the capital punishment system in the United States.[32] And, according to an extensive study by the National Law Journal, a capital trial is more like a random flip of a coin than a balancing of the scales of justice.[33]

Perhaps the legal community's attention to ineffective assistance of counsel especially in capital cases influenced three recent Supreme Court cases finding ineffective assistance of counsel for death row inmates. Historically, the Supreme Court has been highly criticized for the seemingly unreachable *Strickland* standard for ineffective assistance of counsel claims. The Court's decisions in Rompilla v. Beard, Wiggins v. Smith, and Williams v. Taylor marks a critical development in this standard, especially for those facing capital punishment.[34]

In the first of these string of cases, *Wiggins*, the Court overturned a death sentence because of inadequate representation during the sentencing phase of trial.[35] Kevin Wiggins, an inmate on death row for over seven years, was convicted of drowning an elderly woman in her Baltimore apartment. Yet, in the sentencing phase of his trial, his lawyers did not discover or present mitigating evidence that their client was beaten, raped, repeatedly burned by his mother, and further abused in foster care. In a seven-to-two decision, Justice O'Connor, writing for the majority, found this evidence "powerful" and that "[g]iven both the nature and extent of the abuse petitioner suffered, we find there to be a reasonable probability that a competent attorney, aware of this history, would have introduced it at sentencing in an admissible form."[36]

In Williams v. Taylor, the Court found ineffective representation despite the 1996 restrictions on federal habeas corpus.[37] In Rompilla v. Beard, the Court found the defendant's trial counsel incompetent under the *Strickland* test because his lawyer failed to investigate public records, which prosecutors informed her would be used against Rompilla during sentencing. In the Court's opinion, these public files of the defendant's prior convictions would have undoubtedly opened a range of mitigation leads about the defendant's traumatic upbringing and mental

---

30. Texas Department of Criminal Justice, Executions, 1982 through September 25, 2007, available at http://www.tdcj.state.tx.us/stat/annual.htm.

31. Texas Defender Service, Lethal Indifference: The Fatal Combination of Incompetent Attorneys and Unaccountable Courts in Texas Death Penalty Appeals, available at http://www.aba-net.org/moratorium/assessmentproject/texas.html.

32. Ruth E. Friedman & Bryan A. Stevenson, Solving Alabama's Capital Defense Problems: It's a Dollars and Sense Thing, 44 Ala. L. Rev. 1, 32-37 (1992).

33. Marcia Coyle et al., Fatal Defense: Trial and Error in the Nation's Death Belt, Natl. L.J., June 11, 1990, at 30.

34. See Rompilla v. Beard, 125 S. Ct. 2456, 2467-69 (2005); Wiggins v. Smith, 539 U.S. 510, 535 (2003); Williams v. Taylor, 529 U.S. 362, 398-99 (2000).

35. Wiggins v. Smith, 123 S. Ct. 2527 (2003).

36. Id. at 2542.

37. *Williams*, supra note 34.

retardation that no other source had. Without viewing the records, the Court is baffled by how the attorney intended to respond to the prosecution's case. The Court explains that "[t]his evidence adds up to a mitigation case that bears no relation to the few naked pleas for mercy actually put before the jury" and therefore could have changed the decision of the jury.[38]

These cases offer a mere glimpse into the abysmal state of legal representation for indigent defendants facing the death penalty.[39] One egregious example is that of George McFarland, who waits on death row in Texas. McFarland's lawyer actually slept through his trial.[40] The Tennessee Supreme Court found that in a quarter of death penalty cases, counsel did not present evidence that could have been critical to a finding of a prison sentence over the death penalty.[41] A Georgia report presented evidence of the state's inability to provide an adequate defense for those on death row.[42] And in Pennsylvania, the state with the fourth largest death row in the country, 60 percent of all death penalty cases were not adequately investigated, and counsel was largely inexperienced according to the commission's study.[43] Special attention was given to the disproportionate representation of minorities on death row. Sixty-nine percent of death row inmates are minorities, who make up only 12 percent of the state's population.[44] The findings were so profound that the report recommended a moratorium and a Racial Justice Act.

On the other side of the table, prosecutorial misconduct has also been cited as a factor in convicting innocent defendants, many of whom are sentenced to death. An ACLU report highlights that an overwhelming proportion of prosecutors, 97.5 percent, are white and primarily men.[45]

Even new evidence of innocence no longer spares one who has been sentenced to death. The Rehnquist Court has abandoned any commitment to insuring review for innocent people facing execution. In Herrera v. Collins (1993),[46] the Court held that the Constitution does not protect condemned prisoners from execution even if new evidence of their innocence emerges. Calling such protections disruptive of the need for finality in a capital case, the Court ruled against allowing the hearing of appeals based on new proof of a defendant's innocence.[47]

Beyond this, in 1991 the Court held that murder victim's family members may testify at the penalty phase of a capital case.[48] Notably, the Court had called this same practice unconstitutional only four years earlier.[49] This ruling is particularly troubling because victim impact evidence gives more opportunity for jurors to

---

38. *Rompilla*, supra note 34.

39. Rachel King, American Civil Liberties Union Report on the Anniversary of Furman v. Georgia, Three Decades Later: Why We Need a Temporary Halt on Executions, June 2003 at 6-7.

40. http://www.pbs.org/newshour/bb/law/july97/death_penalty_7-30.html. See also King, supra note 39, at 5.

41. King, supra note 39, at 7.

42. Id.

43. Id. at 9.

44. Id.

45. Id. at 10.

46. 506 U.S. 390 (1993).

47. Id. at 417.

48. Payne v. Tennessee, 501 U.S. 808 (1991).

49. Booth v. Maryland, 482 U.S. 496 (1987).

consider arbitrarily the race, character, and social status of the victim in the decision about punishment of the defendant.

Many U.S. citizens remain almost hungry for more executions. In a letter to the editor of USA Today, for example, a man from Massachusetts wrote that a better way than treatment to end illegal drug use is "a quick trial and the death penalty for any dealer, if he or she is found guilty." He continues that this measure will never come into effect because of "bleeding-heart liberals and elite trial lawyers."[50] This man is not alone in believing that enforcement of the death penalty faces too many barriers. As Tony Amsterdam explains, an often-told story in the United States features "a sleazy lawyers' plot to thwart the Nation's Will, weaken its Sovereign Powers of Self-Protection, bamboozle its inferior judges, and thereby nullify the solemn judgments of its Highest Court."[51] And many states have fueled this sentiment by trying to speed up the timeline for executions.

Three possible explanations for why the U.S. public seems to so ardently advocate the death penalty were suggested at the 1995 Conference on the Death Penalty in the Twenty-First Century, held at American University.[52] These include first, a serious lack of trust that life without parole actually means life without parole.[53] Second, the possibility that a sense of justice demands the death penalty in certain circumstances because of the heinous nature of the criminal act.[54] Generally inherent in this is the idea that any punishment short of death discounts the seriousness of some crimes. And third, the possibility that the public may be making a general statement about their fear of crime, meanwhile trying to see the death penalty as a valid response or solution to that fear.[55]

§5.12.2 Growing Momentum to End Injustice in the Administration of the Death Penalty

Recent polls have shown that enthusiasm for the death penalty may be slipping. An ABC News/Washington Post poll in 2003 found that 64 percent of Americans support the death penalty when no other option is presented, which indicates a decline from the late 1990s. Further, the poll shows that the public may be more closely divided when given the option of sentencing a defendant to life in prison for murder convictions. When given the possibility of that alternative sentence, 49 percent would choose imposing the death penalty and 45 percent would choose sentencing to life in prison.[56] Of the 38 death penalty states, 35 offer the option of life without parole, as do 11 of the 12 non–death penalty states.[57]

50. Richard J. Pauley, Death for Drug Dealers, USA Today, Sept. 15, 1999, at 15A.
51. Tony Amsterdam, Selling a Quick Fix for Boot Hill: The Myth of Justice Delayed in Death Cases, in The Killing State 164 (1999).
52. Robert E. Morin, et al., The Death Penalty in the Twenty-First Century, 45 Am. U. L. Rev. 239, 305-310 (1995).
53. Id.
54. Id.
55. Id.
56. See Death Penalty Information website, available at http://www.deathpenaltyinfo.org/article.php?scid=23&did=210#Gallup-5/03, citing ABCNews.com, Jan. 24, 2003.
57. Kansas, New Mexico, and Texas are the only death penalty states without a life without parole sentence. Alaska is the only state that offers neither sentence. For a complete list of the states

The shift in popular opinion reflects a growing movement that has exposed the serious systemic problems that plague death penalty administration. In a Gallup Poll in May 2003, 74 percent of the respondents said they believed an innocent person has been put to death in the past five years.

A leader in raising this question, the American Bar Association has called for a moratorium on executions in recognition of the fact that fairness has been sacrificed in favor of "results" in death penalty cases across the United States.[58] In their report calling for a moratorium, the ABA documents the systematic unfairness in the administration of the death penalty, including demonstration of the influence of race and poverty on whether one is sentenced to death. Unfortunately, the ABA's message about the systematic unfairness of the death penalty has been met with the same indifference as other similar documentation.[59]

States have also come under attack by both abolitionists seeking to end the death penalty and advocates for the death penalty who want to guarantee that the system is not unjust. Since 2000, a number of states have responded to such concerns by commissioning comprehensive investigations of the effectiveness of the death penalty process and have uncovered alarming results.[60] Many of these results point to rampant racial discrimination throughout the system, from inadequate defense attorneys to improper prosecutorial conduct and biased judges to unrepresentative juries.[61]

As a major spark in 2000, Illinois placed a moratorium on death sentences after 13 prisoners on death row were found to be wrongly convicted. In 2003, Governor Ryan commuted the sentences of over 160 persons on death row, stating "[b]ecause the Illinois death penalty system is arbitrary and capricious — and therefore immoral — I no longer shall tinker with the machinery of death."[62] Other states have followed suit by halting executions temporarily. Many states have also considered proposals to abolish the death penalty under growing abolitionist pressure. For example, the New Hampshire House and Senate passed a bill to abolish the state death penalty, but the governor vetoed it.[63] In 1999, bills were introduced in 12 states to abolish the death penalty.

Professor James Liebman of Columbia Law School conducted an initial study that showed a 68 percent error rate in capital sentencing.[64] In a follow-up to this

---

with these sentencing alternatives, see http://www.deathpenaltyinfo.org/article.php?did=555&scid=55/.

58. Stephen B. Bright, The American Bar Association's Recognition of the Sacrifice of Fairness for Results: Will We Pay the Price for Justice? 4 Geo. J. on Fighting Poverty 183 (1996).

59. Id. at 187.

60. Many municipalities have passed bills declaring that a moratorium be recognized in their state. Maryland began a moratorium to study their system, which was recently lifted by a new governor after the study revealed income and racial disparities. North Carolina is trying to pass legislation granting a moratorium. Other states, including Nebraska, Arizona, Indiana, Texas, Pennsylvania, and Kansas, have been studying their death penalty systems with the aim of reform.

61. See Death Row USA, supra note 1; King, supra note 39.

62. Don Babwin, Death Row Move in Ill. Praised by N.H. Official, Union Leader (Manchester, N.H.) Jan. 12, 2003.

63. Catherine Cowan, States Revisit the Death Penalty; Statistical Data Included, State Govt. News, May 1, 2001.

64. James S. Liebman et al., A Broken System: Error Rates in Capital Cases, 1973-1995 i, 4-5 (2000), available at http://justice.policy.net/proactive/newsroom/release.vtml?id=18200.

study, he looked at rates in 2002, which showed error rates that were higher than the national average in states that most frequently use the death penalty, states that have a larger proportion of African Americans in the population.[65] In the past 30 years, 108 death row inmates in 25 states have been released after presenting evidence of their innocence.[66]

Other inmates have had their sentences commuted to life imprisonment or have been released from their death sentences, pleading to a lesser charge. Some advocates have heralded advances in DNA evidence used to exonerate death row inmates and view this technology as a significant factor in changing public opinion about the death penalty.[67] Media and film portrayals of death row, such as Dead Man Walking, The Green Mile, and Monster's Ball, have conveyed real stories about wrongful convictions or raised awareness about the realities of death row.[68]

There are additional signs that evidence about the death penalty's ineffectiveness is affecting public opinion. Jurors who have self-defined prior to selection as "strongly favoring the death penalty" have spared the life of the accused.[69] Death sentences have dropped from 319 in 1996 to 155 in 2001.[70] A recent study showed that in 15 of the past 16 federal capital trials, jurors chose life sentences over death.[71] Changes to the penalty phase allowing defense attorneys to present a range of mitigating factors have been cited as a tremendously influential stage in a juror's decision.[72]

In a law review article, Professor Charles Ogletree examines the racially disproportionate application of the death penalty.[73] Professor Ogletree views capital punishment as a continuation of the extralegal practice of lynching. He notes that "the southern states that together account for over 90% of all executions carried out since 1976 . . . overlap considerably with the southern states that had the highest incidence of extra-legal violence and killings during the Jim Crow era."[74] In addition, he points to ways in which both lynching and the death penalty are discriminatory practices that further racial subordination. Finally, Ogletree concludes:

> The only difference between lynching and capital punishment is the gloss of legality and procedural regularity that the latter enjoys. In this regard, application of the death

---

65. See James S. Liebman et al., A Broken System, Part II: Why There Is So Much Error in Capital Cases, and What Can Be Done About It ii-iii (2002), available at http://justice.policy.net/proactive/newsroom/release.vtml?id=26641.

66. See Death Penalty Information website for a list of those exonerated from death row, available at http://www.deathpenaltyinfo.org/article.php?scid=6&did=110.

67. See Ronald Tabak, Finality Without Fairness: Why We Are Moving Towards Moratoria on Executions, and the Potential Abolition of Capital Punishment, 33 Conn. L. Rev. 733 (2001).

68. Austin Sarat, When the State Kills: Capital Punishment and the American Condition (2001).

69. Alex Kotlowitz, In the Face of Death, N.Y. Times, July 6, 2003.

70. Id.

71. Id.

72. Id.

73. Charles Ogletree, Black Man's Burden: Race and the Death Penalty in America, 81 Or. L. Rev. 15 (2003).

74. Id. at 15.

penalty may be fairer than the vigilante justice that characterized the Jim Crow era, but not by much.[75]

He criticizes the strategy of abolitionists who focus on the flaws in the system and advocate for moratoriums and nationwide death penalty reform, which will be used only to strengthen the system.[76] For example, DNA evidence is currently used to show that innocent individuals have been convicted. If DNA technology is used in all capital trials to confirm identity, this evidence actually strengthens support for the death penalty and destroys the constitutional objection to the death penalty on the grounds that we may kill an innocent person. Ogletree questions: "Are we just chasing these problems down one hole, only to have them reappear, just as virulent and pernicious, from another?"[77] He urges abolitionists to fight for the end to the death penalty by showing that no matter how much we try to reform the system, it cannot be fixed.

The next section reviews the two major Supreme Court cases dealing with racial bias in application of the death penalty and highlights recent cases that may indicate a chipping away at the constitutionality of the death penalty.

§5.12.3   Death Penalty: *Furman* and *McCleskey*

The Supreme Court first visited the issue of racial discrimination in the administration of the death penalty, if only indirectly, in Furman v. Georgia.[78] *Furman*, which consolidated the appeals of three black defendants sentenced to death, involved a challenge to capital punishment in cases of murder and rape on the grounds that application of the death penalty in these cases constitutes cruel and unusual punishment in violation of the Eighth and Fourteenth Amendments. The crux of the defendants' claim was that other defendants who committed equally or more serious crimes were not sentenced to death. Implicit in their argument was the assertion that the arbitrariness related, at least in part, to race.

Splitting five votes to four and with six different opinions, the Court reversed the death penalties in the cases before it. In their precedent-setting opinions, Justices White, Stewart, and Douglas offered the most narrow and least race-conscious basis for relief of all of the opinions. The three argued that the statutes under which the defendants had been sentenced violated due process because they provided no standard for decision-making, leaving to "the uncontrolled discretion of judges or juries the determination of whether defendants committing these crimes should die or be imprisoned."

---

75. Id. at 23. Ogletree states that many scholars and advocates use lynching as a reference point for understanding the underpinnings of our criminal justice system. In particular, he mentions that Jessie Jackson's book about the death penalty was entitled Legal Lynching and that "Professor Emma Coleman Jordan has hypothesized that 'lynching [is] a contemporary civic metaphor for the black experience within the American legal system.'"

76. Id. at 18. See Carol S. Steiker & Jordan M. Steiker, Sober Second Thoughts: Reflections on Two Decades of Constitutional Regulation of Capital Punishment, 109 Harv. L. Rev. 355 (1995).

77. Ogletree, supra note 73, at 38.

78. 408 U.S. 238 (1972).

While still a victory for the defendants, the plurality's opinion fell far short of the goal of eliminating, or even recognizing, the influence of racial prejudice in the imposition of the death penalty. The Justices identified the constitutional violation, but ignored its real harm: discrimination against racial minorities. Because the Court located the constitutional violation in the process itself (whether or not too much discretion inhered in the system) rather than the evil against which the process is intended to guard (the exercise of racial prejudice), the Court committed itself to accepting facially valid procedures without concerning itself with the underlying problem of racism.

Justice Douglas, in his concurring opinion, elaborated an interpretation of the Eighth Amendment colored by equal protection jurisprudence. Influenced by a clearly optimistic view of human nature and social progress, he argued that our conceptions of what is cruel and unusual expands and evolves as society becomes more enlightened. Today, imposition of the death penalty is cruel and unusual if imposed for reasons of "race, religion, wealth, social position, or class, or . . . under a procedure that gives room for the play of such prejudices." Drawing on the common law roots of the Eighth Amendment, Justice Douglas reasoned that the proscription against cruel and unusual punishment applies not only to excessive punishment, but also to the "selective and irregular" imposition of criminal sanctions:

> Those who wrote the Eighth Amendment knew what price their forbears had paid for a system based, not on equal justice, but on discrimination. In those days the target was not the blacks or the poor, but the dissenters, those who opposed absolutism in government, who struggled for a parliamentary regime, and who opposed governments' recurring efforts to foist a particular religion on the people. [Citations omitted.] But the tool of capital punishment was used with vengeance against the opposition and those unpopular with the regime. One cannot read this history without realizing that the desire for equality was reflected in the ban against "cruel and unusual punishments" contained in the Eighth Amendment.[79]

Suspicious that "the death sentence is disproportionately imposed and carried out on the poor, the Negro, and the members of unpopular groups," Justice Douglas argued that the capital statutes under which the defendants were sentenced violate the basic purpose of the Eighth Amendment.[80]

---

79. 408 U.S. at 245.

80. Id. at 249-250. Justice Douglas borrowed this language from a report of the President's Commission on Law Enforcement and the Administration of Justice, which concluded that significant racial discrimination exists in the application of the death sentence. Id. (citing The Challenge of Crime in a Free Society 143 (1967)). For other authorities relied upon by Justice Douglas, see id. at 250-251 and nn.14-17. For decades, commentators had reported evidence of racial disparities in the imposition and administration of the death penalty. These reports are summarized in Comment — Too Much Justice: A Legislative Response to McCleskey v. Kemp, 24 Harv. C.R.-C.L. Rev. 437, 448 & nn.47-48 (1989).

It is also interesting to note that Justice Douglas, advocating a view now disfavored by almost every member of the Court, hinted that the death penalty might also be unconstitutional because it discriminates against the poor. Persons with financial resources, able "to purchase the services of the most respected and most resourceful legal talent in the Nation," are never sentenced to death, while persons who are unable to afford counsel must face the vagaries of their draw. 408 U.S. at 255-256.

Justice Marshall went farther than any of the other Justices, making a strong case that the death penalty is, in all circumstances, cruel and unusual punishment. After reviewing each of the rationales for the death penalty and finding each to come up short, he concluded:

> The point has now been reached at which deference to the legislatures is tantamount to abdication of our judicial roles as fact finders, judges, and ultimate arbiters of the Constitution. We know that at some point the presumption of constitutionality accorded legislative acts gives way to a realistic assessment of those acts. This point comes when there is sufficient evidence available so that judges can determine, not whether the legislature acted wisely, but whether it had any rational basis whatsoever for acting. We have this evidence before us now. There is no rational basis for concluding that capital punishment is not excessive.[81]

Because there is no reasoned basis for imposing the sentence of death, Justice Marshall concluded that capital punishment must offend the morality of an informed citizenry. The fact that capital punishment is discriminatorily imposed against the poor and minorities, Justice Marshall believed, would be sufficient to sway the still unconverted. He asserted, perhaps too optimistically: "If [Justice Powell] is opining that it is only the poor, the ignorant, the racial minorities, and the hapless in our society who are executed; that they are executed for no real reason other than to satisfy some vague notion of society's cry for vengeance; and that, knowing these things, the people of this country would not care, then I most urgently disagree."

Connecting the standard of cruel and unusual punishment to social standards was, to a degree, dangerous. For what seemed cruel and unusual to the Supreme Court in 1972, no longer struck it as impermissible in 1987.[82] In the Court's most significant and lamentable decision on the death penalty in recent years, McCleskey v. Kemp,[83] the Justices upheld the death sentence imposed on a black man despite

---

This favoring of social classes, he continued, is as offensive to the Eighth Amendment as discrimination on the basis of race or ideology. "A law that stated that anyone making more than $50,000 would be exempt from the death penalty would plainly fall, as would a law that in terms said that blacks, those who never went beyond the fifth grade in school, those who made less than $3,000 a year, or those who were unpopular or unstable should be the only people executed. A law which in overall view reaches that same result in practice has no more sanctity than a law which in terms provides the same." Id. at 256.

81. Id. at 355.

82. *Furman* caused a temporary hiatus in executions while states redrafted their death penalty statutes to meet the Supreme Court's mandate. Four years later, in Gregg v. Georgia, 428 U.S. 153 (1976), the Supreme Court approved Georgia's capital punishment statute, which provided for bifurcated guilt and sentencing phases, required findings of aggravating and mitigating factors, and thereby cleared the way for renewed death penalty activity. Without any basis in fact or in common sense, the Court reasoned that allowing juries to consider the character of the defendant through mitigating evidence would allow juries to tailor the sentence to the defendant and exercise mercy where appropriate. 428 U.S. at 197.

Subsequently, in Coker v. Georgia, 433 U.S. 584 (1977), the Court placed additional limits on capital sentencing schemes. In *Coker*, the Court held that death was an excessive penalty for the crime of rape. Although the court never addressed the disproportionate manner in which the death penalty had been applied against black men charged with rape, black offenders were executed eight times more frequently than whites charged with the same crime. William Bowers, Executions in America 74 (1974).

83. 481 U.S. 279 (1987).

clear evidence of racial disparity in the imposition of the death penalty in the defendant's home state of Georgia. Faced squarely with convincing proof of racism in the criminal justice system, the Court was finally confronted with the question of whether it was willing to give official approval to the racial bias which it had unofficially countenanced for years.[84] The Court's answer was unequivocal: It would allow defendants to be sentenced to death for reasons clearly related to race.

Warren McCleskey, a black man, was convicted in 1978 of murdering a white police officer. The jury of eleven whites and one black sentenced McCleskey to die. After his state appeals were exhausted, McCleskey filed a petition for federal habeas corpus, arguing that his sentence was the product of racial discrimination and therefore violated the Eighth and Fourteenth Amendments. To support his claim, McCleskey produced the most complete and unequivocal statistical study of racial discrimination in the death penalty ever compiled.[85]

Writing for the court, Justice Powell found that McCleskey's statistical evidence did not establish a prima facie claim under the due process or equal protection clause or under the Eighth Amendment. Because McCleskey was sentenced under a constitutionally valid post-*Furman* statute that was not enacted "to further a racially discriminatory purpose," the Court refused to infer that the sentence was the intentional product of racial prejudice. Statistical evidence showing a significant racial disparity in the imposition of the death penalty in Georgia, the Court reasoned, was insufficient to "demonstrate a constitutionally significant risk of racial bias." The Court admitted that "there is, of course, some risk of racial prejudice influencing a jury's decision in a criminal case," but found that the level of risk made out by the Baldus study was not "unacceptable."

The Court developed an exacting and seemingly insurmountable standard for proving a constitutional violation in cases such as McCleskey's. Statistical evidence of discrimination alone is not enough to establish that the equal protection rights of a capital defendant have been violated. Justice Powell wrote, "Where the

---

84. The court framed the issue quite bluntly: "This case presents the question whether a complex statistical study that indicates a risk that racial considerations enter into capital sentencing determinations proves that petitioner McCleskey's capital sentence is unconstitutional under the Eighth or Fourteenth Amendment." Id. at 282.

85. In support of his claim, McCleskey proffered a sophisticated statistical study by Professor David Baldus (the "Baldus study"), which showed a disparity in the imposition of the death sentence in Georgia based on the race of the murder victim and, to a lesser extent, the race of the defendant. The Baldus study indicates that black defendants who kill white victims have the greatest likelihood of receiving the death penalty. From his review of over 2,000 cases, Professor Baldus gathered data which showed that the death penalty was imposed in 22 percent of the cases involving black defendants and white victims, 8 percent of the cases involving white defendants and white victims, 3 percent of the cases involving white defendants and black victims, and only 1 percent of the cases involving black defendants and black victims. Id. at 286. Even after factoring in 39 nonracial variables, Professor Baldus found that defendants charged with killing white victims were still 4.3 times as likely to receive a death sentence as defendants charged with killing blacks. Id. at 287. Moreover, 60 percent of the defendants charged with crimes similar to McCleskey's would not have been sentenced to death had their victims been black. Id. at 1784 n.2 (Brennan, J., dissenting).

Since *McCleskey*, evidence of racial discrimination in the application of the death penalty on a nationwide basis has continued to mount. See U.S. General Accounting Office, Death Penalty Sentencing (1990) (finding that the fact that the victim is white influences the likelihood that the defendant will be charged with a capital crime or that the death penalty will be imposed in 82 percent of the 28 studies reviewed).

discretion that is fundamental to our criminal justice system is involved, we decline to assume that what is unexplained is invidious."[86] The defendant must produce the illusive "smoking gun": evidence that the decision-makers in his or her particular case were motivated by racial prejudice. Arguing that the complexity of the criminal process makes it unfair to force the state to defend against claims of discrimination, the Court saw no injustice in requiring the defendant to pinpoint the specific source of the discriminatory effect or die trying.

Obvious in the majority opinion is the fear that acceptance of such statistical proof would, like dominoes, tip not only Georgia's capital system but, indeed, much of this nation's criminal (and even civil) process. Justice Powell wrote that McCleskey's claim will open the floodgates to claims of any arbitrary influence "such as the defendant's facial characteristics, or the physical attractiveness of the defendant or the victim, that some statistical study indicates may be influential in jury decision-making." If arbitrariness or irrationality is the test of the constitutionality of a sentence, the Court reasoned, each of these factors must be screened from decision-making. Faced with the impossible task of making itself even-handed, the criminal justice system would no longer be able to function.

Justice Brennan wrote a strongly worded and eloquent dissent, which Justices Marshall, Blackmun, and Stevens joined. Justice Brennan lamented the callousness of a justice system that would acquiesce in systemic racial discrimination and impose the irreversible sanction of death despite overwhelming evidence that the sanction arises not from a credible determination of guilt but from prejudice. He condemned as illegitimate a process in which race plays a significant, or even predominant, role:[87]

> At some point in [his] case, Warren McCleskey doubtless asked his lawyer whether a jury was likely to sentence him to die. A candid reply to this question would have been disturbing. First, counsel would have to tell McCleskey that few of the details of the crime or of McCleskey's past criminal conduct were more important than the fact that his victim was white. Furthermore, counsel would feel bound to tell McCleskey that defendants charged with killing white victims in Georgia are 4.3 times as likely to be sentenced to death as defendants charged with killing blacks. . . . The story could be told in a variety of ways, but McCleskey could not fail to grasp its essential narrative line: there was significant chance that race would play a prominent role in determining if he lived or died.[88]

86. 481 U.S. at 313. Contrast Justice Powell's statement in *McCleskey* with the Court's opinion just 15 years earlier in *Furman* where Justice Douglas wrote in his concurring opinion, "We cannot say from facts disclosed in these records that these defendants were sentenced to death because they were black. Yet our task is not restricted to an effort to divine what motives impelled these death penalties. Rather, we deal with a system of law and justice that leaves to the uncontrolled discretion of judges or juries the determination whether defendants committing these crimes should die or be imprisoned." 408 U.S. at 253. See also Castaneda v. Partida, 430 U.S. 482, 494 n.13 (1977) (where the Court wrote, in the context of a jury discrimination case: "If a disparity is sufficiently large, then it is unlikely that it is due solely to chance or accident and, in the absence of evidence to the contrary, one must conclude that racial or other class-related factors entered into the selection process.").

87. The Baldus study showed that the race of the victim is more important in explaining the imposition of a death sentence than whether the defendant was a prime mover in the homicide or whether the defendant had a prior conviction for a capital crime.

88. 481 U.S. at 321.

Justice Brennan chastised the Court for its willingness to close its eyes to claims of racial discrimination. By considering the validity of Georgia's capital sentencing statute in only abstract terms, and ignoring the manner in which it is actually applied, the Court ignores the statute's true meaning. Where evidence shows "that there is a better than even chance in Georgia that race will influence the decision to impose the death penalty," it is disingenuous for the Court to base its denial of relief on the existence of procedures which obviously have not worked. The theoretical merit of statutory safeguards is insufficient where that theory fails in practice.

Finally, the dissent condemned Justice Powell for being afraid of "too much justice." Justice Brennan wrote that "[t]he prospect that there may be more widespread abuse than McCleskey documents may be dismaying, but it does not justify complete abdication of our judicial role." He went on to distinguish discrimination based on hair color or beauty, two of the parade of horribles conjured by the majority, from the racial discrimination of which McCleskey complained:

> Race is a consideration whose influence is expressly constitutionally proscribed. We have expressed a moral commitment, as embodied in our fundamental law, that this specific characteristic should not be the basis for allotting burdens and benefits. Three constitutional amendments, and numerous statutes, have been prompted specifically by the desire to address the effects of racism. . . .
>
> Certainly, a factor that we would regard as morally irrelevant, such as hair color, at least theoretically could be associated with sentencing results to such an extent that we would regard as arbitrary a system in which that factor played a significant role. As I have said above, however, the evaluation of evidence suggesting such a correlation must be informed not merely by statistics, but by history and experience. One could hardly contend that this nation has on the basis of hair color inflicted upon persons deprivation comparable to that imposed on the basis of race.[89]

Justice Brennan concluded by warning the Court that racial discrimination cannot yet be relegated to history, to be safely ignored by the Court:

> At the time our Constitution was framed 200 years ago this year, blacks "had for more than a century before been regarded as beings of an inferior order, and altogether unfit to associate with the white race, either in social or political relations; and so far inferior, that they had no rights which the white man was bound to respect." Dred Scott v. Sandford, 19 How. 393, 407 (1857). Only 130 years ago, this Court relied on these observations to deny American citizenship to blacks. Ibid. A mere three generations ago, this Court sanctioned racial segregation, stating that "[i]f one race be inferior to the other socially, the Constitution of the United States cannot put them upon the same plane." Plessy v. Ferguson, 163 U.S. 537, 552 (1896).
>
> In more recent times, we have sought to free ourselves from the burden of this history. Yet it has been scarcely a generation since this Court's first decision striking down racial segregation, and barely two decades since the legislative prohibition of racial discrimination in major domains of national life. These have been honorable steps, but we cannot pretend that in three decades we have completely escaped the grip of an historical legacy spanning centuries. Warren McCleskey's evidence confronts us with the subtle and persistent influence of the past. His message is a disturbing one

89. Id. at 340-341.

to a society that has formally repudiated racism, and a frustrating one to a Nation accustomed to regarding its destiny as the product of its own will. Nonetheless, we ignore him at our peril, for we remain imprisoned by the past as long as we deny its influence in the present.

It is tempting to pretend that minorities on death row share a fate in no way connected to our own, that our treatment of them sounds no echoes beyond the chambers in which they die. Such an illusion is ultimately corrosive, for the reverberations of injustice are not so easily confined. "The destinies of the two races in the country are indissolubly linked together" . . . and the way in which we choose those who will die reveals the depth of moral commitment among the living.[90]

Despite the outcry that the *McCleskey* outcome triggered, the Court's decision is neither surprising nor a departure from the Supreme Court's race jurisprudence. At the doctrinal level, the decision is consistent with the Court's distrust of statistical evidence and its insistence on direct evidence of purposeful discrimination.[91] *McCleskey* makes clear the Court's unwillingness to accept less than direct proof of discrimination, which renders it incapable of recognizing, let alone remedying, the more subtle forms of racism that characterize contemporary institutions.[92] As Professor Charles Lawrence has written:

> [R]equiring proof of conscious or intentional motivation as a prerequisite to constitutional recognition that a decision is race-dependent ignores much of what we understand about how the human mind works. It also disregards both the irrationality of racism and the profound effect that the history of American race relations has had on the individual and collective unconsciousness.[93]

The Court's failure to recognize the pervasive influence of often unspoken racism is a failure to deliver upon the promise of equal protection for black persons in our system of justice.[94] For to require the defendant to produce concrete evidence of discrimination, in effect, is to hold that defendants may almost never prevail in race discrimination cases. If, as the Court argues, the complexities of the justice system make it too onerous for the state to defend itself, it is inconceivable that defendants, without access to the government's operations, its records, or its witnesses, will ever be able to prove in court what we all know happens in practice.

The Court's "see no evil" approach deprives it of any credibility as a vehicle for achieving racial justice in our society. *McCleskey* places in stark relief the Justices' willingness to tolerate racial discrimination in the imposition of the most severe penalty created by law. It is significant that the *McCleskey* majority never disputed the Baldus study and never denied the influence of race in capital sentencing in Georgia. Instead, it accepted the discrimination as a regrettable cost of doing law enforcement's business. When push comes to shove, the Court would

90. Id. at 343-344.
91. See, e.g., Washington v. Davis, 426 U.S. 229 (1976).
92. See Charles Lawrence, The Id, the Ego and Equal Protection: Reckoning with Unconscious Racism, 39 Stan. L. Rev. 317 (1987).
93. Id. at 322-323.
94. See Developments, Race and the Criminal Process, 101 Harv. L. Rev. 1472, 1476 (1988).

rather countenance discrimination against black defendants than risk impairing the efficiency of the present system.[95]

In *McCleskey*, for perhaps the first time, the Supreme Court was forced to acknowledge its commitment to maintaining the status quo and its willingness to engage in utilitarian balancing, rather than positivist reasoning, to arrive at its decisions. The Court's focus on the costs of reckoning with racial injustice makes clear its tendency to reason backwards from the cost of a remedy to the existence of a constitutional right. Only if the Court is willing to tolerate the price of racial equality will it recognize a constitutional mandate for that equality. As Professor Randall Kennedy notes, "Apprehensions over perceived remedial costs have prompted the Court increasingly to narrow the definition of violations. The Justices have made the violations they are willing to recognize dependent upon the remedies they are willing to provide. . . . Unpersuaded in *McCleskey* that an acceptable solution could be found, the Court obviated the remedial question simply by declining to find a constitutional problem."[96]

After denying McCleskey's claims, Justice Powell suggested that McCleskey make his case before Congress and state legislatures which (unlike the Court) are "constituted to respond to the will and consequently the moral values of the people."[97] Unfortunately and despite widespread public dismay with the Court's decision,[98] Congress was no more suited to this task than the Supreme Court.

Within months of the *McCleskey* decision, Congress began fashioning the Racial Justice Act, which was designed to ameliorate the harsh disparities that *McCleskey* had proven.[99] The Act would require Courts to strike down any death sentence where the defendant made an unrebutted statistical showing of racial imbalances in the administration of the capital system in the sentencing jurisdiction. Specifically responding to the Court's holding, the Act would eliminate the requirement that defendants show discriminatory motive or purpose in their particular case. After the defendant offered a prima facie case of discrimination, the burden would shift to the state to rebut the inference that racial discrimination played a role in the defendant's sentence.

The Racial Justice Act was defeated in Congress in short order.[100] Its fate bears out the words of Justice Marshall, concurring in *Furman*:

It is the poor, and the members of minority groups who are least able to voice their complaints against capital punishment. Their impotence leaves them victims of a

95. See Randall Kennedy, McCleskey v. Kemp: Race, Capital Punishment, and the Supreme Court, 101 Harv. L. Rev. 1388, 1403, 1408 (1988).

96. Id. at 1414-1415.

97. 481 U.S. at 315. Ironically, Justice Powell takes this quotation from Furman v. Georgia, 408 U.S. 238, 383 (1972).

98. See Kennedy, supra note 95, at 1389-1390 and nn.6-11 (1988), for other critiques of the Court's decision in *McCleskey*.

99. H.R. 4442, 100th Cong., 2d Sess., 134 Cong. Rec. E1175 (daily ed. Apr. 21, 1988) (House version); 134 Cong. Rec. S15,748 (daily ed. Oct. 13, 1988) (Senate version).

100. While the House of Representatives approved its version of the Racial Justice Act, 134 Cong. Rec. H11108 (daily ed. Oct. 21, 1988), the same provision was stricken from its Senate counterpart, 137 Cong. Rec. S8281 (daily ed. Oct. 27, 1990). The final crime bill was adopted without

sanction that the wealthier, better-represented, just-as-guilty person can escape. So long as the capital sanction is used only against the forlorn, easily forgotten members of society, legislators are content to maintain the status quo, because change would draw attention to the problem and concern might develop. Ignorance is perpetuated and apathy soon becomes its mate, and we have today's situation.[101]

As an example of state legislative action responding to *McCleskey*, Kentucky passed its own version of the Racial Justice Act in 1985.[102] The Act allows defendants to challenge the state's death penalty as unconstitutional using statistical analysis showing racial bias given the disproportionate number of minorities facing death penalty prosecutions. Recently, North Carolina began to push a Racial Justice Act through the state legislature.[103] According to Rev. William Baber, the president of North Carolina's NAACP Chapter, "This is not about emotion. This is about empirical data. Empirical data tells us we have some serious issues."[104] Although only 22 percent of the 8.7 million people in North Carolina are black, currently 53 percent of the 185 people on death row are black.[105] Not surprisingly, though, death penalty states have not followed suit implicitly agreeing with the *McCleskey* decision.

The story told by Warren McCleskey is neither new nor is it yet old. Discriminatory imposition of criminal sanctions upon blacks extends from the earliest days of slavery, when Slave Codes created a separate and more severe set of crimes and punishments for slaves. Although events of the day mandated a change in the statutes' labels, Black Codes perpetuated the same dual system of punishment of the Slave Codes in the years after Reconstruction.[106] Even with the formal

---

the Racial Justice Act. 137 Cong. Rec. S9809 (daily ed. July 11, 1990); 136 Cong. Rec. H13288 (daily ed. July 11, 1990).

In failing to approve the legislation, Congress deferred to the same fears that motivated the Supreme Court's opinion in *McCleskey*. More than one member of Congress expressed concern that a requirement of racial proportionality would effectively halt executions in the United States. Critics characterized the bill as a back-door abolitionist measure and, with the buzzwords of the day, condemned it as an affirmative action measure for convicted killers. Reflecting the tone of the Congressional debate, U.S. Attorney General Richard Thornburgh dismissed the Racial Justice Act as having "very little, if anything to do with racial justice and a great deal to do with wiping out the death penalty through some kind of bizarre death by quota provision that would require courts and prosecutors to match prearranged numbers in order to validate death penalties." Remarks of Bob Martinez, Director, Office of National Drug Control Policy, and U.S. Attorney General Richard Thornburgh to Law Enforcement Officials, Federal News Services, June 18, 1991.

101. Furman v. Georgia, 408 U.S. 238, 366 (1972).

102. North Carolina Could Become Second State to Pass the Racial Justice Act. http://death-penaltyinfo.org/article.php?did=2323

103. Id.

104. Id.

105. Id.

106. The treatment of blacks by the criminal justice system has been well-documented. The statutory system formally mandated the regime that McCleskey complained had arisen in practice: A system in which the legal outcome depended upon the race of the defendant and the victim. See A. Leon Higgenbotham, In the Matter of Color: Race and the American Legal Process: The Colonial Period (1978); Eugene Genovese, Roll, Jordan, Roll: The World the Slaves Made (1972); Kenneth Stampp, Chattels Personal, in Slavery in America 90-96 (1976). Disparities in the enforcement of the criminal laws were nowhere more pronounced than in sex-related crimes. Blacks convicted of raping white women were required by law to be castrated or killed. White men convicted of raping white women, however, could expect much less severe punishments. The rape of black women was not even recognized as a crime. See Bell Hooks, Ain't I a Woman 33-36 (1981).

abolition of racial distinctions in the criminal law, courts did little to ensure that black defendants and victims received the same protections as whites.[107] Instead, the rights of black persons were effectively nullified by the prejudices of judges, prosecutors, and juries, and the summary justice meted out by lynch mobs determined to pick up where the official system left off.

McCleskey falls squarely in line with this history in its devaluation of the lives of both black defendants and black victims. One of the most disturbing facets of the Baldus study was its conclusive evidence that those accused of killing blacks are least likely to receive the death penalty.[108] The pattern of punishment in Georgia and the Supreme Court's willingness to tolerate a risk of discrimination it would never accept with whites or the wealthy is proof of what many have long claimed: The black community is not equally protected or valued by the criminal justice system.[109] McCleskey's statistics and the judiciary's nonresponse to these statistics make clear that in the "marketplace of emotion the lives of blacks simply count for less than the lives of whites."[110]

A number of recent Supreme Court cases, however, have signaled a shift in the Court's death penalty jurisprudence. Although advocates are hopeful about the Court's new precedent, it remains unclear whether the Court aims to simply eliminate unjust convictions and procedural problems or, more fundamentally, to question the constitutionality of the death penalty and ultimately overturn *Furman*.

In 2002, the Supreme Court held that executions of mentally retarded criminals were "cruel and unusual punishment" prohibited by the Eighth Amendment.[111] The majority explained that forms of punishment are not fixed but change according to "evolving standards of decency that mark the progress of a maturing society." Thirteen years prior, in Penry v. Lynaugh, the Court upheld executions of the mentally retarded. Justice O'Connor in *Penry* explained that there was no national consensus against the practice. Since then, 18 death penalty states and 35 states in total currently bar executions of the mentally retarded.[112] Justice Stevens explained that this opinion was informed by a new consensus of the American public, legislators, scholars, and judges about executing the mentally retarded.

The Supreme Court continued to chip away at its pro-death penalty stance on the constitutionality of executing juveniles. Since 1976, 22 juveniles have been

---

107. See generally Daniel J. Flanigan. The Criminal Law of Slavery and Freedom, 1800-1868, 271-276 (1987); Developments, Race and the Criminal Process, 101 Harv. L. Rev. 1472, 1483-1486 (1988).

108. The Baldus study revealed that defendants accused of killing whites were 4.3 times as likely to be sentenced to death than defendants charged with killing blacks, making the race of the victim almost as influential a factor as whether the defendant had been previously convicted of murder. Moreover, fully 95 percent of the defendants on death row were convicted of killing whites, even though blacks are six times more likely than whites to be murdered. The Court Tunes Out, L.A. Times, Apr. 23, 1987, at 4, §2.

109. See, e.g., Stephen Carter, When Victims Happen to Be Black, 97 Yale L.J. 420 (1988); Kennedy, supra note 95, at 1421-1422.

110. Kennedy, supra note 95, at 1441. An array of studies of the role of the race of the victim on the outcome of a criminal case points to the same conclusion. For citations, see id. at 1396 n.27.

111. Atkins v. Virginia, 536 U.S. 304 (2002).

112. See Aimee D. Borromeo, Comment, Mental Retardation and the Death Penalty, 3 Loy. J. Pub. Int. L. 175 (2002).

executed.[113] In 1989, the U.S. Supreme Court held that the imposition of capital punishment on juveniles who were 16 or 17 years old at the time of their crime did not violate the Eighth Amendment.[114] In a 2005 decision, Roper v. Simmons, the Court overruled that decision appearing swayed by society's reconsideration of the death penalty.[115] Justice Kennedy writing for the majority states, "From a moral standpoint, it would be misguided to equate the failings of a minor with those of an adult, for a greater possibility exists that a minor's character deficiencies will be reformed."[116] The largest impact will be felt by Texas and Alabama where 29 and 14 juveniles, respectively, sit on death row.[117] In Roper and Atkins, the Court overruled 1989 precedents based primarily on increases in the headcount of state legislatures barring death sentences for the two categories of offenders and decreases in the number of death sentences jurors had imposed on them since 1989.[118]

Prior to the Court's decision in Miller-El v. Dretke, Professor Ogletree predicted that this case "could provide some much-needed clarity to the Supreme Court's jurisprudence on racial discrimination in jury selection and . . . could also provide one step toward reducing the disparities in sentencing rates of people of color sitting on death row."[119] In a critical decision, the Court with a 6-3 decision found that Miller-El, a Texas death row inmate, prevails on his Batson claim.[120] According to the Court in Miller-El v. Dretke, prosecutors intentionally used preemptory strikes to exclude 10 of 11 qualified black jury panelists.[121] In evaluating the race neutral justifications given by the state, the Court is unconvinced given that the black juror responses are virtually indistinguishable from the responses of white jurors who were selected. Delivering the opinion of the Court, Justice Souter concludes:

> If anything more is needed for an undeniable explanation of what was going on, history supplies it. The prosecutors took their cues from a 20-year old manual of tips on jury selection, as shown by their notes of the race of each potential juror. By the time a jury was chosen, the State had peremptorily challenged 12% of qualified nonblack panel members, but eliminated 91% of the black ones. . . . It blinks reality to deny that the State struck Fields and Warren, included in that 91%, because they were black.[122]

As described in §5.12.1, since 2000, the Supreme Court has placed legal assistance of capital defendants under intense scrutiny. In doing so, these cases

---

113. Death Penalty Information Center, http://www.deathpenaltyinfo.org/article.php?did=204&scid=27#streibstats/.

114. Stanford v. Kentucky, 492 U.S. 361 (1989)

115. Roper v. Simmons, 543 U.S. 551 (2005), See also Vivian Berger, Stop Executing Minors, Nat'l L. J., April 26, 2004.

116. Id.

117. Death Penalty Information Center, supra note 113.

118. 7 CLMLR 1, Slow Dancing With Death: The Supreme Court and Capital Punishment, 1963-2006 (January 2007).

119. Id. at 609 (citing Appendix v. New Jersey, 530 U.S. 466, 494 n.19 (2000)).

120. Miller-El v. Dretke, 545 U.S. 231 (2005).

121. Id.

122. Id.

have raised the bar for effective assistance of counsel in capital cases, especially during sentencing.

Since 1976, Supreme Court Justices have concluded that the Court incorrectly found that the death penalty presented no constitutional problems. Before stepping down from the Court, Justice Blackmun conceded the following in his dissenting opinion in Callins v. Collins:

> For more than 20 years I have endeavored — indeed, I have struggled — along with a majority of this Court, to develop procedural and substantive rules that would lend more than the mere appearance of fairness to the death penalty endeavor. Rather than continue to coddle the Court's delusion that the desired level of fairness has been achieved and the need for regulation eviscerated, I feel morally and intellectually obligated simply to concede that the death penalty experiment has failed.[123]

Echoing Blackmun's sentiment, Justice Powell, when asked by his biographer if he would change any decision he made on the Court, responded that there was only one: *McCleskey.*[124] Professor Ogletree calls on death penalty abolitionists to inspire others to have what he calls a "Blackmun Revelation" — to move from merely trying to tinker with a broken system to recognizing that capital punishment has failed. The more public opinion shifts and this change is reflected in legislative decisions to repeal the death penalty, the more likely that we will see a Supreme Court holding that a death sentence clearly violates "our evolving standards of decency."[125]

§5.12.4 Racially Disproportionate Penalties

The problem of discrimination does not begin or end in capital punishment.[126] Almost 1 in 4 black men between the ages of 20 and 30 are under the supervision of the criminal justice system on any given day. For white men in the same age group, the corresponding statistic is 1 in 16.[127] Black persons are more likely than whites to have been shot at by police, 18 times more likely to be wounded and 5 times more likely to be killed.[128] Prosecutors are more likely to pursue full prosecution, file more severe charges, and seek more stringent penalties in cases involving

123. 510 U.S. 1141 (1994). Blackmun dissented in the decision not to grant certiorari in this case.

124. Ogletree, supra note 73, at 31.

125. Id. at 37.

126. For a comprehensive discussion of the influence of racial prejudice in the criminal process, see Charles Ogletree, Does Race Matter in Criminal Prosecutions? Champion, July 1991, at 7; Developments in the Law — Race and the Criminal Process, 101 Harv. L. Rev. 1472 (1988).

127. The number of young black men under the control of the criminal justice system is greater than the total number of black men of all ages enrolled in college. Marc Mauer, Young Black Men and the Criminal Justice System: A Growing National Problem 3 (The Sentencing Project, Feb. 1990). Blacks comprise almost 50 percent of the prison population, but only 12 percent of the national population. Marc Mauer, Americans Behind Bars: A Comparison of International Rates of Incarceration (The Sentencing Project, Jan. 1989).

128. James Fyfe, Blind Justice: Police Shootings in Memphis, 73 J. Crim. Law & Criminology 707, 718-720 (1982). See also Edward J. Littlejohn, Deadly Force and Its Effect on Police-Community Relations, 27 How. L.J. 1131 (1984).

defendants of color, particularly where the victim is white.[129] Finally, minority offenders are also sentenced to prison more often and receive longer terms than whites convicted of similar crimes and with similar records.[130]

As of 2007, more than 60 percent of the people in prison are now racial and ethnic minorities.[131] For black males in their twenties, 1 in every 8 is in prison or jail on any given day.[132] Of the 2.2 million incarcerated individuals, 900,000 are black.[133] These trends have been intensified by the disproportionate impact of the "war on drugs," in which three-fourths of all persons in prison for drug offenses are people of color.[134]

People of color are also stopped and frisked by police in alarmingly disproportionate numbers.[135] In the two decades since Terry v. Ohio,[136] the power to stop and frisk has been made a powerful tool for harassing and monitoring citizens — particularly black and Latino citizens. In *Terry*, the Supreme Court acquiesced in the possibility of disproportionate intervention as a cost of doing law enforcement's business.[137] Today, it is clear that many police officers, as well as judges, believe that race or poverty are sufficient reasons to detain and search people of color.[138] While the biases that influence an officer's decision to detain a suspect often are unannounced or even subconscious, they occasionally rise to the level of official policy. A sheriff in Louisiana, for instance, reported that all black persons in white neighborhoods would be stopped on sight.[139] Similarly, the Florida

129. Race and the Criminal Process, supra note 112, at 1525-1532 (citing a number of studies that found discrimination in the exercise of prosecutorial discretion); Michael Radelet & Glenn Pierce, Race and Prosecutorial Discretion in Homicide Cases, 19 L. & Soc'y Rev. 587, 615-619 (1985).

130. Joan Petersilia, Racial Disparities in the Criminal Justice System ix (1983); Zimmerman & Frederick, Discrimination in the Decision to Incarcerate, in The Criminal Justice System and Blacks 315, 326 (David Georges-Abeyle ed., 1984). While the arrest ratio of blacks to whites is roughly 3.6 to 1 for serious felonies and 2 to 1 to other crimes, the prison differential is 7 to 1. Arral Morris, Race and Crime: What Evidence Is There That Race Influences Results in the Criminal Justice System?, 72 Judicature 111, 112 (1988). These figures evidence the fact that black offenders are much more likely to be sentenced to jail terms than white offenders.

131. Marc Mauer & Ryan S. King, Uneven Justice: State Rates of Incarceration by Race and Ethnicity, The Sentencing Project, July 2007. Located at www.sentencingproject.org.

132. Id.

133. Id.

134. Id.

135. See Sheri Lynn Johnson, Race and the Decision to Detain a Suspect, 93 Yale L.J. 214 (1983); R. L. McNeely & Carl E. Pope, Race, Crime and Criminal Justice: An Overview, in Race, Crime and Criminal Justice 13-14 (R. L. McNeely & Carl E. Pope eds., 1981).

136. 392 U.S. 1 (1968).

137. Writing for the Court, Chief Justice Warren expressly acknowledged that stops "are a major source of friction between the police and minority groups," particularly "in situations where the 'stop and frisk' of youths or minority group members is motivated by the officers' perceived need to maintain the power image of the beat officer, an aim sometimes accomplished by humiliating anyone who attempts to undermine police control of the streets." Id. at 15 (citing President's Commission on Law Enforcement and Justice, Task Force Report 183 (1967)).

138. Johnson, supra note 135, at 236; Ogletree, supra note 126, at 10-12; Developments in the Law — Race and the Criminal Process, supra note 107, at 1494-1496.

139. J. Michael Kennedy, Sheriff Rescinds Order to Stop Blacks in White Areas, L.A. Times, Dec. 4, 1986, at 1. See also Kolender v. Lawson, 461 U.S. 352 (1983) (discussing the case of a Rastafarian man who was stopped 15 times for taking evening walks in a white neighborhood); State v. Dean, 112 Ariz. 437, 439, 543 P.2d 426, 427 (1975) (where the detaining officer testified: "you know, when we first observed him we could tell that something wasn't correct. He just didn't look, I mean — he was a Mexican male in a predominantly white neighborhood of — oh, middle- to

Highway Patrol relied for some time upon a profile that advised officers to be alert for drivers who "did not fit the vehicle" or who were apparently members of "ethnic groups associated with the drug trade"[140] — meaning black or Latino persons in expensive cars. And in exhibitions of police authority which could only be aimed at humiliating black persons, police officers in Boston stopped and publicly strip-searched residents of a predominantly black neighborhood until public attention and the threat of a class action lawsuit marked the end of this practice.[141]

Like police officers, prosecutors often make decisions that discriminate against African Americans. Meanwhile, because they do not become involved until after an arrest has been made, prosecutors have vast unchecked discretion with which they often profoundly affect the degree of racial equality exhibited in the criminal justice system. So, perhaps it is not surprising that this prosecutorial discretion often becomes a major cause of racial inequality.

Professor Angela J. Davis examines prosecutorial discretion at length in her essay "Prosecution and Race: The Power and Privilege of Discretion."[142] In this work, Davis explains that "through the exercise of prosecutorial discretion, prosecutors make decisions that not only often predetermine the outcome of criminal cases, but also contribute to the discriminatory treatment of African Americans as both criminal defendants and victims of crime."[143] She continues by saying that this discretion, which is usually exercised in private, "gives prosecutors more power than any other criminal justice officials, with practically no corresponding accountability to the public they serve."[144] Thus, Davis maintains, prosecutors "through their overall duty to pursue justice, have the responsibility to use their

---

upper-middle class people."). One police officer candidly admitted that he stops "anyone you see who you wouldn't want your wife, mother or daughter coming in contact with." Bob Woodward, Long Beach Task Force Told to Act within Law, L.A. Times, Oct. 1, 1987, at 1, col. 4.

Terry has the effect of exacerbating relations between the police and communities of color because the discriminatory manner in which it enforces affects entire communities vulnerable to being stopped seemingly at whim. Whenever a suspect is described as black, all blacks — whatever their physical resemblance to the suspect — become targets. Police officers' reliance on race makes entire groups of people or neighborhoods to police interrogation. This was the case in Philadelphia when over 300 black men were stopped or arrested during a police hunt for a rapist who was described as being black. Hentoff, Forgetting the Fourth Amendment in Philadelphia, Wash. Post, Apr. 16, 1988, at A25. See also Davis v. Mississippi, 394 U.S. 721 (1969) (finding unconstitutional the forced detention and fingerprinting of a black man picked up in the course of a dragnet to locate a suspect described as black).

Similarly, whenever crime rates increase, the tendency to point the finger at people of color breeds increased suspicion of all blacks. In Boston, a police crackdown on a crime meant a police crackdown on black and Latino communities. The police department's policy of stopping youths of color, admittedly without cause, was called by one judge "a proclamation of martial law . . . for a narrow class of people, young blacks, suspected of membership in a gang. . . ." Commonwealth v. Phillips & Woody, No. 080275-6, Memorandum and Order, at 3 (Suffolk Sup. Ct., Sept. 7, 1989).

For a discussion of the discriminatory application of *Terry*, see Ogletree, supra note 126, at 12.

140. Developments in the Law — Race and the Criminal Process, supra note 107, at 1503.

141. See Peter Canellos, Black Leaders Find Hope for Reform in Shannon's Report, Boston Globe, Dec. 19, 1990, at 26; Peter Canellos, Youth Decry Search Tactics, Boston Globe, Jan. 14, 1990, at 1.

142. 67 Fordham L. Rev. 13 (1998).

143. Id. at 18.

144. Id.

discretion to help eradicate the discriminatory treatment of African Americans in the criminal justice system."[145]

Note: Why Are So Many African Americans in Prison?

This is the question Professor Glenn Loury raised and answers in a recent article.[146] He notes that in the early 1990s, there was a serious crime wave, particularly in central cities, and so government at every level ramped up law enforcement and prison sentences to meet the challenges. The crime rates peaked in 1992 and have dropped sharply since that time. But as Loury puts it: "Stoked by fear and political opportunism, but also by the need to address a very real social problem, we threw lots of people in jail, and when the old prisons were filled we built new ones." So, though crime rates fell sharply, imprisonment rates remained high and continued to climb to the point that the "current American prison system is a leviathan unmatched in human history." The country now spends $200 billion annually on law enforcement and corrections, and there are now more people employed in corrections than the combined work forces of General Motors, Ford, and Wal-Mart, the three largest employers in the country. Of the 2.25 million persons in 5,000 prisons and jails, one-third are violent criminals, two-thirds are mainly property and drug offenders, and most are black and brown.

Why despite the national decline in crime, Loury asks, has the criminal justice system become crueler and less caring than at any other time in our modern history? Looking at the racial composition of prisons, he suggests: "The punitive turn in the nation's social policy — intimately connected with public rhetoric about responsibility, dependency, social hygiene, and the reclamation of public order — can be fully grasped only when viewed against the backdrop of America's often ugly and violent racial history: there is a reason why our inclination toward forgiveness and the extension of a second chance to those who have violated our behavioral strictures is so stunted, and why our mainstream political discourses are so bereft of self-examination and searching social criticism. This historical resonance between the stigma of race and the stigma of imprisonment serves to keep alive in our public culture the subordinating social meanings that have always been associated with blackness. Race helps to explain why the United States is exceptional among the democratic industrial societies in the severity and extent of its punitive policy and in the paucity of its social-welfare institutions."

Loury cites political scientist Vesla Mae Weaver, who argues that "the punitive turn represented a political response to the success of the civil-rights movement." Weaver describes a process of "frontlash" in which opponents of the civil-rights revolution sought to regain the upper hand by shifting to a new issue. Rather than reacting directly to civil-rights developments, and thus continuing to fight a battle they had lost, those opponents — consider George Wallace's campaigns for the presidency, which drew so much support in states

---

145. Id. See also Angela J. Davis, Arbitrary Justice: The Power of the American Prosecutor (2007).
146. Glenn Loury, Why Are So Many Americans in Prison? Race and the Transformation of Criminal Justice, Boston Review, Mar/Apr. 2007.

like Michigan and Wisconsin — shifted attention to a seemingly race-neutral concern over crime:

Once the clutch of Jim Crow had loosened, opponents of civil rights shifted the "locus of attack" by injecting crime onto the agenda. Through the process of frontlash, rivals of civil rights progress defined racial discord as criminal and argued that crime legislation would be a panacea to racial unrest. This strategy both imbued crime with race and depoliticized racial struggle, a formula which foreclosed earlier "root causes" alternatives. Fusing anxiety about crime to anxiety over racial change and riots, civil rights and racial disorder — initially defined as a problem of minority disenfranchisement — were defined as a crime problem, which helped shift debate from social reform to punishment.

After 1965, Loury points out, public attitudes began associating race with welfare and race with crime with both moving to the right politically with policies falling into lines with the merging of these views. The War on Drugs escalated even as the number of drug users declined with blacks four times more likely to be arrested for a drug offense than whites, usually in the poorest neighborhoods. In his view: "This situation raises a moral problem that we cannot avoid. We cannot pretend that there are more important problems in our society, or that this circumstance is the necessary solution to other, more pressing problems — unless we are also prepared to say that we have turned our backs on the ideal of equality for all citizens and abandoned the principles of justice. We ought to ask ourselves two questions: *Just what manner of people are we Americans? And in light of this, what are our obligations to our fellow citizens — even those who break our laws?*"

Note: Barriers to Re-entry Feed a Vicious Cycle of Recidivism

With a soaring prison population nationally, it is not surprising that nearly 700,000 individuals are released from prison each year.[147] A disproportionate number of these individuals are minorities, who return to a select number of neighborhoods. When inmates are released, especially after years of incarceration, few have families or social networks to help them reintegrate successfully into society. Because record numbers of individuals are returning home to confront many barriers and no safety net, advocates, politicians, former inmates and their families are calling for a solution to this crisis. From the President's State of the Union address to city council hearings, these formerly incarcerated individuals are gaining national political attention.

For example, Congress is responding with the Second Chance Act that funds a number of initiatives to address concerns with housing, family reunification, social services, drug addition, mental health and employment. The Second Chance Act aims to "ensure the transition people make from prison or jail to the community is safe and successful."[148] In doing so it allocates funding for reentry that would include individualized state demonstration projects, a national reentry center, a task force, mentoring and drug rehabilitation programs. All of the initiatives rely heavily on social service agencies to work miracles. This legislative initiative, like

---

147. After Prison: Roadblocks to Reentry, A Report on the State Legal Barriers Facing People with Criminal Records, Legal Action Center Report, 2004.
148. http://www.reentrypolicy.org/reentry/Second_Chance_Act_of_2005.aspx.

their state and city counterparts, does not tackle the larger, and more politically acceptable, legal and economic roadblocks that prevent successful reentry.

The formerly incarcerated face obstacles to getting public assistance, food stamps, a driver's licenses, and student loans. Upon release, some learn that their parental rights were terminated even after only 18 months of incarceration; while others have exponentially accrued child support arrears that can soak up more than 50 percent of an unskilled laborer's paycheck.

Housing may not only be unaffordable for individuals released from prison, but landlords whether public or private can turn people away because of their criminal record. State and federal housing authorities maintain charts defining the length of time individuals will be denied housing based on the type of crime committed and how much time has lapsed since release. Families in public housing run the risk of eviction if they take in a family member after release.

Employment barriers above all severely prevent successful reentry. Without a job, the bills don't get paid. Finding housing, reunifying with children and other goals become merely an illusion. Most states permit employers to deny people jobs because of their criminal records, regardless of how long ago the crime was committed, the date of release and the nature of the offense.[149] Individuals can be denied employment based on a minor violation like disorderly conduct or a conviction that is over a decade old. Compounding this problem, most states make criminal records available to the general public through the internet, without requiring an individual's consent or fingerprints. Facing these seemingly insurmountable legal hurdles, an individual's odds of reintegration seems impossible. Legislation providing social services assistance is a band-aid solution for a much more systemic problem. It is no wonder that the vicious cycle of recidivism continues.

§5.12.5 Contemporary Racial Vigilantes

Yet police and prosecutors are by no means the only actors in the criminal justice system that discriminate against members of minority groups. Defense attorneys, juries, judges, and the public at large are also responsible for the treatment of black persons in the criminal justice system. The assault of three black men in the white New York City neighborhood of Howard Beach offers a telling glimpse of this treatment. The three, who had ventured into Howard Beach after their car broke down on a nearby highway, stopped to eat at a local pizzeria. An anonymous caller summoned the police with a report of "black trouble-makers." The patrol car that responded found no trouble and left. When the black men left the restaurant, they were attacked by a group of white teenagers who beat them with baseball bats and tree limbs. One of the men was permanently blinded in the attack, and another died when he was hit by a car while trying to escape across a highway.[150]

Professor Patricia Williams offers an insightful critique of the Howard Beach incident. As she points out, the legal strategy and the public examination of the case

---

149. LAC Report, supra note 147, at 141.
150. People v. Kern, 75 N.Y.2d 638, 554 N.E.2d 1235, 555 N.Y.S.2d 647 (1990).

had little to do with the wrong committed by the white attackers and much more to do with the wrong committed by the black victims in passing through a white community:

In the heated public controversy that ensued, as much of the attention centered on the community of Howard Beach, where the assault took place, as on the assaulters themselves. The chief cause of such attention was a veritable Greek chorus . . . repeating and repeating that the mere presence of three black men in that part of town at that time of night was reason enough to drive them out: "They had to be starting trouble"; "We're a strictly white neighborhood"; "What were they doing here in the first place?" The pinnacle of legitimacy to which these particular questions rose is, to me, the most frightening aspect of this case. When Mayor Ed Koch was asked why he thought the young men were walking around Howard Beach, he dignified the question with the following answer: "I don't know . . . and neither did the 12 or so people who beat them. Because they didn't ask them. They didn't talk to them." One is left to speculate: If the attackers, those self-appointed gatekeepers, had asked and got an answer like "none of your business," would they then have been entitled to beat and attack out of public spirited zeal? And, one wonders further, what explanation would have been sufficient to allow black males continued unmolested passage into the sanctified byways of Howard Beach?[151]

The defense rested on the proposition that it is reasonable to assume that black persons can have no legitimate reason to walk the streets of Howard Beach.[152] The stereotype that all blacks are criminals was triggered in the minds of a white audience (and jury) to provide legal and moral justification for the attack. The press came to the defendants' aid by reporting the criminal history of one of the victims, as if to say the mob's fear was justified (even though the white residents of Howard Beach could not have known of this history and had no nonracial reason to believe these black men were "troublemakers"). The victims' race, we were told, was reason enough. What happened at Howard Beach, we were to believe, was not an act of racial hatred, but of understandable self-defense.[153]

Similar images of black criminality dominated the treatment of Bernhard Goetz, and undoubtedly led to his acquittal of all charges except unlawful carrying of a firearm. On December 22, 1984, Goetz, a white man, was riding a New York City subway when four young black men approached him to ask for $5.00. According to his subsequent testimony, Goetz believed that they wanted to "play with"

151. Patricia Williams, The Alchemy of Race and Rights 58-59 (1991).
152. Patricia Williams quotes the New York Times report of the defendants' arraignments: "The three defense lawyers also tried to cast doubt on [the prosecutor's] account of the attack. The lawyers questioned why the victims walked all the way to the pizza parlor if, as they said, their mission was to summon help for their car, which broke down three miles away. . . . At the arraignment, the lawyers said the victims passed two all-night gas stations and several other pizza shops before they reached the one they entered. . . . A check yesterday of area restaurants, motels and gas stations listed in the Queens street directory found two eating establishments, a gas station and a motel that all said they were open and had working pay phones on Friday night. . . . A spokesman for the New York Telephone Company, Jim Crosson, said there are six outdoor pay telephones along Cross Bay Boulevard on the way to the pizzeria." Id. at 67.
153. Several of the Howard Beach defendants were ultimately convicted, but only of the lesser charge of second degree manslaughter. People v. Kern, 75 N.Y.2d at 647.

him.[154] So, when one of the youths again asked for money, Goetz pulled out a gun and shot each of them — two of them in the back.

Goetz almost instantly became a hero: a David whose slaying of the Goliath that composites all images of black criminality expressed the fears and fantasies of many whites.[155] As Professor Stephen Carter writes:

> The tragedy of the Goetz case is that a public barely aware of the facts was rooting for him to get away with it. The tragedy is that a public eager to identify transgressors in advance decided from the start that Mr. Goetz was a hero and that his black victims deserved what they got.[156]

The deeper tragedy is that the choice of the hero and the villain was determined solely by the race of each.[157]

To highlight the racist assumptions that animated the public debate over the Goetz case, Professor Patricia Williams paints another scenario:

> A lone black man was riding in an elevator in a busy downtown department store. The elevator stopped on the third floor, and a crowd of noisy white high school students got on. The black man took out a gun, shot as many of them as he could, before the doors opened on the first floor and the rest fled for their lives. The black man later explained to the police that he could tell from the "body language" of the students, from their "shiny eyes and big smiles," that they wanted to "play with him like a cat plays with a mouse." Furthermore, the black man explained, one of the youths had tried to panhandle money from him and another asked him "how are you?"
> "That's a meaningless thing," he said in his confession, "but in certain circumstances, that can be a real threat." He added that a similar greeting had preceded the vicious beating of his father, a black civil rights lawyer in Mississippi, some time before. His intention, he confessed, was to murder the high school students.[158]

Professor Williams is certainly right when she hypothesizes that the black man in the elevator, whose confession almost exactly duplicates that of the real-life Bernhard Goetz, would not have been met with the same sympathy as his white counterpart.

The common thread which runs through these cases — from McCleskey to Goetz to Howard Beach and many others — is the unwillingness to accept the possibility of the black victim. As Professor Carter summarizes:

> All too often, American legal and political culture seems to suggest . . . that there are two varieties of people who are involved in criminal activity, black people and

---

154. People v. Goetz, 68 N.Y.2d at 101, 497 N.E.2d at 44, 506 N.Y.S.2d at 21 (1988).

155. Typical of the public response to the subway shooting were comments to the effect of "blacks commit most crimes" — as if this supposed fact makes the presence of blacks provocation enough for attack. Yet, as Patricia Williams reminds us, U.S. Bureau of Justice Statistics for the same year as the Goetz shooting reveal that whites were arrested for 71.7 percent of all crimes. Williams, supra note 151, at 73 (citing Joan Petersilia, Racial Disparities in the Criminal Justice System, prepared by the Rand Corporation for the National Institute of Corrections, U.S. Dept. of Justice (June 1983), pp. xxiv, 44).

156. Carter, supra note 109, at 424.

157. Id. at 426-427, 425.

158. Williams, supra note 151, at 76.

victims. So perhaps when victims happen to be black, the culture rationalizes the seeming contradiction by denying there has been a crime.[159]

The problem, as Professor Carter begins to suggest, is our differential treatment of the historical experiences of these two races. It is truly remarkable that the relatively recent phenomenon of black crimes against whites fosters a stereotype — rising to the level of legal justification — that all black persons are dangerous, while the long history of white crimes against blacks produces no similar societal assumption. Society all too readily generalizes the wrongs of a few black persons to the entire race, but it is unwilling to make those generalizations which would actually redound to the benefit of black citizens. The long history of exclusion of blacks from almost every arena of social and economic life is conveniently imagined to be confined to its immediate and historically isolatable targets. This rhetorical device has the effect of removing the moral rationale for any race-conscious remedy seeking to compensate blacks today, who have also suffered from the legacy of discrimination. Because we refuse to see the black victim — whether it be in Howard Beach or in a corporate boardroom — we deny that the crime occurred.

Sadly, the stereotype that all blacks are criminals has continued to find lethal force in the last decade with several notorious and tragic episodes of police brutality, two of which took center stage for brief moments in New York City: the cases of Abner Louima and Amadou Diallo. Such cases demonstrate the sad fact that communities tolerate almost any police abuse and torture, particularly when it is inflicted on blacks.

In August 1997, Haitian immigrant Abner Louima alleged that several members of the New York Police Department abused him physically and sexually following his arrest.[160] Louima had been arrested after a scuffle outside a nightclub in Brooklyn on August 9, 1997. After his arrest, he was viciously attacked in the station house by members of the NYPD. One of the officers sodomized him with the wooden handle of a toilet plunger and then forced Louima to hold the blood- and feces-stained wooden handle in his mouth. The violence caused damage to his bladder and intestines so severe that immediate hospitalization was required; months of surgery followed.

Meanwhile, the story of Louima's torture met with brief public outrage in New York City, and four officers and a sergeant were indicted on federal charges ranging from sexual assault to conspiracy.[161] Such a reaction is far from typical. In fact, it remains notoriously difficult to prosecute police brutality cases. In an insightful article on this topic, Professor David Troutt attributes much of the difficulty to the overwhelming power of the racialized narratives mainstream American culture tells about encounters that lead to police violence.[162] Troutt argues that "the apparently

159. Carter, supra note 109, at 447.
160. David Kocieniewski, Injured Man Says Brooklyn Officers Tortured Him in Custody, N.Y. Times, Aug. 13, 1997, at B1.
161. Henri E. Cauvin, Rally for Louima, Daily News (New York), Aug. 10, 1998, at 18.
162. David Dante Troutt, "Screws, Koon, and Routine Aberrations: The Use of Fictional Narratives in Federal Police Brutality Prosecutions," 74 N.Y.U. L. Rev. 18, 1995. In this piece, Troutt examines these racialized authority narratives and demonstrates how they have been used to

intractable problem of police use of excessive force and its relative immunity from federal (or state) criminal prosecution is made possible largely by an enduring mythology that influences normative conceptions of police behavior as well as legal treatment of such cases." We tell a myth of police officers protecting us from random young black men with "little education and uncontrolled impulses" who seek to harm others. Such myths are dangerous with respect to the rights of any suspect in custody because they work to dehumanize him or her. "What happens to the victim of police brutality occurs beyond his own voice and outside his vision; the victim's account, where one exists, is frequently not sought, or it is ignored or forgotten."[163] And, Troutt continues, "the stories of police brutality become articulated and understood primarily as authority narratives, not merely by desk sergeants to complainants or by police chiefs to the public, but, most importantly for these purposes, by courts to the popular culture."[164]

Maybe this explains how four police officers who shot an unarmed man 41 times can be seen as heroic by most of the NYPD and even by some of the citizens of New York City. On February 4, 1999, Amadou Diallo was shot 41 times while standing in the vestibule of his Bronx apartment building.[165] The four police officers responsible later claimed that Diallo looked somewhat like a suspect in a rape case. The four officers were indicted primarily because of serious pressure from outraged protesters. Each of the four officers was charged with two counts of second-degree murder and one count of reckless endangerment.[166] But, as State Supreme Court Justice Patricia Williams noted in her ruling that the evidence against the officers was sufficient to sustain the charges, more than 400 off-duty officers protested, shouting "Free the Bronx 4."[167] Many of these officers claimed that the arrested men were acting heroically, not criminally, when they shot and killed Diallo. Even the supervisor sent to the scene on February fourth failed to ask the officers a single question about what had happened or why they had fired their weapons.[168] Ultimately, the four officers were acquitted.[169]

Such indifference to brutality against black men is only possible because we live in a culture where the lives of black men are repeatedly and relentlessly sacrificed in the war against crime. Such a culture makes every black man a suspect. Is it really any surprise that the cops searched frantically for evidence that the already dead Amadou Diallo might have owned drugs? After all, this was part of their effort to transform the narrative of the events of February 4. If Diallo could be portrayed as a drug-dealer, then the cops who shot him for no reason would not be the only criminals.

---

defeat, if not silence, the counternarratives related by victims and their representatives. He also makes a strong case for the use of literary fiction as a tool for challenging the core of dominant beliefs about race, crime, and social hierarchy.

163. Id. at 22.

164. Id.

165. Amy Waldman, Judge Refuses to Dismiss Charges Against Officers in Diallo Killing, N.Y. Times, Sept. 30, 1999, at B11.

166. Id.

167. Id.

168. Id.

169. Michael Kramer, The World According to Sharpton, Daily News, Apr. 18, 1999, at 47.

§5.12.6 Punishing Black Sexuality

Another strain evident in the treatment of black persons in the criminal justice system has been the particular harshness with which courts have punished black sexuality or parenting. Of most obvious note have been the disproportionate conviction rates and sentences imposed on black men accused of rape.[170] Statistics cited by Justice Marshall in his concurrence in Furman show that disparities in the imposition of the death penalty (1,751 whites to 2,066 blacks sentenced to death between 1930 and 1972) increased exponentially when the crime is rape (48 whites to 405 blacks executed).[171]

More recently, a wave of prosecutions of black women for their conduct during pregnancy has sparked concern over judicial control of black women's sexuality and reproductive choices. In the war against drugs, "fetal endangerment" charges have provided another weapon for the state to penalize those who use drugs.[172] Professor Dorothy Roberts has produced compelling evidence that racial bias has made women of color the overwhelming targets of this prosecutorial zeal.[173] Of the 52 defendants charged with endangering a fetus, 35 are black, 2 are Latino, 1 is Native American, and only 14 are white.[174] Professor Roberts found that underlying this trend is the statistically proven tendency of medical professionals to suspect and report women of color who use drugs during pregnancy.[175] Yet, according to a study by the New England Journal of Medicine, there is no substantial difference in the prevalence of drug abuse by pregnant women either by race or class.[176] The data cited by Professor Roberts makes clear that stereotyped images of the drug dependent and unfit black mother, rather than any public health crisis or statistical predicate, move prosecutors to charge black women in disproportionate numbers.

170. See Gary LaFree, The Effect of Sexual Stratification by Race on Official Reactions to Rape, 45 Am. Soc. Rev. 842, 851-852 (1980). Susan Brownmiller argues that the defendant's race is often the determinative factor in his acquittal or conviction. See Jennifer Wriggins, Rape, Racism, and the Law, 6 Harv. L.J. 103 (1988); Susan Brownmiller, Against Our Will: Men, Women and Rape 230-282 (1975).

171. Furman v. Georgia, 408 U.S. 238, 364 (1972). In Coker v. Georgia, the Supreme Court finally barred the imposition of the death penalty in rape cases. 433 U.S. 584 (1977). The most egregious sentence imposed on a black man convicted of rape, however, occurred seven years after the Court's decision in *Coker*. In South Carolina, a black defendant convicted of rape was given a choice between a 30-year jail term and castration. State v. Brown, 284 S.C. 407, 326 S.E.2d 310 (1985). While the defendant, Roscoe Brown, initially opted for the jail term, several weeks in prison was apparently sufficient to change his mind. The Supreme Court refused to enforce Brown's "choice" of castration, finding the punishment to be cruel and unusual. See Ogletree, supra note 126, at 16.

172. Dorothy Roberts, Killing the Black Body: Race, Reproduction, and the Meaning of Liberty 153 (1997); Paul Marcotte, Crime and Pregnancy, A.B.A. J., Aug. 1985.

173. Dorothy Roberts, Punishing Drug Addicts Who Have Babies: Women of Color, Equality, and the Right to Privacy, 104 Harv. L. Rev. 1419 (1991).

174. Id. at 1421 n.6.

175. Id. at 1433-1436. See also Note, the Problem of the Drug-Exposed Newborn: A Return to Principled Intervention, 42 Stan. L. Rev. 745, 753-754, 782 n.157 (1990). Women of color are ten times more likely than white persons to be reported to public authorities for drug abuse during pregnancy. Roberts, supra note 173, at 1433-1435.

176. Id. at 1433-1434.

Throughout the country, over 200 women in one decade were prosecuted for prenatal substance abuse.[177] In 1990 alone, 34 states introduced and debated bills to criminalize this behavior. Although public support for the issue was strong, by 1995, the fervor around this issue began to subside as "[w]omen's advocates, public health organizations, and physicians successfully campaigned to redefine prenatal drug use as a health problem rather than a crime."[178] Instead of a legal battle between women's rights and fetal rights, the issue became one that could be best treated by social services agencies and doctors, rather than the criminal justice system.

Along the same vein, another controversy was stirred when a California judge offered Darlene Johnson, a black woman convicted of child abuse, an opportunity to avoid a two- to four-year prison term if she agreed to have a new form of birth control called Norplant surgically implanted in her arm.[179] Describing the remarkable nature of the Faustian choice created by the judge, Professor Charles Ogletree writes:

> Though the particular sentence in Johnson was unusual, the paternalistic desire to control the sex lives of minority women is not. This country's long history of sterilization abuse, the unavailability of prenatal care for poor women, the denial of the right to abortion for poor women, and most recently, the denial of information on abortion to poor women, suggest that Norplant is just a sequel to the same old movie. [Citations and emphasis in original omitted.][180]

By incarcerating a large percentage of African Americans, especially black men, there is a dramatic impact on the black community overall. Studies have shown that even upon release the collateral consequences on the lives of convicted criminals is tremendous, including legal obstacles to finding a job, securing housing, reunifying with children, and participating in the political process.[181] In a more recent article, Dorothy Roberts argues that "the racial disparity in criminal justice results in a growing devaluation and disruption of Black families." A recent report of the Justice Department showed that a majority of state and federal prisoners in 1999 reported having a child under age 18, most of whom had lived with their children prior to incarceration.[182] Approximately 2 percent of

177. Laura Gomez, Misconceiving Mothers: Legislators, Prosecutors, and the Politics of Prenatal Drug Exposure (1997). This book takes an extensive look at the prenatal drug problem from a sociological perspective examining the actions of prosecutors, judges, legislators, women's groups, and doctors. It focuses specifically on the experience of the California legislature. Dorothy Roberts, Creating and Solving the Problem of Drug Use During Pregnancy: Book Review, 90 J. Crim. L. & Criminology 1353 (2000).

178. Roberts, supra note 173, at 1354.

179. See Michael Lev, Judge Is Firm on Forced Contraception, But Welcomes an Appeal, N.Y. Times, Jan. 11, 1991, at A17. The controversy was heightened when the introduction of Norplant was greeted by one Chicago newspaper as a remedy to the expansion of the welfare rolls. The editorial suggested that states require that women accept a Norplant as a condition for receiving public assistance. For a response to the editorial, which was later retracted, see Wattleton, Using Birth Control as Coercion, L.A. Times, Jan. 13, 1991.

180. Ogletree, supra note 126, at 14.

181. Marc Mauer & The Sentencing Project, Race to Incarcerate 118-141 (1999).

182. Christopher J. Mumola, U.S. Department of Justice, Incarcerated Parents and Their Children (2000), available at http://www.ojp.usdoj.gov/bjs/pub/pdf/iptc.pdf.

the nation's children — close to 1.5 million children — had a parent in prison that year. Given racially disproportionate prison populations, "[s]even percent of Black children had a parent in prison in 1999, making them nearly nine times more likely to have an incarcerated parent than white children." According to Roberts, the collateral impact of the criminal justice system on black families and communities calls for serious opposition to the imbalanced incarceration of blacks.

§5.12.7 Jury Nullification

Professor Paul Butler argues that the abuse of discretion along racial lines which occurs in the criminal justice system should be combated by self-help strategies among African Americans aimed at keeping some nonviolent offenders from adding to the overwhelming numbers of blacks in prison.[183] He suggests a limited plan of jury nullification, meaning that in some circumstances a jury should acquit a black defendant in spite of evidence of guilt. The black community is better off, according to Butler, when some nonviolent lawbreakers remain in the community rather than go to prison.[184]

Butler does not argue that every black defendant should be acquitted.[185] Instead, he argues that with nonviolent, victimless crimes, such as drug possession, the presumption should be in favor of jury nullification.[186] This is necessary, according to Butler, because nothing else will force the country to offer the same opportunities for community-based drug treatment for poor black drug offenders as are available for wealthy white offenders. He claims that, since a majority of white drug offenders already remain in the community, the community shows willingness to avoid incarceration for such offenders as long as they are white. Butler asks why black drug offenders should not receive the same opportunity for community-based treatment, rather than incarceration, stating that, "when it comes to law enforcement, what is good enough for white people is good enough for African-Americans."[187] Butler recognizes that his rationale for prescribing this use of racially motivated nullification denies the legitimacy of the criminal justice system, and, as a former prosecutor, he claims he has come to this position reluctantly.[188] Still, he argues, blacks must refuse to let the law legitimize the racist criminalization of minorities and should use the system to engage in small acts of acquittal.

Butler contends that jury nullification is perfectly legal. He explains his position this way:

> [T]he power to nullify is based on the Double Jeopardy Clause, but the historical privilege is based on the idea that jurors are an important and necessary check on

183. Paul D. Butler, Race-Based Jury Nullification: Case-in-Chief, 30 J. Marshall L. Rev. 911, 912-913 (1997).

184. Id. at 921.

185. Id. at 920.

186. Id. at 920-921.

187. Id. at 921.

188. Id. at 918.

government power. That is the history and animus of the jury system itself. For much of American history it was expected that jurors would judge the law as much as the facts. After the Industrial revolution, courts started to get uncomfortable with this idea. In 1895, the Supreme Court held that jurors have the power to nullify, but they do not have the right to be instructed on this power. So they can do it, but they cannot be told during the trial about this power that they have: that is still the law today.[189]

Butler offers several historical examples of such selective nullification. First, he mentions the runaway slave cases. It was a crime for slaves to run away, and it was a crime for whites to help slaves escape. These cases were prosecuted in the North, and northern jurors would often nullify, even though both the slaves and their helpers were guilty according to the evidence.[190]

Next, Butler offers as an example the prohibition arrests for possession and distribution of alcohol. Jurors who thought that criminal punishment was an inappropriate way to handle the alcohol problem would often acquit, even though the defendants were legally guilty. Butler notes that many people think that such nullification helped end the unwise policy of prohibition.[191]

Butler has also found negative examples of nullification, and he cites the historical example of the tradition of white juries that refused to convict people guilty of violence against African Americans.[192] So, what does this mean? According to Butler, the meaning is clear: "[L]ike any power, jury nullification can be used for good or it can be used for evil."[193]

Butler notes that financial incentives for adolescents to stay in school, along with parental training for some of the young people having babies, would prevent more crime than do the deterrent effects of prison for any crimes these young people commit. He also notes that the majority knows this and yet still seems to prefer the punishment regime. This is typical, says Butler, when it comes to the way lawmakers deal with the criminal justice system as it applies to African Americans.[194] And, this preference to punish rather than help African Americans is one of the moral reasons why Butler sees selective nullification as appropriate.[195]

Butler concludes his argument with this point:

> If not jury nullification, then what? I do not want to hear that African Americans should write to Congress. We tried that. It did not work. The house that African-Americans live in is on fire, and when your house is on fire, you do not write to Congress. You do not ask the people who set the fire to put it out; you leave the building. That is what my proposal for selective jury nullification encourages.[196]

Professor Andrew Leipold rejects Butler's proposal, stating that "even if the house is on fire, I do not think we should embrace a solution that involves fanning

189. Id. at 917.
190. Id. at 917-918.
191. Id. at 918.
192. Id.
193. Id.
194. Id. at 915.
195. Id. at 919-920.
196. Id. at 922.

the flames and making the fire worse."[197] This is what Leipold fears selective race-based jury nullification will do. He specifically worries that Butler's suggestion may lead to the near absence of blacks on juries.[198]

This is the case, according to Leipold, because potential African American jurors who embrace Butler's plan may be removed from the jury panel for cause. A lawyer may not use a peremptory strike to remove prospective jurors because of their race, but jurors who indicate during voir dire that they will not follow the law contained in the judge's instructions may be removed for cause. So, if the jurors are honest during voir dire, their belief in jury nullification would at least give the prosecutor a race-neutral reason for removing them with a peremptory strike. Beyond this, if the jurors admit that they have a strong presumption against convicting a defendant, regardless of the evidence, such jurors may be excused for cause. And, as challenges for cause are unlimited, Leipold worries that Butler's plan could drastically reduce the number of African American jurors.[199]

Leipold also argues that once the use by African Americans of a cost benefit analysis to decide the outcome of certain case is legitimized, we may find no principled stopping point. He worries that "other groups . . . will feel that they, too, do not get a fair shake from the criminal justice system and they, too, should come to the jury box with an eye toward nullifying the convictions of members of their groups."[200] He continues his argument by saying that once we tell a jury that uniform cost-benefit analysis is acceptable, "we have no moral basis for complaining about any decision that a jury makes."[201]

Professor Randall Kennedy cautions blacks seeking reform to stay away from tactics that lack widespread approval. His apprehension of how whites would react to widespread black jury nullification leads him to urge blacks to choose tactics that, unlike jury nullification, do not offend the white majority. According to Kennedy, as a stigmatized racial minority, blacks must pay attention to how they are perceived by whites in order to avoid facilitating indifference to their plight.[202]

This is in keeping with Kennedy's strategy he calls the "politics of respectability."[203] Along these lines, respectable blacks are uplifted by distancing themselves from "bad blacks," as opposed to aligning with them. Kennedy recognizes a "deeply rooted impulse in African-American culture to distinguish sharply between 'good' and 'bad' Negroes."[204] And, Kennedy readily applies this distinction in the criminal realm, since no one angers him more than violent criminals who are "typically black."[205]

---

197. Andrew D. Leipold, Race-Based Jury Nullification: Rebuttal (Part A), 30 J. Marshall L. Rev. 923 (1997).
198. Id.
199. Id. at 924.
200. Id. at 925.
201. Id.
202. Randall Kennedy, Race, Crime, and the Law (1997).
203. Id. at 12-28.
204. Id. at 17.
205. Id. at 15.

Obviously, Kennedy does not believe the high rate of incarceration of African Americans should make African Americans suspicious of the criminal justice system. In fact, Kennedy claims, instead, that the more that law enforcement is directed at African Americans, the better off the African American community will be. According to Kennedy, blacks "suffer more from the criminal acts of their racial 'brothers' and 'sisters' than they do from [racism]." He continues by noting that racist cops, however problematic, are only "minor irritants" as compared to "black gangs."[206] From this, according to Kennedy, it follows that African Americans should favor the punishment of all blacks whom the law calls "bad." In his text Search and Destroy, Jerome Miller brings a very different perspective to the discussion pointing out that each year more than $31 billion dollars is spent at local, state, and federal levels on a failed drug war that has been mostly directed at African American and Latino citizens.[207] According to Miller, the criminal justice system "has spawned an industry fully capable of producing sufficient numbers of new clientele to validate the need for its existence and justify its growth, demanding more police, arrests, prosecutions, and prisons."[208] This evidence of a $31 billion dollar industry aimed at prosecuting African-Americans and Latinos may lead one to question the role of the criminal justice system itself in the social breakdown of the inner cities.

Miller continues that "though a white suburban jury might buy the sharp difference between the criminal and the law-abiding, such neat distinctions have limited force in communities where most have seen a father, son, brother, or close friend hauled away and labeled as 'criminal.' "[209] In 1990, the D.C.-based Sentencing Project revealed that, on any average day in the United States, one in every four African American men between 20 and 29 was either in jail, in prison, or on probation or parole. And, as Miller insightfully asks in his book, if one in four young African American males are under correctional supervision on any given day, how many have been or will be drawn into the justice system? Nationally, at least 4 to 5 million adults acquire a criminal record each year.[210] Knowing this, is it possible to be comfortable with Kennedy's distinction between "good" and "bad" African Americans?

In an article published in 2003, Butler examines the use of subversion and violence to change laws that discriminate against blacks when more traditional methods prove ineffective.[211] The death penalty and drug penalties are presented as two examples of discriminatory laws that have not been successfully challenged using the judiciary and legislature, regardless of advocates' ceaseless efforts. He argues that African Americans must consider a full range of strategies to alter injustice, but in doing so they must be guided by morality.

As formal legal barriers to equality have been removed, Butler argues that advocates have turned to the criminal justice system. Race plays an important role

---

206. Id. at 17-20.
207. Id. at 5-9.
208. Id.
209. Jerome G. Miller, Search and Destroy 4 (1996).
210. Id. at 7.
211. Paul Butler, By Any Means Necessary: Using Violence and Subversion to Change Unjust Laws, 50 UCLA L. Rev. 721 (2003).

in determining who receives the death penalty. As the Supreme Court in *McCleskey* passed the buck to the legislature, which was unable to pass legislation to remedy the unequal application of the death penalty, the Court appeared "willing to tolerate more severe punishment for blacks, even when that punishment includes killing them."[212]

Butler also discusses the harsh punishments imposed for offenses involving crack cocaine, when compared to powder cocaine. Data from the U.S. Sentencing Commission shows that most people arrested on crack cocaine charges are black and most people accused of powder cocaine are white. Under federal law, upon which most critics focus, a convicted drug offender receives the same five-year sentence for 500 grams of powder as for five grams of crack. The disparity in the law has led to lengthy sentences for "low-level crack sellers, who are almost exclusively African American."[213] Many see this as one more example of how the War on Drugs is targeted at black communities. Appeals to the federal judiciary and Congress have been futile. Even when the Sentencing Commission suggested changes to end the disparity, for the first time in history Congress rejected its recommendation.[214] These examples raise the question of where we can turn to end such unjust policies. One alternative is to use illegal methods to pressure legislatures. Butler rejects Randall Kennedy's "politics of respectability" and contends that morality, not legality, should direct strategic actions. Violence for Butler extends beyond the moral realm because innocent people would be the casualties of such acts of terrorism. Subversion, on the other hand, especially subversion through jury service, can be morally justified. Lying to get on a jury to thwart the application of an unjust law is proportional to the objective of reducing long crack sentences or voting against the death penalty. Throughout his argument, Butler emphasizes that morality over all other concerns should guide the selection of means necessary for ending persistent race-based discrimination.[215]

§5.12.8 Race and Class in the O. J. Simpson Case

In his text, No Equal Justice, David Cole tells of the sharply different reactions to the verdict in the O. J. Simpson case, reactions that almost uniformly broke down along racial lines. In other words, African Americans were pleased with the verdict, while whites were mostly outraged. As Cole explains, given how atypical the Simpson case was, these reactions present a deep irony: Simpson enjoyed every advantage usually reserved for whites. Simpson had unlimited resources, celebrity status, and a jury that identified with him on racial grounds. Most black defendants, by contrast, cannot afford an attorney, let alone the "dream team." Their fate is decided by predominantly white juries; and the image of black defendants is more

212. Id. at 733.
213. Id. at 734.
214. Id. at 735.
215. Id. at 771-772.

commonly linked with criminality than with celebrity.[216] Cole states the implications this way:

> Had Simpson been poor and unknown, as most black (and white) criminal defendants are, everything would have been different. The case would have garnered no national attention. Simpson would have been represented by an overworked and underpaid public defender who would not have been able to afford experts to examine and challenge the government's evidence. No one would have conducted polls on the case, and the trial would not have been televised. In all likelihood, Simpson would have been convicted in short order without any serious testing of the evidence against him or the methods by which it was obtained. Whites would have expressed no outrage that a poor black defendant had been convicted, and blacks would have had nothing to cheer about. That, not California v. O. J. Simpson, is the reality in American courtrooms across the country today.[217]

It took a case this atypical to make whites notice and reach a conclusion based on their fears rather than reality regarding the role that race and class play in the criminal justice system.

§5.13 NONDISCRIMINATORY JURY SELECTION STANDARDS

Almost inexplicably, given the judicial history during the post-Reconstruction period, the Supreme Court's earliest civil rights decisions affirmed the right of blacks not to be systematically excluded from service on juries in criminal cases because of their race and color.[1] Those decisions were handed down three years before the Civil Rights Cases and were never reversed. Over the years, they have been followed and expanded in a lengthy line of Supreme Court decisions.

The principles in these cases, quoted again and again, affirm that the purposeful exclusion or underrepresentation of blacks on a grand or petit jury venire constitutes invidious discrimination violative of the Fourteenth Amendment.[2] Defendants and others alleging discrimination in the jury selection process are seldom in a position to account for the means used to exclude blacks, but they can make out a prima facie case that shifts the burden of proving nonexclusion to the prosecutor. This may be accomplished by proof, usually in statistical form, that a "substantial disparity" exists between the percentage of presumptively qualified blacks in the county and the percentage of blacks actually chosen for jury duty.

---

216. David Cole, No Equal Justice 2-3 (1999).

217. Id. at 3.

§5.13 1. The Court sustained the validity of provisions prohibiting the exclusion of blacks from state juries, finding that the action of a judge charged with such exclusion was state action. Ex parte Virginia, 100 U.S. 339 (1880). A state statute excluding blacks from jury duty was held a violation of the Fourteenth Amendment; this afforded grounds for removal of the case to a federal court under the removal statutes. Strauder v. West Virginia, 100 U.S. 303 (1880). See also Virginia v. Rives, 100 U.S. 313 (1880).

2. Alexander v. Louisiana, 405 U.S. 625 (1972); Sims v. Georgia, 389 U.S. 404 (1967); Whitus v. Georgia, 385 U.S. 545 (1967); Coleman v. Alabama, 377 U.S. 129 (1964).

This disparity is coupled with some positive indication of discrimination or by a showing that the selection procedure provides an opportunity to discriminate.[3] A prima facie case can also be made by showing that blacks have been totally excluded from jury service for many years in the county under attack.[4]

More recent cases indicate that Mexican Americans and other "cognizable groups" are entitled to the same protection against exclusion of members of their groups as are blacks.[5] And even white defendants have been deemed denied their due process rights by the systematic exclusion of minorities from their juries.[6] Similarly, the Supreme Court in Taylor v. Louisiana[7] held that a male defendant could challenge a law excluding women from jury service unless they filed a declaration of intent to serve. There, the Court held that criminal defendants have a constitutional right under the Sixth Amendment to a jury selected from a representative cross-section of the community.[8] *Taylor* represents an almost definitive example of the underlying purpose for the Court's insistence on juries from which no group has been systematically excluded. Fair representation of cognizable groups is deemed essential to the impartiality and legitimacy of the jury system. The jury should include as widespread a set of community attitudes and biases as possible in the hope that the mixture of opinions and viewpoints will result, somehow, in the cancellation of prejudice and the triumph of fairness.[9]

Justice Marshall made this point in explaining why a white defendant was permitted, in Peters v. Kiff,[10] to raise the issue of the exclusion of blacks from his jury:

> When any large and identifiable segment of the community is excluded from jury service, the effect is to remove from the jury room qualities of human nature and varieties of human experience, the range of which is unknown and perhaps unknowable. It is not necessary to assume that the excluded group will consistently vote as a

3. Turner v. Fouche, 396 U.S. 346 (1970).

4. Norris v. Alabama, 294 U.S. 587 (1935); Hill v. Texas, 316 U.S. 400 (1942); Patton v. Mississippi, 332 U.S. 463 (1947).

5. Hernandez v. Texas, 347 U.S. 475 (1954).

6. Peters v. Kiff, 407 U.S. 493 (1972). Persons excluded from jury service as well as defendants may challenge discriminatory selection procedures. Carter v. Jury Comm'n of Greene County, 396 U.S. 320 (1970); Turner v. Fouche, 396 U.S. 346 (1970).

7. 419 U.S. 522 (1975).

8. Id. at 530. To make out a "fair cross-section" challenge under the Sixth Amendment, the defendant must show that: (1) the group alleged to have been excluded is a distinctive group in the community; (2) the representation of the group is not fair and reasonable in relation to the number of its members in the community; and (3) the underrepresentation of the group in the venire is due to the systemic exclusion of the group through the jury selection process. Duren v. Missouri, 439 U.S. 357, 364 (1979).

9. United States v. Ruiz, 894 F.2d 501, 505-506 (2d Cir. 1990) (recognizing Latinos as a cognizable group for purposes of the Sixth Amendment); Roman v. Abrams, 822 F.2d 214, 227-228 (2d Cir. 1987), cert. denied, 489 U.S. 1052 (1989) (holding that whites are a cognizable group); United States v. Iron Moccasin, 878 F.2d 226, 229 (8th Cir. 1989) (Native Americans constitute a cognizable group); United States v. Biaggi, 853 F.2d 89, 96 (2d Cir. 1988) (Italian Americans). But see Murchu v. United States, 926 F.2d 50 (1st Cir. 1991) (Irish Americans are not a cognizable group); United States v. Hamilton, 850 F.2d 1038, 1042 (4th Cir. 1988), cert. denied, 493 U.S. 1069 (1990) (refusing to recognize women as a cognizable group); United States v. Cresta, 825 F.2d 538, 545 (1st Cir. 1987) (rejecting challenge to the exclusion of young adults).

10. 407 U.S. 493 (1972).

class in order to conclude, as we do, that its exclusion deprives the jury of a perspective on human events that may have unsuspected importance in any case that may be presented.[11]

One might assume that, on this line of reasoning, the Court would hold that a defendant's jury, and not simply the venire or panel from which that jury is selected, must reflect a cross-section of the community. But the Court in *Taylor* adhered to a standard first enunciated in the original jury discrimination case, Strauder v. West Virginia,[12] and explicitly refused to impose any requirement that a petit jury must reflect the various distinctive groups in the population.[13] Again and again the Court states that all the Constitution forbids is the systematic exclusion of identifiable segments of the community from the jury panels from which the juries are ultimately drawn. Defendants may not "challenge the makeup of a jury merely because no members of his race are on the jury, but must prove that his race has been systematically excluded."[14]

Reasons suggested for the Court's refusal to carry through the logic of its cross-sectional community balance idea include the fact that the random selection of panels and venires from lists of qualified jurors inevitably will result in juries with no members of particular groups, while any requirement of proportionate representation would pose insurmountable administrative problems. In addition, even if this balance were attained, it could be upset by the removal of a juror for cause or through the exercise of a party's peremptory challenge.[15]

Procedural and administrative problems may be an unenunciated concern, but the Court's opinions suggest the Justices believe that the selection of jurors so as to ensure racial representation in line with the racial population of the jurisdiction would be as constitutionally forbidden as is the systematic exclusion of blacks on a racial basis. All of this would be academic if the process in use — the cross-section representation standard undergirded by the continuing willingness of courts to strike down verdicts arrived at by juries from which blacks have been systematically excluded — resulted in juries able to weigh the facts and reach decisions uninfluenced by personal or societal racial prejudice. Sadly, the evidence to the contrary is overwhelming. Reviewing the brief summary of the evidence that follows, it may be useful to consider other factors that attach the Court to standards for racial fairness in jury selection, which seem so worthwhile in the abstract but which are so woefully inadequate in practice.

11. Id. at 503-504. Note, Limiting the Peremptory Challenge: Representation of Groups on Petit Juries, 86 Yale L.J. 1715, 1729-1730 (1977) (hereinafter cited as Peremptory Challenge) suggests that a similar philosophy motivated the Court in Witherspoon v. Illinois, 391 U.S. 510 (1968). There, the Court held that a rule permitting a challenge for cause in a capital case of any juror who expressed qualms about capital punishment resulted in a jury that fell "woefully short" of the constitutional standard of impartiality with respect to the determination of punishment. Id. at 518. The exclusion of all with reservations about the death penalty resulted in a jury that was partial and therefore unrepresentative on this issue. On the issue of punishment, it had lost its "diffused impartiality."

12. 100 U.S. 303 (1880).

13. 419 U.S. at 538.

14. Apodaca v. Oregon, 406 U.S. 404, 413 (1972).

15. Peremptory Challenge, supra note 11, at 1732.

§5.14   RACISM IN THE JURY BOX

In the major jury study by Professors Harry Kalven and Hans Zeisel,[1] The American Jury, the influence of racist thinking on jury decisions was found in several cases where the juries (and judges) held blacks to a less strict standard of conduct when the victim was also black. The book quotes a judge who presided over a case in which the black defendant was acquitted: "If this had been a white man he would have been convicted. Negroes in cases of this type receive more than equal rights; juries seem to think it's okay for them to cut, if it's another colored person that is cut."[2] A study based on interviews with 225 jurors, conducted in the mid-1950s, shows clearly that many persons brought their racial prejudices to the jury box. As one juror reported: "Niggers have to be taught to behave. I feel that if he hadn't done that, he'd done something else probably even worse and that he should be put out of the way for a good long while."[3]

Perhaps a better and certainly more obvious proof of jury discrimination is the statistics of jury performance in racial cases. For example, the fear on the part of whites that black men pose a serious threat to white women is manifested in jury decisions, as can be seen in statistics prepared by the U.S. Bureau of Prisons for the years 1930-1962: of 446 persons found guilty and executed for rape in the United States, 339 were black, 45 were white, and 2 were of other races. These figures prompted a detailed study of rape convictions in twelve southern states (virtually all of the states which authorized the death penalty for rape are southern), and resulted in findings that, compared to other rape defendants, blacks convicted of raping white women were disproportionately found guilty and sentenced to death. Despite the introduction of this data in support of an argument that the application of the death penalty to blacks charged with rape constituted cruel and unusual punishment, the courts have refused to find that southern juries practice racial discrimination in rape cases.[4]

It has been suggested that if these statistics on executions were applied to the statistical model for determining jury discrimination set out in Castaneda v. Partida,[5] a clear prima facie case could be made out that the death penalty is discriminatorily imposed on racial grounds and is thus unconstitutional.[6] But when, in Furman v. Georgia,[7] the Supreme Court in validated the death penalty imposed

---

§5.14   1. Harry Kalven & Hans Zeisel, The American Jury (1966).

2. Id. at 341.

3. Developments, Race and the Criminal Process, 101 Harv. L. Rev. 1472 (1989); Dale W. Broeder, The Negro in Court, in Race, Crime, and Justice 301 (Charles E. Reasons & Jack L. Kuykendall eds., 1972).

4. See Maxwell v. Bishop, 395 F.2d 138 (8th Cir. 1968); Moorer v. South Carolina, 368 F.2d 458 (4th Cir. 1966).

For an excellent history of jury service by black persons and of the behavior of white juries, see Douglas Colbert, Challenging the Challenge: The Thirteenth Amendment as a Prohibition Against Racial Use of Peremptory Challenges, 76 Cornell L. Rev. 1 (1990).

5. Castaneda v. Partida, 430 U.S. 482 (1977). See §5.15.

6. 2 Emerson, Haber & Dorsen's Political and Civil Rights in the United States 1244 (1979).

7. 408 U.S. 238 (1972).

on three blacks, only Justice Douglas explicitly based his concurrence on the selective application of the penalties to minorities.[8]

Except in the most outrageous cases, in which racial prejudice so reduced the trial to a "mask, — that counsel, jury, and judge were swept to the fatal end by an irresistible wave of public passion,"[9] the Supreme Court has chosen to handle the problem of racism in jury decisions in an oblique and generally ineffective manner. For example, it agreed to review the Maxwell v. Bishop case,[10] but not on the validity of death penalties for blacks convicted of raping white women. As the opinion in Swain v. Alabama[11] indicates, the Supreme Court has adhered to the standard set in the 1880s that black defendants are entitled to be tried by juries from which members of their race have not been systematically excluded. While theoretically available to every criminal defendant, the procedural defense is usually pursued only where the defendant is involved in controversial activities, like civil rights, or when he is charged with a serious offense, such as rape or murder. The defense has served to win reversals and new trials in southern jurisdictions where jury discrimination is blatantly obvious, and has provided federal courts with a means to ameliorate, or at least delay, the harshest aspects of southern racial justice, particularly in those rape cases where the record raises substantial question as to whether the alleged criminal assault was not, in reality, simple seduction.[12]

Thus, civil rights lawyers, at least in a few cause célèbre cases that received national attention, have used the jury exclusion issue not only to gain a reversal of a conviction but to dramatize racial injustice at the place where the defendant was tried.[13] A classic illustration of what can be done is found in United States ex rel. Goldsby v. Harpole.[14] There, a black attorney from Chicago, George N. Leighton (a federal district court judge in the Northern District of Illinois from 1976 to

---

8. Id. at 250-251. Reviewing the studies, Justice Douglas noted that most of those executed are "poor, young, and ignorant" and that blacks are far more likely than whites and Latinos to receive the death penalty. In a Texas study, he reported that "In several instances where a white and a Negro were co-defendants, the white was sentenced to life imprisonment or a term of years, and the Negro was given the death penalty." For citations to more than a dozen studies supporting the conclusion that there is racial discrimination in the administration of the death penalty and in sentencing generally, see supra note 6. For a review of racial disparities in sentencing and other aspects of the criminal justice system, see Derrick Bell, Racism in American Courts: Cause for Black Disruption or Despair?, 61 U. Cal. L. Rev. 165 (1973).

9. Moore v. Dempsey, 261 U.S. 86, 91 (1923).

10. 398 F.2d 138 (8th Cir.), rev'd, 393 U.S. 997 (1968). See supra note 4. See also Rudolph v. Alabama, 375 U.S. 889 (1963).

11. 380 U.S. 202 (1965). Discussed at §5.16.1.

12. See, e.g., the "Scottsboro Boys" cases, Powell v. Alabama, 287 U.S. 45 (1932), and Norris v. Alabama, 294 U.S. 587 (1935); Giles v. Maryland, 386 U.S. 66 (1967); United States ex rel. Montgomery v. Ragen, 86 F. Supp. 382 (N.D. Ill. 1949).

13. Howard Smead, Blood Justice 32 (1986) (discussing the use of poll taxes, literacy tests, and grandfather clauses to keep almost all blacks from becoming voters and, therefore, from serving as jurors). A detailed study documented the actual service of black jurors in counties throughout the South around the turn of the century and found that, despite formal neutrality in the laws, most counties had never had a black juror. Even those blacks who survived rigged election registration procedures to qualify for jury venires were excluded by registrars or clerks who believed that blacks were too ignorant or too irrational to serve as jurors. G. Stephenson, Actual Jury Service by Negroes in the South, in Race Distinctions and American Law 247 (1910).

14. 263 F.2d 71 (5th Cir. 1959).

1987), was called to Mississippi by relatives of Robert Lee Goldsby to represent him on a murder charge growing out of the shooting death of a white woman by blacks firing from an automobile after being ordered to leave the gas station by the husband of the deceased. Ballistics tests showed that a gun found on the defendant at the time of his arrest had fired the fatal shot.

Upon arrival, Leighton appeared with Goldsby at his arraignment and entered a plea of not guilty to the indictment that had been returned the same day. Trial was set for two days later, by which time Leighton had prepared a series of motions to quash the indictment based, inter alia, on the ground that blacks had been systematically excluded from the grand jury. At this point, other relatives of Goldsby retained local white attorneys who told Leighton they could not work with him. Leighton then withdrew, and his motions were not filed. Goldsby was subsequently convicted of murder and sentenced to death. The Mississippi Supreme Court affirmed the conviction.

Attorney Leighton then was brought back into the case and, after unsuccessfully applying for a writ of certiorari to the United States Supreme Court, filed a series of post-conviction remedies in the state and federal courts, each of which served to stay Goldsby's execution. In these petitions, the jury exclusion issue was raised for the first time, and Leighton argued that there had been no effective waiver in that Goldsby had never been told of his right to raise the issue.

Accepting this argument, the Fifth Circuit reversed. Judge Rives admitted that the theoretical right to raise the jury exclusion issue, especially in those areas in the South where no blacks were called for jury service, posed a difficult decision for defense counsel, many of whom feel that the prejudicial effects on their client of raising the issue far outweigh any practical protection it may provide. Because of such concerns, Judge Rives took judicial notice "that lawyers residing in many Southern jurisdictions rarely, almost to the point of never, raise the issue of systematic exclusion of Negroes from juries."[15]

Later, the Fifth Circuit rejected Judge Rives' approach, indicating that defense counsel may appropriately conclude that a guilty plea in return for a prison term of years rather than the death penalty is better than the insistence on a non-discriminatorily selected jury.[16] Reversals on such grounds, Judge Charles Clark concluded after noting that many black defendants were executed after retrial with a proper jury, provided only a "Pyrrhic victory."[17]

---

15. Id. at 82. On the futility of placing a black on a jury in an interracial trial, Judge Rives also quoted Justice Jackson who, concurring in the result in Shepard v. Florida, 341 U.S. 50, 55 (1951), had written: "I do not see, as a practical matter, how any Negro on the jury would have dared to cause a disagreement or acquittal. The only chance these Negroes had of acquittal would have been in the courage and decency of some sturdy and forthright white person of sufficient standing to face and live down the odium among his white neighbors that such a vote, if required, would have brought. To me, the technical question of discrimination in the jury selection has only theoretical importance."

16. Winters v. Cook, 489 F.2d 174 (5th Cir. 1973).

17. Id. at 183. Judge Rives filed a strong dissent. Indicating that in *Winters*, as in *Goldsby*, there was no doubt about the exclusion of blacks from jury service, he rejected the defense attorney's reason for not raising the jury issue, namely that "I have always assumed that jurors try the facts." Such an assumption, Judge Rives said, was "wholly unrealistic and would amount to holding unnecessary all of that long line of jurisprudence forbidding systematic exclusion of persons from jury service because of their race." 489 F.2d at 183-184.

Both Judges Rives and Clark have their points. Rives, the idealist, insists that blacks are entitled to a fairly selected jury while conceding that even in the unlikely event blacks were seated, as Justice Jackson pointed out, they would rarely be able to influence the outcome at the grand jury level and would probably be intimidated to voice objection to a guilty plea at the trial level. One would hope that the situation has improved in even the rural South in the last generation, but progress at that sensitive level is a matter that the defense attorney assumes at his client's peril.

Judge Clark would not assume it, and refuses to question the competence of an attorney who, without providing his client with a lesson in constitutional law, urges acceptance of a bargained guilty plea that will save his life. It is well to keep in mind that most attorneys representing blacks charged with crime today, whether in the South or the North, face a choice that may be less dramatic than those in the Goldsby and Winters cases, but they are no less real.[18] Now, as then, the options are influenced by the fact that a jury that meets constitutional standards is not a jury from which influences of racial prejudice have been removed. These cases, while more than three decades old, reflect in dramatic form the racial facts that continue to challenge defense counsel.

Because there are now few jurisdictions where a black defendant can complain that no member of his race has ever sat on a grand or petit jury, proving exclusion requires reliance on statistical disparities between the percentage of blacks eligible for jury service and the number actually called. The procedure is described in Castaneda v. Partida, a pivotal jury discrimination case reviewed in §5.15.

Judge Rives asserted that the racial composition of the grand and petit juries was of great importance because "the case literally shrieks with racial overtones." The 18-year-old black defendant had been severely slapped by Branch, a middle-aged white man with a bad reputation in the community, for talking to a young black woman employee in Branch's beer joint. Infuriated by the slap, Winters left the beer joint, drove to get a shotgun, and returned to kill Branch. Based on these facts, Judge Rives suggested:

"Perhaps we can better envision the case if in our mind's eye we picture it as one in which the races of the parties are reversed. That is to say, a middle-aged black man with a bad reputation in the community runs a beer joint in which he employs a white girl. A white boy, 18-years old, undertakes to talk to the girl and the black man severely slaps the white boy. The white boy, infuriated by the slap, leaves the beer joint, drives to get a shotgun, and returns to kill the black man. Would any member of this Court be so certain that the white boy would suffer the death penalty unless he entered a bargained plea for a life sentence? Would it be certain that the white boy would be indicted for murder? Would it be fair for that white boy to be indicted for murder by an all-black grand jury and to be tried before an all-black petit jury with whites systematically excluded from jury service? Certainly not. Before this Court, Winters stands on an equal footing with that white boy. Each is entitled to a trial before a jury of his peers from which members of his race have not been systematically excluded."

18. Opportunities for raising jury exclusion issues after the appropriate pretrial stage have been limited by Supreme Court cases. In a federal case, Davis v. United States, 411 U.S. 233 (1973), the Court held that such motions, when not raised prior to trial, were considered waived notwithstanding the petitioner's claim that his counsel had not advised him of his right to make the defense. Similarly, a state murder defendant who pleaded guilty at a time when neither he nor his attorney were aware of the unconstitutional composition of the grand jury, was deemed to have waived the right because the voluntary guilty plea "insulates prior constitutional defects from collateral attack." Tollet v. Henderson, 411 U.S. 258, 266 (1973).

Note: The Racial Composition of Juries: A Matter of Life and Death

The lack of African American jurors may mean the difference between life and death for African American defendants.[19] Using data from the Capital Jury Project, William Bowers shows that a defendant has a better chance of avoiding a death sentence if a black male is on the jury. For African American defendants, the difference is even greater. Prior to presenting the results of juror bias, Bowers explains that blacks and whites have different impressions of the criminal justice system. Blacks are less likely to have confidence in judicial procedure and see many arrests and convictions as tainted with racial bias. As a result:

> The divergent experiences and perspectives of black and white Americans have implications for their service as jurors. Whites are apt to make pro-prosecution interpretations of evidence, especially when defendants are black and particularly on highly determinative issues such as eyewitness identification, probable cause, and resistance to arrest. Blacks may be more critical in their interpretation of factual questions presented at trial, particularly when police testimony is involved. And in capital cases, blacks may be more sympathetic than white jurors to mitigating evidence presented by a black defendant with whom they may be better able to identify and empathize, and whose background and experiences they may feel they understand better than do their white counterparts.[20]

The CJP data showed that one or more black male jurors can reduce a defendant's chance of receiving the death penalty. The most profound influence of race and gender, however, was in cases where the defendant is black and the victim is white. In these cases, Bowers presented a "white male dominance" effect and a "black male presence" effect. If five or more white men sat on a jury, the defendant had significantly higher chance of a death penalty conviction.[21] In stark contrast, the presence of black male jurors substantially reduced the likelihood of a death sentence. Researchers found a dramatic 29-point difference between the absence and the presence of one black male juror.[22] The presence of black and white female jurors did not have a significant impact on sentencing outcomes.

Bowers also showed differences in sentencing decision-making processes over the course of the trial, "reflecting progressive polarization between black and white jurors as the trial proceeded."[23] Unlike their black counterparts, Bowers explains:

> [W]hite jurors were quicker to take a stand on punishment than their black counterparts. Although well over half of the whites thought the punishment should be death at

19. William J. Bowers et al., Death Sentencing in Black and White: An Empirical Analysis of the Role of Jurors' Race and Jury Racial Composition, 3 U. Pa. J. Const. L. 171 (2001); David C. Baldus et al., The Use of Peremptory Challenges in Capital Murder Trials: A Legal and Empirical Analysis, 3 U. Pa. J. Const. L. 3 (2001).

20. Bowers, supra note 19, at 181.

21. Id. at 192-193.

22. Id. at 193. "In the absence of black male jurors, death sentences were imposed in 71.9% of the cases, as compared to 42.9% when one black male was on the jury. The difference rose to thirty-four points when the comparison was between none and one or more black male jurors (71.9% vs. 37.5%)."

23. Id. at 200.

the time of sentencing instructions, it was not until the jury's first punishment vote that most black jurors believed the punishment should be life. By that time whites and blacks were far apart.[24]

A difference emerged when jurors were of the same race as the defendant and victim; here these jurors, presumably identifying with either the defendant or the victim, "were more likely to take early stands on punishment, whether in favor of death or of life imprisonment."[25] The greatest change, however, emerged from cases where the defendant was black and the victim was white. Under this scenario, the percentage of white jurors in favor of a death sentence dropped 25.5 points between the first and final punishment votes.

The CJP data reveal divergent perspectives based on a juror's race by examining "three kinds of punishment considerations: (1) the jurors' lingering doubt about the defendant's guilt, (2) their impressions of the defendant's remorsefulness, and (3) their perceptions of the defendant's future dangerousness."[26] Black and white jurors are sharply divided on these matters in cases where the defendant is black and the victim is white:

> White jurors are particularly likely to see the defendant as a danger to society, and black jurors are especially likely to see the black defendant as remorseful or to have lingering doubts about his guilt. In effect, black and white jurors in cases have different concerns and focus on different considerations, with opposing implications for the defendant's punishment.[27]

In death penalty cases, the underrepresentation of racial minorities in juries makes a difference. Yet, as discussed further in the following sections, working toward a fairer representation of blacks on juries becomes even more complicated when considering racial implications of a prosecutor's use of peremptory strikes. The ample evidence of racial bias in jury selection may require a realization of the suggestion in §5.18 — affirmative action in the jury box to increase black representation in jury pools.

§5.15   THE SYSTEMATIC EXCLUSION STANDARD

Castaneda v. Partida[1] involved an innovative but unsuccessful effort by the state to rebut the defendant's prima facie case. Partida challenged his burglary conviction on the basis of discrimination in the grand jury selection process. In Texas, the relevant state district court judge appoints three to five jury commissioners, who in turn select between 15 and 20 persons each, to make up the list from which the

24. Id.
25. Id. at 201.
26. Id. at 203.
27. Id. at 241-242.
§5.15   1. 430 U.S. 482 (1977).

actual grand jury will be drawn. The district court then tests their qualifications under oath, until 12 qualified grand jurors are found.[2]

Partida testified as to general discrimination against Mexican Americans in the area and introduced statistics that show that the average percentage of Spanish-surnamed grand jurors over a ten-year period was only 39 percent, even though the population was almost 80 percent Spanish-surnamed. The grand jury which indicted plaintiff was 50 percent Spanish-surnamed. The Texas courts rejected these arguments, finding technical difficulties with the statistics.[3] Further, "beyond the uncertainties of the statistics, the court found it impossible to believe that discrimination could have been directed against a Mexican-American, in light of the county and the substantial representation of Mexican-Americans on recent grand juries. . . ." In essence, the court refused to presume that Mexican Americans would discriminate against their own kind.[4] On habeas corpus attack, the U.S. District Court in essence agreed, finding that the prima facie case made out by the statistics was rebutted by the fact that Mexican Americans constituted a "governing majority" in the county. The Fifth Circuit reversed, requiring specific proof explaining the disparity for rebuttal, and finding that proof lacking here.

The Supreme Court affirmed the court of appeals decision. In the context of grand jury selection, Justice Blackmun said, the plaintiff must only show that the procedure employed results in substantial underrepresentation of the identifiable group to which he belongs. This establishes a prima facie case of discrimination, particularly when, as here, the process is subjective or otherwise susceptible to abuse. Then the burden shifts to the state to rebut the inference of discrimination. Here, the state offered no testimony explaining the disparity, and thus failed to carry its burden of proof. The "governing majority" theory was rejected because "it would be unwise to presume as a matter of law that human beings of one definable group will not discriminate against other members of their group," particularly given the fact of statistical disparity.

Four justices dissented. The Chief Justice found fault with the statistics used to show the prima facie case. He felt that eligible rather than gross population figures should have been used. Further, he felt that more recent grand juries were much more representative, and therefore that the ten-year time frame was unreasonable.

Justice Powell also dissented. He said that mere statistical disparity more likely resulted from neutral causes than from discriminatory intent. He found the fact that three of the five jury commissioners (who actually select the grand jury) were Mexican Americans to be highly significant. He accepted the argument that a racial group would not discriminate against its own members, finding this to be the justification for the right to a racially representative jury or grand jury in the first place. Noting also the presence of Mexican Americans in a majority of the

2. The qualifications are state citizenship, be qualified to vote in the county, be literate and "of sound mind and good character," and have no prior convictions, pending indictments, or other legal accusations for theft or other felony. Id. at 486.

3. For instance, they failed to show how many Mexican American women married to Anglo men served on the grand jury, how many met the legal qualifications to serve on the grand jury, etc., 506 S.W.2d 209 (Tex. Crim. 1974).

4. 430 U.S. at 490.

elective positions in the county, Justice Powell reasoned: "In these circumstances, where Mexican Americans control both the selection of jurors and the political process, rational inferences from the most basic facts in a democratic society render improbable respondent's claim of an intent to discriminate against him and other Mexican Americans. . . ."[5]

Justice Marshall concurred, expressly to answer Powell's dissent. As for the statistics, he thought "it is all but impossible that this sizable disparity was produced by chance." He felt there was ample procedural opportunity for discrimination since the juror selection procedure was highly subjective and Spanish-surnamed individuals are easily identified. Most importantly, he rejected Justice Powell's argument "that all Mexican Americans, indeed all members of all minority groups, have an 'inclination to assure fairness' to other members of their group." Rather, he writes, social scientists have shown that, contrary to "common sense," minority group members all too often respond to discrimination and prejudice by attempting to disassociate themselves from the group, and even consciously or subconsciously adopt the prejudices of the majority against their fellow group members. This phenomenon is particularly pronounced in members of the group who have achieved some measure of economic or political success, and thereby have gained some acceptability among the dominant group. Further, even if Justice Powell's assumption were true, Marshall believes it would be wrong to make it a "foundation for a constitutional ruling," since relying on broad generalizations and stereotypes is inherently dangerous, particularly in cases where individual discriminatory intent is present.[6]

§5.15.1   Standards of Proof

Justice Blackmun made it clear in his majority opinion in *Castaneda* that jury discrimination charges could not be supported simply by showing that the selection procedure used resulted in a disparity between the number of the minority persons who might be on the lists and the number whose names actually appear. Referring to recent cases on the point, Justice Blackmun said they had established that "an

5. Id. at 516. Justice Powell does not explain how a minority defendant in Partida's situation can ever show the necessary intent to discriminate if even strong statistics can be set aside because the defendant's race holds a majority of the positions in the jury selection process. It may be, though, that Justice Powell felt that the evidence of Mexican American involvement in this case was too strong. In addition to the factors influencing the Supreme Court dissenters, the district court had viewed as important that 80 percent of the county's population and a majority of its voters were Mexican American. He found that "significant percentages" of Mexican Americans had served on every grand jury in the last decade, and that 50 percent of the jurors summoned to serve on defendant's array as well as the foreman who signed the indictment were Mexican Americans.

6. Id. at 504. Justice Marshall's response to Justice Powell is well taken. Unfortunately, the authorities he cites at notes 2-3 of his opinion are outdated; e.g., Gordon W. Allport, The Nature of Prejudice 150-153 (1953); Arnold Marshall Rose, The Negro's Morale 85-96 (1949); or discredited, e.g., Edward Franklin Frazier, Black Bourgeoisie 213-216 (1957); Abram Kardiner & Lionel Ovesey, The Mark of Oppression 313-316 (1962). Newer studies are needed. They would likely show that (1) blacks are less consumed with self-hate than the earlier studies seemed to indicate, and (2) are more likely to view white racism rather than black inadequacy as a cause of discrimination resulting in more identification with black defendants by black jurors.

official act is not unconstitutional *solely* because it has a racially disproportionate impact."[7] But he said the cases cited recognized that a clear pattern, unexplainable on grounds other than race, can emerge from the effect of the state action even when the governing legislation appears neutral on its face.

Castaneda illustrates that a jury selection system that relies on subjective evaluations such as the selections by the jury commissioners is vulnerable to attack if the result is a pool the racial make-up of which differs significantly from the eligible jurors in the community. The degree of disparity sufficient to make out a prima facie case, though, seems to vary in ways that prove only that most judges were once lawyers rather than statisticians.

For example, a Supreme Court majority in Swain v. Alabama[8] reviewed facts showing that blacks constituted 26 percent of those eligible by age for jury service, with 10 to 15 percent of the blacks whose names were on the venire list, and concluded that "[w]e cannot say that purposeful discrimination based on race alone is satisfactorily proved by showing that an identifiable group in a community is under-represented by as much as 10%."[9] Of course, the disparity was in fact close to 50 percent. In subsequent cases, the Court has done better. In Whitus v. Georgia,[10] the Court found that the disparity between the percentage of blacks on the tax digest (27.1), and that of the grand jury venire (5.1) and the petit jury venire (7.8), strongly indicated that the jury commissioners utilized opportunities in the selection process to discriminate. The Court noted that the mathematical probability of having seven blacks on a venire chosen from a jury list, 27 percent of which consisted of the names of black persons, was only 0.000006, but did not base its holding on statistical analysis. Rather, the defendant's murder convictions were set aside for the second time because the same jury selection procedure had been used in the second trial as had resulted in discrimination in the first.

Based on a record revealing serious disparities between blacks on tax digests and those serving in juries, the Court followed *Whitus* in Jones v. Georgia,[11] and rejected the Georgia Supreme Court's effort to distinguish the two cases on a presumption that because "public officers are presumed to have discharged their sworn official duties . . . we can not assume that the jury commissioners did not eliminate prospective jurors on the basis of their competency to serve, rather than because of racial discrimination."

In Alexander v. Louisiana,[12] the Court again declined to rely solely on statistical improbability. From a population that was 21 percent black, a grand jury list was compiled that was 14 percent black. But only 5 percent of the grand jury venire was black, and there were no blacks on the grand jury that indicted the petitioner. The probability of such a result, had the grand jurors been chosen randomly, was one in 20,000. The holding that the petitioner had made out a prima facie case of

---

7. Washington v. Davis, 426 U.S. 229 (1976); Arlington Heights v. Metropolitan Hous. Dev. Corp., 429 U.S. 252 (1977).
8. 380 U.S. 202 (1965).
9. 380 U.S. at 208-209. See also Akins v. Texas, 325 U.S. 398 (1945).
10. 385 U.S. 545 (1967).
11. 398 U.S. 23 (1967).
12. 405 U.S. 625 (1972).

discrimination, which the state failed to overcome, was based also on the finding that jury selection procedures were not racially neutral.

While, as these cases indicate, judges are willing to rely on intuitive notions of probability in deciding whether the absence of blacks from the jury selection process can be attributed to racial discrimination, they are much more reluctant to apply more advanced mathematical techniques, which are necessary in jury cases where blacks are neither entirely excluded nor included on only a token basis. In these "underrepresentation" cases, courts have not been able to articulate a rationale that defines what is meant by the oft stated notion that some blacks should have been chosen, when in fact some blacks were chosen.

Since *Castaneda* was decided, a number of courts have utilized a variety of complex statistical methods to determine whether the composition of the jury venire can be considered to be the product of discrimination.[13] More significant than the statistical methodology employed by courts is the fact that courts are still willing to accept statistical proof as the sole evidence of discrimination in jury selection. In an era of increasing suspicion of statistical evidence,[14] the federal and state benches have remained relatively steadfast in their commitment to take seriously purely statistical claims of discrimination. It remains to be seen, though, whether jury claims will continue to benefit from this solicitude.

Note: Diversity Brings Out the Best in Jurors

In a 2007 study, the Citizen Action Group investigated the racial composition of Manhattan jurors and found a disturbingly large representation of white jurors.[15] This finding is disappointing in a place where jury pools have the potential to be extremely diverse given the racial make-up of the area, which is only 54 percent white.[16]

These results did not come as a surprise to the President of the New York Association of Criminal Defense Lawyers who said that "the percentage of whites in the jury pool has actually grown larger in recent years, as the court system stopped granting most exemptions." From personal observation, the result is a dramatic influx of middle-class white voters," Mr. Arshack.[17]

The results of the Citizen Action Group's study bore out this anecdotal evidence. Two researchers categorized over 12,000 people in actual pools by observing their race based on their appearance (given that the researchers could not ask the jurors their race).[18] The results showed such a high percentage of white potential jurors that incorrect observations alone could not account for the disparity.

13. See, e.g., Alston v. Manson, 791 F.2d 255 (2d Cir. 1986); Moultrie v. Martin, 690 F.2d 1078 (4th Cir. 1982); Villafane v. Manson, 504 F. Supp. 78 (D. Conn. 1980); Waller v. Butkovich, 593 F. Supp. 942 (M.D.N.C. 1984). See generally David Kairys, Jury Representativeness: A Mandate for Multiple Source Lists, 65 Cal. L. Rev. 776 (1977).

14. See e.g., McCleskey v. Kemp, 481 U.S. 279 (1987); Wards Cove v. Antonio, 490 U.S. 642 (1989).

15. Anemona Hartocollis, Study finds that Whites May Be Overrepresented in Manhattan's Jury Pools, N.Y. Times, June 27, 2007.

16. Id.

17. Id.

18. Id.

Seventy-eight percent of the jury pool were white jurors whereas only about half of the Manhattan population is white.[19] Consequently, only ten percent of the jury pool observed by the researchers was black compared to 17 percent of the population and only 6.5 percent of the pool was Asian compared to 9.5 percent of the population. Hispanics who can be of any race were observed at only 6.3 percent of the pool but they make-up 27 percent of the population.[20]

Such findings raise questions about how to improve the diversity of jury pools so that petite juries can truly reflect a cross-section of the community. The Citizen Action Group suggests: (1) allowing felons to serve on jury pools, (2) sending more jury notices to zip codes with large minority populations (which may raise serious constitutional issues), and (3) sending "motivational" flyers to encourage and educate minority communities about juror participation.[21]

The need for diverse jury pools often centers around the right of defendants to face a jury of their peers including minority jurors who may contribute different perspectives in deliberation. The benefits also include greater information sharing, creativity, flexibility and thoughtfulness.[22] Yet Samuel Sommers of Tufts University explains that very little research has tested the assumptions around diverse juries "or examined the more basic psychological processes through which diversity affects group decision-making."[23] His study actually evidenced not only that minorities made a difference in jury deliberations but also that this difference went beyond information sharing to influencing the participation of their white counterparts.

The study created mock juries from an actual jury pool in a county in Michigan to introduce them to a mock murder case of a black defendant. Twenty-nine juries were selected and each jury consisted of six people, and there were both homogenous (all white) and heterogenous (4 white and 2 black) juries.

The racial composition was significant: 30.7 percent of participants in diverse groups voted guilty, compared to 50.5 percent of participants in all-white groups. Most interesting was the impact of diversity on deliberation:[24]

> [H]eterogeneous groups deliberated longer and considered a wider range of information than did homogeneous groups. However, these differences did not simply result from Black participants adding unique perspectives to the discussions. Rather, White participants were largely responsible for the influence of racial composition, as they raised more case facts, made fewer factual errors, and were more amenable to discussion of race-related issues when they were members of a diverse group.[25]

This study shows that a representational jury can truly make a difference to a defendant's case and seriously requires us to ask what we can do to make our juries look like the communities we live in.

19. Id.
20. Id.
21. Id.
22. Samuel Sommer, On Racial Diversity and Group Decision-Making: Identifying Multiple Effects of Racial Composition on Jury Deliberations, at http://www.apa.org/releases/0406_JPSP_Sommer.pdf, at 3.
23. Id. at 4.
24. Id. at 23.
25. Id. at 30-31.

§5.16   THE PEREMPTORY CHALLENGE: A CHOICE OF INTERESTS

To this point, it is rather clear that the right to be tried by grand and petit juries from which members of minority groups have not been systematically excluded is little more than ethereal when it is considered that allegations of violations of that right must be tested by the loose and unpredictable standards discussed in §5.15. But the chance that black defendants might experience in fact what for a century the Supreme Court has offered in theory was diminished substantially in 1965 when the Supreme Court approved the long-followed prosecutorial practice of striking all blacks from the petit jury through the use of peremptory challenges. Black jurors might be permitted to hear cases without racial questions, particularly those involving a black defendant and black victim, but any crime in which the defendant was black and the victim white was automatically a case with a racial question. In legal terms, a jury peremptorily stripped of all blacks in sight is no less a constitutionally valid jury, but the lay defendant with his fate in the hands of an all white jury may be excused for wondering how he has benefited from the long line of precedent stretching from Strauder v. West Virginia in 1880 to Castaneda v. Partida in 1977.

§5.16.1   Swain v. Alabama

The black defendant in Swain v. Alabama[1] was convicted of rape in Talladega County, Alabama. The jury was all white; the prosecutor had used peremptory challenges to strike from the petit jury venire the only six black men on it eligible for jury service. Swain attacked the conviction on four different grounds. First, for the previous 20 years blacks had been severely underrepresented on grand and petit jury panels in this county. Black adult males were 26 percent of the adult male population, but made up only 10 to 15 percent of the people chosen to be on the panels. Second, the prosecutor in this case struck the six black prospective jurors solely on the basis of race. Third, this technique had been used continuously by prosecutors in the county as far back as anyone could remember; the prosecutors admitted they often used their peremptory challenges, either alone or in cooperation with the defense, to remove all blacks from consideration for jury service. Fourth, and as a result of this governmental practice, "no Negro within the memory of persons now living has ever served on any petit jury in any civil or criminal case tried in Talladega County, Alabama." This total exclusion, the defendant argued, served to make out a prima facie case of discrimination which it is up to the state to rebut, and which they had failed to do.

The Supreme Court denied relief, affirming the conviction. The vote was six to three, Justices Goldberg, Warren, and Douglas dissenting. Justice White in the majority opinion said that first, the underrepresentation of blacks on jury panels was not sufficient in itself to show invidious discrimination. It was only a disparity

§5.16   1. 380 U.S. 202 (1965).

of 10 percent between eligible blacks in the county and those chosen for panels. (Note: It was actually a disparity of close to 50 percent of the eligible blacks.) More convincing evidence of purposeful discrimination was necessary, such as a showing that the jury commissioners intentionally discriminated; this the defendant had failed to prove.

Second, the Court said that the action of the prosecutor in this case in striking all blacks did not of itself violate equal protection. The peremptory challenge system is extremely important in the American system of justice. While not constitutionally mandated, the challenge is one of the most important of the rights secured to the accused. (Note that the Court speaks of the accused's rights, while it was the prosecutor in this case who used the challenge.) The whole basis for the peremptory challenge system is that it allows one to strike a juror for any reason one feels important. The system would no longer serve this purpose if equal protection standards were applicable to one's method of exercising challenges.

However, the Court said in its third point, if the challenge system has been used systematically over many cases to keep blacks from serving on juries in the county, then perhaps a prima facie violation of the Fourteenth Amendment can be shown, because such a systematic use of the peremptory challenge does not serve the purpose for which the system was devised. In any one case, the prosecution may remove all blacks for some legitimate reason related to the case.

While there was evidence in *Swain* to the effect that the prosecutor sometimes agreed with the defense to strike all blacks, there is absolutely none indicating clearly "what the prosecution did or did not do on its own account in any cases other than the one at bar." Any action taken in cooperation with the defense is irrelevant to the discrimination question. As a result, no Fourteenth Amendment violation has been proven.

Finally, the Court held that the mere fact that no blacks have served on juries in the history of the county does not make out a prima facie case of purposeful discrimination. If blacks had been excluded from being on jury panels, a different result would be dictated by Strauder and other prior cases. However, when the issue is the selection of jurors from the panels, it must be noted that defense counsel plays a very crucial part in the challenge process. Thus the absence of blacks from juries is not necessarily the state's fault, and no inference of discrimination can arise.

The dissenters, speaking through Justice Goldberg, took issue with the majority's finding of insufficient evidence as to the involvement of the prosecution in striking blacks. First, the state prosecuting attorney admitted that he struck a jury differently in white-versus-black cases than in white-white or black-black cases. He also stated that many times he would consult with defense attorneys before voir dire to decide whether or not to strike all blacks; often the defense would agree to do so, and all blacks would be struck from the panel first. The prosecutor also said that "only on occasion" did black defendants want all blacks removed.[2]

---

2. Id. at 235.

§5.16.2   Batson v. Kentucky

Swain's insurmountable evidentiary burden made it impossible for defendants to successfully claim that the juries that convicted them were discriminatorily compiled.[3] Moreover, the narrow interpretation imposed upon *Swain* in the years to follow effectively foreclosed equal protection challenges to the composition of a jury. In a remarkable feat of judicial ignorance (or activism), courts read the systematic exclusion requirement of *Swain* to require that the petitioner prove that the prosecutor exercises peremptories against black jurors in all cases, and not solely in cases involving black defendants. Thus, *Swain* was not violated when the government excluded black jurors only in cases where the accused was black. Relief was thus denied in precisely those cases where it was most needed: where prosecutors trying black defendants, foreseeing racially driven leniency, were most likely to strike blacks jurors solely because of their race.[4]

The obstacles which *Swain* placed before those seeking to ensure nondiscrimination in the selection of juries caused many state courts to abandon *Swain* and announce more permissive rules based on their own state constitutions or on the Sixth Amendment.[5] Disagreement with this controlling Supreme Court precedent, oddly enough, was actually invited by the Court. Although the Court passed up the opportunity to overrule *Swain* when it denied certiorari in McCray v. Abrams,[6] a federal case involving the racially motivated use of peremptory challenges by a prosecutor, five of the Justices signaled lower courts to experiment in this area.[7]

---

3. One court noted that a defendant has successfully prosecuted a challenge to the state's exercise of peremptories only twice since Swain was decided. United States v. Childress, 715 F.2d 1313, 1316 (8th Cir. 1983). For a collection of cases in which *Swain* challenges were denied, Note, Affirmative Selection: A New Response to Peremptory Challenge Abuse, 38 Stan. L. Rev. 781, 783 n.8 (1986).

Many commentators condemned the *Swain* decision for the minimal restraints it placed on prosecutors who used their peremptory challenges to exclude black jurors. See, e.g., Developments, Race and the Criminal Process, 101 Harv. L. Rev. 1472, 1573 (1988); George Bundy Smith, Swain v. Alabama: The Use of Peremptory Challenges to Strike Blacks from Juries, 27 How. L.J. 1571 (1984); Sheri Lynn Johnson, Black Innocence and the White Jury, 83 Mich. L. Rev. 1611, 1666 (1985). For a detailed anecdotal account of the use of peremptory challenges to strike persons of color in racially charged cases, see Paula DiPerna, Juries on Trial 151-181 (1984).

4. See Johnson, supra note 3, at 1658 & n.240 and cases cited therein.

5. State appellate courts in New York, California, Florida, and New Mexico announced their unwillingness to follow Swain and adopted rules essentially identical to that adopted by the Court in Batson. Each of these courts rejected what became the largest stumbling block after Swain: the requirement that the petitioner show a history of systematic exclusion of members of her group. Under new state common law, the petitioner need only demonstrate that the prosecutor was motivated by racial animus in her particular case. See State v. Gilmore, 199 N.J. Super. 389, 489 A.2d 1175 (1985); State v. Neil, 457 So. 2d 481 (Fla. 1984); People v. Thomas, 72 A.D.2d 87 (1981); State v. Crespin, 94 N.M. 486, 612 P.2d 716 (N.M. Ct. App. 1980); People v. Wheeler, 22 Cal. 3d 258, 148 Cal. Rptr. 890, 583 P.2d 748 (1978); Commonwealth v. Soares, 377 Mass. 461, 387 N.E.2d 499, cert. denied, 444 U.S. 881 (1979). See also McCray v. Abrams, 576 F. Supp. 1244 (E.D.N.Y. 1983).

6. 461 U.S. 961 (1983).

7. The prosecutor had used seven peremptory challenges to exclude all blacks from the jury.

The defendant, who was black, moved at trial to require the prosecutor to give nonracial reasons for the peremptories. The judge denied the motion, People v. McCray, 429 N.Y.S.2d 158, 159 (N.Y. Sup. Ct., Kings Co. 1980), and the New York Court of Appeals affirmed, relying on *Swain*. New York v. McCray, 57 N.Y.2d 542, 443 N.E.2d 915, 457 N.Y.S.2d 441 (1982), cert. denied, 461 U.S. 961 (1983).

Justices Stevens, Blackmun, and Powell, who voted with the majority to deny review, stated in a separate opinion that they believed that "further consideration of the substantive and procedural ramifications of the problem by other courts" would allow the Supreme Court "to deal with the issue more wisely at a later date." The opinion concluded, "it is a sound exercise of discretion for the Court to allow the various States to serve as laboratories in which the issue receives further study before it is addressed by this Court."[8]

Finally, after more than two decades, the Court in Batson v. Kentucky[9] placed some limits on prosecutors' use of the peremptory challenge to remove potential black jurors under suspicious circumstances that were virtually excluded from judicial review by the proof standards adopted in Swain. The relief was welcome, but as Justice Marshall warns in his concurring opinion, hardly sufficient.

In *Batson*, the prosecutor used his peremptory challenges to strike all four black persons on the venire in a case in which Batson, a black, was charged with second-degree burglary and receipt of stolen goods. A jury composed only of white persons was selected. Defense counsel moved to discharge the jury before it was sworn, on the grounds that the prosecutor's removal of the black veniremen violated petitioner's rights under the Sixth and Fourteenth Amendments to a jury drawn from a cross-section of the community, and under the Fourteenth Amendment to equal protection under the law.

The Supreme Court through Justice Powell held that the state's authority to strike individual jurors through peremptory challenges is subject to the equal protection clause's prohibition on challenging potential jurors solely on account of their race or on the assumption that black jurors as a group will be unable to impartially consider the state's case against a black defendant.

Rejecting the evidentiary formulation in *Swain* as inconsistent with the appropriate standards for assessing a prima facie case under the Equal Protection Clause, Justice Powell said that a defendant may establish a prima facie case of purposeful discrimination in the selection of the petit jury solely on the evidence concerning the prosecutor's exercise of the peremptory challenges at the defendant's trial. To establish such a case, defendant can show that the totality of relevant facts gives rise to an inference of discriminatory purpose. In making this showing, defendant must first show that he is a member of a cognizable racial group capable of being singled out for differential treatment.

Defendant may then make a prima facie case by proving that in a particular jurisdiction members of his race have not been summoned for jury service over an extended period of time. But defendant may also establish in other ways that the prosecutor has exercised peremptory challenges to remove from the venire members of the defendant's race and that the facts and any other relevant circumstances raise an inference that the prosecutor used that practice to exclude the veniremen from the petit jury on account of their race.

Once a defendant makes a prima facie showing of purposeful discrimination in selection of the petit jury, the burden shifts to the state to come forward with a

8. 461 U.S. at 961.
9. 476 U.S. 79 (1986).

neutral explanation for challenging black jurors. The prosecutor may not rebut the defendant's prima facie case of discrimination by stating merely that he challenged jurors of the defendant's race on the assumption that in his intuitive judgment, they would be partial to the defendant because of their shared race. Rather, the prosecutor must articulate a neutral explanation related to the particular case to be tried. Justice Powell expressed confidence that trial judges would be able to decide if the circumstances concerning the prosecutor's use of peremptory challenges creates a prima facie case of discrimination.

Judge Marshall concurred. While joining "Justice Powell's eloquent opinion for the court, which he said takes a historic step toward eliminating the shameful practice of racial discrimination in the selection of juries," he wrote separately to express his view that the "decision today will not end the racial discrimination that peremptories inject into the jury-selection process. That goal, he predicted, can be accomplished only by eliminating peremptory challenges entirely." Justice Marshall then reviewed the history of jury discrimination by prosecutors using their peremptory challenges and warned that it would not require great intelligence for a prosecutor to strike all blacks and then invent nonracial reasons for their exclusion. In his view, the only way to eliminate the practice of racial discrimination in the use of peremptory challenges would be to eliminate peremptory challenges entirely.

Chief Justice Burger, in his dissent, questioned an application of the equal protection clause that singled out racial classifications for special treatment without indicating equal protection limitations on other exclusions in the context of peremptory challenges. He also complained that any change in the challenges use for any reason at all altered its character and might hurt defendants. Justice Rehnquist, also dissenting, objected to the restriction on "the historic scope of the peremptory challenge." Rather than a constitutional violation, he said that the "use of group affiliations, such as age, race, or occupation, as 'proxy' for potential juror partiality, based on the assumption or belief that members of one group are more likely to favor defendants who belong to the same group, has long been accepted as a legitimate basis for the State's exercise of peremptory challenges."

§5.16.3 The Continued Use of Peremptory Challenges after *Batson*

Both Justice Marshall's warning and Justice Rehnquist's disagreement raise fears as to the likely value of the *Batson* reform. Adherence to *Batson* will not much alter the deeply held prosecutorial view that black jurors will be partial to black defendants. Trial courts must be required to perform a more searching review of the prosecutor's reasons than required by Justice Powell. A student of mine, Patricia Perlmutter (J.D. 1989), suggested the following procedure: After defendant makes a prima facie case, prosecutors should then have the burden of showing by a preponderance of the evidence that they would have struck this juror had he or she been white. She explained that judges must compare the reasons offered by the prosecutor for excluding a black person from the jury with the characteristics of the white jurors.

The appropriate instructions for trial courts and the proper standard for reviewing trial court actions can become quite technical without really removing the unmentioned but no less real concern that the "cost of doing justice" on this issue is too great. This unspoken balance seems to undergird the decision in *Swain* — that eliminating the peremptory challenge in order to eliminate its racist use was too high a price to pay. This is an almost predictable outcome when the society — not without some reason — views the potential beneficiaries as mostly black defendants charged with heinous crimes. Thus, the Court's refusal to accept Justice Marshall's suggestion that peremptory challenges be banned may not be based on any realistic belief that prosecutors will stop using their peremptory challenges to discriminate against black jurors, but rather reflects their unspoken conclusion that if this is the "cost of justice" for black defendants, it is too high. Recall that concern is specifically voiced in McCleskey v. Kemp, §5.12.3.

But perhaps we who advocate racial equality cannot have it both ways. If racism is as pervasive in American society as we claim and if in particular the criminal justice system is as racially biased throughout as the statistical studies in *McCleskey* show it is in capital punishment cases, then why should black jurors be "objective" when considering a case against a black defendant, particularly when the victim of the alleged crime is white and those responsible for the prosecution are white? The failure to evidence skepticism based on experience in such cases should raise questions about the individual's sanity, not his or her objectivity.

All the studies serve as mostly ignored proof that white jurors consider race along with all the fears and stereotypes that accompany race in America. And yet for purposes of jury service, all but the flagrantly prejudiced are considered capable of "objective" judgment. Efforts to ferret out the non-obvious but quietly present prejudice via the voir dire process are doomed to minimal success.[10]

So, it is not surprising that *Batson* has proved to be no panacea.[11] Many American juries remain all white or predominantly white.[12] Moreover, persuasive

10. See, e.g., Turner v. Murray, 476 U.S. 28 (1986), where the Court held that in a capital case, a "defendant accused of an interracial crime is entitled to have prospective jurors informed of the race of the victim and questioned on the issue of racial bias." Justice White reasoned that in a capital sentencing proceeding before a jury, the jury is called upon to make a "highly subjective, unique, individualized judgment regarding the punishment that a particular person deserves." He pointed out that "because of the range of discretion entrusted to a jury in a capital sentencing hearing, there is a unique opportunity for racial prejudice to operate but remain undetected." Coming to the present case, he concluded, "we find that risk that racial prejudice may have infected petitioner's capital sentencing is unacceptable in light of the ease with which that risk could have been minimized. By refusing to question prospective jurors on racial prejudice, the trial judge failed to adequately protect petitioner's constitutional right to an impartial jury." Justices Powell and Rehnquist dissented. In their view, the rule in the case "amounts to a constitutional presumption that jurors in capital cases are racially biased. Such presumption unjustifiably suggests that criminal justice in our courts of law is meted out on racial grounds."

11. For criticism of the *Batson* standard, see Albert Alschuler, The Supreme Court and the Jury, Voir Dire, Peremptory Challenges, and the Review of Jury Verdicts, 56 U. Chi. L. Rev. 153 (1989); Note, Due Process Limits on Prosecutorial Peremptory Challenges, 102 Harv. L. Rev. 1013 (1989); Developments in the Law — Race and the Criminal Process, 101 Harv. L. Rev. 1472, 1581 (1988); Note, Batson v. Kentucky: A Half Step in the Right Direction, 72 Cornell L. Rev. 1025 (1987).

12. Johnson, supra note 3, at 1616, 1655-1656; see also National Jury Project, Jurywork: Systematic Techniques §5.01, at 5-2 (2d ed. 1987) (noting that "American jury systems tend to overrepresent white, middle-aged, suburban, middle-class people and underrepresent other groups.").

Litigants' challenges to individual jurors represent an important means of maintaining a predominantly white jury, because of the ease with which racial animus is disguised by seemingly

evidence documents the continued influence of racial prejudice in jury deliberations.[13] White jurors are more likely than black jurors to convict black defendants and less likely to vindicate the rights of black victims or plaintiffs.[14] Discussing the continued homogeneity of American juries, the Harvard Law Review concluded: "The result is that, in spite of the constitutional guarantee that a jury be drawn from a fair cross-section of the community, defendants are judged by juries that are often too homogeneous to recognize and confront their own racial prejudices" (citation omitted).[15]

The limitations of *Batson* are inherent in the Court's refusal to confront the impossibility of removing racial discrimination from a procedure that is fraught with discrimination. The purpose of peremptory challenges is to allow litigants an opportunity to exclude those jurors for whom there is no legitimate cause for dismissal but whom they nonetheless distrust. Race will obviously and inevitably play a role in deciding which jurors a litigant believes will be favorable to her side. When the Court chose to re-affirm the use of the peremptory challenge in *Batson*, it rendered itself impotent to do more than "manifest its symbolic opposition to racial discrimination" in a system that, by its nature, discriminates.[16]

Rather than placing an outright ban on peremptory challenges, *Batson* requires only that the prosecutor offer a racially neutral rationale for the peremptories she exercises. Judicial decisions in the few years since *Batson* have made it crystal clear that the threshold of racial neutrality is a low one. White judges are likely to share the same conscious or subconscious biases as white prosecutors, and are therefore unlikely to recognize the racism of rationale that strikes them as intuitive.[17] Consequently, as Justice Marshall noted in his concurrence in *Batson*, *Swain's* successor will curb only the most flagrant abuses.[18] A recent holding of the Alabama Supreme Court, to name only one instance, provides proof of Justice Marshall's prediction. In *Wallace v. State*,[19] the state court accepted the vague reasons offered by the prosecutor to justify his challenges and found that the prosecutor had not acted from racial prejudice when he excluded black jurors. The prosecutor claimed to have challenged

---

neutral criteria. In Connecticut, one study found that prosecutors struck 55.2 percent of black potential jurors in cases with a white defendant and 84.8 percent in cases where the defendant was black or Latino. United States v. Robinson, 421 F. Supp. 467, 469 (D. Conn. 1976). Likewise, in St. Louis, Missouri, prosecutors used peremptory challenges against 74 percent of the blacks who reported for jury service. DiPerna, supra note 3, at 175.

13. Johnson, supra note 3, at 1616-1650.

14. Id. at 1619-1640. See also Race and the Criminal Process, supra note 11, at 1558. Although white jurors are empirically more likely to favor white defendants, black jurors do not tend to be more lenient towards defendants of the same race. Furthermore, while it is true that black jurors will tend to interpret ambiguous evidence in favor of black defendants, it is also true that black jurors are more likely than whites to convict where the victim is black, regardless of the defendant's race. Johnson, supra note 3, at 1627. See also Miller & Hewitt, Conviction of a Defendant as a Function of Juror-Victim Racial Similarity, 105 J. Soc. Psych. 159, (1978) (noting that white jurors convict black defendants of raping black victims only 32 percent of the time, while black jurors convict in these circumstances 80 percent of the time).

15. Developments in the Law — Race and the Criminal Process, supra note 11, at 1559.

16. Alschuler, supra note 11, at 199.

17. Johnson, supra note 3, at 1693.

18. *Batson*, 476 U.S. at 105-106 (Marshall, J., concurring).

19. 507 So. 2d 466 (Ala. 1987).

one black juror because she was a homemaker, another because she was a student, and a third because she was a "grandmotherly type." Other black jurors were excluded because one wore a beard, another was unemployed, and the last was roughly the same age as the defendant's mother.[20] When courts are willing to accept such non-reasons as rebuttal of an inference of discrimination, even *Batson* will offer no real protection for blacks.

The shortcomings of *Batson* were most clearly illustrated in a petition for certiorari denied by the Supreme Court three years after *Batson* was decided.[21] Richard Wilkerson, a black man, was convicted of murder by an all-white jury and sentenced to death. The prosecution exercised its peremptory challenges to remove all of the potential black jurors. The trial court found that a prima facie case of racial discrimination was established by the racial coincidence of the prosecutors' challenges. But, in a pattern repeated in all too many courtrooms, the judge accepted the prosecutor's justifications as dispositive despite clear evidence that the prosecutor relied on race in making his choices.

The exchange between the judge and one of the prosecutors went as follows:

Q. When you say you felt a little uneasy about [the juror] generally, was it your considered opinion that the fact that she was black and that the defendant was black might have some factor or might be some factor in her decision making process?
A. I was not completely satisfied that it would not, but that was my uneasiness. . . .
Q. Based on [the defendant and the juror] being of the same race?
A. Yeah, that is just a factor.[22]

After this colloquy, the trial judge ruled that the prosecutors "did not exercise peremptory challenges in a discriminatory manner to exclude venire persons based upon racial considerations, nor did they, in any way, purposefully or deliberately deny jury participation to black persons because of race."

The Supreme Court declined to review the trial judge's findings, which were affirmed by two courts of appeal. In his dissent from the denial of certiorari, Justice Marshall expressed his frustration that *Batson*'s guarantee of nondiscrimination will never be realized where courts continue to ignore such "smoking guns."

---

20. Courts have upheld the exclusion of black jurors where the prosecutor claimed to be motivated by a juror's eye contact, perceived hostility, posture and demeanor, poor attitude, and the fact that the juror's last name was similar to the defendant's. See, respectively, United States v. Cartlidge, 808 F.2d 1064, 1071 (5th Cir. 1987); United States v. Matthews, 803 F.2d 325, 331-332 (7th Cir. 1986), rev'd on other grounds, 485 U.S. 58 (1988); United States v. Forbes, 816 F.2d 1006, 1010-1011 (5th Cir. 1987); United States v. Vaccaro, 816 F.2d 443, 457 (9th Cir. 1987); United States v. Tindle, 860 F.2d 125, 129 (4th Cir. 1988), cert. denied, 490 U.S. 1114 (1989). For additional cases, see also Douglas Colbert, Challenging the Challenge: Thirteenth Amendment as a Prohibition Against the Racial Use of Peremptory Challenges, 76 Cornell L. Rev. 1, 97-98 (1990).

Professor Alschuler satirizes courts' application of the racial neutrality requirement: "Although prosecutors may not discriminate against blacks, they may discriminate against unemployed people, people who fail to maintain eye contact with prosecutors, people who stare at prosecutors, liberals, social workers, people who live in public housing, people who have not finished high school, and others who also happen to be black." Alschuler, supra note 11, at 200.

Courts have accepted prosecutors' justifications in all but the most egregious of cases. See, e.g., State v. Tomlin, 299 S.C. 294, 384 S.E.2d 707, 708 (1989) (disallowing prosecutor's exclusion of a black juror who "shucked and jived" in his walk to the jury box).

21. Wilkerson v. Texas, 493 U.S. 924 (1989).

22. Id. at 925.

Justice Marshall concluded that state courts and lower federal courts were applying a but-for causal standard to their analysis of *Batson* claims. Litigants alleging racial discrimination in the selection of the jury may only prevail where they are able to show that those struck would have been seated but-for racial considerations. A *Batson* claim will fail whenever the prosecutor gives her word that she would have challenged the juror regardless of race. When the self-serving justifications of a prosecutor, attempting to preserve a white jury and her own personal reputation, are sufficient to rebut a claim of discrimination, *Batson*'s guarantee of racial fairness in jury selection is made meaningless.

Since 2005, the Supreme Court has handed down three decisions that seem to chastise lower courts for not recognizing "smoking guns." In their attempt to give teeth to the *Batson* standard, the Court found that in all three cases the *Batson* challenge should have succeeded and that the trial courts should have seen through the prosecutors purported race-neutral reasoning. The Court attempts to clarify how a trial court should apply the Batson standard to offer the defendants genuine protection against racially biased peremptories.

One post-*Batson* case, Miller-El v. Dretke, is discussed in §5.12.3. The Supreme Court found *Batson* problems with the prosecution's use of peremptory challenges to exclude black jurors in a capital case. The Court explains that "the rub has been the practical difficulty of ferreting out discrimination in selections discretionary by nature, and choices subject to myriad legitimate influences, whatever the race of the individuals on the panel from which jurors are selected." The majority criticized the prosecution for its race neutral explanations which appear "unlikely" and "reek . . . with afterthought" finding that the explanations would have required exclusion of similarly situated non-minority jurors as well. The result of the *Batson* advance is that it has enabled white men and women to obtain the more fairly constituted juries for which blacks have sought for decades with far less chance of success.

Also in 2005, the Supreme Court in Johnson v. California[23] further explained the defendant's burden of making out a prima facie case in a *Batson* challenge. In *Johnson*, the defendant challenged a prosecutor's use of three peremptory challenges to remove the only three black jurors as a "systematic attempt to exclude African Americans from the jury panel."[24] The Supreme Court reversed and remanded a California Supreme Court's decision to uphold the trial judge decision denying the *Batson* challenge. Justice Stevens held that Batson only required permissible inferences of discrimination to prove a prima facie case of discrimination, which then shifted the burden to the state offer race-neutral reasons for the racial exclusion. The California trial court had required a higher standard — that the objector show the exclusion was more likely than not a result of racial discrimination. Justice Stevens states:

> [I]n describing the burden-shifting framework, we assumed in *Batson* that the trial judge would have the benefit of all relevant circumstances, including the prosecutor's explanation, before deciding whether it was more likely than not that the challenge

23. 545 U.S. 162 (2005).
24. Id. at 165.

was improperly motivated. We did not intend the first step to be so onerous that a defendant would have to persuade the judge — on the basis of all the facts, some of which are impossible for the defendant to know with certainty — that the challenge was more likely than not the product of purposeful discrimination. Instead, a defendant satisfies the requirements of *Batson*'s first step by producing evidence sufficient to permit the trial judge to draw an inference that discrimination has occurred.[25]

Most recently in 2008, the Court found in Snyder v. Louisiana,[26] that the prosecutor's reasons for striking a black juror were a pretext for racial discrimination. In a capital murder case, during voir dire, the prosecutor used peremptory strikes to remove all five black potential jurors who survived challenges for cause. The defendant was convicted of murder and sentenced to death.

The Supreme Court first granted cert, vacated judgment and remanded the case to be reviewed in light of the decision of Miller-El v. Dretke. When the Louisiana Supreme Court rejected petitioner's *Batson* claim again, the Supreme Court again granted cert.

In justifying the use of preemptory strikes, the prosecutor explained that he struck one juror because he looked nervous and was a student teacher which made him more likely to come back with a fast verdict. The Court found that given these reasons the trial court "committed clear error in overruling petitioner's *Batson* objection." The trial judge is required to look at "all of the circumstances that bear upon the issue of racial animosity." The Court rejected the first reason because there was not evidence in the record that the prosecutor would have struck the juror on nervous grounds alone and rejected the second reason because white jurors with family or work conflicts were not struck by the prosecutor. Given this review of the record, the Court disapproved of the trial court's dismissive attitude toward the challenge and finds that the defendant showed purposeful discrimination.

§5.16.4 The Post-*Batson* Era

Batson left open four vital questions with which the Supreme Court has grappled in the years since its decision: its applicability in the civil context, its relevance to discrimination against jurors of a different race than the defendant, the right of other groups to be free from discriminatory jury selection techniques, and the obligations of criminal defense attorneys to abide by requirements of racial neutrality in jury selection.[27]

The Supreme Court's decision to extend *Batson* to civil trials in Edmonson v. Leesville Concrete Co.[28] was arguably the Court's most significant expansion of

---

25. Id. at 170.

26. Snyder v. Louisiana, _____ S. Ct. _____ (2008).

27. See Alschuler, supra note 11, at 180-195.

28. 500 U.S. 614 (1991). Prior to Edmonson, several state courts had already ruled that *Batson* was applicable to civil trials. See, e.g., Thomas v. Diversified Contracters, 551 So. 2d 343 (Ala. 1989); Wilson v. Kauffman, 563 N.E.2d 610 (Ind. Ct. App. 1990); Fludd v. Tiller, 863 F.2d 822 (11th Cir.), cert. denied, 493 U.S. 872 (1989). But see McDaniel v. Mutchnick, 1990 Mo. App. LEXIS, 1565 (Mo. Ct. App., Oct. 30, 1990) (finding no state action in a private litigant's conduct in striking black jurors).

Batson. The petitioner in Edmonson, a black man, sued his employer for its alleged negligence in causing an on-the-job injury. Edmonson objected when the defendant exercised two of its three peremptory challenges to exclude black jurors, raising the issue of whether discrimination by a private litigant in selection of a jury violates the equal protection clause.[29]

Unhesitant in its conclusion that the harm of racial discrimination against jurors is as grave in civil as in criminal cases, the Court faced the question of whether there was sufficient state action to warrant application of the due process clause of the Fifth Amendment. According to the Court's analysis, a private litigant acts as the state when it chooses a jury, "selecting an entity that is a quintessential government body [that] performs the critical governmental functions of guarding the rights of litigants and 'insur[ing] continued acceptance of the laws by all of the people' " (citation omitted). Because private actors are vested with the traditionally governmental function of selecting government officials, they are bound by the same constitutional obligations as the government.[30]

In the same term, the Court took another large step in extending *Batson* in Powers v. Ohio,[31] in which the Court determined that a white criminal defendant may object to the racially motivated exclusion of a black juror. Powers, a white man, had objected at trial when the State exercised seven of its ten peremptory challenges to exclude black persons from the jury. The charges against him, the Court expressly noted, did not implicate race.

---

29. The Fifth Circuit, in its first consideration of the case, had ruled that such challenges are state action, but then reversed itself, 860 F.2d 1308 (5th Cir. 1988), reh'g en banc, 895 F.2d 218 (5th Cir. 1990). The panel opinion contained a strong statement of argument that the state is inextricably involved in a private litigant's exercise of peremptory challenges. "Justice would indeed be blind if it failed to recognize that the [trial] court is employed as a vehicle for racial discrimination when peremptory challenges are used to exclude jurors because of their race. The government is inevitably and inextricably involved as an actor in the process by which a judge, robed in black, seated in a paneled courtroom, in front of an American flag, says to a juror, 'Ms. X, you are excused.' A litigant's decision to provoke the court's action by virtue of a statutorily accorded right does not disguise the official governmental character of the procedure as a whole." 860 F.2d at 1313.

30. Justice Scalia dissented along with Justice O'Connor and Chief Justice Rehnquist. In a biting opinion filed separately, Justice Scalia sarcastically praised the decision as "a magnificent demonstration of this institution's uncompromising hostility to race-based judgments" and bemoaned its contribution to "an increasingly Byzantine system of justice that devotes more and more of its energy to sideshows and less and less to the merits of the case." 500 U.S. at 645.

31. 499 U.S. 400 (1991). The Court had previously rejected a similar claim raised by a white defendant under the Sixth Amendment's right to an impartial jury, rather than the equal protection clause. Holland v. Illinois, 493 U.S. 474 (1990). Apparently, Holland did not press an equal protection claim because he feared that a white person would not have standing to raise the equal protection rights of black jurors. See Arguments Before the Court: Criminal Law and Procedure, 58 U.S.L.W. 3279, 3280 (Oct. 31, 1989); see also United States v. Ruiz, 894 F.2d 501, 506 n.2 (2d Cir. 1990). While the Supreme Court conceded that Holland had standing under the Sixth Amendment to complain of the composition of his jury, the Court held that the exclusion of black jurors did not violate the Sixth Amendment. Justice Scalia, who authored the majority opinion, argued that the antidiscrimination principle of Batson is grounded in the "intransigent prohibition of racial discrimination contained in the Fourteenth Amendment" and does not apply in cases brought under the Sixth Amendment. 493 U.S. at 475. Several of the Justices, however, indicated that a white defendant would be able to challenge the discriminatory exclusions of blacks from his or her jury. See 493 U.S. at 487-489 (Kennedy, J. concurring); id. at 490-493 (Marshall, J., dissenting); id. at 506-508 (Stevens, J., dissenting).

Powers made clear that it is not only the defendant's rights to be judged by an impartial jury that are compromised by discriminatory jury selection practices. Exclusion of jurors on the basis of race harms the excluded juror and the community at large by virtue of the fact that it "condones violations of the United States Constitution within the very institution entrusted with its enforcement, and so invites cynicism respecting the jury's neutrality and its obligation to adhere to the law." Recognizing that jurors are unlikely to have the resources or stake to challenge racial selectivity in their exclusion, the Court reasoned that granting the defendant standing to raise jurors' equal protection claims is the only means of vindicating of jurors' rights and sanctioning impermissible race-based decision making: "To bar petitioner's claim because his race differs from that of the excluded jurors," Justice Kennedy wrote, "would be to condone the arbitrary exclusion of citizens from the duty, honor, and privilege of jury service."

The following year, in Georgia v. McCollum,[32] the Court held that the equal protection clause precludes even criminal defendants from exercising race-based peremptory challenges.[33] Several years later, in J.E.B. v. Alabama ex rel. T.B.,[34] the Court held that the equal protection clause forbids gender-based peremptory challenges. The *J.E.B.* opinion made the limits of *Batson* somewhat clearer. Basically, peremptory challenges can always be used to make any classification subject to a rational basis test, such as employment, but peremptories can never be used to strike jurors according to any strict or heightened scrutiny classifications. So peremptories used to strike women are impermissible, since gender is a heightened scrutiny classification, and peremptories used to strike black are impermissible since race is accorded strict scrutiny.

And, in Campbell v. Louisiana,[35] the Court held that a white criminal defendant has third-party standing to raise equal protection and due process claims based on the racially discriminatory exclusion of nonwhites from serving as his or her grand jury foreperson. The Court relied on *Powers* to establish Campbell's right to challenge the racially discriminatory selection of his grand jury.[36] In applying *Powers*' rules of third-party standing, the Court determined that Campbell proved that he suffered an identifiable injury, established a close relationship with the excluded African Americans through his attempts to eliminate race-based discrimination in the grand juror selection process, and provided evidence that the excluded jurors would not likely have asserted their own right through litigation.[37]

Beyond this, the Court in *Campbell* found that any person, regardless of skin color, could be injured by a racially discriminatory grand jury selection process.[38]

---

32. 505 U.S. 42 (1992).

33. Unfortunately, in the course of extending *Powers* to the defense counsel, the Court impairs the persuasiveness of *Batson* and diminishes motivation to probe facially neutral reasons for strikes that exclude jurors along racial lines. For more on this topic, see Sheri Lynn Johnson, *Batson* Ethics for Prosecutors and Trial Court Judges, 73 Chi.-Kent L. Rev. 475 (1998).

34. 511 U.S. 127 (1994).

35. 523 U.S. 392 (1998).

36. Id. at 397.

37. Id.

38. Id. at 398.

In the majority opinion, Justice Kennedy noted that "the grand jury, like the petit jury, acts as a vital check against the wrongful exercise of power by the State and its prosecutors."[39]

In 2000, a study in the cities of Dallas and Houston, Texas, showed that in both civil and criminal juries, Latinos were severely underrepresented: "Latinos comprised only between 7 percent to 12 percent of the jury pools studied while comprising nearly 33 percent of the population of those cities."[40] The stunning shortage of Latinos in Texas jury pools has drawn the attention of the Texas Supreme Court who is studying this issue and exploring potential reform.[41]

Yet the Supreme Court has not offered *Batson* protection to Latino jurors who are removed from juries with peremptory challenges. In Hernandez v. New York,[42] the Supreme Court held that a prosecutor could use preemptory challenges to remove bilingual jurors without raising a per se violation of the Equal Protection clause. In this case, the "Court promoted a stereotype that bilingual jurors are incapable of following the official translation and being a capable juror."[43] In People v. Morales,[44] the prosecutor eliminated a Latino juror using a peremptory challenge because he lived in a neighborhood with gangs. Also the Court in *Morales* allowed this prosecutorial discretion based on "social categorization and stereotypes." One commentator reflects:

> Due to a juror's address, prosecutors concluded that the juror might be overly sympathetic to and identify too closely with the defendant. Using the social psychology framework, we can see that the prosecutor viewed jurors from gang-infested neighborhoods as "out-group persons" and therefore not suitable for jury service. Moreover, the prosecutor's attempt to strike a Latino juror with a thick Spanish accent in the same case illustrates the depth and breadth of the stereotype and broadens the "out-group persons" to include venire persons with Spanish accents.[45]

As with other areas of its jurisprudence, the Supreme Court has stopped short of requiring that a defendant be tried by a representative jury. *Batson* and its progeny, like *Swain,* only prohibit discrimination and do not require the inclusion of black persons on juries.[46] The Court's refusal to require that petit juries are racially representative is a high mark of the Court's equal opportunity jurisprudence (seen most notably in the Rehnquist Court's employment decisions). The

---

39. Id. at 399.

40. Roger Enriquez & John W. Clark III, The Social Psychology of Peremptory Challenges: An Examination of Latino Jurors, Texas Hispanic Journal of Law and Policy (Spring 2007) at 27. This article provides a summary of post-*Batson* cases. See also Clare Sheridan, Peremptory Challenges: Lessons from Hernandez v. Texas, 25 Chicano-Latino L. Rev. 77 (2005).

41. Id.

42. Hernandez v. New York, 500 U.S. 352, 361 (1991). See also Hernandez v. Texas, 347 U.S. 475 (1954) (holding that the lack of even one Mexican American juror over 25 years violated Equal Protection Clause of the Fourteenth Amendment in a Texas county with a large Mexican American community.

43. Enriquez, supra note 40, at 38.

44. People v. Morales, 719 N.E.2d 261 (1999).

45. Enriquez, supra note 40, at 38.

46. See Lockhart v. McCree, 476 U.S. 162, 173 (1986); Taylor v. Louisiana, 419 U.S. 522, 538 (1975) (both cases holding that a defendant has no right to a jury of a particular composition).

Sixth Amendment and the equal protection clause do not entitle defendants to a jury which is racially inclusive, but only to the opportunity to draw a heterogeneous jury. So long as the venire is composed of a fair cross-section of the community, thereby preserving the potential for drawing an impartial (i.e., diverse) jury in each case, it does not matter that individual juries remain essentially all-white. For this reason, the Court's rhetoric is empty and gives little of substance to the black litigant or witness. Black defendants walking into court to be greeted by twelve white faces in the jury box will take little comfort in the fact that he or she had an equal chance to a racially mixed jury. It matters little to the defendant that she was wrongfully convicted by a jury which was only coincidentally white. For the Court fails to recognize, or is simply unwilling to concede, that discrimination is equally harmful whether it results from design or chance.

Furthermore, neutrality will not generate racially diverse juries. Black persons are already excluded from participation in juries before the prosecutor exercises her first challenge because of underrepresentation of people of color on the voter lists and drivers license registries from which white jury lists are compiled. Because these lists frequently exclude poor people, people of color, and alien residents, these people are denied the opportunity to serve as jurors.[47] In addition, literacy and language requirements, employers who do not compensate employees for jury service, child-care responsibilities, and numerous other factors will screen out persons of color in disproportionate numbers. Patterns of housing segregation also mean that black defendants brought to trial in a white community will be without recourse, since the absence of black jurors in the venire will be attributed to neutral, and hence non-actionable, causes. Consequently, even those jury selection systems which satisfy the mandate of racial neutrality will include only token numbers of people of color. Until the presently unforeseeable day when the Supreme Court is willing to demand representation of black persons on juries, black defendants and complainants will continue to face judgment from all-white juries.

Still, litigation regarding *Batson*'s scope is likely to continue. Professor Jean Montoya suggests another area ripe for the Court's consideration is the exercise of peremptories that can be conceptualized as challenges based on the intersection of race and gender: "challenges based on intersectionality."[48] She explains that such challenges "purposely exclude jurors of a particular race and a particular gender,

---

47. See, e.g., Developments, Race and the Criminal Process, 101 Harv. L. Rev. 1472, 1561-1566 (1988); Joseph Kadane & John P. Lehoczky, Jury Representativeness: A Mandate for Multiple Source Lists, 65 Cal. L. Rev. 776, 788-793 (1977). Courts have unanimously refused to allow challenges to the composition of a jury because of underrepresentation generated by reliance on such facially neutral lists. See United States v. Cecil, 836 F.2d 1431, 1446 (4th Cir. 1988) (the exclusion of persons who have not registered to vote is permissible because no immutable characteristic prevents a person from registering); United States v. Young, 822 F.2d 1234, 1239 (2d Cir. 1987); United States v. James, 528 F.2d 999, 1022 (5th Cir.), cert. denied, 429 U.S. 959 (1976); United States v. Test, 550 F.2d 577, 586-587 & n.8 (10th Cir. 1976); United States v. Biaggi, 680 F. Supp. 641 (S.D.N.Y. 1988). One of the concerns raised by these courts is the difficulty of doing better. Any list — from voter rolls to telephone directories — will likely be linked to wealth and, consequently, to race.

48. Jean Montoya, "What's So Magical About Black Women?" Peremptory Challenges at the Intersection of Race and Gender, 3 Mich. J. Gender & L. 369 (1996).

for example, African American women or Latin men."[49] Professor Paul Lynd suggests another evolving area in his discussion of a continuum of issues relating to the exercise of peremptories based on sexual orientation.[50] He discusses the use of peremptory strikes where one's sexual orientation is known as well as whether a potential juror may be questioned about her sexual orientation during voir dire.[51]

A recent study by Baldus shows that little has changed since *Batson* — discrimination in the use of peremptory challenges is still widespread, and prosecutors who continue to use preemptory challenges to exclude blacks from juries are more successful in controlling jury composition than the defense.[52] Even though prosecutors and defense attorneys have the same number of strikes, and prosecutors, on average, use only 17 of the 20 permitted strikes, the prosecutor's advantage stems from the fact that their prime targets are represented in smaller numbers in the jury venire.

The results indicate that many jurors are removed because of their race and gender. Additionally, a correlation exists between the race of the juror and sentencing decisions, finding that black jurors are often more lenient in sentencing than white jurors. For black defendants, who represent 80 percent of the defendants in their sample, that can have a significant impact on the outcome of a trial. Most dramatically, the report concludes that when discriminatory practices intersect with the death penalty system, the state's advantage may make it more likely for black defendants facing capital charges to be sentenced to death.

As a result of these stark findings, Baldus argues that we consider Marshall's suggestion of totally abolishing the current system of preemptory strikes.[53] Ending this practice, he argues, would "end the systematic exclusion of venire members on the basis of race and gender as well as age and other arbitrary factors that are frequently offered to justify the strikes that have been challenged." In other words, to borrow a phrase a head of General Motors once used, what is good for blacks seeking racial fairness is also good for the country.

In a study of the discriminatory use of peremptory challenges published in 2007, researchers found that in trying a case of a black defendant, the study participants, were college students, law students and attorneys, were more likely to challenge a black prospective juror.[54] Yet, when justifying their judgment to

49. Id. at 371.

50. Paul R. Lynd, Juror Sexual Orientation: The Fair Cross-Section Requirement, Privacy, Challenges for Cause, and Peremptories, 46 UCLA L. Rev. 231 (1998).

51. Id.

52. David C. Baldus et al., Racial Discrimination and the Death Penalty in the Post-*Furman* Era: An Empirical and Legal Overview, with Recent Findings from Philadelphia, 83 Cornell L. Rev. 1638 (1998).

53. Baldus cites other scholars who agree: Raymond J. Broderick, Why the Peremptory Challenge Should Be Abolished, 65 Temp. L. Rev. 369 (1992); Morehead, When a Peremptory Challenge Is No Longer Peremptory: Batson's Unfortunate Failure to Eradicate Invidious Discrimination from Jury Selection, 43 DePaul L. Rev. 625 (1994); David Zonana, The Effect of Assumptions About Racial Bias on the Analysis of Batson's Three Harms and the Peremptory Challenge, 1994 Ann. Surv. Am. L. 203, 243; Alschuler, supra note 11.

54. Samuel R. Sommers & Michael I. Norton, Race-Based Judgments, Race-Neutral Justifications: Experimental Examination of Peremptory Use and the Batson Challenge Procedure, Law and Human Behavior (June 2007) at 9.

strike the juror, the participants cited race-neutral reasons for exclusion and rarely cited the influence of the juror's race.[55] The author of the study explains:

> The practical implications of these findings are clear: even when attorneys consider race during jury selection, there is little reason to believe that judicial questioning will produce information useful for identifying this bias. Because judgments such as those made during jury selection are based on multiple, subjective criteria, myriad justifications are typically available (Norton et al., 2006). In fact, recent Supreme Court decisions have held that a peremptory justification need not be plausible nor even relevant to the case in question for it to comply with *Batson*, as long as it is literally race-neutral. . . . Justifications for peremptories therefore leave judges with little basis for rejecting them. . . . [56]

§5.17   RAISING THE RACIAL ISSUE ON VOIR DIRE

The Supreme Court further narrowed the constitutional right to voir dire on the issue of racial bias in Rosales-Lopez v. United States[1] Drawing a very fine and somewhat arbitrary rule, the Court laid down as near to a *per se* rule as it has been able to develop in this area. It held that judges must question jurors regarding possible racial prejudice only when the defendant is accused of a crime of violence and is a member of a different racial or ethnic group than the victim. In any other case, bias-related voir dire is only necessary when special circumstances suggest a reasonable possibility that racial prejudice will affect the jury's determination.

Rosales-Lopez's rule for limiting voir dire on racial bias quite starkly represents the Court's utilitarian calculus. Although the Court recognized that racial animus still taints jury verdicts in some cases, a concern for efficiency and an unwillingness to face up to the real, daily influence of racism in the courts led the Court to choose to require voir dire only in the most flagrant cases. Yet, as the dissent points out, the Court's rule will not ensure the defendant the opportunity to ferret out racial bias in a vast range of cases where personal prejudice will deny the defendant the right to a fair trial. The dissent raises the example of a member of the Nazi Party being allowed to sit in judgment of a Jewish defendant. Even when the crime is not violent or interracial, the idea that someone predisposed to devalue the life and words of a defendant (or witness) will slip undetected onto the jury is repugnant to basic notions of fair process.[2]

55. Id.
56. Id.
§5.17   1. 451 U.S. 182 (1981).
2. While the right to voir dire on a juror's possible racial bias is an important right, its efficacy in detecting racial bias should not be overestimated. As Professor Albert Alschuler noted, "One doubts that Lester Maddox, Orville Faubus, George Wallace, Theodore Bilbo or anyone else would have responded to the proposed question by confessing a bias likely to affect his or her resolution of a capital murder case." Albert Alschuler, The Supreme Court and the Jury: Voir Dire, Peremptory Challenges, and the Review of Jury Verdicts, 56 U. Chi. L. Rev. 153, 160 (1989). Given that much racial antipathy is unconscious or hidden because of fear of social disapproval, even the most extensive and penetrating voir dire will not screen the vast majority of bigoted jurors.

So, even as the Court announced its decision, its limitations were already clear. Rosales-Lopez, a Mexican American, was charged with smuggling illegal aliens into the United States. Although a juror's feelings towards aliens — particularly Latino aliens — would obviously affect the jury's perception of the gravity of the crime and their sympathy or antipathy for the defendant, the Court would not "hold that there was a reasonable possibility that racial or ethnic prejudice would affect the jury." The denial of voir dire on the issue of bias towards aliens was therefore proper.

The Supreme Court did make one exception to the per se rule of *Rosales-Lopez*. In Turner v. Murray,[3] the Court held that a minority defendant facing capital charges is always entitled to ask jurors regarding potential racial bias. The judge had asked jurors, in general terms, whether they felt that they could render a fair and impartial verdict. He had not, however, informed the jury that the victim in the murder case was white, so that their answers did not reveal whether they would be able to render a verdict free from prejudice in a case in which a black man was accused of killing a white person. In a move that triggered sharp criticism from Justice Brennan, the majority ruled that the failure to allow complete voir dire on the issue of racial prejudice only required reversal of the sentence and not the conviction. The Court reasoned that the range of discretion allowed jurors in determining whether to impose capital punishment made the sentencing phase uniquely susceptible to the influence of racial bias. Moreover, the seriousness of the penalty made necessary the exercise of extreme care in ensuring that the jury's verdict was not based on impermissible factors. But because the guilt phase of a capital trial is no different than in a noncapital case, no special considerations warranted reversal of the conviction.

Justice Brennan concurred in part in a separate opinion, calling the majority's distinction between the role of bias in the defendant's conviction and in his sentencing a "distinction without substance." Prejudice is not selective in the influence it brings to bear on the jury's determination, he argued. The juror who votes at sentencing to impose death because the defendant is black is equally likely to vote for conviction because the defendant is black. Justice Brennan concludes, "A racially biased juror sits with blurred vision and impaired sensibilities and is incapable of fairly making the myriad decisions that each juror is called upon to make in the course of a trial. To put it simply, he cannot judge because he has prejudged. This is equally true at the trial on guilt as at the hearing on sentencing."

Uncomfortable with the message that would be sent by mandatory voir dire, Justice Powell dissented along with Justice Rehnquist. In an opinion remarkable for its concern with form rather than substance, Justice Powell wrote: "The per se rule announced today may appear innocuous. But the rule is based on what amounts to a constitutional presumption that jurors in capital cases are racially biased. Such presumption unjustifiably suggests that criminal justice in our courts of law is meted out on racial grounds."

However the peremptory challenge issue is finally resolved, minority-group defendants will face a panel of prospective jurors all of whom, black and white,

---

3. 476 U.S. 28 (1986).

bring to their task far more in the way of racial prejudices, stereotypes, and unspoken beliefs than most will be willing to admit. It is essential, then, that defense counsel have the opportunity to question each prospective juror fully so as to ascertain hidden biases that could influence the juror's judgment and vote.[4] Rules on voir dire vary from state to state, but in Ham v. South Carolina,[5] the Supreme Court recognized a constitutional right on the part of a black civil rights worker convicted on a marijuana possession charge to ask prospective jurors questions relating to possible racial prejudice during the voir dire examination.

In *Ham*, as in so many civil rights precedents, it is necessary to distinguish recognition of the symbolic right from the degree of substance with which that right is to be endowed. Here, Justice Rehnquist finds a due process requirement for a voir dire question on the subject of racial questions in a case involving a black civil rights worker charged with crime in a southern courtroom. But the number and character of the questions was left entirely to the discretion of the trial court.

Given the unanimous findings of social science studies that race and racism are strong influences in the jury box, the voir dire rights recognized in *Ham* seem of a piece with jury discrimination rights generally, statements that provide far more glitter to the constitutional image than they provide protection to nonwhite defendants charged with crime. Perhaps this is not intentional. There seems to be a belief in the judiciary, as in the country, that if you don't mention racism, it won't manifest itself. Thus, one court, in refusing defense counsel's request on behalf of his black client for voir dire questions on racial prejudice, replied:

> THE COURT: I am not going to ask that. I just feel that I — I may be unfair to you, but I feel that would put undue emphasis on it. I have told them to weigh their own conscience and I believe if they are racially prejudice[d] they ought to come forth and say it; and if they are, they are not going to respond if I ask them. That is just the way I feel about it. I understand your concern but I feel it is better for you.[6]

While perhaps well-intended and in accord with the maxim "let sleeping dogs lie," one would hope that the acquiescence to, if not acceptance of, racial prejudice in potential jurors reflected in this judge's response would not be widespread.

4. Defense attorneys have developed elaborate sets of voir dire questions designed to uncover conscious and unconscious racism in prospective jurors. See Minimizing Racism in Jury Trials (Ann Fagen Ginger ed., 1969). Of course, such procedures require time, dozens (sometimes hundreds) of prospective jurors, and a judge with more patience than can be expected in cases other than those of cause célèbre proportions. Indeed, some judges believe that such questioning implies that they condone racial prejudice in their courts. A black lawyer, seeking to raise the racial issue with a prospective juror in a Bronx, New York court, was held in contempt and fined $50. Wechsler, Whose Contempt?, N.Y. Post, Aug. 31, 1972, at 31. The contempt conviction was reversed by order of a unanimous Appellate Division Court on Oct. 13, 1972. See also National Jury Project, Jury Work: Systematic Techniques 10-18 (2d ed. 1983).

5. 409 U.S. 524 (1973).

6. United States v. Bowles, 574 F.2d 970, 972 (8th Cir. 1978). The Eighth Circuit reversed and remanded for a new trial, indicating that the discretion given the trial court regarding voir dire questions on the subject of racial prejudice did not include discretion not to make any inquiry at all. Virtually every circuit facing this issue has resolved it in accord with the Eighth Circuit's decision. See cases gathered in Annot., Voir Dire Examination of Prospective Jurors Under Rule 24(a) of Federal Rules of Criminal Procedure, §11.28 A.L.R. Fed. 26, 68-76 (1976).

Unfortunately, that hope gets little support from the authorities. Courts have often refused to reverse convictions based on substantial evidence even though the trial court has refused to make voir dire inquiries about racial prejudice. The failure is often criticized, but is deemed "harmless error" in view of the substantial evidence supporting the conviction.[7] In addition, when counsel fails to object to the trial court's failure to inquire into racial prejudice, the inquiry is deemed waived.[8]

After the Supreme Court decision in *Ham*, some courts concluded that its holding established a per se rule requiring reversal whenever the trial court has refused to pose questions on voir dire about racial prejudice without regard to the likelihood of actual prejudice.[9] But then the Supreme Court greatly limited the scope of its *Ham* ruling in Ristaino v. Ross.[10]

Ross, along with two other blacks, was convicted in state court of armed robbery, assault and battery by means of a dangerous weapon, and with intent to murder. The victim was a white security guard. The trial court inquired generally into prejudice during the voir dire of prospective witnesses, but told defendants' counsel, who had requested specific questions about racial prejudice, that he felt "no purpose would be accomplished by asking such questions in this instance." The judge did inquire as to whether any jurors were relatives of police, and he acknowledged that "there was a problem with skin color," but he adhered to his decision not to pose a question directed specifically to racial prejudice. As he told counsel regarding the fact that the victim is white and the defendants black, "all we can hope and pray for is that the jurors . . . take their oaths seriously and understand . . . the spirit of what this Court says to them. . . ."[11]

Justice Powell, speaking for the Court, found the procedure followed did not violate the defendants' constitutional rights. *Ham* was distinguished because of the defendant's prominence in the community because of his civil rights work, and his defense that asserted he had been framed because of his civil rights activities. "Racial issues therefore were inextricably bound up with the conduct of the trial." In those circumstances, Justice Powell explained, "we deemed a voir dire that included questioning specifically directed to racial prejudice, when sought by *Ham*, necessary to meet the constitutional requirement that an impartial jury be impaneled."[12]

---

7. See, e.g., United States v. Grant, 494 F.2d 120 (2d Cir. 1974); United States v. Rivers, 468 F.2d 1355 (4th Cir. 1972), cert. denied, 411 U.S. 969 (1973); United States v. Walker, 491 F.2d 236 (9th Cir.), cert. denied, 416 U.S. 990 (1974). But in United States v. Carter, 440 F.2d 1132 (6th Cir. 1971), and United States v. Booker, 480 F.2d 1310 (7th Cir. 1973), the courts reversed convictions notwithstanding the substantial evidence of guilt. United States v. Williams, 612 F.2d 735 (3d Cir. 1979); Illinois v. Dunum, 537 N.E.2d 898 (Ill. 1989).

8. See, e.g., United States v. Leftwich, 461 F.2d 586 (3d Cir. 1972).

9. United States v. Johnson, 527 F.2d 1104, 1106 (4th Cir. 1975), and referring to United States v. Booker, supra note 7, at 1311, and United States v. Robinson, 485 F.2d 1157 (3d Cir. 1973).

10. 424 U.S. 589 (1976).

11. 424 U.S. at 591. The trial judge did lecture jurors about the importance of impartiality without mentioning racial prejudice. Persons responding affirmatively to the general questions were questioned individually at the bench by the judge. This procedure led to the excusing of 18 veniremen for cause on grounds of prejudice, including one panelist who admitted a racial bias.

12. Id. at 598. There is little doubt that the defendant's counsel could have been more responsive to the trial judge's inquiries regarding special facts that would justify the voir dire questions about racial prejudice. Counsel's general statements about the race of victim and defendant, and the

While disagreeing with the court of appeals, which assumed *Ham* required a reversal in *Ristaino*, and holding that "the need to question veniremen specifically about racial prejudice [did not rise] to constitutional dimensions in this case," Justice Powell indicated that "the wiser course generally is to propound appropriate questions designed to identify racial prejudice if requested by the defendant."

But Powell emphasized, "The mere fact that the victim of the crimes alleged was a white man and the defendants were Negroes was less likely to distort the trial than were the special factors involved in *Ham*." Here, defendant's counsel was unable to point to specific circumstances suggesting a "significant likelihood that racial prejudice might infect . . . [the defendant's] trial."

Justice Marshall, joined by Justice Brennan, dissented. He viewed the decision as an emphatic confirmation "that the promises inherent in *Ham* will not be fulfilled."

And so, with its decision in the *Ristaino* case, the Supreme Court joins the "let sleeping dogs lie" approach of the trial judge in United States v. Bowles, an approach quickly rejected by the Eighth Circuit and most other courts who read *Ham* as requiring at least a specific question concerning racial prejudice. *Ristaino*, as suggested above, is not an insurmountable obstacle to reversal on constitutional grounds where a court has rejected well-constructed questions illustrating how the circumstances of the case raise the possibility of racial prejudice in a trial where a black defendant is charged with crime against a white, or one which threatens white interests.[13]

§5.18 AFFIRMATIVE ACTION IN THE JURY BOX

In Chapter 2, it was noted that despite its symbolic importance, no slaves were freed by the legal effect of the Emancipation Proclamation. Given the rather depressing search in the preceding sections for the jury rights blacks and other minorities are supposed to have, it is appropriate here to ask: How many blacks sat on juries as a result of Strauder v. West Virginia, that first anti-jury discrimination precedent?[1] Whatever the exact number, we can be fairly certain that black jurors did not become fixtures in that state where, just two decades earlier, they and their parents had not been freed, even symbolically, because of the express exemption

---

mention of the victim's identification with the police, provided the ingredients for a far stronger request than was made.

13. The *Ristaino* decision does diminish for the present the importance of discussing the kind of questions defendants might be entitled to ask or have asked during the voir dire. *Ham* had left this to the discretion of the trial judge. In United States v. Bowe, 360 F.2d 1 (2d Cir.), cert. denied, 385 U.S. 961 (1966), the court held that discretion had not been abused by a trial judge who inquired of the sole black juror during the voir dire whether the fact he was black would cause any embarrassment or prevent his rendering an impartial verdict where the black defendant was charged with conspiracy to destroy the Statute of Liberty and to smuggle explosives into the United States.

§5.18 1. 100 U.S. 303 (1880).

the Emancipation Proclamation provided for those slave states, like West Virginia, which had not joined the rebellion.[2]

Strauder then, like the Emancipation Proclamation, the post–Civil War Amendments, and civil rights acts that preceded it, altered the rules without changing the fact that the odds were against blacks actually improving their condition. The subsequent pattern of decisions retains a remarkable fidelity to the original scheme. Thus today, foreign visitors to our shores can be told with pride that our Constitution forbids any person from being tried for crime by a jury from which members of any cognizable minority group have been systematically excluded. Moreover, our guests are informed that courts are obligated to insure that juries, to the extent possible under our random selection system, are a representative cross-section of the many groups that make up this country.

Here is a standard of due process and equal protection that the oppressed of many lands envy. And yet, except for the rare, spectacular case— "Scottsboro Boys," an Angela Davis, a Joanne Little— where media attention, money, and extraordinary talent combine to overcome the odds, most minority defendants and their counsel are stymied by the holdings in *Batson* and *Ristaino*. Unable to surmount the high standards of proof necessary to prove that their rights are violated by the prosecutor's peremptory removal of potential black jurors, and barred except in very narrow circumstances from questioning on voir dire the depths of racial prejudice of white jurors, defendants experience a deprivation of their constitutional right to a fair trial by the simultaneous operation of both rules.

Actually, the situation is much worse than painted here. Achieving true representation of minority groups on criminal jury panels would be extremely difficult, even were the standards for proving systematic exclusion far more liberal than they are. The state lost Castaneda v. Partida, for example, mainly because it didn't really try to rebut the prima facie case of discrimination based on statistics. The Supreme Court did not accept the "governing majority" argument, but Justice Blackmun emphasized "that we are not saying that the statistical disparities proved here could never be explained in another case. . . ."[3]

From the record in *Castaneda*, it would appear that industrious lawyers, aided by the statutory qualifications for jury service in Texas (citizenship, registered voter, literate, no prior felony convictions, no pending indictments, sound mind and good moral character)— all of which are standards rather easily met by the middle-class but which easily ensnare the poor— could greatly reduce and possibly eliminate the disparities upon which the defendant's case was based. Consider that all but the most hardhearted jury commissioners and selectors grant exemptions to working mothers, and poor wage earners who will not be paid and may lose their jobs if they take the time required for jury service. Most jurors are middle-class civil servants and salaried persons, the successfully self-employed, the retired, and the very well-to-do.

---

2. The proclamation excluded from its declaration freeing "all persons held as slaves within any State," portions of those states and "the forty eight counties designated as West Virginia" deemed not in rebellion against the United States.

3. 430 U.S. at 499.

Also, we must place into the equation the growing use of juries composed of less than 12 persons. One need not spend long hours studying social science to understand the increased likelihood of prejudice influencing such smaller jury groups.[4] And finally, even if the picture of upwardly mobile black jurors disidentifying with members of their group in order to curry favor with whites is less prevalent than it was when the studies cited by Justice Marshall were written,[5] it remains a force that cuts against the cross-sectional representation that is our goal.

The answer here, as in other areas of civil rights, could lie in affirmative policies designed to supplement the absence of blacks from jury panels where, but for past racial discrimination, they would normally be found.[6]

§5.19 Racism Hypo: Proposed Model Racial Reality in Jury Selection Act

Following an extensive investigation of the nation's jury selection procedures and an in-depth study of racial discrimination attributable to jury findings, a national commission of experts concluded that (a) nonwhite racial and ethnic minorities are not serving on juries in criminal cases in anything like their percentages in the population; (b) underrepresentation of nonwhite racial and ethnic minorities is due to exclusion from jury lists by blatant and subtle discrimination, artificially high eligibility standards, inadequate jury fee compensation, and similar hardships; and exclusion from the jury box is due to the planned but nonsystematic use by prosecutors of peremptory challenges; (c) jury verdicts, the overwhelming majority of which are returned by all- or mainly white juries, strongly reflect the continued functioning of racial discrimination and racist beliefs in this country.

To remedy quickly as much of this discrimination as possible, the commission has prepared and urges state legislatures to enact the following Model Racial Reality in Jury Selection Act.

> Section 1. Effective immediately, in all criminal cases in which defendants are from nonwhite racial and ethnic minorities and are entitled to a jury trial, the court shall take appropriate steps to insure that the jury impanelled in such trials contains no less than the percentage of the defendant's racial or ethnic minority group in the jurisdiction where the case is tried. Provided, however, that if the defendant's racial or ethnic minority group is less than 50 percent of the population in the jurisdiction where the case is tried, the court shall take appropriate steps to insure that the jury impanelled in such trials contains no less than 50 percent of the defendant's racial or ethnic minority. Notwithstanding this section, a nonwhite racial or ethnic minority defendant, at his or her discretion, may waive this special entitlement provided by this act. Exercise of this waiver

4. The subject is discussed extensively in Richard Lempert, Uncovering Nondiscernible Differences: Empirical Research and the Jury Size Cases, 73 Mich. L. Rev. 643 (1975).

5. Castaneda v. Partida, 430 U.S. 482, 504 (1977). See §5.15.

6. See also, for further discussion, A. Cohn & D.R. Sherwood, The Rise and Fall of Affirmative Action in Jury Selection, Univ. of Mich. J.L. Reform 32 (1999).

will not jeopardize such defendant's right guaranteed by the U.S. Constitution to a jury from which no member of the community is excluded on the basis of race, sex, religion, or ethnic origin.

Section 2. The state Commission Against Discrimination is hereby given authority to promulgate such further regulations as may be necessary to put this act into effect.

Section 3. Failure by the state to comply with this act will result in the reversal of any convictions obtained against any such nonwhite racial and ethnic minority defendants.

Section 4. The results of this act will be evaluated by a team of specialists, designated by the state Commission Against Discrimination. The act will expire in three years. Renewal by legislative reenactment is, of course, possible.

Assume that the model jury selection act has been introduced in the state of your choice, and legislative hearings have been scheduled. As expected, there are many groups who oppose, and others who support, the model act.

Law Firm A can represent the supporters.

Law Firm B can represent the opponents.

§5.20   THE RIGHT TO NONDISCRIMINATORY JURIES IN CIVIL CASES

The Supreme Court in Carter v. Jury Commission[1] held that citizens eligible for service on criminal juries could challenge alleged jury discrimination practices as effectively as defendants facing trial before such juries. The Court reasoned that "People excluded from juries because of their race are as much aggrieved as those indicted and tried by juries chosen under a system of racial exclusion. . . . Once the State chooses to provide grand and petit juries . . . it must hew to federal constitutional criteria in ensuring that the selection of membership is free of racial bias."[2]

If civil petitioners can challenge discrimination in criminal cases based on the entitlement set out in Carter, one would assume such persons would have no less right to challenge exclusionary jury tactics practiced by an opposing party in a civil case. In other words, if one party in a civil matter notices the other party using peremptory challenges to rid the jury panel of prospective black jurors, concerns about fair representation that underlie the criminal jury decisions discussed in previous sections would seem equally applicable. One possible answer is that civil litigants are private parties and are thus not covered by the state action limits of the Fourteenth Amendment, so are able to exclude blacks without raising a constitutional issue. There seems to be virtually no writing on this question.

Judges with whom I have discussed this matter, after conceding that they have given it little thought, generally indicate their conviction that no constitutional questions are involved when private litigants use peremptory challenges to remove

---

§5.20   1. 396 U.S. 320, 329 (1970).
2. 396 U.S. at 329-330.

blacks because they are blacks, or remove prospective jurors for reason of national origin, gender, religion, or color. They argue that the very purpose of peremptory challenges is to allow the litigant to effectuate an arbitrary rejection of various jurors. Here, the peremptory challenge, without the shield of state action that is appropriately applied in criminal cases, is intended to afford each litigant the right to discriminate in any way he or she chooses.

Judges report that in many cases such discrimination is practiced by both sides, and in such cases no one raises an issue. If only one of the litigants uses such challenges to remove blacks from a jury, there remains no constitutional provision that would justify an objection. As one judge put it, "Courts have no oversight over how a private litigant chooses to use his peremptory challenges. Nor, in my judgment, should it. The purpose of the peremptory challenge concept is to afford an unfettered choice, and the state should not now be allowed to intervene and place restraints on how those choices may be exercised."

The quoted statement, while it certainly reflects existing law, is shocking when one considers the abuses that can take place. If, for example, a black plaintiff seeks damages for negligence or other tort, must the plaintiff and the court sit by helplessly and watch the defendant's counsel use the peremptory challenge to remove otherwise qualified blacks from the jury? Suppose, to focus the issue more clearly, the plaintiff is seeking damages under Title VIII of the 1968 Fair Housing Act, where the Supreme Court in Curtis v. Loether[3] held that the defendant is entitled to a jury trial. Surely Justice Thurgood Marshall, who wrote the *Curtis* opinion for a unanimous Court, would not be so sanguine about the possibilities of plaintiffs in fair housing cases receiving a fair trial if it were clear the defendant in such cases could be virtually guaranteed an all-white jury.

Similarly, a black defendant in a civil case should not be placed in jeopardy through the judicial process that rendered him a defendant, and then have that jeopardy worsened by the plaintiff using peremptory challenges to rid the jury of all blacks. Under the doctrine of Peters v. Kiff,[4] where a white criminal defendant successfully challenged the exclusion of blacks from grand and petit juries, I would think that even in civil cases where blacks or other minorities are not involved either white party should be able to challenge the use of peremptory challenges to insure an all-white jury.

Assuming that there is good reason for adopting the fair representation jury rules in criminal cases to civil litigation, the question remains of the legal rationale that will accomplish this result. Here, the theory of Shelley v. Kraemer[5] seems most helpful. While the decision by a civil party to utilize the peremptory challenge to exclude blacks may be "private," it is the state through its judicial process that provides both the means and the approval of this tactic. When successful, the strategy is intended to, and usually has, harmed the other party on the basis of race. Thus, all the arguments made in Shelley v. Kraemer can be utilized in a challenge to the use of the peremptory challenge when racial exclusion seems the sole or primary basis for its use against minority prospective jurors.

3. 415 U.S. 189 (1974).
4. 407 U.S. 493 (1972).
5. 334 U.S. 1 (1948).

In response, it may be said that there is a great divide between a court voiding the sale of property to blacks and denying a black purchaser the fruits of his bargain because of a racially restrictive covenant as in the *Shelley* case, and a court impanelling a jury from which a private litigant has excluded prospective black jurors. In the latter case, it might be said that the court is doing nothing affirmatively to effectuate the discrimination. The attorney who utilizes the peremptory challenges has done that and the court is merely accepting the result.

Even if *Shelley* is distinguishable, there remains an argument that black plaintiffs in civil cases who are seeking vindication of statutory or common law rights, or black defendants who are brought before the judicial process as provided by law, should not be forced to present or defend their cases before juries which do not reflect the racial composition of the community because the other party has systematically excluded all minority jurors from participating. The argument is that such a result seems to fly in the face of basic aspects of due process. As for the judge's role, the court should as readily hear an objection charging the discriminatory use of peremptory challenges as it hears objections to hearsay testimony, leading questions, and the whole array of evidentiary rulings that traditionally have been assumed essential to due process.

Finally, and assuming the courts adopt the theory set out above, there remains the problem of proof. Under Swain v. Alabama, the Court indicated that a prosecutor was entitled to openly remove all blacks from a particular jury, and only if defendant proved that a pattern of exclusion reflected a discriminatory policy would the burden of disproving such a policy shift to the prosecution. In a civil case, of course, proof of such a pattern would be impossible for most litigants. Thus, the civil case presents even more directly than its criminal counterpart the question of whether the value of the peremptory challenge or the right of the litigant to a trial by a jury of peers not sanitized by race should prevail under our system. Given the history of the Fourteenth Amendment in the jury discrimination field, and the clear need of defendants and civil litigants for protection against juries selected by discriminatory means, one would hope that the constitutionally recognized rights would prevail.

Chapter 6

Voting Rights and Democratic Domination

§6.1 INTRODUCTION

Early in his 1984 campaign for the presidential nomination, Jesse Jackson warned that "blacks will no longer be the Harlem Globetrotters of the Democratic Party. We will no longer provide the excitement, tricks and music while white males assume the position of proprietorship."[1] Despite his impressive political skills, Jackson and black people generally remained the source of entertainment and were not the subjects of serious consideration in the Democratic Party either in 1984 or since. Indeed, in subsequent presidential campaigns, the Democrat as well as the Republican parties proved ready to ignore and even insult blacks in a frantic effort to avoid alienating white voters. And as the battle for the Democratic Party nomination in the 2008 campaign boiled down to Senators Hillary Clinton and Barack Obama, race has played an increasingly important role.[2]

§6.1 1. Is the U.S. Ready for a Black President?, U.S. News & World Report, July 25, 1983, at 21-22.

2. Barack Obama has become a household name for many liberal Democrats looking for a serious change in the White House. He rose quickly as a formidable adversary of Hillary Clinton's candidacy, early on deemed inevitable. His base is wide and ranges from young student idealists to professional elites.

Obama's background is unique. Born in Hawaii, he is the son of a white mother from Kansas and a father from Kenya. He was raised primarily in Hawaii by his grandparents and mother but also lived in Indonesia for four years. He is the product of an Ivy League education, including being the first African American President of the Harvard Law Review. After law school, he became a civil rights lawyer and professor until he ran for state Senate where he served for 8 years. He then became the third African American to win an U.S. Senate seat from Illinois in 2004. His charismatic leadership has drawn many to his campaign.

One undeniably symbolic example of how race plays a role in Obama's campaign is a comment by Senator Joseph Biden, also a candidate in the Democrat Presidential primary. In a candid response, Senator Biden described Obama as "articulate and bright." See Peter Applebome, A War of Words, All of Them Hyphenated, N.Y. Times (March 11, 2007).

Many journalists quickly jumped on the racist history associated with categorizing African Americans as "articulate," "bright," and "clean." Comments like Biden's offer a timely reminder of the serious uphill battle for minority leaders who live each day struggling against the remnants of slavery that are still so salient. The Clinton campaign also has drawn criticism for "playing the race card" against Obama. Most notably Bill Clinton came under attack for his demeaning comparison of Obama's crushing victory in South Carolina to the previous overwhelming primary victory of Jesse Jackson in South Carolina.

Given the gravely uncertain state of the economy, many but certainly not all white voters appear more interested in issues of jobs and economic justice than race. In past campaigns, the Democrats have treated black people, the party's most faithful supporters, as though they were a plague. As a result, the Democratic campaign strategists rendered themselves morally and tactically vulnerable to the blatant racism of the Republican campaign. Using "art film" scare tactics like those employed by D. W. Griffith's 1915 film, *Birth of a Nation,* Republicans found they need promise neither to lower the debt nor tell the truth: They need only pledge to keep the Willie Hortons in prison. Varying in style, the two major American political parties signal each presidential election year a readiness — differing only in degree from that of the Constitution's Framers — to sacrifice the rights of blacks in order to advance the political interests and alleviate the security concerns of whites. The reality of the continuing resistance to accepting blacks in the political process is a major reason for the dilution of litigation gains made in the 1960s and 1970s.

Certainly in presidential elections since 1988, but actually in every election where race is a potential issue, Republican candidates have tended to utilize rhetoric and manipulate facts so as to exploit the fears and ignorance of white voters. Democrats, while often dependent on black voters to gain election, go to great pains not to acknowledge that fact — even in those elections where the black vote provided the margin of victory. This willingness to disidentify with black voters is a tactic that both political parties deem necessary in the effort to gain the support of undecided white voters. For Democratic candidates who in their quest for white votes run campaigns well described as "Republican-Lite," success has come far less frequently than defeat.

In a very basic way, rule by the majority, tempered by protections against arbitrary abuse of minority views, is supposedly at the heart of our democratic system. It is assumed and expected that minority political views will lose at election time and will have to give way to "the majority will." The functioning of this process regarding most political issues is understood and generally accepted. The party or interest defeated this year may regroup, hope for more propitious conditions, await the inevitable floundering of office incumbents, and mount a new attack at the next election. There is here a political competition that at least theoretically increases the efficiency of democratic government.[3]

His most serious challenge — at least at the time of this publication — has been the constant media and Internet replaying of snippets of sermons delivered by the Rev. Jeremiah Wright, from the Trinity United Church of Christ, Senator Obama's church for 20 years. Called on to both denounce Rev. Wright and leave the Church, Obama responded on March 18 with his "A More Perfect Union" speech in Philadelphia just across from Constitution Hall. He disagreed strongly with Wright's statements, deeming them the product of an earlier time in American racial history, but did not dissociate himself from Wright or leave the church. He contrasted Wright's angry denunciations with his audacity of hope, his proof that he still believes in the system. He has campaigned as a unifier of races — white, black, Latino, Asian — asking voters to look at his diverse background as an example of what Americans of all backgrounds can offer. Yet this more conservative approach to racial issues does not seem that dramatically different from other black leaders on the national scene. It will be interesting to follow and learn from his Presidential campaign and political life to compare how his candidacy in 2008 differs from those that have come before.

3. Professor Gerhard Casper writes: "That this system has not been subject to controversy before now is, by almost any account, remarkable, for it enables pluralities to elect legislative

But the caste-like status of blacks in the society — the conditions in fact and in strongly held belief that together convince so many whites that blacks as a class are somehow irreparably different from and less worthy than whites — this American mind-set renders it impossible for blacks to participate in the political give and take with any real expectation that their basic goals can prevail. It is not that blacks can never profit from political participation; it is that their gains are almost always the gratuitous dividends of policies that are favored by a controlling white interest or group. When no such fortuitous arrangements are possible, blacks have found that political participation becomes quite difficult. Also, if blacks in a particular area are voting in meaningful numbers they are seen as a political threat, and there is little hesitance to take steps to insure that political outcomes are white-dominated, even if this requires dilution of black voting strength or, as has happened more than once, outright disfranchisement of black voters.

Constitutional protections prove inadequate when, as Justice Holmes found in Giles v. Harris,[4] a "great mass of the white population intends to keep . . . blacks from voting." Thus blacks, while citizens, are always subject to "democratic domination"; their views, aspirations, even basic political rights subject to the prevailing belief that America, and every part of it, must be controlled by whites.

Writing more than three decades ago, Professor Owen Fiss viewed this severely limited political power as deriving from three different sources that act either alternatively or cumulatively, but are, in any event, interrelated.[5] He writes:

> *One* source of weakness is their numbers, the fact that they are a numerical minority; the *second* is their economic status, their position as the perpetual under-class; and the *third* is that, as a "discrete and insular" minority, they are the object of "prejudice" — that is, the subject of fear, hatred, and distaste that make it particularly difficult for them to form coalitions with others (such as the white poor) and that make it advantageous for the dominant political parties to hurt them — to use them as a scapegoat.

Their status as a minority is a political disadvantage, but it is racial prejudice, the third of these factors, that poses the most serious obstacle to effective black representation. Most of the reform efforts reviewed in this chapter are directed toward that end, but even the most far-reaching and controversial judicial decisions and civil rights legislation have not been adequate to overcome the range of interconnected problems enumerated by Professor Fiss.

As the lengthy post-Reconstruction campaign (covered in §§6.2-6.7) shows, securing the right to vote has been so difficult that it is easy to lose sight of the fact

---

majorities and it leaves minorities (which in actuality can be majorities) unrepresented. But the country has apparently felt that some invisible hand, in a rough way, would see to it that the results would not be too inconsistent with the concept of majority rule, 'that [quoting John Stuart Mill] as different opinions predominate in different localities, the opinion which is a minority in some places has a majority in others, and on the whole, every opinion which exists in the constituencies obtains its fair share of voices in the representation.' Underlying this is the further assumption that a communality of interests and the relevant political cleavages are usually defined in territorial terms." Gerhard Casper, Social Differences and the Franchise, Daedalus 103, 108 (Fall 1976).

4. 189 U.S. 475, 488 (1903).

5. Owen Fiss, Groups and the Equal Protection Clause, 5 Philosophy & Pub. Aff. 107, 152 (1976).

that, as Professor Gerhard Casper pointed out also three decades ago, "voting is not merely an act of participation. It is supposedly performed with a goal in mind — representation; but voting does not in itself necessarily entail representation. At its best, representation is a tenuous political reality; at its weakest, a mere legal fiction."[6]

Concern for representation, until recently, received little attention not only in the struggle for black voting rights but also in the universalizing of the franchise through the removal of property and sex qualifications.[7] Now, as Professor Casper indicates, the contemporary demand for reapportionment is not simply a remedy for the traditional problem of "rotten boroughs"; it is an effort to gain for urban areas a fair share of the greatly expanded list of government services and subsidies through the medium of representatives sensitive to the interests and needs of those who elected them, and committed to obtaining their fair share of all the law provides.[8]

Thus, in Professor Casper's view, when "segments" of the community, identifiable in sociological terms, believe the system of representative government has failed adequately to represent their interests by obtaining that level of governmental services to which they feel themselves entitled, the result is voting rights litigation. While the focus and terminology of this litigation is on "legislative representation," with the emphasis on territorial concepts, the real concern is "interest representation."[9] And in giving meaning to the Voting Rights Act of 1965, the federal courts, for a time, moved in the direction of recognizing and sometimes ordering legislative representation on the basis of a racially or ethnically identifiable group.

It is not difficult to predict that many will conclude after reviewing these efforts that more must be done than the courts are able or willing to do. But for more than a century, as the following sections will show, this conclusion could have been reached as easily regarding the law's ability to recognize the right of blacks to simply register and cast their vote. It remains to be seen whether the Obama campaign in 2008, coming as it does during a time of severe economic

6. Casper, supra note 3, at 105.

7. "Nineteenth-century America," Professor Casper reports, "treated the right to vote as a dialectical solution to the actual and potential conflict between equality and freedom. In gradually universalizing the suffrage, civil society made all citizens politically equal, pronounced the vote to be the 'preservative of all rights,' and left social inequalities largely to the free play of forces." Id. at 104.

8. To illustrate that the Supreme Court on occasion has recognized this concept of representation, Professor Casper cites Justice Brennan who, writing for the majority that upheld §4(e) of the 1965 Voting Rights Act, which abolished the English language literacy requirement for Puerto Ricans in New York, said: "The practical effect of §4(e) is to prohibit New York from denying the right to vote to large segments of its Puerto Rican community. . . . This enhanced political power will be helpful in gaining nondiscriminatory treatment in public services for the entire Puerto Rican community. Section 4(e) thereby enables the Puerto Rican minority better to obtain 'perfect equality of civil rights and equal protection of the laws.' " Katzenbach v. Morgan, 384 U.S. 641, 653-656 (1966).

9. Casper, supra note 3, at 108-109. The transition in thinking is difficult, Professor Casper explains, because "[f]or much of its history, and in spite of (or because of) the system of interest representation, the country has avoided theories of legislative representation which tend to confer legal and constitutional status on distinctions such as race, sex, or economic status. These had previously been declared — to use Marx'[s] expression — 'non-political' distinctions. This romantic fiction not only had the advantage of simplicity, but it also served as a normative denominator: it deemphasized differences, calling instead for attention to the citizenship held in common." Id. at 110.

distress at home, the quagmire of an unwinnable war in Iraq, and the growing danger of terrorism by those who are committed to doing us great harm without the need for nuclear weapons, supersonic planes, or smart bombs, will alter the voting patterns described by Fiss, Casper and, to their dismay, experienced by black people in election after election.

§6.2 TO VOTE OR NOT TO VOTE?

White people have always harbored a terrible ambivalence on the subject of black voting rights. On the one hand, blacks are given to understand that it is through the vote that their rights as American citizens will be finally redeemed. And on the other hand, policies are supported or condoned which, depending on the period of history, renders exercise of the franchise by blacks a sometimes dangerous, a sometimes difficult, a sometimes impossible, and never the easy and often rewarding task it is for whites.

The astute nineteenth-century observer, Alexis de Tocqueville, commented on this phenomenon. He knew that blacks in the slaveholding states, whether slave or free, did not vote; but he was more surprised in 1832 to find no blacks voting even in those areas of the North noted for their staunch abolitionist positions:

> I said one day to an inhabitant of Pennsylvania: "Be so good as to explain to me how it happens that in a state founded by Quakers, and celebrated for its toleration, free blacks are not allowed to exercise civil rights. They pay taxes; is it not fair that they should vote?"
>
> "You insult us," replied my informant, "if you imagine that our legislators could have committed so gross an act of injustice and intolerance."
>
> "Then the blacks possess the right of voting in this country?"
>
> "Without a doubt."
>
> "How come it, then, that at the polling-booth this morning I did not perceive a single Negro?"
>
> "That is not the fault of the law. The Negroes have an undisputed right of voting, but they voluntarily abstain from making their appearance."
>
> "A very pretty piece of modesty on their part" rejoined I.
>
> "Why, the truth is that they are not disinclined to vote, but they are afraid of being maltreated; in this country the law is sometimes unable to maintain its authority without the support of the majority. But in this case the majority entertains very strong prejudices against the blacks, and the magistrates are unable to protect them in the exercise of their legal rights."
>
> "Then the majority claims the right not only of making the laws, but of breaking the laws it has made?"[1]

---

§6.2 1. Alexis de Tocqueville, I Democracy in America 261 (Anchor Books ed. 1969), reprinted by Judge Rives in United States ex rel. Goldsby v. Harpole, 263 F.2d 71, 79 n.21 (5th Cir. 1959).

Evidently to conform the law with practice, the Pennsylvania Supreme Court ruled in Hobbes v. Fogg, 6 Watts 553 (1837), that blacks did not have the right to vote even though there was no express

Admittedly, the ambivalence was hard to find prior to the Civil War. Most whites, whether pro- or anti-slavery, saw free blacks as unwelcome companions at the voting booths. Indeed, as Professor Leon Litwack has written, the expansion of political democracy that took place in the first half of the nineteenth century frequently was achieved at the expense of black rights and privileges.[2] By 1840, 93 percent of the northern free black population lived in states which completely or practically excluded them from the right to vote. Only in New England, where many free blacks had lived for decades and where, in any event, their numbers were few, could blacks vote on an equal basis with whites. New York set property and residence requirements for black voters not required for whites, and New Jersey, Connecticut, and, as we have seen, Pennsylvania, eventually barred blacks entirely, although they had at an earlier time had the theoretical right to vote as noted by de Tocqueville.

In several states, the long fight for universal male suffrage was won when opponents and advocates reached compromises based on their generally held view that blacks should not vote. Thus, as Professor Litwack has concluded:

> In several states the adoption of white manhood suffrage led directly to the political disfranchisement of the Negro. Those who opposed an expanded electorate — for both whites and Negroes — warned that it would, among other things, grant the Negro political power.
> . . . But even the friends of equal suffrage had their reservations. One Pennsylvanian, for example, opposed disfranchisement but conceded that Negroes "in their present depressed and uncultivated condition" were not "a desirable species of population," and he "should not prefer them as a matter of choice." Such admissions as these hardly added to the popular acceptance of Negro suffrage, and the advocates of such a dangerous doctrine found themselves labeled as either radical amalgamationists or hypocrites. . . .
> Utilizing various political, social, economic, and pseudo-anthropological arguments, white suffragists moved to deny the vote to the Negro. From the admission of Maine in 1819 until the end of the Civil War, every new state restricted the suffrage to whites in its constitution.[3]

Without formality, whites of widely varying viewpoints on the issue of universal suffrage, through their general agreement that blacks should not be permitted to vote, were able to compromise other differences. It is as though the presence of blacks was a reminder to all whites that, whatever their differences,

---

prohibition in the state's constitution or laws. Relying on reasoning foreshadowing that used by Chief Justice Taney two decades later in Dred Scott v. Sandford, 60 U.S. (19 How.) 393 (1857), the court found that provisions entitling "every freeman" to vote could not include blacks who were slaves when the provisions were adopted and were not freed thereby. Thus, the founders must not have intended to include blacks among citizens entitled to all the rights and privileges of citizenship. The political limbo into which blacks were cast by the Hobbes v. Fogg decision was made certain the following year when the Pennsylvania constitution was amended to give "the rights of an elector" to "every white freeman of the age of twenty-one. . . ." Pa. Const. 1838, art. III, §1. The era is reviewed in Eric Springer, The Unconquerable Prejudice of Caste — Civil Rights in Early Pennsylvania, 5 Duq. L. Rev. 31, 47-50 (1966-1967).

2. Leon Litwack, North of Slavery 74, 79 (1961).

3. Id. at 79.

they must unite to protect themselves against the black citizens in their midst. Thus catalyzed, they moved quickly to resolve their disagreements.

The abrogation of black voting rights by the states in the 1830s and 1840s set the stage for the Hayes-Tilden Compromise in 1876, a unifying action for the North and South that effected a repeal of virtually all black rights, including particularly the voting rights conferred in the Fifteenth Amendment.[4]

The third and last of the Civil War Amendments, designed to grant Negroes the right of suffrage, was enacted only with the greatest difficulty. Those favoring the measure argued that the right to vote was essential if blacks were to participate sufficiently in government to protect their lives against the continuing violence they suffered. News accounts of the time are filled with atrocious stories of blacks who were killed by whites. For example, in June 1868, a Congressional Committee on Lawlessness and Violence reported that 373 freedmen between 1866 and 1868 had been killed by whites.

Black suffrage was far from a popular idea. According to Peter Bergman,

> The Republicans did not include in their [1868] Presidential platform a demand for free negro suffrage in Northern states, since several Northern states had recently rejected the idea. Instead, their platform read: "The guarantee by Congress of equal suffrage to all loyal men in the South was demanded by every consideration of public safety, of gratitude and of justice, and must be maintained; while the questions of suffrage in all the loyal states properly belongs to the people of those states."[5]

After lengthy debate, the Fifteenth Amendment was enacted by Congress in December 1868. Its stated purpose was to safeguard Negroes against a future white supremacy by guaranteeing that their right to vote could not be denied or abridged by the United States or any state. It also guaranteed safe Republican majorities in elections for a dozen years, a fact far from lost on the Amendment's supporters. Ratification of the Fifteenth Amendment was demanded as a condition of readmittance for those few southern states still out of the Union, and it was only with their votes that the amendment was passed. New York rescinded its adoption of the amendment, and the amendment was rejected by California, Delaware, Kentucky, Maryland, Oregon, and Tennessee.[6]

The mobilization of law by the southerners, while the major focus of the discussion here, should be seen as a supplement to the violence, intimidation, and economic pressure which were the major weapons used to disfranchise blacks after the Civil War. If the altruism of all too many radical Republicans who advocated black suffrage was motivated by considerations of political expediency and strategy, southerners, determined to rebuild the Democratic party, were convinced that the achievement of this goal required that blacks be kept from the polls by any means possible.

---

4. "Section 1. The right of citizens of the United States to vote shall not be denied or abridged by the United States or by any State on account of race, color, or previous condition of servitude.
  Section 2. The Congress shall have power to enforce this article by appropriate legislation."
5. Peter Bergman, The Chronological History of the Negro in America 258 (1969).
6. Albert Blaustein & Robert Zangrando, Civil Rights and the American Negro 423 (1968).

It was to this end that secret bands of whites with exotic names — "Regulators," "Jayhawkers," "Knights of the White Camelia," and of course the "Ku Klux Klan" — were organized as early as 1866; and, as the head of the Freedman's Bureau in Georgia reported, they committed the "most fiendish and diabolical outrages on the freedmen," generally with the sympathy of both the populace and the reconstructed governments.

In describing the era, John Hope Franklin writes:

> The Camelias and the Klan were the most powerful of the secret orders. Armed with guns, swords, or other weapons, their members patrolled some parts of the South day and night. Scattered Union troops proved wholly ineffectual in coping with them, for they were sworn to secrecy, disguised themselves and their deeds in many ways, and had the respect and support of the white community. They used intimidation, force, ostracism in business and society, bribery at the polls, arson, and even murder to accomplish their deeds. Depriving the Negro of political equality became, to them, a holy crusade in which a noble end justified any means. Negroes were run out of communities if they disobeyed orders to desist from voting; and the more resolute and therefore insubordinate blacks were whipped, maimed, and hanged. In 1871 several Negro officials in South Carolina were given fifteen days to resign and they were warned that if they failed, "then retributive justice will as surely be used as night follows day."[7]

Much of the violence was far from mindless, and was intended to intimidate blacks who voted or otherwise attempted to become involved in politics. The withdrawal of federal troops from the 1878 elections served as the silent but universally heard signal that electoral contests could more advantageously be waged by bullet than ballot. For those who didn't get the message, it was rebroadcast through the white supremacy campaigns of the 1890s. Evidently, no tale of black atrocity was too bizarre to be given quick credence by the white mind, particularly when elections were near. The retaliatory power mounted by whites in response to rumor was so great as to give the most courageous blacks pause before taking action that would provide white mobs with actual facts. After the election of 1898 in Wilmington, North Carolina, a mob of 400 white men set a black newspaper office on fire and killed 11 blacks.[8] But violence and intimidation were practiced prior to, as well as in the wake of, elections that paved the way toward disfranchisement. A Republican campaigning to be a convention delegate in Mississippi in 1890 was shot. Opposition to the Democrats virtually disappeared thereafter.[9]

7. John Hope Franklin, From Slavery to Freedom 326-328 (1969).
8. C. Vann Woodward, Origins of the New South 350 (1951).
9. During the campaign in 1890 for the election of delegates to Mississippi's constitutional convention, a black convention was held in order to encourage the election of black delegates. Warnings to blacks to desist, at first issued through the newspapers, were later buttressed by the murder of a Republican candidate. Commented the Jackson Clarion-Ledger, "At the time of his death he was canvassing Jasper County as a Republican candidate for the Constitutional Convention, and was daily and nightly denouncing the white people in his speeches and caucuses. . . . Then one or more persons decided that Cook must die. The Clarion-Ledger regrets the manner of his killing, as assassination cannot be condoned at any time. Yet the people of Jasper are to be congratulated that they will not be further annoyed by March Cook." Jackson Clarion-Ledger, July 31, 1890, as quoted in Vernon L. Wharton, The Negro in Mississippi, 1865-1890, at 211 (1947).

And the law? After a few years of mainly federal efforts to control the carnage, the law essentially declared itself unable to halt whites determined to regain control of the former slave states. By 1885, the white supremacy goal was all but accomplished. Despite all, many blacks still voted, but they were no longer the political force they had been in the first years of the Reconstruction. And yet, even this participation was deemed unacceptable. In the decades between 1890 and 1910, 12 states of the Old Confederacy undertook systematic programs that returned the election process to the status of an all-white preserve. The process by which this turn-of-the-century disfranchisement was accomplished, even why it was accomplished, has inherent historical interests; but it has as well a contemporary value, enabling us to compare the procedures used to eliminate the black vote entirely with the techniques utilized today to minimize the political potential of blacks who once again have gained access to the ballot box. While far less overt than the burning torch or the grandfather clause, modern techniques in their own insidious way render it difficult for today's blacks to resolve the question: To vote or not to vote?

§6.3   DISFRANCHISEMENT: POST-RECONSTRUCTION STYLE[1]

Historians for some years have engaged in vigorous debate as to whether the flood of black disfranchisement provisions placed in state statutes and constitutions during the decades after 1890 served as a *fait accompli* for work already accomplished by violence and intimidation, or whether affirmative legal steps were necessary to supplement the courts' silent acquiescence in stripping from blacks rights granted in the Fourteenth and Fifteenth Amendments.[2] The *fait accompli*

In another instance, after Hoke Smith's election on a white supremacy campaign in 1906, there were four days of rioting in Atlanta. Fired by newspaper accounts of four assaults on white women by blacks, white mobs engaged in looting and burning black property and attacking blacks. Four blacks were killed and many injured. Franklin, supra note 7, at 323-324; C. Vann Woodward, The Strange Career of Jim Crow 86-87 (3d ed. rev. 1974).

§6.3   1. The material in this section is adopted from Derrick Bell, The Racial Imperative in American Law, in The Age of Segregation: Race Relations in the South, 1890-1945, 16-19 (Robert Haws ed., 1978). The footnotes are more extensive than those that appeared in the original, and their form has been altered to conform with the style of this book. They provide important details and citations to facilitate further reading in a field still under exploration by historians.

2. See V. O. Key, Jr., Southern Politics in State and Nation 535 (1949), major proponent of the *fait accompli* thesis who states, "[b]efore their formal disfranchisement Negroes had, in most states, ceased to be of much political significance and the whites had won control of state governments." J. Morgan Kousser in The Shaping of Southern Politics 244 (1974) agrees with Prof. Key that there was "a stage previous to disfranchisement in which political activity was muted," but credits the disfranchisement laws themselves with effecting a more significant percentage of actual disfranchisement. He claims that the drop in black voting prior to the enactment of disfranchisement provisions in many southern states, brought about through violence, intimidation, fraud, or preliminary legislative restrictions, was relatively small. Thus these scholars may be seen to disagree on the more fundamental question of the role of law as it applies to this era. Says Prof. Key, supra, at 535, "Oddly enough those who urge an institutional change to enable them to gain power usually first win control without benefit of the procedural or organizational advantage they seek.

theory would seem the more credible approach, particularly in that the legal procedures were themselves accomplished through fraud, bribery, intimidation, and violence. In any event, once the disfranchisement movement began rolling between 1888 and 1893, there is little record that it was greatly slowed by counter-attacks of conscience.

Constitutional conventions and their subsequent deliberations followed a predictable pattern in the five states where they were called — Mississippi, South Carolina, Louisiana, Alabama, and Virginia.[3] An initial step required overcoming opposition from dissenting political groups and the exclusion of blacks from the vote by violence, fraud, or hastily enacted voting restrictions.[4] Having garnered the votes for the calling of a constitutional convention and the election of sympathetic delegates, the conventions proceeded, not as forums for state debate on the pressing problems of the day, but as gatherings of state Democrats eager to solve only one problem — the removal of blacks as a factor in state politics. After these conventions altered the state constitutions to include suffrage restrictions that were neutral as to race but had the effect of barring all blacks and many poor whites as well, the new constitutions were frequently simply proclaimed.[5] The Democrats feared a popular vote might defeat the constitutional changes.

Other southern states adopted disfranchisement provisions without calling a constitutional convention. Between 1900 and 1908, North Carolina, Texas, and Georgia amended the suffrage clauses of their state constitutions through referenda. Florida, Tennessee, and Arkansas, with a combination of the poll tax and

---

Law often merely records not what is to be but what is, and ensures that what is will continue to be." Prof. Kousser, supra, at 264, on the other hand, believes that voting restriction was the result of the ". . . *enforcement* not the nonenforcement of the laws." He thus sees legalized disfranchisement as having a far stronger effect than an informal system of voting restriction; through the withdrawal of even symbolic rights, the black person, the poor person, and the illiterate person were left demoralized and without hope. Id. at 263-264.

3. Constitutional conventions were held in Mississippi (1890), South Carolina (1895), Louisiana (1898), Alabama (1901), and Virginia (1902). For discussions of the conventions, see Vernon L. Wharton, The Negro in Mississippi, 1865-1890, 199-215 (1947); Albert Kirwan, Revolt of the Rednecks, Mississippi Politics: 1876-1925, 58-64 (1964); George Brown Tindall, South Carolina Negroes, 1877-1900, 68-91 (1952); John Brittain, Negro Suffrage and Politics in Alabama Since 1870, 125-170 (1958); Charles Wynes, Race Relations in Virginia, 1870-1902, 51-67 (1961); F. Williams, The Poll Tax as a Suffrage Requirement in the South, 1870-1901, 18 J. S. Hist. 469 (1952); and Kousser, supra note 2, at 139-181.

4. South Carolina, for example, in 1894 passed a new registration law to keep blacks from voting prior to its convention. It retained on the voting rolls all those previously registered, most of whom were white, but set up extremely confusing regulations for those not yet registered. In addition local officials were encouraged to refuse registration blanks to blacks; officials who were unwilling to do so were removed. When a federal district court ruled the registration law unconstitutional, the circuit overturned the decision, stating that the courts lacked jurisdiction over "political questions." Kousser, supra note 2, at 147.

5. In Mississippi, South Carolina, and Virginia, the new constitutions were not submitted to the state at large for ratification but were merely promulgated, largely to avoid a political battle and skirt the embarrassing position of asking a good part of the population to vote for their own disfranchisement. The absence of popular ratification was particularly heinous in Virginia, where the citizens had originally been encouraged to vote for the calling of the convention on the basis of the fact that they would be able to vote on the new constitution. Wynes, supra note 3, at 64-66. See also Tindall, supra note 3, at 88; Wharton, supra note 3, at 214.

registration, multiple-box or secret ballot rules achieved disfranchisement by state legislative action.[6]

Through these legislative proceedings a plethora of restrictive measures were handed down. As J. Morgan Kousser has noted, "Each state became a laboratory for testing one device or another."[7] A number of simple voting restrictions were instituted prior to the passage of more complicated, constitutional provisions. Such basic restrictions as the registration rules, the multiple-box law, and the secret ballot were quite effective in their own right in reducing the popular vote. Registration laws discouraged voting in a number of ways. Either the time or place of voting could be deliberately made inconvenient for registrants. For example, after 1892, Alabama held registration only in May when farmers were the busiest in the field. Registration deadlines were often set months before an election when voters were not interested or aware of campaign issues. Specific information about birth, residency, age, and occupation could be required. These requirements also worked against blacks who, as former slaves, frequently did not know their exact ages and who lived in areas that often lacked house numbers. Sometimes it was required that one bring a registration certificate to the polls. Often the appointees of the state, the puppets of local Democrats, or the subjects of their own political or personal prejudices, the registrars, who had wide discretion in deciding who fulfilled registration requirements, injected further discrimination into the application of the laws. Residency requirements, too, took their toll, usually requiring a tenure of one or two years in the state and some amount of time in the county. These laws disadvantaged farm laborers who frequently moved. The multiple-box laws and the secret ballot put the illiterate at a disadvantage. The multiple-box law required voters to place their ballots in the appropriate box, usually a box being provided for each type of office up for election or for the separation of national and state elections. The secret ballot, heralded as a mechanism of reform in North and South, was also a kind of literacy requirement, substituting an often confusing public ticket for ballots which had been handed out by individual political parties privately to voters. Since in seven out of the 11 southern states, the majority of blacks could be classified as illiterate in 1900, the impact of even an indirect literacy requirement was severe.[8]

Florida, Tennessee, and Arkansas added only the poll tax to these basic provisions in order to effectuate disfranchisement. In many of the other southern states these measures were preliminaries used to mute the opposition vote in the effort to push through more extensive constitutional disfranchisement measures. The poll tax was employed in all the former Confederate states by 1904. Another, less significant provision was that of disqualification for certain crimes,

---

6. In 1900, North Carolina voters agreed to amendments instituting a poll tax and literacy and property tests. In 1902, Texas voters ratified a poll tax amendment. The literacy test, property test, understanding clause, and grandfather clause were accepted in a Georgia referendum in 1908. Kousser, supra note 2, at 182-223.

7. In 1889, Florida adopted the poll tax and multiple-box law. In the same year, Tennessee established registration requirements and the secret ballot, and added the poll tax a year later. Arkansas passed a secret ballot requirement in 1891, and the poll tax in 1892. Id. at 91-138.

8. Id. at 47-56; Key, supra note 2, at 536-539; C. Vann Woodward, Origins of the New South 55-56 (1951).

the list varying from state to state but generally including such acts as bribery, burglary, theft, and obtaining money or goods under false pretenses. Literacy tests, property tests, understanding and character clauses, and the grandfather clause generally completed the disfranchisement arsenal. Still later, as blacks became better educated, more economically secure, and hence more likely to meet the suffrage qualifications, white primaries became popular, restricting the Democratic and only significant primary in those one-party states to white voters.[9]

An intricate weave of sectional and national pressures directed the South toward its disfranchisement programs. Republicans and Populists began to lose strength as the result of the defeat of the Lodge Elections Bill, the death of several key Republican leaders, the shift of the nation's attention to economic problems, and the creation of a stable national Republican majority that no longer needed the South to control the federal government. Without opposition, Democrats were able to pursue suffrage restrictions which they deemed necessary in order to legalize the exclusion of black voters in case voting Republicans, back in power at the national level, might attempt to restore the black vote.

The disfranchising forces chose to act, not only due to a weakening of the opposition, but because they wished to strengthen their own position. White Democrats believed that the elimination of blacks, and some poor whites as well, from the polls would insure Democratic domination of state politics. Fearing, sometimes correctly, that blacks held the balance of power in many elections, they sought to deter them from supporting Republicans or other opposing groups. Rather than continuing efforts to win black votes, which generally required intimidation or fraud. Democrats in most southern states concluded it made more sense to simply prevent blacks, and sometimes some white opposition forces, from voting at all. Moreover, the Democrats were concerned that continued corruption in elections would lead to the inevitable contesting of elections by opposition groups, the possible renewal of federal intervention, and even internal political disintegration if the deceptions became too severe. Paradoxically, disfranchisement of blacks became the key to the elimination of fraud and corruption by whites in the election process. With blacks out of the electorate, there would no longer be the need for fraud. Repeatedly, the adoption of voting restrictions displayed what one commentator termed "the strange picture of one race disfranchising another to save itself from the consequences of its own vices."[10] In addition, efficient government was furthered by disfranchisement, because with this "final solution" to the voting controversy, states could move on to consideration of other important problems.[11] Many of these problems were not race-connected. But as has happened again and again throughout history, adherence by

9. See generally Kousser, supra note 2, passim; Woodward, supra note 8, at 321-349; Key, supra note 2, at 535-539; and Williams, supra note 3, at 469.

10. Charles Mangum, The Legal Status of the Negro 411-412 (1940).

11. See William Alexander Mabry, The Negro in North Carolina Politics Since Reconstruction, in Thirteen Historical Papers of the Trinity College Historical Society at 62 (1940). Wharton, supra note 3, at 208.

the socioeconomically privileged (in this case the white Democrats) to the Racial Imperative enabled them to protect and further their interests against competing whites as well as blacks.[12]

The crusade of Democratic southerners for suffrage restriction also harmonized with changes in the national political philosophy. In the late nineteenth century, mass suffrage became suspect and a move for a literate and propertied electorate was begun. Suffrage restriction was aimed toward immigrants as well as blacks. Thus the voices of Democrats calling for "white supremacy" were joined by the more genteel intonations of upper-class reformers who embraced Darwin's notion of survival of the fittest and a return to a Federalist philosophy which championed the propertied classes. Imperialism abroad was also consonant with these elitist leanings and buttressed the arguments of those withholding rights from minorities at home.[13]

Litigation protesting the disfranchisement provisions and the white primaries was filed in state and federal courts. The decisions, in the main, upheld the rights of states to fashion their own suffrage provisions. Often ruling on technical grounds or declaring the Reconstruction amendments and legislation inapplicable to state legislation, most disfranchisement devices were allowed to stand.[14]

There can be little argument about the presence of powerful political pressures that fueled the disfranchisement movement. The willingness of political policymakers to respond to these forces by systematically denying to blacks their basic citizenship right may not come as a surprise given the history of the region, but the cavalier disregard for the voting rights of thousands of poor whites should convey more of a message than it did then or does now. It would appear that as long as the mass of whites are willing to forego their rights if they can be assured blacks are being denied theirs, then, when future political pressures dictate, both blacks and poor whites can expect nullification of their constitutional rights.

---

12. The leaders of the disfranchisement movements in the southern states generally came from the black belt, were the sons or grandsons of plantation owners, and were generally affluent and well-educated. Kousser, supra note 2, at 246-250.

13. For a discussion of U.S. imperialism, see Harold Faulkner, The Quest for Social Justice, 1898-1914, 29, 308-332; Woodward, supra note 8, at 324-326; Rayford W. Logan, The Betrayal of the Negro, 271-273 (1965); and Thomas Gossett, Race: The History of an Idea in America 310-338 (1963).

14. The Alabama provisions remained in effect after a challenge under the federal civil rights statutes in Giles v. Harris, 189 U.S. 475 (1903). In contending that the Court as a court in equity could not require registration of blacks under a state law which plaintiffs alleged was unconstitutional, and that a court of equity cannot grant political rights, the Supreme Court ignored the fact that the civil rights statute also provided for an action at law. When later the Alabama Supreme Court dismissed a voting rights suit on similar grounds, the Supreme Court refused to review what it deemed an independent state basis for decision. Giles v. Teasley, 193 U.S. 146 (1903).

See also the Mississippi cases contesting the suffrage provisions of the 1890 constitutional convention. The restrictions were upheld by both the state court in Dixon v. State, 74 Miss. 271 (1896), and Sproule v. Fredericks, 69 Miss. 898 (1892), and by the Supreme Court in Williams v. Mississippi, 170 U.S. 213 (1898). See also Breedlove v. Shuttles, 302 U.S. 277 (1937), in which the Supreme Court ruled that the poll tax did not violate any constitutional rights.

§6.4   SYMBOLIC VOTING RIGHTS

Beginning about 1915, the Supreme Court started a long, slow process of responding to civil rights litigation by invalidating a few of the more odious disfranchisement provisions. In this category, the grandfather clauses were first to fall.[1] But by this point there was little need to bar blacks by virtue of the fact that their forefathers had been unable to vote because of their slave status. Every southern state had in place far more effective barriers to the exercise of the franchise by citizens who were black.[2] Two main points of attack for civil rights lawyers were the white primary and the poll tax.

§6.4.1   The White Primary

For almost 30 years, the NAACP and other civil rights groups labored in the courts to strike down the white primary. This was an ingenious device that took advantage of the one-party politics that prevailed in the South and effectively frustrated the desire to vote, at least in the primary — the only election that counted — of even the most persistent blacks. But litigation tends to be a slow method of reform, and the courts were often a few steps behind the newest procedure devised to shield the critical part of the election process from the Court's constantly shifting state action standard.

In Nixon v. Herndon,[3] the Supreme Court held that a Texas statute forbidding the participation of blacks in primary elections violated the petitioners' constitutional rights under the Fourteenth Amendment. Texas then changed the statute, delegating to the State Executive Committee of the Democratic Party the right to fix qualifications for voting in the primary. The committee promptly adopted a resolution designed to effect the same result as the voided statute. The Court rejected this arrangement in Nixon v. Condon,[4] holding that the committee operated as the state's representative in the discharge of the state's authority. But in 1932, the State Convention of the Democratic Party passed a resolution

---

§6.4   1. Guinn v. United States, 238 U.S. 347 (1915). The provisions gave all those who had the franchise before a certain date and their descendants the right to register permanently before a certain time had elapsed without complying with the educational qualifications required of all other voters. The Court found the date was fixed at a time when blacks were not permitted to vote, thereby allowing all illiterate whites to vote while disfranchising ignorant blacks in circumvention of the Fifteenth Amendment. *Guinn* involved a provision in Oklahoma's constitution. A similar clause in a Maryland local act applying only to the city of Annapolis was also invalidated in Myers v. Anderson, 238 U.S. 368 (1915).

2. By the time the Supreme Court declared the grandfather clause unconstitutional, the time limits for these temporary measures had expired in every state in which they were adopted. Charles Mangum, The Legal Status of the Negro 399-400 (1940). And, a year after *Guinn*, the Oklahoma legislature enacted a statute requiring registrars to enroll all those persons who had voted in 1914, while all other persons, were to be registered only if officials "shall be satisfied" of their qualifications. Id. at 398. That rather obvious evasion was not voided until 1939 in Lane v. Wilson, 307 U.S. 268 (1939).

3. 273 U.S. 536 (1927).

4. 286 U.S. 73 (1932).

limiting membership in the state party and thus limiting qualifications for voting in the primary; and in Grovey v. Townsend,[5] the Supreme Court held that the determination by the state convention of the membership of the Democratic party made a significant change from a determination by the Executive Committee, because the convention action was not state action but party action, "voluntary in character" and protected as an exercise of private associational rights by the Texas Bill of Rights. Later in United States v. Classic,[6] the Court held that corrupt acts of election officials in a Louisiana primary were subject to congressional sanctions "where the primary is by law made an integral part of the election machinery."

In Smith v. Allwright,[7] the Court reopened the question of whether discrimination effected by the state convention, which denied to blacks the right to participate in primaries, was private or state action when in conducting the primary the party was fulfilling duties delegated to it by a statutory electoral scheme. The Texas statutes regulating primaries were substantially similar to the Louisiana statutes considered in *Classic;* and the Court said, "Such a variation in the result from so slight a change in form influences us to consider anew the legal validity of the distinction which has resulted in barring Negroes from participating in the nominations of candidates of the Democratic party in Texas." Then, after reviewing the importance of the primary to the election process, the Court concluded: "We think that this statutory system for the selection of party nominees for inclusion on the general election ballot makes the party which is required to follow these legislative directions an agency of the state in so far as it determines the participants in a primary election." There was thus the state action requisite to a finding of a violation of Fourteenth and Fifteenth Amendment rights.

The decision in Smith v. Allwright did not discourage Texas officials. In Terry v. Adams,[8] the Supreme Court reviewed still another scheme designed to divorce the effective election process from the nondiscrimination standards of the Fourteenth and Fifteenth Amendments. The Jaybird Association, a private organization whose membership included all the white members of the Democratic party appearing on the voting rolls of Fort Bend County, Texas, followed a "three-step" electoral process to select county officials. There was first a Jaybird primary; next, the Jaybird selections appeared on the ballot in the Democratic party primary; finally the Democratic nominees appeared as such on the general election ballot. The Jaybirds claimed that their exclusion of blacks from their primaries did not violate the Fifteenth Amendment, because it did not involve any action on the part of the state, inasmuch as their primary was not provided for or regulated by any state statutes. The candidates victorious in the Jaybird primaries, with few exceptions, proceeded to success in the general elections. Justice Black, for the Court, held that the scheme violated the Fifteenth Amendment, reversed the court of appeals, and reinstated the decree granted by the district court declaring that the

---

5. 295 U.S. 45 (1935).
6. 313 U.S. 299 (1941).
7. 321 U.S. 649 (1944).
8. 345 U.S. 461 (1953).

plaintiffs and others similarly situated had the right to vote in the Jaybird Association's primaries.

The Court relied upon recently decided cases, voiding the South Carolina white primary: Rice v. Elmore[9] and Baskin v. Brown,[10] in which South Carolina's Democratic primaries were held to violate the Fifteenth Amendment, even though South Carolina had repealed all statutory control of the primaries, and had left them ostensibly in private hands.[11] The Court quoted *Allwright* for the principle that "the constitutional right to be free from racial discrimination in voting . . . is not to be nullified by a state through casting its electoral process in a form which permits a private organization to practice racial discrimination in the election."

§6.4.2   The Poll Tax

For the 11 southern states that enacted poll taxes, the tax served less as a financial deterrent to the prospective black voter than as a grant of administrative discretion to registration officials, who used the device in myriad ways, all designed to bar the ballot to blacks. The tax, usually $1 to $2 and payable annually, had little revenue-raising value. Indeed, blacks in one Mississippi county alleged in a suit that the sheriff and tax collector had simply refused to accept their poll tax payments (United States v. Dogan).[12] But since presentation of poll tax receipts (often for a few years back) was required, and deadlines for payment of the tax were set on dates far from election time and at times and places inconvenient for the black voter, the tax was worth its weight in gold for whites who wished to discourage the black (and a goodly part of the white) electorate from voting. At the least, payment of the poll tax alerted registration officials (and others) as to which blacks might actually be contemplating registration and voting.

Over the years, efforts to end the poll tax through national legislation and judicial action failed. The Supreme Court in 1937 found that poll taxes did not violate any rights protected by the Constitution. (Breedlove v. Shuttles.)[13] But almost three decades later, the Court acknowledged the barriers to voting posed by such taxes. In Harmon v. Forssenius,[14] Virginia, seeking to avoid the effect of the Twenty-fourth Amendment (barring use of taxes to deny or abridge the exercise of voting rights in federal elections), enacted a provision enabling citizens either to pay the tax or to file a notarized or witnessed certificate of residence six months

---

9. 165 F.2d 387 (4th Cir. 1947), cert. denied, 333 U.S. 875 (1948).

10. 174 F.2d 391 (4th Cir. 1949).

11. The federal district judge in both South Carolina cases was J. Waties Waring. In Brown v. Baskin, 80 F. Supp. 1017 (E.D.S.C. 1948), he told the voting officials, "It is time to realize that the people of the United States expect [you] to follow the American way of elections." These decisions won Judge Waring national fame and local notoriety, and when in 1951 he dissented from the ruling of a three-judge court that South Carolina's segregation laws were constitutional, he became the target of intense local abuse, his life was threatened, his wife slandered, and he soon retired from the bench and moved to New York. J. W. Peltason, Fifty-eight Lonely Men 10 (1961).

12. 314 F.2d 767 (5th Cir. 1963).

13. 302 U.S. 277 (1937).

14. 380 U.S. 528 (1965).

before election. The Court voided the measure, concluding that the certificate requirement posed an obstacle to voting more onerous than the poll tax.

Then in 1966 the Court overruled Breedlove v. Shuttles, and declared that to the extent that it required payment as a condition for voting, Virginia's poll tax provision violated the Fourteenth Amendment's equal protection clause. (Harper v. Virginia Board of Election.)[15] Observing that the right to vote in federal elections is conferred by Art. 1, §2 of the federal Constitution, the Court conceded that the right to vote in state elections is nowhere expressly mentioned. But once the franchise is granted, the equal protection clause of the Fourteenth Amendment prohibits the states from drawing artificial and discriminatory lines among the voters. "We conclude that a State violates the Equal Protection Clause of the Fourteenth Amendment whenever it makes the affluence of the voter or payment of any fee an electoral standard."[16] Voter qualifications are for the state to determine, but the state may not draw arbitrary lines, and affluence or the payment of the poll tax bears no reasonable relationship to qualification for voting. In justifying its action the Court pointed to its overruling of Plessy v. Ferguson[17] in Brown v. Board of Education,[18] stating: "In determining what lines are unconstitutionally discriminatory, we have never been confined to historic notions of equality. . . ." Poll taxes in Texas and Alabama were invalidated in, respectively, United States v. Texas[19] and United States v. Alabama.[20] Both courts found that the poll taxes were instituted as a means of subverting the Fifteenth Amendment.

Opponents of Voter ID laws, enacted or being considered in several states, maintain that they will discourage voting and in particular black and Latino voting for reasons quite similar to those that led to invalidation of poll taxes. In 2005, Indiana's Republican-controlled legislature enacted a new law requiring voters to show a current, government-issued photo ID at the polls in order to be allowed to vote, allegedly to prevent voter fraud. The plaintiffs in these two consolidated cases have challenged the law, claiming that it imposes an unconstitutional burden on the right to vote. In particular, the plaintiffs contend that the poor and the elderly will be unduly burdened by the requirement to show this type of identification. They also contend that concerns about voter fraud have been exaggerated.

In a 2-1 ruling in January, the United States Court of Appeals for the Seventh Circuit upheld the law, rejecting the plaintiffs' claims that it imposes an unconstitutional burden on the right to vote. In a majority opinion written by Judge Richard Posner (a Reagan appointee) and joined by Judge Diane Sykes (a George W. Bush appointee), the court was dismissive of the notion that requiring current photo IDs is an undue burden on certain groups of voters, including lower income voters. Judge Terence Evans (a Clinton appointee) dissented, bluntly stating "Let's not beat around the bush: The Indiana voter photo ID law is a not-too-thinly-veiled attempt to discourage election day turnout by certain folks believed to skew

15. 383 U.S. 663 (1966).
16. 383 U.S. at 666.
17. 163 U.S. 537 (1896).
18. 347 U.S. 483 (1954).
19. 252 F. Supp. 234 (W.D. Texas), aff'd mem., 384 U.S. 155 (1966).
20. 252 F. Supp. 95 (M.D. Ala. 1966).

Democratic." Judge Evans noted that "no one — in the history of Indiana — had ever been charged" with the crime of voter fraud.[21]

§6.4.3   Overt Racial Designations

A few states have attempted blatant as well as neutral-on-their-face schemes in efforts to dilute the effect of increased voting by blacks in the period prior to enactment of the Voting Rights Act of 1965. Again, as with the white primary and poll tax cases, the affirmative response of the courts to these petitions for relief probably helped black morale more than it increased the actual number of black voters.

In Anderson v. Martin,[22] two black candidates for the school board in East Baton Rouge Parish, Louisiana, brought suit in the United States District Court for the District of Louisiana to enjoin the Louisiana secretary of state from effectuating a state statute requiring that, in all primary, general, or special elections, the nomination papers and ballots designate the race of candidates for elective office. A three-judge federal district court denied injunctive relief on the ground that the statute was constitutional.

Justice Clark, per curiam, held that the statute operated as a discrimination against the black candidates and was therefore violative of the equal protection clause of the Fourteenth Amendment. The right of the voters to vote for whomever they chose for whatever reason they chose was not involved; what was involved was the right of the state to "require or encourage" voters to discriminate on the basis of race. The statute placed a "racial label" on the candidates "at the most crucial stage in the electoral process — the instant before the vote is cast"; this encouraged voters to pick out a single issue or consideration on which to make their choice. The results for the Negro plaintiffs would differ, depending upon whether the electoral unit was predominantly white or predominantly black, but "The vice lies not in the resulting injury but in the placing of the power of the state behind a racial classification that induces racial prejudice at the polls."

The provision in the statute was added in 1960, at a time when pressure on blacks was great and hence could not help but have a "repressive effect" which was "brought to bear only after the exercise of government power." Nor can the provision be deemed to be reasonably designed to meet legitimate governmental interest in informing the electorate. The state's contention that the provision was nondiscriminatory because it applied both to whites and blacks was rejected as superficial. "Race is the factor upon which the statute operates and its involvement promotes the ultimate discrimination which is sufficient to make it invalid."

In Hamm v. Virginia State Board of Elections,[23] an action was brought to attack the validity of Virginia statutes requiring designation of persons by races.

---

21. Crawford v. Marion County Election Board; Indiana Democratic Party v. Rokita, 472 F.3d 949 (7th Cir. 2007). The Supreme Court has granted review and heard arguments in January 2008.
22. 375 U.S. 399 (1964).
23. 230 F. Supp. 156 (E.D. Va.), aff'd per curiam sub nom. Tancil v. Wools, 379 U.S. 19 (1964).

A three-judge district court held that Virginia's constitutional and statutory provisions requiring separation of white and black persons on poll tax, residence-certificate and registration lists, and on assessment rolls were invalid under the equal protection clause of the Fourteenth Amendment, but that the Virginia statute requiring inclusion in divorce decrees of recitation showing race of husband and wife is not constitutionally objectionable. Citing Anderson v. Martin, supra, the court said, "To be within the condemnation, the governmental action need not effectuate segregation of facilities directly. . . . The result of the statute or policy must not tend to separate individuals by reason of difference in race or color." But designation of race may serve some useful purposes in areas where it will not operate discriminatorily: "Vital statistics, obviously, are aided by denotation in the divorce decrees of the race of the parties," so the divorce provisions were sustained.

The language in *Hamm* is somewhat contradictory, reflecting the ambivalence at the judicial level observable in many current voting rights cases. When is a racial classification invalid for tending "to separate individuals by reason of difference in race or color," and when are they valid because they "serve some useful purposes in areas where it will not operate discriminatorily . . ."? As the next sections will show, recognition of race is of some importance in securing the individual right to vote, but it is of critical importance in evaluating schemes that dilute black voting strength. Before the latter issue could assume real importance, far more blacks had to be made eligible to vote than had been put on the rolls by all the litigation up to 1964.

§6.4.4   Gomillion v. Lightfoot[24]

In 1957, the Alabama legislature passed Act No. 140, which redefined the boundaries of the city of Tuskegee. The statute transformed the city from one whose municipal limits formed a square into one which took on the shape of what Justice Frankfurter later called an "uncouth" and "strangely irregular" 28-sided polygon. "The essential inevitable effect of this redefinition of Tuskegee's boundaries [was] to remove from the city all save only four or five of its 400 Negro voters while not removing a single white voter or resident."[25]

Initially, the exclusion of Tuskegee's black voters by the Alabama legislature's action appeared beyond the reach of judicial relief because of the Court's oft-repeated unwillingness to "enter the political thicket." Yet a group of civil rights lawyers under the direction of then NAACP General Counsel Robert L. Carter proceeded on the assumption that, in the post-*Brown* era, the Court would have to provide a remedy for so flagrant a denial of the right to vote.

The Court reversed the district court's dismissal of the complaint. Justice Frankfurter wrote for the Court that the complaint "amply allege[d] a claim of racial discrimination" in violation of the Fifteenth Amendment. The Court further

---

24. 364 U.S. 339 (1960).

25. Id. at 341. In an appendix to its opinion, the Supreme Court printed a map showing Tuskegee before and after Act 140. 364 U.S. at 348.

found that although a state's power "to establish, destroy, or reorganize by expansion or contraction . . . its cities, counties and other local units" was broad, the exercise of that power was nonetheless subject to the restrictions of the Fifteenth Amendment.

Although the Court did not rule on the merits of the complaint, Justice Frankfurter remarked that if the allegations were true, "the conclusion would be irresistible, tantamount for all practical purposes to a mathematical demonstration, that the legislation [was] solely concerned with segregating white and colored voters by fencing Negro citizens out of town so as to deprive them of their pre-existing municipal vote."[26] "The inescapable human effect of this essay in geometry and geography is to despoil colored citizens, and only colored citizens, of their theretofore enjoyed voting rights."[27]

Two aspects of the *Gomillion* decision are noteworthy. First, the relief granted was not premised upon the petitioner's showing intent or malevolent purpose. The Court assumed that there were no rightful aims in the legislative mind when it so radically altered the boundaries of Tuskegee, one of the few areas in the state where blacks — many of them associated with Tuskegee College and the federal hospital there — were beginning to vote in substantial numbers.

Second, the relief could be granted without in any way limiting the power of state entities to alter or enlarge their boundaries for arguably legitimate reasons. No whites would lose either their vote or the proper power of their vote by a court order requiring Tuskegee to retain its original boundaries. The relief also served as proof, rather inexpensively obtained, that courts would correct state efforts to deny blacks the right to vote because of their race or color.

Gomillion has proven of little precedential value in subsequent gerrymander or other vote-dilution challenges, even in cases where the impact on black voting power is as severe. Judicial commitment to the eradication of discrimination in the electoral process has often faltered when confronted with challenged actions that appear normal but for their effect on the black vote, and when the relief requested would undermine white voting power legitimately obtained.

Indeed, the Court seems to have forgotten that the case was decided under the broad (because limited to voting) mandate of the Fifteenth Amendment, and not, as Justice Whittaker suggested in his opinion concurring in the judgment, under the much more nebulous standard of the Fourteenth Amendment's equal protection clause. In other voting cases the Court consciously or unconsciously has shifted the standard for review from the Fifteenth to the Fourteenth Amendment. For example, in Whitcomb v. Chavis,[28] the Court not only used the Fourteenth Amendment as its standard, but also cited *Gomillion* as though it had been decided on Fourteenth Amendment grounds.

An additional and important though not frequently acknowledged aspect of *Gomillion* deserves mention. Professor Paul Freund has observed that the quest by blacks for racial justice has resulted in dozens of major court decisions that led

26. Id. at 341.
27. Id. at 347.
28. 403 U.S. 124, 149 (1971).

to social reforms of general significance.[29] Gomillion v. Lightfoot represents perhaps the definitive example of this phenomenon. Heartened by the lesson of the *Gomillion* experience that the needs of justice might require invasion of the political thickets regardless of the inevitable thorns, the Court in the very next term determined that apportionment issues were justiciable by federal courts to review charges of arbitrary and capricious state action under the Fourteenth Amendment.[30] Soon thereafter, the Court had held as to both congressional and state districts that every individual has the right to have his or her district represented in proportion to the overall population,[31] or, as Justice Stewart phrased it while concurring in Gray v. Sanders, "[w]ithin a given constituency, there can be room for but a single constitutional rule — one voter, one vote."[32]

But there has been a divergence between the apportionment cases alleging mathematical inequality and those in which blacks charge racial inequality. In the first, proof of representational disparity between districts of similar size is sufficient to trigger relief.[33] But in the second, when blacks seek to show that election districts are drawn, or policies such as at-large voting are followed that dilute seriously the value of their votes, relief depends on a showing that the lines or policies were intended to have a racially discriminatory effect.[34] There are, to be

29. Paul Freund, The Civil Rights Movement and the Frontiers of Law, in Talcott Parsons & Kenneth Clark, The Negro American 363 (1967).

30. Baker v. Carr, 369 U.S. 186, 226 (1962).

31. See, e.g., Gray v. Sanders, 372 U.S. 368 (1963) (holding Georgia's county unit method of tallying votes in Democratic party primary elections for statewide offices violated the equal protection clause by wasting citizens' votes when small pluralities in a given county were translated into sweeps of all of the county's votes); Wesberry v. Sanders, 376 U.S. 1 (1964) (apportionment of Atlanta so as to limit its 20 percent of the state's population to electing 10 percent of the state's congressional representatives violates Article 1, §2's requirement that representatives shall be chosen "by the People."); Reynolds v. Sims, 377 U.S. 533 (1964) (The "individual's right to vote for State legislators is unconstitutionally impaired when its weight is in a substantial fashion diluted when compared with votes of citizens living in other parts of the State." Id. at 568.).

32. 372 U.S. at 382.

33. See, e.g., Lucas v. Colorado Gen. Assembly, 377 U.S. 713 (1964) (the state has the burden of justifying deviations from the equal protection standard); Kirkpatrick v. Preisler, 394 U.S. 526 (1969) (the equal protection standard in reapportionment cases allows only minuscule deviations from numerical equality, and these only if unavoidable despite good faith efforts to achieve absolute equality). But see Mahan v. Howell, 410 U.S. 315 (1973) (a less strict de minimis standard for deviations is permissible in state legislative reapportionment cases).

34. Other cases that illustrate the thesis that civil rights precedents in the long run better serve white interests than those of blacks include Dixon v. Alabama State Bd. of Educ., 294 F.2d 150 (5th Cir. 1961) (recognized entitlement of students in public colleges to specific due process protections when faced with serious disciplinary action); and NAACP v. Button, 371 U.S. 415 (1963) (civil rights litigation recognized as a form of political association and expression protected by the Constitution).

Cases like *Dixon* led to the general recognition of due process rights for public school students in decisions like Goss v. Lopez, 419 U.S. 565 (1975). These precedents have been of only minimal value to the thousands of black students suspended or otherwise unfairly disciplined in the school desegregation process. See Children's Defense Fund, School Suspensions: Are They Helping Children? 12 (1975). *Button* was an important victory for blacks, protecting them from harassment by state bar units, but it led to the overturning of state bar restrictions against group legal practice with potential benefits for millions of middle class Americans. See United Transp. Union v. State Bar of Mich., 401 U.S. 576 (1971); UMWA, Dist. 12 v. Illinois State Bar Assn., 389 U.S. 217 (1967); Brotherhood of R.R. Trainmen v. Virginia ex rel. Virginia State Bar, 377 U.S. 1 (1964).

sure, differences in the two categories of cases, but consider in reviewing them whether those differences justify such widely varying standards for relief.

§6.4.5   Criminal Disenfranchisement Laws

As seen through earlier sections, history is wrought with examples of states devising laws that block minority vote.[35] Most insidious are those disguising discriminating intent with race-neutral language, like the poll tax. Falling into this category are laws that disenfranchise groups of citizens from participating in the political process based on their criminal convictions.[36] Given the disproportionate number of minorities represented in state and federal prisons, this type of voter disenfranchisement undeniably impacts minority voters' ability to participate in our political processes.

The statutory voting restrictions vary from state to state. Over 4 million felons cannot vote: "[F]orty-seven states disenfranchise offenders while they are incarcerated. Thirty-two states go farther and disenfranchise parolees while twenty-nine states disenfranchise probationers."[37] Twelve states have lifetime bans on voting for individuals convicted of some or all criminal convictions.[38] Only two states have no restrictions.[39] All of these state laws, however, are facially neutral with respect to race. Consequently, federal courts are split when challenged with the question of whether a criminal disenfranchisement law violates the Voting Rights Act, Equal Protection or the Fifteenth Amendment.[40]

The Second and Eleventh Circuits found that voter disenfranchisement laws do not violate the VRA, while the Ninth Circuit used a totality of the circumstances analysis using Section 2 of the VRA to find a violation without a showing of racial animus or intent.

In Muntaqim v. Coombe,[41] challenging New York State's disfranchisement law,[42] which bars people with felony convictions from voting while in prison or on parole, the Circuit Court affirmed the District Court, which found that the VRA is

---

35. For full coverage on this issue see the NAACP LDF's section on Felon Disenfranchisement: http://www.naacpldf.org/issues.aspx?issue=4.

36. The Sentencing Project, "Felony Disfranchisement Laws in the United States" at http://www.sentencingproject.org/Admin/Documents/publications/fd_bs_fdlawsinus.pdf ("48 states and the District of Columbia prohibit inmates from voting while incarcerated for a felony offense. 35 states prohibit felons from voting while they are on parole and 30 of these states exclude felony probationers as well.")

37. John Calmore, Race-Conscious Voting Rights and the New Demography in a Multiracing America, 79 N.C. L. Rev. 1253, 1273 (2001).

38. After Prison: Roadblocks to Reentry: A Report on State Legal Barriers Facing People with Criminal Records, Legal Action Center, 2004 available at http://www.lac.org/lac/index.php.

39. Id.

40. Jason Schall, "The Consistency of Felon Disenfranchisement with Citizenship Theory," The Sentencing Project publication available at http://www.sentencingproject.org/PublicationDetails.aspx?PublicationID=355.

41. Muntaqim v. Coombe, No. 94-CV-1237, slip op. (N.D.N.Y. Jan. 24, 2001). A part of this section was excerpted with permission from the paper "Disenfranchisement Laws in the United States" by Eun Ju Jung.

42. New York Election Law §5-106.

inapplicable to felony disenfrancisement.[43] The Plaintiffs agrued that because the criminal justice system "targets African Americans and Latinos for arrest, prosecution, and conviction . . . these groups are disenfranchised at much higher rates than whites."[44]

Hayden v. Pataki took a different approach, arguing that New York State's law which denies the vote to currently incarcerated felons and felons on parole[45] violates the VRA, more so in combination with historic and systemic discrimination in the criminal justice system.[46] The Court of Appeals reasoned that "Congress did not intend the Voting Rights Act to cover such provisions, and Congress made no clear statement indicating an intent to modify the federal balance by applying the Voting Rights Act to these provisions." Thus, the court remarked that the control of the franchise is a matter of state concern.

The Eleventh Circuit used similar analysis to find that the provisions of the Voting Rights Act do not encompass felon disenfranchisement laws.[47] Plaintiffs in this case sought to have Florida's disfranchisement statutes declared to be in violation of the VRA for denying convicted felons who have completed their sentences the right to vote, but the court concluded that "applying the VRA's plain text would not automatically draw into question state disenfranchisement statutes in general. Rather, it would only constrain states from enacting felon disenfranchisement regimes that result in the 'denial . . . of the right . . . to vote on account of race or color.' "[48]

The Ninth Circuit, on the other hand, reversed the District Court, in Farrakhan v. Locke,[49] finding that the lower court did not properly apply Section 2 analysis to Washington state's disenfranchisement statute. The District Court relied on the fact that the law was not "motivated by racial animus" and that it did not have discriminatory effect by itself.[50] The Ninth Circuit[51] explained that a law violates Section 2 when it can be shown by a "totality of the circumstances" that the challenged voting practice results in vote dilution or vote denial on account of race.[52] Evidence of discrimination within the criminal justice system is relevant to Section 2 analysis and discriminatory intent is not required to establish a Section 2 violation.[53]

One of the main hurdles to finding felon disenfranchisement laws unconstitutional is Section 2 of the Fourteenth Amendment, which provides that "when the right to vote at any [federal] election . . . is denied to any of the male inhabitants of

43. Muntaqim v. Coombe, 366 F.3d 102, 104 (2d Cir. 2004).
44. See http://www.brennancenter.org/stack_detail.asp?key=102&subkey=7177.
45. New York Election Law §5-106.
46. Plaintiffs' claims under Section 2 of the Voting Rights Act were dismissed in light of the decision in Muntaqim v. Coombe, 366 F.3d 102 (2d Cir. 2004).
47. Johnson v. Gov. of State of Florida, 405 F.3d 1214 (11th Cir. 2005) (en banc).
48. Id.
49. 987 F. Supp. 1304 (E.D. Wash. 1997).
50. Id.
51. Farrakhan v. Washington, 338 F.3d 1009 (9th Cir. 2003).
52. Cf. Hunter v. Underwood, 471 U.S. 222, 233 (holding that disproportionate impact of disenfranchisement is not sufficient grounds to utilize Equal Protection unless discriminatory intent is proven).
53. Id.

[a] State . . . or in any way abridged, except for participation in rebellion, or other crime, the basis of representation therein shall be reduced. . . ."[54] Courts, like the dissenting opinion on *Farrakhan*, can use this language to conclude that contrary to a constitutional violation these laws were "explicitly endorsed by the text of the Fourteenth Amendment."[55] The U.S. Supreme Court in Richardson v. Ramirez[56] stated that

> the understanding of the framers of the Fourteenth Amendment, as reflected in the express language of Section 2 of the Amendment, which exempts from the sanction of reduced congressional representation resulting from the denial of citizens' right to vote, the denial of such right for 'participation in rebellion, or other crime,' and in the historical and judicial interpretation of the Amendment's applicability to state laws disenfranchising felons, is of controlling significance in distinguishing such laws from those other state limitations on the franchise that this Court has held invalid under the Equal Protection Clause.

In making arguments in favor of felon disenfranchisement, Roger Clegg invokes Article I, section 2 of the Constitution to argue that Congress lacks authority to prohibit felon disenfranchisement, and that it is for the state legislatures to determine elector qualifications.[57] Other proponents of these laws use Article I, section 4 in the same way saying that the Constitution restricts the authority of Congress to the regulation of the time, the place and the manner of elections.[58] Lastly, proponents make a move similar to that of the Second and Eleventh Circuit by emphasizing that intentional racial discrimination is not present in disfranchisement statutes.[59] These arguments, however, conveniently dismiss that the laws have a discriminatory impact on minorities and overlook the fact that in some southern states felon disenfranchisement laws were historically adopted to exclude blacks from the political process by calling for disenfranchisement for crimes believed to be committed primarily by blacks.[60]

Those opposing felon disenfranchisement recognize the historical context of these laws, the undeniable statistical impact on minority voters, and the public policy arguments in favor of removing these laws. Marc Mauer projected that if this trend of voter disenfranchisement continues, "thirty to forty percent of black males born today will lose the right to vote for at least part of their adult lives."[61]

---

54. U.S. Const. amend. XIV, §2.

55. Alex Kozinski, Judge, U.S. Ninth Circuit Court of Appeals, in his dissent of the order denying a Ninth Circuit Court of Appeals rehearing en banc in Farrakhan v. State of Washington.

56. Richardson v. Ramirez, 418 U.S. 24 (1974).

57. Roger Clegg, "Felon Disenfranchisement is Constitutional and Justified," available at http://www.constitutioncenter.org/education/ForEducators/Viewpoints/FelonDisenfranchisementIs Constitutional,AndJustified.shtml/.

58. Article I, section 4 of the U.S. Constitution reads: "The Times, Places and Manner of holding Elections for Senators and Representatives, shall be prescribed in each State by the Legislature thereof; but the Congress may at any time by Law make or alter such Regulations, except as to the Places of choosing Senators."

59. Richard L. Hansen, The Uncertain Congressional Power to Ban State Felon Disenfranchisement Laws (2005).

60. See Ratliff v. Beale, 74 Miss. 247, 265-66 (1896).

61. Quoted in Calmore, supra note 37, at 1276.

Such data may not only impact election results in a real way, but it raises larger questions about how a democracy can eliminate such a substantial number of minority voters simply because they lack political support.

Practically, felon disenfranchisement laws are "in sharp conflict with the goal of promoting public safety" because a way to "reduce the likelihood that [an ex-offender] will re-offend is through instilling within the offender a sense of obligation and responsibility to the community."[62] Similarly, Jeffrey Reiman argues that including felons in the political process might not only "provide valuable civic education to the general public" but also "promote responsible engagement in society."[63]

Ryan Haygood, an assistant council at NAACP Legal Defense Fund, views disenfranchisement based on criminal convictions as vestiges of slavery that exclude groups of citizens — especially African-American citizens — from the ballot box and the political process altogether.[64] He concludes that since a disproportionate number of blacks are incarcerated, felon disenfranchisement laws are nothing but a way of blocking blacks from voting.[65] In "The Color of Justice,"[66] Haygood explains that America's criminal justice system's treatment of whites and blacks is "as stark as day and night." Comparing two similar situations with different outcomes based on race, Haygood shows how a wealthy white offender's crime related to drugs is treated as a "public health problem requiring treatment and rehabilitation," whereas the law enforcement strategy toward the same crimes committed by "low-income Black and Brown people" is mass incarceration.[67] Given this disparity, minorities' disproportionate burden from the felon disenfranchisement laws is inextricably linked to racist application of criminal law. With this background scenario, the only way that "the promise of increased political participation by Blacks and other racial minorities created by the Voting Rights Act [will reach] its full potential" is, according to Haygood, to reach "the last excluded segments of our society: Americans with felony convictions."[68]

§6.5   TWENTIETH-CENTURY VOTING RIGHTS ACTS

As indicated in the preceding section, the effort by blacks to remedy voting discrimination through legal attacks on barriers such as the poll tax and the white

62. Marc Mauer, "Disenfrachisement of Felons: The Modern-Day Voting Rights Challenge," Civil Rights Journal (Winter 2002).

63. Jeffrey Reiman, "Liberal and Republican Arguments Against the Disenfranchisement of Felons," Criminal Justice Ethics (Winter/Spring 2005).

64. Ryan P. Haygood, "Vestiges of Slavery Seen in Voting Rights," The Birmingham News (June 10, 2007). See also "Felon Disenfranchisement — Free the Vote" available at http://www.naacpldf.org/content.aspx?article=1178.

65. Comment made by Ryan P. Haygood, "Should Felons Have the Right to Vote?," available at http://www.justicetalking.org/transcripts/061023_felonvoting_transcript.pdf.

66. Ryan P. Haygood, "The Color of Justice," available at http://www.blackcommentator.com/107/107_haygood_justice.html.

67. Id.

68. Ryan P. Haygood, "Millions Still Can't Vote," available at http://www.blackcommentator.com/129/129_think_vote.html.

primary had little effect on the overall problem of voter discrimination, which remained widespread throughout many parts of the country. In 1947, President Truman's Committee on Civil Rights recommended new federal legislation to protect voting rights. There was little response from a Congress that, session after session, refused to enact even an anti-lynching law. Nevertheless, both Presidents Truman and Eisenhower recommended new civil rights legislation to protect voting rights; and Congress, shocked by the flouting of federal law by the states in the wake of the school desegregation cases, overcame determined filibusters by southern members and enacted the Civil Rights Act of 1957.[1] This was the first modern legislation designed to enforce the right secured by the Fifteenth Amendment.

The 1960 Civil Rights Act[2] provided that if injunctive relief were granted in a suit brought by the Attorney General under the provisions of the 1957 Act, to which the state could now be made a party defendant,[3] the Attorney General could ask the court to find a "pattern or practice" of discrimination. Upon such a finding, any individual within the jurisdiction of the defendant could apply to the court for an order that he was qualified to vote in any election. The applicant was required to prove that he was qualified to vote under state election laws, and that he had been denied the opportunity to register or vote by persons acting under color of law subsequent to the court's finding of "pattern or practice." The court was authorized to appoint referees to hear the evidence on such applications ex parte.[4] The act also contained provisions for the preservation, production, and inspection of voting records.[5]

The voting rights provisions of the 1964 Civil Rights Act[6] were directed largely at the standards applied by state election officials in the voter registration process. The act required that registration standards, practices, and procedures for federal elections be uniformly applied. The right to vote could not be denied because of immaterial errors or omissions in registration forms, and literacy tests were to be conducted in writing, with a certified copy made available to the applicant. The use of literacy tests was further limited: in any action brought by the Attorney General in a jurisdiction where literacy tests were used, a sixth-grade education would create a rebuttable presumption of sufficient literacy to vote in federal elections. To expedite review of voting rights cases, the Attorney General could request hearing by a three-judge district court. None of these

---

§6.5   1. 43 U.S.C. §§1971, 1975(d) (1964).

Under the 1957 Act the Attorney General of the United States was authorized to institute civil actions on behalf of one or more named individuals for injunctive relief against proscribed deprivations of the right to vote in federal elections. 42 U.S.C. §1971(c)-(d) (1964). Penalties were provided for interference with federal voting rights (42 U.S.C. §1971(b) (1964)), and criminal contempt cases arising under the act could be tried without a jury where the sentence was less than a $300 fine or 45 days imprisonment. 42 U.S.C. §1995(c) (1964). Finally, a six-member bipartisan Civil Rights Commission was created to investigate deprivations of voting rights on account of race, religion or national origin. 42 U.S.C. §1975(c) (1964).

2. 42 U.S.C. §§1971(c), (e), 1974(e), 1975(h) (1964).

3. 42 U.S.C. §1971(c) (1964).

4. 42 U.S.C. §1971(e) (1964).

5. 42 U.S.C. §§1974-1974(c) (1964).

6. 42 U.S.C. §§1971, 1975(a)-(d), 2000(a) to 2000(h)-(4) (1964).

legislative efforts to remedy voting discrimination through use of the judicial process proved successful.

Most southern district courts provided fairly inhospitable environments for the voting cases brought by the federal government under the new civil rights acts. The extent to which local voting officials were willing and able to delay and circumvent compliance with both the law and federal court orders is reflected in decisions like United States v. Duke.[7] There, the Fifth Circuit's most civil rights–sensitive judges, Chief Judge Tuttle with Judges Rives and Wisdom, reviewed a long history of official intransigence in Panola County, Mississippi, where there were about 7,000 whites and about the same number of blacks of voting age. Over 5,300 of the whites were registered, and only one black — a 92-year-old man who had registered in 1892.

The record revealed that the county voting registrar used every conceivable device to avoid registering blacks, including making himself unavailable when blacks tried to register, and applying wildly varying standards to black and white applicants. While whites had for years been able to register simply by "signing the book," blacks were asked to interpret arcane provisions of the state constitution including sections on the interest rate of the Chickasas School Fund, alluvial land, restrictions on state office holding, and the validity of recognizances and other obligations entered into before the adoption of the 1890 Constitution.

Reviewing these and several similar discriminatory tactics, Judge Tuttle applied the principle of "freezing" fashioned in other voting cases. This principle recognizes that blacks illegally excluded from registering when standards were low are effectively frozen out of the process when new, higher registration standards are adopted, theoretically applicable to all, but in actuality imposing a heavy burden on black applicants. To cure this problem, the court ordered the old standards frozen so that blacks would have an opportunity to register under the former, lower standards.[8]

But tactics of delay and intimidation that had discouraged blacks earlier served more in the 1960s to increase their determination to vote. Moreover, exclusionary policies that the courts had so frequently condoned during the first 60 years of the twentieth century were now seen as not only a denial of black rights but a challenge to judicial authority. As the inadequacies of the 1957, 1960, and 1964 Acts became more apparent, and the often violent response to peaceful voting rights marches and protests first embarrassed then alarmed the nation, political pressure increased for what was to become the Voting Rights Act of 1965.

In January 1965 Dr. Martin Luther King, leading several civil rights organizations, initiated demonstrations in Selma, Alabama, in support of a registration

7. 332 F.2d 759 (5th Cir. 1964).

8. In forbidding for five years the application of voter qualifications, tests, or devices other than requirements of age, residency, and lack of felony conviction, the 1965 Voting Rights Act, 42 U.S.C. §§1973 et seq. (1965), adopted and expanded the "freezing" principle evolved by the Fifth Circuit in United States v. Duke, 332 F.2d 759 (5th Cir. 1964). But enforcing the act was not simply a matter of judicial pronouncement followed by willing — or even grudging — compliance. Protracted and repeated litigation was usually required in order to obtain meaningful relief, and even then, some forms of discriminatory behavior were not controlled. See Hamer v. Campbell, 358 F.2d 215 (5th Cir. 1966), and Hamer v. Ely, 410 F.2d 152 (5th Cir.), cert. denied, 390 U.S. 942 (1969).

drive designed to increase the percentage of black registration from the two percent of voting-age blacks who had been permitted to register. Local officials responded with vicious attacks in which marchers were beaten with clubs and whips, kicked by horses, and attacked with tear gas. During this campaign, two white activists — the Reverend James J. Reeb, a Unitarian minister from Boston, and Mrs. Viola Liuzzo, a Michigan housewife — were killed by local whites. All of this activity received wide coverage by the media.[9]

President Johnson urged new voting legislation in an emotional speech to the nation on March 15, 1965, and was able to sign the new Act in August of that year.[10] The Supreme Court upheld its constitutionality the following year.[11] For reasons, and under circumstances, not unlike those that had led to the enactment of a series of civil rights statutes in the 1860s, the nation had again attempted by specific federal law to prevent whites from barring blacks from participation in the most important function of the democratic process. There was one question, and few were asking it during a time when the President of the United States had identified himself with the civil rights movement by ending his March 15 address to Congress with the words to their marching song, "We Shall Overcome." Would the historic process of disfranchisement (the 1830s), enfranchisement (the 1860s), disfranchisement (the 1890s), and enfranchisement (1960) again come full circle?

Note: Persistent Racial Injustice in Voting: Technology Failures, Felon Disenfranchisement, and the Electoral College

Bush v. Gore,[12] the closely watched Supreme Court case that decided the 2000 presidential election, brought to light election procedures that disproportionately barred blacks from voting. The Supreme Court, in particular, held that the equal protection clause afforded a political candidate the right to have each vote counted by a single standard.[13] In this unique application of equal protection doctrine, the Court did not address how the principle of one person, one vote was impacted by the divergent rules and procedures throughout the country that affect how a citizen's vote is counted. The protections afforded by the Voting Rights Act discussed in this chapter focusing on redistricting and vote dilution do not tell the whole story of racial injustice on the local level.

In Florida, differing local rules made it difficult for some voters to cast their votes, uncovering a serious inequality in ballot access and technology. Many academics criticized the Supreme Court for failing to examine this issue "while invoking the Equal Protection Clause at the moment of recounting ballots," which "created nothing more that a false patina of legitimacy."[14] In the end, African Americans, the elderly, and the poor were disenfranchised with no response. Professor Lani Guinier likened these obstacles to literacy tests: "[Voters]

---

9. See Rayford W. Logan & Michael Winston, 2 The Negro in the United States 27-29 (1971).
10. Voting Rights Act of 1965, Pub. L. No. 89-110, 79 Stat. 437, 42 U.S.C. §§1971, 1973 to 1973p (1970).
11. South Carolina v. Katzenbach, 383 U.S. 301 (1966).
12. 531 U.S. 98 (2000) (per curiam).
13. Id.
14. Lani Guinier, Supreme Democracy: Bush v. Gore Redux, 34 Loy. U. Chi. L.J. 23, 32 (2002).

had to pass a test to have their votes counted, and the implicit suggestion was that only those who passed this test actually deserve to participate in the democratic process."[15] Guinier criticized the Court for their "ambivalence toward the basic principles, and its longstanding preference for order over participation."[16] This issue is more profound when such ambivalence has a disproportionate impact on those with historically little political power, like minorities.

More generally, the Bush-Gore election raised questions about the role of the electoral college and the highly racialized underpinnings of our democratic political structures. The electoral college has been a form of vote dilution that has made the African American vote negligible for presidential candidates. Calmore believes that this fact made the 2000 election even more difficult for black voters because, for a change, black votes could have made a difference in the results. Findings by the U.S. Commission on Civil Rights showed that "black voters in Florida were rejected 14.4 percent of the time, compared with a 1.6 percent rate of rejection for non-black voters."[17] This is not surprising, though, when one considers the historical underpinnings of the electoral college, which was deliberately created to give the South a political advantage. Professor Akhil Amar contends that the same "compromise" that gave Southern states more House members by counting slaves as three-fifths of a person for purposes of apportioning representation (while giving the slaves none of the privileges of citizenship), gave those states electoral college votes in proportion to their congressional delegation.[18] As a result of treating slaves as a "political asset," Southern Presidents were much more likely to be elected in our country's early history.[19] From the beginning, the rights of blacks were traded to bring together the country. As the development of the electoral college illustrates, the institution of slavery helped determine many of our presently functioning democratic structures.

§6.6 JUDICIAL REVIEW AND THE 1965 VOTING RIGHTS ACT

Chief Justice Warren swept aside all arguments questioning the validity of the Voting Rights Act of 1965, in South Carolina v. Katzenbach.[1] He noted the voluminous legislative history of the Act, which reflected that Congress felt itself (1) "confronted by an insidious and pervasive evil which had been perpetuated in certain parts of our country through unremitting and ingenious defiance of the Constitution; and (2) that the unsuccessful remedies prescribed in the past would have to be replaced by "sterner and more elaborate measures in order to satisfy the clear commands of the Fifteenth Amendment."

15. Id.
16. Id.
17. John Calmore, Race-Conscious Voting Rights and the New Demography in a Multiracing America, 79 N.C. L. Rev. 1253, 1273 (2001) at 1270.
18. Guinier, supra note 14, at 30.
19. Id.
§6.6 1. 383 U.S. 301 (1966).

Reviewing the black voting experience from the enactment of the Fifteenth Amendment, and the inability of case-by-case litigation to eliminate the massive opposition to black suffrage, he concluded that the 1965 Act "reflects Congress' firm intention to rid the country of racial discrimination in voting." Enumerating the new remedies, he found:

> The heart of the Act is a complex scheme of stringent remedies aimed at areas where voting discrimination has been most flagrant. Section 4(a)(d) lays down a formula defining the States and political subdivisions to which these new remedies apply. The first of the remedies, contained in §4(a), is the suspension of literacy tests and similar voting qualifications for a period of five years from the last occurrence of substantial voting discrimination.[2] Section 5 prescribes a second remedy, the suspension of all new voting regulations pending review by federal authorities to determine whether their use would perpetuate voting discrimination. The third remedy, covered in §6(b), . . . is the assignment of federal examiners by the Attorney General to list qualified applicants who are thereafter entitled to vote in all elections.

South Carolina challenged each of the sections with an array of arguments, all of which Chief Justice Warren said could be resolved using the Fifteenth Amendment as the standard. The Amendment, he said, is self-executing as to state voting qualifications that discriminate on a racial basis. And §2 of the Amendment expressly gives Congress the power to enforce §1 by appropriate legislation, so that both the courts and Congress have remedial powers to insure against discrimination in voting. Congress can exercise its power in any way that is appropriate for achieving legitimate ends within the scope of the Constitution.

In the Voting Rights Act of 1965, Chief Justice Warren found Congress had exercised its power in an "inventive manner." Remedies that could take effect without case-by-case litigation were essential as shown by experience under earlier acts. Confining the remedies to a small number of states and political subdivisions was also appropriate in that reports and litigation indicated that here the evil was most severe. Similar findings were reached as to the coverage formula, the use of examiners, and the necessity of obtaining approval of changes in election laws from the Attorney General or the federal court in the District of Columbia.[3]

---

2. Section 4(b) provided originally that subsection (a), requiring the suspension of tests or devices in determining eligibility to vote, would apply to any state or political subdivision which maintained any test or device on November 1, 1964, and where less than 50 percent of the voting age residents were registered on November 1, 1964, or less than 50 percent of such persons voted in the presidential election of November 1964. By congressional amendments, this standard was extended on and after August 6, 1970, using November 1, 1968 and the November 1968 presidential election to measure, respectively, registration and voting percentages, and then further extended, using November 1, 1972 and the presidential election of November 1972 as the measuring dates for areas that would be barred from using tests or devices on and after August 6, 1975. The 1975 amendments also added "membership in a language minority" to race and color as categories protected under the Act against deprivation of the right to vote.

3. In the Voting Rights Act Amendment of 1970, 42 U.S.C. §1973aa (1976), Congress extended to the whole country its ban on the use of literacy tests. This provision, together with other sections of the 1970 Amendment lowering the minimum age of voters in both state and federal elections from 21 to 18, and abolishing state durational residency requirements with respect to voting for president and vice-president, except for a 30-day period for advanced registration, were considered by the Court in Oregon v. Mitchell, 400 U.S. 112 (1970). In several opinions, the justices all

Despite the reservations of Justice Black, the majority of the Court was initially unswervingly liberal in its interpretations of §5's coverage, particularly in the scope of election changes that must be submitted to the Attorney General for review. Having very early concluded in Allen v. State Board of Elections[4] that Congress intended the section to reach any state enactments which altered the election law of a covered state in even a minor way, the *Allen* Court held that any enactment which burdens independent candidates by increasing the difficulty for them to gain a position on the general election ballot is subject to §5, since such a measure could undermine the effectiveness of voters who wish to elect nonaffiliated representatives.[5]

Because of the language of §5 requiring that new provisions not have "the purpose and . . . the effect of denying or abridging the right to vote on account of race or color. . . ." The protection against switches to atlarge elections or other election changes that dilute or submerge the black vote are easier to attack than under the constitutional standards set out in Whitcomb v. Chavis and White v. Regester.

Expectations in this regard were strengthened by the Court's decision in Gaston County v. United States.[6] There, the Court affirmed the District of Columbia Court's refusal to approve a North Carolina statute that would reinstate a literacy test as a qualification for voting. The government had argued that the use of the literacy test coupled with the county's segregated school system, which the lower court found was not only segregated but highly inferior, would discriminatorily deprive blacks of the franchise in violation of the 1965 Voting Rights Act. On behalf of the Court, Justice Harlan concluded from a study of the Voting Rights Act's legislative history that a principle reason for adoption of the test

---

concurred that the provision abolishing literacy tests was an appropriate exercise of congressional power to enforce the Fifteenth Amendment by eliminating a device that served to discriminate against voters on the basis of race or color. With the exception of Justice Harlan, the justices agreed that the provision abolishing state durational residence requirements was an appropriate exercise of congressional power to protect freedom of travel and freedom to establish new residences as privileges of national citizenship.

The members of the Court differed sharply on the provision reducing the voting age. Four members of the Court agreed with Justice Black that the provision was valid as to federal elections, and four agreed with his view that the provision was invalid with respect to voting in state and local elections. None of the eight agreed with Justice Black that the provision was valid as to federal, but could not regulate state elections. Constitutional authority for state and local voting by 18-year-olds was provided by the Twenty-sixth Amendment, adopted in 1971, §1 of which reads: "The right of citizens of the United States, who are eighteen years of age or older, to vote shall not be denied or abridged by the United States or by any State on account of age." Residence barriers to voting were further lowered in Dunn v. Blumstein, 405 U.S. 330 (1972). Tennessee laws requiring one year's residence in the state and three months' residence in the county as prerequisites for registration were found to violate the equal protection clause and unnecessary to further any compelling state interests. Noting the serious penalty that the statutes imposed on bona fide residents who have recently traveled from one jurisdiction to another, the Court concluded that a period of 30 days is ample to complete whatever administrative tasks are needed to prevent fraud and ensure the purity of the ballot box.

4. 393 U.S. 544, 566 (1969).

5. See also Hadnott v. Amos, 394 U.S. 358 (1969) (statute requiring independent candidates to declare their intention to seek office two months earlier than under prior procedures imposed "increased barriers" and was subject to §5 scrutiny); Perkins v. Matthews, 400 U.S. 379 (1971) (preclearance required for change in the location of polling places).

6. 395 U.S. 285 (1969).

suspension provisions was "the potential effect of unequal educational opportunities upon the exercise of the franchise." The segregated and unequal public
school system Justice Harlan found "deprived its black residents of equal educational opportunities, which in turn deprived them of an equal chance to pass the
literacy test."[7]

The Court has applied §5 obligations to "political subdivisions" even though
they are not counties or other units of state government that register voters as defined
in §14(c)(2) of the Act. In United States v. Board of Commissioners of Sheffield,
Ala.,[8] the Court upheld a city's use of a referendum to adopt a mayor-council form of
government. And in Dougherty County, Ga. v. White,[9] a school board requirement
that employees take unpaid leaves of absence while campaigning for elective office
was a "standard, practice, or procedure with respect to voting" within the meaning
of §5.

Most voter discrimination cases have focused on what Congress did rather
than on its power to do it.[10] Congressional power was considered again in United
Jewish Organizations of Williamsburgh v. Carey,[11] a case where the relief seen as
appropriate for blacks served to dilute the voting strength of plaintiffs, a Hasidic
Jewish group. Although Katzenbach v. Morgan was the first case in which the
Supreme Court indicated clearly that Congress could employ the flexible tools
of administrative procedure to protect constitutional rights, Professor Laurence
Tribe suggests that the reliance on the Fifteenth Amendment, which protects a
well-defined and difficult to dispute right, renders the decision constitutionally
non-controversial.[12]

Such is not the case when Congress relies on the much more open-ended
provisions of the Fourteenth Amendment, which have been construed to affect
many of the most important aspects of the nation's economic, political, and social
life. Thus, in reviewing legislation enacted under §5 of the Fourteenth Amendment, the Court, according to Professor Tribe, must ask:

> Does Congress possess a power to define constitutional rights unencumbered by
> judicial conceptions of those rights, at least insofar as the congressional definitions
> rationally relate to the language of the fourteenth amendment and violate none of the
> restrictions which the Bill of Rights impose on Congress? Or rather, do judicially
> defined rights fix the limits of the congressionally possible by serving as relatively
> detailed descriptions of the ends that congressional action protecting fourteenth
> amendment rights must further?[13]

7. Id. at 289, 291.

8. 435 U.S. 410 (1978).

9. 439 U.S. 812 (1978). Rejecting the school board's contention that the policy was a neutral
rule intended simply as "a means of getting a full days work for a full days pay — nothing more and
nothing less," the Court found the rule operates like a filing fee and is subject to §5 review. "By
imposing substantial economic disincentives on employees who wish to seek elective office, the Rule
burdens entry into elective campaigns and, concomitantly, limits the choices available to Dougherty
County voters."

10. See, e.g., Beer v. United States, 425 U.S. 130 (1976); City of Richmond v. United States,
422 U.S. 358 (1975).

11. 430 U.S. 144 (1977). The case is discussed in §6.13.2.

12. Laurence Tribe, American Constitutional Law §5-14, at 265 (1978).

13. Id.

These issues were raised in Katzenbach v. Morgan,[14] a challenge to §4(e) of the 1965 Voting Rights Act, providing that states may not prohibit registration because of the inability of persons to read, write, or understand English, if they were educated in "American-flag" schools in which the dominant classroom language was other than English. New York constitutional and statutory provisions requiring literacy tests in English were invalidated, the Court ruling that §4(e) could be viewed as a measure to secure nondiscriminatory treatment by the government for the Puerto Rican community in New York. It ruled that Congress could reasonably have found that prejudice played a prominent role in the enactment of the New York English literacy tests, and that denial of the franchise is not a justifiable means of encouraging persons to learn the English language.[15]

In view of its earlier finding that the Fourteenth Amendment did not bar states from setting literacy requirements for voting, it would seem that the *Morgan* result acknowledges a power in Congress to reach a view of the Fourteenth Amendment contrary to that held by the Supreme Court. Writing for the majority in *Morgan*, Justice Brennan suggested that this was one of two alternative theories on which the decision could be based.[16] Both Justices Harlan and Stewart dissented from this position, contending that under Marbury v. Madison it is the Court's responsibility to determine the scope of the Fourteenth Amendment. In their view, the amendment did not reach state laws which are not so arbitrary or irrational as to offend the command of the equal protection clause.[17]

Courts have found little difficulty in upholding the 1982 Amendments to the Voting Rights Act of 1965 against constitutional challenge.[18]

§6.7 THE AFTERMATH OF DISFRANCHISEMENT

The ravages of the first disfranchisement of black voters during the post-Reconstruction years remain apparent. Years of long, hard effort were required to re-win in the 1960s and 1970s the voting rights which the Civil War amendments and statutes had guaranteed blacks a century before. But voting reform could not alone undo the interim generations of acute economic hardship, and racist-based deprivation that sparked one exodus after blacks moved away from the South to mainly urban areas across the country. The black diaspora dissipated the potential for majority black

14. 384 U.S. 641 (1966).

15. The Supreme Court had earlier held that a state's literacy requirement did not violate the Fourteenth Amendment's equal protection clause. Lassiter v. Northampton County Bd. of Elections, 360 U.S. 45 (1959).

16. 384 U.S. at 653-656. In the alternative, Justice Brennan ruled that Congress may have concluded that by granting Puerto Ricans the right to vote, they would gain a political weapon with which to fight for nondiscriminatory treatment in the distribution of political services. This Congress could do under its authority to find facts and fashion remedies.

17. In a lengthy discussion as to whether Katzenbach v. Morgan "stood Marbury v. Madison on its head" by judicial deference to congressional interpretation of the Constitution, Professor Tribe finds several theories that justify the decision without posing a threat to judicial supremacy. Tribe, supra note 12, at 267-272.

18. See Major v. Treen, 574 F. Supp. 325 (E.D. La. 1983).

voting power in the South. And even where large percentages of blacks remained, they were reconstituted in the growing black ghettoes of the North, where poverty and deprivation, combined with the manipulation of election procedures, enabled whites to retain effective political control in all but a few locations.

Effective voting has three prerequisites: (1) Access to the ballot. This is the basic hurdle addressed by the new voting rights acts, and is discussed in §§6.5-6.6. (2) Availability of political power. An election structure that does not dilute or fragment the group's potential voting strength. Problems in this area are reviewed in the sections that follow. (3) Motivation to participate in the political process as affected by past and present discrimination. Courts have given little direct attention to this critically important area.

For many blacks, mired at the bottom of the economic ladder, the duty to go out and register within the proper period and go to the polls and vote on election day occupies a very low priority in their problem-filled lives. Their experience, influenced and reinforced by poverty, inadequate education, and long-term unemployment, teaches that the exercise of the right to vote is a waste of precious energy and time.[1] It should be noted that immigrant groups from Ireland, Italy, and Eastern Europe were organized around the local political machines that could and did use patronage, food, fuel, and even dollars to provide voters with an immediate, tangible benefit for taking the trouble to register and vote. Civil service laws, social welfare programs, and more restrictive election laws have removed virtually all of these "encouragements" from politicians trying to organize poor black communities.

The "anti-dilution" cases discussed in §§6.10-6.12 present a veritable maze of conflicting rules and standards. Close readers of earlier chapters will recognize the judicial tendency to become hyper-concerned about standards of intent and purpose if the challenged practice is less obvious and odious than a blatant redrawing of a town's boundaries to virtually exclude black voters.[2] But when the challenged practice is an ordinary annexation by a city of additional territory,[3] or when another city decides to reapportion its councilmanic districts,[4] and the effect of

---

§6.7 1. Courts are not unaware that racial discrimination, particularly in employment and education, renders "participation in community processes extremely difficult." White v. Regester, 412 U.S. 755, 768 (1973). See also Kendrick v. Walder, 527 F.2d 44 (7th Cir. 1975). Social scientists have studied these difficulties. Dr. Gunnar Myrdal found a "striking relationship between nonvoting and poverty." He found that in some cities the black vote percentage is far smaller than that for whites, but in others, where opportunities for participation and election are better, the black voting percentage could surpass the whites. Gunnar Myrdal, An American Dilemma 493 (1944).

And yet the comforting myth that black apathy unrelated to economic condition is the root cause for underrepresentation persists in even the highest places. While blacks gave Jimmy Carter their overwhelming support in the 1976 presidential elections, and are generally credited with having made the difference in his narrow victory, President Carter subsequently chided black Americans for failing to exercise their voting rights to help conquer "the cancer of racial injustice" that he said "has always been near the heart of America." Martin Tolchin, President Criticizes Blacks Who Neglect to Use Voting Right, N.Y. Times, May 21, 1979, at A1. "How," the President asked a commencement audience at predominantly black Cheyney State College, "are we going to have the leadership to fight for equal opportunity and affirmative action in jobs, schools and housing if even the act of voting is too great an effort?" Id.

2. Gomillion v. Lightfoot, 364 U.S. 339 (1960).
3. City of Richmond v. United States, 422 U.S. 358 (1975).
4. Beer v. United States, 425 U.S. 130 (1976).

both actions is to limit or reduce black voting power, the seemingly firm judicial resolve not to let it happen again[5] waivers badly. And even when the requested relief is given in voter dilution cases, the failure to consider the third factor — voter motivation as afflicted by discrimination-related disadvantage — tends to nullify the effectiveness of the relief granted.

§6.7.1 The Voting Rights Act: 1982 Amendments

In City of Mobile v. Bolden,[6] a plurality of the Supreme Court found that §2 of the Voting Rights Act of 1965[7] did not authorize relief in vote dilution cases absent proof that the discrimination was *intentionally imposed*. The Court claimed that this treatment would be similar to requirements for protection under the Fifteenth Amendment, which bars only direct, purposeful denial to blacks of the right to vote. Soon after the Supreme Court announced the *Bolden* decision, civil rights groups began lobbying Congress to consider amending §2 of the Voting Rights Act, which provides a private right of action to challenge state practices that affect minority voting power.[8] After lengthy consideration Congress approved amendments clarifying whether proof of discriminatory intent or purpose is necessary.[9]

The revised version of §2 resurrects the principles applied in voting cases prior to *Bolden*. Plaintiffs who are able to show denial of opportunity to participate in the electoral process on an equal basis need not prove discriminatory intent. The Report of the Senate Committee on the Judiciary states:

> In pre-*Bolden* cases plaintiffs could prevail by showing that a challenged election law or procedure, in the context of the total circumstances of the local election process,

5. South Carolina v. Katzenbach, 383 U.S. 301 (1966).
6. 446 U.S. 55 (1980).
7. 42 U.S.C. 1971, 1973 (1981).
8. The original §2 provided that:

> No voting qualification or prerequisite to voting, or standard, practice, or procedure shall be imposed or applied by any State or political subdivision to deny or abridge the right of any citizen of the United States to vote on account of race or color, or in contravention of the guarantees set forth in section 1973b(f)(2) of this title.

42 U.S.C. §1973 (1976).

9. Section 2 of the Voting Rights Act of 1965, 42 U.S.C. §1973 (1982). 42 U.S.C.A. §1973b (Supp. 1983), provides:

> (a) No voting qualification or prerequisite to voting or standard, practice, or procedure shall be imposed or applied by any State or political subdivision in a manner which results in a denial or abridgment of the right of any citizen of the United States to vote on account of race or color, or in contravention of the guarantees set forth in §4(f)(2) [42 U.S.C. §1973(f)(2)], as provided in subsection (b).
>
> (b) A violation of subsection (a) is established if, based on the totality of circumstances, it is shown that the political processes leading to nomination or election in the State or political subdivision are not equally open to participation by members of a class of citizens protected by subsection (a) in that its members have less opportunity than other members of the electorate to participate in the political process and to elect representatives of their choice. The extent to which members of a protected class have been elected to office in the State or political subdivision is one circumstance which may be considered: *Provided*, That nothing in this section establishes a right to have members of a protected class elected in numbers equal to their proportion in the population.

had the result of denying a racial or language minority an equal chance to participate in the electoral process. Under this results test, it was not necessary to demonstrate that the challenged election law or procedure was designed or maintained for a discriminatory purpose.

In *Bolden*, a plurality of the Supreme Court broke with precedent and substantially increased the burden on plaintiffs in voting discrimination cases by requiring proof of discriminatory purpose. The Committee has concluded that this intent test places an unacceptably difficult burden on plaintiffs. It diverts the judicial inquiry from the crucial question of whether minorities have equal access to the electoral process to a historical question of individual motives.[10]

The Amendments did not significantly affect the sections of the Act relating to "preclearance" of changes in voting procedures. Some southern jurisdictions, given a history of racial discrimination, had to submit their redistricting plans to comply with §5 of the Voting Rights Amendment. The Supreme Court has decided a number of cases concerning the preclearance requirements of Section 5 of the Voting Rights Act, with mixed results.

In City of Rome v. United States,[11] a Georgia city with no history of voting discrimination was unable to "bail out" of the preclearance system imposed by Section 5 of the Voting Rights Act because the state of Georgia as a whole is subject to Section 5.

The 1982 Amendments to the Voting Rights Act specifically deny "a right to have members of a protected class elected in numbers equal to their proportion in the population," but provide that for purposes of establishing a §2 violation, courts may consider as one circumstance the extent to which "members of a protected class have been elected to office in the State or political subdivision. . . ."

The Court in Gingles v. Thornburgh applied this standard to a vote dilution claim in North Carolina based on the use of multi-member districts. To prevail on this claim, the Court held that plaintiffs were able to show that a bloc-voting

---

10. S. Rep. No. 97-417 at 16, U.S. Code Cong. & Admin. News, p. 193. The value of the amended §2 has been debated extensively. Compare James Blumstein, Defining and Proving Race Discrimination: Perspectives on the Purpose vs. Results Approach from the Voting Rights Act. 69 Va. L. Rev. 633 (1983), with Frank R. Parker, The "Results" Test of Section 2 of the Voting Rights Act: Abandoning the Intent Standard, 69 Va. L. Rev. 715 (1983).

The Voting Rights Act Amendments of 1982 also extended the special enforcement provisions of the Act, including the preclearance requirements in §5, for an additional 25 years. 42 U.S.C. §1973(c). The Amendments extend the bilingual voter registration and election assistance provisions until 1992. 42 U.S.C. §1973aa-1a.

For content and results of committee hearings, see Extension of the Voting Rights Act: Hearings Before the Subcommittee on Civil and Constitutional Rights of the Committee on the Judiciary, 97th Cong., 1st Sess. 2053 (1981). The extensive Senate and House floor debates on the amendments are summarized in Thomas Boyd & Stephen Markman, The 1982 Amendments to the Voting Rights Act: A Legislative History, 40 Wash. & Lee L. Rev. 1347 (1983), and Note, Amending Section 2 of the Voting Rights Act of 1965, 32 Case W. Res. L. Rev. 500 (1982).

The amended Act (Pub. L. No. 97-205) was signed by President Reagan on June 29, 1982. The amended sections can be found at 42 U.S.C.A. §§1973, 1973b, and 1973aa-1a, aa-6 (1983).

For a discussion of the effect of the amendments on the Voting Rights Act, see The Rise and Fall of Supreme Court Concern for Racial Minorities, 36 Wm. & Mary L. Rev. 345 (1995); Who Are to Be the Electors? A Reflection on the History of Voter Registration in the United States, 9 Yale L. & Pol'y Rev. 370 (1991); Note, Eradicating Racial Discrimination in Voter Registration: Rights and Remedies Under the Voting Rights Act Amendments of 1982, 52 Fordham L. Rev. 93 (1983).

11. 446 U.S. 156 (1980).

majority would "*usually* be able to defeat candidates supported by a politically cohesive, geographically insular minority group." That group, the Court said, must demonstrate that it is sufficiently large and compact to constitute a majority in a single-member district, that it was politically cohesive, and that the white majority votes sufficiently as a bloc to defeat any minority candidate. Under this standard, the Court upheld all but one of the district court's findings that "use of multi-member electoral structure resulted in black voters [having] less opportunity than white voters to elect representatives of their choice."

§6.8   POST-*GOMILLION* GERRYMANDERS: PROBLEMS OF PROOF

While in Gomillion v. Lightfoot[1] the Court assumed hostile legislative intent, in subsequent cases black plaintiffs have been hampered both by the difficulty of proving such intent and by judicial preoccupation with population equality among districts.

The earliest example is Wright v. Rockefeller,[2] which was decided a mere four years after *Gomillion. Wright* presented a variation on the theme of racial segregation of voters. In 1961 the New York legislature reapportioned the state's congressional districts according to the 1960 decennial census. Plaintiffs — a class of nonwhite and Puerto Rican origin citizens — challenged the concentration of black voters in three Manhattan congressional districts and their exclusion from the predominantly white seventeenth congressional district. They alleged that the district lines were irrational, discriminatory, and unequal, and that they segregated eligible voters by race and place of origin. This, they alleged, violated the Fourteenth and Fifteenth Amendments and various civil rights statutes including 42 U.S.C. §1983.

The three-judge district court found that plaintiffs had failed to prove that any boundaries were drawn on racial lines or that the legislature was motivated by racial, religious, or ethnic considerations while drawing the districts.[3] District Judge Murphy, in his dissent, found that the plaintiffs' uncontroverted statistical evidence showed that the district lines could only have been drawn with impermissible motivation of fostering racial segregation, and found the Manhattan redistricting unconstitutional as a clear parallel to *Gomillion.*

---

§6.8   1. 364 U.S. 339 (1960), discussed in §6.4.4.

2. 211 F. Supp. 460, 461 (S.D.N.Y. 1962), aff'd, 376 U.S. 52 (1964).

3. The district court observed "[w]herever areas have to be divided into districts, there will be voters who may prefer to vote in districts other than their own, but such deprivation is not a constitutional deprivation. In any large city it is not unusual to find that persons of the same race or place of origin have a tendency to settle together in various areas. Often this understandable practice enables them to obtain representation in legislative bodies which otherwise would be denied to them. Where geographical boundaries include such concentrations there will be a higher percentage of one race in one district than in others. To create districts based on equal proportions of the various races inhabiting metropolitan areas would indeed be to indulge in practices verging upon the unconstitutional." 211 F. Supp. at 467-468.

The Supreme Court accepted the district court's finding that plaintiffs failed to prove that the state contrived to segregate on the basis of race or country of origin, and affirmed its dismissal of the complaint. Justice Black wrote for the Court that "the concentration of colored and Puerto Rican voters in one area of the county made it difficult, even assuming it to be permissible, to fix districts so as to have anything like an equal division of these voters among those districts. Undoubtedly, some of these voters, as shown by this law suit, would prefer a more even distribution of minority groups among the four congressional districts, but others, like the intervenors in this case, would argue strenuously that the kind of districts for which appellants contended would be undesirable and, because based on race or place of origin, would themselves be unconstitutional."[4]

Justice Douglas, joined by Justice Goldberg, dissented. In his view, even if, as intervenors contended, the existing district lines resulted in "separate-but-better-off," "[r]acial segregation that is state-sponsored should be nullified whatever may have been intended."[5] He regarded the arrangement of the seventeenth and eighteenth districts as "comparable to the Electoral Register System which Britain introduced into India," variants of which were also used in other countries. An electoral register allocates electoral constituencies on the basis of religion, race, ethnic or national origin, or even political party, rather than according to geography. In India, "[t]hat system gave a separate constituency to Sikhs, Muslims, Anglo-Indians, Europeans, and Indian Christians." In the United States, as well, the "government has no business designing electoral districts along racial or religious lines."[6]

Reading the opinions in *Gomillion* and *Wright* back to back, one is surprised to find that only four years separates the two decisions. The sense of constitutional violation was so clear in *Gomillion* that the Court was quite ready to assume intent. The issue before the Court was whether the plaintiffs' allegations that the state was using the redrawn boundaries to disfranchise blacks was sufficient to avoid a motion to dismiss. Justice Frankfurter left little doubt that the allegations, if true, ended all discussion and entitled the plaintiffs to relief.

In *Wright*, however, where evidence of racial gerrymanders seemed equally strong, the Court divided because it was far less clear that the gerrymandering had been based on race rather than party affiliation. The Court may have been thrown into confusion by the dramatically opposite views regarding voting rights as between plaintiffs (seeking a color-blind apportionment that would better spread black votes in three districts), and intervenors (defending the concentration of black voters in the eighteenth district). Neither the majority nor the dissent discussed whether race might be a relevant guide for line drawing, and the Court, by failing to address this unstated issue in a decision that simply condemned plaintiffs' case as "unproved," created a new and difficult proof standard for subsequent racial gerrymander cases.

4. 376 U.S. 57-58.
5. Id. at 61. He further stated that the "fact that Negro political leaders find political advantage in this nearly solid Negro and Puerto Rican district is irrelevant. Rotten boroughs were long a curse of Democratic processes. Racial boroughs are also at war with Democratic standards." Id. at 62.
6. Id. at 66.

In later cases where the racial gerrymandering that benefited whites at the expense of blacks was less blatant than in *Gomillion*, the harm done by this new proof standard, along with subsequent Courts' use of neutral equal protection standards (with their requirement of illegal state action and inherent balancing of interests) as opposed to the Fifteenth Amendment's explicit mandate to protect the voting rights of blacks when addressing plaintiffs' charges of vote dilution, became apparent. As illustrated by the following cases, it became difficult to defeat the distribution of black population centers among several white-majority districts because defendants could usually provide a rational nonracial explanation for such "cracking."

§6.9 POLITICAL GERRYMANDERS WITH RACIAL IMPLICATIONS

§6.9.1 Davis v. Bandimer

In Davis v. Bandimer,[1] an Indiana reapportionment case in which the record rather clearly indicated a legislative dedication to purely political gerrymandering, the Court indicated that it might consider whether such activity constituted an equal protection violation. Writing on the issue of justiciability, Justice White said the political question doctrine would not bar an equal protection challenge to political gerrymandering. There were, he said, "judicially discernible and manageable standards" based on judicial experience in both "one man-one vote" cases as well as racial gerrymandering cases.

Writing for only a plurality on the merits, Justice White (with Justices Brennan, Marshall, and Blackmun) rejected the equal protection claim in this case on the basis that "the mere fact that a particular apportionment scheme makes it more difficult for a particular group in a particular district to elect the representatives of its choice does not render that scheme constitutionally infirm." There is an assumption that those who vote for a losing candidate are adequately represented by the winning candidate and have as much opportunity to influence that candidate as other voters in the state. At least, absent proof, Justice White was unwilling to assume the contrary: that the elected candidate would entirely ignore the interests of those voters.

On the other hand, Justice White indicated that the Court might depart from earlier cases denying political gerrymandering claims where "unconstitutional discrimination occurs [when] the electoral system is arranged in a manner that will consistently degrade a voter's or a group of voters' influence on the political process as a whole." This finding, he said, must be supported by evidence of continued frustration of the will of a majority of the voters or effective denial to a minority of voters of a fair chance to influence the political process.

Justice Powell, with Justice Stevens, found the issue justiciable while dissenting from the denial of the claim in this case. Justice O'Connor, with Chief Justice

§6.9 1. 478 U.S. 109 (1986).

Burger and Justice Rehnquist, concurred in the judgment, but believed all political gerrymandering cases present nonjusticiable political questions.

Despite the clear distaste for the idea Congress expressed in the 1982 Voting Rights Act, a guarantee of racial representation remains an untried but still tempting route to fair and effective representation for African Americans.

In *Davis*, the Court held partisan gerrymandering claims justiciable, but "no districting plan for Congress or for either house of a state legislature has ever been invalidated under *Bandemer*."[2] It is difficult to imagine a future case in which plaintiffs can provide sufficient proof to entitle them to relief against a gerrymandered district. In all likelihood, the gerrymandering will have been accomplished without violating the Court's one person, one vote mandate. In that case, what form should the remedy take?

At that time, only a few writers discussed the possibility of proportional representation, but Professor Sanford Levinson raised the possibility of such relief.[3] He argued that if "one emphasizes political entitlement to vote as derived directly from notions of rights, whether individual or group, proportional representation becomes attractive, for it may well be the most rights-sensitive system of legislative selection available to us."

The racial significance of Professor Levinson's approach is obvious. If the successful suit charged gerrymandering to dilute minority-group votes, could the Court find constitutional support for relief that guarantees minority voters a certain percentage of legislative seats? Consider both the result in *Davis* and the computer-based obsolescence of the one person, one vote test in Karcher v. Daggett.[4]

§6.9.2   Vieth v. Jubelirer[5]

Eighteen years after *Davis*, the Court decided Vieth v. Jubelirer, which reflects a deeply divided Court that found ultimately that political gerrymandering cases were justiciable but could not agree on the standard set forth in *Davis* to adjudicate these claims. Perhaps because of the scattered opinions, *Vieth* has drawn little attention.[6]

In readdressing the question of the justiciability of political gerrymandering, a plurality of the Court found such claims non-justiciable. Scalia writing for the plurality argued that partisan gerrymandering was not justiciable given that "no judicially discernable or manageable standards for adjudicating political gerrymandering claims have emerged." Scalia, with the Chief Justice, Justice O'Connor, and Justice Thomas, voted to overrule *Davis* given that no standard was agreed upon over a decade ago. Scalia looked to Congress, where the plurality argues the Constitution places the power to address political gerrymandering.

2. Sam Hirsch, The United States House of Unrepresentatives: What Went Wrong With the Latest Congressional Round of Redistricting?, 2 Election L.J. 19, 204 (2003).
3. Sanford Levinson, Gerrymandering and the Brooding Omnipresence of Proportional Representation: Why It Won't Go Away, 33 UCLA L. Rev. 257 (1985).
4. 462 U.S. 725 (1983).
5. 541 U.S. 267 (2004).
6. Note, 117 Harv. L. Rev. 2598 (June 2004).

Pointing to Article 1, section 4 of the Constitution, the plurality opinion explains, "[s]ometimes, however, the law is that the judicial department has no business entertaining the claim of unlawfulness — because the question is entrusted to one of the political branches . . ."[7]

Justice Kennedy wrote the controlling opinion that saved *Davis* from being overturned. He agreed with the plurality that the gerrymander at issue in *Vieth* was constitutional but would not go as far as the plurality to find the issue non-justiciable. Kennedy did not believe that "all possibility of judicial relief should be foreclosed in cases such as this because a limited and precise rationale may yet be found to correct an established constitutional violation."

Writing separate dissents, Justices Stevens, Souter, and Breyer all agreed that the issue is justiciable but presented four different standards for adjudicating the claims.

Professor Karlan argues that part of the reason the Supreme Court has grappled with the justiciability of political gerrymandering claims for nearly 40 years is precisely because the issue calls on Courts to decide among hotly contested principles of political philosophy.[8] An example of this that Karlan provides is the strong debate political actors have over whether political fairness is better guaranteed when drawing hotly contested districts where each vote counts or drawing blocs of identifiable voters which secure predictable results but the votes feel wasted.[9] The Court does not want to engage in these decisions and therefore tries to deflect it to Congress.

The Court's failure to set a standard in *Vieth* has created the type of entrenched political results that it wants to avoid. District Courts without guidance from the Supreme Court unsurprisingly deny most political gerrymander claims. The Court leaves no place for Democrats to challenge harms in political gerrymandering, causing them

> to file influence dilution claims, thereby placing undue strain on the Voting Rights Act by improperly forcing the Act to accommodate partisan as well as racial harms. Moreover, requiring plaintiffs to identify as racial the harm in partisan gerrymandering will further inflame the already heated debate over the role of race in politics.[10]

§6.9.3 LULAC v. Perry[11]

In 2006, League of United Latin American Citizens (LULAC) v. Perry represented the third time the Court failed to settle on a standard for the adjudication of partisan gerrymander claims.[12] In this case, the Court did not rehash the question of

7. Vieth v. Jubelirer, 541 U.S. 267, 277 (2004) (plurality opinion) (citing Nixon v. United States, 506 U.S. 224 (1993).

8. Testimony of Professor Pamela Karlan, Stanford Law School, on the continuing need for Section 5 preclearance, 5 Election L.J. 331 (2006).

9. Id.

10. Note, supra note 6, at 2617.

11. 548 U.S. 399, 126 S. Ct. 2594 (2006).

12. Aaron Brooks, The Court's Missed Opportunity to Draw the Line on Partisan Gerrymandering: LULAC v. Perry, 126 S. Ct. 2594 (2006), 30 Harv. J.L. & Pub. Pol'y 781 (2007).

justiciability. Instead, it simply used Davis v. Bandemer to say that political gerrymandering claims are justiciable, but still found that the Texas legislatures redistricting action was constitutional given that there was no standard to adjudicate the claim.

LULAC developed out of the gerrymandering frenzy in Texas as the Republican Party utilized a questionable strategy in an attempt to gain Congressional seats between redistricting cycles. The Republican-dominated state legislature redrew district lines after the 2000 census changes had already taken place. The original post-2000 census lines were drawn by the federal courts, which the Republicans later argued was a violation of the Constitution. Professor John Alford of Rice University explains: "Republicans used the court-drawn plan as a place to park redistricting until they could address the issue when they were in control of the House and obviously better off in the Senate."[13]

The Texas political uproar made national headlines. The drama began when State House Democrats chartered a bus to Oklahoma to avoid the first vote on the new redistricting plan. When the Governor called for a second special session, 11 Democrat Senators fled to New Mexico for over a month to avoid a quorum on the issue. Both sides accuse the other of acting in a manner that demeans the democratic process. Critics of the Republican move to redistrict point out that race underlies the confrontation as whites attempt to gain more political power in a state that may realize a majority of minorities in the next decade.[14] They highlight the fact that of the 11 Senators in the New Mexico standoff, 10 were minorities and the eleventh represents a district with a high minority concentration.[15] This Texas showdown exemplifies the high stakes of redistricting and how race is intricately linked to the actions of the country's two major political parties.

In January 2004, a special three-judge panel in federal court heard the case against the Republican redistricting, finding no constitutional problem with the legislature's action. Most importantly, "[t]he judges ruled that there was no bar to mid-decade redistricting, even though redistricting normally occurs after the once-a-decade census."[16] Additionally, they indicated that "politics — not illegal racial discrimination — prompted the redrawing of district lines."[17]

The Supreme Court in a splintered decision reminiscent of *Vieth* did nothing to override the District Court's decision on political gerrymandering. Justice Kennedy, writing in part for the majority, in part for a plurality and in part for himself, used the holding in *Davis* to say that an equal protection challenge to political gerrymandering was a justiciable case but acknowledged that the Court has not determined a standard for analyzing these cases. The Appellants argued that "a legislature's decision to override a valid, court-drawn plan mid-decade

---

13. David M. Halbfinger, Across U.S., Redistricting as a Never-Ending Battle, N.Y. Times, July 1, 2003, at A1.

14. Michelle Goldberg, The Texas stalemate: It's all about race. Few are saying it openly, but the DeLay-Rove power grab in Austin is all about keeping white control of an increasingly Hispanic state, September 3, 2003 at http://archive.salon.com/news/feature/2003/09/03/texas/index_np.html.

15. Id.

16. Ralph Blumenthal, Texas G.O.P. Is Victorious in Remapping, N.Y. Times, January 7, 2004, at A12.

17. Id.

is sufficiently suspect to give shape to a reliable standard for identifying unconstitutional political gerrymanders." Kennedy disagreed and found the Texas
Republicans gerrymandering constitutional.[18]

Justice Stevens narrowed the question presented to whether Texas can replace
a lawful redistricting plan with one that "maximizes partisan advantage."[19] He
argued that the plan is invalid as a violation of "the State's duty to govern impartially."[20] Justice Breyer, similar to Stevens, argued that the redistricting was a
violation of the Equal Protection Clause as an "unjustifiable use of purely partisan
line-drawing."[21]

As a separate challenge, Appellants also argued that the redistricting of
District 23 presented an unconstitutional violation of Section 2 of the Voting
Rights Act and the Equal Protection Clause of the Fourteenth Amendment. District
23 covered a large area in West Texas. District 23 was an "increasingly powerful
Latino population that threatened to oust the incumbent Republican."[22] The legislature aimed to change the district lines by splitting Webb County, which was 94
percent Latino, removing 100,000 people into District 28. The Latino share of the
citizen population of voting age fell to 46 percent in the newly drawn District 23,
from 57.5 percent. The resulting new District 25 presents a long narrow strip
covering communities from the Mexican border towns to Austin 300 miles away.

Finding the three *Gingles* conditions present, the Court held that District 23
represented unconstitutional vote dilution in violation of Section 2 of the Voting
Rights Act. Even if the Court found that the basic drive behind the changes was
politics and not race, Kennedy explains that the Court cannot ignore how damaging
the changes would be to Latino voters. In finding for the Appellants, the Court
ordered that District 23 be redrawn so it did not reach the Constitutional question
about District 25, which would consequently need to be redrawn.

Chief Justice Roberts and Justice Alito found the political gerrymandering
claim constitutional while taking no position on whether it was justiciable. Justice
Scalia and Thomas, on the other hand, argued that the issue of the constitutionality
of political gerrymandering in this case did not present a justiciable case or controversy. All four Justices found that the recreation of District 23 did not rise to the
level of unconstitutional vote dilution. The Chief Justice specifically pointed to
the fact that Latinos constitute 58 percent of the voting population but controlled
85 percent of the voting districts in the area. To Scalia, redistricting District 23 was
a political, not racial, decision.

One serious problem with *LULAC* is that although the Court had the opportunity, it did not take on the issue of justiciability, leaving lower courts in the same
quagmire they faced post-*Davis* and -*Vieth*. But more interestingly, the decision
evidences how political gerrymander claims will be redefined as racial
gerrymander claims where possible to increase the likelihood of a favorable result.

---

18. Supra note 11, at 548 U.S. ___, 126 S. Ct. 2594, 2613.
19. Id. at 2631.
20. Id. at 2626.
21. Id. at 2652.
22. Id. at 2613.

Note: Political Gerrymandering Translates into Less Democracy

With each new census, political gerrymandering ensures that elections are decided before the first campaign ads hit the billboards or voters cast a single ballot. The impact of political gerrymandering can profoundly stymie competitive campaigning, which effectively disenfranchises citizens who have no voting options to choose among. The dominant political party conducting the redistricting process secures even greater and long-lasting advantage, while incumbents are the real winners with essentially guaranteed district seats. With the dramatic rise of the Republican Party's influence in the South over the past 20 years, one political commentator attributed the success of this conservative revolution more to the redistricting that followed the 1990 census than popular support for the Republican "Contract with America."

On the national level, President Bush's pollster predicted accurately that the "latest round of redistricting would give each party almost 200 safe congressional seats out of a total of 435."[23] Only an estimated 25 to 50 congressional seats will be genuinely contested in upcoming elections.[24] The result is significant: "In the 1990s, the juggernaut of radical gerrymandering meant that almost 75% of United States House seats did not change hands once, and the parties appeared to have eliminated even more competitive seats in their quest to maximize incumbent protection in the 2000 round of redistricting."[25] After the 1980 reapportionment, California turned a one-seat advantage to an 11-seat advantage (28-17 seats). After the recent round, Michigan Republicans forced incumbent Democrats to square off against each other, while Pennsylvania simply eliminated Democratic-leaning seats. As a result, "the legislative agenda is shaped more to energize the political base than to advance the common good."[26]

On the state level, the picture appears bleaker. Ballots in over 40 percent of state elections listed candidates from only one political party. Increasingly low voter turnout may simply reflect a rational decision not to vote when options to choose from are nonexistent.

Placing the role of redistricting in the hands of those who currently control political power harms minority voters, who often face even greater obstacles. Yet there are options for redistricting that can enhance competition within districts. Take Iowa for example. The state constitutes only 1 percent of the U.S. population, granting it only five congressional seats.[27] Yet its elections are highly competitive, primarily because an independent redistricting commission sets new boundaries, and it is not permitted to take incumbent interests into account.[28]

After the 1990 census, the Republicans have effectively used the mandates of the Voting Rights Act to justify the creation of intensely concentrated black voting districts, which in effect increased their control over southern legislatures. The stronghold of the Democratic Party in many Southern states became

---

23. Lani Guinier, Supreme Democracy: Bush v. Gore Redux, 34 Loy. U. Chi. L.J. 23, 40 (2002), citing Republican Party of N.C. v. Martin, 980 F.2d 943 (4th Cir. 1992).
24. Id.
25. Id. at 40-41.
26. Earl Blumenauer, Redistricting, A Bi-Partisan Sport, N.Y. Times, July 8, 2003, at A23.
27. Id.
28. Id.

predominantly confined to the decreasing number of districts that elected black representatives.[29]

As the Democrats in the past few years began to regain control over legislatures in the South, they desired to unpack some of the majority-minority districts in order to elect more Democrats, who in turn would substantively represent the black voters who comprised a voting population of less than 50 percent.[30] After Census 2000, Democrats tried to reverse the Republican strategy of minority concentration. As witnessed by the redistricting under the Court's scrutiny in Ashcroft v. Georgia, Democrats feared violating voting rights mandates as the populations in the supermajority minority districts were reduced. Their seemingly uphill battle with §§2 and 5 of the Voting Rights Act, however, may have been eliminated by this 2003 decision, which receives greater attention in §6.14.7.

§6.10 BLACK VOTE DILUTION VIA AT-LARGE ELECTIONS

The most common type of legislative districting used in this country is the *single-member district*, a district drawn so as to enable the voters residing there to elect one representative to the legislative body.

A *multi-member district*, on the other hand, is one where the district's voters elect more than one representative to the legislative body. Rather than divide a city or county entitled to more than one representative into single-member districts, the legislature instead assigns all of the representatives to the whole district, with each candidate running *at-large*.[1]

Because in multi-member districts the party or interest able to control 51 percent of the votes will win 100 percent of the seats, multi-member districts have a long history of use as vehicles for diluting the votes of minority groups and interests. Congress in 1842 outlawed at-large elections for Congress by requiring that each member be elected by a separate district of contiguous territory.[2] By this action, Congress conceded that the at-large system for electing a state's delegation to the House of Representatives, with every elector voting for as many names as the state was entitled to representatives in the House, worked an injustice by giving "an undue preponderance of power to the political party which had a majority of votes in the State, however small. . . ."[3]

---

29. Id.
30. Many commentaries pointed out that the same five Justices that decided Bush v. Gore also wrote the majority opinion in Ashcroft v. Georgia.

§6.10 1. Multi-member districts are one means of meeting the Supreme Court's "one person, one vote" standard, particularly in large or heavily populated districts.

2. Act of June 25, 1842, ch. 47, §2, 5 Stat. 491. In recent years, state legislatures have been moving to abandon the use of multi-member districts. Robert Dixon & Hatheway, The Seminal Issue in State Constitutional Revisions: Reapportionment Method and Standards, 10 Wm. & Mary L. Rev. 888, 903 (1969).

3. Ex parte Yarbrough, 110 U.S. 651, 660-661 (1884). See generally Eric Van Loon, Representative Government and Equal Protection, 5 Harv. C.R.-C.L. L. Rev. 472 (1970).

Studies indicate that the effect of multi-member districts on black voting strength is particularly invidious at the city level, where representatives are elected at-large in well over half of American

The Supreme Court is not unaware of the disadvantages and dilutive effect at-large districts pose for minority groups. Having held that apportionment schemes which give the same number of representatives to unequal numbers of constituents unconstitutionally dilute the value of the votes in the large districts,[4] the Court has questioned the constitutional validity of multi-member districts in several cases. As Justice White pointed out in Whitcomb v. Chavis,[5] "these questions have focused not on population-based apportionment but on the quality of representation afforded by the multi-member district when compared with single-member districts." In these cases, the Court has refused to find multi-member districts a per se violation of equal protection.[6] But it has acknowledged that they may "operate to minimize or cancel out the voting strength of racial or political elements of the voting population."[7] Such districts are subject to challenge, but plaintiffs must carry the burden of "proving that multi-member districts unconstitutionally operate to dilute or cancel the voting strength of racial or political elements."[8]

---

cities. Barbara Berry & Thomas Dye, The Discriminatory Effects of At-Large Elections, 7 Fla. St. L. Rev. 85, 86 (1979). "Concentrated in a few ghetto areas, blacks often have the votes to determine the outcome of an election in a ward system. But in an at-large system, they remain a minority and their candidates are defeated, . . . [and] because of racial hostility, blacks have generally been unable to form effective coalitions with other minority groups." Id. at 88.

While at-large elections at the state level are on the decline, they are increasing at the city level as a reform mechanism to encourage citywide rather than parochial focus on issues by city councilpersons. Id. at 87. But what may be a reform in general is a deterrent to blacks required to appeal to a citywide electorate. At-large elections require greater financial resources, a more efficient campaign team, and they put a premium on the endorsement of civic associations and local newspapers. Those blacks able to overcome these obstacles and gain the white voter support necessary for election are often not the most effective advocates of black interests. Id. at 88, citing, at note 20, Kannig, Black Representation on City Councils: The Impact of District Elections and Socioeconomic Factors, 12 Urb. Aff. Q. 223, 237 (1976).

Significantly, black representation is greater in cities with ward elections than in cities with at-large elections. A study of all cities with more than 50,000 population in which blacks constitute 15 percent of the population revealed that blacks received only 42 percent of the representation their population warranted in at-large election cities and 85 percent of their deserved representation in ward cities. Id. at 93. The authors report: "We looked at a variety of socioeconomic variables that might have explained the disparity in black representation [e.g., education, income, size, and percentage of population which was black], and found that at-large elections were the single most influential variable." Id. at 93, 113-122.

4. Reynolds v. Sims, 377 U.S. 533 (1964).

5. 403 U.S. 124, 142 (1971).

6. Fortson v. Dorsey, 379 U.S. 433 (1965); Burns v. Richardson, 384 U.S. 73 (1966). The Burns Court indicated that an invidious effect can be shown if "districts are large in relation to the total number of legislators, if districts are not appropriately subdivided to assure distribution of legislators that are resident over the entire district, or if such districts characterize both houses of a bicameral legislature rather than one." Id. at 88.

7. Whitcomb v. Chavis, 403 U.S. 124, 143 (1971).

8. Id. at 144. Fortson foreshadowed the affirmative action challenges brought by whites unwilling to introduce proof of racial discrimination. See, e.g., Regents of Univ. of Cal. v. Bakke, 438 U.S. 265 (1978). The plaintiffs, Goldwater Republicans, were challenging the 1962 reapportionment of the Georgia Senate, which did them no good but was ostensibly intended to prevent the election of a black senator from Atlanta. Gordon E. Baker, Gerrymandering: Privileged Sanctuary or Next Judicial Target?, in Reapportionment in the 1970s 121, 125 (Nelson W. Polsby ed., 1971). Plaintiffs wanted to stress the theoretical possibility of dilution, but were unwilling to press the invidious racial discrimination that, in fact, had resulted from the at-large dilution. Thus, blacks were saddled with a Supreme Court dictum when a careful presentation of available facts might have resulted in a clear precedent finding a multi-member district in violation of their right to vote.

Obviously, diminished quality can dilute votes as effectively as reduced quantity, but while statistical data provides an easy means of ascertaining defects in population-based apportionment, it is more difficult to define violations in multi-member districts. This is particularly true when they serve legitimate political ends, were in place before the arrival of the minority group allegedly harmed by their retention, and do not totally obviate the political influence of that group. Two decisions, *Whitcomb* and White v. Regester,[9] illustrate the difficulty in challenging multi-member districts that possess these characteristics. Proof of dilution was difficult enough, but *Whitcomb* and *White* increased the difficulty by requiring plaintiffs to prove the dilution was the result of invidious intent. Given these standards, the decisions reveal how narrow the range of protection courts will be able to provide against multi-member district dilution actually is as long as existing definitions of voting rights remain in place.

The result in Perkins v. City of West Helena[10] is typical when the facts are strongly indicative of discriminatory purpose. The city has a 40 percent black and 60 percent white population. Since 1920, it has elected a council of eight aldermen (two each from four wards, two all-white and two racially mixed). Candidates must specify post or seat, and then run at-large with each voter having two votes for each ward. No blacks have been elected and the elected white officials were unresponsive to minority interests. The court reviewed the law, finding the system discriminatory, particularly given the city's unsavory record of efforts to prevent blacks from voting.[11]

The Supreme Court adopted this approach with Rogers v. Lodge.[12] The Court declared Burke County, Georgia's at-large election system invalid, finding that although the system had no discriminatory purpose when it was enacted in 1911, the electoral structure was maintained after 1965 for discriminatory reasons. Intent was inferred from the fact that no blacks had ever been elected to the county commission, officials were unresponsive to minority interests, and segregation and discrimination were rife in other areas of public conduct (education, housing, civil service employment).

Some courts welcomed the Supreme Court's return to pre-*Mobile* proof standards.[13] The cases that have upheld at-large election districts have found that neither discriminatory purpose nor effect was proven.[14]

---

9. 412 U.S. 755 (1973).

10. 675 F.2d 201 (8th Cir.), aff'd without opinion, 459 U.S. 801 (1982).

11. See also Political Civil Voters Org. v. City of Terrell, 565 F. Supp. 338 (N.D. Tex. 1983) (citing history of severe segregation and interference with black voting).

12. 458 U.S. 613 (1982), aff'g Lodge v. Buxton, 639 F.2d 1358 (5th Cir. 1981). The case is noted at 96 Harv. L. Rev. 106 (1982). The editors found that while the opinion gave lip service to the *City of Mobile* holding that at-large districts are not per se unconstitutional, they concluded, "*Rogers* seems inconsistent with much of the language and analysis of the plurality in *Mobile.*"

13. McMillan v. Escambia County, Fla., 688 F.2d 960 (1982).

14. Leadership Roundtable v. City of Little Rock, 661 F.2d 701 (8th Cir. 1981) (plaintiffs did not show sufficient dilution of black votes); United States v. Dallas County Commn., 548 F. Supp. 794, 875 (S.D. Ala. 1982) (court held that despite past discrimination black voters now are able to participate fully in elections).

For more discussion of the future of at-large elections, see Crosby, At-Large Congressional Elections: A By-Gone Proposition, 38 J. Mo. B. 266 (1982); O'Rourke, Constitutional and Statutory

In the wake of the 1982 Voting Rights Act Amendments, several courts have eschewed requiring any showing of intentional discrimination when an at-large system acts to dilute black voting power.[15] In Jordan v. City of Greenwood,[16] the Fifth Circuit remanded a challenge to an at-large system for reconsideration in light of the 1982 Amendments.

§6.11   THE SUPREME COURT AND MULTI-MEMBER DILUTION STANDARDS

Admitting that multi-member districts could operate to dilute the voting strength of racial or political elements proved far easier for the Supreme Court than setting standards for determining when such dilution would violate constitutional rights of black voters.

§6.11.1   Whitcomb v. Chavis

In Whitcomb v. Chavis,[1] plaintiffs attacked the Indiana legislative apportionment statutes as violative of the equal protection rights of the residents of Marion County. Indiana had both single-member and multi-member districts; Marion County was multi-member, electing 8 senators and 15 members of the House. First the plaintiffs challenged that the multi-member plan diluted the votes of "ghetto area" residents within the county. Mostly black and poor, they constituted a minority interest group with distinctive interests in specific areas of substantive law, urban renewal, health care, and welfare. Unlike multi-member districts that neutralize their impact, single-member districts would allow these people to elect representatives with those interests in mind. The plaintiffs' second claim was that multi-member districts are inherently unconstitutional in that they overrepresent their residents relative to those who reside in single-member districts.

The three-judge district court convened for the case found for the plaintiffs. It ruled that the multi-member plan and the other factors mentioned had combined to "minimize and cancel out the voting strength of this minority racial group . . . and to deprive them of equal protection of the laws." The Court also stated that in drawing up a new apportionment plan, the state should favor uniform single-member districts.

Challenges to Local At-Large Elections, 17 U. Rich. L. Rev. 39 (1982). See also Comment, Constitutional Significance of the Discriminatory Effects of At-Large Elections, 91 Yale L.J. 974 (1982).

15. See, e.g., Buchanan v. City of Jackson, 708 F.2d 1066 (6th Cir. 1983), which reversed dismissal of a challenge to at-large election, allowing plaintiffs to amend the complaint to reflect the 1982 Amendments. The court found that intentional discrimination was an alternate ground for hearing the case.

16. 711 F.2d 667 (5th Cir. 1983).

§6.11   1. 403 U.S. 124 (1971).

After determining that the new apportionment did not render the case moot, the Supreme Court's slim five-to-four majority addressed whether these multi-member districts were violative of equal protection. Relevant factors in this assessment included: "if the district is large and elects a substantial proportion of the seats of either house of a bicameral legislature, if it is multi-member for both houses of the legislature, and if it lacks provision for at-large candidates running from particular geographical sub-districts." While all of these elements were present here, the Court insisted more was required to strike down the plan.

The Supreme Court disagreed with the district court's ruling that the "ghetto voters" lacked adequate representation. First, the fact that the ghetto voters' partial influence on the electoral process was not enough for their candidates to win did not make their underrepresentation unconstitutional. Second, there was no evidence that the ghetto's interests were that different from those of everyone else, or that their representatives had disregarded their interests. Third, the Court feared the principle espoused by the district court could easily lead to every ethnic, social, economic, or religious group demanding its own "safe" seats for the representation of its own distinctive interests. While there are many problems with the multi-member district (winner-take-all effect, underrepresentation of minorities, lack of connection with community interests, etc.), the Court did not find such plans unconstitutional per se, or this particular plan invalid.

Justice Douglas, joined by Justices Brennan and Marshall in concurring in part and dissenting in part, took issue with the majority's holding that the multi-member district in Marion County did not unconstitutionally dilute the votes of the ghetto residents. First of all, he said, it does not follow from giving their own "safe" representation that every special interest group in society must be accorded like rights. "Our Constitution has a special thrust when it comes to voting; the Fifteenth Amendment says the right of citizens to vote shall not be 'abridged' on account of 'race, color, or previous condition of servitude.' " Second, it is irrelevant whether the blacks can show that their "actual voting power" has been reduced. Whatever their political affiliation, "once their identity is purposely washed out of the system, the system . . . has a constitutional defect."

§6.11.2   White v. Regester

In White v. Regester,[2] plaintiffs charged that the reapportionment of the Texas House of Representatives performed after the 1970 census was violative of equal protection on two counts. First, the variations in population between districts made the plan "unjustifiably remote from the ideal of 'one man, one vote' " that is required by the Fourteenth Amendment. Second, the use of multi-member districts in Dallas and Bexar Counties served to impermissibly dilute the voting power of racial and ethnic minorities (blacks in Dallas County and Mexican

---

2. 412 U.S. 755 (1973).

Americans in Bexar County). The three-judge district court declared the apportionment statutes unconstitutional on both grounds.[3]

The Supreme Court, in addressing this claim, indicated that plaintiffs were required to prove that the members of the minority group in question "had less opportunity than did other residents in the district to participate in the political processes and to elect the legislators of their choice."[4] The mere fact that the minority group was not represented proportionately among the district's legislators would not suffice to show invidious discrimination. Some showing of actual palpable denial of the right to participate must be shown.

The Court found such proof that the Dallas County multi-member district was unconstitutional. First, Texas had a long history of official racial discrimination, "which at times touched the right of Negroes to register and vote and to participate in the democratic processes." Second, since Reconstruction there had been only two blacks in the county delegation to the state House of Representatives. Third, a white-dominated political organization controlled the slating of Democratic Party candidates in the county, and by extension, the election of the county's representatives. Given that it did not need black support, it disregarded the needs of the black community, even at times using racist campaign tactics to defeat the black community's candidates. These circumstances, supplemented by the existence of several technical rules of the county electoral process that served to make it even harder for blacks to gain office, sufficed to prove that blacks in Dallas County had indeed been "not permitted to enter into the political process in a reliable and meaningful manner."

The Court also found that the burden of proof had been met in Bexar County. First, it found, this group had been subjected to discriminatory treatment, as had many other Mexican Americans in Texas. Second, as to the nomination and electoral processes, "a cultural incompatibility . . . conjoined with the poll tax and the most restrictive voter registration procedures in the nation have operated to effectively deny Mexican-Americans access to the political processes in Texas even longer than the Blacks were formally denied access by the white primary." Third, voting registration for the group was very low and only five members of the group had represented the county in the legislature since 1880. Thus, this minority group had been effectively excluded from participation in the political processes in the county.

§6.11.3   Thornburgh v. Gingles

In Thornburgh v. Gingles,[5] the court established a three-part test under the 1982 amendments to the Voting Rights Act for a racial vote dilution claim based on the use of multi-member districts. *Gingles* requires that a minority group claiming racial vote dilution show that it is sufficiently large and compact to constitute a majority in a single-member district, that it is politically cohesive, and that the

---

3. Graves v. Barnes, 343 F. Supp. 704 (W.D. Tex. 1972).
4. This is the test set out by the Court in *Whitcomb*.
5. 478 U.S. 30 (1986).

white majority votes sufficiently as a bloc to defeat any minority candidate. The *Gingles* Court expressly limited the three-factor test to the facts stated in the claim addressed in that case — a minority group sufficiently large and geographically compact to constitute a majority in a single member district alleging that the selection of a multi-member electoral scheme impaired their ability to elect representatives of their choice. The Court stated:

> "[w]e have no occasion to consider whether §2 permits, and if it does, what standards should pertain to, a claim brought by a minority group, that is not sufficiently large and geographically compact to constitute a majority in a single-member district, alleging that the use of a multi-member district impairs its ability to influence elections [or whether these standards] are fully pertinent to other sorts of vote dilution claims, such as a claim alleging that the splitting of a large and geographically cohesive minority between two or more multimember or single-member districts resulted in the dilution of the minority vote."

Since *Gingles*, lower federal courts have continued to struggle with issues raised by racial vote dilution claims in at-large, multi-member electoral districting schemes. One commentator stated that such claims "necessarily force the federal courts to resolve a direct conflict between two constitutional criteria of fair representation: majority rule and nondiscrimination against racial minorities."[6] Justice Blackmun observed that "[e]qual apportionment is a majoritarian principle, but racial representation is a question of minority rights. [There is] dissonance between the one person, one vote ideal and a goal of fair representation for minorities."[7] This dissonance is reflected in the conflicts between and among the circuits as to the meaning and proper application of the *Gingles* standards.

§6.12   SECTION 5 AND ANNEXATION CHALLENGES

The language of §5 places the burden on the state to prove that requested changes in election procedure will not have the intent or purpose of denying blacks the right to vote. This seemingly clear congressional direction has been read quite differently by judicial interpreters.

§6.12.1   City of Petersburg v. United States

In City of Petersburg v. United States,[1] the city sought a declaratory judgment to gain approval of an annexation that would alter the racial balance of the

---

6. James U. Blacksher & Larry T. Menefee, From Reynolds v. Sims to City of Mobile v. Bolden: Have the White Suburbs Commandeered the Fifteenth Amendment?, 34 Hastings L.J. 1, 54 (1982).

7. Connor v. Finch, 431 U.S. 407, 427 (1977) (Blackmun, J., concurring).

§6.12   1. 354 F. Supp. 1021 (D.C. Cir. 1972), aff'd, 410 U.S. 962 (1973).

population, as well as approval of the city's decision to keep its at-large method of electing the city council in the face of challenging proposals to move to single-member districts. In reaching its conclusion, the Court noted that the annexation proposal had initially enjoyed biracial support. The court also recognized that Virginia had a long history of racial segregation, which included some restrictions on the ability of blacks "to wield effective political influence in relation to their actual numerical strength." These restrictions had been reflected in the fact that "an informal white political structure has wielded a controlling influence in city politics and runs only white candidates." The court also noted that in recent years, a black political structure has arisen which slates only black candidates. Also, racial polarization had increased so much that virtually total bloc voting by race had become the well-established pattern in the city. In recent council elections, where black candidates ran opposite white candidates, there had been unusually large turn-outs of white voters in the white wards, as a result of which, black candidates generally were defeated. In fact, the court found that even the black councilman who introduced the annexation ordinance had been defeated. So, the annexation had resulted in a transformation of a potential black voting majority into a clear minority.

The court specifically found that the city must bear the burden of proving both that the annexation did not have the *purpose* of denying or abridging the right of blacks to vote, and that it did not have the "effect of such a denial." The court found no evidence of purpose in the annexation, but held the city failed to show that the effect of the enlarged boundary line had not significantly diluted black voting power. In conclusion, the court found that:

> [T]his annexation, insofar as it is a mere boundary change and not an expansion of an at-large system, is not the kind of discriminatory change which Congress sought to prevent; but . . . this annexation can be approved only on the condition that modifications calculated to neutralize to the extent possible any adverse effect upon the political participation of black voters are adopted, i.e., that the plaintiff shift from an at-large to a ward system of electing its city councilmen.[2]

§6.12.2   City of Richmond v. United States

The Supreme Court's affirmance of *Petersburg* was in a brief per curiam statement, but the result was specifically approved in City of Richmond v.

---

2. Id. at 1031. While the court felt the change to a ward system of electing councilmen would increase black representation on the City Council, and thus improve voting strength over results obtainable under the present system, even with a majority of the voters, it added: "We recognize that it is arguable that black citizens might be able to obtain even greater representation in old Petersburg if the annexation were prohibited, but the smaller city would not be as viable a political unit and the percentage figures which represent the relative voting strengths of the two races after the annexation are not so disparate that, given the proven defection from absolute bloc voting that exists here, the resulting representation and government would not be fairly representative of both races. Under the annexation, the relative voting strengths of the two races are close to being equal and control of the City Council could go either way and might shift from election to election, depending on the interests of the voters in any given election, the qualifications of the candidates, and the apportionment of the Council districts." 354 F. Supp. at 1031.

United States.[3] In the late 1960s, the City of Richmond, Virginia, had annexed territory which reduced the proportion of blacks from 52 percent to 42 percent. Complex litigation resulted, which paralleled the legal action in the *Petersburg* case. The Attorney General had refused to grant §5 approval on grounds quite similar to those given in the *Petersburg* case, but after the district court's decision in *Petersburg*, Richmond developed and submitted to the Attorney General its annexation supplemented by plans for establishing single-member districts for the election of Council members. The Attorney General approved a plan providing for nine wards, four of which would have substantial black majorities, four wards of substantial white majorities, and a ninth with a racial division of approximately 59 percent white and 41 percent black. Both the city and the Attorney General submitted this plan to the District Court for the District of Columbia in the form of a consent judgment. When black intervenors opposed it, the matter was referred to a special master, who disapproved it on the basis that the ward plan did not cure the dilution of black voting power resulting from the annexation. The district court accepted these findings, holding that the annexation was discriminatory in purpose and in effect in violation of §5, and that "the invidious racial purpose underlying the annexation had not been eliminated since no 'objectively verifiable, legitimate purpose for annexation' had been shown and since the ward plan does not effectively eliminate or sufficiently compensate for the dilution of the black voting power resulting from the annexation." The Court also found the city had not minimized "to the greatest possible extent," the dilution through its fashioning of the ward system.

In reversing the district court's decision, Justice White explained that *Petersburg* was correctly decided because the consequences of the annexation were satisfactorily obviated by the replacement of at-large elections of councilmen with a ward system. The fact that blacks would nevertheless constitute a lesser proportion of the population after the annexation than before would not, in Justice White's view, have the effect of denying or abridging the right to vote in violation of §5.

Justice White acknowledged that here, unlike *Petersburg*, the lower court found that when the annexation was approved in 1969 it was adopted by the city with a discriminatory racial purpose. The master had found that there were no current, legitimate economic or administrative reasons warranting the annexation. But even accepting the master's findings, Justice White was persuaded "that if verifiable reasons are now demonstrable in support of the annexation, and the ward plan proposed is fairly designed, the city need do no more to satisfy the requirements of §5."

Justice Brennan dissented, along with Justices Douglas and Marshall. According to Brennan, the record clearly indicated that the motive and desire of city officials in 1969 was to "acquire 44,000 additional white voters for Richmond, in order to avert a transfer of political control to what was fast becoming a black-population majority."[4] Justice Brennan would not permit Richmond to "purge the

---

3. 422 U.S. 358 (1975).
4. Id. at 382.

taint of its impermissible purpose by dredging up supposed objective justifications for the annexation and by replacing its practice of at-large councilmanic elections with a ward-voting system."

§6.13   SECTION 5 AND REDISTRICTING CHALLENGES

Despite its difficulty with the special problems presented in annexation cases, the Supreme Court's standards for judging electoral changes under §5 seemed clear enough to insure the protection of black rights. But litigation results have been mixed, with divided courts and controversial outcomes.

§6.13.1   Beer v. United States

In Beer v. United States,[1] the district court reviewed a proposed redistricting plan for New Orleans councilman elections. The court found of critical importance the city's decision to draw the city council's zones from north to south even though predominantly black neighborhoods generally ran from east to west. As a result, blacks were placed in a minority in each area. In addition, two councilmen were elected on an at-large basis. In finding no justification for the city's plan, the district court stated that blacks were not entitled to districts in which there would be a safe majority, "[b]ut just as surely, 'neither may [the group] be enveloped in a structure which will necessarily minimize its potential for meaningful access to the political process.'"

Justice White, who had written the majority opinion in Richmond v. United States, agreed with the district court's finding.[2] But in the New Orleans case, Justice White found himself dissenting along with Justices Marshall and Brennan. In the majority's view, according to Justice Stewart, the requirements of §5 were met by the new apportionment plan in that blacks will constitute a population majority in two of the five districts and a clear voting majority in one. Under the old plan, none of the five districts had a clear black voting majority and no black had been elected to the council under this plan. Thus, said Justice Stewart, "a legislative reapportionment that enhances the position of racial minorities with respect to their effective exercise of the electoral franchise can hardly have the 'effect' of diluting or abridging the right to vote on account of race within the meaning of §5. We conclude, therefore, that such an ameliorative new legislative apportionment cannot violate §5 unless the new apportionment itself so discriminates on the basis of race or color as to violate the Constitution."[3]

---

§6.13   1. 374 F. Supp. 363 (D.D.C. 1974).

2. Beer v. United States, 425 U.S. 130 (1976).

3. The majority in *Beer* did not define what an "effective exercise of the electoral franchise" meant. In Georgia v. Ashcroft, over two decades later, the Supreme Court discussed this phrase further (see §6.14.6).

In reviewing the facts, Justice Stewart acknowledged that block voting along racial lines was the rule in New Orleans elections, and that because of it, blacks would likely be able to elect only one councilman from the district in which a majority of the voters were black. Even so, he found that §5 did not enable rejection of the New Orleans plan simply because it did not eliminate the two at-large councilmanic seats. These seats had existed since 1954, while §5 applies only to proposed changes in voting procedures.

In his dissent, Justice White expressed the view that §5 is not satisfied by enhancement of the black vote but requires that lines be drawn so as to afford the minority the opportunity of achieving fair representation in the legislative body. Justice Marshall in his dissent also criticized the majority's failure to address the question of when a redistricting plan has the effect of "abridging" the right to vote on account of race or color.

§6.13.2 United Jewish Organizations of Williamsburgh, Inc. v. Carey

With the exception of the affirmative action decisions in Regents of University of California v. Bakke[4] and United Steel Workers of America v. Weber,[5] few decisions of the 1970s stirred more controversy than United Jewish Organizations of Williamsburgh, Inc. v. Carey.[6] The multiplicity of opinions accurately reflected the state of judicial confusion over the appropriate standards for reviewing §5 redistricting cases.[7] In the *UJO* case, Justice White found himself again writing a majority opinion, but he could garner support of all seven justices who concurred in the result only in Part I, where he reviewed the case history. New York State, subject to §§4 and 5 of the Voting Rights Act of 1965, submitted its 1972 reapportionment statute through the Attorney General, who concluded that certain districts in Kings County could not be approved because the state had not met its burden of showing the redistricting had neither the purpose nor the effect of abridging the right to vote on the basis of race or color. Rather than challenging the Attorney General's objections by filing a declaratory judgment action, New York attempted to meet these objections so that its 1974 primary and general elections could go forward under the 1972 redistricting plan. To this end, a revised plan was prepared and submitted to the Attorney General which changed the size of the nonwhite majorities in several districts in the Bedford-Stuyvesant area of Brooklyn, which had been the focus of the Attorney General's concern.[8]

The *UJO* litigation, intended to challenge the legality of the 1974 revisions, was filed on behalf of the Hasidic Jewish community of Williamsburgh after the

4. 438 U.S. 265 (1993).
5. 436 U.S. 948 (1979).
6. 430 U.S. 144 (1977).
7. Justice White announced the Court's judgment in an opinion in which Justice Stevens joined in all but Part IV. Justices Brennan and Blackmun joined in Part IV. Justice Brennan filed an opinion concurring in part, while Justice Stewart filed an opinion concurring in the judgment, in which Justice Powell joined. Only Chief Justice Burger dissented. Justice Marshall did not participate in the decision.
8. The revised plan did not change the size of the number of districts with nonwhite majorities, but did change the size of nonwhite majorities in most of those districts.

state senate and assembly districts where about 30,000 Hasidic Jews lived were split in two in order to create substantial nonwhite majorities. Under the 1972 plan, the Hasidic community was located in an assembly district that was 61 percent nonwhite and a senate district that was 37 percent nonwhite. Revisions in 1974 split the Hasidic community between two senate and two assembly districts. A staff member of the legislative reapportionment community testified that he "got the feeling" from meetings and telephone conversations with Justice Department officials "that 65 percent would be probably an approved figure" for the nonwhite population in the assembly district in which the Hasidic community was located. Thus a district that was about 61 percent nonwhite under the 1972 plan was altered to the 65 percent figure; to achieve this, a portion of the white population including part of the Hasidic community was reassigned to an adjoining district.

The district court ruled against the plaintiffs, reasoning that they enjoyed no constitutional right in reapportionment to have separate community recognition as Hasidic Jews. The Court also held that the redistricting did not disenfranchise plaintiffs, and that racial considerations were permissible to correct past discrimination.[9]

In response, Justice White reviewed the history of the Voting Rights Act of 1965, noting that Congress, in renewing §5, was aware of the danger posed to the newly gained voting strength of minorities by reason of redistricting plans that divided minority areas among predominantly white districts. White said that implicit in *Beer* and *City of Richmond* was the proposition "that the Constitution does not prevent a State subject to the Voting Rights Act from deliberately creating or preserving black majorities in particular districts in order to insure that its reapportionment plan complies with §5. . . . Contrary to petitioners' . . . argument[s], neither the Fourteenth nor the Fifteenth Amendment mandates any per se rule against using racial factors in redistricting and apportionment nor is . . . [t]he permissible use of racial criteria . . . confined to eliminating the effects of past discriminatory districting or apportionment."[10]

In Part III of his opinion, Justice White approved the revision creating the 65 percent nonwhite majorities in two additional senate and two additional assembly districts. First, he ruled that New York had done no more than the Attorney General was authorized to require it to do under the non-retrogression principle of *Beer*, and he pointed out that there was no evidence that the 1972 plan either increased or decreased the number of districts with substantially nonwhite majorities. The revisions may have done no more than restore the nonwhite voting strength to the levels enjoyed prior to the 1972 revision. Given the facts of the case and the standards set in *Beer*, Justice White thought it was "reasonable for the Attorney General to conclude in this case that a *substantial* nonwhite population majority — in the vicinity of 65% — would be required to achieve a nonwhite majority of eligible voters."[11]

9. United Jewish Orgs. v. Wilson, 377 F. Supp. 1164 (E.D.N.Y. 1974), aff'd, 510 F.2d 512 (2d Cir. 1975).

10. 430 U.S. at 161.

11. Id. at 164. The Court did not address the additional argument of New York and the United States that, wholly aside from the state's obligation under the Voting Rights Act to preserve minority

In Part IV, Justice White indicated that a second and independent ground for sustaining the challenged 1974 revisions could be based on the fact that, whether or not the plan was authorized by or was in compliance with §5, New York was free to act as it did as long as it did not violate the Fourteenth and Fifteenth Amendments. In Justice White's view neither Amendment was infringed. Nonwhite majorities in certain districts were increased so as to improve the opportunity for the election of nonwhite representatives, but there was no fencing out of the white population from participation in the political processes of the county, and the plan did not minimize or unfairly cancel out white voting strength.[12]

Justice Brennan joined Parts I, II, and III of Justice White's opinion, although he expressed his concern that in using an overt racial number, the case carried the Court closer to race-centered remedial devices than earlier litigation. He agreed, somewhat reluctantly, that even in the absence of the Voting Rights Act, New York's action might be justified as a preferential policy designed to overcome nonwhite disadvantages in voter registration or turnout. He would prefer to leave this thorny question rather than address it as did Justice White in Part IV of his opinion.

Chief Justice Burger dissented. First, he argued that the use of a strict 65 percent quota violated the "clearcut principles established in *Gomillion*." He pointed out that keeping the Hasidic community within a single district would have resulted in a 63.4 percent nonwhite concentration as opposed to the 65 percent suggested by the Justice Department. Second, he disputed the necessity of using the quota to achieve compliance with the Voting Rights Act, and noted that four of the five districts with 65 percent or more nonwhite populations had since elected white representatives. Finally, he advocated the use of neutral districting principles.[13]

---

voting rights, the Constitution permits it to deliberately draw district lines so that a percentage of districts with a nonwhite majority roughly equals the percentage of nonwhites in the county.

12. New York's revision was seen by Justice White as no different than a decision by a state in which a racial minority is unable to elect representatives from multi-member districts to change to single-member districting so as to increase minority representation. Id.

13. The racial cases have developed along a different and more exacting line of proof than those alleging mathematical inequality in the apportionment process. In the latter, proof of representational disparity between districts of similar size sufficed to entitle relief, but in racial cases, plaintiffs' allegations of gerrymandered districts or adherence to at-large voting must be supported by proof that such policies were intended to have a racially discriminatory effect.

In 1983 the Supreme Court decided a pair of reapportionment cases that seem explainable on the new "good faith" approach. First, a 5-4 majority overturned the 1980 New Jersey state legislative reapportionment scheme in Karcher v. Daggett, 462 U.S. 725, even though the maximum population deviation between districts was less than one percent. The Court held that the state had not shown a good faith effort to achieve equality. The state contended that the districts were drawn so as to preserve the voting strength of minority groups, but the Court held that no relationship had been shown between the district lines chosen and minority voting power. A companion case, Brown v. Thompson, 462 U.S. 835 (1983), upheld Wyoming's reapportionment of state representatives, despite an average population deviation of 15 percent and a maximum deviation of 89 percent. This result was justified by Wyoming's long-standing and nondiscriminatory policy of allocating at least one representative to each county. Also, the entire system was not challenged, but only the allocation of one representative to Wyoming's smallest county, which by itself did not cause such a large deviation between districts.

§6.14   SHAW v. RENO LINE OF CASES

In the 1993 case of Shaw v. Reno (*Shaw I*),[1] the Supreme Court created a new cause of action to remedy a newly located constitutional injury. The injury, as elucidated by the *Shaw* line of cases, was the action of a state in sending the message, through the predominant use of race in redistricting, that racial identity is and should be an American citizen's most salient political characteristic. Since *Shaw*, the Court has struggled with the question of whether such an injury even exists and, if it does, whether individual districts causing the injury should be struck down as violative of the Constitution. The Court has had several opportunities to provide more satisfying answers to the vexing questions raised by *Shaw* and to offer an acceptable justification for striking down districts. Unfortunately, the Court has failed to articulate a threshold test for applying strict scrutiny that is consistent with the Court's definition of the *Shaw* injury. The Court's persistent interference with redistricting, despite its continuing inability to devise a satisfying test, creates an appearance of arbitrary judicial interference in state activity, damages the legitimacy of the Court, and unjustifiably prevents good-faith efforts to remedy this country's ugly history of discrimination in voting.

§6.14.1   *Shaw I*

In *Shaw I*, the Court announced its new objective of enforcing a color-blind approach to electoral redistricting. The case in *Shaw* arose from the 1990 Census figures, which entitled North Carolina to an additional congressional district. Since 40 of North Carolina's counties were covered districts under the Voting Rights Act, North Carolina had to submit its reapportionment plan for preclearance. The legislature's first plan failed to preclear. Although the plan included a majority minority district, the Justice Department believed that a state in which 20 percent of the population was black could and should create an additional majority black district. The General Assembly redrew the district, and the plan was precleared by the Justice Department. White voters challenged the second majority black district, arguing that the deliberate segregation of voters into separate districts based on race violated their constitutional right to participate in a color-blind electoral process.

The Court held that the allegation that the reapportionment plan could be understood only as a racial classification, stated a claim under the equal-protection clause, and noted that such a plan would be subject to strict judicial scrutiny. The district in question, District 12, was described as:

> [U]nusually shaped[, it] is approximately 160 miles long and, for much of its length, no wider than the [Interstate]-85 corridor. It winds in snakelike fashion through tobacco country, financial centers, and manufacturing areas "until it gobbles in enough enclaves of black neighborhoods." Northbound and southbound drivers on

§6.14   1. 509 U.S. 630 (1993).

[Interstate]-85 sometimes find themselves in separate districts in one county, only to 'trade' districts when they enter the next county. Of the 10 counties through which District 12 passes, 5 are cut into 3 different districts; even towns are divided. At one point the district remains contiguous only because it intersects at a single point with two other districts before crossing over them.

The Court, in an opinion written by Justice O'Connor, found that the district was drawn so bizarrely that it "could not be understood as anything other than an effort to separate voters into different districts on the basis of race and that the separation lacks sufficient justification." The harm caused by these districts was not that any individual was denied access to the voting booth; nor was any one group's voting power diluted. Instead, according to the Court, the harm was a representational one. The Court argued that a district drawn solely based on race "reinforc[es] racial stereotypes and threaten[s] to undermine our system of representational democracy by signaling to elected officials that they represented a particular racial group rather than their constituency as a whole." O'Connor described these districts as "political apartheid," "segregation," and "balkanization."[2] She chose to ignore the integrative nature of this district, which had a population 55 percent black and the rest white.

Justice Stevens dissented, and he was joined by Justices Ginsburg and Breyer on Parts II-V. In Part I, Justice Stevens argued that the Court lacked jurisdiction over both the District 1 and District 12 claims because the record shows that the appellants' real grievance was not racial gerrymandering, but rather that they were represented in Congress by Democrats when they would have preferred to be represented by Republicans. Stevens concluded that the equal-protection clause was not violated because the appellants had not been shut out of the electoral process on account of their race, nor had their voting power been diluted as a consequence of race-based districting. The appellants only allegation was that the state's failure to legislate in a color-blind manner violated the Constitution.

In Part II, Stevens claimed that strict scrutiny should not have been the standard used in evaluating this case because "the legitimate consideration of race in a districting decision is usually inevitable under the Voting Rights Act when communities are racially mixed." He continued by noting that the Court had recognized that, in the context of redistricting, before strict scrutiny could be applied a plaintiff must demonstrate that race had been used in a particularly determinative manner. Thus, the mere facts that the state had sought to create two congressional districts with effective black voting majorities and that, geographically, District 12 was not compact should not trigger strict scrutiny.

In Part III, Stevens contended that even if strict scrutiny were applicable to this case, the state had presented satisfactory compelling interests so as to meet its burden. He cited the legislature's claims that poor race relations in the state necessitated a move to increase black leadership in the political process, as well as the state's efforts to avoid litigation with the Attorney General.

---

2. See also Holder v. Hall, 512 U.S. 874, 905-906 (1994) (quoting Justice Thomas describing the creation of majority/minority districts as "an enterprise of segregating the races into political homelands that amount in truth to nothing short of political apartheid").

In Part IV, Stevens argued that the creation of District 12 would preclude a §2 action against the state; meanwhile, the Court's requirement that to avoid a §2 action district lines must be drawn around the affected area would have "the perverse consequence of requiring states to inflict the very harm that supposedly renders racial gerrymandering challenges constitutionally cognizable." Finally, in Part V, Stevens contended that, absent a demonstration that voters were being denied fair representation as a result of their race, the Court should not intervene in a process that federal and state actors, black and white, had instituted to alleviate past wrongdoing.

§6.14.2   Miller v. Johnson

The Supreme Court's next major voting rights case, Miller v. Johnson,[3] involved Georgia's additional congressional district. Until the 1990s, although Georgia had a significant black population, it had not sent a black representative to Congress since Reconstruction. The Justice Department refused preclearance until Georgia designed a reapportionment plan that added three majority minority districts. White voters challenged the redrawn districts as racial gerrymandering under *Shaw*.

In *Miller*, the Court held that evidence that a legislature had used race as the predominant or controlling rationale for reapportionment was enough to state a claim under the equal-protection clause. This use of race would trigger strict scrutiny of the plan. As a threshold matter, a plaintiff must show that "the legis-lature subordinated traditional race-neutral districting principles, including but not limited to compactness, contiguity, and respect for political subdivisions or com-munities defined by actual shared interests, to racial considerations." The Court explicitly rejected the idea that "individuals of the same race share a single polit-ical interest," claiming that this view is "based on the demeaning notion that members of the defined racial group ascribe to certain minority views that must be different from those of other citizens." Using as its new test "race as a pre-dominant factor," the Court concluded that race was the predominant rationale behind the *Miller* redistricting plan. The Court then invoked strict scrutiny to ascertain whether the plan was narrowly tailored to served a compelling state interest. Deciding that complying with the Voting Rights Act might be a compel-ling interest, the Court concluded that the plan was not narrowly tailored. The Court, therefore, found the districts unconstitutional.

Justice Ginsberg, in her dissent, took issue with the Court's assertion that voting rights were about individuals, not groups. She argued that it is the nature of redistricting plans to organize people into political groups. Pointing to our history of accommodating the reality of ethnic bonds, she argued that the creation of these districts is not demeaning.

3. 515 U.S. 909 (1995).

§6.14.3 *Shaw II*

In the next round of cases, in 1996, the Court continued to refine the *Shaw* standard and to consider majority minority districts drawn in after the 1990 Census. Shaw v. Hunt (*Shaw II*)[4] marked the return of North Carolina's District 12. In *Shaw I*, the Court had remanded the case to the district court to consider whether evidence existed of racial gerrymandering in the challenged district. At that time, the district court found that while race played a predominant role in the creation of District 12, the legislature had a compelling interest in designing the reapportionment plan and that the district was narrowly tailored to its purpose.

In *Shaw II*, the Court, in an opinion written by Chief Justice Rehnquist, rejected the argument that the legislature's proffered interests were compelling. The appellees offered three compelling interests. The legislature's first interest was seeking to eradicate the effects of past and present discrimination. The Court rejected this claim, finding no evidence that the district was created to ameliorate past discrimination. The second compelling interest was compliance with §5 of the Voting Rights Act. Relying on *Miller*, the Court dismissed the Department of Justice's interpretation of §5. The third compelling interest was compliance with §2 of the Voting Rights Act. The appellees argued that failure to create a second majority minority district would leave North Carolina vulnerable to attacks of voter dilution under §2. Assuming arguendo that compliance with §2 could be a compelling interest, the Court found that the tortured shape of District 12 did not contain a geographically compact population of any race. Without this threshold finding, no voting dilution injury could be found; without an injury, no harm could occur.

§6.14.4 Bush v. Vera

The following case, Bush v. Vera,[5] arose in Texas when the state was found to be entitled to three additional districts. The Texas legislature's plan included three additional districts (two majority black and the other majority Latino). Six white voters challenged 24 of Texas's 30 congressional districts on racial gerrymandering grounds. Since the voters only had standing to challenge the districts in which they lived, the Court dismissed the case against the 21 other districts. In a case with a plurality opinion, three concurrences and two dissents, the Court invalidated all three of the districts.

Justice O'Connor, writing for the plurality, began by explaining that using race as a factor in drawing electoral districts does not in itself give rise to strict scrutiny. Here, however, she argued that race was the predominant factor in the creation of the three districts. Unlike the previous cases, the predominant factor analysis was complicated by Texas's claim that the legislature had drawn the district lines heavily influenced by the desire to protect incumbents. Acknowledging that this was a mixed motive case, O'Connor disagreed, finding that the

---

4. 517 U.S. 899 (1996).
5. 517 U.S. 952 (1996).

legislature had "substantially neglected traditional districting criteria such as compactness, that it was committed from the outset to creating majority/minority districts and that it manipulated district lines to exploit unprecedentedly detailed racial data." O'Connor, following her reasoning in *Shaw I*, described the districts as being bizarre in shape. She also described the computer program used to draw the district lines, which superimposed racial and other socioeconomic data on maps, concluding that the program made more intricate refinements on the basis of race than on the basis of other demographic information.

O'Connor next considered whether the district lines were narrowly tailored to further a compelling state interest. The state's three compelling interests were the same as those in *Shaw II*. O'Connor assumed, without deciding, that compliance with the results test of §2's voting dilution claim could be a compelling state interest, and she added that the "narrow tailoring requirement of the strict scrutiny analysis allows states a limited degree of leeway in furthering such interests." A State would need a strong basis for belief that the threshold conditions for §2 liability were present.[6] Focusing on the districts' lack of compactness, O'Connor found that the districts were not narrowly tailored to avoid liability under §2. O'Connor then rejected the state's argument that the districts were created to remedy past and present racial discrimination. Although the state cited a long history of discrimination against minorities in the electoral process, O'Connor did not find this history to be significant. Instead, she admonished: "A State's interest in remedying discrimination is compelling when two conditions are satisfied. First, the discrimination that the State seeks to remedy must be specific, 'identified discrimination'; second, the State must have had a 'strong basis in evidence' to conclude that remedial action was necessary, 'before it embarks on an affirmative action program.'" Here, she found no need for remedial action. Consistent with entire *Shaw* line of cases, O'Connor found §5 did not require maximizing majority minority districts.

O'Connor also wrote a concurrence to her plurality opinion. She emphasized that compliance with the results test of §2 of the Voting Rights Act constituted a compelling state interest. She also described her belief that in a situation in which a state faces potential liability in a vote dilution claim, the state may intentionally create a majority minority district.

Justice Thomas, concurring in the result, argued that strict scrutiny applies to all governmental classifications based on race. He would have gone further than O'Connor did, by holding that all intentionally created majority minority districts are subject to strict scrutiny.

In his dissent, Justice Stevens argued that since this case involved political, not racial gerrymandering, strict scrutiny did not apply. He asserted that the "predominant influence" test ignores the reality of the legislative process. If irregularity were a constitutional fault, and if the Texas districts suffered from this fault, the cause was protection of incumbents and political gerrymandering. Stevens

---

6. See Thornburg v. Gingles, 478 U.S. 30, 50-51 (1986). The *Gingles* factors are: first, that the minority group is sufficiently large and geographically compact to constitute a majority in a single-member district; second, that it is politically cohesive; and third, that the white majority votes sufficiently as a bloc to enable it usually to defeat the minority's preferred candidate.

declared that "decisions issued today serve merely to reinforce my conviction that the Court has, with its 'analytically distinct' jurisprudence of racial gerrymandering, struck out into a jurisprudential wilderness that lacks a definable constitutional core and threatens to create harms more significant than any suffered by the individual plaintiffs challenging these districts."

Justice Souter in his dissent began by noting that the Court found no injury here that required redress. He argued that when the Court devises a new cause of action to enforce a constitutional provision, it must identify an injury and should describe the elements necessary to make out this new claim. After the three rounds of *Shaw* cases, he found that "a helpful statement of a *Shaw* claim still eludes this Court." He contended that the reason that use of the "predominant motive" standard in reviewing a districting decision is bound to fail is that, in the political environment in which race can affect election results, many of these traditional districting principles cannot be applied without taking race into account; they are, thus, as a practical matter, inseparable from the supposedly illegitimate racial considerations. *Shaw I*'s recognition of a misuse of race in districting, even when no vote dilution results, thus rests upon two basic deficiencies. First, it fails to provide a coherent concept of equal protection injury. No separable injured class exists, and no concept of harm exists that would not also condemn a constitutionally required remedy for past dilution as well as call into question many of the districting practices that the Court seeks to preserve. Second, it fails to provide a coherent test for distinguishing a "predominant" racial consideration from the application of traditional districting principles in a society in which racial mixture remains politically significant and in which racial-bloc voting exists. The necessary consequence of these shortcomings is arbitrariness; the distinction between what is valid from what is not becomes impossible to make, as does the decision of how much members of racial minorities may engage "in the same sort of pluralist electoral politics that every other bloc of voters enjoys."

§6.14.5   Hunt v. Cromartie

In Hunt v. Cromartie,[7] the Court denied the appellees' motion for a summary judgment on the claim that the new District 12, like the old one, is the product of an unconstitutional racial gerrymander. Justice Thomas wrote the opinion, in which Rehnquist, O'Conner, Scalia, and Kennedy joined. Stevens filed a concurring opinion, in which Souter, Ginsburg, and Breyer joined.

Appellees had filed suit seeking to enjoin elections under the state's plan, which had been enacted in response to the Court's decision in *Shaw II*. The district court granted appellees' motion and granted an injunction, stating that "the General Assembly, in redistricting, used criteria with respect to District 12 that are facially race driven" and which thereby violated the equal-protection clause of the Fourteenth Amendment.

7. 526 U.S. 541 (1999).

Appellees offered evidence in support of their claim, including maps of District 12 that showed its size and shape to lack continuity, as well as evidence of the district's low scores with respect to traditional measures of compactness and expert affidavit testimony explaining that this statistical evidence proved the state had ignored traditional districting criteria in crafting the new district. Appellees further claimed that the state had disrespected political subdivisions and communities of interest. Appellees also presented statistical and demographic evidence.

Appellants argued that the General Assembly drew the district intending to make a strong Democratic district. In support of this claim, appellants presented affidavits from two members of the General Assembly responsible for developing the state's 1997 plan. The legislators stated that they attempted to protect incumbents, to adhere to traditional districting criteria, and to preserve the existing partisan balance in the state's congressional delegation.

Appellants also supplied the affidavit of an expert, Dr. David W. Peterson, who reviewed racial demographics, party registration, and election result data from three recent elections for the precincts included within District 12. He also examined the district's entire border — all 234 boundary segments. This expert testified to "a strong correlation between racial composition and party preference" so that "in precincts with high black representation, there is a correspondingly high tendency for voters to favor the Democratic Party" but that "[i]n precincts with low black representation, there is much more variation in party preference . . ." such that the data tended to support both a political and racial hypothesis. Peterson therefore focused on "divergent boundary segments," those where numbers of blacks were greater inside District 12 but numbers of Democrats were greater outside and those where numbers of blacks were greater outside the district but numbers of Democrats were greater inside. He concluded that the state had included in the District 12 the more heavily Democratic precinct much more often than the more heavily black precinct, and, therefore, that the data as a whole supported a political explanation at least as well as, and somewhat better than, a racial explanation for the composition of the district.

The Court held that appellees were not entitled to judgment as a matter of law. The Court noted that prior decisions had made clear that a jurisdiction may engage in constitutional political gerrymandering, even if it so happens that the most loyal Democrats happen to be black. Evidence that blacks constitute even a supermajority in one congressional district while amounting to less than a plurality in a neighboring district will not, by itself, suffice to prove that a jurisdiction was motivated by race in drawing its district lines, when the evidence also shows a high correlation between race and party preference.

The Court continued that, while appellees' evidence might allow the District Court to find that the state acted with an impermissible racial motivation, it does not require that the Court do so. "All that can be said on the record before us is that motivation was in dispute. . . . The District Court nevertheless concluded that race was the 'predominant factor' in the drawing of the district. . . . [I]t was error in this case for the District Court to resolve the disputed fact of motivation at the summary judgment stage."

§6.14.6   Georgia v. Ashcroft

Georgia v. Ashcroft,[8] decided in 2003, will have a dramatic impact on the protections for African Americans under §5 of the Voting Rights Act. The Georgia Senate devised a redistricting plan using the 2000 census data that aimed to unpack the "most heavily concentrated majority-minority districts" where the black population exceeded 60 percent.[9] As compared to the earlier 1997 plan, the approved 2001 plan aimed at increasing the influence of black voters statewide by creating three more districts where the black voting age population exceeded 50 percent and five additional districts where the black voting population fell between 30 and 50 percent. Through the creation of these latter districts, which they called influence districts, the plan increased Democratic strength in areas where black voters constituted smaller percentages of the population.

The district court denied preclearance under §5, finding the plan retrogressive because it diminished the ability of African Americans to elect candidates of their choice in three districts. The Supreme Court, in a five-to-four decision, vacated the lower court's decision and remanded the case for a rehearing, holding the District Court did not apply the proper retrogression analysis. Justice O'Connor explained that §5 requires that a new plan cannot lead to retrogression that would diminish the position of African Americans with "respect to their effective exercise of the electoral franchise."[10] An effective exercise of the electoral process, according to the majority, is broader than the ability of a racial minority to elect a candidate of their choice. O'Connor explained that although this can be one factor in a §5 inquiry, it "is not dispositive or exclusive."[11]

The proper retrogression analysis, instructed Justice O'Connor, would assess the totality of the circumstances that influenced a state's redistricting decisions. A proper examination of a new plan would consider the ability of minorities to participate in the political process, the extent to which they can elect a candidate of their choice, and the feasibility of a nonretrogressive plan given demographic changes. For example, a decline in minority voters' effective exercise of the electoral process in one or two districts does not necessarily present a violation of §5. A violation would occur only if the losses in some districts are not offset by the gains in "the plan as a whole."[12] The district court "failed to consider all the relevant factors when it examined whether Georgia's Senate plan resulted in a retrogression of black voters' effective exercise of the electoral franchise."[13]

According to the majority, §5 permits states to choose from a number of redistricting strategies that would provide minorities with effective representation. A state may choose to establish safe districts with large percentages of minority voters who are likely to elect a candidate of their choice at the risk of isolating these voters. Or a state may opt to establish districts where the minority population is less

8. 539 U.S. 461 (2003).
9. Id. at 470.
10. Id. at 473, quoting Beer v. United States, 425 U.S. 130, 141 (1976).
11. Id. at 480.
12. Id.
13. Id. at 485.

likely to elect a candidate of their choice but plays a significant role in the electoral process, enhancing the potential for greater substantive representation in a larger number of districts.

Even though the majority insists that the district court is in a "better position to reweigh all the facts," Justice O'Connor argued that "[g]iven the evidence submitted in this case, we find that Georgia likely met its burden of showing nonretrogression."[14] Using the 2000 census numbers, the Court listed numerous factors, including the position of African American legislators, the overall increase in majority-minority districts, and the manner in which the plan offsets the decline in some districts by increasing the black voting population in others.

Concurring, Justice Kennedy identified a "discord and inconsistency" in the voting rights precedents that has gone unaddressed.[15] Considerations of race as a predominant factor in drawing district lines, as in this case, that "would doom a redistricting plan under the Fourteenth Amendment or §2 seem to be what save it under §5." Dismissing the comparison between §2 and §5 raised by Georgia, the majority simply concluded that they "combat different evils and, accordingly . . . impose very different duties on the States."[16] Kennedy believes that the issue must be confronted: "There is a fundamental flaw, I should think, in any scheme in which the Department of Justice is permitted or directed to encourage or ratify a course of unconstitutional conduct in order to find compliance with a statutory directive."[17]

The dissent found that the district court committed no error. Justice Souter, writing for the four dissenting justices, characterized the majority opinion as drastically redefining "effective voting power" under §5.[18] The impact for the dissent is profound: §5's requirement that voting changes be nonretrogressive is "substantially diminished and left practically unadministrable."[19] The dissent agrees that reducing the number of minority-majority districts does not automatically violate §5. But Justice Souter takes issue with the Court's conclusion that a state can carry its burden of showing nonretrogression by simply showing minority "influence" in a district. The majority is content to find no retrogression when the "power of the voting majority of minority voters is eliminated, so long as elected politicians can be expected to give some consideration to minorities."[20]

The legislative history of §5 shows that Congress intended more than that, according to Justice Souter. After redistricting, minority candidates should not be left with less power to elect a candidate of their preference. The dissent argued that when redistricting reduces voting power in majority-minority districts, it must show coalition districts are created, where nonminorities will reliably vote with the minority. The state must show that "minority voters in new districts may have some influence, but that minority voters will have effective influence translatable into probable election results comparable to what they enjoyed under the existing

---

14. Id. at 487.
15. Kennedy concurring at 491.
16. Georgia v. Ashcroft, supra note 8, at 493, citing Reno v. Bossier Parish School Bd., 520 U.S. 471, 477 (1997).
17. Kennedy, supra note 15.
18. Souter dissenting at 492-508.
19. Id.
20. Id.

district scheme."[21] Such evidence must indicate that the nonminorities will make coalitions a serious prospect and cannot simply rely on inferences from minority voting percentages or party allegiances in the district. The dissent believes that the district court properly applied this analysis and did not find the state could show that racial polarization in the new districts would be unlikely or continued minority effectiveness probable. Short of such evidence, Justice Souter contended, a redistricting plan would be retrogressive.

§6.14.7   An Assault on the Voting Rights Act?

The political backdrop of this case provides an interesting aside. As discussed more generally in the note in §6.9, the Republican Party in Georgia packed majority-minority districts to increase the number of Republican districts that could be created. Once the power of the political parties switched hands before the Census 2000 redistricting efforts, state Democratic leaders, 20 percent of whom are African American, looked to unpack these safe districts to increase Democratic seats. The assumption was based on the fact that "white voters no longer abandon the party when it nominates black candidates" or exhibit racist block voting.[22] The natural connection was that Democratic candidates who were elected would be influenced by the African American voters living in their districts even if they were not a supermajority. Or, in an even more extreme sense, "what good are seats in a political body more hostile overall to the interests of black voters?"[23]

As a result, some legal scholars have described Georgia v. Ashcroft as a means to access greater representation, while others view it as a means of effectively diluting the black vote. For the former, the Court's new precedent signals progress. The South of 2003 is a different South than the one that refused to register black voters, devised literacy tests to keep blacks away from the ballot box, and presented the most ingrained patterns of racial block voting. From this perspective, the Voting Rights Act has served its purpose.

In fact, both the majority and dissent in *Ashcroft* cite an article by Professor Richard Pildes that looks to social science data to demonstrate the change that would permit the reduction of safe districts.[24] He views the voting behavior change in the past decade as radical. The 1980s data used for the previous round of redistricting showed that "racially polarized voting . . . was a pervasive fact of political life" throughout much of the South.[25] Only 1 percent of districts with white majorities in the South elected a black legislator.[26] Studies showed that unless the black population reached 65 percent, the minority community remained woefully unrepresented.[27]

21. Id. at 2518.
22. Richard Pildes, Less Power, More Influence, N.Y. Times, Aug. 2, 2003, at A23.
23. Id.
24. Richard Pildes, Is Voting Rights Law Now at War with Itself? Social Science and Voting Rights in the 2000s, 80 N.C. L. Rev. 1517 (2002).
25. Id. at 1524.
26. Id. at 1525.
27. Id.

Recent studies present a different picture indicating that the severe racial polarization may have declined: "By 1990, the 65% rule was considered exceptional."[28] A 55 percent black population could defeat racial block voting. One-third of white voters in the South regularly support black congressional candidates. This crossover vote in comparison to the 1980s looks astounding. And studies suggest that even minority populations as low as 33 to 39 percent could elect a black congressional representative. Consequently, researchers called for a change in the supermajority minority districts created in the 1990s.

Unlike Pildes who sees the Supreme Court's color-blind decisions as a sign of racial progress, other scholars view it as an attempt to effectively kill the Voting Rights Act. John Calmore contends that "[t]hrough an imposition of colorblind *in*justice, the Supreme Court is undermining the Voting Rights Act by rearticulating its antidiscrimination principles to 'diminish minority political power.' "[29] He sees the Court as incapable of recognizing the extent to which whites employ racially polarized block voting and "therefore will not permit black bloc voting in what really amounts to self-defense."[30]

Looming over the *Shaw* line of cases, and particularly Georgia v. Ashcroft, are unanswered, profound questions. For example: Will attaining political equality require black candidates to give up safe seats? Does the Court utilize racist blinders that endorse racial subordination of political rights of blacks? Does "effective enfranchisement" mean electing someone who looks like me? Of course, the larger question remains: What power will be left in the Voting Rights Act to guarantee blacks effective enfranchisement?

Note: Vote Dilution and the Creation of an Aggregate Right

The doctrine developed in the *Shaw* line of cases raises many questions about the Supreme Court's equal protection jurisprudence and the determination of individual rights in the context of voting rights claims. In one analysis of *Shaw*, Professor Heather Gerken develops a conceptual framework for resolving two distinct approaches to equal protection that she views as being on "a collision course: the highly individualistic view of rights developed by the Rehnquist Court and the group-based conception of harm evident in many other areas of law."[31] At risk is not only equal protection but also many civil rights protections. She views the redistricting context, specifically the right to an undiluted vote, as one of the most immediate areas of concern, and she chastises the Supreme Court for proving "ill equipped" to address the tension.[32]

One vote does not elect a representative but groups of votes do. A central function of redistricting is to group people by shared interests so that those interests

---

28. Id. at 1527.

29. John Calmore, Race-Conscious Voting Rights and the New Demography in a Multiracing America, 79 N.C. L. Rev. 1253, 1270 (2001).

30. Id. at 1273.

31. Heather Gerken, Understanding the Right to an Undiluted Vote, 114 Harv. L. Rev. 1663, 1665 (2002).

32. See also Calmore, supra note 29. Calmore makes similar points about the Court's jurisprudence and raises the tension between individual and group rights in less depth.

can influence the people who represent them.[33] For Gerken, vote dilution claims present a unique injury in that a court must consider the relative treatment of groups to determine an individual harm. Dilution does not yield a clear-cut picture of individual or group rights. A vote dilution claim "cannot be established simply by examining the treatment of the individual voter. Such an inquiry will reveal only whether that person had an equal opportunity to cast a vote. It will not tell us whether she had an equal opportunity to aggregate her vote."[34]

Although the Court continues to apply strict scrutiny analysis to these cases, Gerken cannot see how the vote dilution context does not trigger what she terms "aggregate rights." An aggregate right is distinguished from an individual right because of its group-based characteristics: Fairness is measured in group terms, the right rises and falls with the treatment of the group, and no group member is more or less injured than another. She views rights on a continuum with individual rights on one end and group rights at the other.

Gerken applies her new approach to show the danger of the Court's current trajectory. She claims that aggregate harms were taken into account prior to *Shaw* but have been lost in the strict scrutiny analysis of "traditionalist" Justices post-*Shaw*.[35] The Court's hesitancy is, according to Gerken, most likely, a concern about essentialism — "the drawing of inferences about an individual's substantive preferences based on her group membership."[36] But can the Court continue to easily dismiss the group aspect inherent in a vote dilution claim? Although the Court appears to recognize the tension, their limited doctrine leads to no "quick fix." More drastically, it may place the constitutionality of §2 in question and jeopardize other civil rights contexts where the identification of injury depends on the relationship of the individual to the group.

§6.15 RESERVED RACIAL REPRESENTATION

It must now be obvious that the various forms of "enhancing" opportunities for blacks to gain racial representation are subject to many forms of political and economic dilution. The Court reached far in *United Jewish Organizations* to accomplish this goal.

Various minority admissions programs to colleges and professional schools and affirmative action programs in employment are premised upon the "intergroup contact hypothesis" that posits that prejudice is overcome by individuals interacting informally as equals.[1] The need and the purpose for elected officials who can

---

33. Gerken, supra note 31, at 1679.

34. Id. at 1684.

35. Id. at 1718. Gerken presents an interesting and in-depth interpretation of the *Shaw* line of cases.

36. Id.

§6.15 1. Lani Guinier. No Two Seats: The Elusive Quest for Political Equality, 77 Va. L. Rev. 1413, 1445 n.116 (1991).

represent the interests of blacks are quite similar to those already approved in these contexts. Those blacks admitted or hired are not necessarily better than rejected white applicants, but it is expected that they will be the "pump primers" who level past barriers, real and psychological, in the hope that within a reasonable period all can hope to seek and gain admittance without fear of racial exclusion.

Professor Lani Guinier notes, however, that the efficacy of the intergroup contact hypothesis is not supported by empirical evidence within the context of small, informal deliberative bodies. She states that the combination of enduring white prejudice with decisional rules that do not require the members of the legislative majority to obtain minority support often results in minority and dissenting views being ignored.[2]

The intergroup contact rationale presumably was the basis for University of North Carolina's approval of a provision in its student constitution that allowed the president of the student body to appoint, from among the general student body, up to two minority, two male, and two female additional council members to the 18-member council in the event the annual election failed to result in that minimal degree of racial or gender representation.[3] The Fourth Circuit Court of Appeals first ruled that this appointive structure impermissibly classified students based on race. It later stated that the structure also impermissibly barred majority students from appointment to the council, in effect disfranchising majority students based on race. The court did not explain how any white students were excluded from participation because black or other minority students were guaranteed extra seats if necessary.[4]

In the *United Jewish Organizations* case, Justice Frankel dissented from the lower court's decision to approve the creation of a 65 percent nonwhite district.[5] He noted the number of black mayors elected by mainly white majorities, to underscore the electorate's willingness to erase race as the sole test for selecting leaders. In response, it should be noted that in most of these instances, black mayors assume the titular heads of local governments that are close to bankruptcy,

2. Id. at 1445 and nn.115-118.

3. Uzell v. Friday, 401 F. Supp. 775 (M.D.N.C. 1975), rev'd in part, 547 F.2d 801 (4th Cir.), confirmed en banc, 558 F.2d 727 (4th Cir. 1977), vacated and remanded for further consideration in light of Regents of Univ. of Cal. v. Bakke, 438 U.S. 265 (1978), reversal aff'd, 591 F.2d 997 (4th Cir. 1979).

4. Although a university is distinguishable from a general election because it stands in a special relationship to its students and thus may, to enhance its overall educational aims, adopt policies that would be subject to far closer scrutiny if utilized off-campus, courts have approved remedies to ensure minority representation in noneducational contexts. In Local 10 v. Federation of Musicians. 57 L.R.R.M. (BNA) 2227, 1 Fair Empl. Prac. Cas. (BNA) 56, 2 Empl. Prac. Dec. (CCH) ¶ 10, 212 (ND. Ill. 1964) the district court approved a merger plan designed to ensure black representation on the policy-making board of the merged union because its purpose was to promote integration, and it would not affect any member's status. The court found the fact that the racial makeup of the two locals was different irrelevant because the classification was designed to protect the interest of the smaller local. Id. at 2236. See also Pittsburgh Black Musicians v. Local 60-471, Fed'n of Musicians, 442 F. Supp. 855 (W.D. Pa. 1977).

5. United Jewish Orgs. of Williamsburgh, Inc. v. Wilson, 510 F.2d 512, 531-532 (2d Cir. 1975). Chief Justice Burger dissented from the Court's approval of the intentionally created 65 percent nonwhile district, and warned that race conscious gerrymandering, "endorsed by the Court today, moves us one step further away from a truly homogeneous society." 430 U.S. 144, 186-187 (1977).

are controlled by city councils that remain predominantly white, and are burdened by problems that require state and federal funds that may or may not be more available because the mayor is black.

The reality of the black political condition, and the remedial goals of the Voting Rights Act, argue for voting rights remedies that result not only in desegregation of legislative and executive positions but also in meaningful access to participation in power. This is the objective that Professor Guinier's theory of proportionate interest representation is designed to achieve.[6]

Professor Guinier identifies three generations of voting rights litigation strategies.[7] The first generation lawsuit was concerned with formal challenges to disfranchising laws and practices, conceptualized the right to vote as access to the ballot, and sought to establish formally fair rules for voting. The second generation lawsuit, particularly after the 1982 amendments, reconceptualized the right to vote as the right to cast a meaningful vote (the right to elect a candidate of the minority groups' choice) and sought to extend the fairness principle to the level of election outcomes.[8] The subdistricting model is associated with the second generation strategy. The third generation litigation strategy, which Professor Guinier proposes as the next step for voting rights litigation, seeks to extend the fairness principle to policy formulation and implementation once minority-preferred candidates are elected. She reconceptualizes the right to a "meaningful vote" as the right to "proportionate interest representation" of the minority group's interests in legislative outcomes, guaranteed by procedural mechanisms designed to prevent majoritarian tyranny within the legislative body.[9]

6. Lani Guinier, The Triumph of Tokenism: The Voting Rights Act and the Theory of Black Electoral Success, 89 Mich. L. Rev. 1077, 1136-1144 (1991).

7. Guinier, supra note 1, at 1424.

8. Id.

9. Recently, the Supreme Court decided two "legislative gerrymandering" cases that illustrate Professor Guinier's concern about the "majoritarian tyranny" that can effectively overturn the value of gaining black, elected officials. In Pressley v. Etowah County Comm'n, 502 U.S. 491 (1992), the Court, speaking through Justice Kennedy in a 6-3 vote, held that changes in the authority of elected officials made in anticipation of the first black elected officials in modern times did not require preclearance under the 1965 Voting Rights Act.

In Etowah County, Alabama, voters elect members of a county commission whose principal function is to supervise and control county road maintenance, repair, and construction. Without seeking preclearance, the Commission passed, inter alia, its "Common Fund Resolution," which altered the prior practice of allowing each commissioner full authority to determine how to spend funds allocated to his own road district. The resolution was passed by the four holdover members of the Commission adopted a "Unit System," which abolished individual road districts a transferred responsibility for all road operations to the county engineer a Commission appointee. Neither the Commission's resolution nor implementing state legislation was submitted for preclearance.

Refusing to defer to the Attorney General's interpretation that the challenged structural alterations should have been precleared, the Court found the changes concern only the internal operations of an elected body and the distribution of power among officials and, thus, have no direct relation to, or impact on, voting Justice Kennedy argued that to agree with the appellants' position (requiring preclearance for any act diminishing or increasing a local official's power) would work an unconstrained expansion of §5's coverage beyond the statute's language and Congress's intent by including innumerable enactments, such as budget measures, that alter the power and decisionmaking authority of elected officials but have nothing to do with voting. The appellants' position, Justice Kennedy continued, also fails to provide a workable standard for distinguishing between governmental decisions that involve voting and those that do not. Some standard is necessary, the Court found, for in a real sense every decision taken by government implicates voting, yet no one would contend that

Notwithstanding the statutory proportional representation disclaimer[10] in the 1982 amendments to the Voting Rights Act, the courts appear to have adopted a principle that seems very like proportional representation in the context of reme-dying minority vote dilution caused by the use of multi-member districting schemes. Professor Guinier observes:

> [T]he courts have ignored statutory language providing for "the opportunity . . . to participate [equally] in the political process" and instead have focused exclusively on language securing the "opportunity . . . to elect representatives of [the protected group's] choice." Especially since 1986 the courts have measured black political representation solely by reference to the number and consistent election of black candidates. The submergence of black electoral potential and the subsequent emer-gence of black voting majorities capable of electing black candidates have become the preferred indicia of a statutory violation. Issues of voter participation, effective representation, and policy responsiveness are omitted from the calculus."[11]

This single-member district, or subdistricting model for analyzing and rem-edying racial vote dilution, can succeed in integrating previously all-white legis-latures that have been maintained as such through the use of at-large systems. Thornburgh v. Gingles[12] established a three-part test for a racial vote dilution claim in the particular context of the use of multi-member districts to submerge geographically concentrated minority voting strength. The test requires a minority group to show that it is sufficiently large and compact to constitute a majority in a single-member district, that it is politically cohesive, and that the white majority votes sufficiently as a bloc to defeat any minority candidate.

In a more recent article, Guinier discusses other possible approaches to lev-eling the playing field for minority voters.[13] She finds that there are lessons to be learned from democracies throughout the world that score better in engaging voters to play a role in their political system. Acknowledging that serious structural change is required to improve the United States' electoral process, Guinier sees a dramatic need to explore different paths that can lead to the revitalization of American voting. She points first to the possibilities of effective campaign finance reform in varying degrees — in public financing, mandating free advertising access, and increasing voting through 24-hour voting or a weekend election day.[14]

She then sets out a hypothetical plan for a serious third-party challenge to our seemingly impenetrable two-party system. She suggests that a new independent party could take a deliberately local approach and specifically target minority-majority

---

Congress meant the Act to subject all or even most government decisions in covered jurisdictions to federal supervision.

Justice Kennedy's opinion makes no mention of Alabama's history of efforts to bar blacks from voting and to dilute the effect of black votes. This history is the major focus of Justice Stevens' dissent contending that "this is a case in which a few pages of history are far more illuminating than volumes of logic and hours of speculation about hypothetical line-drawing problems."

10. "Nothing in this section establishes a right to have members of a protected class elected in numbers equal to their proportion in the population." 42 U.S.C. §1973(b) (1988).
11. Guinier, supra note 6, at 1093.
12. 478 U.S. 30 (1986).
13. Lani Guinier, Supreme Democracy: Bush v. Gore Redux, 34 Loy. U. Chi. L.J. 23 (2002).
14. Id. at 53.

districts where its platform can be shaped by unaddressed issues of minorities and the working class.[15] Ideally, the new party could attract a current leader in state or national office to switch parties and draw serious attention, Guinier explains. Although she recognizes that many attempts by third parties have been intentionally thwarted by the two monolithic national parties and even by the judicial branch, she argues that a successful third party, like the Labour Party in Britain, can add new voices to the mainstream political fray.

Ultimately, Guinier advocates for a participatory democracy that can transform politics by engaging citizens in a real way, which translates into legislative efforts for change. She concludes by discussing the successful attempts in Brazil of Augusto Boal, who used "legislative theatre" to win multiple terms as a city councilman and then to advise other politicians on how to take his strategy to a national level.[16] In running his campaign, Boal hired not trained political advisors, but his acting troupe. Forming issue groups led by a couple of actors, local voters would join groups that addressed issues affecting them and then create dramas that would depict real problems and potential solutions. As the plays traveled throughout the voting district, Boal would ask for audience feedback that was used to improve the skits and help him develop his legislative strategies.

The goal of Guinier's "thought experiment" is to "demonstrate once again just how poorly the country currently represents the interests of the poor and working class people of all races" and, in doing so, to call on leaders to heed John Dewey's solution: "the cure for ailments in democracy is more democracy."[17]

Professor Guinier notes that:

> [a]s a result of the judicially perceived importance of establishing proximate cause between the form of election and the challenged dilution, courts define the violation itself narrowly as the submergence of potential majority black voting districts. By articulating its proximate cause reasoning in the context of single-member districts, the *Gingles* analysis has begun in fact to superimpose a single-member district model on the statutory totality-of-the-circumstances approach at both the liability and remedy phases.[18]

She notes further that the subdistricting strategy "could magnify the legislative strength of the Republican Party if concentrating blacks in a few districts gives the party a statewide electoral advantage. If this occurs, then Republicans, even if a minority of the electorate, may elect a bare numerical majority of representatives yet wield 100 percent of the power in the legislature."[19]

The result of subdistricting is often that moderate white voters are submerged in a conservative-white majority district, and separated from black voters who might join with them in electoral coalitions but for the new districts. Guinier notes that this is apparently the Republican districting strategy for the 1990s, because by supporting majority black districts, they drain potential Democratic

15. Id. at 55.
16. Id. at 63.
17. Id. at 52.
18. Guinier, supra note 1, at 1426-1427 n.47 (emphasis in original).
19. Id. at 1442-1443, n.108.

allies and create majority conservative white districts.[20] White domination may thus continue to be preserved in spite of a litigation strategy and judicial decisions that attempt to empower blacks.[21]

Professor Guinier further critiques the subdistricting strategy because:

> [It] presupposes an unresponsive decision-making body and then builds in appropriately limited alternatives without ever defining what "better off" means. In order to redefine "better off" we need to reformulate our understanding of equal political participation to emphasize both the political equality and political empowerment goals of the Voting Rights Act. . . . [E]mpowerment should contemplate sustained political organization and mobilization leading to fair treatment within and by the council or commission — not merely success in desegregating it."[22]

The fact that black representatives are present in a particular legislative body does not necessarily mean that any of the laws enacted will reflect the policy preferences of the black representative's single-member district constituency. Thus the subdistricting strategy fails to ensure meaningful participation in the legislative process.

Central to Professor Guinier's recognition of the need for, and her proposed reconceptualization[23] of, vote dilution under the Voting Rights Act is the frequent failure of the subdistricting strategy to ensure such meaningful participation. The key problem addressed by her redefinition of vote dilution is the interaction of legislative racism with the "winner take-all" features of majority legislative voting processes[24] that results in the consistent and permanent submergence of the minority group's interests.[25] She defines legislative racism as " 'racism infecting political judgments about how organized society should allocate scarce resources.' Legislative racism describes a pattern of actions persistently disadvantaging a fixed, legislative minority and encompasses conscious exclusion as well as marginalization that results from 'a lack of interracial empathy.' "[26] She defines

---

20. Id. at 1454 and n.108.

21. One wonders whether David Duke's strong showing in Louisiana's gubernatorial election on November 16, 1991, is in part attributable to single-member districting remedies in Louisiana voting rights cases. See Cajun Voters Stop Duke, Calgary Herald, Nov. 17, 1991, at A1; Peter Applebome, Duke: The Ex-Nazi Who Would Be Governor, N.Y. Times, Nov. 10, 1991, at 1, col. 1; Don Terry, Blacks See Old Hate Behind Duke's New Strength, N.Y. Times, Nov. 9, 1991, at 8, col. 1; Frances Frank Marcus, White Supremacist Group Fills a Corner in Duke Campaign, N.Y. Times, Nov. 14, 1991 at B12. Duke is a former leader of the Ku Klux Klan and former member of the American Nazi party. Of course, Klan influence on public officials is nothing new, and it is more likely than not that Klan members have held public office. See William Katz, The Invisible Empire: The Ku Klux Klan Impact on History 99-106 (1986); William Patterson, We Charge Genocide: The Crime of Government Against the Negro People 160-171 (1952).

22. Guinier, supra note 1, at 1458.

23. Id. at 1458-1492.

24. She states "a winner-take-all approach legitimated by majority rule actually exacerbates marginalization of minorities. It is an especially thin version of pluralism that allows a racially homogenous majority disproportionate representation at the expense of an historically oppressed racial minority." Id. at 1447.

25. Professor Guinier defines "interests," for the purposes of her theory of proportionate interest representation, as "voluntary constituencies that self-identify their interests[, and they] would be recognized to the extent they conceptually organize and attract sufficient numbers of like-minded voters." Id. at 1468.

26. Id. at 1444-1445 (footnote citations omitted).

interests as "those high salience needs, wants and demands articulated by any politically cohesive group of voters."[27]

Professor Guinier's theory of proportionate interest representation redefines "dilution" as:

> the "marginalization" of minority interests. Marginalization expands the definition of vote dilution to include any set of techniques used to dilute or nullify the effects of votes cast by minorities or their representatives, is the third-generation claim of resegregation within the walls of a formally integrated legislature. Marginalization focuses on discrimination in the distribution of procedural resources such as votes, not on the specific outcomes of public policy debates such as the unfair and unequal distribution of [non-procedural] resources. . . . [28]

The right to be enforced using this concept of vote dilution would be the right to recognition throughout the political process of distinctive group interests that the group's numbers alone would presumptively give black voters or their representatives in the absence of racial polarization.[29] An interest representation theory would identify a violation of the right to a meaningful vote where it found a politically cohesive minority's interests submerged because of winner-take-all voting structures. It would demonstrate interest submergence by showing that alternative electoral systems capable of eliciting not only the existence, but also the intensity, of minority voter preferences, would result in greater minority interest representation and satisfaction.[30] Under both §2 and §5 of the 1965 Voting Rights Act,

> . . . the interest representation complaint would be that black voting strength is diminished unfairly where because of particular electoral or legislative voting practices, standards or procedures blacks do not enjoy the same opportunity as other voters to use their vote to influence a governmental decision. Political effectiveness would be measured by the actual ability to affect legislative decision-making [and the] statutory right would become the right to elect representatives who have the same opportunity as other representatives to influence the legislative process by casting a "decisive" vote. Depending on the nature of the violation, the remedy could be a restructured electoral, or legislative decision-making arrangement.[31]

Professor Guinier proposes cumulative voting[32] as a method for ensuring proportionate representation of minority interests both at the legislative and

---

27. Id. at 1462.

28. Id. at 1481-1482. She later states that under §2, "dilution occurs where electoral or legislative processes permit a bloc-voting majority over a substantial period of time, consistently to defeat claims publicly identified with the interests of, and supported by, a politically cohesive, statutorily protected minority group or their representatives." Id. at 1496.

29. Id. at 1496.

30. Id. at 1462.

31. Id. at 1494.

32. This is a nonexclusive remedy. She also discusses minority vetoes, supermajority requirements, weighted voting and rotation in office as methods of protecting minority interests. Id. at 1502-1503, 1512. The purpose of cumulative voting is to allow members of a numerical minority to elect a proportionate share of representatives to a governing body. Each voter in the electorate is allowed as many votes as there are positions available, and the threshold of exclusion for election is reduced

electoral levels. By aggregating their votes, "voluntary minority interest constituencies could . . . express the intensity of their distinctive group interest"[33] or vote
strategically to enforce reciprocal coalitions. The benefits of this proposal would
include an enhanced level of fairness in terms of minority interest participation in
power[34] and an avoidance of the resentment caused by race-conscious districting
among the groups that are not statutorily protected.[35] Since the basis of representation would no longer be territorial, the power of non-statutory groups such as
women, poor people, or others would likely increase because their electoral coalition options would be less restricted.[36]

The goal of proportionate interest representation theory, namely a more fair
distribution of political power, requires an evaluation of decisional rules based on
their effectiveness in promoting shared respect and shared power.[37] This involves
using a proportionality principle as a measure of fairness. While conceding the
legitimacy of majority rule, this principle argues that when a permanent homogenous majority of white voters exercises either all or a disproportionate amount of
that majority power, and ignores and marginalizes minority interests, it delegiti-
mates majority rule to the extent that minority group interests are consistently
submerged.[38] Although Congress rejected the *election* of protected group members

---

from a simple majority (50%) to something less. The numerical minority would be able to express the
intensity of its preference for a particular candidate through aggregating or "plumping" all their votes
on that candidate, and thereby achieve a measure of representation proportional to their relative
numbers in the population. See hypothetical example at Guinier, 89 Mich. L. Rev 1077, 1138-
1140 and nn.296-303 (1991). "Cumulative voting is a semiproportionate electoral [mechanism]
widely used in the corporate context to protect minority shareholders' interests . . . [whereby] minority interests . . . gain proportional representation on the board of directors roughly commensurate
with their share of ownership; each shareholder has a number of votes equal to the number of shares
multiplied by the number of directors to be elected; shareholders may distribute votes among many
candidates; by strategic distribution of votes, minority shareholders may attain roughly proportionate
representation on board." Id. at 1139 n.298.

33. Guinier, supra note 1, at 1460.

34. Professor Guinier argues that "simple-minded notions of majority rule or winner-take-all
procedures interact with racial bloc voting to make statutorily protected groups perennial legislative
losers" thus submerging fair representation of minority interests. Id. at 1476.

35. Id. at 1474. The fear that racial electoral quotas would foster racial divisiveness was one of
the arguments against the subdistricting strategy — that in effect what it produced was a number of
seats for minority group members proportional to the minority group's population in the relevant at-
large electoral district. In fact, proportionate interest representation advocates could argue that, to the
extent the subdistricting strategy seeks proportionate election of members of the protected class, it
violates the statute's express disclaimer of the "right [to elect] members of a protected class . . . in
numbers equal to their proportion in the population." 42 U.S.C. §1973(b) (1988). The danger of this
argument, of course, is that it could result in the undoing of the gains of the second-generation
litigation model in integrating previously segregated legislatures. Even if a minority legislator experiences legislative racism, and the consequent inability to affect policy, his or her presence in the
legislature alone does have symbolic value. However, the question of who benefits from integration
without shared power would remain, because the minority legislator's presence and presumptive
participation in the deliberative process may help to legitimate policy outcomes distinctively unfavorable to her interest constituency.

36. Id. at 1417, 1452-1454, 1457, 1464, 1474-1475. Thus the type of resentment at "white"
voter interest submergence which resulted in the protracted litigation challenging the 65 percent
black population majority district approved in United Jewish Orgs. of Williamsburgh, Inc. v. Carey,
430 U.S. 144 (1977), would likely be avoided.

37. These goals are consistent with the political empowerment objectives of the Voting Rights
Act. Id. at 1477.

38. Id. at 1478-1480, 1497.

in proportion to their population as a permissible §2 remedy, it "did not reject proportional electoral opportunity or legislative influence as a *measure* of minority group voting rights."[39]

Although there is no parallel to it under current vote dilution jurisprudence, a *legislative* interest representation challenge would seek to prove that the black representative's potential to cast decisive votes in the challenged system was less than his or her potential to do so in a system where the majority did not consistently exercise disproportionate legislative power because of the interaction of racial polarization with winner-take-all majoritarian decisional rules. On the other hand, an *electoral* interest representation challenge would be very similar to current vote dilution challenges, except that "a modified at-large election alternative would be used as a baseline to establish a violation on the grounds that black voters are a politically cohesive, voluntary interest constituency whose voting strength is submerged within the winner-take-all at-large system."[40]

Proportionate interest representation theory thus proposes, consistent with the political equality and political empowerment norms of the 1965 Voting Rights Act, a remedial ideal that includes a qualitative approach to minority representation both at the electoral and legislative levels.

Steven Mulroy agrees with Guinier that traditional "winner-take-all" elections, by definition, serve to dilute the votes of members of minority groups. In "Alternative Ways Out: A Remedial Road Map for the Use of Alternative Electoral Systems as Voting Rights Act Remedies," Mulroy argues that jurisdictions attempting to correct minority vote dilution should employ alternative electoral systems.[41] He explains three such systems, each of which uses special voting rules designed to enhance the ability of voting minorities to obtain representation: limited voting, cumulative voting, and preference voting.[42]

In a limited voting system, a voter casts one vote per candidate to fill a number of seats, but the total number of votes one may cast is less than the total number of seats to be filled. For example, a voter may be allowed to vote for two people when three seats need to be filled. This limitation is designed to prevent the majority from sweeping up all of the seats. Several jurisdictions already use limited voting systems, including North Carolina, Alabama, Connecticut, and Pennsylvania.[43] Still, Mulroy opines that meanwhile such systems offer simplicity, they are short on flexibility, and they may not remedy minority vote dilution as well as do some other systems.[44]

In a cumulative voting system, voters have a given number of votes that they may distribute among candidates in any way they choose. The number of votes is usually equal to the number of seats to be filled, but this need not be the case. So, if a voter in this system has a total of three votes, she may give one vote to each of

---

39. Id. at 1496 (emphasis added).
40. Id. at 1500.
41. 77 N.C. L. Rev. 1867, 1876 (1999) [hereinafter, "Alternative Ways Out"].
42. Id. at 1877.
43. Id.
44. Id. at 1907-1908.

three candidates, all three to one candidate, or two to one candidate and one to another. Cumulative voting is in use in some jurisdictions across Texas, Alabama, and Illinois.[45] Mulroy suggests that while cumulative voting offers flexibility and enhanced voting strength for cohesive minorities, it requires a lot of group organization if much systemic change is to occur. And, as Mulroy suggests, if different minority groups cannot agree to consolidate their voting power, the majority may continue to sweep all the seats.[46]

In a preference voting or single transferable voting system, a voter ranks the candidates in order of preference, putting a number beside each candidate's name for as many candidates as are on the ballot. In the first round, candidates with a set minimum number of first-choice designations win a seat. Votes they receive in excess of the required minimum are reallocated in accordance with that voter's second-choice designation. After this reallocation, any candidates with the required minimum number of first-choice votes win a seat. If no such candidates emerge, the candidate who received the fewest votes is disqualified, and her votes are reassigned according to the voter's original ranking. This process continues until all of the seats are filled.[47] Several countries already use preference voting, including Ireland and Australia. Preference voting is also used to elect city council and school board members in Cambridge, Massachusetts.[48]

Mulroy offers three arguments for his personal favorite — preference voting. First, according to Mulroy, preference voting leads to the closest proportional results. Second, Mulroy claims that intragroup competition is not a problem, because once a candidate has met the minimum requirement for election, her excess votes are transferred to the candidate ranked next by the voter. And third, strategic voting is unnecessary to maximize the number of elected minority candidates.[49] Still, according to Mulroy, any of these alternative voting systems will result in a more diverse body of elected officials who are more closely aligned with the populations they represent. And, unlike redistricting along racial lines, these alternative systems allow proportional representation of minorities without the associated cost of limiting the strength of the minority vote to only one area.

Of course, these alternative systems have their critics. One fundamental policy argument against alternative systems is that they do away with geographically based representation. This argument is based on two assumptions: first, that geography is a useful proxy for a community of interests; second, that geography is a better proxy than is the self-selected preferences of voters themselves.[50] Along these lines, critics also argue that alternative systems make constituent-incumbent interaction more problematic because they do away with the connection between a representative and her neighborhood of constituents. According to this line of argument, when a representative is not tied to a specific geographical location, she has less incentive to perform constituent services and generally less patience

---

45. Id. at 1878.
46. Id. at 1908-1911.
47. Id. at 1878-1879.
48. Id. at 1879.
49. Id. at 1893-1895.
50. Id. at 1900.

for constituent interaction. In other words, the relationship becomes less "neighborly."[51] One response to these latter concerns has offered the suggestion that, where a district is large, the need for geographically local representation might be satisfied by combining the district system with an alternative system.[52] Lani Guinier suggests another way of looking at the situation when she questions the fundamental assumption that whoever lives in a district is represented by that district's representatives.

Another common criticism of alternative systems is that they encourage racial bloc voting and thus fragment voters into competing racial and ethnic factions, a development that can lead to the "balkanization" that Justice O'Connor was concerned about in Shaw v. Reno. At an ABA conference in 1997, "The Geography of Race in Election: Color-Blindness and Redistricting," Charles Cooper made this argument by quoting Justice Thomas (who was quoting William O. Douglas in Wright v. Rockefeller):

> The principle of equality is at war with the notion that District A must be represented by a [black], as it is with the notion that District B must be represented by a Caucasian, District C by a Jew, District D by a Catholic and so on . . . That system, by whatever name it is called, is a divisive force in a community, emphasizing differences between candidates and voters that are irrelevant.[53]

He continues by saying that he thinks Justice O'Connor put it well in Shaw when she stated, "When a district obviously is created solely to effectuate the perceived common interests of one racial group, elected officials are more likely to believe that the primary obligation is to represent only members of that group, rather than their constituency as a whole. This is, altogether antithetical to our system of representative democracy."[54]

Guinier responds, "The issue of race-conscious districting puts the issue of race on the table; even more importantly, it puts the issue of representation on the table; and, most fundamentally, it puts the issue of democracy on the table."[55] She continues her argument by stating that democracy is already fundamentally about groups; we aggregate people into geographic districts based on the idea that people gain power on the basis of where they live. The Court believes that people are represented by being a member of a group defined by a district, but Guinier and others suggest that collective identity makes more sense along racial lines than geographic ones.[56]

A related criticism of alternative systems is that they allow the election of "radical" or "fringe" candidates. Daniel Troy makes this point by quoting political scientist Quintin Quade: "[P]lurality voting encourages the competing parties to adopt a majority-forming attitude. The parties incline to be moderate, to seek

51. Id. at 1901.
52. Id.
53. Charles Cooper, Gerald Torres, Lani Guinier, Daniel Troy & Pamela Karlan, "The Geography of Race in Elections: Color-Blindness and Redistricting," 14 J.L. & Pol. 109, 112 (1998).
54. Id. at 116-117.
55. Id. at 121.
56. Id.

conciliation, to round off their rough edges — in short, to do before the election, in public view, the very tasks that . . . PR systems . . . do after the elections."[57] By contrast, Troy continues, proportional representation promotes extremism.[58] Mulroy suggests that any fear of extremism may be eliminated by using a mandatory minimum percentage of the vote in the primary before one can enter the general election.[59]

> Fairness requires that there be some level of support at which a candidate's share of the vote is high enough — say, 10%, 20%, or 30% — that he or she must be viewed as deserving a seat at the table. While individuals may differ about what the minimum is, voters can collectively decide what the threshold ought to be and set it accordingly.[60]

Beyond this, Mulroy makes an interesting claim that while our current election results may reflect the moderation of a very middle-of-the road American electorate, the moderation may be merely a reflection of the narrow range of choices currently offered voters. He continues,

> The will of the people should not be thwarted to promote an artificial stasis: If greater ideological diversity is a truer reflection of the electorate's overall preferences, then such diversity ought to be allowed to exist. If, on the other hand, ideological moderation truly results from the inherent middle-of-the road nature of the electorate, then adopting a system which more accurately measures the nature should not unduly change political results.[61]

§6.16   THE RACIAL FUTILITY COMPONENT IN BLACK VOTING

Why is it that while the black vote has often been crucial in electing Democratic party candidates (particularly in national elections, but often in state and local elections as well), Democratic party leaders are reluctant to acknowledge the importance of the black vote and will often go out of their way to distance themselves from issues and individuals associated with black people? Professor Paul Frymer offers a detailed response to this question in his book, *Uneasy Alliances.*[1]

Citing as example the presidential election of 1992, in which the country elected Bill Clinton, the first Democratic party presidential nominee to gain the White House in 16 years, Frymer traces the party's move to the right, with emphasis on Clinton's call for welfare reform and for cutbacks on "excessive" employment benefits, both widely perceived as benefiting "undeserving blacks." Other examples of this "distancing" included failing to mention in the party platform the

---

57. Id. at 126.
58. Id.
59. Alternative Ways Out, supra note 41, at 1905.
60. Id.
61. Id. at 1906.
§6.16   1. Paul Frymer, Uneasy Alliances: Race and Party Competition in America (1999).

redress of racial injustice and of Clinton's public criticism of rap performer Sister Souljah for allegedly advocating black-on-white violence.

These actions deeply troubled many blacks but were deemed necessary by party elites and, as Professor Frymer shows, were only the latest instance of a tradition of "efforts of national party leaders to downplay the interests of their black constituents in order to broaden the party's electoral base and increase its chances in presidential campaigns. At most moments in American history, the desire of political parties to elect candidates to national office has meant marginalization for African Americans."[2] This does not mean that, once elected, a Democratic president entirely ignores blacks, but the rewards tend to be individualized—judicial appointments, cabinet and other high level offices—rather than a generalized push for policy changes of particular value to blacks, such as changes in draconian drug laws; increased employment opportunities for the unskilled or underemployed; elimination of the death penalty; and meaningful implementation, funding, and enforcement of civil rights laws and legal services programs.

Frymer acknowledges that a party can identify closely with blacks, as the Democratic party did during the civil rights movement of the 1960s. He notes, though, that this was a period when some leaders were moved by ideological principle, and public support was widespread for eliminating racially segregated public facilities. By the late 1960s, the public enthusiasm for civil rights had changed dramatically, as did the incentive for party leaders to be inclusive rather than exclusive.

As a political matter, given the likelihood that blacks would vote Democratic, advocating blacks' basic rights—including the right to vote—would certainly accrue to the benefit of the Democratic party. The Republicans for quite similar reason pushed for black rights during the Reconstruction era. Frymer pointed out that the two examples are quite exceptional and occurred during periods notable for the absence of a strong, competitive two-party system.

In general, though, Frymer does not believe that the competitive two-party system produces a more democratic and inclusive society. In fact, he contends that given the role of race and racism in American society, parties trying to win elections have politically compelling reasons to resist mobilizing and incorporating blacks into the political system. At times, parties will go so far as to deny black Americans their democratic rights completely, thereby exacerbating rather than diminishing this historically disadvantaged minority group's marginalized position. In ways unique to our country, Frymer notes:

[T]he founders of our modern party system understood and, in some ways, even intended for party competition to have this negative impact on African American political interests. More than 150 years ago, party leaders conceived of a party system that would avoid, or at least minimize, racial and sectional conflict. . . . [T]he Democratic party was founded to a significant degree with this in mind. In the mid-1820s, northern and southern elites agreed to put existing differences on the slave issue aside for the sake of combining forces to elect candidates to national office. They formed

2. Id. at 6.

the Democratic party, a powerful electoral agency that influenced any potential opposition to follow a similar strategy in order to compete effectively for national office.
Both the Democratic and Whig parties in the period prior to the Civil War derived a
great deal of legitimacy and strength from their ability to keep slavery off the political
agenda. The leaders of the two-party system not only structured electoral competition
around the average voter. Over the long run, they structured competition around the
white voter.[3]

Frymer uses the phrase "electoral capture" to explain how the competitive
two-party system leads party leaders to deemphasize black interests in order to
create broad-based electoral coalitions. This occurs when blacks have no choice
but to remain in the party because the opposing party does not want the blacks'
votes and, in fact, asserts positions hostile to blacks and their interests. In this
situation, the party leadership can take blacks for granted, neglect their interests,
and even distance itself from black leaders and their issues. This happens, in
particular, when the party fears that identification with black issues will cost it
the support of moderate and conservative whites or disrupt the party's electoral
coalition. No matter that blacks remain loyal to the party and that their votes can
make the difference in an election.

It is tough for black leaders to move out of their captured position and gain
support for the economic and social issues that, because of the legacy of slavery
and discrimination, require dramatic action not easily taken by a government that
favors incrementalism. When blacks have made overtures to the Republican or
independent parties, those parties have been reluctant to make even the most
general of political appeals to respond to blacks.

Frymer differs with scholars who contend that the presence of two
majoritarian parties and the competition between them insures all groups a hearing
and representation. While this may be true for the many issues on which the United
States population normally aligns itself on a left-right continuum, it is not true for
race-specific issues about which the majority of blacks tend to be skewed strongly
to one side and the majority of whites tend to be skewed, often equally strongly, to
the other. He writes:

> Party theorists champion the concept of a majority interest only because they believe
> an individual who is in the minority on one issue will be in the majority on another
> issue. Yet, when it comes to race issues, black Americans continue to be in the
> minority and white Americans are in the majority. Unable to form coalitions with
> other groups facing similar socioeconomic concerns, or even to become junior part-
> ners of the majority interest, blacks often lack the substantive power to persuade party
> leaders to take their interests seriously. Moreover, racial cleavage makes party elites
> hesitant about attracting African Americans to an existing party coalition. They fear
> that mobilizing black votes will lead to a decrease in the overall votes of the coalition.
> If voter hostility to black political interests is great, then the threat of defections
> among the party's current supporters will likely diminish the party's efforts to appeal
> to black voters. As long as political party leaders believe that racial appeals to whites

---

3. Id. at 7. The Civil War eliminated two-party competition in the 1850s and 1860s; it
reemerged little more than a decade later when the Republicans and Democrats resumed "normal"
electoral competition.

are a successful method of gaining votes and attaining office, it will remain in their interests to continue such efforts, and it will remain in the interests of the other party to try to take race issues off the agenda entirely.[4]

§6.17 Racism Hypo: The Democratic Party v. The State

In preparation for the upcoming Presidential Election, one southern state legislature, motivated by a determination to avoid the breakdown during the 2004 election that effectively disenfranchised thousands of the state's voters, enacted "No Voter Left Behind." This Act, supported predominantly by Republicans, who make up over 65% of the state legislature, allocated millions of dollars in funding toward revamping the state's voting process, including the creation of state-of-the-art computerized voting booths that enabled the elimination of all paper ballots. It also launched a massive voter registration drive that registered hundreds of new voters. The voting machines will use touch-pad computer screens akin to many ATM machines to make candidate selections during voting. The machines will be placed in shopping malls as well as schools, libraries, and firehouses for a week prior to the election. Most dramatically, individuals with access to the Internet will be able to vote from home or work. New voter ID cards have been distributed to all registered voters with voter ID numbers that can be used to log in to an election website to place votes over the Internet. An elaborate back-up system is in place to resolve voting challenges.

The Democratic Party, voter rights groups, and the AARP immediately challenged the No Voter Left Behind law as a violation of the right to vote for poor, elderly and minority voters. Comparing the computer technology to literacy tests, the lawsuit argued that voting with this technology for those they represented—and the plaintiffs included numbers of each group—was akin to reading a foreign language. The advanced computer voting would deter elderly voters and voters of color in poor rural areas where over 35 percent of this small state's population lives. The complaint read, "over 72 percent of these citizens are African American or Latino and almost all of them are registered Democrat. Only 2 percent of the population located in the southwest rural region of the state own computers. Few schools and libraries have any computer equipment. There are no large shopping malls and few ATM machines." At the same time, Republican-dominated portions of the state were ready to vote with their laptops and blackberries. The plaintiff's constitutional right to vote could only be protected if voters in all regions have an option to use a paper ballot.

The state responded by arguing that this system enhanced the right of each citizen to vote, making it easy and more convenient. The response presented detailed plans for equipping the Southwest region with trainings on how to vote using the new machines. Following a hearing, the district court ruled with the state, a decision affirmed on appeal. The Supreme Court has granted review.

Group A represents the Democratic Party, NAACP, and the AARP. Group B represents the state.

4. Id. at 20.

Chapter 7

Property Barriers and Fair Housing Laws

§7.1 INTRODUCTION

In 1968, the Kerner Commission named segregated housing as among the ingredients of the explosive mixture accumulating in cities since World War II. It is in the black ghettos, said the commission, that "segregation and poverty converge on the young to destroy opportunity and enforce failure. Crime, drug addiction, dependency on welfare, and bitterness and resentment against society in general and white society in particular are the result."[1]

It seemed the right approach to point out the harm to blacks and the potential danger to whites traceable to racial ghettos, and to hope that the society's sense of justice as well as its concern for self-interest would lead to policies that would open housing markets that have remained closed to blacks despite a host of antidiscrimination laws. But segregated housing serves several interests. Housing is not only shelter — it represents status — and the general view is that nonwhites residing in a neighborhood will lower its status and hence the value of the property in the area. To the extent that such views limit the housing opportunities for minorities, the cost of available housing is artificially inflated. Landlords and realtors profit by exploiting the preference of whites to live in all or mostly white neighborhoods and by exploiting the inability of most blacks to seek housing wherever it is available because of economic limitations, racial exclusion, and hostility. Also, fair housing laws, by relying for enforcement on the filing of actions by victims of housing discrimination, serve to further insulate landlords and realtors from punishment for discrimination.

Professor Leon Litwack, reviewing the history of housing discrimination in the middle of the nineteenth century, found that "economic exploitation and segregation produced the Negro ghetto."[2] There were, he reports, a remarkable number of fine houses owned by blacks in attractive neighborhoods, but most lived in wooden shacks and shanties in crowded sections with picturesque names: "Nigger Hill" and "New Guinea" in Boston; "Little Africa" in Cincinnati;

---

§7.1 1. National Advisory Comm'n on Civil Disorders 5 (1968).
2. Leon Litwack, North of Slavery: The Negro in the Free States 1790-1860 at 168-170 (1961).

"Five Points" in New York. The foul living conditions adversely affected the general health of blacks. Mortality rates, particularly from diseases like tuberculosis, were twice as high for blacks as for whites. Blacks suffered from exposure and malnutrition. "[V]igorous exclusion of Negroes from white residential neighborhoods made escape from the ghetto virtually impossible. The fear of depreciated property values overrode virtually every other consideration." Efforts by successful blacks to purchase or rent homes in white neighborhoods usually met with stiff resistance and occasional violence.

Whites frequently deprecated these slums, but Professor Litwack indicates that whites also profited from most of them. They owned most of the wooden shacks and shanties in Cincinnati's Little Africa and protested the attempt of municipal authorities to bar further construction of wooden buildings in the center of town. While critics continued to deplore black housing conditions, white landlords made few, if any, improvements. Litwack advises that "both conveniently concluded that Negroes naturally lived that way."

The law's posture did not vary much from the society's convenient conclusions regarding black housing until a few cities and states enacted relatively innocuous fair housing ordinances and laws in the post-World War II era. Surprisingly, the Supreme Court had set a Fourteenth Amendment limitation on state-mandated housing segregation as early as 1917. In Buchanan v. Warley,[3] a unanimous Court declared unconstitutional the provisions of a city ordinance that denied blacks the right to occupy houses in blocks in which the greater number of houses were occupied by white persons. Similar restrictions were imposed on whites with respect to blocks in which the greater number of houses were occupied by blacks. In its opinion, the Court found that the Fourteenth Amendment and those federal statutes enacted in furtherance of its purpose "operate to qualify and entitle a colored man to acquire property without state legislation discriminating against him solely because of color." The asserted purpose of the ordinance was to maintain public peace and keep down racial disorders. The Court acknowledged that both were worthwhile and appropriate goals, but that they could not be achieved through the violation of constitutional rights.[4]

Of course, the precedents did little more than bar the states from giving de jure status to segregated housing patterns rigidly maintained on a de facto basis throughout most of the country. As a part of this "societal conspiracy," many deeds for private housing contained provisions restricting the sale or conveyance to whites only. In the 1940s, civil rights groups launched a concerted legal attack on these restrictive covenants. The result was Shelley v. Kraemer,[5] a major victory that, somehow, was never translated into terms that would significantly ease housing discrimination, which continued to narrow to a trickle the housing opportunities available to black citizens.

3. 245 U.S. 60 (1917).
4. See also Harmon v. Tyler, 273 U.S. 668 (1927) (voiding ordinance requiring written consent from majority of majority-race inhabitants in community before member of minority race could establish home); City of Richmond v. Deans, 281 U.S. 704 (1930) (voiding *Buchanan*-type ordinance).
5. 334 U.S. 1 (1948).

§7.1.1   Housing Discrimination Today

Discrimination in housing, with its vices of segregated housing patterns and inadequate and overpriced housing for minorities, continues to be one of those areas where the law is unable and not really willing to keep up with conditions in the real world. Despite the multiplicity of federal and state statutes designed to deal with housing discrimination, the law is not structured to provide effective relief. Furthermore, black homeownership continues to lag behind white homeownership, 47.9 percent to 75.8 percent.[6] Much of the United States remains racially segregated — nearly one third of the African-American population reside in blocks that are more than 90 percent black, and nearly half of the white population live on blocks that are more than 90 percent white.[7] As Joan Magagna, acting chief of the Housing and Civil Enforcement Section of the Justice Department has said. "It is quite unusual to live next door to someone of a different color."[8]

A study performed by the nonpartisan Urban Institute for the United States Department of Housing and Urban Development found that white "testers" who inquired about rental units were consistently favored over black testers in 21.6 percent of tests and were consistently favored over Hispanics in 25.7 percent of tests.[9] Whites were more likely to receive information about housing units and have the opportunity to inspect housing units than both blacks and Hispanics. White homebuyers were consistently favored over black homebuyers in 17 percent of tests and over Hispanic homebuyers in 19.7 percent of tests.[10] Whites were more likely to be able to inspect available homes, and were more likely to receive information and assistance with financing and encouragement.[11] Moreover, white and black homebuyers were consistently steered to neighborhoods that promoted or perpetuated segregation.[12]

The issue is not only one of white versus black, or even white versus nonwhite. In a Los Angeles study, all ethnic groups showed some willingness to live in mixed neighborhoods; but the comfort level dropped for Asians and Latinos if more than a third of their hypothetical neighbors were blacks.[13] Conversely, in the late 1990s Asians in predominantly black public housing in San Francisco settled a lawsuit that charged harassment by black residents,[14] and in

6. United States Census Bureau, Annual Statistics: 2006, Table 20, available at http://www.census.gov/hhes/www/housing/hvs/annual06/ann06t20.html.

7. Lois M. Quinn & John Pawasarat, Racial Integration in Urban America: A Black Level Analysis of African American and White Housing Patterns 3 (2003), available at http://www.uwm.edu/Dept/ETI/integration/integration.pdf.

8. Victoria A. Roberts, With a Handshake and a Smile: The Fight to Eliminate Housing Discrimination, 73 Mich. B.J. 276, 278 (1994).

9. The Urban Institute, Discrimination in Metropolitan Housing Markets: National Results from Phase I HDS 2000, iii-iv (2002).

10. See id.

11. See id.

12. See id. at 6.

13. Larry Gordon, Prejudice Called Main Cause of Housing Segregation Study: Angelenos Have Become More Open to Diverse Neighborhoods, But Evidence of Racial "Hierarchy" Is Found, L.A. Times, Dec. 23, 1996, at B1.

14. See Yumi Wilson, Consent Decree Ends Asians' Housing Bias Case, Accord Settles Suit Over Strife in Projects, San Fran. Chron., July 19, 1999, at A15.

Los Angeles some black and Latino neighborhoods are perceived as least inviting to Asians.[15]

Most state statutes, like the federal Fair Housing Act,[16] are not self-enforcing but rely on implementation by overburdened agencies or injured individuals who typically have few resources. Given the traditionally low damage awards in housing discrimination suits, the existing law serves neither to discourage wrong-doers nor compensate the injured. Housing laws and agencies are even less well suited to deal with the complicated issues that surround urban renewal and low-income housing projects where the parties are not individuals but rather munici-palities, agencies, and large classes of affected citizens. The difficulty of fashioning plans to effectively break up segregated housing patterns and provide low-income housing is exacerbated by the ease with which legal tactics and dilatory ploys can be used by opponents to thwart such plans.

Despite this pessimistic assessment of the existing laws, the potential exists to make these laws the framework for more effective enforcement. The impetus for enforcement, however, lies with a strong public desire for change, recognized and supported by the government and the courts.

§7.2   THE RESTRICTIVE COVENANT CASES

Shelley v. Kraemer[1] was the landmark case which declared state judicial enforcement of restrictive covenants aimed at preventing blacks from purchas-ing property in white neighborhoods to be state action in violation of the Four-teenth Amendment. The cases decided by the opinion arose in Missouri and Michigan. Both enforced covenants that forbade occupancy by non-Caucasians, and the Missouri courts had gone so far as to require that a black who purchased in good faith, without actual knowledge of the covenant, divest his title. The Court had no difficulty in finding that this agreement was directed at blacks solely because of race. It cited Buchanan v. Warley for the proposition that the state could not interfere with the right of a black person to purchase property in a white area, even if the state action was taken with the benign motive of protecting the public, both black and white, from racial violence. Given these clear principles, the only remaining question was whether judicial enforcement of a private contract or covenant would rise to the level of state action.

The Court reaffirmed the principle that the Fourteenth Amendment could extend only to state action, and could not prevent purely private action, no

---

15. Gordon, supra note 13. For a more in-depth analysis of the various barriers and issues facing specific ethnic groups in the housing context, see John O. Calmore, Race/ism Lost and Found: The Fair Housing Act at Thirty, 52 U. Miami L. Rev. 1067 (1998).

16. Fair Housing Act of 1968, 42 U.S.C. §§3601-3619 (1976 & Supp. IV 1981) (also known as Title VIII).

§7.2   1. 334 U.S. 1 (1948).

matter how discriminatory. Therefore, restrictive covenants voluntarily adhered to did not violate the Fourteenth Amendment. However, once the covenant was violated and the aggrieved parties sought to enforce its terms through the state courts, the Court found that state action in violation of the Fourteenth Amendment had taken place. It pointed to a series of cases where procedural judicial irregularities had been declared state action for Fourteenth Amendment purposes, and even to cases where state judicial enforcement of common law principles was held to violate Fourteenth Amendment rights. But for the state enforcement, the Court reasoned, the plaintiffs would have been free to buy the property. Therefore, the state action had in fact deprived them of equal protection of the laws. The Court rejected the argument that no equal protection violation had occurred because the state courts would also enforce restrictive covenants by blacks aimed at keeping whites out. Not only was this possibility unrealistic but, more fundamentally, in each case an individual's right to be free from discrimination would be violated. The fact that courts also stood ready to deny whites' constitutional rights did not cure the violation.[2]

In Barrows v. Jackson,[3] the Court extended Shelley v. Kraemer by holding that damages could not be awarded by a state court for a breach of a racial restriction. The plaintiffs in the damage suit were white owners of property subject to the covenant, while the defendant, a former white owner, had violated the agreement by selling her land to a black. Thus, while blacks were not directly involved in the litigation, the Court concluded that an award of damages would effectively punish the defendant for failure to continue discriminating against non-Caucasians in the use of her property, which punishment would be the equivalent to state encouragement of restrictive covenants depriving blacks, "unidentified but identifiable," of equal protection of the laws, in violation of the Fourteenth Amendment. To prevent such result, the Court permitted the white defendant to raise a defense resting on the assertion of another person's right, because "it would be difficult if not impossible for the persons whose rights are asserted to present their grievance before any court."

In response to Shelley and its progeny, white property holders determined to bar blacks from their neighborhoods devised a seemingly inexhaustible list of restrictions, many of which took advantage of the Shelley holding that such restrictions were valid between the parties. All manner of self-operating cooperatives, associations, and leasing arrangements were devised to protect the racial exclusiveness of white residential areas. Such arrangements were not foolproof, but they added to the barriers facing those few blacks in a position to take advantage of the Shelley decision.[4] Shelley Ross Saxer suggests that rather than finding such

---

2. Hurd v. Hodge, 334 U.S. 24 (1948), was a companion case to *Shelley*, involving a restrictive covenant in the District of Columbia, where, of course, the Fourteenth Amendment had no application. Nevertheless, the Supreme Court held the covenant unenforceable, relying on 42 U.S.C. §1982. See Jones v. Alfred H. Mayer Co., 392 U.S. 409 (1968). This statute was held to prohibit enforcement by the courts of racial covenants within the district. The Court did not reach the constitutional question of whether judicial implementation violated the Fifth Amendment's due process clause, but determined that enforcement of the covenants would violate federal public policy.

3. 346 U.S. 249 (1953).

4. Charles Abrams, Forbidden Neighbors 224-225 (1955).

covenants unenforceable under the state action theory, courts should revisit this area and instead find that such contracts violate public policy and are an unreasonable restraint on alienation and, therefore, void.[5] Saxer suggests that this would both clarify the doctrine of state action and, combined with state and federal legislation, eliminate the ability of private individuals to create self-enforcing discriminatory covenants.

§7.3 METHODS OF RESISTANCE TO INTEGRATION

Few expected that housing discrimination would be eliminated through use of the Shelley v. Kraemer principle. Efforts to enact fair housing laws at the state and local levels began in the 1940s. Few were actually enacted until the 1950s, and none without great resistance, particularly from real estate groups. The measures generally required the filing of individual complaints before commissions, which, when "probable cause" was found, had to exhaust efforts to secure voluntary compliance before imposing penalties or seeking judicial relief.[1] Although their effectiveness was never impressive, a number of efforts were made in the late 1960s to repeal these legislative attempts to curb discrimination in housing, or to use municipal zoning ordinances from preventing the integration of white neighborhoods.

Whatever their sympathies for southern blacks concerning the historic campaign of the 1960s to gain the right to vote and use public facilities on a nonsegregated basis, most northern whites' commitment to racial tolerance stopped somewhere short either of wanting blacks as neighbors or of countenancing the growing number of local ordinances and state laws that forbade whites from discriminating against nonwhites in the sale or lease of houses and apartments.[2]

§7.3.1 Referenda as a Threat to Civil Rights

Spurred by the conviction that state fair housing provisions violated their fundamental rights to absolute discretion in the sale or lease of their property, California voters responded in 1964 with the famous Proposition 14, which initiated an amendment to the state constitution providing:

> Neither the State nor any subdivision or agency thereof shall deny, limit or abridge, directly or indirectly, the right of any person, who is willing or desires to

5. See Shelley Ross Saxer, Shelley v. Kraemer's Fiftieth Anniversary: "A Time for Keeping: A Time for Throwing Away"?, 47 U. Kan. L. Rev. 61, 102-120 (1998).

§7.3 1. See, e.g., Laurence Pearl & Benjamin Terner, Fair Housing Laws: Halfway Mark, 54 Geo. L.J. 156 (1965).

2. For a discussion of the resistance to desegregation in Chicago, see Arnold R. Hirsch, Massive Resistance in the Urban North: Trumball Park, Chicago, 1953-1966, 82 J. Am. Hist. 522 (1995).

sell, lease or rent any part or all of his real property, to decline to sell, lease or rent such property to such person or persons as he, in his absolute discretion, chooses.

When in two separate cases plaintiffs charged that they had been denied housing due to their race in violation of the state fair housing law, defendants asserted the new constitutional amendment as a defense. The California Supreme Court ruled that the amendment violated the federal Constitution, and by a close five-to-four decision, the Supreme Court affirmed in Reitman v. Mulkey.[3]

Justice White, speaking for the majority, acknowledged that the state had the right to remain neutral in matters of housing discrimination, and was not required by the federal Constitution to use its police power to enforce a nondiscriminatory housing policy. The California amendment, however, had the effect of "encouraging" private discrimination and therefore unconstitutional state action was present. By enacting the provision, and thus in effect nullifying previous fair housing laws, the state had taken affirmative action to make discrimination legally possible.[4] Answering the dissent's argument, the Court stated that this encouragement went beyond mere repeal of an antidiscrimination statute, since it did not just remove barriers against discrimination: "The right to discriminate . . . on racial grounds, was now embodied in the State's basic charter, immune from legislative, executive, or judicial regulation. . . ."[5]

Justice Harlan, joined by Justices Black, Clark, and Stewart, dissented. He stated that in effect the amendment had merely repealed the previous statutes. He argued that the amendment was facially neutral, so the only way to find it encouraged discrimination was to question the motives of the legislators and voters, an improper and impossible inquiry. Further, the concept of "encouragement" was so vague and ill-defined that it could lead to a point where " 'state action' in the form of laws that do nothing more than passively permit private discrimination could be said to tinge *all* private discrimination with the taint of unconstitutional state encouragement."[6]

Concurring in *Reitman*, Justice Douglas argued that the covenants in *Shelley* were one means by which the dominant interests kept a neighborhood white, and Proposition 14 was simply another device of the same character. Zoning is a state and municipal function, and to delegate the zoning function to groups which

3. 387 U.S. 369 (1967).

4. Cautioning that the Court had not attempted the "impossible task" of formulating an infallible test to determine when a state has become significantly involved in private discrimination, Justice White indicated that the Court had relied heavily on the state supreme court's findings in this regard. He did cite Burton v. Wilmington Parking Auth., 365 U.S. 715 (1961), and several sit-in decisions, including Peterson v. City of Greenville, 373 U.S. 244 (1963), and Lombard v. Louisiana, 373 U.S. 267 (1963).

5. Compare the Court's reasoning in Romer v. Evans, 517 U.S. 620 (1996), discussed in §7.3.4. In that case, the Court decided that an amendment to Colorado's constitution forbidding local ordinances that protected gays and lesbians from discrimination did not meet the rational basis test. The Colorado amendment, like the California amendment in *Reitman*, embodied the right to discriminate — although the choice to use the rational-basis test meant that the Court did not decide whether sexual orientation qualified as a protected class worthy of strict or of intermediate scrutiny.

6. 387 U.S. at 395.

practice racial discrimination and are licensed by the states constituted state action in the most narrow sense in which Shelley v. Kraemer could be construed.[7]

Although it was not apparent at the time, a subsequent case, Hunter v. Erickson,[8] while relying on *Reitman*, provided a means by which the "encouragement" standard could be circumvented. In 1964, the Akron, Ohio, City Council enacted a fair housing ordinance. Subsequently, an amendment to the city charter was passed requiring that any law dealing with the rental or sale of real property which pertained to race, color, religion, national origin, or ancestry must first be approved by a majority of the electors at the next regular city election.

The Supreme Court invalidated the charter amendment on the ground that it discriminated, on racial or religious grounds, against groups seeking the law's protection by setting up a new procedure of lawmaking which was more complex than the method used with regard to any other group. Although the law purported to apply to all races and religions, the Court held that its effect was to make it virtually impossible for certain minorities to secure protective legislation. The Court stated further that it was unimpressed with the state's justification of its action as simply a public decision to move slowly in the delicate area of race relations.

Interestingly, between 1960 and 1968 (when the federal Fair Housing Act was passed, preempting state and local action in the housing discrimination area) nine anti-fair housing initiatives and referendums were voted on — and 90 percent of them won.[9] This would seem to indicate that without some judicial scrutiny of "direct democracy," at least during that time period, referendums and initiatives served only to harm minority interests.

For Justice Black, though, it was not enough that the protection of *Reitman* and *Hunter* might be rendered inapplicable by a "neutral" referendum repealing a fair housing law. Exercises in direct democracy, in his view, should be held valid because they "demonstrate devotion to democracy, not to bias, discrimination, or prejudice." And it was this principle, one with which most Americans (whether or not legally trained) would agree, that provided the main theme in Justice Black's majority opinion in James v. Valtierra.[10]

In that case, black and Mexican American indigents had challenged Article 34 of the California Constitution, which required prior approval in a local referendum before a state public body could develop a federally financed low-rent housing project. They argued that Article 34 unreasonably discriminated (explicitly against the poor and implicitly against minority groups) because it mandated special voter approval for low-income housing.

Justice Black, writing for a five-to-three majority, distinguished *Hunter* as involving a referendum that specifically burdened racial minorities. He perceived little evidence that the housing referendum required by Article 34 relied on

7. Id. at 381.
8. 393 U.S. 385 (1969).
9. Sylvia R. Lazos Vargas, Judicial Review of Initiatives and Referendums in which Majorities Vote on Minorities Democratic Citizenship, 60 Ohio St. L.J. 399, 426 (1999).
10. 402 U.S. 137, 141 (1971). The referendum discussion that follows is adopted from Derrick Bell, The Referendum: Democracy's Barrier to Racial Equality, 54 Wash. L. Rev. 1 (1978).

"distinctions based on race."[11] Noting that mandatory referenda were required by California law for other actions, albeit not connected with housing, Justice Black viewed the referendum as a legitimate vehicle for ensuring "that all the people of a community will have a voice in a decision which may lead to large expenditures of local governmental funds for increased public services and to lower tax revenues."[12]

The burden that Article 34 imposed on the poor who rely on public housing seems clear. Yet the *Valtierra* majority ignored the de jure wealth classification created by the referendum requirement, despite the chiding of the dissenters, who, speaking through Justice Thurgood Marshall, thought it "far too late in the day to contend that the Fourteenth Amendment prohibits only racial discrimination." In Justice Marshall's view, the amendment was equally violated by laws singling out the poor to bear burdens not placed on other classes of citizens.[13]

The Supreme Court's approval of the "neutral" referenda in *Valtierra* and *City of Eastlake* illustrates the effectiveness in the post-civil rights era of adopting standards that are facially neutral as to race and arguably legitimate in purpose. Even the most unsophisticated voters recognize these measures are intended to exclude poor and nonwhite groups. Here, as in other instances, the referendum as a medium for perpetuating discrimination is effective because so many whites, particularly those in the lower classes, are convinced that their own insecure social status may best be protected by opposing equal rights for blacks.

Even if the use of the referendum were confined to the repeal of relatively ineffective state and local fair housing laws, there would be ample basis for concern, but the referendum's potential for undermining the rights of minority groups is much greater. Consider, as a start, how unpopular fair housing measures were enacted in the first place. Public officials, even those elected in more or less overtly racist campaigns, may prove responsive to minority pressures for civil rights measures once in office or, at least, be open to the negotiation and give-and-take that constitutes much of the political process. Thus, legislators may vote for, or executive officials may sign, a civil rights or social reform bill with full knowledge that a majority of their constituents oppose the measure.[14] They are in the spotlight and do not wish publicly to advocate racism; they cannot openly attribute their opposition to "racist constituents." The more neutral reasons for

---

11. 402 U.S. at 140-141.

12. Id. at 143. The three mandatory referenda cited by Justice Black, id. at 142, constitutional amendments, certain municipal annexations, and local issuance of general-obligation, long-term bonds, are unexceptional and clearly distinguishable from Article 34. Moreover, it is obvious that low-income housing is not the only change in existing land uses that may adversely affect property owners and residents or lead to large expenditures of public funds. Even governmental construction projects, including mental hospitals and prisons, are not subject to popular veto.

13. 402 U.S. at 145.

14. The dilemma for public officials is not recent. Between 1865 and 1870 proposals for black voting were defeated in at least 14 northern states. See Robert R. Dykstra & Harlan Hahn, Northern Voters and Negro Suffrage: The Case of Iowa, 1868, 32 Pub. Op. Q. 202 (1968). The authors advise: "Rejection of Negro suffrage by Northern states in the Reconstruction era placed the Republican 'radicals' in Congress in a serious dilemma. At the same time that most of them demanded the right to vote for Southern Negroes, some on the grounds of principle, others to establish a Republican foothold in the South, their constituents blocked similar plans in the North." Id. at 203.

opposition are often inadequate in the face of serious racial injustices, particularly those posing threats not confined to the minority community.[15]

When the legislative process is turned back to the citizenry either to enact laws by initiative or to review existing laws through the referendum, few of the concerns that can transform the "conservative" politician into a "moderate" public official are likely to affect the individual voter's decision. No political factors counsel restraint on racial and other passions emanating from long-held and little-considered beliefs and fears. Far from being the pure path to democracy that Justice Black proclaimed, direct democracy, carried out in the privacy of the voting booth, has diminished the ability of minority groups to participate in the democratic process. Ironically, because it enables the voters' beliefs and fears to be recorded and tabulated in their pure form, the referendum has been a most effective facilitator of that bias, discrimination, and prejudice which has marred American democracy from its earliest day.[16]

While "direct democracy" is often touted as a means for the average person to have a real say in public policy, initiatives and referendums are more and more the province of those who have the resources to conduct the necessary campaign — currently estimated at about $1 million. Signatures are rarely gathered by grass-roots organizations working for the love of the cause. Instead, initiatives and referendums appear on the ballot as a result of efforts by paid signature gatherers,

---

15. See Raymond Wolfinger & Fred Greenstein, The Repeal of Fair Housing in California: An Analysis of Referendum Voting, 62 Am. Pol. Sci. Rev. 753, 768-769 (1968). The authors note that the legislative decision-making process is characterized by compromises between the initial demands of groups of varying size and intensity. They continue as follows: "In referenda, of course, compromise is impossible once the issue has been formally posed. A second, closely related advantage of legislatures is that they typically take account of the intensity of demands as well as their numerical support, while in referenda every voter's preference, no matter how casual, is equally weighted. The legislative process is responsive to intensity because legislators (consciously or unconsciously) ask themselves how much the interested parties care about the issue since they want to find out what the cost in votes and other forms of campaign support will be of disappointing one side or the other. "Calculations about intensity are relevant to considerations other than electoral advantage. First, a politician may feel on principle that, all things being equal, he would rather respond to an intense minority than a more or less lukewarm majority particularly if he thinks the minority's claim is legitimate. It appears that Governor Brown's strong support of the Rumford Act was based on such a view, along with a belief that fair housing was essential to any strategy of coping with the Negro problem. Second, as the history of California race relations since Watts reminds us, judgments about intensity are crucial data for the enterprise of making policies designed to minimize civil strife. A key consideration in assessing civil rights proposals is whether their passage or failure will increase or reduce the likelihood of racial disturbance." Id. For other studies reaching generally similar conclusions, see Clubb & Traugott, National Patterns in Referenda Voting: The 1968 Election, in 6 Urban Affairs Annual Review, People and Politics in Urban Society 137 (Harlan Hahn ed., 1972); Kendall & Carey, The Intensity Problem and Democratic Theory, 62 Am. Pol. Sci. Rev. 5 (1968).

16. Between 1963 and 1968, ten cities and the state of California conducted open housing referenda. All were initiated by opponents of fair housing measures who were successful in every case until 1968, when the Flint, Michigan, ordinance was upheld by a paper-thin margin on recount. Charles Hamilton, Direct Legislation: Some Implications of Open Housing Referenda, 64 Am. Pol. Sci. Rev. 124, 125 (1970). Another critical analysis of the referendum found: "Not only does the referendum hold great potential for racial divisiveness and for worsening inter-group relations, but it can also be employed by relatively small, organized groups to prevent achievement of the legitimate hopes and aspirations of underprivileged minorities." Scott & Nathan, Public Referenda: A Critical Reappraisal, 5 Urb. Aff. Q. 313, 319 (1970).

and through direct mass campaigns and media exposure. Money is also a strong predictor of the ability to get good legal help in drafting an initiative and of the ability to successfully advertise and pass an initiative or referendum.[17]

Sylvia R. Lazos Vargas suggests that in light of Romer v. Evans,[18] where the Supreme Court struck down an amendment to the Colorado Constitution that prohibited localities from passing antidiscrimination laws that included gays and lesbians, the Supreme Court needs to clarify its stance on review of voter initiatives and referendums. Her recommendation is as follows:

> [T]hat the Court has implicitly employed, and should employ, a strict scrutiny analysis to determine whether direct democracy measures have violated the Equal Protection Clause by unduly infringing on minorities' participation rights. The appropriate analysis has two major components. First, the Court must determine whether the particular democratic initiative or referendum severely jeopardizes minorities participation rights. Second, where such a harm exists, the Court should use standard strict scrutiny analysis and allow the direct democracy measure to stand, notwithstanding the harm it has caused, only if the measure is necessary to serve a compelling state interest. . . . [T]he Court has implicitly identified, and should explicitly recognize, a fundamental right to civic participation.

Courts, however, have been reluctant to grapple with or even to acknowledge the plethora of racist influences and status and class concerns that come into play when the future of a fair housing or other law is to be decided at the voting booth, or when the electorate must approve a legislative or administrative decision to construct a low-income housing project. Any serious consideration of the degree to which prejudice affects the outcome of referenda must at the very least bring an end to the uncritical acceptance and repetition of the unproved assumptions that direct voting techniques are fair and faithful reflections of the country's highest democratic values.

During its 2002 term, the Supreme Court unanimously found that the City Council of Cuyahoga Falls' decision to submit to a public referendum a petition to repeal an ordinance authorizing the construction of a low-income housing project, and the city engineer's refusal to issue building permits for the project while the referendum was pending, did not constitute an equal protection or due process violation.[19] The referendum ultimately passed, repealing the ordinance. The Supreme Court found that the equal protection clause was not implicated because the evidence did not sufficiently support "proof of racially discriminatory intent or purpose" on the part of the city officials.[20] The submission of a referendum to the public was viewed as a facially neutral act prompted by the city charter. Even though statements during the petition drive suggested discriminatory voter sentiment, these potentially racist private motives did not in and of themselves

---

17. Id. at 419-420. In California, 60 percent of one successful initiative campaign was funded by a single donor. This belies the idea that initiatives truly represent the voice of the people.
18. 517 U.S. 620 (1996).
19. City of Cuyahoga Falls, Ohio v. Buckeye Community Hope Found., 538 U.S. 188 (2003).
20. Id. at 193.

constitute state action. The Court also found that the referendum process did not constitute arbitrary or capricious government conduct in violation of due process.

§7.3.2 Municipal Resistance to Integrated Housing

Municipal zoning ordinances provide another method of perpetuating segregation. Towns often limit the zoning of multifamily homes to largely minority areas. Because minorities families may be less likely to be able to afford single-family homes, this essentially prevents minority families from finding affordable housing outside the neighborhoods in which they are the majority, perpetuating the existence of separate white neighborhoods and minority neighborhoods.

This was the case in Huntington, New York, in the 1980s. In the 1960s, as part of Huntington's urban renewal effort, the town had created zoning classifications permitting the construction of multifamily housing projects, but restricted the construction of such housing to the area around Huntington Station.[21] By the 1980s, Huntington had approximately 200,000 residents, 95 percent of whom were white and less than 4 percent of whom were black. Nearly 75 percent of the black population was clustered in six census tracts in the Huntington Station and South Greenlawn areas. Of the remaining census tracks, most were at least 99 percent white. [22]

Housing Help, Inc., a private developer looking to foster residential integration, acquired an option to purchase a site in a 98 percent white section of the town that was zoned for single family residences. Housing Help requested that the town board amend the Town Code to permit multifamily rental construction in their zone, which it refused to do. Housing Help filed suit, arguing that the town board had violated the Fair Housing Act by perpetuating zoning laws that had a disproportionate discriminatory impact on minorities and promoted segregation. In response, the town argued that restriction of multifamily projects to the urban renewal area was necessary to encourage developers to invest in a deteriorated section of town. The Court of Appeals ruled in favor of the plaintiffs, finding evidence of a discriminatory impact on minorities, and rejecting the town's proffered justification. Without detailing its reasoning, the Supreme Court affirmed.[23]

Unfortunately, there has not been a significant amount of similar litigation. This is primarily due to the difficulty in finding willing plaintiffs. Developers who have worked in underdeveloped segregated communities for decades looking for places to build would be obvious candidates. However, such developers often prefer to avoid making such unpopular choices in wealthier, white communities who have expressed their clear desire, through zoning ordinances, to keep their neighborhood "theirs."

---

21. See Town of Huntington, New York v. Huntington Branch, NAACP, 488 U.S. 15, 16 (1988) (per curiam).
22. See id.
23. See id. at 16-18.

Another method of perpetuating segregation is through affordable public housing or housing aid attached to residency preferences. In New York, new affordable public housing often gives priority for 50 percent of the units to residents of the community district in which the apartments are being constructed, perpetuating segregation.[24] For example, an Upper East Side, Manhattan, housing project expresses a preference for a community district in which, compared to the city as a whole, blacks are underrepresented by 87 percent and Hispanics by 78 percent.[25] The Second Circuit rejected such housing preferences in Comer v. Cisneros, stating that

> [w]hile a local preference may be neither *per se* unconstitutional nor *per se* unfair, where a government erects a local preference that has the effect of filtering only a small percentage of minorities to the locally preferred area, such government action is suspect to being a proxy to race and therefore a barrier to racial minorities who wish to integrate into [the neighborhood].[26]

The District Court in Massachusetts reached a similar conclusion with regard to a housing policy with a residency preference:

> All of the communities in this case have significantly lower percentages of minority residents than their urban neighbors; all of them have fewer minority residents *per capita* than the state average. If follows logically, then, that any policy that factually favors the residents of these communities will disproportionately favor whites over minorities in the long run. . . . [W]here a community has a smaller proportion of minority residents than does the larger geographical area from which it draws applications to its . . . program, a selection process that favors its residents *cannot but* work a disparate impact on minorities.[27]

More recently, antidiscrimination advocates have sought alternative means of fighting housing segregation perpetuation by municipalities. The Anti-Discrimination Center of Metro New York has filed a suit against Westchester County under the False Claims Act. As an applicant for funds under the Community Development Act, Westchester was required to certify that it was furthering, and would affirmatively further, fair housing.[28] However, Westchester has failed to take such steps to affirmatively further fair housing, despite its knowledge of the extremely segregated nature of Westchester's housing.[29] The complaint argues that, despite its affirmative obligation, Westchester failed to push communities to desegregate as a condition of providing them a share of the funds. As of the time

24. See Anti-Discrimination Center of Metro New York, Inc., Affordable Housing Listings, at http://www.antibiaslaw.com/today/affordablehousing.html.

25. See id.

26. 37 F.3d 775, 793 (2d Cir. 1994).

27. See Langlois v. Abington Housing Authority, 234 F. Supp. 2d 33, 56, 58 (D. Mass. 2002).

28. See U.S. ex rel. Anti-Discrimination Center of Metro New York, Inc. v. Westchester County, 06-cv-2860, Complaint, filed Apr. 12, 2006 (S.D.N.Y.).

29. Over 60 percent of Westchester's 45 municipalities are less than 3 percent black, while other towns are 58 percent black and 10 percent Hispanic, 34 percent black and 22 percent Hispanic, 19 percent black and 20 percent Hispanic, and 15 percent black and 26 percent Hispanic. See id.

of publication, the case is still pending, and the district court has denied the county's motion to dismiss.[30]

§7.4 SECTION 1982

In the period between the *Reitman* and *Hunter* decisions, the Supreme Court resurrected a post–Civil War civil rights statute by liberating it from the constraints of state action requirements, thereby transforming it into a federal fair housing law more formidable than anything Congress was considering and, according to the Court's critics, far more vigorous than anything the nineteenth-century Congress had in mind.

§7.4.1   Jones v. Alfred H. Mayer Co.

The decision in Jones v. Alfred H. Mayer Co.[1] made the threat to state and local fair housing measures posed by post-*Hunter* referendums appear less serious, and led many civil rights advocates to predict that housing discrimination would soon disappear. Optimism of that character has not proven justified, although the extension to private action of the Civil Rights Act of 1866, now codified in 42 U.S.C. §1982 (1994), sought to give victims of housing discrimination a prompt and possibly effective remedy.

Section 1982 provides: "All citizens of the United States shall have the same right, in every State and Territory, as is enjoyed by white citizens thereof to inherit, purchase, lease, sell, hold, and convey real and personal property."[2] Relying on this act, plaintiffs filed suit alleging that they had been denied a house they sought to purchase solely because they were black. The Supreme Court held that "Section 1982 bars *all* racial discrimination, private as well as public, in the sale or rental of property, and that the statute, thus construed, is a valid exercise of the power of

30. See U.S. ex rel. Anti-Discrimination Center of Metro New York, Inc. v. Westchester County, 495 F. Supp. 2d 375 (S.D.N.Y. 2007).
§7.4 1. 392 U.S. 409 (1968).
2. Justice Stewart made clear early in his opinion that §1982 was a different remedy than that which the Congress had only recently enacted as the Fair Housing Title (Title VIII) of the Civil Rights Act of 1968, Pub. L. No. 90-284, 82 Stat. 81 (42 U.S.C. §§3601-3619, 3631 (1970, Supp. 1975)). He noted that §1982 protects only against racial discrimination and does not address discrimination based on religion or national origin. It does not deal with bias in the provision of services or facilities in connection with the sale or rental of housing, nor does it bar discriminatory preferences in advertising, financing arrangements, or brokerage services. No federal agency is empowered to assist aggrieved parties, and there is no provision for intervention by the Attorney General, nor an express authorization for a federal court to order the payment of damages. Title VIII provides for all the above, but also contains several exemptions not mentioned in §1982. In addition, relief under §1982, unlike Title VIII, does not depend on the bureaucratic uncertainties of a governmental agency that, as experience has shown, may lack adequate staff, suffer political interference, and hinder its own effectiveness with overcautious procedures, unnecessary delays, protracted conciliation efforts and efficiency-killing jurisdictional wrangles with state and local commissions.

Congress to enforce the Thirteenth Amendment."[3] The Court examined the legislative history to find support for this revolutionary reading of the statute. It found that Congress meant to secure the right to purchase property from private as well as official interference. The criminal provisions of the Act of 1866 were limited to those acting "under color of state law," but the civil provisions, including §1982, extended to all citizens.

The Court pointed to congressional recognition of the widespread evil of race prejudice, embodied not just in anti-Negro legislation but in the customs of the people. Having determined that meaning of the bill, as supported by the legislative history, all that was left for the Court was to determine its constitutionality. Since the act was based on the Thirteenth, instead of the Fourteenth, Amendment, there was no "state action" limitation on congressional enforcement power. The Thirteenth Amendment abolished slavery, and its enabling clause empowered Congress, according to the Civil Rights Cases, "to pass all laws necessary and proper for abolishing all badges and incidents of slavery in the United States." The Court had no difficulty concluding that the inability to purchase property freely could rationally be determined to be a badge or incident of slavery, since it restrained a fundamental right. "[W]hen racial discrimination herds men into ghettos and makes their ability to buy property turn on the color of their skin, then it too is a relic of slavery."

Justice Harlan, joined by Justice White, wrote a lengthy dissent to what he considered a "most ill-considered and ill-advised" decision. He suggested that the enactment of a fair housing statute "so diminishes the public importance of this case that by far the wisest course would be for this Court to refrain from decision and to dismiss the writ as improvidently granted."[4] Although conceding that the coverage of the new law would not provide petitioner with relief, he concluded, "The political process now having taken hold again in this very field, I am at a loss to understand why the Court should have deemed it appropriate or in the circumstances of this case, necessary to proceed with such precipitate and insecure strides."[5]

3. 392 U.S. at 412-413.
4. 392 U.S. at 450.
5. Id. at 478. The *Jones* decision brought out in full force the legal commentators, many of them taking widely divergent views as to the decision's validity, wisdom and likely scope. One writer said, "It may well be that this decision, by infusing new vitality both into the early Reconstruction statutes and into the thirteenth amendment, will prove to be the most far-reaching race relations case since the Civil War." Arthur Larson, The New Law of Race Relations, 1969 Wis. L. Rev. 470, 486. Typically, concern was expressed that, without the "state action" qualification, congressional power to regulate private conduct under the Thirteenth Amendment would be unlimited. While conceding that the right to discriminate, taken alone, should not outweigh the right of blacks to fair treatment, commentators were concerned that discrimination often occurs in conjunction with interest in privacy, free association or free expression. One article suggests the possible resurrection of the "social rights" formula, developed by Justice Bradley in his [Civil Rights Cases] opinion, a formula which courts could use to encompass rights considered to be less than "fundamental" to blacks but denoting a sphere in which the discriminators' personal interests are especially strong. See Note, The "New" Thirteenth Amendment: A Preliminary Analysis, 82 Harv. L. Rev. 1294, 1313 (1969).

§7.4.2   The *Jones* Progeny

The potential of §1982 to provide an all-encompassing remedy for housing discrimination was illustrated two years after *Jones*. In Sullivan v. Little Hunting Park, Inc.,[6] the defendant was a nonstock corporation formed to operate a community park and playground for the benefit of neighborhood resident members. A person owning a membership share was entitled to transfer the membership to his tenant if he leased his home. Sullivan rented his home to a black, Freeman, and assigned him his membership share. The Board of Directors, acting under the corporation's bylaws, refused to accept this assignment of membership, and Sullivan was expelled from the organization, which offered him cash for his membership share. The Court reaffirmed its holding in *Jones* that §1982 applied to private as well as public discriminatory conduct, reiterating that the enactment of Title VIII in no way impaired the sanctions of §1982. Since membership was a component of the property's value, the refusal to recognize Freeman's membership interfered with his ability to lease property and thus violated §1982. The Court further held that Sullivan, the white who rented the house to Freeman, was also entitled to relief, and thus his expulsion from membership was invalid. If the expulsion, backed by the state court judgment, was allowed to stand, the state in effect would be in the position of encouraging discrimination. Further, the Court held that it was free to award damages if necessary to remedy the invasion of §1982 rights.[7]

The next year, the Court decided Tillman v. Wheaton-Haven Recreational Association Inc.[8] In *Tillman*, defendant was a nonprofit corporation organized for the purpose of operating a swimming facility in Silver Spring, Maryland. Funds for the pool were privately raised, and membership was largely keyed to a three-quarter-mile radius around the pool. The record shows that the defendant discouraged membership by a black who had purchased a home within the preference area, and that after a white member had brought a black friend as a guest, the guest policy was limited to relatives of members. Suit was filed by the white member whose black guest was denied admission and by the black resident who was refused an application form. Jurisdiction for the case was based on Title II of the Civil Rights Act of 1964 and 42 U.S.C. §§1981 and 1982. The district court granted a summary judgment for the defendant, which was affirmed by the court of appeals, one judge dissenting.

Justice Blackmun, speaking for a unanimous Court, found that the refusal to admit a black resident of the preference area to membership abridges and dilutes a property right on the basis of race. Justice Blackmun wrote, "When an organization links membership benefits to residency in a narrow geographical area, the decision infuses those benefits into the bundle of rights for which an

---

6. 396 U.S. 229 (1969).

7. Justice Harlan, joined by Chief Justice Burger and Justice White, dissented. As he had done in his *Jones* dissent, Justice Harlan argued that governmental enactment of the 1968 Fair Housing Act removed any necessity for the Court's reliance upon the 1866 antidiscrimination statute. He again pointed out that the new law contained specific provisions for relief and obviated the need for fashioning remedies, as the majority had done in this case.

8. 410 U.S. 431 (1973).

individual pays when buying or leasing within the area." At that point, the mandate of §1982 operates to ensure that the nonwhite resident is guaranteed the same rights as are enjoyed by a white resident. Justice Blackmun also found that under the provisions of §§1981 and 1982, the defendant could not validly exclude black guests of white members.[9] Most courts followed *Tillman*'s interpretation of §1982 as to plaintiff's entitlement to damages and also took a similarly broad view as to attorney's fees.[10]

Despite the line of cases affirming the Court's holding in *Jones*, the composition of the Court has changed dramatically to one much less favorable to holding private entities responsible for racial discrimination under §1982. The Roberts Court has not been afraid to call into doubt the Court's past decisions or put forth decisions completely at odds with the Court's previous holdings.[11] Moreover, Justice Stevens has explicitly stated that he believes *Jones* to be wrongly decided.[12] Given this line-up of predictable opponents, civil rights advocates may avoid bringing a §1982 case before the Supreme Court for fear that it would do more harm than good.

§7.4.3   Section 1982 and the Thirteenth Amendment

In the late 1970s, the city of Memphis, at the request of a group of white neighbors, decided to restrict the volume of traffic on a street leading into city center by closing the street at the point where the white neighborhood ended and a largely black neighborhood began. The decision was not part of a citywide traffic control program and was in fact the first residential street closure in Memphis. The closure was accomplished by deeding a strip of land across the street to the white neighborhood association. The effect was to restrict black access to the white neighborhood and to require residents of the black neighborhood to take an alternate route to city center. Residents of the black neighborhood filed a class action under the Thirteenth Amendment and §1982, charging that the barrier's creation of racially separate neighborhoods was a "badge of slavery," and that it reduced

9. Following remand of the *Tillman* case, the district court awarded compensatory damages under §1982 but refused punitive damages on the ground that there was no proof that defendants had acted "willfully and wantonly." The district court also refused to hold the Association directors personally liable, reasoning that they could not have known that the exclusionary policy was illegal, 367 F. Supp. 860 (D. Md. 1973).But the 1866 Civil Rights Act, the Fourth Circuit found on appeal, governs those who are insensitive to the racial discrimination abolished by the act as well as those who are aware of its scope. Plaintiffs here were seeking redress of a tort and there is no doubt that the directors acted voluntarily and intentionally, proof of which is ordinarily sufficient to support liability or tort when the action invades an interest that the law protects. It is not necessary that a plaintiff relying on §1981 or §1982 prove that the defendant knew the duties that the statute imposed. Ignorance of the rights secured by these statutes is not a defense to an action brought to enforce them.

10. See Lee v. Southern Home Sites Corp., 444 F.2d 143 (5th Cir. 1971). A whole series of cases since *Jones* has tested the scope and effectiveness of relief under §1982. Although the *Jones* case itself involved only injunctive relief, cases citing 28 U.S.C. §1343(4) as creating federal jurisdiction for granting damages under §1982 have held that damages and equitable relief are available. 517 F.2d 1141 (4th Cir. 1975).

11. Compare Gonzales v. Carhart, 127 S. Ct. 1610 (2007), with Stenberg v. Carhart, 530 U.S. 914 (2000).

12. See Runyon v. McCrary, 427 U.S. 160, 189-192 (1976) (Stevens, J., concurring).

property values in the black community for the benefit of the white neighborhood.[13]

The Supreme Court granted certiorari to City of Memphis v. Greene to investigate the standard of intent required to show discrimination under §1982 and the Thirteenth Amendment, but found it unnecessary to reach that issue, holding that black citizens did not suffer a significant property injury by the closure.[14] Justice Marshall, joined by Justices Brennan and Blackmun, dissented strongly, arguing that the Court ignored evidence of historic segregation in Memphis, that there was evidence of discriminatory intent in this situation, and that the erection of a barrier to carve out racial enclaves within a city is precisely the kind of injury that §1982 and the Thirteenth Amendment were enacted to prevent.

Greene attracted a good deal of comment in the law reviews, and few have found much to commend in it. The gentlest criticisms focus on the Court's failure to establish an intent standard for §1982 and Thirteenth Amendment cases.[15] The decision, the first §1982 case heard by the Court since 1973, represented an ominous retreat from the liberal scope of §1982 envisioned by cases like *Tillman* and *Jones*.[16] Though the opinion did not reach the issue of intent, it seemed to set the stage for a requirement that plaintiffs prove intentional discrimination in §1982 cases.[17] The Court majority gave little weight to the injury and inconvenience suffered by the black community because of the barrier, and its refusal to take into account evidence of historic[18] and contemporary[19] discrimination by the city of Memphis. As one commentator put it, the *Greene* decision may become the

13. City of Memphis v. Greene, 451 U.S. 100, 102 (1981); 610 F.2d 395, 396-400 (6th Cir. 1979).

14. Compare the result in Evans v. Tubbe, 657 F.2d 661 (6th Cir. 1981). Evans was one of several landowners who relied on a road running through Tubbe's land to reach their property. Tubbe erected a gate across the road and gave a key to all white landowners but refused to give a key to Evans, who is black. The Sixth Circuit held that the maintenance of such a barrier on racial grounds was an incident of slavery under §1982. This may have been an injury of greater magnitude than that in *Greene*, but similar interests were involved.

15. Comment, City of Memphis v. Greene: A Giant Step Backwards in the Area of Civil Rights Enforcement. 48 Brooklyn L. Rev. 621, 622 (1982).

16. See Note, Civil Rights — Racial Discrimination and Property Rights — the Scope of 42 U.S.C. §1982, 29 Wayne L. Rev. 203 (1982).

17. Comment, Dead-end Street: Discrimination, the Thirteenth Amendment, and Section 1982, City of Memphis v. Greene, 58 Chi.-Kent L. Rev. 873, 904 (1982). The Comment analyzes Washington v. Davis, *Arlington Heights*, and *Greene* as a trio representing a shift away from broad construction of the Civil Rights Act of 1866.

18. Id. at 895.

19. Casenote, Constitutional Law — Civil Rights — Memphis Street Closing: Minimal Inconvenience or Monument to Racial Hostility?, 22 Santa Clara L. Rev. 931, 941 (1982). While discrimination in Memphis, as in the rest of the country, is not as obvious as it was 20 years ago, signs of it remain prominent. Although Memphis has a black mayor and the majority of both the city council and the school board is black, 40 percent of African Americans in Memphis live below the poverty line (compared with only 8 percent of whites); only 12 percent of blacks in Memphis have professional careers, and 68 percent are in service positions. See Jan Crawford Greenburg. Memphis Blues: Slow Progress Despite Gains, Racism Remains an Obstacle, Chi. Trib., Sept. 3, 1996, at 1, WL 2704411. Additionally, as in many areas, combating racism has become an issue of increasing profits for white businesses rather than one of decreasing black poverty. While this tactic may get more white people involved in the problem, it is unlikely to come up with solutions for those who most need them.

"prototype of facially neutral actions used as smokescreens to cloak discrimination."[20]

The Supreme Court seems to have decided not that there was no injury to black residents, but, as in so many other areas of racial conflict, including electoral districts, seniority policies, and educational testing, that such injury must be borne if it arguably can be explained on some racially neutral ground. Even when, as in *Greene*, the discriminatory intent seems palpable, one reads an unspoken concern that, some other time, in some other case, blacks might be able to thwart some legitimate municipal policy decision because of its adverse impact on them. It is this fear and the complex, unspoken but generally accepted reasoning out of which the fear emanates, that civil rights advocates view as posing a barrier to racial equality far more massive than anything erected on a Memphis city street.

Despite its usefulness, §1982 has not been used to combat housing discrimination in the same way as §1981 has been used in the employment setting. Several factors have contributed to the lack of legal action in this area, and many of those factors spill over into litigation under fair housing laws. The need for housing is generally immediate, and the pool of available housing tends to be large enough so that those turned away from a specific place will find alternate housing quickly rather than sue the discriminating landlord or owner. Further, people often do not realize that they have been discriminated against, as many factors play into the decision to sell or rent housing. Additionally, the historical difficulty in getting large damage awards[21] has prevented attorneys from pursuing most housing discrimination cases.[22] These factors, coupled with the national apathy toward the need for adequate housing and toward discrimination in the housing context have led to few cases under §1982. Thus, the law has not been the equalizer in the housing field that proponents thought it would be once the state action requirement was removed.

§7.5 Racism Hypo: Town and Country Fair Housing, Inc. v. RIGHT ON Home Mortgage Co.

A group of black realtors and savings and loan companies have organized a special home-financing plan called the Righteous in Getting Homes Together Organization for Negroes (RIGHT ON). The purpose of the organization, as explained by its founders, is to assist black families living in the ghetto to finance the purchases of homes. The persons eligible for financial assistance are generally stable individuals with low- to middle-incomes, good credit, and steady jobs. They generally are unable to obtain mortgage loans through the usual channels, because of very high qualifying standards for such loans, and also because of obvious, but almost impossible to prove, racial discrimination, much of it of the "institutional" character.

---

20. 48 Brooklyn L. Rev. at 641.
21. See §7.7.
22. See Victoria A. Roberts, With a Handshake and a Smile: The Fight to Eliminate Housing Discrimination, 73 Mich. B.J. 276 (1994).

The RIGHT ON Financing Company has been operating for about three years, during which time it has assisted hundreds of black families in obtaining mortgage loans at reasonable rates. It should be said that all the mortgage loans made are secured by guarantees from a major foundation, and there is, thus, little risk of serious loss to the participants in the mortgage operation. Officers of RIGHT ON have generally received the approbation of the community as well as the lasting appreciation of the black families they have helped.

The membership of Town and Country Fair Housing, or T&C Inc. as they are usually called, is not counted among RIGHT ON's admirers. For two decades, T&C Inc. (an integrated, volunteer group) has worked untiringly to break down biased housing policies. They advise and assist persons seeking integrated housing, serve as testers to verify complaints of discrimination, lobby for legislation, support builders seeking to construct low and moderate income housing in the suburbs, and fight assiduously against realtors who practice blockbusting, steering, and other policies that they deem anti-integration.

After a lengthy investigation and some fruitless negotiation, T&C has concluded that RIGHT ON's lending policy is anti-integration and in violation of §1982. They have filed a suit on behalf of white applicants for RIGHT ON mortgages, all of whom were turned down even though they sought to purchase housing in the ghetto, and of black applicants now living in the ghetto who wished to purchase homes in all-white areas.

In a long affidavit appended to a motion to dismiss or, in the alternative, a motion for summary judgment, RIGHT ON acknowledges that they have limited their loans to blacks seeking housing in the ghetto or in changing areas. In defense of this policy, they assert that: (1) statistics show that blacks experience far more difficulty in obtaining mortgages than do whites because of "institutional racism"; (2) because of "redlining" practices of finance agencies, it is very difficult to obtain mortgages in all-black areas; (3) because the mortgage funding available to them is limited, they wish to use it in an "affirmative action" way to counteract the effects of still-prevalent discriminatory policies; (4) the RIGHT ON mortgage policy does not undermine integration or perpetuate ghettos as T&C charges. Rather, the loans enable blacks who wish to live in black neighborhoods to purchase and rehabilitate their homes. RIGHT ON argues that the creation of a strong black community, living in decent housing owned by the occupants, should not be held in violation of any civil rights law.

Law Firm A will represent T&C Inc. in a motion for a preliminary injunction.

Law Firm B will oppose the injunction and seek dismissal of the case on behalf of the RIGHT ON Home Mortgage Co.

§7.6   THE FAIR HOUSING ACT OF 1968

Section 1982, as revived in Jones v. Alfred H. Mayer Co., has provided a remedy for those victims of obvious, provable housing discrimination with the energy and resources to obtain legal assistance. But the availability of remedies for those instances of discrimination that can be proven could not be expected to alter widespread and pervasive patterns of housing discrimination. An all-encompassing and vigorously enforced government policy based on clear-cut legislation will be required for that task. Whatever its merits, Title VIII of the Civil Rights Act of 1968[1] is not that legislation.

The Act's inadequacies are not apparent in its opening "declaration of policy," which proclaims: "It is the policy of the United States to provide, within constitutional limitations, for fair housing throughout the United States."[2] In furtherance of this policy, Title VIII generally bans discrimination on grounds of race, color, religion, or national origin in the sale or rental of housing. Owners and realtors are prohibited from refusing to sell or rent covered housing or evidencing discriminatory preferences among prospective customers. Blockbusting (the creation of a panic by real estate agents and others among residents in a neighborhood who then rush to sell their property — all because one nonwhite family has moved into the area) is made illegal, and lending agencies are barred from discriminating against applicants covered in the Act.[3]

While Title VIII covers all property transactions of dwellings owned, operated, financed or otherwise insured by the federal government, single family dwellings and owner-occupied buildings of no more than four units are exempt from the act's coverage if the owner does not own more than three such single-family houses, meets other limitations set out in the Act, and does not utilize a realtor or advertise in violation of the prohibition in §3604(c).[4]

It has been suggested that under the "encouragement of racial discrimination" rubric of Reitman v. Mulkey,[5] Title VIII's exemption of private owners amounts to an abandonment of a position of government "neutrality" on the discrimination issue, and the provision is thus unconstitutional.[6] A possible response might focus on the availability to victims of housing discrimination of 42 U.S.C. §1982, which contains no exemptions. It might be argued that since Title VIII involves an administrative process, Congress restricted coverage to "institutionalized" forms of discrimination so as to provide a manageable work load. A more honest answer would concede that whatever the constitutional problems with exemption, exclusion of single-family dwelling owners (§3603(b)(1)) and the so-called "Mrs. Murphy's boarding house" exemption (§3603(b)(2)) were essential if the act was to be passed.

Nearly 40 years later, "the standard in the fair housing/fair lending arena continues to be sketchy and haphazard."[7] As in the §1982 context, courts cannot decide whether to use the "disparate impact" test or to demand intentional

---

§7.6 1. 42 U.S.C. §§3601-3619 (1994).

2. 42 U.S.C. §3601. As one commentator put it, this act "explicitly, if less than emphatically, refined a commitment Congress made more than two decades [earlier] in the Housing Act of 1949, that 'every American family' be provided 'a decent home and a suitable living environment . . . as soon as feasible.' " Spencer, Enforcement of Federal Fair Housing Law., 9 Urb. Law. 514 (1977).

3. See 42 U.S.C. §§3604-3606 (1994).

4. Id. at §3603(b).

5. 387 U.S. 369 (1967).

6. Morris & Powe, Constitutional and Statutory Rights to Open Housing, 44 Wash. L. Rev. 1, 79 (1968).

7. Peter E. Mahoney, The End(s) of Disparate Impact: Doctrinal Reconstruction, Fair Housing and Lending Law, and the Antidiscrimination Principle, 47 Emory L.J. 409, 411 (1998).

discrimination. Where disparate impact is used, the test required remains muddled, and the trend seems to be toward a strict test that demands a great deal from any potential housing discrimination plaintiff.[8]

Regardless of the test used, however, it appears that racism in the context of the Fair Housing Law has persisted, and this leads one to question whether laws are ever capable of making a dent in societal norms.[9] A case in point is the difficulty black families often have when selling their homes. While the Fair Housing Law covers sellers and realtors, it is difficult to construe the law to cover purchasers, especially before any contract has been entered. Thus, around the country, realtors will often "suggest" that black families remove art, family pictures, and other indicators of the family's race.[10] While realtors claim that they suggest to everyone trying to sell a home that they depersonalize it, blacks who need to move may have even more reason to do so, since many potential purchases are likely to be unable to picture themselves in a home owned by someone of another race. (See §7.6.1 Racism Hypo below.)

In 1988, Congress amended the FHA's authority to strengthen the government's enforcement power, in addition to its authority to investigate and settle complaints. In circumstances where no conciliation is reached, the federal agency can bring charges before an administrative law judge, who can impose penalties for discriminatory behavior.[11] However, little evidence shows that the strengthened enforcement mechanism and increased penalties have had a widespread impact on the housing market. Like most government agencies, HUD's resources are overburdened, and the system continues to rely on individual complaints. Yet, advocates like the Fair Housing Council of Greater Washington argue that the worst way to enforce the Fair Housing Act and combat housing discrimination nationwide is through private parties. To deter housing discrimination, the government needs to make the consequences for racial housing practices real, which it has yet to accomplish.

It is increasingly clear that the FHA does not adequately address the practical realities of housing discrimination. For example, in Halprin v. Prairie Single Family Homes, the Seventh Circuit held that the FHA did not prohibit post-acquisition harassment.[12] In *Halprin*, the homeowners alleged that the president of the homeowner's association and the association engaged in an ongoing campaign of harassment against the plaintiffs, including the vandalization of the plaintiffs' property by writing an ethnic slur on the wall of the plaintiffs' property, damaging trees and plants, and cutting down strings of holiday lights.[13] However, the court held that there was no cause of action under the FHA because the Act

---

8. Id. at 495-496.

9. See generally John O. Calmore, Race/ism Lost and Found: The Fair Housing Act at Thirty, 52 U. Miami L. Rev. 1067 (1998), for a discussion of the complexities involved in trying to obtain fair housing practices and integration.

10. Kevin Helliker, Hidden Roots: Some Blacks Must Hide Their Race to Sell Their Houses, San Diego Union & Trib., Apr. 19, 1998, at H2, 1998 WL 4003911.

11. Veronica Reed, Fair Housing Enforcement: Is the Current System Adequate?, in Residential Apartheid: The American Legacy 222-224 (Robert Ballard et al. eds., 1994).

12. 388 F.3d 317 (7th Cir. 2004).

13. See id. at 328.

"contains no hint either in its language or its legislative history of a concern with anything but *access* to housing."[14] As Craig Gurian, Executive Director of the Anti-Discrimination Center of Metro New York notes, this doctrine was created after HUD Regulations had been passed that specifically prohibited failing or delaying the maintenance or repair of a dwelling or limiting the "use of privileges, services or facilities associated with a dwelling," prohibitions that clearly extend beyond the acquisition of property.[15]

Another issue that has arisen in the past few years is the liability of online housing list serves under the FHA. Courts have held a variety of media outlets liable for publishing discriminatory housing advertisements, including newspapers, advertising brochures, and multiple listing services.[16] However, it is not clear to what extent a corporation may escape liability merely by offering a website on which discriminatory advertisements can be placed, unedited, by the advertiser. Of particular note is a lawsuit brought against Craigslist, Inc., a company that runs a website allowing individuals or groups to post notices for housing, items for sale, personal ads, and various other miscellaneous announcements. Craigslist's housing section allows anyone to post an advertisement announcing a unit for rent or sale, or seeking a roommate. Such advertisements often indicated a preference or limitation on the basis of race, color, religion, sex, familial status, or national origin, such as "African Americans and Arabians tend to clash with me so that won't work out," "NO MINORITIES," "Non-women of Color NEED NOT APPLY," or "Requirements: Clean Godly Christian Male."[17] In response to a suit brought by the Chicago Lawyers' Committee for Civil Rights Under the Law, Inc., the Northern District of Illinois held that Craigslist could not be held liable for the postings of third parties under the FHA and dismissed the case.[18] Specifically, the court found that Craigslist's role in the postings was not as a publisher, but merely as an "interactive computer service that serves as a conduit for information provided by another information content provider."[19] The plaintiffs are currently appealing.

§7.6.1 Racism Hypo: A Right of Racial Disclosure

Mike and Michelle Middleton, a black couple living in an upper class, mainly white community have decided to sell their home. They call in a series of real estate brokers. Each broker compliments them on the beauty of their home and

---

14. Id. at 329.

15. Craig Gurian, A Return to Eyes on the Prize: Litigating Under the Restored New York City Human Rights Law, 33 Fordham Urb. L.J. 255, 314 (2006) (citing 24 C.F.R. §100.65 (2005)).

16. See, e.g., Ragin v. New York Times Co., 923 F.2d 995, 999-1000 (2d Cir. 1991); Saunders v. Gen. Servs. Corp., 659 F. Supp. 1042, 1057-59 (E.D. Va. 1987); Wheatley Heights Neighborhood Coalities v. Jenna Resales Co., 447 F. Supp. 838, 842 n.3 (E.D.N.Y. 1978).

17. Chicago Lawyers' Committee for Civil Rights Under the Law, Inc. v. Craigslist, Inc., 06-cv-00657 (N.D. Ill. Nov. 14, 2006).

18. See id.

19. See id. (quotation marks omitted).

its immaculate condition. Each also assures them that the house will sell quickly for close to a million dollars — if they remove their family photographs and black art from the walls and arrange to be absent when the house is shown.

The realtors explain that because their home is located in a mainly white community and because most of the potential buyers will be whites, many of these people will not wish to purchase a home from blacks or will not offer top dollar for it. Some whites may view such a purchase as demeaning, the purchase of a black's hand-me-down. Others will worry about the title, assuming that the blacks must be drug dealers or otherwise engaged in illegal activity if they can afford such a fine house. Most potential purchasers will not articulate any of these reasons; they will simply wish to look elsewhere.

Insulted, the Middletons initially bridled at the realtors' requests and refused to take down their family photographs and black art. While at least a dozen white families were shown the house, no offers were made. Finally, after three months, the Middletons relented. They took down their pictures and art, and within a week a white couple, the Winthrops, submitted an offer that the Middletons accepted.

At the closing, the Middletons and Winthrops met for the first time. The Winthrops were shocked, and after a heated discussion with their lawyer, they refused to go through with the deal. They claimed misrepresentation, in that they were not told that the house was owned by blacks. They contended that the house was of less value because blacks owned it, and added that they simply would not be comfortable living there. The Middletons, having just closed on a new home the previous day, filed suit charging a breach of the purchase and sales contract and a violation of the federal Fair Housing Act.

The Winthrops countersued for return of their deposit, based on their misrepresentation claim. They asserted that their action was not discrimination covered by federal civil rights law but an exercise of a personal substantive due process right of privacy and of a right of association under the First Amendment. They asserted, too, the right of a choice to buy from a black or a white family. They had been led to believe when they made the offer that the house, located in a white neighborhood, was owned by whites. This deception was furthered by the Middletons' removal of their photos and art.

A federal trial judge sitting without a jury determined that he could not enforce the Winthrops' claim, citing Shelley v. Kraemer and Barrows v. Jackson. He thus ordered specific enforcement of the Middletons' purchase and sales agreement, but denied their request for damages under the federal Fair Housing Act, finding the Winthrops' refusal to buy did not violate that Act. The appellate court affirmed without comment, and both parties seek certiorari.

§7.7 DAMAGES FOR INTANGIBLE INJURY IN HOUSING DISCRIMINATION CASES

When compared to the astronomical awards often returned in contemporary tort cases, the relatively small recovery available to plaintiffs in housing discrimination cases until recently simply added insult to injury. Damage remedies are available under both Title VIII and §1982, and they have ranged from $14.5 million to $2.[1] Before 1988, however, 42 U.S.C. §3612(c) entitled plaintiffs to "not more than $1,000 punitive damages." The cap on punitive damages was eliminated by the Fair Housing Amendments Act of 1988.[2] The Amendments also aided individuals pursuing housing discrimination claims by making attorney's fees recoverable without regard to the plaintiff's financial status[3] and by instituting civil penalties ranging from $10,000 to $50,000 in cases enforced by the Secretary of Housing or the Attorney General.[4]

As in tort cases, financial damage resulting from the wrong is compensated. Seldom, however, does a major out-of-pocket loss in a housing discrimination case occur. Usually the real injury suffered by the plaintiffs is the deep humiliation of racial rejection that is no less painful because it is deemed to be an intangible harm. Some courts have recognized this form of injury as a compensable type of damage through awards for emotional distress or embarrassment.[5] Courts have had a relaxed standard of proof for emotional distress, permitting it to be proved by

§7.7   1. Daniel W. Barkley, Beyond the Beltway: Compensatory and Punitive Damages in Fair Housing Cases, 7-SPG J, Affordable Housing & Community Dev. L. 218 (1998), citing United States v. American Family Mut. Ins. Co., Fair Hou.-Fair Lending (P-H) 19,386 (E.D. Wis. Apr. 12, 1995) (consent decree for $5 million in monetary compensation and $9.5 million for community-based housing programs), and Fort v. White, 530 F.2d 1113 (2d Cir. 1976). Barkley points out that some awards exceed $4.5 million once the value of nonmonetary services and benefits is included. Id. at 218 n.1.

2. Pub. L. No. 100-430, 102 Stat. 1619 (codified as amended at 42 U.S.C. §§3601-3631 (1988)). Sections 3613(c)(1) and 3614(d)(1)(b) eliminate caps on punitive damages in private suits and suits brought by the Attorney General, respectively. Recognizing the critiques raised by fair housing advocates, H.R. Rep. No. 100-711 — discussing the amendments — states, [Title VIII of the Civil Rights Act of 1968] proscribes housing practices that discriminate on account of race, color, national origin or religion, but it fails to provide an effective enforcement system to make that promise a reality. This bill seeks to fill that void by creating an administrative enforcement system, which is subject to judicial review, and by removing barriers to the use of court enforcement by private litigants and the Department of Justice. The Amendments did not address criticisms focused on the ineffectiveness of relying on private individuals to police discriminatory practices. Now, however, no damage limits exist unless a plaintiff opts for an administrative adjudication. See infra.

3. 42 U.S.C. §§3613(c)(2) & 3614(d)(2).

4. 42 U.S.C. §§3612(3) & 3614(d)(1)(c).

5. Plaintiffs' reaction to the trauma involved when they are discriminated against varies widely. In Seaton v. Sky Realty Co., 491 F.2d 634 (7th Cir. 1974), the plaintiff testified that he was "humiliated . . . [and] intimidated, not only as a person but as a man. He stripped me of my right as a father to my kids." 491 F.2d at 636. The court said that the racial indignity to which Mr. Seaton was subjected "is one of the relics of slavery which 42 U.S.C. §1982 was enacted to eradicate." Id. Rather than intimidation, the experience of discrimination spurred another plaintiff to action. After repeated incidents of discrimination while seeking housing in college towns across the country, plaintiff became "very tired of it" and "upset" over such treatment and was "determined to do something about it." Steele v. Title Realty Co., 478 F.2d 380, 384 (10th Cir. 1973). The court did not construe plaintiff's reaction of vindication as a disqualification for relief for mental distress. On occasion, plaintiffs are able to show substantial damage that resulted from the mental distress caused by the discriminatory experience. In McNeil v. P-N&S, Inc., 372 F. Supp. 658 (N.D. Ga. 1973), defendant's biased action not only embarrassed plaintiffs but left them unable to find suitable housing. Forced to remain in a small apartment, they suffered great anxiety, which placed a strain on their marriage. A well-known civil rights attorney, Nathaniel S. Coley, in Civil Actions for Damages Arising out of Violations of Civil Rights, 17 Hastings L.J. 189, 201 (1965), points out that even a relatively innocuous case of discrimination in the denial of goods or services is not merely the deprivation of goods themselves but also "an abrupt, traumatic confrontation with a form of racial discrimination."

the testimony of the victim and by inference from the circumstances rather than requiring corroboration by medical testimony.[6]

Some courts have indicated that a violation of the Fair Housing Act raises a presumption of compensable harm due to humiliation.[7] Most courts, however, are less willing to see harm without proof from the victim of discrimination. Instead, most courts hold that they "may not presume emotional distress from the fact of discrimination. A plaintiff must actually prove that he suffers from emotional distress and that the discrimination caused the distress."[8] The same court also stated, however, that "The more inherently degrading or humiliating the defendant's action is, the more reasonable it is to infer that a person would suffer humiliation or distress from that action; consequently, somewhat more conclusory evidence of emotional distress will be acceptable to support an award of emotional distress."[9] Still, a plaintiff need not generally show medical evidence of emotional distress in order to recover, and some courts go farther, holding that even where no damages can be proven, nominal damages should be granted.[10] Perhaps to compensate for this relaxed standard of proof, damage awards until recently have tended to be lower than is usual in emotional distress injuries.[11] Recent cases show a trend toward more reasonable awards, although most remain in five figures.[12]

Several commentators have urged recognition that the degree of emotional damage to discrimination victims may be more severe than the level that is usually compensated.[13] It is possible that the generally low level of these damages is in part

6. See, e.g., Seaton v. Sky Realty Co. and Steele v. Title Realty Co., supra note 5.

7. Barkley, supra note 1, at 220. Barkley cites Harrison v. Otto G. Heinzeroth Mortgage Co., 430 F. Supp. 893, 897 (N.D. Ohio 1977), in which the court stated that "[c]ompensatory damages for a violation of civil rights in general must be more than nominal."

8. United States v. Balistrieri, 981 F.2d 916, 931 (7th Cir. 1992).

9. Id. at 932.

10. See Gore v. Turner, 563 F.2d 159 (5th Cir. 1977).

11. See Jay L. Lichtman, The Cost of Housing Discrimination: Assessment of Damages and Attorney's Fees for Violations of the Civil Rights Act of 1866 and the Fair Housing Act of 1968, 10 Suffolk U. L. Rev. 963, 975 (1976), where the author cites (at 967) compensatory damages awards in civil rights cases, including $500 in Seaton (supra note 5); $1,500 in Hughes v. Dyer, 378 F. Supp. 305 (W.D. Mo. 1974); $1,500 in Stevens v. Dobs, 373 F. Supp. 618 (E.D.N.C. 1974); $3,500 in Allen v. Gifford, 368 F. Supp. 317 (E.D. Va. 1973).

12. Portee v. Hastava, 853 F. Supp. 597, 614 n.9 (E.D.N.Y. 1994), provides an excellent breakdown of awards since 1988. In the case, Mr. and Mrs. Portee, an interracial couple, had been denied a rental apartment after the defendant discovered Mr. Portee was black. The jury in the case awarded general compensatory damages for emotional distress of $100,000 to Mrs. Portee, $100,000 to Mr. Portee, and $80,000 to their five-year-old son Justin. Finding $280,000 an excessive award, the court reviewed Second Circuit court decisions on emotional distress damages. The awards ranged from $500 (male denied housing because of his gender, Baumgardner v. Secretary, U.S. Dep't of Housing & Urban Dev., 960 F.2d 572 (6th Cir. 1992)) to $75,000 (victim of false arrest suffered from post-traumatic stress disorder, Rodriguez v. Comas, 888 F.2d 899 (1st Cir. 1989)). They included one award for $50,000 where the landlord made harassing phone calls to the renter at home and at work, left a note threatening the life of the white renter's black boyfriend ("By THE Time you read this message Kiss your Niger [sic] friend goodbye Bitch — he's dead!!!"), and called the renter's sister saying he was a member of the Ku Klux Klan and asking how the renter "could have [gone] to bed with a nigger." Littlefield v. McGuffey, 954 F.2d 1337 (7th Cir. 1992). In the Portee case, the court ordered a new trial on damages.

13. See, e.g., Coley, supra note 5, at 203-204; Lichtman, supra note 11, at 970-971.

due to the fact finders' lack of personal experience with this type of injury.[14] It may also be due to an effort to find a middle ground between the progressive legislation which is in some ways in advance of social realities, and the residual racism which makes it difficult to enforce such legislation fully. It is also worth noting, however, that occasionally juries are willing to grant more than the norm in compensatory damages, but courts may set them aside, being unwilling or unable to see discrimination as causing severe enough distress to warrant six figure awards, particularly without medical evidence.[15]

Ideally, courts should reconsider the nature and scope of the intangible damage to victims of discrimination. Acts of discrimination can not only cause severe momentary distress and humiliation, they can also limit an individual's freedom of action and diminish his or her self-perception as an autonomous human being and a secure and equal member of society. Damage to the autonomy and freedom of action — the badges and incidents of citizenship — is the threshold damage which always occurs in a race discrimination case, and would merit compensation greater than it has generally received.

Traditionally, emotional distress law was geared toward limiting the situations in which tort damages could be recovered in order to avoid making legal action a solution to emotional upsets in the normal interactions among people.[16] Often they were available only as "parasitic damages" when mental distress arose from the commission of some other compensable tort.[17] Even then, there has generally been a requirement that the distress for which compensation is sought be shown to be severe, often by medical testimony or accompanying physical injury.[18]

But as one commentator put it, the arguments for limiting emotional distress damages to strictly delineated categories is unpersuasive in the context of racial discrimination, a form of behavior which has been recognized as offensive to society and is likely to induce considerable distress in the victim.[19] Certainly the public policy of vindicating individual victims of housing discrimination embodied in §1982 and Title VIII, and the need for an emotional distress remedy to compensate victims for the widespread though subtle damage involved, argues against limiting relief to the most obvious and acute cases in order to weed out false claims.

While this position has gained fairly broad judicial acceptance, the cases reveal wide variation in the perception of how important such damages are, of how closely emotional distress is tied into the deprivation of rights, and of what

14. See Coley, supra note 5, at 201.

15. See *Portee*, supra note 12. See also Darby v. Heather Ridge, 827 F. Supp. 1296 (E.D. Mich. 1993) ($187,160 jury award for emotional distress lowered to $37,160 where black plaintiffs testified that they were very sad and depressed, that they suffered a loss of self-esteem, and that they did not like to be with other people anymore).

16. See generally William Prosser, The Law of Torts §11 (4th ed. 1971); Note, Torts — Mental Distress Damages for Racial Discrimination, 49 N.C. L. Rev. 221, 226 (1970).

17. Prosser, supra note 16, at §12.

18. Id.

19. Note, supra note 16. See also John Duda, Damages for Mental Suffering in Discrimination Cases, 15 Clev.-Mar. L. Rev. 1 (1966).

level of proof of emotional distress damage is required for recovery. In addition, faced with claims for emotional damage and requests for punitive damages, there is some judicial ambivalence perhaps growing out of the feeling that because racial discrimination remains widespread, it is not fair to impose large sanctions on otherwise decent people who practice discrimination without personal malice but occasionally because they feel some pressure to do so from owners, other tenants, and the community in general.

Some judges would give such arguments short shrift, but others are moved by them to adopt an "it was just one of those things" attitude. In Stevens v. Dobbs, Inc.,[20] the district judge dismissed a suit in which the defendant, after checking the plaintiff's credit, employment, and character, turned him down for the apartment he sought because he had an "offensive odor." In reversing, the court of appeals noted that beliefs that blacks have a peculiar odor have long been used to justify discrimination. On remand, the district judge found that the plaintiff had been embarrassed and humiliated by the defendant's rejection, and had been further humiliated at trial by questions concerning his personal hygiene habits. The award was $500, but a request for punitive damages was denied because the judge found that the acts complained of, "while certainly not in good taste, were not wanton, reckless, malicious, or oppressive."[21]

From the plaintiff's standpoint, the defendant's action was all of these, and once the alleged discriminatory act is proved, courts would do well to focus on the harm suffered by the plaintiff rather than to probe further into the nature of the defendant's evil that caused the harm. Civil rights statutes, after all, provide the individual with only a small degree of protection against specific forms of infringement of their autonomy and personal security. The expectation of this autonomy and security should be vindicated where it exists and fostered where it does not.[22] Judicial misunderstanding of the most basic concepts of the FHA, at least at the trial level, is so widespread, however, that plaintiffs bringing even simple housing complaints must be prepared to follow the case to the appellate level.[23] This has the effect of making every housing case a test case. Not only does this discourage plaintiffs from using the existing laws, the uncertainty inherent in such claims discourages defendants from settling before trial.

Punitive damages may also be awarded under §1982 and §3612. The standard for punitive damages in civil rights cases is the same as the standard in tort cases: malicious, willful, and wanton, or reckless or oppressive conduct. Application of the standard is somewhat uncertain, depending on the factfinder's perceptions of how malicious it is to racially discriminate. Courts have also indicated that the standard does not require a showing of malice or personal animosity in awarding punitive

20. 483 F.2d 82 (4th Cir. 1973).
21. 373 F. Supp. at 623.
22. Portions of this section were contained in an unpublished student paper by Emily Cheslow, J.D., Harvard Law School, 1979. For another critical analysis of the FHA's strengths and weaknesses, see Charles Lamb, Congress, the Courts, and Civil Rights: The Fair Housing Act of 1968 Revisited, 27 Vill. L. Rev. 1115 (1982).
23. See Woods-Drake v. Lundy, 667 F.2d 1198 (5th Cir. 1982); McDonald v. Verble, 622 F.2d 1227 (6th Cir. 1980).

damages and that reckless disregard for another's rights is sufficient.[24] The elimination of the $1,000 limit on punitive damages, coupled with a liberal standard and with fees to the government on a finding of discrimination, could help move housing discrimination legislation from simply being about compensating a harmed victim into the realm of punishing those who discriminate — thus more effectively pursuing the goals of civil rights advocates. Moreover, recent Supreme Court jurisprudence has indicated that higher ratios between punitive and compensatory damages may be permissible where "a particularly egregious act has resulted in only a small amount of economic damages."[25]

Also, an important consideration in private housing discrimination claims is the availability of attorneys' fees. Before the 1988 Amendments, only those who demonstrated financial need could obtain attorneys' fees from the defendant, even where the defendant lost on the merits. As stated by one commentator,

> The former provision had the unfortunate effect of discouraging litigation by imposing the cost of FHA enforcement upon those most likely to encounter discrimination. Minority homeseekers who were income eligible for middle class housing, and more likely than poorer minorities to seek housing in white neighborhoods and encounter discrimination, were forced to subsidize enforcement of the law under this provision.[26]

The Civil Rights Attorney's Fees Act of 1976[27] increased the chances that federal claimants, particularly those who could include a §1982 claim with their FHA claim, would receive attorneys' fees, thus making litigation somewhat more viable for middle-class minorities.[28] But it was not until the 1988 Amendments eliminated the financial need requirement on Title VIII FHA claims that attorneys could depend on fees in the event of successful litigation. Again, this provision displays Congress's increased willingness to encourage private litigation in housing discrimination and to actively punish violators of the FHA. In some state courts, however, plaintiffs still run the risk of having to pay the costs of their own litigation, even where they are victorious on the merits.[29]

Despite the 1988 Amendment to the Fair Housing Act, the dual goals of discouraging discrimination and of creating integrated housing have not been met. Violators often simply receive a fine, which some realtors and owners can simply roll into the cost of doing business. Some commentators have suggested that increasing judicial use of injunctive relief in connection with FHA claims, while

24. United States v. Tropic Seas, Inc., 887 F. Supp. 1347, 1365 (D. Haw. 1995); Miller v. Apartments & Homes of N.J., Inc., 646 F.2d 101, 112 (3d Cir. 1981); Gore v. Turner, 563 F.2d 159, 164 (5th Cir. 1977); Fountila v. Carter, 571 F.2d 487, 491 (9th Cir. 1978).

25. State Farm Mut. Auto. Ins. v. Campbell, 538 U.S. 408, 410 (2003).

26. Margalynne Armstrong, Desegregation through Private Litigation: Using Equitable Remedies to Achieve the Purposes of the Fair Housing Act, 64 Temp. L. Rev. 909, 924 n.82 (1991).

27. 42 U.S.C.A. §1988 (1983).

28. See Price v. Pelka, 690 F.2d 98 (6th Cir. 1982); Williams v. City of Fairburn, 640 F.2d 635 (5th Cir. 1981) (plaintiff who obtained desired relief in pretrial settlement entitled to attorneys' fees as prevailing party).

29. See, e.g., Miles v. F.E.R.M. Enters., Inc., 29 Wash. App. 61, 627 P.2d 564 (1981) (trial court refused to grant attorney's fees where jury found that the defendant had discriminated but returned a verdict of no damages).

not a perfect solution, may help further integrate the nation's housing stock and thus decrease future discrimination.[30]

Margalynne Armstrong suggests both temporary and permanent injunctions to aid integration of housing. Temporary injunctions provide a means for those who have been discriminated against to place a hold on the housing they desire. Because housing often moves quickly, landlords, sellers, and realtors are often able to dispose of the disputed property before litigation even begins. Thus, the plaintiff is unable to obtain the housing, and the only penalty involved is a fine. Temporary injunctions provide a means for the plaintiff to hold on to the space (or possibly the landlord's next available space) until the litigation is decided and have the added effect of further punishing the defendant by reducing the income from any possible sale or rental.

Even more potentially useful are permanent injunctions, which could be used in a wide variety of ways to enforce integrated housing and nondiscriminatory real estate practices. Armstrong suggests that injunctions should be used to compel affirmative action by proven discriminators. She points out that "[b]ecause the essence of racially discriminatory behavior is that the victim's individual identity is irrelevant to the perpetrator, the victim's individuality should not shelter the discriminator from effective fair housing violation sanctions."[31]

Even if injunctive relief is available, plaintiffs must find a place to live during the process of litigation. Once alternative, acceptable housing has been found, a court order offering the plaintiffs the original space will not be of much help. Thus, the plaintiff does not serve to integrate the defendant's housing, and because no other injunction has been issued, the housing will generally remain segregated. Armstrong recommends injunctions that require the discriminator to hold the space for applicants of the plaintiff's minority group. As she puts it, this "removes the incentive to gamble that any individual plaintiff will acquire other housing prior to the judgment."[32] Injunctions of this sort not only serve to integrate the discriminator's housing, but they also open up one more unit of housing for people in the minority group, who generally have fewer housing options than do whites. Additionally, injunctions could be issued to multiple violators to integrate their entire housing stock. In a housing market increasingly dominated by large corporations with multiple properties, these types of injunctions could be extremely effective in integrating large portions of the housing market relatively quickly.

Further, Armstrong suggests that discriminating realtors should not be exempt from injunctions. Rather than allowing them simply to consider fines as a cost of doing business, realtors could "be required to engage in 'corrective steering,' whereby they affirmatively seek and recruit minority purchasers/renters for housing in areas that have traditionally excluded minorities."[33] Realtors could also be required to show plaintiffs who have lost housing in a specific area other housing in the same area. Also, and perhaps most dramatically, Armstrong suggests that realtors who have proven to be discriminatory could be required to

---

30. The following section relies heavily on Armstrong, supra note 26, at 925-935.
31. Armstrong, supra note 26, at 931.
32. Id.
33. Id. at 933.

provide neighborhood education about fair housing laws and the benefits of deseg-regation. Since realtors are often in the best position to educate sellers and land-lords, such a requirement could further diminish the amount of discrimination occurring in segregated areas.

Professor Armstrong's injunctive recommendation is interesting but overly optimistic, given courts' reluctance to grant more than minimal damages in the face of clear and humiliating discrimination.

Note: Limiting Punitive Damages; Silencing Defendants

District courts often deny plaintiffs punitive damages in housing discrimina-tion cases under the FHA when no other damages are granted.[34] In doing so, these courts act without clear guidance from the circuit courts, which have either yet to determine the issue or put forth a clear interpretation of Congress's intent concerning punitive damages under the FHA.[35] This fact surprises proponents of awarding punitive damages because congressional history appears to favor such awards even in the absence of damages. For example, in amending the FHA in 1988, Congress was concerned that a lack of enforcement resulted in no serious progress in eliminating housing discrimination.[36] One factor noted by Congress was that the $1,000 cap on punitive damages failed to serve as an effective deterrent to discrimination.[37] Thus, the amendment eliminated this stat-utory limit and permitted courts to award both punitive and actual damages to housing discrimination plaintiffs.

Under other civil rights statutes, the Supreme Court has held that punitive damages should be permitted even in the absence of other damages.[38] In Smith v. Wade,[39] the Court looked to the intent of 42 U.S.C. §1983 and common law prin-ciples to permit an award of punitive damages to an incarcerated youthful offender.[40] Under Title VII of the Civil Rights Act of 1964, the Supreme Court also allowed punitive damages in Kolstad v. American Dental Association[41] for intentional dis-crimination in an employment action.[42] Again looking to common law doctrine, the Court found that such an award should be based on "a defendant's motive or intent."

However, circuit courts are split as to whether the FHA permits punitive damages in situations when neither nominal nor compensatory damages are awarded. The Third Circuit has found such an award can be granted and that barring a punitive award in the absence of other damages would fail to give effect to the plain language of the FHA and other civil rights statutes.[43] However, the

---

34. Timothy J. Moran, Punitive Damages in Fair Housing Litigation: Ending Unwise Restric-tions on a Necessary Remedy, 36 Harv. C.R.-C.L. L. Rev. 279, 283 (2001).
35. Id. at 284.
36. Johanna M. Lounger, Capstones: A Weakened Enforcement Power: The Fifth Circuit Lim-its Punitive Damages Under the Fair Housing Act in Louisiana Acorn Fair Housing v. LeBlanc, 46 Loy. L. Rev. 1325 (2000).
37. Moran, supra note 34, at 280.
38. Moran, supra note 34, at 290.
39. 461 U.S. 30 (1983).
40. Id.
41. 527 U.S. 526 (1999).
42. Id.
43. See Alexander v. Riga, 208 F.3d 419 (2000).

Fourth Circuit in People Helpers Foundation, Inc. v. Richmond[44] has held that punitive damages may not be granted in the absence of actual damages. Doing so, the court felt, would permit potential monetary windfalls for plaintiffs in future cases.[45] Similarly, in Louisiana Acorn Fair Housing v. LeBlanc, the Fifth Circuit vacated an award for punitive damages under the FHA.[46] In *LeBlanc*, an African American resident of Lake Charles, Gene Lewis, sued a private landlord who refused to rent an apartment to him because of the color of his skin. When Mr. Lewis answered by phone an ad to rent a one-bedroom apartment, the owner stated that he would hold the apartment for him if he brought a deposit at the time when he viewed the apartment. When Lewis attempted to offer the deposit, the owner responded that he "don't rent to you people."[47] When Lewis asked him to explain the comment, LeBlanc replied, "Black, colored, negro, whatever you call yourself, I don't rent to y'all."[48] A jury found for Mr. Lewis and granted a $10,000 award in punitive damages. But the Fifth Circuit overturned this award on the basis that it did not accompany other damages. Because the Fifth Circuit only permits punitive damages to be granted in the absence of other damages where there is a constitutional violation, the Fifth Circuit has allowed such damages to be recovered in a housing discrimination action taken pursuant to Section 1982.[49]

With holdings similar to that of *LeBlanc*, landlords have virtually no incentive to change their racist behavior. Academics argue that punitive damages are necessary to enforce civil rights statutes, especially the FHA.[50] Housing discrimination is difficult to prove, and actual damages are often not calculable. As a result, the actual harms of housing discrimination cannot be captured in these cases, and landlords can get away with the behavior. Without punitive damages awards, the statute would essentially offer no recourse for changing discriminatory behavior. Consequently, Congress removed the cap on punitive damages in 1988 when the FHA was amended. In addition, attorneys and plaintiffs facing difficult cases would have little incentive to file cases under the FHA if punitive damages cannot be awarded without other awards. Punitive damages are particularly important for providing such incentives to private parties and the private bar because under resourced government programs cannot meet the demands of plaintiffs with housing discrimination claims to properly enforce the statute.

Another potential source of confusion is the type of conduct that can support an award of punitive damages. Several circuits have adopted in the context of the FHA the standard outlined in Kolstad v. American Dental Association, which held

---

44. 12 F.3d 1321 (4th Cir. 1993).

45. This holding has not been followed by other circuits in subsequent housing discrimination cases, but the Second Circuit followed the Fourth Circuit's *LeBlanc* analysis in the employment context under Title VII and Section 1981.

46. 211 F.3d 298 (5th Cir. 2000). The Supreme Court denied certiorari.

47. Id. at 299-300.

48. Id.

49. Hog v. Sealer, 588 F.2d 284 (5th Cir. 1977). Professor Moran argues that since both statutes are silent on the punitive damages question, the Fifth Circuit should have applied the same holding to both cases. Moran, supra note 34, at 310, nn.175-176.

50. See Moran, supra note 34; Lounger, supra note 36. See also Justin W. Ristau, Should Punitive Damages Be Recoverable Absent a Finding of Actual Damages Under the Federal Fair Housing Act?, 70 U. Cin. L. Rev. 343 (2001).

that an award of punitive damages under Title VII did *not* require a showing of egregious or outrageous discrimination.[51] However, *Kolstad* left open to question the precise mental state that *is* required. The Court compared the standard to the requirement that defendants act with "knowledge of falsity or reckless disregard for the truth" and concluded that, for punitive damages to be awarded, "an employer must at least discriminate in the face of a perceived risk that its actions will violate federal law."[52] This requirement means that intentional discrimination will not give rise to punitive damages liability where "the employer may simply be unaware of the relevant federal prohibition" or "discriminates with the distinct belief that its discrimination is lawful."[53] Basing an award of punitive damages on a defendant's knowledge of the law creates perverse incentives for defendants. Defendants may seek to insulate themselves from potential punitive damages by insulating themselves from knowledge of the law; to the extent that they remain liable for any compensatory damages, such damages may be minor costs of doing business. Those defendants that do hire attorneys may do so in order to be mis-informed, creating a defense that they were merely improperly informed about whether their actions were legal. This gives an advantage to those who choose to shelter themselves from their legal responsibilities. A system that awards punitive damages for knowledge that their actions may cause *harm*, on the other hand, targets reckless discriminatory conduct without providing an incentive for defen-dants to shirk their obligations to understand the laws prohibiting discrimination.[54]

Another issue *Kolstad* raises is that of the liability of the defendants who employ agents that engage in discriminatory conduct. *Kolstad* departed from the general agency principal law as outlined in the Restatement of Agency.[55] The Restatement of Agency had allowed punitive damages to be imposed on a principal only where: (a) the principle authorized the doing and the manner of the act; (b) the agent was unfit and the principal was reckless in employing him; (c) the agent was employed in a managerial capacity and was acting in the scope of employment; or (d) the principal or a managerial agent of the principal ratified or approved the act.[56] *Kolstad* narrowed the limited circumstances where a principal may be held liable even further, holding that, "in a punitive damages context, an employer may not be vicariously liable for the discriminatory employment decisions of manage-rial agents where these decisions are contrary to the employer's 'good faith efforts to comply with Title VII.' "[57] This standard allows employers to escape *all* liability for punitive damages if they put forth evidence of a good faith effort to comply with

51. See *Kolstad*, 527 U.S. at 536-539; see also United States v. Space Hunters, Inc., 429 F.3d 416, 427-28 (2d Cir. 2005); Lincoln v. Case, 340 F.3d 283, 290-292 (5th Cir. 2003); Preferred Properties, Inc. v. Indian River Estates, Inc., 276 F.3d 790, 800 (6th Cir. 2002); Badami v. Flood, 214 F.3d 994, 997 (8th Cir. 2000); *Alexander*, supra note 43, at 430-431.

52. *Kolstad*, supra note 51, at 536.

53. Id. at 536-537.

54. This discussion is based on a discussion with Craig Gurian as to the workings of *Kolstad* in the litigation practice.

55. In the context of non-punitive damages, the Supreme Court has held that normal agency-principal rules apply when holding an employer liable for an agent's action under the FHA. See Meyer v. Holley, 537 U.S. 280 (2003).

56. See id. at 542-543.

57. See id. at 545.

antidiscrimination laws. Another approach, not discussed by the *Kolstad* Court, would involve holding employers liable for punitive damages under the already narrow rules of the Restatement, but allowing evidence of good faith effort to comply with antidiscrimination laws to act as a mitigating factor in the determination of their liability. This allows a more considered approach of the extent to which the employer made efforts to prevent the discriminatory action rather than giving employers a free pass based on any such efforts.

§7.8   Racism Hypo: Trudy Trustwell v. Have-A-Hart Realty Co.

It was like a dream come true. Trudy Trustwell had opened with a sense of foreboding the large envelope with the impressive return address, "Harvard Law School, Cambridge, Mass. 02138." But her years of work and sacrifice were returning a most welcome dividend. The letter informed Trudy that she had been admitted to the Harvard Law School class for the following fall. Now she was indeed on her way to achieving her goal of becoming a lawyer and eventually a law school professor.

Ambitions on this order are hard for anyone to fulfill, but for a black woman raised in a small, Midwestern town, the obstacles appeared insurmountable. But this black woman had read and been enthralled by Holmes's *The Common Law* at age 12 and had set her career plans at about that time. In addition, Trudy had received tremendous help and inspiration from her father, a self-taught man who had read widely in philosophy during his long runs as a Pullman car porter. He had instilled in her his belief that anyone in this country could go as high as his talents and efforts would take him.

"You cannot," he would often tell her, "blame failure on racism. There are good and bad in all races, and every person is a child of God."

In keeping with this belief, there was much Bible reading in the Trustwell home, but no discussion of racial issues. An early exception came when Trudy, at age 9, returned from her first trip to summer camp. The girls there, she told her father, had been discussing the countries from which their parents had come. They had decided that Trudy, with her long black hair and rich brown complexion, must be a descendent of Polynesians. Judy had asked her father whether the girls were correct.

"You come from people who belonged to many races," her father replied simply, "but I doubt that there were any Polynesians among them." Trudy accepted the answer and no more was said on the subject. Even on that dreadful day, only a few weeks after she received the admissions letter from Harvard, he didn't mention race. He had been cheered by the Harvard news, though a long illness had taken away his once-boundless energy.

"Don't forget, Trudy," he told her. "You are God's child and can achieve whatever you decide to do. Choose well." A few hours later, Mr. Trustwell died.

Arriving in Cambridge a week before her first-year classes were scheduled to begin, Trudy found the usual expensive, tight housing market typical of college communities. She also found racial discrimination. Convinced after several days of fruitless searching that she could not find an apartment on her own,

Trudy called the Have-A-Hart Realty Company, responding to their ads in the college paper promising "Special Spaces For Special People."

Two days later, after another long and unsuccessful day of apartment searching in a drenching rain, Trudy found a phone message reporting that Have-A-Hart had found her a small apartment. She was delighted, and after returning the call and obtaining more details, she was certain that her search was over. She provided the agent with information for credit and reference checking purposes, and arranged to see the apartment on the following day.

When Trudy awoke, it was still raining, and she had sniffles and a splitting headache. She called and explained her reluctance to go out in the bad weather to Sandra Hauphstead, another entering law school student whom she had met on the apartment search circuit. Sandra seemed amazed that Trudy had gotten so quick a response from the real estate agency, but she promised to keep Trudy's appointment and reported back later that it was the perfect place, and that Trudy was lucky to get it.

The credit and reference checks were completed, Trudy signed and returned the lease by mail, and on the day before classes began, she moved into the apartment which proved to have everything she had hoped for, including a view of the Charles River.

"If my good fortune continues," Trudy thought as she reviewed her preparations for her first day's classes, "I am certain to do well here." But her good fortune ended with a heavy knock on the door late that evening.

"Where is the Trudy Trustwell who rented this apartment?" Trudy had opened the door to find a large, heavy-set man so angry that he didn't identify himself as Harold A. Hart.

"I am Trudy Trustwell. I signed the lease. Who are you?"

"Trustwell was a blond," the man sputtered. "You are not blond, but black, and you will have to get out of this apartment immediately."

The man's anger frightened Trudy.

"But I am Trudy Trustwell," she repeated. "I signed a year lease, and if you don't leave immediately, I'll call the police."

"If you do, it will simply save me the trouble. My company manages this building. We are careful about our tenants. I agreed to lease this place to a young white woman with impeccable credentials. I most certainly didn't lease it to you."

"Here." Trudy reached into her handbag. "My driver's license and my copy of the lease. You can see the picture is me, and the signatures on the license and on the lease are identical." Harold Hart glanced at the documents just long enough to see that Trudy's description was correct. The realization added a dimension of panic to his fury.

"Go live with your own kind," he screamed at her. "You tricked me, but I'll be damned if you'll turn tricks in my building. Your lease is worthless. I want you out of here. And I want you out now."

Sooner than he could have known, Hart came to regret his angry attack. He said later that he had been forced to leave his own child's birthday party to respond to several calls from long-term tenants in the building, all of whom expressed dismay and indignation at the "change" in the building's rental policy.

Trudy's years of growing up in isolation from racial discrimination left her ill prepared for Hart's insulting and racially derogatory language. She was hurt too deeply either to fight back or to cry. Her only option, or so it seemed then, was to pack her belongings and leave as Hart had ordered. Her efforts lacked direction, and it seemed she had lost all her strength. Trudy's silence and ineffective packing efforts finally got to Hart.

"I am sorry this happened, Miss." He relaxed his menacing, arms-folded stance in the still-open doorway.

"It's the tenants here. They are terribly afraid of narcotics and crime. You understand? Can I take you anywhere? I'll return your rent and security deposit tomorrow."

Trudy hardly heard Hart. She certainly didn't answer him. She picked up the phone, but there was no one she could call at this hour. The great weight that had inhibited her packing grew heavier, pressing until she collapsed.

Trudy spent the first few days of her law school career in the university hospital. After her release, she was unable to read her assignments or the class notes that the black students' association brought to her until three weeks later. She did not feel able to attend classes until yet another week later. While Trudy qualified for the free mental health program offered by the university, she felt embarrassed by her reaction and did not seek further medical assistance after she left the hospital. Trudy will now be able to complete the academic year, but her teachers doubt that her performance will equal the high standards they had predicted on the basis of her A-average college grades and almost perfect score on the Law School Admissions Test.

By the time Trudy left the hospital, Sandra Hauphstead had found her a new, albeit more expensive, apartment, and a lawyer with experience in the civil rights field. Based on a thorough investigation of the facts, the lawyer has filed a civil action against the Have-A-Hart Company, charging them with violating Trudy's civil rights as protected by §1982 and §712 of Title VIII. The suit seeks injunctive relief (including holding the next available apartment at the rent Trudy would have paid on the original apartment and gradual integration of all of Have-A-Hart's properties), $5,000 in out-of-pocket expenses (including medical costs), $200,000 in damages for emotional distress, and $20,000 in punitive damages.

Hart had expected that his actions, which he admitted were "precipitous," might result in a lawsuit. He had even talked to the company lawyer about a settlement. The lawyer urged him to resist the suit. A good defense, he pointed out, could be based on a contention that the apparent fraud, and not racial discrimination, had evoked Hart's wrath and led to the eviction. Moreover, the lawyer added, little precedent existed for damages exceeding more than a few thousand dollars for emotional distress in a civil rights case. The lawyer also suggested that, later in the litigation process, they could offer to settle for a small dollar amount and consent to the injunction, which would not cost Hart much money. If awarded, the full money judgment would put Hart on the edge of bankruptcy. The company's insurance did not cover liability for intentional torts.

Hart has decided to seek further advice from a downtown law firm. After reviewing the facts and the applicable law, this firm recommends that Hart attempt a settlement by offering as large a cash award as his company can afford. They suggest that this will not only end the litigation, which has the possibility of bankrupting Hart in light of recent jury awards higher than those typical in the past, but will also avoid the hassle and tenant resentment he would face under the injunction.

To help him decide, Hart has scheduled a conference at which both the "stand fast" arguments of the company lawyer and the "settle at any cost" position of the downtown firm will be represented.

Student A will present the arguments in support of the company lawyer position.

Student B will present the arguments available to the downtown law firm.

As an alternative, assume that Hart has offered a settlement of a consent decree regarding the firm's discriminatory policies, and $25,000 to cover all damages, together with a reasonable sum for attorney's fees and court costs. A conference then can be held in which Trudy's lawyer urges taking the case to trial, and a committee of law school teachers urges acceptance of the settlement offer.

§7.9 FEDERAL FAIR HOUSING LAW AND THE "STANDING" ISSUE

Both §1982 and Title VIII are intended to provide relief to individuals who have been the victims of housing discrimination. With few exceptions, courts have interpreted these statutes liberally. The opinions provide a sense that courts recognize housing bias as a serious evil and that, because of Title VIII's weak enforcement provisions and the government's woefully inadequate staff, enforcement of both laws must rely on legal action initiated by the victims or those, including whites, who represent them. The issues in these cases fall into now-predictable categories, but one that has created perhaps more than its share of litigation is the issue of standing to sue.

In Trafficante v. Metropolitan Life Insurance Co.,[1] a group of white tenants, who charged that defendant owner's racially discriminatory policy "stigmatized" them in a white ghetto and denied them the benefits of being in an integrated community, were held by the District Court to lack standing to sue under both §1982 and the Fair Housing Act of 1968. The Fourth Circuit affirmed on the basis that the acts were limited to the direct victims of discriminatory housing practices.

The Supreme Court reversed, Justice Douglas wrote that the definition of "persons aggrieved" in Title VIII, §810(a), is defined broadly as "any person who claims to have been injured by a discriminatory housing practice." Noting both that compliance with the act depends primarily on complaints by private persons, and that HUD has no enforcement powers and its Civil Rights division has less than two dozen lawyers, he concluded that Congress intended coverage to extend to tenants of the housing unit that is charged with discrimination. Again, the Court emphasized the important role of complainants as "private attorneys general."[2]

§7.9 1. 409 U.S. 205 (1972).

2. The *Trafficante* decision represents one of several instances in which the Supreme Court has granted whites standing, the effect of which was to protect the rights of blacks to nondiscrimination in the housing field. This tendency parallels the advance of equal rights for women. In those cases, men have often been the plaintiffs in test cases, pointing out that even when oppressed minorities make

Trafficante left open the question of whether the "persons aggrieved" language of §810[3] suits could be interpreted to cover indirect victims of housing discrimination who came into federal court under §812, which does not contain the "persons aggrieved" language. In Gladstone v. Village of Bellwood,[4] the Court decided that §§810 and 812 provide alternative remedies to precisely the same class of plaintiffs, and that standing under §812, like that under §810, is as broad as is permitted by Article III, as described in *Trafficante.*

In the *Gladstone* case, one black and four white residents of Bellwood, the Village itself, and a black resident of a neighboring town, filed a §812 suit against two realty firms charging that they had violated §804 by "steering" prospective black homeowners to houses in a specified 12 by 13 block, the integrated "target" area of Bellwood, and by "steering" white customers away from this area. The Village claimed that these practices had resulted in the wrongful manipulation of its housing market to the detriment, both economic and social, of its citizens. The individual plaintiffs said they had been "deprived of the social and professional benefits of living in an integrated society." Prior to filing suit, each of these plaintiffs had served as "testers" of the realtors' policies. That is, they had presented themselves as potential home buyers to obtain proof of the realtors' steering policies.[5]

In ruling for plaintiffs, Justice Powell first reviewed the Court's basic standing policies, particularly as set out in Warth v. Seldin.[6] Standing involves both constitutional limitations on federal court jurisdiction, and prudential limitations on its exercise. As to the former, Article III requires a plaintiff to show that there is a case or controversy between him or herself and the defendant resulting from some actual or threatened injury suffered by plaintiff as a result of the alleged illegal

---

progress in our society, it is partially due to the willingness of members of the majority to fight on their behalf. The society is more willing to grant relief to men seeking to enter traditionally women's schools and to white people who have sued to integrate housing than to acknowledge an independent right of women and racial minorities to be equal to the majority. Lower courts have also permitted whites to assert racial bias charges against other whites. In Walker v. Pointer, 304 F. Supp. 56 (N.D. Tex. 1969), jurisdiction under §1982 was extended to whites who suffer racial discrimination because of their association with blacks. Two white college students, who had been evicted because they entertained blacks in their apartment, were able to obtain compensatory damages for loss and damage to personal property and exemplary damages for being evicted in a malicious manner. The court alternatively upheld its exercise of jurisdiction as protecting the freedom of blacks to come and go at the invitation of whites lawfully in control of their property.

3. Section 810(a) begins, "Any person who claims to have been injured by a discriminatory housing practice or who believes that he will be irrevocably injured by a discriminatory housing practice that is about to occur (hereafter 'person aggrieved') may file a complaint with the Secretary. . . ." 42 U.S.C. §3610(a).

4. 441 U.S. 91 (1979).

5. The mechanics of testing are fairly simple. A minority tester (or actual potential buyer or renter) and a majority-group tester are matched on all relevant characteristics, such as age, income, education, and attire. They each visit a targeted apartment building or realtor within a short time of one another and ask about the availability of housing. Both testers (or sets of testers, if they go as a couple) then report on their entire experience on a standardized tester report form. If the organization conducting the testing then determines that a realtor, landlord, or building or group of buildings is discriminating, it may bring suit under *Havens.* See generally Stephen E. Haydon, A Measure of Our Progress: Testing for Race Discrimination in Public Accommodations 44 UCLA L. Rev. 1207, 1216-1217 (1997).

6. 422 U.S. 490 (1975).

conduct of the defendant. As to the latter, the Court would prefer not to decide broad social questions where no individual rights would be vindicated, and thus a plaintiff must assert an injury that is peculiar to himself or herself, or to a distinct group of which he or she is a part, rather than one shared in substantially equal measure by all or a large class of citizens. Congress, though, may expand standing to the full extent permitted by Article III.[7]

In *Gladstone*, Justice Powell, rejecting the defendant realtors' argument that Article III, as construed in *Trafficante*, provided extended standing only to suits under §810, found the argument inconsistent with the legislative history of Title VIII. Congress, he found, intended to provide *all* victims of Title VIII violations with two alternative mechanisms by which to seek redress.

As to the Village, Justice Powell said:

> The adverse consequences attendant upon a "changing" neighborhood can be profound. If petitioner's steering practices significantly reduce the total number of buyers in the Bellwood housing market, prices may be deflected downward. This phenomenon would be exacerbated if perceptible increases in the minority population directly attributable to racial steering precipitate an exodus of white residents. A significant reduction in property values directly injures a municipality by diminishing its tax base, thus threatening its ability to bear the costs of local government and to provide services. Other harms flowing from the realities of a racially segregated community are not unlikely. As we have said before, "[t]here can be no question about the importance" to a community of "promoting stable, racially integrated housing. . . ." If, as alleged, petitioners' sales practices actually have begun to rob Bellwood of its racial balance and stability, the Village has standing to challenge the legality of that conduct.[8]

The plaintiffs in *Gladstone* did not press the claim that they had standing as testers, and Justice Powell found the Bellwood residents had standing as homeowners. In Havens Realty Co. v. Coleman,[9] however, the Supreme Court recognized the standing of housing testers and housing associations to sue in their own right as injured parties. Suit was brought against a realty corporation for racial

---

7. Plaintiffs in *Warth* charged that through its zoning ordinance the defendant town officials (of Penfield, a suburb of Rochester, New York) were excluding low and moderate income persons, the effect of which was to exclude minority racial and ethnic groups, most of whom have only low or moderate incomes. The plaintiffs included: (1) nonresident racial or ethnic minority persons of low or moderate income, claiming that they would have moved to the defendant city but for its exclusionary policies barring housing they could afford; (2) City of Rochester taxpayers claiming an increased tax burden by reason of Penfield's exclusionary policies; and (3) various associations representing prospective builders and buyers of low and moderate income housing. Justice Powell responded that while allegations of indirect harm do not preclude standing, it then becomes more difficult to meet the minimum Article III requirement "to establish that, in fact, the asserted injury was the consequence of the defendant's actions, or that prospective relief will remove the harm." 422 U.S. at 505. The Rochester taxpayers were simply asserting rights of third parties said to have been excluded from Penfield. And they did not show that standing was required to prevent the violation of third parties' rights. As to the associations, they may have had standing to represent their members, NAACP v. Alabama, 357 U.S. 449 (1958), but Justice Powell held that the "association must allege that its members, or any one of them, [were] suffering immediate or threatened injury as a result of the challenged action of the sort that would make out a justiciable case had the members themselves brought suit." 422 U.S. at 511.

8. 441 U.S. at 110-111 (citations omitted).

9. 455 U.S. 363 (1982).

steering in violation of FHA §804 by one black person (Coles) who had attempted to rent, two testers (one, Coleman, was black, one was white), and HOME (Housing Opportunities Made Equal), a nonprofit housing group. The district court dismissed the testers and HOME for lack of standing, trying only Coles's claim. The Fourth Circuit reversed, finding that all plaintiffs made sufficient allegations of injury to have standing.[10]

The Supreme Court affirmed in part and reversed in part, holding that courts may not create prudential barriers to standing under §812 and that only a minimum of injury in fact is required to create standing.[11] By alleging that the realtor misrepresented facts about the availability of housing to him, the black tester gained standing. The white tester could not allege such misrepresentation, and so had no standing to sue. However, both testers had standing to assert that the defendant deprived them, as residents of the community, of the benefits of interracial association. HOME had standing to sue for damages on its own behalf through its claim that steering tactics interfered with its efforts to guide members to integrated housing. Since the *Havens* decision testing has been one of the few ways civil rights organizations could gather evidence of discrimination in the housing context. Indeed, some commentators have suggested that testing should be expanded to other public accommodations areas in order to create more definite proof that blacks are being turned away from hotels, restaurants, and employment based solely on their race.[12] As the Seventh Circuit pointed out:

> It is frequently difficult to develop proof in discrimination cases and the evidence provided by testers is frequently valuable, if not indispensable. The evidence provided by testers both benefits unbiased landlords by quickly dispelling false claims of discrimination and is a major resource in society's continuing struggle to eliminate the subtle but deadly poison of racial discrimination.[13]

The *Havens* court, however, only allowed HOME, the organization, to claim standing to sue because it demonstrated injury to itself. An organization can demonstrate this in two ways: (1) by demonstrating that it expended resources to investigate and uncover discrimination *and* that those expenditures diverted resources from other activities the organization might have otherwise performed, or (2) by demonstrating that the organization's mission was frustrated because the organization had attempted to counteract or remedy the discrimination it uncovered.[14] As Craig Gurian of the Anti-Discrimination Center of Metro New York

---

10. Coles v. Havens Realty Corp., 633 F.2d 384 (4th Cir. 1980).

11. 455 U.S. at 371. The Court indicated that it was guided by its decision in Gladstone v. Village of Bellwood, 441 U.S. 91 (1979).

12. See generally Stephen E. Haydon, A Measure of Our Progress: Testing for Race Discrimination in Public Accommodations, 44 UCLA L. Rev. 1207 (1997).

13. Richardson v. Howard, 712 F.2d 319, 321 (7th Cir. 1983). For a discussion of the ethical implications for lawyers who engage in testing, see David B. Isbell & Lucantonio N. Salvi, Ethical Responsibility of Lawyers for Deception by Undercover Investigators and Discrimination Testers, 8 Geo. J. Legal Ethics 791 (1995).

14. See Craig Gurian, Using Local and State Legislation to Preserve and Expand the Ability of Fair Housing Organizations to Prosecute the Discrimination They Uncover, Harv. L. & Pol'y Rev. Online (2007), available at http://www.hlpronline.com/Gurian.pdf.

notes, each of these paths poses unnecessary obstacles to fair housing organizations.[15] Many fair housing organizations cannot realistically engage in other activities as necessary to demonstrate a diversion of resources because "it may neither
be possible as a matter of funding, nor desirable as a matter of policy, for the
organization to do anything other than focus all of its limited resources on investigation."[16] This may also be prohibited by the fact that such organizations have
funding that is specifically earmarked for conducting testing and other investigative activities, such as United States Department of Housing and Urban Development "Private Enforcement Initiative" funds.[17] Moreover, a minority of circuits
have held that standing cannot be grounded in litigation-related expenses incurred
by the suit against the defendant.[18] It may also be difficult for organizations to
demonstrate an attempt to remedy the situation because they lack the funds to begin
remedial efforts that entail the "significant resources" expended in *Havens.*[19]

Gurian suggests that more fair housing organizations consider gaining
standing based on the deprivation of a statutorily protected right. Section
3604(d) of the FHA prohibits falsely representing to any person that a dwelling
is unavailable if the misrepresentation is based on protected class membership.
In *Havens*, the Court found that, by creating a private right of action to enforce
the prohibition on status-based misrepresentations, "Congress has thus conferred on all 'persons' a legal right to truthful information about available
housing."[20] As Gurian notes, non-profit fair housing corporations are "persons" under the FHA who act through their agents:

> A tester is unquestionably the agent of the fair housing organization, and thus, each
> time a tester is deprived of truthful information due to protected class basis, the
> organization is itself so deprived. Moreover, as the fair housing organization is the
> person that has the ongoing, institutional interest in identifying, punishing, and rem-
> edying violations of the FHA, it is the party whose interest is most substantial.[21]

Since the *Havens* case, testing and auditing to uncover housing discrimination
have proven critical devices to enforcing the FHA. (See §7.15.) Federal funding for
local testing projects permit fair housing organizations to increase their testing and
auditing capacities. Professor Veronica Reed argues that these practices of local
testing have provided a means for ferreting out and prosecuting discriminating
landlords.[22] But ultimately, FHA amendments, which strengthened its enforcement mechanisms and increased penalties against offenders, depend predominantly on private litigation for enforcement. These cases, which are in short

15. See id. at 2.
16. See id.
17. See id. at 2-3.
18. See id. at 3 (citing Spann v. Colonial Village, Inc., 899 F.2d 24, 27 (D.C. 1990)).
19. See id.
20. *Havens*, supra note 10, at 373.
21. Gurian, supra note 14, at 4-5.
22. Veronica Reed, Fair Housing Enforcement: Is the Current System Adequate?, in Residential
Apartheid: The American Legacy 225-231 (Robert Ballard et al. eds., 1994). See also Veronica Reed,
Civil Rights Legislation and the Housing Status of Black Americans: Evidence from Fair Housing
Audits and Segregation Indices, 19 Review of Black Political Economy 29 (1991).

supply given the obstacles to awarding punitive damages discussed in §7.7, will never act as a sufficient deterrent of housing discrimination. Professor Reed points to a need for greater federal action to provide the teeth that the FHA intended on creating. She advocates for an increased federal role in identifying housing discrimination and suggests that the government engage in a nationwide campaign of random testing that aims to identify and prosecute offenders.[23] She contends that "only with an ever-present threat of prosecution and the cost of discriminating outweigh[ing] any perceived benefit will equal housing opportunity become a reality in the United States."[24]

§7.10 CONTINUING SEGREGATION AND OCCUPANCY CONTROLS

While, for the lawyer and legal scholar, issues of standing may have an inherent interest that remains no matter how they are resolved, it must be said that even if the decision in Gladstone v. Village of Bellwood became the gateway for a whole host of plaintiffs alleging more or less dubious interest in housing litigation, the result would hardly change current patterns of discrimination in the sale and rental of housing. There is a lesson in this fact: Although existing laws against individual housing discrimination have teeth and can provide quick and effective relief, even if these remedies were expanded to group efforts through a more liberal reading of the rules of standing, they would not overcome the pressures that cause individual owners and realtors to maintain discriminatory practices, and that motivate suburban zoning boards and city councils to enact exclusionary policies.

It is hard-headed pragmatism and not inordinate pessimism that underlies a prediction that even the most vigorous enforcement of anti-housing discrimination laws can hardly hope to overcome the tremendous economic, social, and psychological motivations that result in a society whose residential patterns are becoming more, rather than less, racially segregated. And, as will be shown in this section, approaches to the problem that would limit the entry of blacks in a given area through "benign" policies, require, for their approval, interpretations of the fair housing laws that the courts have steadfastly refused to give when more overtly discriminatory exclusionary schemes were under attack.

§7.10.1 Downs's Middle-Class Dominance Theory

In his 1970 Senate testimony, economist Anthony Downs summarized some of the motivating factors for racial exclusion in predominantly white neighborhoods.[1] His critique, now almost four decades old, retains its relevance for a problem that has lessened but far from disappeared.

---

23. Reed, Fair Housing Enforcement, supra note 22, at 234.
24. Id.
§7.10 1. Senate Select Committee on Equal Educational Opportunity, Part 5: De Facto Segregation and Housing Discrimination 2966 (Sept. 1, 1970).

Professor Downs concedes that racism and the desire not to associate with people perceived to be in a lower class strongly motivate exclusionary practices that he would condemn as "illegitimate"; but there are, he argues, other factors at work which he deems "legitimate." For example, most middle class Americans want their children to attend schools in which the majority of students have characteristics that will be a good influence on their own children. This objective implies that children who do not possess the traits that parents like somehow will be screened out of the schools. Because screening is illegal in public schools, the parents resort to residential screening devices, the chief of which are racial discrimination and practices that raise the cost of living in the school area. He explains that the undesirable traits perceived by middle-class people to be associated with low-income people — including middle-class blacks as the cases in this chapter indicate — include relatively high crime rates, high juvenile delinquency rates, high drug addiction rates, and a high illegitimacy rate, even though most low-income people do not have these attributes. Other exclusionary motivations, according to Professor Downs, are the desire to maintain the high property value of one's home, to keep down real estate taxes, and to maintain the quality of life (e.g., safety, public comportment) in one's neighborhood — that is, a "middle-class environment." Many whites, he says, confuse ethnic and socioeconomic status because a high proportion of blacks and Latinos live in low-income households. Thus, he believes, most white parents are unwilling to send their children to schools where blacks or Puerto Ricans are a majority or even a significant minority. In such settings, whites would not dominate most aspects of school life.

Professor Downs sees what is apparently an irreconcilable conflict of interest between two major groups:

> On the one hand, the relatively established middle class has a right to protect the quality of life it has won for itself through past striving and effort. On the other hand, the presently deprived lower-income group has an equally valid right to upgrade itself by trying to gain access to many of the benefits now enjoyed mainly by members of middle- and upper-income groups. Such access requires a significant entry of low-income households into residential areas now occupied exclusively — or nearly exclusively — by middle-income and upper-income groups.[2]

He believes that the conflict can be resolved because middle-class goals do not require completely excluding members of lower-income groups, so long as middle-class dominance in the neighborhood is maintained. Emphasizing that, for a majority of middle-class Americans, the perception of race and color are relevant to the kind of neighborhood homogeneity they desire, Professor Downs, in a later book detailing an urban strategy for America,[3] argues that white insistence on what amounts to "neighborhood racial dominance" does not bar the establishment of stable, racially integrated areas.

---

2. Id. at 2976.
3. Anthony Downs, Opening Up the Suburbs 98-102 (1973).

§7.10.2 The "Tipping Point" Phenomenon

The attitude of whites who treat all nonwhites as "others" is "demeaning and unjustified," but Professor Downs asserts such white attitudes "must be recognized as real if we are to understand why residential segregation by race has persisted so strongly in the United States. . . ."[4] It is these attitudes and beliefs surrounding "others" that cause whites to move out as blacks begin to move into a previously all-white area, particularly if it is adjacent to a racial ghetto. Whites who flee are convinced the area will become all-black, because that has happened so frequently in the past. Other whites are unwilling to fill vacancies because they too are willing to move only where whites seem likely to remain the dominant majority.[5] It is this conviction on the part of current white residents of an area, and the corresponding reluctance of potential white residents, that leads inevitably to an area changing from all-white to all-black. And, just as an airliner on its take-off run reaches a "point of no return," so a neighborhood reaches a point of black occupancy that causes whites to abandon or avoid it so that all vacancies must be filled by other blacks. In housing, this point of no return is known as the "tipping point."

Professor Bruce Ackerman offers a dynamic illustration of the tipping phenomenon at work:

> Envision a 100-house neighborhood with 1 vacant unit and 99 units occupied by white families with the following characteristics: 19 white families can tolerate no black neighbors; 20 white families can live with blacks as long as they believe that there will be 2 white families for each black family; and 60 white families will remain until the black population actually reduces the white dominance to less than 2 white families for each black family. Also, assume black families are anxious to live in this neighborhood.
>
> If a black family moves into the vacant unit, 19 white families will flee the neighborhood because they have no tolerance for the presence of black families in their neighborhood. Assuming that black families fill the vacant units, another 20 white families will leave because the rapid influx of black families triggers an expectation that the neighborhood will "go black." Once these newly vacated units are filled by black families, the remaining 60 white families will abandon the neighborhood because they cannot tolerate a situation in which there are fewer than 2 white families for each black family.
>
> In the example above, 80 of the 99 white families could tolerate a substantial degree of integration, but because of the interaction of varying individual tolerances and uncontrolled expectations every white family eventually will abandon the hypothetical neighborhood. The numbers can be varied, but as long as problems of racial intolerances and uncontrolled expectations persist, interracial neighborhoods will lose their white families as the actions of the least tolerant and least stable families tip, or appear about to tip, the neighborhood to a point that is racially unacceptable to some of the more tolerant and more stable families.[6]

---

4. Id. at 98.
5. Id. at 99.
6. Bruce Ackerman, Integration for Subsidized Housing and the Question of Racial Occupancy Controls, 26 Stan. L. Rev. 245, 251-253 (1974). Ackerman notes that the area may not become 100 percent black because some whites may have an unlimited tolerance for black neighbors. In poorer

Studies indicate that tipping points range from 25 percent to 60 percent black, although in some situations, a single family can tip a neighborhood.[7] The actual point at which stable integrated housing becomes impossible is difficult to predict because the departure of whites and the refusal of others to replace them depends on a wide range of factors. These include income level of the area, the percentage of the overall community that is black, the availability of alternative all-white housing, the openness of the overall housing market to blacks, and the vigor with which fair housing laws, particularly anti-blockbusting policies, are controlled. Consider whether Professor's illustration written more than 30 years ago has lost any relevance with the passage of time.

§7.10.3   Residential Preferences of Blacks

An alternative explanation for the continuing prevalence of segregated communities is the preference of blacks to live among other blacks. Scholars in this view contend that post-*Brown* mainly black housing area represent a "voluntary phenomenon" reflecting the strong preference of many blacks to live among their own race because of feelings of "cultural similarity and positive in-group attraction."[8] Others argue that such preferences are explained by racial pride and a desire to preserve black institutions; still others suggest that it is the result of a desire to avoid other groups rather than to preserve the integrity of their own.[9]

Recent empirical evidence, however, calls this theory into doubt. A recent study conducted in communities throughout the nation asked black participants to choose between neighborhoods that were all white, overwhelmingly white with a black population of 14 percent, split evenly between blacks and whites, split fairly evenly with a black majority of 64 percent, or all black. Overall, the results showed a desire for integration, but a reluctance to move into neighborhoods in which the participants would be the sole black residents or one of very few black residents.[10] The typical black participant, if given the opportunity, preferred a neighborhood with a 50-50 ratio of blacks to whites.[11] The next most popular choices were neighborhoods that were either nearly evenly split with a narrow majority of blacks, or all-black.[12] Of the participants that selected the neighborhoods that were 50-50 or nearly evenly mixed, most preferred these neighborhoods specifically because they were racially mixed.[13] Overall, few reported racial pride as a

---

areas, whites may remain because of attachment to their homes or facilities in the area, or they may not be able to afford a move to other all-white areas.

7. Id. at 254. See also Margalynne Armstrong, Race and Property Values in Entrenched Segregation, 52 U. Miami L. Rev. 1051 (1998); Bill Dedman, For Black Home Buyers, a Boomerang; Segregation, Persists Despite Fair Housing Act, Chicago Study Finds, N.Y. Times, Feb. 13, 1999, at A15; Victor Navasky, The Benevolent Housing Quota, 6 How. L.J. 30, 34-37 (1960).

8. Maria Krysdan & Reynolds Farley, The Residential Preferences of Blacks: Do They Explain Persistent Segregation?, 80 Social Forces 937, 938-939, 941 (2002).

9. See id. at 941.

10. See id.

11. See id. at 949, 969.

12. See id. at 949-950.

13. See id. at 951-953.

reason for their selection, and a sizable minority cited the improvement of race relations as an impetus for wanting to live on a block that included whites.[14]

Surveys of white participants demonstrated white preferences to live in segregated communities. Almost all whites surveyed expressed a willingness to move into a neighborhood that was either all white or had a 1 black to 13 white ratio.[15] As the ratio of blacks to whites increased, whites became less and less willing to move to the neighborhood. Seventy-three percent of whites would move into a neighborhood that had a 3 black to 11 white ratio, 47 percent would be willing to move to a neighborhood with a 5 black to 9 white ratio, only 31 percent was willing to enter a neighborhood with a slight black majority of 8 to 6.[16]

Placed side by side, these results help explain how preferences perpetuate segregation. While blacks prefer to live in 50-50 neighborhoods, such neighborhoods are nearly impossible to find. Meanwhile, blacks prefer not to become pioneers in all white or nearly all-white neighborhoods because of fears of hostility from whites.[17] Whites, on the other hand, are unlikely to enter or remain in neighborhoods that reach the 50-50 ratio that is preferred by most blacks.

A problem with these surveys involving racial questions is that so many respondents are unwilling to tell the full truth about their preferences. In addition, such surveys raise hypothetical "what if" questions that might differ substantially were they to pose real-life situations. For example, if 60 percent of a prestigious community were black, but they were all of the caliber of Oprah Winfrey, Tiger Woods, or Kenneth Chenault, chairman and CEO of American Express, would not their answers differ from those they gave in the survey?

§7.10.4   Racism Hypo: Co-op Practices

New York City contains over 300,000 housing cooperatives, or "co-ops." In a co-op, a corporation owns and manages the building. Rather than buying an apartment in the building, residents buy shares in the co-op and are granted the right to occupy a specific unit in the building. The co-op is managed by a board of residents/shareholders—often voted in among the other residents/shareholders or, in smaller co-ops, consisting of all residents/shareholders. Because cooperative housing involves each member having a share of the building, shareholders/residents rely on each other's financial stability. For example, if common areas need repair, all shareholders/residents must be able to contribute to the costs. Similarly, all shareholders/residents must be able to contribute to the monthly maintenance, which usually includes a payment toward the mortgage underlying the building. Moreover, co-op members resolve disputes before the board, involving much more interaction among neighbors than the average condominium or house owner.

14. See id. at 951-953.
15. See id. at 959.
16. See id. at 959-960.
17. See id. at 969-970

As a result, those seeking to sell their apartment must have the buyer approved by the co-op board, as the buyer will become the new shareholder/resident with all the attendant responsibilities and powers. Co-op boards interview prospective applicants and usually require significant amounts of financial information and even personal information. Co-op boards routinely have preferences based on race, religion, age, and marital status, often rejecting applicants who they feel would "change the character" of the building. While New York City's Human Rights Law does not allow co-ops to discriminate on these bases, it fails to require co-op boards to provide applicants with the reason for their rejection. Co-op boards do not customarily provide rejected applicants with a reason for their decision, leaving applicants with little understanding of their rejection. Thus, it is nearly impossible for rejected applicants to prove discrimination.

As a result, the Anti-Discrimination Center of Metro New York advocated in 2007 that New York City adopt Intro 119, the Fair and Prompt Coop Disclosure Law. Intro 119 would require co-ops to disclose in a timely fashion their specific reasons for rejecting an applicant, and would permit co-ops to defend themselves against discrimination charges only based on the reasons provided to the applicant rejected, and not based on new reasons produced after the fact.

While a substantial number of co-op boards support the measure, several of them are lobbying against Intro 119. These co-ops argue that privacy is essential to the co-op decision-making process. They note that their decisions are sometimes based on personal, non-discriminatory reasons regarding the personalities of prospective neighbors, and that Intro 119 would create a chilling effect on the frank discussions involved in the selection process and will deter co-op members from taking board positions. They also argue that Intro 119 requires greater expenses and record-keeping, as it requires boards to disclose the number of rejections and total applications in the prior three-year period. They also argue that the bill will not deter those who want to discriminate from putting forth non-discriminatory, pretextual reasons; thus it will only punish those co-op members who are not discriminating by increasing their expenses and chilling their discussion of potentially embarrassing personal reactions to their potential neighbors. The City Council has opened the debate up to advocates from the community.

Student A will represent a co-op board that opposes the bill.

Student B will represent the Anti-Discrimination Center.

§7.10.5   Racial Occupancy Controls

Recognizing that the use of quotas and other "racial balancing" techniques in housing is deplored by many who support racial integration, Professor Downs asserts that, under present conditions, some form of racial selection process is absolutely required to avoid expanding the concentration of blacks that results from reliance on "color-blind" policies. The foundation of Professor Downs's argument is that "almost all racially integrated neighborhoods and housing developments that have remained integrated for very long have used deliberate management to achieve certain numerical targets as to the proportion of minority-group occupants."[18]

In the seminal 1988 case of United States v. Starrett Associates,[19] the Second Circuit found that a "ceiling" quota[20] had a significant discriminatory effect on black applicants for an apartment complex. Despite the argument that the quota existed to prevent tipping, the court found that the quota-related extended waits for apartments imposed on blacks (as compared to the wait time for white applicants) amounted to an illegal denial of housing. As has happened in the educational and occupational fields, the court found that race-conscious quotas must be based on a narrow history of racial discrimination and must be temporary, with a defined termination point. Because the housing developer involved in the *Starrett* case had not discriminated in the past (in any provable way), and because the purpose of the quota was to permanently maintain integration with no definite end date, the Court found the occupancy controls illegally denied housing to black applicants, and were therefore deemed illegal.

Given the current Supreme Court trend to use strict scrutiny review whenever a racial distinction is made, regardless of the histories surrounding segregation and integration, it is unlikely that other courts will differ from the Second Circuit on the matter of benign quotas. While some indications show that quotas may be permissible to achieve racial balance, they probably may not be utilized to achieve lasting integration — a fact that helps explain why lasting integration continues to be elusive.

Finally, even before the courts intervene, proponents of benign housing quotas in cities and towns must expect massive opposition from white homeowners and the real estate industry. Managers of a project or development who decide to further racial balance goals with a quota policy have voluntarily imposed restraints on their ability to sell or lease their housing properties, and will likely incur only those legal challenges based on their apparent violation of fair housing laws. When governmental units, on the other hand, legislate similar quota restrictions, they affect countless owners by restricting (albeit for a worthy cause) the free alienation of their land — a principle of law with a history even longer than the struggle to impose workable sanctions on racial hostility.[21]

18. Downs, supra note 3, at 99.

19. 840 F.2d 1096 (2d Cir.), cert. denied, 488 U.S. 946 (1988).

20. A "ceiling quota" is one that sets a limit on the number of nonwhite people that can live in a given dwelling; its aim is preserving integration. The alternative, an "access quota," sets a minimum number of nonwhites that must be included in a dwelling, a measure that does not prevent a dwelling from becoming completely black, or "tipping."

21. The benign housing quota in Racism Hypo §7.11 is based on similar legislation drafted but later rejected by Oak Park, Illinois, in 1973. The ordinance and the events that led to its proposal are summarized in Note, The Use of Racial Housing Quotas to Achieve Integrated Communities; The Oak Park Approach, 6 Loy. L.J. 164 (1975). See also Boris Bittker, The Case of the Checker-Board Ordinance: An Experiment in Race Relations, 71 Yale L.J. 1387 (1962); John Kaplan, Equal Justice in an Unequal World, 61 Nw. U. L. Rev. 363 (1966).

§7.11 Racism Hypo: Blackright v. Village of New Day

The Village of New Day City Council has enacted a benign quota amendment to its fair housing ordinance.[1] In compliance with the terms of that ordinance, a sector of the Village comprising approximately 25 percent of its total area was set aside as a "designated area," and sales and rentals of homes and apartments to nonwhite persons were forbidden once a 30 percent "quota" had been reached on any given block in the designated area.[2] Likewise, rentals to black persons in any given apartment building (of four or more units) were forbidden once the number of blacks in that apartment building had reached 30 percent or more. Any person attempting to purchase or lease housing who was refused under the terms of the ordinance was to be referred to the Community Relations Department of the village, which was charged with the responsibility of locating comparable housing for the refused applicant in other areas of the village. The penalty for violation of the ordinance was a fine upon the seller of up to $1,000.[3]

§7.11   1. An Ordinance Amending the Fair Housing Ordinance of the Village of New Day and Establishing Procedures for Achieving Stable Integrated Housing Patterns: *Be it ordained* by the Mayor and City Council of the Village of New Day, Sunrise County, Illinois, that the Code of the Village of New Day is amended to read as follows: *Section 1. Designated Area.* That part of New Day shown on the official village map as the "East End," is hereby established as a "designated area," where there is a danger of said area, or parts thereof, becoming a black segregated area. *Section 2. Limitation on Sales in Designated Area.* It shall be unlawful for any seller or any agent for any seller knowingly to sell any real property to a black person on any block in the designated area after official notice by the village Community Relations Service that 30 percent or more of the block between two intersecting streets on both sides of the street has been occupied by black persons. *Section 3. Rentals in Designated Area.* It shall be unlawful for any owner or any agent for an owner knowingly to rent any apartment in a multiple family dwelling of four or more units in the designated area to a black person if 30 percent or more of the multiple family dwellings in the building have been rented to or have been occupied by black persons. This section shall not apply to the renewal of an existing lease. *Section 4. Alternate Housing To Be Made Available.* Any black person attempting to purchase or lease housing in New Day and refused pursuant to paragraph two or three hereof, shall be referred to the village Community Relations Department. The department is charged with the responsibility of locating comparable housing for the refused applicant in other areas of the village. The department is also charged with the responsibility of assisting owners to find white persons to purchase or lease real estate in the designated area. *Section 5. Limitation of Area.* The limitations in this ordinance are to be applicable only to the portion of the village referred to in §1 as the designated area. This Ordinance is not intended to state any limitation on the sale or rental of property to any person other than in said designated area, it being the intent of this ordinance that there shall be no limitation on any block or building in the Village of New Day as to the percentage of population of any race other than in the designated area. *Section 6. Penalty.* Any person, firm or corporation violating any provisions of this chapter shall be punished by a fine not to exceed $1,000. A copy of this ordinance shall be forthwith mailed to each taxpayer listed on the most current tax rolls of properties in the designated area and shall be in full force and effect from and after its adoption, approval, mailing and publication as provided by law. *Section 7. Definitions.* For the purposes of this ordinance, a black person is defined as any person designated as Negro or black for the purpose of the United States Census.

2. Experience and sociological studies in the metropolitan area and elsewhere indicate a trend such that, when it appears to white persons that they may become a minority in a block, a building, or a school, they leave the area, resulting in completely segregated blocks, buildings or schools. These studies indicate that a "tipping" point comes when the percentage of blacks in an area reaches 30 percent, making it likely that the area will ultimately become entirely black.

3. Since 1954, the Village of New Day has enforced a policy of fair housing for black persons. New Day has vigorously prosecuted owners or agents for owners of real estate who have denied housing to black persons. Said litigation has been filed pursuant to the New Day Fair Housing

The designated area of the village is situated on the northern border of the City of Metropolis, at the edge of an all-black area that had been inexorably expanding from the center of that city. The suburbs surrounding New Day are almost completely white, and have shown consistent, intense hostility toward the entry of any blacks. New Day, on the other hand, has taken steps to encourage the integration of the village, including the formation of an active Community Relations Department, the passage of a local open housing law, and the vigorous prosecution of cases involving discrimination against blacks under local and federal laws.

As a result, a "funnel effect" began to develop. Blacks, for whom the housing market in the Metropolis area was (and still is) desperately congested, began in increasing numbers to look to New Day for housing. Although at the time the ordinance was passed, the black population of the village was only 10 percent, it was clear that unless some action was taken, black immigration into the village would inevitably "tip" it and result in the creation of yet another all-black community. It was this result that the present ordinance was designed to prevent.[4]

Three years after the passage of the ordinance, the black population of the designated area had reached the 30 percent limit. At about that time, the black plaintiff in this action, Ben Blackright, attempted to purchase a house in the area. The owner of the house, Owen P. Owner, refused to sell to Blackright, stating that such a sale would place him in violation of the ordinance. The Community Relations Department offered Blackright an alternative house in another section of the village, but he refused, stating, "I do not object to and, in fact, prefer living near black people. Moreover," he added, "New Day's integration scheme is no benefit to blacks, but a last-ditch measure to maintain white dominance. It is a measure which demeans blacks while it guarantees control to whites."[5] When the City Council determined to enforce the quota amendment Blackright brought

---

Ordinance, the Federal Fair Housing Act and the 1866 Federal Civil Rights Act. The Village has also enacted anti-blockbusting and anti-steering laws.

4. The Mayor and City Council, in a report widely endorsed by village leaders, found that: "A. The area immediately east of New Day in the City of Metropolis is a segregated area. Approximately 98 percent of its occupants are black. B. Black persons have been discouraged from seeking housing in communities to the north, south and west of New Day and said communities have practically no black persons residing therein. C. Because of the more friendly environment in the Village of New Day, and because of the excellence of New Day schools, government, transportation and other community services, many black persons residing in the segregated area of Metropolis east of New Day have chosen to move to New Day. D. The citizens of New Day have come to recognize that it is in their best interests to reside in a heterogeneous and racially integrated community. Aided by Village subsidies, they have organized neighborhood fair housing groups to further by education, communication, and cooperation their goals of a racially balanced community. Now, additional steps must be taken to prevent a segregated area in our Village. E. Such segregated areas are contrary to the policies of the United States, as set forth in the United States Constitution and Fair Housing Act and are contrary to the policy of the Village of New Day." It was this report that sparked the drive leading to the passage of the amendment to the village's fair housing ordinance.

5. At a special town meeting called to discuss whether the amendment should be enforced or repealed in the face of the threatened litigation, Ben Blackright addressed the overflow crowd: "My friends and, I hope, my future neighbors: Dr. Martin Luther King had a dream. His was a vision of interracial brotherhood that kindled a new light in an already bright land. His dream was majestic in its sweep and magnetic in its attraction to the best in all of us. I have a more humble, more personal dream. I am black and proud of my race, its heritage, and its potential. I am also an American and, despite my country's many flaws, I would not trade and do not intend to abandon my citizenship. But my dream, my goal, is to get this country to recognize me as a man who is respected for his

suit in federal court against Owner and villagers claiming a violation of his civil rights under the Fourteenth Amendment of the U.S. Constitution, under 42 U.S.C. §1982 (the 1866 Civil Rights Act), and under 42 U.S.C. §3604 (the Fair Housing Act). On these facts, a preliminary injunction hearing has been set.

Law Firm A will represent Ben Blackright.

Law Firm B will represent the Village of New Day.

§7.12 URBAN RENEWAL AND BLACK HOUSING

Clearly, slum clearance has not been for the benefit of slum residents, nor has slum rehabilitation benefited families of low and modest incomes. Instead, cities have substituted their own goals for national housing goals because solving the housing problem of the poor does not improve the tax rate; does not improve the cities' competitive position vis-à-vis the suburbs; and does not gain national recognition for leadership in creating symbols of civic grandeur.

Urban renewal has eliminated pockets of dilapidated housing and blight in core cities and suburbs, reaped windfall profits for real estate investors, and paved the way for new public monuments. But urban renewal has hurt and scattered those who are poor and nonwhite, while subsidizing the right of the more affluent to replace them, as the "highest and best use of the land." Except in private, the federal government refuses to admit this fact: slum clearance has failed to provide decent housing for slum-dwellers. Urban renewal and public housing programs have intensified segregation of blacks in inner city ghettos.[1]

Professor Schuchter's summary of the burden borne by blacks in most urban development projects remains valid. In blatant situations, the victims can access court and win some procedural victories but, unless a compromise settlement can be effected, the chances of actually gaining orders requiring that the project be halted or that the displaced residents be adequately compensated are not great.

---

accomplishments, blamed for his failures, and as entitled as any white to be compensated for what he gives just as I expect to pay for whatever I receive. As I would not discriminate on the basis of race, so I do not wish to be discriminated against. Discrimination, masquerading as an affirmative action experiment, remains discrimination when, for whatever reason, it denies me a house that I desire in my heart, and that, with the product of my labor, I am able to afford. That I should be denied this house because of the racism of whites (descriptively sanitized in your debate of "tipping points") is a double evil. First, it legitimates the worst in you, and second, it raises an unnecessary barrier between me and my goal. That you should voluntarily do the first is regrettable. That you would do the second is, I humbly submit, illegal, immoral, and personally intolerable. It is said that I must sacrifice my house for another just as good so that other blacks may obtain better housing. If this were true, no sacrifice on my part would be too great. But were I offered a palace, I would not alter my present course if it meant, as I believe it does, that blacks once again must obtain rights twisted and warped to conform to prevailing views by whites as to where, when, how, and under what circumstances, they will suffer the presence of blacks. No black has gained from enactment of your law. Its enforcement, I predict, will diminish us all."

§7.12 1. Arnold Schuchter, White Power/Black Freedom 36-37 (1968).

One of the most frequently cited cases in the field is Norwalk CORE v. Norwalk Redevelopment Agency.[2] This complex case illustrates the difficulties courts have encountered with housing discrimination in the class-wide context, as opposed to the discrete claims of individuals, particularly in the area of urban renewal. Federal law required the agency undertaking a redevelopment project to accept responsibility for providing adequate housing to families displaced by the urban renewal project. Plaintiffs, tenant organizations representing low-income black and Puerto Rican families, filed a class action claiming that the Norwalk Redevelopment Agency had not met this obligation. They alleged that the agency had not provided for any new, low-rent replacement housing on the grounds that existing housing would adequately meet the displaced families' needs, while in fact the agency was aware that there was a long waiting list for public housing, and that the private housing market discriminated against the blacks and Puerto Ricans who made up the bulk of the displaced families. Rental prices to blacks were twice as high as those for comparable housing available to whites. Further, the complaint stated, the agency had entered into a contract to provide housing for medium-income families to be built on the only lot suitable for low-income housing development. As a result of these policies, plaintiffs alleged that displaced blacks and Puerto Ricans were forced to move into substandard housing, and some had been driven out of the city entirely, all of which violated their entitlement to equal protection of the laws.

The district court dismissed for lack of standing, and also seemed to indicate a belief that the claim was nonjusticiable due to the seeking of inappropriate relief. The court of appeals reversed, holding that the plaintiffs did have standing, since their stake in the outcome of the case was immediate and personal, and they had a right to be free from discrimination in government programs, a right they asserted was one which courts should protect. The court, however, separated the political issue of what the requisite standard for housing for displaced persons was to be, from the legal and justiciable question of whether that standard was administered in a discriminatory manner because relocated minority group members were being placed in worse areas and dwellings than relocated whites.

> Since the plaintiffs are admittedly displaced as a result of the redevelopment project, there is no question of the presence of "state action" within the meaning of the Fourteenth Amendment. Where the relocation standard set by Congress is met for those who have access to any housing in the community which they can afford, but not for those who, by reason of their race, are denied free access to housing they can afford and must pay more for what they can get, the state action affirms the discrimination in the housing market. This is not "equal protection of the laws."[3]

It was not for the court to determine what the standard should be, but it was the court's duty to require that whatever standard Congress adopted was administered equally without regard to race. Therefore, plaintiffs' equal protection claim was remanded to the district court for a trial on the merits.

2. 395 F.2d 920 (2d Cir. 1968).
3. Id. at 931.

But while lawyers and courts cited the language as evidence of the Constitution's commitment to remedying past discrimination at least to find standing, the plaintiffs and the class they represented received no relief. Returning to the district court, the Norwalk CORE lawyers were unable to obtain an injunction, and the area was developed in basic conformance with the plan. The process of dispersal was completed.[4] Professor Henry McGee attributes judicial reluctance to provide substantive relief to displaced plaintiffs to many factors, including:

> reluctance to unravel a plan that has been many years in the making, that has built up community expectations, and that has presented several opportunities for discussion, persuasion and attack during its years of preparation. This unwillingness, in turn, is responsive to the widely shared opinion that the courtroom is the improper milieu for planning (or unplanning) the physical and human development of a community. Moreover, even the delay of such a plan for the course of a trial and inevitable appeals might set in motion a wave of repercussions that would be difficult to foresee and which few judges would risk unleashing on a community. During this interim, while condemnation is stayed, land values might rise, increasing project costs beyond the limits of local and federal funds committed or even available to the venture; demand conditions might change, so as to undo the reuse assumptions that underpin the renewal scheme; the terms and availability of construction financing or municipal borrowing might become less advantageous; existing community or political support for the program might despair and vanish: federal moneys might be diverted to citizens ready to proceed; urgently needed public improvements such as schools and neighborhood centers, which depend upon the urban renewal scheme for their financing, might be indefinitely delayed; and assuming the neighborhood is indeed a "blighted" one, the deterioration might get far worse and even spread.[5]

But Professor McGee suggests that judicial abdication occurs because "the political strength of the displacees is too diffused and lacks sufficient economic support to withstand the larger and more powerful forces that compel the adoption of the renewal scheme." He suggests that urban renewal cases are no more complex than reapportionment, school desegregation, and welfare cases, but in the latter cases there is a "sufficiently powerful social and political consensus" for such action.

Whatever the basis for judicial reticence, requests for judicial intervention that are deemed tardy have little chance. In Nashville I-40 Steering Committee v. Ellington[6] an integrated group sought to enjoin construction of a highway that would destroy Nashville's black business community and erect a physical barrier between the predominantly black area and other parts of the city. In affirming dismissal, the court first found that procedural requirements had been met by defendants. Then, the court expressed its concern about the delay that would attend granting relief requested by plaintiffs, claiming:

> It would be virtually impossible to select a route for an interstate highway through a congested metropolitan area without working hardships upon many citizens.

---

4. Henry McGee, Urban Renewal in the Crucible of Judicial Review, 56 Va. L. Rev. 826, 866 (1970).
5. Id. at 878.
6. 387 F.2d 179 (6th Cir. 1967).

Appellants suggest possible alternative routes which they contend would avoid the unfortunate economic consequences which the proposed route will impose upon the North Nashville area. Alternative routes undoubtedly would impose hardships upon others. The minimizing of hardships and adverse economic effects is a problem addressing itself to engineers, not judges. The providing of just compensation to property owners falls within the purview of the laws of eminent domain.[7]

A final difficulty worth noting occurs when private developers or affluent individuals buy and displace low-rent tenants in order to redevelop the land or rehabilitate the buildings. In such cases, tenants have no legal claim, or so the Eighth Circuit found in Moorer v. U.S. Department of Housing & Urban Development.[8] There, federal relocation benefits were denied to displacees where a private developer purchased property for rehabilitation under a HUD program for FHA-insured mortgage financing and rental assistance. The court determined that the federal involvement did not qualify the displacees as "displaced persons" within the definition in 42 U.S.C. §4601(6) (The Uniform Relocation and Assistance and Real Property Acquisition Policies Act), which provides for federal assistance.

A similar result would probably occur if tenants in a black ghetto area such as that in the Capitol Hill area of Washington, D.C., sought judicial relief or relocation benefits because upper class buyers had decided to take over the area. In dozens of individual transactions, rundown dwellings are purchased, gutted to the exterior walls, and rebuilt into townhouses that are far beyond the financial reach of tenants — and even of owners no longer able to afford the increased taxes or unable to resist the large offers for their houses. As the poor depart, they can often observe streets being repaired and regularly cleaned, new street lighting and trees being installed, and regular visits by garbage trucks taking place — all the municipal services whose long absence was a major factor in the black residential area becoming a slum.

While not a racial case, the Court's 5-4 decision in Kelo v. City of New London,[9] provided another incentive for developers seeking to renew blighted or under-utilized area. The city had used its eminent domain authority to transfer land from private owners to a corporate entity to further economic development. The much criticized decision found that the promised economic growth in a city that needed it badly, justified the redevelopment as a permissible "public use" permitted under the Fifth's Amendment's Takings Clause.

The four dissenters asserted that the takings had a "reverse Robin Hood" effect in that the city was taking homes from the poor and turning the land over to a

---

7. Id. Compare the *Nashville I-40* result with Powelton Civic Homes Owners Ass'n v. HUD, 284 F. Supp. 809 (E.D. Pa. 1968), where a project still in the condemnation stage was enjoined to enable plaintiffs to have a hearing on the adequacy of relocation shelter. Further compare Western Addition Community Org. v. Weaver, 294 F. Supp. 433 (N.D. Cal. 1968), where an urban renewal project in the cultural, political, and economic center of the black community was actually enjoined. The injunction was only temporary, however, and once the project met with approval from HUD, the court felt itself no longer capable of interfering. No. 45,053 (N.D. Cal. 1969). See also McGee, supra note 4.

8. 561 F.2d 175 (8th Cir. 1977).

9. 545 U.S. 469 (2005).

rich corporation for promises of jobs and economic improvement, thereby setting a dangerous precedent. Criticism from many levels of government and housing groups have slowed development in the New London project to the point that it may never take place.

Note: Economic Revitalization Continues to Threaten Black Neighborhoods

Over the past decade, a number of the most blighted neighborhoods in major metropolitan areas have been experiencing an unprecedented surge of investment.[10] Over a wide range of economic measures, low-income neighborhoods actually outpaced the United States as a whole, according to a new study of the 100 largest inner cities by Boston's Initiative for a Competitive Inner City, a group founded by Professor Michael E. Porter of Harvard University. From a business perspective, investors have been willing to take a chance on reinvigorating these areas and have been encouraged by the initial results.[11] "Smart business-people gravitate toward good opportunities, and it has become clear that inner cities are just that," says David W. Tralka, chairman of Merrill Lynch & Co.'s Business Financial Services Group.

Dilapidated brownstones and rundown housing stock have been transformed and major corporations have moved in — from Starbucks and Disney to Pathmark. From this vantage point, the change looks like signs of economic vitality. But that does not reveal the complete story.

From the perspective of the residents who have raised their families for generations in these communities, the change may seem frightening and an unwanted intrusion that can result in squeezing them out of the housing market.[12] An increase in economic indicators may merely be an indication that more affluent residents are moving in without any real change for the residents who are left behind. Unlike white flight, where white residents deliberately left their community as minority families moved in, the minorities in these urban neighborhoods feel pushed out of their homes, without affordable alternatives.

Harlem is a prime example of this transformation. As the empowerment zones clean up the neighborhood, residents are angered by the exorbitant real estate values and rents that follow. They have not felt adequately included in the conversation about what happens to their community. Even as the wealthier move in, they see no change in their job prospects or the schools for their children. "Exactly who is the Empowerment Zone empowering?" asks Nellie Bailey of the Harlem Tenants Council. "Why is it that developers bring in businesses that raise real estate rates, but don't offer jobs that enable people to remain in the community?"

Residents have used political rallies at city hall to protest the changes and have devised a housing task force to voice their complaints. But the most frustrating aspect is that the Harlem political machine enabled this development without looking to community needs beyond the demands of big business. Developers have received land for virtually nothing or have been given city subsidies for upscale

10. Aaron Bernstein et al., An Inner-City Renaissance, Business Week, Oct. 27, 2003.
11. Id.
12. White Flight, This Time Toward Harlem; Newcomers and Good Times Bring Hope, and Fears of Displacement, N.Y. Times, Feb. 5, 2001.

housing construction without being required to give anything back to the community.

Harlem is only one example where corporate interests in the name of economic vitality have marginalized African American community members and excluded their participation. Gentrification or urban renewal efforts need to recognize the human costs implicated as big business and the wealthy move in, leaving nowhere for the current community to go.

§7.13   PUBLIC HOUSING AND THE INTEGRATION IDEOLOGY

Originally, the federally funded public housing program was intended to help the "submerged middle class" survive the rigors of the Depression. It was a short-term solution for those deemed the innocent victims of the economic crisis. Most of the early projects were low-rise row houses, often suburban in location and design.[1]

The beneficiaries of the program have changed. Indeed, the attitudes of those who fund and administer public housing programs, as well as the public, have shifted. For some time, the perception that public housing is intended for the poor, particularly the nonwhite poor, has served to decrease interest in and support for it. As Professor Kenneth T. Jackson writes, the location and funding of public housing served to reinforce white flight to the suburbs and perpetuate segregation:

> Because municipalities had discretion on where and when to build public housing, the projects invariably reinforced racial segregation. A suburb that did not wish to tarnish its exclusive image by having public housing within its precincts could simply refuse to create a housing agency. . . . As a result, low-income housing did not go up on the cheaper, vacant land of the suburbs, but in the heart of cities. . . . [B]ecause determination of need and site selection were left up to localities, public housing was confined to existing slums. It further concentrated the poor in the central cities and reinforced the image of suburbia as a place of refuge from the social pathologies of the disadvantaged.[2]

In opting for more public housing in the ghetto rather than no new public housing at all, governmental agencies may have made the better choice for less than the best reasons. Academicians as well as black militants have argued the positive benefits of ghetto living for its inhabitants. Other studies indicate that, despite all the difficulties of slum living, social benefits are derived from the close association with people in the community and the sense of identity in the neighborhood. It is felt that these sources of residential satisfaction help provide a "framework for personal and social integration."[3] This view of

---

§7.13   1. See Lawrence M. Friedman, Public Housing and the Poor: An Overview, 54 Cal. L. Rev. 642-654 (1966).

2. Kenneth T. Jackson, Crabgrass Frontier: The Suburbanization of the United States 225, 227 (1985).

3. Marc Fried & P. Gleicher, Some Sources of Residential Satisfaction in an Urban Slum, 27 J. Am. Inst. Planners 305 (Nov. 1961).

"home" as an area or community rather than simply a place is so at variance with typical middle-class orientations that appreciation for the basic sense of identity involved, and particularly for the loss felt when an individual leaves the area, is very difficult. One writer, however, reports that "grieving for a lost home is evidently a wide-spread and serious phenomenon following in the wake of urban dislocation."[4] Public housing officials report that they frequently meet with resistance when they assign black families to outlying projects far removed from their accustomed living area. Certainly, concern about transportation to work, church, and shopping, as well as fear of reactions from a white neighborhood, may spark some of this resistance, but identification with the familiar neighborhood may also be involved. To the extent that integration policies, whether or not prompted by court orders, require them to leave a black neighborhood in order to obtain public housing, blacks may be deprived of the liberty to decide where to live, just as they were under the former segregation policies.[5]

Not every observer of ghetto life would view the isolation of its residents as a blessing. It is assumed that those who see strengths in the sense of community would not condone decrepit housing, high rents, crime, poor health conditions, and inadequate city service, all of which tend to be a part of life in the overcrowded black and Latino ghettos in this country. There can be little doubt that Dr. Kenneth Clark's forty-year-old statement is still accurate not only for blacks, but for all people living in projects:

> Housing is no abstract social and political problem, but an extension of man's personality. If the Negro has to identify with a rat infested tenement, his sense of personal inadequacy and inferiority already aggravated by job discrimination and other forms of humiliation, is reinforced by the physical reality around him. If his home is clean and decent and even in some way beautiful, his sense of self is stronger. A house is a concrete symbol of what the person is worth.[6]

The bad reputation of most projects is a result of decades of neglect and mismanagement by politically well-placed but administratively incompetent officials. "Poorly maintained, segregated, cheaply constructed, and often physically dangerous, the projects [became] 'the dumping ground for the poor.' "[7] Many families who are eligible for public housing never place their names on the usually lengthy waiting lists, preferring to take their chances in the private housing market.[8]

---

4. Fried, Grieving for a Lost Home: Psychological Costs of Relocation in Urban Renewal, in The Record and the Controversy 359 (J. Wilson ed. 1966).

5. Comment, 5 Harv. C.R.-C.L. L. Rev. 150, 156 (1970).

6. Kenneth Clark, Dark Ghetto 32-33 (1965).

7. See Jackson, supra note 2, at 228.

8. The term "public housing" now refers to several types of projects, but traditionally described housing owned and operated by local housing authorities. Construction was financed by long-term bond issues. The Note adds, "[s]ince the operating income of conventional public housing is derived from a pegged system under which the tenant pays a certain proportion of his income as his monthly rent, the income of the housing authority is tied closely to tenant income. Unfortunately, even in an era of economic expansion, the income level of the poor has not increased proportionately. At the same time, the housing authorities are caught in an inflationary squeeze, forcing use of reserves for operation." Id. at 895. In a summary of all federally subsidized housing programs, Martin Sloane,

Those eligible for public housing do not usually set policy in litigation brought to vindicate their constitutional rights. Middle-class lawyers and their supporting organizations that do set such policies view the squalor in a typical, segregated project and conclude that the evil is the housing authority policy that initially placed the project in the ghetto, and then originally assigned only blacks to live there. Such policies certainly are illegal, but do not alone explain why so much of this housing is so rundown, unhealthy, and unsafe. Some explanation is required in view of the fact that there are predominantly black projects, often those in which tenants' groups have taken over the management role, which are functioning well.[9]

Public housing litigation has relied on Brown v. Board of Education, with the presumption that desegregation will result in quality housing. As the cases reviewed in this section show, federal and local agencies have traditionally taken the path of least resistance in meeting public housing needs: first, authorizing segregated housing when this was legally permissible; and then, after *Brown* and civil rights laws mandated desegregation, failing to enforce the letter and spirit of their own nondiscriminatory regulations whenever opposition to integrated housing appeared — as it generally did.

As Burney v. Housing Authority of the County of Beaver[10] makes clear, the advent of low-income public housing did not greatly alleviate residential segregation. Though economic and social factors often militate against integration, local and federal agencies, whether intentionally or unwittingly, often assist these impersonal forces in maintaining segregation.

Efforts intended to desegregate public housing developments through court action were waged vigorously in the 1970s with results hardly better than the decades-long campaign to desegregate public schools.[11]

General Counsel of the National Committee Against Discrimination in Housing, found that most of these programs contained two basic weaknesses. First, they have not produced enough low-income housing "to come close to satisfying the need." Second, they contain provisions that permit exclusion of low-income housing by communities that seek to keep out the poor, in which category minorities are over-represented. Norman Dorsen et al., 2 Emerson, Haber and Dorsen's Political and Civil Rights in the United States 947 (4th Law School ed., 1979).

9. Experience has shown, for example, that high-rise public housing projects are particularly difficult to manage and maintain. Even a small percentage of "problem families or individuals" can render such buildings unlivable. The Pruitt-Igoe project in St. Louis, consisting of 33 eleven-story buildings, was finally written off as a disaster and the structures were demolished. Meanwhile, a single eleven-story building, managed by a tenant's group only a few blocks away, was functioning well. N.Y. Times, June 4, 1970, at 45, col. 4.

10. 551 F. Supp. 746 (W.D. Pa. 1982).

11. Hills v. Gautreaux, 425 U.S. 284 (1976). Earlier aspects of the decade-long litigation are reported at 342 F. Supp. 827 (N.D. Ill. 1972), aff'd, 480 F.2d 210 (7th Cir. 1973). Professor Henry McGee summarized the *Gautreaux* case in the following terms: "A decade of litigation in which the central issue of discrimination was uncontested . . . failed to disestablish racial segregation or produce desperately needed low-income housing for Chicago blacks. . . . [T]he first-named plaintiff in the suit, Dorothy Gautreaux, did not survive the Supreme Court decision. . . ." Henry McGee, Illusion and Contradiction in the Quest for a Desegregated Metropolis, 1976 U. Ill. L. Forum 948, 949. See also, John Calmore, Fair Housing vs. Fair Housing: The Conflict Between Providing Low-Income Housing in Impacted Areas and Providing Increased Housing Opportunities Through Spatial Deconcentration, 9 Housing L. Bull. 1, 4 (Nov.-Dec. 1979) (hereinafter cited as Fair Housing vs. Fair Housing).

§7.13.1   Black Opposition to Public Housing Projects

While the *Gautreaux* litigation well illustrates the tenacious resistance that can be expected when whites and those governmental officials who represent them fear that public housing will be located in their neighborhoods, it does not illustrate another source of such resistance: middle-class blacks. In several cases, black plaintiffs, often represented by civil rights organizations, opposed government plans to place public housing in their communities. A typical case is Shannon v. U.S. Department of Housing and Urban Development.[12] The case involved a renewal plan that was to be changed so that government-subsidized housing would be placed in a neighborhood of predominantly middle-class blacks, many of whose homes were themselves relatively new federally assisted or insured units. Residents strongly opposed the change because it would have brought a lower-income group into a middle-class island surrounded by a large area of low-income units. Noting that all federally assisted housing in the city was heavily concentrated in minority areas, the court ordered HUD to consider the racial impacts of the location of any HUD-assisted housing. The *Shannon* decision is often cited because of the strong language the court used in rejecting HUD arguments that no relief was necessary, in that some rent-subsidy housing had been distributed in non-ghetto areas. The court said that whatever the federal government's responsibilities were prior to the enactment of the Civil Rights Act of 1964, law and housing regulations now required a higher standard. No longer, the court warned HUD, could it carry out its responsibilities by focusing on land use controls, building code enforcements, and physical conditions of buildings, and thereby "remain blind to the very real effect that racial concentration has had in the development of urban blight. Today such color blindness is impermissible."[13]

Evidently political pressures have more impact on HUD than does judicial lecturing. Almost a decade after the *Shannon* decision, an interracial group of neighborhood residents and community organizations, including the NAACP, challenged HUD's approval of a low-income, high-rise building in a racially balanced area of Staten Island. Plaintiffs claimed that the complex would further minority concentration in the area and upset the racial balance presently existing there. The court agreed in King v. Harris.[14] The court noted that HUD had violated several of its own regulations in approving the low-income project and agreed with plaintiffs that the project would have a "tipping" effect on the neighborhood, further noting that HUD had also violated its affirmative duty to integrate low-income housing; the court granted a permanent injunction against construction.

The discussion of opposition by blacks to low-income housing projects does not, and is not intended to, prove the similarity of white and black discrimination. On the other hand, it does indicate that there are components of white opposition that cannot be attributed to racism in its purest form. From the standpoint of those

12. 436 F.2d 809 (3d Cir. 1970).

13. 436 F.2d at 820. Similar relief was sought and obtained by blacks in Crow v. Brown, 332 F. Supp. 382 (N.D. Ga. 1971); Banks v. Perk, 341 F. Supp. 1175 (N.D. Ohio 1972); Hicks v. Weaver, 302 F. Supp. 619 (E.D. La. 1969).

14. 464 F. Supp. 827 (E.D.N.Y. 1979).

in need of low-income housing, it illustrates the wide range of opposition that can, and often does, make allies of the most reactionary conservatives and the middle-class leadership of the NAACP. The developments do not surprise those who maintain that class and not race is the more significant basis for categorizing people in contemporary America.[15] The irony of middle class blacks joining with middle class whites to oppose any housing project intended to benefit poor blacks may not surprise, but will likely appall, those who, like Professor Freeman, fear that the probable long-term result of the integrationist civil rights drive will result in the bourgeoisification of some blacks who will be, more or less, accepted into white society. The great mass of blacks will remain in a disadvantaged status, but their plight will be said to be the result of their class, and, by implication, their lack of ability and ambition, rather than race.[16]

Note: Public Housing Policies Exclude Black Tenants

The large concentration of tenants have made public housing complexes fertile ground for organizing tenants around issues of serious concern. Some efforts have focused on women organizing for their children's education; others have sought to clean up the physical surroundings of the project. In one tenant campaign to create safer projects and reduce drug trafficking, tenants pushed to rid their community of neighbors engaging in criminal drug activity from their buildings. And they saw a real change. Local housing authorities throughout the country seized such an opportunity to enact lease provisions that empowered the housing authority, not the tenants, with a tremendous amount of discretion in subjecting tenants to eviction for criminal actions. For example, some housing policies permit the initiation of eviction proceedings against a tenant and her family if her oldest son is arrested outside the housing project (even if the son is not convicted of a drug crime). For many living in public housing, these policies were emboldened by a tenant's campaign, comprised predominantly of minority housing residents, but they have disproportionately affected minority families living in these public housing units.

In a 2002 unanimous opinion, the Supreme Court enabled local housing authorities with such discretion to evict tenants under a policy commonly known as "One Strike; You're Out." In Department of Housing and Urban Development v. Rucker,[17] the Court upheld these housing regulations as permitted under an interpretation of the language of federal legislation. Under the regulations, public housing tenants and their families may be evicted from their homes because of drug-related criminal acts of family members, guests, or visitors. The eviction can proceed even in situations where the tenant has no knowledge of the criminal activity or has taken all steps possible to prevent the problem.[18]

15. William Julius Wilson, The Declining Significance of Race (1978). See also William Julius Wilson, The Truly Disadvantaged: The Inner City, the Underclass, and Public Policy (1987); Richard D. Bahrenberg, The Remedy: Class, Race, and Affirmative Action 83-120 (1996) (arguing for affirmative action based on class rather than race).

16. Alan David Freeman, Legitimizing Racial Discrimination Through Anti-Discrimination Law: A Critical Review of Supreme Court Doctrine, 62 Minn. L. Rev. 1049 (1978).

17. 535 U.S. 125 (2002).

18. Michael Balboa, Symposia: Layering at the Margins, 11 Am. U. J. Gender Soc. Pol'y & L. 135 (2003).

As homelessness rates across the country increase, an additional housing policy passed by many local housing authorities concerning both public housing and Section 8 vouchers excludes one of the most marginalized segments in low-income communities. These policies mandate the automatic denial of subsidized housing to convicted criminals.[19] As these individuals — predominantly black males comprising a significant percentage of the prison population — return home after serving their sentences, they confront serious legal obstacles and cannot find adequate housing. Many family members or friends living in public housing or receiving Section 8 vouchers cannot offer support without jeopardizing their lease. With few options for transitional living or shelters available, ex-offenders are also unable to access one of the most affordable housing options in their communities. Over 650,000 individuals will return from prison this year, mostly to urban areas where rents have skyrocketed and supply is slim. Consequently, the lack of housing has become a leading factor that contributes to increasing rates of recidivism, creating a vicious cycle of crime and punishment for these individuals.

§7.14 PROOF STANDARDS IN MUNICIPAL LAND USE CHALLENGES

Whatever the difficulties of fashioning realistic and enforceable relief in *Gautreaux*, courts hearing the case found little need to devote energies to problems of proof. It was quite obvious that the policy discriminated against blacks and could only be justified on the basis that it was better to provide segregated public housing for blacks than no public housing at all. In many housing cases though, plaintiffs, assuming they survive the barriers of standing (see §7.9), face formidable obstacles of proof. There are several reasons for this. A number of federally subsidized housing programs require some form of local government approval. In addition, planning and zoning committees sensitive to a community's opposition to low-income housing try to hide exclusionary intentions behind a neutral facade of facially legitimate factors which have an exclusionary effect. This strategy was often used in the urban renewal cases (see §7.12) where a quite justified desire to obtain federal funds for a new highway, downtown shopping center, or a park, effectively eliminated a black ghetto neighborhood. The problem of proof is also present in the referendum cases (see §7.3), but to some extent the difficulties there are subordinated to the greater difficulties stemming from judicial obeisance to the processes of direct democracy.

§7.14.1   Village of Arlington Heights v. Metropolitan
Housing Development Corp.

Staggering under defeats in a whole series of housing cases, civil rights proponents were hopeful that the Supreme Court might agree to review the

---

19. This denial can be appealed but often appeals are merely denied.

proof problem and set a more reasonable standard. These hopes were dashed by the Supreme Court's decision in Village of Arlington Heights v. Metropolitan Housing Development Corporation.[1] In the *Arlington Heights* case, the issue was rezoning. The Metropolitan Housing Development Corporation (MHDC) had applied to the Village of Arlington Heights, Illinois, to rezone a 15-parcel area from single-family to multiple-family classification in order to enable MHDC to construct 190 townhouse units for low- and moderate-income tenants. When the village denied the request, MHDC filed suit alleging violations of the Fourteenth Amendment and the Fair Housing Act of 1968.

Justice Powell, speaking for the Supreme Court, noted that Arlington Heights is a suburb of Chicago, populated mainly by whites and primarily consisting of detached, single-family homes. The religious order that owned an 80-acre parcel decided to make available some of the land for low- and moderate-income housing. The order contracted with a nonprofit developer, MHDC, in order to gain a federal housing subsidy. The request for rezoning resulted in three public hearings which drew large crowds, and some opposition was voiced to low-income housing that would probably be racially integrated. Other opponents focused on the zoning aspects of the petition, citing the fact that the area had always been zoned for single-family dwellings and neighboring citizens had built or purchased in reliance on that classification. Rezoning threatened a measurable drop in property values for neighboring sites. In addition, the zoning restriction on minimum acreage was intended to create a buffer between single-family developments and land uses thought to be incompatible with residential use.

Justice Powell attacked the major finding in the court of appeals' decision, its reliance on the disproportionate impact on minorities of the adverse zoning decision as sufficient proof of discrimination. He first cited the Court's decision (during the previous term) in Washington v. Davis,[2] which held that official action will not be held unconstitutional solely because it results in a racially disproportionate impact. While this disproportionate impact was not irrelevant, the Court held that proof of racially discriminatory intent or purpose is required to show a violation of the equal protection clause. Plaintiffs need not prove that discrimination was the "dominant" or "primary" motive, and once evidence of its presence is introduced, judicial deference is no longer justified. The impact of an action may suffice, as in Gomillion v. Lightfoot,[3] but cases providing so stark a pattern are rare.

Thus, courts must look to other evidence, Justice Powell declared, including the historical background of the decision; the specific sequence of events leading up to the challenge decision; departures from the normal procedural sequence; or substantive departures by policymakers, particularly if factors usually considered important strongly favor a decision contrary to the one reached. Reviewing the *Arlington Heights* record, Justice Powell acknowledged that the impact of the

§7.14   1. 429 U.S. 252 (1977).
2. 426 U.S. 229 (1976).
3. 364 U.S. 339 (1960).

village's decision not to rezone placed a heavier burden on racial minorities, but that much of the evidence focused on the wisdom of altering zoning that had long been established. Plaintiffs claimed simply that discrimination motivated the zoning action, Justice Powell concluded, but they failed to carry their burden of proving that discriminatory purpose was a motivating factor in the village's decision. He pointed out that had this burden been carried, the case would not have been made, but the burden would then have shifted to the village to establish that the same decision would have resulted even had the impermissible purpose been considered. If the village succeeded in this effort, there would again be no justification for judicial interference with the challenged decision.

Finally, Justice Powell noted that plaintiffs had alleged that the defendants violated their rights under Title VIII, as well as the Fourteenth Amendment, and that the court of appeals had proceeded in a somewhat unorthodox fashion by not deciding the statutory question. The case was therefore remanded for consideration of the plaintiffs' statutory claims. On remand, the Seventh Circuit decided that, under some circumstances, discriminatory effect may be enough to make out a violation of the Fair Housing Act of 1968.[4] The Seventh Circuit's standard for identifying statutory violations contained four critical factors: (1) the strength of plaintiffs' showing of discriminatory effect; (2) some evidence of discriminatory intent; (3) the defendant's interest in taking the action complained of; and (4) whether the plaintiff seeks affirmative action or merely restraint from interference. The Seventh Circuit held that where the land rezoned by defendants is the only land suitable for federally subsidized low-cost housing, then a refusal to rezone violates the act.[5]

---

4. 558 F.2d 1283 (7th Cir. 1977). The court noted that the Washington v. Davis decision, while announcing its new intent requirement for equal protection cases, reaffirmed the viability of Griggs v. Duke Power Co., 401 U.S. 424 (1971), in which it had earlier held that an employment practice which produced a discriminatory effect was invalid under Title VII, unless it was shown to be job-related. Concluding from a comparison of Titles VII and VIII that Congress intended both to be construed expansively in order to implement their nondiscriminatory goals, the Seventh Circuit held that, "[a] strict focus on intent permits racial discrimination to go unpunished in the absence of evidence of overt bigotry. As overtly bigoted behavior has become more unfashionable, evidence of intent has become harder to find. But this does not mean that racial discrimination has disappeared. We cannot agree that Congress in enacting the Fair Housing Act intended to permit municipalities to systematically deprive minorities of housing opportunities simply because those municipalities act discreetly." 558 F.2d at 1290.

5. The Seventh Circuit remanded the case to the district court for determination of the facts based on its standard. Subsequently, the Supreme Court denied certiorari, 434 U.S. 1025 (1978). After seven years of litigation, there would seem to be a happy ending in the *Arlington Heights* case. After the litigation was remanded to the district court, the two parties agreed to construct the housing development on an alternate site. The alternate site is not in Arlington Heights, but is located in an unincorporated area of the county between Arlington Heights and the village of Mt. Prospect. As one might imagine, the village was quite willing to have the project built on what the district judge described as "land on the fringe of the village." And, as might have been predicted, the village of Mt. Prospect was not pleased and raised all the arguments against the project which Arlington Heights had interjected at an earlier stage of the litigation. The district judge rejected all objections and approved a consent order. 469 F. Supp. 836 (N.D. Ill. 1979).

§7.14.2   The Re-Emergence of Pre–*Arlington Heights* Standards

The *Arlington Heights* standard, both the intent-oriented measure promulgated by the Supreme Court for Fourteenth Amendment cases, and the effect-oriented measure developed by the Seventh Circuit for housing challenges under Title VIII, has a strangely circular character. In this litigation, the fundamentals of housing discrimination law apparently underwent a traumatic metamorphosis only to emerge in almost the same form they held prior to the cataclysmic event. Prior to *Arlington Heights*, few housing cases were decided strictly on whether a challenged action would have a disproportionate impact on minorities.[6] And, in cases decided by lower courts, no significant change in standards of proof seems to have occurred, despite a certain amount of verbal genuflecting in the direction of the *Arlington Heights* language. In lower court decisions handed down both before and after the "big case," plaintiffs, to prevail, had to prove that the challenged action discriminated against them and was, at least to a significant extent, intended to discriminate against them. The post–*Arlington Heights* cases indicate that this task is more easily carried out in some cases than in others.

For example, it was relatively easy in Resident Advisory Board v. Rizzo.[7] This case easily met all the various measures suggested by Justice Powell for proving discriminatory intent and purpose. The litigation had a history extending back 20 years, during all of which time efforts had been made to develop a low-income housing project in the Whitman Urban Renewal Area of South Philadelphia. A site had been selected in 1956, the result of which was that a number of black families living in the area were forced to move to blocks adjacent to the project or to other neighborhoods. Subsequent modifications to the project required the condemnation of additional land, requiring many black families relocated to this area to again move. As a result of the clearance efforts, every black family was removed from an area that initially had been slightly less than 50 percent black. Thus, a previously integrated area was transformed into an entirely segregated white community.[8]

In 1970, the property was conveyed to a private developer for the construction of the low-income housing, but community residents conducted a protest that prevented the delivery trucks and construction equipment from entering the site. The company obtained a court injunction against the demonstrations, but the Philadelphia police failed to enforce it, and subsequently the city obtained an

---

6. See Dailey v. City of Lawton, 425 F.2d 1037 (10th Cir. 1970) (defendant city's refusal to rezone land to permit federally subsidized project to be constructed in a white neighborhood deemed "racially motivated" and unconstitutional); Kennedy Park Homes Ass'n v. City of Lackawanna, 436 F.2d 108 (2d Cir. 1970) (city's refusal to issue building permits for subsidized housing in a predominantly white area deemed purposefully discriminatory under both the Fourteenth Amendment and Title VIII).

7. 564 F.2d 126 (3d Cir. 1977).

8. 564 F.2d at 131-132. A detailed report of the city of Philadelphia's harassment of the construction company is set out in the district court's opinion. Resident Advisory Bd. v. Rizzo, 425 F. Supp. 987 (E.D. Pa. 1976). Philadelphia exceeded anything attributed to Chicago in opposition to the public housing policies ordered in *Gautreaux*, and equaled, in its disregard for the law and its own contractual promises, policies emanating from Selma, Alabama, or Mississippi during the early 1960s.

injunction to prevent the company from resuming construction. The city subsequently initiated legal action claiming the company had breached its contract. Under this barrage of opposition, the company finally withdrew from the project.[9]

In the federal suit, plaintiffs charged that the city and various agency defendants had violated their rights under Title VIII as well as under the Constitution. The district court agreed with the plaintiffs with regard to a violation of Title VIII because the defendants' activities had a racially discriminatory impact which was not justified by compelling government interest. In addition, the district court found that the city had acted with discriminatory intent in violation of the Thirteenth and Fourteenth Amendments.[10] In affirming, the Third Circuit cited the Seventh Circuit's decision on remand in *Arlington Heights*, and held that discriminatory effect was the proper test under Title VIII, and that plaintiffs had satisfied that test. Acknowledging that the burden of proof to justify a case of prima facie discrimination then shifted to the defendants, the court declined to rule that the compelling interest test applied. Rather, the court of appeals said that the defendants must show "a legitimate, bona fide interest," and "that no alternative course of action could be adopted."[11]

Here, as with the decisions in the school desegregation area, one is left with the distinct impression that when courts become overly involved in providing detailed standards for the proof necessary to find liability for racial discrimination, it indicates either judicial unease with the character of the remedy requested or, more likely, prudential concern over the expected resistance to implementation of that remedy by defendants and those citizens defendants represent. As urged by its proponents, the disproportionate impact theory of racial discrimination had much to commend it as a basic standard in a world where discrimination utilizing neutral, nonracial standards is widely used.[12] It is seldom the case that plaintiffs, relying on the disproportionate impact theory, would not be able to supplement their proof with evidence of historic discrimination, procedural irregularities, or substantive decisions and statements reflecting racial motivation. The Court's insistence on these additional factors of proof in Washington v. Davis may merely reflect its reaction to an inadequately prepared and possibly ill-advised lawsuit. At the least, the Court's application of its Washington v. Davis test in the *Arlington Heights* case was strained, and served to confuse more than clarify the proof issue. The seeming greater willingness to accept adverse effect in Title VIII suits may serve as an acceptable solution to the proof dilemma, but as indicated in *Resident Advisory Board*, many cases will provide more than enough discriminatory evidence to meet both constitutional as well as statutory standards.

9. 425 F. Supp. at 1021-1025.
10. 564 F.2d at 140. Facts similar to those of the *Resident Advisory Board* case were present in Joseph Silken & Co. v. City of Toledo, Ohio, 380 F. Supp. 228 (N.D. Ohio 1974), rev'd, 528 F.2d 867 (6th Cir. 1975). The Supreme Court, following its *Arlington Heights* decision, vacated the court of appeals' ruling that defendant's conduct blocking construction of public housing for minorities in white areas of the city was not racially discriminatory. But when the court of appeals, on remand, reaffirmed its earlier ruling without discussion, the Supreme Court denied certiorari.
11. 564 F.2d at 149.
12. See Michael Perry, The Disproportionate Impact Theory of Racial Discrimination, 125 U. Pa. L. Rev. 540 (1977).

§7.14.3   Exclusionary Zoning Litigation in State Courts

During the 1970s, state courts evidenced their recognition of the housing crisis and the impact of exclusionary zoning practices in a series of decisions which utilized the state's police powers, both to void zoning and other exclusionary schemes that seriously limited low-income housing construction, and to impose inclusionary requirements designed to encourage suburban communities to accept their "fair share" of low-income housing projects.

The fair share principle was first enunciated by the New Jersey Supreme Court in Southern Burlington County NAACP v. Township of Mt. Laurel.[13] In a decision hailed by civil rights activists, the New Jersey Supreme Court affirmed a voiding of a restrictive ordinance and approved an affirmative order requiring the municipality to provide low- and moderate-income housing. Speaking through Justice Hall, the court held that the provision of adequate housing for all categories of people is an "absolute" essential in promoting the general welfare, and is "required in all land use regulation." The court concluded that a developing municipality may not, by a system of land use regulations, make it physically and economically impossible to provide low- and moderate-income housing in the municipality for the various categories of persons who need and want it, thereby excluding such people from living within its confines because of the limited extent of their incomes and resources. Rather, the court found that every municipality must make realistically possible an appropriate variety and choice of housing. The Court held that "[t]hese obligations must be met unless the particular municipality can sustain the heavy burden of demonstrating peculiar circumstances that dictate that it should not be required so to do."[14]

Cases like *Mt. Laurel* have been litigated under a state rather than the federal constitution, a strategy that avoids review, and possible reversal, by the Supreme Court on a federal constitutional issue. Placing the decision on state constitutional grounds also renders difficult, if it does not entirely foreclose, effective amendment of the state zoning law by state legislatures who might respond to the opposition of suburban constituents. But insulating decisions requiring fair share zoning from judicial attack is one thing; setting meaningful standards for compliance and obtaining more than token implementation of the principle is quite another.

Mt. Laurel II demonstrates how, in several areas of constitutional and civil rights law, state courts have taken the initiative once reserved to federal courts and agencies. In 1982, the New Jersey Supreme Court made a valiant effort to attack exclusionary zoning in Southern Burlington County NAACP v. Mt. Laurel

---

13. 67 N.J. 151, 336 A.2d 713 (1975).
14. Id. at 174, 336 A.2d at 724. The New Jersey court reviewed Mt. Laurel Township's justifications for its land use regulation, to determine whether the municipality had carried its heavy burden of showing "peculiar circumstances" that would exempt it from the fair share standard. This burden, the court concluded, could not be carried by the assertion of concerns over maintaining a rural environment and protecting the local tax base. Rather, the need to adequately house all categories of people is of such importance "that the general welfare which developing municipalities like Mt. Laurel must consider extends beyond their boundaries and cannot be parochially confined to the claimed good of the particular municipality." 67 N.J. at 79, 336 A.2d at 727-728.

Township.[15] The case represented the reopening, after eight years, of the *Mt. Laurel* controversy.[16] In response to lower court decisions approving narrow interpretations of the *Mt. Laurel* doctrine and minor rezoning and other limited remedies, the court accepted cases concerning six New Jersey municipalities. The court reiterated its commitment to the *Mt. Laurel* doctrine and expressed unhappiness with the lack of progress since 1975. Though the doctrine has had some practical effect — numerous municipalities have amended ordinances to allow low- and moderate-income housing — many cases have dragged on in unending litigation.[17]

The court put teeth into the *Mt. Laurel* doctrine by recognizing a "builder's remedy" that allows judges to approve increased housing densities if a town's zoning does not provide for a fair share of low- and moderate-income housing. In addition, incentives were provided to towns that voluntarily rezone in the form of a grace period from builders' suits. Though local reaction to the decision had been mixed, legal commentators greeted *Mt. Laurel II* as a "landmark" and a major leap in housing law.[18] The case did, to some extent, provide a major leap in New Jersey. As one writer has said, "Developers took *Mt. Laurel II* seriously."[19] The decision led to numerous court cases, many of which were settled in ways that provided new housing for low-income people in New Jersey. The wave of litigation, however, also led to state litigation that created the Council on Affordable Housing (COAH) — an agency to whom all pending cases under *Mt. Laurel II* would be transferred absent "manifest injustice," but which lacks the teeth necessary to actually create housing for people who need it.

It is clear, even from the brief summaries, that state courts are aware of the serious societal problem imposed by the great and growing shortage of low-income housing, but that even their efforts are not likely to substantially lessen a shortage based far more on socioeconomic and political pressures than on shortcomings in the law. If communities saw that it was in their interest to include and encourage low-income housing, there is little doubt that they would do so without government subsidy, and without the rather than the limited prodding provided by judicial orders. But all too many suburban communities grew out of a desire of those who built and resided there to separate themselves from what they considered urban problems, and to congregate in a racially and economically homogeneous circle, resisting with all the considerable political power at their disposal encroachment by those that they had come together to exclude.

---

15. 92 N.J. 158, 456 A.2d 390 (1983).

16. Southern Burlington County NAACP v. Township of Mt. Laurel, 67 N.J. 151, 336 A.2d 713, cert. denied, 423 U.S. 808 (1975).

17. 92 N.J. at 170, 456 A.2d at 402.

18. See Leonard Zax & Jerold Kayden, A Landmark in Land Use, Nat'l L.J., Mar. 14, 1983, at 11.

19. Kenneth E. Meiser, The *Mt. Laurel* Doctrine: A 25 (Plus)-Year Personal Perspective, 188 N.J. Law. 8 (1997).

§7.15   MORTGAGE DISCRIMINATION

Civil rights advocates maintain that one of the barriers perpetuating both the residential segregation of, and inadequate housing provided for minorities, is discrimination in mortgage lending.[1] "Until 1949, FHA official policy was to refuse to insure any unsegregated housing. It was not until . . . 1962 that the agency required nondiscrimination pledges from loan applicants."[2] When the FHA shifted its policies in 1966 towards making more mortgages available for inner-city neighborhoods, the effect was only to further white flight and segregation. As Professor Kenneth T. Jackson writes:

> Ironically, the primary effect of the change was to make it easier for white families to finance their escape from areas experiencing racial change. At the same time, the relaxed credit standards for black applicants meant that home improvement companies could buy properties at low cost, make cosmetic improvements, and sell the renovated home at inflated prices approved by FHA. Many of the minority purchasers could not afford the cost of maintenance, and FHA had to repossess thousands of homes. The final result was to increase the speed with which areas went through racial transformation and to victimize those it was designed to help. The only people to benefit were contractors and white, middle-class homeowners who were assisted in escaping from a distress position.[3]

An authoritative report released by the Federal Reserve Board in 1991 revealed a wide gap between the mortgage denial rates for whites and those for minorities.[4] While for many years racial discrimination in mortgage lending was

---

§7.15   1. Black Groups Speak Out on America's Homeownership Gap, Wash. Informer, Mar. 18, 1998, v. 34, n.21 (an appeal by several African American groups to the U.S. Justice and Housing and Urban Development departments to investigate the growing gap in African American home-ownership). See also Jesse Jackson, Racism Is the Bottom Line in Home Loans: After Rejection by Banks, Blacks and Latinos Are Driven to Private Lenders Who Charge 30% Using the Same Bank Capital, L.A. Times, Oct. 28, 1991, at B5, col. 1 [hereafter "Racism Is Bottom Line"]. Discriminatory lending practices are not a new phenomenon. See, e.g., Theodore Rosengarten, All God's Dangers: The Life of Nate Shaw 266-269, 327-330 (1974) (detailing the collaboration of local banker with white landholder to appropriate to the latter's benefit illiterate Alabama tenant farmer/sharecropper's personal property through unfair repayment requirements on loans extended for agricultural purposes).

2. Report of the National Advisory Commission on Civil Disorders (Kerner Commission Report) 474 (1968); see also Kenneth T. Jackson, Crabgrass Frontier 206-217 (1985).

3. Jackson, supra note 2, at 214-215.

4. The study examined 5.3 million mortgage applications made to 9,300 banks and other lenders in 1990. The report found that, nationwide, 33.9 percent of black applicants and 21.4 percent of Hispanic applicants were denied home mortgages, compared with 14.4 percent of whites. Among the highest-income applicant group, the denial rate nationally for blacks was 21.4 percent; for whites, 8.5 percent; and for Asians, 11.2 percent. Racial Gap Detailed on Mortgages, N.Y. Times, Oct. 22, 1991, at D1, col. 3 (quoting Maud Hurd, president of Association of Community Organizations for Reform Now, who stated that "if you're a minority, our nation's banks want only your deposits, not your loan applications"); Minorities Strike Out with Banks; Mortgage Rejection Rates High for Blacks, Hispanics, N.Y. Newsday, Oct. 22, 1991, at 45 (quoting attorney Richard Marsico of the Citywide Responsible Banking Alliance, that the Federal Reserve study results "certainly show what community advocates have been saying all along").

conceptualized as a problem of geographic "redlining,"[5] the new study showed that race is more significant than wealth in determining the likelihood of loan approval.

In 1993, Comptroller Stephen R. Steinbrink announced a new procedure for fair-lending exams, which involved comparing the loan files of minority applicants who were rejected to those of non-minority applicants who were approved. Finally, the nation's chief banking regulator began using testers or "mystery-shoppers" to test institutions' sincerity when making loans to low-income and minority families.[6]

After acknowledging that race discrimination is a significant indicator of the likelihood of mortgage loan denial, federal enforcement agencies under the Clinton Administration stepped up efforts to discover discrimination and enforce the Home Mortgage Disclosure Act (HMDA), which permits both private and public actions.[7] The Departments of Justice (DOJ) and Housing and Urban Development (HUD) proceeded to bring a series of high profile actions charging banks and other lenders with discrimination in lending on the basis of race and national origin.[8] On Martin Luther King Day of 1998, President Clinton triumphantly announced a $6.5 billion settlement between HUD and the Columbia National Mortgage Company.[9] The settlement would be used to help 78,000 minority and low- and moderate-income families "unlock the door to homeownership." Thirty-one years after Congress passed the Fair Housing Act, Clinton proudly hailed the Columbia settlement as a sign that housing discrimination had ended.[10] Unfortunately, the sizeable Columbia settlement seemed to indicate only the continued depth and pervasiveness of discrimination in mortgage lending.

A 2001 study released by the Association for Community Organizations for Reform Now (ACORN) indicates that African Americans were 2.31 times more likely than white applicants to be turned down for a conventional mortgage, while Hispanics were rejected 1.53 times more often. The study, based on the Federal Financial Institutions Examiners Council data from over 7,800 lenders covered by

---

5. "Redlining" has been defined as "mortgage credit discrimination based on the characteristics of the neighborhood surrounding the would-be borrower's dwelling." Buycks-Robereson v. Citibank Fed. Sav. Bank, 162 F.R.D. 322, 323 (N.D. Ind. 1995), quoting Thomas v. First Fed. Sav. Bank of Ind., 653 F. Supp. 1330, 1337 (N.D. Ind. 1987); see also AACP v. AFMI Co., 978 F.2d 287, 290 (7th Cir. 1992), cert. denied, 508 U.S. 907 (1993); Cartwright v. American Sav. Ass'n, 880 F.2d 912, 922 (7th Cir. 1989).

6. Earl Golz, Regulator's "Mystery-Shoppers" Find Loan Disparity, Regulator Still Finding Inequalities; Regulator Says Loan Disparity Still an Issue, Austin Am.-Statesman, Mar. 12, 1998, at D1.

7. Home Mortgage Disclosure Act, 12 U.S.C. §2801 et seq., as amended by the Financial Institutions Reform, Recovery, and Enforcement Act of 1989 (FIRREA), Pub. L. No. 101-73, §1211, 103 Stat. 183, 524-526 (1989).

8. See, e.g., U.S. v. Decatur Fed. Sav. & Loan Ass'n (N.D. Ga. 1992) (consent decree); U.S. v. Shawmut Mortgage Co. (D. Conn. 1993) (consent decree); U.S. v. Chevy Chase Fed. Sav. Bk., (D.D.C. 1994) (consent decree); U.S. v. The Northern Trust Co. (N.D. Ill. 1995) (consent decree); U.S. v. Fleet Mortgage Corp. (E.D.N.Y. 1996) (consent decree).

9. William J. Clinton, Remarks to AmeriCorps Volunteers, 1/25/99 Weekly Compilation of Presidential Documents 74, vol. 35, issue 3.

10. Id.

HMDA, found that the disparity is "greater than it was in 2000 and an even bigger increase from what it was in 1996."[11] Minorities are disadvantaged in the lending process both by the service they receive and by differential pricing.[12] Individuals living in minority neighborhoods with few banks to choose from may be forced to accept unfair lending terms.

The denial of mortgages by banks to minority borrowers has extremely pernicious effects. Funds to buy houses, and to maintain them once bought, are difficult to obtain. Many minority applicants go to private lenders, who borrow money from the same banks that denied the minority applicants mortgages or loans, and who in turn charge the applicants interest rates as high as 34.09 percent. If the borrower falls behind in her payments, these secondary lenders may foreclose.[13] Thus, long-term, stable homeowners with no intention of selling are often forced to give up their homes. Bernard Frieden, professor of urban development at MIT, stated that "[i]t's very circular. People can't fix up their homes because they can't get a mortgage, so you get buildings aging and falling apart, and that leads to a belief that the neighborhood is a poor investment risk, because the buildings are falling down. It all runs together."[14]

Note: Predatory Lending Targets Minorities

Although recent studies suggest that discrimination in lending is declining as loans to minorities increase, consumer advocates caution that such information is incomplete because it fails to account for the prevalence of loans with unfair terms or high interest rates. Even when African Americans secure mortgages, many become victims of predatory lending. Using suspect practices, lenders target consumers who do not realize the traps in the fine print of loans, including hidden charges and inflated interest rates. Subprime lenders, companies that specialize in loans for people or businesses with blemished credit records or other financial problems, can potentially provide loans for individuals who would not otherwise have access to institutional lenders. But many have been accused of disproportionately providing loans at very high rates to minorities, many of whom could qualify for prime rate loans. Freddie Mac and Fannie Mae, two large institutional lenders, "estimate that 35 percent to 50 percent of all homeowners with subprime

11. Amilda Dymi, Discrimination Down for Some Minorities?, Nat'l Mortgage News, Nov. 25, 2002, at 22.

12. David E. Teitelbaum & Clarke D. Camper, Developments in Fair Lending, 51 Bus. Law. 843 (May 1996); Warren W. Traiger, New York Seizes Fair Lending Initiative, v. 219, n.49, 3/16/98 N.Y.L.J. 1, col. 1. Lending discrimination settlements by the department include a $2.1-billion agreement with AccuBank Mortgage of Dallas and $1.3-billion with Temple-Inlan Mortgage of Austin, Tex. See Rob Wells, Columbia Reaches $6.5 Billion Settlement: Mortgage Lender Accused by Minorities, Low Income Buyers, Nat'l Post, Jan. 19, 1999, at C10.

13. Racism Is Bottom Line, supra note 1; Boston Minority Areas Found Trapped by Credit Squeeze, Boston Globe, Oct. 23, 1991, at 1 [hereafter "Credit Squeeze"] (describing Massachusetts "second-mortgage scandal" where, because of the lack of bank branches in their neighborhoods, minority homeowners were found more likely to fall prey to the "bottom-dwellers" of the financial world, i.e., the high-interest mortgage lenders and the high-fee check cashing outlets).

14. Justice Using Off-Duty Agents for Lending Tests, Reg. Compliance Watch, May 11, 1998, at 1.

loans might have qualified for lower-cost financing had they known what to look for and how to shop for a loan."[15]

Consumer advocates argue that predatory lending has become an epidemic for low-income communities of color and the elderly.[16] A 2002 study of home refinancing conducted by ACORN presented findings that African Americans "were 4.4 times more likely than whites to end up with a subprime loan, while Hispanics were more than twice as likely to do so." Even with growing attention to the problem, the practice will be difficult to eliminate, leaving African Americans seeking home loans with virtually no fair-lending options.

Perverse interests, combined with a lack of oversight, has generated an enormous market of predatory lending. Brokers are paid on commission and receive kickbacks from lenders for funneling business to them.[17] It is more profitable for these brokers to steer a borrower toward a loan with a higher interest rate than the borrower qualifies for.[18] Such brokers often steer prospective borrowers toward "exploding" adjustable rate mortgages that offer an immediate reduction and then jump to 30-50 percent beyond the initial payments, pushing the payments well beyond the range of the borrower's budget.[19]

The consequences of subprime lending and the foreclosures it entails are widespread. Areas with high proportions of minorities have a disproportionate number of foreclosures. One foreclosure decreases the value of all other homes on the block by about 1.5 percent.[20] As property loses value, homeowners are forced to refinance, perpetuating the cycle throughout entire neighborhoods. The problem has become so prevalent that many states, including Florida, North Carolina, and New York, have passed laws designed to curb predatory lending. In 2007, Congressional members introduced the "Mortgage Reform and Anti-Predatory Lending Act of 2007" to protect families from abusive subprime mortgages. However, even if this legislation does successfully curtail future predatory lending, support must be provided for the borrowers that have already been victimized by questionable lending practices. Throughout 2007, foreclosures on subprime loans continued to mount to the highest levels ever recorded in the modern mortgage market. Over $600 billion in loans will have interest rate resets within the next two years, indicating that things are likely to worsen for subprime borrowers before they improve.[21]

As this edition goes to press, the excesses of the sub-prime market, particularly as these instruments have been bundled and sold to large investors, hedge funds, have now caused billions in losses to major banking and investing institutions. Credit markets in general both in the United States and other countries have

15. See ACORN Urges Scrutiny Before Celebrating Growth in Minority Lending Increases—May Be Due to Harmful Predatory Loans, available at http://www.acorn.org/acorn10/predatorylending/plreleases/scrutiny.htm.
16. Id.
17. See Delvin Davis, Here Today, Gone Tomorrow: The Impact of Subprime Foreclosures on African-American and Latino Communities, 16 Poverty & Race 1, 2 (2007).
18. Id.
19. Id. at 1-2.
20. Id. at 12.
21. Id.

been shaken and there are predictions that the unacknowledged recession that is all too real in minority communities, will spread and further undermine the U.S. economy.[22]

22. For a general explanation of the situation, see James Grant, The Fed's Subprime Solution, N.Y. Times, Aug. 26, 2007.

Chapter 8

Interracial Intimate Relationships and Racial Identification

§8.1 DEFINING THE CONTEMPORARY MISCEGENATION PROBLEM

Society's attraction-repulsion ambivalence to interracial sex not only preceded the array of prohibitions on such unions, but survives their repeal. This chapter examines the origins of the hostility to interracial unions, its development and incorporation into law, and the residue of racial problems that have accompanied the new sexual freedom, whether within or outside the bounds of matrimony. Based on the paucity of litigation now engendered over the issue, one might conclude that the barriers to interracial sex and marriage had been leveled permanently. Since the Supreme Court struck down such provisions in Loving v. Virginia[1] and McLaughlin v. Florida,[2] states, in the main, have sought neither to enforce statutes barring interracial marriage nor to exact more onerous penalties for interracial cohabitation. Yet interracial unions in this country, while far more common than even two decades ago, are far from the generally accepted norm.

Despite or perhaps because of continuing societal concerns, interracial dating has become common on at least the more progressive college and high school campuses and, according to U.S. Census reports, the number of interracial marriages in this country is growing. Between 1960 and 1970, the number of interracial marriages jumped by 108 percent (from 148,000 to 310,000). It doubled again in the 1970s, climbing to 639,000 in 1981. By 1992, the United States had 1,161,000 interracial married couples, 246,000 of them black/white couples.[3] For the first time in the history of the Census, reflecting a strong debate among minority

§8.1   1. 388 U.S. 1 (1967).
2. 379 U.S. 184 (1964).
3. Source: U.S. Bureau of the Census, Current Population Reports: Population Characteristics — Perspectives on American Husbands and Wives (Mar. 1970); Current Population Reports: Population Characteristics — Household and Family Characteristics (Mar. 1981); Current Population Reports: Population Characteristics — Material Status and Living Arrangements (Mar. 1992).

The number of interracial couples increased steadily throughout the 1970s and 1980s, and black/white couples increased by 20 percent in the 1970s (65,000 in 1970 to 132,000 in 1981) and by another 20 percent in the 1980s (132,000 in 1981 to 231,000 in 1991). Eighty percent of all black/white couples in 1981 consisted of a black husband and a white wife. By 1992, the percentage of black

communities, Census 2000 presented respondents with a different list of racial categories[4] yet permitted them to select more than one race.[5] Of the total population, 2.4 percent indicated more than one race.[6] As a result, it has been difficult to quantify interracial marriages using the more recent data. However, the number has continued to increase, reported by news sources as well over two million.

The steadily increasing figures do not much alter the fact that the increase in interracial couples represents only a small percentage of all married couples. Interracial married couple households in 2000 were only 6 percent of the total married population.[7] The highest concentration of these couples was in the West, with 11 percent, not surprisingly in areas with high concentrations of Native populations.[8] Even so, the acceptance level, if not the legality, of interracial sex and marriage remains a controversial area of American life for both whites and nonwhites. Why this should be so in a heterogeneous society where marriages across ethnic and religious lines are both common and often a basis for pride is the issue examined in this chapter.

The cases and topics summarized here reflect the strong feelings that continue to characterize the discussion, to say nothing of the fact, of interracial relationships. Reservations about, opposition to, and support of mixed marriages and sexual liaisons can be found in black as well as white communities. It is also a controversial subject in the Asian and Latino communities. One would hope that four decades after *Loving,* reservations might be limited to family-level matters and no longer manifest themselves in discriminatory public policies. But as the cases indicate, charges of employment discrimination based on interracial marriage or relationships remain a source of litigation. The alterations of adoption and custody statutes, along with a sharp increase in litigation of these issues, are indicative of local and national concern about the race relations of the next generation. To the extent that debate continues in the legislature, in courtrooms, and in popular culture on the topic of interracial and international adoption, the underlying anxiety about interracial marriage has clearly not dissipated.

---

husband–white wife couples had dropped to two-thirds. Id.

Perhaps reflective of the trend, in 2005, 422,000 black/white marriages took place; in 1990 211,000, that is, 4 out of every 1,000. In 1970, 1.5 of every 1,000 marriages were interracial.

4. In 1990, the following list of racial categories existed: White, black, Indian (American), Eskimo, Aleut, Chinese, Filipino, Hawaiian, Korean, Vietnamese, Japanese, Asian Indian, Samoan, Guamanian, Other (API), Other Race. The 2000 Census combined American Indian and Alaska Native and asks for those self-identifying as such to indicate, by writing in, their tribal affiliation.

5. Nicholas A. Jones and Amy Symens Smith, The Two or More Races Population: 2000, Census 2000 Brief, Nov. 2001 at 1.

6. Tavia Simmons & Martin O'Connell, Married-Couple and Unmarried-Partner Households: 2000, Census 2000 Special Rep., Feb. 2003, at 11. The report categorized a couple as interracial if either partner or spouse was not in the same single race as the other partner, or if at least one partner was multiracial. The 2000 Census included many racial categories that were reduced to seven for reporting purposes: white alone; black/African American alone; American or Alaska Native alone; Asian alone; Native Hawaiian and other Pacific Islander alone; some other race alone and two or more races.

7. Id. This 6 percent figure does not include households with only one partner of Hispanic origin, which constituted 3.1 percent of all married couples in the United States.

8. A higher percentage of partners from different races, 12 percent, were found amongst unmarried partner households.

§8.2 THE RISE AND DECLINE OF MISCEGENATION LAWS

According to historian Winthrop Jordan,[1] the sense that Africans were not only different but inferior to Englishmen was prevalent in Shakespeare's time. Certainly, this feeling had not lessened when Europeans and Africans met in America. No one thought intermixture was a good thing, but interracial sex was extensive in all the English colonies. Professor Jordan estimates that sex between the races was most common among the lower classes, but that white men of every social rank engaged in sex with black women. In most colonies, the offspring of interracial unions were illegitimate, but legally recognized interracial marriages did occur. Nevertheless, while the private desire for sexual relationships across race lines was evident, the public distaste became sufficiently strong to be reflected in the statutes of Maryland and Virginia as early as the 1660s.

Tracing the history of the Maryland anti-miscegenation statute is revealing. The 1664 provision entitled "An Act Concerning Negroes and Other Slaves"[2] provided that all blacks and other slaves either within the colony or thereafter imported into the colony, as well as their children, shall be slaves for life. Within the same provision, the law provided that any "freeborne (white) woman who thereafter married a slave would be required to serve the master of such slave during her husband's life, and that any children born of this union would be slaves."[3] Thus, in a statute designed to make official the increasingly common practice of requiring Negroes to remain indentured servants for life (that is, slaves), the law sought to control interracial unions as a mechanism of making clear the distinction between whites and blacks. Subsequent laws indicate that the goals of the original measure often backfired. In 1681, the earlier 1664 state statute was repealed and replaced by a new provision that continued the status of blacks as slaves, but added:

> And for as much a[s] diverse ffreeborne Englishe or Whitewoman *sometimes* by the Instigation Procurement or Conievance of theire Masters Mistres or dames, & *always* to the Satisfaction of their Lascivious & Lustfull desires, & to the disgrace not only of the English butt allso of many other Christian Nations, doe Intermarry with Negroes & Slaves by which means diverse Inconveniencys Controversys & suits may arise. . . . [4]

To frustrate such schemes the 1681 law provided that if any master contrived to get a white woman to marry a slave, then that servant would be absolutely discharged from her indentured service, and all her children would be born free. Masters who permitted such marriages, as well as ministers who performed them, were subject to fines of 10,000 pounds of tobacco.[5]

---

§8.2   1. Winthrop Jordan, White Over Black: American Attitudes Toward the Negro 1550-1812, 8, 37-39, 136-140 (1968).

2. 1 Md. Archives 533-534.

3. The statute and its successors are reviewed in Jon Alpert, The Origin of Slavery in the United States — The Maryland Precedent, 14 Am. J. Legal Hist. 189 (1970).

4. Id. at 209.

5. Id.

Subsequently, the Maryland legislature realized that the 1681 statute, while discouraging masters from promoting interracial unions between slaves and white servants, encouraged those servants to marry slaves in order to terminate their service obligations. Thus, in 1692, the legislature forbade all interracial marriages and sexual relations.[6] Penalties were provided for persons involved whether slave, servant, or free. White women who had a child by a black man were required to serve for seven years, and if the black man were free, he was required to serve for seven years. The children of such unions were required to be servants until they were 31 years old. It is clear from the provisions of this statute[7] that its basic intent was to define status as much as to discourage interracial sex and marriage. The need for such definition and division is made clear in Professor Edmond Morgan's discussion of the origins of slavery in this country.[8]

§8.2.1   Supreme Court Evasion of Miscegenation Issues

While there was no ban on mixed marriages at common law or by statute in England, virtually all the American colonies, and later the states, enacted such measures. According to one study,[9] 38 states had miscegenation statutes at one time or another during the nineteenth century, and as late as 1951, 29 statutes were still on the books.[10] Prior to the Supreme Court's decision in the Loving v. Virginia case striking down all such laws, only the California Supreme Court in 1948 had declared its miscegenation statute unconstitutional.

No stampede followed the California precedent. The U.S. Supreme Court, by 1954, had reviewed miscegenation legislation only once, in 1883. (In Pace v. Alabama, 106 U.S. 583 (1883), it upheld an Alabama statute because blacks and whites were punished equally for interracial adultery or fornication.) For several years after *Brown*[11] was decided in 1954, the Supreme Court exercised "prudent avoidance" of miscegenation cases. In fact, a few months after its decision, the Court denied certiorari for the Alabama conviction of a black

---

6. Id. at 210.

7. Id. at 210-211.

8. Edmond Morgan, American Slavery, American Freedom (1975), see §1.8. The double standards in interracial sex that prevailed during the slavery era are detailed by Eugene Genovese in his book, Roll, Jordan, Roll: The World the Slaves Made 413-431 (1974).

9. Harvey Applebaum, Miscegenation Statutes: A Constitutional and Social Problem, 53 Geo. L.J. 49 (1964).

10. Id. at 50-51. In Perez v. Sharp, 32 Cal. 2d 711, 198 P. 2d 17 (1948) (Perez v. Lippold), the California Supreme Court voided the state's miscegenation statute in a close 4-3 decision. The majority found the statute violated the Fourteenth Amendment's equal protection clause in that it represented neither a reasonable classification by the legislature, nor was it a response to a clear and present danger. Moreover, the court found it unconstitutionally vague. Concurring opinions found the statute denied due process on the basis that marriage is a Fourteenth Amendment liberty, and found the interests allegedly protected by the statute of evidently little importance in that California recognized so-called "carfare" marriages by local residents who married in neighboring states to avoid the California statute. Moreover, California imposed no criminal sanctions.

11. 347 U.S. 483 (1954) (declaring "separate but equal" black and white school systems unconstitutional).

woman, Linnie Jackson, who was prosecuted for marrying a white man.[12] A provision in the Alabama Constitution of 1965 directed the legislature to pass anti-miscegenation statutes.[13] Interestingly, in 1872, the Alabama Supreme Court in Burns v. State[14] held that state statutes prohibiting the intermarriage of white and black partners violated the Fourteenth Amendment, Civil Rights Bill, and state constitution. The justice writing for the court expressed that "it is self-evidence that an inhabitant of a country, proscribed by its law, approaches equality with the more favored population in proportion as the prescription is removed." Given that this view was not self-evident to the high court in deciding Cox v. Alabama, the Supreme Court of Alabama overturned *Burns*, and interracial marriages were prohibited under state law. Linnie Jackson served her prison sentence.

A half century later, n November 2000, Alabama became the last state to remove formal legal impediments to interracial marriages. The Alabama electorate voted to strike the clause forbidding the legislature from authorizing interracial marriages from the 1965 state constitution.[15] Forty percent of the voters, however, voted not to remove the provision. Just two years earlier, South Carolina repealed its anti-miscegenation provision with 38 percent of voters voting not to remove the language. In some counties, a majority of voters voted to keep the anti-miscegenation passage.[16]

In 1955, the Court went out of its way to avoid invalidating Virginia's anti-miscegenation statute. In Naim v. Naim[17] the Virginia Court distinguished marriage from education, finding that the legislature had complete power to control marriage. In a decision that was "wholly without basis in law,"[18] the Supreme Court found the record incomplete with respect to domicile. The Court dismissed an appeal from the remanded Virginia judgment for lack of a substantial federal question.[19] According to Professor Randall Kennedy, the Justices felt it imprudent to consider *Naim* "on the heels of the Court's recent invalidation of de jure segregation in public schooling."[20] One unreported Justice is quoted as saying, "One bomb shell at a time is enough."[21]

---

12. Jackson v. State, 37 Ala. App. 519, 72 So. 2d 114, cert. denied, 348 U.S. 888 (1954). Randall Kennedy, Interracial Intimacies: Sex, Marriage, Identity, and Adoption 270 (2003). See also Peter Wallerstein, Race, Marriage and the Law of Freedom: Alabama and Virginia, 1860s-1960s, 70 Chi.-Kent L. Rev. 371 (1994); Julie Novkov, Racial Constructions: The Legal Regulation of Miscegenation in Alabama 1890-1934, 20 Law & Hist. Rev. 225 (2002).

13. Wallerstein, supra note 12, at 375.

14. 48 Ala. 195 (1872).

15. Kennedy, supra note 12, at 270.

16. George A. Yancey & Michael O. Emerson, An Analysis of Resistance to Racial Exogamy: The 1998 South Carolina Referendum, Journal of Black Studies, Vol. 32 No. 1, 134 (Sept. 2001).

17. 179 Va. 80, 87 S.E.2d 749 (1955); 349 U.S. 294 (1955).

18. Herbert Wechsler, Toward Neutral Principles of Constitutional Law, 73 Harv. L. Rev. 1, 34 (1959).

19. 350 U.S. 985 (1956).

20. Kennedy, supra note 12, at 270.

21. Id., citing Walter Murphy, Elements of Judicial Strategy 193 (1964).

§8.2.2   McLaughlin v. Florida

The Supreme Court did not review the continued validity of anti-miscegenation laws until the late 1960s, more than a decade after *Brown*. The only argument put forth by the states containing even surface merit, the point in *Pace* (that miscegenation statutes were applied evenly to blacks and whites) had been rejected almost two decades before in Shelley v. Kramer.[22] There, in rejecting a suggestion that restrictive covenant clauses should be found valid because blacks as well as whites could use the courts to enforce their provisions, the Court responded that "equal protection of the laws is not achieved through indiscriminate imposition of inequalities."[23]

Perhaps by the late 1960s the Court felt that the societal myths, fears, and economic concerns that led to the enactment of miscegenation statutes some three centuries before had abated, even though for many such concerns were now so deeply entrenched that they would not likely be altered by rational argument or weakened by further judicial delay.

Professor Ariela Dubler has argued that McLaughlin v. Florida[24] is a "watershed" case which lay the groundwork upon which future cases to invalidate anti-miscegenation statutes would build.[25] In it, the Court invalidated a Florida statute authorizing more severe penalties for interracial cohabitation and adultery than for those crimes committed by persons of the same race. Specifically, section 798.05 of the Florida Statutes made it a crime for "[a]ny negro man and white woman, or any white man and negro woman, who are not married to each other" to "habitually live in and occupy in the nighttime the same room."[26]

The Florida court had upheld the provision relying solely on the Supreme Court's decision in *Pace*. Justice White, writing for the Court, stated that *Pace* had been overturned and applied "most rigid scrutiny" to the racial classification. In addition, White rejected the state's position that the law was necessary to prevent breaches of the basic concepts of sexual decency. Without reaching the validity of the state's miscegenation statute, White found that the anticohabitation law was subject to independent examination under the Fourteenth Amendment. To be upheld, such a law must be necessary, and not merely rationally related, to the accomplishment of a permissible state policy. White reasoned that the general statutes outlawing interracial cohabitation and adultery did not serve the state's policy against interracial marriage.

Most of the Court found that Florida simply failed to show any overriding statutory purpose that would justify a racial classification. In a concurring opinion, Justices Stewart and Douglas expressed doubt that any constitutional purpose could justify a law that "makes the color of a person's skin the test of whether his conduct is a criminal offence." Stewart conceded the constitutionality of keeping racially

---

22. 334 U.S. 1 (1948).
23. Id. at 22.
24. 379 U.S. 184 (1964).
25. Ariela R. Dubler, From McLaughlin v. Florida to Lawrence v. Texas: Sexual Freedom and the Road to Marriage, 106 Colum. L. Rev. 1165, 1174 (June 2006).
26. Fla. Stat. Ann. §798.05 (repealed 1969), quoted in McLaughlin, 379 U.S. at 186 n.1.

segregated records for valid public purposes,[27] but he concluded, "Discrimination of that kind is invidious per se." Professor Dubler writes that the Court's decision signals, "a dramatic renunciation of deeply embedded cultural views of interracial sex as particularly illicit in a way that was different in kind from non marital sex between people of the same race because of the unique threat it posed to the socio-political order."[28] She brings attention to writing from the press including a New York Times article which reflected on McLaughlin with, ". . . the case could determine the validity of anti-miscegenation laws in general,"[29] and a Washington Post story which wrote, "it was clear that one more push would probably finish the job."[30] That extra push was Loving v. Virginia.

§8.2.3   Loving v. Virginia

Three years after the *McLaughlin* case, the Supreme Court delivered the legal coup de grace to laws prohibiting interracial marriage in Loving v. Virginia.[31] By this time, whatever their personal views as to its wisdom or appropriateness, most thoughtful citizens were ready to concede that statutes barring interracial marriage clearly violated the post-*Brown* interpretation of the Fourteenth Amendment's equal protection clause. Speaking for a unanimous Court, Chief Justice Warren made it official. Significantly, for those members of the Court perhaps still smarting from criticism of the *Naim* "prudent tactic," it was Virginia's comprehensive statutory scheme prohibiting and punishing interracial marriages that the Court found violated both the equal protection and due process clauses of the Fourteenth Amendment.

Mildred Jeter, a black woman, and Richard Loving, a white man, like the Naim couple, were married outside Virginia and then returned to the state and established their residence. They were subsequently indicted for violating Virginia's ban on interracial marriages, pled guilty to the charge, and were sentenced to one year in jail with sentence suspended for 25 years on condition that the Lovings leave the state and not return for that period.[32] Leaving the state, the Lovings challenged their conviction. The Virginia Court of Appeals affirmed.

Chief Justice Warren, noting that 16 states continued to prohibit and punish marriages on the basis of racial classifications, traced all of such provisions back to

---

27. Tancil v. Wools, 379 U.S. 19 (1964). The decision affirmed, per curiam, Hamm v. Virginia State Board of Elections, 280 F. Supp. 156 (E.D. Va. 1964), a voting case that, while invalidating provisions for racially separate voting lists, upheld a requirement that divorce decrees contain the race of husband and wife.

28. Dubler, supra note 25, at 1175.

29. Id. at 1179 (quoting Anthony Lewis, Court to Review Racial Sex Curb, N.Y. Times, Apr. 28, 1964, at A7).

30. Id. at 1180 (quoting John P. MacKenzie, Precedents Shattered in "Quiet" Court Term, Wash. Post, July 2, 1967, at B4).

31. 388 U.S. 1 (1967).

32. Id. at 3. The trial judge stated in his opinion that,

Almighty God created the races white, black, yellow, Malay and red, and He placed them on separate continents. And but for the interference with His arrangement there would be no cause for such marriages. The fact that he separated the races shows that He did not intend for the races to mix.

the colonial period, when they had been incident to slavery. He noted that the Virginia court, in *Naim,* had concluded that the state's object under such provisions was "to preserve the racial integrity of its citizens," and to prevent "the corruption of blood," "a mongrel breed of citizens," and "the obliteration of racial pride." Finding all of these arguments "obviously an endorsement of the doctrine of white supremacy," he acknowledged that marriage traditionally has been subject to state regulation without federal intervention, but that obviously state discretion was not unlimited.

As in *McLaughlin,* Chief Justice Warren rejected the state's "equal application" of the statute argument. He dismissed the scientific and social science authorities because few of them were modern and many were published in the early decades of the century. And as in *McLaughlin,* the Court found that racial classifications, to survive, must pass most rigid scrutiny and must be shown to be necessary to the accomplishment of some permissible state objective independent of the racial discrimination which it was the object of the Fourteenth Amendment to eliminate. Chief Justice Warren found no such legitimate overriding purpose in the Virginia statutory scheme. He said that it "prohibits only interracial marriages involving white persons," and that this demonstrates that the racial classifications are "designed to maintain white supremacy" and are a clear denial of the equal protection clause. The statutes, he found, also denied the Lovings liberty without due process of law. "The freedom to marry," he said, "has long been recognized as one of the vital personal rights essential to the orderly pursuit of happiness by free men." Citing marriage as one of the "basic civil rights of man," the Court concluded that the Fourteenth Amendment "requires that the freedom of choice to marry not be restricted by invidious racial discriminations." "Under our Constitution," Chief Justice Warren concluded, "the freedom to marry, or not marry, a person of another race resides with the individual and cannot be infringed by the state."[33]

Certainly, the state interests for retaining barriers to interracial sex and marriage suggested by the arguments of Florida and Virginia constituted, as Chief Justice Warren observed, little more than "an endorsement of the doctrine of white supremacy." At the very least, these arguments seemed archaic and more than a little out-of-place in the midst of the greatest civil rights upheaval in the nation's history. By the time *Loving* was decided in 1967 blacks were shifting their emphasis from peaceful sit-ins at lunch counters to more disruptive protests. School desegregation litigation was moving from the South to the rest of the country, and the fiery urban rebellions that began in the Watts section of Los Angeles in 1965 had spread across the nation's urban centers. In the face of racial challenges of this magnitude, letting down the legal barriers to interracial sex and marriage, particularly when these restrictions had not served to prevent interracial sex and

---

33. A key issue to be discussed in this chapter is whether justice requires, and the Constitution can be read to permit, exceptions to the bar against state interference with interracial marriage, particularly if the exceptions take the form of provisions recognizing the continuing hostility to interracial marriages, or the need to limit the rights of such couples to further important interests of the minority community.

marriage, must have seemed to the Court and to some of the country an overdue but not very momentous step.

There was no massive resistance to *Loving,* but legislatures did not rush to repeal miscegenation statutes, and from time to time a lower court vainly attempted to enforce them. Courts have tended to view any state interference with interracial marriage with great suspicion. Those charged with defending provisions that arguably interfere with the right to interracial marriage seem reluctant to present even reasonable defenses.[34]

Despite the protection of interracial association provided in the above cases, there have been several instances in which white women (particularly school teachers) have lost jobs because they married or associated with black men. Usually some nonracial basis for the discharge is given, and the resulting problems of proof make contesting the dismissal difficult. Consistent with the trend in race relations at the end of the twentieth century, discrimination against interracial couples is thinly veiled by nonracial or "race-neutral" motivations. Although the 1990s have seen little litigation of miscegenation policy, the issues underlying the old anti-miscegenation laws remains unresolved.

§8.3   THE MOTIVATIONS OF MISCEGENATION POLICY

It has long been the general view that the desire to maintain the purity of the white race, and the odiousness of interracial intercourse, motivated not merely laws prohibiting interracial sex and marriage but the whole scheme of racial segregation. In Gunnar Myrdal's famous work, *An American Dilemma,* six items are listed in what Dr. Myrdal refers to as the "white man's order of discriminations."[1] Highest in this order stands the bar against intermarriage and sexual intercourse involving white women. Myrdal places lower on the list social conventions, use of public facilities, political franchise, legal equality, and employment. Miscegenation statutes were supposedly the legislative expressions of this principal concern, and the basis for American racial prejudice. Certainly, as one commentator has observed,[2] geographical distribution of miscegenation statutes followed the lines of racial feeling against blacks in the South and Asians in the western states. But Dr. Myrdal found that even in the early 1940s blacks did not view miscegenation as the crux of racial prejudice. Indeed, miscegenation was listed as the least significant among the barriers of segregation.[3]

---

34. For example, in Pederson v. Burton, 400 F. Supp. 960 (D.D.C. 1975), a three-judge court found without rational basis, and thus violative of the equal-protection clause, a statutory requirement that marriage license applicants in the District of Columbia disclose their race or color. Initially, District officials confessed that the provisions served no useful purpose. Later, they attempted to argue that it had great statistical value and should be retained.

§8.3   1. Gunnar Myrdal, An American Dilemma 60 (1964).

2. Harvey Applebaum, Miscegenation Statutes: A Constitutional and Social Problem, 53 Geo. L.J. 49, 51-53 (1964).

3. Myrdal, supra note 1, at 61.

Professor Oliver Cox, a black sociologist, rejected the conclusions of Dr. Myrdal regarding the white man's discrimination priorities. In his major work, *Caste, Class and Race,*[4] Dr. Cox asserted that Dr. Myrdal was also wrong in concluding that blacks reverse the white list of racial grievances (that is, Cox placed employment at the top of the list and sex at the bottom). As Cox stated, "[B]oth the Negroes and their white exploiters know that economic opportunity comes first and that the white woman comes second; indeed, she is merely a significant instrument in limiting the first."[5] Dr. Cox explained that the elements of social discrimination are intermeshed in a definite pattern intended to maintain whites in a dominant position and to facilitate the exploitation of blacks forced into a subordinate position. If intermarriage were allowed, Cox argued, those able to exploit race would no longer be able to direct mass hatred against blacks. "Sexual obsessions," according to Cox, "function in the fundamental interest of economic exploitation."[6] Economic exploitation was the basis for miscegenation prohibitions, and the cultural advantage they secured for whites motivated miscegenation policy. Protection of the "honor and sanctity of white womanhood" only shielded their basic purpose: refusing blacks the opportunity to become the cultural peers of whites. Cox dismissed the idea that opposition to interracial marriage was intended to preserve white women for white men. He pointed out that whites are not particularly disturbed by intermarriage in foreign countries; but, when white women come into the area with American black husbands, whites are equally hostile whether the women are foreigners or relatives.

Finally, Dr. Cox suggested that black leaders and blacks generally were merely being politic when they told Dr. Myrdal and other polltakers that black men were not interested in white women. He points out that whenever whites are in a ruling-class situation, there is a very strong urge among black men to marry or have sex with white women. He does not view this urge as an "ungovernable sexual craving" for white flesh, as many whites believe. As he rather drolly puts it, "[w]omen of any color are totally sufficient for the satisfaction of any such simple desire."[7] Evidently, he adds, under the heat of passion, men have found colored women of every race quite adequate. Thus, he concludes "[i]t must not be supposed that it is the white woman as a mere sexual object which is the preoccupation of colored men, it is rather her importance to him as a vehicle in his struggle for economic and cultural position."[8]

Dr. Cox's theory of economic exploitation as the moving force behind the opposition to intermarriage is not widely accepted, though others who have written on the subject share his view.[9] Dr. Myrdal's position that a basic fear and abhorrence

---

4. Oliver Cox, Caste, Class, and Race (1948).
5. Id. at 526-527.
6. Id.
7. Id. at 386.
8. Id.
9. Particularly impressive is the documentation gathered in Charles Herbert Stember's Sexual Racism: The Emotional Barrier to an Integrated Society (1976). Mr. Stember quotes several black spokesmen, including Frantz Fanon, Malcolm X, and Eldridge Cleaver, who acknowledged the political implications in the black man's attraction for the white woman. He points out that the phenomenon is not limited to black men, quoting Philip Roth in his novel, *Portnoy's Complaint,*

of interracial sex motivated the sanctions, legal and extra-legal, imposed on blacks for 300 years, is still pervasive in the scholarly world. It is reasonable to assume that attitudes about sex are imbedded in a given cultural and historical context, and that even if sexuality is basically biological, its form of expression is influenced by variables including economics, status, and access to power.[10]

Loving v. Virginia has become the definitive precedent for the equal protection standard that racial classifications are suspect, and that absent a compelling state interest, they will not be upheld. The *Loving* Court made clear, though, that racial classifications are not absolutely void, thereby keeping open the possibility that, under certain circumstances, a statute might be upheld as a necessary exercise of the state's police power, even though it had a discriminatory effect on a racial group.[11] While the state's police power in the area is clearly not unlimited, Chief Justice Warren acknowledged in *Loving* that "[m]arriage is a social relation subject to the state's police power. . . ."[12] Marriages between relatives are barred both because they are deemed abhorrent by society and because offspring of such unions may be defective. Given the serious political and economic connotations of mixed marriage discussed by Dr. Myrdal and Dr. Cox, and with the continuing aversion to interracial unions by so many members of the society, might a state not meet the heavy burden placed on racial classifications if it cited these bases in support of provisions that required interracial partners to receive special training, or otherwise differentiated them from couples applying for marriage licenses who were of the same race? Your answer may be, "Certainly not!" But such demands have been made by interracial adoption policies. Consider whether the testimony of psychiatrists and social scientists set out below could undermine your skepticism and strengthens the likelihood that a state might appropriately and legally impose different standards for interracial marriages.

While social scientists like Cox and Myrdal have focused their attention on societal factors that explain prohibitions on mixed marriages, other writings suggest that some of the same social factors tend to draw couples together across racial lines. Calvin Hernton, for example, rejects the "economic" explanation for whites' resistance to interracial unions as too mechanical. He argues that both white women and black men belong to a "semioppressed" class, facing social and economic pressures that draw them together. In their book, *Black Rage,* two black psychiatrists, William Grier and Price Cobbs, developed Hernton's theme, suggesting a range of conscious and unconscious emotions accompanying interracial unions that defy society's conventions. The analysis in *Black Rage* examines the possible unconscious attractions of individuals using four scenarios.[13]

---

in which the main character discusses his fascination with gentile girls. Id. at 114-118. See also Calvin Hernton, Sex and Racism in America 32-33 (1965).

10. See Frantz Fanon, The Wretched of the Earth 39 (1963).

11. Hirabyashi v. United States, 320 U.S. 81 (1943); Korematsu v. United States, 323 U.S. 214 (1944).

12. 388 U.S. at 7.

13. William Grier & Price Cobbs, Black Rage 91-100 (1968).

These racialized sexual perceptions are revisited and reexamined by Paul R. Spickard, in Mixed Blood, at 252-267, 312-314 (1989). After a long discussion of sexualized images, Spickard notes that personal attraction has become increasingly important since the civil rights movement.

The Grier-Cobbs analysis has been dismissed by many individuals, and particularly by interracial couples, as a worthless generalization of what motivates
individuals to accept mates across racial lines. Without doubt, however, from the
days of their slave origins in this country, black women and men have been highly
sexualized by whites. Consider the black family under slavery. Neither marriage
nor paternity were recognized, and offspring became the property of whoever
owned the mother, just as with livestock. The biological paternity of slave children
had no social significance.[14] Dr. Joel Kovel has explored the origins of the myth
that blacks have supersexual powers. He found that "archetypal lynching in the old
[post–Civil War] South was for the archetypal crime of having a black man rape
(touch, approach, . . . etc.) a white lady." Such lynchings often included castration,
and even when they didn't, the idea of castration was present in the entire procedure.[15] Kovel agrees with Grier and Cobbs that issues of sexuality and racism are

---

Black Man, White Woman. The white woman still represents the "socially identified" female
ideal, and it is she, according to Grier and Cobbs, who has been barred to the black man by every
social institution. Her forbiddenness adds to her sexual desirability, and it makes her a natural object
for the projection of Oedipal fantasies. In addition, the black man "conquers" the white man through
the white woman, thus reversing roles and balancing the scales of his humiliation and emasculation in
other areas. According to Grier and Cobbs, if the relationship progresses to marriage, the black man is
forced to recognize that outside the bedroom his manhood remains compromised. Even so, when
society gives interracial marriages a chance to grow, they can flourish even between people of
disparate origins.

White Woman, Black Man. There is again a projection of Oedipal fantasies by the white
woman, who finds her black lover particularly exciting because he has been forbidden to her by
society. Moreover, the difference in appearance of blacks adds to this excitement, because anyone
who is not Caucasian in appearance has been deemed subhuman and therefore capable of an especially intense animal sexuality. The white woman in an interracial marriage, Grier and Cobbs hypothesized, becomes more concerned with her partner's economic prospects and faces contempt, both of
her and of her children, from many whites.

Black Woman, White Man. Grier and Cobbs describe this relationship as the oldest and most
complex interracial relationship. During slavery, white owners commonly used black women slaves
sexually. Unable to protect herself, the black woman's only recourse was to bind herself sexually to
one white man who might then protect her against others. Although the utter helplessness of slavery is
no longer the danger, the modern black woman is attracted to the white man as "a part and
representative of the powerful white majority." By aligning herself with him, the black woman
shares in his strength and prestige; no matter how weak and poor he is, the white man is more
powerful than any black man. In addition, through this liaison, the black woman loses some of
the sense that society deems her ugly. While the black man is aroused by the societal significance
of subduing and possessing the white female, the black woman is similarly aroused by being subdued
and possessed by the powerful white man. In marriage, the black woman fears abandonment.

White Man, Black Woman. The white man continues to act out the traditional exploitative role
of using black women as sexual objects. Similar to the way in which the white woman views the black
man as a dangerous sex-animal, the white man views the black woman as a debased and sex-hungry
subhuman beast. A relationship with the black woman may represent defiance of the social order,
generally. If the white man develops an emotional attachment to her, he faces societal condemnation,
and to the extent he accepts societal stereotypes, he may feel inferior to the black man as a sexual
partner.

14. Herbert Gutman, Black Family in Slavery and Freedom, 1750-1925 (1976); Eugene Genovese, Roll, Jordan, Roll: The World the Slaves Made (1974); John Blassingame, The Slave Community (1972).

15. Joel Kovel, White Racism: A Psychohistory 67-71 (1970). Dr. Kovel's point is illustrated
by another writer who recalled William Bradford Huie's investigation of the lynching of Emmitt Till
in 1955. She indicated that Till's real sin was less his audacity at wolf-whistling at a Mississippi white
woman than his bullheaded persistence in behaving like a man. His abductors, the husband of the
offended woman and the husband's half brother, had actually first thought only to scare the boy and

linked with power and dominance. Because whites feared that any slave revolt would result in the rape of white women, they insisted on black submission, and white men gave white women undue protection. The perception of black women as more passionate than white women, and the fact that they had served as black "mammies" during the youth of many white men, contributed to the complicated racial culture of the South.

Dr. Kovel suggests that sexuality remains the core of the race problem. Some writers discerned a racist fear of the black male in the rape scare of the white feminist movement in the 1970s. Winthrop Jordan and John Dollard suggest that the rape fixation reflects white men's fear of retaliation, coupled with a projection onto black men of white men's guilt feelings for their own sexual abuse of black women.[16]

Whatever their modern manifestations, the historical associations of sex and race in our society must influence contemporary thinking, and, arguably, they are proper subjects of state concern in its exercise of its police powers over the legal status of marriage. It should be added, though, that critics of the psychological theories summarized above reject the argument that sexuality is the core of society's racial problem. As two authorities point out, if racism is predicated on the sexual tensions caused by the "Oedipal conflict," the whole struggle by blacks against political and economic oppression is hopeless or, at best, of limited usefulness. "[B]lack liberation becomes contingent on emancipation from the id."[17] Even the critics do not entirely discount the relationship between sex and racial attitudes, however, and they do not argue that its influences are only negligible. Thus, it may be appropriate at this point to examine how these factors may be utilized in a legal argument to justify a statute intended in good faith both to recognize the special nature of interracial marriages and to provide some state assistance to interracial couples entering into marriage.

§8.4 EVOLVING PERCEPTIONS OF INTERRACIAL LOVE AND MARRIAGE

During the 1970s and early 1980s, periodicals and books aimed at black readers published a number of articles reflecting the debate in the black community as to whether interracial marriage would further or retard the development of ethnic pride and solidarity. More recently, scholars have examined trends, patterns and experiences of interracial married couples looking less at how the increase in interracial marriage would affect ethnic pride and solidarity, and more at

---

"chase his black ass back to Chicago," but when Till refused to cry out when they beat him, or to show fear, grovel, or plead for mercy, the brother reportedly told the court, "What else could we do except kill him?" Beth Day, The Hidden Fear, in The Black Male in America 193, 194 (Doris Wilkinson & Ronald Taylor eds., 1977).

16. Spickard, supra note 13, at 254.

17. Alexander Thomas & Samuel Sillen, Racism and Psychiatry 106 (1972).

underlying motivations, sociological theories, geographic and historic trends, and the impact of growing numbers of interracial marriages on public policy.[1] This is not to say however, that concerns over ethnic pride and solidarity are any less important within the black community. They have just been surrounded by a more complex analysis of the issues. Few modern studies on intermarriage are complete without a discussion of the racial marriage gap, described by Professor Richard Banks as "the likelihood of ever marrying, the likelihood of divorce, and the likelihood of remarriage after divorce."[2] Black women are less likely to ever marry, more likely to get a divorce and less likely to remarry after the divorce, when compared to white women.[3] Given these statistics, it is no wonder that black women tend to be less tolerant of a mixed couple than their black male counterparts (particularly between a black male and white female).

Among black men, those who see the availability of white women as a civil rights gain may discount the argument that such romances or marriages will lessen black pride by pointing to militant black leaders such as Frederick Douglass, Walter White, and James Farmer, who married white women. Some black men feel that interracial romance and marriage represent one hope for lessening the racial separation and conflicts in this society, which are based on ignorance and the adherence to racial myth. Others still, view their relationships with white women as apolitical and purely a function of color-blind love. Few, if any, black men however are not influenced or aware of the many in the society who disapprove of intermarriage.

Black women until fairly recently have been more uniform in their pragmatic and philosophical opposition to interracial relationships, particularly interracial marriage. On the practical side, according to the 2000 census, black women over the age of 15 outnumber black males over the age of 15 in the United States by almost two million, and they argue that the statistical chances for black women to form strong relationships with black men should not be further decreased by the black males' choice of white women as mates.[4] When looking at population statistics from

§8.4   1. See, e.g., Rachel Moran, Interracial Intimacy: The Regulation of Race & Romance (2001); Randall Kennedy, Interracial Intimacies: Sex, Marriage, Identity, and Adoption (2003); R. Richard Banks & Su Jin Gatlin, African American Intimacy: The Racial Gap in Marriage, 11 Mich. J. Race & L. 115 (Fall 2005); Kyle D. Crowder & Stewart E. Tolnay, A New Marriage Squeeze for Black Women: The Role of Racial Intermarriage by Black Men, Journal of Marriage and the Family 62 (August 2000).

2. Banks & Gatilin, supra note 1, at 118.

3. Id. at 119.

4. The concern of black women that black men are increasingly marrying white women is borne out by census figures. In 1960, the number of black males married to white females roughly equaled the number of white males married to black females (according to a 1966 Census Bureau bulletin on marital status). See Carter, Racial-Caste Hypogamy: A Sociological Myth?, 29 Phylon 347 (1968). During the decade of the 1960s, there were more than twice as many black man-white woman marriages than white man–black woman marriages.

In recent years, 65 to 75 percent of marriages between blacks and whites have been between a black man and a white woman in states where more than 8 percent of all marriages included black partners, while this combination ranged from about 80 to well over 90 percent of marriages between blacks and whites in states where not more than 1.2 percent of marriages included a black partner. See Robert E. T. Roberts, Black-White Intermarriage in the United States, Inside the Mixed Marriage 72 (Walter R. Johnson & D. Michael Warren eds., 1994).

another angle, the number of unmarried black women exceeds the number of unmarried black men by 2.5 million. As marriage rates for all races continue to decline, rates of intermarriage are increasing. Indeed, because of high rates of unemployment among black men, lower earnings and lower education levels, educated and accomplished black women find fewer socioeconomic peers among black men than do less educated black women.[5]

Moreover, some black women have said that honest feeling for a white man is difficult, because they can't forget the centuries of white exploitation of black women.[6] Sociologist Erica Chito Childs writes that, "black women frame their view of intermarriage within a historical context of slavery, sexual abuse, and exploitation. For black women in particular, there exists an explicit and immediate sense of connectedness with the past."[7]

On the one hand, they see the black man's choice of a white woman as a rejection of them, an indication of racial abandonment. On the other hand, many black women view interracial marriage as an option not available to them because they cannot conform to white standards of beauty — neither appealing to white men nor the black men who tend to choose white women. "Probably the most painful part of being a black woman . . . is the rape of the short male supply by white woman. . . . What is worse, black women take it as a personal insult, a denunciation of their own black beauty. . . . Invariably, black women feel, the union is rooted in pathology and/or white subterfuge."[8]

Professor Childs writes that for a black person "to engage in an intimate relationship with a white person means that one is selling out to white society and in the process has sold out the black community . . . blacks who cross the color line are often accused of sacrificing their blackness for a white ideal."[9]

A study of 17 states in 1980 indicates that both white and black partners in interracial marriages have more education than those who marry endogamously. Only 9 percent of black men who married black women had completed college, while 13 percent of black men who married white women held college degrees. See id. See also William Chapman, Marriage and Race, Wash. Post, Feb. 14, 1973, at F1, col. 8 (citing data revealing that the black man who marries a white woman tends to have a higher level of income than the average black male).

According to the 2000 census, there are 86 unmarried men for every 100 unmarried women for the general population and yet there are over 2.5 million more unmarried black women than black men.

5. According to a 1993 study, for every 100 marriageable black women, there are only 66 black men active in the labor force. M.A. Fossett & K. J. Kiecolt, Mate Availability and Family Structure among African Americans in U. S. Metropolitan Areas. Journal of Marriage and the Family, 55, 288-302 (1993).

6. The number of white man–black woman marriages did increase from about 10 percent of black-white marriages in 1980 to 30 percent in 1987; this count included a number of famous entertainers. In comparison, 40.6 percent of Japanese women and 53.7 percent of Native American women marry men (mostly white) outside their group. See Reger C. Smith, Two Cultures, One Marriage 2-3 (1996).

7. Erica Chito Childs, Navigating Interracial Borders: Black-White Couples and Their Social Worlds, 95 (2005).

8. A conversation among a group of married and single black women in the Spike Lee film *Jungle Fever* demonstrates the continuing frustration and bitterness of black women in the 1990s, who still feel betrayed when black men choose white women.

9. Childs, supra note 7, at 87.

Not all discourse on interracial unions has been negative. Recently, the dialogue has expanded to include more voices that support these unions, the private choices of individuals that lead to them, and the change in society's attitudes. Dr. Alvin Poussaint, a psychiatry professor at Harvard attributes the increase in interracial marriages to the dissolution of social barriers and taboos surrounding interracial dating and marriage.[10] Pointing towards popular culture, he highlights the prevalence of mixed race couples on television and the music industry. Today, society sees not only mixed race couples in their own communities, on television and in magazines, but we are also seeing the offspring of these interracial couples in those media as well. Athletes like Tiger Woods and Derek Jeter, politicians like Barack Obama and Oscar-winning actress Halle Berry all illuminate the products of interracial unions.

Looking toward the white community, the greatest opposition to interracial unions was correlated with older-age, lower-educational and income levels, being Anglo and politically and religiously conservative.[11] One of the limitations of this micro-level survey research, is the risk that people, especially younger, highly educated, middle- and upper-class, liberal individuals will answer questions about race in the way they feel they are supposed to, rather than how they actually feel or what they actually believe. In a study following the South Carolina Referendum of 1998, a more macro-level study found that education level has the strongest effect on support of racial intermarriage, followed by urban setting and a lower amount of status difference between groups. In communities where socioeconomic status levels between blacks and white was less, approval for interracial marriage was greater. Where the status gap was larger, disapproval was greater.[12]

Even though the United States has witnessed an increase in interracial marriages over the past five decades, these marriages are a small percentage of all marriages in this country.[13] Ninety-two percent of whites and blacks choose partners of the same race.[14] Such data raises questions about the condition of interracial marriage four decades after the Supreme Court's decision in Loving v. Virginia. Especially in light of Professor Poussaint's commentary, does such marriage remain a serious social taboo? What kind of progress toward breaking racial barriers can be made through interracial intimacy? How does interracial marriage compare across different color lines? In a number of recently published books, scholars and journalists have delved deeply into the history of black-white marriage, revealing a rich history and new insights into the power of these relationships to deconstruct social constructs of race.

---

10. Lynn Norment, Black Women White Men, White Women Black Men — Interracial Relations, Ebony, Nov. 1999.

11. George A. Yancy & Michael O. Emerson, An Analysis of Resistance to Racial Exogamy: The 1998 South Carolina Referendum, Journal of Black Studies, Vol. 32 No. 1, September 2000, 132-133, 147.

12. Id. at 144.

13. Rachel Moran, Interracial Intimacy: The Regulation of Race & Romance 6 (2001).

14. Id.

Professor Rachel Moran at UC-Berkeley School of Law and Professor Randall Kennedy at Harvard Law School both explore the legal and social history of interracial marriage in the United States and tie this issue to more contemporary debates around racial relationships. Moran's book, *Interracial Intimacy: The Regulation of Race & Romance,*[15] raises the question of whether thirty years after the decision *Loving* can be seen as a success. She begins by looking at the legal obstacles that led to *Loving*, presenting a detailed analysis of court decisions, examining the interracial marriage question, and then looking to more contemporary reactions to types of interracial intimacy, including adoption, custody battles, and multiracial identities.

Professor Kennedy's book, *Interracial Intimacies: Sex, Marriage, Identity, and Adoption,*[16] takes an extensive look at the history of black-white intimacy. Yet, in Chapter Four, Kennedy presents a rich discussion that reminds us that the story of racial relationships has been anything but peaceful. He explores the demonization of black male sexuality, the lynching of black men for a mere suspicion of lusting after white women and white men's sexual coercion and rape of black women. Kennedy also explores in detail the phenomena of racial passing and the case for biracial adoption. Painting the picture of the foster care system in the United States and the difficulty of adoption, Kennedy advocates strongly for an end to race-matching in adoption, which he argues is not for government officials to determine. Although he recognizes that it is no panacea, Kennedy sees interracial intimacy as a means toward racial progress.

In *Race Mixing: Black-White Marriage in Postwar America,*[17] Renee Romano, a white professor of African American Studies who is married to a black man, presents a social and cultural history of black-white relationships since World War II. She examines how different attitudes have been depicted in popular culture from music to children's books to magazines.[18] She emphasizes the perspective of black women who feel marginalized by interracial marriages.[19] One of the most powerful elements of the book comes from actual interviews she conducted with interracial couples. Romano tells their stories to show how individuals can create supportive communities to overcome racist sentiment. For Romano, love, however, does not conquer all. She recognizes racism as deeply imbedded in the structure of our culture which will continue to persist in our society without more systemic remedies.

In *Mulattas and Mestizas: Representing Mixed Identities in the Americas, 1850-2000,*[20] Suzanne Bost also analyzes a large range of cultural images of

---

15. Id.

16. Randall Kennedy, Interracial Intimacies: Sex, Marriage, Identity, and Adoption (2003).

17. Renee Romano, Race Mixing: Black-White Marriage in Postwar America (2003).

18. For a more detailed book review, see Kate Manning, Crossing the Color Line, review of Interracial Intimacies: Sex, Marriage, Identity, and Adoption, by Randall Kennedy; Race Mixing: Black-White Marriage in Postwar America, by Renee C. Romano; Mulattas and Mestizas: Representing Mixed Identities in the Americas, 1850-2000, by Suzanne Bost; and Mulatto America: At the Crossroads of Black and White Culture: A Social History, by Stephan Talty, L.A. Times (March 30, 2003).

19. Id.

20. Suzanne Bost, Mulattas and Mestizas: Representing Mixed Identities in the Americas, 1850-2000 (2003).

interracial marriages, expanding her analysis beyond the black-white color line. She looks specifically to race mixing in the Southwest as a model that allows individuals to transcend their history of domination. The mestiza model created a fluid mixture of races, languages and cultures. She also goes further in her study than the other authors by comparing biracial individuals with individuals who blur gender lines. Both, she believes, play an important role in challenging social constructions — one of race, the other of gender. She examines ways that race mixing can expose and restructure power through this deconstruction.

Stephan Talty's work, *Mulatto America: At the Crossroads of Black and White Culture: A Social History from White Slaves, W.E.B. Du Bois and the Jazz Revolution to Dorothy Dandridge, Elvis, Sam Cooke, Civil Rights and Eminem*,[21] presents the intertwining of blacks and whites that goes beyond sexual relationships to include connections in almost every area of human experience, including art, religion, music and sports. Talty shows that both races borrow from each other in ways that develop a shared American culture, which can help overcome racism.

With each author's intense look at race relationships in the United States, a similar theme about black-white relationships emerges: While America's pigmentocracy persists, the taboo of mixed-race marriages is eroding, and that signals progress for race relations. Yet, intimate relationships in and of themselves cannot be expected to completely eradicate racism, which is deeply rooted in the economic structure of American society.

§8.4.1   Race as Biology

The biological definition of race that prevailed at the onset of modernity took account of genetic or morphological differences between groups of individuals. Under this approach, persons sharing a common ancestral line are thought to belong to a single race while those emerging from distinct lines are thought to belong to a different race. Physical character traits are assumed to vary little among races and greatly between races. Because race is tied to ancestry or genetics, society at large perceives differences in skin color, hair texture, and facial features between groups as outward signs of racial difference.[22] As a result, racial boundaries are marked by the surface features shared among groups of people and become proof that racial categories are real, fixed, and naturally determined.

At first blush, a biological conception of race appears unassailable given its scientific foundation. What happens then, if genetic patterns in fact do not correlate with racial categories? If racial assignments are based on a shared genetic background, how does one account for genetic variations among individuals within a single race or, for that matter, genetic conformity among individuals of different

---

21. Stephan Talty, Mulatto America: At the Crossroads of Black and White Culture: A Social History (2003).

22. See Anthony Appiah, Race, Culture, Identity: Misunderstood Connections, in Color Conscious: The Political Morality of Race 296 (1998) [hereinafter Misunderstood Connections]; see also Jayne Lee, Navigating the Topology of Race, 46 Stan. L. Rev. 747, 759 (1994).

races? Because physical character traits are influenced by individual DNA sequences, racial differences from a biological perspective should be discernible at the chromosomal level.[23] Yet scientific advancements have shown that physical and genetic similarities are more likely to be found among individuals of different races than among those of the same race. Moreover, although an individual's genetic pattern is influenced by an infinite number of variables, only a fraction of one's genetic composition determines the physical characteristics used to define race.

This disconnect between racial categories and genetic makeup or morphology undermines the legitimacy of contemporary racial categories. Anthony Appiah argues that using characteristics as malleable as skin color or hair texture to define racial categories yields a classification scheme so arbitrary that it becomes essentially meaningless. To Appiah, "trying to classify people into a few races is like trying to classify books in a library: You may use a single property — size, say — but you will get a useless classification, or you may use a more complex system of interconnected criteria, and then you will get a good deal of arbitrariness."[24] Given the extreme variations in DNA markers among members of a particular race, a racial classification based on DNA does not say much. In the end, any significance among individual group members in terms of shared DNA patterns is overshadowed by DNA differences.

Jayne Lee provides additional ammunition against a biological conception of race.[25] For instance, how does one categorize an individual who self-identifies with a particular race, but who displays the physical traits or ancestry generally associated with another? In the United States, millions of self-proclaimed white Americans are actually descendants of black ancestors. Should these individuals be categorized as white or black? What happens to an individual whose physical appearance does not fit neatly into predetermined racial categories? Most physical features vary along a gradient. Communities blend into one another and physical characteristics overlap among neighboring populations. To the extent that this is true, an infinite number of racial categories would have to be created to adequately accommodate the diversity of the human species.

Perhaps the critical flaw in a biological conception of race is not the manner by which races are classified, but the normative judgments that flow from the classification. As Lee suggests, the danger lies in the ideology of racial difference, not in the methodology by which racial difference itself is defined. In other words, the correlation of physical difference with racial difference is meaningless unless physical traits are used as stand-ins for cultural and moral values. In turn, these associations influence our perception about and attitudes toward individuals in particular racial categories.

---

23. See Anthony Appiah, The Uncompleted Argument: Du Bois and the Illusion of Race, in "Race," Writing, and Difference 36 (Henry Louis Gates, Jr., ed., 1989) [hereinafter Illusion of Race]; see also Christine Hickman, The Devil and the One Drop Rule, 95 Mich. L. Rev. 1161, 1203 (1997); Misunderstood Connections, supra note 22 at 21-22; Lee, supra note 22, at 759-760.

24. Illusion of Race, supra note 23, at 38; see also Lee, supra note 22, at 760.

25. Lee, supra note 22, at 760-763.

The presumed correlation between racial designations, physical features, and moral characteristics creates a dynamic by which appearance and behavior among members of a single racial category are expected to remain constant. Skin color, hair texture, and other physical aspects are taken as visible evidence of moral, intellectual, and personality differences among individuals of different races. Eventually, however, expectations collide with reality, and we confront individuals whose appearance and behavior do not conform with prevailing stereotypes. When this occurs, we experience what Michael Omi and Howard Winant term a "crisis of meaning."[26] A response along the lines of "Funny, you don't look black" from a white individual introduced to a "well-spoken" and handsomely dressed black individual provides an example of such a crisis in operation. Moreover, using physical characteristics as the basis for ordering the human social hierarchy makes it appear as though racial inequality is a natural phenomenon. The problem, as Lee describes, is that "physical differences are invoked to refer to moral qualities that are coupled to them. It is through its self-evident visibility that biological race accomplishes its most damaging work. Because race seems to function as a description, we fail to question its work as a normative judgment."[27] That normative judgment has been the tool of minority oppression and white privilege since the inception of the biological theories of racial difference.

Any discussion about the concept of race merits mentioning the related concepts of racialization and racism. Roger Sanjek defines "race" as the "the framework of ranked categories segmenting the human population."[28] "Racialization," on the other hand, reflects the process by which individuals are assigned membership in those categories. "Racism" is the product of the two — the assignment of negative value to the traits commonly associated with a disfavored race, and the subordinate ranking of that race on the social hierarchy. These three concepts operate in unison to form the basis for social ordering in the modern world.

Omi and Winant chart the interplay between race, racialization, and racism as the basis for social ordering in modern society.[29] They explain that ancient communities settled in close proximity to one another and were inhabited by people who displayed similar physical characteristics. The resulting relative uniformity in skin tone, hair texture, and facial features made distinctions based on physical difference irrelevant. As a result, caste or ethnicity emerged as the basis for social ordering in the primitive world. That changed in the 1400s when western Europeans "discovered" the "New World." The economic and political exploitation of native peoples became the order of the day, but that agenda could not be rationalized through old perceptions about caste and ethnicity alone. Instead, European explorers began to assign social meaning to the physical differences between themselves and newly encountered peoples, thus creating an ideology of racial difference that enabled them to propagate the genocide of African and

---

26. Michael Omi & Howard Winant, Racial Formation in the United States 71 (2d ed. 1994).
27. Lee, supra note 22, at 763.
28. Roger Sanjek, The Enduring Inequalities of Race, in Race 1 (Steven Gregory & Roger Sanjek eds., 1994).
29. Omi & Winant, supra note 26.

Native Americans as a natural, inevitable, and divinely predetermined phenomenon. Later scientific efforts to develop a sophisticated classification scheme that segregated the human species according to anatomical distinctions lent an air of objectivity to the cause. Race thereafter became accepted as a mark of social and cultural differences that could be attributed to natural physical distinctions.

§8.4.2 Racial Essence

Lee describes a second conception of race that is related to, but ideologically distinct from, a biological conception. That is the concept of "racial essence."[30] Like biological race, race as essence assumes that members of the same race share distinctive physical features and inherit corresponding moral and character traits. In theory, both race as biology and racial essence assume that morphology provides a visible indicator of the essential and inheritable components of each race. In practice, however, adherents of a biological conception of race exploit race as a justification for minority oppression whereas proponents of race as essence appeal to race as a basis for political solidarity.

The unifying theme of racial essence has played a critical role in the success of liberatory movements throughout the twentieth century. A premise of Pan-Africanist discourse, Lee explains, is the supposition that membership in a particular race serves as the basis for political unity. Such an ideology unites people in a common cause notwithstanding tribal, ethnic, or national differences within the group. Despite its unifying potential, however, the theory of racial essence has been critiqued as a precursor to racism. According to Appiah, for example, in the case of black liberation, the theory is both morally questionable and politically dangerous because it exalts all blacks without considering the attributes that individual blacks share with each other. All blacks are treated similarly even if they share no moral characteristics other than race. At the same time, nonblacks are treated differently from blacks even when they share all other moral characteristics except race.[31] Both Appiah and Lee predict devastating political consequences for oppressed peoples who appeal to a racial essence. A push towards intrinsic unity, they argue, might very well destabilize anti-racist efforts by discouraging coalitions among entities with overlapping agendas. A case in point is the attention to issues affecting women of color given jointly by civil rights advocates and feminist organizations. In a similar vein, attributing unity to members of a particular race sets the stage for intergroup ideological conflicts.

As an example, Lee points to the dilemma faced by anti-racist advocates during U.S. Supreme Court Justice Clarence Thomas's confirmation hearings. Despite his lack of experience and conservative record, some black leaders hesitated to publicly criticize the appointment for fear of condoning racist stereotypes about the intellectual inferiority of blacks. At the same time, they knew that the

30. Lee, supra note 22, at 766-770.
31. See Anthony Appiah, In My Father's House, Africa in the Philosophy of Culture 18 (1993); Lee, supra note 22, at 769.

appointment of a neo-conservative of any race meant surrendering many of the advancements toward equality made in the past half-century. Lee saw Thomas's nomination as presenting a conflict in racial identification. As she explains, "to the extent that racial identity is defined biologically or essentially, Thomas is obviously black; to the extent that it is defined politically, as a firm commitment to anti-racist struggles, Thomas's claim to racial authenticity flounders."[32] Perhaps the Thomas nomination best exemplifies the political dangers that ensue when group identity is defined in terms of race as opposed to shared values regarding race, justice, and equality.

The Thomas nomination dilemma, though, may be the example that tests rather than destroys the rule. Without black support, few black politicians could win elections. Even so, the most competent blacks regularly lose elections against unimpressive white opponents based on racist considerations by white voters. This phenomenon occurs in the North as well as in the South.

§8.4.3   Sociohistorical Construction of Race

Today, most cultural anthropologists and social historians see human categorization and social ordering as products of political, social, economic, and historical developments rather than of immutable and inheritable character traits.[33] Unlike a biological conception of race, a sociohistoric explanation of race takes account of the context in which racial categories arise along with the larger influences that shape racial meaning.

Omi and Winant suggest that race, at least in the United States, is an indeterminate social construct that is constantly reinvented and manipulated to enhance white privilege. They explain that during the early seventeenth century, the existing social order was organized around a class-based system of indentured servitude under which race was largely insignificant. With the transition to a color-coded slave society, however, both Africans and European settlers took on specific and mutually exclusive racial identities. This process is revealed through the use of self-identifiers claimed by early European settlers. English, Dutch, and French settlers originally identified themselves in religious terms as "Christian." By the mid-seventeenth century, however, Anglo settlers began to view identity in terms of race and status, referring to themselves as "English" or "free" and eventually settling on the more general designation of "white." Slaves were also classified in racial terms, although they were denied the capacity to self-identity. European settlers stripped slaves of their previous affiliations with Ibo, Fulani, or Mandingo tribes and began to identify Africans simply as "black."

32. Lee, supra note 22, at 769.
33. Not all efforts to discern a biological or essential meaning of race have been abandoned, however. See also Kenneth L. Karst, Myths of Identity: Individual and Group Portraits of Race and Sexual Orientation, 43 UCLA L. Rev. 263, 272-273 (1995) (discussing biological conception s of race in employment discrimination doctrine); Neil Gotanda, A Critique of Our Constitution Is Color-Blind, 44 Stan. L. Rev. 1, 28-32 (1991) (examining jurisprudence linking racial categories with physiognomy and ancestry); Omi & Winant, supra note 26, at 63-64 (discussing studies in areas of genetics and educational psychology).

Other historical events demonstrate how changing patterns of racial categorization operate to maintain white privilege. Consider the rule of matrilineage adopted in the antebellum South. At common law, a child's racial status was based on patrilineage and inherited through his or her father. Carrying that rule over to the American colonies, which operated on a system of slavery, would have had devastating consequences given that white male slaveholders regularly sired children with black female slaves. Those children would have been classified as white and thus could have stated claims to freedom under the laws of slavery. Anxious to avoid this result, state lawmakers discarded the rule of patrilineage in favor of a system under which a child inherited the racial status of his or her mother. This approach not only fortified the institution of slavery, it also provided a financial boon to white slaveholders who could then regenerate their holdings without the cost of purchasing additional slaves. The malleability of race in this circumstance demonstrates how racial categories are manipulated to reify existing racial inequalities.

The emergence of slavery and the resulting correlation between race and social status supports the argument that race in America is a socially constructed concept. Consider also how the color line was preserved after the abolition of slavery. One might predict that if slavery gave rise to a race-based social order, emancipation would herald its demise. Even after the end of slavery, however, the terms "black" and "white" held their position as substitute vocabulary for relative social status.[34] The only thing that changed was the composition of the two groups.

Compare the number of individuals who qualify as white today with the number who qualified at the turn of the century. The original western European immigrants to the New World initially saw themselves — to the exclusion of other Europeans — as members of a distinct Anglo caste that constituted the white race.[35] Immigrants from across Europe and other nations who came to America with different languages, religious tenets, and cultural traditions were initially cast in a single lot as "nonwhites." Popular conception agreed with Benjamin Franklin's description of European differences: "The number of purely white People in the World is proportionally very small. All Africa is black or tawny. Asia chiefly tawny. America (exclusive of the new comers) wholly so. And in Europe, the Spaniards, Italians, French, Russians and Swedes, are generally of what we call a swarthy Complexion; as are the Germans also, the Saxons only excepted, who with the English, make the principle Body of White People on the Face of the Earth."[36] But Franklin's hyperpurified conception of whiteness eventually faded. Western European settlers ultimately formed alliances with new eastern European, Irish, and to some extent Jewish immigrants in order to amass additional power for themselves vis-à-vis a shared disdain for blacks.[37] For their part, the new immigrant working class exploited their

---

34. See John A. Powell, The Racing of American Society: Race Functioning as a Verb Before Signifying as a Noun, 15 Law & Ineq. 99, 105 (1997).

35. Omi & Winant, supra note 26, at 61-62.

36. Powell, supra note 34, at 107.

37. See Roger Sanjek, The Enduring Inequalities of Race, in Race 8-9 (Steven Gregory & Roger Sanjek eds., 1994).

racial affiliations with the aristocracy, despite the class differences dividing the two groups, as a way to court favor with wealthy capitalists who controlled access to the labor market. The end result was a mutually beneficial arrangement that guaranteed ethnic immigrant assimilation into the white race.

Soon after working class alliances among newly arrived immigrants formed along racial lines, a new anti-black and anti-immigrant sentiment took hold. Physical violence, political intimidation, and the economic exploitation of non-European laborers became an organizational priority, while institutionalized patterns of segregated unions, dual labor markets, and exclusionary legislation perpetuated the color line between whites and nonwhites within the working class.

These developments took their toll on nonwhite workers. Excluded from the industrialized labor force, African Americans, Latinos, Asians, and other non-European immigrants were left to contend with high rates of unemployment and impoverished living conditions. Whites, on the other hand, including the new white ethnics, benefited from continued access to job opportunities and self-sustaining work. This dichotomy set up the social conditions underlying the perception that productivity and responsibility were the virtues of whiteness while laziness and dependence were the vices of all other racial affiliations. Together, the organization of the working class and the assimilation of selected immigrants into the white race demonstrate the mutability of racial categories. Both developments exemplify how race is manipulated for the political and economic advantage of those belonging to the white race.[38] The manipulation, though, affected whites as well as blacks. Identifying across ethnic lines and united in the determination to maintain blacks in a subordinate state, whites were vulnerable to exploitation both economically and politically. The commitment to white dominance blinded many whites to the reality that their actual status, while better than blacks', was far from ideal. Legal forms, often supported by whites, have served to rationalize racial boundaries with fictions that, in fact, conceal exploitation and marginalization that do not observe the color line.[39] Today, many whites oppose all social reform as "welfare programs for blacks." They ignore the fact that poor whites have employment, education, and social service needs that differ from the condition of poor blacks by a margin that, without a racial scorecard, becomes difficult to measure. In summary, the blatant involuntary sacrifice of black rights to further white interests, so obvious in early American history, remains viable and, while somewhat more subtle in its contemporary forms, is as potentially damaging as it ever was to black rights and the interests of all but wealthy whites.

Just as the composition of racial categories evolves in a manner that promotes white privilege, the justification supporting these classifications also shifts in order to reconcile white privilege with democratic egalitarianism. As discussed above, biological conceptions of racial difference associating subhuman characteristics

---

38. Noel Ignatiev, How the Irish Became White (1995); Karen Brodkin, How Jews Became White Folks & What That Says About Race in America (1999).

39. See, e.g., David R. Roediger, The Wages of Whiteness: Race and the Making of the American Working Class (1991); Howard Winant, Racial Conditions: Politics, Theory, Comparisons (1994).

with blacks emerged to justify slavery. As scientific developments began to discredit a biological conception of racial difference, however, equally pernicious ideologies arose.

Consider, for example, the argument described in John Powell's *The Racing of American Society*.[40] Powell suggests that in the modern era of de facto segregation, white domination survives without the prevalence of overt racism. It does so through ideologies such as the "culture of poverty." This theory discounts the impact of systemic discrimination or structural racism, and instead attributes the inferior social, economic, and political status of minority groups to cultural tenets prevailing in minority communities that conflict with the norms of hard work and lawful behavior. As Powell explains, when explicit racist discourse falls out of fashion, a new discourse consistent with conventional understandings of race but articulated in race-neutral terms emerges as a way to rationalize the status quo.

At that time, masses of white male workers abandoned the manual labor force in pursuit of emerging business opportunities. The labor shortages left in their absence, the automation of Southern agriculture, and the demands of the post–World War II industrial boom presented blacks with never-before-seen job opportunities. As blacks migrated into urban industrial fields, however, they became susceptible to the ensuing economic recession of the mid-1970s. Black unemployment skyrocketed to unprecedented levels eclipsing unemployment rates among whites. But society at large, rather than attribute this phenomenon to global and national economic shifts or changing employment patterns that disfavored labor intensive work, cited deviant black cultural norms and family disorganization as reasons for deteriorating conditions in black communities.

Economic conditions in the first years of the twenty-first century present similar challenges for blacks. With minimal political opposition, manufacturing and textile companies in search of cheap labor have relocated factories overseas.[41] Because black men and women dominate in many of these industries, black communities are hardest hit by rising unemployment rates. As in the 1970s, unemployment rates rose twice as fast among blacks than among whites. Unlike previous recessions, however, economists caution that unemployed blacks are not likely to benefit from the speedy recovery that accompanied previous cyclical downturns because corporations have removed whole swaths of industrial labor opportunities from the national market. Thus, a significant slide in living standards for middle-class black families is taking place. One would be well-advised not to wager anything of significance on the likelihood that society will correctly attribute this unfortunate phenomenon to profit-based occupational patterns rather than to malicious stereotypes about black work ethics.

40. Powell, supra note 34, at 99.
41. See Louis Uchitelle, Blacks Lose Better Jobs Faster as Middle-Class Work Drops, at http://cgi.cnn.com/2003/US/07/12/nyt.uchitelle.

§8.5   CHOICE IN RACIAL IDENTITY

Racial identity might also be a function of individual choice. Such is the position taken by Ian Haney Lopez.[1] To Lopez, the process of racial identification involves considerations of ancestry, social context, and choice, each element taking on overlapping and inseverable significance in influencing the way race is experienced and perceived. In this sense, Lopez sees the significance of race not as a mark of external proscription but, at least in part, as a source of chosen social affiliations.

As evidence that race is a matter of choice, Lopez points to the practice of passing — adopting another group's racial affiliation as one's own.[2] In the period immediately following the Civil War, tens of thousands of individuals sought to abandon their black race by adopting a white identity. For many reasons, passing, while no longer a major way of dealing with discrimination, has certainly not disappeared. For those individuals able to do so, passing became a way to access the benefits — property rights associated with whiteness. But crossing the color line came with a high price. Raising children, maintaining family ties, and perpetuating community relations are no longer options for those blacks wanting to hide their "true," albeit socially prescribed, racial identity.[3] Lopez admits that because America's racial caste system is grounded in physical appearance, passing is unavailable to the majority of individuals of color whose appearance attests to their race. To Lopez, however, this limitation does nothing to undermine his argument because passing is only one manifestation of racial self-identification. According to Lopez, race is also deployed voluntarily through a host of everyday decisions that take on racial meaning, ranging from the clothes we wear, music we listen to, foods we consume, speech patterns and dialects we emphasize, vocabulary we invoke, and subjects we publicly address and respond to.[4]

To the extent that particular fashions, cuisines, and art forms are associated with a certain race, our choice of food, clothing, and music provides a marker of racial identification. Surely most individuals proceed through their day without consciously investigating ways to declare their racial identity. Still, everyday choices take on racial meaning and serve as mediums for continually reinventing race. Indeed, to the extent that races are socially prescribed at all, each individual must, to a certain degree, learn to conform to a given racial category. Perhaps this observation lends credence to Lopez's theory. At the same time, it begs the question: What if some individuals are more skilled at adopting a particular racial categorization? Does this again bring us back to biology?

Lopez does more than simply describe the relationship between choice and one's individual racial identity. He suggests that choice, when expressed in the

---

§8.5   1. See Ian Haney Lopez, The Social Construction of Race: Some Observations on Illusion, Fabrication and Choice, 29 Harv. C.R.-C.L. L. Rev. 1, 39-40 (1994).

2. See id. at 47-49; see also Kenneth L. Karst, Myths of Identity: Individual and Group Portraits of Race and Sexual Orientation, 43 UCLA L. Rev. 263, 268-269 (1995).

3. See Adrian Piper, Passing for White, Passing for Black, in Passing and the Fictions of Identity 244 (Elaine K. Ginsberg ed., 1996).

4. See Lopez, supra note 1, at 49.

aggregate, can rework the social fabric and significance of race.[5] Take rap music, for example. Lopez suggests that although a diverse group of people listens to, enjoys, and performs rap music, its association with the inner city has led to its identification as black music. In this respect, an affinity for rap music, another artistic genre, or any other race-coded experience serves as a medium for racial affiliation and identification.

Public aversion to racialized experiences can be equally effective. Such was the case when Bill Clinton chided rapper Sister Souljah for her violent rap lyrics during his first presidential campaign. As a pioneer of rap music, Sister Souljah provided Clinton with a means of distancing himself from African Americans in an appeal to moderate whites who considered him overly sympathetic to minority interests. For Lopez, Clinton's decision to reject the violent content of certain rap lyrics, rather than to directly renounce his allegiance to black Americans, reflects how the aggregate expression of choice alters social context by coding experiences, activities, and intentions according to race.

One might add that Clinton was not the first Democratic politician who had to rely on the black vote to win elections but who did not want to acknowledge that reliance. Clinton, like so many other Democrat politicians, was willing to insult blacks — as he surely did by his public criticism — in order to curry favor with "undecided" whites.

Lopez's assertion that race is deployed voluntarily through everyday decisions is not universally accepted. Christine Hickman criticizes Lopez's theory. She admits that some daily actions do take on racial meaning but argues that it is nearly impossible to actually reinvent race through daily activities, political views, or economic achievements. According to Hickman, Lopez's theory is flawed because it is decidedly one-sided. While whites regularly make choices without relinquishing their racial identity, Hickman argues, blacks are not entitled to the same privilege. White Americans can "freely occupy any point on the political spectrum" and can "straighten or curl their hair, darken their skin, change the color of their eyes, and have collagen injected into their lips" without implicating their racial identity.[6]

Blacks, on the other hand, are denied such choice by the assumption that their daily activities take on racial significance. Under Lopez's theory, blacks cannot amass wealth, enjoy classical music, or support certain political initiatives without abandoning their claim to racial authenticity. In the end, Hickman is convinced that associating every act or expression with a racial connotation ironically denies the role of choice in constructing racial identity.

Hickman further argues that the role of history in dictating one's racial identity overpowers the influence of choice.[7] To make her point, she alludes to the discourse surrounding W. E. B. Du Bois's self-proclaimed black identity. Many scholars cite Du Bois's experience to demonstrate the power of choice in fabricating racial identity. Anthony Appiah, for example, uses Du Bois to ground his discussion of race as a historical component derived from the "common

5. See Lopez, supra note 1, at 50-53.
6. Christine Hickman, The Devil and the One Drop Rule, 95 Mich. L. Rev. 1161, 1252 (1997).
7. See id. at 1244-1251.

experiences" of certain peoples.[8] According to Appiah, Du Bois shared a history with both the people of Holland and America on account of his combined black and Dutch ancestry, but it was his decision to embrace his African American experiences that determined which race formed the core of his identity.[9] According to Hickman, however, Appiah mistakenly overlooks the role of history on Du Bois's choice.[10] In reality, she argues, Du Bois's decision to self-identify as black was externally driven given that the prevailing racist ideology of the day prevented the alternative. Any attempt by Du Bois to identify with his Dutch heritage, perhaps by joining a white civic organization or fostering relations with a white woman, would have been ineffective, not to say illegal and potentially deadly. Moreover, Du Bois lacked any social or cultural ties with his European forebears and therefore had little incentive to cultivate a Dutch identity. Finally, adopting a Dutch identity would have required Du Bois to abandon his oppressed brothers and sisters and join ranks with the oppressor. Legally and culturally, therefore, Du Bois was black, and any attempt to appropriate a competing identity would have been wholly ineffective.

It could be, however, that choice today plays a more significant role in fabricating racial identity than it did several decades ago when Du Bois was claiming membership in, or was assigned to, the black race. Kenneth Karst speaks almost exclusively in terms of self-identification and offers contemporary evidence that race is primarily self-determined. As an example, Karst points to transracial adoption where black children are defined as "children of birth parents self-identified as Black."[11] But perhaps this too overlooks the effects of human intervention. According to Hickman, when a women who is pregnant with a black child goes to an adoption agency, what matters is not how the birth parents identify themselves or the child, but how society will identify the child and the child's parents.[12] The consequences are significant given that the demand for an adopted child increases exponentially according to whether that child is classified as black, biracial, or white.[13] According to Hickman, therefore, while the malleability of racial identity allows for some contribution from choice, racial identification is still a choice others make for us.

§8.6   CHOICE AND THE IMPLICATION OF MULTIRACIALITY

Despite Hickman's sound criticism, an argument can be made that the mechanics of racial identification still involve some element of choice, at least in specific contexts. In addition to passing and undertaking racially coded activities, more

---

8. See id. at 1236; see also Jayne Lee, Navigating the Topology of Race, 46 Stan. L. Rev. 747, 763 (1994).

9. See Hickman, supra note 6, at 1245-1246.

10. See id. at 1246-1248.

11. Id. at 347.

12. See Hickman, supra note 6, at 1250.

13. See id.; see also Karst, supra note 2, at 347.

nuanced methods of invading racial boundaries are available. Consider the process of self-identification that takes place when individuals participate in the U.S. census. Census forms provide an opportunity for each individual to designate his or her own race, and although each person must choose from a list of preselected categories, the sheer multitude of informally defined choices provides an opportunity for modern-day passing.

Some scholars applaud the inclusion of a multiracial census category because it accurately recognizes that most people do not fit neatly into a single racial group.[1] In this respect, the multiracial category stands in stark contrast to traditional racial categories that promote a false ideology of racial purity. In practical terms, it allows children born of parents from different races to claim relationship to both, rather than forcing them to choose one.[2] It also accommodates many multiracial people, especially those raised by white parents or those who have very light skin, who feel uncomfortable asserting a racial affiliation with blacks.

Despite these benefits, the inclusion of a multiracial category has been the subject of criticism. The late Professor Trina Grillo, a self-proclaimed black-Latina-white law professor, feared that multiraciality would be used like other racial categories as a way to stratify persons on a race-based social hierarchy.[3] She argued against a multiracial consciousness that, in her mind, severed affiliations between individuals and their oppressed brothers and sisters and introduced the potential for subordinating individual minorities to "multiracials."

The lack of stable conventions for describing multiracial persons also complicates the debate. Consider Grillo's anecdotal description of jurors in the O. J. Simpson trial. One newspaper described "eight Blacks, one Anglo, one Hispanic and two persons of mixed race." Another counted "eight Blacks, two Hispanics, one Anglo and one person who identified himself as half white and half American-Indian." Grillo later found out that one of the Hispanics was an Hispanic-black, classified as mixed race by one paper and as Hispanic by another. In a more personal account, Grillo explained that the reason she grew up considering herself black was because society at large described her in that way. Her own self-conception dictated, however, that in biological terms, she should be considered at least half white.[4] Should Grillo have checked the multiracial box?

Not only can mixed race people check different boxes on the census, they may also navigate in and out of different racial groups depending on social context with dexterity afforded to them via their own physical appearance and socioeconomic status.[5] Social scientists have explored the malleability of racial boundaries

§8.6 1. See, e.g., Tanya Kateri Hernandez, Multiracial Discourse: Racial Classifications in an Era of Color-Blind Jurisprudence, 57 Md. L. Rev. 97, 101-103, 106-113 (1998); Kenneth L. Karst, Myths of Identity: Individual and Group Portraits of Race and Sexual Orientation, 43 UCLA L. Rev. 263, 328 (1995).

2. See Trina Grillo, Anti-Essentialism and Intersectionality: Tools to Dismantle the Master's House, 10 Berkeley Women's L.J. 16, 23-25 (1995).

3. See id.

4. See Grillo, supra note 2, at 24.

5. The material that follows by Sarah Marie Blanton, N.Y.U. J.D. '07, is derived from her Sociology Honors Thesis, Dartmouth College, 2000 (on reserve at either the sociology department or Baker Library).

especially for those individuals who are mixed race. Robin Miller writes that, "... a theory of ethnic identity development that could accommodate multiethnic or multiracial people would need to incorporate rules governing the rigidity or fluidity of boundaries surrounding social groups, principals for accommodating structural change, and rules to describe situational views of self."[6] Whereas Lopez writes about the practice of passing, more and more individuals do not conform to the phenotypic ideas that society has about what someone of a certain race should look like. Thus, "passing" is not comprehensive enough when applied to racially ambiguous individuals. A growing number in the population are challenging the legal concept of race as an immutable and visible characteristic and often doing so unbeknownst to the society which tends to think of race as a binary.

Robin Miller writes that "[t]raditionally, biracial, Black-White people have been actively socialized as Black and considered part of the spectrum of the community, increasing the likelihood of identification with Black experiences."[7] It is also the case in contemporary times that "... the multiracial person may select behavior, labels, and perspectives based on their immediate utility in a given context."[8] Theories on situational ethnicity underscore Lopez's argument that racial choice is based on social situations. John C. Turner writes, "Social situations which switch on or increase the prepotency of social identity should tend to produce their very own behavioral effects."[9]

Professor Kenji Yoshino has written on the process by which racial minorities and homosexuals assimilate via conversion, passing and covering.[10] He writes, "If individuals have multiple ways of modulating their identities, discrimination against them will take multiple forms, including demands to convert, to pass, and to cover."[11] From this perspective, the fluidity of racial boundaries is exploited not only by those who can assimilate for their own benefit and comfort, but also by those whose personal prejudice imposes conformity or compliance on the racial minority. He highlights an experience of Professor Patricia Williams where she was asked to cover, "... he is not asking Williams to convert to being white, or to pass as white. He is, rather, asking her to perform her racial identity in ways that make it easy for him to ignore her race."[12] Thus, the situational, contextual options for racial minorities may undermine and break down certain racial barriers. At the same time, however, removing some of the racial boundaries that have defined our

---

6. Robin Miller, "The Human Ecology of Multiracial Identity," in Racially Mixed People in America 30 (Maria P. P. Root ed., 1992).

7. Id. at 29.

8. Id. at 32.

9. John C. Turner, "Towards a Cognitive Redefinition of the Social Group," in Social Identity and Intergroup Relations (Henri Tajfel ed., 1982).

10. Kenji Yoshino, Covering, 111 Yale. L. J. 769, 772 (Jan. 2002) ("Conversion means the underlying identity is altered. Conversion occurs when a lesbian changes her orientation to become straight. Passing means the underlying identity is not altered, but hidden. Passing occurs when a lesbian presents herself to the world as straight. Covering means the underlying identity is neither altered nor hidden, but is downplayed. Covering occurs when a lesbian both is, and says she is, a lesbian, but otherwise makes it easy for others to disattend her orientation.").

11. Id. at 774.

12. Id. at 887.

culture does not remove racist tendencies of those who prefer whiteness in whatever form they can create it.

§8.7 SUMMARY

The foregoing is intended to show why those who contend that race is just a social construct underestimate its significance in the lives of all people of color, particularly those whose parentage requires that they answer the question: "What are you?" posed by others as well as those to themselves. It is a general overview of the development of racial meaning in the United States and explores the viability of competing theories of race and racialization. It is by no means expected to serve as a definitive account. Its utility comes in providing the backdrop against which the cases and policies in this text can be discussed and analyzed. Consider asking whether judicial constructions of race take on the same malleable properties as the theoretical constructions. Consider whether those concepts have evolved in practice to account for shifting demographics or changes in social, political, or economic circumstances in a manner that reifies racial difference and maintains the status quo. Are changing conceptions of race and racial meaning being invoked to dismantle or reify white privilege? Is there real reason to hope that increasing numbers of whites will come to recognize the substantial costs to them of white privilege, which so often is actually a different form of subordination? Perhaps as racially conscious legal advocates, we cannot supply the answers. We must consider the questions responsibly, however, so that our course toward racial equality under law might be charted strategically and with due regard to the essentially cyclical character of policies and practices that perpetuate racial subordination.

§8.8 INTERRACIAL COUPLES AND EMPLOYMENT DISCRIMINATION

In addition to the more general attention to employment discrimination issues covered in Chapter 4, the cases and readings set out below provide an appropriate focus on job barriers faced by interracial couples even as acceptance among the general public continues to grow. The most common cases arise because interracial couples are denied job opportunities for reasons similar to those reflected in the anti-miscegenation laws. In the 1970s and 1980s, some courts protected private and public employees from racial discrimination based on fear of a possible community reaction. Fear of public disfavor does not justify racial discrimination, even when the employee involved is in a public position.[1] Although both black and white

§8.8 1. See Faraca v. Clements, 506 F.2d 956 (5th Cir.), cert. denied, 422 U.S. 1006 (1975) (granting damages against Georgia Retardation Center for denying a white man and his black wife live-in administrator positions in a home for retarded children; evidence indicates that Faraca was the

employees have suffered discrimination for interracial relationships, courts initially applied Title VII only to cases involving a white plaintiff. In Gutwein v. Easton Publishing Co.,[2] a state court noted that the Equal Employment Opportunity Commission (EEOC) had interpreted Title VII as protecting the white employee's interracial associations.[3] Several courts applied a "but for" analysis to uphold white plaintiffs' claims under Title VII.[4] If the plaintiffs in these cases had been black, the alleged discrimination would not have occurred: "In other words, *but for* their being white, the plaintiffs in these cases would not have been discriminated against."[5] Similarly, in Parr v. Woodmen of the World Life Insurance Co.,[6] the Eleventh Circuit reversed a lower court and held that plaintiff's complaint did state a cause of action under Title VII and federal statutes guaranteeing equal rights under the law. Citing the rule of liberal construction, the court held that Parr's claim that he "was not hired because of race" was sufficient to allege discrimination based on his interracial marriage. It further stated that there was "no requirement that plaintiff specifically state that he was discriminated against because of *his* race to allege discrimination based on his interracial marriage."[7] Following the precedent set in *Faraca*,[8] the court also recognized Parr's §1981 claim and, employing an argument

---

best candidate for the job and would have been hired except that one supervisor voiced "grave concern about the effects of the racially mixed couple on visitors and possible adverse reactions from state legislators").

In Langford v. City of Texarkana, Ark., an Eighth Circuit court reversed dismissal of a suit by a black community development leader who had been discharged from his Model Cities position, along with a white woman he had hired, allegedly because neither of them could gain the confidence of the people in the black community where they worked. The City denied that the close social relationship between the two was a factor in the dismissal, but the district court's failure to make factual findings on this point led to reversal by the Court of Appeals: "The fact that interracial associations are frowned on by some in a community cannot serve as a justification to discourage or prohibit such associations by public employees." Langford v. City of Texarkana, Ark., 478 F.2d 262 (8th Cir. 1973).

2. See Gutwein v. Easton Publishing Co., 272 Md. 563, 325 A.2d 740 (Md. 1974), cert. denied, 420 U.S. 991 (1975) (upholding the order of a human relations commission that found an unlawful employment practice where a white employee was discharged because of his association with his fiancée, who was black).

3. See EEOC Dec. No. 71-1902, 3 F.E.P. ¶1244 (Apr. 28, 1971); EEOC Dec. No. 71-969 (Dec. 24, 1970); see also EEOC Decision No. 76-23, 1983 EEOC Dec. (CCH) ¶6615 (Aug. 25, 1975); Decision No. 79-03, 1983 EEOC Dec. (CCH) ¶6734 (Oct. 6, 1978).

4. See Holiday v. Belle's Restaurant, 409 F. Supp. 904 (W.D. Pa. 1976); Whitney v. Greater N.Y. Corp. of Seventh Day Adventists, 401 F. Supp. 1363 (S.D.N.Y. 1975).

But see Parr v. United Family Life Ins. Co., Civil Action no. C83-26G (N.D. Ga. 1983) (O'Kelley, J.); Adams v. Governor's Comm. on Post-secondary Educ., 26 Fair Empl. Prac. Cas. (BNA) 1348 (N.D. Ga. 1981) (Evans, J.); Rip v. Dobbs Houses Inc., 366 F. Supp. 205, 208-209 (N.D. Ala. 1973), all rejecting that allegations of discrimination resulting from interracial marriage can constitute a Title VII claim.

5. Gresham v. Waffle House, Inc., 586 F. Supp. 1442, 1445 (N.D. Ga. 1984) (finding that a white female had a claim under Title VII by alleging that she had been fired because she was married to a black man).

6. 791 F.2d 888 (11th Cir. 1986). During Parr's job interview, Woodmen told him that the company neither hired nor sold insurance to black people. Parr told the employment service that he was married to a black woman, and when Woodmen learned this, the company manager said that he would not recommend Parr for the job. Despite his experience and strong qualifications, Parr was not in fact hired.

7. Id. at 890 (emphasis in original).

8. See *Faraca*, supra note 1. See also Canterbury v. West Virginia Human Rts. Commn., 382 S.E.2d 338 (W.V. 1989). The suit alleged that Canterbury, the owner of a restaurant, fired his cook/

parallel to that in *Gresham* (and citing the case), determined that plaintiff had a Title VII action as well.

While courts have continued to hold that Title VII prohibits discrimination against Caucasians based on interracial association,[9] Title VII protection has not been accorded to blacks who face discrimination based on interracial association. In 1991, a district court extended Title VII protection to an allegation of hostile work environment by a white woman who claims she was subjected to denigrating remarks because her husband is Hispanic.[10] Denise Chacon claimed her supervisor made periodic derogatory comments about Hispanics, made fun of Hispanics, and repeated offensive Mexican jokes. Following her complaint, plaintiff alleges that her supervisor called her a "demon" during a supervisors' meeting, wrote a negative work evaluation about her, and encouraged other supervisors to "write her up" at every opportunity. As in *Woodmen*, plaintiff did not need to show discrimination based on *her* race to allege Title VII discrimination based on her interracial association.[11]

Most of the decisions summarized above seemed to provide protection appropriate under the Loving v. Virginia precedent, but a district court decision in Ohio demonstrates that, lacking hard to obtain proof, not every court will find a Title VII violation when interracial couples experience harassment. In Eperesi v. Envirotest Systems Corp. the court granted summary judgment in a Title VII wrongful discharge action because the plaintiff failed to establish that her discharge was based on her interracial relationship with another employee.[12] Ms. Eperesi claimed that her immediate supervisors told her employer that they would not tolerate interracial relationships and that she was handed transfer papers and told that she and her partner could no longer be employed there at the company because they were in a relationship together. The court reasoned that because no company policy forbids interracial relationships, and because a number of them existed within the employer's work force, plaintiff failed to meet her burden of persuasion.[13] This Ohio case is not alone. Numerous plaintiffs have brought Title VII suits against employers alleging discrimination and/or harassment on account of their interracial marriages

---

chef (Richardson) when he discovered that he was involved in an interracial marriage. Richardson is black and his wife is white. The Supreme Court of Appeals of West Virginia found that extrajudicial statements by an employee that the owner "didn't like interracial marriages" was admissible hearsay. Based on that evidence and testimony that the owner would not allow the white waitresses to bring food orders into the kitchen to Richardson and testimony that Richardson had been warned by a former co-owner of the restaurant to be careful of Canterbury, the court reinstated the Commission's finding of discrimination.

9. See, e.g., Tetro v. Elliott Popham Pontiac, Oldsmobile, Buick, 173 F.3d 988 (6th Cir. 1999) (holding that the discharge of a white employee for having a biracial child violates Title VII), Rosenblatt v. Cohen, 946 F. Supp. 298 (S.D.N.Y. 1996) (denying summary judgment against a white employee who claimed that he was fired for being married to a black woman, in violation of Title VII, §1983 and New York antidiscrimination law); Reiter v. Center Consol. Sch. Dist., 618 F. Supp. 1458, 1459-1460 (D. Colo. 1985) (finding that "discriminatory employment practices based on an individual's association with people of a particular race or national origin is prohibited under Title VII," where (white) plaintiff alleged she was refused employment because of her association with the Hispanic community).

10. See Chacon v. Ochs et al., 780 F. Supp. 680 (C.D. Cal. 1991).

11. Id. at 682.

12. 999 F. Supp. 1026 (N.D. Ohio 1998).

13. Id. at 1033-1034.

and have met varying degrees of success. In Smith v. Century Concrete, Inc, the plaintiff brought an action against his former employer for racial discrimination, retaliation and a hostile work environment. It granted in part and denied in part the defendant's motion for summary judgment. The court pointed out the threshold matter that no cases exist in the Tenth Circuit where the plaintiff successfully brought a Title VII case against an employer for associational discrimination. The Court stated that, "based on three racial comments made by [defendant] coupled with the three examples of facially neutral acts of harassment, a reasonable jury may find that this harassment was objectively severe or pervasive . . ."[14] and denied the summary judgment on this issue.

In the Texas case of Wooten v. Federal Express Corporation, a white woman married to a black man, who both had worked for the same employer, brought a claim alleging disparate treatment race discrimination, retaliation, and hostile work environment. The former employer moved for summary judgment which the court granted in part and denied in part. The court denied summary judgment on plaintiff's claim of discriminatory termination under Title VII and §1981 and her claim of retaliation. In granting summary judgment the court held that a "reasonable jury could not find that [defendant's] 'snide jokes' to a coworker about white women taking the black men . . . were sufficiently severe and pervasive as to alter a term or condition of [plaintiff's] employment" or that "without piling one inference on another inference, that [defendant's] allegedly harassing actions were motivated by plaintiff's interracial relationship." These comments were accompanied by "cursing at her, throwing her purse, duffle bag, and water bottle . . . using an expletive to tell her to stay out of his truck" and were found to be unrelated to her interracial relationship.[15]

Chapter 4 provides statistics that make clear how difficult it is for blacks to obtain relief under Title VII for alleged racial bias. Based on the materials reviewed here, those difficulties are not eased because the discrimination was the result of an interracial relationship.

§8.9   INTERRACIAL COUPLES AND HOUSING DISCRIMINATION

While the exclusion of blacks, including some cases where rejection was based on the plaintiffs' interracial relationship, are covered in Chapter 4, some special attention to this issue is set out here where hostility to mixed race couples is particularly clear. For example, Ku Klux Klan members expressed their opposition to interracial relationships by firing into a residence that was the home of two black men and two white women. This action, together with other harassment of NAACP officials, led to the conviction of Klan members for intimidating and interfering

14. Smith v. Century Concrete, Inc. No. 05-2105-JAR (D. Kan. 2006).
15. Wooten v. Federal Express Corporation, Civil Action No. 3:04-CV-1196-D (N.D. Tex. 2007) (slip op., 2007 WL 63609 (N.D. Tex.)).

with persons exercising rights protected by the Fair Housing Act of 1968.[1] It is easy to dismiss such totally irresponsible behavior as "typical of the Klan," but those robes conceal human beings with emotions and fears, just like the rest of us. What is it about a black person cohabiting with a white person that motivates some human beings to sally forth and shoot blindly into their home? What, precisely, were they trying to kill? What message were they trying to convey?

Fortunately, few Americans feel as strongly about interracial cohabitation as did the Klan members in the *Johns* case, but prejudice against interracial couples still makes it difficult for them to obtain housing. Like the employers discussed above, landlords offer pretextual excuses for thinly veiled discrimination against interracial couples.[2] In Oliver v. Shelly,[3] the landlord candidly admitted that one factor in his decision to refuse to rent an apartment to an interracial couple was "concern of tension caused by their presence."[4] It was not remarkable that the court there found a violation of both §1982 and the Fair Housing Act (FHA); nor were the landlord's concerns without basis, even 30 years after enactment of the Fair Housing Act. Indeed, the presence of an interracial couple, especially if the man is black, will give rise to more "tension" than if both spouses were black.

The "tensions" so feared by the landlord may simply be the normal reaction to what for many tenants will be the new, the unusual, and, for some, the bizarre. For those whites who do not move, the interracial couple will likely be little cause for special concern after a few months. Unhappy white tenants might respond that they could probably adjust to a halfway house in their residential neighborhood, too, but they are living where they are precisely to avoid the necessity for such adjustments.

In Meyers v. Holley,[5] an interracial couple alleged discrimination in buying a house under the FHA, which forbids racial discrimination in connection with the sale or rental of a dwelling. The couple sued the real estate corporation, the discriminating agent, and the corporation's president and sole shareholder in his individual capacity. The Court viewed the action brought under the FHA as a tort action and applied the legal background of ordinary tort-related vicarious liability rules. Justice Breyer, writing for a unanimous court, stated that the FHA "imposes vicarious liability upon the corporation but not upon its officers or owners."[6] The Court reversed the Ninth Circuit's holding that the criteria for the FHA extend beyond tort law analysis "so that owners and officers of corporations" are "absolutely liable for an employee's or agent's violation of the Act."[7] In doing

---

§8.9 1. United States v. Johns, 615 F.2d 672 (5th Cir. 1980). The court relied on §3631 of the Act.

2. See, e.g., Kane v. Oak Trust & Sav. Bank, 1995 WL 683820 (N.D. Ill.); Cato v. Jilek, 779 F. Supp. 937 (N.D. Ill. 1991) (at trial landlord claimed he rejected plaintiffs because they were unmarried); Pollitt v. Bramel, 669 F. Supp. 172 (S.D. Ohio 1987) (owners of trailer park falsely stated nothing was available); Stewart v. Furton, 774 F.2d 706 (6th Cir. 1985) (trailer park manager claimed innocence because plaintiffs decided not to rent, after discovering his racism).

3. 538 F. Supp. 600 (S.D. Tex. 1982).

4. Id.

5. 123 S. Ct. 824 (2003).

6. Id. at 827.

7. Id. at 828, citing 258 F.3d 1127, 1134-1135 (2001).

so, the Court limited the potential sources of remedy for plaintiffs alleging housing discrimination under the FHA.

§8.10   RELIGIOUS BELIEF AND INTERRACIAL SOCIAL CONTACT

The Court has not defined the extent to which churches operating private schools with racially discriminatory policies are exempt from the desegregation mandate of Brown v. Board of Education. And, while churches and civil rights groups discuss the issue in terms that intersperse statutory and First Amendment questions, during the Reagan administration that discussion became blatantly political.[1] Litigation on this subject stretches back to the late 1960s, but the Supreme Court took a definitive position in 1983, in Bob Jones University v. United States.[2] This decision answered two challenges filed by fundamentalist church sects. Both presented one basic question to the court: Can the Internal Revenue Code be read to require the denial or the revocation of tax-exempt status to private religious schools that engage in racial discrimination based on religious belief?

The Supreme Court responded with a firm "Yes," in an opinion written by Justice Berger, to which only Justice Rehnquist dissented. The Court found the governmental interest in eradicating racial discrimination in education compelling, fundamental, overriding, and substantially outweighing whatever burden denial of tax benefits places on petitioners' exercise of their religious beliefs. These beliefs, the Court found, cannot be accommodated with the government's compelling interest, and no "less restrictive means" are available to achieve the governmental interest.

Bob Jones University, at the time of this litigation, offered schooling from kindergarten through graduate school. It adhered to fundamentalist religious beliefs that might charitably be defined as judiciously diluted white supremacy.

§8.10   1. The Internal Revenue Service was under strong pressure to conform its regulations to decisions such as Green v. Connally, 330 F. Supp. 1150 (D.D.C.), aff'd sub nom. Coit v. Green, 404 U.S. 997 (1971), barring federal tax-exempt status unless the schools demonstrated a publicized nondiscriminatory admissions policy. The Internal Revenue Service announced that it could "no longer legally justify allowing tax-exempt status to private schools which practice racial discrimination. . . ." Then, in 1982, as it developed the government's position in the *Bob Jones* and *Goldsboro Christian School* cases pending before the Supreme Court, the Treasury Department, with the advice of the Justice Department, reversed its interpretation of the Internal Revenue Code. It announced that, in the absence of specific statutes authorizing such a policy, it would no longer revoke or deny tax-exempt status for religious, charitable, educational, or scientific organizations on the grounds of their nonconformity with fundamental policies — including the national policy against racial discrimination.

The change in policy evoked strong protests from civil rights groups, and when the government withdrew from the appeals in the *Bob Jones* and *Goldsboro Christian School* cases, the Supreme Court appointed former Department of Transportation secretary, William Coleman, to represent the interests opposed to approval of tax-exempt status for the two schools.

2. 461 U.S. 574 (1983), aff'g 468 F. Supp. 890 (D.S.C. 1978), rev'd, 639 F.2d 147 (4th Cir. 1980). The decision also consolidated and affirmed the lower court's decision in Goldsboro Christian Sch., Inc. v. United States, 436 F. Supp. 1314 (E.D.N.C. 1977), aff'd per curiam, No. 80-1473 (4th Cir. Feb. 24, 1981) (unpublished opinion).

The university was absolutely opposed to interracial sex and marriage, and it enforced a prohibition on such unions within its community, first by barring the enrollment of black students and then later by admitting only married black students. Only after the Fourth Circuit upheld an administrative ruling that terminated all Veterans Administration assistance to the university[3] did Bob Jones amend its admissions policy to permit unmarried black students to enroll. At the same time, however, the school adopted a disciplinary rule providing that students who advocate or engage in interracial dating or marriage would be subject to expulsion.[4] The Goldsboro Christian School had been more steadfast in its racially discriminatory policy and from its inception had absolutely prohibited the enrollment of black students. The Goldsboro school had opened in 1963 in evident response to the perceived need for a private, fundamentalist religious school. The school received financial support from and used the facilities of the Second Baptist Church of Goldsboro, North Carolina.

Both Bob Jones and Goldsboro argued that the Fourth Circuit erroneously applied the tax-exemption provisions of the Internal Revenue Code by requiring that they eschew all racial discrimination in the operation of their schools. They claimed infringement of their First Amendment rights to the free exercise of religion and violation of the establishment clause.

The Court noted that similar issues had earlier been decided against schools practicing racial discrimination, but Green v. Connally did not specifically reach the First Amendment issues raised by the Bob Jones and Goldsboro schools. Chief Justice Burger's opinion dwelled on the validity of withholding §501(c)(3) status to a private church school because of discriminatory racial policies mandated by religious beliefs. The opinion reviewed federal income tax law provisions, including the current Internal Revenue Code providing tax-exempt status for several charitable entities that "operate exclusively for religious . . . or educational purposes."[5] "Charitable exemptions are justified," the Court found, "on the basis that the exempt entity confers a public benefit—a benefit which the society or the community may not itself choose or be able to provide, or which supplements and advances the work of public institutions already supported by tax revenues."[6] In this case, the institution's policy was "so at odds with the common community conscience as to undermine any public merit that might otherwise be conferred." The Court recognized the serious impact on an institution that loses its tax-exempt status, but it found the history of school desegregation compelling evidence that "racial discrimination in education violates deeply and widely accepted views of elementary justice." Citing a long list of actions by both Congress and the Executive branch intended to eliminate racial segregation, particularly in education, the Court concluded: "Whatever may be the rationale for such private schools' policies, and however sincere the rationale may be, racial discrimination in

---

3. Bob Jones Univ. v. Johnson, 529 F.2d 514 (4th Cir. 1975). See also Runyon v. McCrary, 515 F.2d 1082 (4th Cir. 1975), aff'd, 427 U.S. 160 (1976).

4. Bob Jones Univ. v. United States, 639 F.2d 147, 149 (4th Cir. 1980).

5. 330 F. Supp. 1150 (D.D.C.), aff'd mem. sub nom. Coit v. Green, 404 U.S. 997 (1971).

6. I.R.C. §§501(a), (c)(3). Tax deductions are permitted for contributions to §501(c)(3) tax-exempt charitable organizations. I.R.C. §170(c).

education is contrary to public policy."[7] Finally, the Court pointed out that the First Amendment's free exercise clause does not absolutely prohibit governmental regulation of religious beliefs. The state may justify a limitation on religious liberty by showing that it is essential to accomplish an overriding governmental interest. The governmental interest in ending racial discrimination is compelling and substantially outweighs whatever burden denial of tax benefits places on petitioners' exercise of their religious beliefs.[8] The Court's decision in *Bob Jones University* was hailed as a hard-won victory by civil rights adherents. The opinion was sufficiently broad (too broad for Justice Powell's tastes) to establish the balance between racial justice and religious freedom. The Court affirmed the Fourth Circuit decisions on the First Amendment claims in strong terms. Even so, civil rights adherents may only have won another Pyrrhic victory. Consider:

1. The serious undermining of school desegregation efforts occurred during the late 1960s and early 1970s; the litigation resulting in *Green* was intended to address this problem.
2. Many of these schools that came to life as alternatives to school desegregation have long since faded from the scene. Those that survive with discriminatory policies in place that have been maintained too often without loss of their tax-exempt status.
3. Few, if any, black parents are breaking down the doors and seeking admission for their children to schools like Bob Jones University.

Without underestimating the continuing danger, as well as the societal insult, posed for blacks by policies based on antimiscegenation philosophies, it is at least worth speculating whether the time and resources focused on the Bob Jones University litigation might not have been more profitably devoted to providing educationally effective alternative schools to minority youngsters, all to many of whom are achieving no more impressively in nominally desegregated schools than their parents did in "separate but equal" school systems.

---

7. 461 U.S. at 595. The Court rejected the contention by the petitioners, and indirectly that of the federal government, that only Congress could alter the scope of §§170 and 501(c)(3). The Internal Revenue Service had the authority to interpret these provisions and, given the strong actions by all three branches of government, it would have been anomalous for the IRS to blissfully ignore what the government had declared.

In this regard, the Court noted that Congress had not only failed to alter the IRS interpretation of the statutory provisions, but had rejected 13 bills introduced to overturn the IRS reading of §501(c)(3). Id. at 600.

8. Justice Powell concurred in the decision, but questioned whether entitlement to tax-exempt status depends on organizations providing a clear "public benefit" as defined by the Court. Id. at 602. He doubted that all or even most of the 106,000 organizations that filed §501(c)(3) tax returns in 1981 could demonstrate that they serve and are in harmony with the public interest. He also felt that the petitioners likely served the public interest through the substantially secular character of the curricula despite their racially discriminatory policies.

In this regard, he expressed concern about the "element of conformity" in the Court's analysis suggesting that tax-exempt entities must not act in a manner at odds with the declared position of the government. Such a view, Powell maintains, ignores the important role played by tax exemptions in encouraging diverse, and even sharply conflicting, activities and viewpoints. Id. at 603.

Given the above, I may be barred by expository estoppel from concurring with the media that Allen v. Wright was a significant defeat for the civil rights movement.[9] In a five-to-three ruling, the majority held that private citizens may not go to court to prod the federal government into denying or rescinding tax breaks for racially discriminatory schools.

While the controversy over barring religious-based schools that practice discrimination from receiving tax-exempt status has occupied the Supreme Court, determined private school forces have been attacked from an unexpected quarter. In 1980, in Fiedler v. Marumsco,[10] a white father brought suit against the private, fundamentalist religious school that had expelled his daughter because of her "romantic relationship" with a black classmate. The school had admitted blacks since 1972, but its interpretation of the Bible caused it to bar interracial dating, romance, and marriage. The district court cited the free-exercise clause as its basis for dismissing the suit. The Fourth Circuit reversed.[11] Reviewing the rationale of Runyon v. McCrary, the court held that the school could not, under §1981, discriminate on the basis of race, in either in its admissions or its operating policies. Moreover, the school failed to show that the pastor's actions were consistent with the church's beliefs.[12]

§8.11   INTERRACIAL INFLUENCES ON CUSTODY CASES

The growing acceptance by society of interracial relationships is mirrored by an increasing number of biracial and multiracial children.[1] Due to rising national

---

9. 468 U.S. 737 (1984). The black parents who filed the suit charged that racially segregated private schools, with a total enrollment exceeding 750,000, enjoy tax-exempt status that is illegal under IRS policy affirmed in the *Bob Jones University* case and that directly harms their children's chances to receive a desegregated education. Justice O'Connor said people seeking more aggressive enforcement of the IRS policy should turn to Congress, not the federal courts, for help. But Justice Brennan, in dissent, accused the Court of displaying "a startling insensitivity to the historical role played by the federal courts in eradicating race discrimination from our nation's schools."

10. 631 F.2d 1144 (4th Cir. 1980).

11. 486 F. Supp. 960 (E.D. Va. 1979).

12. The church's position was not helped when it expelled the sister of the expelled girl after the father contacted the NAACP about the original expulsion. The court found the sister's expulsion retaliatory and also barred by §1981.

§8.11   1. Although the number of children born to two white or two black parents changed little between 1968 and 1988, the number of births of children of interracial white and black parentage increased at a marked and steady rate. The number of biracial children in 1988 reached 41,308, compared to 8,758 biracial births reported in 1968. National Center for Health Statistics (1988 and previous years). According to the U.S. Census, 3.7% of children were bi or multiracial in 2004, 3.8% in 2005 and 4.0% in 2005 which equals nearly 3,000,000 children. Assessing statistics prior to 1990 by way of the U.S. Census is difficult because prior to 1980, a mixed race child was assigned the race of the father. From 1980 to 1990 the child would have been assigned the race of the mother. Sharon M. Lee, "Racial Classification in the U.S. Census: 1890-1990," Ethnic and Racial Studies, vol. 16, no. 1, 75-94, 83 (1993).

In 2004, statistics were available for the percentage of mothers who listed more than one race on the birth certificate of their children. Statistics were collected from CA, HI, ID, KY, MN, NY, OH, PA,

divorce rates for all races, family courts confront more frequently than ever before the dissolution of racially mixed families. Custody disputes arise over biracial children in three ways: (1) when an interracial couple divorces; (2) when the child's mother remarries outside her race; and (3) when black or biracial children are put up for adoption.

In custody disputes between divorcing parents, biracial children were historically placed with the parent that they most resembled, although this tendency was changing by the late 1970s.[2] If the custodial parent remarried outside the child's race, courts were sympathetic to petitions for modification of a custody settlement. In Blackburn v. Blackburn,[3] the child's white paternal grandparents obtained an order awarding them custody when the white mother had an affair with a married black policeman that produced a second child. Although the court insisted that race was not a factor in the verdict, the judge told one reporter, "This town just isn't ready for that kind of integration."[4] Several outside organizations petitioned the Georgia Supreme Court on behalf of the mother, arguing that custody cannot be terminated because the child might have more advantage with other guardians. The grandparents claimed that the mother "failed to provide necessaries" and was raising the child with "influences likely to degrade his moral character." Ultimately, the Georgia Supreme Court found insufficient evidence to justify severance of a parent-child custodial relationship and avoided the interracial overtones of the case. While lacking legal grounds, the grandparents' concern that the mother was unfit would have gained moral strength if they had sought custody of both children. But perhaps this is more than one could expect of grandparents, even if race was not the motive for their action.

A few years later, a Florida court faced with similar facts awarded a white father custody of his child after his former wife first lived with and then married a black man. When Linda Sidoti Palmore and Anthony Sidoti, both white, were divorced, Linda was awarded custody of her daughter. When she later married Clarence Palmore, a black man, Mr. Sidoti applied for a change of custody.

The Circuit Court for Hillsborough County, Florida, ruled that though both parents had chosen "respectable" new spouses and though society had made strides in "bettering relations between the races," it was inevitable that Melanie would suffer from "social stigmatization" if she remained with her mother.[5] The Florida Court of Appeals affirmed without opinion, and Mrs. Palmore appealed to the U.S. Supreme Court, arguing that the custody decision violated the equal protection clause by punishing her for marrying outside her race. The U.S. Solicitor General, the NAACP, the Women's Legal Defense Fund, and other organizations filed amicus briefs on behalf of Mrs. Palmore.

TN, UT, and WA. The total number of women who indicated more than one race for themselves was nearly 1.4 million which is 1.9% of all births in 2004. National Center for Health Statistics (2004).

2. See Gayle Pollack, The Role of Race in Child Custody Decisions Between Natural Parents Over Biracial Children, 23 N.Y.U. Rev. L. Soc. Change 612-619 (1997). But see Farmer v. Farmer, 109 Misc. 2d 137, 140 (N.Y. Sup. Ct. 1981) (granting custody to the white mother rather than the black father, but noting that the child would "endure identity problems" related to her black appearance).

3. 249 Ga. 689, 292 S.E.2d 821 (1982).

4. Newsweek, May 17, 1982, at 105.

5. 426 So. 2d 34 (Fla. Ct. App. 1982), rev'd, 466 U.S. 429 (1984).

Writing for the Court, Chief Justice Burger acknowledged that state court custody decisions are unlikely candidates for Supreme Court review, but important federal concerns were raised by the lower court's finding regarding the damaging impact on the child of remaining in a racially mixed home. Taking the court's findings and rationale at face value, he found it clear that "outcome would have been different had petitioner married a Caucasian male of similar respectability." The state, Chief Justice Burger said, has a duty of the highest order to protect the interests of minor children and has a substantial governmental interest for purposes of the equal protection clause. And, a child living with a stepparent of another race may face a variety of stresses and pressures due to the fact that racial and ethnic prejudices do exist. But citing the early residential neighborhood segregation case of Buchanan v. Warley,[6] the Chief Justice wrote that the reality of private biases and the possible injury they might inflict are not permissible considerations for removal of an infant child from the custody of its natural mother.

"Whatever problems racially-mixed households may pose for children in 1984," Chief Justice Burger said, "can no more support a denial of constitutional rights than could the stresses that residential integration was thought to entail in 1917. The effects of racial prejudice, however real, cannot justify a racial classification removing an infant child from the custody of its natural mother found to be an appropriate person to have such custody."[7] Despite what seemed the clear message of *Palmore,* courts continue to deny custody awards on the basis of racial assumptions and a continuing abhorrence of a white child raised in a setting with substantial contact with blacks.

McWilliams v. McWilliams[8] seems typical. Mrs. McWilliams had filed suit under 42 U.S.C. §1983, claiming that enforcement of the custody provisions of a divorce decree would violate her First and Fourteenth Amendment rights. The district court dismissed her complaint. Mr. McWilliams was granted custody of their children in the final divorce decree, and Mrs. McWilliams was granted visitation rights with the further restriction that she discontinue taking the children to a predominantly black church with which she was affiliated. Despite testimony "replete with racial references manifestly intended to prejudice judge and jury" against plaintiff, her counsel made no objection.

Furthermore, after the decree was handed down, counsel neither filed a motion for reconsideration nor a motion for a new trial, and took no appeal. Though Mrs. McWilliams had surely relied upon *Palmore* in her complaint, the court of appeals search of the record in the state action showed that her counsel failed to mention any constitutional issues. The court found this omission "astonishing," especially in view of what it considered to be prima facie violations of the First, Thirteenth, and Fourteenth Amendments. However, the Fifth Circuit found itself

---

6. 245 U.S. 60 (1917). In *Buchanan,* the Court had said, "It is urged that this proposed segregation will promote the public peace by preventing race conflicts. Desirable as this is, and important as is the preservation of the public peace, this aim cannot be accomplished by laws or ordinances which deny rights created or protected by the Federal Constitution." 466 U.S. 429, 433 (1984).

7. 466 U.S. at 434.

8. 804 F.2d 1400 (5th Cir. 1986).

bound to affirm dismissal of the plaintiff's action by the claim-preclusive effects of the Texas court's judgment.[9]

Holt v. Holt[10] is a complicated case that involves manifested societal prejudices against interracial coupling and the influence of these prejudices on custody decisions. The primary issue in *Holt* was whether the trial judge considered race in his decision, a consideration of which would be incorrect after *Palmore*. When the Holts, both white, divorced, the mother, Barbara, was awarded custody of their infant daughter. Several years later, Barbara married a black man and became pregnant, at which time her former husband petitioned for change of custody of their daughter, Dawn. At the custody hearing, Dawn testified that she was taunted at school when her mother married a black man and had been further taunted about her mother's "black baby." Dawn was so upset that she finally did leave school to go to her father's, refusing to return to her mother's.

The trial court approved modification of custody based on the "willful reactions to manifestations of racial prejudice" expressed by Dawn. This decision was reversed by both the Court of Appeals and Kentucky Supreme Court, which ruled that it did not comport with Kentucky law and *Palmore*. The case was remanded for further findings of fact that did not reflect racial concerns.

A 1996 federal court decision may indicate that, although the role of racial considerations is made plain in the *Williams* and *Holt* decisions, other courts may simply be less candid about the role race plays in child custody determinations.[11] The general standard applied is the "best interests of the child," which is, at best, an ambiguous test. Jones v. Jones[12] is the first published case to expressly recognize the significance of racial identity to a child's best interests. Although the trial court cited racially neutral factors in granting custody to the Native American father over the white mother, the South Dakota Supreme Court held it proper for a trial court to "consider the matter of race as it relates to the child's ethnic heritage" and to consider also which parent is "better able to expose the child to it."

In the 2000 Massachusetts case, Adoption of Vito,[13] the court acknowledged the role that race plays in the identity development of a child and the extent to which that should play in custody hearings. It found that the best interests standard

9. See Charles Wisdom, Will Palmore v. Sidoti Preclude the Use of Race as a Factor in Denying an Adoption?, 24 J. Fam. L. 497-521 (1986), suggesting that had the trial court's racial standard been less blatant, *Palmore* might have reached a different result. In answering the question posed in the article's title, Professor Charles Wisdom first differentiates adoption proceedings and custody awards, emphasizing the voluntarily severed rights of both natural parents in the Wisdom adoption context and the generally involuntary interruption of the relationship between a child and at least one parent in custody cases. He then turns to the Supreme Court's findings in *Palmore,* pinpointing the Court's identification of race as the Florida's sole basis for determining custody. *Palmore* at 432. He feels that the case might have been decided differently had the Florida court relied on race *and* other factors, Wisdom at 506, and argues such a decision would be consistent with other cases holding that race may be a factor in the state proceedings if used nondiscriminatorily. It is not a large leap, then, to his conclusion that *Palmore* does not toll the bell for race as a nonexclusive factor in determining a child's best interests in an adoption proceeding.

10. 722 S.W.2d 897 (1987).

11. See generally Pollack, supra note 2.

12. 542 N.W. 2d 119 (S.D. 1996).

13. 431 Mass. 550 (2000).

is one that requires decision-making on the individual level for each particular child and that child's needs, and not on essentialist generalizations about race.[14] That said, it does permit race to be considered as a factor among others in a consideration of the best interests of the child standard.

For as much progress has been made to focus on the developmental, emotional and physical needs of children in custody hearings, cases still exist which ignore *Palmore*, allow racist testimony to go unchallenged and are resolved by judges' findings that a child's placement in an interracial household, "will create problems for him in the future."[15] In Tipton v. Aaron, a white father initiated paternity proceedings for his seven year old son who was living with the child's white mother and black stepfather. Also in the household was a biracial three-year-old. The circuit court awarded custody to the father, despite his history of drug use and the allegations of domestic violence against him, following extensive testimony by individuals expressing concern over a white child growing up in an interracial home. The father did not want his son growing up in an interracial household because "it's not right" and he "did not believe in the interracial thing and the mixing."[16] The Court of Appeals held that the evidence presented to the trial court was insufficient to support a finding for granting custody to the father and held that it was in the best interest of the child to grant custody to the mother. In a concurring opinion, five judges joined to illuminate the point that the trial court judge improperly based his determination on racial bias contrary to *Palmore*.[17]

> It is not asking too much of lawyers and judges to confront racial bias during court proceedings. To the contrary, one would ordinarily consider a court proceeding to be the most likely secular forum where racial bias would be immediately and firmly met with vigorous objections from legal counsel and a stern rebuke from judges sworn to uphold equal protection of the law. It seems ironic that, as we celebrate the fifty-year anniversary of Brown v. Board of Education, appellee's counsel in the instant case elicited, without limitation of objections, testimony regarding racial bias that would have compelled reversal if a proper objection had been raised. Sadly, this demonstrates that fifty years after *Brown* and more than two decades after *Palmore*, we have not come as far regarding interracial understanding as some observers would believe or hope. [internal citations omitted][18]

§8.12 Racism Hypo: The Color-Blind Adoption Act

Tamara Toussaint and Brad McGregor met during their doctoral studies at a large university, Arcadia State. Soon they began to date, quickly becoming quite serious. Brad's family was of Scots-Irish descent, and Tamara's was an African

---

14. Id. at 556-557 (generalities about what may be in the best interests of some children, without more, cannot be the basis of judicial orders concerning post-adoption contact of a particular child; the best interests of the child standard is one grounded in the particular needs and circumstances of the individual child in question).

15. Tipton v. Aaron, 87 Ark. App. 1, 185 S.W.3d 142, 144 (2004).

16. Id. at 148.

17. Id at 150-151.

18. Id. at 154.

American family. Although both families expressed strong reservations, Tamara and Brad were married. Within the year, Tamara gave birth to Alice, whom both sets of grandparents adored. Both traveled to visit, and both had the young family for extended visits over summer vacations. When Alice was six, her parents went out for the evening and never came back. They were in a car crash and were killed instantly. Both sets of grandparents fought bitterly over who should have custody of Alice.

In administrative hearings initiated by both sets of grandparents, the Arcadia Social Service Agency ruled that it was in the best interest of a child of mixed racial heritage to be placed with the grandparental family granted statutory preference by the state legislature. On appeal, the trial court invalidated the portions of the state's adoption statute that granted preference in adoption proceedings to relatives or other members of a racial minority, asserting that these provisions impermissibly classified children on the basis of race and thus failed strict scrutiny. The Arcadia Court of Appeals and Supreme Court of Arcadia both affirmed the trial court, even though the National Association of Black Social Workers had filed an amicus brief stating that "Black children belong in Black families. . . ." The United States Supreme Court denied certiorari, thus putting the competing grandparents back where they started.

Due to the heart-touching factual circumstances, the case received a tremendous amount of media coverage. Pressure from groups favoring transracial adoption and from groups opposing such adoptions made life miserable for the Toussaints and the McGregors. They came to recognize that race was an inappropriate surrogate for their love of Alice, and they proclaimed, "Our love for Alice is color-blind; and so, we think, should all custody and adoption criteria be." Aided by Richard Banks, a young law teacher, they drafted and submitted to friends in the state legislature the Color-Blind Adoption Act. Both couples roamed the halls of the legislature lobbying on behalf of the bill. The two couples, one black, one white, united in their commitment to the legislation, were a tremendous influence on the legislators and on the public, which followed their efforts through the media and demonstrated great enthusiasm and broad support. In significant part, the bill provided as follows:

> I. A person, agency, or government entity involved in adoption or foster child placement may not:
> (A) deny, delay, or otherwise obstruct the opportunity of any individual to become an adoptive or a foster parent, on the basis of the race, color, or national origin of the individual, or of the child, involved.
> (B) facilitate, aid, or otherwise accommodate the racial preferences of any individual wishing to become an adoptive or foster parent and who seeks to select or reject a child on the basis of the race, color, or national origin of the individual, or of the child, involved.
> II. The Department of Child Protective Services is authorized to promulgate and implement appropriate regulations under this statute.

Arcadia's legislature, like much of the nation, caught-up in the color-blind mania, easily passed the Color-Blind Adoption Act, and the governor signed it into law. It was only when the Department of Child Services issued regulations under the new act that a storm of opposition appeared. The regulations provided that adoption agencies could no longer classify children by race, nor could they take any action to facilitate the racial preferences of individuals seeking to adopt.

In effect, race-matching was banned. Preferences would be limited to age, sex, and physical and mental health.

The Toussaints and McGregors were pleased. Pointing to the large number of minority children who languished in orphanages and foster placements because most adopting parents were white and wished to adopt white children, they hailed a new day when many people would come to see love, and not color, as the only meaningful basis for adoption.

The Arcadia Association of Independent Adoption Agencies and a wide range of persons seeking to adopt took a much harsher view of the Color-Blind Adoption Act, asserting in quickly filed litigation that it unconstitutionally denied them liberty, privacy, associational rights, and rights of autonomy in the intimate adoption process, in which freedom of choice is critical. As a policy matter, they warned that if the new adoption law were to be upheld, adoptions in Arcadia would cease.

In response, the State argued that the new adoption law complied with the antidiscrimination principle by barring both the limitation of adoptions to persons of the child's race and the facilitation of adoptions based on the racial preferences of the adopting parents. Each possibility constituted a racial situation subject to strict scrutiny and for which no compelling state interest existed.

Arcadia's state courts approved the statute. The state Supreme Court drew an analogy with segregated schools, finding that granting adopting parents' racial preferences produces state-sanctioned discrimination and inequality and denies black children access to a pool of potential adoptive parents comparable to that available to white children.

The United States granted certiorari.

§8.13 INTERRACIAL ADOPTIONS

Adopting a child is not a simple matter. A complicated system regulates the termination of parental rights by biological parents or the courts and balances adoptive parents' interests in adopting a child with the consideration of the child's "best interests." The subject of interracial adoption, commonly a euphemism for white parents adopting black babies, has been the center of heated debate and controversy for more than three decades.

Historically, adoptive parents wanted the children to become their "own" — to be disconnected from their birth parents as much as possible.[1] Beginning in the 1960s, several factors contributed to the rise of interracial adoption. First, the increasing number of unwed mothers who decided to keep their babies and the introduction of birth control pills reduced the number of white babies available. Second, the acceptance of transnational adoption, the Civil Rights Movement, and

---

§8.13 1. The sealing of adoption records and reissuing of birth certificates was common practice, consistent with contemporary perceptions of the child's best interest (as well as with the interest of the birth mother, who was usually young and unwed). Ruth-Arlene W. Howe, Transracial Adoption (TRA): Old Prejudices and Discrimination Float Under a New Halo, 6 B.U. Pub. Int. L.J. 385, 394 (1997), citing Ann Hartman, Practice in Adoption, in A Handbook of Child Welfare: Context, Knowledge, and Practice 640, 667 (Joan Laird & Ann Harman eds., 1985).

the first significant inclusion of African American children in the foster care system also contributed to the initial rise in interracial adoption.[2] In 1971, almost 35 percent of 7,420 black children adopted were adopted by white parents.[3]

In 1973, the practice declined sharply when the National Association of Black Social Workers (NABSW) took a firm stand against interracial adoptions, characterizing them as "a growing threat to the preservation of the black family"[4] and "a form of race and cultural genocide."[5] The NABSW expressed concern both for the welfare of black children raised by white families and for the larger black community. In response to this concern, the number of interracial adoptions in 1973 declined to half the 1971 statistic.[6] In the five years following the NABSW's statement, while Americans were pursuing fewer domestic, interracial adoptions, international adoptions increased by 200 percent.[7]

It is difficult to obtain comprehensive figures stating the number of children available for adoption, the races of those children, or the races of those interested in adopting them. The accuracy of the figures that are available is clouded by definition issues, such as how to count the number of children, in some years a little less than half of all children adopted, who are adopted by relatives.[8] With this caveat, of the 523,000 children estimated to be in foster care in 2003, 58 percent were children of color. Black children represented 35 percent of the foster care population but only 16 percent of the general population.[9] 17 percent of adoptions in the United States are transracial but only between 2-3 percent are of white parents adopting black children.[10] These figures fuel the controversy over interracial adoption. The high demand for children, and the visibility of available children who would be adopted but for their race, conflict with the social norms regulating the process of adoption. Coverage of the issue in the popular press provides anecdotal evidence supporting both sides in the cross-race adoption debate.[11] The judicial and legislative treatments of interracial adoption suggest policies in transition.

2. Howe, supra note 1, at 442.

3. Jennifer Ruark, What Makes a Family? A Historian Traces the Rise and Fall of Adoption in America, Chron. of Higher Ed., Oct. 25, 2002, at 12; Randall Kennedy, Interracial Intimacies: Sex, Marriage, Identity and Adoption 452 (2003).

4. National Association of Black Social Workers News, Jan. 1973, at 1. The group's position has changed only slightly since then. "There is a lot of confusion about choosing a role model if your parents are white and your skin is black," Gerald Smith, the group's president, told a reporter, "Children come out better when they're able to look up at their parents and look at a mirror." Carol Castenada, Transracial Adoption Ban Runs into Parents' Backlash, Gannett News Serv., Nov. 19, 1990.

5. Rita Simon & Howard Alstein, Adoption Across Borders 30 (2000) (quoting William T. Merritt, President of NABSW).

6. Kennedy, supra note 3, at 423.

7. David Rosettenstein, Transracial Adoption in the U.S. and the Impact of Considerations Relating to Minority Population Groups, 9 Int'l J.L. & Fam. 131, 141042 (1995).

8. David S. Rosettenstein, Trans-Racial Adoption and the Statutory Preference Schemes: Before the "Best Interests" and after the "Melting Pot," 68 St. John's L. Rev. 137, 141 (1994) (citing Nat'l Comm. for Adoption, 1989 Adoption Factbook 60).

9. Children's Defense Fund, Child Abuse and Neglect Fact Sheet (August 2005).

10. Solangel Maldonado, Discouraging Racial Preferences in Adoptions, 39 U.C. Davis L. Rev. 1415, 1460 (April 2006).

11. See, e.g., When White Parents Adopt Black Babies, Race Often Divides, Wall St. J., Sept. 12, 1990, at A1; Black Kids, White Parents: Debating What's Best for the Kids, USA Today, Aug. 15,

Courts have been troubled by issues of interracial adoption. The Fifth Circuit court expressed more than a little uncertainty in Drummond v. Fulton County Dept. of Family and Children's Services.[12] White foster parents argued that the department's denial of their request to adopt their mixed-race foster child was based solely on racial grounds and violated their equal protection and due process rights. Department records indicated preference for a black home that would teach the child "how to protect himself in difficult situations." The district court dismissed the complaint; on appeal, a divided panel reversed.[13] On rehearing, the Fifth Circuit, en banc, affirmed the district court decision, stating that, although an application could not automatically be denied because of race, "the difficulties inherent in interracial adoption justify the consideration of race as a relevant factor in adoption." The court recognized that even if a government activity has a racially disproportionate impact, the impact alone does not sustain a claim of discrimination without "proof of racially discriminatory intent or purpose."[14] Consideration of race was used merely to determine the best interests of the child. The court granted discretion to unbiased professionals to find the best home for a child, and it recognized that duplication of biological features enables a child to best adjust to a normal family relationship.

Palmore[15] set a strong precedent against the use of race as a substantial factor in child placement decisions. Nevertheless, courts have not uniformly supported interracial adoption.[16] In 1993, a Western Tennessee district court heard a case with facts very similar to *Drummond,* but held that racial considerations were unconstitutional.[17] In *Reisman,* white foster parents sought custody of a biracial child. Analogizing to marriage and education, the court found that changes in society made race an inappropriate factor in adoption decisions. A twenty-year study of biracial children in white homes convinced the bench that "children who were adopted across racial lines grow up healthy" and comfortable with their identities. Finding for the plaintiff, the court concluded that biracial children should be classified as such and placed in the most suitable homes that would provide "love and nurture with a commitment to assist the children." Similarly, in the Matter of the Welfare of D.L.,[18] a Minnesota law requiring that children be placed with families of the same race was found unconstitutional.

1991, at 1D [hereafter Black Kids, White Parents]; Jerry Thomas, Should White Parents Adopt Black Children?, Chi. Trib., June 23, 1991, at 1; Thomas, Adoption Isn't as Simple as Black, White, Chi. Trib., June 2, 1991, at 1.

12. 563 F.2d 1200 (5th Cir. 1977).

13. 547 F.2d 835 (5th Cir. 1977) (indicating that a policy requiring that mixed-race children be placed with black families would be unconstitutional and remanding to determine the precise basis for the agency's decision).

14. Citing Arlington Heights v. Metropolitan Hous. Dev. Corp., 429 U.S. 252, 265 (1977).

15. See §8.11.

16. See, e.g., DeWees v. Stevenson, 779 F. Supp. 25, 29 (E.D. Pa. 1991) (denying white foster parents' claims of due process and equal protection violations; and finding that consideration of racial attitudes is constitutionally permissible in determining the best interests of child); Tallman v. Tabor, 859 F. Supp. 1078 (E.D. Mich. 1994) (finding that race was not the dominant factor in decision to remove African American child from white foster parents' care and return foster child to the birth mother).

17. Reisman v. State of Tenn. Dept. of Human Servs., 843 F. Supp. 356, 365 (W.D. Tenn. 1993).

18. 479 N.W.2d 408 (Minn. 1992).

§8.13.1   Adoption Legislation

Across the country, adoption legislation is in transition. While a few jurisdictions have quite recently changed their mandatory preferences for same-race placement,[19] other states have implemented balancing tests that include race as only one of several factors to be considered in making adoption decisions.[20] In jurisdictions that require determination of the "best interests of the child," without mentioning the factors involved,[21] the role of race appears to be indeterminate.

In 1994, Congress passed the Multiethnic Placement Act (MEPA) to limit race as only one of multiple factors that is to be considered when placing children in adoptive homes or foster placements. One purpose of MEPA was to ensure that fulfilling race-matching priorities did not lead to long delays in placing children. The Act, however, failed to define an impermissible delay and, in effect, condoned waiting indefinitely for a same-race placement.

Although this initial version fell short of eliminating race as a consideration in adoption placements, an amendment passed in 1996 took a further step. In 1996, the Interethnic Adoption Provisions (IEP), added to MEPA, prohibited agencies that receive federal funding from using race as a factor at all. Such organizations cannot use race, ethnicity, or national origin to deny a placement or adoption.[22] The IEP, however, has no teeth to it.[23] First, the IEP applies only to agencies receiving federal funding, allowing private organizations to continue to race-match. Second, no federal agency is devoting any resources to its enforcement. The legislation fails to abolish race-matching entirely, a dramatic reversal in current practices that would require a level of color-blindness that society, regretfully, has not yet achieved.

Scholars disagree on the clarity and effectiveness of MEPA and the IEP. While Kennedy believes IEP has no teeth, Bartholet predicts once the law becomes established as "part of the nation's basic civil rights commitment" the evasion and resistance to the law will diminish.[24] Professors Ezra Griffith and Rachel Bergeron point towards the Department of Health and Human Services documents issued to

---

19. See, e.g., Ark. Code Ann. §9-9-102 ((b) "The Department of Human Services and any other agency or entity which receives federal assistance and is involved in adoption or foster care placement shall not discriminate on the basis of the race, color, or national origin of the adoptive or foster parent or the child involved nor delay the placement of a child on the basis of race, color, or national origin of the adoptive or foster parents; . . . (d) The court shall not deny a petition for adoption on the basis of race, color, or national origin of the adoptive parent or the child involved)."

20. See, e.g., Cal. Fam. Code §8708 (West 1997); Colo. Rev. Stat. §19-5-104(1) (Bradford 1996); Conn. Gen. Stat. §45a-727(c)(3) (1995); Ill. Ann. Stat. ch. 750, para. 50/15.1(b)(8) (Smith-Hurd Supp. 1996); Ky. Rev. Stat. Ann. §199.471 (Michie 1995); Md. Code Ann. Fam. Law §5-311(b)(2) (Michie Supp. 1996); N.J. Stat. Ann. Supp. §9:3-40 (West 1996); 23 Pa. Cons. Stat. Ann. §2724(b) (West 1991); S.C. Code Ann. §20-7-1740(B) (Law Co-op. Supp. 1996).

21. See, e.g., Ga. Code Ann. §19-8-17(a)(5) (Michie 1991 & Supp. 1993); Idaho Code §16-1506 (Michie Supp. 1993); Neb. Rev. Stat. §43-109 (1988 & Supp. 1992); R.I. Gen. Laws §15-7-4 (Michie Supp. 1988); W.Va. Code §48-4-9(a)(4) (Michie 1992).

22. Kennedy, supra note 3, at 400. Similar antidiscrimination statutes in Pennsylvania, Texas, and Wisconsin were designed to combat race-matching policies.

23. Id. at 434.

24. Elizabeth Bartholet, Commentary: Cultural Stereotypes Can and Do Die: It's Time to Move on with Transracial Adoption, J. Am. Acad. Psychiatry Law 34: 315-20, 319, 2006.

provide compliance guidance with the IEP as allowing for race-matching under certain circumstances. "Any consideration of these factors must be done on an individualized basis where special circumstances indicate that their consideration is warranted."[25]

In 1997 Congress created the Adoption and Safe Families Act (ASFA) which eliminated the "reasonable efforts" requirement that previous legislation had included for reunification within the family structure, and focused on adoption as the solution for children in foster care.[26] This policy contrasts to the position of the National Association of Social Workers (NASW) who in 2003 stated, "The placement of choice should be within the child's family of origin, among relatives. . . ."[27] The ASFA prioritizes adoptions over reunification, which may mean disincentives to keep a child within his or her family of origin and incentives to keep a child in foster care until an adoptive family is ready. Thus, given that black children represent an overwhelmingly disproportionate percentage of children in the foster care system, and yet white children are five times more likely to be adopted, many black children are left behind to languish in a system that works against them.[28]

§8.13.2   Race-Matching and Accommodation

Regardless of the legislative standard, race-matching is the norm practiced both unofficially and officially by adoption placement offices across the country. Adoption officials probably attempt to achieve the traditional goal of creating "believable" family units. Many adoptive parents enter the system because they are unable to produce their own biological family. The biological family they desire would, exhibit racial commonality. The National Association of Black Social Workers (NABSW) argues that, regardless of the adoptive parent's interests, matching black children with black adoptive families is in the child's best interests. The social workers argue that black children raised by white parents will be deprived of their ethnic identification and the survival skills necessary to live in a racially conscious society.[29] It is always in the best interests of the child, therefore, to be raised by a black family, where the child will absorb a sense of racial identity, cultural inclusion, and pride.

25. Ezra E.H. Griffith & Rachel L. Bergeron, Cultural Stereotypes Die Hard: The Case of Transracial Adoption, J. Am. Acad. Psychiatry Law 34: 303-14, 309 (2006) (citing Questions and Answers Regarding Multiethnic Placement Act of 1994 and Section 1808 of the Small Business and Job Protection Act of 1996. Office for Civil Rights, Department of Health and Human Services. Available at http://www.hhs.gov/ocr/gaoreply.htm).

26. Adoption and Safe Families Act of 1997, Pub. L. No. 105-89, 111 Stat. 2115 (1997).

27. National Association of Social Workers: Foster care and adoption, in Social Work Speaks: National Association of Social Workers Policy Statements, 2003-2006 150 (6th ed. 2003).

28. Ruth G. McRoy, Overrepresentation of Children and Youth of Color in Foster Care, in Child Welfare for the 21st Century: A Handbook of Practices, Policies, and Programs 623, 628 (Gerald P. Mallon & Peg McCartt Hess eds., 2005).

29. See supra note 4.

In addition, the NABSW characterizes interracial adoptions as "a growing threat to the preservation of the black family." They consider transracial adoption a route to the expression of white imperialism through the domination and subversion of black culture and heritage. Black nationalists, too, describe the need to preserve the community's most valuable resources — its children. Relinquishing black babies to white families signals the failure of the black community in its struggle for group status. Race-matching, on the other hand, reinforces the perceived strength of community.

Although often cited for their assertion that transracial adoption is a form of "cultural genocide," the NABSW softened its position in 1994.[30] The new statement continued to maintain that the best options for a black child would be to either (1) remain with a biological parent or other relatives or (2) receive a placement with a family of the same race. However, NABSW recognized that a transracial family could be seen as a "last resort" after a documented failure to find an African American home.[31] The NABSW's altered position does not indicate how long an agency should search for a race match to "document a failure" and has been criticized as merely a tactical "public relations strategy aimed at improving the NABSW's public image."[32]

Professor Ezra E. H. Griffith and Dr. Rachel Bergeron co-authored an article presented at the ABA's Conference on Children and the Law (2007) featuring the positions of other national organizations. The Child Welfare League of America (CWLA) established its position in support of race as a consideration in adoption placements in its *Standards of Excellence for Adoption Services* (2000). CWLA believes that placement in a same-race family is best:

> All children deserve to be raised in a family that respects their cultural heritage. . . . If aggressive, ongoing recruitment efforts are unsuccessful in finding families of the same race or culture as the child, other families should be considered to ensure that the child's adoptive placement is not delayed.[33]

Similarly, the National Association of Social Workers (NASW) issued a statement in 2003 supporting the use of race and ethnicity in placement:

> Agencies must . . . respect the integrity of each child's ethnicity and cultural heritage. . . . The social work profession stresses the importance of ethnic and cultural sensitivity. An effort to maintain a child's identity and his or her ethnic heritage should prevail in all services and placement actions that involve children in foster care and adoption programs.[34]

---

30. Leora Neal, The Case Against Transracial Adoption, citing National Association of Black Social Workers, Position Statement: Preserving African-American Families (1994). See also Rita Simon, Should Transracial Adoption Rules Change? Don't Let Race Keep Children in Foster Care, Chi. Sun-Times, Apr. 16, 1994.

31. Neal, supra note 30.

32. Kennedy, supra note 3, at 394.

33. Griffith & Bergeron, at 311 (citing Child Welfare League of America: Standards of Excellence for Adoption Services (rev. ed. 2000)).

34. Id. at 311-12.

Professor Twila Perry writes that black women often seem ambivalent toward transracial adoption because of its political ramifications for black families and communities and its implications for the satisfaction of the needs of all black children. She notes that black women scholars focus on the political and racial issues in transracial adoption, whereas white women, such as Elizabeth Bartholet, prioritize the individual parent/child relationships involved.[35] For many black women, the controversy is not simply about white families adopting black children; it is also about white women mothering black children. Perry suggests that black women are concerned about the competence of white women to raise black children; but they also believe that the role of race in parenting is minimized, effectively devaluing "what motherhood means to them — a historical and contemporary struggle to raise black children successfully in a racist world." Transracial adoption emerges as part of a larger system of racial hierarchy and privilege that advantages white women while it devalues and subordinates women of color.

Like advocates of race-matching, supporters of interracial adoption argue that it is the best practical and philosophical solution for the children and for society. Scholars like Elizabeth Bartholet point to the high numbers of black children in the foster care system as an urgent reason to support interracial adoption. She recognizes that a same-race placement may be preferable in some cases, but she also calls attention to the close family relationships that can develop between white parents and their black children. In response to concerns about children's cultural identity and self-actualization, Bartholet cites empirical studies that suggest black children raised by white families are well-adjusted and cared for. "The children are doing well in terms of achievement and self esteem."[36] A 1997 report indicates that transracial adoptees demonstrate insight, tolerance, and sensitivity. Although many might praise these qualities, the NABSW argues that these children grow up with unrealistic, naive perceptions that do not prepare them to survive in a racialized society. Bartholet acknowledges the imbalance of racial power as an additional reason to integrate the family; yet she perceives the ultimate goal of race matching as perpetuation of race separatism through the family.

§8.13.3 Nonaccommodation

Many maintain that race should not be dispositive in adoption placements; Professor R. Richard Banks argues that race should not even be a consideration.[37] According to Banks, "facilitative accommodation" amounts to an impermissible racial classification of children by state adoption agencies. As a result, children are

---

35. Twila Perry, Transracial and International Adoption: Mothers, Hierarchy, Race, and Feminist Legal Theory, 10 Yale J.L. & Feminism 101, 112-113 (1998).

36. Elizabeth Bartholet, Where Do Black Children Belong? The Politics of Race Matching in Adoption, 139 U. Pa. L. Rev. 1163, 1209 (citing Joan Shireman, Growing Up Adopted: An Examination of Major Issues (1988) and Ruth McCroy & Louis Zurcher, Transracial and Inracial Adoptees: The Adolescent Years (1983)).

37. R. Richard Banks, The Color of Desire: Fulfilling Adoptive Parents' Racial Preferences Through Discriminatory State Action, 107 Yale L.J. 875, 881 n.20 (1997).

labeled as having "special needs" because of their classification as members of a minority, and they are denied equal opportunities for placement. Only a "color-blind" system, one that does not accommodate the racial preferences of adoptive parents, is constitutionally sound. Banks posits that forbidding "facilitative accommodation" serves the best interests of individual minority children by making them available for adoption by the most suitable family. If race is considered as a factor in a balancing test, Banks says, the test becomes a front for race matching.

Banks accuses Bartholet and others of politicizing the debate over transracial adoption to the detriment of the child's best interests. Banks recognizes that under the current politics of race, people of color have an interest in racial identification and in the recognition of African American culture as unique and valuable. The white hegemony, on the other hand, has an interest in subverting "difference" under blankets of "neutral" policies and color-blind laws. He notes that ideological events such as the Nazi rise to power in Germany and the civil rights movement contribute to whites' perception of race as a dirty word. Blacks, on the other hand, were empowered by the civil rights movement and, in a manner of speaking, exist only where their voices are distinguishable from those of the dominant white race. The irony is that blacks can argue for measures (such as affirmative action) that are designed to achieve equality, but because such measures are packaged as differential treatment, the blacks will be perceived as grasping, greedy, or, at the least, instruments of racial separatism. Whites, on the other hand, can uphold facially neutral laws that perpetuate inequalities, but because these laws are perceived as evenly applied, they will be considered just. Therefore, the harder blacks fight for a separate, independent cultural community, the more they become marginalized by the white society that seeks to subjugate them.

Banks holds out hope for an integrated community, even as he admits that "neutrality" is a white male standard in today's society. The only hope for black survival is to undermine pernicious, race-based treatment that perpetuates a cycle of poverty and prejudice. The goal of nonaccommodation in adoption is to undermine a "pernicious type of race-based treatment," thereby eradicating the undervaluation of minority babies and their communities.

Banks acknowledges that a nonaccommodation standard could not prevent adoptive parents, with complicit adoption agencies, from considering the child's race; he notes that wealthier couples leave the government-funded system, thereby reducing the overall number of available homes. Finally, a nonaccommodation policy may find little political support, because its benefits are diffuse and because those helped the most — minority children awaiting adoption — are politically disenfranchised. Without strong interest group support, any new limitation on personal autonomy and privacy interests will be difficult to effect.

The state's responsibility in an adoption case is far greater than its responsibility in validating a marriage; perhaps judicial recognition of the special problems involved justifies a heightened level of sensitivity to these issues may also be needed to adequately translate the feelings of substantial portions of the black community regarding interracial marriages. Any assumption that blacks view interracial marriage or adoption as merely one more step in the long civil rights campaign for full equality is a position that would receive little support in the literature on the subject written by blacks.

A survey of 87 adoption agencies (64 private and 23 public) released in August 1991, prepared by the North American Council on Adoptable Children, found that four out of five adoption officials believe certain institutional barriers keep blacks from adopting, thus supporting a claim made by the National Association of Black Social Workers.[38] "Insistence upon young, two-parent, materially endowed families eliminates many potentially viable minority homes," the report says. "More minority family recruiters, deeper penetration into the black community and lower fees also could allow more blacks to adopt kids of their own race."[39] Another report indicates that following years in which many adoption agencies rejected or discouraged white parents seeking to adopt minority children, anecdotal evidence suggests that the number of transracial adoptions is increasing.[40] Prospective white parents are challenging racial restrictions with civil rights complaints and lawsuits. Behind many of the fights is the National Coalition to End Racism in America's Child Care System, a group that has filed numerous complaints challenging bans on transracial adoptions.[41] Preventing white parents from adopting black children means that, given the small number of black parents seeking to adopt, many minority children will spend their childhood years in foster homes. The Color-Blind Adoption Act proposed by the Toussaints and the McGregors (see §7.9) is well-intentioned, but as Patricia Williams points out, "the social reality of unbalanced race relations and racial power suggest some constraints on complete color-blindness as a possibility."[42]

§8.13.4 International Adoption

As children languish in the United States foster care system, adoptions from countries with international adoption policies such as Guatemala, Russia, Korea, and China remain a desirable option. Stories in the newspapers with captions like "Ni Hao, Everyone!" "Blessed by Adoption," "Love Trumps Fear of SARS: Adoptions from China Continue," and "The Adoption Revolution"[43] abound, describing how parents travel thousands of miles to orphanages in other countries to bring home their new family additions. They may spend anywhere between $7,000 to $25,000 according to The Adoption Institute.[44] These adoptions seem so prevalent because families with international children are often multi-ethnic or

---

38. Black Kids, White Parents, supra note 11.

39. Id.

40. Transracial Adoption Ban Runs Into Parents' Backlash, Gannett News Serv., Nov. 19, 1990.

41. Id.

42. Patricia Williams, In Search of Pharaoh's Daughter, The Rooster's Egg 214, 218, 221-222 (1995).

43. Jenny Gordon, Ni Hao, Everyone!, Macon Telegraph (Ga.), section d, Oct. 7, 2007; Jennifer Wilson, Blessed by Adoption, Better Homes & Gardens, Feb. 2003; Kay Lazar, Love Trumps Fear of SARS: Adoptions from China Continue, Boston Herald, Apr. 20, 2003; The Adoption Revolution — It's Fueling Changes Throughout Society, Providence-Journal Bulletin, Mar. 4, 2001.

44. Jennifer Wilson, Blessed by Adoption: More Americans Are Adopting Than Ever Before, Better Homes & Gardens, Feb. 1, 2003.

multiracial, making them more readily identifiable. In addition, international adoptions have doubled in the past decade. In 1990, about 8,500 children were granted orphan visas; in 2002, that number totaled 20,099. Federal legislation has contributed to this rapid increase by making it easier for parents to apply for orphan visas.

Not all reports have been positive. As initial popularity in international adoption increased so did stories of exploitation. Adoption laws in other countries are not always as strict as those in the United States and the potential to profit from selling children has led to kidnapping and child trafficking.[45] Following the tsunami that struck Southeast Asia in 2004, the U.S. State Department announced its opposition to adoptions from those countries until the countries were stabilized to the point of being able to properly identify legitimate orphans. Then and only then, adoptions could proceed in countries that decided to make orphans available for international adoption.[46]

Advocates who represent families pursuing international adoptions present a number of incentives for international adoptions many of which are myths according to some scholars. One of the most common is that adoptive parents like the security of knowing that a child's biological parent will not seek to regain custody of the adopted child. As Professor Solangel Maldonado notes, the risks of biological parents seeking the return of their children are present for both domestic and international adoptions. As noted earlier, not all children put up for international adoption are, in fact, orphans in the first place. Further, few domestic birth parents revoke consent to adoption and even fewer would succeed in getting their children back.[47]

Another includes a perception that adopting a child in the foster care system is uncertain and time-consuming with many strings attached. Also, parents with international adoptees desire the opportunity to adopt infants or young children. Lastly, parents recognize a need and desire to exercise a desire to help children they perceive to be suffering, with over 2.1 million orphans in China alone.[48] Maldonado points out that 80 percent of American couples seeking to adopt through the private system cite infertility as their primary reason for wanting to adopt. They are seeking to satisfy their needs to be parents, more so than to save children. Further, it is no less humanitarian to adopt a child domestically than internationally especially in light of the inability for US policy to regulate adoption policies in foreign countries.[49]

---

45. U.S. State Dep't, Department of State Urges Citizens Not to State Adoptions in Guatemala (Sept. 2007); Solangel Maldonado, Discouraging Racial Preferences in Adoptions, 39 U.C. Davis L. Rev. 1415, 1442 (April 2006) (citing Sergiu Verona, Cong. Research Serv., Romanian Policy Regarding Adoptions, at CRS-3 (1994) (3000 Romanian children adopted by Americans prior to July 1991 were poor children coming directly from their biological families as a result of a baby market where large sums of money were used to purchase children from illiterate, unsophisticated parents)).

46. Evan B. Donaldson Adoption Institute, Intercountry Adoption in Emergencies: The Tsunami Orphans, Policy Brief (citing U.S. State Department, 2005 January 3). Available at http://www.adoptioninstitute.org.

47. Maldonado, supra note 45, at 1442.

48. Chris Jones, Chosen One for the Unchosen, Daily Oklahoman, Apr. 21, 2003.

49. Maldonado, supra note 45, at 1452.

Child abduction rings have been broken up everywhere from Guatemala to Vietnam and Cyprus to Mexico. The commercial rhetoric of auctions and market price in Romania has since caused the government to suspend adoptions. Some countries, such as Cambodia, do not maintain a centralized database of death or birth records, so corruption in the adoption process can run rampant without much chance of detection. As a result, the United States has placed a moratorium on adoptions from Cambodia and most recently Guatemala.

Although adoptions in the United States still outnumber international adoptions, the margin is shrinking. Even with federal reforms like MEPA that encourage adoption, in 2006 alone, 126,000 children in foster care were waiting to be adopted, 58 percent of these children are children of color, and most were older children.[50] This stark statistic raises questions about the actual hurdles to domestic adoption that may drive potential adoptive parents to look internationally. More generally, though, the trend in international adoption presents a new complexity to the growing number of interracial and interethnic family relations in the United States.

§8.14   INTERRACIAL ADOPTIONS AND THE AMERICAN INDIAN CHILD WELFARE ACT OF 1978

The problems minority groups face as they seek to maintain their cultural uniqueness within a dominant, different, and often hostile society are universal. Section 8.10 referred to writings by black social workers who condemned interracial adoptions as "a growing threat to the preservation of the black family." They urge that standards for adoption be eased so that black families, willing to adopt, would not be excluded because they are unable to meet traditional qualifications on age, health, income, marital status, home size, and other criteria that exclude those who are not substantial members of the middle class.

Native American groups have experienced similar problems in preserving their cultural heritage. According to one commentator, Manuel P. Guerrero,[1] the policy of destroying Indian culture and tribal integrity by removing Indian children from their families and tribal settings was set even before the country became a nation. By the end of the nineteenth century, sending Indian children away to distant boarding schools to "civilize" and educate them had become customary among the tribes. Often the removal of children was coerced by agents of the Department of Indian Affairs.

Currently, the removal of Indian children to boarding schools continues, but even larger numbers of children are removed from their homes for purposes of foster care and adoption. Studies in 1969 and 1974 of states with large Indian

---

50. Maldonado, at 1452; Child Abuse and Neglect Fact Sheet, August 2005, Policy Report from the Children's Defense Fund, available at www.childrensdefense.org.

§8.14   1. Manuel Guerrero, Indian Child Welfare Act of 1978, 7 Am. Ind. L. Rev. 51 (1979).

populations indicate that 25-35 percent of all Indian children are separated from their families and placed in foster homes or institutions.

According to one writer, "American Indian families face vastly greater risks of involuntary separation than are typical of society as a whole."[2] Mr. Guerrero concurs, stating that the wholesale separation of Indian children from their families ranks among the most tragic and destructive aspects of contemporary Indian life. He reports:

> State intrusion in parent-child relationships within the Indian culture impedes the ability of the tribe to perpetuate itself and is ultimately an unjustified coerced assimilation into the large society. . . . [T]he Indian way of life is a unique expression of an identifiable but highly complex culture apart from the non-Indian world. It is a culture which has at its core a persistent talent for preservation and survival. Among other aspects, it is inculcated with the concept known as the extended family, which is largely misunderstood by white America.[3]

Black social workers opposed to interracial adoption of black children would likely adopt Mr. Guerrero's statement in whole. They would certainly recognize his reports that social workers, untrained in Indian cultural values and social norms, make decisions inappropriate to Indian family patterns, judge the fitness of an Indian family by white middle-class values, and thus discover neglect and abandonment where none exists.

In late 1978, Congress, responding to recommendations of the American Indian Review Commission, enacted the Indian Child Welfare Act (ICWA).[4] The Act is premised on the fact that Indian tribes, as sovereign governments, have a vital interest in any decision as to whether Indian children should be separated from their families. With a few exceptions, the Act gives the Indian tribe, and more specifically the Indian tribal court, exclusive jurisdiction over child custody proceedings where the Indian child is residing or domiciled on the reservation.

State courts having jurisdiction over an Indian child custody proceeding are directed by the Act to transfer such proceeding to an appropriate tribal court. Either parent may veto such transfer so as to enable the state court to insure that the rights of the child, the parents, and the tribe are fully protected. Various procedural protections are provided, including adequate notice and right to counsel, to further the goals of the Act.

Parental rights may not be easily terminated, and a party seeking foster care placement or termination of parental rights over an Indian child must satisfy the court that positive efforts have been made to provide assistance designed to prevent the breakup of Indian families. Section 1915 of the Act addresses the adoptive placement of Indian children subsequent to the termination of parental rights, and provides that "a preference shall be given, in the absence of good cause to the contrary, to a placement with (1) a member of the child's extended family; (2) other

---

2. Gaylene McCartney, The American Indian Child Welfare Crisis: Cultural Genocide or First Amendment Preservation, 7 Colum. Hum. Rts. L. Rev. 529, 530 (1975).

3. See Guerrero, supra note 1, at 53.

4. 25 U.S.C. §§1901-1963 (1982).

members of the Indian child's tribe; or (3) other Indian families."[5] Although the Act may help preserve the ethnic identity of Indian children who are placed out for adoption, its provisions are largely procedural and deal only with children who have been removed from their families. Professor Russel Barsh stresses the need for substantive support to Indian families and the tribes to prevent the breakup of existing families.[6] Since its passage, the ICWA has come under fire from all sides. Randall Kennedy challenges the validity of expert testimony relied on by Congress (and state courts) to show that Indian children "suffer psychological damage when adopted by non-Indians."[7] As a result, he strongly advocates for serious reform of the ICWA, including abolishing the mandatory race-matching system. He argues that the preference given to "other Indian families" is unacceptable "racial bias."[8] Other academics argue the legislation did not go far enough and creates great leeway for state court resistance.[9] Professor Jeanne Carriere discusses in detail ICWA's "good cause" exception to the statutory provision of transferring cases to tribal court, which has been "manipulated by state court judges to thwart tribal jurisdiction."[10] For many critics, the ICWA's limited definition of Indian child is both under- and overinclusive.[11] In Professor Barbara Atwood's comprehensive review of the ICWA and recent attempted amendments, she suggests that "developing new language for resolving the hard cases that arise under the ICWA may mean the authorization of new, more fluid conceptions of adoption and guardianship."[12] As Kennedy points out, when "one finds oneself praying that judges will interpret a statute narrowly, emphasize its exceptions and discern limitations that are otherwise absent, one surely is in the presence of a statute in need of reform."[13]

5. 25 U.S.C. §1915(a) (1982). Under §1915(a), the quoted provision is to be read as a preference for keeping the Indian child in the tribe rather than a preclusion of placement with a non-Indian family. Similar provisions are provided for foster care or preadoptive placements. For a detailed review of all the provisions of the Act, see Guerrero, supra note 1.

6. Russel Barsh, Indian Child Welfare Act of 1978: A Critical Analysis, 31 Hastings L.J. 1287 (1980). Barsh takes a more pessimistic view of the Act than Guerrero. He agrees with the aims of the Act, but feels that it does not do enough, is poorly drafted, and will be ineffective even within its too-limited scope.

7. Randall Kennedy, Interracial Intimacies: Sex, Marriage, Identity, and Adoption 518 (2003).

8. Id.

9. Barbara Ann Atwood, Flashpoints Under the Indian Child Welfare Act: Toward a New Understanding of State Court Resistance, 51 Emory L.J. 587 (2002).

10. Id. at 589, citing Jeanne Louise Carriere, Representing the Native American: Culture, Jurisdiction and the Indian Welfare Act, 79 Iowa L. Rev. 585 (1994).

11. Id. at 589. See also Christine Metteer, A Law Unto Itself: The Indian Child Welfare Act as Inapplicable and Inappropriate to the Transracial/Race-Matching Adoption Controversy, 38 Brandeis L.J. 47 (1999-2000).

12. Atwood, supra note 9, at 675.

13. Kennedy, supra note 7, at 488.

Chapter 9

Public Facilities: Symbols of Subordination

§9.1 SEGREGATION STATUTES: METHODS AND MOTIVATIONS

It is now general knowledge that the state segregation statutes in the South (which, in fact, parallel quite similar practices followed on a de facto basis in much of the North) were not the products of post–Civil War racial hostility, but rather were enacted in the period from about 1890 to 1910, long after the Reconstruction period had ended. Scholarship making this clear appeared during the 1950s, just in time to dampen pro-segregation arguments that separate facilities represented laws that had lasted a century and thus should not be upset.[1] But the enactment of Jim Crow statutes, whether early or late, usually had political significance far beyond the often paranoid racial requirements in their provisions.

The nature and steady extension of segregation laws has been traced by Professor John Hope Franklin.[2] In the late 1880s, soon after the Supreme Court invalidated the federal civil rights laws in the Civil Rights Cases, segregation laws began to proliferate. Public carriers were an early target. By 1900, all the southern states had segregated railroad trains, and the laws were being extended to cover all travel facilities, even local street cars. Then, quite quickly, separation of the races in all facilities open to the public was mandated. Parks, hospitals, prisons, courthouses: All had segregated toilets, drinking fountains, seating, stairways, entrances, and exits—even telephone booths.[3] As Professor Franklin put it, no detail was too small in the frantic effort to seal off social contact between blacks and whites.

The law had created two worlds, so separate that communication between them was almost impossible. State-mandated or condoned separation bred suspicion and hatred, fostered rumors and misunderstanding, and created conditions that made extremely difficult any steps toward its reduction. Legal segregation was so complete that a white southern minister was moved to remark that it

---

§9.1 1. Particularly influential was C. Vann Woodward's The Strange Career of Jim Crow (1955).

2. John Hope Franklin, History of Racial Segregation in the United States, in Annals Am. Acad. Political & Soc. Sci. 34, at 1 (Mar. 1956).

3. Id. Segregation of cemeteries was de rigueur, and New Orleans even deemed it in the public welfare to enact an ordinance separating black and white prostitutes.

made every activity, from eating and drinking to even "our very institutions of religion, a problem of race as well as a problem of maintenance."[4]

If segregation statutes represented merely a massive retaliatory spasm by a defeated South, or even the honest manifestation of the oft-cited belief that blacks were so inferior to whites that the latter should be shielded from contact with them whenever public interchange was possible, Jim Crow laws could be mentioned briefly and then dismissed as the twisted product of a better-forgotten age. But we know better. The enactment of laws requiring the racial separation of blacks and whites in every conceivable activity did not occur in an ideological vacuum. Rather, they were like an enameled finish on a well-crafted piece of furniture intended for quite utilitarian purposes. They were the highlight of a political structure that also included violence, disfranchisement, and economic exploitation. And finally, like slavery, segregation laws represented an economic-political compromise between elite and working-class whites. Blacks, once again, served as the involuntary sacrifices in a bargain that gave to the poor the sense of superiority, while retaining for the rich economic and political dominance.

Professor William J. Wilson, in reviewing this era, rejects the view of Marxist scholars that the Jim Crow system was instituted by the planter class when blacks tried to take advantage of their legal freedom to organize with poor whites in the Populist movement.[5] He concedes that the planters were mainly responsible for the Black Codes enacted immediately after the Civil War to restrict and control the black population so as to insure an adequate and cheap labor supply for the plantations. But Prof. Wilson claims the Black Codes both reignited the dying flames of abolitionist sentiment in the North and played into the hands of Republicans looking for an excuse to defer reentry of the southern states until the dominance of the Republican party was assured. Congress nullified the Black Codes with the series of civil rights acts, the Fourteenth and Fifteenth Amendments, and statutes dividing the southern states into five military districts under Northern supervision.

---

4. Id. at 8. During the era of "separate but equal," the problem of who was black and who was white created serious difficulties, and for carriers a considerable amount of litigation was initiated by whites who, having been mistaken for blacks, were required to ride in segregated cars. In a typical case, Chicago R.I. & P. v. Allison, 120 Ark. 54, 178 S.W. 401 (1915), a white woman who was directed by a train conductor to the "colored" end of a segregated train coach, where she was required to ride three miles in about fifteen minutes, was held entitled to recover; but an award of $875 was found excessive, considering that there was no noise or misbehavior and that other whites were riding with the sole black in the coach. The court did find that a jury in estimating damage in such a case may consider the white woman's age, degree of refinement, and her mortification and humiliation, if any, as well as her fear and nervous shock.

See also Missouri, K. & T. Ry. v. Ball, 25 Tex. Civ. App. 500, 61 S.W. 327 (1901). But a Kentucky court approved an award of $3,750 for a white woman required to ride in a "colored" car by a conductor who was insulting in his conduct and who pushed her into it, causing her nervous shock and anguish. Louisville & N.R.R. Co. v. Ritchel, 148 Ky. 701, 147 S.W. 411 (1912). See also Norfolk & W. Ry. v. Stone, 111 Va. 730, 69 S.E. 927 (1911) (awarding $400 to a white woman who rode 10 to 15 minutes in a segregated car with one black man and one black woman, because the conductor seated her there).

5. William Wilson, The Declining Significance of Race 52-61 (1978). The Marxist writers referred to are Oliver Cox, Caste, Class and Race: A Study in Social Dynamics (1948); and Paul Baran & Paul Sweezy, Monopoly Capital: An Essay on the American Economic and Social Order 247 (1966).

As industrialization of the South began, the large planters learned to share their power with a rising class of merchant-bankers and with the owners and operators of factories, mines, and railroads. These groups were not fearful of blacks, and indeed formed loose alliances with them, receiving their votes in return for which the elites sometimes spoke out in paternalistic terms against segregation laws as a "needless affront to our respectable and well behaved colored people."[6]

The Populists, on the other hand, tried strenuously to win the black vote, realizing that this goal was essential for a working-class party strong enough to overcome the economic exploitation of the ruling classes. For a time, both the Populists and the conservative Democrats tried to attract the black vote, but when both realized that neither was assured of control they decided to exclude blacks entirely through state constitutional amendments, thereby leaving whites to fight out elections among themselves. With blacks no longer a force at the ballot box, conservatives dropped even the semblance of opposition to Jim Crow provisions pushed by lower-class whites. As Professor Wilson put it, "[a]s long as poor whites directed their hatred and frustration against the black competitor, the planters were relieved of class hostility directed against them."[7] Thus, he concludes, the racial caste system which encompassed all aspects of black life was solidified both by the ruling class's support of disfranchisement and by the working class's drive (with tacit approval of the ruling class) toward racial exclusiveness in occupation, education, and political power.

§9.2 THE SUPREME COURT'S NINETEENTH-CENTURY APPROVAL OF SEGREGATION

By the time challenges to the growing network of segregation statutes reached the Supreme Court, the Reconstruction era had been effectively brought to an end. The Court's almost total rejection of the freedmen's claims gave legal sanction to what was already an accomplished political fact. Was there any alternative to Justice Holmes' view, expressed in Giles v. Harris,[1] that the Court lacked power to protect the voting rights of blacks when whites in overwhelming numbers determined to violate them?

The Civil Rights Cases[2] arose under the provisions of the Civil Rights Act of March 1, 1875, which provided that all persons within the jurisdiction of the United States "shall be entitled to the full and equal enjoyment of the accommodations, advantages, facilities, and privileges of inns, public conveyances on land or water, theatres, and other places of public amusement; subject only to the conditions and limitations established by law, and applicable alike to citizens of every race and color, regardless of any previous condition of servitude."

6. Wilson, supra note 5, at 58.
7. Id. at 54.
§9.2 1. 189 U.S. 475 (1903).
2. 109 U.S. 3 (1883).

Justice Bradley saw the Civil Rights Act of 1875 as a code for the regulation of private rights beyond what Congress had power to enact. The Fourteenth Amendment only effected the "prohibition" of "state action" of a particular character; the fifth section of the Amendment, the enabling provisions, did "not authorize Congress to create a code of municipal law for the regulation of private rights." The Fourteenth Amendment, therefore, does not guard against private wrongs. Nor does the Thirteenth Amendment grant Congress the power to enact such legislation. Justice Bradley conceded that the amendment grants Congress power to enact all laws necessary to obliterate slavery "with all its badges and incidents," but concluded that full and equal access to public accommodations was not implied by the elimination of "badges of slavery." Justice Harlan dissented, unable "to resist the conclusion that the substance and spirit of the recent Amendments of the Constitution have been sacrificed by a subtle and ingenious verbal criticism."[3]

In Plessy v. Ferguson,[5] Plessy brought suit for a writ of prohibition against the judge who was to try him for the violation of a Louisiana statute, adopted in 1890, which provided for separate facilities for white and black passengers on trains, and which prescribed criminal penalties for violators.

For the Court, Justice Brown affirmed the Supreme Court of Louisiana's denial of the writ and upheld the statute as not violative of the Fourteenth Amendment's prohibition of unequal protection of the laws. The object of the Fourteenth Amendment was to "enforce absolute equality of the races before the law," but not "to abolish distinctions based on color" or to enforce social equality or "a commingling of the races upon terms unsatisfactory to either."

It is, said the Court, a generally recognized power of the state legislatures to enforce racial segregation, especially in schools.[6] Plaintiff's claim that he had

---

3. "Were the States against whose protest the institution [of slavery] was destroyed, to be left free, so far as national interference was concerned, to make or allow discriminations against that race, as such, in the enjoyment of those fundamental rights which by universal concession, inhere in a state of freedom? . . .

"I do not contend that the Thirteenth Amendment invests Congress with authority, by legislation, to define and regulate the entire body of the civil rights which citizens enjoy, or may enjoy, in the several States. But I hold that since slavery, as the court has repeatedly declared, [citations omitted] was the moving or principal cause of the adoption of that amendment, and since that institution rested wholly upon the inferiority, as a race, of those held in bondage, their freedom necessarily involved immunity from, and protection against, all discrimination against them, because of their race, in respect of such civil rights as belong to freemen of other races. Congress, therefore, under its express power to enforce that amendment, by appropriate legislation, may enact laws to protect that people against the deprivation, because of their race, of any civil rights granted to other freemen in the same State; and such legislation may be of a direct and primary character, operating upon States, their officers and agents, and, also, upon, at least, such individuals and corporations as exercise public functions and wield power and authority under the State. . . ." 109 U.S. 34, 36 (1883). In addition, Justice Harlan found that §§1 and 5 the Fourteenth Amendment have a "distinctly affirmative character" that enables Congress to protect citizens by direct legislation. Corporations running railroads or public inns are regulated by the state and operate as the state's agents, and may be subjected to the federal government's newly granted power to protect the privileges and immunities of the citizens of the various states. Harlan cited the provision in §1 of the Fourteenth Amendment that all persons are citizens of the United States as an affirmative statement; he thus construed the enabling provisions of §5 as granting Congress the power to legislate.

5. 163 U.S. 537 (1896).

6. The Court cited Roberts v. City of Boston, a Massachusetts case dating back to the early 1850s, which upheld the right of the Boston School Committee to make separate provision for the instruction of colored children. Roberts v. City of Boston, 59 Mass. (5 Cush.) 198 (1850).

a property right, protected by the Fourteenth Amendment, to be treated as a white man was denied because he was black. A black man "is not lawfully entitled to the reputation of being a white man." With an equally circular argument, the Court said that this principle of segregation was not arbitrary because the state statute must be a "reasonable regulation." According to the Court, the state reasonably could "act with reference to the established usages, customs and traditions of the people, and with a view to the promotion of their comfort, and the preservation of the public peace and good order."[7]

Justice Harlan, as he did in the Civil Rights Cases, again dissented strongly, saying that the legislation was inconsistent not only with the equality of rights of citizenship guaranteed by the Fourteenth Amendment, but with the personal liberty enjoyed by "everyone in the United States." He foresaw great social evils resulting from the decisions.[8]

§9.3 JUSTICE BRADLEY RECONSIDERS THE FOURTEENTH AMENDMENT

One legal historian, Professor John Anthony Scott,[1] has pointed out that Justice Bradley's highly restrictive interpretation of the Fourteenth Amendment in the Civil Rights Cases represented a total change from the very broad reading he gave that amendment in the Slaughterhouse Cases.[2] In 1870, when Justice Bradley was "riding circuit" in New Orleans, he heard the first of several challenges to an 1869 Louisiana statute that chartered a private corporation and essentially gave it a twenty-five year monopoly on slaughtering operations in a broad area that included the City of New Orleans. The legislation, justified as a health measure, was challenged by local butchers under the Thirteenth and Fourteenth Amendments. Justice Bradley agreed with the butchers, in effect, holding that citizens enjoyed Fourteenth Amendment rights to pursue a trade. While he acknowledged that a state was

---

7. 163 U.S. at 550-551.
8. As Justice Harlan stated:

The present decision, it may well be apprehended, will not only stimulate aggressions, more or less brutal and irritating, upon the admitted rights of colored citizens, but will encourage the belief that it is possible, by means of state enactments, to defeat the beneficent purposes which the people of the United States had in view when they adopted the recent amendments of the Constitution. . . . Sixty millions of whites are in no danger from the presence here of eight millions of blacks. The destinies of the two races, in this country, are indissolubly linked together, and the interests of both require that the common government of all shall not permit the seeds of race hate to be planted under the sanction of law. What can more certainly arouse race hate, what more certainly create and perpetuate a feeling of distrust between these races, than state enactments, which, in fact, proceed on the ground that colored citizens are so inferior and degraded that they cannot be allowed to sit in public coaches occupied by white citizens? That, as all will admit, is the real meaning of such legislation as was enacted in Louisiana.

163 U.S. at 560.
§9.3 1. John Anthony Scott, Justice Bradley's Evolving Concept of the Fourteenth Amendment from the Slaughterhouse Cases to the Civil Rights Cases, 25 Rutgers L. Rev. 552 (1971).
2. 83 U.S. (16 Wall.) 36 (1873).

entitled to make police regulations to protect the public health, such regulations could not abridge fundamental rights of citizens. Bradley concluded that the federal government had a duty to protect the individual rights of citizens, and found congressional authorization for federal jurisdiction in such cases under the Civil Rights Act of 1866 (even though it was passed before the Fourteenth Amendment). The Act provided direct protection to white citizens in the enjoyment of their rights.[3]

Justice Bradley's decision was overruled, and he dissented when the Slaughterhouse Cases reached the Supreme Court. The majority, rejecting the Bradley position, ruled that the principal purpose of the Fourteenth Amendment was to admit black people to citizenship. The Court said, "We doubt very much whether any action of a State not directed by way of discrimination against the negroes as a class, or on account of their race, will ever be held to come within the purview of this provision." Even so, the Court held that the primary authority for protection of civil rights was the state. The federal role was considered to be a secondary or corrective one that would only arise in the event that states failed to provide equal protection. In his dissent, Justice Bradley said that state citizenship had become secondary to U.S. citizenship, and the whole power of the nation was pledged to sustain equality of rights among citizens.

Why was Justice Bradley's ruling in the Civil Rights Cases precisely the opposite of the position taken thirteen years before? Professor Scott suggests that both positions represent the philosophy of the Republican party during the two periods. He points out that the turmoil created in 1877 by the Hayes-Tilden crisis had been settled by a special electoral commission, including five members of the Supreme Court with Justice Bradley one of the members. The Republican, Hayes, was awarded the disputed returns and was immediately inaugurated. In the years that followed, the Republicans sought to put aside their differences with the South by granting the latter "home rule" with respect to the freed slaves. The decisions in the Civil Rights Cases fit that policy to perfection.

Whether or not the Court could have enforced orders based on Justice Bradley's earlier view of the Fourteenth Amendment, the decision in the Civil Rights Cases served as an important stimulus to the enactment of segregation statutes. The requirement in the Civil Rights Cases that the state must be involved in discriminatory behavior to evoke the Fourteenth Amendment has been expanded but never overturned, even though discrimination in many private areas of activity has been rendered illegal by contemporary civil rights laws.[4]

---

3. Live-Stock Dealers' & Butchers' Ass'n v. Crescent City Live-Stock Landing & Slaughter-House Co., 15 F. Cas. 649, 652-653 (No. 8,408) (C.C.D. La. 1870).

4. While the Civil Rights Cases are today important chiefly for Justice Bradley's analysis of the state action clause, Professor Laurence Tribe asserts that the result of the case — the invalidation of the Civil Rights Act of 1875 and the denial of federal power to prevent the emergence of Jim Crow statutes — "was plainly wrong, not only morally and politically, but as a matter of constitutional law." Laurence Tribe, American Constitutional Law §18-2 n.16 (2d ed. 1988). In Professor Tribe's view, Justice Bradley offered no response to Justice Harlan's argument in dissent that §1 of the Fourteenth Amendment, by granting state citizenship to all persons born or naturalized in the United States, afforded Congress a constitutional basis for guaranteeing to all state citizens an equal right to common law protections.

§9.4 THE SUPREME COURT'S MID-TWENTIETH-CENTURY REJECTION OF SEGREGATION

The 1954 decision in Brown v. Board of Education[1] did not expressly overrule Plessy v. Ferguson. The Court simply concluded "that in the field of public education the doctrine of 'separate but equal' has no place." In the years that followed, the Supreme Court delayed its implementation of public school desegregation, but experienced no difficulty in ordering the immediate end of state-sponsored racial segregation in a wide variety of facilities. Many of these decisions were summary per curiam orders in which the only authority cited by the Court was *Brown*.

The Court voided "Jim Crow" policies in streetcars and buses, public parks, beaches and bathhouses, municipal golf courses, cafeterias, auditoriums, and courtroom seating. Lower courts followed suit, with the result that in the first half dozen years after Brown, civil rights lawyers experienced far more success in desegregating state-operated recreational facilities, such as golf courses and swimming pools, than in litigation involving public schools, where the Court had found separate facilities "inherently unequal."

Why did it happen? Had the Court and the country come to recognize that blacks were equal and that segregation was wrong? C.J. Warren wrote in *Brown* that "we cannot turn the clock back," but segregation had not always been the law. Nineteenth-century federal statutes specifically made segregation illegal. When they were voided by the Civil Rights Cases, Justice Harlan's dissent (heard again in *Plessy*) put the Court on notice as to the real purpose and harm done blacks under the "separate but equal" doctrine. Thus, *Brown* could be simply the completion of a cycle begun by the enactment of the post–Civil War Reconstruction Acts.

This possibility may be tested by isolating factors that may have influenced the Court and country's abandonment of segregation. A list of these factors might include:

1. the difficulty in justifying official segregation and its implications of racial superiority after defeating, in World War II, forces that espoused super-race ideologies and resorted to racial genocide in their name;
2. the perceived need to compete with Communist powers for the friendship of emerging Third World nations without the handicap of explaining official apartheid policies at home;
3. the refusal of more and more blacks, particularly those who had fought in the war, to return home to life under segregation;
4. the unacceptable restraints on full industrialization of the South imposed by rigid segregation laws; and
5. the perception by those in policymaking positions that they could no longer afford to honor the compromises of the past, in which poorer whites won segregation laws as an alternative to demands for social reform legislation and greater political power.

§9.4 1. 347 U.S. 483 (1954).

None of these factors are acknowledged in the statutes or judicial decisions that ended the laws protection for Jim Crow policies.

§9.4.1   Prison Segregation

Consider the possible events that might prompt acceptance of racial segregation in prisons. The prevention of violence might be one justification. In 1968, the Supreme Court approved a lower court order that, while requiring the desegregation of Alabama's prisons, recognized that, in some instances, "prison security and discipline necessitates segregation of the races for a limited period."[2] Consider that for more than two decades, the California Department of Corrections (CDC) has followed a policy of racially segregating prisoners in double cells in reception centers for up to 60 days each time they enter a new correctional facility.

Garrison Johnson, an African-American inmate, filed suit alleging that this unwritten policy violated his Fourteenth Amendment right to equal protection because it used race as a factor in determining housing assignments for the first 60 days of incarceration.[3]

In Johnson v. California,[4] the United States Supreme Court held that prison racial-segregation policies are subject to strict scrutiny even when all prisoners are "equally" segregated,[5] thus reversing the decision of the liberal Ninth Circuit, which had stated that using racial qualifications to assign cellmates was a reasonable measure to avoid violence caused by racial gangs in prisons.[6] The Supreme Court refused to apply the standard applied by the "liberal Ninth Circuit"[7] because it would allow "prison officials to use race-based policies even when there are race-neutral means to accomplish the same goal, and even when the race-based policy does not in practice advance that goal."[8]

According to Erwin Chemerinsky, "there is a time when segregation benefits prison race riots or the behavior of particular inmates, but routine segregation

---

2. Washington v. Lee, 263 F. Supp. 327, 331 (M.D. Ala. 1966), aff'd, 390 U.S. 333, 334 (1968).

The basic problem in the Alabama prison system remained segregation and discrimination based on race. Affirmative hiring programs and other corrective steps were ordered in 1978. McCray v. Bennett, 467 F. Supp. 187 (M.D. Ala. 1978). See also Holt v. Sarver, 309 F. Supp. 362 (E.D. Ark. 1970), aff'd, 442 F.2d 304 (8th Cir. 1971).

The refusal to permit visitation privileges because the visitor and the visitee are of different races was held illegal discrimination in Martin v. Wainwright, 525 F.2d 983 (5th Cir. 1976).

3. Johnson v. California, 543 U.S. 499 (2005).

4. Id.

5. Id.

6. "The use of race as a predominant factor in assigning cellmates for 60 days . . . is reasonably related to the administrator's concern for racial violence." Johnson v. California, 321 F.3d 791 (2003). The Ninth Circuit applied the deferential standard articulated in Turner v. Safley, 482 U.S. 78, 89 (1987) (requiring judges to defer to prison administrators' safety and disciplinary decisions, even if they would be unconstitutional outside prison walls, as long as the policy is reasonably related to legitimate penological interests).

7. See Erwin Chemerinsky, The Myth of the Liberal Ninth Circuit, 37 Loy. L.A. L. Rev. 1, 1 (2003).

8. *Johnson*, supra note 6, at 803.

doesn't meet strict scrutiny,"[9] and as Justice O'Connor stated in *Grutter*, "[c]ontext matters when reviewing race-based governmental action under the Equal Protection Clause."[10] But in any event, there is no doubt that "[f]rom the beginning, nearly everyone has agreed that the central purpose of the Equal Protection Clause is to outlaw certain kinds of discrimination."[11] Because "racial classifications receive close scrutiny even when they may be said to burden or benefit the races equally"[12] the *Johnson* Court stated that the segregation based on race was constitutionally suspect and thus should be evaluated by the same judicial scrutiny that applies to other racial classifications, leaving the CDC with the burden of demonstrating that the policy was narrowly tailored to serve a compelling state interest.[13] The CDC decided to reach a settlement instead of producing such evidence.[14] The Settlement and Release Agreement states that the CDC "shall integrate the Reception Centers by creating a housing protocol that assigns inmates to cells using several criteria, rather than race as the determinative factor."[15]

As Justice Thomas pointed out, the Court was faced with two conflicting lines of precedent when deciding Johnson: one stating that all government actions that expressly classify individuals according to their race must be reviewed under strict scrutiny,[16] and another applying a deferential standard every time a prison policy limits a prisoner's constitutional rights.[17] For instance, it has been held that "racial segregation, which is unconstitutional outside prisons, is unconstitutional within prisons, save for 'the necessities of prison security and discipline,'"[18] but it has also been held that since courts are "ill-equipped to deal with the increasingly urgent problems of prison administration and reform" courts must give deference to the prison administrators.[19]

The deferential standard in Turner v. Safley requires (1) that there be a valid, rational connection between the regulation and the government's legitimate interest, (2) that the inmates have alternative means of exercising their constitutional rights, (3) the analysis of the impact that the accommodation of

---

9. See "The Defiant Ones," Supplement of the L.A. Daily Journal and San Francisco Daily Journal, published on March 28, 2005, available online at http://www.proskauer.com/news_publications/itn/data/001334/_res/id = PDF/Proskauer%20Rose-DJ%20EXTRA%203.28.05.pdf.

10. See Grutter v. Bollinger, 539 U.S. 306, 327 (2003), citing Gomillion v. Lightfoot, 364 U.S. 339, 343-344 (1960).

11. See David A. Strauss, Discriminatory Intent and the Taming of *Brown*, 56 U. Chi. L. Rev. 935, 937 (1989).

12. See Shaw v. Reno, 509 U. S. 630, 651 (1993).

13. Id. at 642.

14. See Assembly Budget Subcommittee No. 4 of May 23, 2006, available online at http://www.assembly.ca.gov/acs/committee/c22/hearing/2006/may%2023%20%202006%20-%20public-jn.doc

15. Id. The Administration submitted a finance letter requesting $5.9 million and roughly two dozen positions to fund staff, physical plant, training and equipment expenses to implement in-cell racial integration as required in the settlement agreement for Johnson v. California.

16. See Adarand Constructors, Inc. v. Pena, 515 U.S. 200 (1995).

17. See Turner v. Safley, 482 U.S. 78 (1987) (holding that deference to prison officials is appropriate for "all circumstances in which the needs of prison administration implicate constitutional rights").

18. See, e.g., Cruz v. Beto, 405 U.S. 319, 321 (1972) (quoting Lee v. Washington, 390 U.S. 333, 334 (1968)).

19. *Turner*, supra note 17, at 84 (quoting Procunier v. Martinez, 416 U.S. 396, 405 (1974)).

the right would have on other inmates, guards and prison resources, and (4) the existence of another alternative to the regulation. The Ninth Circuit held that temporary racial segregation of inmates is rationally related to furthering the state's penological interest in protecting the safety of inmates and staff. It also reasoned that inmates could exercise their right to be free from this policy after 60 days. It found that race was a factor that had to be considered in order to avoid racial violence. Finally, the court concluded that Johnson failed to show that there were alternative solutions to the issue of violence.

The Supreme Court did not decide whether the CDC's policy violated equal protection. Instead of striking down the segregation policy and declaring it unconstitutional under any legal standard as Justice Stevens insisted in his dissent, the majority simply remanded the case to the Ninth Circuit instructing it to apply strict scrutiny.[20]

The Equal Protection Clause provides that no State shall "deny to any persons within its jurisdiction the equal protection of the laws"[21] and the U.S. Supreme Court ruled that segregation is a denial of the equal protection of the laws in Brown v. Board of Education.[22] Title VI of the Civil Rights Act of 1964[23] prohibits racial classifications that would violate the Equal Protection Clause because racial classifications are antithetical to the Fourteenth Amendment, whose purpose was "to eliminate racial discrimination emanating from official sources in the States."[24]

State Senator Gloria Romero reiterated in a proposed bill intending to reform the California Penal Code that the state "should neither defend nor practice racial segregation. . . . People — regardless of whether they are inmates or not — should not be judged by the color of their skin."[25] The other side of the coin is, however, that California began temporary segregation with the intent to protect prisoners from the growing interracial violence and not to impose a new Jim Crow. After all, as Justice Thomas remarked in his dissent, "[t]he Constitution has always demanded less within the prison walls."[26] He also pointed out that deference was appropriate, for "whatever the Court knows of administering educational institutions, it knows much less about administering penal ones."[27]

Brandon N. Robinson criticized the decision in *Johnson*, stating that by explicitly establishing the application of the strict scrutiny standard of review for any government policy of racial segregation,[28] the court "free[d] government

20. Justice Stevens stated his view that "the conclusion that CDC's policy is unconstitutional is inescapable regardless of the standard of review that the Court chooses to apply."

21. U.S. Const. amend. XIV, §1.

22. Brown v. Board of Education, 347 U.S. 483 (1954).

23. 42 U.S.C. §§2000d et seq.

24. McLaughlin v. Florida, 379 U.S. 184, 192 (1964).

25. See SB 814 Senate Bill introduced by Senator Gloria Romero, available online at http://info.sen.ca.gov/pub/05-06/bill/sen/sb_0801-0850/sb_814_cfa_20060619_103106_asm_comm.html.

26. *Johnson*, supra note 3, at 524.

27. Id. at 543.

28. Id. at 505 (quoting Adarand Constructors, Inc. v. Pena, 515 U.S. 200, 227 (1995)). The court in Adarand held that "all racial classifications, imposed by whatever federal, state, or local governmental actor, must be analyzed by a reviewing court under strict scrutiny. In other words, such classifications are constitutional only if they are narrowly tailored measures that further compelling governmental interests."

bodies to adopt measures that would have previously been struck down from the start, in hopes that they can subsequently compile a record establishing a factual basis for a claim of compelling interest."[29] This is so because "although all governmental uses of race are subject to strict scrutiny, not all are invalidated by it."[30]

The Court has previously applied a heightened standard in reviewing racial segregation in prisons[31] and racial segregation policies in prison have been declared unconstitutional in the past, rejecting the notion that separate can ever be equal, or "neutral,"[32] a notion that is also linked to human dignity.[33]

It seems to be clear now that in order for a racial classification to be legitimate it must further a compelling governmental interest and the means for achieving it must be narrowly tailored to the interest.[34] Nevertheless, as the Ninth Circuit had pointed out, "particularized circumstances" and the "necessities of prison security and discipline" that can justify racial segregation have not been defined yet.[35] Suppose, as in the Racism Hypo that follows, the legislature decides on an alternative tack that results in segregated prison units, but without the mandatory component of the *Plessy* approach?

§9.5 Racism Hypo: ACLU v. Harmonia Prison Authority

Harmonia, a large northern state with a nonwhite population of approximately 20 percent, has a serious problem in maintaining order at Big House, its fully integrated, maximum security prison. The inmate population at Big House is 30 percent white and 70 percent black. In the last few years, 12 white and three black inmates have been killed and dozens of both races injured in racial clashes. There have been two serious racial riots within the last year, during both of which Big House officials, in order to gain control, found it necessary to isolate inmates by race for short periods. News of the riots tended to increase racial tensions, violence, and disruption in Harmonia's largest cities.

---

29. See Brandon N. Robinson, Note, Johnson v. California: A Grayer Shade of *Brown*, 56 Duke L. J. 343, 374 (2006).

30. *Grutter*, supra note 10, at 306, 326-327.

31. See *Lee*, 390 U.S. at 333 (rejecting the contention that desegregation would undermine prison security and discipline, thus striking down Alabama's policy of segregation in its prisons).

32. *Brown*, supra note 22.

33. See Peter J. Rubin, Reconnecting Doctrine and Purpose: A Comprehensive Approach to Strict Scrutiny after *Adarand* and *Shaw*, 149 U. Pa. L. Rev. 1, 18-19 ("The only adequate explanation — as both a descriptive and a normative matter — for application of strict scrutiny to classifications based on race must be that the government's use of race is frequently inconsistent with notions of human dignity.") In November 2001, Viet Mike Ngo petitioned the Marin County Superior Court for a writ of habeas corpus regarding San Quentin's racial segregation of inmates in housing and discipline, a violation of the Fourteenth Amendment of the U.S. Constitution. See "Inmates protest 'de facto segregation' at San Quentin," published on July 19, 2002. Though Ngo's case went all the way up to the Supreme Court, the decision only dealt with the need to exhaust administrative remedies, dodging the issue of segregation. See Woodford v. Ngo, 548 U.S. 81 (2006).

34. *Johnson*, supra note 3. *Grutter*, supra note 10, at 326. *Adarand*, supra note 16, at 227.

35. See *Johnson*, 321 F.3d at 797.

Following an investigation and report by a blue-ribbon legislative commit-tee, the Harmonia legislature passed, and the governor signed into law, the Peace of Mind Prison Statute (PMPS).

The statute provides:

> Upon the effective date of this statute, and annually thereafter, each inmate at Big House will have the absolute freedom to choose either (a) a cell with a person of his race, or (b) a cell assigned without regard to race. Those selecting the (a) option will be provided eating, working, and recreational facilities with persons of their race. Those selecting the (b) option will be provided facilities on a nonracial basis.

Exercises of choice under the statute have resulted in the prison population being entirely separated on the basis of race. The Big House has been quite calm for six months, and inmates from the prison's black wings have met in intramural sporting events with inmates from the white wings. Competitive feeling has been high, but there have been no racial incidents. In addition, officials in charge of rehabilitation programs report that the effectiveness of these programs, particularly for black inmates, has been increased due to the adoption of techniques perfected over the years by the Black Muslims. As used in Big House, these programs do not have a political or religious component, but strive to improve self-image, diminish self-hate, and convey the sense that societal success and self-esteem can be gained through legitimate enterprise. Guards and other Big House employees have continued to be hired and assigned on a nonracial basis, but over time, most black employees have requested assignment to black wings and most white employees have chosen to work in white wings.

Seven months after PMPS went into effect, the local chapter of the American Civil Liberties Union, supported by a broad coalition of civil rights groups (all of whom opposed the law from the outset) filed a federal court suit challenging the validity of PMPS. Suit was filed on behalf of five ACLU members, all white, who were convicted and sentenced to two years in Big House for their participation in a disruptive protest that did serious damage to Harmonia's nuclear power facility. The ACLU members claim that Big House is a segregated facility, that the so-called freedom of choice provision is a sham that will not enable desegregation of the facility, and that the present policy will violate their rights under federal statutes and the federal Constitution to assign-ment without regard to race or color.

ACLU lawyers argue that if PMPS is held valid on the basis that racial segregation to prevent prison violence is acceptable, it will lead inevitably to school, job, and even neighborhood segregation to maintain racial peace. Law-yers for Harmonia reject this "slippery slope" argument, maintaining that Big House is a special problem, that each inmate does have absolute freedom of choice, and that if even prestigious colleges regularly assign freshmen to dor-mitory rooms on the basis of race, the state, dealing as it is with persons con-victed of felonies, should be able to provide a choice of cellmates when such provision has been shown to substantially reduce serious violence and disorder.

Law firm A will represent the ACLU.

Law firm B will represent the State of Harmonia.

§9.6   TITLE II, ITS DEVELOPMENT AND POTENTIAL

A full decade after the *Brown* decision, and following three years of civil rights protests against the continued maintenance of segregated facilities (see discussion in Chapter 3), Congress enacted the Civil Rights Act of 1964, which banned racial discrimination in a number of areas, including public accommodations, employment, voting, education, and other federally financed activities. The prohibition against racial bias in public facilities is included as Title II[1] of the 1964 Act. By the time of its enactment, many of the larger public facilities in the south had desegregated in order to halt the disruptive sit-in protests that had captured the interest and the support of peoples all over the world and had (perhaps more importantly) resulted in serious economic loss to many business interests.

In Heart of Atlanta Motel, Inc. v. United States,[2] the Court established the validity of Title II. Plaintiff hotel sought an injunction restraining enforcement of the Act on grounds that it was unconstitutional. The 216-room hotel, serving an interstate clientele, had followed a policy of refusing to rent rooms to blacks. After examining the history of Title II and describing its contents, the Court found that the Heart of Atlanta Motel clearly came within the provisions of §201(a)(1) ("any inn, hotel, motel, or other establishment which provides lodging to transient guests . . .") leaving the sole question one of the Act's constitutionality. Although Congress based the Act on §5 of the Fourteenth Amendment as well as the power to control interstate commerce, the Court found that the commerce power alone was adequate grounds for congressional action. The Court distinguished the 1875 Civil Rights Act because it had been enacted and rejected without consideration of the commerce power granted by Article I. The 1964 Act, on the other hand, appropriately limited its scope to business affecting interstate commerce. Finding ample evidence that discrimination places serious burdens on interstate travel and thus interstate commerce, the Court recognized the need to regulate local incidents of discrimination that might "have a substantial and harmful effect upon that commerce."[3] The 1964 Act provided "reasonable and appropriate" means to eliminate interference with commerce, without depriving the owner of liberty or property under the Fifth Amendment or subjecting him to involuntary servitude. While recognizing that the fundamental object of Title II was to vindicate "the deprivation of personal dignity that surely accompanies denials of equal access to public establishments," the Court relied on the affirmative commerce power, rather than the Fourteenth Amendment, to establish its legal validity. The Court refused to find any violation of the motel owner's liberty or property under the Fifth Amendment,[4] and it rejected as frivolous appellant's contention that being forced to lodge blacks subjected him to involuntary servitude.[5]

§9.6   1. 78 Stat. 243, 42 U.S.C. §§2000a et seq.

2. 379 U.S. 241 (1964).

3. Id. at 258. The Court relied heavily on Gibbons v. Ogden, 22 U.S. 1 (1824).

4. Id. at 258-259 (finding that discrimination interfered with commerce, and "reasonable and appropriate means were enacted to eliminate that interference").

5. Id. at 261, quoting from Butler v. Perry, 240 U.S. 328, 332 (1916) (requiring an innkeeper to furnish accommodation to travelers was not "akin to slavery"). In a companion case, Katzenbach v.

The Supreme Court strategy adopted in the *Heart of Atlanta* case of avoiding direct conflict with the holding in the Civil Rights Cases and basing the constitutionality of Title II on commerce clause grounds led, as might have been expected, to a great deal of straining in subsequent cases to find the necessary impact on commerce.[6] Whenever at all feasible, the use of interstate materials or the possible service of interstate passengers was used to extend coverage to places of public accommodation not specifically enumerated in §201(b) of Title II.[7]

McClung, the Court upheld the application of §201 against a restaurant that had purchased 46 percent of its meat from a local supplier who had procured it from out of state. This provided sufficient nexus with interstate commerce for Congress to act. In a concurrence applying to both cases, Justice Black recognized that certain isolated local businesses might be beyond the reach of Congress's commerce power; but Justices Douglas and Goldberg, concurring separately, emphasized that Congress had authority under the Fourteenth Amendment's equal protection clause, as well as the commerce power, to protect blacks from discrimination. 379 U.S. 294 (1964). Title II does not represent the first effort to utilize the commerce clause to attack racial segregation in public facilities. In fact, the provision of the Interstate Commerce Act prohibiting common carriers from giving "undue or unreasonable preference or advantage to any particular person . . . in any respect whatsoever, or [subjecting] any particular person . . . to any unreasonable or undue prejudice or disadvantage" became the basis of a complaint filed by a black minister before the commission in 1887, the same year the act took effect. Interstate Commerce Act, Part I, 24 Stat. 380 (1887), 49 U.S.C. §3(1) (1958). In this proceeding, the commission found that racial segregation on terms of equality is permissible, but that the act barred provision of second-class accommodations to blacks who paid a first-class fare. Council v. Western & A.R.R., 1 I.C.C. 339 (1887). Earlier, state courts had reached conflicting results as to whether state laws requiring segregation in travel facilities violated the commerce clause. Some of these cases were influenced by the Supreme Court's decision in Hall v. DeCuir, 95 U.S. 485 (1878), which held invalid a state law forbidding racial segregation on an interstate steamboat plying the Mississippi River and serving states where the law might vary between requiring and forbidding segregation.

In a series of cases in the 1930s and 1940s, the Court struck down segregation practices of interstate carriers as a direct burden on commerce or because they violated antidiscrimination provisions of the Interstate Commerce Act. See Mitchell v. United States, 313 U.S. 80 (1941) (failure to provide blacks with first-class accommodations equal to those furnished whites violated the Interstate Commerce Act notwithstanding the carrier's contention that racial segregation was required by state law and that there were insufficient black passengers to justify providing a separate car for them); Morgan v. Virginia, 328 U.S. 373 (1946) (a state statute requiring segregation on interstate buses was held an unconstitutional burden on commerce, despite arguments that state police power justified segregation to "keep down racial frictions"); Henderson v. United States, 339 U.S. 816 (1950) (a railroad's practice of providing segregated dining facilities on its cars was held invalid under the Interstate Commerce Act in situations where blacks were delayed in receiving dining service because of limited accommodations for them, while seats were vacant in the section of the dining car reserved for whites); Boynton v. Virginia, 364 U.S. 454 (1960) (the trespass conviction of a black bus passenger who had refused to leave the premises of a restaurant located in the bus terminal was held invalid as a violation of the nondiscrimination provision of the Interstate Commerce Act; the Court found that the restaurant, while privately owned, was part of the facility devoted to interstate transportation as defined by the act).

6. In Daniel v. Paul, for example, the Supreme Court held that since a snack bar in a private country club (the Lake Nixon Club in Arkansas) was principally engaged in selling food on the premises, and since it served interstate travelers with food that moved in commerce, the club was a "public accommodation" covered by Title II. Equipment, furniture, and alcohol purchased out of state also indicated a public accommodation. The Court also found the club a "place of entertainment" under the Civil Rights Act of 1964, and subsequent efforts to privatize the facility were deemed a subterfuge. 395 U.S. 298 (1969).

7. In Newman v. Piggie Park Enterprises, Inc., 395 U.S. 1969, the Supreme Court, per curiam, held Title II applicable to drive-in restaurants. The Piggie Park case has generally been cited though for its reading of §204(b): the attorneys' fee provision. The Court interpreted "prevailing party" broadly to provide "a reasonable attorneys' fee" in every case unless special circumstances would

Note: Buckhannon: *Limiting Attorneys' Fees for "Prevailing Parties"*

Over the past 15 years in more than a half dozen cases, the Supreme Court has signaled a trend of limiting attorneys' fees authorized by federal statutes for prevailing parties in civil rights and environmental cases.[8] In one of most recent cases, Buckhannon v. West Virginia Department of Health and Human Resources,[9] the Court's narrow definition of a prevailing party has the potential to dramatically reduce the number of civil rights cases, including Title II claims, that the private bar could afford to bring.[10]

In *Buckhannon*, the Supreme Court held that the fee-shifting provisions of the Fair Housing Amendments Act (FHAA) and Americans with Disabilities Act (ADA) required a party to secure a judicial decision or court-approved settlement to qualify for attorneys' fees as a "prevailing party." The Court in *Buckhannon* rejected the more inclusive meaning of "prevailing party" accepted by the majority of appellate courts under the catalyst theory. Under this theory, courts award attorneys' fees if the litigation served as a catalyst for the intended relief or settlement sought by the plaintiff. The Court determined that permitting this more expansive interpretation would impermissibly extend beyond Congress's intent. Quoting Black's Law Dictionary, the Court explained that the term "prevailing party" is a term of art that is limited to "a party in whose favor a judgment is rendered."[11]

Justice Ginsburg's dissent, however, argued that the Court's "insistence that there be a document filed in court . . . upsets long-prevailing Circuit precedent applicable to scores of federal fee shifting statutes."[12] Congress adopted these provisions to "advance the enforcement of civil rights."[13]

The dissent describes the distorted incentives that the majority's decision would encourage. First, defendants could draw out a meritorious lawsuit, causing the plaintiffs to amass exorbitant fees, but then avoid the statutory obligation at the

---

render such an award unjust. The court below had awarded counsel fees only to the extent that defendants' defenses had been advanced "for purposes of delay and not in good faith." Enforcement of Title II, the Court explained, is dependent in part on private litigation, and thus such suits are private in form only. When a plaintiff brings an action under that title, he cannot recover damages. If he obtains an injunction, he does so not for himself alone, but also as a "private attorney general" vindicating a policy that Congress considered of the highest priority. If successful plaintiffs were routinely forced to bear their own attorneys' fees, few aggrieved parties would be in a position to advance the public interest by invoking the injunctive powers of the federal courts. Congress therefore enacted the provision for counsel fees — not simply to penalize litigants who deliberately advance arguments they know to be untenable but, more broadly, to encourage individuals injured by racial discrimination to seek judicial relief under Title II. See also United States ex rel. Clarke v. Gramer, 418 F.2d 692 (5th Cir. 1969). See also United States v. Boyd, 327 F. Supp. 998 (S.D. Ga. 1971) (enjoining a restaurant from seating whites in a front dining room and blacks in the back, and further requiring the restaurant to eliminate the back room when customers voluntarily continued to use the rooms on a racially segregated basis).

8. David Luban, Taking Out the Adversary: The Assault on Progressive Public-Interest Lawyers, 91 Cal. L. Rev. 209, 240 (2003). See also Sylvia A. Law, In the Name of Federalism: The Supreme Court's Assault on Democracy and Civil Rights, 70 U. Cin. Law Rev. 367, 389-390 (2002).

9. 532 U.S. 598 (2001).

10. Mary D. Fan, Case Note: Textual Imagination, 111 Yale L.J. 1251 (2002).

11. 532 U.S. at 603 (quoting Black's Law Dictionary 1145 (7th ed. 1999)).

12. Id. at 623 (Ginsberg, J., dissenting).

13. Id.

last minute when the defendant decides to change the improper behavior. Second, the decision will impede access to the courts "for the less well heeled, and shrink the incentive Congress created for the enforcement of federal law by private attorneys general."[14]

After *Buckhannon*, advocates have grown concerned about the Supreme Court's erosion of attorneys' fees, a crucial component to enforcing a range of federal protections.[15] *Buckhannon* may have a silencing effect on Title II enforcement, in particular, given that its "prevailing party" provision served as the model for other civil rights legislation, including the ADA and FHAA.

§9.6.1   Evaluating Public Accommodations Statutes

Even hard-line critics of the civil rights movement are likely to concede that if the early years of protests accomplished anything, they achieved a breakdown of the system of segregation and exclusion of blacks from businesses open to the public. Laws have been passed, and the public generally assumes that such behavior is no longer acceptable. Yet racial discrimination in public places is still with us, often in quite blatant forms. Despite the abolition of de jure segregation, and despite changed attitudes in a substantial portion of the populace, the desire of some whites to exercise dominance over blacks — even on the meanest grounds — remains strong.

To take just a few examples from the many cases reported in the past three decades, black people are still suffering discrimination ranging from outright denial of service to grudging service or lower standards of service. A taxicab driver who refused to stop for a black student, picked up his white friend, but then refused to drive both students when the driver realized they were traveling together;[16] a national motel chain told a black marine that there were no rooms available for the night and then offered a room a few minutes later to his companion, a white marine;[17] black guests attending a reunion faced discriminatory treatment that included requiring only these guests to prepay their rooms in full, limiting the rooms available to them, and requiring them to wear orange wrist bands that were not required of white guests;[18] a black businessman agrees to rent an office and is later told that the office is unavailable;[19] a black customer is first insulted and then refused service when he challenges an increase in a price that he had checked over the phone;[20] black patrons are segregated on the second floor of a motel and are discouraged from using the motel's recreational facilities;[21] a black man who tries to return his bus ticket for a refund is racially abused and accused of

---

14. Id.
15. Luban, supra note 8, at 240.
16. Bolden et al. v. J&R Inc., 1:99CV01255 (D.D.C. June 21, 2000).
17. Powell v. Super 8 Motels, Inc., 181 F. Supp. 2d 561 (E.D.N.C. 2000).
18. Gilliam v. HBE Corp., 204 F.R.D. 493 (M.D. Fla. 2000). AACT, Adam's Mark Hotels Reach Settlement, 19 Black Issues 16 (Dec. 5, 2002).
19. Phiffer v. Proud Parrot Motor Hotel, Inc., 648 F.2d 548 (9th Cir. 1980).
20. Ledsinger v. Burmeister, 114 Mich. App. 12, 318 N.W.2d 558 (1982).
21. Director, Division on Civil Rights v. Slumber, Inc., 82 N.J. 412, 413 A.2d 603 (1980).

stealing the ticket;[22] a white woman with a black date is refused admission to a nightclub on the ground that she cannot produce proof of age, though she has offered four pieces of ID;[23] a black man is refused admission to a disco because of the dress code, though he can see that some white customers are dressed more casually than he;[24] yet another disco discourages black patronage by charging lower admission fees for whites.[25] These cases are at once shocking and mundane. They are unusual only in that complaints were actually filed and taken through the court system.

If the subject of public accommodations is no longer a high priority for civil rights crusaders, perhaps it is because all the battles have already been fought at least once, and seemingly adequate statutes have been enacted. We are now in the long, often painfully slow, process of using the existing law to modify ingrained social attitudes. This process can be accomplished only through prompt, effective enforcement of rights. The threat of legal penalties may not change the hearts of those who have been raised in prejudice, but it may modify their behavior, and it will reassure the victims of discrimination that society disapproves of such behavior.

The effectiveness of public accommodations statutes is often vitiated by small or token damage judgments for prevailing plaintiffs,[26] as well as the uncertainty of damages for non-economic injuries. Small judgments indicate lack of respect for the non-economic aspects of the damage, including injury to an individual's sense of self-worth and personal integrity.[27] Though some courts recognize and compensate these injuries, no uniform method exists for calculating damages in public accommodations cases. Because a purely moral victory is not generally sufficient motivation to pursue a lawsuit, this discourages victims from seeking legal solutions.

Even with clients who are able to pay, many lawyers do not encourage litigation in an area of law with which they are unfamiliar and where a victory may

22. King v. Greyhound Lines, Inc., 61 Or. App. 197, 656 P.2d 349 (1982).
23. Gaudry v. Bureau of Labor & Indus., 48 Or. App. 589, 617 P.2d 668 (1980).
24. McCuller v. Gaudry, 59 Or. App. 13, 650 P.2d 148 (1982).
25. McDaniel v. Cory, 631 P.2d 82 (Alaska 1981).
26. A typical award may include general damages, punitive damages, and attorneys' fees. Judgments tend to fall between $1,000 to $2,000. See Director, Division of Civil Rights v. Slumber, Inc., 82 N.J. 412, 413 A.2d 603 (1980) ($1,500 to couple complaining of segregation in motel); King v. Greyhound Lines, Inc., 61 Or. App. 197, 656 P.2d 349 (1982) ($500 general damages, $1,000 punitive damages and reasonable attorneys' fees to man accused of stealing bus ticket presented for refund).

Plaintiffs who suffer economic losses seem to gain higher overall judgments, whereas plaintiffs who suffer only inconvenience or humiliation may receive nothing or a token award, despite favorable judgment on the discrimination issue. See Phiffer v. Proud Parrot Motor Hotel, Inc., 648 F.2d 548 (9th Cir. 1980) (insurance agent and wife who tried unsuccessfully to rent an office granted $7,500 general damages, $1,000 for emotional distress, $2,000 punitive damages, and $2,500 in attorneys' fees for a total of $13,000). See also McDaniel v. Cory, 631 P.2d 82 (Alaska 1981) (judgment of $600 for disco patron who was insulted and refused admission, settlement of $25 to another patron who did not press complaint; both judgments later overturned).

27. King v. Greyhound Lines, Inc., 61 Or. App. 197, 203, 656 P.2d 349, 352 (1982) (recognizing that injury to a person's self-worth and personal integrity caused by discrimination in a public accommodation is a greater evil than monetary loss). (See Chapter 7 for further discussion of emotional distress resulting from acts of discrimination.)

alienate potential business clients. In addition, defeat on a technicality can prevent lawyers from being compensated.[28] Further difficulties are caused by the numbers of federal, state, and administrative remedies on the books. Plaintiffs with a good case sometimes lose simply because they filed under the wrong statute.[29] In response, plaintiff attorneys have become overly cautious and burden the courts with pleading every conceivable statutory and common law claim.[30]

§9.6.2 The Value of the Dramatic Instance

In 1993, a group of six black Secret Service agents, on assignment guarding the President, entered a Denny's Restaurant in Annapolis, Maryland. They sat for almost an hour, ignored and made to feel unwanted, while their white colleagues received friendly greetings and prompt service. The incident was widely reported and led to a Department of Justice investigation, the filing of several lawsuits, and a customer boycott that brought national attention to a company-wide problem.

Consequently, Denny's Restaurants agreed to pay $45 million to over 4,500 discrimination victims, the largest reported public accommodation settlement to date. Determined to repair its damaged image, Denny's underwent a massive restructuring to expand its minority recruiting and employment efforts, aired a series of commercials focusing on diversity, and contributed over $1.5 million to civil rights organizations and the Negro College Fund.[31]

Denny's efforts have yielded positive results. In 1993, only one franchise was owned by an African American. In 2002, African Americans owned 66 Denny's restaurants, and 199 minority franchisees collectively owned 450 Denny's restaurants, representing 42 percent of all Denny's franchise restaurants. In 1992, Denny's had no minority contract suppliers; by 2001, minority purchasing contracts represented 17 percent of all purchases. In 2002, 45 percent of Denny's more than 30,000 company employees were minorities and 20 percent of the company's board was African American.[32]

---

28. In one case, the Alaska Supreme Court held that the Alaska State Commission for Human Rights did not have the power to award compensatory damages to claimants. McDaniel v. Cory, 631 P.2d 82 (Alaska 1981). No unanimity exists among the various states as to the remedies that may be granted in administrative proceedings. In contrast to *McDaniel*, the New Jersey Supreme Court has specifically held that the state Division on Civil Rights may grant damages to nonparty complainants in its hearings on public accommodations offenses. Director, Division on Civil Rights v. Slumber, Inc., 82 N.J. 412, 413 A.2d 603 (1980).

29. See, e.g., Human Rights Comm'n of N.M. v. Board of Regents of the Univ. of N.M. Coll. of Nursing, 95 N.M. 576, 624 P.2d 518 (1981) (claim of racial and sexual discrimination in treatment of students; filed under Title II, should have been filed under Title IV).

30. In Ledsinger v. Burmeister, 114 Mich. App. 12, 318 N.W.2d 558 (1982), plaintiffs sued a merchant who shouted racial epithets at Mr. Ledsinger under 42 U.S.C. §1983, two Michigan civil rights statutes, and common law theories of slander, publication of embarrassing private facts, intentional infliction of emotional distress, and loss of consortium.

31. Most recently, Denny's is partnering with the NAACP to raise $1 million to expand the civil rights museum. See Chris Carter, Denny's Raising Funds to Expand Civil Rights Museum, Greenville News, Jan. 10, 2002, at 6B.

32. Hugh Morley, Study Touts 9 Firms on Race Issues, Bergen County, N.J., Record, Feb. 27, 2003, at 5.

Denny's has been recognized for its progress.[33] Since 1998, Fortune magazine has ranked Denny's among the top 10 leaders in corporate diversity in its annual ranking of America's 50 Best Companies for Minorities and ranked Denny's no. 1 in 2000 and 2001. Former chairman and CEO of Advantica, Denny's parent company, Jim Adamson, received the CEO of the Year Award from the NAACP in 1996.

The lesson seems plain. Denny's discriminatory policies had been motivated by fears that if they attracted blacks, whites would stop patronizing their restaurants. Their current actions stem from the recognition that antidiscrimination policies are good business. One can applaud Denny's positive, even enthusiastic, policies without forgetting that while racial policies based on hoped-for financial profit prove both fragile and unreliable, they tend to be as effective as those relying on the law and morality.

Even with Denny's high-profile example of the damaging legal and economic consequences of discrimination in public accommodations, such discrimination still persists. In April 2002, the NAACP filed a $100 million class action lawsuit against Cracker Barrel restaurants on behalf of 42 plaintiffs in 16 states with 96 witnesses alleging discrimination against African American patrons. Violations reported in over 200 cities include turning away black customers, placing minorities in segregated seating areas, and withholding proper service.[34]

Hotel chains can also be a source of discriminatory treatment of blacks.[35] In 1999, African American guests brought a Title II action alleging discriminatory treatment during their stay at an Adam's Mark Hotel in Daytona, Florida. The NAACP joined the lawsuit and organized a boycott of the hotel chain, while the U.S. Department of Justice filed a lawsuit against the entire chain "for engaging in discriminatory practices against minorities."[36] Adam's Mark Hotel agreed to pay the biggest discrimination settlement by a hotel chain: $1.1 million to Florida's historically black colleges and to the hotel guests who were mistreated at the 1999 Black College Reunion.[37] The guests were required to prepay rooms in full, were limited in the selection of rooms available to them, and were required to wear orange wrist bands that were not required of white guests. Economic motivations for discrimination continue to be strong in areas where racial stereotypes persist.

---

33. Yet, such strides are no guarantee for an open atmosphere of inclusion at all Denny's establishments. Denny's restaurants continue to receive complaints from minority patrons about discriminatory treatment. A Vermont franchise has settled with African American customers who were not served for over an hour after being seated.

34. Larry Bivins, More Plaintiffs Added to Discrimination Lawsuit, Gannett News Serv., Apr. 11, 2002. See also http://www.naacp.org/news/releases/crackerbarrel041102.shtml.

35. Powell v. Super 8 Motels, Inc., 181 F. Supp. 2d 561 (E.D.N.C. 2000). This lawsuit alleges that an African American marine was turned away from a Super 8 Motel because there were no vacancies, while the same desk clerk minutes later offered a room to a white fellow marine.

36. Gilliam v. HBE Corp., 204 F.R.D. 493 (M.D. Fla. 2000). AACT, Adam's Mark Hotels Reach Settlement, 19 Black Issues 16 (Dec. 5, 2002).

37. Partially in response to this lawsuit, the Florida legislature passed legislation that would permit lawsuits identifying a pattern or practice of discrimination in education, in jobs, or at businesses serving the public that is due to "race, color, religion, gender, national origin, age, disability or marital status."

§9.6.3 Government Services and Facilities

Most public accommodations statutes, whether state or federal, are aimed at private entities offering goods or services to the public. Government services, such as education are not covered by Title II or by state public accommodations laws. Moreover, public accommodations statutes are really designed to furnish remedies for individuals experiencing acts of discrimination, rather than the large classes of people affected when public officials discriminate. However, minority individuals or groups suffering from discrimination in provision of government facilities or services may have a constitutional claim or a right of action under one of many federal statutes: 42 U.S.C. §1981 or 1983, Title VI (barring discrimination in programs receiving federal funds),[38] the Revenue Sharing Act, the Housing and Urban Development Act. The difficulty, as always, is in judging which provision to use and in presenting a set of facts and arguments that compel a legal remedy.

The cities and towns of America, both north and south, still reflect the historical realities of segregation. As James Kushner notes in his guide to fair housing law, the minority neighborhoods are still on the "wrong side of the tracks" for

---

38. Alexander v. Sandoval, 532 U.S. 275 (2001). Alexander v. Sandoval limited the scope of Title VI, which bars recipients of federal funding from discriminating on the basis of race, ethnicity, or national origin. Sandoval arose as a challenge to the Alabama Department of Public Safety's policy to administer driver's license examinations in English only. Through a class action lawsuit, the Sandoval plaintiffs argued that the policy constituted discrimination against non-English speakers in violation of DOJ regulation passed pursuant to §602 of Title VI. Professor Sylvia Law views this case as part of the Court's "revolutionary new interpretations of federal statutes that drastically undermine federal statutory and regulatory protection of individual rights to liberty and equality." (Law, supra note 8, at 387.)

In *Sandoval*, the Supreme Court held in a five-to-four decision that private plaintiffs do not have an implied private right of action to enforce disparate impact regulations under Title VI. Although the court left the disparate impact regulations undisturbed, the Court's opinion suggests that a majority of the Court may be willing to entertain a future challenge to the regulations. See John Arthus Laufer, Alexander v. Sandoval and Its Implications for Disparate Impact Regimes, 102 Colum. L. Rev. 1613 (2002). Speaking for the majority, Chief Justice Rehnquist wrote, "it is most certainly incorrect to say that language in a regulation can conjure up a private cause of action that has not been authorized by Congress. Agencies may play the sorcerer's apprentice but not the sorcerer himself." 532 U.S. at 291. After *Sandoval*, private plaintiffs can sue under Title VI only if they can prove intentional discrimination, a difficult standard to meet. Federal agencies, which remain the sole means to enforce disparate impact regulations, lack the resources to file suit on behalf of all the individuals now barred from bringing suit.

In his dissent, Justice Stevens describes the majority opinion as "unfounded in our precedent and hostile to decades of settled expectations," and therefore "carv[ing] out an important exception to the right of private action long recognized under Title VI." Id. at 294. Stevens argues, however, that denying a private right of action under Title VI would not foreclose all remedies: "[l]itigants who in the future wish to enforce the Title VI regulations against state actors in all likelihood must only reference §1983 to obtain relief." Id. at 300. Section 1983 provides in relevant part:

"Every person who, under color of any statute, ordinance, regulation, custom, or usage, of any State or Territory or the District of Columbia, subjects, or causes to be subjected, any citizen of the United States or other person within the jurisdiction thereof to the deprivation of any rights, privileges, or immunities secured by the Constitution and laws, shall be liable to the party injured in an action at law, suit in equity, or other proper proceeding for redress."

Since *Sandoval*, two district courts have held that §1983 can be used to enforce Title VI disparate impact regulations. South Camden Citizens in Action v. New Jersey Dept. of Envt'l Protection, 145 F. Supp. 2d 505 (D.N.J. 2001); Lucero v. Detroit Pub. Sch., 160 F. Supp. 2d 767 (E.D. Mich. 2001). However, the case law on this issue remains relatively undeveloped.

receiving municipal services.[39] Although systematic discrimination in the provision of services violates the Fourteenth Amendment[40] and federal laws,[41] a walk across the railroad tracks in many towns still takes one from a community with street lights and modern plumbing to an area where many roads are little more than unpaved alleys and drainage is provided by open ditches.

In Johnson v. City of Arcadia,[42] the Eleventh Circuit found conditions that indicated intentional discrimination in the provision of municipal services, violating both the Fourteenth Amendment and Title VI.[43] Arcadia had a population of 7,000, about 32 percent black, when suit was filed in 1976. At that time, all black residents lived in a poor area with inadequate services and many unpaved roads. Their community center was a one-room basketball gym that could be reached only by crossing an unbridged ditch. This was in striking contrast with the community center on the white side of town, which was extensive, fully equipped, and well-maintained.[44]

For many years city officials had ignored complaints from the black community and refused to act upon a consulting firm's report that the black area was severely blighted and should receive priority in allocations of city funds. The court found that the dramatic inequalities in services and facilities provided by the city to black and white residents were the result of systematic racial discrimination, and included in its order a plan to distribute federal revenue sharing funds so as to upgrade facilities in the black community.[45]

Cases such as these might have set powerful precedents, but their influence has been limited by two developments in civil rights law.[46] First, under Washington v. Davis,[47] the violation must be demonstrated by proof of intent and not just by discriminatory impact. In the absence of published statements proclaiming city officials' intention to discriminate, intent is most easily proved in small towns with a clear history of segregation. In large urban areas, measurement of service delivery is difficult, and officials can simply argue that the limited

---

39. James Kushner, Fair Housing: Discrimination in Real Estate, Community Development and Revitalization 565 (1995) (1998 Supp.).

40. Hawkins v. Town of Shaw, 437 F.2d 1286 (5th Cir. 1971), aff'd en banc, 461 F.2d 1171 (5th Cir. 1972) (97 percent of the town's unpaved streets were in the black community, no high-power mercury vapor lights had been installed in the area, parts of the black community had no sewer system and had open ditches for a drainage system).

41. The HUD regulations implementing the Fair Housing Amendments of 1988 expressly prohibit bias in the provision of municipal services. 24 C.F.R. §100.70(d)(4).

42. 450 F. Supp. 1363 (M.D. Fla. 1978).

43. 42 U.S.C.A. §2000d (1988).

44. 450 F. Supp. at 1368.

45. See also Dowdell v. City of Apopka, 511 F. Supp. 1375 (M.D. Fla. 1981), modified, 698 F.2d 1181 (11th Cir. 1983) (finding the City liable for intentional discrimination under the Fourteenth Amendment, Title VI, and the Revenue Sharing Act, 31 U.S.C. §12 (1982), because the City failed to provide adequate services to black neighborhoods, even though $800,000 had just been poured into newly annexed white neighborhoods); Pleasant Grove v. United States, 479 U.S. 462 (1987) (finding discriminatory annexation of only white neighborhoods violated the Voting Rights Act, 42 U.S.C. §1973, and claim of higher service costs in the black area were pretextual).

46. This discussion owes a large debt to James Kushner's analysis of municipal services in Kushner, supra note 39, at 565-571.

47. 426 U.S. 289 (1976).

funds available have been allocated on a rational basis and that inequities in services are a product of economic forces rather than prejudice.

Secondly, plaintiffs may have difficulty proving that they have received unequal services. Under Beal v. Lindsay[48] the measure of comparability of services is input, not results. Because a greater investment may be needed to maintain services and facilities in poorer communities, especially where theft and vandalism are prevalent, an equal allocation of funds may result in deterioration. Similarly, a funding system based on extent of use may result in shrinking budgets for facilities that cannot be fully used because they are already rundown, poorly equipped, and inadequately staffed. Such systems, though based on a seemingly neutral standard, tend to result in the improvement of well-maintained facilities and the deterioration of poorer ones.[49]

Finally, poor (disproportionately black and Hispanic) neighborhoods suffer when community services are funded by special assessment of property rather than citywide taxes. Although assessment funding or "pay as you go" programs facilitate the disparate delivery of municipal services, it has been upheld because of its objectively equal terms.[50] If, however, a segregated city attempts to rely on assessment funding pendente lite, liability may not be avoided.[51]

Kushner predicts an enhanced role for special assessment funding in response to the national fiscal austerity movement. The reduction in federal funds for community development indicates that special assessment funding, and municipal immunity for disparate delivery of services, may rise.[52]

Issues concerning municipal services are most complicated in our cities. The misery in our inner cities is attributable to social and economic factors, as well as to racial prejudice. These forces combine to perpetuate segregated, poor neighborhoods; it is not disputed that blacks and other minorities constitute a high percentage of city dwellers. When city officials must balance the competing claims of

---

48. 468 F.2d 287 (2d Cir. 1972).

49. Kushner, supra note 39, at 322.

50. *Hawkins*, supra note 40; see also Citizens for Underground Equality v. City of Seattle, 6 Wash. App. 338, 492 P.2d 1071 (1972) (residents of low-income neighborhood opposed plan to fund installation of underground utility lines through assessment of property owners; the court held that although some sections of the city might be unable or unwilling to pay such assessments, the plan was constitutional).

51. See Kushner, supra note 39, at 567; Williams v. City of Dothan, 745 F.2d 1406 (11th Cir. 1984) (upholding street paving and sewer assessments of white neighborhoods on summary judgment), subsequent proceedings, 818 F.2d 755 (11th Cir. 1987) (enforcing order for remedy based on lower city contribution to black neighborhoods and order to apply effects test to future policies); Baker v. Kissimmee, 645 F. Supp. 571 (M.D. Fla. 1986) (holding that special assessment funding is no defense to intentional inequality); but see Crenshaw v. City of Defuniak Springs, 891 F. Supp. 1548 (N.D. Fla. 1995) (failing to find a §1982 or §1983 violation where the city closed a street and refused to collect garbage from the "private property"; holding that there is no racial discrimination because residents on the closed street are treated the same as white citizens).

52. The Housing and Community Development Act of 1974 provides large communities with automatic entitlement funds. However, 1981 Amendments eliminated the annual application process and generally weakened program standards. Throughout the 1980s, federal funding for community development dropped. In addition, no regulation funds target minority neighborhoods. Litigation challenging block grant programs is likely to succeed only in egregious situations; relief often may include allocation of entitlement grants for poor and minority neighborhoods. Courts have not specifically found a fundamental right to receive a minimum level of municipal services.

many interest groups, however, the interests of minorities rarely seem to weigh as heavily as those of other groups. The closure and relocation of inner-city hospitals illustrates the difficulties minority groups face in challenging municipal decisions that adversely affect them.[53]

Though closing and relocation of hospitals is a continuous process reflecting population change and growth, "runaway" hospitals have disproportionately left black neighborhoods with reduced medical services — or with no services at all.[54] Urban healthcare providers become overburdened for several reasons, including overcrowding in hospitals, clinic closures, and a shortage of doctors and dentists willing to practice in the inner city. When the income level of the inner-city clientele drops, hospitals hit financial trouble and physicians follow well-heeled patients out to the suburbs. Old and inadequate facilities only become problems when hospitals lack the resources to remodel and update.[55] When a hospital is closed, it leaves a vacuum; residents without access to healthcare often substitute emergency treatment for preventative care.[56] Hospitals also serve other community functions — they are, for example, large employers and symbols of neighborhood identity — that may not be replaced when the hospital leaves. Minority and low-income groups have challenged hospital relocation strategies, but without success.[57]

53. See John Charles Boger, Race and the American City: The Kerner Commission in Retrospect — An Introduction, 71 N.C. L. Rev. 1289, 1349 n.179 (1993).

54. Gwendolyn Robert Majette, Access to Health Care: What a Difference Shades of Color Make, 12 Ann. Health L. 121 (2003). Urban Hospital Closings in the Face of Racial Change, a statement on Hospital Financing Problems to the Subcommittee on Health, Committee on Ways and Means, U.S. House of Representatives, March 14, 1980, by Alan Sager, Ph.D., Assistant Professor of Urban and Health Planning, Brandeis University. Reprinted in Civil Rights Issues in Health Care Delivery (a consultation sponsored by the United States Commission on Civil Rights), Washington, D.C., April 15-16, 1980, p. 383.

"As the minority proportion of the neighborhood increases, so does the proportion of hospitals closing or relocating from 1937 to 1977. In neighborhoods 0-25 percent black in 1970, for example, only 14.1 percent of the 1937 hospitals had closed or relocated by 1977. But in neighborhoods 76-100 percent black in 1970, fully 46.9 percent of hospitals — almost half — had disappeared." Id. at 388. See also Boger, supra note 53, at 1349 n.179.

55. See Sager, supra note 54, at 395.

56. See Sager, supra note 54, at 396.

57. Courts fail to recognize the removal of services as a violation of constitutional rights or of civil rights legislation. In NAACP v. The Medical Center, the Third Circuit upheld a reorganization plan as the most feasible and least expensive option, in spite of its disparate impact on minority and low-income people. See 657 F.2d 1322 (3d Cir. 1981), aff'g 491 F. Supp. 290 (D. Del. 1980) (allowing the Delaware Medical Center to relocate 75 percent of the beds from three central city hospitals out to a new suburban facility; while recognizing that the burdens of travel to and from the suburban facility would fall on minorities and low-income city dwellers, the court found that no more accommodation to these groups' needs could be expected). Likewise, the Second Circuit in Bryan v. Koch held that Title VI does not require consideration of alternatives beyond a rational assessment of all hospitals in the system, noting that courts should be wary of substituting their judgment for that of government officials. 627 F.2d 612 (2d Cir. 1980), aff'g 492 F. Supp. 212 (S.D.N.Y. 1980) (finding no evidence of discriminatory intent in the closure of Harlem's Sydenham Hospital. Again, despite disproportionate inconvenience to minority patients, closure of a St. Louis hospital was also upheld, because projections showed that the overall healthcare in the city would be improved. Jackson v. Conway, 620 F.2d 680 (8th Cir. 1980), aff'g 476 F. Supp. 896 (E.D. Mo. 1979) (upholding the closure of the Homer G. Phillips Hospital on the north side of St. Louis, despite a showing that minority residents would be disproportionately inconvenienced). The Eleventh Circuit continues to hear cases

In addition to being deprived of necessary public services, minority neighborhoods have been targeted for unpopular land uses, such as those carrying environmental hazard.[58] The location of highways and mass-transit intensify segregated
housing patterns and actually diminishes access to employment for the poor
and minorities as plants relocate to the suburbs. Nevertheless, city planners
have embraced mass- and rapid-transit as a convenience to their commuting
constituents.[59]

§9.7   THE PRIVATE CLUB EXEMPTION

§9.7.1   Using Title II to Protect Racist Clubs

Section 201(e) of Title II excludes from coverage "a private club or other
establishment not in fact open to the public." As could have been expected, this
provision has encouraged proprietors of hitherto open facilities to form "private
clubs" which, in many instances, have only one membership criterion — race. In
the obvious instances, the courts have branded such schemes as "shams" and have
enjoined the discriminatory policies.[1]

Neighborhood associations that provide facilities such as swimming pools,
tennis courts, and golf courses are not exempt as "private clubs." Courts have
found that under 42 U.S.C.A. §1982, which guarantees property rights of all

---

charging racial discrimination in the distribution of goods and services. In an analysis paralleling that in
Dowdell, the Ammons court identified four factors as "highly probative" of a municipality's intent to
discriminate. Ammons v. Dade City, Fla., 783 F.2d 982 (11th Cir. 1986), aff'g per curiam 594 F. Supp.
1274 (M.D. Fla. 1984). First, the nature and size of the disparity are relevant. Second, if allocation of
greater resources to the white community foreseeably would result in "a deprived black community,"
discriminatory purpose is shown. Third, a history of racial discrimination in the allocation of a
particular resource may be sufficient evidence of discriminatory intent. Finally, if the discriminatory
impact of the municipality's practices is visible in the physical condition of the black community, the
municipality cannot claim lack of knowledge. 594 F. Supp. at 1300; see also Williams v. City of
Dothan, Ala., 818 F.2d 755 (11th Cir. 1987) (applying an intent test, but finding that the city violated
equal protection by contributing a lower percentage of municipal funds to pay for street paving and
sewer improvement projects in black neighborhoods than in predominantly white areas).

58. See Kushner, supra note 39, at 539; see also Jon C. Dubin, From Junkyard to Gentrification: Explicating a Right to Protective Zoning in Low-Income Communities of Color, 77 Minn. L.
Rev. 739 (1993); Symposium: Urban Environmental Justice, 21 Fordham Urb. L.J. 425 (1994).

59. The City of Los Angeles, for example, has poured enormous transportation funds into
commuter rails and suburban buses, while its city buses have deteriorated. At least 90 percent of all
the riders of public transportation in L.A. County ride the bus. In 1994, however approximately 90
percent of the MTA budget went to the commuter rail lines. See the "Bus v. Rail" case brought by
Legal Defense and Educational Fund (LDF) in 1994. Although LDF, working with grass roots
organizations, has won equal protection and Title VI victories, change is slow. In 1998, 79 buses
were monitored, and 75 were still not in compliance with the MTA's promise to reduce overcrowding
to fewer than 15 standees.

§9.7 1. United States v. Richberg, 398 F.2d 523 (5th Cir. 1968) (restaurant transformed into
the "Dixie Dinner Club"); United States v. Johnson Lake, Inc., 312 F. Supp. 1376 (S.D. Ala. 1970)
(previous patronage was the only qualification for membership to formerly all-white recreational
facility); United States v. Northwest La. Restaurant Club, 256 F. Supp. 151 (W.D. La. 1966) (club
consisted of 90 white-owned restaurants formerly operated on a segregated basis).

citizens, a community recreational corporation open to all white residents can not deny membership to or use by black residents.[2]

In spite of judicial diligence in ferreting out public facilities in fact that try to exclude blacks under the private club exemption, hundreds of such operations continue to exist and to discouraging black membership in subtle ways. The few blacks who seek admission are turned away with a "this is a private club" excuse so flimsy that the victims, enraged and demeaned, conclude that litigation to affirm their rights would add farce to what, in any event, is injury no court order can heal.

There are also the thousands of "bona fide" clubs and organizations which, by the grace of congressional exemption, continue policies and practices that deny the personal dignity of all blacks simply because they are not open to all whites. Section 201(e) is not justified by any First Amendment right of privacy or association argument. The fraternal groups that lobbied for this exemption include those with thousands of members. The sponsors of Title II were led to believe that without a private club exemption the whole of Title II might go down to defeat. The private club exemption then stands less as a monument to First Amendment rights than as a still viable and damaging holdover of the *Plessy* philosophy, most frightening in its reminder of the anti-black political power still available to mainstream whites, aided by white elites, when both are determined to protect what they deem are joint interests.

Even the exclusive small club and fraternal groups that arguably may have protected interests in privacy and association may be adequately protected by due process rights enabling them to rebut a discriminatory presumption by showing that the basis for rejecting a black complainant was nonracial.

Although the Supreme Court and lower courts have discussed the requisite features of a private club,[3] the dimensions of the exemption remain undefined.[4] The very presence of §201(e) reflects the congressional intention to permit private clubs to use race as one criterion of membership, but if the black applicant has the

2. Sullivan v. Little Hunting Park, Inc., 396 U.S. 229 (1969); see also Tillman v. Wheaton-Haven Recreational Ass'n, Inc. 410 U.S. 431 (1973) (finding that a swimming pool association comprised of neighbors who joined together to build the pool for use by persons living within a three-quarter-mile radius of the facility could not deny membership to a black family that purchased a home within that area; denial of membership would violate rights protected by both Title II and 42 U.S.C. §1982); Wright v. The Salisbury Club, Ltd., 632 F.2d 309 (4th Cir. 1980) (holding that a club offering sports and dining facilities to all members of a subdivision, as well as to some nonresidents, was not a private club under Title II); Daniel v. Paul also involved allegations rejected by the Court that the facility was a private club.

3. See, e.g., Sullivan v. Little Hunting Park, Inc., 396 U.S. 229, 236 (1969) (indicating that a club must follow some "plan or purpose of exclusiveness"); Daniel v. Paul, 395 U.S. 298 (1969) (indicating that the presence of a profit motivation reflects a public accommodation rather than a club; see also Wright v. Cork Club, 315 F. Supp. 1143, 1153 (S.D. Tex. 1970) (suggesting guidelines for distinguishing a bona fide club from subterfuge: 1. specific screening process for applicants; 2. controlled by the membership; 3. nonprofit, existing for the benefit and pleasure of its members; and 4. directs publicity and newsletters only to its membership); Cornelius v. Benevolent Protective Order of the Elks, 382 F. Supp. 1182 (D. Conn. 1974) (examining the size of club dues and circumstances of the club's origin).

4. Welsh v. Boy Scouts, 993 F.2d 1267 (7th Cir.), cert denied, 510 U.S. 1012 (1993) (concluding that the Boy Scouts are not covered by Title II, and if it were, it would be within the private club exception).

same qualifications as white applicants, including the often necessary sponsorship of one or more members, his rejection would seem to be solely on the basis of race, an inadequate defense under *Sullivan*.[5]

Thus, more than three decades after the enactment of Title II, private clubs continue to occupy an anomalous position in the scheme of public accommodations laws. At the same time, however, present legal action seeking relief under Title II for discrimination in private clubs has become more and more rare. With the state of the law so uncertain, organizations feel little pressure to change discriminatory membership policies until forced to do so by legal action.[6]

§9.7.2 Fighting Exclusion in Private Business Clubs

Efforts to get Congress to distinguish between private social clubs and groups organized primarily for business purposes have gained little support. Business-related groups are largely adjuncts of the marketplace, organized to provide business-related services and funded by dues paid by businesses and employers. The impressive lobbying power of these clubs and the cooling of congressional ardor for civil rights makes it unlikely that even a limited amendment would pass.[7]

In the face of Title II's private club exemption, courts have distinguished business-supported clubs from so-called private clubs in upholding state or municipal laws barring discrimination against women. The Supreme Court has found that under these more expansive antidiscrimination laws the public's interest in affording individuals equal opportunity outweighed the private club members' rights to private association.[8]

In Rotary International v. Rotary Club of Duarte,[9] for example, women invoked state antidiscrimination laws to successfully challenge the exclusionary policies of a large private club whose dining and other social facilities were places

5. See Watson v. Fraternal Order of Eagles, 915 F.2d 235 (6th Cir. 1990) (finding that §1981 reached racial discrimination by a private club that was exempt under Title II).

6. Rotary International v. Rotary Club of Duarte, 481 U.S. 537 (1987). James Durham realized that he faced an uphill battle when he brought a suit after being denied admission into an 80-member fishing, hunting, and boating club. Durham was recommended highly by another member as "the son of Walter Durham" who had worked for the Club since its inception in 1938. But Durham received five negative votes and that, under Club rules, mandated his rejection. The Club rejected only two applicants in its history.

After an almost too-careful consideration of the facts and applicable law, the district court found for Durham. Thirty years ago, such a victory would have seemed another milestone in the long effort to eradicate islands of racial discrimination that stubbornly remained after the enactment of Title II. Unfortunately, the Red Lake Hunting and Fishing Club represents similar groups all over the country whose members' sense of racial superiority requires the exclusion of even a black man whose father has served the club for more than 40 years. Durham v. Red Lake Fishing & Hunting Club, Inc., 666 F. Supp. 954 (W.D. Tex. 1987).

7. See United States v. Glass Menagerie, Inc., 702 F. Supp. 139 (E.D. Ky. 1988) (holding that nonselective use of VIP entrance cards to exclude blacks from a restaurant-nightclub was a violation of rights under Title II).

8. New York State Club Ass'n v. City of New York, 487 U.S. 1 (1988). The Court upheld a New York City law that prohibited clubs from practicing discrimination based on race, creed, or sex, stating that the law did not interfere with club activities or selectivity, except insofar as is necessary to prevent invidious discrimination.

9. 481 U.S. 537 (1987).

where business was conducted. Upholding the California statute that required an international nonprofit corporation of professional men to admit women members,[10] the Supreme Court found that the state statute did not violate the Rotarian's First Amendment right of expressive association.

Even in the face of such progress for women, discrimination continues. Challenges to discriminatory practices, however, may require advocacy that circumvents the confines of legislation, especially when seeking litigation remedies becomes time-consuming, expensive, and futile given the narrowness of the range of clubs to which Title II applies.

One such example is a one-woman crusade to use a nonlitigation strategy to pressure Augusta National, the elite all-male golf course that hosts the Masters tournament, to open its doors to women. Martha Burk, President of the National Council of Women's Organizations, sparked a debate over the club's men-only policy by sending a single letter to the club's chairman, William Johnson, which drew an unexpectedly hostile response.[11]

Johnson, the club's autocratic leader, announced publicly that women members are not in the club's foreseeable future and that the club would not capitulate to Burk's threats. Johnson's reaction fed directly into Burk's strategy. Because the majority of the public either favor or are indifferent about Augusta National's all-male policy, Burk's campaign intentionally targeted reporters, columnists, editorialists, and others whom Burk calls a part of the "thinking class."[12]

While Johnson argued that the private club had the right to selective association, Burk's response framed the discussion in terms of protecting women's basic civil rights.[13] Regardless of the legal viability of her argument under federal protections, it has attracted supportive editorials and op-eds criticizing the policy. A New York Times story suggested that Augusta members settled for a sexist exclusionary policy because "no prominent, powerful business leader can afford to be labeled a racist."[14] The first black golf player was invited to join Augusta National in 1975.

Burk's campaign tried to recruit the support of Tiger Woods, urging him to go as far as boycotting the 2003 tournament. When his silence about the controversy began hurting his image, Woods stated publicly, "Do I want to see a female member? Yes. . . . It would be nice to see everyone have an equal chance to participate, but there's nothing you can do about it."[15]

Woods's response reflects the fact that while he is one of the most popular men of color in the nation, his "acceptance" would be diminished by taking a

---

10. Unrue Civil Rights Act, Cal. Civ. Code Ann. §51 (West 1982). The Unrue Act is a California statute that entitles all persons, regardless of sex, to full and equal accommodations, advantages, facilities, privileges, and services in all business establishments in the state.

11. Peter Boyer, Club Rules: The Antagonists in the Augusta Controversy Are More Complicated Than You'd Think, New Yorker, Feb. 17, 2003, at 78. Bill Saporito, Getting Teed Off: A Women's Group Is Targeting Top CEO's Who Are Members of All-Male Augusta National Golf Club, Time, Sept. 17, 2002, at 50.

12. Id.

13. Id.

14. Id. See also Boyer, supra note 11; Saporito, supra note 11.

15. Lawrence Donegan, Britian's Craven Role in Golf War, Guardian Unltd., Dec. 15, 2002.

strong stand in support of an obviously correct democratic principle. Although the
ultimate result of this pressure is uncertain, it has taken a toll on Augusta National's
reputation. Republican party members seeking political appointments have withdrawn their memberships. Prominent Augusta member, Thomas Wyman, former
CEO of CBS, the network that hosts the Masters each year, resigned in protest of
the policy, calling Johnson "pigheaded" in a New York Times article. And perhaps
most significantly, Augusta National released prospective sponsors from their
contracts for the April 2003 Masters tournament, requiring the club to pick up
the tab.[16] The Augusta National showdown highlights an alternative means for
fighting discrimination in private clubs where legislation has failed women and
minorities. Regardless of the outcome, Burk has already declared victory:
"Augusta National has now become emblematic of sex discrimination."[17]

§9.8   ALTERNATIVE LEGAL APPROACHES TO ELIMINATE
PRIVATE CLUB DISCRIMINATION: STATE ACTION,
TAX SUBSIDIES, AND SECTION 1981

Because Title II does not prohibit all private activity that is discriminatory, civil
rights advocates have devised additional legal arguments to challenge the legality
of such practices. Although these approaches have not been overwhelmingly
successful, the following subsections briefly summarize three major strategies
deployed by advocates to attack discriminatory membership practices: (1) attempting to uncover a significant nexus to state action, (2) challenging the tax exempt
status of discriminating private organizations, and (3) using §1981 to circumvent
Title II's private club exemption.

§9.8.1   State Action and Private Clubs

Advocates have mounted several investigations of discriminating facilities to
uncover significant "state action" in the contacts between the defendants' objectionable policies and the government's insistence on or acquiescence in these
policies. The outcome of this litigation has been as indeterminate as the state action
concept itself. Increasingly subtle forms of discrimination and ever more complex
theories of state involvement have led to divided courts and unsatisfactory results.
From a doctrinal standpoint, the state action cases are, as Professor Charles Black
described them, "a conceptual disaster area."[1]

---

16. Patrick McGeehan, Low Profiles and No-Shows at Golf's Showcase, N.Y. Times, Mar. 30,
2003.
17. Id.
§9.8 1. Charles Black, The Supreme Court, 1966 Term — Foreword: "State Action," Equal
Protection, and California's Proposition 14, 81 Harv. L. Rev. 69, 95 (1967). Professor Laurence Tribe
makes a heroic effort to make order out of chaos by accepting that the state action cases make no

The major post-*Brown* public accommodation cases presenting state action issues illustrate Professor Black's criticism and provide an appropriate prelude for an examination of state action challenges to private clubs whose racially discriminatory policies are beyond the scope of Title II.

In Burton v. Wilmington Parking Authority,[2] the Court held that the leasing of government-owned facilities to private operators is sufficient state involvement to require the operation of the restaurant on a desegregated basis. The Court warned, however, that this decision was based on the "facts and circumstances" of the record and that, in other cases, "sifting and weighing of the circumstances" should determine the true significance of "non-obvious involvement of the state in private actions."

The restaurant's policy was deemed state action because the parking authority had so insulated itself into a position of interdependence with the coffee shop that they had to be regarded as a joint venture between the public authority and private lessee. But in other situations seemingly involving governmental connections as clear and critical as those in *Burton*, the Court has refused to find discriminatory state action. The Court has declined to recognize a constitutional violation when a state merely applies "race neutral" laws or acts in a racially neutral manner even if that conduct has direct discriminatory consequences.[3]

Within an array of less than precise and consistent standards, the Court addressed the issue of state action specifically in the context of a private club. In Moose Lodge No. 107 v. Irvis,[4] the majority in a six-to-three decision concluded that the licensing of Moose Lodge by the Pennsylvania Liquor Control Board did not create a "symbiotic relationship" between state and private entity as in *Burton*,

---

sense. In this way, he explains, it is possible "to construct an 'anti-doctrine,' an analytical framework which, in explaining why various cases differ from one another, paradoxically provides a structure for the solution of state action problems." Laurence Tribe, American Constitutional Law §18-1 (2d ed. 1988).

Professor Tribe's approach is itself complex, but at bottom, he views the basic flaw in the present approach to be the single-minded search by courts for a government actor whenever the state action challenge is raised. This is appropriate, but Professor Tribe warns that the characterization of an actor as private or governmental properly depends upon external symbols no less than upon the government's internal criteria for identifying agents as its own. In addition, courts must ask the question "whether federal or state law can validly distribute authority between governmental and private actors as it purports to do." Id.

2. 365 U.S. 715 (1961).

3. See Evans v. Abney, 396 U.S. 435 (1970). In the context of public accommodations, Palmer v. Thompson serves as such an example. 403 U.S. 217 (1971). This case grew out of a 1962 district court order to desegregate all public recreational facilities of Jackson. Although the city complied with more facilities, the pools were not one of them. The Court upheld a decision of the City of Jackson, Mississippi, to close rather than desegregate five public swimming pools. Justice Black, writing for the majority, conceded that closing public pools was state action but reasoned that there was no equal protection problem because both blacks and whites were deprived of swimming facilities. Although this opinion has been widely criticized, it foreshadowed the civil rights decisions of the past two decades, which emphasize neutral impact as an affirmative defense to equal protection claims. In dissent, Justice Douglas observed that "abolition of a designated public service becomes a device for perpetuating a segregated way of life." Justice White, joined in his dissent by Justices Brennan and Marshall, stressed the state action involved in closing public pools: "The fact is that closing the pools is an expression of official policy that Negroes are unfit to associate with whites."

4. 407 U.S. 163 (1972).

so as to hold the Lodge's policy of refusing service to black guest of members unconstitutional.

Irvis, a respected state legislator, did not dispute the right of private clubs to choose members on a racially exclusive basis, but relying on Burton, he argued that the licensing process involving extensive regulation and control by the Liquor Control Board constituted adequate state involvement to render his exclusion illegal. Speaking for the Court, Rehnquist said that the mere receipt of a state service could not be enough to constitute state action.

In a sharply worded dissent, Justice Douglas found that the complete and pervasive nature of the state regulation, coupled with the limited number of liquor licenses available, created state action. Justices Brennan and Douglas, in a separate dissent, agreed that the pervasive state regulation "intertwines the state with the operation of the Lodge bar in a significant way [and] lend[s] [the State's] authority to the sordid business of racial discrimination." Justice Marshall joined both dissents.[5]

With the Supreme Court conveying so many signals in state action challenges to discriminatory practices in private facilities receiving government subsidies, lower courts have found themselves reaching different results on fairly similar factual situations. Yet, for the most part, state action has proven an uncertain means to breaking down such discrimination barriers.

§9.8.2   Private Clubs and Public Tax Subsidies

The cases proceeding from *Burton* and *Moose Lodge* trace a wavering line between what constitutes a "private club," and what "state action" creates liability under Title II. Rather than directly attacking discriminatory membership policies, proponents of open membership have attempted to pry open club doors by eliminating tax benefits conferred upon these organizations.

The most frequently cited of these cases is McGlotten v. Connally.[6] In McGlotten, a black male who was denied membership in Local Lodge 142 of the Benevolent and Protective Order of the Elks (BPOE) sought a permanent injunction of federal tax benefits under the Internal Revenue Code to BPOE and other social clubs with racially discriminatory membership policies. Under the IRC, the Elks were exempt from the payment of income taxes and contributions made to the organization were tax deductible.

The court found for the plaintiff arguing that granting tax benefits to the Elks represented government approval and encouragement of private discrimination

---

5. Several weeks after the Supreme Court's *Moose Lodge* decision, the Pennsylvania Supreme Court, acting on the appeal of an order by the state's Human Relations Commission, held that the Lodge was a place of public accommodation for guests subject to the state's antidiscrimination law. Commonwealth v. Loyal Order of Moose Lodge 107, 448 Pa. 451, 294 A.2d 594 (1972). The court explained that its law exempted private club membership and guests on a racial basis, but that the lodge for years had opened its dining room and bar facilities to public organizations for banquets and dinners on a nondiscriminatory basis, and had thereby diminished its status as a purely private club. An appeal to the Supreme Court was dismissed for lack of a substantial federal question. Loyal Order of Moose Lodge No. 107 v. Pennsylvania Human Relations Comm'n, 409 U.S. 1052 (1972).

6. 338 F. Supp. 448 (D.C. Cir. 1972).

that was also contrary to the strong national policy against providing federal financial support to those practicing discrimination.[7] Distinguishing *Moose Lodge* (see §9.8.1), the court noted that because a "symbiotic relationship" is created by tax exemptions, which did not exist for state liquor licenses in *Moose Lodge*, the state could not "effectively abdicate" its duty to uphold the Fourteenth Amendment.[8]

Although several courts have applied something like the "encouragement" test,[9] the question of whether state tax exemptions "encourage" discrimination,

7. The *McGlotten* court further recognized the following: "We have no illusion that our holding today will put an end to racial discrimination or significantly dismantle the social and economic barriers that may be more subtle, but are surely no less destructive. Individuals may retain their own beliefs, however odious or offensive. But the Supreme Court had declared that the Constitution forbids the Government from supporting and encouraging such beliefs. By eliminating one more "nonobvious involvement of the State in private conduct," we obey the Court's command to quarantine racism."

8. *McGlotten*, citing Burton v. Wilmington Parking Auth., 365 U.S. 715, 888-889 (1961).

For a highly critical analysis of the *McGlotten* decision, see Boris Bittker & Kaufman, Taxes and Civil Rights: "Constitutionalizing" the Internal Revenue Code, 82 Yale L.J. 51 (1972). Basically, the authors, while sympathetic to the goal of eliminating governmental involvement in private discrimination, feel that the court failed to fully comprehend the complexities of the tax structure. In addition to serious technical failings, the authors fear that the *McGlotten* decision represents poor policy. They concede that the objectives and membership qualifications of many groups and clubs are invidious but warn that

> "a governmental program to discover and eradicate them necessarily imposes social costs; a society that tries to punish every instance of man's inhumanity to man may lose its humanity while crusading against the enemy. The 'right of free association' and 'the right of privacy' . . . are labels recognizing the social value of membership organizations and the dangers inherent in governmental controls. Like free speech and the privilege against self-incrimination, however, the rights of free association and privacy cannot be reserved for the noblest among us.
>
> "If full sway is given to the *McGlotten* theory the tax allowances are equivalent to direct grants of public funds and hence impose constitutional obligations on the recipient, no one will be immune. As we have pointed out, the Internal Revenue Code is a pudding with plums for everyone. In theory, the 'tax subsidy' theory does not constrict the right of free association or the right to privacy, because the tax allowances can be renounced by the recipient or eliminated by Congress. But the former remedy, by distinguishing among associations by reference to their ideologies, would make some pay a high price for their enjoyment of the rights in question. On the other hand, the congressional remedy of repeal, resting on the dubious premise that there is a 'constitutionally neutral' definition of taxable income, would be costly to all associations.
>
> "The *McGlotten* court sought to minimize these consequences by picking and choosing among tax subsidies. But its distinctions, in our opinion, are unworkable and, as adumbrated by the court, impose or withhold constitutional obligations in a puzzling fashion."

Unlike the state action standards under the equal protection clause, application of which depends upon a review of appropriate facts, the article concludes that the tax subsidy theory — even "as watered down" by *McGlotten* — "turns on technical niceties of tax law that are unrelated to the impact of the organization's behavior on the persons excluded by its membership rules or other restrictive practices. It would, therefore, be a mistake to use this theory to 'constitutionalize' the Internal Revenue Code." 82 Yale L. Rev. 86-87.

9. Pitts v. Wisconsin Dept. of Revenue, 333 F. Supp. 662 (E.D. Wis. 1971) (finding that a property tax exemption to a segregated fraternal order was significant state action in violation of the Fourteenth Amendment); see also New York City Jaycees, Inc. v. United States Jaycees, Inc., 377 F. Supp. 481 (S.D.N.Y. 1974) (granting a preliminary injunction against the expulsion of the local chapter for admitting women, finding state action in the control exercised over the Jaycees through

thereby creating a symbiotic relationship with private actors, has not been conclusively determined.[10]

It is not certain whether the Supreme Court would have distinguished the liquor license involved in the *Moose Lodge* case from the tax exemptions involved here, but perhaps there is a clue in Bob Jones University v. Simon.[11] The Internal Revenue Service announced in 1970 that it would no longer allow tax-exempt status under §501(c)(3) to private schools maintaining racially discriminatory admissions policies, and would no longer treat contributions to such schools as tax-deductible.

Bob Jones University is devoted to the teaching and propagation of fundamentalist religious beliefs that include a ban on interracial relationships. In 1971, the school informed the IRS that it had no intention of admitting blacks and filed suit to enjoin revocation of its tax-exempt status. The Supreme Court affirmed that the IRS decision is not enjoinable under the Code unless it is clear that under no circumstances could the government ultimately prevail. Noting the decisions in cases like McGlotten v. Connally and Green v. Connally, the Court concluded that no such finding was possible in this case.[12]

The denial of tax exempt status will not end discriminatory practices, but it does make such policies more apparent and costly. Even though the Court has not set clear parameters for removing tax exemption status for discriminatory practices of private organizations, these cases and IRS regulations send a message that such exclusion will not, at the very least, benefit from federal subsidization.

§9.8.3 Private Facilities and Section 1981

Title 42 U.S.C. §1981 provides in part that: "[a]ll persons within the jurisdiction of the United States shall have the same right in every State . . . to make and enforce contracts . . . as is enjoyed by white citizens. . . ."

On its face, §1981 would seem available to all victims of racial discrimination in groups or accommodations upon a showing that, but for race, they would have

---

the federal funding process); but see Junior Chamber of Commerce of Rochester, Inc. v. Jaycees, 495 F.2d 883 (10th Cir. 1974) (holding that the federal organization could expel the local chapter for admitting women, because the expulsion policies did not relate directly to the group's administration of federal funds in a variety of national programs).

10. But see Cornelius v. Benevolent Protective Order of the Elks, 382 F. Supp. 1182 (D. Conn. 1974) (dismissing prayer for revocation of state tax exemptions, and redistribution of $11 million from the Elks and Moose Lodges to the class of black men the plaintiff claimed to represent).

An alternate means of attacking discrimination in private organizations is suggested in Hawthorne v. Kenbridge Recreation Ass'n Inc., 341 F. Supp. 1382 (E.D. Va. 1972) (holding that a rural recreational association that received a direct federal loan must consider membership applications without regard to race, creed, or national origin, citing Title VI of the Civil Rights Act of 1964, 42 U.S.C. §2000(d) and 7 U.S.C. §1926 (permitting loans to nonprofit corporations for recreational development by rural residents). The court determined that Congress intended to support public not private, groups for uses that would not further racial segregation.

11. 416 U.S. 725 (1974).

12. In 1982, Bob Jones University and Goldsboro Christian Schools, Inc., both sought a refund of unemployment taxes paid, and the Internal Revenue Service counterclaimed for back taxes. In an opinion that addressed both cases, the Supreme Court found that both schools had been denied tax-exempt status, and it declared them liable for these ordinary taxes. Bob Jones Univ. v. United States 461 U.S. 574 (1983).

been admitted. While specifically excluding from its decision some of the most interesting aspects of §1981's scope, the Supreme Court in Runyon v. McCrary[13] did utilize the provision to narrow somewhat the ambit of what had been considered private discrimination shielded from law.

In Runyon, the parents of black children made applications for admission to private schools in response to brochures mailed to "resident" and advertisements directed to the general public. Suits were filed under §1981 after the applications were denied because of the children's race. Based on the authority of Jones v. Alfred H. Mayer, Co.,[14] Justice Stewart found that the plaintiff's rights under §1981 were violated by the private school's racially based restrictions. Application of §1981 did not violate defendant's rights of privacy because these rights are subject to reasonable government regulation, and the Constitution places no value on discrimination.[15]

Justice Stewart indicated that Runyon only presented the question of racial discrimination in schools, not by social organizations. The case, he said, did not raise the issue of whether the "private club" exemption of §201(e) operates to narrow §1981. But he suggested that personal contractual relationships that are based on the close association of parties, or that are the foundation of a close association, reflect a "purpose of exclusiveness" other than racial discrimination. These purposes "would invoke associational rights long respected."

The preceding cases most of which, significantly, are decades old, suggest that established private clubs, based largely on racial exclusiveness, are not being challenged and, thus unless younger members push for at least a few black members, are continuing to practice discrimination with impunity. Private schools, however, may have difficulty barring blacks if they seek students from the public at large, as most private schools must do.

In the Civil Rights Act of 1991,[16] Congress declared that it fully intends for §1981 to reach nongovernmental as well as governmental discrimination.

---

13. 427 U.S. 160 (1976).

14. 392 U.S. 409 (1968).

15. "The prohibition of racial discrimination that interferes with the making and enforcement of contracts for private educational services furthers goals closely analogous to those served by §1982's guarantee that 'a dollar in the hands of a Negro will purchase the same thing as a dollar in the hands of a white man.' " Runyon v. McCrary, 427 U.S. at 179, citing Jones v. Alfred H. Mayer, Co., 392 U.S. 443 (1968).

As to freedom of association, the First Amendment right to "engage in association for the advancement of beliefs and ideas . . ." recognized in NAACP v. Alabama, 357 U.S. 449 (1958), enables the white parents to send their children to schools that promote the belief that racial segregation is desirable, but the right does not include the practice of excluding racial minorities, because, as indicated in Norwood v. Harrison, 413 U.S. 455, 469 (1973), "the Constitution . . . places no value on discrimination." Invidious private discrimination may be protected, but it has never been accorded affirmative constitutional protections.

As to parental rights, the First Amendment recognizes the parents' right to send their children to a private school, Meyer v. Nebraska, 262 U.S. 390 (1923), and Pierce v. Society of Sisters, 268 U.S. 510 (1925), and application of §1981 does not infringe on these rights.

As to rights of privacy, application of §1981 will implicate parental interests similar to those protected in Roe v. Wade, 410 U.S. 113 (1973), and Griswold v. Connecticut, 381 U.S. 479 (1965), but while parents have a constitutional right to select private schools that offer specialized instruction, they have no constitutional right to provide their children with private school education unfettered by reasonable government regulation. Wisconsin v. Yoder, 406 U.S. 205 (1972).

16. Pub. L. No. 102-166, 105 Stat. 1071 (1991).

The Act added a new subsection (c) that flatly declares "[R]ights protected by this section are protected against impairment by nongovernmental discrimination and impairment under color of State law."[17] This new section in the 1991 Act was enacted under Congress's Thirteenth Amendment powers, and specifically responded to the Court's decision in Patterson v. McLean Credit Union.[18] Although Congress expressly intended the 1991 Act to expand the scope of civil rights statutes in order to provide adequate protection for victims of discrimination, its effectiveness has been limited. Section 1981 has been applied in a variety of contexts;[19] however, proving intentional discrimination remains a high bar for those challenging discrimination.[20]

Without attempting to give this area of race law a priority it may not deserve, it should be profitable to review the scope of private discrimination still permitted by the law, trying at the same time to understand how conduct which Congress and the courts have found deeply hurtful and humiliating to blacks can be equated with concepts of liberty, privacy, and freedom of association. That they were, and are, conveys a message with too much clarity to ignore.

The 40-year history of efforts to implement the public accommodations provisions of Title II and to supplement the judicially revived language in §1981 were not — as was generally believed during the course of those efforts — a sure-fire antidote to racially biased policies. Rather, the decisions in the Jackson, Mississippi swimming-pool closing case, *Palmer*, the insulation from state action concepts of the private club in *Moose Lodge No. 107*, represent devices to retain remnants of racial exclusivity.

Today, lower status whites, while without the law's protection, can — and often do — discriminate against black patrons. Middle- and upper-class whites sometimes rely on the racially insulating potential of "privacy," but generally find that economic status is sufficient to insure that no more than a few "token" blacks gain access to facilities that retain the prestige of color exclusivity. This is all very sad and not less so because it is far from clear that the current trend is not a retreat toward more segregation, even though current barriers rely more on economic than openly racial factors. The remedies, aimed at controlling what is assumed a nonconforming, biased few, are thus rendered relatively ineffective because they ignore the temptations and tendencies to exclude or otherwise discriminate that are obviously deeply ingrained, widespread, and incapable of easy analysis on grounds of racial animus or economic

17. 42 U.S.C. §1981; see Wicks v. Mississippi State Employment Serv., 41 F.3d 991 (5th Cir. 1995).

18. 491 U.S. 164 (1989) (applying §1981 to a private discrimination issue based primarily on stare decisis).

19. See, e.g., Rivers v. Roadway Express, Inc., 511 U.S. 298 (1994) (holding that §1981 is not limited to employment; it covers all contracts); Homan v. Resading, 963 F. Supp. 485 (E.D. Pa. 1997) (plaintiffs, interracial couple, stated a §1982 claim based on city's enforcement of ordinances against them that were not enforced against white property owners in a similar manner; survived motion to dismiss); Bermudez Zenon v. Restaurant Compostela, Inc., 790 F. Supp. 41 (D.P.R. 1992); Cook v. Twin Oaks Country Club, 122 F. Supp. 1064 (W.D. Mo. 2000); Crawford v. Willow Oaks Country Club, Inc., 66 F. Supp. 2d 767 (E.D. Va. 1999) (holding that private membership club exemptions of Title VII and Title II did not apply to §1981 in the context of employment discrimination).

20. See National Ass'n of Gov't Employees v. City Pub. Serv. Bd., 40 F.3d 698 (5th Cir. 1994) (proof of intentional discrimination is an essential element of §1981).

advantage. The study of discrimination by new car dealers against black and white female buyers summarized in the next section, and the discussion of mortgage discrimination, exemplify the depth of the phenomenon.

§9.9 RACIAL DISCRIMINATION IN THE MARKETPLACE: A FOCUS ON CAR SALES AND THE HOUSING MARKET

§9.9.1 Retail Car Sales

Even seasoned civil rights veterans have been profoundly disturbed by the discovery that white males seeking to purchase a car receive significantly better prices than do blacks. Even before the enactment of the civil rights protections in the 1960s, most blacks assumed that whatever their vulnerability to racial prejudice when they sought a job, a place to live, or a service in a facility open to the public, they could at least purchase a car without the burden of color either barring them at the door or disadvantaging them in the bargaining process. This assumption was likely always naive, but Professor Ian Ayres's Chicago-based research destroys it entirely.[1] In his groundbreaking research, he has demonstrated that retail car dealerships systematically offered substantially better deals on price to whites than they did to blacks.

Professor Ayres's original study found that automobile retailers react differently to black than to white testers of both genders who utilize a uniform negotiation strategy. A second, broader audit confirms the pricing discrimination, but the ordering is changed. While in the initial study the final offers to black females were $500 higher than to black males, the later study indicates that black males received offers that were $686 higher than those made to black females. In addition, the disparate treatment of white females is less significant: The first study suggested that white females received a final offer 40 percent higher than the one made to white males; in the second study, this difference was a statistically insignificant 2 percent. Because of the limited scope of the first study, it is difficult to determine whether variations in the results of the two studies were caused by Ayres's method or by changes in the car dealers' bargaining strategies. The second study, however, may be considered authoritative. It involved 38 testers, including 5 black males, 7 black females, and 8 white females, who negotiated for more than 400 automobiles at 242 dealerships. The testers entered new car dealerships separately and bargained to buy a new car, using a uniform negotiation strategy (detailing script, language, dress, and responses). Testers even arrived in similar rented cars. After the initial offer, testers followed a uniform bargaining script, using either a "split-the-difference" strategy or a "fixed concession" strategy.

Professor Ayres analyzes several possible causes of discrimination within the parameters of game theory. He concludes that the evidence supports several possible explanations for price discrimination.

§9.9 1. Ian Ayres, Further Evidence of Discrimination in New Car Negotiations and Estimates of Its Cause, 94 Mich. L. Rev. 109 (1995); Ian Ayres, Fair Driving: Gender and Race Discrimination in Retail Car Negotiations, 104 Harv. L. Rev. 817 (1991).

A.   Animus-Based Theories

Sellers may have higher costs of bargaining with a disfavored group, or they may wish to disadvantage a disfavored group. The results of Ayres's second study do not provide strong support for the theory that racial animus causes the disparate treatment of black buyers. Contrary to what one might expect,[2] the race of the salesperson, dealership owner, and the other customers had no effect on the treatment received by the black and white test buyers. The one exception was that black women received worse treatment from black salesmen.

B.   Statistical Discrimination Theories

Stemming from a seller's desire to maximize profits, discrimination occurs because of rational statistical inferences about average types of customers among different groups. Sellers may believe that a disfavored group has higher costs of bargaining or higher reservation prices. By charging high-risk groups a higher mark-up, the dealership seeks to cover its default risk with a higher average profit per customer.

Salespersons seem to exercise statistical discrimination when they "qualify the buyer," that is, estimate how much the buyer is willing or able to pay. This is done by direct observation and through the answers to questions about the customer's experiences with other dealerships and other cars. Sellers may perceive that race and gender affect buyers' costs of searching for a car and for information about the car market.

Studies find many of these statistical inferences irrational and based on erroneous stereotypes. But if market experience does not teach sellers that their preconceptions are false, disparate treatment that is inequitable and inefficient will persist. The uniformity of discrimination in different neighborhoods suggests that salespeople may bring many of their racial conceptions to the job and that these beliefs are not learned through their bargaining experiences. Ayres suggests that dealers' behavior is motivated largely by informational disparities among different groups. Manufacturers also prefer a sales process that allows their dealers to get the most money from consumers.

§9.9.2   Discrimination Lawsuits Pressure Car Industry

Six African Americans filed a lawsuit alleging discriminatory treatment when they were denied credit entirely when they shopped for cars at two dealerships in Chicago and Midlothian, Illinois. One executive used a racial slur to drive away one potential customer. Additionally, 70 cars purchased from the Chicago Marquette Chrysler Jeep dealership were repossessed because of the race of the

---

2. John Yinger, for example, concludes that, in the housing market, discrimination against blacks is motivated by realtors' perceptions that other renters or house buyers dislike having a black neighbor. See John Yinger, Measuring Racial Discrimination with Fair Housing Audits: Caught in the Act?, 76 Am. Econ. Rev. 881 (1986).

purchaser. Many of the customers, according to the lawsuit, were not behind on payments. A boycott of the dealerships has been threatened if management is not fired and such practices do not cease.[3]

Similar lawsuits have been filed against the financing arms of Toyota, Ford, General Motors, and Nissan.[4] A study accompanying one lawsuit looked at over 300,000 car loans financed by Nissan dealers from March 1993 to September 2000. The study, currently the largest statistical analysis of car loan data examining racial patterns, showed that black customers in 33 states where over one-third of blacks reside consistently paid more for cars than whites, regardless of their credit histories. In the more populous states, the black-white gap was substantial. In New York, the gap was $405; in Texas, it was $364; and in Florida, it was $533.

None of the lawsuits allege that the lenders are intentionally discriminating by race, but as a Justice Department brief for the plaintiffs argues, lenders can be held responsible for the actions of the dealers. The argument calls into question an industry-wide practice that allows car dealers rather than lenders to determine the ultimate interest rates offered to customers. The lender provides a rate based on income and credit history, and the dealer can mark up these rates and even bump consumers into higher lending credit tiers without the consumer's knowledge of the disparity. As a result, black consumers are often informed that they do not qualify for advertised discount financing that attracted them into the dealership in the first place.

One study conducted by Mark Cohen, a professor at Vanderbilt University, presents the significance of the markups. Two female customers from Louisiana qualified to borrow in the same first credit tier. The white female was given the preferential interest rate, while the black consumer received a 1 percentage point dealer markup, resulting in higher monthly payments even though she borrowed less than her white counterpart.[5] As this example illustrates, blacks, according to the study, were twice as likely to receive dealer markups, blacks paid more overall than whites, and when black consumers fell into the top credit tier, they were less likely to be offered lender's special preferential rates.[6]

Under a proposed settlement of the 1998 lawsuits from Tennessee and Florida by black and Hispanic car buyers, Nissan's financing arm has agreed to stop marking up loan rates offered to qualified minority buyers and agreed to inform car buyers their interest rate may be negotiable. NMAC would also pay $5,000 to

3. DaimlerChrysler Threatened with Boycott, Chi. Sun-Times, Feb. 28, 2003.

4. Diana B. Henriques, Review of Nissan Car Loans Finds That Blacks Pay More, N.Y. Times, July 4, 2001, at A1.

5. Id. According to Professor Cohen, dealer markup is a big-ticket issue for the industry, and the new Nissan data show why. He estimates that Nissan's share of the dealer markup paid by black consumers alone since 1990 was more than $210 million. Based on fee-splitting formulas in place during much of that time, the dealers' aggregate share would have been roughly three times that amount.

6. Id. In looking at the Cohen data, Professor Ayres pointed out that the seemingly race-neutral policies of allowing less of a markup on individuals falling in the top tier or on shorter loans also have discriminatory effects. Whites are more likely to fall in the top credit tier and therefore avoid the largest dealer markups. In addition, black customers tend to borrow for slightly longer terms than whites, which can also contribute to larger markups. Such statistical analysis supporting legal arguments provides a vehicle for exposing and challenging discriminatory practices in the market place.

$20,000 to each plaintiff named in the suit plus $1 million to America Saves, a Washington-based consumer agency.[7]

The lawsuits and academic studies have intensified nationwide advocacy to eliminate discrimination in car sales. California passed a Car Buyers Bill of Rights, which took effect on July 1, 2006 with hopes to curb the abuses that have affected California car buyers.[8] However, research already shows widespread non-compliance with the new law.[9] Law and economics scholars suggest that people will tend to negotiate whenever resources are misallocated. Common experience tells us that many people in the United States are averse to bargaining, largely because of the great inefficiency in the way cars are marketed. The studies of car sales challenge the efficiency of car negotiations and expose the pervasive discrimination against blacks and women that characterize them.

§9.9.3   Ensnaring Consumers with Tricks of the Trade

Blacks are the special targets of car dealers, but the unscrupulous among the latter group are quite willing to use what Consumer Reports describes as the "Tricks of the Trade" to maximize profit in their dealings with white as well as black and Latino customers.[10] While possible explanations are discussed above, it

---

7. Nissan OKs Lending Changes, Orlando Sentinel, Feb. 21, 2003, at C3.

8. See Car Buyer's Bill of Rights — Important Facts about a New Law That Substantially Impacts the Purchase of New and Used Vehicles, available at http://www.dmv.ca.gov/pubs/brochures/fast_facts/ffvr35.htm.

9. See Looking under the Hood — Preliminary Report (March 7, 2007), available at http://www.carconsumers.com/CBBR_PrelimReport.pdf.

10. Tricks of the Trade: Resist These Dealer Ploys That Squeeze You for More Cash Than You Should Pay, Consumer Rep., Apr. 2003, at 17. Mirroring discriminatory dealer markups detailed above, the vast majority of car dealership schemes perpetrated on car buyers regardless of their race distort financing, which translates directly into larger profits. Rather than deceptively marking up interest rates, a dealer may sell consumers a car on the spot at a good credit rating, only to call a few days later explaining that they did not qualify for the low financing rates. The actual contract price was subject to financing approval, which, the dealer points out, is in the fine print of the contract. The consumer is informed that the new rate must be paid or the contract is breached.

The fine print often reveals misleading offers, which go unnoticed until the contract is signed and the consumer drives the car home. Take, for example, the program that many dealerships widely advertise as a "0-0-0" financing deal. Consumers believe they are buying a car for a steal, with a 0 percent interest rate and without making any payments, including a down payment, for an entire year. In reality, this "deal" often requires car buyers to make up a year's worth of payments in one lump sum at an extremely high interest rate at the end of the first year. Ultimately, the payments greatly exceed the car's sticker price. Another "special offer" urges consumers to buy a new car by guaranteeing that the dealership will assume the consumer's current car debt or lease. The truth is that the dealer simply incorporates the cost of the old car loan into the new purchase price.

Aside from financing problems, car contracts can also contain mandatory arbitration clauses, which consumers are unaware of until a problem arises. By requiring any dispute between a customer and dealer to be decided through arbitration, the dealerships limit a consumer's available legal remedies.

More generally, dealers can also ratchet up prices through simple sales pitch strategies. Rather than negotiating the overall cost of the car, the dealer asks how much the consumer is hoping to pay monthly. The dealer then adjusts the term of the car loan and the interest rate to reach that monthly figure without having to discuss outright the overall price of the car or disclose markups. Consumers who see these payments as reasonable because they are within their expected range fail to see the exorbitant profit the dealer is making.

remains unclear why blacks and Latino customers are so frequently the special marks of salespeople, including those of their race? There is likely no definitive answer, but it is not difficult that their status in the society, the damaged level of confidence and self-assurance based on that status, leads to a readiness to accept whatever the salesperson tells them. At least, he or she is willing to sell the car without racial hassles.

Additionally, dealers may falsely tell consumers that their bank requires any car buyer to purchase a three-year extension on the warranty. Although the practice is illegal in some states, it is difficult to prove if it is not in writing. Dealers may also include expensive amenities into the cost of the car without prior mention. Costs for fabric protection, rustproofing, or the addition of a Vehicle Identification Number (VIN) on car windows may total over $1,000 even though they cost the dealer only $90.

To protect themselves from dealer markups, some consumers secure financing from banks or credit unions other than those offered by the dealership. Despite the fact that dealers have no uniform policy against such arrangements, some dealers respond by refusing this financing to protect their profit margin. Dealerships will also coerce consumers unnecessarily into mandatory credit checks even after financing is secured through outside lenders.

The bottom line is that these car dealer ploys put the onus on consumers to resist being cheated. Consumers must be highly informed about their car purchases — informed of manufacturing prices, their credit rating, and competitive financing options. They must read the fine print and strike needless charges or a mandatory arbitration clause. Ultimately, though, the consumer's best leverage may be a willingness to walk out when dealers refuse to back down.

Providing the details on new car dealer trickery in a race, racism text serves as a dramatic illustration that the racial discrimination that dramatically plagues blacks in many areas also disadvantages whites in less visible but hardly less damaging forms. Even so, there is a question as to why blacks and Latino buyers are particularly vulnerable to tactics intended to exploit them and unfairly enrich sellers.

Chapter 10

The Parameters of Racial Protest

§10.1 INTRODUCTION

As this edition enters the publication process, the media is reporting that thousands of lawyers in Lahore and other cities are demonstrating against the emergency rule imposed by the Pakistani president, General Pervez Musharraf, who has suspended the Constitution, dissolved the Supreme Court and the four provincial High Courts, and silenced privately owned television news channels. According to one report, "At one point, lawyers and police officers clashed in a pitched battle, with lawyers standing on the roof of the High Court throwing stones at the police below, and the police hurling them back. Some of the lawyers were bleeding from the head, and some passed out in clouds of tear gas.[1]

Adding to the chaos in Pakistan, Benazir Bhutto, a prominent woman who was an opposition leader and twice serving prime minister, was assassinated by a suicide bomber in December 2007.[2] Returning from exile, she was again seeking to return to politics, running for prime minister. She was a "politician who presented herself on public platforms as the standard-bearer for Pakistan's impoverished masses, for civil liberties and for an unfettered democracy."[3] Hearing of her death, protests erupted.

Musharraf was trounced in the Parliamentary elections in February 2008. Some view the defeat as a response to Bhutto's assassination and others "said the vote was a protest against government policies and the rise in terrorism."[4] The election results leave more questions than answers about Pakistan's democratic future.

During the 1960s, civil rights protestors in this country generally observed the rules of nonviolence, but often met with quite violent responses by both police and citizens. Peaceful protests turned violent, particularly in the wake of Dr. Martin

---

§10.1 1. Jane Perlez & David Rohde, Pakistan Attempts to Crush Protests by Lawyers, N.Y. Times, Nov. 6, 2007.

2. John F. Burns, Benazir Bhutto, 54, Who Weathered Pakistan's Political Storm for 3 Decades, Dies, N.Y. Times, Dec. 28, 2007.

3. Id.

4. Carlotta Gall & Jane Perlez, Pakistanis Deal Severe Defeat to Musharraf in Election, N.Y. Times, Feb. 19, 2008.

Luther King's murder, and the harsh response of police and courts were on the order of those utilized by Pakistani police and authorities. Generally, civil rights lawyers have not engaged in such direct confrontations. This chapter examines the self-help methods blacks have utilized to gain access to opportunities closed or limited by reason of race, reviewing the degree to which the law has either protected or condemned these activities. The extent and character of this protection and the limits set by law can then be profitably measured against the reactions, surveyed in Chapter 5, of legal authorities to illegal and often violent activities by whites intended to deny or discourage blacks from exercising their rights. The juxtaposition of the legal rules developed in black protest litigation and those precedents evolved from cases in which blacks were victims of summary punishment may raise questions as to why courts seem more alarmed at the disruptive potential of a relatively peaceful protest by blacks than they are with all but the most shocking acts of intentional violence perpetrated by whites as a means of denying the civil rights of blacks. Perhaps this seeming disparity in concern can be explained by the fact that the law tends to treat gingerly any protest activity that exceeds the bounds of speech clearly protected under the First Amendment. On the other hand, the very limited range of statutory authority available for prosecuting or obtaining civil remedies against those charged with violating the civil rights of blacks may have diluted what otherwise might have been a more purposeful judicial response to those violations. If that is the case, then that judicial limitation should perhaps become the basis for affording greater protection to efforts by blacks to protest and through self-help activity to achieve the protection against societal discrimination that the courts are unable and the political structure is unwilling to provide. This, of course, has not happened. Indeed, First Amendment protection has been more available to those whose hostile expressions and actions toward minorities are challenged as being in violation of regulations and laws punishing "hate speech."

Given the measures the federal government has taken in the wake of the 9/11 attacks and the Iraqi war to protect security, actions reviewed in §10.9, there is reason to wonder whether the series of peaceful protests mounted across the country by U.S. lawyers supporting their Pakistani counterparts might be as appropriately focused on the devaluation of the rule of law in this country.

§10.2   THE LAWFUL PROTESTOR'S DILEMMA

Every constitutional law student knows that judicial determinations of what "free speech" activities are protected under the First Amendment resemble the shifting sands of a desert. Attempting to predict in advance how courts will rule requires consideration of many factors that are not likely to be acknowledged in the decisions. Blacks and other minority groups in this country, though, lacking economic and political power, and subject to continuing — if increasingly subtle — racial discrimination, have often turned to protests in one form or another as the only available mechanism for airing their grievances. And during each "direct action" campaign, civil rights leaders have wrestled with the dilemma of how to structure demonstrations that will dramatize their plight to the majority community so as to spur action that will improve rather than worsen conditions for the black community. Protest actions clearly entitled to protection, such as a non-disruptive speech at an appropriate time and place, a petition properly filed with a governmental body, or a parade that conforms with all rules and regulations, are likely to gain little attention when they are not ignored entirely. On the other hand, more vigorous protests — those that cannot be ignored — are likely to contravene either existing laws or laws that are promptly enacted or interpreted to transform what was arguably legal protest into criminal activity. In addition to this risk, there is general uncertainty as to whether or not protest activity actually helps to bring about racial reform. Indeed, there is a tendency by those in policymaking positions to separate reform from protest activity even when the latter was fairly clearly the major motivation for the former. Thus, university officials have seen nothing inconsistent in proceeding with disciplinary action against student protesters at the same time as steps are taken to reform the conditions about which the protest was mounted.

One would have thought that when then Federal Judge A. Leon Higginbotham, serving as a member of the National Commission on the Causes and Prevention of Violence in 1969, indicated that the sit-ins and other nonviolent protests paved the way for the elimination of Jim Crow practices throughout the South, he would have been stating the obvious. But he was speaking as one of the minority in a seven-to-six decision by the Commission when he wrote:

> Recent advances in the field of civil rights have not come about and could never have come about solely through judicial tests "by one individual" while all others in the silent black majority waited for the ultimate constitutional determination.
>
> Rather, the major impetus for the Civil Rights Acts of 1957, 1960, 1964 and 1965, which promised more equal access to the opportunities of our society, resulted from the determination, the spirit and the nonviolent commitment of the many who continually challenge the constitutionality of racial discrimination and awakened the national conscience.[1]

The Commission majority had expressed the view that the constitutionality of a law could be effectively challenged in a test case brought by one individual or a small group. "While the judicial test is in progress," the majority urged, "all other dissenters should abide by the law involved until it is declared unconstitutional." And yet, without the drama and confrontation of direct action protest, the basic mandate of *Brown,* ending the "separate but equal" doctrine of Plessy v. Ferguson, might never have been implemented. Certainly, there had been little voluntary compliance from 1954 until the sit-in era in the early 1960s. So, while the majority of the President's Commission on the Causes and Prevention of Violence was not ready, even in 1969, to accept Judge Higginbotham's assessment of the limitations

---

§10.2   1. Additional Statement of Judge Higginbotham, Commission Statement on Civil Disobedience, Nat'l Comm'n on the Causes & Prevention of Violence 16 (Dec. 1969).

of litigation as an effective challenge to racial discrimination, thousands of blacks had reached Higginbotham's conclusion that the long awaited promise of Brown v. Board of Education would not be self-executing.

Even President John F. Kennedy admitted to civil rights leaders privately in June 1963 "that the demonstrations in the streets had brought results, they had made the executive branch act faster and were forcing Congress to entertain legislation which a few weeks before would have had no chance."[2] It should be noted that Kennedy's statement was "off the record." Violence, as H. Rap Brown once said, may be as American as cherry pie, but few boast of the centrality of violence in American history. Coercive tactics, even peaceful ones for the most justifiable cause, are deplored. The absence of an effective alternative gains only minimum sympathy for protests with disruptive potential, particularly if they are mounted by blacks.

§10.2.1 Protest as a Revelation of Law

A politics of dissimulation seems involved here. The tenor of the legal institution's opposition to protests and boycotts suggests that more is at stake than just the weighing of First Amendment rights and limits. Also at stake could be the status of protesting as a form of political expression (opposition to which would contradict a fundamental element of Americans' self-image, given that it was often violent protest against England that led to the American Revolution), or perhaps an unconscious rejection of the potential inherent in protests and boycotts. At some level, protest actions place in issue the relationship of "the law" to peace and social order. Legal analysis of protests would have to change if the law was recognized as a kind of violence rather than as the antithesis of violence.

Thus, it should not surprise us that the rhetorical definition of certain protest traditions as "coercive" both casts them as "violent" or potentially "violent" and insulates state institutions in general and the judiciary in particular from interrogation. Many of the protests discussed in this chapter were aimed at challenging state racism and state-sanctioned racism. To call these protests "coercive" is to simultaneously (albeit, implicitly) position the state practices being challenged, if not the state itself, as the "coerced."

Martin Luther King, in his famous "Letter from Birmingham City Jail,"[3] tried to address this issue by distinguishing between just and unjust laws. He would obey the former because they square with moral law or the law of God, but he would disobey the latter because they are out of harmony with moral law. In King's view,

2. Arthur Schlesinger, A Thousand Days 970 (1965). Kennedy was not the first President who "got religion" on racial issues in the face of a massive civil rights protest in the nation's capital. In 1941, Franklin D. Roosevelt feared his effort to gear up the nation for war would be disrupted by a march on Washington by 100,000 blacks under the leadership of A. Philip Randolph, head of the Brotherhood of Pullman Car Porters. To get the march called off, Roosevelt agreed to issue an Executive Order barring discrimination in war industries and apprenticeship programs. Using similar tactics, Randolph later pressured President Truman to issue two Executive Orders. One provided for "equal treatment and equal opportunity" in the armed services and the other sought to abolish "racial discrimination in federal employment." Lerone Bennett, Before the Mayflower 366-370 (5th ed. 1982).
3. Martin Luther King, Why We Can't Wait (1963).

segregation laws are immoral for they distort the soul and damage the personality of both the segregator and the segregated. Segregation laws are also evil, King said, because the majority inflicts on a minority standards it would not impose on itself. Dr. King provided additional examples, but his key distinction was made at that point where he said:

> In no sense do I advocate evading or defying the law as the rabid segregationist would do. This would lead to anarchy. One who breaks an unjust law must do it openly, lovingly (not hatefully as the white mothers did in New Orleans when they were seen on television screaming "nigger, nigger, nigger") and with a willingness to accept the penalty. I submit that an individual who breaks a law that conscience tells him is unjust, and willingly accepts the penalty by staying in jail to arouse the conscience of the community over its injustice, is in reality expressing the very highest respect for law.[4]

Impressive, but many legal commentators were troubled by Dr. King's philosophy. Professor Charles Fried expressed concern that the protestors expected others to abide by the law but were unwilling to contribute like sacrifice by abiding by the principle of "institutional settlement" of claims determined against them by some fair procedure.[5] Moreover, Professor Fried claims, if the demonstrators get the law changed to suit them, their tactics would enable those who think the former law justified to resist the "remedial" laws. Standing ready to pay the penalty for civil disobedience does, he concedes, evidence an affirmation of law in general, and he emphasized his belief that the law protested against is not simply disadvantageous, but wrong. "This is a gamble," he concludes, "but civil disobedience is a risky, maybe a desperate course."[6]

Professor Fried speaks of the resolution of differences by a *fair procedure.* This hardly fits the history of segregation laws enacted at a time when most blacks were disenfranchised, and enforced by a legal structure from which blacks were almost entirely excluded. And yet the law, at least at the Supreme Court level, did

---

4. Id. at 84-86. The famous Montgomery bus boycott, which brought Dr. King to national prominence, provided a definitive model for combining a committed community protest action with effective litigation. According to Dr. King, the months of walking and the constant harassment of local officials had taken their toll, and the boycott was about to collapse. Martin Luther King, Stride Toward Freedom 151-153, 157-160 (1958). The Supreme Court then affirmed a three-judge court order that voided the state and local laws requiring segregation on Montgomery's motor buses. Browder v. Gayle, 142 F. Supp. 707 (N.D. Ala.), aff'd per curiam, 352 U.S. 903 (1956). The Supreme Court's decision came on the same day that an Alabama judge enjoined the protestors from operating an alternative car pool system to replace bus services — a ruling which may have marked the end of the boycott. For an extensive discussion of the Montgomery bus boycott, see Randall Kennedy, Martin Luther King's Constitution: A Legal History of the Montgomery Bus Boycott, 98 Yale L.J. 999 (1989). And even after the decision, Alabama officials continued vehemently to enforce segregation. Mayor Gayle's response to the decision that carried his name was typical of this reaction: "The recent Supreme Court decisions . . . have seriously lowered the dignified relations which did exist between the races in our city and in our state. . . . The difficulties [which the segregation laws were] meant to prevent and the dignities which they guard are not changed here in Alabama by decisions of the Supreme Court. . . . To insure public safety, to protect people of both races, and to promote order in our city we shall continue to enforce segregation." Quoted in Kennedy, supra, at 1056-1057.

5. Charles Fried, Moral Causation, 77 Harv. L. Rev. 1258, 1268-1269 (1964).

6. Id. at 1269.

provide crucial support to the racial reforms achieved during the 1960s. This support, however, tended to reinforce the characterization of the protests as "coercive." While reversing convictions of protesters arrested during clearly nonviolent protests, the Court seemed to adopt Fried's postion that the law should be *beyond* coercion, that is, the law should be absolute and transcendentally present. By Fried's account, the law should not countenance any violence. This position casts law as the antithesis of violence. Robert Cover, however, suggests that law operates in a field of violence. In particular, he refers to the law in the following terms:

> I believe the more general term "legal interpretation" is warranted, for it is my position that the violence which judges deploy as instruments of a modern nation-state necessarily engages anyone who interprets the law in a course of conduct that entails either the perpetration or the suffering of this violence.[7]

Jacques Derrida went even farther in asserting that the law *is* violence. It is through the imposition of "order" that law functions as authority. Derrida wrote that "law is always an authorized force, a force that justifies itself or is justified in applying itself, even if this justification may be judged from elsewhere to be unjust or unjustifiable."[8] "Enforceability," Derrida indicates, is not a second order condition; it structures the very possibility of law. We are trained to think about law as referencing itself for authority (precedent, and so on). Initially, however, law had to install itself without its own prior approval. Derrida refers to this installation as an "originary violence."[9] This "originary" violence replays itself over and over. Thus, according to Derrida, to categorically equate law with justice is to participate in the elaboration of a fiction that posits the law as the dyadic opposite of violence. It is a fiction to which the courts are committed. To quote Montaigne, who referred to this phenomenon as the "mystical foundation" of the authority of laws, "[L]aws keep up their good standing, not because they are just, but because they are laws: that is the mystical foundation of their authority, they have no other."[10]

Much of this chapter reviews protests and judicial decisions resulting from those protests that took place during the civil rights movement of the 1960s and 1970s. These events occurred two generations ago. They remind us of the importance of direct action in racial reform efforts. Reviewing the civil rights protests against often blatantly biased practices provides an experiential background enabling contemporary protesters and those who provide them with legal counsel as to which tactics are likely to prove effective and which may garner judicial approval. These are often two different questions. As a result of literally hundreds of conservative federal judges appointed during Republican administrations, racial protesters are likely to receive little sympathy and mostly adverse rulings in the courts.

7. Robert M. Cover, Violence and the Word, 95 Yale L.J. 1601 n.1 (1986).
8. Jacques Derrida, Force of Law: The "Mystical Foundation of Authority" in Deconstruction and the Possibility of Justice 5 (Drucilla Cornell et al. eds., 1992).
9. Id. at 6.
10. Id. at 12.

§10.3   "CREATIVE DISORDER" AND THE COURTS

Unfortunately, history shows that the courts are as likely to decline as to provide relief when blacks involved in protest activity seek judicial protection from white retaliation. Justices of the Supreme Court have been motivated less by their conceptions of First Amendment guarantees than by their sympathy with the underlying goals of protest activity. During the first half of the 1960s, when the civil rights movement sought the most basic civil rights and liberties, demonstrators were protected against the frequently violent challenges of white groups and white governments.[1] But after 1965, weary of the tactics of the civil rights movement and ambivalent about its goals, the Court began to withdraw its support from protest demonstrations.

Even though demonstrations can lead to fairly dramatic change, and even conceding that in the area of racial discrimination there is at least reason to hope that the Court will be supportive, civil rights demonstrations, particularly those involving serious risk of arrest or reactionary violence, are not easy to mount. Frances Fox Piven and Richard A. Cloward put it well:

> However hard their lot may be, people usually remain acquiescent, conforming to the accustomed patterns of daily life in their community, and believing those patterns to be both inevitable and just. Men and women till the fields each day, or stoke the furnaces, or tend the looms, obeying the rules and rhythms of earning a livelihood; they mate and bear children hopefully, and mutely watch them die; they abide by the laws of church and community and defer to their rulers, striving to earn a little grace and esteem. In other words, most of the time people conform to the institutional arrangements which enmesh them, which regulate the rewards and penalties of daily life, and which appear to be the only possible reality.[2]

The human tendency to hope for a better day rather than working and risking for it is particularly strong when the injustice involves racial violence. James Weldon Johnson, the NAACP Field Secretary, reportedly suggested in a 1919 speech that "the negroes in a city like Jacksonville, Florida could send a committee representing 10,000 negroes to the city government and tell them that if they did not receive protection [against white violence] they would not cook or work in any way. . . . Such a course," Johnson emphasized, "would be a method more effective than the shotgun."[3] There is no indication that blacks in Jacksonville were ready to

---

§10.3   1. Davidson Douglas suggests that the more "moderate" southern states (North Carolina, Tennessee, and Texas) were more successful in evading integration than were those that defiantly resisted the *Brown* ruling. The white political establishment in the "moderate states," he contends, identified the question not as one of whether to desegregate, but how much. By rhetorically accepting and making tokenistic steps toward integration, these states limit more successfully limited court orders for extensive pupil desegregation than did their more "defiant" counterparts. While focusing on school desegregation, Davidson's article discusses how business leaders utilized the rhetoric of moderation to attract out-of-state business and facilitate economic growth. Davidson M. Douglas, The Rhetoric of Moderation: Desegregating and the South during the Decade after *Brown*, 89 Nw. U. L. Rev. 92, 93-97 (1994).

2. Frances Fox Piven & Richard A. Cloward, Poor People's Movements: Why They Succeed, How They Fail 6 (1977).

3. Arthur Waskow, From Race Riot to Sit-in, 1919 and the 1960s, 226-228 (1967).

follow Johnson's suggestion in a year when 76 blacks were lynched and hundreds more were killed or wounded in race riots.[4] It would be many years before tactics such as Johnson's "creative disorder" would seem feasible. Blacks in the North had utilized sit-in tactics for years in their efforts to desegregate facilities that usually excluded blacks more for business policy reasons than in compliance with local law. But frustrated by the seeming determination of most southern whites to retain segregation in all its forms, black students in February 1960, launched a sit-in movement in a Greensboro, North Carolina, lunch counter. The pattern was quickly set. Seeking service where they had never been served, and denied it, the blacks refused to leave. They attracted shouted curses and whispered support from white bystanders. Arrests and prosecutions followed, but the sitting-in tactic was expanded to every imaginable public facility that refused to serve blacks on a basis of racial equality.[5] Within a year, the sit-ins caused restaurants in 108 southern or border cities to end racial segregation, but in other areas, particularly in the Deep South, resistance remained strong.[6]

Fortunately for hundreds of sit-in protesters who were arrested and convicted of trespass, disorderly conduct, breach of the peace, or various other "neutral laws," the first sit-in case to reach the Supreme Court, Boynton v. Virginia,[7] presented a sympathetic set of facts and was resolved on an extension of existing law that, while it offered little help for most sit-in cases, did set the tone of "legal innovation" that found methods of reversing convictions on a range of procedural grounds. *Boynton* involved a black law student who had been convicted for trespass when he refused to leave the white section of a restaurant in the Richmond, Virginia, Trailways Bus Terminal. The record was slim; Boynton had been arrested under the state's trespass statute, not a segregation measure; whatever his right to ride an interstate bus on a desegregated basis, he was arrested in a privately operated restaurant which merely leased the premises from Trailways. Indeed, as two Justices pointed out in dissent, Boynton's attorneys had at no point challenged the trespass conviction as in violation of the Interstate Commerce Act.

But the majority, evidencing the sympathy for blacks convicted in nonviolent efforts to use public facilities on a nonsegregated basis that was to prevail for five years, found little difficulty in deciding the case under §316(d), the nondiscrimination clause of Part II of the Interstate Commerce Act, dealing with motor carriers. Although the Act, by its express wording, includes only terminal facilities owned, operated, or controlled by interstate carriers — seemingly excluding the privately leased restaurant in *Boynton* — the Court reasoned pragmatically to extend the statute to facilities made available by carriers. Justice Black, speaking for the

---

4. Peter Bergman, The Chronological History of the Negro in America 387-388 (1969).

5. Waskow, supra note 3. For extensive, more recent histories of the civil rights movement, see also Taylor Branch, Parting the Waters: America in the King Years 1954-63 (1988); Eyes on the Prize: America's Civil Rights Years — A Reader and Guide (Clayborne Carson et al. eds., 1987); David J. Garrow, Bearing the Cross: Martin Luther King, Jr., and the Southern Christian Leadership Conference (1986).

6. Waskow, supra note 3. For an extensive examination of a protest movement which, because of strong resistance, failed to achieve most of its goals, see John Hart Ely, Negro Demonstrations and the Law: *Danville* as a Test Case, 27 Vand. L. Rev. 927 (1974).

7. 364 U.S. 454 (1960).

majority, wrote, "if the bus carrier has volunteered to make terminal and restaurant facilities and services available to its interstate passengers as a regular part of their transportation, and the terminal and restaurant have acquiesced and cooperated in this undertaking, the terminal and restaurant must perform these services without discriminations prohibited by the Act."[8]

Justice Black, whose ambivalence about the legality of sit-in protests grew with the passing years, indicated in *Boynton* the mixed blessing that the Court provided in decisions reversing sit-in convictions. As in *Boynton,* the Court's uncertainty was manifested by quite narrow decisions that offered little precedent or encouragement for future protest. In *Boynton,* for example, the Court's exclusion of an independent roadside restaurant was potentially mischievous as well as legally inconsistent. At the point when such a proprietor opened his doors to a whole busload of passengers, it is difficult to understand why Congress lacked the power to extend coverage under the Interstate Commerce Act or what rights of the private proprietor the Court was seeking to protect. Certainly, the "roadside exception" exposed black bus riders to discrimination at just those isolated stops where it would not be possible for them to find unsegregated food service.[9]

§10.4 JUDICIAL SANCTIONING OF THE SIT-INS WHILE PRESERVING RACIAL HIERARCHY

Even as the Court overturned the convictions of sit-in demonstrators, it demonstrated qualified endorsement of the protest activity but refused to create a consistent and generally applicable right to relief for the activists. The Court both declined to extend the rationale of its restrictive covenant cases to bar the prosecution of those who challenged discriminatory customs or to declare their activity protected First Amendment speech. In addition, the Supreme Court reversed protestors' convictions on only the narrowest grounds. By refusing to articulate general principles to protect civil rights activists, the Court limited the tactics available to protestors, avoided the full-scale wrath of many opposed to the protests' aims, and left itself an avenue of retreat.

8. 364 U.S. at 460. The *Boynton* decision marked the end of a long series of efforts to utilize the Interstate Commerce Commission to specifically prohibit all racial segregation on interstate carriers. Later that year, the ICC issued an order (49 C.F.R. §180(a)) that specifically prohibited motor carriers from in any way utilizing terminal facilities that segregate on the basis of race, color, creed, or national origin.

9. Inconsistent or not, the *Boynton* decisions spurred civil rights groups who determined that the combined enforcement of segregation in interstate travel must be exposed. Organized first by the Congress of Racial Equality (CORE), and continued later by the Student Nonviolent Coordinating Committee (SNCC), racially mixed groups rode interstate buses into the South. In a repetition of the violence that blacks had experienced when they integrated streetcars in Savannah 89 years before, the freedom riders were attacked and beaten. Police harassed and arrested the protestors instead of providing them protection. Then, as later, white protestors were singled out for violent attacks by police and spectators. Finally, the federal government took action to end the violence in United States v. United States Klans, Knights of the Ku Klux Klan, Inc., 194 F. Supp. 897 (N.D. Ala. 1961).

Over a decade before the initial cases of the 1960s civil rights movement, the Supreme Court decided in principle that judicial assistance in enforcing the segregatory policies of private parties violated the equal protection clause.[1] Civil rights lawyers marshalled these precedents to argue that when police officers arrested black patrons at the behest of lunch counter proprietors and when local courts prosecuted these sit-in protestors, the Fourteenth Amendment was also violated. They contended that it is impossible to draw any meaningful distinction between the judicial enforcement of racially discriminatory private real estate contracts which had been condemned in *Shelley* and judicial enforcement of racial segregation in private businesses. Eleven Justices consistently disagreed.

In Garner v. Louisiana,[2] for instance, a majority of the Court rejected the argument that the prosecution of black patrons who refused to abide by segregated seating patterns in privately owned restaurants constituted state action. While the Court reversed the convictions of 16 blacks who refused requests by lunch-counter proprietors to move from seats reserved for whites, it did so on the narrow ground that the protestors' conduct was orderly and therefore did not constitute a disturbance of the peace. The majority refused to adopt Justice Douglas' opinion, set forth in his concurrence to *Garner,* that the arrests constituted state action since they were in response to the coercive state custom of segregation. Justice Douglas also contended, and the Court denied, that the restaurants licensed by the state had become property affected with a public interest and hence could not segregate.[3]

Again in Peterson v. City of Greenville,[4] the Court refused to extend the state action doctrine of *Shelley* to reverse the conviction of sit-in protestors. *Peterson* involved the appeal of ten blacks who seated themselves at the lunch counter of the city's S.H. Kress store. Upon seeing them, the store manager promptly announced that the counter was closed and asked everyone to leave the area. When the black would-be patrons refused to leave, they were arrested.

Avoiding petitioners' arguments that they were engaged in constitutionally protected free speech and that the Fourteenth Amendment prohibited their prosecution for violating segregation rules, the Supreme Court reversed the trespass convictions on the narrower ground that the segregation complained of was not private discrimination. The Court held that the manager was acting pursuant to a local ordinance which commanded that blacks and whites be served in separate rooms. Because the existence of the ordinance provided a clear basis for finding state action, the Court did not reach respondent's arguments that the convictions alone violated the Fourteenth Amendment.

The Supreme Court's protest decisions seem designed to localize bias conceptually. The Court's refusal to create a generally applicable right to relief for activists appears temporally if not ideologically coextensive with its reluctance to

<hr>

§10.4   1. Shelley v. Kraemer, 334 U.S. 1 (1948); Barrows v. Jackson, 346 U.S. 249 (1953).
2. 368 U.S. 157 (1961).
3. See also Taylor v. Louisiana, 370 U.S. 154 (1962) (reversing the breach of peace convictions of blacks arrested for a sit-in in a bus terminal waiting room on *Garner*'s "lack of evidence" rationale).
4. 373 U.S. 244 (1963). Similar results were reached in Fields v. South Carolina, 375 U.S. 44 (1963), Henry v. Rock Hill, 376 U.S. 776 (1963), and South Carolina v. Edwards, 372 U.S. 229 (1963) (187 black students protested segregation at the state house).

extend Shelley v. Kraemer. The Court's reluctance or skepticism seems partially explained by its investment in the ideas articulated by Professor Fried. For the Supreme Court to have conceded broad protection to activists would have been tantamount to recognizing the failings of legal procedure as a general matter. That is, such protection would acknowledge that "fair procedures" might systematically operate to the disadvantage of particular categories of people. That legal procedures are structurally biased is not at all surprising if one looks upon the law through the optic proposed by Derrida.[5] For the judicial mind, however, the more comforting view would be that the law can be purged of racism and other forms of social bias by striking explicitly racist laws. In other words, the law is (or can be made to be) the perfect antithesis of violence. Justice Black's interpretation of the First Amendment in Bell v. Maryland seems to be an almost reflexive judicial resistance to legitimating protest as a political activity *unless* operating in the free-speech context. In the First Amendment context, courts sometimes have the leverage to decouple protest from its political objectives. Courts, however, become very skittish when free speech is used to rationalize a protest that appears outwardly violent, disruptive, or coercive. Perhaps judicial fears are related to the sense that protest often — implicitly if not explicitly — questions the extent to which courts represent a neutral forum for arbitrating certain political-legal contests.

The consensus the Supreme Court had built in favor of civil rights protesters showed signs of tension as early as 1964. In Bell v. Maryland,[6] the Court first confronted the issue of whether passage of a public accommodations law (quite likely prompted by the sit-in demonstrations), vitiated the criminal convictions of protestors who had violated segregatory orders. Although the Court reversed the convictions and remanded the case, its decision revealed deepening divisions over the extent of constitutional protection for demonstrators who refused to leave private property.[7] Justice Douglas urged the outright reversal of the convictions, on the basis that the right to be served at places of public accommodations is a privilege of national citizenship protected from state interference by the Fourteenth Amendment. Under the *Shelley* doctrine, Justice Douglas asserted that state judicial action, in the form of prosecution of demonstrators, served to enforce the private property owner's racially discriminatory policies and thus denied the affected Negroes the equal protection of the laws.

Justice Goldberg, citing the Civil Rights cases,[8] said that the Fourteenth Amendment was intended to obligate a state, either by statutory law or by common law, to guarantee all citizens access to places of public accommodation. The failure of a state to protect the constitutional right of blacks is no justification, in Justice Goldberg's view, for its judiciary's participation in prosecutions of citizens for exercising such rights.

---

5. See Jacques Derrida, Force of Law: The "Mystical Foundation of Authority" in Deconstruction and the Possibility of Justice (Drucilla Cornell et al. eds., 1992).

6. 378 U.S. 226 (1964).

7. The signals were not uniform. The Court continued to reverse convictions in peaceful sit-ins. Abernathy v. Alabama, 380 U.S. 447 (1965) ("freedom riders" arrested at a lunch counter in a Montgomery, Alabama, bus station).

8. 109 U.S. 3 (1833).

Justice Black, joined by Justices Harlan and White, dissented, in an opinion concluding that the convictions should have been affirmed, and the effect of intervening changes in state law left for independent consideration by the Maryland courts. Justice Black asserted that the rights of property include the right to select business associates or patrons, subject to regulation by proper state or federal legislation. The Fourteenth Amendment was not intended to assure access to privately owned accommodations, and a license to do business by the state should not be considered to convert private activity into state action for Fourteenth Amendment purposes, so long as there is no official state action or policy coercing or encouraging discrimination by private parties. As to arguments based on rights of free speech and protest, Justice Black contended that such rights do not include a right to force a private owner to furnish his property as a platform for criticism of his use of that property. The use of judicial proceedings to enforce trespass laws was therefore justified on the ground that the Fourteenth Amendment permits a state to prosecute crime committed against a person or his property, regardless of the prejudice or bigotry of the victim of the crime.

The Court issued an even stronger warning when it reviewed the conviction of Reverend B. Elton Cox, a civil rights leader convicted of disturbing the peace, obstructing public passages, and picketing before a courthouse.[9] As in the past, the Court reversed the convictions on the ground that the Reverend had been well-behaved and nondisruptive and struck down the state statutes as overly vague. But the Court departed from routine when the *majority* emphasized the limits of its tolerance.

The *Cox* decision is an appropriate point to note that the Court's concern over the potential for violence in civil rights demonstrations, and the threat posed thereby to the traditional concepts of private property, was observable not only in judicial warnings but also in its unwillingness to grant review in a number of cases involving disorder. In such cases, convictions were permitted to stand by the procedural techniques of denying certiorari, dismissal of appeal, or summary affirmance. This was the fate of Ford v. Tennessee,[10] where defendants were reported to have run down the aisles and seated themselves during a segregated outdoor religious service, despite requests to stay in the rear.

During this period, the nonviolent, prayer-oriented southern protests of the early 1960s were becoming more militant, and the North was experiencing a succession of urban race riots. The views expressed earlier by a minority of the Court now became those of a new majority. More and more places and tactics of protest were declared off-limits to demonstrators. There was a continuance of the earlier practice of denying review to convictions, and adverse judgments where protests had been accompanied by violence or where they posed serious threats of disorder.[11]

In Brown v. Louisiana,[12] the Court again reversed convictions, under Louisiana's Breach of the Peace Statute, of protesters who sat in a public library that

9. Cox v. Louisiana, 379 U.S. 536 (1965).
10. 377 U.S. 994 (1964).
11. McLaurin v. Greenville, 385 U.S. 1011 (1967); NAACP v. Overstreet, 21 Ga. 16, 142 S.E.2d 816 (1965), cert. denied, 384 U.S. 118 (1966).
12. 383 U.S. 131 (1966).

barred blacks.[13] As in the earlier cases, the Court found no support in the records for the state's charges of disorderly conduct and concluded that it was the defendant's race and not their behavior that led to their arrest. Nevertheless, Justice Fortas, writing for the majority, felt constrained to admonish:

> It is an unhappy circumstance that the locus of these events was a public library — a place dedicated to quiet, to knowledge, and to beauty. It is a sad commentary that this hallowed place in the Parish of East Feliciana bore the ugly stamp of racism. It is sad, too, that it was a public library which, reasonably enough in the circumstances, was the stage for a confrontation between those discriminated against and the representatives of the offending parish. Fortunately, the circumstances here were such that no claim can be made that use of the library by others was disturbed by the demonstration. Perhaps the time and method were carefully chosen with this in mind. Were it otherwise, a factor not present in this case would have to be considered. Here, there was no disturbance of others, no disruption of library activities, and no violation of any library regulations.[14]

Four justices dissented. Speaking for them, Justice Black refused to concede "that a state must measure disturbances in its libraries and on the streets with identical standards. . . ." He felt that the state's use of its breach of peace statute was appropriate, warning that, if one group can take over libraries for one cause, other groups will assert the right to do so for other less appealing causes. He predicted that the rights to paralyze libraries would lead to assertion of the right to paralyze schools, adding that efforts to this effect had already been made all over the country. Justice Black concluded:

> I am deeply troubled with the fear that powerful private groups throughout the Nation will read the Court's action, as I do — that is, as granting them a license to invade the tranquility and beauty of our libraries whenever they have quarrel with some state policy which may or may not exist. It is an unhappy circumstance in my judgment that the group, which more than any other has needed a government of equal laws and equal justice, is now encouraged to believe that the best way for it to advance its cause, which is a worthy one, is by taking the law into its own hands from place to place and from time to time.[15]

In Walker v. City of Birmingham,[16] the majority upheld the contempt conviction of Dr. Martin Luther King, Jr. and others for having violated an injunction forbidding the celebrated Good Friday and Easter Sunday Birmingham marches, which many believe were crucial to the demonstrations that led to passage of the 1964 Civil Rights Act.[17] The Court did not rule on the validity of the injunction or the statute under which the request for parade permits had been denied. (In fact, the statute was later invalidated in Shuttleworth v. City of Birmingham.) Rather, the majority emphasized the critical importance of order and orderly judicial

13. See Garner v. Louisiana, Taylor v. Louisiana, and Cox v. Louisiana, supra.
14. 383 U.S. at 142.
15. 383 U.S. at 167-168.
16. 388 U.S. 307 (1967).
17. Jack Greenberg, The Supreme Court, Civil Rights and Civil Dissonance, 77 Yale L.J. 1538.

procedure, holding, in effect, that such procedure takes precedence even over freedom of speech. The majority concluded: "One may sympathize with the petitioner's impatient commitment to their cause. But respect for judicial process is a small price to pay for the civilizing hand of law, which alone can give abiding meaning to constitutional freedom."[18]

In dissent, Justice Brennan criticized the majority's overriding concern with public order:

> We cannot permit fears of "riots" and "civil disobedience" generated by slogans like "Black Power" to divert our attention from what is here at stake — not violence or the right of the State to control its streets and sidewalks, but the insulation from attack of ex parte orders and legislation upon which they are based even when patently impermissible prior restraints on the exercise of the First Amendment rights. . . .[19]

Although the holdings in Brown v. Louisiana and Walker v. City of Birmingham appear to be progressive, the language deployed in each of the cases betrays a sensibility that is far from it. Consider these points:

A. The imagery Justice Fortas evokes in the excerpt from Brown v. Louisiana quoted above begins by fixing the public library as the site of "quiet . . . peace" and intellectualism; the library is a "hallowed place," a private refuge. The passage implicitly positions the law as the public library's defender. The fact that the library discriminates on the basis of race is secondary. That is to say, the law's primary duty is to defend "hallowed places." The passage is careful to note that, had the protesters actually disturbed the hallowed place (or its use), things might have turned out very differently for the protesters — even though the protest was about the public library's failure to comply with the Court's findings of a decade earlier.

Through its representation of the law's relationship with the library, the passage imputes a kind of existential peacefulness to the law itself. The invocation of such imagery is peculiar, given that the public library was a site of racist exclusion; racist exclusion is a kind of violence. The library's racist exclusion, however, is cast as almost incidental to its hallowedness. Brown v. Louisiana leaves the distinct impression that it is the protesters who pose the real threat to existential calm, not racism.

B. The majority opinion in Walker v. City of Birmingham represents law as a "civilizing hand." The petitioners (protestors), on the other hand, are represented as "impatient." The majority held that the petitioners were not "constitutionally free to ignore all the procedures of the law and carry their battle to the streets."[20] The Alabama law, in other words, rightly restricted the impatient protesters from carrying their battle into public space (presumably inhabited by white people). The majority's language is evocative of an entirely familiar racist/colonial trope. The racialized other is cast as lawlessly barbaric; he is literally unable to lead a structured, human existence without assistance. Historically, "assistance" has taken the

---

18. 388 U.S. at 321.
19. 388 U.S. at 349.
20. 388 U.S. at 321.

rhetorical form of a "civilizing mission"; in this formulation, "civilizing" is interpreted in terms of "bringing law to" those without it. Law is, thus, positioned as the antithesis of barbarism. By representing the relationship between black protestors and white ("civil") society through this familiar rhetorical framework, the *Walker* majority racializes and consolidates the law-protest opposition. Through *Walker,* law is positioned (or repositioned) as the cultural endowment of white civil society.

Even during the period when the Supreme Court was most protective of civil rights demonstrations, the most peaceful protest at a religious service was deemed beyond the pale. Thus, when college students refused to stand quietly in the rear of a segregated outdoor religious service held at a publicly owned stadium and moved down the aisle, seating themselves with the white audience, the Supreme Court summarily affirmed convictions under a state statute prohibiting interference with a worship service.[21] It is hard to imagine protests by blacks less likely to be viewed sympathetically by whites or to be found entitled to constitutional protection by the courts.

But without judicial sanction and despite the predictable cries of outrage that followed his action, James Forman, then President of the Student Non-Violent Coordinating Committee (SNCC), interrupted the Sunday morning service at New York's famed Riverside church on May 4, 1969, and read his "black manifesto." The statement, which condemned racism in the church and in the country, and stated the failure of antidiscrimination programs, demanded $500,000,000 from the "Christian white churches and the Jewish synagogues." The money was to be used, inter alia, to establish a Southern Land Bank that would assist blacks in organizing cooperative farms; to set up publishing firms, television networks and other audiovisual agencies to provide blacks with an alternative to racist propaganda; and to start a skills center for research on the problems of blacks, training centers to teach marketable skills, and a "National Black Labor Strike and Defense Fund" to protect black workers and their families. To justify his demands, Forman claimed, "We are not unaware that the exploitation of colored peoples around the world is aided and abetted by the white Christian churches and synagogues."

The protest is reviewed thoroughly by Alan Schuchter[22] who writes, "Forman's violation of the most 'sacred' hour of the week and his violent anti-American rhetoric against America, capitalism and the church touched millions of nerve ends like a multi-pronged cattle prod."[23] Some churchmen were extremely critical, but during the next year various churches and denominational groups gave several million dollars to black church programs, generally specifying that the money not go to Forman or the group he represented.

---

21. Ford v. Tennessee, 377 U.S. 994 (1964). See also Jones v. Georgia, 379 U.S. 935 (1964), where defendants were reported to have acted in a disorderly fashion in and about a church.

22. Alan Schuchter, Reparations, the Black Manifesto and Its Challenge to White America (1970). See also Black Manifesto (Robert S. Lecky & H. Elliott Wright eds., 1969).

23. Schuchter, supra note 22, at 5.

Despite some vocal opposition, it is evident that many churchmen shared the view of Dr. Ernest Campbell, the minister of Riverside Church, whose service was interrupted by James Forman. Dr. Campbell commented on the incident:

> . . . the shame of it all was not that a service of worship was interrupted, indefensible as that action was. The shame centers in the fact that in the population of this most prosperous nation there are people who feel, rightly or wrongly, that they have to use such tactics to draw attention to their grievances. . . . Let's be done with rationalizing. Wherever you go in this country the white man rides higher than the black. He lives in better parts of town, sends his children to more desirable schools, borrows books from finer libraries, holds down higher paying jobs. . . . And where has the church been in all of this? By its silence it has blessed these arrangements and given them an extra aura of divine approval. It has conveniently exalted the virtue of obedience and order — getting fat in the process. . . . Reparations, restitution, redress, call it what you will. We subscribed to the conviction that given the demeaning and heinous mistreatment that black people suffered in this country at the hands of white people in the slave economy, and given the lingering handicaps of that system that still works to keep the black man at a disadvantage in our society, it is just and reasonable that amends be made by many institutions in society — including, and perhaps especially the church. . . .[24]

James Forman was not arrested and the legality of his demonstration was not tested in the courts. Other groups who mounted similar church demonstrations modeled on Forman's well-publicized interruption of a worship service were less fortunate.

In Gannon v. Action,[25] the minister of a Catholic church in St. Louis filed suit seeking an injunction from a federal district court against black activists, who during a period of several weeks had interrupted church services with demands based on asserted racism in the church.

Although the defendants were private individuals, the district court found that it had jurisdiction to grant the requested relief under the Civil Rights Statutes, 42 U.S.C. §§1981, 1982, 1983, and 1985(3). Ignoring questions of "state action," the court granted broad injunctive relief.[26]

The Eighth Circuit affirmed, but narrowed the injunction so as not to deprive the defendants of their First Amendment rights which, the court held, included reasonable picketing and pamphleting. In the period between the district court's order and the appeal, the Supreme Court had decided Griffin v. Breckenridge,[27] reversing an earlier decision that §1985(3) could not be used to reach private conspiracies. The appellate court found that the injunction was properly based on §1985(3), avoiding discussion of whether there was jurisdiction under the other civil rights statutes.[28]

---

24. Id. at 6.

25. 303 F. Supp. 1240 (E.D. Mo. 1969).

26. In a similar suit brought by another church, the court granted similar relief on similar jurisdictional grounds. Central Presbyterian Church v. Black Liberation Front, 303 F. Supp. 894 (E.D. Mo. 1969).

27. 403 U.S. 88, 91 (1971).

28. Action v. Gannon, 450 F.2d 1227 (8th Cir. 1971).

The Supreme Court's decision in United Brotherhood of Carpenters & Joiners of America v. Scott,[29] however, severely curtailed the scope of §1985(3), rendering the statute virtually powerless. The Court, without explicitly overturning Griffin v. Breckenridge, held that §1985 did not cover private conspiracies. A more complete history of civil remedies under §1985 is discussed in §5.8.

§10.5 THE JUDICIAL ROLE IN SOCIAL REFORM THROUGH PROTESTS

Whatever the value of the Supreme Court's decisions in the early 1960s supporting the sit-in protests, it is clear that most communities experiencing anti-segregation protests, as well as the lower courts that served them, did not feel bound to conform their decisions in protest cases within the standards set by the High Court. The civil rights forces actually lost many, if not a majority, of these suits. Lower court cases were marked by several almost predictable components: The responsibility for disturbances or disruption was generally placed on the protesters, even though disorder was frequently the result of action by police or hostile spectators; there was a presumption that police and city officials were enforcing the laws impartially and with fairness, although this was seldom the case; federal courts in suits filed by city officials often assumed jurisdiction and granted injunctive relief, even though there was clearly no basis for federal jurisdiction; there was a markedly greater concern for property than for personal rights; extraordinary restrictions were placed on picketers; and even when the protesters were clearly entitled to injunctive relief, it was delayed (often by refusal of district courts to grant it, and the unwillingness of courts of appeal to provide injunction pending appeal) until arrests and harassment had seriously damaged the protest movement. There is some question whether these decisions reflect a breakdown of stare decisis, or whether the Supreme Court decisions were so narrow that lower courts were able to distinguish them easily.

Whatever their practical and precedential effect, many commentators have emphasized the merely symbolic value of the Supreme Court decisions. Judicial orders barring segregation, long thought to be a moral as well as legal imperative, confirmed that the oppression of blacks was not inevitable. They encouraged both whites and blacks in their belief that blacks had rights to fight for, both in and out of the courts. In the setting of the courtroom, blacks could stand with their white opponents as equals and not as supplicants, demanding rights to which they were entitled, rather than pleading for judicial favor. But perhaps even more importantly, legal decisions striking down segregative laws and customs deprived segregation of the moral force of its lawfulness. Professor Randall Kennedy expressed this idea when he wrote, "By winning in court and forcing segregationists to go outside the law to maintain their power, the Movement's litigators helped to erode

29. 463 U.S. 825 (1983).

the facade of inevitability that surrounded the segregation regime and to create the perception of a gap between right and reality, authority and force."[1]

Militants might condemn the utilization of litigation in direct action campaigns as worse than a waste of time and resources, since protest leaders put more emphasis in their planning on the potential effectiveness of their tactics. Civil rights lawyers, though, would contend that legal action was essential to defend against criminal charges and civil actions brought to frustrate protest activities, and that affirmative litigation — whether or not successful as to relief — served to publicize the protests, and, more important, involved the courts as monitors of counter-protest activities. With varying degrees of reluctance, even state tribunals and unsympathetic federal courts could be expected to enjoin the most flagrant denials of constitutional rights.

Still, there is little agreement as to what role courts played in the civil rights protests of the 1960s, and even less of a consensus on what role they should play in protecting direct action protest activity. There are writers who reject the view that the courts protected civil rights protests against anti–civil rights violence, and withheld protection only when the protests themselves were disruptive. Lewis Steel, a civil rights attorney, suggested in a controversial magazine article[2] that the Supreme Court's decisions in the protest cases were intended to harmonize with the views of the white community rather than the needs of blacks. He wrote:

> When Negroes and their white supporters began demonstrating, they were considered to be humble supplicants seeking succor from white America. Toward the middle of the 1960s, civil rights demonstrators, rather than playing a humble role, proclaimed that they would not be moved. Negroes had become assertive in a society which considered such behavior anathema, and repression became the order of the day. White America, without any basis in fact, decided that demonstrations and riots were synonymous. . . .[3]

Although Lewis Steel's observations appear to be correct, cases like Brown v. Louisiana suggest that more might have been going on in the protest cases than just accommodating "the views of the white community." A certain *concept* of law appears to have been at stake. To the extent that the inconsistency between earlier and later protest cases could be interpreted in terms of a "judicial concession to white anxieties," it seems important not to represent the judiciary as self-consciously extending concessions to "white anxieties." Rather, the "white anxieties" that Steel speaks about probably mirrored the judiciary's own anxieties. The "civilizing" language in Brown v. Louisiana begins to suggest the extent to which racial fear-fantasies informed the Supreme Court's protest-jurisprudence (if not its interpretation of "the law," more generally).

§10.5   1. Randall Kennedy, Martin Luther King's Constitution: A Legal History of the Montgomery Bus Boycott, 98 Yale L.J. 999, 1065 (1988).

2. Lewis Steel, Nine Men in Black Who Think White, N.Y. Times Magazine, Oct. 13, 1968, at 56.

3. Id. at 115.

From the viewpoint of a great many whites, there really were no peaceful, non-disruptive civil rights protests. Each represented a most threatening challenge to an important aspect of the local status quo. Without the history and odiousness of racial segregation that motivated the sit-in demonstrations and influenced how "neutral" observers viewed their actions, one would suspect that any group who refused to leave privately owned premises after a demand by an owner or agent would be liable for arrest and prosecution under a disturbing-the-peace-type statute. The disorderliness would be in the simple refusal to leave, which in the case of lunch counter protests effectively closed down the facility. Rather clearly, the Supreme Court in the early cases was influenced to seek means of reversing protestors' convictions for reasons other than their character, which, while not aggressively violent, certainly were not nondisruptive.

Assuming Steel's analysis is correct, is it reasonable to expect leaders of black and other minorities to mount effective protests that accord with majority interests and concerns? The sit-ins did not directly support white interests, and they threatened directly both the economic and political interests of whites in the areas where they were conducted. But lunch-counter-type protests were tailored to and were carried out simply by presenting individuals seeking to purchase services readily available to whites. The injustice of refusing to serve blacks, despite the incipient breach of peace and trespass violations inherent in the sit-in activity, struck a sympathetic chord in most whites outside the South, who saw no reason to continue Jim Crow policies that embarrassed the nation, disadvantaged blacks, and violated the spirit if not the letter of the *Brown* decision.

More important than sympathy, though, was the disruption of business as usual resulting from the protests. In the most peaceful sit-in, crowds gathered, police were called, traffic was tied up. Predictably, regular customers began staying away to avoid involvement in the confusion, generated less by the protests than by the reaction to them from bystanders, hecklers, and the police. When even the fear that protestors might appear resulted in business lost to both lunch counters and other stores not involved in the protest activity, pressure to correct the problem became substantial. It was this pressure that ended segregation policies in public facilities in some cities even before enactment of any civil rights laws.

It is not clear that courts can easily give constitutional weight to the possibility that particular protests, if protected, will lead to the reform sought by the protesters. For example, the other side of Judge Higginbotham's position (§10.2 supra) that protests led to the enactment of civil rights statutes is that without the pressure of mass protests, little civil rights progress can be expected. Thus the observation made by the famous theologian Reinhold Niebuhr in the 1930s retains its validity:

> It is hopeless for the Negro to expect complete emancipation from the menial social and economic position into which the white man has forced him, merely by trusting in the moral sense of the white race. . . . However large the number of individual white men who do and who will identify themselves completely with the Negro cause, the white race in America will not admit the Negro to equal rights if it is not forced to do so. Upon that point one may speak with a dogmatism which all history justifies.[4]

4. Reinhold Niebuhr, Moral Man and Immoral Society 252-253 (1932).

Compare Dr. Niebuhr's conclusion with that of Justice Black, who warned:

> Those who encourage minority groups to believe that the United States Constitution and federal laws give them a right to patrol and picket in the streets whenever they choose, in order to advance what they think to be a just and noble end, do no service to those minority groups, their cause, or their country. I am confident from this record that this appellant violated the Louisiana statute because of a mistaken belief that he and his followers had a constitutional right to do so, because of what they believed were just grievances. But the history of the past 25 years if it shows nothing else shows that his group's constitutional and statutory rights have to be protected by the courts, which must be kept free from intimidation and coercive pressures of any kind.[5]

Assuming that Justice Black is wrong and Dr. Niebuhr right about the necessity of forceful protests to effect improvement in the status of blacks in America, courts would not seem likely to condone disruptive demonstrations, even those conducted to protest serious racial injustices. But courts have implicitly and sometimes expressly measured the disruption of the protest by the seriousness of the wrongs protested. Thus, after reciting the brutal treatment of the protesters at Selma, Judge Johnson said: "It seems basic to our constitutional principles that the extent of the right to assemble, demonstrate and march peaceably along the highways and streets in an orderly manner should be commensurate with the enormity of the wrongs that are being protested and petitioned against. In this case the wrongs are enormous."[6] All but the hardest heart would be moved by the events at Selma. But using Judge Johnson's standard, what must blacks or other disadvantaged minorities do when those against whom they protest peacefully are not so obligingly vicious in their response, or when the cause is less symbolic and more practical than voting (if more threatening), such as employment rights or the administration of criminal justice?

Few courts actually acknowledged considering the "enormity of the wrongs" in determining how disruptive protest might be and still receive judicial protection, and yet it is likely that such factors influenced decisions as much as unnecessarily violent police action. Perhaps, as well, courts should consider that poor minorities are likely to be as effective in pressing for reform in the streets as at the ballot box or even in the courtroom.

Frances Fox Piven and Richard A. Cloward go further. In a study of several twentieth-century protest movements — the unemployed workers, the industrial workers, the civil rights, and welfare rights movements — they conclude that the poor gain more through mass defiance and disruptive protests than by organizing for electoral politics and other more acceptable reform policies.[7] Indeed, they suggest that the effort by protest leaders to organize for political activity undermines the effectiveness of the protest and creates formally structured organizations that are unable to sustain the pressure on public or private elites possible

5. Cox v. Louisiana, 379 U.S. 536, 584 (1965) (dissenting).
6. William v. Wallace, 240 F. Supp. 100, 106 (M.D. Ala. 1965).
7. Frances Fox Piven & Richard A. Cloward, Poor People's Movements: Why They Succeed, How They Fail (1977).

through mass disruptions. Without this pressure, the concessions required to sustain and enlarge the mass organizations cannot be obtained.[8]

Piven and Cloward found that during those always brief and usually unpredictable periods when large numbers of lower class people are roused to indignation and defiance, the victories needed to sustain an organization seem ready to be won. Elites seem responsive and seek out the new groups, encouraging them to present their grievances before the courts or other formal bodies of the state. However, Piven and Cloward note that this responsiveness is not to the groups but to the underlying force and threat of insurgency. When the masses leave the streets and "normalcy" is regained, elites lose interest in the organizations which they earlier had encouraged and helped to sustain. In a comment with deep significance for some old-line civil rights organizations, the authors note: "As for the few organizations which survive, it is because they become more useful to those who control the resources on which they depend than to the lower class groups which the organizations claim to represent. Organizations endure, in short, by abandoning their oppositional politics."[9]

Except in extraordinary situations, courts are unlikely to consider what Piven and Cloward view as the reality of poor peoples' politics. Certainly First Amendment doctrine is sufficiently complex without attempting to factor in such considerations, but there is an advantage in making judges aware of *all* the reasons why the poor and minorities may have determined to take their grievances into the streets.

Whatever their political sophistication, courts are certainly aware that law enforcement officers during the sit-in period often harassed, arrested, and prosecuted civil rights adherents. In some instances they virtually joined those onlookers who opposed the protests. It was not difficult to conclude that officials generally served the interests of whites and the status quo, rather than the blacks who sought change. But for some white people, official efforts were not enough, and acting in private groups (sometimes with the help of public officials), they sought to maintain by force racial policies in lunch counters and elsewhere that the courts had determined could no longer be justified by law.

In the main, white "self-help" resistance took the form of economic coercion. A black employee might have the constitutional right to vote, send his child to a white school, or protest peacefully, but he had no right to his job, credit, or lease. At least, so those whites who were employers, bankers, and landlords believed. The difficulties in proving racial discrimination gave actual, if not legal, validity to their beliefs in most cases.

Not infrequently, whites supplemented economic coercion with physical threats, harassment, and violence. It is impossible to ascertain the amount of loss, suffering, and sacrifice resulting from the extra-legal actions of whites willing to demonstrate their opposition to equality for blacks.[10]

8. Id.
9. Id.
10. In Haywood County, Tennessee, a well-organized group of white landowners, merchants, bankers, and public officials — including the mayor of Brownsville, the sheriff, and school superintendent — sought to interfere with voting rights of blacks by exerting economic pressures

In summary, courts reviewing the convictions of civil rights protesters, or determining whether injunctive relief should be granted to either halt or protect such demonstrations, probably at least considered the wide range of factors discussed in this section. As indicated here, there seems to have been an initial step in the process of judicial review in which courts rejected all claims by protesters if the record indicated they had been responsible for violence or aggressively disruptive behavior. Assuming the protesters survived this step, courts then inquired whether the protest sufficiently involved First Amendment rights so as to entitle the protesters to a presumption of validity, even though their conduct, examined alone, seemed violative of peace and order. In effect, the Supreme Court weighed both the quality and manner of civil rights communication versus the interests and manner of state interference.

The problem with this analysis of judicial behavior in the civil rights protest era is that the grounds of possible decision are so broad that it is difficult to ascertain which factors the Court is relying on in any given case. Thus, the Court retained an extremely broad range of discretion under which they either gave or withheld protection, and protestors had difficulty ascertaining in advance whether their activities would be deemed constitutionally protected. The dangers this presented in a sit-in or protest march were quite real, but if a civil rights boycott was involved in the demonstration campaign, the process of trying to predict judicial reaction was fraught with peril.

§10.6   CIVIL RIGHTS BOYCOTTS AND COUNTERATTACKS

Many of the civil rights protest demonstrations examined thus far in this chapter were staged to gain support for consumer boycotts of segregated facilities. Indeed, the ability to organize blacks to selectively withhold their patronage from white businesses that relied on it became one of the most important weapons in the civil

---

and evicting black sharecroppers. Relief was sought by the United States under the 1957 Voting Rights Act. The district court with some reluctance enjoined defendants from interfering with efforts by blacks to register and vote, but found the Civil Rights Act did not "vest the courts with authority to adjudge contracts and property rights." The Sixth Circuit reversed and granted relief against the threatened evictions and economic pressures. United States v. Beaty, 288 F.2d 653 (6th Cir. 1961). The various orders in the case are set out in 6 Race Rel. L. Rep. 200-206 (1961-1962), 7 Race Rel. L. Rep. 484-487 (1962).

The government was less successful in a suit under the 1965 Voting Rights Act to prevent the eviction of sharecroppers and tenant farmers in West Feliciana Parish, Louisiana, Judge West ruling that the evidence failed to show any intimidation or coercion. United States v. Harvey, 250 F. Supp. 219 (E.D. La. 1966). Blacks failed to obtain relief against alleged evictions in Lowndes County, Alabama, and Judge Johnson not only granted summary judgment for the defendants, but even taxed the attorneys for the blacks with court costs, asserting that the evidence indicated that few, if any, of the plaintiffs had specifically authorized the suit, and finding that it was instigated by certain "civil rights organizations," from whom he suggested plaintiffs' attorneys could secure reimbursement. Miles v. Dickson, 40 F.R.D. 386 (M.D. Ala. 1966). On appeal, the assessment of costs was reversed, but the summary judgment was affirmed. Miles v. Dickson, 387 F.2d 716 (5th Cir. 1967).

rights arsenal. The successes achieved were impressive despite the uncertainty of judicial support.

— The Montgomery, Alabama, bus boycott, led by Dr. Martin Luther King, provided impetus for the whole civil rights movement of the next several years.[1]

— Blacks in Macon, Georgia, stopped riding buses in 1962 to protest segregated seating. Their action cost the bus company a 50 percent loss in fares, precipitating a surrender to the protest demands.

— In 1963, Birmingham, Alabama, retailers estimated they were losing $750,000 per week because of a boycott by black customers and the added loss of business of whites who were afraid to come downtown.

— In Nashville, Tennessee, the black population stopped buying from downtown stores prior to Easter in 1960. Formerly, blacks had spent about $7,000,000 per year in these stores. As a result of the boycott, there were serious losses at all stores and at the local transit company as well. Within a few weeks, white merchants had met with black leaders and subsequently opened formerly segregated eating facilities to blacks.[2]

— In Chicago, a 16-week boycott of all A&P stores led by Rev. Jesse Jackson ended when A&P promised 286 more jobs for blacks.[3]

Consumer boycotts have become a potent means of "sending a message" to manufacturers that they ignore at their peril. When a group of sports-bar owners threatened to mount a national boycott of network sponsors over plans of CBS and NBC to scramble their satellite transmissions of professional football games, the two networks promptly delayed their plans.[4] And, in the five months after the tanker *Exxon Valdez* dumped 10 million gallons of oil into Alaska's Prince William Sound in March 1988, nearly 40,000 of Exxon's 7 million credit card holders returned their cards to protest the spill and the company's cleanup effort.[5]

§10.6 1. Martin Luther King, Stride Towards Freedom (1958). As a result of the boycott, Dr. King was convicted of violating a state law that prohibited conspiracies to hinder business without a "just cause," and fined $500.

2. Consumer boycotts are not limited to racial issues. A nationwide boycott of table grapes in 1968, sponsored by Cesar Chavez's farmworkers union, resulted in a 12 percent decline in sales. See Time, July 4, 1969, at 16, 18.

The boycott has become an instrument of foreign diplomacy. The United States boycotted the 1980 Olympics in Moscow when the Soviet Union invaded Afghanistan. There is now general acceptance of the argument that sports and politics are intertwined, a position adamantly rejected when it was asserted by black athletes who wished to boycott the 1968 Olympic games to protest racial discrimination in this country. See Harry Edwards, The Revolt of the Black Athlete (1969). John Carlos and Tommie Smith, whose "clenched fist" protest at the 1968 Olympics (see photograph in front of this volume) became famous, were themselves boycotted for years in sports and in the job market by outraged whites.

More recently, companies that did business in South Africa faced a widely supported consumer boycott. The threat to image and profits posed by such boycotts led many American companies to halt doing business in South Africa or disguise their corporate activities there. Thus, boycotts — along with international sanctions against the pro-apartheid government — were critical factors in moving the South African government in the direction of political reform.

3. These and other boycott campaigns are discussed in Note, The Consumer Boycott, 42 Miss. L.J. 226-227, 239-242 (1971).

4. Mark Stencel, The Boycott Comes of Age, Wash. Post, Sep. 26, 1990, at F1.

5. Id. Exxon responded with newspaper ads in 100 newspapers emphasizing that because most Exxon stations were privately owned, these businesses rather than Exxon would bear the brunt of

The enormous potential for disruption in a free market economy of combinations who agree not to do business with particular firms and to urge others not to do so has led to a number of common law and statutory limitations on such activity. Participants in civil rights boycotts maintain that their actions are not intended to obtain economic advantage, but are aimed at communicating group displeasure at the discriminatory policies that victimize the group. As such, the argument goes, the First Amendment protects their right of peaceful protest, including selective withholding of patronage and urging others to do the same. Often, boycott campaigns last for months, during which time there are incidents involving violence, charges of undue coercion, and, usually, growing losses of revenue to the businesses the boycott targets.

Litigation by local businesses, generally initiated in sympathetic state courts, has posed a serious challenge to civil rights boycotts and has often resulted in large judgments that effectively destroyed the campaign and threatened the organizational sponsors. During the 1960s, the Supreme Court did not review any of these cases. It came closest to doing so in NAACP v. Overstreet.[6] Four Justices would have heard and reversed the judgment against the NAACP in the *Overstreet* case. Speaking for the dissenters, Justice Douglas reviewed the litigation instituted by a store in Savannah, Georgia, which had, because of alleged mistreatment of blacks, become the focus of a customer boycott organized by the local branch of the National Association for the Advancement of Colored People (NAACP). To publicize the campaign, pickets were established around the store who urged customers to withhold their patronage. There was no indication of misconduct by NAACP members or officers, but the picketing attracted large crowds. Incidents involving the intimidation of customers were reported, sidewalks were blocked, and there were scattered incidents of violence. The state court judge in the suit for damages filed by the store instructed the jury that if the picketing was the "proximate cause" of the misconduct of others, the jury could hold both the branch NAACP and the national NAACP liable, if the branch were found to be the "agent" of the national office. Accordingly, the jury held both the branch and the national office liable. Damages totalling $85,793 were assessed, including $50,000 in punitive damages. The Georgia Supreme court affirmed, and initially the Supreme Court had granted certiorari to review whether the judgment against the national office "for acts performed without its knowledge and by persons beyond its control" denied it rights secured by the Fourteenth Amendment.[7]

---

the boycott. Similarly, Nike Inc. responded to the boycott against its products launched by Operation PU by claiming that PUSH's action was motivated by donations from its leading competitor, Reebok International Ltd.

The greater constitutional protection granted by courts to boycotts deemed for "political" ends than to those seen as seeking "economic" advantage is examined in M. B. Gorrie, Per Se Can You See? The Superior Court Trial Lawyers and Their Perilous Fight, 24 Colum. J.L. & Soc. Probs. 203 (1991); James Gray Pope, Republican Moments: The Role of Direct Popular Power in the American Constitutional Order, 139 U. Pa. L. Rev. 287 (1990); Jeffrey Webb, Political Boycotts and Union Speech; A Critical First Amendment Analysis, 4 J.L. & Pol'y 579 (1988).

6. 221 Ga. 16, 142 S.E.2d 816, cert. dismissed as improvidently granted, 384 U.S. 118 (1966).
7. 382 U.S. 937.

Justice Douglas conceded that the market had suffered economic loss as a result of those who blocked its sidewalk and threatened its customers. He noted that the lower court's findings that the local NAACP could be held liable for these injuries posed no constitutional issues.[8] But, Justice Douglas maintained, the record contained not one iota of proof that the local NAACP official was an agent of the national office as alleged by the suit. The local branch is an affiliate of the national organization and a portion of its membership dues are forwarded to the national, thereby making members of the local branch automatically members of the national organization. The local branch also makes an annual report of its activities to the national NAACP. But the trial court's instructions seemed to make this connection between the local and the national sufficient both for agency and conspiracy.

In this precedent, Justice Douglas saw the seeds by which southern states could achieve their long-desired goal: the destruction of the NAACP. "To equate the liability of the national organization with that of the Branch, in the absence of any proof that the national authorized or ratified the misconduct in question could ultimately destroy it." He observed that the rights of political association are fragile enough without this additional danger of destruction through litigation, and warned that juries hostile to the aims of an organization in the educational or political field could deliver crushing verdicts that would stifle organized dissent, unless their discretion was carefully confined by meticulous instructions and judicial supervision.[9]

8. Giboney v. Empire Storage Co., 336 U.S. 490 (1949).

9. Justice Douglas, in the course of his dissent in *Overstreet*, refers to several efforts by southern states to suppress the activities of civil rights organizations, principally the NAACP, through their authority to regulate corporations. Most of these efforts were ultimately defeated in the courts, but not without doing great harm to the organizational structure of the civil rights groups. For example, in the wake of the Supreme Court's "freedom of association" decision in NAACP v. Alabama, 357 U.S. 449 (1958), which dissolved a $100,000 civil contempt fine levied against the association for its refusal to disclose its membership lists to state authorities, the NAACP was banned from doing business in Alabama by a state court from 1961 until the Supreme Court's final vindication of the group's activity on First Amendment grounds in 1964. NAACP v. Alabama, 377 U.S. 288 (1964). See also NAACP v. Thompson, 357 F.2d 831 (5th Cir.), cert. denied sub nom. Johnson v. NAACP, 385 U.S. 820 (1966), ending a three-year effort by state officials in Mississippi to bar the group.

In Virginia, in addition to NAACP v. Button (cited by Justice Douglas), there was a long history of litigation in which the state legislative committees sought to hamstring NAACP legal programs. The cases are reviewed in Jordan v. Hutchinson, 323 F.2d 597 (4th Cir. 1963). Louisiana statutes requiring annual filing of names and addresses of members, and requiring certain "non-trading" associations to file annual affidavits that none of its officers were Communists or members of subversive organizations, were voided in Louisiana ex rel. Gremillion v. NAACP, 181 F. Supp. 37 (E.D. La. 1960), aff'd, 366 U.S. 293 (1961).

In the wake of the *Brown* decision, eleven southern states acted separately through legislation or litigation to restrict NAACP efforts to end segregation through court cases. See 2 Race Rel. L. Rep. 892 (1957). Other groups espousing civil rights causes were also attacked. Dombrowski v. Pfister, 380 U.S. 479 (1965), was an unsuccessful effort by Louisiana to use its Subversive Activities and Communist Control law as a basis for harassing and prosecuting the Southern Conference Educational Fund (SCEF), a group active in fostering civil rights for blacks in Louisiana and other southern states. Legislative harassment of civil rights groups was not limited to the states. In Braden v. United States, 365 U.S. 431 (1961), the Supreme Court affirmed a contempt conviction obtained by the House Committee on Un-American Activities against an official of a pro-integration organization who refused to answer questions concerning his alleged Communist connections.

The NAACP's loss in the *Overstreet* case pointed the way to similar litigation in other places. In SCLC v. A.G. Corp.,[10] the plaintiff charged another civil rights organization (SCLC) and 39 individual defendants with liability for $115,000 in damages because of what was alleged as "illegal and unlawful conspiracy and with a secondary boycott the malicious and unlawful object of which was to ruin and cause injury to the businesses of the complainant and others." The court here held the defendants liable although it reversed and remanded the damages awarded as excessive. In the court's view, the plaintiff was an "innocent victim" of the black struggle for political and economic power. Since there was no showing that the plaintiffs had any authority to correct the racial discrimination complained of by defendants, and indeed had not even received a demand that it do so from defendants, the court characterized the picketing and the withdrawal of trade as an illegal and unlawful conspiracy through a secondary boycott.[11]

Lengthy efforts by blacks in Port Gibson, Mississippi, to protest racial discrimination through a boycott against local merchants led to a judgment against the NAACP for $1.25 million.[12] The case is an example of the conflict between the rights of freedom of expression and the traditional protection offered economic interests against coercive interference.

More than 15 years after the initiation of the Port Gibson boycott, the suit by white merchants seeking to end that very successful effort, and to cripple, if not destroy, the NAACP, was resolved by the Supreme Court in NAACP v. Claiborne Hardware Co.[13] In a unanimous decision (Justice Marshall abstaining), the Court vacated a permanent injunction against the boycott and overturned a massive state court judgment awarded against the NAACP and individual boycott participants. Justice Powell's strong opinion emphasized that nonviolent political boycotts are protected under the First Amendment and that organizers of such boycotts may not be held liable for individual acts of violence without proof that they condoned such illegal acts and that the damages were proximately caused by the violence.

The trial court in *Claiborne* granted a permanent injunction against the Port Gibson boycott and a judgment of more than $1.25 million against the NAACP and 129 individual defendants on three theories. First, the trial court found that the boycott participants had conspired to commit the tort of malicious interference

10. 241 So. 2d 619 (Miss. 1970).
11. See Henry v. First Nat'l Bank of Clarksdale, 444 F.2d 1300 (5th Cir. 1971). In the *Henry* case, an early skirmish in the major litigation (Claiborne Hardware, Inc. v. NAACP), the civil rights group was able to obtain a federal court order requiring banks to release funds which had been attached by the plaintiffs through a state court order shortly after their suit for damages was filed. Efforts by the NAACP to secure an injunction against continued prosecution of the anti-boycott suit were unsuccessful. Generally, federal courts have been reluctant to interfere with state court actions in this field unless the injunctive relief granted by the state court clearly infringes on protected First Amendment rights. Macheski v. Bizzell, 414 F.2d 283 (5th Cir. 1969), is a good example of relief granted in this situation.
12. Claiborne Hardware, Inc. v. NAACP, 78,353 (Miss. Ch. Ct. Aug. 9, 1976). Note, Political Boycott Activity and the First Amendment, 91 Harv. L. Rev. 659 (1978); the facts of the case are discussed in Sandifer & Smith, The Tort Suit for Damages: The New Threat to Civil Rights Organizations, 41 Brooklyn L. Rev. 559 (1975). For other writing on the subject, see Isaiah Madison, Mississippi's Secondary Boycott Statute: Unconstitutional Deprivation of the Right to Engage in Peaceful Picketing and Boycotting, 18 How. L.J. 583 (1975).
13. 458 U.S. 886 (1982).

with business.[14] Second, the boycott was held to violate a Mississippi statute prohibiting secondary boycotts that was enacted two years after the Port Gibson boycott began.[15] Third, the boycott was held to violate a Mississippi antitrust statute because it diverted patronage from white merchants to black. Because the second and third theories prohibited even nonviolent boycotts, the trial court neither made extensive fact findings linking the defendants with the several incidents of violence and coercion that had occurred, nor required proof that defendants had conspired to use violence or coercion to enforce the boycott. The judgment represented the entire loss in business to plaintiff merchants over the seven years of the boycott, plus generous attorneys' fees, costs, and interest.

On appeal, the Mississippi Supreme Court ruled that the statute prohibiting secondary boycotts did not apply to boycotts commenced before its enactment and that the Mississippi antitrust act, like the Sherman Act, did not apply to political boycotts. However, the court affirmed the injunction and the damages award on the common law theory of malicious interference with business, though it did question the methods used to calculate damages. Without remanding for further fact finding, the court found that "many" black citizens were "intimidated" by "threats" of "social ostracism, vilification, and traduction" and that the entire boycott was tainted by this use of force. The court held that liability could be imposed on defendants who acted as "store watchers" or otherwise participated in the boycott, or merely attended meetings of the Claiborne County branch of the NAACP, and against the national NAACP because it had not "repudiated" the boycott. Thirty-eight defendants were dismissed for lack of proof, leaving 92 defendants jointly and severally liable. The effect of this decision was to impose draconian penalties against all organizers and participants in a political boycott for any isolated incident of violence or coercion, thus effectively chilling the use of boycotts in Mississippi.

The Supreme Court's opinion by Justice Stevens refused to accept the Mississippi Supreme Court's ambiguous findings, emphasizing that the record showed that incidents of violence were few and limited to the early years of the boycott, that the victims of such incidents had continued patronizing white merchants, and that the success of the boycott was due to widespread support in the black community.

Though any defendants who used force could be held liable for damages proximately caused by that force, the Supreme Court held that they would not be liable for the consequences of their nonviolent, protected activity. Civil liability may not be imposed merely because an individual belongs to a group, some members of which commit acts of violence, without proof that the group itself possesses

14. Miss. Code Ann. §97-23-85 (1972), provides in relevant part: "If two (2) or more persons conspire to prevent another person or other persons from trading or doing business with any merchant or other business and as a result of said conspiracy said persons induce or encourage any individual or individuals to cease doing business with any merchant or other person, and when such a conspiracy is formed and effectuated because of a reasonable grievance of the conspirators over which the said merchant or place of business boycotted or against which a boycott is attempted has no direct control or no legal authority to correct . . . then each of such persons shall be guilty [of violating the statute and] liable in civil action."

15. Miss. Code Ann. §75-21-1 (1972).

unlawful goals. Likewise, liability cannot be imposed on an organization such as the NAACP because its agents organized a political boycott, or even participated in unauthorized acts of violence. The case was remanded to determine the liability of the few defendants who allegedly participated in violent or coercive incidents.

The *Claiborne* decision makes it virtually impossible for a state or local court to discourage boycotts by imposing tort liability for lost business on participants. Though it is a striking victory for the NAACP, freed from the threat of a massive judgment after many years; for the majority of the individual defendants whose cases were dismissed; and for all those who would use boycotts as a tool for change, the victory came at great cost. The NAACP was forced to spend massive amounts of time and money to defend this case. While attorneys' fees and legal costs may be recovered, initially the NAACP had to absorb the entire cost of its defense (and of the many defendants represented by NAACP counsel). In the meantime, the Port Gibson boycott, though effective, was not allowed to accomplish its goals, and many other substantive causes have been neglected during the long years of organization-threatening litigation.

Historically, courts have equated boycotts with violence and murder.[16] As a general matter, we probably shouldn't be surprised that courts remain inclined to equate boycotts with violence. As in protest cases, courts are intent upon establishing whether appropriate, nonviolent motives animated any particular boycott. The courts' willingness to draw the equation between boycotts and violence probably has much to do with the judiciary's almost visceral compulsion to position the "law" as the "antithesis of violence." The assumption that the courts have a profound interest in maintaining a law-violence opposition, helps make sense of, first, the courts' comfort with boycotts that seek to further constitutional values, as was seemingly the case in the Port Gibson case; and second, the courts' reliance upon the (ultimately untenable) distinction between "political" and "economic" boycotts. As suggested above, the courts work so assiduously to preserve the law-violence opposition just because it is so dubious.

In his very interesting article, Gary Minda tries to make sense of the confusion in the area of boycott law. In particular, he is concerned with the apparent contradiction between the results in the Port Gibson case, NAACP v. Claiborne Hardware, in which the Court eventually found First Amendment protection for boycotts mounted to end racial discrimination, and International Longshoremen's Ass'n v. Allied International, Inc., considered in the same term, in which the image of force projected in federal labor laws seemingly led the Court to find a labor union's secondary boycott illegal.[17] Minda wonders how it is that judges equate

16. Gary Minda, The Law and Metaphor of Boycott, 41 Buff. L. Rev. 807, 809, 820 (1993). Characterizing boycott law as "mired in indeterminancy," Minda suggests that the early hostility of courts to labor union boycotts continues to influence decisions. See Gompers v. Bucks Stove & Range Co., 221 U.S. 418 (1911) (holding that the mere promotion of a threatened boycott could be enjoined because "verbal acts" are like the "use of any other force whereby property is unlawfully damaged"). The decision, never reversed despite heavy criticism, has deeply influenced the meaning of boycotts and has led state and federal courts to regulate peaceful labor boycotts to protect society from their feared economic disruptions.

17. 456 U.S. 212 (1982). Even though the International Longshoremen's Association argued that their actions were premised on a purely political objective to communicate a message about

boycotts with "violence" in certain contexts, but not in others. He contends that it has to do with how courts characterize or interpret the protestors and their objects of protest. Methodologically, Minda looks to the semantic processes by which judges make sense of boycotts. His argument is that boycott law is best understood by considering how "language and power are mediated by the metaphoric structure" of the ideas about boycotts on which judges rely.[18]

As illustration, Minda cites FTC v. Superior Court Trial Lawyers' Ass'n[19] where a group of public defender lawyers representing indigent criminal defendants pursuant to the District of Columbia Justice Act conducted a boycott in an effort to extract higher hourly fees from the District of Columbia government. They asserted their action was protected by a First Amendment right to petition the government and was necessary to advance effectively the Sixth Amendment rights of their clients. Justice Stevens, writing for the Court majority, found the boycott constituted an illegal price fixing conspiracy, and he distinguished his opinion from that in *Claiborne Hardware* holding that First Amendment protection for civil rights boycotts are limited to instances where the boycotters seek no special economic advantage for themselves and advance a constitutional principle that transcends the interests of the individual. The District of Columbia lawyers were seen as motivated by an economic incentive to fix the price of their services rather than by an altruistic or idealistic motive of advancing a transcendent constitutional value.[20]

The Court eschewed a rule that would protect expressive boycotts unless they in fact caused economic harm. Analogizing antitrust laws to speed limits, the Court reasoned that the possibility of danger to the community from boycotts warranted enforcement of general laws even where the particular rule-breaker caused no actual damage.

The dissent, joined by Justices Marshall, Brennan, and Blackmun, sharply disagreed with the majority's content-blind approach to boycotts. Justice Brennan wrote:

> I cannot countenance this reasoning, which upon examination reduces to the Court's assertion that since the government may prohibit airplane stunt-flying and reckless

---

foreign trade and international justice, the Court held illegal the longshoremen's secondary boycott of a ship bound for Russia, mounted, according to the union, to protest the Soviet Union's invasion of Afghanistan. As an illegal act, the Court ruled, it could be enjoined.

18. Minda, supra note 16, at 827-828.

19. 493 U.S. 411 (1990).

20. For further critical comment on the *Superior Court Trial Lawyers' Ass'n* decision, see Jennifer L. Dauer, Political Boycotts: Protected by the Political Action Exception to Antitrust Liability or Illegal Per Se?, 28 U.C. Davis L. Rev. 1273 (1995); and Kay P. Kindred, When First Amendment Values and Competition Policy Collide: Resolving the Dilemma of Mixed-Motive Boycotts, 34 Ariz. L. Rev. 709 (1992).

The Court's reliance on an unstructured and ad hoc form of policy-balancing in civil rights boycotts has a lengthy history. Compare New Negro Alliance v. Sanitary Grocery Co., 303 U.S. 552 (1938) (finding protection under the Norris-LaGuardia Act as a "labor dispute" for blacks who urged boycott of grocery store that did not hire black clerks, even though many blacks shopped there), with Hughes v. Superior Court, 339 U.S. 460 (1950) (upholding a state court injunction of a civil rights boycott demanding that a grocery store located near a black housing project hire blacks in proportion to the percentage of black customers — estimated at 50 percent — on the basis that the boycott was contrary to the judicially stated California public policy of nondiscrimination in employment; at the time of the boycott, California had no law barring discrimination based on race).

automobile driving as categorically harmful, it may also subject expressive political boycotts to a presumption of illegality without even inquiring as to whether they actually cause any of the harms that the antitrust laws are designed to prevent. This non sequitur cannot justify the significant restriction on First Amendment freedoms that the majority's rule entails.[21]

The First Amendment's command that regulations on speech be no greater than necessary argues against a rule which bars boycotts whether or not they cause the damage against which the rule protects.

The dissent emphasized that the boycott was political rather than economic in both its means and aim. Economic boycotts generally seek to operate without detection and to persuade no one but its target. And as a matter of common sense, it is unrealistic that a small coalition, without any significant market power, would hope to change the practice of the government through exclusively, or even primarily, economic means. The lawyers' campaign was political, using a dramatic form of protest to communicate the justness of their cause and the seriousness of their commitment, and thereby generate reform:

> By sacrificing income that they actually desired, and thus inflicting hardship on themselves as well as on the city, the lawyers demonstrated the intensity of their feelings and the depth of their commitment. The passive nonviolence of King and Gandhi are proof that the resolute acceptance of pain may communicate dedication and righteousness more eloquently than mere words ever could. A boycott, like a hunger strike, conveys an emotional message that is absent in a letter-to-the-editor, a conversation with the mayor, or even a protest march. In this respect, an expressive boycott is a special form of political communication.[22]

Even more importantly, it is a form of communication essential to those who, because they have little money, cannot generate change without dramatic forms of protest. By enforcing a broad ban on boycotts, the Court's decision would not only controvert long-standing First Amendment jurisprudence, but deprive those in need of their most effective political weapon.

§10.7   DEFAMATORY STATEMENTS AND PROTEST RIGHTS

Even when they do not contain threats, militant statements against whites may subject blacks to legal liability where such statements can be interpreted as defamatory. This danger is real despite the tremendous extension given freedom of expression in New York Times v. Sullivan.[1] There, the Supreme Court reversed a judgment of $500,000 in damages awarded by Alabama courts to the elected police commissioner of Montgomery, who charged that a full-page

---

21. *Superior Court Trial Lawyers'Ass'n*, 493 U.S. at 437.
22. Id. at 450-451.
§10.7   1. 376 U.S. 254 (1964).

advertisement soliciting funds for various civil rights groups constituted libel, in that it imputed improper conduct to him and contained statements that were untrue in a number of respects. He alleged that the statements damaged his reputation, and tended to bring him into public contempt. The Supreme Court determined that the list of racial abuses contained in the advertisement was not "commercial," but was an expression protected by the First and Fourteenth Amendments, the suppression of which would discourage newspapers from providing an important outlet for the promulgation of information and ideas by persons who do not themselves have access to publishing facilities. Speaking through Justice Brennan, the Court concluded, "The constitutional guarantees require, we think, a federal rule that prohibits a public official from recovering damages for a defamatory falsehood relating to his official conduct unless he proves that the statement was made with 'actual malice' — that is, with knowledge that it was false, or with reckless disregard of whether it was false or not. . . ."

As happened in Gomillion v. Lightfoot,[2] the *New York Times* case, while protecting the rights of blacks, established a precedent which substantially increased the First Amendment rights of all citizens.[3] Based on this success in providing breathing space for civil rights speech in an area traditionally deemed subject to tort liability for defamation, the NAACP should perhaps have expected an unfavorable response to their demand that a political candidate broadcasting racial epithets be silenced.

§10.8 RACIAL DEMONSTRATIONS SINCE THE SIT-IN PERIOD

It is important to remember that by 1965-1966, when the Supreme Court was reflecting its unwillingness to provide further support of civil rights protests by

2. 364 U.S. 339 (1960).

3. The *New York Times* rule has been extended (1) to prohibit punishment under a state criminal defamation statute based on charges respecting district court judges, Garrison v. Louisiana, 379 U.S. 364 (1964); (2) to bar a suit for seditious libel based on impersonal criticism of the government's operations, Rosenblatt v. Baer, 383 U.S. 75 (1966); and (3) to hold that an invasion of privacy action would not lie against a publication which erroneously stated that a play was based upon a true incident involving the plaintiff's family, Time, Inc. v. Hill, 385 U.S. 374 (1967). In Rosenbloom v. Metromedia, Inc. 403 U.S. 29 (1971), the Court held that the *New York Times* rule of knowing or reckless falsity applied in a state civil libel action, which was brought by a private individual for a defamatory falsehood that had been uttered in a radio news broadcast about his involvement in an event of public or general interest.

Subsequently, in Gertz v. Robert Welch, Inc., 418 U.S. 323 (1974), the Court, rejected the extension of the *New York Times* test proposed by the three-justice plurality in Rosenbloom v. Metromedia, and held that the states may impose liability on a publisher upon a showing of simple negligence where (1) the defamed individual is neither a public official nor a public figure but rather a private individual; (2) the statement is such as to make substantial danger to reputation apparent; and (3) actual injury is proved. The *Gertz* holding limits plaintiffs who do not establish *New York Times* malice to compensation for actual injury; punitive damages will not be recoverable upon a showing of simple negligence.

affirming some convictions and denying review in others, most of the "sat-in" facilities had long since been desegregated, either by "voluntary" action or as a result of the Civil Rights Act of 1964. In a sense, the protesters' ends had been attained despite the Court's subsequent condemnation of some of their means.

It is doubtful whether the mass of blacks locked in northern urban ghettos were aware of the Court's hardened position on civil rights protests, but it is certain that they had little reason to believe they would share in the progress made in the South. The urban riots, unlike the sit-ins and marches in the South, were generally unplanned (if not unprovoked), violent, destructive, and costly in both human and financial terms. Neither the rioting itself nor the often totally arbitrary and vindictive response of the courts to the rioters can be evaluated in traditional legal terms.[1] Many of the protests after the sit-in period were not prayerfully nonviolent, but neither were they riots. Rather, they fell somewhere between these two extremes. The courts, though, generally condemned all but those close to the classical nonviolent model; where the demonstrators resorted to violence, questions of provocation and even of self-defense did not serve as restraints to prompt judicial condemnation.

As open resistance to black demands spread from the South to the rest of the nation, blacks became increasingly unwilling to play a deserving, nonviolent, supplicant role. James Meredith, whose courage had thrilled the nation in 1962, was shot on a protest walk through his home state in June 1966; and in the demonstrations that followed, Stokely Carmichael coined the phrase "Black Power," which in one fell swoop cost blacks millions of dollars in white contributions and other support, while providing them with a new sense of racial pride not measurable in financial terms.[2] On April 4, 1968, Martin Luther King, Jr., was killed by a white assassin, precipitating racial violence in scores of cities. Although the revolution that some blacks called for did not come, clearly the era of prayerful nonviolence was at an end. The protests that followed were intended to end racial injustices no less serious than those which had been opposed with much of the nation's support in the early 1960s. Indeed, the injustices were frequently more serious, but the protests were also more threatening.

As might have been predicted by their tendency during the early 1960s to withhold protection to those civil rights protests that were aggressively disruptive or violent, the courts in the main took a judicial "hard line" on the more militant black protests of the late 1960s. Sympathy for these demonstrations had been drained both by concern over the urban riots and the sense that federal laws addressed to legitimate black grievances had been enacted — albeit tardily — and should be utilized.

---

§10.8   1. The major racial confrontations, from East St. Louis in 1917 to the killings at Jackson State University in 1970, as seen by the official commissions appointed to investigate them, are summarized together with critical analyses of those reports in Anthony Platt, The Politics of Riot Commissions, 1917-1970 (1971).

2. Stokely Carmichael Peter became known as Kwame Ture. The Black Power movement, represented by Carmichael and CORE leader Floyd McKissick, rejected the moderate integrationist aims of the civil rights movement and advocated separatism and, where necessary, self-defense. See Stokely Carmichael & Charles V. Hamilton, Black Power: The Politics of Liberation in America (1967). For the contribution of Black Power to the civil rights movement, see Lucius Barker &

§10.9 RESPONDING TO ACTS OF PROTEST

§10.9.1 Silencing Protest and Dissent in 2003 and Beyond

The events of September 11, 2001 sparked a national policy response that exploited the fear of terrorist attacks to curtail liberties of all citizens. The U.S.A. Patriot Act was passed immediately by Congress, with little time for public debate. Professor Orin Gross explains that "the panoply of counterterrorism measures put in place since September 11th has created 'an alternate system of justice' aimed at dealing with suspected terrorists."[1] He describes some of the most egregious elements: "allowing the monitoring of exchanges between suspected terrorists and their lawyers, the aggrandizement of powers of the federal government, combating the financial infrastructure of terrorism, racial profiling, the refusal to release information about hundreds of persons arrested since September 11th, expanding the scope of government surveillance, and the Total Information Awareness project."[2] In addition, major institutional changes have included the creation and establishment of the Department of Homeland Security and structural changes to the FBI.[3] According to supporters of the legislation, secrecy and heightened surveillance were justified by the need for strong national security and ferreting out terrorist enemies, rationales reflecting those given for the Japanese internment during World War II and the federal policing of groups like the Communist Party or the Black Panthers. The legislation provides yet another historical example of how in times of war or serious crisis supposedly "democratic nations tend to race to the bottom as far as the protection of human rights and civil liberties, indeed of basic and fundamental legal principles, is concerned."[4] Suspending basic civil rights and free speech enormously impacts the ability of any group of individuals to use protest as a meaningful form of disagreement with government action.[5] Immediately after September 11, the Bush administration framed any opposition to its response as unpatriotic. White House spokesperson Ari Fleischer warned Americans to "watch what they say." Even reporters have found they cannot speak out against administration policy without jeopardizing their jobs.

D. Jansiewicz, Coalitions in the Civil Rights Movement, in Black Americans and the Political System 231-235 (Lucius Barker & Jesse McCorry eds., 1976).

§10.9   1. Orin Gross, Chaos and Rules: Should Responses to Violent Crises Always Be Constitutional?, 112 Yale L.J. 1011, 1017 (2003). Gross describes a model for responding to times of crisis through innovative legal structures. In doing so, he suggests that constitutionality guide our actions: "[C]onstitutionality tells us that whatever responses are made to the challenges of a particular exigency, such responses are to be found and limited within the confines of the constitution. While terrorists are lawless and operate outside the sphere of legal principles, rules, and norms, democratic governments must be careful not to fight terrorism with lawless means. Otherwise, they may only succeed in defeating terrorism at the expense of losing the democratic nature of the society in whose defense they are fighting."

2. Id. at 1017-1018.

3. Id. at 1018.

4. Id.

5. For a more expansive discussion, see ACLU, Freedom Under Fire: Dissent in Post-9/11 America (2003).

The U.S.A. Patriot Act defines domestic terrorist activity broadly to consist of acts that are "dangerous to human life."[6] Many activist organizations fear that they will find themselves under investigation and prosecution for acts of terrorism that arise from protest.

In addition, the legislation, like most emergency responses, increased federal surveillance while removing certain checks and balances to ensure basic constitutional protections. The U.S.A. Patriot Act makes it easier for federal officials to look into an individual's records held by third parties and to make secret searches of personal property without the knowledge of the owner. Wiretapping laws have also been expanded. Agency regulations are released daily, curtailing rights of citizens and immigrants in the name of national security.[7] Requests by Congress to learn how the law's provisions have been implemented have gone largely unanswered because the answers are deemed classified information. Any answers have been criticized for highlighting the least problematic uses of agencies' new powers.[8] Even against this uncertain background, some congressional leaders are lobbying for more drastic measures in Patriot Act II.

In one specific example, the Act compels libraries and bookstores to help federal investigators monitor the reading selections of their customers.[9] Some libraries are responding by posting signs that warn customers about the law; others are going as far as destroying borrowing records. Over 90 municipalities have passed resolutions condemning this provision.[10] One town, Arcata, California, has subjected those who voluntarily comply with a fine.[11]

In response to the war against Iraq, individuals have used varying forms of protest from marches to actions of civil disobedience. Yet, in trying to subvert these dissenting opinions, some municipalities have made it more difficult to receive protest permits. In New York City, after September 11, the police department had an unwritten policy to prevent any public permits for protests or marches, other than those that have traditionally been given parade routes.[12] The police department failed to plan adequately for a major anti-war protest. The area designated for a rally proved far too small. Hundreds of thousands of protesters, uninformed by the police as to where to go, were forced into adjoining streets. There they were charged by police horses and many persons were

---

6. How the U.S.A. Patriot Act redefines "Domestic Terrorism," Dec. 6, 2002, available at http://www.aclu.org/newsprint.cfm.

7. Dan Eggen, Laws Evoked Against Crimes Unrelated to Terror, Report Says, Wash. Post, May 21, 2003.

8. Id.

9. Rene Sanchez, Librarians Make Some Noise over Patriot Act, Wash. Post, Apr. 10, 2003.

10. Clarence Page, Defending Our Privacy Rights Against an All-Out Assault, Balt. Sun, Apr. 25, 2003.

11. Id.

12. Andrew Chow, NYPD Monitoring Irks Civil Liberties Union, Wash. Sq. News, Apr. 21, 2003. The New York City police used arrest interrogations to record information about individuals and their organizing activity strategies to develop a protester's database. Given serious public criticism, the police commissioner, who denied any knowledge of the database, released a formal apology to ensure that it was destroyed. Advocates feared that information was shared with federal officials before this action was taken.

arrested.[13] Even when permits are granted, police action has been questionable. In Vermont, police authorized undercover officers to film protest activities to get a sense of unlawful actions. In many other municipalities, officers have gone undercover to investigate organizing strategies, even going as far as creating a database with details about protesters and their direct actions.[14]

These examples are only a few of the recent deliberate attacks on civil rights and liberties that have been largely accepted by courts and much of the country as necessary responses to a national threat. This abridgement of rights has no end in sight. In countless times since the passage of the U.S.A. Patriot Act, Americans have been reminded of Benjamin Franklin's wisdom: "They that can give up essential liberty to obtain a little temporary safety deserve neither liberty nor safety." Those who are willing to give up essential liberty also rarely suffer from its deprivation. As the federal policy curtails our ability to protest effectively and express dissenting views, it jeopardizes the ability to use protest and speech to resist unjust and racist laws.

§10.9.2 Racial Issues and the Flag-Burning Cases

As indicated above, the liberty-threatening responses to the September 11, 2001, attacks follow an all too familiar response to national threats.[15] Consider the general hostility that early met opponents to the Vietnam War. Americans who supported the country's involvement were outraged when opponents resorted to tactics that included burning draft cards, despoiling Selective Service records with animal blood, and burning the American flag. A poignant chapter in this era is reported in Street v. New York.[16] A state statute made it a misdemeanor to "publicly mutilate, deface, defile, or defy, trample upon, or cast contempt upon either by words or act [any flag of the United States]." In this case, according to the Court:

> Appellant testified that during the afternoon of June 6, 1966, he was listening to the radio in his Brooklyn apartment. He heard a news report that civil rights leader James Meredith had been shot by a sniper in Mississippi. Saying to himself, "They didn't protect him," appellant, himself a Negro, took from his drawer a neatly folded, 48-star American flag which he formerly had displayed on national holidays. Appellant left his apartment and carried the still-folded flag to the nearby intersection of St. James Place and Lafayette Avenue. Appellant stood on the northeast corner of the intersection, lit the flag with a match, and dropped the flag on the pavement when it began to burn.
>
> Soon thereafter, a police officer halted his patrol car and found the burning flag. The officer testified that he then crossed to the northwest corner of the intersection, where he found appellant "talking out loud" to a small group of persons. The officer

13. Christopher Dunn et al., Arresting Protest: A Special Report of the New York City's Civil Liberties Union on New York City's Protest Policies at the February 15, 2003 Antiwar Demonstration in New York City, Apr. 2003.

14. Police Filming of the Vermont Protests Revives Anger, Fears, Burlington Free Press, Apr. 7, 2003.

15. See generally Geoffrey Stone, Perilous Times: Free Speech in Wartime from the Sedition Act of 1798 to the War on Terrorism (1905).

16. 394 U.S. 576 (1969).

estimated that there were some 30 persons on the corner near the flag and five to 10 on the corner with appellant. The officer testified that as he approached within 10 or 15 feet of appellant, he heard appellant say, "We don't need no damn flag," and that when he asked appellant whether he had burned the flag appellant replied: "Yes; that is my flag; I burned it. If they let that happen to Meredith we don't need an American flag." Appellant admitted making the latter response, but he denied that he said anything else and asserted that he always had remained on the corner with the flag.

In a five-to-four decision, the Court reversed a conviction by the New York Supreme Court because it was unclear whether conviction was based on the act of burning or on the spoken words. If based on the latter, or on a combination of act and words, it was violative of rights of free expression. At the conclusion of his majority opinion, Justice Harlan added, "disrespect for our flag is to be deplored no less in these vexed times than in calmer periods of our history."

Chief Justice Warren and Justices Black, White, and Fortas each wrote dissenting opinions, totaling 23 pages in the official reports. Each believed that the issue of whether appellant could be convicted of burning the flag was properly before the Court, and that the conviction should be affirmed.

On remand, the New York Court of Appeals, while asserting its opinion that defendant had been tried and convicted solely for the act of burning the flag, conceded that the conviction must be reversed under the Supreme Court's mandate. A new trial was ordered at which defendant was "to be tried solely for his act of burning the flag."[17]

In *Street,* the Court's opposition to flag burning, even when done with great provocation, was shown more by the opinion than the result. None of the opinions expressed any sympathy for Street, who, the record shows, was clearly patriotic, but who, upon hearing of the Meredith shooting, had simply lost control. The New York Court of Appeals had recognized the situation, but, concerned about the threat to public order posed by Street's act, said:

> The violation of the statute may not be condoned simply because the defendant's agitation resulted from the distressing news he had heard on the radio or because no violence actually did occur as a result of the flag burning. These were mitigating circumstances that were properly taken into account by the trial court when it suspended sentence for the conviction. [People v. Street.][18]

17. 24 N.Y.2d 1026, 250 N.E.2d 250 (1969).

18. 20 N.Y.2d 231, 229 N.E.2d 187, 282 N.Y.S.2d 491 (1967). Upon remand of the case, Street was retried and convicted in Criminal Court, Kings County, of burning the flag. During the pendency of his appeal to the appellate term, Street died and the prosecution was abated. Letter to author dated Sept. 21, 1972, from Burt Neuborne, N.Y. Civil Liberties Union, 84 Fifth Ave., New York, N.Y. 10011. In subsequent flag desecration cases, the Court seemed more sympathetic of human rights. See Smith v. Goguen, 415 U.S. 566 (1974) (conviction for wearing a small U.S. flag sewn onto the seat of his trousers reversed as violative of the due process clause because statute subjected to criminal liability anyone who "publicly treats contemptuously the flag of the United States."); Spence v. Washington, 418 U.S. 405 (1974) (the display of an American flag with large peace symbols attached with removable tape was held protected expression that was impermissibly infringed on by a state statute barring such a display); Texas v. Johnson, 491 U.S. 397 (1989) (invalidated a state statute making burning the flag a criminal offense).

Professor Melville Nimmer believes that a basic problem in these cases arises from the judicial effort to accord symbolic speech less protection than is given verbal speech. The purpose of both is the same, and, in fact, both are subject to regulation under present rules. For example, words which presage an imminent and likely breach of the peace will justify abridgment as much as if the idea had been conveyed in nonverbal terms. Professor Nimmer concludes that adoption of this equality would prevent a protester from being penalized because of his choice of method or his inability to communicate in a language other than that of conventional words.[19]

Though long recognized as rich in symbolic content, protests involving the American flag remain likely to provoke reprisals from employers and bystanders and hostile reactions from the courts. In Leonard v. City of Columbus,[20] black policemen who were improperly discharged after demonstrations that included removing a United States flag patch from their uniforms sued for wrongful discharge and reinstatement, only to have their suit dismissed by the District Court for the Middle District of Georgia. On appeal the Eleventh Circuit recognized that the flag incident constituted symbolic speech which is protected under the First and Fourteenth Amendments and granted the officers a chance to try their case.

Leonard stemmed from an incident in 1971 when black policemen, protesting discriminatory practices within the force and by police officers in the treatment of black citizens, formed an "Afro-American Patrolmen's League" and submitted a list of complaints and requests to the police department. After attempts to pursue the matter with department officials failed, black officers began to picket the police station in a peaceful and orderly manner. At a meeting with civic leaders the officers agreed to cease picketing, but when police officials violated this "cooling down period," League members resumed picketing and removed the American flag patch from their uniforms, announcing that they could not wear it because of injustice on the force. Subsequently, the officers were discharged on the grounds that their removal of an official part of their uniforms was conduct unbecoming officers. After their discharge other reasons were given, including "making baseless allegations of racism and discrimination" and violating police regulations regarding demonstrations.

The Eleventh Circuit found that the League members' dismissal did not follow established Columbus procedures, and that though many officers neglected to wear the flag patch, no police officer had been disciplined for this infraction before the League incident. Apparently, up to that time, few Columbus policemen had been aware of a 1969 directive making the flag an official part of the uniform. From these facts the court concluded that the officers were dismissed less for the act of removing the flag patch than for the symbolic meaning expressed by that action.[21]

19. Melville Nimmer, The Meaning of Symbolic Speech under the First Amendment, 21 UCLA L. Rev. 29 (1973).

For a contrary view, see Tinsley E. Yarbrough, Justice Black and His Critics on Speech-Plus and Symbolic Speech, 52 Texas L. Rev. 257 (1974). See also John Hart Ely, Comment, Flag Desecration: A Case Study in the Roles of Categorization and Balancing in First Amendment Analysis, 88 Harv. L. Rev. 1482 (1975).

20. 705 F.2d 1299 (11th Cir. 1983).

21. Id. at 1306.

Although many in Congress recognized the potential political value in the flag burning issue, there was some resistance to the idea of tampering with the Constitution based on this concern.[22] But, rather than directly refusing to change the Constitution, Congress choose another, arguably politically safer approach — the Flag Protection Act of 1989.[23] The Flag Protection Act of 1989 was almost immediately challenged by two groups on opposite ends of the country. In the West, in Seattle, Washington, seven people burned flags to protest the new law.[24] In the East, protesters against various U.S. domestic and foreign policies burned flags on the steps of the Capitol to drive home their concerns as well as to confront the new law.[25] Both groups challenged the constitutionality of the new flag burning statute on its face and as applied in their cases. The district court judges in each case[26] found the statute unconstitutional in light of Texas v. Johnson. The Justice Department utilized a provision in the new law which allowed for direct appeal to the United States Supreme Court of the first case to challenge this law.[27] The court declined to reconsider its decision in *Johnson,* and considered only whether the Flag Protection Act is "sufficiently distinct from the Texas statute that it may constitutionally be applied to proscribe appellees' expressive conduct."[28] Justice Brennan, writing for the majority, concluded that the Act was not distinct and therefore was unconstitutional; "the Act still suffers from the same fundamental flaw: it suppresses expression out of concern for its likely communicative impact."[29] Justice Brennan noted that although the government denied that the statute sought to place content-based limits on the flag burning conduct, that was clearly its intent.[30] He stated that the "Government's perceived interest in protecting the 'physical integrity' of a privately owned flag [footnote omitted] rests upon a perceived need to preserve the flag's status as a symbol of our Nation and certain national ideals." But he argued that "mere destruction . . . of a particular physical

22. See Norman Dorsen, Flag Desecration in Courts, Congress and Country, 17 T.M. Cooley L. Rev. 417 (2000), describing the flag burning debate, including a discussion of Supreme Court precedent and the political fight that ensued in response to the Court's 1989 decision.

23. 18 U.S.C.S. §700 (1991). Desecration of the flag of the United States; penalties, was amended under this Act effective October 28, 1989. The statute has existed on the books since 1968. The 1989 Act was drafted to correct perceived constitutional problems raised by the earlier statute.

24. United States v. Haggerty, 731 F. Supp. 415 (W.D. Wash. 1990).

25. United States v. Eichman, 731 F. Supp. 1123 (D.C. 1990), aff'd, 496 U.S. 310 (1990).

26. *Haggerty,* supra note 24; *Eichman,* supra note 25.

27. 18 U.S.C.S. §700(d) (1991).

28. *Eichman,* 496 U.S. at 315.

29. Id. at 317. The breakdown of the Court decision in this case was identical to the breakdown in *Johnson.* Brennan wrote for the majority. He was joined by Justices Marshall, Blackmun, Scalia, and Kennedy. The dissent was written by Stevens and joined by Chief Justice Rehnquist and Justices White and O'Connor.

30. The Court noted that the government's action was related to both the content and suppression of free speech. 496 U.S. at 315-316. Further, Justice Brennan stated, the words of the statute itself "confirms Congress' interest in the communicative impact by flag destruction. . . . Each of the specified terms [of the statute] — with the possible exception of 'burns' — unmistakably connotes disrespectful treatment of the flag and suggests a focus on those acts likely to damage the flag's symbolic value." (footnote omitted) Id. at 310-311.

Moreover, the Act excluded disposal of "worn or soiled" flags, indicating its aim to exempt acts associated with respect for the flag. Id.

manifestation of the symbol, without more, does not diminish or otherwise affect the symbol itself. . . ." Justice Brennan concluded his analysis of the statute by noting that "[a]lthough Congress cast the Flag Protection Act in somewhat broader terms than the Texas statute at issue in *Johnson,* the Act still suffers from the same fundamental flaw: it suppresses expression out of concern for its likely communicative impact." Since the Act's restrictions were directly related to the content of the regulated speech, the Court applied "the most exacting scrutiny" standard established in Boos v. Barry.[31] Then, for the reasons noted in *Johnson,* the Court held "the Government's interest cannot justify its infringement on First Amendment rights." Brennan recognized that flag desecration was offensive to many people but argued that "punishing such desecration of the flag dilutes the very freedom that makes this emblem so revered, and worth revering." The dissent focused on the symbolic value of the flag as it argued that the government did have a "legitimate interest in protecting . . . the American flag." This interest arises because "the flag is a reminder both that the struggle for liberty and equality is unceasing, and that our obligation of tolerance and respect for all of our fellow citizens encompasses those who disagree with us. . . ."[32]

The dissent revealed a deep discomfort with the disrespect flag burning implies. Seeking to restore the symbol as a means of restoring all that it symbolized harkened back to an earlier era of unquestioning patriotism: "The symbolic value of the American flag is not the same today as it was yesterday. Events during the last three decades have altered the country's image in the eyes of numerous Americans, and some now have difficulty understanding the message that the flag conveyed to their parents — whether born abroad and naturalized or native born." The dissent also argued that this statute sought to "protect the symbolic value of the flag without regard to the specific content of the flag burner's speech." Since there were other means by which protesters could relay their messages, the dissent stated that the protesters' right to expression was not unconstitutionally infringed upon by the Flag Protection Act.

With the Court's ruling that the Flag Protection Act was unconstitutional, the cry went up again for a constitutional amendment. There had been some speculation prior to this decision, that the political pressures raised by this issue would have an effect on the Justices.[33] One commentator said that the political pressures were noted by the dissent when Justice Stevens stated, "the integrity of the [flag] has been compromised by those leaders who seem to advocate compulsory worship of the flag even by individuals whom it offends, or who seem to manipulate the symbol of national purpose into a pretext for partisan disputes about meaner ends."

---

31. 485 U.S. 312 (1988).

32. *Eichman*, 496 U.S. at 321. The dissenters' position seems contradictory. They argue in favor of the government's interest in regulating the treatment of the flag because it represents, among other things, tolerance of differing views, yet punishing people with differing views as to the flag is the apparent intent of the statute. This form of intolerance by the flag burning statute advocates seems to contradict the dissent's view of what the flag represents.

33. "Privately, several justices expressed surprise at the intense reaction to their ruling . . . in Texas v. Johnson. Some legal experts speculated that one or more justices might switch votes this time. . . . In fact, however, none of the justices switched positions." High Court Voids Law Against Burning Flag, L.A. Times, June 12, 1990, at A1.

Legislation to amend the Constitution regarding the flag was raised in both the House and Senate, but failed to gain the two-thirds majority votes required as a first step in the ratification of a constitutional amendment.[34]

In addressing the merits of protecting the flag through a constitutional amendment, Professor Norman Dorsen contends that a high burden should be placed on supporters of the amendment.[35] He rejects the notion that history can be a solid source of support for anti-flag burners, mentioning the often-cited case of George Washington defacing the English flag, and points to serious problems with the vagueness of flag desecration prohibitions. More significantly, he responds to the argument that our democratic system of law should respond to the flag amendment's tremendous popular support. Dorsen argues that "the whole purpose of the Bill of Rights is to protect minorities."[36] Although popular sovereignty is an important aspect of democracy, "equally important is the concept of individual liberty, which need not yield to majority sentiment."[37] It is tempting to believe that the flag-burning controversy of the late 1980s and early 1990s represented little more than politicians manipulating what, for most Americans, was not a serious issue.[38] It is, however, difficult to reconcile the "political manipulation" argument with the fervent popular support for legal restrictions on flag burning. Might it be that the period's fervent anti-flag-burning sentiments were related to a kind of collective visual trauma? The late twentieth century is replete with images of the American flag aflame. In many instances, these images attach to hazy memories of America's military "emasculation" at the hands of some demonized racial other. In the wake of the Iranian hostage crisis, flag-burning was routinely associated with so-called Islamic fundamentalism and with hostage-taking in the Middle East. It also seems worth noting that the flag debate played out during an historical moment in which America's economic and political position in the world seemed terribly unclear.

The issue has yet again been raised in Congress's 2003 session, even amidst issues of homeland security, budget deficits, tax breaks, and political unrest throughout the world.[39] This attempt to push forward the amendment arises in the wake of a revival of U.S. patriotism since the tragedy of September 11, 2001, as flags fly outside homes and renditions of "America the Beautiful" and "God Bless America" seem to pervade public ceremonies and sporting events. In sharp contrast to the Iran hostage crisis, the flag amendment issue has come to the floor of Congress immediately after the United States unilaterally asserted its military muscle in the Middle East to overthrow Iraq's dictator and began to reconstitute the state under the singular control of U.S. military forces. Simultaneously, at home the civil liberties of U.S. citizens and especially Arabs and

34. After a constitutional amendment is passed by Congress, the measure must be passed by three-fourths of the state legislatures.

35. See Dorsen, supra note 22.

36. Id. at 437.

37. Id. at 438.

38. Robert Justin Goldstein asserts as much in his book, The Great 1989-1990 Flag Desecration Controversy 370 (1996). See a review of Goldstein's book by Travis, Wall, Burning the Flag, 84 Cal. L. Rev. 1719 (1996).

39. Editorial, Burnt Out, Wash. Post, May 13, 2003.

Muslims have come under attack through the passage of the U.S.A. Patriot Act of 2002 (see §10.9.1) and regulations emanating from the newly formed Department of Homeland Security. Such circumstances, like the flag amendment itself, undermine the democratic foundations upon which this country, and the symbol of the flag, rests.

§10.10 CROSS BURNING BY WHITES AS EXPRESSIVE CONDUCT

For all of the political play given to flag burning, another type of incendiary activity — cross burning — is noticeably absent from the national political scene.[1] Many states have taken action on their own to address this type of hate crime.[2] In two Supreme Court rulings, the Court has addressed the constitutionality of these laws to determine whether cross burning, a symbol plagued with a history of violence and terror, is afforded First Amendment protection. Each case hinged on whether the proscribed activity was a permissible content-based restriction on speech.

§10.10.1 R.A.V. v. City of St. Paul

In the first Supreme Court case addressing the issue, R.A.V. v. City of St. Paul, Minnesota,[3] the Court invalidated a Minnesota statute aimed at hate-motivated expressive conduct as an invalid content-based restriction on speech.[4]

§10.10 1. The incidence of hate crimes, including cross burning, is substantial each year: Law enforcement agencies reported nearly 8,000 incidents of bias-motivated acts of violence to the FBI; over 4,000 were racially motivated. See Rob Hiassen, Faith and Forgiveness, Balt. Sun, Jan. 21, 2003. This hatred continues to be expressed through cross burning, as reflected in the articles of local newspapers across the country. See David Reyes, Panel Sees Big Drop in Bigotry Reports, L.A. Times, May 16, 2003 (discussing an African American couple in Orange County who found an eight-foot cross burning outside their home after hearing cheers outside); Woman, 28, Sentenced in KKK Cross-Burning, State Times/Morning Advocate, Apr. 19, 2003 (cross-burning in front of the home of an African American family on September 1, 2002, resulted in the conviction of five individuals, with sentences ranging from 12 to 21 months and fines over $1,500); New Mexico: Air Force Cross-Burning Case, N.Y. Times, Apr. 9, 2003; Randy Ellis, Three Sentenced in Burning of Crosses, Daily Oklahoman, Dec. 19, 2002; Holly Zachariah, FBI Looking into West Jefferson Cross-Burning, Columbus Dispatch, Oct. 24, 2002 (interracial married couple with two children found a five-foot cross burning in their yard); Michael Novick, Leading Edge of the Wedge: Anti-Immigrant Racism & Repression, Ethnic News, Fall 2002; Charles Keeshan, Men Convicted in Cross Burning Back in Jail, Chi. Daily Herald, Aug. 2, 2002; Newswatch, Seattle Times, Mar. 24, 2002; Rain, Drums Drown Out Klan's Words, Deseret News, Jan. 20, 2002; Michelle Gerise Godwin, Cross Burning a Hateful Act, Capital Times, Jan. 2, 2002.

2. Although cross burnings are discussed here (especially when they are used to promote racial hatred), such statutes also address crimes against persons based on creed, sexual orientation, and religion.

3. 505 U.S. 377 (1992).

4. The ordinance read:

Whoever places on public or private property a symbol, object, appellation, characterization or graffiti, including but not limited to, a burning cross or Nazi swastika, which one knows or has reasonable grounds to know arouses anger, alarm, or resentment in others on

In January 1990, Robert A. Viktora was one of several white teenagers involved in burning a cross within the fenced yard of the home of the only black family in his St. Paul, Minnesota, neighborhood.[5] He was a minor at the time of the incident and was described as a "skin-head."[6] Viktora was charged with violating the ordinance. The defendant did not contest the city's ability to charge him for his action, but rather, he argued that the ordinance under which he was charged was overbroad on its face and therefore, unconstitutional. By providing a narrow reading of the statute, the Minnesota Supreme Court held the statute to be valid. All nine Supreme Court Justices voted to overturn the conviction and hold the ordinance unconstitutional as overbroad. Justice Scalia wrote the majority opinion, which was joined by Rehnquist, Kennedy, Souter, and Thomas. While the Court has sometimes said that unprotected categories of speech are not protected, Scalia asserted that these statements must be taken in context, and even within categories of unprotected speech, the government is limited in its ability to draw content-based distinctions unrelated to their distinctively proscribable content. A government may proscribe libel, for example, but it may not make the further content discrimination of proscribing only libel critical of the government.

As to fighting words as a category of unprotected speech, Justice Scalia denied that their content is in all respects worthless and undeserving of First Amendment protection. Government cannot, however, regulate use based on hostility — or favoritism — toward the underlying message expressed. In short, Scalia said no absolute prohibition existed.

Under this reasoning, Scalia found that content-based distinctions within a category of unprotected speech have to meet strict scrutiny, with two exceptions: if the content-based distinction directly advances the reason why the category of speech is unprotected (an obscenity law that bans the most sexually explicit material without banning everything that is obscene); and if it is directed at remedying secondary effects of speech and is justified without respect to content. Applying these principles to invalidate the St. Paul ordinance, Scalia said the law distinguished varying expressions of hate, prohibiting hate speech based on

---

the basis of race, color, creed, religion, or gender commits disorderly conduct and shall be guilty of a misdemeanor. 609 Minn. Stat. §2231 (1990) (offense of assault in the fourth degree when assault motivated by bias due to race, ethnicity, religion, disability, or sexual orientation).

5. Unfortunately, this incident was not the only reported cross burning during the period. Despite President Reagan's proclamations in the early 1980s that racism no longer exists, the increasing number of incidents of cross burnings, as well as other forces of direct violence on people of color, sends a different and frightening message. See, e.g., Minorities Rally Against Hate, L.A. Times, Aug. 16, 1991, at B9, col. 1 (Metro) (California community responds to 1988 cross burning and recent incidents of increased violence against people of color); Ban on Cross Burning Unconstitutional, Judge Says, UPI, Apr. 22, 1991 (Regional) (cross burning conviction of Virginia high school student overturned when statute fails review); Richard Seven, Racist Acts Spurs Town, Officials into Action — Oak Harbor Incident "Won't Be Shrugged Off," Seattle Times, Oct. 12, 1990, at E1 (burning cross and painted swastikas placed outside home of black family in Washington state); Hearing Set in Cross-Burning Case, UPI, Mar. 1, 1990 (Regional) (prosecution suspects in cross burning in front of predominantly black church in Missouri).

6. Clarence Page, The Myth of "Fighting Words," Chi. Trib., July 7, 1991, at 3.

race, religion, or gender, but not that based on political affiliation or sexual orientation. Fighting-word "[d]isplays containing abusive invective, no matter how vicious or severe, are permissible unless they are addressed to one of the specified disfavored topics. Those who wish to use 'fighting words' in connection with other ideas — to express hostility, for example, on the basis of political affiliation, union membership, or homosexuality — are not covered."[7] Concurring on the basis of the majority holding that the ordinance was over-broad, Justice White, joined by Blackmun, O'Connor, and Stevens, objected to the majority's conclusion that content-based distinctions within categories of unprotected speech generally must meet strict scrutiny. After R.A.V., he feared, should governments wish to criminalize certain fighting words, they would have to criminalize all fighting words. In separate concurring opinions, Justices Blackmun and Stevens argued that government should have latitude to draw distinctions within categories of unprotected speech. And Justice Blackmun, who felt the decision was regrettable whether or not it was followed, was concerned that the Court had used this case to decide issues of "politically correct" speech and "cultural diversity," neither of which is present in R.A.V. Justice Stevens felt conduct that created special risks or caused special harms should be prohibitable by special rules; content-based distinctions within categories of unprotected speech are thus often justified. These concurring opinions appear to have significant influence on the Supreme Court's 2003 cross burning decision, Virginia v. Black.

Professor Erwin Chemerinsky suggests that the situation in R.A.V. actually met the exceptions that Justice Scalia recognized where content-based discrimination is allowed. Scalia held that an exception existed where the distinction advances the reason why the category is unprotected. This was true in the St. Paul ordinance, which was based on a judgment that fighting words based on race, religion, or gender are most likely to cause the harms that the fighting-words doctrine means to protect against.[8] Judith Butler offers a critical reading of R.A.V., arguing that the Court's speech constitutes a violence in its own right.[9] She demonstrates this argument by tracking how the R.A.V. majority opinion displaces the metaphor of "burning" from the cross onto the First Amendment. By Butler's reading, the decision erases the "historical correlation between cross-burning and marking a community." The majority opinion deplores the burning of a cross in "someone's front yard" rather than the burning of a cross in a black family's front yard.[10] Butler notes that "[t]he stripping of blackness and family from the figure of the complainant is significant." It is this strategic "stripping," in part, that allows the Court to displace the designation "threatened" from the black family onto the First Amendment.

The Supreme Court's decisions in church-related protest cases also reflects this transformation in which the First Amendment rather than the victim becomes the object the Court seeks to protect. The Supreme Court's rhetoric in Brown v. Louisiana reveals this tendency when it comes to protests that disrupt church

---

7. 505 U.S. at 391.
8. Erwin Chemerinsky, Constitutional Law: Principles and Policies 821 (1997).
9. Judith Butler, Excitable Speech: A Politics of the Performative 52-65 (1997).
10. 505 U.S. at 377, 396.

services or schools. In *Brown,* the Court implicitly positioned law as the protector of hallowed places. The Court idealized the library in terms suggesting spirituality and sanctity: the library as the site of monistic intellectual pursuits. The Court, in effect, articulated the law's social purpose by likening the protested library to a church. In *Brown* the Court overturned the protesters' conviction (on technical grounds) only because they had been careful not to disturb the library's functioning. By this logic, the Court's summary affirmation in Ford v. Tennessee should not be surprising. To protest during a service is certainly to disrupt the functioning of a "hallowed place" while in use.

§10.10.2   Virginia v. Black

In Virginia v. Black,[11] however, Justice O'Connor, writing for a majority of the Court, held that a state may ban cross burning with the intent to intimidate without violating the First Amendment.[12] Yet, the provision of the Virginia statute that makes the burning of a cross prima facie evidence for an intent to intimidate renders the Virginia statute unconstitutional. The Virginia statute reads:

> It shall be unlawful for any person or persons, with the intent of intimidating any person or group of persons, to burn, or cause to be burned, a cross on the property of another, a highway or public place. . . . Any such burning of a cross shall be prima facie evidence of an intent to intimidate a person or group of persons.[13]

On May 2, 1998, Richard Elliott and Jonathan O'Mara attempted to burn a cross on the front lawn of their African American neighbor James Jubilee, who had moved in four months earlier. The men set the cross on fire one night to be found the next morning by Jubilee, who was "very nervous" because cross burning "tells you that it's just the first round."[14] The cross burning appeared to be an act of retaliation. Jubilee had spoken to Elliot's mother about hearing shots fired from the backyard, which his mother explained Elliot used as a firing range. After Elliot and O'Mara were arrested, O'Mara pleaded guilty and Elliot's case went to trial. The jury was not instructed as to the meaning of intent to intimidate or on the prima facie evidence provision of the cross burning statute in Elliot's case. The jury found him guilty.

On August 22, 1998, Barry Black led a Ku Klux Klan rally in Carroll County, Virginia, on private property with the permission of the owner. With 20 to 35 people in attendance, the speakers at the rally addressed what they believed in, speaking poorly about African Americans and Mexicans, according to one observer.[15] One

---

11. 123 S. Ct. 1536 (2003).
12. Tony Mauro, American Lawyer Media, Apr. 8, 2003. Currently, the following states have anti-cross burning statutes similar to Virginia: California, Connecticut, Delaware, Florida, Georgia, Idaho, Montana, North Carolina, South Carolina, South Dakota, Vermont, Washington, and the District of Columbia.
13. Id. at 1541-1542.
14. Id at 1543 (quoting Jubilee).
15. Id. at 1542.

Klan member told the audience that he wished he could "take a .30/.30 and just randomly shoot the blacks."[16] The rally concluded with the burning of a 25- to 30-foot cross that could be viewed approximately 300 feet from the road. Black, the rally organizer, was arrested and charged under the Virginia cross burning statute. In his trial, the jury was instructed that an intent to intimidate described the motivation of the accused to put another person in fear of bodily harm, and that "the burning of the cross by itself is sufficient evidence from which you may infer the required intent."[17] Black was convicted.

All three defendants appealed to Virginia's Supreme Court, arguing that the statute is facially unconstitutional. The state supreme court consolidated the cases and found the statute unconstitutional. The statute, the Virginia Supreme Court argued, was impermissible content-based discrimination that was "indistinguishable from the ordinance found unconstitutional in RAV v. St Paul."[18] The prima facie evidence provision rendered the statute overbroad because it increased the likelihood of arrest and prosecution of individuals engaged in legal cross burning, resulting in a chilling effect on this form of expression and raising a serious First Amendment problem. The Supreme Court granted certiorari to hear the case.

Justice O'Connor's majority opinion in Virginia v. Black launches into a brief history of cross burning, concluding that:

> while a burning cross does not inevitably convey a message of intimidation, often the cross burner intends that the recipients of the message fear for their lives. And when a cross is used to intimidate, few if any messages are more powerful.[19]

Given that cross burning is a particularly virulent form of intimidation, Justice O'Connor states that upholding the constitutionality of a statute banning cross burning with the intent to intimidate is entirely consistent with the First Amendment and particularly with the Court's analysis in R.A.V.

The majority opinion, in which Chief Justice Rehnquist and Justices Scalia, Breyer, and Stevens join Sections I, II, and III, made a clear distinction between the Virginia statute and the ordinance in R.A.V. because the Virginia statute did not limit protection to a group of persons based on religion, race, or gender, but more generally banned only a particular kind of threat. The Court in Virginia v. Black compared the cross burning ban to the permissible speech restrictions of prohibiting threats against the President or prohibiting the only most "lascivious displays of sexual activity."[20] The majority found that the Virginia statute fell within the types of content discrimination that did not violate the First Amendment, quoting R.A.V.: "[w]hen the basis for the content discrimination consists entirely of the reason the entire class of speech at issue is proscribable, no significant danger of idea or viewpoint discrimination exists."[21] Rather than prohibiting all intimidating

16. Id.
17. Id. at 1542, quoting trial transcript.
18. Id. at 1543, quoting Black v. Commonwealth, 262 Va. 764 (2001).
19. Id. at 1546-1547.
20. Id. at 1549, quoting R.A.V. v. City of St. Paul, 505 U.S. 377 (1992).
21. Id. at 1549.

messages, a government may prohibit only "a subset of messages in light of cross-burning's long and pernicious history of impending violence."[22]

Yet, in the final two sections of her opinion, Justice O'Connor, writing for a plurality, which includes Chief Justice Rehnquist and Justices Stevens and Breyer, argues that the prima facie provision, specifically as interpreted in the model jury instruction, rendered the statute overbroad and therefore facially invalid. The prima facie provision would create "an unacceptable risk of suppression of ideas."[23] The plurality was concerned that the provision as interpreted by the jury instruction would silence protected speech because of a high likelihood that the provision would permit the prosecution and potentially the conviction of a person or group who is engaging in permissible political speech. Justice O'Connor discusses an example of the danger of prosecuting a person who burns a cross for artistic purposes, such as in the filming of *Mississippi Burning*. The plurality leaves room, however, for the Virginia Supreme Court to save the statute by interpreting the prima facie evidence provision in a manner that would not conflict with the First Amendment or by severing the provision from the rest of the statute.

Justice Scalia argues that the statute in its entirety does not pose any First Amendment problems. He agrees with the majority that a statute can constitutionally ban cross burning with the intent to intimidate and that the prima facie evidence provision should be remanded to the state supreme court for an authoritative interpretation of the provision. Scalia takes issue with the jury instruction and not the statute itself. He criticizes the plurality for a "baffling" interpretation of overbreadth jurisprudence.[24] A problematic jury instruction interpreting the prima facie evidence provision, he contends, should not result in the invalidation of the entire statute on its face.

Justice Stevens's concurrence states that " 'cross burning with an intent to intimidate,' unquestionably qualifies as the kind of threat that is unprotected by the First Amendment."[25] He refers specifically to the rationale in the opinions that he and Justice White wrote in *R.A.V.* to explain his justification for upholding this content-based prohibition without including all types of threatening expressive conduct.

Justice Souter, joined by Justices Kennedy and Ginsburg, concur in the judgment in part and dissent in part, arguing that the Virginia statute does not fall under any of the exceptions described in *R.A.V.* Justice Souter finds that the cross burning statute is an unconstitutional content-based regulation constituting an "official suppression of ideas." Yet, he also argues that the prima facie evidence provision furthers this problem by allowing constitutionally permissible speech to be curtailed by the statute.

Although Justice Thomas agrees with the majority that banning cross burning with the intent to discriminate is constitutionally permissible, his dissent argues

---

22. Id. at 1549.
23. Id. at 1561, citing R.A.V. v. City of St. Paul, 505 U.S. 377 (1992).
24. Id. at 1558 (Scalia joined by Thomas in Parts I and II, concurring in part, concurring in the judgment in part, and dissenting in part.)
25. Id. at 1562, (Stevens, concurring).

that the majority incorrectly analyzes the statute as expressive conduct, which could be protected by the First Amendment.[26] The Virginia legislature, according to Justice Thomas, "simply wrote [any expressive value] out of the statute by banning only intimidating conduct undertaken by a particular means."[27] In describing the connection of cross burning and violence throughout the history of the KKK in Virginia, Thomas argues that the legislature, dominated by segregationists who supported resistance to school desegregation, passed the statute at issue to criminalize terrorizing *conduct* as an "instrument of intimidation."[28] Even for segregationists, cross burning was an intolerable act.

As for the statute's prima facie evidence provision, Justice Thomas finds that it raises no constitutional issue. The inference, he explains, is rebuttable and the jury has to find each element by proof beyond a reasonable doubt. Even in the First Amendment context, the Court has upheld regulations, as in the case of child pornography, where conduct appears culpable but may through further investigation or trial result in an acquittal or dismissed charges. And the First Amendment in the context of protests at abortion clinics has given way to "unwanted communication" directed at patients with "vulnerable physical and emotional conditions."[29] Justice Thomas is critical of the plurality's decision to strike down the statute because of a concern for the "fate of an innocent cross-burner who burns a cross, but does so without an intent to intimidate."[30] Thomas points out, reflecting Judith Butler's critique of *R.A.V.*, that "cross burning subjects its targets, and, sometimes, an unintended audience . . . to extreme emotional distress."[31] As a consequence, he indicts the plurality for placing less value on physical safety than the right to be free from unwanted communications.

The fate of the Virginia statute remains in the hands of the Virginia Supreme Court, which must determine whether the prima facie provision can be severed from the statute or whether there is an interpretation of the provision that will not raise the constitutional concerns implicated in the jury instructions. This opinion sheds little light on how far the Court's holding will extend. Will restrictions for using other symbols of hate, such as the swastika, to intimidate be upheld under this analysis? Or will they be distinguished because of the unique history of cross burning? Could Virginia v. Black be used to alter the constitutionality of anti-flag burning statutes? Will it be more difficult to use the First Amendment to shield racist speech?

A new test case for the Supreme Court may arise from recent cases of noose hangings used as a vivid reminder that from the 1880s to the 1960s, 4,700 men and women were lynched in this country with black people making up 70 percent of this total. While there have been about a dozen such incidents a year in the past

26. Interestingly, in his opening paragraphs, Justice Thomas quotes from Chief Justice Rehnquist's dissent in Texas v. Johnson, drawing similarities between prohibiting cross burning and prohibiting flag burning.

27. Id. at 1563, Thomas dissenting.

28. Id. at 1566, quoting W. Wade, The Fiery Cross: The Ku Klux Klan in America 185, 279 (1987).

29. Id. at 1569, quoting Hill v. Colorado, 530 U.S. 703, 729 (2000).

30. Id. at 1568.

31. Id. at 1569.

decade, white high school students in Jena, Louisiana made national headlines by hanging nooses off their school's "white tree," a tree where historically only white students sit in the shade. The noose hanging, in retaliation for black students who dared sit under the tree, resulted in mere suspensions for the white kids involved. The District Attorney in Jena said he could not find a single criminal law to prosecute the white students, but charged six black students with felonies following a fight with white students. On September 20, 2007, thousands of civil rights protesters traveled to Jena and marched to protest the town's racism. Since then, over 60 noose hangings have surfaced around the country.[32] A noose was even hung on the door of a black Columbia University professor, Madonna Constantine.[33] As a result, states are debating the passage of statutes criminalizing the hanging of nooses in the same manner as a ban on cross burning.[34] In light of the Court's holdings in R.A.V. v. City of St. Paul, Minnesota and Virginia v. Black, how can states draft the statutes to avoid the constitutional problems that surfaced in these cases? Do such anti-hate laws discourage statements or actions intended to intimidate, or does rendering the actors subject to penalty or prosecution add an element of thrill to the actions?

§10.11   BALANCING SCHOOL PROTEST RIGHTS

The post-1960s cases in this area tend to follow the principles of those decided at the height of the civil rights era. While some convictions are reversed, the reversals are, as with the earlier sit-in cases, on technical grounds, and no special right of racial protest is recognized. The opinion by Justice Marshall in Grayned v. City of Rockford[1] sufficiently illustrates the pattern to justify a fairly detailed summary.

The *Grayned* case involved a demonstration on the part of approximately 200 public school students, members of their families, and friends, to protest the racially discriminatory practices and policies at a public high school in Rockford, Illinois. The demonstrators marched around on a sidewalk about 100 feet from the school building, some of them carrying signs stating their grievances, while others made symbolic "clenched fist" gestures. Richard Grayned, one of the demonstrators, was arrested, tried, and convicted for violating, through his participation in the demonstration, the city's "anti-picketing" and "anti-noise" ordinances. Grayned appealed the convictions, arguing that the ordinances on which they were based were unconstitutional.

32. Mark Potok, Luke Viscont, Barbara Frankel, and Nigel Holmes, The Geography of Hate, N.Y. Times, Nov. 25, 2007. The writers suggest that the September rally in Jena was not the start of a new social movement as civil rights activists hoped, "but a surprisingly broad and deep white backlash against the gains of black America."

33. Dr. Constantine, 44, is a professor of psychology and education who specializes in the study of how race and racial prejudice can affect clinical and educational interactions. Elissa Gootman, Noose Case Puts Focus on a Scholar of Race, N.Y. Times, Oct. 12, 2007.

34. Christopher Dunn, Hanging Nooses: Hateful Crime or Protected Speech, New York Law Journal, Oct. 29, 2007.

§10.11   1.   408 U.S. 104 (1972).

With regard to the anti-picketing ordinance, the Supreme Court, referring to its decision in Police Department of Chicago v. Mosley,[2] agreed that the ordinance was unconstitutional. In the *Mosley* case, the Court had held a virtually identical Chicago ordinance unconstitutional because it made an impermissible distinction between picketing over a labor dispute and other peaceful picketing. Grayned's conviction under the anti-picketing ordinance was therefore reversed.

With regard to the anti-noise ordinance, however, the Court rejected appellant's claims that the ordinance was, on its face, both vague and overbroad, and therefore unconstitutional. Addressing itself first to the claim that the anti-noise ordinance was unconstitutionally vague, the Court noted that "[c]ondemned to the use of words, we can never expect mathematical certainty from our language," and that, while the specific words of Rockford's anti-noise ordinance "are marked by 'flexibility and reasonable breadth, rather than meticulous specificity' . . . we think it clear what the ordinance as a whole prohibits."[3] In view of the Illinois Supreme Court's construction of what the Court apparently took to be a substantially similar phrase, the Court concluded "that the Supreme Court of Illinois would interpret the Rockford ordinance to prohibit only actual or imminent interference with the 'peace or good order' of the school." The Court then distinguished the cases of Cox v. Louisiana[4] and Coates v. Cincinnati[5] on which *Grayned* had relied, stating that Rockford's anti-noise ordinance does not permit punishment for the expression of an unpopular point of view (as in *Cox*), and it contains no broad invitation to subjective or discriminatory enforcement (as in *Coates*). In the Court's view, the Rockford ordinance, unlike those involved in the *Cox* and *Coates* decisions, simply did not support any assertion of an unlimited power to prohibit or punish all "noises" and "diversions." Rather, as the Court emphasized, "[T]he vagueness of these terms, by themselves, is dispelled by the ordinance's requirements that (1) the 'noise or diversion' be actually incompatible with normal school activity; (2) there be a demonstrated causality between the disruption which occurs and the 'noise or diversion'; and (3) the acts be 'willfully' done."[6] In view of these qualifications, which had the effect of confining or properly restricting the exercise of police judgment which is "always" required in enforcement of such ordinances, the Court concluded that the City had "given fair warning as to what is prohibited" and that therefore, the ordinance was not impermissibly vague.

2. 408 U.S. 92 (1972). The challenge to the Chicago ordinance involved in the *Mosley* case was brought by a black who, for seven months prior to the passage of the ordinance, had been peacefully picketing a high school with a sign that read "Jones High School practices black discrimination. Jones High School has a black quota."

3. 408 U.S. at 110.

4. In the *Cox* case, the Court held that a "breach of the peace" ordinance that had been construed by state courts to mean "to agitate, to arouse from a state of repose, to molest, to interrupt, to hinder, to disquiet" was unconstitutional since, as construed, persons could be punished under the statute simply for expressing unpopular views.

5. 402 U.S. 611 (1971). The ordinance involved in the *Coates* case prohibited the sidewalk assembly of three or more persons who conducted themselves in any manner "annoying" to passersby. Since enforcement of the ordinance depended on the completely subjective judgment of police officers as to what constituted an "annoyance," the Court held that the ordinance was impermissibly vague.

6. 408 U.S. at 113.

Turning to Grayned's contention that the anti-noise ordinance was unconstitutionally overbroad, because it "unduly [interfered] with First and Fourteenth Amendment rights to picket on a public sidewalk near a school," the Court made careful note of the fact that a government has no power to restrict its citizens' uses of public streets and parks for purposes of "assembly, communicating thoughts between [themselves], and discussing public questions" on the basis of the content of those discussions and communications. As the Court stated, "peaceful demonstrations in public places are protected by the First Amendment."[7]

The Court went on to say, however, that its earlier cases had made "equally clear . . . that reasonable 'time, place and manner' regulations may be necessary to further significant governmental interests, and are permitted." In determining the reasonableness of a particular governmental regulation, "[t]he crucial question is whether the manner of expression is basically incompatible with normal activity of a particular place at a particular time." Of particular relevance to the Court in answering this question was its earlier decision in the case of Tinker v. Des Moines Independent Community School District,[8] where it had held "that the Des Moines School District could not punish students for wearing black armbands to school in protest of the Vietnam War." The Court stated:

> Just as *Tinker* made clear that school property may not be declared off limits for expressive activity by students, we think it clear that the public sidewalk adjacent to school grounds may not be declared off limits for expressive activity by members of the public. But in each case, expressive activity may be prohibited if it "materially disrupts classwork or involves substantial disorder or invasion of the rights of others."[9]

Since the City's anti-noise ordinance was directed only at "[n]oisy demonstrations which disrupt or are incompatible with normal school activities" — specifically, at noisy demonstrations occurring "next to a school, while classes are in session" — and since the ordinance did not impose restrictions on noisy demonstrations occurring "at other places or other times" where, as the Court noted, "[s]uch expressive conduct may be constitutionally protected" from such restrictions, the Court held that the anti-noise ordinance was not invalid, despite the fact that its reach extended to picketing "that is neither violent nor physically obstructive."[10] Hence, the Court affirmed Grayned's conviction under the anti-noise ordinance.

Justice Douglas, who joined the Court's opinion insofar as it reversed Grayned's conviction under Rockford's anti-picketing ordinance, would also have reversed Grayned's conviction under the anti-noise ordinance, in view of the

---

7. Without elaborating at what point a demonstration could be said to "turn violent" — nor indeed, offering any guidelines for distinguishing between merely vigorous protests and violent demonstrations (or stating whether any distinction would be made on the basis of *who* was being violent — demonstrators or spectators) — the Court added that "[o]f course, where demonstrations turn violent, they lose their protected quality as expression under the First Amendment." [Emphasis supplied.]

8. 393 U.S. 503 (1969).

9. 408 U.S. at 118.

10. 408 U.S. at 120.

fact that, although the dispute itself "doubtless disturbed the school," and the noise from the police officers' loudspeakers "was certainly a 'noise or diversion' in the meaning of the ordinance," there simply "was no evidence that [Grayned himself] was noisy or boisterous or rowdy." In Justice Douglas' view of the record, as expressed in his partial dissent, "the disruptive force loosened at this school was an issue dealing with race — an issue that is preeminently one for solution by First Amendment means . . . and the entire picketing, including [Grayned's] part in it, was done in the best First Amendment tradition."[11]

While student demonstrations around schools are not treated with as much suspicion as protest in and around churches, it is clear that demonstrations of this character are not favored by the Supreme Court.[12] On the other hand, the strong emotional component in racial issues almost guarantees that any protest involving this area will lead to noisy confrontations. Under the standards in the *Grayned* case, it is difficult to imagine how a meaningful protest can be mounted around a school protected by an ordinance of the type involved there. Even before the Supreme Court's decision in *Grayned,* black school protests received only limited protection from the courts.[13]

Few would contend that violence and destruction of property can be protected by assertion of First Amendment rights. The difficulty is that even in peaceful protests, such as those in *Grayned* and *Tinker,* there is a tendency by lower courts to look primarily to the actual impact of the protest activity, and to sanction disciplinary action whenever the protest in question results in disruption. Thus, while Supreme Court standards seem to impose a heavier burden on school authorities, that is, the responsibility of showing that a rule entrenching on First Amendment rights is justified in the circumstances, lower courts tend to make no serious attempt to balance the students' right of expression against the interest of the state in preventing and punishing conduct that interferes with discipline. Nor is there the searching review of the challenged school rule needed to determine whether its enforcement, in fact, was intended to suppress speech rather than protect against disorder.

As schools across the country become more and more segregated, the opportunity to challenge racial inequality through protest is also becoming greatly restricted. For example, lower courts have applied *Tinker* differently to student expression through messages on their clothing, particularly T-shirts.[14] Some have looked at additional factors, such as a student's age, to justify suppression of

11. Id. at 124. (Douglas, J. dissenting, in part).

12. Through legislation or judicial interpretation of state constitutions, some states provide greater protection than the U.S. Constitution to encourage student speech. These states include Arkansas, California, Colorado, Iowa, Kansas, and Massachusetts. A New Jersey court found that although the U.S. Constitution would not protect the speech at issue, the New Jersey Constitution did. See Scott Andrew Felder, Stop the Presses: Censorship and the High School Journalist, 29 J.L. & Educ. 433, 458 (2000).

13. See, e.g., Jackson v. Ellington, 316 F. Supp. 1071 (W.D. Tenn. 1970) (approving, despite First Amendment protest rights, the use of statutes prohibiting absenting of children from school and contributing to the delinquency of a minor against parents who kept their children home to protest racial policies of the board of directors).

14. Clay Weisenberger, Constitution or Conformity: When the Shirt Hits the Fan in Public Schools, 29 J.L. & Educ. 51 (2000).

speech.[15] In addition, several cases have addressed whether schools can punish students for critical statements about school policies or student harassment over e-mail or through websites.[16] Supreme Court precedents have left lower courts with vague standards for evaluating student speech, often resulting in conflicting decisions, many of which simply defer to the decisions of school administrators.

Regardless of state statutory or constitutional protections for students, on a daily basis school administrators use disciplinary power to silence student speech, especially if it is expressing views that may be deemed unpopular by mainstream society, even if the speech has little potential for disruption. Given this reality, it becomes more and more difficult to see how schools can become places that teach citizenship and respond to a concern by the Fifth Circuit in 1972:

> One of the great concerns of our time is that our young people, disillusioned by our political processes, are disengaging from political participation. It is most important that our young become convinced that our Constitution is a living reality, not parchment preserved under glass.[17]

With raging inequalities in our education system nationwide — inequalities that disproportionately impact racial minorities — it is difficult to see how protest can help achieve greater racial equality in schools when this arena is closing the door to all forms of political expression.

§10.11.1　Post-*Tinker* Cases: Leaving Freedom of Speech at the Schoolhouse Gate

> In the three decades since *Tinker*, the courts have made it clear that students leave most of their constitutional rights at the schoolhouse gate. The judiciary's unquestioning acceptance of the need for deference to school authority leaves relatively little room for protecting student's constitutional rights.[18]

In *Tinker*, the Supreme Court famously proclaimed that students do not "shed their constitutional rights to freedom of speech or expression at the schoolhouse gate." The *Tinker* majority found that high school students had the right to wear armbands to convey a political message protesting the Vietnam War, even if that message was offensive to the school administration. The Court explained that the First Amendment prohibits schools from silencing student speech, unless that speech would disrupt school activities. Three themes emerge from Justice Fortas' opinion: "the importance of protecting students' free speech rights, the need for

---

15. See Broussard v. School Bd. of Norfolk, 801 F. Supp. 1526 (E.D. Va. 1992); McIntire v. Bethel Indep. Sch. Dist. No. 3, 804 F. Supp. 1415 (W.D. Okla. 1992); Pyle v. South Hadley Sch. Comm., 861 F. Supp. 157 (D. Mass. 1994).

16. Susan H. Kosse, Student Designed Home Web Pages: Does Title IX or the First Amendment Apply?, 43 Ariz. L. Rev. 905 (2001).

17. Shanley v. Northeast Indep. Sch. Dist., 462 F.2d 960 (5th Cir. 1972).

18. Erwin Chemerinsky, Students Do Leave Their First Amendment Rights at the Schoolhouse Gates: What's Left of *Tinker*?, 48 Drake L. Rev. 527 (2000), at 530.

proof of significant disruption of school activities, and the role of the judiciary in monitoring schools' decisions to ensure compliance with the Constitution.[19]

Although *Tinker* has never been explicitly overturned, the Court has chipped away at it's holding, raising the question whether, and to what extent, the First Amendment protects student speech and protest. Indeed, in the three times since *Tinker* that the Court has addressed restrictions on student speech — Bethel School District No. 403 v. Fraser,[20] Hazelwood School District v. Kuhlmeier,[21] and Morse v. Frederick[22] — it has upheld the restrictions, based largely on the rationale in the *Tinker* dissent: the need for courts to defer to the decisions of school authorities. Lower courts have followed the Court's lead; "in the thirty years since *Tinker*, schools have won virtually every constitutional claim involving students' rights."[23]

A.   Silenced at a School Assembly: Bethel School District No. 403 v. Fraser[24]

Fraser, a high school student, was punished for a "lewd" speech nominating a classmate at a school election assembly. The school suspended Fraser for three days and removed his name from a list of potential graduation speakers. Consequently, Fraser and his parents sued the school district, arguing it had violated his First Amendment right to free speech.

Chief Justice Burger's majority opinion did not spell out what Fraser said in his speech, but characterized the speech as having inappropriate sexual innuendo. Burger explained that such sexual speech can be punished given the critical mission of schools to teach students appropriate behavior: "The determination of what manner of speech in the classroom or school assembly is inappropriate properly rests with the school board."[25] Further, Burger distinguished this speech from the constitutionally protected speech in *Tinker* because a school has an obligation to protect students from sexually explicit and vulgar speech. Although Burger noted that students do not leave all of their First Amendment rights outside the school doors, he made clear that First Amendment rights of students in public schools "are not automatically coextensive with the rights of adults in other settings."[26] His divergence from *Tinker* was explicit as he concluded his opinion with a quote from Justice Black's dissent in *Tinker*: " 'I wish therefore, . . . to disclaim any purpose . . . to hold that the Federal Constitution compels the teachers, parents, and elected school officials to surrender control of the American public school system to public school students.' "[27] Although it lacks a well-defined standard for when schools may restrict student speech, the decision has been read by lower courts to permit schools to restrict speech at "school-sponsored" events.

---

19. Id. at 539.
20. Bethel School District No. 403 v. Fraser, 478 U.S. 675 (1986).
21. Hazelwood School District v. Kuhlmeier, 484 U.S. 260 (1988).
22. Morse v. Frederick, 127 S. Ct. 2618 (2007).
23. Chemerinsky, supra note 18, at 530.
24. *Bethel*, supra note 20.
25. Id. at 683.
26. Id. at 682.
27. Id. at 686.

Justice Brennan, in his concurrence, did directly quote Fraser's speech, but he did not find it offensive.[28] Nevertheless, he agreed that the speech was not constitutionally protected because it failed a key *Tinker* factor: It was disruptive. Justice Stevens' dissent, on the other hand, states, "Frankly, my dear, I don't give a damn."[29] He argued that the case made a big deal of nothing, and therefore Fraser's speech should be protected.

B.   No Freedom for the School Press: Hazelwood School District v. Kuhlmeier[30]

In *Kuhlmeier*, three journalism students writing for a school newspaper sued the school for pulling two articles prior to printing. The articles, which had teacher approval, discussed the pregnancies of three students and the impact of divorce on students at the school. The articles did not name any students. The principal removed the articles, however, out of concern that they would identify students, and because he thought they contained content inappropriate for younger students, and lacked a response from divorced parents.

The Supreme Court upheld the principal's decision. Justice White, writing for the Court, deferred to the school's decision to determine what manner of speech is appropriate for a newspaper published as a part of the curriculum. Because the school newspaper was not a public forum, "school officials were entitled to regulate the content[ ] . . . in any reasonable manner."[31] White distinguished this case from *Tinker*:

> The question whether the First Amendment requires a school to tolerate particular student speech — the question that we addressed in *Tinker* — is different from the question whether the First Amendment requires a school affirmatively to promote particular student speech. The former question addresses educators' ability to silence a student's personal expression that happens to occur on the school premises. The latter question concerns educators' authority over school-sponsored publications, theatrical productions, and other expressive activities that students, parents, and members of the public might reasonably perceive to bear the imprimatur of the school.[32]

Echoing Fraser, White concluded that "the education of the Nation's youth is primarily the responsibility of parents, teachers, and state and local school officials, and not of federal judges."[33]

C.   More Tinkering: Morse v. Frederick[34]

Morse v. Frederick held that schools can suppress student speech at a school-sponsored or school-sanctioned event that advocates or promotes the use of illegal

28. Id. at 687, dissenting.
29. Id. at 691.
30. *Kuhlmeier*, supra note 21.
31. Id. at 270.
32. Id. at 271.
33. Id. at 273.
34. *Morse*, supra note 22.

drugs.[35] The majority opinion, written by Chief Justice Roberts, found that a 14-foot banner stating "BONG HiTS 4 JESUS" did just that.[36]

In January of 2002, the Olympic torch, on its way to the winter games in Salt Lake City, Utah, passed by Juneau-Douglas High School. Deborah Morse, the principal, permitted students to line up outside the school to watch the torch relay. As the torch and cameras passed, Frederick, a high school student, and a few friends unfurled a 14-foot banner with the words "BONG HiTS 4 JESUS." The students across the street could plainly read the sign. Morse immediately crossed the street and ordered the students to remove the banner. When Frederick refused, Morse confiscated the banner and suspended Frederick for 10 days.[37] When asked why he created the banner, Frederick explained that he wanted to get the attention of the cameras.

In the majority opinion, Roberts outlined three points leading to the conclusion that the school did not violate Frederick's constitutional rights.[38] The first point is unquestioned: This is a case of student speech at a school-sponsored event. Viewing the torch was "sanctioned by the principal 'as an approved social event or class trip,'" and teachers and administrators supervised the students.[39]

The Court's second point is more contentious: The banner promotes illegal drug use. Although Roberts described the message on the banner as "cryptic," and he acknowledged that it could be interpreted in various ways — including to mean nothing at all — he agreed with Morse that the banner endorsed drug use.[40] Roberts noted that "the pro-drug interpretation of the banner gains further plausibility given the paucity of alternative meanings."[41]

For Roberts, the final point simply follows from the first two: Because the words advocate drug use, which is against school policy, they are not protected student speech. Roberts did state that this decision is not about silencing political speech, even advocacy for legalizing drugs. But the distinction between a political statement that drug use should be legal and a statement merely endorsing drug use is not entirely clear, especially since student protest (or any protest, for that matter) is not always couched in explicitly legal or political rhetoric. For an earlier generation of protesters, "fuck the draft" seemed more effective than "the draft should not be legal."

Justice Alito, with Justice Kennedy in concurrence, viewed the Morse holding narrowly: "(a) it goes no further than to hold that a public school may restrict speech that a reasonable observer would interpret as advocating illegal drug use and (b) it provides no support for any restriction of speech that can plausibly be interpreted as commenting on any political or social issue, including speech on

35. Id.
36. Id.
37. Id. at 2623. On appeal to the school superintendent, the suspension was reduced to time served or 8 days.
38. See Martin Schwartz, Supreme Court Restricts Student Speech, N.Y.L.J., Oct. 16, 2007.
39. *Morse*, supra note 22, at 2624.
40. Id.
41. Id. at 2625.

issues such as 'the wisdom of the war on drugs or of legalizing marijuana for medicinal use.' "[42]

Justice Thomas advocated that the Court overturn *Tinker*. Looking at the evolution of public schools, he found that: "the Constitution does not afford students a right to free speech in public schools."[43]

Justice Breyer concurred in the judgment of the Court, arguing that the majority should not have addressed the First Amendment issue at all. The Court could have simply held that Morse was not liable for damages because her disciplinary action was rational under the qualified immunity standard. Deciding that issue would have allowed the Court "to avoid resolving the fractious underlying constitutional question" and "to avoid the risk of interpretations that are too broad or too narrow."[44]

Joined by Justices Ginsburg and Souter, Justice Stevens dissented, arguing that: "the school's interest in protecting its students from exposure to speech 'reasonably regarded as promoting illegal drug use' cannot justify disciplining Frederick for his attempt to make an ambiguous statement to a television audience simply because it contained an oblique reference to drugs.[45] He views BONG HiTS 4 JESUS as "a nonsense message, not advocacy."[46] He also suggested that if the banner mentioned alcohol — also an illegal substance for high school students — the opinion would have been different. He finds it "hard to believe the Court would support punishing Frederick for flying a 'WINE SiPS 4 JESUS' banner — which could quite reasonably be construed as a protected religious message or as a pro-alcohol message."[47] The only speech that the dissent would proscribe is speech that conforms with *Tinker*'s standard — speech that "neither violates a permissible rule nor expressly advocates conduct that is illegal and harmful to students."[48] He criticizes the majority for abdicating its "constitutional responsibility" by outright rejecting the "foundations of *Tinker*, because, in its view, the unusual importance of protecting children from the scourge of drugs supports a ban on all speech in the school environment that promotes drug use."[49]

The recent student speech cases seem to reduce the Court's holding in *Tinker* to protecting a student's right to wear armbands to communicate antiwar political speech provided that no serious school disruption occurs. As the Court gives greater and greater deference to schools, and takes away the school assembly, school-sponsored activities and the school newspaper as forums for protest and speaking about unpopular ideas, it is hard to imagine where within the schoolhouse gates a student's constitutional right for free speech can be found. While none of these school cases raised racial issues, it should be noted that they undermine not only *Tinker*, but a much earlier case, discussed below, that provided constitutional

---

42. Id. at 2636 (Alito concurring, joined by Kennedy).
43. Id. at 2634 (Thomas concurring).
44. Id. at 2640 (Breyer concurring in the judgment in part and dissenting in part).
45. Id. at 2643 (Stevens dissenting, joined by Ginsburg and Souter).
46. Id. at 2649.
47. Id. at 2650.
48. Id. at 2644.
49. Id. at 2646.

protection to college students expelled for protesting segregated facilities in a state building.

§10.11.2 Racism Hypo: Protest Rights and Students

On March 26, 2003, a group of five high school seniors decided to make a political statement, to protest the war against Iraq. They all decided to wear matching shirts depicting the face of President George Bush with the words "International Terrorist" written below the picture. They attended a nationally recognized magnet school in Manhattan and were all well known as part of the top 10 percent of their graduating class.

The students attended classes as usual from 8:30 A.M. to 11:45 A.M. without any reaction from students or teachers about the message on their shirts. As they were eating lunch in the school cafeteria, they were approached by Vice Principal Cowers, who requested that they follow him to the principal's office.

Principal Jane Little explained that the students had a choice. "You can turn your T-shirts inside out and attend classes for the rest of the day or refuse to change your shirt and go home." One student, Claudia Ramirez, ranked second in her class, asked why they had to remove the shirts. The vice principal responded immediately that the T-shirt promoted terrorism, especially at a time when the entire nation was under high alert, code orange. Jessica piped up that the shirts were just emphasizing a message of peace during an important historical moment. The principal answered her by explaining that there was a Supreme Court case called Tinker v. Des Moines that permitted school administrators to restrict students' ability to express themselves in the classroom. Another student, James Bolden, who was an aspiring constitutional lawyer, responded by saying, "You are summarizing the dissent in *Tinker*. We are no different from the students wearing the black armbands to protest the Vietnam War whose punishment was overturned by the court. *Tinker* actually states that 'students or teachers do not shed their constitutional rights to freedom of speech or expression at the schoolhouse gate.'" Principal Little snapped in response that they all had a simple choice—turn the T-shirts inside out or leave.

All of the students went home for the remainder of the day, but they decided not to wear the shirts again. They did not want to risk interrupting their education or jeopardizing graduation awards.

The students' T-shirts, however, became the talk of the school, partially sparked by the administration's harsh response. Many students commented that they supported the students. The students were interviewed for an article in the school newspaper, even though the principal would not comment. Some teachers used the example as a teaching moment to discuss the T-shirts, the school's reaction, and the curtailing of constitutional rights, especially during times of war.

The message and the spotlight on these students, however, infuriated a student group called Patriotic Students in Action (PSIA). PSIA, which was founded in response to the attacks on September 11, believed that the T-shirt-wearing students were traitors during a time requiring extreme American vigilance. The 40-member group decided to respond by wearing identical flag T-shirts that read, "United We Stand, Divided We Fall" only three weeks after the original political statement. The administration did not respond at all.

The unequal treatment did not go unnoticed by the anti-war students. Increasing their ranks by 10, 15 students decided to wear the "International Terrorist" T-shirts one week later. Within an hour into the school day, the administration responded without much discussion. The 10 new students were sent home with a warning not to return wearing the T-shirts; the five original offenders were suspended for three days and stripped of all graduation privileges. A memo from the principal was distributed to all teachers forbidding them from discussing the matter with students during or outside of class time.

Represented by the local ACLU, the five honor students responded by filing a lawsuit against the high school officials for violating the First Amendment rights of the students. The brief argued that the "school could have ensured a safe school environment without banning the students' political speech." Citing a number of recent circuit cases, the brief described the administration's response as "a rash decision, which was plainly unconstitutional viewpoint discrimination and did not provide the students their right to due process." The school, represented by counsel for the school board, responded that the First Amendment rights of high school students are not co-extensive with those of adults. Citing *Tinker*, they argued that schools are legally permitted to take action to avoid "a significant fear of disruption."

§10.11.3   School Speech and the Internet

The hypothetical below in §10.11.4 is based on a student speech scenario involving the Internet. Dozens of state and federal circuit courts have addressed the boundaries of student speech on the internet both inside and outside the classroom. Their outcomes are unpredictable, as highlighted by a few recent decisions where students challenged their schools' disciplinary action as a violation of their First Amendment rights:[50]

- *J.S. v. Bethlehem Area School District*[51] — A student was disciplined for creating a website using his home computer that used defamatory and offensive comments toward a teacher and the school principal. Overturning the lower court, the Pennsylvania Supreme Court, applying both *Fraser* and *Tinker*, found no constitutional barrier to the school's disciplinary action. The website, which the court said had a nexus to the school and could be considered on-campus speech, was not protected speech because it contained lewd language and caused disruption in that the teacher was unable to complete the school year.
- *Beussick v. Woodland R-IV School District*[52] — A high school student was suspended for creating a website that used vulgar language to criticize school administrators. No evidence showed that he used school resources to make the website. Finding that the speech was not on-campus, the court applied *Tinker* and found the speech protected because it did not materially upset school activities.

50. For a more extensive analysis of the first four cases, see Sandy Li, The Need for a New, Uniform Standard: The Continued Threat to Internet-Related Student Speech, 26 Loy. L.A. Entmt. L. Rev. 65 (2005).

51. J.S. v. Bethlehem Area Sch. Dist., 807 A.2d 847 (Pa. 2002).

52. Beussink v. Woodland R-IV Sch. Dist., 30 F. Supp. 2d 1175 (E.D. Mo. 1998).

- Emmett v. Kent School District No. 415[53] — A high school student created a website prompted by his critical writing class where he began writing fake obituaries for his friends and asking others to vote on who would get the next obituary. The site was reported in the news and discussed in class. The district court held that the case stood outside Supreme Court precedent because it was not school speech. The website was not viewed as a serious threat and was therefore constitutionally protected.
- Mahaffey ex. rel Mahaffey v. Aldrich[54] — Two students created a website for 'fun' that listed people they wished would die. The district court did not apply Tinker because the speech was determined to be off-campus speech and the students had a constitutional right to the speech because a reasonable person would not find the website to be a true threat.
- Layshock ex rel. Layschock v. Hermitage School District[55] — A student was punished for creating a website that parodied the school principal. According to the court, the website, although created at home, became on-campus speech when the student showed it to friends at school. Nevertheless, the court held that the school violated the student's First Amendment right to speak because there was no connection between the website and a substantial disruption of the school environment.
- Wisniewski v. Board of Education of Weedsport Central School District[56] — While using his parents' home computer, an eighth-grade student sent his friends an instant message over the internet with "a small drawing crudely, but clearly, suggesting that a named teacher should be shot and killed." The picture could be viewed for three weeks. School authorities learned of the picture, which is an icon on instant messenger, and suspended the eighth-grader, interviewed other students, and replaced the teacher named in the message. Even though the initial speech was made at home, the court found that sharing the picture with friends created school speech that caused disruption of the school environment that was foreseeable. The student's claim against the school was dismissed.

As these cases indicate, courts have disagreed about what speech constitutes in-school speech and also what standard to apply. Using the Internet for hate speech against students would add another layer of complexity to the court's analysis. It is likely that the Supreme Court will have to address this issue to create greater uniformity of lower courts throughout the country. In discussing the hypothetical below, it may be useful to look at the full opinions of these and other Internet speech cases to help frame your argument.

§10.11.4 Racism Hypo: School Racism and the Internet

A teacher of a high school computer course presented students with an assignment to create their own website, expressing personal views that were

53. Emmett v. Kent Sch. Dist. No. 415, 92 F. Supp. 2d 1088 (W.D. Wash. 2000).

54. Mahaffey ex. rel. Mahaffey v. Aldrich, 236 F. Supp. 2d 779 (E.D. Mich. 2002).

55. Layshock ex rel. Layschock v. Hermitage School Dist., 496 F. Supp. 2d 587 (W.D. Pa. 2007).

56. Wisniewski v. Bd. of Educ. of Weedsport Cent. Sch. Dist., 44 F.3d 34 (C.A. 2 N.Y. 2007).

important to them. The class had spent the entire semester learning basic HTML programming and creating individual webpages. For this final assignment, the students could work on the project at home or after school in the computer lab.

One 15-year-old student, Theodore Johnson, was a computer wiz. He worked for many hours on his website at school and home, and posted it on his private Internet address, www.patriotkid.net. His Web site displayed his opinion that the United States needed to take terrorism seriously. He described the need for restrictions on our liberty to "fight the evil of terrorism, especially as espoused through the teaching of Islam." He chronicled the United States' actions toward Arabs since September 11, focusing on the need for increased detention and use of torture to "get them to talk." The Web site featured actual Arab and Muslim students in the school who he felt were "probably engaged in terrorist plans and warned" other students to "keep a close eye on them and be ready to act in your country's name." The site also had links to many white supremacist organizations.

Theo then decided to make his website interactive. On a Friday afternoon, before the project was due, he distributed his website address to other students in the class so that they could add their comments and viewpoints. Over the weekend more than a dozen students posted additional derogatory remarks and expanded their attacks to other racial minority students in the school. One student wrote, "The Black Students Honor Society is a joke. It lets blacks get away with being lazy and still getting credit. Just look at Michelle Dodson." The site became out of control before the administration got wind of it.

The following Monday, parents of some of the targeted students came to speak to the principal. They demanded that the website be shut down, that the student fail the computer class, and that he be suspended. Looking at the website with the parents, the principal was stunned. He promised the parents the school would do something about it.

Without contacting the school's general counsel, the principal called Theo to his office and expressed his concern about the website. He demanded that he shut down the website and prepare an entirely new one for the final project. The principal contacted Theo's parents to tell him that he would be suspended for two weeks.

Theo, represented by the ACLU, argued that the school infringed on his constitutional right to free speech. The public high school, represented by its general counsel, responded that such disciplinary action was permissible restriction on speech that would cause serious disruption of the school day.

§10.12   FAIR HEARINGS FOR STUDENT PROTESTORS

The major breakthrough from the traditional concept that students attending public colleges were not entitled to due process rights prior to the imposition of disciplinary action came in Dixon v. Alabama State Board of Education.[1]

---

§10.12   1. 294 F.2d 150 (5th Cir. 1961).

The six plaintiffs were expelled from Alabama State College, a state-owned institution, without notice or hearing. Between February 25 and March 1, 1960, black students at the college had engaged in a series of civil rights demonstrations, including a sit-in, a march, and a sing-in. All of the plaintiffs had participated in at least one of these events, but, in instructing the college president to expel them, the Board of Education did not assign specific grounds for its action. School regulations authorized expulsion for willful disobedience of school rules, failure to meet academic standards, and conduct "prejudicial to the school." The plaintiffs brought an action for injunctive relief. The district court dismissed the complaint, and the court of appeals reversed, holding that due process required that a student at a state college or university not be expelled without notice and hearing.

The court began with the premise that "[w]henever a governmental body acts to injure an individual, the Constitution requires that the act be consonant with due process of law. The minimum procedural requirements necessary to satisfy due process depend upon the circumstances and the interests of the parties involved."[2] In the court's view, the balance weighed heavily in favor of plaintiffs. Earlier cases holding that college students were not entitled to due process before expulsion were distinguished, on the grounds that either they involved a private institution, where the relationship between the student and the school was one of contract and where procedural rights had been waived, or there was a question whether the hearing that had been provided was adequate.

The court concluded by setting forth the standards regarding notice and hearing that state colleges would be required to meet. Students should be apprised of "the specific charges and grounds which, if proved, would justify expulsion under the regulations of the Board of Education." Although the type of hearing required would depend upon the circumstances of each case, more than an "informal interview" would be necessary where misconduct was charged.

> In such circumstances, a hearing which gives the Board or the administrative authorities of the college an opportunity to hear both sides in considerable detail is best suited to protect the rights of all involved. This is not to imply that a full-dress judicial hearing, with the right to cross-examine witnesses, is required. . . . Nevertheless, the rudiments of an adversary proceeding may be preserved without encroaching upon the interests of the college [in maintaining an atmosphere consonant with its educational functions].[3]

The "rudiments of an adversary proceeding" were to include advance notice of the names of witnesses against the student and a statement of the facts to which each testifies; an opportunity to appear before the board, or at least before an administrative official, and present a defense by way of oral testimony or affidavits of witnesses; and a statement of the board's findings and decision.[4]

2. 294 F.2d at 155.
3. Id. at 159.
4. *Dixon* was preceded by a long line of cases that denied procedural rights to students. Several theories were advanced in support of such holdings: (1) Schools, whether public or private, stand in loco parentis and thus have inherent authority to discipline. (2) The relationship between a student and a privately owned school is a matter of contract, and the school may condition admission upon a

Representative of the narrower reading given to *Dixon* is Scott v. Alabama Board of Education.[5] This case involved students from the same Alabama State College where expulsions of protesting students in 1960 were reversed by the *Dixon* case. Almost a decade later, Alabama State College students were still being expelled for demonstrations at the college. They filed suit, alleging violation of both due process and First Amendment rights. The college officials filed a counterclaim, charging that the students had (1) refused to quit the campus after being dismissed or suspended as students; (2) intimidated students desiring to attend classes and prevented their attendance at classes; (3) intimidated faculty members desiring to conduct classes; (4) damaged college property; and (5) otherwise disrupted the orderly operation of Alabama State College as an educational institution.[6] Applying the standard set in *Dixon,* the district court found the school's action justified. Considering the plaintiffs' contention that the charges were vague, the court agreed that some of the charges lacked the specificity required to enable a student to adequately prepare defenses against them, but felt that certain other charges, "when viewed in the circumstances of the case, make quite clear the basis upon which the college proposes to take disciplinary action." It rejected plaintiffs' argument that one vague charge, like one bad apple, spoils the entire barrel, holding that *Dixon* requires only the rudimentary elements of fair play.

Plaintiffs challenged the impartiality of the committee which heard the evidence, but the court found that "this Committee was selected in a reasonable fashion considering the emotional circumstances which tended to render nearly everyone at the college at least mildly partisan." Turning to the First Amendment, the court took the view that, if a student was found guilty of a specific charge of conduct not protected by the First Amendment, his suspension or dismissal could stand even though activities in other charges might be protected. A demonstration including the takeover of the college dining hall was held not protected. It was not symbolic speech, and did not achieve protected status simply because it was largely peaceful and nonviolent and involved little if any destruction of college property. In entering a broad injunction against further demonstrations, the court said:

> There seems to be a tendency in this country — and it is especially prevalent among
> students — toward the view that if one only believes strongly enough that his cause is

---

promise to abide by school regulations and upon waiver, express or implied, of procedural rights. (3) Education is a privilege, not a right, and therefore due process requirements do not apply, even in the case of a student at a state-owned or state-supported school. *Dixon* was compatible, however, with later Supreme Court decisions that have discredited the privilege-right distinction and given wider application to due process requirements. In the school discipline cases that followed, *Dixon* was frequently taken as the starting point.

The *Dixon* decision represents another instance where blacks, using the courts to combat racial discrimination, have established new precedents that strengthen the rights of all citizens — in this case, students who traditionally were powerless to defend against arbitrary and even malicious actions of school officials. The issue remains, though, of whether the procedural rights found in *Dixon* can be translated into substantive value for students, in cases where protest activity is deemed disruptive by school officials whose broad authority to discipline students is not directly limited by the *Dixon* case.

5. 300 F. Supp. 163 (M.D. Ala. 1969).
6. Id. at 165.

right, then one may use in advancing that cause any means that seem effective at the moment, whether they are lawful or unlawful and whether or not they are consistent with the interests of others. The law, of course, cannot and does not take that position, and those who do must not expect to receive substantive protection from the law; to the contrary, they must expect to be punished when they violate laws and college regulations which are part of a system designed to protect the rights and interests of all.[7]

Judge Johnson, who decided the *Scott* case, undercut the gains in due process won by students in *Dixon;* a decision which reversed Judge Johnson's dismissal of the protesters' suit. By finding that if some of the several charges were sufficiently clear, all charges were not invalidly vague, and by asserting that the review committee was fairly selected, "considering the emotional circumstances" rendering nearly everyone on campus "mildly partisan," and finally by holding that the students facing expulsion were responsible for the consequences of their attorney's decision to boycott the hearing, Judge Johnson in effect returned to school authorities virtually all the discretion they exercised in disciplinary matters prior to the *Dixon* precedent. His comments do raise a serious question as to the extent that the whole concept of "fair hearing" turns on the presence of an impartial hearing body, i.e., a tribunal removed sufficiently from direct interest in the outcome so that neither party can reasonably charge bias. One might argue that a truly impartial body is more important in a student disciplinary hearing than in a criminal trial. In the latter, the jury is usually limited to determining the defendant's guilt; in the student disciplinary hearing, the tribunal usually both determines guilt and fixes the penalty. At neither phase of the proceeding is a tribunal dominated by college administrators and faculty likely to give much weight to student arguments that the actions or inactions of college officials served as a provocation for the student demonstrations. Finally, a panel made up of college-affiliated personnel is likely to have an understandably strong vested interest in peace and order on the campus. Considering the fact discussed above, that First Amendment standards in *Tinker* tend to provide protection only to those protesters whose activities don't upset anyone, and keeping in mind that racial issues in this society tend to be inherently upsetting, campus protests, even with the protection of *Dixon,* tend to resemble a form of "ultrahazardous activity."

Scott didn't require much for a hearing body to be deemed "impartial." In Jenkins v. Louisiana State Board of Education, the Fifth Circuit held that students would have to demonstrate that proceedings had actually been biased in order to prove that the hearing body was not "impartial."[8] The hearing body in *Jenkins* consisted of people appointed by the university president, one of the main witnesses against the *Jenkins* students. Yet this was found insufficient to support the argument that the hearing body was partial.

An interesting parallel is to be found between Professor Fried's assessment of protest movements (from §10.2) and Judge Johnson's pronouncement on protests in Scott v. Alabama Board of Education. Judge Johnson implies that something is

---

7. Id. at 168.
8. 506 F.2d 992, 1003-1004 (5th Cir. 1975).

intrinsically coercive about unlawful protests. His words appear to leave room for "lawful protest." It is not clear, however, how "lawful protest" could ever meaningfully challenge the law itself. Judge Johnson's rhetoric positions the law as fundamentally neutral; the law sees to it that an individual's actions are "consistent with the interest of others." In an ironic twist, however, *Scott* eviscerates the due process requirements created by *Dixon*. In effect, *Scott* denies the protestors what is supposed to be the law's hallmark: due process. That is, in effect, to deny the law's benefit to those who challenge the social order it consolidates.

§10.13   PROTEST RIGHTS IN RESIDENTIAL AREAS

The argument for exempting residential areas from the ambit of public places where First Amendment free speech rights prevail is precisely why protests in such areas are likely to be both effective and unpopular. In the PACE v. Doorley case,[1] the plaintiff, the Reverend James Ford, together with seven members of his group, picketed the residence of Abraham Konoff, carrying signs which read, "Mr. Konoff fix your property on Dudley Street." Other signs contained pictures of the Dudley Street property, showing what were termed violations of the housing code. The group was advised that their action was in violation of an anti-residential-picketing ordinance, and they were ordered to disperse. Fearing arrest and prosecution, the plaintiffs departed.

Then, in a suit against Mayor Joseph A. Doorley, plaintiffs challenged the validity of the ordinance in federal court. The ordinance prohibited picketing "before or about the residence or dwelling of any individual," but not "lawful picketing during a labor dispute at the place of employment" involved, or assembly on any premises "commonly used for the discussion of subjects of general interest." The district court declared the ordinance constitutional and not in violation of either First or Fourteenth Amendments. Rather, the court found that the ordinance reflects a legislative judgment that residential picketing is meant to harass and cause emotional stress, destroying tranquility and the privacy of the home.

The court concluded that residential picketing is not a conventional means for the exercise of First Amendment rights. "On the contrary, it is an instrument of harassment and oppression, pregnant with 'physical intimidation and coercion.' . . . I find this undemocratic and violative of constitutional protection belonging to all citizens — innocent or otherwise." Concerning the plaintiffs' equal protection argument, growing out of the ordinance's exemption of picketing during labor disputes, the court stated that "such exemption is necessary so as not to deny an employee the right of picketing at the subject matter of his dispute." The court found that the home is protected unless it is a place of employment.

§10.13   1. People Acting Through Community Effort (PACE) v. Doorley, 338 F. Supp. 574 (D.R.I. 1972).

On appeal, the *Doorley* decision was reversed.[2] Without reaching the question of whether residential picketing would have been constitutionally protected in the absence of the discriminatory clause in the ordinance exempting labor picketing, the court found the labor exemption in the ordinance a fatal defect, citing both Police Dept. of Chicago v. Mosley and Grayned v. City of Rockford.[3] Inveighing against the interference with privacy that occurs when protesters seek out public figures at their homes rather than at their offices is not a concern felt only at the district court level. Two Supreme Court liberals, Justices Black and Douglas, admonished state officials that the First Amendment had not rendered them powerless to protect against protest demonstrations conducted whenever and however they pleased. If this were the case, Justice Black wrote:

Homes, the sacred retreat to which families repair for their privacy and their daily way of living, would have to have their doors thrown open to all who desired to convert the occupants to new views, new morals, and a new way of life. Men and women who hold public office would be compelled, simply because they did hold public office, to lose the comforts and privacy of an unpicketed home. I believe that our Constitution, written for the ages, to endure except as changed in the manner it provides, did not create a government with such monumental weaknesses. Speech and press are, of course, to be free, so that public matters can be discussed with impunity. But picketing and demonstrating can be regulated like other conduct of men. I believe that the homes of men, sometimes the last citadel of the tired, the weary and the sick, can be protected by government from noisy, marching, tramping, threatening picketers and demonstrators bent on filling the minds of men, women, and children with fears of the unknown.[4]

The motivation for this display of constitutional conservatism was the usual stumbling block for Justice Black's liberalism: blacks who refused to follow his admonition that in seeking redress for racial injustices, their "constitutional and statutory rights have to be protected by the courts. . . ."[5] In this instance, black humorist and advocate Dick Gregory demanded that Chicago mayor Richard Daley seek the ouster of the Superintendent of Chicago's public schools. Gregory led a march that first picketed the Mayor's office, and then proceeded to Daley's home five miles away. Arriving about 8 P.M., the demonstrators, with the police and an Assistant City Attorney looking on, began marching around and around near the Mayor's home. Neighborhood spectators gathered and the crowd's "language and conduct" toward the protesters as described in Justice Black's concurring opinion, became "rougher and tougher." The record shows that the police did all they could to maintain order, and that the protesters maintained their decorum in the face of jeers, insults, and assaults with rocks and eggs. Finally, about 9:30 P.M., fearful that the ever more threatening crowd could not be contained, the police asked Gregory and his marchers to leave the area. They refused and were arrested and convicted of disorderly conduct. The Supreme Court reversed.

2. 468 F.2d 1143 (1st Cir. 1972).
3. See Comment, Picketers at the Doorstep, 9 Harv. C.R.-C.L. L. Rev. 95 (1974).
4. Gregory v. City of Chicago, 394 U.S. 111, 125 (1969).
5. Cox v. Louisiana, 879 U.S. 536, 584 (1965) (dissenting).

Without questioning police motives, the Supreme Court held that the convictions violated due process in that they were "totally devoid of evidentiary support." The Court also found that the trial judge's charge permitted the jury to convict for acts clearly entitled to First Amendment protection, and that this independently required reversal.[6] In the majority opinion, Chief Justice Warren had described *Gregory* as a "simple case" because the record contained no indication that the protester-petitioners had been disorderly, but Justice Black disagreed. In his concurring opinion, in which Justice Douglas joined, Justice Black viewed the case as "highly important" requiring more detailed consideration than given it by the majority's opinion, and posing the dilemma of whether the country can both protect the constitutional rights to protest racial injustice and maintain peace and order. In noting that the *Gregory* demonstrators themselves had not been unruly or disorderly, Justice Black said

> [t]he so-called "diversion tending to a breach of the peace" here was limited entirely and exclusively to the fact that when the policeman in charge of the special police detail concluded that the hecklers observing the march were dangerously close to rioting and that the demonstrators and others were likely to be engulfed in that riot, he ordered Gregory and his demonstrators to leave, and Gregory — standing on what he deemed to be his constitutional rights — refused to do so.[7]

On the basis of these facts, Justice Black was led "unerringly" to the conclusion that:

> . . . when groups with diametrically opposed, deep-seated views are permitted to air their emotional grievances, side by side, on city streets, tranquility and order *cannot* be maintained even by the joint efforts of the finest and best officers and of those who desire to be the most law-abiding protestors of their grievances.
>
> It is because of this truth, and a desire *both to promote order and to safeguard First Amendment freedoms,* that this Court has repeatedly warned States and governmental units that they cannot regulate conduct connected with these freedoms through use of sweeping, dragnet statutes that may, because of vagueness, jeopardize these freedoms. In those cases, however, we have been careful to point out that the Constitution does not bar enactment of laws regulating conduct, even though connected with speech, press, assembly, and petition, if such laws specifically bar only the conduct deemed obnoxious and are carefully and narrowly aimed at that forbidden conduct.[8]

Specifically, Justice Black noted that nothing in the Constitution prevented either state or local governments from enacting laws designed "to protect the

---

6. *Gregory*, supra note 4, at 112. The Chicago disorderly conduct ordinance under which Gregory and his fellow demonstrators had been convicted provided that "[a]ll persons who shall make, aid, countenance, or assist in making any improper noise, riot, disturbance, breach of the peace, or diversion tending to a breach of the peace, within the limits of the city; all persons who shall collect in bodies or crowds for unlawful purposes, or for any purpose, to the annoyance or disturbance of other persons; . . . shall be deemed guilty of disorderly conduct, and upon conviction thereof, shall be severally fined not less than one dollar nor more than two hundred dollars for each offense." Municipal Code of Chicago, Sec. 193-1.

7. Id. at 120.

8. Id. at 117-118 (emphasis added).

public from the kind of boisterous and threatening conduct that disturbs the tranquility of spots selected by the people either for homes, wherein they can escape the hurly-burly of the outside business and political world, or for public and other buildings that require peace and quiet to carry out their function, such as courts, libraries, schools, and hospitals." Here, neither the state legislature nor the Chicago city council had enacted any narrowly drawn laws forbidding disruptive demonstrations in residential areas: As a result, the petitioners' conduct could properly be deemed "disorderly" only if the policeman's order to disperse was considered "a law which the petitioners were bound to obey at their peril." To hold that the policeman's order constituted such a law would, however, run contrary to the nation's democratic system of government; as Justice Black stated, "lawmaking is not entrusted to the moment-to-moment judgment of the policeman on his beat. Laws, that is valid laws, are to be made by representatives chosen to make laws for the future, not by police officers whose duty is to enforce laws already enacted and to make arrests only for conduct already made criminal." Since the First Amendment freedoms here involved had been impermissibly subjected "to such a clumsy and unwieldy weapon" — that is, to the police officer's unfettered and arbitrary discretion — Justice Black concurred in the reversal of the petitioners' convictions.

Having stated what police may not do, it is not the Court's responsibility to suggest how a state legislature or city council should draft "narrowly-drawn laws forbidding disruptive demonstrations in residential areas." To ban all protests in residential neighborhoods raises the equal protection problem with federal labor law provisions that defeated the anti-picketing ordinance in the PACE v. Doorley case. On the other hand, a law defining a "disruptive disturbance" as one where hostile spectators threaten to get out of control provides those opposed to the protest aims with a potential statutory "heckler's veto" exercisable by violent actions for which the protesters, unless they cease protesting, can be held criminally liable.[9]

Notions of the sanctity of the home inform judicial anxiety about protecting protestors. The majority opinion in Gregory v. City of Chicago deftly sidestepped the profound limitations that inhere in the Court's protest-law jurisprudence. Justice Black's concurring opinion, however, reveals the limitations quite clearly. The way in which Justice Black characterizes private space resonates with language deployed by the Supreme Court in its Brown v. Louisiana opinion. Justice Black characterizes one's residence as a place of "tranquility" and peace; it is, he says, a place to take refuge from "threatening conduct" and "the hurly-burly of the outside. . . . political world." In a rhetorical gesture evocative of *Brown*, Justice Black asserted a link among homes, libraries, schools, and so on. Protest and protestors,

---

9. "Heckler's veto" is how Professor Harry Kalven referred to this problem. See The Negro and the First Amendment 140-145 (1965). Professor Laurence Tribe, in reviewing the authorities, observes several recurring themes in the Court's decisions on the issue: (1) speakers can't be silenced if their identity as blacks seeking service in facilities reserved for whites is the primary factor offered to justify a fear that audience violence is imminent; (2) speech may not be suppressed if reasonable crowd control techniques can be used to prevent or curb spectator violence; and (3) where such techniques cannot curb threatened violence, government authorities may suppress otherwise constitutionally protected speech. Laurence Tribe, American Constitutional Law 621-622 (1978).

on the other hand, are equated with "hurly-burly" and "threatening conduct." Notions of political "hurly-burly" during the mid- to late-1960s, of course, were often racially inflected. By insisting upon the insularity of private space, Black's concurrence foreclosed consideration of the extent to which the "peace" and "tranquility" afforded by a particular private space functions to ensure racist exclusion. As in *Brown,* Black's concurrence in *Gregory* seems to limit the capacity of a protest to directly challenge practices that transpire in tranquil "private space." Unfortunately, it is often the case in our society that one's capacity to feel "peace" and "tranquility" in a particular space is predicated upon the systematic exclusion of *others,* of those not like oneself, from that space. It would seem that part of what antiracist protests seek to do is to challenge not only the materiality of racist exclusion, but the structure of "comfort" underguided by it. Insisting upon a rigid private-public dichotomy effectively shields the structure of comfort from scrutiny or interrogation.

In the sit-in cases, the Court rejected state arguments that the very presence of blacks in all-white facilities was a provocation to violence.[10] Assuming a continuing sensitivity to spectator anger aroused mainly because blacks are protesting racial injustice adds to the difficulty of drafting a valid anti-disruptive demonstration law.

Injunctions against residential protests present constitutional problems of their own. In Organization for a Better Austin v. Keefe,[11] a state court had granted the motion of a real estate broker for an order enjoining a racially integrated community organization from further distributions of leaflets charging the broker with "block-busting" and "panic peddling"; the leaflets had been distributed throughout the Chicago suburb in which the broker lived. The state court found that the organization's leafletting activities invaded the realtor's right of privacy, and were coercive and intimidating rather than informative.

The Supreme Court disagreed, finding the leafletting within the organization's First Amendment right to freedom of expression, and further finding that issuance of the injunction constituted an unjustified prior restraint. According to the Court, the Organization's members "were engaged openly and vigorously in making the public aware of [Keefe's] real estate practices," and although their tactics may have been offensive to him and to others, "so long as the means [were] peaceful, the communication need not meet standards of acceptability." The Court further noted that no prior decisions supported "the claim that the interest of an individual in being free from public criticism of his business practices in pamphlets or leaflets warrants use of the injunctive power of a court."[12] An Illinois statute prohibiting residential picketing was struck down by the Supreme Court in Carey v. Brown.[13] The Court held that the statute was "constitutionally indistinguishable" from the one invalidated in Police Department of Chicago v. Mosley[14] and that by exempting picketing involving a labor dispute, it impermissibly discriminated

---

10. See, e.g., Garner v. Louisiana, 368 U.S. 157 (1961).
11. 402 U.S. 415 (1971).
12. Id. at 419.
13. 447 U.S. 455 (1980), aff'g Brown v. Scott, 602 F.2d 791 (1979).
14. 408 U.S. 92 (1972). The Illinois provisions involved were Ill. Rev. Stat., ch. 38, §21.1-2.

between lawful and unlawful conduct based upon the content of the demonstrator's communication. The controversy arose when members of the Committee Against Racism participated in a peaceful demonstration on the public sidewalk in front of the home of Chicago Mayor Michael Bilandic to protest his failure to support the busing of school children to achieve integration. The picketers were arrested and charged with unlawful residential picketing in violation of Illinois statutes.[15] Though similar statutes have consistently been overturned,[16] it is important to note that the cases do not support any substantive right to picket or demonstrate in residential areas. In the *Carey* opinion the Supreme Court cautions, "[w]e are not to be understood to imply, however, that residential picketing is beyond the reach of uniform and nondiscriminatory regulation."[17] The opinion goes on to discuss the state's high interest in protecting the well-being, tranquility, and privacy of the home. But as with earlier reassurances of this kind,[18] the Court provided no guidelines as to how all residential picketing might be banned without violating federal statutes authorizing picketing when a labor dispute is involved.

Other groups, however, have not looked for guidance before claiming constitutional authority for protests that transform the free speech shield into a sword of intimidation through terror. The governing body of Skokie, Illinois, in an effort to avoid spectator intimidation and possible violence, sought an injunction to restrain the defendant, a "neo-Nazi" organization, from conducting a demonstration in that town.[19] Skokie had a population of some 70,000 people, of whom over 40,000 were Jewish; included within the town's Jewish population were "hundreds of persons" who had survived Nazi concentration camps and "many thousands" whose families and close relatives had been murdered by Nazis. In view of these and other facts, the circuit court of Cook County issued a decree that enjoined the defendants from engaging in any of the following acts within the village of Skokie:

> Marching, walking or parading in the uniform of the National Socialist Party of America; Marching, walking or parading or otherwise displaying the swastika on or off their person; Distributing pamphlets or displaying any materials which incite or promote hatred against persons of Jewish faith or ancestry or hatred against persons of any faith or ancestry, race or religion.

On appeal, the appellate court of Illinois upheld only that portion of the injunction decree which prohibited the wearing or display of swastikas, holding that such display fell within the "fighting words" exception to free speech.

The Illinois Supreme Court rejected the theory that the display or wearing of swastikas in connection with the defendants' proposed demonstration constituted "fighting words." Relying heavily upon the U.S. Supreme Court's decision in Cohen v. California,[20] the Illinois court held that "use of the swastika is a symbolic

---

15. 447 U.S. at 460.
16. See also People Acting Through Community Effort (PACE) v. Doorley, 468 F.2d 1143 (1st Cir. 1972).
17. 447 U.S. at 466.
18. See Gregory v. City of Chicago, 394 U.S. 111 (1969).
19. Village of Skokie v. National Socialist Party of Am., 69 Ill. 2d 605, 373 N.E.2d 21 (1978).
20. 403 U.S. 15 (1971).

form of free speech entitled to first amendment protections." In addition, the court rejected the plaintiffs' alternative argument that "the swastika, while not representing fighting words, is nevertheless so offensive and peace-threatening to the public that its display can be enjoined." As the court stated, the possibility that such display might provoke a violent reaction by spectators did not, under the decisions of the U.S. Supreme Court, "justify enjoining defendants' speech"; rather, under *Cohen* and *Erznoznik,*[21] the burden was placed upon the *viewers* to "avoid further bombardment." Hence, the court held that that portion of the appellate court's decision enjoining the defendants from displaying or wearing the swastika must be reversed. The remainder of the appellate court's opinion was affirmed.

Not satisfied in their efforts to utilize First Amendment doctrine gained by civil rights groups, anti-abortion protesters, in their attempt to seek the moral high ground on the abortion issue, have tried to link their protests to the civil rights movement. Thus, activists such as Operation Rescue, an anti-abortion group known for its willingness to use threats, intimidation, and violence in order to get its message across, have invoked the name of Dr. Martin Luther King to justify their lawbreaking activities.[22] Pro-choice activists argue that the actions of anti-abortion protesters are antithetical to the goals of Dr. King and the civil rights movement. Former state senator and civil rights activist Julian Bond said, "Civil rights tried to expand life for everyone. These people [such as Operation Rescue members] want to restrict life for women."[23] In Frisby v. Schultz,[24] the Court upheld a municipal ordinance prohibiting picketing before or about the residence of any individual against a challenge brought by "pro-life" protestors who sought to picket on a public street outside the residence of a doctor who allegedly performed abortions. The Court concluded that the ordinance did not ban all picketing in residential areas, but prohibited only focused picketing taking place solely in front of a particular residence. The Court further held that the ordinance did not violate the First Amendment because it was narrowly tailored to serve the significant governmental interest of protecting residential privacy.

§10.14 PROTECTING PATIENTS OR SILENCING UNWANTED SPEECH: RESTRICTING PROTEST ACTIVITIES OUTSIDE HEALTH FACILITIES

Between 1986 and 2000, over 3,000 incidents of violence were linked to anti-abortion protests outside of clinics, including "murder, arson, bombing,

---

21. Erznoznik v. City of Jacksonville, 422 U.S. 205 (1975).
22. See, e.g., Operation Rescue: Soldier in a "Holy War" on Abortion, L.A. Times, Mar. 17, 1989, at 1, col. 1.
23. Id. See also Pro-Lifers Claim King as Model, Wash. Times, Aug. 16, 1991, at A3 (leaders of Operation Rescue claim to follow "higher law" than civil law).
24. 487 U.S. 474 (1989).

vandalism, and anthrax threats."[1] As a result, federal and state action has placed boundaries around anti-abortion protest activities intended to harass and obstruct patients' entry into clinics. The Supreme Court has been confronted with these restrictions because they walk a fine line between protecting patients' rights and restricting speech.

The Court has upheld the validity of anti-abortion protest restrictions beyond the residential sphere to provide protection for unwilling listeners entering health clinics for an abortion. Although the Court found no statutory protection under §1985 in Bray v. Alexandria,[2] the Court in more recent decisions permitted judicial injunctions creating a buffer zone around clinic entrances and upheld a state statute placing content neutral restrictions on protestors outside health care facilities.

In *Bray*[3] the Court had to decide whether anti-abortion protestors could be prevented from blocking an entrance to an abortion clinic under 42 U.S.C. §1985(3), which affords a federal cause of action against anyone who conspires to deny equal protection under the law to a person or class of persons. The Court also had to decide whether the anti-abortion activists' tactics impinged upon the women's right to interstate travel. (They had traveled to Washington, D.C. for abortions.) Justice Scalia wrote for a divided Court. He stated that because the anti-abortion protestors did not invidiously intend to discriminate against women as a class, §1985(3) afforded clinics (and women seeking abortions therein) no protection. The Court also held that the anti-abortion activists' tactics did not impinge upon the women's right to interstate travel.[4] Following *Bray*, the Court heard additional cases regarding prohibitions of protests outside clinics.[5] The first two cases addressed judicial injunctions on protest activities at specific clinics. The third case, Hill v. Colorado, examined the constitutionality of a state statute that limited the obstruction of entrances to any health care facilities.[6] Specifically, the statute passed in 1993 prohibited anyone within 100 feet of an entrance to a health care facility from approaching within 8 feet of a person to hand out a leaflet, display a sign, or engage in counseling, education, or oral protest.

---

§10.14 1. See Jamie Edwards, McGuire v. Reilly: The First Amendment and Abortion Clinic Buffer Zones in the Wake of Hill v. Colorado, 36 U.C. Davis L. Rev. 787 (2003). Twelve states and the District of Columbia prohibited activities near facilities that prevent safe, public access to health care.

2. 506 U.S. 263 (1993).

3. Id.

4. In 1994, Congress passed the Freedom of Access to Clinic Entrances (FACE) Act, 18 U.S.C. §248 (1994), which criminalized the obstruction of abortion clinic entrances. In addition, the Act subjects to criminal liability those who attempt to "intimidate" or "interfere" with a person's (or a class of person's) efforts to obtain reproductive health services. It is not clear whether the Supreme Court's ruling in *R.A.V.* bears upon the terms of the FACE Act's application (or its constitutionality, for that matter). For an interesting discussion of this question, see Alan E. Brownstein, Rules of Engagement for Cultural Wars: Regulating Conduct, Unprotected Speech, and Protected Expression in Anti-Abortion Protests, 29 U.C. Davis L. Rev. 553 (1996).

5. See Schenck v. Pro-Choice Network, 519 U.S. 357, 376 (1997); Medtronic, Inc. v. Lohr, 518 U.S. 470, 475 (1996), upholding an injunction creating a buffer zone around a clinic's entrances but rejecting a 15-foot "floating" buffer zone around people leaving and entering the clinic; see also Madsen v. Women's Health Center, Inc., 512 U.S. 753, 767 (1994), upholding an injunction that restricted abortion protestors from entering a 36-foot buffer zone around a clinic's entrances.

6. 530 U.S. 703 (2000).

Writing for the majority, Justice Stevens framed the question as "whether the First Amendment rights of the speaker are abridged by the protection the statute provides for the unwilling listener."[7] In applying the test in Ward v. Rock Against Racism[8] for time, place, and manner restrictions, the Court held that the statute serves legitimate and significant state interests, is narrowly tailored to serve that interest, restricts only content-neutral speech, and leaves alternate avenues for communication. Justice Stevens did not find the statute to necessarily impede the communication of protestors and observed that restrictions may actually assist them in communicating their message while moderating confrontational and harassing conduct.[9]

Justice Scalia argued in dissent that the statute is an unconstitutional content-based regulation "directed against the opponents of abortion."[10] He characterizes the majority opinion as an example of the " 'ad hoc nullification machine' that the Court has set in motion to push aside whatever doctrines of constitutional law stand in the way of that highly favored practice."[11] He found that the non-speech-related obstruction prohibitions would be sufficient to protect the state's interest.[12] Justice Kennedy, also dissenting, reasoned that the "Court approves a law which bars a private citizen from passing a message in a peaceful manner on a profound issue, to a fellow citizen on a public sidewalk."

Perhaps the most significant general problem with the *Hill* decision is that it applies a very ambiguously defined narrow-tailoring analysis for content-neutral restrictions of speech.[13] This opinion adds to the criticism that the time, place, and manner doctrine is eroding, "depriving the Court's First Amendment jurisprudence of a valuable tool for the protection of speech."[14]

One critique from Professors Jamin Raskin and Clark LeBlanc argues that "[t]he Court's decision last year in Hill v. Colorado, a case deeply colored by abortion politics, has opened the door widely to a new era of restrictive speech regulation within traditional public fora."[15] In their view, the Court's decision makes it easier for "government entities to discriminate against disfavored viewpoints . . . provided that their enactments maintain the thinnest façade of neutrality."[16] The protection of the unwilling listener, derived from cases like *Schultz*, could become an instrument for silencing the messages of unpopular groups or individuals. In response, the authors advocate for the creation of a more objective content and viewpoint discrimination analysis — an analysis that looks "not only

---

7. Id at 708.

8. 491 U.S. 781 (1989).

9. See The Supreme Court 1999 Term, Leading Cases, 114 Harv. L. Rev. 279, 289 (2000). See also James J. Zych, Note: Hill v. Colorado and the Evolving Rights of the Unwilling Listener, 45 St. Louis U. L.J. 1281 (2001).

10. 530 U.S. at 741 (Scalia, J. dissenting).

11. Id.

12. Supreme Court 1999 Term, supra note 9, at 293.

13. Id. at 294-296.

14. Id. at 299.

15. Jamin B. Raskin & Clark L. LeBlanc, Disfavored Speech about Favored Rights: Hill v. Colorado, The Vanishing Public Forum and the Need for an Objective Speech Discrimination Test, 51 Am. U. L. Rev. 179, 182 (2001).

16. Id.

at the facial character of a statute and its stated purpose, but the substantive character in social, historical, and political context as well."[17] The goal of a structured approach would be to "prevent government from dressing up speech-discriminatory regulations in the clothing of official neutrality."[18]

§10.15 RACE, RAP, AND THE REGULATION OF FREE SPEECH

While attention so far has been focused on the First Amendment's protection (or lack of protection) for the protest activities of blacks, the treatment of the most traditional First Amendment activity — speech — has also had significant impact on blacks and other historically oppressed groups. The extent to which the First Amendment has been invoked to shelter speech which attacks blacks is as telling a story of the courts' concern for the rights of blacks as the protest cases discussed above.

It is an unfortunate truth that free speech has largely meant free speech for white people and the wealthy. As Professor Laurence Tribe notes:

> The reality of First Amendment jurisprudence has never been — nor is it now — consistent application of that charter's blanket guarantees. Instead, constitutional protection for free speech emerges as a patchwork quilt of exceptions. And . . . the Supreme Court has been all too willing to endorse doctrinal rubrics that protect the speech of corporations but not workers, or that zealously guard the preferred expressive methods of the wealthy while tolerating restrictions on the means of communication upon which the less fortunate must rely.[1]

As will be illustrated, even the seemingly neutral speech regulations held to be consistent with the First Amendment have disproportionately burdened blacks and other excluded groups.

An approach to the First Amendment that is equally protective of blacks requires a delicate and clear-sighted balancing act. It calls upon courts to sensitize themselves to the particular concerns of blacks as speakers *and* as listeners. It demands, on the one hand, *restricting* the field of constitutionally guarded speech in order to shelter blacks from the oppressive and degrading impact of racist speech. At the same time, it counsels *broadening* our conception of speech to include and protect the distinctive voices of black persons. It requires, at the most basic level, an understanding that "neutral" free speech principles rarely operate in a neutral fashion.

To cope with a society that all too frequently ignores and demeans them, blacks often resort to speech which challenges or subverts the norm — speech least likely to win judicial favor. The response to black musicians typifies the hostile response of predominantly white judges to typically black modes of

---

17. Id. at 217.
18. Id. at 218.
§10.15 1. Laurence Tribe, Constitutional Choices 220 (1985).

expression. Rather than understanding or even tolerance, this music is often met with a narrow cultural single-mindedness. Little Richard, who sang of the unspoken topics of teenage pregnancy and interracial dating, was an early victim of private censorship by radio stations that simply refused to play his music. Today, the boisterous and often controversial music of rap artists is pulled from record store shelves, pasted with warning labels, denied concert locations, and even banned by courts. One rap group, 2 Live Crew, became the center of controversy when its first album became the first album to be judged obscene by a federal court.[2] The swift judicial response to this rap album stood in sharp contrast to society's tolerance of the most outrageous music by whites.

The treatment of 2 Live Crew prompted many to question the ability of a predominantly white judiciary to evaluate fairly the work of black artists. Evaluating the speech of nondominant groups in terms of legal norms set by the larger society means that black speakers often will find themselves outside of the First Amendment's shelter. Translations by those unfamiliar with or hostile to speech codes of many blacks distort the meaning of this speech and misjudge the effect it will have on audience members well-versed in this language. Professor Henry Gates, urging courts to "become literate in the vernacular tradition of African-Americans," describes their uninformed judgments as "the equivalent of intellectual prior restraint." Considering the racial overtones of courts' decisions, Professor Gates is certainly right when he warns that "censorship is to art what lynching is to justice."[3]

At least one court, though, has recognized that even seemingly neutral restrictions on First Amendment freedoms have disproportionately burdened members of excluded groups. The city of Pomona enacted an ordinance which prohibited signs on the premises of commercial or manufacturing establishments with advertising copy in foreign alphabetical characters unless at least one half of the sign area is devoted to advertising copy in English alphabetical characters. This regulation was struck down in Asian American Business Group v. City of Pomona.[4] Requiring English characters, the court found, regulates the cultural expression of the sign owner. Choice of language is a form of expression as real as the textual message conveyed. Language is an expression of culture, directly related to and constitutive of a person's national origin, culture and ethnicity. Because the ordinance regulates the cultural speech of the sign owner, it is a content regulation which must survive strict scrutiny. The ordinance failed to pass muster because it was not narrowly tailored to serve the apparent governmental interest at stake — the identification of buildings to facilitate the reporting of emergencies.

Failure to engage in the inquiry mapped out by *Pomona* court — to look behind the laws to their intent and impact — is the failure to afford blacks the equal protection of the law. It is a selective exercise of judicial blindness which allows courts to hide behind their own insensitivity while clinging to underinclusive and race based conventions of normality.

2. Jon Pareles, An Album Is Judged Obscene; Rap: Slick, Violent, Nasty and Maybe Hopeful, N.Y. Times, June 17, 1990, at 1, col. 4.
3. Henry Louis Gates, Jr., 2 Live Crew Decoded, N.Y. Times, June 19, 1990, at A23.
4. 716 F. Supp. 1328 (C.D. Cal. 1989).

§10.16   PROTESTING POLICE BRUTALITY

Police departments throughout the country have come under intense public scrutiny because of police brutality and fatal shootings in minority neighborhoods. Angry citizens from Los Angeles to Chicago and Cincinnati to New York City have voiced their opinions by filling streets to protest a lack of police accountability.[1] As protestors demand reform of police practices, many cities have attempted to investigate police misconduct by setting up special commissions or strengthening civilian review boards. But few have any teeth and major progress has not been made.[2] Many civil rights advocates fear that this leaves urban populations increasingly distrustful of police. A report by the National Organization of Black Law Enforcement Executives warned that "[t]here are numerous cities . . . in crisis — powder kegs waiting to be ignited by a single incident."[3]

A great deal of national attention was directed specifically at police brutality and shootings in New York over the past five years. In one example, Amadou Diallo, an unarmed man, was killed outside his Bronx apartment as he reached for his wallet. In response to the shooting, Rev. Al Sharpton arranged massive protests, including "two weeks of civil disobedience that resulted in the arrest of hundreds, including the state comptroller, Carl McCall, and the actress Susan Sarandon."[4] Sharpton stated that the protests pressured the administration to empanel a grand jury for the four officers involved in the incident, who were subsequently indicted and acquitted.[5] Today, the New York City Civilian Complaint Review Board reports that civilian complaints of police abuse have been rising over the past two years, increasing to 4,616 in 2002.[6]

As an unexpected response to the daily Diallo protests, the Police Department issued an official policy that resulted in protestor arrests and overnight jail stays.[7] Traditionally, protestors were issued a summons to appear in court at a later date and released. Challenging the new policy, protestors won over $350,000 in a 2002 settlement that also formally ended the policy.[8]

Anti-war protestors in 2003, however, were again arrested and detained for over 24 hours. New lawsuits have been filed.[9] These cases may turn on whether

§10.16   1. Salim Muwakkil, The Global Costs of Police Brutality in the U.S., Chi. Trib., May 28, 2001, at 15; Geov Parrish, Calling for a Crackdown, Seattle Weekly, June 29, 2000; Daniel Wood, Police Incident Shows How L.A. Has Changed, Christian Sci. Monitor, July 15, 2002, at 2.

2. Muwakkil, supra note 1, at 15.

3. Id.

4. Elizabeth Kolbert, The People's Preacher: Al Sharpton Would Rather Walk Naked Than Wear Your Wretched Dress, New Yorker, Feb. 18, 2002.

5. Michael Kramer, The World According to Sharpton, Daily News, Apr. 18, 1999, at 47.

6. William Rashbaum, Police Abuse Cases Rising, Complaint Review Board Says, N.Y. Times, June 3, 2003, at B4.

7. Robert Worth, City Agrees to End the Giuliani Policy of Jailing Most Protestors for the Night, N.Y. Times, Mar. 28, 2003, at B4.

8. Robert Gearty, Protesters Get 350G from City for Jailings, Daily News, Mar. 28, 2002, at 8. The police policy seems tame compared to Al Sharpton's 90-day sentence and three Bronx politicians' 40-day sentences for protesting Navy bombing exercises in Vieques, Puerto Rico.

9. Anthony Ramirez, Metro Briefing New York: Manhattan: Protesters Sue City, N.Y. Times, July 2, 2003, at B4.

the courts will agree that such detention is necessary to protect us from national security threats, an argument that helped to severely limit the location for anti-war rallies. The police action in New York City continues to send the message that the consequences of protesting makes expressing one's political opinion a costly activity.

§10.17   PROTESTING PROSECUTORIAL ZEAL TO PUNISH STUDENTS OF COLOR

As this discussion of protesting the police makes clear, the criminal justice system exemplifies persistent racial inequality in this country. One aspect of that system gaining greater national attention is the excessively punitive approach to policing and prosecuting students of color. Protests around the overzealous prosecution of the "Jena 6," helped to expose this issue.

The period of mounting racial tension in Jena, Louisiana, began after an African American student and his friend, with the permission of the school principal, sat under the "white tree," where only white students historically would gather. Some white students retaliated by hanging nooses on the tree. The white school board viewed the nooses as a student prank and the students were suspended for a couple of days. Over the following months, fights broke out among the black and white students. In one altercation, six black students attacked a white student who was said to be bragging about racist acts of white students. Jena's district attorney overcharged the students with attempted murder, and decided to try them as adults.

Mychal Bell, the first to be tried, was found guilty of reduced charges by an all white jury. An appeals court reversed the conviction on the ground that he should not have been tried as an adult. Bell remained in jail for 10 months, and was released only after his bail was reduced to $45,000 from $90,000. He awaits a new trial.

In response, "local civil rights groups objected to what they saw as a throwback to the worst kind of Deep South justice, and that protest has escalated into a nationwide campaign, through Web sites, bulk e-mail and instant messages, black radio stations, and YouTube."[1] On September 20, 2007, over 20,000 protesters traveled to Jena and marched through town to protest law enforcement's treatment of the students.[2] Additional rallies, marches, and a national student walkout at more than 100 colleges have taken place in solidarity with the Jena 6. The protests have sparked media commentary and garnered the attention of Congress.

§10.17   1. Richard Jones, In Louisiana, a Tree, a Fight and a Question of Justice, N.Y. Times, Sept. 19, 2007.

2. Paul Krugman, Politics in Black and White, N.Y. Times, September 24, 2007. See also "NAACP Jena Branch President Testifies Before House Judiciary Committee on Hate Crimes and Racially Discriminatory Prosecution of Six African American Youth," http://www.naacp.org/news/press/2007-10-18/index.html.

Testifying before the House Judiciary Committee, Professor Charles Ogletree urged that Congress provide funding to the states and localities that would "educate professionals about racial disparities and the bias and prejudice that likely plays a role in disparate treatment."[3] He argued that "[t]he immediate lessons of Jena should be clear. . . . A public educational system should not be allowed to punish anyone in disparate ways where it appears to have racial implications."[4] These activists and academics showed how protest can ferret out the injustices pervading our criminal justice system, especially for students of color.

§10.18   THE FIRST AMENDMENT AND RACIST SPEECH

While the First Amendment may be "the Constitution's most majestic guarantee," it is nonetheless a limited guarantee.[1] Defamation, obscenity, and speech which threaten the social order — bomb threats, incitements to riot, and "fighting words" — are all limited by law.[2] In the world of business, false advertisements, insider information, and suggestions that prices be fixed, are also off-limits. Yet hate speech — expressions which abuse, insult, or belittle a person because of his or her race, ethnicity, national origin, gender, religion, sexual orientation, or physical abilities — is still tolerated and even protected.[3] Debate over restrictions on racist speech has been triggered by renewed publicity surrounding hate-motivated slurs against members of target groups.[4] In one recent case, a black student

3. Charles J. Ogletree, Jr., Testimony: Jena 6 and the Role of Federal Intervention in Hate Crimes and Race-Related Violence in Public Schools, available at http://www.law.harvard.edu/news/2007/10/ogletree_testimony.pdf.

4. Id.

§10.18   1. Laurence Tribe, American Constitutional Law §12-1 at 576 (1978).

2. See, e.g., Chaplinsky v. New Hampshire, 315 U.S. 568 (1942) (fighting words); Brandenburg v. Ohio, 395 U.S. 444 (1969) (clear and present danger); Gertz v. Robert Welch, Inc., 418 U.S. 323 (1974) (libel).

3. See Mari Matsuda, Public Response to Racist Speech: Considering the Victim's Story, 87 Mich. L. Rev. 2320 (1989) (arguing that the law's ability to recognize the reputational injury to the person who has been libeled or defamed, for instance, "and yet to fail to see that the very same things happen to the victims of racist speech," is selective vision.) In a highly publicized case, the Seventh Circuit considered whether statements of the National Socialist Part, a neo-Nazi group which planned a demonstration in the predominantly Jewish town of Skokie, Ill., could be considered libel. The National Socialist Party maintains that blacks are biologically inferior and that Jewish people are linked to an international community conspiracy. The court held that these assertions are not libel because they are ideas, not factual statements which can be judged true or untrue. Village of Skokie v. National Socialist Party, 373 N.E.2d 21 (Ill. 1978).

4. The National Institute Against Prejudice and Violence estimates that one fifth of all minority students attending college are physically or verbally harassed. America's Youthful Bigots, U.S. News & World Report, May 7, 1990, vol. 208, no. 18, at 59. See also Racism Flares on Campus, Time, Dec. 8, 1980, at 28 ("stinking black monkeys" and other messages sent to African American students at Williams College; an African American student at Harvard found her office calendar defaced with racist slogans; crosses burned at Purdue University; letter addressed to African American student dormitory at Wesleyan University spoke of "wip[ing] all g.d. niggers off the face of the earth") (cited in Richard Delgado, Words That Wound: A Tort Action for Racial Insults, Epithets, and Name-Calling, 17 Harv. C.R.-C.L. L. Rev. 133, 135 n.12 (1982)).

at Emory University was hospitalized for "emotional traumatization" and rendered literally mute by a campaign of racist harassment.[5] Racial epithets were scrawled in her dormitory room, bleach poured onto her clothing, and death threats sent to her through the campus mail. When the student refused to be relocated, the university installed a motion detector and alarm system in her room and assigned police to patrol the hallway outside of her room.

This guarded exile, many would argue, is sadly but necessarily the only constitutionally acceptable remedy for those like the Emory student. They warn that suppressing racist speech leads us down a slippery slope towards totalitarianism, vesting in the government a censorship power over unpopular ideas which is inconsistent with the First Amendment and the most basic precepts of a democratic society. They point to the instrumental role that the First Amendment played in protecting the civil rights movement in its often angrily greeted advocacy for social change as proof of the necessity of an absolute free speech guarantee. Courts have almost unanimously accepted these arguments.[6]

In the face of a rising tide of racism on university campuses and as a result of demands by minority students, many schools have enacted free speech policies

5. Racial Attacks Leave Freshman in Severe Shock, N.Y. Times, Apr. 22, 1990, at 44. For a collection of other incidents, see Richard Delgado, Campus Antiracism Rules: Constitutional Narratives in Collision, 85 Nw. L. Rev. 343, 349-358 (1991); Charles Lawrence, If He Hollers Let Him Go: Regulating Racist Speech on Campus, 1990 Duke L.J. 431, 431-434. Professors as well as students have been targets of racial invectives. A black professor at Dartmouth college was called "a cross between a welfare queen and a bathroom attendant." See Lawrence, supra, at 432.

6. See, e.g., Doe v. University of Mich., 721 F. Supp. 852 (E.D. Mich. 1989) (finding unconstitutional university's restriction on racist speech); Collin v. Smith, 447 F. Supp. 676 (1978); Village of Skokie v. National Socialist Party, 373 N.E.2d 21 (Ill. 1978) (both cases striking down city ordinances limiting the dissemination of racist materials and display of racist symbols, such as the swastika); Irving v. J. L. Marsh, Inc., 46 Ill. App. 3d 162, 360 N.E.2d 983 (1977) (holding that plaintiff failed to state a claim of intentional infliction of emotional distress where salesperson wrote on sales slip: "Arrogant Nigger refuses exchange"); Bradshaw v. Swagerty, 1 Kan. 2d 213, 563 P.2d 511 (1977) (holding that epithets like "nigger" are "mere insults of the kind which must be tolerated in our roughened society"). See also Court Voids Wisconsin U.'s Ban on Hate Speech, N.Y. Times, Oct. 13, 1991, at A25 (reporting that a federal district court voided the university's rule barring speech intended to create a hostile learning environment).

It is ironic that courts unwilling to bar speech that harasses people of color have not felt the same compunctions in barring speech that more privileged groups find bothersome. In one recent case, the Court of Appeals for the Second Circuit upheld a transit authority regulation banning panhandling in the New York City subways. Young v. New York City Transit Auth., 903 F.2d 146 (2d Cir.), cert. denied, 498 U.S. 984 (1990). The court's ruling rested upon its doubt that panhandling constitutes protected speech and its conclusion that the regulation, in any event, still allowed alternative methods of communicating this social critique. The state's interest in protecting subway riders from conduct which the court analogized to extortion justifies this narrow limitation on speech. The majority's reasoning represents a 180-degree shift from the hate-speech cases. In rejecting the idea that beggars may intend to convey a message regarding poverty, the court wrote: "A majority of the subway's over three million daily passengers perceive begging and panhandling to be 'intimidating', 'threatening', and 'harassing'. . . . [I]t is fair to say that whether intended as so, or not, begging in the subway often amounts to nothing less than assault. . . ." Id. at 158. The dissent was harshly critical. One judge wrote: "In the seclusion of a judge's chambers, it is tempting to assume that beggars could obtain jobs and spend their free time distributing leaflets or buttonholding passersby in the subway to further the cause of the homeless and poor. . . . [But to] suggest that these individuals, who are obviously struggling to survive, are free to engage in First Amendment activity in their spare time ignores the harsh reality of the life of the urban poor." Id. at 166. See also Clark v. Community for Creative Non-Violence, 468 U.S. 288 (1984).

which limit students' rights to verbally harass blacks and members of other target groups.[7] The University of Michigan, for instance, adopted a Policy on Discrimination and Discriminatory Harassment of Students in the University Environment in response to a number of racist incidents.[8] The policy prohibited individuals from "stigmatizing or victimizing" individuals or groups on the basis of race, ethnicity, religion, sex, sexual orientation, creed, national origin, ancestry, age, marital status, handicap, or Vietnam-era veteran status.[9] One student, whose name was withheld, successfully challenged the constitutionality of the regulation.[10] The student, enrolled in a graduate psychology program, apparently feared that "certain controversial theories positing biologically-based differences between sexes and races might be perceived as 'sexist' and 'racist' by some students" and might therefore be sanctionable.[11] Writing that the dissemination of ideas, however offensive, may not be foreclosed to protect conventions of decency, the court held that the regulation was overbroad. The court refused to hold that hate speech could be punished under one of the many exceptions to free speech guarantees, as fighting words or libel, for instance. The court cited two instances which it believed illustrated the potential of the school's policy to reach protected speech. In the first case, a complaint was filed against a student on the grounds that he openly stated his belief that homosexuality was a disease. In another incident, a professor complained of a student's remarks that she did not treat minority students fairly. That such complaints were even entertained, the court concluded, showed that the policy

7. See Delgado, supra note 5; William Wilson, Colleges' Anti-Harassment Policies Bring Controversy over Free-Speech Issues, Chron. Higher Educ., Oct. 4, 1989, at A1, col. 2.

8. Unknown persons distributed a flier declaring "open season" on blacks, which it referred to as "saucer lips, porch monkeys, and jigaboos." A student disc jockey at an on-campus radio station allowed racist jokes to be broadcast. At a demonstration protesting these incidents, a Ku Klux Klan uniform was displayed from a dormitory window. See Doe v. University of Mich., 721 F. Supp. 852 (E.D. Mich. 1989).

9. The Michigan regulation is unusually broad. A regulation more likely to find constitutional acceptance was recently accepted by Stanford University. Under that regulation, speech constitutes sanctionable harassment when: (1) it is intended to insult or stigmatize an individual . . . on the basis of discrete and insular characteristics including sex, race, color, handicap, religion, sexual orientation, or national and ethnic origin; (2) it is addressed directly to the individual, and not to the general public (i.e., in a book, lecture or newspaper); and (3) it makes use of fighting words or symbols which convey direct or visceral hatred or contempt. Words that Wound: Free Speech for Campus Bigots, The Nation, Feb. 26, 1990, vol. 250, no. 8, at 272. Most university hate-speech regulations, like that of Stanford, track the fighting words exception to the First Amendment.

10. Doe v. University of Mich., 721 F. Supp. 852 (E.D. Mich. 1989). For a thoughtful critique of the *Doe* decision, see Recent Cases: Racist and Sexist Expression on Campus — Court Strikes Down University Limits on Hate Speech: Doe v. University of Michigan, 103 Harv. L. Rev. 1397 (1990). The author notes that the court's decision was predetermined by its categorical rejection of content regulation and its refusal to consider competing interests. However, the Supreme Court has considered the interest in eradicating discrimination and held that this value outweighed rights of expressive association. See Roberts v. United States Jaycees, 468 U.S. 609 (1984) (upholding state antidiscrimination law forbidding the exclusion of women from a civic group); Meritor Sav. Bank v. Vinson, 477 U.S. 57 (1986) (holding, without considering first amendment arguments, that Title VII forbids the creation of a hostile work environment even where speech creates that environment). Charles Lawrence argues that even Brown v. Board of Education can be interpreted to bar racist speech, since the harm of racial segregation is not the physical separation but the message of inferiority that separation conveys. Charles Lawrence, If He Hollers Let Him Go: Regulating Racist Speech on Campus, 1990 Duke L.J. 431, 439-441.

11. Id.

could be used to preclude serious classroom discussion. The costs of hate speech, it was reasoned, are more than outweighed by the costs of using the law to prevent the discussion.[12]

What the *Doe* court forgot to weigh in the balance it struck was the equally valid, though most usually forgotten, right of blacks to equal protection of the law — a right which is sacrificed by oppressive hate speech. Racist speech, more than any other extremist speech, subjects its already-weakened victim to humiliation, isolation, and self-hate.[13] As Professor Mari Matsuda writes:

> [A]t some level, no matter how much both victims and well-meaning dominant group members resist it, racial inferiority is planted in our minds as an idea that may hold some truth. The idea is improbable and abhorrent, but it is there before us, because it is presented repeatedly. "Those people" are lazy, dirty, sexualized, money-grubbing, dishonest, inscrutable, we are told. We reject the idea, but the next time we sit next to one of "those people" the dirt message, the sex message, is triggered. We stifle it, we reject it as wrong, but it is there, interfering with our perception and interaction with the person next to us. For the victim, similarly, the angry rejection of the message of inferiority is coupled with absorption of the message. . . .[14]

Professor Patricia Williams describes racist expression as "a crime, an offense so deeply painful and assaultive as to constitute something I call 'spirit-murder.' Society is only beginning to recognize that racism is as devastating, as costly, and as psychically obliterating as robbery or assault; indeed they are often the same."[15] These acts of hierarchy and racial inferiority harm not only the immediate victims, but all blacks. They also injure all those who care for the victims and who are committed to the establishment of an equal, tolerant society.

The refusal to withdraw protection from racist speech stems from a failure to give weight to the claims of blacks, claims which may be fairly balanced against

---

12. After the University of Michigan's policy against hate speech was struck down, the school enacted a new, narrower policy which bars slurs directed at specific persons, but exempts statements made during classroom discussion. Heller, U. of Michigan Scales Back Its Rules on Discrimination and Harassment, Chron. Higher Educ., Sept. 27, 1989, at A3, col. 1.

13. The damage caused by racist speech is in many ways analogous to the injury sustained by women as a result of pornography. Feminist scholars, most notably Catherine MacKinnon and Andrea Dworkin, have forcefully argued that pornography is "an institution of gender inequality" that not only causes discrete acts of sexual violence against individual women but, more fundamentally, that hurts "individuals, not as individuals in a one-at-a-time sense, but as members of the group 'women,'" Catherine MacKinnon, Feminism Unmodified: Discourses on Life and Law 148, 156 (1987); see also Andrea Dworkin, Men Possessing Women (1981). Women as a group are harmed because "pornography constructs the social reality of gender," and all women are "defined in pornographic terms" as sexually unequal. MacKinnon, at 166. For a general discussion of the First Amendment and pornography, see Paul Brest & Ann Vandenberg, Politics, Feminism, and the Constitution: The Anti-Pornography Movement in Minneapolis, 39 Stan. L. Rev. 607 (1987); Robert Post, Cultural Heterogeneity and Law: Pornography, Blasphemy, and the First Amendment, 76 Cal. L. Rev. 297 (1988); Geoffrey Stone, Anti-Pornography Legislation as Viewpoint-Discrimination, 9 Harv. J.L. & Pub. Pol'y 461 (1986); Cass Sunstein, Pornography and the First Amendment, 1986 Duke L.J. 589.

14. Matsuda, supra note 3. See also Delgado, supra note 4, at 135-136.

15. Patricia Williams, Spirit Murdering the Messenger: The Discourse of Fingerpointing as the Law's Response to Racism, 42 U. Miami. L. Rev. 127, 129 (1987); see also Lee Bollinger, The Tolerant Society 65-66.

what has been held to be a nonabsolute free speech interest. It is a failure to recognize that oppressive speech is as much a badge of servitude as segregation or employment discrimination. It is, in short, a failure to consider "the victim's story."[16] It is no accident, as Professor Mari Matsuda writes that the law fails to provide redress for blacks victimized by hate speech. "The absence of law," she writes, "is itself another story with a message, perhaps unintended, about the relative value of different human lives."[17] Its message is not lost to those forced to suffer the effects of racist speech:

> When hundreds of police officers are called out to protect racist marchers, when the courts refuse redress for racial insult, and when racist attacks are officially dismissed as pranks, the victim becomes a stateless person. Target-group members can either identify with a community that promotes racist speech, or they can admit that the community does not include them.[18]

An absolutist interpretation of the free speech guarantee is rooted, in part, in the idea that uncensored discourse is necessary to protect the open traffic of opinions essential to any reasoned and just democracy.[19] As Justice Holmes wrote:

> But when men have realized that time has upset many fighting faiths, they may come to believe even more than they believe the very foundations of their own conduct that the ultimate good desired is better reached by free trade in ideas — that the best test of truth is the power of the thought to get itself accepted in the competition of the market, and that truth is the only ground upon which their wishes safely can be carried out."[20]

It is only through the mutual toleration and comparison of diverse opinions, the theory goes that the truth will emerge.[21] Because our ideas of a just society are changing and emergent, it is impossible to say for certain that particular ideas are unacceptable. Ideas once rejected as immoral or blasphemous, including ideas underlying major advances in civil rights, eventually become the majority position. As it is impossible with certainty to distinguish good from bad ideas, the only choice is to protect all ideas.

It is also argued that confrontation with falsehood renews our commitment to our beliefs. When we censor speech, we "lose, what is almost as great a benefit [as truth], the clearer perception and livelier impression of truth produced by its collision with error."[22] Without exercise, truth atrophies into dogma. Even false speech is of value because it reveals the underlying current of dissatisfaction

---

16. See Matsuda, supra note 3.

17. Id.

18. Id.

19. See, e.g., Bollinger, supra note 15; Thomas Emerson, Toward a General Theory of the First Amendment, 72 Yale L.J. 877, 878-886 (1963).

20. Abrams v. United States, 250 U.S. 616, 630 (1919) (Holmes, J., dissenting).

21. See Carl Becker, Freedom and Responsibility in the American Way of Life 33 (1945) (cited in Bollinger, supra note 15, at 45 n.3; Thomas Emerson, The System of Freedom of Expression 7 (1970); Alexander Meiklejohn, Free Speech and Its Relation to Self-Government, in Political Freedom: The Constitutional Powers of the People 24-27 (1964).

22. John Stuart Mill, On Liberty 21 (C. V. Shields ed., 1956).

and dissent. It is preferable to have hate groups operating in public rather than in private:

> Where the unwanted weeds of frustration and revolt may grow more rapidly from inattention and where the falsehoods being propagated may less easily be exposed for their error. A policy of near complete openness to speech, in this sense, provides us with a social thermometer for registering the presence of disease within the body politic and the best opportunity of administering a speedy cure.[23]

Mill's advice resounds in the argument of civil libertarians who claim that it is tactically wise to permit hate speech since that speech galvanizes the opposition and sparks protest, which history often has proved to be the only effective vehicle of change. A focus on racist speech diverts attention from the real problem, which is the intolerant attitudes which underlie that speech; it deals only with the symptom, and not the disease itself.

If we are threatened or offended by certain ideas, we can employ less costly and more effective remedies than censorship. Justice Louis Brandeis's advice of over 50 years ago still proves true: "If there be time to expose through discussion the falsehood and fallacies, to avert the evil by the processes of education, the remedy to be applied is more speech, not enforced silence."[24] Protest, debate, confrontation, and shunning are but a few of the sanctions which may be applied to deter racist speech. Attaching the stigma of social disapproval to the speaker who seeks to stigmatize others is as effective as any legal remedy, and is more empowering and poetically just than repression.[25] The marketplace theory, however, rests upon a naive or convenient assumption that in our democratic society all speakers occupy a level playing field in which all speech is presumptively equal. It assumes that free speech exists and that segments of society are not systematically silenced even before the government enters the arena. Yet, like all social goods, speech is not equally and freely accessible to all. The battle which blacks have fought simply to have their voices heard makes this assumption untenable.

In addition, the regulation of racist speech is qualitatively different from other speech restrictions. Racism is not simply an unpopular view which requires special governmental solicitude — it is, sadly, the majority view.[26] Protection of racism and its expression in racial invectives has favored the powerful against the powerless. To provide redress for persons of color and other excluded groups is not to

23. Bollinger, supra note 15, at 55.

24. Whitney v. California, 274 U.S. 357, 377 (1927) (Brandeis, J., concurring); see also Franklin Haiman, Speech and Law in a Free Society 86 (1981).

25. Each court which considered the National Socialist Party's plan to march in Skokie affirmed the group's right to demonstrate. The march, however, never happened; the Party abandoned the march because of threatened counter-demonstrations. See Donald Downs, *Skokie* Revisited: Hate Group Speech and the First Amendment, 60 Notre Dame L. Rev. 629, 630 (1985).

26. It is ironic, as Catherine MacKinnon notes, that unbending free speech principles are justified as necessary to protect divergent or extremist views. But First Amendment absolutists fail "to notice that pornography (like the racism, in which I include anti-Semitism, of the Nazis and the Klan) is not at all divergent or unorthodox. It is the ruling ideology. Feminism, the dissenting view, is suppressed by pornography." Catherine MacKinnon, Not a Moral Issue, 2 Yale L. & Pub. Pol'y Rev. 321, 337 (1984).

open the floodgates of censorship but to identify a specific group uniquely vulnerable to majoritarian oppression in need of government intervention simply to
balance the scales.

The marketplace analogy also presumes that the discourse of all speech is in
fact a dialogue. But racist invectives are one-sided; they neither invite nor permit
response. How can the student who receives a card reading "the Ku Klux Klan is
watching you" be expected to speak back?[27] Hate speech silences its victim and
mars his or her response as presumptively unequal. Professor Charles Lawrence
writes:

> Assaultive racist speech functions as a preemptive strike. The invective is experienced
> as a blow, not as a proffered idea, and once the blow is struck, it is unlikely that a
> dialogue will follow. Racial insults are particularly undeserving of First Amendment
> protection because the perpetrator's intention is not to discover truth or initiate
> dialogue but to injure the victim. In most situations, members of minority groups
> realize that they are likely to lose if they respond to epithets by fighting and are forced
> to remain silent and submissive.[28]

Furthermore, the marketplace theory avoids the fundamental question of
whether there is certain speech whose role in social decision-making is either
detrimental or so marginal that it should never be countenanced. There are
some ideas which simply are so repugnant to any concept of civilized society
that they are not entitled to entry into the marketplace. To permit an idea to be
advocated is to concede its legitimacy and to accept the possibility that it may
become the governing system. There are some policies, though, whose implementation would be so unacceptable in a democratic society that their advocacy should
not be permitted.[29] The Fourteenth Amendment reflects our choice not to permit
absolute freedom at the expense of equality and equal personhood.

While a great many states have responded to the hate speech issue with hate-
crime laws prohibiting and punishing such speech, some commentators fear that
the Court's confused decision in R.A.V. v. St. Paul sounded the death knell
for hate-crime laws directly targeting speech and cast the constitutionality of all
hate-crime laws into doubt.[30] The continued validity of penalty-enhancing laws in
hate-crime cases was confirmed in 1993, the year after *R.A.V.*, in Wisconsin v.
Mitchell.[31] In *Mitchell*, the Court unanimously upheld the enhanced sentence for
aggravated assault given to a young black man who, inflamed by the racism
portrayed in the film *Mississippi Burning,* asked a friend if they were ready to

27. Lawrence, supra note 10, at 432.
28. Charles Lawrence, The Debate Over Placing Limits on Racist Speech Must Not Ignore the
Damage It Does to Victims, Chron. Higher Educ., Oct. 25, 1987, at B1; see also Delgado, supra note
4, at 177. Justice Jackson has written, "These epithets come down to our generation weighted with
hatreds accumulated through centuries of bloodshed. . . . They are always, and in every context,
insults which do not spring from reason and can be answered by none." Kunz v. New York, 340 U.S.
290, 299 (1951) (Jackson, J., dissenting).
29. Alexander Bickel, The Morality of Consent 70-77 (1975).
30. See Terry Maroney, The Struggle Against Hate Crime: Movement at a Crossroads, 73
N.Y.U. L. Rev. 564, 592 (1998).
31. 508 U.S. 476 (1993).

"move on some white people" and, seeing the victim in the street, said "There goes a white boy: go get him." The Court said that the special harms posed by hate crimes — creating fear in the community — justified greater punishment. Speech, the Court held, is often evidence of motive, and factors such as motive can be taken into consideration in sentencing decisions.[32] The Court sought to distinguish *Mitchell* from *R.A.V.* by noting that the St. Paul ordinance was aimed at speech, while the Wisconsin statute was aimed at pure conduct and would have no "chilling effect" on speech.

Black people unable to decipher the Court's distinguishing complexities but well aware of racial history may wonder how the act of whites burning a cross in the yard of a black family newly arrived in a neighborhood is deemed protected speech, while a black person who attacks a white person is convicted of assault and has his sentence enhanced by a hate-crime statute. A part of the problem is that the law in general, and existing hate-crime statutes in particular, finds it difficult to target accurately the unique harm these actions cause to subordinated groups. Judith Butler addresses some of these problems.[33] Butler points out that proponents of hate-speech regulation, including Mari Matsuda, Charles Lawrence, and Richard Delgado, liken hate speech to physical injury. In drawing the analogy, however, they implicitly concede that an injury related to hate speech is distinct from a physical injury. That is to say, Matsuda, Lawrence, and Delgado never assert that hate speech is physical violence. Butler, therefore, theorizes on the nature of the injurious quality of hate speech. She contends that hate speech derives its violent efficacy by echoing "prior actions." Hate speech "accumulates the force of authority through the repetition of a prior and authoritative set of practices. It is not simply that the speech act takes place within a practice, but that the act is itself a ritualized practice."[34] In the case of cross-burning, for instance, the violent efficacy of the expressive gesture lies in the fact that it promises further acts of violence against the black family towards whom it is directed. The efficacy of a violent gesture, then, is not a function of the cross-burner's intent per se. (Butler, however, does not argue that the cross-burner should bear no responsibility for his speech-act.) Rather, the expressive act derives its efficacy from its genealogical relationship to a particularized set of historical practices. Given this understanding, trying to locate "final accountability" in a single person (or group of persons) is rather problematic. Hate-speech regulation, however, proposes doing exactly that.[35] According to Butler, hate-speech regulation consolidates the subjective position of the articulator of the hateful utterance. Hate-speech regulation necessarily assumes that the injury inflicted by hate speech is complete; that is it assumes that the hateful speech can in no way be turned against its speaker. This, according to Butler, concedes an unjustified authority (power) to the person delivering the hate speech. In addition, it constructs the courts as neutral sites of adjudication. This is ironic because recirculating the hateful speech is a necessary component of adjudication. Hate-speech regulations empower the courts to participate in the

---

32. 508 U.S. at 487-490.
33. Judith Butler, Excitable Speech: A Politics of the Performative (1997).
34. Id. at 51.
35. Id. at 51-52.

furtherance of discussion as to what constitutes consequential speech — as if the courts' speech itself were not violently consequential.[36] The Supreme Court's decisions in *R.A.V.* and Mitchell v. Wisconsin reveal how shallow these notions of legal neutrality are.

Butler contends that Mari Matsuda, by advocating hate-speech regulation in the introduction to *Words that Wound: Critical Race Theory, Assaultive Speech, and the First Amendment,* argues that despite its racist formation, the law can be constructively used against hate speech. According to Butler, this notion, in effect, reinscribes the fantasy of law's neutrality or instrumentality. Butler takes issue with this privileging of judicial space (given its history) as the staging site for the antiracist struggle (or the ant-sexist struggle, in the case of pornography).[37] The very idea of legal redress, in Butler's view, stabilizes hate speech. She therefore advocates for critical, nonjudicial modes of intervention. Given that hate speech derives its violent efficacy from the promise of doing future harm, the speech's efficacy is contingent. Butler contends that, therefore, the speech can be made to "fail." The ostensibly hateful speech can be interdicted and redirected before the violence it promises can manifest. Indeed, a lot of antiracist/sexist/homophobic contemporary art seeks to do exactly that.

Amy Adler explores the possible consequences for art if hate-speech regulations were enacted.[38] She refers to critical race theorists like Delgado and Matsuda, who advocate against hate speech, as "left censors" who "fail to recognize that central to the contemporary activism emanating from their own communities are techniques that make leftist speech almost indistinguishable from the hate speech and pornography it questions."[39] She fears that censorship will threaten ways in which artists and writers have used language to deconstruct harmful speech by working from "within the system that it criticizes, revealing internal contradictions by using the conceptual apparatus of the very thing it wishes to subvert."[40] Adler presents numerous examples of activist speech to show how "[h]ate speech, it seems, can play dual roles."[41] She describes how the gay movement has used the pink triangle as a symbol of empowerment, a symbol appropriated by the inverted pink triangle, which, like the yellow star for Jews, was used by the Nazis to mark homosexuals. She describes the artwork of Andres Serrano, a black Hispanic artist who takes glorified photographs of Ku Klux Klan leaders, and the controversial appropriation of the word "nigger" by rap artists. She argues from these examples that subversion and reversal are the central mode of the outsider's discourse — a mode that would be lost if the speech codes desired by hate-speech activists were implemented.

She accuses "left censors" of an inability to recognize the complexity of speech. Their theories of censorship do not recognize that "words and images

---

36. Id. at 97-98.
37. Butler, supra note 33, at 47, 98-99.
38. Amy Adler, What's Left? Hate Speech, Pornography, and the Problem for Artistic Expression, 84 Cal. L. Rev. 1499 (1996).
39. Id. at 1541.
40. Id. at 1519, quoting J.M. Balkin, Deconstructive Practice and Legal Theory, 96 Yale L.J. 743 (1987).
41. Id. at. 1520.

are arbitrary and that the conditions of interpretation, themselves unpredictable, are all that gives words and images meaning."[42] She problematizes the approach of theorists who recommend considering factors such as the intent of the speaker or the speech's impact on its victims to identify hate speech. The difference between subversive and oppressive speech, she contends, is often elusive. She concludes by supporting an approach that offers "full protection to activism,"[43] rather than a code of regulation, warning leftists that they must make a choice and cannot have it both ways.

§10.19   Racism Hypo: Speech Codes on University Campuses

Kimberly Gibson, a first-year law student, was searching her school's website for a Criminal Law outline. She was shocked and angered by what she discovered. An Asian American classmate in her section posted a Criminal Law outline using the word "nigger" whenever he described African Americans. Gibson, an African American student, immediately brought a printed copy to the attention of the school's disciplinary committee. The Dean of Students who heads the committee assured her that there would be a prompt response.

A few days after the news about the outline hit general campus gossip, Gibson received a threatening e-mail from another student saying, "This is a private law school where anyone wishing to use the word 'nigger' should not be prevented from doing so. If you, as a race, want to prove that you should not be called that word, work hard and you will be recognized. Complaining will only lead to trouble." Merely one day later, flyers containing racist statements with numerous swastikas were placed in all student mailboxes.

The Black Law Student Association held an emergency four-hour meeting to draft a response to the school administration that had remained silent until that point. In a letter to the Dean, BLSA demanded immediate action, which included (1) punishing the students responsible for the racist outline, e-mail, and flyers, and (2) creating a diversity committee to draft a Racial Harassment Policy modeled after the Sexual Harassment Policy that raised a controversy only six years earlier. The seven African American law professors on the faculty sent a letter to the Dean, which was published as a full-length ad in the student newspaper, discussing their reasons for endorsing BLSA's demands.

Unsurprisingly, the administration was slow to respond. In its first effort, three months after the student reported the e-mail, the Dean sent a school wide e-mail that emphasized a need for greater sensitivity and understanding in an academic environment. She noted that a Diversity Committee was being recruited to recommend how to foster a better community.

Needless to say, BLSA was disappointed by the response. So they organized a series of actions to express their concerns. One of the most successful was an all-school walkout planned intentionally at noon on admitted students' day. Over 300 students, faculty, and staff lined the main walkway

42. Id. at 1542.
43. Id. at 1548.

running through the law school's campus to protest in silence. "Incoming students always ask about the racial climate of the school," stated the President of BLSA, Laura Smith, "They should know that this is a particularly bad time for us."

In the last few weeks of the semester, *The Daily Legal Times* reported that the school's disciplinary committee held a hearing for two students who were identified as the perpetrators of the outline and the racist e-mail. The committee's response was unanimous: The students were asked to leave for one semester and were given a formal reprimand that was added to their official files and would show up on their transcripts. The students were incredulous that they did not have the right to freely express their opinions and could be censored so easily. Represented by a professor who had defended the most notorious criminal defendants, the students sued the school, arguing that the school's action violated their right to free speech.

At the end of the semester, a Diversity Committee, which consisted of 12 faculty members and four students, was formed. Their first decision was to hire a professor to host a series of sensitivity trainings to discuss how professors should talk about difficult topics in an academic setting. The following fall, the school hosted "building a safe community" workshops for all incoming students.

In its most controversial move, the Diversity Committee drafted a policy that became quickly dubbed a speech code. The policy received enormous criticism at a number of public debates about the issue, which were hosted by Students for Free Speech (SFFS), the local ACLU student group. SFFS doubled its membership as a result of the controversy. At every chance they could seize, SFFS organized to lobby faculty and protest the policy as an infringement on academic freedom and expression. Nevertheless, the policy with only minor amendments was distributed for a faculty vote and passed unanimously.

Represented by the state ACLU, SFFS, on behalf of the law school student body, sued the school arguing that the policy was unconstitutional. The university, represented by its general counsel, responded that as a private institution they could establish such restrictions to foster an unoppressive and open learning environment.

Chapter 11

Racism and Other "Nonwhites"

§11.1 INTRODUCTION

This book is concerned primarily with American racism initiated by whites against blacks, and it reviews the extent to which racial discrimination is legitimated by the law, as well as many of the efforts to utilize the law to remedy racial bias. African Americans, of course, are not the only victims of racial discrimination. Other minorities who are identifiably nonwhite — Indians, Chinese, Japanese, Mexicans, and other nonwhite Spanish- and French-speaking people — have suffered exploitation and discrimination in ways quite similar to those experienced by blacks and often for similar purposes. America has exported racism to the foreign territories that have come under its control, including the Philippines, Hawaii, Puerto Rico, Cuba, and Hispaniola (Haiti and the Dominican Republic).[1] Color as the basis of racist policy is not limited to the United States. White supremacy and greed drove the European invasion and three-centuries'-long exploitation of Africa, the ill effects of which remain all too visible. But racism is not a uniquely American outlook. By the mid-1990s South Africa ended apartheid aimed at total physical and political separation of racial groups. Great Britain's history of imperialism included involvement in the slave trade and the creation of segregated colonial societies. British patterns of racism against nonwhites have been visible in restrictive immigration laws and housing and employment discrimination not unlike those found in urban America.

Merely as exemplar, §11.3 includes a brief summary of the fate of peoples of color in Australia and New Zealand. Adequate treatment of racial bias suffered by nonwhites in the United States and around the world is deserving of book-length treatment, far beyond the limits of this text. The summaries and excerpts that follow review the history of discrimination against other nonwhites. They are brief and are not intended to convey fully either the extent or the complexity of racial discrimination experienced by peoples of color the world over or the current

---

§11.1 1. See Rubin F. Weston, Racism in U.S. Imperialism (1972); II To Serve the Devil: Colonials and Sojourners (Paul Jacobs, Saul Landau & Eve Pell eds., 1971). For a discussion of the U.S. policy toward Haitian refugees that returned thousands to certain persecution, see Jean-Pierre Benoit & Lewis A. Kornhauser, Unsafe Havens, 59 U. Chi. L. Rev. 1421 (1992).

controversies in which they are involved. The intention is to permit a clearer understanding of the factors of racism that serve to rationalize exploitation, discrimination, forced removal, and genocide both in America and elsewhere. Such a comparative reading may serve to illuminate both those aspects of the construction of race and racism that uniquely reflect the American context and those that seem to transcend national boundaries.

§11.2 AMERICA AND THE INDIANS

Building on models already tested by the Spanish, the French, and the British, America advanced its takeover of the lands held by Indians[1] through resort to treaties — easily made and as easily abandoned — open warfare waged with, first, superior weapons and, later, with overwhelming numbers, and, ultimately, through genocide.[2] Professor Ward Churchill in opening his monumental history of the eradication of the Indians wrote:

> During the four centuries spanning the time between 1492, when Christopher Columbus first set foot on the "New World" of a Caribbean beach, and 1892, when the U.S. Census Bureau concluded that there were fewer than a quarter-million indigenous people surviving within the country's claimed boundaries, a hemispheric population estimated to have been as great as 125 million was reduced by something over 90 percent. The people had died in their millions of being hacked apart with axes and swords, burned alive and trampled under horses, hunted as game and fed to dogs, shot, beaten, stabbed, scalped for bounty, hanged on meathooks and thrown over the sides of ships at sea, worked to death as slave laborers, intentionally starved and frozen to death during a multitude of forced marches and internments, and, in an unknown number of instances, deliberately infected with epidemic diseases.[3]

Throughout American history, the law was manipulated to justify whatever was necessary to get rid of the Indians, who refused to depart from what whites felt were lands that were part of the "manifest destiny" of this nation. Indeed, American Indian law developed with and was closely tied to the means by which whites displaced Indians. The Court adopted a number of policies that to

§11.2   1. There is much discussion about what term should be used to refer to Indians. Many people, including people who are themselves Indians, use the term "Indian" or "American Indian" and see such use as preferable to what they deem an oppressive colonial nomenclature. Others prefer "Native American" or "First American," which for them reflect the fact that Native peoples are indigenous to America and move away from the often stereotypically used term "Indian." When other scholars or sources are cited, the terms they use are not altered, which accounts for the variation throughout the chapter.

2. The traditional myths about the winning of the West have been deromanticized. The virtual eradication of the Western Indian is painfully detailed, for example, in Dee Brown, Bury My Heart at Wounded Knee (1970). Indian politics is surveyed with insight, wit, and militancy in Vine Deloria, Custer Died for Your Sins (1969).

3. Ward Churchill, A Little Matter of Genocide 1 (1997).

the observant were hardly more than rationalizations for that displacement. As one article put it, a cynic would not be far off the mark who defined Indian law as

> based on the separative premise when it was possible to move the Indians to other territory and on the assimilative premise when land scarcity required that the Indian and his lands be brought into the totally alien private-property system of the white man, where the Indian could easily be dispossessed by such devices as inflated tax appraisals and long-term leases returning minimal rents.[4]

In reviewing the major cases summarized below, consider Professor Robert Williams position that these decisions were influenced heavily by the widespread and comforting belief that the Indians were uncivilized and lawless savages who did not know the value of the lands they surrendered for trinkets or signed away in treaties, duly made in one period and then violated, reinterpreted, or simply ignored in another.[5]

The examples of these self-serving stereotypes are set out without shame in decisions from those of the first Chief Justice, John Marshall, down to the present day. In his 1823 opinion in the critically important case, Johnson v. McIntosh, Marshall referred to Indians as "heathens" and as "fierce savages, whose occupation was war, and whose subsistence was drawn chiefly from the forest."[6] Throughout the nineteenth century, Supreme Court justices spoke about Indians in similar tones of disrespect that were little changed by the middle of the twentieth century. Indeed, in 1955, the year after Brown v. Board of Education, the Court handed down Tee-Hit-Ton v. United States, what Professor Williams describes as "one of the most racist Indian rights decisions of all time."[7] Later Justice William Rehnquist in 1978, writing in Oliphant v. Suquamish Indian Tribe, quoted more than a dozen nineteenth-century Court precedents, executive policy statements, and congressional enactments, reflecting the general view that Indians were "lawless, uncivilized, unsophisticated, hostile, or warlike savages. . . . an inferior race and as therefore entitled to lesser rights than whites."[8]

Professor Williams asserts that the stereotypes of Indian savagery must be challenged at every level including in litigation presenting issues of Indian land, civil, and cultural rights. He recognizes the difficulty of the task and cites with approval a statement (admission really) of Justice Sandra Day O'Connor who wrote that "real change comes principally from attitudinal shifts in the population at large. Rare indeed is the legal victory — in court or legislature — that is not a

4. D.H. McMeekin, Red, White, and Grey: Equal Protection and the American Indian, 21 Stan. L. Rev. 1236, 1238-1240 (1969). Chief Joseph, one of the last great Indian leaders observed, "The white men made us many promises. They only kept one. They said they would take our land and they took it."

5. Robert A. Williams, Jr., Like a Loaded Weapon: The Rehnquist Court, Indian Rights, and the Legal History of Racism in America (2005).

6. Id. at xviii. Later in the landmark case of Cherokee Nation v. Georgia, Marshall described Indians as a race of people who were "once numerous, powerful, and truly independent," but who had gradually sunk "beneath our superior policy, our arts and our arms."

7. Id. at xxi. Writing for a six-person majority, Justice Reed declared that every schoolboy knows "that the savage tribes of this continent were deprived of their ancestral ranges by force and that, even when the Indians ceded millions of acres by treaty in return for blankets, food and trinkets, it was not a sale but the conqueror's will that deprived them of their land."

8. Id. at xxiii.

careful byproduct of an emerging social consensus."[9] In reviewing summaries of the major cases involving Indian rights set out below, consider both the likely influences of stereotypes about Indians as an inferior people properly deemed subordinate to whites, and the significance of Justice O'Connor's observation about the social prerequisite for political and legal change.

§11.2.1   Federal Power over Indians: Its Sources, Scope, and Limitations[10]

The mystique of plenary power has pervaded federal regulation of Indian affairs from the beginning. While the Articles of Confederation contained a general power over Indian affairs, the Constitution enumerates only one power specific to these affairs: the power "[t]o regulate Commerce . . . with the Indian tribes."[11] The Plenary Power Doctrine, a fixture of American Indian law since John Marshall provided its first justification in 1832,[12] can be traced not only to this commerce power but also to the treaty, war, and other foreign affairs powers,[13] as well as to the property power.[14] Each has been characterized, historically, as vesting Congress (or the President) with almost unlimited power in contexts not involving Indians.

A.   The Treaty Era: Foreign Affairs and Indian Commerce (1776-1871)

The absence from the Constitution of a general power over Indian affairs is not surprising to students of history, for at the time the Constitution was drafted, the Framers regarded Indian tribes as sovereign nations, albeit nations that would soon either move west, assimilate, or become extinct. Thus, the same powers that sufficed to give the federal government a free rein in the international arena were viewed as sufficient to enable the new government to deal adequately with the Indian tribes. In formulating federal policy toward Indian tribes in the early years of the Constitution, President Washington and Secretary of War Knox followed the policy promulgated by the British Crown — though not always followed by individual colonies — of dealing with Indian tribes as sovereign nations. Their principal reason was practical: Earlier attempts by individual colonies and some states under the Articles of Confederation to assert power over Indian tribes, especially the power to seize tribal lands, had caused conflicts. According to one historian, "[T]he country, precariously perched among the sovereign nations

---

9. Sandra Day O'Connor, The Majesty of the Law: Reflections of a Supreme Court Justice, 166 (2003).

10. Nell Jessup Newton, Federal Power over Indians: Its Sources, Scope, and Limitations, 132 U. Pa. L. Rev. 195 (1984). In a lengthy article, a major portion of which is excerpted here with her permission, University of Denver Law School Dean Newton traces the judicial "flexibility" that categorized American Indian law. Footnotes, where included, are renumbered to conform with those in this chapter.

11. U.S. Const. art. I, §8, cl. 3.

12. Worcester v. Georgia, 31 U.S. (6 Pet.) 515, 557-562 (1832).

13. U.S. Const. art. II, §2 (treaty); id. art. I, §8, cls. 11-16 (congressional war powers).

14. U.S. Const. art. IV, §3 (property clause).

of the world, could not stand the expense and strain of a long drawn-out Indian war."[15] Washington and Knox advocated a policy of respect for existing treaty promises. In addition, they recommended that a series of new treaties be negotiated for the purpose of acquiring Indian land by consent in an orderly fashion; the treaties would contain promises to protect Indian tribes and tribal land from white incursions in exchange for the land cessions. This policy of dealing with Indian tribes as nations capable of executing treaties continued until 1871.

The treaty powers of Congress and the executive branch were sufficient to carry out this early policy. In addition to ratifying treaties, Congress also affected Indian affairs by means of the Trade and Intercourse Acts, first enacted in 1790. These laws originally were designed to effectuate treaty promises of protection by imposing sanctions on individuals and states that had infringed on Indian land or dealt with Indians in violation of treaties.

The judiciary further solidified the analogy of Indian affairs to foreign affairs. In Worcester v. Georgia,[16] Chief Justice John Marshall upheld the supremacy of federal over state power regarding Indian tribes, an issue that threatened to split the nation apart at that time, but which has never seriously been open to question since then. Chief Justice Marshall premised much of his eloquent defense of federal power on his view of the Indian tribes as sovereign nations whose rights of self-government predated the Constitution and whose dealings with the United States were governed by principles of international as well as constitutional law.

Although the Court in *Worcester* recognized that Indian tribes possess inherent sovereignty rights, the decision was really a defense of federal over state power, not a defense of Indian tribal sovereignty — the tribe was not even a party to the suit. Indeed, by relying on federal foreign relations power to free tribal sovereignty from state control, *Worcester* subjugated that sovereignty to the will of Congress. This set the stage for a tradition of deference to Congress in Indian affairs analogous to that deference accorded Congress (or the President) in foreign affairs.

One legacy of *Worcester*, then, is that courts applied to Indian affairs doctrines peculiar to the federal foreign affairs power without necessarily distinguishing the special status of Indian tribes as domestic rather than foreign nations. Under the last-in-time rule, for example, Congress can abrogate a treaty with a foreign country, merely by passing a later statute conflicting with it. Early on, this doctrine was applied to treaties with Indians; moreover, courts continue to apply the doctrine today when Indian tribes are no longer regarded as foreign nations.[17] Another

15. Francis Prucha, American Indian Policy in the Formative Years 44 (1962). See also A. Wallace, The Death and Rebirth of the Seneca 159-162 (1969) (Indian battles resulting in high U.S. casualties).

16. 31 U.S. (6 Pet.) 515 (1832). Georgia had attempted to assert jurisdiction and ownership rights over the gold-rich lands of the Cherokee Nation. Invalidating the Georgia law, the Court held that the Constitution assigned to the federal government exclusive power to deal with Indians. Consequently, the Court concluded that the exclusivity of federal power alone would bar any state law and that federal laws as well as treaties preempted state laws. Id. at 561-562.

17. See, e.g., Yankton Sioux Tribe v. United States, 623 F.2d 159, 181 (Ct. Cl. 1980) (statute permitting Secretary of Interior to pay out shares of tribal funds to individuals abrogated a treaty promise that payment for land sale be held in a tribal trust fund); see also Rosebud Sioux Tribe v. Kneip, 430 U.S. 584 (1977) (statutes opening parts of a treaty reservation to settlers disestablished reservation). For a thorough discussion of this controversy, see Comment, Statutory Construction — Wildlife

example of the uncritical borrowing of foreign affairs doctrines was the frequent invocation of the political question doctrine, relatively common in foreign affairs, as a justification for failing to question congressional power in Indian cases,[18] even those raising individual rights concerns.[19] For instance, although the integrity of tribal sovereignty was protected from state incursions in *Worcester*, the federal government later forced the Cherokee Nation to march to Indian territory by negotiating a treaty with a minority faction of the tribe.[20] Despite the immediate protest of nearly all of the Cherokee people to the President and to Congress, removal was ordered.[21] Judicial recourse would have been unavailing: The political question doctrine would have barred the courts from questioning the procedures leading up to the treaty.

Although courts analogized Indian nations to foreign nations in finding congressional power to deal with them, it is important to note that the Court did not view Indian tribes as possessing all the attributes of sovereignty of a foreign nation. In the first Cherokee case, Cherokee Nation v. Georgia,[22] the Court held that Indian nations were not foreign states for the purpose of invoking the Supreme Court's original jurisdiction. The Court reasoned that the Cherokee Nation was "a distinct political society, separated from others, capable of managing its own affairs, and governing itself. . . ." Nevertheless, the nation was neither a state of the union nor a foreign state, but a "domestic dependent nation" incapable of conducting foreign relations with countries other than the United States. Instead, "[t]heir relation to the United States resembles that of a ward to his guardian."

In sum, from the beginning, Indian tribes were in a truly anomalous position. Congress and the President viewed them as separate nations in some respects. Furthermore, individual Indians were regarded as domestic subjects, more akin to aliens than citizens, until Congress granted them universal citizenship in 1924.[23]

Protection Versus Indian Treaty Hunting Rights, 57 Wash. L. Rev. 225 (1981); see also Charles F. Wilkinson & John M. Volkman, Judicial Review of Indian Treaty Abrogation: "As Long as Water Flows, or Grass Grows Upon the Earth" — How Long a Time Is That?, 63 Cal. L. Rev. 601 (1975).

18. See, e.g., United States ex rel. Hualpai Indians v. Santa Fe Pac. R.R., 314 U.S. 339, 347 (1941) ("The manner, method and time of such extinguishment [of aboriginal Indian title] raise political, not justiciable, issues."); Beecher v. Wetherby, 95 U.S. 517, 525 (1877) ("[A]ction towards Indians with respect to their lands is a question of governmental policy. . . .").

19. See e.g., Tee-Hit-Ton Indians v. United States, 348 U.S. 272, 281 (1955) (Indians not entitled to compensation under Fifth Amendment for taking of timber by United States from aboriginal lands. The "power of Congress is supreme.").

20. Treaty with the Cherokees at New Echota, Dec. 29, 1835, 7 Stat. 478. The pressures from state and public officials created two factions among the Cherokee Nation: the Treaty Party, comprising the elite mixed bloods, and the Ross faction, supporters of Chief John Ross. Ross, who had the support of most of the Cherokee people, was incarcerated while the Treaty Party representatives negotiated the treaty. The treaty, ratified at New Echota, the capital of the Cherokee Nation, by only 20 persons, ceded all the tribal land in Georgia in exchange for 7 million acres of land in Indian Territory. French, The Death of a Nation, 4 Am. Ind. J. 2, 3-4 (1978).

21. A petition protesting the treaty, signed by nearly sixteen thousand of the seventeen thousand members of the Cherokee people, was presented to Congress. Grant Foreman, Indian Removal 269 (new ed. 1953). More than four thousand of sixteen thousand Cherokees died in the camps where they awaited removal and along the Trail of Tears, as the route to Indian Territory came to be called. Id. at 294-312; see also Grant Foreman, The Last Trek of the Indians (1946).

22. 30 U.S. (5 Pet.) 1, 16-17 (1831).

23. Citizenship Act of 1924, ch. 233, 43 Stat. 253 (current version at 8 U.S.C. §1401(b) (1982)).

The judicial deference traditionally accorded the political branches of the federal government in conducting foreign affairs and dealing with aliens attached to federal regulation of Indian affairs. As domestic dependent nations, Indian tribes possessed sovereignty, but could not invoke the jurisdiction of the federal courts. Indeed, the broad language in *Cherokee Nation* about the peculiar status of Indian tribes, created doubt that tribes had standing to sue in federal court, a matter that was subject to some question for many years. In short, the integrity of tribal sovereignty rested precariously on the whim of Congress, owing, in the early years, to the Court's extraordinary deference to the political branches' exercise of the foreign affairs power in their dealings with the Indians.

B. The End of the Treaty Era (1865-1871)

In the years preceding the Civil War, especially during the 1830s to the 1850s, Congress had sought to remove the eastern Indian tribes west of the Mississippi, but as settlers began opening up the west, continued removal began to be viewed as impossible. After the Civil War and the pacification of the last tribes of the plains, a movement began to assimilate Indians into American culture, by force if necessary. A policy of treating Indian tribes as separate nations with power over their own people on their own land was seen as antithetical to this new policy.

Divergent groups coalesced for very different reasons behind this assimilationist policy. Some regarded Indians as barbarians who had to be civilized for their own security and the security of those living near them. It was believed that if Indians were citizens, individually owning small tracts of land, they would come under the civilizing effects of the life of a farmer or a rancher and would abandon their nomadic and barbaric habits. Large portions of surplus reservation land could then be sold to settlers, who were clamoring for it. In addition, with the end of the reservations, promises that reservation land would never be contained within a state's limits would become meaningless; thus, for the remaining territories, individual ownership would remove this barrier to statehood. Other advocates of assimilation, members of the "Friends of the Indians" movement, were moved by more benign motives. They argued that only by becoming citizens, voters, and individual landowners would Indians be able to protect themselves and their land from the settlers and from the federal government's dishonorable practice of "breaking . . . several hundred treaties, concluded at different times during the last 100 years. . . ."[24] The House of Representatives ushered in the new "Era of Allotment and Assimilation," when it decreed in a rider to the Appropriations Act of 1871 that henceforth "[n]o Indian nation or tribe within the territory of the United States shall be acknowledged or recognized as an independent nation, tribe, or power with whom the United States may contract by treaty."[25] The legislators were motivated by the belief that Indian affairs should no longer be a matter of foreign affairs now that the last remaining Indian tribes of a warlike

---

24. Helen Hunt Jackson, A Century of Dishonor 26 (1881 & photo. reprint 1965). Jackson's indictment of federal policy sparked the reform movement.
25. Act of Mar. 3, 1871, ch. 120, §1, 16 Stat. 566 (codified at 25 U.S.C. §71 (1976)).

nature had been subdued. Thus, the treaty-making era came to an end. Indian law became more a matter of domestic law, with Indians regarded as subjects to be governed, rather than as foreign nationals.

With the end of the treaty-making era came statutes designed to implement the new assimilationist policies. Many of these statutes could not be viewed as either effectuating treaty promises or regulating trade. Thus the Court was forced to develop new rationales to justify federal actions concerning Indians. From two concepts — property interest and guardianship — the Court in the late nineteenth century gradually developed a guardianship power over Indian tribes, a power that it frankly acknowledged to be extraconstitutional.

C. Plenary Power: Its Genesis and Exercise (1870s-1930s)

The notion that the federal government had a property interest of some sort in Indian land provided the central element in the analysis resulting in guardianship power. Thus, to understand the guardianship power asserted by the federal government, it is necessary to briefly trace the history of the Doctrine of Discovery, the source of the property interest. Johnson v. McIntosh,[26] decided in 1823, was the first major case directly concerning the validity of Indian property interests to reach the Court. Drawing inspiration from international law regarding the sovereign rights of the nations that had colonized the New World, Chief Justice Marshall held that by virtue of discovering a nation inhabited by non-Europeans, the discovering nations (and America as their successor) obtained a property interest, described as "ultimate title," to that discovered land. According to Chief Justice Marshall: "[D]iscovery gave title to the government by whose subjects, or by whose authority, it was made, against all other European governments, which title might be consummated by possession." This title gave the government the preemptive right to purchase Indian land or to confiscate it after a war. The Indians, on the other hand, remained "the rightful occupants of the soil, with a legal as well as just claim to retain possession of it." Until the sovereign exercised its preemptive right to extinguish Indian title, the Indians' right to the land was sacrosanct. Thus, a purchaser from the Indians could not obtain a fee simple absolute title without obtaining the government's interest as well.

The Doctrine of Discovery protected federal, individual, and tribal interests. Federal power to control acquisition of new land was supreme. Individuals tracing title to past grants had their title confirmed, although, if Indians still inhabited the land, extinguishment of the Indian title was necessary to perfect their interests. Finally, tribal rights to aboriginal land were confirmed and protected to some extent.[27] Although the Doctrine of Discovery was a concept designed in part to

---

26. 21 U.S. (8 Wheat.) 543 (1823).

27. See Felix S. Cohen, Original Indian Title, 32 Minn. L. Rev. 28, 48-49 (1947); accord Russel Lawrence Barsh & James Youngblood Henderson, Contrary Jurisprudence: Tribal Interests in Navigable Waterways Before and After Montana v. United States, 56 Wash. L. Rev. 627, 635-636 (1981); Howard R. Berman, The Concept of Aboriginal Rights in the Early Legal History of the United States, 27 Buffalo L. Rev. 637, 644-645 (1978). See generally Henderson, Unraveling the Riddle of Aboriginal Title, 5 Am. Indian L. Rev. 75 (1977).

protect Indian rights to land as well as to protect the principle of federal exclusivity in dealing with Indians regarding their land, later judicial misinterpretations of the doctrine are in large part responsible for arguments in favor of virtually unreviewable federal power over Indian lands. These arguments were prevalent in the late eighteenth and early nineteenth centuries and are still present to some extent in Indian law today.

While the early decisions of the Marshall Court viewed the government's property interest in land as a preemptive right to purchase, or a sort of glorified option to buy the land, subsequent decisions denominated the government's interest as a title interest and the tribal interest as a possessory one. The more the government's interest was characterized as an ownership interest, the more it became possible to regard the ownership of land alone as giving the government power to govern Indians.

Acknowledging that no existing constitutional provision granted Congress this right to govern Indian affairs, the Court found it to be inherent, first by analogy to early decisions regarding the power to regulate activities within the territories. Drawing support from cases upholding congressional power to govern territories before statehood, the Court in *Kagama* stated that the power over territories derived "from the ownership of the country in which the Territories are."[28] The Court quoted an earlier opinion by Chief Justice Marshall regarding territorial government: "[T]he right to govern may be the inevitable consequence of the right to acquire territory."[29] By parity of reasoning, the Court found inevitable the right to govern activities of reservation Indians whether within or without state boundaries. The Doctrine of Discovery gave the United States "ultimate title" over Indian land wherever located and the exclusive right to acquire that land. Thus the federal government owned the country in which the Indian tribes lived, and this ownership interest in turn vested the government with the right to govern them. Finally, the Court relied on the history of federal supremacy over the states in Indian affairs and the historic, protective role that the government played toward Indians. These Indian tribes (the Court held) are the wards of the nation. They are communities dependent on the United States: dependent largely for their daily food and dependent for their political rights. They owe no allegiance to the states and receive from them no protection. Because of the local ill feeling, the people of the states where the Indians are found are often their deadliest enemies. From the Indians' very weakness and helplessness, so largely due to the course of the federal government's dealings with them and to the treaties through which the government made its promises to them, there arises the duty of protection and, with it, the power.

At first glance the practical solution seems a happy one. The states had proven themselves to be the greatest enemies of the Indian tribes, and the federal government had insisted on the exclusive right to deal with the tribes since the founding of the republic. Moreover, the practical solution did no violence to the allocation of powers between nation and states in the Constitution. Although the Court might

---

28. United States v. Kagama, 118 U.S. 375, 380 (1886).
29. Id. (quoting American Ins. Co. v. Canter, 26 U.S. (1 Pet.) 511, 542 (1828)).

have taken greater care to demonstrate that the continued power to legislate regarding Indian affairs was a necessary inference from the history and the text of the Constitution, still the narrow result of *Kagama*—the supremacy of federal over state power—was a just one. Yet the Court in *Kagama* failed to consider tribal rights. Consent of the governed had been a cardinal principle of the founders. Nevertheless, that Indians were not citizens and could not vote did not seem relevant to the Court. Once again, by concentrating on justifying federal power, the Court reinforced earlier precedents abdicating its role in accommodating the legitimate but competing interests raised by the federal government's interference with tribal rights. Such accommodation was left to the political arena: an arena from which Indians were excluded.

Kagama and its nineteenth-century precedents reflect a laissez-faire judicial attitude toward federal regulation of Indian affairs more than a prescription concerning the proper balance of the interests at stake. It is unnecessary at this late date to argue that such a deferential attitude was inappropriate in nineteenth-century jurisprudence, when nonintervention in the cause of individual liberties was a hallmark of judicial policy.[30] What is important, however, is the tenaciousness of the deferential attitude, manifested in the Court's subsequent reliance on *Kagama* well into the twentieth century.

From the time of *Kagama* until well into the twentieth century, policy makers denied tribal Indians the basic freedoms accorded other Americans, on the theory that their relation to the United States was "an anomalous one and of a complex character."[31] Although nominally protected by the individual rights provisions of the Constitution, like other noncitizens, Indians and Indian tribes in fact could not vindicate their rights in the courts. While the Fourteenth Amendment had been held to guarantee all persons equal access to the state courts, irrespective of their race,[32] Elk v. Wilkins[33] and subsequent cases cast considerable doubt on whether the Fourteenth Amendment's equal protection clause extended to Indians. Moreover, the 1866 Civil Rights Act guarantee that "citizens . . . shall have the same right . . . to sue, be parties, and give evidence" explicitly excluded Indians from citizenship. Even when access to the courts was granted, this lack of familiarity with state law and procedures, state laws excluding them from juries and declaring them incompetent as witnesses, and state juries' anti-Indian prejudice were powerful disincentives to their filing suit in state courts.

Access to federal courts was also problematic. First, being neither citizens nor true aliens, individual Indians and Indian tribes could not sue in federal court on nonfederal questions. Although Indian tribes and individuals bringing class actions on behalf of tribes did raise federal questions in federal courts, their status as wards

---

30. See, e.g., Mormon Church v. United States, 136 U.S. 1, 44 (1890) (upholding law breaking up Mormon Church and providing for seizure of Church property); Dred Scott v. Sandford, 60 U.S. 393, 451-452 (1857) (fundamental property rights of slave owners); cf. William E. Nelson, The Impact of the Antislavery Movement upon Styles of Judicial Reasoning in Nineteenth Century America, 87 Harv. L. Rev. 513 (1974) (the formalistic "rules" approach of the late nineteenth century was in part a reaction to freewheeling instrumentalist opinions like *Dred Scott*).

31. *Kagama*, 118 U.S. at 381.

32. Yick Wo v. Hopkins, 118 U.S. 356 (1886).

33. 112 U.S. 94 (1884).

of the government sometimes confused the issue of tribal and individual standing to sue.

Undoubtedly, racial and cultural prejudice played no small role in federal actions toward Indians during this period. The reported justifications for these federal actions rested on the guardianship theory of United States v. Kagama, cited frequently in the cases of that era. Yet one key to the Court's finding of a congressional guardianship power over Indians was its view of their racial and cultural inferiority. Repeatedly, the decisions of that era invoked this inferiority in terms that would be intolerable in a judicial opinion today. The undisguised contempt for the native culture was unrelieved by an open-minded assessment in any of the principal cases studied. Rather, the Indians were described as semibarbarous, savage, primitive, degraded, and ignorant.

The relationship between the federal government and the Indian was frequently termed as one between a superior and inferior. The white race was called more intelligent and highly developed. The government's representatives held the implicit belief that a higher civilization justly replacing that of a passing race whose time was over and whose existence could no longer be justified. The very weakness of the Indians in resisting the tide seemed to be one of their greatest moral shortcomings, but one not as serious as the Indian communal tradition. To the white observer, the lack of proprietary interest generally displayed by tribal members was repulsive and backward. Removing the "herd" instinct was deemed by some to be the key to civilizing the Indian. The ethnocentric outlook of the times may well have tainted the Court's view of the legitimacy of Indian rights claims and may explain, if not excuse, some of the more egregious violations of tribal and individual fundamental rights that have continued to occur.

Forced allotment of Indian lands and assimilation of Indians into the dominant culture became the primary policy of the federal government during the years following *Kagama*. Tribal land was subdivided, some apportioned to individuals with no compensation to the tribe, and the rest sold to non-Indian settlers, often at far less than fair market value. The Court aided this process, holding that the plenary power of Congress, derived from the Indians' "condition of dependency," somehow converted Indian property, even fee simple property, into quasi-public land "subject to the administrative control of the government." This authority permitted Congress, acting through the Secretary of the Interior, to lease, sell, or allot any tribal land without tribal consent, even in violation of solemn treaty promises. The money gained by these ventures was placed in trust funds managed by the government and disbursed as the government believed wisest, often for the purpose of assimilating and civilizing the Indians. For example, tribal trust money was often spent to pay missionaries to educate Indian children in the ways of white society and Christianity — without consulting the tribe. Furthermore, money promised the tribe as an entity in treaties could be paid to members per capita, thus drastically diminishing the tribe's resources.

The Court supported these federal actions by eschewing any role in accommodating the competing interests at stake. Congress had decided in 1871 to govern Indians by statute, and its actions were not justiciable: Plenary authority over the tribal relations of the Indians has been exercised by Congress from the beginning, and the power has always been deemed a political one, not subject to be controlled by the judicial department of the government. Indians abandoned the attempt to restrain federal action. Instead, tribes used what resources they had to persuade Congress to pass statutes permitting them to sue for compensation for land that was taken.

The legacy of *Kagama* dominated Indian sovereignty issues, and citation of *Kagama* frequently signaled judicial deference to Congress. Chief Justice John Marshall had regarded Indian tribes as possessing a "right of self-government" and having a protectorate relationship with the federal government, like "that of a nation claiming and receiving the protection of one more powerful: not . . . submitting as subjects to the laws of a master." Nevertheless, in *Kagama*, the Court interpreted the 1871 statute ending the practice of making treaties with Indian tribes as establishing the premise that the federal government intended to govern the tribes by acts of Congress. Thus, the Court upheld federal power to take from Indian tribes jurisdiction over crimes among Indians, the first major federal inroad into tribal internal affairs. The court subsequently invoked the *Kagama* guardianship power and the political question doctrine as justifying judicial nonintervention when Congress abrogated tribal self-government rights. Tribes largely shunned litigation as a strategy to protect their political sovereignty interests after these early judicial defeats.

Having obtained such a judicial seal of approval for the exercise of its power, Congress proceeded to treat the previously semi-independent Indian tribes as subject peoples. The dissolution of tribal governing structures was a cardinal aim of the Allotment Period. For instance, in 1906, Congress denied the legislatures of the Five Civilized Tribes the right to meet more than 30 days per year, and their legislative action was made subject to veto by the President of the United States. Legislative intervention even extended to federal power over tribal money. Statutes provided that money due to tribes from tribal assets could be appropriated at the discretion of Congress. The Secretary of the Interior's power over disbursement of Indian money enabled him to manipulate the tribe with a concomitant weakening effect on tribal sovereignty. Moreover, Congress, not the tribes, had the ultimate authority to determine who was a tribal member for purposes of distributing property, annuities, and trust money and to determine, further, how that money was spent. Finally, Congress even authorized the consolidation of tribes with no ethnological ties — even some who were ancient enemies.

As one commentator has noted, by these and other measures, "the Indian Agent and his staff were 'the government' for most tribes from the cessation of treaty-making to the 1930's."[34] While the courts did not explicitly endorse every erosion of tribal political sovereignty occurring during this time, they certainly shared responsibility for it, because *Kagama* and its progeny had eviscerated any litigation strategy to protect tribal sovereignty rights.

Judicial abandonment of Indians was not limited to rights asserted by tribes. The Court also treated individual Indians as constitutional castaways. For instance, according to *Kagama*, Indians were within the geographical limits of the United

---

34. Theodore W. Taylor, The States and Their Indian Citizens 17 (1972).

States and thus were subject to whatever laws Congress deemed appropriate. A year and a half before *Kagama*, however, the Court had held in Elk v. Wilkins[35] that Indians were not citizens, thereby upholding a state's denial of the right to vote to an Indian who had severed relations with his tribe and become a lawful resident of the state. Over the dissent of the first Mr. Justice Harlan, the Court reasoned that, although the petitioner was born in the United States, he was not "subject to the jurisdiction" of the United States for the purposes of the Fourteenth Amendment, because all Indians "owed immediate allegiance to their several tribes, and were not part of the people of the United States." Indians might be subject to United States jurisdiction in some respects, but the Fourteenth Amendment required more: They must be "completely subject to [United States] political jurisdiction, and owing them direct and immediate allegiance." While the Court in *Elk* reaffirmed salutary principles of tribal sovereignty, it undermined individual rights, because Indians, even those who had assimilated, could not become citizens of the United States without permission of Congress. Many other noncitizen aliens who claimed direct allegiance to other nations had a choice that Indians never had: They could go home and remain subject to the sole jurisdiction of the country of their birth. Indians, on the other hand, were alien subjects of a federal power they had not chosen and could not escape.

Eventually, those who favored the assimilationist policy because of concerns for Indian well-being urged successfully that Indians who received allotments should be made U.S. citizens.[36] This grant of citizenship permitted Indians to take part in the political process. Nevertheless, those Indians whose lands escaped allotment remained noncitizen subjects.

Even after the bestowal of citizenship on all Indians,[37] Congress continued to legislate pervasively on Indian matters. The Court supported this exercise of power, holding that conferral of citizenship did not end the guardian-ward relationship. Moreover, the Court held that an individual Indian had no power to terminate the guardian-ward relationship unilaterally.

Legislation of this era curtailed individual Indian property rights by placing restraints on the alienation of allotted land, including fee simple allotted land. The right of Indians to make contracts affecting trust property and to dispose of trust property was conditioned on approval by the Secretary of the Interior. Furthermore, individual Indian beneficiaries of congressional allotment schemes could not rely on the congressional largess bestowed on them. Statutes granting individuals property rights in the most explicit language were overturned by later statutes enlarging the class of beneficiaries and even, when congressional policy favoring tribal self-government resurfaced in the 1930s, giving the land back to the tribe.

First Amendment rights, too, were curtailed drastically. Indian religions were banned upon threat of criminal prosecution in the Courts of Indian Offenses set up

---

35. 112 U.S. 94 (1884).

36. The General Allotment Act provided that Indians receiving allotments under any treaty or statute would become citizens; General Allotment Act of 1887, ch. 119, §6, 24 Stat. 388, 390 (codified as amended at 25 U.S.C. §349 (1976)). The act also declared Indians living separate and apart and "adopting the habits of civilized life" to be citizens.

37. Indian Citizenship Act of 1924, ch. 233, 43 Stat. 253 (current version at 8 U.S.C. §1401(b) (1982)).

by the Bureau of Indian Affairs. Children were forced to attend boarding schools to receive rations promised in return for land cessions. Moreover, the children were denied the right to speak their own language at the schools. They were educated only in English, and then only about American values. This coerced education in Indian boarding schools continued even after the Supreme Court recognized the fundamental right of non-Indian families to oversee the education of their children by sending them to private schools or to schools where foreign languages were taught. Finally, individual Indians were subject to liquor laws, whether or not they had severed tribal relations and whether or not they lived on a reservation.[38] In modern times, the Supreme Court has apparently repudiated both the ethnocentric overtones of the doctrine of plenary power and the doctrine itself, at least as far as the doctrine suggests it has an extraconstitutional source or is a power unlimited by other constitutional provisions. Nevertheless, the concept of plenary power continues to influence contemporary Indian law by conditioning the courts to defer to congressional power over Indian affairs.

D.   The Modern View of Congressional Power over Indians: The Development of a More Restrictive View of the Guardian-Ward Relationship (1930s to the Present)

As demonstrated above, barriers to the Indian tribes' access to the judicial system and that system's deference to Congress, coupled with indifference to tribal and individual rights on the rare occasions when Indians were allowed into court, marked the plenary power era, which lasted at least until the 1930s. In the 1930s and 1940s, Congress repudiated the allotment and assimilation policy, which had come under much criticism, and adopted a policy of protecting tribal cultures and encouraging tribal self-government. This shift in policy undoubtedly affected the Court, as demonstrated by an increased receptivity to Indian claims.

First, both Congress and the judiciary opened the doors to the courthouses to which Indians had long denied ready access. For instance, the Court finally clarified the murky question of whether tribal Indians had standing to sue in federal court absent a congressional grant. During the allotment era, the Court had upheld the power of the executive to bring suit on behalf of Indian wards and had intimated that Indians not only could have no say in the litigation, but might also have no right to sue on their own behalf once the United States had undertaken their representation. In 1943, the Court entertained a suit brought under a statute expressly permitting an aggrieved tribe to seek appellate review of a determination of the value of land taken by railroads. The Court held that the statute gave the tribe the right to sue, but added that Indian tribes also have "a general legal right" to bring lawsuits.[39] Finally, in 1968, the Court made plain that an individual Indian's status

---

38. See, e.g., Hallowell v. United States, 221 U.S. 317 (1911) (upholding prosecution for violation of law against selling liquor to an Indian or Indian allottee). These liquor laws were explicitly racial. In *Hallowell*, for instance, despite the fact that the defendant had been active in county and state governments as a judge, county attorney, county assessor, and director of a public school district, he was still subject to the law because of his status as an Indian. See id. at 320, 324.

39. Creek Nation v. United States, 318 U.S. 629, 640 (1943).

as a ward of the United States did not preclude him or her from bringing suit on his or her own behalf.[40]

More important, Congress, by enacting the Indian Claims Commission Act of 1946, finally removed the barrier of sovereign immunity to money claims against the government that had hindered tribes in the 83 years since the Court of Claims was created. Within five years, tribes filed more than five times as many claims against the government as they had during the entire 65 previous years. Finally, the 1976 passage of an amendment to the Administrative Procedure Act, waiving sovereign immunity for claims based on that statute, enabled Indians and Indian tribes to seek review of wrongful agency actions.[41]

As more Indian claims reached the judiciary, the Court began to narrow the Plenary Power Doctrine and repudiated the notion that Congress's plenary power could prevent the courts from reaching the merits of specific constitutional claims by Indian tribes. It held that plenary authority over Indians did not enable the United States to give the tribal lands to others, or to appropriate them to its own purposes, without rendering, or assuming an obligation to render, just compensation for them; for that "would not be an exercise of guardianship, but an act of confiscation."[42]

Concurrently, the Court began to rely on specific provisions of the Constitution in place of inherent authority as the source of congressional power over Indians. The process was a gradual one. By 1965, the Court relied solely on the Indian commerce clause in holding that a federal law regulating trading activities on Indian reservations preempted state taxation of those activities. Since the 1960s, the Court has looked increasingly to enumerated powers, especially the power to effectuate treaties, the Indian commerce clause, or both. Moreover, the Court repudiated the notion that Congress's plenary power was extraconstitutional, ruling rather that it was "drawn both explicitly and implicitly from the Constitution itself."[43]

Subsequently, the Court adjudicated an equal protection challenge to the distribution of judgment funds by the Secretary of the Interior. The Court noted that power over tribal property, while plenary, is "rooted in the Constitution" and may be challenged when it infringes constitutional rights. Moreover, the Court served notice that the political question doctrine, which had been invoked often in the past as a bar to reviewing congressional action adverse to Indian claims, had no place in cases raising individual rights guarantees. By 1980, the Court had dismissed the political question doctrine.[44]

During this process of narrowing the Plenary Power Doctrine, the Court also began to redefine its source — the guardian-ward relationship. Although the guardian-ward relationship of *Kagama* was the basis for the power to impose

40. Poafpybitty v. Skelly Oil Co., 390 U.S. 365, 370-371 (1968) (construing Heckman v. United States, 224 U.S. 413 (1912), as implying that standing to sue existed).
41. Act of Oct. 21, 1976, Pub. L. No. 94-574, 90 Stat. 2721 (codified at 5 U.S.C. §702 (1982)). For a discussion of pitfalls in suing the federal government, see Newton, Enforcing the Federal-Indian Trust Relationship after Mitchell, 31 Cath. U. L. Rev. 635 (1982).
42. United States v. Creek Nation, 295 U.S. 103, 110 (1935).
43. Morton v. Mancari, 417 U.S. 535, 551-552 (1974).
44. United States v. Sioux Nation, 448 U.S. 371, 413 (1980).

federal criminal laws on tribal Indians, *Kagama* itself and other allotment era cases also referred to duties toward Indians imposed on the government by the guardian-ward relationship. These decisions treated the duties as self-imposed moral obligations, not legally enforceable. Nevertheless, in cases in which Congress had waived sovereign immunity, the judiciary began to impose duties on the government, akin to those imposed on ordinary fiduciaries, to manage Indian money and land responsibly. Indian breach of trust cases proliferated, and many were successful. Courts rendered specific relief or assessed money damages for breaches of a trustee's duties of care and loyalty in a number of cases involving mismanagement of money or natural resources. The result is that, in modern-day Indian law, the trust relationship, although not constitutionally based and thus not enforceable against Congress, is a source of enforceable rights against the executive branch and has become a major weapon in the arsenal of Indian rights.

Perhaps the success of breach of trust claims has obscured the fact that neither Congress nor the courts have expunged completely the Plenary Power Doctrine from Indian law. Tribes wishing to impose fiduciary duties on the government did not challenge the government's power to manage and control Indian resources, but argued that the power carried duties along with it. Moreover, with the taming of the doctrine in recent years, most commentators have come to regard the term "plenary power" as referring only to the notion that the existing, fairly sketchy references to sources of power over Indians in the Constitution are to be read broadly, much as are the references to foreign affairs, and thus as giving the federal government primary power over Indian affairs.

Nevertheless, vestiges of the judicial attitude of nonintervention developed and nurtured in the plenary power era remain, especially in the areas of tribal sovereignty and property rights where the Court continues to rely on an inherent Indian affairs power of almost unlimited scope. For instance, the Court characterizes tribal sovereignty as existing "only at the sufferance of Congress," which has "plenary authority to limit, modify or eliminate the powers of local self-government." As to property, the Court continues to recognize Congress's "paramount power over the property of the Indians." The Court, moreover, quite frankly explains that this power is derived "by virtue of [Congress's] superior position over the tribes" or even "the conquerors' will" — the kind of might-makes-right argument that resonates of nineteenth-century Indian law jurisprudence. The following is a partial list of the congressional actions receiving the Court's sanction in modern times, often in decisions citing the major cases of the plenary power era. The Court has upheld congressional power to reduce the boundaries of a reservation without tribal consent or compensation, thereby reducing, for all practical purposes, a tribe's power to govern. In addition, the Court has upheld power to divest a tribe of all criminal, civil, or regulatory jurisdiction; to abrogate treaties; and to subject tribal laws and constitutions to federal approval. As to tribal property rights, congressional power remains as sweeping as it was during the plenary power era. Congress may require the Secretary of the Interior to approve land sales and leases by tribes and contracts obligating money held by the federal government but owed to the tribe. Congress may abrogate without liability future interests in Indian lands granted by earlier statutes and may enlarge or decrease the class of beneficiaries of tribal trust funds or lands. Congress may take one kind of tribal property, aboriginal Indian property, without paying compensation; it may, without consent, dispose of recognized-title tribal property under the guise of management and sell it at less than fair market value without liability, as long as the tribe receives some proceeds. According to some observers, it may even extinguish legal land claims of Indian tribes by retroactively extinguishing both title to the land and any claims based on that title. The Court's continued failure to attempt to define the extent of Congress's power over Indian affairs has encouraged further undue assertions of that power.

Though a full discussion of the concept of native or aboriginal title lies outside the scope of this section, a few notes on U.S. law in this area should be considered.[45] Native or aboriginal title refers to the ability of indigenous peoples to successfully claim ownership of or title to their historical homelands within the legal system of a colonizing power. The claim for title grounds itself in the historical, cultural, and spiritual connection between indigenous peoples and the land they inhabited both before and after the arrival of colonial regimes. In countries such as Canada and Australia, both of which recognize native title, if a group of indigenous peoples shows a particular form of historical, non-colonial connection to disputed lands, the legal ownership of that land under the domestic law of the colonial power flows to the indigenous peoples or tribe.[46] Though fraught with legal complications, the recognition of native title has been hailed as a crucial step in the liberation of indigenous peoples from the continuing effects of colonization and conquest.

In opposition to growing trends in international law, the U.S. does not recognize the right of Native Americans to native title in their historical lands. In the case of Tee-Hit-Ton Indians v. United States,[47] the U.S. Supreme Court rejected a Fifth Amendment takings claim brought by Indian tribes. In order to make a takings claim, the land taken must have been the legal property of the claimant. The Court explicitly rejected native title as the basis for land ownership and held that Native American tribes could claim only lands not already held by the tribe in fee simple if an explicit act of Congress granted the land to the tribe.[48] The *Tee-Hit-Ton* decision continues to vigorously function as good law within the United States.[49] Although state disenfranchisement of Indians continued into the twentieth century, individual Indians now facially enjoy the same constitutional rights as other Americans. It is, however, important to note that, in certain instances, federal

---

45. Thank you to Elizabeth Loeb, J.D./Ph.D. candidate at New York University School of Law, for her assistance on researching Native American title claims.

46. See Mabo v. State of Queensland, 107 A.L.R. 1 (1992); Guérin v. Canada, S.C.R. 335 (1984).

47. 348 U.S. 272 (1955).

48. Id. at 274.

49. See Green v. Rhode Island, 398 F.3d 45 (1st Cir. 2005); Lac Courte Oreilles Band of Lake Superior Chippewa Indians v. Voight, 700 F.2d 341, 351 (7th Cir. 1983); Karuk Tribe of Calif. v. Ammon, 209 F.3d 1366, 1374 (Fed. Cir. 2000); Alabama-Coushatta Tribe of Tex. v. United States, 2000 WL 1013532 *11 (Fed. Cl. 2000); Zuni Indian Tribe of N.M. v. United States, 16 Cl. Ct. 670, 671 (1989).

constitutional provisions may not apply on "Indian country."[50] While on Native land, persons, both Native and non-Native, may be subject to the jurisdiction of tribal courts and laws, which do not mirror exactly federal constitutional protections.[51] The application of tribal law, as opposed to federal or state law, on Native lands is too complex to summarize here, and involves many contested issues.

The jurisdiction of tribal courts over non-Native Americans, or over all non-tribal members, has been the subject of much recent litigation in tribal and federal courts. Tribal property and political sovereignty rights are a different matter, however. Attempts to assert constitutional protection for these rights have been largely unsuccessful.

The task of constructing a constitutional framework that will protect tribal rights finds its most formidable barrier in the legacy of the plenary power era — the long tradition of judicial analysis justifying extraordinary federal power over Indian tribal property and sovereignty that created powerful precedents impeding the application of meaningful judicial scrutiny of federal actions affecting tribal claims. Such a task is also hampered by the long and invidious history of discrimination against Indian peoples that has yet to be fully acknowledged and dealt with by the dominant society and whose tentacles extend into the present day.

---

50. "Indian country," as defined at 18 U.S.C. §1151, means "(a) all land within the limits of any Indian reservation under the jurisdiction of the United States Government, notwithstanding the issuance of any patent, and, including rights-of-way running through the reservation, (b) all dependent Indian communities within the borders of the United States whether within the original or subsequently acquired territory thereof, and whether within or without the limits of a state, and (c) all Indian allotments, the Indian titles to which have not been extinguished, including rights-of-way running through the same." The Court has held that this definition applies to questions of both criminal and civil jurisdiction. California v. Cabazon Band of Mission Indians, 480 U.S. 202, 208 n.5, citing DeCoteau v. District County Ct., 420 U.S. 425, 427 n.2. The applicability of these doctrines in Alades Hawaii involves additional complexities.

51. The relationship between Indian lands and the Constitution, and the Bill of Rights in particular, is a complicated as well as somewhat ambiguous one, as Lucy A. Curry writes:

> An unavoidable tension results from recognizing tribes as sovereign entities with the powers of self-government that are necessarily diminished under the historic and pervasive control of the dominant Anglo-American norms and prejudices. The inherent conflicts arising from this arrangement are most apparent when Indian tribes assert their sovereign powers over non-Indians living or transacting on tribal lands. For example, Congress passed the Major Crimes Act, extinguishing tribal jurisdiction over all major crimes, and passed both the IRA and the ICRA, respectively giving tribes the official power of self-governance and statutorily restricting tribal exercise of its powers based on the Anglo-American liberties of the Bill of Rights. Read together these laws allow tribes to operate as separate sovereigns with the jurisdiction to prosecute only minor crimes occurring on Indian land with the due process protections of the Bill of Rights, including habeas corpus relief in federal courts. With this status of the relevant law in mind, it is difficult to understand why the Supreme Court, in Oliphant v. Squamish Indian Tribe, chose to impliedly divest tribes of what remained of its sovereign power to prosecute and punish non-Indians for the minor crimes they commit on Indian territory. Not only does the status of the law render it puzzling, the Court's reasoning revived principles hundreds of years old found in the Doctrine of Discovery, which had remained dormant in the Court's Indian law jurisprudence for nearly 150 years.

A Closer Look at Santa Clara Pueblo v. Martinez: Membership by Sex, by Race, and by Tribal Tradition, 16 Wis. Women's L.J. 161 (2001).

Federal Indian policy in the past 20 years has been marked by a devolution of congressional power to states.[52] Jurisprudentially, the Supreme Court has regularly acted to diminish the legal sovereignty of Native peoples and to restrict Native self-government upon reservations.[53] Legal issues affecting Native people that are at the current forefront of debate include[54] the scope of federal regulations such as Title 7 on Indian land; the whaling rights of the Makah Indian tribe;[55] and Native water rights, particularly in western lands.[56] In addition, the contested issue of defining "Indian-ness" through biological measures such as "blood quantum" provide an interesting perspective on the American construction of race.[57]

§11.2.2 Legal Gambling on Native American Lands

No legal issue affecting Native Americans may be more controversial than that of gaming on Indian lands. This issue is a complex one whose scope is beyond the purposes of this text. A brief overview is useful, however, both because the issue is so important and because it highlights the ongoing tensions between state and tribal sovereignty as well as the political and economic plight facing many tribes.

Seminole Tribe of Florida v. Butterworth[58] and California v. Cabazon Band of Mission Indians[59] were critical to the development of current Indian gaming law.[60] In *Seminole*, the Court of Appeals for the Fifth Circuit held that a Florida bingo statute could not be enforced against the Seminole Indian tribe. The court further held that Native Americans as well as non-Native Americans could play bingo on Indian land.[61] In *Cabazon*, the Supreme Court reaffirmed "attributes of

---

52. See Tracy Becker, Traditional American Indian Leadership: A Comparison with U.S. Governance (DL 8/27/01), available at http://www.airpi.org/research/tradlead.html.

53. For a more in-depth analysis of Native American policy and jurisprudence, see generally Robert Williams, Like a Loaded Weapon: The Rehnquist Court, Indian Rights, and the Legal History of Racism in America (2005); Frank Pommersheim, Coyote Paradox: Some Indian Law Reflections from the Edge of the Prairie, 31 Ariz. St. L.J. 439 (1999); John Fredericks, America's First Nations: The Origins, History and Future of American Indian Sovereignty, 7 J.L. & Pol'y 347 (1999); Derek C. Haskew, Federal Consultation with Indian Tribes: The Foundation of Enlightened Policy Decisions, or Another Badge of Shame?, 24 Am. Indian L. Rev. 21 (2000).

54. Thank you to Damien Pfister, Ph.D. candidate at the University of Pittsburgh, for his research assistance on current Native American issues.

55. See generally William Bradford, Save the Whales v. Save the Makah: Finding Negotiated Solutions to Ethnodevelopmental Disputes in the New International Economic Order, 13 St. Thomas L. Rev. 155 (2000).

56. See generally Rebecca Tsosie, The Challenge of Differentiated Citizenship: Can State Constitutions Protect Tribal Rights?, 64 Mont. L. Rev. 199 (2003). For further discussion of the contest over Native American water rights, see Taiawagi Helton, Indian Reserved Water Rights in the Dual-System State of Oklahoma, 33 Tulsa L.J. 979 (1998).

57. See generally Steve Russell, A Black and White Issue: The Invisibility of American Indians in Racial Policy Discourse, 4 Geo. Pub. Pol'y Rev. 129 (1999). For further discussion of blood quantum, see Scott L. Gould, Mixing Bodies and Beliefs: The Predicament of Tribes, 101 Colum. L. Rev. 702 (2001).

58. 658 F.2d 310 (5th Cir. 1981).

59. 480 U.S. 202 (1987).

60. See Jeffrey A. Dempsey, Surfing for Wampum: Federal Regulation of Internet Gambling and Native American Sovereignty, 25 Am. Indian L. Rev. 133 (2000); Gary C. Anders, 556 Annals 98 (Mar. 1998).

61. *Seminole*, supra note 58.

sovereignty"[62] retained by Indian nations in some matters and held that a state could not regulate gaming on Indian lands so long as gaming is permitted in that state for any other purpose.[63]

In 1988, after *Cabazon* was decided, Congress passed Public Law Number 100-497, the Indian Gaming Regulatory Act (IGRA).[64] The act was intended to strike a balance between tribal sovereignty and state interests.[65] Also at play were the powerful interests of the gaming industry.[66] The IGRA divides Indian gaming activities into three distinct classes, each with separate rules.[67] The distinctions are generally based on the type of game and the size of the potential prizes. The IGRA also creates a regulatory framework for gaming operations.[68] Under this framework, regulatory authority is allocated at four separate levels: tribal, state, federal, and National Indian Gaming Commission.[69]

In general, under the IGRA, tribes have greater regulatory authority over gaming then they had previously. The IGRA mandates that all tribal gaming revenue be used exclusively for the welfare of the tribe and its members, tribal government operations, local government agencies, and charitable purposes.[70] In addition, a tribe may petition the Secretary of the Interior to allow per capita distributions to its members.[71]

Although the IGRA generally protects Native sovereignty over gaming, it also imposes some forms of state control. For this reason, some tribal members and leaders object to the act's infringement on total sovereignty and call attention to the fact that, under the IGRA, an individual state is allowed to exercise power over Indian land that they are not allowed to exercise over another individual state.[72] The act is even more broadly contested by many states, which argue that the IGRA violates the Tenth and Eleventh Amendments.[73]

The advantages and disadvantages of gaming on Indian lands, as judged from the perspective of Native Americans as well as the states, is a complex and nuanced topic. Briefly, it is worth noting that gaming has often provided desperately needed revenues for tribes living in abject poverty. Gaming revenues have been used to build houses, provide drug and alcohol treatment programs, allow tribal members to go to college, fund retirements, build hospitals and clinics, and provide other social services.[74] In addition, gaming revenues have increased the general economic well-being of many tribes. Such assistance is greatly needed given the harshness of conditions facing many Indians today, particularly those living on

62. 480 U.S. at 207, citing United States v. Mazurie, 419 U.S. 544, 557 (1975).
63. Id.
64. Pub. L. No. 100-497, Oct. 17, 1988, 102 Stat. 2467, United States Public Laws 100th Cong., 2d Sess., convening Jan. 25, 1988 (S. 555).
65. Dempsey, supra note 60; Anders, supra note 60.
66. Anders, supra note 60.
67. Id.
68. Dempsey, supra note 60; Anders, supra note 60.
69. Anders, supra note 60.
70. Id.
71. Id.
72. Dempsey, supra note 60.
73. Anders, supra note 60.
74. Id.

reservations. According to the U.S. Census Bureau, 31 percent of American Indians in general and 51 percent of American Indians living on reservations or trust lands live below the official poverty line; more than 20 percent of American Indian housing units on reservations or trust lands lack complete plumbing facilities; and major disparities in educational attainment exist between American Indians and the total population.[75] In addition, many Native American communities, particularly those on reservations, are plagued by disproportionately high rates of drug and alcohol abuse, suicide, and unemployment.[76] Gaming has been successful at generating tribal revenues virtually every place it has been established.[77] Gaming has also been credited with creating jobs, increasing Native American choice over economic development, elevating the status of tribes, and increasing political mobilization.[78]

The lack of resources and troubling social conditions facing many Indians is viewed by many as a clear indicator of the need for the revenue generated by gaming on Indian lands. There are also, however, disadvantages to gaming, some of which are more difficult to precisely quantify.[79] Commentators such as Gary Anders have noted disadvantages, for example, spousal and child abuse and neglect; missed workdays; gambling addictions; increased drug and alcohol abuse; increased opportunities for theft, embezzlement, and criminal infiltration; the undermining of the cultural integrity of Indian communities; economic disparities between small and large tribes; the prevalence of casino jobs, which are "low-wage, high-turnover positions"; and the possibility that gaming may draw money from other local businesses.[80] Gaming may also open tribes up to organized crime involvement. Although most commentators agree that Indians are disproportionately impacted by many social ills, whether gaming helps or exacerbates the problem is a matter for debate.

The issue of gaming on Native lands, then, is one that calls attention both to the plight of many tribes and to the ongoing tensions between state and tribal sovereignty. As the heated debate over gaming draws on, how courts and legislators continue to act will have far-reaching implications for Indian peoples.

§11.3 NONWHITE NATIVES IN OTHER LANDS

Racism is not a uniquely American practice. In 1994, South Africa's peoples ended generations of apartheid aimed at complete physical and political separation of racial groups. Great Britain's history of imperialism included intense involvement in the slave trade and the creation of segregated colonial societies. In England,

75. "We the . . . First Americans," U.S. Dep't of Commerce, Economics and Statistics Administration, Bureau of the Census (Sept. 1993), available at http://www.census.gov/apsd/wepeople/we-5.pdf.
76. Anders, supra note 60.
77. Id.
78. Id.
79. Id.
80. Id. at 104.

patterns of racism against nonwhites were visible in restrictive immigration laws and discrimination in housing and employment, not dissimilar to those found in urban America.

Another example is the half-century of conflict between Israelis and Palestinians, who believe that the land of Israel belongs to them and who claim the "right to return," based on their residence in British Mandatory Palestine prior to the establishment of the State of Israel. This is the cornerstone of the Palestinian struggle against Israel. By contrast, Zionism, the modern movement for the return of Jews to their ancient homeland, views a Palestinian right to return as antithetical to the Jews' special, even God-given, historical and religious relationship with the land of Israel. Many argue that the return of Palestinians to Israel poses direct ideological and existential threats to the Israeli State. Israel has dominated the region by its superior arms and, in the process, views the Palestinians as a conquered people on whom it has imposed military rule. By denying the Palestinians basic rights and subjecting them to impoverished living conditions, the Israeli position has sparked revolts such as the Intifada and terrorist attacks.[1]

The following discussion, to create a context for a deeper understanding of the plight of Indians in America when overwhelmed by European invaders, sets out a brief description of the experiences of the natives of Australia and of New Zealand under similar pressures. Both summaries were researched and drafted by Rebecca Kavanagh.[2]

§11.3.1   Aboriginal Australians

Roberta Sykes is one of Australia's foremost black activists.[3] She is a world-renowned poet and writer and was the first black Australian to be awarded a doctoral degree from Harvard University. Yet, in her seminal text, *Black Majority: An Analysis of Twenty-one Years of Black Australian Experience as Emancipated Australian Citizens*, Dr. Sykes recounts being led off a plane in Europe because the

---

§11.3   1. For scholarly works supporting the Palestinian position, see Edward W. Said, Peace and Its Discontents: Essays on Palestine in the Middle East Peace Process (1995); Edward W. Said, The Politics of Dispossession: The Struggle for Palestinian Self Determination, 1969-1994 (1994); Noam Chomsky & Edward W. Said, The Fateful Triangle: The United States, Israel, and the Palestinians (1999). For a quick overview that provides a good background on the controversy, see Ron David, Arabs and Israel for Beginners (1993). Also see Justus Weiner, The Palestinian Refugees' "Right to Return" and the Peace Process, 20 B.C. Int'l & Comp. L. Rev. 1, 1-2 (1997). For more discussion, see Ved Nanda et al., Self-Determination: The Case of Palestine, 82 Am. Soc'y Int'l L. Proc. 334 (1988); Burns Weston et al., International Law and Solutions to the Arab-Israeli Conflict, 83 Am. Soc'y Int'l L. Proc. 121 (1989).

2. B.A. (First Class Honors) University of Sydney 1994; LL.B. (First Class Honors) University of Sydney 1996; Awarded Lionel Murphy Overseas Postgraduate Scholarship 1997; LL.M. New York University 1998, JSD, 2004.

3. Aboriginal Australians are black and identify as such, so these terms are used interchangeably throughout this section. This identification is not questioned in Australia and elsewhere outside the United States, but it seems to confuse some Americans because Aboriginal Australians are not of African descent.

authorities suspected she was an Ethiopian terrorist.[4] Why had she aroused suspicion? Because she is black and was traveling on an Australian passport.

When Ralph Ellison wrote *The Invisible Man* in 1952, he could have been describing the Aboriginal experience in Australia as easily as the African American experience in the United States. Indeed, some 50 years after it was written, this trope of invisibility resonates strongly in the experiences of modern-day Aboriginal Australians. Few non-Australians are aware that Australia has a significant black population. Even those who are aware would probably not find Dr. Sykes's story surprising, since their impression of Aboriginal Australians is that they are a tribal people who live in the outback, and they certainly do not travel across the European continent. Indeed, the problem of invisibility is a defining element of the black experience in Australia — and it is not just about perceptions overseas. Few white Australians have meaningful contact with black Australians, and many hold the same misconceptions as do non-Australians. Like non-Australians, white Australians' contact with Aboriginality is often limited to movies like *Crocodile Dundee* and to documentaries on the Discovery Channel.

But while Aboriginal Australians themselves are largely invisible on the world stage, Aboriginal culture (or at least the white co-opted version of it) is everywhere. Aboriginal art adorns Qantas planes; Aboriginal dance featured prominently in the opening ceremony for the Sydney 2000 Olympic games and as part of the 2003 Rugby World Cup opening spectacular; Aboriginality has become Australia's "cultural mascot," replacing the koala and kangaroo. This use (or, rather, misuse) of Aboriginal culture is not unintentional. Indeed, it is part of a very deliberate (and clever) attempt by the Australian government to control what the world sees of the black experience in Australia. Writing in the lead-up to the Sydney 2000 Olympic games, expatriot journalist John Pilger described this phenomenon in the *Guardian*.

> In Monaco, when the IOC met to decide on the winning city, Australia was presented as an oasis of human harmony, in marked contrast to China, its main rival for the games. Delegates were treated to street performances by Aboriginal dancers and didgeridoo-players in full body paint, together with cavorting giant kangaroos and wombats. Of course, white Australia has long appropriated the art and artifacts of the Aboriginal Dreaming. It was no surprise that the boomerang was adopted as the motif for the Sydney Games. Two Qantas aircraft have been repainted in indigenous designs, and there is an "indigenous advisory committee," headed by the affable former rugby star, Gary Ella, himself an Aborigine. When foreign VIPs arrive next year, they will be met by Aboriginal elders: "official greeters." And when the Olympic torch is first carried on Australian soil by Nova Peris-Kneebone, winner of the 200m at the 1998 Commonwealth Games, all those revelations of kickbacks, junkets, and gifts of $10,000 necklaces will be subsumed in the glow of an opening ceremony devoted to "mutual respect and reconciliation."[5]

Pilger's analysis proved prescient. Black activists had long planned, and did manage to some degree, to use the games to draw international media attention to

---

4. Roberta Sykes, Black Majority: An Analysis of Twenty-One Years of Black Australian Experience as Emancipated Australian Citizens (1989).

5. John Pilger, "Fixed Race," The Guardian, Aug. 21, 1999.

the plight of their people. But the carefully orchestrated government counterstrategy ensured that, when issues such as the stolen generations (discussed below) were covered in the international media, Australia was more often presented as a nation grappling with its past maltreatment of its Native people rather than as one dealing with the present-day consequences of that maltreatment.

The media darling of the games was Cathy Freeman, the Aboriginal Australian runner who lit the Olympic torch during the opening ceremony and who was later victorious in the 400-meter sprint. Of the 400-meter dash, *Time* magazine commented, "not since African American Jesse Owens ran upside Hitler at the 1936 Olympics in Berlin has a footrace been freighted with so much extra-athletic significance."[6] Indeed, anyone who watched the race can attest to the enormous outpouring of emotion from the crowd, whose chants of "Cathy" reached fever pitch in the last hundred meters. Clearly something about this slight, elegant, and gracious young woman touched the soul of white Australia in a way that even they did not understand. Freeman completed her victory lap of the arena carrying both the Australian and Aboriginal flags. (A few years earlier, her decision to carry only the Aboriginal flag at the Commonwealth Games had sparked a national controversy.) In a phenomenon not dissimilar from the way in which African American athletes such as Michael Jordan become national heroes (almost, though not completely, transcending their race — witness O. J. Simpson), so too Cathy Freeman became the quintessential Australian heroine of the new millennium. And while most white Australians chose to bask in the glory of her victory against insurmountable odds, perhaps reassuring themselves that all was right in the new Australia, at least one Australian — then–Prime Minister John Howard — chose not to participate. When asked if he was proud of Freeman's win, Howard replied that he was proud of all the Australian athletes competing in the games. He had shown no such reserve when praising white Australian swimmer Ian Thorpe's victory a few days prior.[7]

Putting aside all of the hoopla surrounding Cathy Freeman's victory, however, just what is the reality of the black experience in Australia?

The Australian continent has a human history of between 50,000 and 150,000 years, making Aboriginal Australians representatives of the oldest surviving cultures in the world. At the time of the European invasion in 1788, there were more than two hundred Aboriginal tribes, each with a distinct culture and language, and the total Aboriginal population was probably more than one million. Despite this, and in contrast to other British colonies, such as New Zealand, the British acquired sovereignty over the Australian continent based on the lie that it was uninhabited — "terra nullius" or nobody's land — and no treaty was ever negotiated with the Aboriginal peoples. By the early twentieth century, the Aboriginal population had declined to fewer than 20,000 due to the efforts of the white invaders to rid themselves of what they termed the "Aboriginal problem."

6. For Her People, Time Magazine: The Year in Pictures, Dec. 2000.
7. On November 24, 2007, Australians defeated John Howard and elected a Labor Party leader, Kevin Brown as the new prime minister. He was elected on a platform of major reforms in education, health care, and environmental issues, particularly climate change.

Today, according to the 2001 census, Aboriginal people comprise 2.7 percent of Australia's population, or close to 500,000 people, with the highest concentration of Aborigines choosing to live in Australia's largest city, Sydney.[8] The real figure is undoubtedly much higher — probably closer to 5 percent — due to historical undercounting. In recent years, there has been a massive national indigenous population surge. Indeed, in the last decade alone, the national Aboriginal population increased 55 percent.[9] Historically and to this day, Aboriginal people have lived on mainland Australia, Tasmania, and many of the continent's offshore islands; however, in all but the most remote areas of Australia, Aboriginal people have over the past 200 years been dispossessed of their traditional lands. Today, more than three-quarters of black Australians live in urban areas, and, of those who live in rural areas, only a small number live in remote traditional communities.[10] Still, the idea of the tribal Aborigine is the image paraded to the world (and to white Australia) in countless documentaries and news stories.

Good reason exists, of course, for why the plight of Aboriginal Australians living in remote communities should garner international media attention — many communities have deplorable living conditions, lacking access to clean water or sanitation — but, sadly, the real needs of these communities are seldom part of the spin put on stories about the experience of Aboriginal Australians living in the outback.

One of the most shocking examples of institutional discrimination and racism in the provision of basic services to indigenous Australians was documented in a report by the Human Rights and Equal Opportunity Commission, a federal government agency, on the living conditions of a remote Aboriginal community in an area known as Toomelah. The report found that the Aboriginal people in Toomelah lived without access to clean water; that the communities had hopelessly inadequate sewage systems; and that housing, often in the form of tin sheds more reminiscent of something one might find in a South African township than in a wealthy nation such as Australia, was dilapidated. The problem, according to the report, was not the remoteness of the community; it noted that a nearby white community had access to all these amenities. The report was so shocking that it received saturation media coverage, but some ten years later, a television crew visiting Toomelah found that little had changed.[11]

The state of Aboriginal health is, or should be, a matter of national shame. Many Aboriginal people die of diseases otherwise eradicated in Australia, such as tuberculosis. The Aboriginal infant mortality rate is five times that of white Australians, and Aboriginal people have a life expectancy some 20 years less than

8. Native Titles in Private Housing, Canberra Times, Oct. 26, 2007; Tim Johnston, Australian Leader Wants "New Reconciliation" with Aborigines, New York Times, Oct. 26, 2007, at A9.

9. Debra Jopsen, "White as a Ghost" But One of a Growing Aboriginal Nation, Sydney Morning Herald, June 18, 2002. A significant part of this increase can be attributed to people raised without awareness of their Aboriginal heritage reclaiming their black identity and roots.

10. Australian Bureau of Statistics, Population Distribution: Indigenous Australians (1997).

11. Human Rights and Equal Opportunity Commission, Report on the Problems and Needs of Aborigines Living on the NSW-Queensland Border (Toomelah Report), 1988.

other Australians.[12] Perhaps surprisingly, these appalling statistics apply not only to black Australians living in remote communities but to *all* black Australians, most of whom, of course, live in urban areas. The problem, then, is not access to resources but the decades of neglect and the entrenched racism that is as much a part of Australian society as it is of society in the United States.

The interplay of race and racism in Australia in many ways echoes the American experience, with, of course, vitally important differences. The same stereotypes that George Frederickson identifies in *The Black Image in the White Mind* (which examines racist attitudes in nineteenth-century America) were — and are — very much a part of Australia's culture of racism. The idea that black Australians are uncivilized savages draws on constructs similar to those that shaped the treatment of blacks in the United States. In 1844, for instance, W. C. Wentworth, speaking on the Aborigines Evidence Bill, which would have allowed Aborigines to testify in courts of law, claimed that it would "be quite as defensible to receive evidence in a court of justice the chatterings of the ourang-outang as of this savage race."[13] Henry Reynolds writes,

> Many early settlers probably arrived in Australia with, or soon acquired, a view of savagery compounded of godless anarchy, violence, cannibalism and sexual depravity. . . . Thus ideas from many sources — scientific and popular, old and new — fostered the growth of racial prejudice in the Australian colonies. Such attitudes influenced the course of race relations, encouraging and ultimately sanctioning the use of violence and vitiating the officially favored policy of assimilating the indigenes into white society.[14]

Many scholars draw links between this racist ideology and the horrific violence that has been inflicted upon black Australians in the eighteenth, nineteenth and, indeed, twentieth centuries. Reverend William Yate, for instance, declared in 1830, "They were nothing better than dogs, and . . . it was no more harm to shoot them than it would be to shoot a dog when he barked at you."[15] As in the United States, the idea of the black man as a sexual predator and threat to white women was a central part of this mythology and led to many lynchings in late nineteenth- and early twentieth-century Australia. (In fact, John Pilger claims that "nigger hunts" continued well into the 1960s.[16]) This appalling history of lynchings, massacres, and other violence toward Aboriginal Australians is well documented.[17] Despite this, a recent book by a previously little-known right wing academic, Keith Windschuttle, *The Fabrication of Aboriginal History* (2002), claims that orthodox historians had deliberately fabricated or exaggerated evidence of massacres and ill treatment of Aborigines by the early colonialists in order to assuage "white guilt

12. Heather McRae, Garth Nettheim & Laura Beacroft, Indigenous Legal Issues 10ff. (1997).
13. Cited in Henry Reynolds, Racial Thought in Early Colonial Australia 45-53 (1974).
14. Id.
15. Cited in Bruce Elder, Blood on the Wattle: Massacres and Maltreatment of Australian Aborigines since 1788 1 (2003).
16. John Pilger, Australia Is the Only Developed Country Whose Government Has Been Condemned as Racist by the United Nations, Oct. 13, 2000, available at http://pilger.carlton.com/print/30056.
17. Id. See also Elder, supra note 15.

for genocide." He focuses in particular on the destruction of the Aboriginal population of Tasmania, off the southeast coast of mainland Australia: The island's Native population was virtually wiped out in the early days of British colonial rule. Windschuttle dismisses as ideologically motivated the accepted estimates of the number of Aborigines killed by settlers. For instance, he categorizes the bitter clashes between settlers and Aborigines in the 1830s known as the "Black war" as "an outbreak of robbery, assault and murder by tribal Aborigines." Employing the narrowest standards possible, he also accepts as evidence of deliberate killings only those cases that were publicly reported or recorded. In doing so, as one critic, Dirk Moses (see below), points out, he uses the same standards of evidence as Holocaust deniers such as David Irving who argue that "because there are no direct surviving eyewitnesses of gas chambers . . . therefore they did not exist or we cannot prove they exist." Ordinarily this sort of ideological drivel would be dismissed as the ranting of the lunatic fringe, but Windschuttle's work was praised by the Australian prime minister — who has used it to refute what he has termed the "black armband" view of Australian history — and received widespread coverage in Australian newspapers owned by Rupert Murdoch's News Limited. Windschuttle declares in the introduction to his book that what is at stake is "our understanding of the character of our nation and of the caliber of the British civilization we brought here in 1788," and as such, his book fans the flames of the "culture wars" set in motion with the 1996 election of the now former Australian prime minister, John Howard. A new collection of essays by some of the most esteemed historians of Australian history (edited by Robert Manne and including a contribution from Dirk Moses), *Whitewash: On Keith Windschuttle's Fabrication of Aboriginal History* (2003), comprehensively tears apart his analysis. But Windschuttle's book has already done tremendous damage to the reconciliation movement.

As in the United States, white Australians are profoundly ignorant of both the modern-day and historical black experience. One could argue that such ignorance is a matter of choice. While few white Australians have meaningful contact with black Australians, the media, at least in Australia, does cover issues pertaining to Aboriginal Australia. Few Australians could feign ignorance, for instance, of the substandard living conditions of many Aboriginal people. The Toomelah Report, for example, received saturated media coverage. Similarly, the University of Sydney, Australia's oldest and most prestigious university, is located in the heart of Redfern, an inner-city neighborhood of Sydney with a majority black population. Each and every day, thousands of the children of the power elite make the 15-minute walk from Redfern Station to the university through streets lined with what can be described only as slum housing. Most choose to look away. Interestingly, Redfern is prime Sydney real estate, located just five minutes from the city center. The state government, keenly aware of this, has offered to buy up the land and relocate the families to other Sydney neighborhoods. While this proposal is attractive to some Aboriginal people living in Redfern who no doubt would like their families to grow up in more salubrious surroundings, it also threatens to scatter Redfern's black population all over Sydney, thereby breaking up the one majority black neighborhood in the city.

Just as white America refuses to understand the modern-day consequences of slavery, many white Australians see the invasion of Australia two hundred years ago, and the consequent dispossession of Aboriginal people from their land, as an historical event of limited relevance to an understanding of the experience of black Australians today. Since the invasion of the Australian continent, black Australians have been subject to government policies that attempted variously to kill off, displace, convert, isolate, or assimilate them. It was not until 1967 that black Australians were recognized as fully fledged Australian citizens, and many nefarious government policies continued well into the 1970s. In a report by the Australian Human Rights and Equal Opportunity Commission, Australian government policies towards Aborigines were labeled "genocide."[18]

Dr. Rosalind Kidd, who has extensively researched the policies and practices of the administration of the state of Queensland, concludes from her work that, for all of this century, "Aborigines have been the most intensively supervised sector of the population, and if we are to understand why present social indicators for Aborigines — health, education, employment, family cohesion — are so appallingly deficient, we must investigate how the machinery of government has created these circumstances."[19] After the white invasion in 1788, an extremely large number of indigenous Australians died, whether as the result of massacres by white Australians or as the result of introduced diseases or government neglect. The remnants of the black population were rounded up by the white authorities and moved away to reserves or missions where they were forbidden to speak their languages or practice their culture. Aboriginal people were used as a source of cheap labor for farmers, and Aboriginal women were often employed as domestics.

The Australian states had a myriad of laws that prevented black Australians from entering hotels, marrying without permission, and living within town boundaries. Those Aborigines who were allowed to leave the missions were issued with papers known colloquially as "dog tags." One such law was the Native Administration Act enacted in Western Australia in 1936. This blatantly racist law provided, among other things, that:

(a) No native, except adult half-caste males who do not live as Aborigines, can move from one place to another without the permission of a protector and the giving of sureties;

(b) No native parent or other relative living has the guardianship of an Aboriginal or half-caste child;

(c) Natives may be ordered into reserves or institutions and confined there;

(d) The property of all minors is automatically managed by the Chief Protector, while the management of the property of any native may be taken over by consent or if considered necessary to do so to provide for its due preservation;

---

18. Human Rights and Equal Opportunity Commission, Bringing Them Home: A Guide to the Findings and Recommendations of the National Inquiry into the Separation of Aboriginal and Torres Strait Islander Children from Their Families (1997).

19. Rosalyn Kidd, cited in Aboriginal and Torres Strait Islander Commission, As a Matter of Fact: Answering the Myths and Misconceptions about Indigenous Australians 11 (1998).

(e)   Natives may be ordered out of town or from prohibited areas; and
(f)   Subject to the right of appeal, the Commissioner of Native Affairs may object to the marriage of any native.

Many historians have compared these laws to the apartheid regime as it existed in South Africa. The last of the laws listed above was not repealed until the 1970s. Antimiscegenation laws existed as well, though the rate of intermarriage and (consensual) sexual relations between black and white Australians has always been much higher than in the United States; currently almost 50 percent of black Australians marry outside their race.

The idea of invisibility was central to these government policies. The official government policy was to assimilate the black population into the wider community. The belief was that this would mean that the Aboriginal "problem" would eventually disappear, as black Australians lost their identity within the wider community. In 1947, A. O. Neville, a Western Australian Commissioner of Native Affairs, claimed that he had a "scientific solution" to the "Aboriginal problem." He argued that research showed that skin pigmentation could be bred out of Aborigines in two or three generations, and, if he were given the money to start a selective breeding program, he declared that he would solve the Aboriginal problem by breeding a race of white Aborigines.[20] The scariest thing about this proposal is that it was not seen as outlandish or bizarre by the powers that be at the time: After all, it was really just an extension of what they were already doing.

Though the official aim of government policy was assimilation, no one suggested that Aboriginal Australians should have equal citizenship rights, and they remained subject to strict government supervision. The most devastating part of the policy of assimilation was the forced removal of Aboriginal children from their families. These children, fostered out to white families or raised in institutions, are known as the "stolen generations," and the practice, begun in the earliest days of the British occupation, continued until the 1970s. At its peak from 1910 to 1970, between one in three and one in ten black children were removed from their families and communities.[21]

While racism is no longer officially sanctioned in Australian law, it continues to have a destructive effect on the lives of black Australians and to manifest in their contacts with the legal system and government. The welfare system continues to remove Aboriginal children from their families at a rate far higher than white children are removed from theirs. Aboriginal people make up almost 20 percent of the Australian prison population (a rate of imprisonment higher than that of any other people in the world, including blacks in the United States and apartheid-era South Africa). The rate of imprisonment among Aboriginal women is even higher — some 32 percent of women in prison nationally are Aboriginal. In

20. See further Elder, supra note 15, at 179.
21. See Human Rights and Equal Opportunity Commission, Bringing Them Home, supra note 18. This policy is the subject of the critically acclaimed film by director Philip Noyce, *Rabbit Proof Fence*, about three Aboriginal children who escaped from the reserve, where they were placed after having been stolen from their families. The children found their way home by following the so-called rabbit proof fence that runs the length of the Australian continent.

Western Australia, the rate is higher still — there, one-half of the female prison population is black, and in the Northern Territory, the figure is two-thirds.[22]

The number of black deaths in custody is so alarming that the government instituted a Royal Commission to examine the problem. Some 15 years after that commission released its recommendations, little if anything has changed, and, in fact, Aboriginal deaths in custody continue at a rate higher than during the period that was examined by the commission. Police brutality toward Aborigines is a huge problem in inner-city and rural areas. While Australia has no equivalent to the harsh drug laws that impact so greatly on black communities in the United States, black Australians are subject to a far higher rate of arrest than are other Australians for all crimes. They are also far more likely to be arrested for minor offenses, such as resisting arrest and disorderly conduct, than are white Australians.

Few white Australians have any understanding of the impact of racism on the everyday lives of black Australians. As Elliot Johnston, who oversaw part of the Royal Commission into Aboriginal Deaths in Custody, has commented,

> Until I examined the files of the people who died and other material which has come before the commission and listened to Aboriginal people speaking, I had no conception of the degree of pinpricking domination, abuse of personal power, utter paternalism, open contempt and total indifference with which so many Aboriginal people were visited on a day to day basis.[23]

Regrettably, this is a sentiment understood and shared by a seeming minority of white Australians. Although an increasing number of Australians seem to recognize the devastation that official government policies have wrought upon black Australia (there have been huge marches in support of reconciliation), a larger number seem to subscribe to the sentiments held by former Australian prime minister Howard, who has rejected what he terms the "black armband" view of Australian history. Whereas the former Labor party prime minister, Paul Keating, argued that white Australians needed to accept their culpability for the devastation wrought on Australia's indigenous people, Howard would absolve white Australia of all responsibility, instead proclaiming that the country has a proud history. The contrast between the two leaders could not be more complete. In a famous speech in 1992, launching the Council for Aboriginal Reconciliation, then–prime minister Keating passionately argued that reconciliation

> begins, I think, with the act of recognition. Recognition that it was we who did the dispossessing. We took the traditional lands and smashed the traditional way of life. We brought the disasters. The alcohol. We committed the murders. We took the children from their mothers. We practiced discrimination and exclusion. It was our ignorance and our prejudice. And our failure to imagine these things being done to us. With some noble exceptions, we failed to make the most basic human response and enter into their hearts and minds. We failed to ask — how would I feel if

---

22. Australian Institute of Criminology Study, cited in Aboriginal Justice Advisory Council, News, Mar. 2001.
23. Elliot Johnson, Report of the Royal Commission into Aboriginal Deaths in Custody (1991).

this were done to me? As a consequence, we failed to see that what we were doing degraded all of us.[24]

By contrast, Howard was dragged kicking and screaming into making what was termed "an historic statement of regret" to the Australian parliament in 1999 for Australia's past treatment of its Aboriginal peoples. The power of the resolution was diluted because the prime minister made clear that this was not an apology and that it would entail no compensation. Some victims of the most terrible government policies — such as those who were removed from their natural families as children — have brought cases before the courts at a state and federal level. So far these claims have not been successful, but hope persists in some quarters that eventually Aboriginal people will get legal redress.

Thus far, at least, the judiciary has had a better record than the legislature at upholding Aboriginal rights, but, considering how little the Australian parliament has done, that is not really saying a lot. In 1992, in the *Mabo* decision, the High Court for the first time recognized that in certain circumstances where Aborigines could demonstrate a "continuous connection" to a piece of land they could then assert native title to that land.[25] The case was considered a landmark because it overturned the doctrine of "terra nullius," but its practical effect was limited because of the stringent test the court established as necessary to prove a "continuous connection" to a piece of land. So while the decision was widely praised, for the vast majority of Aboriginal Australians, who had long been dispossessed of their land, including the more than 80 percent who live in urban areas, it had, at most, symbolic significance. A later decision in the *Wik* case generated more controversy.[26] In that case, the court extended its earlier ruling and held that native title was not extinguished by pastoral leases, a decision that caused a furor among the landed aristocracy and that resulted in government legislation that effectively overruled the decision.

This legislation prompted a group of black Australians to bring a claim before the United Nations, arguing that Australia was in violation of the United Nations Convention against Racial Discrimination. In a controversial decision, the United Nations Committee on the Elimination of Racial Discrimination found that Australia was indeed in violation of the convention — the first western nation ever to be found in violation — and asked the government to "please explain" its conduct; the Australian government has refused to consider this invitation. In a reaction not unlike that of many white South Africans when the international community imposed economic sanctions in their country, many white Australians expressed resentment at the United Nations' intervention in their "domestic affairs."

Many white Australians, who have little if any contact with black Australians, are appallingly ignorant of the condition of blacks in Australia, and myths about black identity, in particular, abound. Because of the systematic rape of black Australian women by white men, for instance, as well as the official government policy of assimilation and the high rate of intermarriage between black and white

---

24. Paul Keating, Dec. 10, 1992, available at http://apology.west.net.au/redfern.html.
25. Mabo v. Queensland (No. 2), 175 C.L.R. 1 (1992).
26. Wik Peoples v. Queensland, 134 A.L.R. 637 (1996).

Australians, many Aborigines, particularly those who live in urban centers, are of light complexion. Many white Australians believe that these Aborigines are not really "black" and that they claim to be Aboriginal only to gain special privileges. Historically, the federal and state governments have used definitions of Aboriginality based on percentages of blood, producing results that were both brutal and inconsistent. Child removal policies often targeted children with lighter skin, as they were thought to be more "assimilable."

In contrast to the United States, however, and in parallel with South Africa, a person of some black heritage was historically much more likely to be defined as white than as black. Australia had no equivalent to the "one drop" rule. This was in keeping with the policy of assimilation, and it means that today many Australians have Aboriginal heritage of which they are unaware. Because of the enormous disadvantage associated with being defined as black, many Aboriginal people historically have "passed" as white. Many are only now reclaiming the heritage that was denied to them for so long, which explains why the percentage of people identifying themselves as Aboriginal has increased in recent census counts. (Although, in any case, as for blacks in the United States, black Australians have historically been undercounted.) Today, the government uses a three-part definition of Aboriginality that is generally accepted by black Australians; it provides that "an Aboriginal or Torres Strait Islander person is a person of Aboriginal or Torres Strait Islander descent who identifies as an Aboriginal or Torres Strait Islander and is accepted as such by the community in which he or she lives."

The question of black Australian identity at the dawn of the twenty-first century is a complex one. Aboriginal leaders throughout the 1960s and up to today have looked to the black struggle in the United States for inspiration. Today, however, many younger Aboriginal leaders question this identification and have aligned themselves more closely with indigenous peoples around the world, such as with Native Americans, for example. This trend has been reflected in the political struggles on which Aboriginal leaders have focused. In recent years, they have increasingly focused on land rights and a treaty, though, of course, civil rights issues are still very much a part of the black agenda.

Dr. Sykes points to the uniqueness of the Aboriginal identity: Aboriginal Australians are at once black and indigenous. Their struggle is likewise unique, at once having similarities and differences with the struggles of black Americans and Native Americans. Nothing better illustrates the current debate over Aboriginal identity than the controversy that currently surrounds Dr. Sykes herself. It has long been known that Dr. Sykes's mother was white and, although her father was not personally known to her, she always maintained that he was Aboriginal. In fact, it has emerged that Dr. Sykes's father was more likely an African American serviceman stationed in Australia during World War II. In the wake of this revelation, Dr. Sykes has faced a barrage of criticism from both black and white Australians. That this should be an issue of controversy at all is interesting, since for a long time black Australians identified almost completely with black Americans. That it is controversial speaks to the fact that Aboriginal Australians now wish to assert an identity separate and different from that of African Americans.

This is not to deny the very strong pull that the African American experience has for many Aboriginal Australians. Young black Australians often dress in a manner similar to that adopted by young black Americans; they listen to hip-hop and admire black American athletes. In 1998, Minister Louis Farrakhan visited Australia for the specific purpose of meeting with Aboriginal leaders, and he clearly saw the plight of Aboriginal Australians as analogous to that of American blacks. When Minister Farrakhan visited the inner-city neighborhood of Redfern in Sydney, he was greeted with cries of "Brother" and received an exceptionally warm welcome.[27] Minister Farrakhan's visit was enormously controversial within Australia because of his reputation for anti-Semitism. Indeed, he was almost denied a visa because the government claimed they feared he would make statements in violation of Australia's racial vilification laws. Clearly, the government's real concern was that Farrakhan would draw unfavorable media attention to the plight of Aboriginal Australians. In reality, the visit drew little coverage in either the Australian or international press. Notwithstanding this, the plight of Aboriginal Australians has definitely become more visible in the wake of the Sydney 2000 Olympic games and the international success of movies such as *Rabbit Proof Fence*. Australia is also currently the country du jour in the United States, with Australian actors and musicians more visible than ever before on the world stage. The country itself is experiencing a surge in international tourism. With visibility, of course, comes power, and black Australians are hoping they can use the attention trained on their country to finally gain the redress to which they are entitled.

§11.3.2 The Maori of New Zealand

Like Australia, New Zealand is a majority white nation located in the heart of the Asia-Pacific. New Zealand shares much in common with its larger neighbor, although, with a total population of just over 3 million,[28] it is much smaller. (Sydney, Australia's largest city, has a population of more than 4 million, and the total Australian population is more than 20 million.[29]) Today, New Zealand's population is more than 80 percent white.[30] The oldest inhabitants of New Zealand are the Maori, a people whose ancestors settled the previously unoccupied land in a series of migrations from eastern Polynesia starting some thousand years ago. Ethnically and linguistically, the Maori share much in common with other Polynesian peoples who inhabit South Pacific islands such as Hawaii and Fiji.

The Maori are made up of more than 40 distinct tribes sharing a common language (in contrast to Australia, with more than 200 Aboriginal languages). Before the white colonization of New Zealand in the late eighteenth century, and despite their shared language, there was considerably less sense of shared Maori identity than there is today. Today, while important differences remain in

27. Nadia Jamal, "Aboriginal Misery Is Shame of Australia Says Farrakhan," Sydney Morning Herald, Feb. 16, 1999.
28. United Nations, Population and Vital Statistics Report, 1983.
29. Id.
30. Richard Mulgan, Politics in New Zealand 29 (1994).

the interests and culture of the Maori people, a much stronger sense of Maori solidarity has developed, partly as a means of defending Maori culture and institutions against the white colonizers. (In the Maori language, New Zealanders of European origin are called "Pakeha" and New Zealand is known as "Aotearoa," meaning the land of the long white cloud.)

The Maori make up almost 15 percent of the New Zealand population.[31] Other minorities, such as Pacific Islanders and Asian immigrants, together make up another 5 percent of the population.[32] For a long time, the view persisted that the history of race relations in New Zealand was a harmonious one in which the interests of Maori were taken into account and respected. This view is wrong and ignores the massive injustices suffered by the Maori population both historically and in the present day. It is true that the Maori were able to negotiate a better deal than many indigenous peoples, but, given the deplorable treatment of indigenous peoples in general, this is not saying a great deal.

The critically acclaimed movie, *Once Were Warriors*, searingly portrays the contemporary condition of Maori in New Zealand. The movie depicts, in unflinching terms, the devastating impact of European colonization on Maori institutions and the Maori way of life. Today, using most indicators of socioeconomic well-being, Maori are considerably worse off than most New Zealanders. The Maori unemployment rate is almost three times the national average; they comprise almost half the prison population; the infant mortality rate is far higher than for white New Zealanders; and life expectancy is much lower than for the white population.[33]

It is clear then — and today most New Zealanders would accept this proposition — that white colonization has had a devastating impact on the Maori. Many important differences, however, distinguish the Maori experience from that of other colonized peoples. Unlike Australian Aborigines, the Maori experienced no widespread genocide, and Maori children were not forcibly removed from their families. Maori were also not systematically removed from their lands; more commonly, land was relinquished to the colonists in trades (the terms of which were often, however, disadvantageous to the Maori). The rate of intermarriage between Maori and European New Zealanders is higher than for any indigenous people anywhere, and overt racism against the Maori is far less common than against black Australians and Americans.

Like Aboriginal Australians, and unlike Native Americans, today more than 80 percent of Maori live in urban areas. Unlike Aboriginal Australians, Maori do not identify themselves as black, nor do they look to the black struggle in the United States as a model for their own struggle. In New Zealand, as in Australia, the race debate is less formalized, and minorities are not as easily fitted into constructed categories such as "black" and "white." If Maori identify themselves as anything other than Maori, it would be as indigenous, Polynesian, or "brown." Maori often call themselves "tangata whenua," or "people of the land." While they might define themselves in opposition to the predominant white culture, it is

31. Id. at 32.
32. Id.
33. Id. at 26.

more common for them to speak in terms of partnership. Within that concept, however, the idea of a distinct, coequal Maori culture is central. Increasingly, that notion is being expressed through the idea of "Maori sovereignty" or "Maori self-determination."

While the idea that New Zealand has had a harmonious history in the area of race relations is clearly false, it is certainly true that the Maori are better integrated into New Zealand politics and society than are the Aborigines in Australia. This is undoubtedly partly due to the fact that the Maori comprise a larger percentage of the population. Maori hold a number of seats in the New Zealand parliament (some seats are especially reserved for Maori representatives), although still in numbers far less than their proportion of the general population. A recent deputy prime minister, Winston Peters, is Maori. In Australia, by contrast, only two Aborigines have served as senators at the federal level (only one is currently in office) and no Aborigine has been a member of the federal House of Representatives.

Unlike the United States and Australia, New Zealand has no history of de jure legal discrimination. Under the Treaty of Waitangi ("Te Tiriti.o Waitangi") of 1840, the Maori acquired the full rights and privileges of British subjects. The Treaty of Waitangi comprises just three short articles and, despite New Zealand's essentially Westminster-style democracy, it is regarded by many today as one of New Zealand's most important founding constitutional documents. By the first article, Maori transferred sovereignty to Queen Victoria; the second article retained to Maori the "full and undisturbed possession of their lands, forests, fisheries and other properties"; and by the third, all Maori were declared to be British subjects.

Two versions of the treaty were made: one in English, the other in Maori. Crucially, they didn't say the same thing. Under the Maori version of the treaty, Maori ceded something rather less than sovereignty and retained "rangatiratanga" — full and complete chieftainship or authority — over their lands. In the aftermath of the treaty, protracted land wars took place between the colonizers and the Maori, the end result of which was further devastating confiscation or loss of tribal lands. The Maori population declined dramatically over the course of the nineteenth century, primarily due to introduced diseases, although in recent decades the population has grown considerably.

For a long time, so far as the legal system was concerned, the treaty had no status at all. In an infamous nineteenth-century case, it was declared a "simple nullity."[34] Over time, however, Maori came to focus on the treaty as the measure of the wrongs that must be repaired in respect of land, forests, water, fisheries, and human rights for the Maori people. In the 1960s and 1970s, widespread demonstrations in protested the injustices suffered by the Maori people. In an attempt to meet some of the protestors' claims, the government in 1975 set up the Waitangi Tribunal as an independent statutory body charged with hearing and inquiring into claims by Maori of injustice on the part of the Crown. It had the power only to make recommendations to the government, not to make final decisions. To begin with,

---

34. Wi Pa Rata v. Bishop of Wellington, 3 Jur (N.S.) SC 72, 78 (1877).

it was limited to investigating grievances that occurred after its establishment in 1975. A decade later, in 1985, the government responded to political pressure from Maori groups by extending its jurisdiction to cover all grievances arising since the Treaty of Waitangi was signed in 1840. Within two years of this change, the number of claims awaiting hearing went from around 40 to 200; by 1993, the number of outstanding claims awaiting hearing totaled 350.[35]

In the late 1980s, the New Zealand government began a process of selling off government assets, many of which were already, or could be in the future, subject to Maori claims before the tribunal. The Maori were concerned that once the assets were out of government hands they would have no means of redress. They brought a case challenging the legality of proposed sales by seeking enforcement of a provision of the legislation that the government had thought relatively ineffectual.[36] As a result of prior negotiations, the statute had been amended to include the phrase, "Nothing in this Act shall permit the Crown to act contrary to the principles of the Treaty of Waitangi."

The Court held that this prohibited the government from carrying out sales of certain crown assets without negotiating with the Maori a mechanism for protecting present and future claims to those assets. The Court enumerated a number of important principles derived from the treaty. First, they held that the government had the right to make laws, but that it must accord Maori appropriate priority in that process; second, the Maori retained the right to manage their resources and treasures; and, third, the government was required to respect the principles of equality, of cooperation, and of redress. All of this meant that the Crown had to accept that it had failed its treaty partner and was legally obligated to make redress.

In response to this decision and subsequent decisions extending the application of the principles, the government decided that it needed to institute a political solution, and, in 1994, it proposed a "fiscal envelope" of one billion dollars for full and final settlement of all Maori claims. This proposal was unpopular with Maori who found problematic the idea that all claims were to be finalized (particularly since the total dollar amount of the claims was far in excess of $1 billion). They also resented that the government thought it could dictate terms of the settlement. In the aftermath of the offer, a number of claims have been negotiated with the government, which appears to be accepting the Maori position that no dollar cap should apply to the settling of claims.

Clearly then, the New Zealand government has been more responsive to Maori claims than the Australian government has been to aboriginal claims, though New Zealand has a long way to go to in recognizing the devastating impact of white colonization on the Maori people. The recognition by both the New Zealand Court of Appeal and the parliament that a substantial settlement is called for — and that any compensation has to go beyond just land rights — should, however, not be underestimated. The Australian government has yet to recognize this reality.

---

35. Id. at 167ff.
36. NZ Maori Council v. Attorney General (1987).

§11.4 NONBLACK RACIAL MINORITIES IN THE UNITED STATES

§11.4.1 The Chinese

The Chinese were the first Asians to immigrate to California. Primarily laborers from Kwantung Province, they emigrated from China to escape the great hardships that followed the Taiping Rebellion of 1850 to 1864. The discovery of gold at Sutter's Mill in 1848 greatly increased the attractiveness of California for the Chinese. By 1879, the Chinese population of California exceeded 111,000.[1] Much of the immigration was the product of the "coolie trade," an arrangement by which Chinese laborers were imported under contracts that amounted to a form of slavery.[2]

The laborers quickly filled California's existing labor vacuums, and they provided an exceedingly cheap, efficient labor force. Responsible for the completion of such construction as the Central Pacific Railroad, the Chinese have been credited with much of California's subsequent prosperity. By 1860, however, they outnumbered the other immigrant groups in California and had earned the animosity of white labor groups by being "too efficient."[3]

The Democratic and Republican parties were evenly matched at this period, and the labor vote of California was crucial to them. A contest soon developed as to which party was more anti-Chinese. Not surprisingly, a correlation existed between the economic situation and the level of anti-Chinese agitation.[4] The California legislature passed laws and regulations designed specifically to create social and economic hardships for the Chinese. The statutes ranged from a "foreign miner's tax" to a "police tax" and a "cubic air" ordinance. Virtually all of these laws were eventually declared unconstitutional, including the San Francisco ordinance requiring operators of frame laundries to obtain a license. This law, which appeared fair on its face but which actually was applied only to Chinese, resulted in the famous equal protection decision Yick Wo v. Hopkins.[5]

Two important court decisions, however, were the source of great trouble to the Chinese. In 1854, the California Supreme Court ruled that the laws of the state intentionally excluded all people of color from giving evidence in court either for or against a white person, and, in 1867, a federal court held that the Chinese aliens

§11.4   1. See S. W. Kung, Chinese in American Life, 3, 30, 66 (1962).

2. Gunther Barth, Bitter Strength 56-58 (1964).

3. Kung, supra note 1, at 68; Carey McWilliams, Brothers Under the Skin 102 (rev. ed. 1964).

4. See generally Ronald Takaki, Strangers from a Different Shore 79-130 (1989) (documenting the treatment of Chinese immigrants in nineteenth-century America).

5. 118 U.S. 356 (1886). See also United States v. Wong Kim Ark, 169 U.S. 649 (1898), establishing that a Chinese born in the United States is a citizen, regardless of whether his parents are aliens. Ho Ali Kow v. Noonan, 12 F. Cas. 252 (No. 6,546) (C.C.D. Cal. 1876), invalidated the infamous "queue ordinance." Kung, supra note 1, at 22, explains that under this ordinance every male imprisoned in the county jail was required to have his hair cut to a uniform length of one inch from the scalp. As was well known, the custom of wearing queues was observed by practically every Chinese. The Chinese community aggressively posed sophisticated legal challenges to the grossly discriminatory legal restrictions imposed on them. See Charles J. McClain, In Search of Equality (1994) (reviewing their ultimately losing efforts to fight law with law).

were not eligible for naturalization.[6] To achieve their objective of excluding Asians, the anti-Chinese forces realized that federal action was necessary. As a result of their political pressure, a joint special committee was appointed by Congress to study the "Chinese problem" in California. This committee concluded, in an oft-quoted report, that the presence of Chinese in California was advantageous to the capitalists but deleterious to the laboring classes. It also concluded that the intelligence of the Chinese was inferior to that of other races, including Negroes, and that coolies were men of vice; it recommended that they be denied naturalization and suffrage. The Fifteen Passengers Bill, which limited to 15 the number of immigrants that a ship could bring from China, was proposed and passed by Congress. It was vetoed, however, by the President, who considered it a violation of the Burlingame Treaty with China. This 1868 treaty did not give the Chinese the right to enter the United States (no treaty was needed for this purpose, since it was not until 1875 that Congress began to restrict immigration), but it recognized the "inalienable right" of man to change his home and allegiance as well as the "mutual advantage of the free migration of their citizens and subjects respectively from the one country to the other for purposes of curiosity, of trade, or as permanent residents."[7] This treaty was negotiated in 1880 to permit the United States to "regulate, limit, or suspend" the entrance of Chinese laborers, but "not to absolutely prohibit it." The power of interpretation was left to Congress, although it was provided that "the limitation or suspension shall be reasonable."[8]

The Chinese Exclusion Act of 1882[9] became the first exclusively racial immigration law.[10] It was meant to carry into effect the treaty of 1880 by "suspending" the immigration of Chinese laborers for 10 years. It provided, however, that the Chinese laborers who had been in the United States since 1880 or who were to come within 90 days of the act's passage had the right to depart from the United States and reenter with an identifying certificate. In 1884, it was established that these certificates were the only permissible evidence in establishing a right of reentry.[11]

The Scott Act of 1888 declared void all outstanding certificates (at the time, numbering at least twenty thousand) and barred from reentering the United States all Chinese laborers who had not done so before its passage.[12] The Supreme Court upheld this act in the "Chinese Exclusion Case."[13] Although the Court conceded that the act contravened the treaties made with China, it held that treaties are not

---

6. People v. Hall, 4 Cal. Rep. 399 (1854). The Californian Supreme Court overturned the conviction of a white man convicted of killing a Chinese American because the conviction was based on the testimony of Chinese persons.

7. See Milton Konvitz, The Alien and the Asiatic in American Law 5 (1946).

8. Act of May 6, 1882, 22 Stat. 826.

9. 22 Stat. 58.

10. The second session of the first Congress, on March 26, 1790, enacted a naturalization law confining the right of becoming citizens to "aliens being free white persons." The law was cited by Chief Justice Taney in Dred Scott v. Taney, 60 U.S. (19 How.) 393, 419 (1857), supporting his conclusion that Africans, whether free or slave, were not intended by the Founding Fathers to hold citizenship.

11. Act of July 5, 1884, 9, 3 Stat. 115.

12. Act of Sept. 13, 1888, 25 Stat. 476.

13. Chae Chan Ping v. United States, 130 U.S. 581 (1889).

superior but equal to acts of Congress, and, therefore, the last expression of sovereign will controlled. It ruled that the power to exclude aliens is incident to sovereignty, which is delegated by the Constitution. The Court also held that the vested property rights are unaffected by the abrogation of a treaty, finding that it would be most mischievous if vested property rights could be so nullified.

The Geary Act of 1892 extended the suspension for an additional 10 years, and, in 1902, the suspension was converted into permanent exclusion.[14] The Act of 1892 provided that all Chinese laborers lawfully in the United States were required to obtain certificates of residence or face deportation. The Chinese raised large sums of money to sponsor litigation challenging the constitutionality of the act, but the Supreme Court upheld the Geary Act. The Court held that the determination of Congress was conclusive on the judiciary, and that the government has the inalienable right to expel all of any class of aliens, "absolutely or upon certain conditions, in war or in peace."[15] In its opinion, the Court referred to the unassimilable character of the Chinese in the United States. In 1927, the Court found that no equal protection violation resulted from the exclusion of a child with some Chinese blood from white schools under state law.[16] The United States entered the Second World War as an ally of China, and, the wrath of the nation being turned on Japan, American hostility to the Chinese was reduced. This change of heart, together with a goodwill visit by Madam Chiang Kai-shek, led to the repeal of the exclusion acts, although not without strenuous opposition. The Act of 1943 repealed all previous exclusion acts and established a token quota of one hundred Chinese immigrants.[17] This act was also a counter to Japanese propaganda against the United States. The Chinese gained the right of naturalization and were thus taken out of the category of citizens "ineligible for naturalization," a phrase used in discriminatory laws against Asians. The law remained prejudicial, however, in that only Asians did not fall under the "national origins" system. A Chinese immigrant was put under the Chinese quota even though his national origin was English or Malayan. In 1952, the Walter-McCarren Act was passed over bitter debate and a presidential veto.[18] The act retained the national origins system, but special racial quotas were established for Chinese and other Asians indigenous to a geographical Pacific triangle, drawn to include most Asian nations.

It was not until 1965 that an amendment to the 1952 Act eliminated the discrimination against Asians in the immigration laws.[19] Specifically, the 1965 Act abolished the special immigration restrictions relating to Asians and forbade discrimination because of race, sex, nationality, place of birth, or place of residence. These amendments, as well as special provisions to allow Chinese immigrants to enter the country as refugees, have enabled the number of Chinese entering the United States to increase tremendously. Ironically, the sudden flow

14. Act of May 5, 1892, 27 Stat. 25, 26, repealed, Dec. 17, 1943.
15. Fong Yue Ting v. United States, 149 U.S. 698 (1893).
16. Gong Lum v. Rice, 275 U.S. 78 (1927).
17. Act of Dec. 17, 1943, 57 Stat. 600.
18. Act of June 27, 1952, Pub. L. No. 82-414, 66 Stat. 163, 8 U.S.C. §§1101 et seq. See Higham, American Immigration Policy in Historical Perspective, 21 Law & Contemp. Prob. 235 (1956).
19. Act of Oct. 3, 1985, Pub. L. No. 89-236, 79 Stat. 911.

of immigrants has severely strained the social fabric of Chinese communities, to the point of disintegration, but this problem stems from a different source than racial discrimination against immigrants, unless, of course, Chinatowns themselves are viewed as products of discrimination.[20] The "Chinese Exclusion Cases," as they are called, have been brought to attention in the wake of September 11 and the anti-Asian/anti-immigrant backlash that resulted. This topic is discussed in more detail in §11.5.

Presently, it appears that all the racial discrimination in the immigration and nationality laws has been eliminated. In a sense, the Chinese alien's problems have been diffused and have become a part of the general "alien's problem." As for the immigration laws as a whole, serious issues of due process and equal protection remain.[21] In administering immigration laws, administrative agencies have much discretion. The Department of State, which issues the visas to aliens, has almost complete control over the number of aliens entering, since applicants have no recourse against a consul's denial of a visa. Thus, as with the Native Americans, the Court's willingness to defer to Congressional "plenary power" remains a serious problem.[22]

Beyond problems of immigration, the Chinese in the United States are still widely thought to be intimately tied to China, and, as their history would seem to indicate, the discrimination faced by Americans of Chinese ancestry is in large part determined by Americans' attitudes towards China.[23] Professor Taunya Banks discusses interminority racial bias by tracing how the Chinese in Mississippi, who while a marginalized group when imported to work in the post–Civil War period gained status as shopkeepers serving the black community, subsequently developed the prejudices against blacks held by the whites who dominated them both.[24]

§11.4.2   The Japanese

The Japanese, who in 1890 began immigrating to the United States in large numbers, arrived on the West Coast at one of the most inopportune periods in American history. Anti-Chinese feeling had reached its peak, and this hostility was easily transferred to the new Asian arrivals. Japan stunned the world with her victory in the Russo-Japanese War of 1905, and the military strength that Japan had displayed aroused fears of a "Yellow peril" in the United States.[25]

In 1906, the San Francisco Board of Education, then controlled by the Labor party, decided to enforce an ordinance passed the previous year that would segregate the city's Asian children. In the context of events, the school board's action

20. See Chin, New York Chinatown Today: Community in Crisis, 1 Amerasia J. (Mar. 1971).
21. See Rosenfield, 1 Immigration Law (rev. 1970).
22. See Gabriel J. Chin, Segregation's Last Stronghold: Race Discrimination and the Constitutional Law of Immigration, 46 UCLA L. Rev. 1 (1998).
23. See Paula C. Johnson, The Social Construction of Identity in Criminal Cases: Cinéma Vérité and the Pedagogy of Vincent Chin, 1 Mich. J. Race & L. 347 (1996).
24. Taunya Lovell Banks, Both Edges of the Margin: Blacks and Asians in Mississippi Masala, Barriers to Coalition Building, 5 Asian L.J. 7 (1998).
25. McWilliams, supra note 3, at 142-145.

was highly, and intentionally, provocative. Protests were lodged in Washington, and President Theodore Roosevelt denounced the ordinance as a "wicked absurdity."

A suit by the Attorney General to enjoin the enforcement of the ordinance was never brought to trial, since President Roosevelt had negotiated the Gentlemen's Agreement (by which the Japanese government had agreed to restrict the flow of Japanese immigrants entering the United States), and the appeased school board agreed not to enforce the ordinance. California racists were not satisfied, however, and began to scream about a loophole in the agreement that allowed the importation of Japanese "picture brides." The fears of a Mongoloid invasion and contamination rose, and the Japanese immigrants, seeing this, petitioned the Japanese government not to allow any more Japanese women to come to the United States, in order to preserve the status quo of the Gentlemen's Agreement.[26]

But racism and exclusion need not take the form of exclusion acts; in 1913, California enacted the Alien Land Laws. Many states followed suit. The laws were designed to prevent Japanese immigrants from earning a living in agriculture, thereby driving them out of the state. The Japanese had filled the agricultural labor vacuum in California, and again their fault was that they were "too efficient" and provided stiff competition for other agricultural laborers. The first Alien Land Law was enacted in 1913, and its constitutionality was established during the following decade. Nevertheless, for a number of years prior to World War II, enforcement was only halfhearted. Legal loopholes, administrative inactivity, and public indifference enabled Japanese aliens to circumvent many of the prohibitions. Although they were excluded from the labor movement and from many businesses, their ingenuity and hard work nevertheless enabled the Japanese to do well in small farming and merchandizing.

But in the 1920s, the Alien Land Laws did not seem sufficiently restrictive to many Americans, and in 1924 an exclusion act was passed. The Quota Act of 1924 excluded from immigration "aliens ineligible to citizenship."[27] Japanese aliens were not to gain the right to citizenship until the Walter-McCarren Act of 1952. Since the Chinese were already excluded, the 1924 Act was obviously aimed at Japanese immigrants. Japan's sense of honor was greatly offended. She was still suffering from the Tokyo earthquake, and the exclusion act was viewed as the direct opposite of Japan's response to America's similar tragedy. (Japan had sent generous assistance to San Francisco in the aftermath of *its* earthquake, just before the San Francisco School Board incident.) This direct affront has been cited many times as one of the major factors that enabled the military to gain the upper band in the Japanese government, leading eventually to World War II.[28]

The Japanese attacked Pearl Harbor on December 7, 1941. The next day, December 8, 1941, the United States declared war on Japan, and all Japanese aliens were classified as "enemy aliens." On February 19, 1942, President Franklin Roosevelt issued Executive Order 9066, "giving authority to certain military commanders to prescribe military areas from which any or all persons may be excluded,

26. Id. at 146.
27. Act of May 26, 1924, 43 Stat. 153, 8 U.S.C. §§201 et seq.
28. See William Hosokawa, Nisei: The Quiet American 112-113 (1969).

and with respect to which the right to enter, remain in, or leave, shall be subject to the discretion of the military commander," Lieutenant General John L. DeWitt.[29] Executive Order 9102 established the War Relocation Authority on March 18, 1942.[30] Significantly enough, certain pressure groups—the Western Growers Protective Association, the American Legion, the Native Sons of the Golden West, and various other groups—actively promoted the campaign to evacuate the Japanese. Some other pressure groups were the Grower-Shipper Vegetable Association, the Associated Farmers, and the California Farm Bureau. Carey McWilliams has written:

> There is an irony about mass evacuation which has somehow escaped attention. The economic vulnerability of the Japanese on the West Coast made their removal possible and this vulnerability had been brought about largely by external pressures and discriminations. In Hawaii the Japanese were not nearly so vulnerable; indeed they were the mainstay of the economic life of the Islands and hence could not be evacuated. . . . Mass evacuation was not the product of wartime hysteria; it was the logical end-product, the goal, of a strategy of dominance which began forty years earlier and which was closely related to a similar strategy of American dominance in the Pacific. The resident Japanese were always the hostages of this larger strategy.[31]

Three cases were brought before the Supreme Court to test the constitutionality of the orders in three aspects: the curfew, the evacuation, and the internment. The first case, Hirabyashi v. United States,[32] presented the question whether the curfew restriction of March 24, 1942, adopted by General DeWitt, was based on an unconstitutional delegation by Congress of its legislative power and whether it unconstitutionally discriminated between citizens of Japanese ancestry and those of other ancestries, in violation of the Fifth Amendment. The Court acknowledged the hardships imposed by the exclusion order on a large group of American citizens, but it affirmed the validity of the restriction, stating:

> We cannot say that these facts and circumstances, considered in the particular war setting, could afford no ground for differentiating citizens of Japanese ancestry from other groups in the United States. . . . We cannot close our eyes to the fact, demonstrated by experience, that in time of war residents having ethnic affiliations with an invading enemy may be a greater source of danger than those of a different ancestry.

In Korematsu v. United States,[33] the Court sustained the constitutionality of the evacuation order in a six-to-three decision. In Justice Murphy's dissenting opinion, DeWitt was quoted as saying before a congressional committee: "I don't want any of them here. They are a dangerous element. . . . It makes no difference whether he is an American citizen, he is still a Japanese. . . . But we must worry about the Japanese all the time until he is wiped off the map."

---

29. Executive Order No. 9066, 7 Fed. Reg. 1407.
30. Executive Order No. 9102 and Executive Order No. 9066, 7 Fed. Reg. 1407.
31. McWilliams, supra note 3, at 164.
32. 320 U.S. 81, 101-102 (1943).
33. 323 U.S. 214, 235 n.2 (dissenting opinion) (1944).

The same day that the *Korematsu* case was decided, the Supreme Court also considered the case of Ex parte Endo,[34] which tested the internment order. Endo sought release, on a writ of habeas corpus, from a War Relocation Authority camp. The Court upheld the writ, but only on extremely narrow grounds: that the detention was not authorized by the Congress or the President. The constitutional question was expressly avoided.

Subsequent research by Peter Irons has revealed that the government fraudulently concealed its actual reasons for the internment of Japanese-American citizens from the Supreme Court during the litigation challenging the internment orders.[35] While the Japanese were interned, much of their property was confiscated, stolen, or escheated. Little compensation was given. One writer reports:

> On July 2, 1948, President Truman signed into law the Japanese American Evacuation Claims Act. The evacuees were given until January 3, 1950, to file claims against the government. By that deadline they filed 23,689 claims asking a total of $131,949,176 — one third of the sum the Federal Reserve Bank had estimated they had lost. . . . In all, some, $38,000,000 was paid out in evacuation claims — less than 10 cents for every dollar lost. Furthermore, claims were made on the basis of 1942 prices, and payment was made in inflated postwar dollars. In terms of reduced purchasing power, the evacuees were paid only a nickel in compensation for every dollar they had lost as a direct consequence of the evacuation.[36]

In addition to loss of freedom, property, educational opportunities, businesses, and employment income, the 120,000 people of Japanese ancestry interned, more than two-thirds of whom were native-born American citizens, were subjected to onerous living conditions. They were forced to wear identification tags; and many suffered disease and hardship from exposure to the elements, poor sanitation, and an inadequate diet. Exposed to such conditions for up to four years, many died. In addition to disruption of familiar life and customs, they lost all rights to privacy, even to the extent of performing ordinary bodily functions. The interns had no freedom of expression or ability to communicate freely with others outside the camps and were denied the right to use the Japanese language or to read Japanese literature other than the Bible and the dictionary. Nevertheless, they had to swear an oath of loyalty to the United States as a condition of their release.[37] In analyzing the overall effect of the wartime cases, Eugene Rostow has written:

> What the Supreme Court has done in these cases, especially in *Korematsu v. U.S.*, is to increase the strength of the military in relation to civil government. It has upheld an act of military power without a factual record in which the justification for the act was analyzed. Thus, it has created doubt as to the standards of responsibility to which the

34. 323 U.S. 283 (1944).
35. See Peter Irons, Justice at War vii-ix (1983).
36. Hosokawa, supra note 28, at 445-447. Compensation under the act was paid only for loss of property that could be proved by records, 50 U.S.C. app. §1983(b). And once a claim was paid, the claimant waived all rights to make any further claims against the United States arising out of the evacuation. 50 U.S.C. app. §1984(d).
37. See Robert Wesley, Symposium: The Long Shadow of *Korematsu*, Many Billions Gone: Is It Time to Reconsider the Case for Black Reparations?, 40 B.C. L. Rev. 429, 449-450 (1998).

military power will be held. For the first time in American legal history, the Court has seriously weakened the protection of our basic civil right, the writ of habeas corpus.[38]

The ease with which federal authorities had succumbed to old wives' tales about Black Dragon societies, emperor worship, and sabotage cults endowed anti-Nipponism with an intellectual acceptability that it had not possessed during earlier periods. Moreover, the federal program for relocation of the Japanese in 1942 provided an unparalleled opportunity for the state governments to conduct investigations and to adopt plans for systematic discrimination against the Japanese upon their return. Both the *Korematsu* decision itself and the United States' shameful history of internment of Japanese Americans has taken on new relevance, unfortunately, in light of the post–September 11 increase in anti-Asian violence and the institutionalization of ethnically motivated government processes such as the Special Registration Program, which is discussed in detail at the end of the chapter.

Accordingly, both the California and Oregon legislatures amended their laws during the war years so as to provide for stricter control of Japanese land ownership, and in 1945 the Attorney General of California was given an appropriation to expedite: investigation by the counties of evasion of the Alien Land Law. Upon ascertainment of evasion, the state, in conjunction with the county, was to institute escheat proceedings divided between state and county.

Such proceedings received judicial sanction by California courts but were struck down by the Supreme Court in Oyama v. California.[39] By a six-to-three decision, the Court ruled that the escheat action was unconstitutional because it was a denial of equal protection to the citizens in whose name the alien father had placed his property. The *Oyama* case established the escheat action as unconstitutional. Later litigation voided the Alien Land Law.

In another important case, Takahashi v. Fish and Game Commission,[40] the right of Issei (first-generation Japanese immigrants) to engage in commercial fishing was upheld by the Supreme Court. California had denied commercial fishing licenses to "aliens ineligible to citizenship" on the pretext that this was a conservation measure. The question presented was: Can California, consistently with the Constitution, use this federally created racial ineligibility for citizenship as a basis for barring Takahashi from earning his living as a commercial fisherman? The Supreme Court held that this violated the Equal Protection Clause and conflicted with the federal power to regulate immigration.

After great pressure was brought, President Reagan signed the Civil Liberties Act of 1988, setting in motion the statutory means by which Japanese Americans would begin to receive federal reparations payments.[41] Government implementation of the measure has been slow, and it is estimated that only about 60,000

---

38. Eugene Rostow, The Japanese-American Cases — A Disaster, 54 Yale L.J. 489 (1945); see also Konvitz, supra note 7, at 244-276.

39. 332 U.S. 633 (1948). See The Alien Land Laws: A Reappraisal, 56 Yale L.J. 1017-1036 (1946-1947); Anti-Japanese Land Laws of California and Ten Other States, 35 Cal. L. Rev. 7 (1947).

40. 334 U.S. 410 (1948).

41. 50 U.S.C. app. §§1984(b)(4), (d).

survivors or their next of kin will be paid. About half of the internment survivors died before the legislation was passed.[42]

§11.4.3   The Mexicans

When the Mexican American War ended in 1848, approximately 75,000 Spanish-speaking people lived in the borderlands that were now U.S. territory. In these areas (later to become the states of Texas, New Mexico, California, Arizona, and Colorado), immigrants from the south had begun establishing settlements in the early sixteenth century. Santa Fe had been functioning as the capital of "Nuevo Santander" (the Spanish name for New Mexico) for some 20 years before Jamestown was established in 1607. Living in isolation on land that was as yet hardly penetrated by traders and explorers from the eastern states, the settlers had until the 1820s only infrequent contact with Anglos (non-Spanish-speaking people), and this contact had not been antagonistic.

The Southwest Territories passed from Spanish rule to Mexican sovereignty in 1821, when Mexico declared its independence from Spain. Mexico experienced severe internal political problems for about the next twenty years, and these problems culminated with the secession of Texas from Mexico in 1836. Mexico considered the 1845 Act of Annexation, under which Congress allowed Texas to enter the Union, an act of war, and armed conflict ensued in 1846.

The result for the United States of the Mexican American War was the annexation of Texas and the rest of the southwest Territories. The Treaty of Guadalupe Hidalgo, signed on February 2, 1848, codified the secession and annexation of the Southwest Territories. The treaty further guaranteed both the civil and property rights of the Mexicans who agreed to become American citizens. An estimated 75,000 Mexicanos accepted American citizenship, but, as with other "nonwhite" Americans, neither citizenship nor treaties provided protection. Certainly, the treaty failed to protect the Chicano.[43] The borderlands of Mexico, part of a country long regarded by many Americans as poor, degenerate, and uncivilized, fell quickly to the surge of Anglos who migrated there. The war with Mexico had left a heritage of hatred, hostility, and contempt. The Anglos who flooded the southwest had little appreciation for the economic, cultural, and political history of the Chicanos, who fell victim to all the sufferings endured by a conquered people.

The pattern of oppression and discrimination that has characterized Anglo-Hispano relations for more than a century emerged in the course of westward expansion. Anglos were determined to take possession of the land. The pattern was reinforced when the demands of economic development created a need for

42. Wesley, supra note 37, at 451.

43. "Chicano," a diminutive of "mejicano," was first used as a sobriquet, "given in sympathy and exasperation," for the refugees from the Mexican Revolution in the years following 1910. On the inspiration of Rudolfo "Corky" Gonzales, the militants have adopted it to "announce a distinct people, once suppressed but now reclaiming their integrity." John Womack, The Chicanos, N.Y. Review of Books, Aug. 31, 1972, at 12, 14. In the "barrio" (that is, the Mexican American community), the word had long been used to distinguish Mexican Americans from Mexican citizens.

cheap labor, a demand easily filled by successive waves of immigrants from Mexico. In the competition for land and for control over other resources, the provisions of the Treaty of Guadalupe Hidalgo guaranteeing the cultural autonomy and property rights of the Spanish-speaking inhabitants were forgotten.

The arrival of the transcontinental railroads created strong pressures for economic development and increased the competition for control over the land. Mexican Americans were disadvantaged in their struggle for survival, not only by their small numbers (in 1860 they constituted only one tenth of the population of the southwest as a whole), but also by the cultural and geographical isolation they had experienced for generations. The "Spanish Colonials," descendants of the earliest Spanish-speaking settlers, acted as a buffer group between more recent arrivals and the dominant Anglo culture; while they thus helped to soften the impact of an alien and antagonistic social environment, they also impeded the development of group consciousness and self-organization among the Chicano masses.

Protest was not lacking in the nineteenth century, but it was unsuccessful. Courtroom battles were lost, and the few organizations that fought for Mexican American rights — the Knights of Labor, the Gorras Blancos — fought in vain.[44] According to Carey McWilliams, political participation was suppressed by such techniques as withholding statehood from Arizona and New Mexico until 1912 — until, that is, Anglos had achieved numerical superiority. In New Mexico, California, and Texas, the native upper-class Hispanos collaborated with the Anglos and bought off the Chicano masses with favors and minor patronage.[45]

Organizing efforts were more successful after the Mexican Revolution of 1910, which produced a flood of new migrants — some 800,000 between 1910 and 1920. Even so, economic conditions continued to favor the exploitation of cheap labor. Federally financed irrigation of desert lands, which began in 1902, was felt in the mid-1920s when changes in American eating habits created a great demand for fruits and vegetables and new packaging methods made mass production feasible. One writer estimates that Mexican Americans provided about 75 percent of the labor that grew these crops. In addition, between 1910 and 1930, most of the cotton field-workers in Arizona, Texas, and California; 60 percent of the mine workers; and 80 percent of the railroad workers in the western states were Mexican Americans.[46]

With the advent of "agri-business," the farm-village economy disintegrated, and the isolation that had rendered unity difficult came to an end. In addition, self-perception was influenced by revolutionary foment in Mexico: A new pride and self-confidence was born out of identification with the Mexican Indian, rather than from spurious links with the Spanish heritage. The League of Latin American Citizens (LULAC), a "self-improvement" group, was established in 1927, and in 1928 and 1930 migrant workers, organized as the Confederación de Uniones Obreras Mexicanas, staged strikes in southern California. "But the tougher the fights, the uglier the defeats; though LULAC citizened along, the Confederation

44. See Womack, supra note 43, at 12.
45. McWilliams, supra note 3, at 134.
46. Cohen, The Failure of the Melting Pot, in The Great Fear: Race in the Mind of America 150 (Gary Nash & Richard Weiss eds., 1970).

was busted with tear gas and clubs."[47] Strikers were arrested or kidnapped and beaten by the growers' henchmen, and strike leaders were deported. Organized labor discriminated against Mexican Americans by excluding them from established unions and by creating ethnic wage differentials. The availability of "cheap Mexican labor" caused resentment among Anglos who could not exploit it for their own benefit. By the mid-1920s immigration laws were being enforced by "border patrols." Nevertheless, at least half a million Mexicans entered the United States between, 1920 and 1929; this is a conservative estimate, because nothing officially records the number of illegal entrants, which may have reached into in the hundreds of thousands. Agitation increased during the Depression; nearly 500,000 Mexican Americans, probably half of them American citizens, were deported.

World War II marked a turning point: The manpower shortage created by the war meant new opportunities for Chicanos, as did the postwar boom. But entry into higher echelons of the economy did not ensure an end to discrimination or vigilante action. On the contrary, Anglos reacted violently. Shortly after the "relocation" of Japanese Americans, Californians directed their xenophobia at Mexican Americans in a "Campaign of Terror" that culminated in the "Zoot-Suit Riots" of June 1943. For a week, Anglo soldiers, policemen, and civilians rampaged in the Mexican American ghetto of Los Angeles, beating and stabbing their victims, many of whom were then arrested.

Token social reform followed in the wake of economic progress. In 1947, segregated schools for Mexican Americans were outlawed.[48] The Community Services Organization (founded in 1947) and the G1 Forum (1948) reflected increasing self-awareness and self-assertiveness. By the early 1960s, Chicanos were participating with some success in the political process. "Viva Kennedy" clubs brought out the Chicano vote for John F. Kennedy, and Mexican American organizations helped to elect a few congressmen.

Militancy increased in the wake of the civil rights movement. Some money became available to Chicano activists in 1964 and 1965 as a result of the War on Poverty, but the Delano grape strike led by César Chávez undoubtedly had a greater impact on Chicanos than on American society at large. Activism has ranged from unionization of migrant workers to organization of Brown Beret self-defense units in the barrios and walkouts by high school students in protest against racist teachers and curricula. The rallying cry for protest was *la raza* "the people." Later, the movement split into "integrationist" and "separatist" branches. Internal ideological disputes evidenced a sense of success or at least of increased self-confidence.

Response at the federal level has consisted of the Bilingual Education Act[49] — eliminated under No Child Left Behind — and the appointments by the Nixon and subsequent administrations of some Spanish-speaking persons to

---

47. Womack, supra note 43, at 13.

48. Westminster Sch. Dist. v. Mendez, 161 F.2d 774 (9th Cir. 1947); similar action was taken in Texas in 1948, Delgado v. Bastrop Indep. Sch. Dist., Civ. No. 388 (W.D. Tex., June 15, 1948). See Rachel F. Moran, Bilingual Education as a Status Conflict 75 Cal. L. Rev. 321 (1987) (analyzing controversy over bilingual education as conflict over status between Anglos and Latinos).

49. 20 U.S.C. §§880(a) et seq. (1968).

government posts. But a great many Mexican American families still earn a median income of only two-thirds that of Anglo families in the southwest, and millions of Chicanos in that region are living at a subsistence level. Now about 80 percent urbanized, Chicanos are still crowded into "Mextown" ghettos.

In a series of school cases, courts have recognized Mexican American students as a cognizable ethnic group who have been the victims of segregated schools no less than have blacks and who are thus as entitled as blacks to the protection afforded by the Fourteenth Amendment and Title VI of the Civil Rights Act of 1964. Not surprisingly, the position of Chicanos in terms of both earning power and employment is analogous to the deprivation and discrimination they have suffered in the area of education. The Mexican American Legal Defense and Educational Fund initiated a number of lawsuits based on Title VII, the employment discrimination section of the Civil Rights Act of 1964. The group cites statistics showing that employment discrimination directed against the Chicano remains prevalent. In the southwest, the unemployment rate of Chicanos is twice that of Anglos; Fund members maintain that even this figure does not reflect the true situation, since chronically underemployed farm workers are not included in the statistics. Because of the long tradition of economic and social deprivation, the Chicano has been denied a basic opportunity to participate in the political process.

And American immigration policy as directed at Mexican Americans retains the hallmarks of racism that mark the history of U.S. immigration policy in general. Professor Kevin Johnson, in a lengthy article reviewing U.S. immigration policy visited on people of color, reports:

> Despite the fact that undocumented persons come from nations all over the world, the near exclusive focus of governmental and public attention at the tail end of the twentieth century has been on undocumented immigration from Mexico. The racial impact of the push to crack down on "illegal aliens" is unmistakable. Well-publicized border enforcement operations, little different from military operations, in El Paso, Texas (Operation Blockade, later renamed Operation Hold the Line due to protests from the Mexican Government) and San Diego, California (Operation Gatekeeper) have been aimed at sealing the U.S.–Mexico border and keeping undocumented Mexican citizens from entering the United States. Indeed, U.S. military forces assisted the Immigration & Naturalization Service (INS) in policing the border. At the same time, reported abuses against Mexican nationals along the border continue unabated. For example, in 1997, a U.S. Marine on patrol shot and killed a teenager, Esequiel Hernandez, Jr. (a U.S. citizen who had no criminal record) while he was herding his family's goats near the border. The U.S. General Accounting Office found that, despite the border enforcement buildup, the evidence was inconclusive about whether the strategy had proven effective.[50]

The United States Border Patrol reported 1013 migrants died between 1997 and mid-2001 trying to cross the southwest border. The number of deaths increased

---

50. Kevin R. Johnson, Race, the Immigration Laws, and Domestic Race Relations: A "Magic Mirror" into the Heart of Darkness, 73 Ind. L.J. 1111, 1137-1138 (1998). See also Cecelia M. Espenoza, The Illusory Provisions of Sanctions: The Immigration Reform and Control Act of 1986, 8 Geo. Immigr. L.J. 343 (1994) (arguing for elimination of sanctions because of their ineffectiveness and because they have increased discrimination against persons of Mexican ancestry).

as the border patrol efforts intensified.[51] In the last few years, the Border Patrol has instituted a "zero-tolerance" policy in some areas along the southwest border only, in which apprehended illegal immigrants are prosecuted by federal authorities for a misdemeanor, sent to jail for 15 to 180 days and then deported. If they are caught illegally entering the country a second time, they are eligible for a felony charge of illegal entry and as much as two years in federal prison.[52]

The comparison of how the law has addressed racial issues with other non-whites offers a fearsome insight into how the dominant society, even today, would treat African Americans given sufficient political and economic motivation. The legal protections, barely adequate in normal times, would provide little insulation against the racial hostility against blacks that seems always lurking just beneath an all too thin veneer of racial civility.

In addition to demonstrating how U.S. law treats those it considers "foreign," the differential treatment of citizens and noncitizens serves as a "magic mirror," revealing how dominant society might treat domestic minorities if legal constraints were abrogated. Indeed, the harsh treatment of noncitizens of color reveals terrifying lessons about how society views citizens of color.

§11.5 SEPTEMBER 11, 2001

The events of September 11, 2001, have had a dramatic impact on U.S. racial policies and practices. Issues such as racial profiling have taken on new meanings in the public discussion;[1] race and ethnicity have been used as proxies for affiliation with terrorism; and the numbers of immigration-based detentions, including purely "preventive" based detentions, of persons from certain countries or ethnic or religious backgrounds has risen tremendously.[2] The federal government has also imprisoned a large number of foreign persons in Guantánamo Bay, Cuba, and in unknown locations abroad without formal charges or access to lawyers. In addition, the government has failed to extend traditional legal procedures to three U.S. citizens being held as "enemy combatants."[3] In addition to the detentions of foreign nationals and a small number of U.S. citizens, the federal government

---

51. Wayne A Cornelius, Death at the Border: The Efficacy and "Unintended Consequences" of U.S. Immigration Control Policy 1993-2001, Working Paper for the Center for Comparative Immigration Studies, available at http://www.ccis-ucsd.org/PUBLICATIONS/wrkg27.PDF.

52. Sylvia Moreno, Along the Border, a Zero-Tolerance Zone, Washington Post, June 18, 2006, at A03. In November 2007, the zero-tolerance zone was expanded in Texas.

§11.5 1. See generally Deborah A. Ramirez, Jennifer Hoopes & Tara Lai Quinlan, Defining Racial Profiling in a Post-September 11 World, 40 Am. Crim. L. Rev. 1195 (2003).

2. See David Cole, Enemy Aliens: Double Standards and Constitutional Freedoms in the War on Terrorism (2003).

3. This area of the law is one that is both highly secretive and evolving. While every effort has been made to ensure accuracy and up-to-dateness, the information contained in this section may not reflect changes made since the time of publication nor information that was not made generally available to the public.

has conducted secret wiretapping and secret searches without a showing of probable cause of criminal wrongdoing.[4]

The Attorney General of the United States, John Ashcroft, publicly announced that he was willing to engage in preventative detentions in the name of fighting terrorism, and his administration has followed through.[5] Under the rubric of fighting terrorism, the federal government has preventively detained a total of what is conservatively estimated to be over 5,000 foreign nationals (non-U.S. citizens).[6] This figure includes 1,182 persons admitted by the government to have been arrested in the first seven weeks of "sweeps" conducted by the Bush government after September 11, 2001;[7] 1,100 persons detained in the Absconder Apprehension Initiative,[8] which explicitly prioritizes for deportation Arabs and Muslims among all foreign nationals living in the U.S. with outstanding deportation orders;[9] 2,747 persons detained in connection with the Special Registration Program discussed in more detail later in this section;[10] and approximately 50 persons detained as material witnesses. Of these over 5,000 persons, a total of five (three foreign nationals and two U.S. citizens) have been charged with terrorism-related crimes.[11] Out of the five charged, two were acquitted of all terrorism charges, one was convicted of conspiracy to support terrorism, one had all charges dropped by the government when he pled guilty to a minor infraction, and one is awaiting trial.[12] Professor David Cole argues that while it may currently be politically expedient and easy to maintain a double standard and target foreign nationals (who do not vote or generally carry much political weight in the United States), this strategy carries tremendous risks for the civil rights and liberties of all persons, both citizen and noncitizen. Professor Cole also argues that such strategies are both unconstitutional and very dangerous for our collective security.[13]

In addition, the conditions of detention have come under criticism, even from government sources. For example, the Office of the Inspector General (OIG), an independent organization reporting to Congress and the Attorney General, released two reports relating to the post–September 11 immigration detentions.[14] The OIG's 2003 Report looks at 762 detainees who were held in U.S. facilities on immigration violations as part of anti-terrorism initiatives and finds "significant evidence" that physical and verbal abuse by correctional officers occurred.[15] In addition, persons were detained for long periods of time without charges, access to

---

4. Id.

5. Cole, supra note 2. See generally Editorial, The Constitution Turned Upside Down, Pittsburgh Post-Gazette, Oct. 12, 2003, at E2.

6. Cole, supra note 2, at 25.

7. Id.

8. Id.

9. Id.

10. Id.

11. Cole, supra note 2, at 26.

12. Id.

13. See generally Cole, supra note 2.

14. See Anita Ramasastry, How the U.S. Has Mishandled the Post-Sept. 11 Detention Process, CNN.com, Sept. 26, 2003.

15. Id.

lawyers, or information about their futures.[16] Many of these detentions have continued even after immigration issues have been resolved.[17]

Much criticism has also been leveled at the detention of persons outside of domestic facilities. Nearly 400 persons are currently detained at Guantánamo Bay, Cuba, although the population was once double its current size.[18]

There were also at least two known U.S. citizens detained there at some time, Jose Padilla and Yasser Esam Hamdi, who, like the other detainees at Guantanamo, were being held as "enemy combatants" based on allegations of terrorist involvement.[19] It has been reported that at least three children are among those being held in Guantánamo, a claim that sparked an international outcry.[20] The American Bar Association's Task Force on Treatment of Enemy Combatants' Preliminary Report notes that the term "enemy combatant" "is not a term of art which has long established meaning."[21] The U.S. government has maintained that persons labeled as "enemy combatants" may be detained indefinitely and "have no right under the law and customs of war or the Constitution to meet with counsel concerning their detention."[22] The ABA Task Force notes that the government has taken the position that "with no meaningful judicial review, any American citizen alleged to be an enemy combatant could be detained indefinitely without charges or counsel on the government's say-so."[23] The Task Force argues that more comprehensive legal protections must be provided to such persons. Specifically, the Task Force recommends that the "administration should explain the basis and scope of its authority to detain U.S. citizens as enemy combatants; Congress should establish clear standards and procedures governing detention of U.S. citizens; citizen detainees should have access to judicial review to challenge their detention; citizen detainees should not be denied access to counsel; and consideration should be given to the international impact of our treatment of enemy combatants."[24]

In addition to the Guantánamo detainees, an unknown number of noncitizen prisoners are being held by the military in secret foreign locations.[25] Guantánamo Bay is the site of a U.S. naval base; its location outside of the United States means that prisoners, according to the United States government, are not entitled to the

16. Id.
17. Id.
18. David Bowker & David Kaye, Guantanamo by the Numbers, N.Y. Times, Nov. 10, 2007, at A15; Guantanamo Sheds Inmates, Wash. Post, Dec. 18, 2006, at A25.
19. After being detained in 2002, Padilla was eventually transferred to civilian custody in 2006 and tried in 2007. Hamdi was transferred to an American jail and eventually released when it became apparent that he was not a threat to national security.
20. Alice Wignall, The Prisoners of Guantánamo Bay, The Guardian (London), May 6, 2003, at 63. See also Neil A. Lewis, More Prisoners to Be Released from Guantánamo, Officials Say, N.Y. Times, May 6, 2003, at A21.
21. American Bar Association Task Force on Treatment of Enemy Combatants, Preliminary Report (Aug. 8, 2002), available at http://www.abanet.org/leadership/enemy_combatants.pdf.
22. Id. at 7.
23. Id. at 3, referencing Hamdi v. Rumsfeld, 337 F.3d 335 (4th Cir. 2003).
24. Id. at 21, Summary of Recommendations.
25. Neil A. Lewis, Threats and Responses: The Tribunals; Six Detainees Soon May Face Military Trials, N.Y. Times, July 4, 2003, at A1.

same legal protections, such as access to a lawyer,[26] as they would be if detained domestically.[27] Although initially very limited outside access to the detention camp in Guantánamo Bay was allowed, early photos showed prisoners kneeling in the scorching Cuban sun, shackled in chains and hooded.[28] These photos were taken when prisoners were detained in a makeshift camp entitled Camp X-Ray, which housed prisoners not in cells but in cages with link-chain "walls" and sheet metal roofs.[29] Camp X-Ray's prisoners had only buckets for toilets, and harsh lights were kept on every hour of the day.[30] Camp X-Ray has since been replaced by a newer camp, Camp Delta. Camp Delta is better equipped; it has toilets, cells, and beds equipped with arrows that point the way to Mecca.[31] Media access to Camp Delta is more open than was access to Camp X-Ray.[32] Despite somewhat better conditions in Camp Delta, its prisoners still remain in a vast legal limbo.[33] Reports of poor treatment still persist along with 41 reported suicide attempts among prisoners.[34] The U.S. government contends that the Guantánamo detainees are "unlawful combatants" and thus do not qualify for prisoner of war status[35] and attendant judicial protections under the Third Geneva Convention.[36] International lawyers have argued that, as prisoners of war, the detainees were entitled to release when the war in Afghanistan ended.[37] The United States claims that the prisoners are not entitled to any of the legal protections, such as access to a lawyer, the existence of formal charges, and the right to a fair and speedy trial, rights that are extended to prisoners held on U.S. soil.[38]

On June 28, 2004, in Rasul v. Bush, the Supreme Court held that the nearly 600 men imprisoned in Guantánamo Bay at the time had a right of access to the federal courts, via habeas corpus and otherwise, to challenge their detention and conditions of confinement.[39] Reversing the U.S. Court of Appeals for the D.C. Circuit, the Court held that the right to habeas does not depend on citizenship, and affirmed the right of non-citizen detainees held at Guantánamo to challenge their detention in U.S. courts.

26. As of the time of publication, two of the detainees have been granted access to lawyers. One is Australian detainee David Hicks and the other is Yaser Esam Hamdi, a U.S.-born suspect. These two cases are discussed in more detail later in this section. See Lawyer Says Cuba Appeal Prompted Pentagon, New York Times, Dec. 9, 2003.

27. Wignall, supra note 20, at 63; Marcia Coyle, Relief Denied, Challenging the Limits of Executive Authority, Cases over Guantánamo Bay Detainees Move Toward Supreme Court, Palm Beach Daily Bus. Rev., May 5, 2003, at A8.

28. Wignall, supra note 20, at 63.

29. Id.

30. Id.

31. Id.; Caroline Overington, Camp Delta Lacks Nothing but Freedom, Sydney Morning Herald, May 29, 2003, at 16.

32. Overington, supra note 31, at 16.

33. Id.

34. David Bowker & David Kaye, Guantanamo by the Numbers, N.Y. Times, Nov. 10, 2007, at A15.

35. Neil A. Lewis, Aftereffects: Prisoners; Detainees from the Afghan War Remain in a Legal Limbo in Cuba, N.Y. Times, Apr. 24, 2003, at A21.

36. Id. See Coyle, supra note 27, at A8.

37. Lewis, Aftereffects, supra note 35, at A21.

38. Wignall, supra note 20, at 63; Coyle, supra note 27, at A8.

39. 542 U.S. 466 (2004).

Little over a week later, in another effort to avoid providing the detainees access to United States courts, the government authorized the establishment of Combatant Status Review Tribunals (CSRT) at Guantánamo. In the CSRTs, the military officers could review each detainee's "enemy combatant" status without the involvement of lawyers for the detainees and with numerous procedural short-cuts. For example, the CSRT procedures permitted the inclusion of evidence obtained under coercion or torture and denied detainees access to classified evidence, which in some cases constituted the majority of the evidence presented to the tribunal. In December 2005, Congress passed the Detainee Treatment Act of 2005, which stripped courts of jurisdiction over habeas corpus petitions filed on behalf of Guantánamo detainees and vested exclusive review of final decisions of CSRTs and military commissions in the D.C. Circuit Court.

The following June, in Hamdan v. Rumsfeld,[40] the Supreme Court considered a challenge by a Guantánamo detainee charged under military commissions established by executive order. The Court held that the DTA did not preclude federal jurisdiction of pending habeas actions. It also ruled that the military commissions, as defined under the President's 2001 executive order, violated military law and the Geneva Conventions. In doing so, the Court rejected the arguments of Government representatives, including Pentagon officials and Defense Secretary Rumsfeld, that the detainees may be lawfully and indefinitely held until the effort against terrorism ends.[41]

The largest public response to the U.S. anti-terrorism initiatives may, however, be in response to the Guantánamo detentions. International and domestic criticism of the status of Guantánamo detainees has been severe, especially from human rights groups,[42] and some of the battles on behalf of the detainees are taking place outside of courtrooms. A senior official of the International Committee of the Red Cross, the only group outside of the government allowed to meet the detainees and inspect the main detention center, recently broke from its standard policy of silence[43] and criticized the United States for holding the detainees indefinitely and without proper legal process.[44] One of the chief concerns cited by the Red Cross is the complete uncertainty about the future shared by all detainees.

In response to the *Hamdan* decision and Congress' prohibition of cruel, inhuman and degrading treatment during interrogations in the McCain Amendment to the DTA, the Military Commissions Act (MCA) was enacted in 2006. The MCA amends the War Crimes Act to immunize from punishment officials who engaged in, supervised, or condoned various forms of "torture lite" — outrages on personal

40. 126 S. Ct. 2749 (2006).
41. Lewis, Aftereffects, supra note 35, at 63.
42. Lewis, Threats and Responses, supra note 25, at A1. See also Wignall, supra note 20, at 6; Overington, supra note 31, at 16.
43. Lewis, Threats and Responses, supra note 25, at A1. The International Red Cross Committee generally operates under an agreement by which they exchange access for the promise that they will not publicize their findings but will instead bring their complaints to the government in charge. The Red Cross publicizes their views only when it feels that there is a distinct lack of action in response to their criticisms.
44. Id. See also International Red Cross website, available at http://www.icrc.org/web/ eng/ siteeng0.nsf/html/5QRC5V?OpenDocument, where the views of the Red Cross official who went public with his findings are available.

dignity, or cruel, inhuman, humiliating, and degrading treatment — and allows the admission of evidence obtained through these methods.[45] The MCA also severely limits the avenues of judicial review for non-citizens held in U.S. custody, eliminating judicial review for any claims challenging any aspect of detention or treatment of all non-citizen detainees determined to be "enemy combatants" or "awaiting such determination." Moreover, the MCA ratifies the limited CSRT review process that the DTA established as a substitute for habeas corpus.

Shortly following the passage of the MCA, the Department of Justice notified the District Court for the District of Columbia that under the MCA the district court lacked jurisdiction to consider habeas corpus petitions brought on behalf of Guantánamo detainees. The plaintiff in *Hamdan* challenged the MCA's applicability to his habeas corpus petition, relying on the Supreme Court holding in *Hamdan*. The District Court held that the MCA prohibited the federal courts from exercising jurisdiction over his habeas petition. The Court of Appeals of the D.C. Circuit also ruled against the detainees in the consolidated cases of Boumediene v. Bush and Al Odah v. United States, holding that Guantánamo detainees had no constitutional right to habeas corpus review of their detentions in federal court. The court reasoned that the common law habeas did not extend to noncitizens captured abroad and held outside the United States and that the MCA eliminated any statutory right to habeas corpus.

At first, the Supreme Court declined to hear the case. However, a few months later, in its first reversal in 60 years, the Supreme Court announced that it would hear the consolidated *Al Odah* and *Boumediene* cases. At the time of publication, both sides were briefing the case before the Supreme Court.

There have also been lower court cases challenging other aspects of the U.S. government's anti-terrorism tactics. On the same day in which it announced the granting of certiorari in *Al Odah* and Rasul v. Bush, the Supreme Court announced the denial of certiorari in Global Relief Foundation v. Snow.[46] In this case, the Court rejected without comment an appeal from The Global Relief Fund, an Illinois-based Islamic charity whose assets were frozen by the government three months after September 11, 2001.[47] Global Relief has not been charged with any terror-related crime and argues that it is purely a humanitarian organization with no links to terrorist activities.[48]

Another important case in the anti-terrorism arena, MKB v. Warden,[49] is one about which very little is known and that previously did not seem to even exist. The plaintiff, known only by his initials, was arrested and charged with unknown federal crimes. The federal court made everything about the case secret. Two different federal courts have held hearings and issued rulings, yet there is no public

45. See Jenny S. Martinez, The Military Commissions Act and "Torture Lite": Something to Be Proud Of?, 48 Harv. Int'l L. J. Online 58 (2007), available at http://www.harvardilj.org/print/109#_ftnref2.
46. 315 F.3d 748 (7th Cir.), cert. denied, 124 S. Ct. 531 (2002).
47. Anne Gearan, High Court Will Hear Appeals from Guantánamo Prisoners, Associated Press, Nov. 10, 2003.
48. Id.
49. No. 03-6747.

record of any action and no files or documents are available.[50] Lawyers are required not to speak about the case, and the filed documents and docket sheet are sealed from the public.[51] Furthermore, the very *existence* of a legal proceeding itself was hidden.[52] Its existence was only discovered when the case was briefly and accidentally listed on a federal court docket. There was no record that this case had ever arisen or that it was being heard until a docketing mistake resulted in a newspaper report that identified the defendant by name.[53] This case is an important one because it indicates that the Justice Department is engaging in tactics of complete secrecy even in federal habeas cases.[54] The case, which is currently on petition to the Supreme Court, would allow the Court to explicitly rule on whether such secret judicial proceedings are constitutional.[55]

Those not suspected of terrorism who merely belong to certain ethnic and racial groups have also been the target of recent government policies.[56] In 2002, reviving provisions that have rarely been used since they were enacted in 1952, the Attorney General announced a policy requiring nonimmigrant men from certain designated countries to appear at their local Immigration Naturalization Services/Department of Homeland Security offices[57] to submit to fingerprinting, photographs, and periodic registration under oath.[58] The Attorney General announced that these provisions were pursuant to already existing U.S. law.[59] The Attorney General targeted nonimmigrant men from primarily Arab and Muslim countries and required that they alone participate in a Special Registration Program.[60]

While the Special Registration Program was announced as part of the general National Security Entry-Exit Registration System (NSEERS), the call-in registration procedures established for nationals and citizens of certain countries differed substantially from the more general policy of registration and fingerprinting that

50. Warren Richey, Secret 9/11 Case Before High Court, Christian Sci. Monitor, Oct. 30, 2003.
51. Id.
52. Id.
53. Id.
54. See id.
55. See id.
56. The section on the Special Registration Program and NSEERS draws heavily from research done by Benita Jain, Melissa Goodman, Gabrielle Prisco, and Kathryn Sabbeth under the auspices of the Arthur Garfield Hays Civil Liberties Program at New York University School of Law.
57. On March 1, 2003, the Immigration and Naturalization Services transitioned into the Department of Homeland Security. See http://www.usdoj.gov/immigrationinfo.htm.
58. See Attorney General Prepared Remarks on the National Entry-Exit Registration System 1 (June 6, 2002), available at http://www.usdoj.gov/ag/speeches/2002/060502agpreparedremarks.htm.
59. Id.
60. All males from designated countries who were 16 years or older as of the date that registration began for the relevant call-in group had to register. See, e.g., 67 Fed. Reg. 67766, 67767 (Nov. 6, 2002). The first group subject to the Special Registration Program comprised certain nationals or citizens of Iran, Iraq, Libya, Sudan, or Syria. See 67 Fed. Reg. 67766 (Nov. 6, 2002). The second Special Registration Program group included certain nationals and citizens of Afghanistan, Algeria, Bahrain, Eritrea, Lebanon, Morocco, North Korea, Oman, Qatar, Somalia, Tunisia, United Arab Emirates, and Yemen. See 67 Fed. Reg. 70525 (Nov. 22, 2002). The third group subject to the Special Registration Program covers nationals and citizens of Pakistan and Saudi Arabia. See 67 Fed. Reg. 77642 (Dec. 18, 2002). The fourth group required to participate in the Special Registration Program includes nationals and citizens of Bangladesh, Egypt, Indonesia, Jordan, and Kuwait.

was taking place at the borders or other ports of entry.[61] Contrary to statements suggesting that periodic registration would be required for all nonimmigrants who stay in the country over 30 days, the Special Registration Program applied only "to those individuals of elevated national security concern who stay in the country more than thirty days."[62] Specifically, the Special Registration Program applied only to nonimmigrants from Arab and Muslim countries, with the exception of nationals and citizens of North Korea.[63] Since its implementation, the general rule that all such foreign nationals must periodically register has been suspended, but such registration may still be required by the Department of Homeland Security.[64] The process of registration calls to mind two cases from the not-so-distant past, Korematsu v. United States[65] (upholding the internment of U.S. citizens of Japanese ancestry during World War II) and Narenji v. Civiletti[66] (unsuccessfully challenging the process by which Iranian students were forced to register with the U.S. government during the Iranian hostage crisis). All call attention to the ways in which race, ethnicity, and national origin take on new national meanings in light of the perception of an external security threat.

In addition, since September 11, 2001, hate crimes against Asian Pacific Americans, Muslims, persons of Arab or Middle Eastern descent, and persons incorrectly perceived to be Arab or Muslim, such as Sikhs, abound. Although by no means an exhaustive list, the Department of Justice has released a list of bias-motivated crimes that are being treated as a response to September 11. For example, on December 12, 2001, the U.S. Attorney's Office for the Central District of California filed a criminal complaint against two defendants for "conspiring to damage and destroy, by means of an explosive, the King Fahd mosque and for possessing an explosive bomb to carry out the conspiracy."[67] The two defendants were also indicted under additional charges related to their alleged attempts "to damage and destroy, by means of an explosive, the office of the Muslim Public Affairs Council and the district office of U.S. Representative Darrell Issa."[68] In addition, many community groups have reported bias-motivated violence, including beatings, street harassment, and shootings.[69] According to a report put out by

61. Attorney General, supra note 58. The Attorney General announced that the NSEERS program consists of three components: first, fingerprinting and photographing at the border; second, periodic registration of individuals who stay in the United States for 30 days or more; third, exit procedures that track when nonimmigrants leave the country. The Special Registration Program was apparently part of the second component.

62. Attorney General, supra note 58.

63. Supra note 60.

64. Department of Homeland Security, NSEERS 30 Day and Annual Interview Requirements to Be Suspended, Dec. 1, 2003, available at: http://www.dhs.gov/xnews/releases/press_release_0306.shtm.

65. 323 U.S. 214 (1943).

66. 481 F. Supp. 1132 (D.D.C.), reversed, 617 F.2d 745 (D.C. Cir. 1979).

67. Department of Justice, Civil Rights Division, Enforcement and Outreach Following the September 11th Attacks, available at http://www.usdoj.gov/crt/legalinfo/discrimupdate.htm.

68. Id.

69. See Backlash: When America Turned on Its Own, A Preliminary Report to the 2001 Audit of Violence Against Asian Pacific Americans, available at http://www.napalc.org/literature/ annual_report/Post9_11.pdf. See also statements from the Asian American Legal Defense Fund, available at http://www.aaldef.org/violence.html; 2000 Audit of Violence Against Asian Pacific Americans, available at http://www.napalc.org/literature/annual_report/2000Audit.pdf.

the National Asian Pacific American Legal Consortium (NAPALC), in the three months following September 11, 2001, there were almost 250 "bias-motivated incidents targeting Asian Pacific Americans generally and South Asians particularly, [a] number [that] stands in stark contrast to the approximately 400-500 anti-APA incidents annually that NAPALC has reported in previous years."[70] At least two Asian Pacific Americans were murdered as a result of the backlash,[71] and many of the incidents involved a high degree of physical violence.[72] The domestic repercussions of policies such as the Special Registration Program and the increasing hostilities faced by persons of Middle Eastern or Arab descent exist in a larger geopolitical framework in which tensions between the United States and other countries, particularly those considered "non-Western," is increasing. Issues of race, ethnicity, religion, and culture all figure prominently in these tensions. Although a thorough discussion of these issues is far beyond the scope of this text, it is critical to note that any current discussion of race in America takes place within the context of and is shaped by these current events.

For many years, discussions of race in America have taken place in a context that emphasizes the racial categories of black and white. Although these categories are still highly relevant ones that carry much social meaning, issues of race and ethnicity have become ever more complex and nuanced. At the same time, the United States' history of race and racism can greatly inform current struggles for nonblack persons of color. Within the domestic United States, as well as within its foreign policy, South Asians, Arabs, Palestinians, and other persons of Middle Eastern descent are implicated by the United States' understandings of race and by its racism.

70. Backlash, supra note 69.
71. Id. at 2.
72. Id.

Table of Cases

Italics indicate principal cases and the locations of major discussions of these cases.

Index